PRINTED IN U.S.A.

GREEK LITERATURE IN TRANSLATION

GREEK
LITERATURE
IN
TRANSLATION

By

WHITNEY JENNINGS OATES
PRINCETON UNIVERSITY

and

CHARLES THEOPHILUS MURPHY
OBERLIN COLLEGE

DAVID McKAY COMPANY, INC.
New York

OATES & MURPHY

GREEK LITERATURE IN TRANSLATION

COPYRIGHT · 1944

BY DAVID MCKAY COMPANY, INC.

First Edition February 1944
Reprinted April 1945
June 1946, September 1946
December 1947, June 1949
May 1951, August 1952
October 1953
May 1956
August 1958
July 1961
August 1963
January 1966

PRINTED IN THE UNITED STATES OF AMERICA

PREFACE

Anyone who faces the task of selecting from the range of Greek literature those portions which are unfailingly important for man's wisdom and judgment, finds it in one sense difficult and in another sense easy. It is easy, for there are certain masterpieces which could not possibly be overlooked by the anthologist. On the other hand, it is difficult because of the proverbial richness of the Greek creative spirit in letters. The editors therefore submit their selections with profound humility and with the hope that no egregious omissions have been made. If such omissions have occurred, they perhaps may plead the limitation of size placed upon the volume.

At the outset it might be well to indicate in outline the philosophy of the present book. All too frequently anthologies are cursed by the fact that their individual selections are short, merely snippets cut arbitrarily from larger wholes. Consequently, wherever possible, the editors have sought to give total units. Thus, for example, in the drama they have not selected brief gems from Aeschylus, Sophocles or Euripides, but have included complete plays. Though this means a sacrifice perhaps in the extent which the volume covers, still there is some satisfaction for the editors in being able to offer the complete texts of nine plays. The editors also have determined to give a systematic rather than an historical arrangement to the selections. If an anthology is arranged historically, *e.g.,* by placing together the selections taken from a given historical epoch, there is the inevitable temptation for the reader to regard the selection as merely an historical document and not as a work of art or piece of literature. The purpose of the volume is to present these works as pieces of literature primarily and through them to acquaint the reader with the wisdom of Greece. Hence the editors have divided Greek literature into ten different categories, and have arranged the selections within the categories chronologically. The first category includes Homer, and from the *Iliad* will be found five complete books which should acquaint the reader with the core of this great epic and its delineation of the tragic figure of Achilles. From the *Odyssey* are included the introduction of the first book plus seven other complete books which contain the most brilliant passages of the narrative and drama of Odysseus' adventure. The second category contains the tragic plays. Here the editors were faced with an embarrassment of riches and cannot hope that their choice will receive unanimous approval. In the third category of comedy, they present one example from the Old Comedy of Aristophanes and one from the New Comedy of Menander. The editors hope that the selections from philosophy will give as complete a conspectus as possible of the four great philosophical systems which have emerged from Greek antiquity. In choosing these selections it was thought best not to include many of the political passages of Plato and Aristotle which seem on the surface to be most applicable to modern life, such as the description of the so-called communism of the *Republic* or the constitutional theories of Aristotle's *Politics,* but rather to give the reader the core of these two philosophers' systems and the fundamental premises from which their political principles are ultimately derived. History is represented by Herodotus, Thucydides, Xenophon and Polybius. Then follow four short categories which present in limited form representative works in oratory, the mime, romance, the satirical dialogue and biography. The concluding section of the book is devoted entirely to poetry. Here the editors have attempted to include the most significant portions of the didactic poetry of Hesiod and the later epic of Apollonius, the hymns of Homer and of Callimachus, the satire of Archilochus and Semonides, and the pastoral verse of Theocritus, Bion and Moschus. In the field of lyric and reflective poetry the editors have tried to include every important and well-known piece that can be found in this widely varied field.

Thus the reader, if he follows through these pages from the passages from Homer to the selections from the Greek Anthology, should gain a full-length picture of the rich heritage of the Greek literary genius. He can see it in its philosophical perspective where the values and principles of life are dealt with systematically by the minds of Plato or Aristotle. Also he can see the Greek mind as it viewed itself in time in the writings of those who invented history. And thirdly, in all the remaining selections he can see in their concrete artistic forms the embodiment of Greek insight into values, principles, human nature and life in its infinite complexity and multiplicity. There is no more profitable undertaking for a man in the modern age with all its desperate tensions and catastrophes than to return to these sources of wisdom which appeared in the world so long ago, but which no custom has ever been able to stale.

In selecting the translations for this anthology, the editors have tried to keep in mind the needs of the contemporary reader, and have used, whenever possible, those versions which seemed most readily comprehensible without sacrificing too much of the spirit of the originals. The practice found in many anthologies of giving samples of several translations of different portions of the same work has been deliberately avoided in this volume; works like the *Iliad* and *Odyssey,* for example, are unified works of art, and the reader's comprehension of them as artistic wholes would be seriously hampered if he read, *e.g.,* Book I of the *Iliad* in an Elizabethan verse translation, Book VI in nineteenth-century prose, and so on. The translations selected for this anthology are, for the most part, the standard modern versions. Since, however, no really adequate version of Aristophanes' *Lysistrata* was available, one of the editors prepared for this volume a new translation which appears here in print for the first time.

In conclusion, the editors wish to express their deepest gratitude to Professors Charles Osgood and Francis R. B. Godolphin of Princeton University for compiling the Appendix on influences in English literature, a section which, it is hoped, will add greatly to the usefulness of the work. They are also indebted to President Howard Lowry of the College of Wooster for his helpful suggestions and advice, and to Mr. Robert L. Straker of Longmans, Green and Company for his invaluable assistance in the preparation of this volume.

W. J. O.
C. T. M.

ACKNOWLEDGMENTS

For permission to reprint selections in this book, the editors thank the following translators and publishers:

George Allen — Sappho's Andromache's Wedding (Atlantic Monthly, Feb. 1937).

George Allen & Unwin — Homeric Hymns, and Euripides' Hippolytus and The Bacchae.

Edward Arnold & Company — Sappho's Evening.

G. Bell & Sons — Marcus Aurelius' Meditations, and Isocrates' Panegyricus.

Basil Blackwell — Archilochus' There is Nothing Strange, Simonides' The Poet's Friend, and Palladas' Naked I Came.

Edmund Blunden and the Beaumont Press — Anacreontea Cicada.

Cambridge University Press — Sophocles' Antigone and Oedipus Rex, Sappho's To a Bride, and Simonides' A Hound.

Jonathan Cape — Asclepiades' There is no Loving after Death.

The Clarendon Press — The selections from Aristotle, Demosthenes, Epictetus, Epicurus, and Lucian; Callimachus' Epigrams; and sixty-five poems from The Oxford Book of Greek Verse in Translation.

The Clarendon Press and the Jowett Trustees — The selections from Thucydides and selections from Plato.

J. M. Dent & Sons —The selections from Apollonius of Rhodes' Argonautica.

J. M. Edmonds — Sappho's Night, Theognis' Immortality Conferred in Vain, and Agathias Scholasticus' Leave a Kiss within the Cup.

Kathleen Freeman — The selections from Solon.

The Golden Cockerel Press — Alcman's The Halcyons and Night.

Gowans & Gray — Simonides of Ceos' The Spartan Monument, Anacreon's On a Slain Warrior, Asclepiades' Love is Best, and Aeschylus' An Epitaph on Himself.

Harper & Brothers — Mimnermus' The Son's Golden Bowl.

Harvard University Press — The selections from Herodas, Hesiod, Semonides of Amorgus, Theophrastus, and Longus' Daphnis and Chloe; selections from Anacreontea, Asclepiades, and Meleager.

Henry Holt & Company — Adaptation of map from Shepherd's Historical Atlas.

John Lane, The Bodley Head — Swallow Song, and Meleager's The Bride.

Macmillan & Company — The selections from Xenophon's Anabasis, and Cleanthes' Hymn to Zeus.

The Macmillan Company — Aeschylus' Agamemnon and The Eumenides, and the selections from The Iliad and The Odyssey, Bacchylides, Bion, Moschus, Polybius, and Theocritus.

Methuen & Company — Mimnermus' Sine Amore nil est Jucundum.

Mrs. Harry Fine — Paul Elmer More's translation of Aeschylus' Prometheus Bound.

Nonesuch Press — Pindar's Fourth Pythian Ode.

The Poetry Review — Simonides' Lost at Sea, i.

Levi A. Post — Menander's The Arbitration.

Richards Press —Simonides' Archedike and Lost at Sea, iii.

George Routledge & Sons — Swallow Song and Mimnermus' We all do Fail as a Leaf.

Benj. H. Sanborn — Archilochus' The Poet's Shield.

The Wessex Press — Pindar's First and Second Olympian Odes and Callimachus' To Apollo.

Yale University Press — Simonides' The Athenian Monument.

CONTENTS

ix

CONTENTS

ORATORY

PAGE

ISOCRATES: PANEGYRICUS. 19–53; 170–189 [*J. H. Freese*] 802

DEMOSTHENES . . . . [*A. W. Pickard-Cambridge*]
PHILIPPIC I 811
ON THE CROWN. 199–210; 322–324 819

CHARACTER STUDY, MIME, AND ROMANCE

THEOPHRASTUS . . . . [*J. M. Edmonds*]
GARRULITY 825
LOQUACITY 825
SUPERSTITIOUSNESS 826
NASTINESS 826

HERODAS . . . . [*A. D. Knox*]
THE JEALOUS LADY 828
A PRIVATE CHAT 829

LONGUS . . . [*George Thornley — J. M. Edmonds*]
DAPHNIS AND CHLOE. I. 22–27 832

THE SATIRICAL DIALOGUE

LUCIAN . . . . [*H. W. and F. G. Fowler*]
DIALOGUES OF THE GODS 836
  II. Eros and Zeus 836
  VI. Hera and Zeus 836
  VIII. Hephaestus and Zeus 838
  XVI. Hera and Leto 838
  XX. The Judgment of Paris 839
DIALOGUES OF THE DEAD 844
  I. Diogenes and Pollux 844
  XXII. Charon and Menippus 845

BIOGRAPHY

PLUTARCH . . [*John Dryden — Arthur Hugh Clough*] 847
LIVES
  Lycurgus. 13–18; 24–28. On Sparta 849
  Solon. 15–16. Athens. 27–28. Croesus 858
  Pericles. 24. Aspasia 862
  Marius. 37–39. The Exile of Marius 864
  Alexander. 26–28. Trip to Zeus Ammon. 75–76. Death 866
  Julius Caesar. 60–69. Death 869
  Antony. 75–79; 82–86. Deaths of Antony and Cleopatra 876

CONTENTS

LYRIC AND REFLECTIVE POETRY

HOMER

[Date Unknown]

Greek literature is unique in that the first works appearing in its chronology, the epics of Homer, are virtually the finest monuments in letters which the Greek tradition produced. The so-called Homeric age falls roughly between the thirteenth and the ninth centuries B.C. For this epoch, part of which lies within the last years of the Minoan-Mycenaean civilization and the rest within the limits of the so-called Greek Dark Ages, we have two sources of information, the *Iliad* and *Odyssey,* and evidence derived from archaeology. By using these two sources in combination, scholars have attempted to reconstruct the essential character of that age. The results of such investigations have thrown great light on the interpretation of the Homeric poems, although many of the emergent problems have never been definitely solved.

One of these problems concerns the authorship of the *Iliad* and the *Odyssey.* We can indicate here only in brief the nature of this question. In antiquity the various inconsistencies in the poems did not cause individuals like Plato or Horace to doubt that Homer was an individual poet who composed the two epics, nor in antiquity was there any general disposition to doubt the historicity of the poems. People believed that there had been a Trojan war, that the various human characters actually lived, and some even thought that it was an age when the gods walked on earth and frequently intermingled with men. However, in the late eighteenth and early nineteenth centuries studies in the rise and development of saga poetry led scholars to advance the thesis that the *Iliad* and *Odyssey* had grown gradually out of poetry of folk origin and were handed down and increased by the oral tradition of bards and roving minstrels. This view of multiple authorship has had many supporters. The advances in archaeology, stimulated at first by the brilliant career of Schliemann in the nineteenth century, have enabled us to define with some precision the extent to which the poems reflect history. More recently, however, literary criticism has emphasized the extraordinary unity and artistic perfection which are to be found in the poems. This literary approach indicates that a single poet must have imposed artistic unity upon the epics, although he was, to be sure, considerably indebted to an oral poetic tradition. Consequently the tendency in recent years among scholars has been to accept in some form a theory of single authorship.

Even though the problem of authorship will always be debated, it seems safe to conclude that the poems themselves reflect the main outlines of an actually existing social structure. It resembled a feudal society with "barons" ruling over large estates. Government was carried on by a council of these chiefs according to traditional unwritten laws, and their rulings were communicated to the people in general assemblies. Beyond doubt some "barons" were more powerful than others, as we can gather from Agamemnon's leadership of the Greek expedition. Although the common man did not possess much significance in the social structure, still amongst the leaders there was a rudimentary democratic spirit. Each leader had a modicum of independence and could speak freely in the council, while the commander-in-chief was to all intents and purposes bound by the decisions of the council.

The epics of Homer have held their place in the front rank of western tradition not only because of their structural excellence but also because of the universal scope of their content. One need only review what critics from the time of antiquity have seen in Homer in order to realize the extent of his range. Homer has been regarded as the first great dramatist, particularly in his manipulation of plot and in his characterizations. The Greeks themselves called him the first historian. Quintilian, the great theorist of oratory at Rome, examined Homer's speeches and maintained that he had discovered all the essential principles of oratory. Doctors have scrutinized his descriptions of wounds and their treatment, and conclude that the poet must have been a trained physician. Military experts read his accounts of battles and agree that Homer possessed a knowledge of tactics. Anyone who is acquainted with the sea and with ships realizes that Homer in the *Odyssey* is delineating something of which he himself had a wide experience. His references to the world of external nature reveal great keenness of observation. Nor can we overlook Homer's mastery of the simile, in which he exhibits an almost unrivaled excellence of the poetic imagination. In addition to these qualities, Homer established once and for all the form of epic poetry and all the regular devices and the technique of the epic tradition. Among these are, of course, the divine machinery, the device of plunging the reader *in medias res* at the outset of the poem, and the effective use of retrospective narrative.

Combined with all these other powers Homer's most notable achievement is his view of man. It would be difficult to deny that the poet attributes dignity to man, despite the fact that Homeric man is controlled in his behaviour by the force of convention and by the interference of the gods, who are often capricious. Nevertheless, man is conceived not merely as a puppet of the gods but as an individual who possesses free will and who is responsible for his actions. The tragedy of Achilles is ample evidence for this point. Achilles' free choices have involved him in a situation which results in the death of his closest friend and the loss of his own personal honour. The hero ultimately comes to realize the consequences of his deeds in the last book of the *Iliad,* where the whole Homeric view of life and of man is expressed most powerfully. When Priam pleads with Achilles to ransom the body of his slain son, Hector, Achilles gains sufficient stature to realize not only his own position but also that of the bereaved Trojan king. The *Odys-*

sey does not contain as profound an interpretation of human life as does the *Iliad,* yet centuries of readers have admired its narrative excellence, its poetic unity and variety. Here more than in the *Iliad* we have the story for the story's sake, which, withal at its own level, reflects the same attitude toward life which is found in the *Iliad.*

The selections from the two epics will give the reader a grasp of the essential structure of each poem. It is hoped, however, that the remaining books will be read in order to obtain a knowledge of Homer in his entirety, for his comprehensiveness is the closest analogue in Greek literature to the all-embracing poetry of Shakespeare.

THE ILIAD

How Agamemnon and Achilles fell out at the siege of Troy; and Achilles withdrew himself from battle, and won from Zeus a pledge that his wrong should be avenged on Agamemnon and the Achaians.

Sing, goddess, the wrath of Achilles Peleus' son, the ruinous wrath that brought on the Achaians woes innumerable, and hurled down into Hades many strong souls of heroes, and gave their bodies to be a prey to dogs and all winged fowls; and so the counsel of Zeus wrought out its accomplishment from the day when first strife parted Atreides king of men and noble Achilles.

Who then among the gods set the twain at strife and variance? Even the son of Leto and of Zeus; for he in anger at the king sent a sore plague upon the host, that the folk began to perish, because Atreides had done dishonour to Chryses the priest. For he had come to the Achaians' fleet ships to win his daughter's freedom, and brought a ransom beyond telling; and bare in his hands the fillet of Apollo the Far-darter upon a golden staff; and made his prayer unto all the Achaians, and most of all to the two sons of Atreus, orderers of the host: "Ye sons of Atreus and all ye well-greaved Achaians, now may the gods that dwell in the mansions of Olympus grant you to lay waste the city of Priam, and to fare happily homeward; only set ye my dear child free, and accept the ransom in reverence to the son of Zeus, far-darting Apollo."

Then all the other Achaians cried assent, to reverence the priest and accept his goodly ransom; yet the thing pleased not the heart of Agamemnon son of Atreus, but he roughly sent him away, and laid stern charge upon him, saying: "Let me not find thee, old man, amid the hollow ships, whether tarrying now or returning again hereafter, lest the staff and fillet of the god avail thee naught. And her will I not set free; nay, ere that shall old age come on her in our house, in Argos, far from her native land, where she shall ply the loom and serve my couch. But depart, provoke me not, that thou mayest the rather go in peace."

So said he, and the old man was afraid and obeyed his word, and fared silently along the shore of the loud-sounding sea. Then went that aged man apart and prayed aloud to king Apollo, whom Leto of the fair locks bare: "Hear me, god of the silver bow, that standest over Chryse and holy Killa, and rulest Tenedos with might, O Smintheus! If ever I built a temple gracious in thine eyes, or if ever I burnt to thee fat flesh of thighs of bulls or goats, fulfil thou this my desire; let the Danaans pay by thine arrows for my tears."

So spake he in prayer, and Phoebus Apollo heard him, and came down from the peaks of Olympus wroth at heart, bearing on his shoulders his bow and covered quiver. And the arrows clanged upon his shoulders in his wrath, as the god moved; and he descended like to night. Then he sate him aloof from the ships, and let an arrow fly; and there was heard a dread clanging of the silver bow. First did he assail the mules and fleet dogs, but afterward, aiming at the men his piercing dart, he smote; and the pyres of the dead burnt continually in multitude.

Now for nine days ranged the god's shafts through the host; but on the tenth Achilles summoned the folk to assembly, for in his mind did goddess Hera of the white arms put the thought, because she had pity on the Danaans when she beheld them perishing. Now when they had gathered and were met in assembly, then Achilles fleet of foot stood up and spake among them: "Son of Atreus, now deem I that we shall return wandering home again — if verily we might escape death — if war at once and pestilence must indeed ravage the Achaians. But come, let us now inquire of some soothsayer or priest, yea, or an interpreter of dreams — seeing that a dream too is of Zeus — who shall say wherefore Phoebus Apollo is so wroth, whether he blame us by reason of vow or hecatomb; if perchance he would accept the savour of lambs or unblemished goats, and so would take away the pestilence from us."

So spake he and sate him down; and there stood up before them Kalchas son of Thestor, most excellent far of augurs, who knew both things that were and that should be and that had been before, and guided the ships of the Achaians to Ilios by his soothsaying that Phoebus Apollo bestowed on him. He of good intent made harangue and spake amid them: "Achilles, dear to Zeus, thou biddest me tell the wrath of Apollo, the king that smiteth afar. Therefore will I speak; but do thou make covenant with me, and swear that verily with all thy heart thou wilt aid me both by word and deed. For of a truth I deem that I shall provoke one that ruleth all the Argives with might, and whom the Achaians obey. For a king is more of might when he is wroth with a meaner man; even though for the one day he swallow his anger, yet doth he still keep his displeasure thereafter in his breast till he accomplish it. Consider thou, then, if thou wilt hold me safe."

And Achilles fleet of foot made answer and spake to him: "Yea, be of good courage, speak whatever soothsaying thou knowest; for by Apollo dear to Zeus, him by whose worship thou, O Kalchas, declarest thy soothsaying to the Danaans, no man while I live and behold light on earth shall lay violent hands upon thee amid the hollow ships; no man of all the Danaans, not even if thou mean Agamemnon, that now avoweth him to be greatest far of the Achaians."

Then was the noble seer of good courage, and spake: "Neither by reason of a vow is he displeased, nor for any hecatomb, but for his priest's sake to whom Agamemnon did despite, and set not his daughter free and accepted not the ransom; therefore hath the Fardarter brought woes upon us, yea, and will bring. Nor will he ever remove the loathly pestilence from the Danaans till we have given the bright-eyed damsel to her father, unbought, unransomed, and carried a holy hecatomb to Chryse; then might we propitiate him to our prayer."

So said he and sate him down, and there stood up before them the hero son of Atreus, wide-ruling Agamemnon, sore displeased; and his dark heart within him was greatly filled with anger, and his eyes were like flashing fire. To Kalchas first spake he with look of ill: "Thou seer of evil, never yet hast thou told me the thing that is pleasant. Evil is ever the joy of thy heart to prophesy, but never yet didst thou tell any good matter nor bring it to pass. And now with soothsaying thou makest harangue among the Danaans, how that the Far-darter bringeth woes upon them because, forsooth, I would not take the goodly ransom of the damsel Chryseis, seeing I am the rather fain to keep her own self within mine house. Yea, I prefer her before Klytaimnestra my wedded wife; in no wise is she lacking beside her, neither in favour nor stature, nor wit nor skill. Yet for all this will I give her back, if that is better; rather would I see my folk whole than perishing. Only make ye me ready a prize of honour forthwith, lest I alone of all the Argives be disprized, which thing beseemeth not; for ye all behold how my prize is departing from me."

To him then made answer fleet-footed goodly Achilles: "Most noble son of Atreus, of all men most covetous, how shall the great-hearted Achaians give thee a meed of honour? We know naught of any wealth of common store, but what spoil soe'er we took from captured cities hath been apportioned, and it beseemeth not to beg all this back from the folk. Nay, yield thou the damsel to the god, and we Achaians will pay thee back threefold and fourfold, if ever Zeus grant us to sack some well-walled town of Troyland."

To him lord Agamemnon made answer and said: "Not in this wise, strong as thou art, O godlike Achilles, beguile thou me by craft; thou shalt not outwit me nor persuade me. Dost thou wish, that thou mayest keep thy meed of honour, for me to sit idle in bereavement, and biddest me give her back? Nay, if the great-hearted Achaians will give me a meed suited to my mind, that the recompense be equal — but if they give it not, then I myself will go and take a meed of honour, thine be it or Aias', or Odysseus' that I will take unto me; wroth shall he be to whomsoever I come. But for this we will take counsel hereafter; now let us launch a black ship on the great sea, and gather picked oarsmen, and set therein a hecatomb, and embark Chryseis of the fair cheeks herself, and let one of our counsellors be captain, Aias or Idomeneus or goodly Odysseus, or thou, Peleides, most redoubtable of men, to do sacrifice for us and propitiate the Far-darter."

Then Achilles fleet of foot looked at him scowling and said: "Ah me, thou clothed in shamelessness, thou of crafty mind, how shall any Achaian hearken to thy bidding with all his heart, be it to go a journey or to fight the foe amain? Not by reason of the Trojan spearmen came I hither to fight, for they have not wronged me;

never did they harry mine oxen nor my horses, nor ever waste my harvest in deep-soiled Phthia, the nurse of men; seeing there lieth between us long space of shadowy mountains and sounding sea; but thee, thou shameless one, followed we hither to make thee glad, by earning recompense at the Trojans' hands for Menelaos and for thee, thou dog-face! All this thou reckonest not nor takest thought thereof; and now thou threatenest thyself to take my meed of honour, wherefor I travailed much, and the sons of the Achaians gave it me. Never win I meed like unto thine, when the Achaians sack any populous citadel of Trojan men; my hands bear the brunt of furious war, but when the apportioning cometh then is thy meed far ampler, and I betake me to the ships with some small thing, yet mine own, when I have fought to weariness. Now will I depart to Phthia, seeing it is far better to return home on my beaked ships; nor am I minded here in dishonour to draw thee thy fill of riches and wealth."

Then Agamemnon king of men made answer to him: "Yea, flee, if thy soul be set thereon. It is not I that beseech thee to tarry for my sake; I have others by my side that shall do me honour, and above all Zeus, lord of counsel. Most hateful art thou to me of all kings, fosterlings of Zeus; thou ever lovest strife and wars and fightings. Though thou be very strong, yet that I ween is a gift to thee of God. Go home with thy ships and company and lord it among thy Myrmidons; I reck not aught of thee nor care I for thine indignation; and this shall be my threat to thee: seeing Phoebus Apollo bereaveth me of Chryseis, her with my ship and my company will I send back; and mine own self will I go to thy hut and take Briseis of the fair cheeks, even that thy meed of honour, that thou mayest well know how far greater I am than thou, and so shall another hereafter abhor to match his words with mine and rival me to my face."

So said he, and grief came upon Peleus' son, and his heart within his shaggy breast was divided in counsel, whether to draw his keen blade from his thigh and set the company aside and so slay Atreides, or to assuage his anger and curb his soul. While yet he doubted thereof in heart and soul, and was drawing his great sword from his sheath, Athene came to him from heaven, sent forth of the white-armed goddess Hera, whose heart loved both alike and had care for them. She stood behind Peleus' son and caught him by his golden hair, to him only visible, and of the rest no man beheld her. Then Achilles marvelled, and turned him about, and straightway knew Pallas Athene; and terribly shone her eyes. He spake to her winged words, and said: "Why now art thou come hither, thou daughter of aegis-bearing Zeus? Is it to behold the insolence of Agamemnon son of Atreus? Yea, I will tell thee that I deem shall even be brought to pass: by his own haughtiness shall he soon lose his life."

Then the bright-eyed goddess Athene spake to him again: "I came from heaven to stay thine anger, if perchance thou wilt hearken to me, being sent forth of the white-armed goddess Hera, that loveth you twain alike and careth for you. Go to now, cease from strife, and let not thine hand draw the sword; yet with words indeed revile him, even as it shall come to pass. For thus will I say to thee, and so it shall be fulfilled; hereafter shall goodly gifts come to thee, yea in threefold measure, by reason of this despite; hold thou thine hand, and hearken to us."

And Achilles fleet of foot made answer and said to her: "Goddess, needs must a man observe the saying of you twain, even though he be very wroth at heart; for so is the better way. Whosoever obeyeth the gods, to him they gladly hearken."

He said, and stayed his heavy hand on the silver hilt, and thrust the great sword back into the sheath, and was not disobedient to the saying of Athene; and she forthwith was departed to Olympus, to the other gods in the palace of aegis-bearing Zeus.

Then Peleus' son spake again with bitter words to Atreus' son, and in no wise ceased from anger: "Thou heavy with wine, thou with face of dog and heart of deer, never didst thou take courage to arm for battle among thy folk or to lay ambush with the princes of the Achaians; that to thee were even as death. Far better booteth it, forsooth, to seize for thyself the meed of honour of every man through the wide host of the Achaians that speaketh contrary to thee. Folk-devouring king! seeing thou rulest men of naught; else were this despite, thou son of Atreus, thy last. But I will speak my word to thee, and swear a mighty oath therewith: verily by this staff that shall no more put forth leaf or twig, seeing it hath for ever left its trunk among the hills, neither shall it grow green again, because the axe hath stripped it of leaves and bark; and now the sons of the Achaians that exercise judgment bear it in their hands, even they that by Zeus' command watch over the traditions — so shall this be a mighty oath in thine eyes — verily shall longing for Achilles come hereafter upon the sons of the Achaians one and all; and then wilt thou in no wise avail to save them, for all thy grief, when multitudes fall dying before manslaying Hector. Then shalt thou tear thy heart within thee for anger that thou didst in no wise honour the best of the Achaians."

So said Peleides and dashed to earth the staff studded with golden nails, and himself sat down; and over against him Atreides waxed furious. Then in their midst rose up Nestor, pleasant of speech, the clear-voiced orator of the Pylians, he from whose tongue flowed discourse sweeter than honey. Two generations of mortal men already had he seen perish, that had been of old time born and nurtured with him in goodly Pylos, and he was king among the third. He of good intent made harangue to them and said: "Alas, of a truth sore lamentation cometh upon the land of Achaia. Verily Priam would be glad and Priam's sons, and all the Trojans would have great joy of heart, were they to hear all this tale of strife between you twain that are chiefest of the Danaans in counsel and chiefest in battle. Nay, hearken to me; ye are younger both than

I. Of old days held I converse with better men even than you, and never did they make light of me. Yea, I never beheld such warriors, nor shall behold, as were Peirithoos and Dryas shepherd of the host and Kaineus and Exadios and godlike Polyphemos [and Theseus son of Aigeus, like to the immortals]. Mightiest of growth were they of all men upon the earth; mightiest they were and with the mightiest fought they, even the wild tribes of the mountain caves, and destroyed them utterly. And with these held I converse, being come from Pylos, from a distant land afar; for of themselves they summoned me. So I played my part in fight; and with them could none of men that are now on earth do battle. And they laid to heart my counsels and hearkened to my voice. Even so hearken ye also, for better is it to hearken. Neither do thou, though thou art very great, seize from him his damsel, but leave her as she was given at the first by the sons of the Achaians to be a meed of honour; nor do thou, son of Peleus, think to strive with a king, might against might; seeing that no common honour pertaineth to a sceptred king to whom Zeus apportioneth glory. Though thou be strong, and a goddess mother bare thee, yet his is the greater place, for he is king over more. And thou, Atreides, abate thy fury; nay, it is even I that beseech thee to let go thine anger with Achilles, who is made unto all the Achaians a mighty bulwark of evil war."

Then lord Agamemnon answered and said: "Yea verily, old man, all this thou sayest is according unto right. But this fellow would be above all others, he would be lord of all and king among all and captain to all; wherein I deem none will hearken to him. Though the immortal gods made him a spearman, do they therefore put revilings in his mouth for him to utter?"

Then goodly Achilles brake in on him and answered: "Yea, for I should be called coward and man of naught, if I yield to thee in every matter, howsoe'er thou bid. To others give now thine orders, not to me [play master; for thee I deem that I shall no more obey]. This, moreover, will I say to thee, and do thou lay it to thy heart. Know that not by violence will I strive for the damsel's sake, neither with thee nor any other; ye gave and ye have taken away. But of all else that is mine beside my fleet black ship, thereof shalt thou not take anything or bear it away against my will. Yea, go to now, make trial, that all these may see; forthwith thy dark blood shall gush about my spear."

Now when the twain had thus finished the battle of violent words, they stood up and dissolved the assembly beside the Achaian ships. Peleides went his way to his huts and trim ships with Menoitios' son and his company; and Atreides launched a fleet ship on the sea, and picked twenty oarsmen therefor, and embarked the hecatomb for the god, and brought Chryseis of the fair cheeks and set her therein; and Odysseus of many devices went to be their captain.

So these embarked and sailed over the wet ways; and Atreides bade the folk purify themselves. So they purified themselves, and cast the defilements into the sea and did sacrifice to Apollo, even unblemished hecatombs of bulls and goats, along the shore of the unvintaged sea; and the sweet savour arose to heaven eddying amid the smoke.

Thus were they busied throughout the host; but Agamemnon ceased not from the strife wherewith he threatened Achilles at the first; he spake to Talthybios and Eurybates that were his heralds and nimble squires: "Go ye to the tent of Achilles Peleus' son, and take Briseis of the fair cheeks by the hand and lead her hither; and if he give her not, then will I myself go, and more with me, and seize her; and that will be yet more grievous for him."

So saying he sent them forth, and laid stern charge upon them. Unwillingly went they along the beach of the unvintaged sea, and came to the huts and ships of the Myrmidons. Him found they sitting beside his hut and black ship; nor when he saw them was Achilles glad. So they in dread and reverence of the king stood, and spake to him no word, nor questioned him. But he knew in his heart, and spake to them: "All hail, ye heralds, messengers of Zeus and men, come near; ye are not guilty in my sight, but Agamemnon that sent you for the sake of the damsel Briseis. Go now, heaven-sprung Patroklos, bring forth the damsel, and give them her to lead away. Moreover, let the twain themselves be my witness before the face of the blessed gods and mortal men, yea and of him, that king untoward, against the day when there cometh need of me hereafter to save them all from shameful wreck. Of a truth he raveth with baleful mind, and hath not knowledge to look before and after, that so his Achaians might battle in safety beside their ships."

So said he, and Patroklos hearkened to his dear comrade, and led forth from the hut Briseis of the fair cheeks, and gave them her to lead away. So these twain took their way back along the Achaians' ships, and with them went the woman all unwilling. Then Achilles wept anon, and sat him down apart, aloof from his comrades on the beach of the grey sea, gazing across the boundless main; he stretched forth his hands and prayed instantly to his dear mother: "Mother, seeing thou didst of a truth bear me to so brief span of life, honour at the least ought the Olympian to have granted me, even Zeus that thundereth on high; but now doth he not honour me, no, not one whit. Verily Atreus' son, wide-ruling Agamemnon, hath done me dishonour; for he hath taken away my meed of honour and keepeth her of his own violent deed."

So spake he weeping, and his lady mother heard him as she sate in the sea-depths beside her aged sire. With speed arose she from the grey sea, like a mist, and sate her before the face of her weeping son, and stroked him with her hand, and spake and called on his name: "My child, why weepest thou? What sorrow hath entered into thy heart? Speak it forth, hide it not in thy mind, that both may know it."

Then with heavy moan Achilles fleet of foot spake to her: "Thou knowest it; why should I tell this to thee that knowest all! We had fared to Thebe, the holy city of Eëtion, and laid it waste and carried hither all the spoils. So the sons of the Achaians divided among them all aright; and for Atreides they set apart Chryseis of the fair cheeks. But Chryses, priest of Apollo the Far-darter, came unto the fleet ships of the mail-clad Achaians to win his daughter's freedom, and brought a ransom beyond telling, and bare in his hands the fillet of Apollo the Far-darter upon a golden staff, and made his prayer unto all the Achaians, and most of all to the two sons of Atreus, orderers of the host. Then all the other Achaians cried assent, to reverence the priest and accept his goodly ransom; yet the thing pleased not the heart of Agamemnon son of Atreus, but he roughly sent him away and laid stern charge upon him. So the old man went back in anger; and Apollo heard his prayers, seeing he loved him greatly, and he aimed against the Argives his deadly darts. So the people began to perish in multitudes, and the god's shafts ranged everywhither throughout the wide host of the Achaians. Then of full knowledge the seer declared to us the oracle of the Far-darter. Forthwith I first bade propitiate the god; but wrath gat hold upon Atreus' son thereat, and anon he stood up and spake a threatening word, that hath now been accomplished. Her the glancing-eyed Achaians are bringing on their fleet ship to Chryse, and bear with them offerings to the king; and the other but now the heralds went and took from my hut, even the daughter of Briseus, whom the sons of the Achaians gave me. Thou therefore, if indeed thou canst, guard thine own son; betake thee to Olympus and beseech Zeus by any deed or word whereby thou ever didst make glad his heart. For oft have I heard thee proclaiming in my father's halls and telling that thou alone amid the immortals didst save the son of Kronos, lord of the storm-cloud, from shameful wreck, when all the other Olympians would have bound him, even Hera and Poseidon and Pallas Athene. Then didst thou, O goddess, enter in and loose him from his bonds, having with speed summoned to high Olympus him of the hundred arms whom gods call Briareus, but all men call Aigaion; for he is mightier even than his father — so he sate him by Kronion's side rejoicing in his triumph, and the blessed gods feared him withal and bound not Zeus. This bring thou to his remembrance and sit by him and clasp his knees, if perchance he will give succour to the Trojans; and for the Achaians, hem them among their ships' sterns about the bay, given over to slaughter; that they may make trial of their king, and that even Atreides, wide-ruling Agamemnon, may perceive his blindness, in that he honoured not at all the best of the Achaians."

Then Thetis weeping made answer to him: "Ah me, my child, why reared I thee, cursed in my motherhood? Would thou hadst been left tearless and griefless amid the ships, seeing thy lot is very brief and endureth no long while; but now art thou made short-lived alike and lamentable beyond all men; in an evil hour I bare thee in our halls. But I will go myself to snow-clad Olympus to

tell this thy saying to Zeus, whose joy is in the thunder, if perchance he may hearken to me. But tarry thou now amid thy fleet-
faring ships, and continue wroth with the Achaians, and refrain
utterly from battle: for Zeus went yesterday to Okeanos, unto the
noble Ethiopians for a feast, and all the gods followed with him;
but on the twelfth day will he return to Olympus, and then will I
fare to Zeus' palace of the bronze threshold, and will kneel to him
and think to win him."

So saying she went her way and left him there, vexed in spirit
for the fair-girdled woman's sake, whom they had taken perforce
despite his will: and meanwhile Odysseus came to Chryse with the
holy hecatomb. When they were now entered within the deep
haven, they furled their sails and laid them in the black ship, and
lowered the mast by the forestays and brought it to the crutch with
speed, and rowed her with oars to the anchorage. Then they cast
out the mooring stones and made fast the hawsers, and so themselves went forth on to the sea-beach, and forth they brought the
hecatomb for the Far-darter Apollo, and forth came Chryseis withal
from the seafaring ship. Then Odysseus of many counsels brought
her to the altar and gave her into her father's arms, and spake unto
him: "Chryses, Agamemnon king of men sent me hither to bring
thee thy daughter, and to offer to Phoebus a holy hecatomb on the
Danaans' behalf, wherewith to propitiate the king that hath now
brought sorrow and lamentation on the Argives."

So saying he gave her to his arms, and he gladly took his dear
child; and anon they set in order for the god the holy hecatomb
about his well-builded altar; next washed they their hands and took
up the barley meal. Then Chryses lifted up his hands and prayed
aloud for them: "Hearken to me, god of the silver bow that standest over Chryse and holy Killa, and rulest Tenedos with might;
even as erst thou heardest my prayer, and didst me honour, and
mightily afflictedst the people of the Achaians, even so now fulfil
me this my desire; remove thou from the Danaans forthwith the
loathly pestilence."

So spake he in prayer, and Phoebus Apollo heard him. Now
when they had prayed and sprinkled the barley meal, first they
drew back the victims' heads and slaughtered them and flayed them,
and cut slices from the thighs and wrapped them in fat, making a
double fold, and laid raw collops thereon, and the old man burnt
them on cleft wood and made libation over them of gleaming wine;
and at his side the young men in their hands held five-pronged
forks. Now when the thighs were burnt and they had tasted the
vitals, then sliced they all the rest and pierced it through with spits,
and roasted it carefully, and drew all off again. So when they
had rest from the task and had made ready the banquet, they
feasted, nor was their heart aught stinted of the fair banquet. But
when they had put away from them the desire of meat and drink,
the young men crowned the bowls with wine, and gave each man
his portion after the drink-offering had been poured into the cups.

So all day long worshipped they the god with music, singing the beautiful paean, the sons of the Achaians making music to the Far-darter; and his heart was glad to hear. And when the sun went down and darkness came on them, they laid them to sleep beside the ship's hawsers; and when rosy-fingered Dawn appeared, the child of morning, then set they sail for the wide camp of the Achaians; and Apollo the Far-darter sent them a favouring gale. They set up their mast and spread the white sails forth, and the wind filled the sail's belly and the dark wave sang loud about the stem as the ship made way, and she sped across the wave, accomplishing her journey. So when they were now come to the wide camp of the Achaians, they drew up their black ship to land high upon the sands, and set in line the long props beneath her; and themselves were scattered amid their huts and ships.

But he sat by his swift-faring ships, still wroth, even the heaven-sprung son of Peleus, Achilles fleet of foot; he betook him neither to the assembly that is the hero's glory, neither to war, but consumed his heart in tarrying in his place, and yearned for the war-cry and for battle.

Now when the twelfth morn thereafter was come, then the gods that are for ever fared to Olympus all in company, led of Zeus. And Thetis forgat not her son's charge, but rose up from the sea-wave, and at early morn mounted up to great heaven and Olympus. There found she Kronos' son of the far-sounding voice sitting apart from all on the topmost peak of many-ridged Olympus. So she sat before his face and with her left hand clasped his knees, and with her right touched him beneath his chin, and spake in prayer to king Zeus son of Kronos: "Father Zeus, if ever I gave thee aid amid the immortal gods, whether by word or deed, fulfil thou this my desire: do honour to my son, that is doomed to earliest death of all men: now hath Agamemnon king of men done him dishonour, for he hath taken away his meed of honour and keepeth her of his own violent deed. But honour thou him, Zeus of Olympus, lord of counsel; grant thou victory to the Trojans the while, until the Achaians do my son honour and exalt him with recompense."

So spake she; but Zeus the cloud-gatherer said no word to her, and sat long time in silence. But even as Thetis had clasped his knees, so held she by him clinging, and questioned him yet a second time: "Promise me now this thing verily, and bow thy head thereto; or else deny me, seeing there is naught for thee to fear; that I may know full well how I among all gods am least in honour."

Then Zeus the cloud-gatherer, sore troubled, spake to her: "Verily it is a sorry matter, if thou wilt set me at variance with Hera, whene'er she provoketh me with taunting words. Even now she upbraideth me ever amid the immortal gods, and saith that I aid the Trojans in battle. But do thou now depart again, lest Hera mark aught; and I will take thought for these things to fulfil them. Come now, I will bow my head to thee, that thou mayest be of good courage; for that, of my part, is the surest token amid the immortals; no word of mine is revocable nor false nor unfulfilled when the bowing of my head hath pledged it."

Kronion spake, and bowed his dark brow, and the ambrosial locks waved from the king's immortal head; and he made great Olympus quake.

Thus the twain took counsel and parted; she leapt therewith into the deep sea from glittering Olympus, and Zeus fared to his own palace. All the gods in company arose from their seats before their father's face; neither ventured any to await his coming, but they stood up all before him. So he sate him there upon his throne; but Hera saw, and was not ignorant how that the daughter of the Ancient of the sea, Thetis the silver-footed, had devised counsel with him. Anon with taunting words spake she to Zeus the son of Kronos: "Now who among the gods, thou crafty of mind, hath devised counsel with thee? It is ever thy good pleasure to hold aloof from me and in secret meditation to give thy judgments, nor of thine own good will hast thou ever brought thyself to declare unto me the thing thou purposest."

Then the father of gods and men made answer to her: "Hera, think not thou to know all my sayings; hard they are for thee, even though thou art my wife. But whichsoever it is seemly for thee to hear, none sooner than thou shall know, be he god or man. Only when I will to take thought aloof from the gods, then do not thou ask of every matter nor make question."

Then Hera the ox-eyed queen made answer to him. "Most dread son of Kronos, what word is this thou hast spoken? Yea, surely of old I have not asked thee nor made question, but in very quietness thou devisest all thou wilt. But now is my heart sore afraid lest thou have been won over by silver-footed Thetis, daughter of the Ancient of the sea, for she at early morn sat by thee and clasped thy knees. To her I deem thou gavest a sure pledge that thou wilt do honour to Achilles, and lay many low beside the Achaians' ships."

To her made answer Zeus the cloud-gatherer: "Lady, Good lack! ever art thou imagining, nor can I escape thee; yet shalt thou in no wise have power to fulfil, but wilt be the further from my heart; that shall be even the worse for thee. And if it be so, then such must my good pleasure be. Abide thou in silence and hearken to my bidding, lest all the gods that are in Olympus keep not off from thee my visitation, when I put forth my hands unapproachable against thee."

He said, and Hera the ox-eyed queen was afraid, and sat in silence, curbing her heart; but throughout Zeus' palace the gods of heaven were troubled. Then Hephaistos the famed craftsman began to make harangue among them, to do kindness to his dear mother, white-armed Hera: "Verily this will be a sorry matter, neither any more endurable, if ye twain thus fight for mortals' sakes, and bring wrangling among the gods; neither will there any more be joy of the goodly feast, seeing that evil triumpheth. So I give

counsel to my mother, though herself is wise, to do kindness to our
dear father Zeus, that our father upbraid us not again and cast the
banquet in confusion. What if the Olympian, the lord of the lightning, will to dash us from our seats! for he is strongest far. Nay,
approach thou him with gentle words, then will the Olympian forthwith be gracious unto us."

So speaking he rose up and set in his dear mother's hand the
twy-handled cup, and spake to her: "Be of good courage, mother
mine, and endure, though thou art vexed, lest I behold thee, that
art so dear, chastised before mine eyes, and then shall I not be able
for all my sorrow to save thee; for the Olympian is a hard foe to
face. Yea, once ere this, when I was fain to save thee, he caught me
by my foot and hurled me from the heavenly threshold; all day I
flew, and at the set of sun I fell in Lemnos, and little life was in me.
There did the Sintian folk forthwith tend me for my fall."

He spake, and the white-armed goddess Hera smiled, and smiling took the cup at her son's hand. Then he poured wine to all the
other gods from right to left, ladling the sweet nectar from the
bowl. And laughter unquenchable arose amid the blessed gods to
see Hephaistos bustling through the palace.

So feasted they all day till the setting of the sun; nor was their
soul aught stinted of the fair banquet, nor of the beauteous lyre that
Apollo held, and the Muses singing alternately with sweet voice.

Now when the bright light of the sun was set, these went each
to his own house to sleep, where each one had his palace made with
cunning device by famed Hephaistos the lame god; and Zeus the
Olympian, the lord of lightning, departed to his couch where he was
wont of old to take his rest, whenever sweet sleep visited him.
There went he up and slept, and beside him was Hera of the golden
throne.

[tr. LANG, LEAF, MYERS]

[The next day, at the instigation of Zeus, Agamemnon leads the Greek
forces out for a general engagement. An attempt is made to settle the
war by single combat between Menelaus and Paris, but Aphrodite rescues
Paris as he is being defeated, and Menelaus is wounded by an arrow
treacherously shot by one of the Trojans. A general battle follows, in
which the Greeks are at first successful; Aphrodite and Ares intervene to
rally the Trojans, but are wounded and driven off the field by Athene and
Diomedes.]

BOOK VI

How Diomedes and Glaukos being about to fight, were known to each
other, and parted in friendliness. And how Hector returning to the city
bade farewell to Andromache his wife.

So was the dread fray of Trojans and Achaians left to itself, and
the battle swayed oft this way and that across the plain, as they
aimed against each other their bronze-shod javelins, between Simoeis
and the streams of Xanthos.

First Aias son of Telamon, bulwark of the Achaians, brake a battalion of the Trojans and brought his comrades salvation, smiting a warrior that was chiefest among the Thracians, Eussoros' son Akamas the goodly and great. Him first he smote upon his thick-crested helmet-ridge and drave into his forehead, so that the point of bronze pierced into the bone; and darkness shrouded his eyes.

Then Diomedes of the loud war-cry slew Axylos Teuthranos' son that dwelt in stablished Arisbe, a man of substance dear to his fellows; for his dwelling was by the roadside and he entertained all men. Howbeit of all these was there then not one to meet the foe before his face and save him from fell destruction; but Diomedes took the life of both of them, even of him and Kalesios his squire that now was the driver of his chariot; so passed both below the earth.

And Euryalos slew Dresos and Opheltios, and followed after Aisepos and Pedasos whom erst the fountain-nymph Abarbarea bare to noble Boukolion. Now Boukolion was son of proud Laomedon, his eldest born, begotten of a mother unwedded; and as he tended his flocks he had converse with the nymph in love, and she conceived and bare twin sons. And lo, the strength of these and their glorious limbs Mekisteus' son unstrung, and stripped the armour from their shoulders. And stubborn Polypoites slew Astyalos, and Odysseus with spear of bronze laid low Pidytes of Perkote, and so did Teukros to goodly Aretaon. Then was Ableros killed by the glistening spear of Antilochos, Nestor's son, and Elatos by Agamemnon king of men; beside the banks of fair-flowing Satnioeis dwelt he in steep Pedasos. And Leïtos the warrior caught Phylakos, as he fled; and Eurypylos slew Melanthios.

Now did Menelaos of the loud war-cry take Adrestos alive; for his horses took flight across the plain, and stumbling in a tamarisk bough brake the curved car at the pole's foot; so they themselves fared towards the city where the rest were fleeing in rout, and their lord rolled from out the car beside the wheel, prone in the dust upon his face. Then came Atreus' son Menelaos to his side bearing his far-shadowing spear. Thereat Adrestos caught him by his knees and besought him: "Take me captive, thou son of Atreus, and accept a worthy ransom; many a treasure is stored up in my father's rich palace, bronze and gold and smithied iron; thereof would my father yield thee ransom beyond the telling, if he but heard that I am alive at the ships of the Achaians."

So spake he, and moved the spirit in his breast. And now had he forthwith given him to his squire to lead him to the Achaians' fleet ships, but that Agamemnon came running to meet him, and spake a word of chiding to him: "Good Menelaos, why art thou so careful of the foeman? Have then such good deeds been wrought thee in thy house by Trojans? Of them let not one escape sheer destruction at our hands, not even the man-child that the mother beareth in her womb; let not even him escape, but all perish together out of Ilios, uncared for and unknown."

So spake the hero and turned his brother's mind with righteous persuasion; so with his hand he thrust the hero Adrestos from him, and lord Agamemnon smote him in the flank, and he was overthrown, and Atreus' son set his heel upon his chest and plucked forth his ashen spear.

Then Nestor called to the Argives with far-reaching shout: "My friends, Danaan warriors, men of Ares' company, let no man now take thought of spoils to tarry behind, that he may bring the greatest burden to the ships; but let us slay the foemen. Thereafter shall ye at your ease also strip of their spoil the dead corpses about the plain."

So spake he and stirred the spirit and soul of every man. Now had the Trojans been chased again by the Achaians, dear to Ares, up into Ilios, in their weakness overcome, but that Priam's son Helenos, far best of augurs, stood by Aineias' side and Hector's, and spake to them: "Aineias and Hector, seeing that on you lieth the task of war in chief of Trojans and Lykians, because for every issue ye are foremost both for fight and counsel, stand ye your ground, and range the host everywhither to rally them before the gates, ere yet they fall fleeing in their women's arms, and be made a rejoicing to the foe. Then when ye have aroused all our battalions we will abide here and fight the Danaans, though in sore weariness; for necessity presseth us hard: but thou, Hector, go into the city, and speak there to thy mother and mine; let her gather the aged wives to bright-eyed Athene's temple in the upper city, and with her key open the doors of the holy house; and let her lay the robe, that seemeth to her the most gracious and greatest in her hall and far dearest unto herself, upon the knees of beauteous-haired Athene; and vow to her to sacrifice in her temple twelve sleek kine, that have not felt the goad, if she will have mercy on the city and the Trojans' wives and little children. So may she perchance hold back Tydeus' son from holy Ilios, the furious spearman, the mighty deviser of rout, whom in good sooth I deem to have proved himself mightiest of the Achaians. Never in this wise feared we Achilles, prince of men, who they say is born of a goddess; nay, but he that we see is beyond measure furious; none can match him for might."

So spake he, and Hector disregarded not his brother's word, but leapt forthwith from his chariot in his armour to earth, and brandishing two sharp spears passed everywhere through the host, rousing them to battle, and stirred the dread war-cry. So they were rallied and stood to face the Achaians, and the Argives gave ground and ceased from slaughter, and deemed that some immortal had descended from starry heaven to bring the Trojans succour, in such wise rallied they. Then Hector called to the Trojans with far-reaching shout: "Oh high-souled Trojans and ye far-famed allies, quit you like men, my friends, and take thought of impetuous courage, while I depart to Ilios and bid the elders of the council and our wives pray to the gods and vow them hecatombs."

So saying Hector of the glancing helm departed, and the black hide beat on either side against his ankles and his neck, even the rim that ran uttermost about his bossed shield.

Now Glaukos son of Hippolochos and Tydeus' son met in the mid-space of the foes, eager to do battle. Thus when the twain were come nigh in onset on each other, to him first spake Diomedes of the loud war-cry: "Who art thou, noble sir, of mortal men? For never have I beheld thee in glorious battle ere this, yet now hast thou far outstripped all men in thy hardihood, seeing thou abidest my far-shadowing spear. Luckless are the fathers whose children face my might. But if thou art some immortal come down from heaven, then will not I fight with heavenly gods. Nay moreover even Dryas' son mighty Lykurgos was not for long when he strove with heavenly gods, he that erst chased through the goodly land of Nysa the nursing-mothers of frenzied Dionysos; and they all cast their wands upon the ground, smitten with murderous Lykurgos' ox-goad. Then Dionysos fled and plunged beneath the salt sea-wave, and Thetis took him to her bosom, affrighted, for a mighty trembling had seized him at his foe's rebuke. But with Lykurgos the gods that live at ease were wroth, and Kronos' son made him blind, and he was not for long, because he was hated of all the immortal gods. So would neither I be fain to fight the blessed gods. But if thou art of men that eat the fruit of the field, come nigh, that anon thou mayest enter the toils of destruction."

Then Hippolochos' glorious son made answer to him: "Great-hearted Tydeides, why enquirest thou of my generation? Even as are the generations of leaves such are those likewise of men; the leaves that be the wind scattereth on the earth, and the forest buddeth and putteth forth more again, when the season of spring is at hand; so of the generations of men one putteth forth and another ceaseth. Yet if thou wilt, have thine answer, that thou mayest well know our lineage, whereof many men have knowledge. There is a city Ephyre in the heart of Argos, pasture land of horses, and there dwelt Sisyphos that was craftiest of men, Sisyphos son of Aiolos; and he begat a son, even Glaukos, and Glaukos begat noble Bellerophon. To him the gods granted beauty and lovely manhood; but Proitos in his heart devised ill for him, and being mightier far drave him from the land of the Argives, whom Zeus had made subject to his sceptre. Now Proitos' wife, goodly Anteia, lusted after him, to have converse in secret love, but no whit prevailed she, for the uprightness of his heart, on wise Bellerophon. Then spake she lyingly to king Proitos: "Die, Proitos, or else slay Bellerophon, that would have converse in love with me against my will." So spake she, and anger gat hold upon the king at that he heard. To slay him he forbare, for his soul had shame of that; but he sent him to Lykia, and gave him tokens of woe, graving in a folded tablet many deadly things, and bade him shew these to Anteia's father, that he might be slain. So fared he to Lykia by the blameless convoy of the gods. Now when he came to Lykia and the stream of

Xanthos, then did the king of wide Lykia honour him with all his heart; nine days he entertained him and killed nine oxen. And when on the tenth day rosy-fingered Dawn appeared, then he questioned him and asked to see what token he bare from his son-in-law, even Proitos. Now when he had received of him Proitos' evil token, first he bade him slay Chimaira the unconquerable. Of divine birth was she and not of men, in front a lion, and behind a serpent, and in the midst a goat; and she breathed dread fierceness of blazing fire. And her he slew, obedient to the signs of heaven. Next fought he with the famed Solymi; this, said he, was the mightiest battle of warriors wherein he entered. And thirdly he slew the Amazons, women peers of men. And as he turned back therefrom, the king devised another cunning wile; he picked from wide Lykia the bravest men, and set an ambush. But these returned nowise home again; for noble Bellerophon slew them all. So when the king now knew that he was the brave offspring of a god, he kept him there, and plighted him his daughter, and gave him the half of all the honour of his kingdom; moreover the Lykians meted him a domain pre-eminent above all, fair with vineyards and tilth to possess it. And his wife bare wise Bellerophon three children, Isandros and Hippolochos and Laodameia. With Laodameia lay Zeus the lord of counsel, and she bare godlike Sarpedon, the warrior with arms of bronze. But when even Bellerophon came to be hated of all the gods, then wandered he alone in the Aleian plain, devouring his own soul, and avoiding the paths of men; and Isandros his son was slain by Ares insatiate of battle, as he fought against the famed Solymi, and his daughter was slain in wrath of goldgleaming Artemis. But Hippolochos begat me, and of him do I declare me to be sprung; he sent me to Troy and bade me very instantly to be ever the best and to excel all other men, nor put to shame the lineage of my fathers that were of noblest blood in Ephyre and in wide Lykia. This is the lineage and blood whereof I avow myself to be."

So said he, and Diomedes of the loud war-cry was glad. He planted his spear in the bounteous earth and with soft words spake to the shepherd of the host: "Surely then thou art to me a guestfriend of old times through my father: for goodly Oineus of yore entertained noble Bellerophon in his halls and kept him twenty days. Moreover they gave each the other goodly gifts of friendship; Oineus gave a belt bright with purple, and Bellerophon a gold twyhandled cup, the which when I came I left in my palace. But of Tydeus I remember naught, seeing I was yet little when he left me, what time the Achaian host perished at Thebes. Therefore now am I to thee a dear guest-friend in midmost Argos, and thou in Lykia, whene'er I fare to your land. So let us shun each other's spears, even amid the throng; Trojans are there in multitudes and famous allies for me to slay, whoe'er it be that God vouchsafeth me and my feet overtake; and for thee are there Achaians in multitude, to slay whome'er thou canst. But let us make exchange of arms between us, that these also may know how we avow ourselves to be guest-friends by lineage."

So spake the twain, and leaping from their cars clasped each the other by his hand, and pledged their faith. But now Zeus son of Kronos took from Glaukos his wits, in that he made exchange with Diomedes Tydeus' son of golden armour for bronze, the price of five score oxen for the price of nine.

Now when Hector came to the Skaian gates and to the oak-tree, there came running round about him the Trojans' wives and daughters, enquiring of sons and brethren and friends and husbands. But he bade them thereat all in turn pray to the gods; but sorrow hung over many.

But when he came to Priam's beautiful palace, adorned with polished colonnades — and in it were fifty chambers of polished stone, builded hard by one another, wherein Priam's sons slept beside their wedded wives; and for his daughters over against them on the other side within the courtyard were twelve roofed chambers of polished stone builded hard by one another, wherein slept Priam's sons-in-law beside their chaste wives — then came there to meet him his bountiful mother, leading with her Laodike, fairest of her daughters to look on; and she clasped her hand in his, and spake, and called upon his name: "My son, why hast thou left violent battle to come hither? Surely the sons of the Achaians — name of evil! — press thee hard in fight about thy city, and so thy spirit hath brought thee hither, to come and stretch forth thy hands to Zeus from the citadel. But tarry till I bring thee honey-sweet wine, that thou mayest pour libation to Zeus and all the immortals first, and then shalt thou thyself also be refreshed if thou wilt drink. When a man is awearied wine greatly maketh his strength to wax, even as thou art awearied in fighting for thy fellows."

Then great Hector of the glancing helm answered her: "Bring me no honey-hearted wine, my lady mother, lest thou cripple me of my courage and I be forgetful of my might. Moreover I have awe to make libation of gleaming wine to Zeus with hands unwashen; nor can it be in any wise that one should pray to the son of Kronos, god of the storm-cloud, all defiled with blood and filth. But go thou to the temple of Athene, driver of the spoil, with offerings, and gather the aged wives together; and the robe that seemeth to thee the most gracious and greatest in thy palace, and dearest unto thyself, that lay thou upon the knees of beauteous-haired Athene, and vow to her to sacrifice in her temple twelve sleek kine, that have not felt the goad, if she will have mercy on the city and the Trojans' wives and little children. So may she perchance hold back Tydeus' son from holy Ilios, the furious spearman, the mighty deviser of rout. So go thou to the temple of Athene, driver of the spoil; and I will go after Paris, to summon him, if perchance he will hearken to my voice. Would that the earth forthwith might swallow him up! The Olympian fostered him to be a sore bane to the Trojans and to great-hearted Priam, and to Priam's sons. If I but saw him going down to the gates of death, then might I deem that my heart had forgotten its sorrow."

So said he, and she went unto the hall, and called to her hand-maidens, and they gathered the aged wives throughout the city. Then she herself went down to her fragrant chamber where were her embroidered robes, the work of Sidonian women, whom godlike Alexandros himself brought from Sidon, when he sailed over the wide sea, that journey wherein he brought home high-born Helen. Of these Hekabe took one to bear for an offering to Athene, the one that was fairest for adornment and greatest, and shone like a star, and lay nethermost of all. Then went she her way and the multitude of aged wives hasted after her.

Now when they came to the temple of Athene in the citadel, fair-cheeked Theano opened them the doors, even Kisseus' daughter, wife of horse-taming Antenor; for her the Trojans had made priest-ess of Athene. Then lifted they all their hands to Athene with lamentation: and fair-cheeked Theano took the robe and laid it on the knees of beauteous-haired Athene, and lifted up her voice and prayed to the daughter of great Zeus: "Lady Athene, saviour of the city, fair among goddesses, break now Diomedes' spear, and grant moreover that himself may fall prone before the Skaian gates; that we may sacrifice thee now forthwith in thy temple twelve sleek kine, that have not felt the goad, if thou wilt have mercy on the city and the Trojans' wives and little children." So spake she pray-ing, but Pallas Athene denied the prayer.

So were these praying to the daughter of great Zeus; and Hector was come to Alexandros' fair palace, that himself had builded with them that were most excellent carpenters then in deep-soiled Troy-land; these made him his chamber and hall and courtyard hard by to Priam and Hector, in the upper city. There entered in Hector dear to Zeus, and his hand bare his spear, eleven cubits long: before his face glittered the bronze spear-point, and a ring of gold ran round about it. And he found Paris in his chamber busied with his beauteous arms, his shield and breastplate, and handling his curved bow; and Helen of Argos sate among her serving-women and ap-pointed brave handiwork for her handmaidens. Then when Hec-tor saw him he rebuked him with scornful words: "Good sir, thou dost not well to cherish this rancour in thy heart. The folk are perishing about the city and high wall in battle, and for thy sake the battle-cry is kindled and war around this city; yea thyself would-est thou fall out with another, didst thou see him shrinking from hateful war. Up then, lest the city soon be scorched with burning fire."

And godlike Alexandros answered him: "Hector, since in meas-ure thou chidest me and not beyond measure, therefore will I tell thee; lay thou it to thine heart and hearken to me. Not by reason so much of the Trojans, for wrath and indignation, sate I me in my chamber, but fain would I yield me to my sorrow. Even now my wife hath persuaded me with soft words, and urged me into battle; and I moreover, even I, deem that it will be better so; for victory shifteth from man to man. Go to then, tarry awhile, let me put on my armour of war; or else fare thou forth, and I will follow; and I think to overtake thee."

So said he, but Hector of the glancing helm answered him not a word. But Helen spake to him with gentle words: "My brother, even mine that am a dog, mischievous and abominable, would that on the day when my mother bare me at the first, an evil storm-wind had caught me away to a mountain or a billow of the loud-sounding sea, where the billow might have swept me away before all these things came to pass. Howbeit, seeing the gods devised all these ills in this wise, would that then I had been mated with a better man that felt dishonour and the multitude of men's reproachings. But as for him, neither hath he now sound heart, nor ever will have; thereof deem I moreover that he will reap the fruit. But now come, enter in and sit thee here upon this bench, my brother, since thy heart chiefly trouble hath encompassed, for the sake of me, that am a dog, and for Alexandros' sin; on whom Zeus bringeth evil doom, that even in days to come we may be a song in the ears of men that shall be hereafter."

Then great Hector of the glancing helm answered her: "Bid me not sit, Helen, of thy love; thou wilt not persuade me. Already my heart is set to succour the men of Troy, that have great desire for me that am not with them. But rouse thou this fellow, yea let himself make speed, to overtake me yet within the city. For I shall go into mine house to behold my housefolk and my dear wife, and infant boy; for I know not if I shall return home to them again, or if the gods will now overthrow me at the hands of the Achaians."

So spake Hector of the glancing helm and departed; and anon he came to his well-stablished house. But he found not white-armed Andromache in the halls; she with her boy and fair-robed handmaiden had taken her stand upon the tower, weeping and wailing. And when Hector found not his noble wife within, he came and stood upon the threshold, and spake amid the serving-women: "Come tell me now true, my serving-women. Whither went white-armed Andromache forth from the hall? Hath she gone out to my sisters or unto my brothers' fair-robed wives, or to Athene's temple, where all the fair-tressed Trojan women propitiate the awful goddess?"

Then a busy housedame spake in answer to him: "Hector, seeing thou straitly chargest us tell thee true, neither hath she gone out to any of thy sisters or thy brothers' fair-robed wives, neither to Athene's temple, where all the fair-tressed Trojan women are propitiating the awful goddess; but she went to the great tower of Ilios, because she heard the Trojans were hard pressed, and great victory was for the Achaians. So hath she come in haste to the wall, like unto one frenzied; and the nurse with her beareth the child."

So spake the housedame, and Hector hastened from his house back by the same way down the well-builded streets. When he had passed through the great city and was come to the Skaian gates, whereby he was minded to issue upon the plain, then came his dear-won wife, running to meet him, even Andromache daughter of great-hearted Eëtion, Eëtion that dwelt beneath wooded Plakos, in Thebe under Plakos, and was king of the men of Kilikia; for his daughter was wife to bronze-harnessed Hector. So she met him now, and with her went the handmaid bearing in her bosom the tender boy, the little child, Hector's loved son, like unto a beautiful star. Him Hector called Skamandrios, but all the folk Astyanax; for only Hector guarded Ilios. So now he smiled and gazed at his boy silently, and Andromache stood by his side weeping, and clasped her hand in his, and spake and called upon his name. "Dear my lord, this thy hardihood will undo thee, neither hast thou any pity for thine infant boy, nor for me forlorn that soon shall be thy widow; for soon will the Achaians all set upon thee and slay thee. But it were better for me to go down to the grave if I lose thee; for never more will any comfort be mine, when once thou, even thou, hast met thy fate, but only sorrow. Moreover I have no father nor lady mother: my father was slain of goodly Achilles, for he wasted the populous city of the Kilikians, even high-gated Thebe, and slew Eëtion; yet he despoiled him not, for his soul had shame of that, but he burnt him in his inlaid armour and raised a barrow over him; and all about were elm-trees planted by the mountain nymphs, daughters of aegis-bearing Zeus. And the seven brothers that were mine within our halls, all these on the selfsame day went within the house of Hades; for fleet-footed goodly Achilles slew them all amid their kine of trailing gait and white-fleeced sheep. And my mother, that was queen beneath wooded Plakos, her brought he hither with the other spoils, but afterward took a ransom untold to set her free; but in her father's halls was she smitten by the Archer Artemis. Nay, Hector, thou art to me father and lady mother, yea and brother, even as thou art my goodly husband. Come now, have pity and abide here upon the tower, lest thou make thy child an orphan and thy wife a widow. And stay thy folk beside the fig-tree, where best the city may be scaled and the wall is assailable. Thrice came thither the most valiant that are with the two Aiantes and famed Idomeneus and the sons of Atreus and Tydeus' valiant son, and essayed to enter; whether one skilled in soothsaying revealed it to them, or whether their own spirit urgeth and biddeth them on."

Then great Hector of the glancing helm answered her: "Surely I take thought for all these things, my wife; but I have very sore shame of the Trojans and Trojan dames with trailing robes, if like a coward I shrink away from battle. Moreover mine own soul forbiddeth me, seeing I have learnt ever to be valiant and fight in the forefront of the Trojans, winning my father's great glory and mine own. Yea of a surety I know this in heart and soul; the day shall come for holy Ilios to be laid low, and Priam and the folk of Priam of the good ashen spear. Yet doth the anguish of the Trojans hereafter not so much trouble me neither Hekabe's own, neither king Priam's, neither my brethren's, the many and brave that shall fall in the dust before their foemen, as doth thine anguish in the day when some mail-clad Achaian shall lead thee weeping and rob thee of the light of freedom. So shalt thou abide in Argos and ply the loom at another woman's bidding, and bear water from fount Messeis or Hypereia, being grievously entreated, and sore constraint shall be laid upon thee. And then shall one say that beholdeth thee weep: 'This is the wife of Hector, that was foremost in battle of the horse-taming Trojans when men fought about Ilios.' Thus shall one say hereafter, and fresh grief will be thine for lack of such an husband as thou hadst to ward off the day of thraldom. But me in death may the heaped-up earth be covering, ere I hear thy crying and thy carrying into captivity."

So spake glorious Hector, and stretched out his arm to his boy. But the child shrunk crying to the bosom of his fair-girdled nurse, dismayed at his dear father's aspect, and in dread at the bronze and horse-hair crest that he beheld nodding fiercely from the helmet's top. Then his dear father laughed aloud, and his lady mother; forthwith glorious Hector took the helmet from his head, and laid it, all gleaming, upon the earth; then kissed he his dear son and dandled him in his arms, and spake in prayer to Zeus and all the gods, "O Zeus and all ye gods, vouchsafe ye that this my son may likewise prove even as I, pre-eminent amid the Trojans, and as valiant in might, and be a great king of Ilios. Then may men say of him, 'Far greater is he than his father' as he returneth home from battle; and may he bring with him blood-stained spoils from the foeman he hath slain, and may his mother's heart be glad."

So spake he, and laid his son in his dear wife's arms; and she took him to her fragrant bosom, smiling tearfully. And her husband had pity to see her, and caressed her with his hand, and spake and called upon her name: "Dear one, I pray thee be not of oversorrowful heart; no man against my fate shall hurl me to Hades; only destiny, I ween, no man hath escaped, be he coward or be he valiant, when once he hath been born. But go thou to thine house and see to thine own tasks, the loom and distaff, and bid thine handmaidens ply their work; but for war shall men provide and I in chief of all men that dwell in Ilios."

So spake glorious Hector, and took up his horse-hair crested helmet; and his dear wife departed to her home oft looking back, and letting fall big tears. Anon she came to the well-stablished house of man-slaying Hector, and found therein her many handmaidens, and stirred lamentation in them all. So bewailed they Hector, while yet he lived, within his house: for they deemed that he would no more come back to them from battle, nor escape the fury of the hands of the Achaians.

Neither lingered Paris long in his lofty house, but clothed on him his brave armour, bedight with bronze, and hasted through the city,

trusting to his nimble feet. Even as when a stalled horse, full-fed
at the manger, breaketh his tether and speedeth at the gallop across
the plain, being wont to bathe him in the fair-flowing stream, exultingly; and holdeth his head on high, and his mane floateth about
his shoulders, and he trusteth in his glory, and nimbly his limbs bear
him to the haunts and pasturage of mares; even so Priam's son
Paris, glittering in his armour like the shining sun, strode down
from high Pergamos laughingly, and his swift feet bare him. Forthwith he overtook his brother noble Hector, even as he was on the
point to turn him away from the spot where he had dallied with his
wife. To him first spake godlike Alexandros: "Sir, in good sooth
I have delayed thee in thine haste by my tarrying, and came not
rightly as thou badest me."

And Hector of the glancing helm answered him and said: "Good
brother, no man that is rightminded could make light of thy doings
in fight, seeing thou art strong: but thou art wilfully remiss and
hast no care; and for this my heart is grieved within me, that I hear
shameful words concerning thee in the Trojans' mouths, who for
thy sake endure much toil. But let us be going; all this will we
make good hereafter, if Zeus ever vouchsafe us to set before the
heavenly gods that are for everlasting the cup of deliverance in our
halls, when we have chased out of Troy-land the well-greaved
Achaians."

[tr. LANG, LEAF, MYERS]

[The day's battle ends with an inconclusive single combat between
Hector and Ajax. The next day is spent in burial of the dead, and the
Greeks build a wall to protect their beached ships. When the battle
is resumed on the day following this, Zeus begins to fulfil his promise to
Thetis, and the Trojans are everywhere so successful that at the end of the
day they encamp on the field instead of retiring to Troy for the night.]

BOOK IX

How Agamemnon sent an embassage to Achilles, beseeching him to be
appeased; and how Achilles denied him.

Thus kept the Trojans watch; but the Achaians were holden of
heaven-sent panic, handmaid of palsying fear, and all their best were
stricken to the heart with grief intolerable. Like as two winds stir
up the main, the home of fishes, even the north wind and the west
wind that blow from Thrace, coming suddenly; and the dark billow
straightway lifteth up its crest and casteth much tangle out along
the sea; even so was the Achaians' spirit troubled in their breast.

But Atreides was stricken to the heart with sore grief, and went
about bidding the clear-voiced heralds summon every man by name
to the assembly, but not to shout aloud; and himself he toiled amid
the foremost. So they sat sorrowful in assembly, and Agamemnon
stood up weeping like unto a fountain of dark water that from a
beetling cliff poureth down its black stream; even so with deep

groaning he spake amid the Argives and said: "My friends, leaders and captains of the Argives, Zeus son of Kronos hath bound me with might in grievous blindness of soul; hard of heart is he, for that erewhile he promised and gave his pledge that not till I had laid waste well-walled Ilios should I depart, but now hath planned a cruel wile, and biddeth me return in dishonour to Argos with the loss of many of my folk. Such meseemeth is the good pleasure of most mighty Zeus that hath laid low the heads of many cities, yea and shall lay low; for his is highest power. So come, even as I shall bid let us all obey; let us flee with our ships to our dear native land, for now shall we never take wide-wayed Troy."

So said he, and they all held their peace and kept silence. Long time were the sons of the Achaians voiceless for grief, but at the last Diomedes of the loud war-cry spake amid them and said: "Atreides, with thee first in thy folly will I contend, where it is just, O king, even in the assembly; be not thou wroth therefor. My valour didst thou blame in chief amid the Danaans, and saidst that I was no man of war but a coward; and all this know the Argives both young and old. But the son of crooked-counselling Kronos hath endowed thee but by halves; he granted thee to have the honour of the sceptre above all men, but valour he gave thee not, wherein is highest power. Sir, deemest thou that the sons of the Achaians are thus indeed cowards and weaklings as thou sayest? But and if thine own heart be set on departing, go thy way; the way is before thee, and thy ships stand beside the sea, even the great multitude that followed thee from Mykene. But all the other flowing-haired Achaians will tarry here until we lay waste Troy. Nay, let them too flee on their ships to their dear native land; yet will we twain, even I and Sthenelos, fight till we attain the goal of Ilios; for in God's name are we come."

So said he, and all the sons of the Achaians shouted aloud, applauding the saying of horse-taming Diomedes. Then knightly Nestor arose and said amid them: "Tydeides, in battle art thou passing mighty, and in council art thou best among thine equals in years; none of all the Achaians will make light of thy word nor gainsay it; but thou hast not made a full end of thy words. Moreover thou art a young man indeed, and mightest even be my son, my youngest-born; yet thou counsellest prudently the princes of the Achaians, because thou speakest according unto right. But lo, I that avow me to be older than thou will speak forth and expound everything; neither shall any man despise my saying, not even the lord Agamemnon. A tribeless, lawless, homeless man is he that loveth bitter civil strife. Howbeit now let us yield to black night and make ready our meal; and let the sentinels bestow them severally along the deep-delved fosse without the wall. This charge give I to the young men; and thou, Atreides, lead then the way, for thou art the most royal. Spread thou a feast for the councillors; that is thy place and seemly for thee. Thy huts are full of wine that the ships of the Achaians bring thee by day from Thrace across the wide sea; all entertainment is for thee, being king over many. In the gathering of many shalt thou listen to him that deviseth the most excellent counsel; sore need have all the Achaians of such as is good and prudent, because hard by the ships our foemen are burning their watch-fires in multitude; what man can rejoice thereat? This night shall either destroy or save the host."

So said he, and they gladly hearkened to him and obeyed. Forth sallied the sentinels in their harness, around Thrasymedes Nestor's son, shepherd of the host, and Askalaphos and Ialmenos son of Ares, and Meriones and Aphareus and Deïpyros and Kreion's son noble Lykomedes. Seven were the captains of the sentinels, and with each went fivescore young men bearing their long spears in their hands; and they took post midway betwixt fosse and wall, and kindled a fire and made ready each man his meal.

Then Atreides gathered the councillors of the Achaians, and led them to his hut, and spread before them an abundant feast. So they put forth their hands to the good cheer that lay before them. And when they had put away from them the desire of meat and drink, then the old man first began to weave his counsel, even Nestor, whose rede of old time was approved the best. He of good intent spake to them and said: "Most noble son of Atreus, Agamemnon king of men, in thy name will I end and with thy name begin, because thou art king over many hosts, and to thy hand Zeus hath entrusted sceptre and law, that thou mayest take counsel for thy folk. Thee therefore more than any it behoveth both to speak and hearken, and to accomplish what another than thou may say, when his heart biddeth him speak for profit: wheresoever thou leadest all shall turn on thee, so I will speak as meseemeth best. No other man shall have a more excellent thought than this that I bear in mind from old time even until now, since the day when thou, O heaven-sprung king, didst go and take the damsel Briseis from angry Achilles' hut by no consent of ours. Nay, I right heartily dissuaded thee; but thou yieldedst to thy proud spirit, and dishonouredest a man of valour whom even the immortals honoured; for thou didst take and keepest from him his meed of valour. Still let us even now take thought how we may appease him and persuade him with gifts of friendship and kindly words."

And Agamemnon king of men answered and said to him: "Old sir, in no false wise hast thou accused my folly. Fool was I, I myself deny it not. Worth many hosts is he whom Zeus loveth in his heart, even as now he honoureth this man and destroyeth the host of the Achaians. But seeing I was a fool in that I yielded to my sorry passion, I will make amends and give a recompense beyond telling. In the midst of you all I will name the excellent gifts; seven tripods untouched of fire, and ten talents of gold and twenty gleaming caldrons, and twelve stalwart horses, winners in the race, that have taken prizes by their speed. No lack-wealth were that man, neither undowered of precious gold, whose substance were as great as the prizes my whole-hooved steeds have borne me off. And seven women will I give, skilled in excellent handiwork, Lesbians whom I chose me from the spoils the day that he himself took stablished Lesbos, surpassing womankind in beauty. These will I give him, and with them shall be she whom erst I took from him, even the daughter of Briseus; moreover I will swear a great oath that never I went up into her bed nor had with her converse as is the wont of mankind, even of men and women. All these things shall be set straightway before him; and if hereafter the gods grant us to lay waste the great city of Priam, then let him enter in when we Achaians be dividing the spoil, and lade his ship full of gold and bronze, and himself choose twenty Trojan women, the fairest that there be after Helen of Argos. And if we win to the richest of lands, even Achaian Argos, he shall be my son and I will hold him in like honour with Orestes, my stripling boy that is nurtured in all abundance. Three daughters are mine in my well-builded hall, Chrysothemis and Laodike and Iphianassa; let him take of them which he will, without gifts of wooing, to Peleus' house; and I will add a great dower such as no man ever yet gave with his daughter. And seven well-peopled cities will I give him, Kardamyle and Enope and grassy Hire and holy Pherai and Antheia deep in meads, and fair Aipeia and Pedasos land of vines. And all are nigh to the salt sea, on the uttermost border of sandy Pylos; therein dwell men abounding in flocks and kine, men that shall worship him like a god with gifts, and beneath his sway fulfil his prosperous ordinances. All this will I accomplish so he but cease from wrath. Let him yield; Hades I ween is not to be softened neither overcome, and therefore is he hatefullest of all gods to mortals. Yea, let him be ruled by me, inasmuch as I am more royal and avow me to be the elder in years."

Then knightly Nestor of Gerenia answered and said: "Most noble son of Atreus, Agamemnon king of men, now are these gifts not lightly to be esteemed that thou offerest king Achilles. Come therefore, let us speed forth picked men to go with all haste to the hut of Peleus' son Achilles. Lo now, whomsoever I appoint let them consent. First let Phoinix dear to Zeus lead the way, and after him great Aias and noble Odysseus; and for heralds let Odios and Eurybates be their companions. And now bring water for our hands, and bid keep holy silence, that we may pray unto Zeus the son of Kronos, if perchance he will have mercy upon us."

So said he, and spake words that were well-pleasing unto all. Forthwith the heralds poured water on their hands, and the young men crowned the bowls with drink and gave each man his portion after they had poured the libation in the cups. And when they had made libation and drunk as their heart desired, they issued forth from the hut of Agamemnon son of Atreus. And knightly Nestor of Gerenia gave them full charge, with many a glance to each, and chiefest to Odysseus, how they should essay to prevail on Peleus' noble son.

So the twain went along the shore of the loud-sounding sea, making instant prayer to the earth-embracer, the Shaker of the Earth, that they might with ease prevail on Aiakides' great heart. So they came to the huts and ships of the Myrmidons, and found their king taking his pleasure of a loud lyre, fair, of curious work, with a silver cross-bar upon it; one that he had taken from the spoils when he laid Eëtion's city waste. Therein he was delighting his soul, and singing the glories of heroes. And over against him sate Patroklos alone in silence, watching till Aiakides should cease from singing. So the twain came forward, and noble Odysseus led the way, and they stood before his face; and Achilles sprang up amazed with the lyre in his hand, and left the seat where he was sitting, and in like manner Patroklos when he beheld the men arose. Then Achilles fleet of foot greeted them and said: "Welcome; verily ye are friends that are come — sore indeed is the need — even ye that are dearest of the Achaians to me even in my wrath."

So spake noble Achilles and led them forward, and made them sit on settles and carpets of purple; and anon he spake to Patroklos being near: "Bring forth a greater bowl, thou son of Menoitios; mingle stronger drink, and prepare each man a cup, for dearest of men are these that are under my roof."

So said he, and Patroklos hearkened to his dear comrade. He cast down a great fleshing-block in the fire-light, and laid thereon a sheep's back and a fat goat's, and a great hog's chine rich with fat. And Automedon held them for him, while Achilles carved. Then he sliced well the meat and pierced it through with spits, and Menoitios' son, that godlike hero, made the fire burn high. Then when the fire was burned down and the flame waned, he scattered the embers and laid the spits thereover, resting them on the spit-racks, when he had sprinkled them with holy salt. Then when he had roasted the meat and apportioned it in the platters, Patroklos took bread and dealt it forth on the table in fair baskets, and Achilles dealt the meat. And he sate him over against godlike Odysseus by the other wall, and bade his comrade Patroklos do sacrifice to the gods; so he cast the first-fruits into the fire. Then put they forth their hands to the good cheer lying before them. And when they had put from them the desire of meat and drink, Aias nodded to Phoinix. But noble Odysseus marked it, and filled a cup with wine and pledged Achilles: "Hail, O Achilles! The fair feast lack we not either in the hut of Agamemnon son of Atreus neither now in thine; for feasting is there abundance to our heart's desire, but our thought is not for matters of the delicious feast; nay, we behold very sore destruction, thou fosterling of Zeus, and are afraid. Now is it in doubt whether we save the benched ships or behold them perish, if thou put not on thy might. Nigh unto ships and wall have the high-hearted Trojans and famed allies pitched their camp, and kindled many fires throughout their host, and ween that they shall no more be withheld but will fall on our black ships. And Zeus son of Kronos sheweth them signs upon the right by light-ning, and Hector greatly exulteth in his might and rageth furiously, trusting in Zeus, and recketh not of god nor man, for mighty madness hath possessed him. He prayeth bright Dawn to shine forth with all speed, for he hath passed his word to smite off from the ships the ensigns' tops, and to fire the hulls with devouring flame, and hard thereby to make havoc of the Achaians confounded by the smoke. Therefore am I sore afraid in my heart lest the gods fulfil his boastings, and it be fated for us to perish here in Troy-land, far from Argos pasture-land of horses. Up then! if thou art minded even at the last to save the failing sons of the Achaians from the war-din of the Trojans. Thyself shalt have grief hereafter, and when the ill is done is there no way to find a cure therefor; in good time rather take thou thought to ward the evil day from the Danaans. Friend, surely to thee thy father Peleus gave commandment the day he sent thee to Agamemnon forth from Phthia: 'My son, strength shall Athene and Hera give thee if they will; but do thou refrain thy proud soul in thy breast, for gentlemindedness is the better part; and withdraw from mischievous strife, that so the Argives may honour thee the more, both young and old.' Thus the old man charged thee, but thou forgettest. Yet cease now at the last, and eschew thy grievous wrath; Agamemnon offereth thee worthy gifts, so thou wilt cease from anger. Lo now, hearken thou to me, and I will tell thee all the gifts that in his hut Agamemnon promised thee: seven tripods untouched of fire, and ten talents of gold and twenty gleaming caldrons and twelve stalwart horses, winners in the race, that have taken prizes by their speed. No lack-wealth were that man, neither undowered of precious gold, whose substance were as great as the prizes Agamemnon's steeds have borne him off. And seven women will he give, skilled in excellent handiwork, Lesbians whom he chose him from the spoils the day that thou thyself tookest Lesbos, surpassing womankind in beauty. These will he give thee, and with them shall be she whom erst he took from thee, even the daughter of Briseus; moreover he will swear a great oath that never he went up into her bed nor had with her converse as is the wont of mankind, O king, even of men and women. All these things shall be set straightway before thee; and if hereafter the gods grant us to lay waste the great city of Priam, then enter thou in when we Achaians be dividing the spoil, and lade thy ship full of gold and bronze, and thyself choose twenty Trojan women, the fairest that there be after Helen of Argos. And if we win to the richest of lands, even Achaian Argos, thou shalt be his son and he will hold thee in like honour with Orestes, his stripling boy that is nurtured in all abundance. Three daughters are his in his well-builded hall, Chrysothemis and Laodike and Iphianassa; take thou of them which thou wilt, without gifts of wooing, to Peleus' house; and he will add a great dower such as no man ever yet gave with his daughter. And seven well-peopled cities will he give thee, Kardamyle and Enope and grassy Hire and holy Pherai and Antheia deep in meads, and fair Aipeia and Pedasos land of vines. And all are nigh to the sea, on the uttermost border of sandy Pylos; therein dwell men abounding in flocks and kine, men that shall worship thee like a god with gifts, and beneath thy sway fulfil thy prosperous ordinances. All this will he accomplish so thou but cease from wrath. But and if Agamemnon be too hateful to thy heart, both he and his gifts, yet have thou pity on all the Achaians that faint throughout the host; these shall honour thee as a god, for verily thou wilt earn exceeding great glory at their hands. Yea now mightest thou slay Hector, for he would come very near thee in his deadly madness, because he deemeth that there is no man like unto him among the Danaans that the ships brought hither."

And Achilles fleet of foot answered and said unto him: "Heaven-sprung son of Laertes, Odysseus of many wiles, in openness must I now declare unto you my saying, even as I am minded and as the fulfilment thereof shall be, that ye may not sit before me and coax this way and that. For hateful to me even as the gates of hell is he that hideth one thing in his heart and uttereth another: but I will speak what meseemeth best. Not me, I ween, shall Aga-memnon son of Atreus persuade, nor the other Danaans, seeing we were to have no thank for battling with the foemen ever without respite. He that abideth at home hath equal share with him that fighteth his best, and in like honour are held both the coward and the brave; death cometh alike to the untoiling and to him that hath toiled long. Neither have I any profit for that I endured tribula-tion of soul, ever staking my life in fight. Even as a hen bringeth her unfledged chickens each morsel as she winneth it, and with her-self it goeth hard, even so I was wont to watch out many a sleep-less night and pass through many bloody days of battle, warring with folk for their women's sake. Twelve cities of men have I laid waste from ship-board, and from land eleven, I do you to wit, throughout deep-soiled Troy-land; out of all these took I many goodly treasures and would bring and give them all to Agamemnon son of Atreus, and he staying behind amid the fleet ships would take them and portion out some few but keep the most. Now some he gave to be meeds of honour to the princes and the kings, and theirs are left untouched; only from me of all the Achaians took he my darling lady and keepeth her — let him sleep beside her and take his joy! But why must the Argives make war on the Trojans? why hath Atreides gathered his host and led them hither? is it not for lovely-haired Helen's sake? Do then the sons of Atreus alone of mortal men love their wives? surely whatsoever man is good and sound of mind loveth his own and cherisheth her, even as I too loved mine with all my heart, though but the captive of my spear. But now that he hath taken my meed of honour from mine arms and hath deceived me, let him not tempt me that know him full well; he shall not prevail. Nay, Odysseus, let him take coun-sel with thee and all the princes to ward from the ships the con-suming fire. Verily without mine aid he hath wrought many things, and built a wall and dug a fosse about it wide and deep, and set a palisade therein; yet even so can he not stay murderous Hector's might. But so long as I was fighting amid the Achaians, Hector had no mind to array his battle far from the wall, but scarce came unto the Skaian gates and to the oak-tree; there once he awaited me alone and scarce escaped my onset. But now, seeing I have no mind to fight with noble Hector, I will to-morrow do sacrifice to Zeus and all the gods, and store well my ships when I have launched them on the salt sea — then shalt thou see, if thou wilt and hast any care therefor, my ships sailing at break of day over Hellespont, the fishes' home, and my men right eager at the oar; and if the great Shaker of the Earth grant me good journey, on the third day should I reach deep-soiled Phthia. There are my great possessions that I left when I came hither to my hurt; and yet more gold and ruddy bronze shall I bring home hence, and fair-girdled women and grey iron, all at least that were mine by lot; only my meed of honour hath he that gave it me taken back in his despitefulness, even lord Agamemnon son of Atreus. To him declare ye everything even as I charge you, openly, that all the Achaians likewise may have indignation, if haply he hopeth to beguile yet some other Danaan, for that he is ever clothed in shamelessness. Verily not in my face would he dare to look, though he have the front of a dog. Neither will I devise counsel with him nor any enterprise, for utterly he hath deceived me and done wickedly; but never again shall he beguile me with fair speech — let this suffice him. Let him begone in peace; Zeus the lord of counsel hath taken away his wits. Hateful to me are his gifts, and I hold him at a straw's worth. Not even if he gave me ten times, yea twenty, all that now is his, and all that may come to him otherwhence, even all the revenue of Orchomenos or Egyptian Thebes where the treasure-houses are stored fullest — Thebes of the hundred gates, whence sally forth two hundred warriors through each with horses and chariots — nay, nor gifts in number as sand or dust; not even so shall Agamemnon persuade my soul till he have paid me back all the bitter despite. And the daughter of Agamemnon son of Atreus will I not wed, not were she rival of golden Aphrodite for fairness and for handiwork matched bright-eyed Athene — not even then will I wed her; let him choose him of the Achaians another that is his peer and is more royal than I. For if the gods indeed preserve me and I come unto my home, then will Peleus himself seek me a wife. Many Achaian maidens are there throughout Hellas and Phthia, daughters of princes that ward their cities; whomsoever of these I wish will I make my dear lady. Very often was my high soul moved to take me there a wedded wife, a help meet for me, and have joy of the possessions that the old man Peleus possesseth. For not of like worth with life hold I even all the wealth that men say was possessed of the well-peopled city of Ilios in days of peace gone by, before the sons of the Achaians came; neither all the treasure that the stone threshold of the archer Phoebus Apollo encompasseth in rocky Pytho. For kine and goodly flocks are to be had for the harrying, and tripods and chestnut horses for the purchasing; but to bring back man's life neither harrying nor earning availeth when once it hath passed the barrier of his lips. For thus my goddess mother telleth me, Thetis the silver-footed, that twain fates are bearing me to the issue of death. If I abide here and besiege the Trojans' city, then my returning home is taken from me, but my fame shall be imperishable; but if I go home to my dear native land, my high fame is taken from me, but my life shall endure long while, neither shall the issue of death soon reach me. Moreover I would counsel you all to set sail homeward, seeing ye shall never reach your goal of steep Ilios; of a surety far-seeing Zeus holdeth his hand over her and her folk are of good courage. So go your way and tell my answer to the princes of the Achaians, even as is the office of elders, that they may devise in their hearts some other better counsel, such as shall save them their ships and the host of the Achaians amid the hollow ships: since this counsel availeth them naught that they have now devised, by reason of my fierce wrath. But let Phoinix now abide with us and lay him to rest, that he may follow with me on my ships to our dear native land to-morrow, if he will; for I will not take him perforce."

So spake he, and they all held their peace and were still, and marvelled at his saying; for he denied them very vehemently. But at the last spake to them the old knight Phoinix, bursting into tears, because he was sore afraid for the ships of the Achaians: "If indeed thou ponderest departure in thy heart, glorious Achilles, and hast no mind at all to save the fleet ships from consuming fire, because that wrath hath entered into thy heart; how can I be left of thee, dear son, alone thereafter? To thee did the old knight Peleus send me the day he sent thee to Agamemnon forth from Phthia, a stripling yet unskilled in equal war and in debate wherein men wax pre-eminent. Therefore sent he me to teach thee all these things, to be both a speaker of words and a doer of deeds. So would I not be left alone of thee, dear son, not even if god himself should take on him to strip my years from me, and make me fresh and young as in the day when first I left Hellas the home of fair women, fleeing from strife against my father Amyntor son of Ormenos: for he was sore angered with me by reason of his lovely-haired concubine, whom he ever cherished and wronged his wife my mother. So she besought me continually by my knees to go in first unto the concubine, that the old man might be hateful to her. I hearkened to her and did the deed; but my sire was ware thereof forthwith and cursed me mightily, and called the dire Erinyes to look that never should any dear son sprung of my body sit upon my knees; and the gods fulfilled his curse, even Zeus of the underworld and dread Persephone. [Then took I counsel to slay him with the keen sword; but some immortal stayed mine anger, bringing to my mind the people's voice and all the reproaches of men, lest I should be called a father-slayer amid the Achaians.] Then would my soul no more be refrained at all within my breast to tarry in the halls of mine angered father. Now my fellows and my kinsmen came about me with many prayers, and refrained me there within the halls, and slaughtered many goodly sheep and shambling kine with crooked horns; and many swine rich with fat were stretched to singe over the flames of Hephaistos, and wine from that old man's jars was drunken without stint. Nine nights long slept they all night around my body; they kept watch in turn, neither were the fires quenched, one beneath the colonnade of the fenced courtyard and another in the porch before the chamber doors. But when the tenth dark night was come upon me, then burst I my cunningly fitted chamber doors, and issued forth and overleapt the courtyard fence lightly, unmarked of watchmen and handmaidens. Then fled I far through Hellas of wide lawns, and came to deep-soiled Phthia, mother of flocks, even unto king Peleus; and he received me kindly and cherished me as a father cherisheth his only son, his stripling heir of great possessions; and he made me rich and gave much people to me, and I dwelt in the uttermost part of Phthia and was king over the Dolopians. Yea, I reared thee to this greatness, thou godlike Achilles, with my heart's love; for with none other wouldest thou go unto the feast, neither take meat in the hall, till that I had set thee upon my knees and stayed thee with the savoury morsel cut first for thee, and put the wine-cup to thy lips. Oft hast thou stained the doubtlet on my breast with sputtering of wine in thy sorry helplessness. Thus I suffered much with thee and much I toiled, being mindful that the gods in nowise created any issue of my body; but I made thee my son, thou godlike Achilles, that thou mayest yet save me from grievous destruction. Therefore, Achilles, rule thy high spirit; neither beseemeth it thee to have a ruthless heart. Nay, even the very gods can bend, and theirs withal is loftier majesty and honour and might. Their hearts by incense and reverent vows and drink-offering and burnt-offering men turn with prayer, so oft as any transgresseth and doeth sin. Moreover Prayers of penitence are daughters of great Zeus, halting and wrinkled and of eyes askance, that have their task withal to go in the steps of Sin. For Sin is strong and fleet of foot, wherefore she far out-runneth all prayers, and goeth before them over all the earth making men fall, and Prayers follow behind to heal the harm. Now whosoever reverenceth Zeus' daughters when they draw near, him they greatly bless and hear his petitions; but when one denieth them and stiffly refuseth, then depart they and make prayer unto Zeus the son of Kronos that sin may come upon such an one, that he may fall and pay the price. Nay, Achilles, look thou too that there attend upon the daughters of Zeus the reverence that bendeth the heart of all men that be right-minded. For if Atreides brought thee not gifts and foretold thee not more hereafter, but were ever furiously wroth, then I were not he that should bid thee cast aside thine anger and save the Argives, even in their sore need of thee. But now he both offereth thee forthwith many gifts, and promiseth thee more here-

after, and hath sent heroes to beseech thee, the best men chosen
throughout the host of the Achaians and that to thyself are dearest
of the Argives; dishonour not thou their petition nor their journey
hither; though erst it were no wrong that thou wast wroth. Even
in like manner have we heard the fame of those heroes that were
of old, as oft as furious anger came on any; they might be won by
gifts and prevailed upon by speech. This tale have I in mind of
old time and not of yesterday, even as it was; and I will tell it
among you that all are friends. The Kuretes fought and the
staunch Aitolians about the city of Kalydon, and slew one another,
the Aitolians defending lovely Kalydon, the Kuretes eager to lay it
waste in war. For Artemis of the golden throne had brought a
plague upon them, in wrath that Oineus offered her not the harvest
first-fruits on the fat of his garden land; for all the other gods had
their feast of hecatombs, and only to the daughter of great Zeus
offered he not, whether he forgat or marked it not; and therein
sinned he sore in his heart. So the Archer-goddess was wroth and
sent against him a creature of heaven, a fierce wild boar, white-
tusked, that wrought sore ill continually on Oineus' garden land;
many a tall tree laid he low utterly, even root and apple blossom
therewith. But him slew Meleagros the son of Oineus, having
gathered together from many cities huntsmen and hounds; for
not of few men could the boar be slain, so mighty was he; and
many an one brought he to the grievous pyre. But the goddess
made much turmoil over him and tumult concerning the boar's
head and shaggy hide, between the Kuretes and great-hearted Aitolians. Now so long as Meleagros dear to Ares fought, so long
it went ill with the Kuretes, neither dared they face him without
their city walls, for all they were very many. But when Meleagros
grew full of wrath, such as swelleth the hearts of others likewise
in their breasts, though they be wise of mind, then in anger of
heart at his dear mother Althaia he tarried beside his wedded wife,
fair Kleopatra, daughter of Marpessa fair-ankled daughter of Eue-
nos, and of Ides that was strongest of men that were then upon
the earth; he it was that took the bow to face the king Phoebus
Apollo for sake of the fair-ankled damsel. And she was called
Alkyone of her father and lady mother by surname in their hall,
because her mother in the plight of the plaintive halcyon-bird wept
when the far-darter Phoebus Apollo snatched her away. By her
side lay Meleagros, brooding on his grievous anger, being wroth by
reason of his mother's curses: for she, grieved for her brethren's
death, prayed instantly to the gods, and with her hands likewise
beat instantly upon the fertile earth, calling on Hades and dread
Persephone, while she knelt upon her knees and made her bosom
wet with tears, to bring her son to death; and Erinys that walketh in darkness, whose heart knoweth not ruth, heard her from
Erebos. Now was the din of foemen about their gates quickly
risen, and a noise of battering of towers; and the elders of the
Aitolians sent the best of the god's priests and besought him to

come forth and save them, with promise of a mighty gift; to wit, they bade him, where the plain of lovely Kalydon was fattest, to choose him out of a fair demesne of fifty plough-gates, the half thereof vine-land and the half open plough-land, to be cut from out the plain. And old knightly Oineus prayed him instantly, and stood upon the threshold of his high-roofed chamber, and shook the morticed doors to beseech his son; him too his sisters and his lady mother prayed instantly — but he denied them yet more — instantly too his comrades prayed, that were nearest him and dearest of all men. Yet even so persuaded they not his heart within his breast, until his chamber was now hotly battered and the Kuretes were climbing upon the towers and firing the great city. Then did his fair-girdled wife pray Meleagros with lamentation, and told him all the woes that come on men whose city is taken; the warriors are slain, and the city is wasted of fire, and the children and the deep-girdled women are led captive of strangers. And his soul was stirred to hear the grievous tale, and he went his way and donned his glittering armour. So he saved the Aitolians from the evil day, obeying his own will; but they paid him not now the gifts many and gracious; yet nevertheless he drave away destruction. But be not thine heart thus minded, neither let heaven so guide thee, dear son; that were a hard thing, to save the ships already burning. Nay, come for the gifts; the Achaians shall honour thee even as a god. But if without gifts thou enter into battle the bane of men, thou wilt not be held in like honour, even though thou avert the fray."

And Achilles fleet of foot made answer and said to him: "Phoinix my father, thou old man fosterling of Zeus, such honour need I in no wise; for I deem that I have been honoured by the judgment of Zeus, which shall abide upon me amid my beaked ships as long as breath tarrieth in my body and my limbs are strong. Moreover I will say this thing to thee and lay thou it to thine heart; trouble not my soul by weeping and lamentation, to do the pleasure of warrior Atreides; neither beseemeth it thee to cherish him, lest thou be hated of me that cherish thee. It were good that thou with me shouldst vex him that vexeth me. Be thou king even as I, and share my sway by halves, but these shall bear my message. So tarry thou here and lay thee to rest in a soft bed, and with break of day will we consider whether to depart unto our own, or to abide."

He spake, and nodded his brow in silence unto Patroklos to spread for Phoinix a thick couch, that the others might bethink them to depart from the hut with speed. Then spake to them Aias, Telamon's godlike son, and said: "Heaven-sprung son of Laertes, Odysseus of many wiles, let us go hence; for methinks the purpose of our charge will not by this journey be accomplished; and we must tell the news, though it be no wise good, with all speed unto the Danaans, that now sit awaiting. But Achilles hath wrought his proud soul to fury within him — stubborn man, that recketh naught of his comrades' love, wherein we worshipped him beyond all men amid the ships — unmerciful! Yet doth a man accept recompense of his brother's murderer or for his dead son; and so the man-slayer for a great price abideth in his own land, and the kinsman's heart is appeased, and his proud soul, when he hath taken the recompense. But for thee, the gods have put within thy breast a spirit implacable and evil, by reason of one single damsel. And now we offer thee seven damsels, far best of all, and many other gifts besides; entertain thou then a kindly spirit, and have respect unto thine home; because we are guests of thy roof, sent of the multitude of Danaans, and we would fain be nearest to thee and dearest beyond all other Achaians, as many as there be."

And Achilles fleet of foot made answer and said to him: "Aias sprung of Zeus, thou son of Telamon, prince of the folk, thou seemest to speak all this almost after mine own mind; but my heart swelleth with wrath as oft as I bethink me of those things, how Atreides entreated me arrogantly among the Argives, as though I were some worthless sojourner. But go ye and declare my message; I will not take thought of bloody war until that wise Priam's son, noble Hector, come to the Myrmidons' huts and ships, slaying the Argives, and smirch the ships with fire. But about mine hut and black ship I ween that Hector, though he be very eager for battle, shall be refrained."

So said he, and they took each man a two-handled cup, and made libation and went back along the line of ships; and Odysseus led the way. And Patroklos bade his fellows and handmaidens spread with all speed a thick couch for Phoinix; and they obeyed and spread a couch as he ordained, fleeces and rugs and fine flock of linen. Then the old man laid him down and tarried for bright Dawn. And Achilles slept in the corner of the morticed hut, and by his side lay a woman that he brought from Lesbos, even Phorbas' daughter fair-cheeked Diomede. And on the other side Patroklos lay, and by his side likewise fair-girdled Iphis, whom noble Achilles gave him at the taking of steep Skyros, the city of Enyeus.

Now when those were come unto Atreides' huts, the sons of the Achaians stood up on this side and on that, and pledged them in cups of gold, and questioned them; and Agamemnon king of men asked them first: "Come now, tell me, Odysseus full of praise, thou great glory of the Achaians; will he save the ships from consuming fire, or said he nay, and hath wrath yet hold of his proud spirit?"

And steadfast goodly Odysseus answered him: "Most noble son of Atreus, Agamemnon king of men, he yonder hath no mind to quench his wrath, but is yet more filled of fury, and spurneth thee and thy gifts. He biddeth thee take counsel for thyself amid the Argives, how to save the ships and folk of the Achaians. And for himself he threateneth that at break of day he will launch upon the sea his trim well-benched ships. Moreover he said that he would counsel all to sail for home, because ye now shall never reach your goal of steep Ilios; surely far-seeing Zeus holdeth his hand over her and her folk are of good courage. Even so said he, and here are

also these to tell the tale that were my companions, Aias and the
two heralds, both men discreet. But the old man Phoinix laid him
there to rest, even as Achilles bade him, that he may follow with
him on his ships to his dear native land to-morrow, if he will; for
he will not take him perforce."

So said he, and they all held their peace and were still, marvelling
at his saying, for he harangued very vehemently. Long were the
sons of the Achaians voiceless for grief, but at the last Diomedes of
the loud war-cry spake amid them: "Most noble son of Atreus,
Agamemnon king of men, would thou hadst never besought Peleus'
glorious son with offer of gifts innumerable; proud is he at any
time, but now hast thou yet far more encouraged him in his
haughtiness. Howbeit we will let him bide, whether he go or
tarry; hereafter he shall fight, whenever his heart within him biddeth and god arouseth him. Come now, even as I shall say let us
all obey. Go ye now to rest, full to your hearts' desire of meat and
wine, wherein courage is and strength; but when fair rosy-fingered
Dawn appeareth, array thou with all speed before the ships thy
folk and horsemen, and urge them on; and fight thyself amid the
foremost."

So said he, and all the princes gave assent, applauding the saying of Diomedes tamer of horses. And then they made libation
and went every man to his hut, and there laid them to rest and took
the boon of sleep.

[tr. LANG, LEAF, MYERS]

[During the night Odysseus and Diomedes make a raid on the Trojan
camp; they slay a Trojan spy, Dolon, and capture the horses of Rhesus,
a king of the Thracians.

The Greeks continue the battle without Achilles. In the third great
battle that fills up the next day, the Trojans win their greatest success:
while most of the major Greek heroes are wounded and out of the fray,
Hector breaks through the wall of the Greeks and throws fire on one of
the Greek ships. This marks the high point of the Trojan advance.
Patroklos now enters the battle out of pity for the Greeks; clad in the
armour of Achilles and leading the Myrmidons, he drives the Trojans
back to the walls of Troy, where he is slain by Apollo and Hector. Hector
strips him of his armour, but his body is rescued by Menelaus and Ajax,
as the day ends.

Achilles, overcome with remorse and rage at the death of his friend,
decides to enter the fray and seek revenge on Hector, although his mother
warns him that his own death is fated straightway after Hector. During
the night Hephaistos makes new armour for Achilles, and the next morning Agamemnon and Achilles are publicly reconciled. Achilles then leads
the host forth to battle and after a series of superhuman feats drives the
Trojans back to the city-walls. All the Trojans except Hector manage to
enter the gates while Achilles is pursuing Apollo who has taken on the
form of Agenor to divert his attack.]

BOOK XXII

How Achilles fought with Hector, and slew him, and brought his body to the ships.

Thus they throughout the city, scared like fawns, were cooling their sweat and drinking and slaking their thirst, leaning on the fair battlements, while the Achaians drew near the wall, setting shields to shoulders. But Hector deadly fate bound to abide in his place, in front of Ilios and the Skaian gates. Then to the son of Peleus spake Phoebus Apollo: "Wherefore, son of Peleus, pursuest thou me with swift feet, thyself being mortal and I a deathless god? Thou hast not even yet known me, that I am a god, but strivest vehemently. Truly thou regardest not thy task among the affliction of the Trojans whom thou affrightedst, who now are gathered into the city, while thou hast wandered hither. Me thou wilt never slay, for I am not subject unto death."

Then mightily moved spake unto him Achilles fleet of foot: "Thou hast baulked me, Far-darter, most mischievous of all the gods, in that thou hast turned me hither from the wall: else should full many yet have bitten the dust or ever within Ilios had they come. Now hast thou robbed me of great renown, and lightly hast saved them, because thou hadst no vengeance to fear thereafter. Verily I would avenge me on thee, had I but the power."

Thus saying toward the city he was gone in pride of heart, rushing like some victorious horse in a chariot, that runneth lightly at full speed over the plain; so swiftly plied Achilles in his feet and knees. Him the old man Priam first beheld as he sped across the plain, blazing as the star that cometh forth at harvest-time, and plain seen his rays shine forth amid the host of stars in the darkness of night, the star whose name men call Orion's Dog. Brightest of all is he, yet for an evil sign is he set, and bringeth much fever upon hapless men. Even so on Achilles' breast the bronze gleamed as he ran. And the old man cried aloud and beat upon his head with his hands, raising them on high, and with a cry called aloud beseeching his dear son; for he before the gates was standing, all hot for battle with Achilles. And the old man spake piteously unto him, stretching forth his hands: "Hector, beloved son, I pray thee await not this man alone with none beside thee, lest thou quickly meet thy doom, slain by the son of Peleus, since he is mightier far, a merciless man. Would the gods loved him even as do I! then quickly would dogs and vultures devour him on the field — thereby would cruel pain go from my heart — the man who hath bereft me of many valiant sons, slaying them and selling them captive into far-off isles. Ay even now twain of my children, Lykaon and Polydoros, I cannot see among the Trojans that throng into the fastness, sons whom Laothoë bare me, a princess among women. If they be yet alive amid the enemy's host, then will we ransom them with bronze and gold, for there is store within, for much goods gave the old man famous Altes to his child. If they be dead, then even in the house of Hades shall they be a sorrow to my soul and to their mother, even to us who gave them birth, but to the rest of the folk a briefer sorrow, if but thou die not by Achilles' hand. Nay, come within the wall, my child, that thou preserve the men and women of Troy, neither give great triumph to the son of Peleus, and be thyself bereft of sweet life. Have compassion also on me, the helpless one, who still can feel, ill-fated; whom the father, Kronos' son, will bring to nought by a grievous doom in the path of old age, having seen full many ills, his sons perishing and his daughters carried away captive, and his chambers laid waste and infant children hurled to the ground in terrible war, and his sons' wives dragged away by the ruinous hands of the Achaians. Myself then last of all at the street door will ravening dogs tear, when some one by stroke or throw of the sharp bronze hath bereft my limbs of life — even the dogs I reared in my halls about my table and to guard my door, which then having drunk my blood, maddened at heart shall lie in the gateway. A young man all beseemeth, even to be slain in war, to be torn by the sharp bronze and lie on the field; though he be dead yet is all honourable to him, whate'er be seen: but when dogs defile the hoary head and hoary beard and the secret parts of an old man slain, this is the most piteous thing that cometh upon hapless men."

Thus spake the old man, and grasped his hoary hairs, plucking them from his head, but he persuaded not Hector's soul. Then his mother in her turn wailed tearfully, loosening the folds of her robe, while with the other hand she showed her breast; and through her tears spake to him winged words: "Hector, my child, have regard unto this bosom and pity me, if ever I gave thee consolation of my breast. Think of it, dear child, and from this side of the wall drive back the foe, nor stand in front to meet him. He is merciless; if he slay thee it will not be on a bed that I or thy wife wooed with many gifts shall bewail thee, my own dear child, but far away from us by the ships of the Argives will swift dogs devour thee."

Thus they with wailing spake to their dear son, beseeching him sore, yet they persuaded not Hector's soul, but he stood awaiting Achilles as he drew nigh in giant might. As a serpent of the mountains upon his den awaiteth a man, having fed on evil poisons, and fell wrath hath entered into him, and terribly he glareth as he coileth himself about his den, so Hector with courage unquenchable gave not back, leaning his shining shield against a jutting tower. Then sore troubled he spake to his great heart: "Ay me, if I go within the gates and walls, Polydamas will be first to bring reproach against me, since he bade me lead the Trojans to the city during this ruinous night, when noble Achilles arose. But I regarded him not, yet surely it had been better far. And now that I have undone the host by my wantonness, I am ashamed before the men of Troy and women of trailing robes, lest at any time some worse man than I shall say: 'Hector by trusting his own might undid the host.' So will they speak; then to me would it be better far to face Achilles and either slay him and go home, or myself die gloriously before the city. Or what if I lay down my bossy shield and my stout helm, and lean my spear against the wall, and go of myself to meet noble Achilles and promise him that Helen, and with her all possessions that Alexandros brought in hollow ships to Troy, the beginning of strife, we will give to the sons of Atreus to take away, and therewithal to divide in half with the Achaians all else that this city holdeth: and if thereafter I obtain from the Trojans an oath of the Elders that they will hide nothing but divide all in twain [whatever wealth the pleasant city hold within]? But wherefore doth my heart debate thus? I might come unto him and he would not pity or regard me at all, but presently slay me unarmed as it were but a woman, if I put off my armour. No time is it now to dally with him from oak-tree or from rock, like youth with maiden, as youth and maiden hold dalliance one with another. Better is it to join battle with all speed: let us know upon which of us twain the Olympian shall bestow renown."

Thus pondered he as he stood, but nigh on him came Achilles, peer of Enyalios warrior of the waving helm, brandishing from his right shoulder the Pelian ash, his terrible spear; and all around the bronze on him flashed like the gleam of blazing fire or of the Sun as he ariseth. And trembling seized Hector as he was aware of him, nor endured he to abide in his place, but left the gates behind him and fled in fear. And the son of Peleus darted after him, trusting in his swift feet. As a falcon upon the mountains, swiftest of winged things, swoopeth fleetly after a trembling dove; and she before him fleëth, while he with shrill screams hard at hand still darteth at her, for his heart urgeth him to seize her; so Achilles in hot haste flew straight for him, and Hector fled beneath the Trojans' wall, and plied swift knees. They past the watch-place and windwaved wild fig-tree sped ever, away from under the wall, along the waggon-track, and came to the two fair-flowing springs, where two fountains rise that feed deep-eddying Skamandros. The one floweth with warm water, and smoke goeth up therefrom around as it were from a blazing fire, while the other even in summer floweth forth like cold hail or snow or ice that water formeth. And there beside the springs are broad washing-troughs hard by, fair troughs of stone, where wives and fair daughters of the men of Troy were wont to wash bright raiment, in the old time of peace, before the sons of the Achaians came. Thereby they ran, he flying, he pursuing. Valiant was the flier but far mightier he who fleetly pursued him. For not for beast of sacrifice or for an ox-hide were they striving, such as are prizes for men's speed of foot, but for the life of horse-taming Hector was their race. And as when victorious whole-hooved horses run rapidly round the turning-points, and some great prize lieth in sight, be it a tripod or a woman, in honour of a man that is dead, so thrice around Priam's city circled those twain with flying feet, and all the gods were gazing on them. Then among them spake first the father of gods and men: "Ay me, a man beloved I see pursued around the wall. My heart is woe for Hector, who hath burnt for me many thighs of oxen amid the crests of many-folded Ida, and other times on the city-height; but now is goodly Achilles pursuing him with swift feet round Priam's town. Come, give your counsel, gods, and devise whether we shall save him from death or now at last slay him, valiant though he be, by the hand of Achilles Peleus' son."

Then to him answered the bright-eyed goddess Athene: "O Father, Lord of the bright lightning and the dark cloud, what is this thou hast said? A man that is a mortal, doomed long ago by fate, wouldst thou redeem back from ill-boding death? Do it, but not all we other gods approve."

And unto her in answer spake cloud-gathering Zeus: "Be of good cheer, Trito-born, dear child: not in full earnest speak I, and I would fain be kind to thee. Do as seemeth good to thy mind, and draw not back."

Thus saying he roused Athene, that already was set thereon, and from the crests of Olympus she darted down.

But after Hector sped fleet Achilles chasing him vehemently. And as when on the mountains a hound hunteth the fawn of a deer, having started it from its covert, through glens and glades, and if it crouch to baffle him under a bush, yet scenting it out the hound runneth constantly until he find it; so Hector baffled not Peleus' fleet-footed son. Oft as he set himself to dart under the well-built walls over against the Dardanian gates, if haply from above they might succour him with darts, so oft would Achilles gain on him and turn him toward the plain, while himself he sped ever on the city-side. And as in a dream one faileth in chase of a flying man — the one faileth in his flight and the other in his chase — so failed Achilles to overtake him in the race, and Hector to escape. And thus would Hector have avoided the visitation of death, had not this time been utterly the last wherein Apollo came nigh to him, who nerved his strength and his swift knees. For to the host did noble Achilles sign with his head, and forbade them to hurl bitter darts against Hector, lest any smiting him should gain renown, and he himself come second. But when the fourth time they had reached the springs, then the Father hung his golden balances, and set therein two lots of dreary death, one of Achilles, one of horse-taming Hector, and held them by the midst and poised. Then Hector's fated day sank down, and fell to the house of Hades, and Phoebus Apollo left him. But to Peleus' son came the bright-eyed goddess Athene, and standing near spake to him winged words: "Now verily, glorious Achilles dear to Zeus, I have hope that we twain shall carry off great glory to the ships for the Achaians, having slain Hector, for all his thirst for fight. No longer is it possible for him to escape us, not even though far-darting Apollo should travail sore, grovelling before the Father, aegis-bearing Zeus. But do thou now stand and take breath, and I will go and persuade this man to confront thee in fight."

Thus spake Athene, and he obeyed, and was glad at heart, and stood leaning on his bronze-pointed ashen-spear. And she left him and came to noble Hector, like unto Deiphobos in shape and in strong voice, and standing near spake to him winged words: "Dear brother, verily fleet Achilles doth thee violence, chasing thee round Priam's town with swift feet: but come let us make a stand and await him on our defence."

Then answered her great Hector of the glancing helm: "Deiphobos, verily aforetime wert thou far dearest of my brothers, whom Hekabe and Priam gendered, but now methinks I shall honour thee even more, in that thou hast dared for my sake, when thou sawest me, to come forth of the wall, while the others tarry within."

Then to him again spake the bright-eyed goddess Athene: "Dear brother, of a truth my father and lady mother and my comrades around besought me much, entreating me in turn, to tarry there, so greatly do they all tremble before him; but my heart within was sore with dismal grief. And now fight we with straight-set resolve and let there be no sparing of spears, that we may know whether Achilles is to slay us and carry our bloody spoils to the hollow ships, or whether he might be vanquished by thy spear."

Thus saying Athene in her subtlety led him on. And when they were come nigh in onset on one another, to Achilles first spake great Hector of the glancing helm: "No longer, son of Peleus, will I fly thee, as before I thrice ran round the great town of Priam, and endured not to await thy onset. Now my heart biddeth me stand up against thee; I will either slay or be slain. But come hither and let us pledge us by our gods, for they shall be best witnesses and beholders of covenants: I will entreat thee in no outrageous sort, if Zeus grant me to outstay thee, and if I take thy life, but when I have despoiled thee of thy glorious armour, O Achilles, I will give back thy dead body to the Achaians, and do thou the same."

But unto him with grim gaze spake Achilles fleet of foot: "Hector, talk not to me, thou madman, of covenants. As between men and lions there is no pledge of faith, nor wolves and sheep can be of one mind, but imagine evil continually against each other, so is it impossible for thee and me to be friends, neither shall be any pledge between us until one or other shall have fallen and glutted with blood Ares, the stubborn god of war. Bethink thee of all thy soldiership: now behoveth it thee to quit thee as a good spearman and valiant man of war. No longer is there way of escape for thee, but Pallas Athene will straightway subdue thee to my spear; and now in one hour shalt thou pay back for all my sorrows for my friends whom thou hast slain in the fury of thy spear."

He said, and poised his far-shadowing spear and hurled. And noble Hector watched the coming thereof and avoided it; for with his eye on it he crouched, and the bronze spear flew over him, and fixed itself in the earth; but Pallas Athene caught it up and gave it back to Achilles, unknown of Hector shepherd of hosts.   Then Hector spake unto the noble son of Peleus: "Thou hast missed, so nowise yet, godlike Achilles, hast thou known from Zeus the hour of my doom, though thou thoughtest it.   Cunning of tongue art thou and a deceiver in speech, that fearing thee I might forget my valour and strength.   Not as I flee shalt thou plant thy spear in my reins, but drive it straight through my breast as I set on thee, if God hath given thee to do it.   Now in thy turn avoid my spear of bronze. O that thou mightst take it all into thy flesh!   Then would the war be lighter to the Trojans, if but thou wert dead, for thou art their greatest bane."

He said, and poised his long-shadowed spear and hurled it, and smote the midst of the shield of Peleus' son, and missed him not: but far from the shield the spear leapt back.   And Hector was wroth that his swift weapon had left his hand in vain, and he stood downcast, for he had no second ashen spear.   And he called with a loud shout to Deiphobos of the white shield, and asked of him a long spear, but he was nowise nigh.   Then Hector knew the truth in his heart, and spake and said: "Ay me, now verily the gods have summoned me to death.   I deemed the warrior Deiphobos was by my side, but he is within the wall, and it was Athene who played me false.   Now therefore is evil death come very nigh me, not far off, nor is there way of escape.   This then was from of old the pleasure of Zeus and of the far-darting son of Zeus, who yet before were fain to succour me: but now my fate hath found me.   At least let me not die without a struggle or ingloriously, but in some great deed of arms whereof men yet to be born shall hear."

Thus saying he drew his sharp sword that by his flank hung great and strong, and gathered himself and swooped like a soaring eagle that darteth to the plain through the dark clouds to seize a tender lamb or crouching hare.   So Hector swooped, brandishing his sharp sword.   And Achilles made at him, for his heart was filled with wild fierceness, and before his breast he made a covering with his fair graven shield, and tossed his bright four-plated helm; and round it waved fair golden plumes [that Hephaistos had set thick about the crest].   As a star goeth among stars in the darkness of night, Hesperos, fairest of all stars set in heaven, so flashed there forth a light from the keen spear Achilles poised in his right hand, devising mischief against noble Hector, eyeing his fair flesh to find the fittest place.   Now for the rest of him his flesh was covered by the fair bronze armour he stripped from strong Patroklos when he slew him, but there was an opening where the collar bones coming from the shoulders clasp the neck, even at the gullet, where destruction of life cometh quickliest; there, as he came on, noble Achilles drave at him with his spear, and right through the tender neck went the point.   Yet the bronze-weighted ashen spear clave not the windpipe, so that he might yet speak words of answer to his foe. And he fell down in the dust, and noble Achilles spake exultingly: "Hector, thou thoughtest, whilst thou wert spoiling Patroklos, that thou wouldst be safe, and didst reck nothing of me who was afar, thou fool. But away among the hollow ships his comrade, a mightier far, even I, was left behind, who now have unstrung thy knees. Thee shall dogs and birds tear foully, but his funeral shall the Achaians make."

Then with faint breath spake unto him Hector of the glancing helm: "I pray thee by thy life and knees and parents leave me not for dogs of the Achaians to devour by the ships, but take good store of bronze and gold, gifts that my father and lady mother shall give to thee, and give them home my body back again, that the Trojans and Trojans' wives give me my due of fire after my death."

But unto him with grim gaze spake Achilles fleet of foot: "Entreat me not, dog, by knees or parents. Would that my heart's desire could so bid me myself to carve and eat raw thy flesh, for the evil thou hast wrought me, as surely is there none that shall keep the dogs from thee, not even should they bring ten or twenty fold ransom and here weigh it out, and promise even more, not even were Priam Dardanos' son to bid pay thy weight in gold, not even so shall thy lady mother lay thee on a bed to mourn her son, but dogs and birds shall devour thee utterly."

Then dying spake unto him Hector of the glancing helm: "Verily I know thee and behold thee as thou art, nor was I destined to persuade thee; truly thy heart is iron in thy breast. Take heed now lest I draw upon thee wrath of gods, in the day when Paris and Phoebus Apollo slay thee, for all thy valour, at the Skaian gate."

He ended, and the shadow of death came down upon him, and his soul flew forth of his limbs and was gone to the house of Hades, wailing her fate, leaving her vigour and youth. Then to the dead man spake noble Achilles: "Die: for my death, I will accept it whensoever Zeus and the other immortal gods are minded to accomplish it."

He said, and from the corpse drew forth his bronze spear, and set it aside, and stripped the bloody armour from the shoulders. And other sons of Achaians ran up around, who gazed upon the stature and marvellous goodliness of Hector. Nor did any stand by but wounded him, and thus would many a man say looking toward his neighbour: "Go to, of a truth far easier to handle is Hector now than when he burnt the ships with blazing fire." Thus would many a man say, and wound him as he stood hard by. And when fleet noble Achilles had despoiled him, he stood up among the Achaians and spake winged words: "Friends, chiefs and counsellors of the Argives, since the gods have vouchsafed us to vanquish this man who hath done us more evil than all the rest together, come let us make trial in arms round about the city, that we may know somewhat of the Trojans' purpose, whether since he hath fallen they will forsake the citadel, or whether they are minded to abide, albeit Hector is no more. But wherefore doth my heart

debate thus? There lieth by the ships a dead man unbewailed, unburied, Patroklos; him will I not forget, while I abide among the
living and my knees can stir. Nay if even in the house of Hades
the dead forget their dead, yet will I even there be mindful of my
dear comrade. But come, ye sons of the Achaians, let us now, singing our song of victory, go back to the hollow ships and take with
us our foe. Great glory have we won; we have slain the noble
Hector, unto whom the Trojans prayed throughout their city, as
he had been a god."

He said, and devised foul entreatment of noble Hector. The
tendons of both feet behind he slit from heel to ankle-joint, and
thrust therethrough thongs of ox-hide, and bound him to his chariot,
leaving his head to trail. And when he had mounted the chariot
and lifted therein the famous armour, he lashed his horses to speed,
and they nothing loth flew on. And dust rose around him that was
dragged, and his dark hair flowed loose on either side, and in the
dust lay all his once fair head, for now had Zeus given him over
to his foes to entreat foully in his own native land.

Thus was his head all grimed with dust. But his mother when
she beheld her son, tore her hair and cast far from her her shining
veil, and cried aloud with an exceeding bitter cry. And piteously
moaned his father, and around them the folk fell to crying and
moaning throughout the town. Most like it seemed as though all
beetling Ilios were burning utterly in fire. Scarcely could the folk
keep back the old man in his hot desire to get him forth of the
Dardanian gates. For he besought them all, casting himself down
in the mire, calling on each man by his name: "Hold, friends, and
though you love me leave me to get him forth of the city alone and
go unto the ships of the Achaians. Let me pray this accursed
horror-working man, if haply he may feel shame before his age-
fellows and pity an old man. He also hath a father such as I am,
Peleus, who begat and reared him to be a bane of Trojans — and
most of all to me hath he brought woe. So many sons of mine hath
he slain in their flower — yet for all my sorrow for the rest I mourn
them all less than this one alone, for whom my sharp grief will
bring me down to the house of Hades — even Hector. Would that
he had died in my arms; then would we have wept and wailed our
fill, his mother who bore him to her ill hap, and I myself."

Thus spake he wailing, and all the men of the city made moan
with him. And among the women of Troy, Hekabe led the wild
lament: "My child, ah, woe is me! wherefore should I live in my
pain, now thou art dead, who night and day wert my boast through
the city, and blessing to all, both men and women of Troy throughout the town, who hailed thee as a god, for verily an exceeding
glory to them wert thou in thy life: — now death and fate have
overtaken thee."

Thus spake she wailing. But Hector's wife knew not as yet, for
no true messenger had come to tell her how her husband abode
without the gates, but in an inner chamber of the lofty house she

was weaving a double purple web, and broidering therein manifold
flowers. Then she called to her goodly-haired handmaids through
the house to set a great tripod on the fire, that Hector might have
warm washing when he came home out of the battle — fond heart,
and was unaware how, far from all washings, bright-eyed Athene
had slain him by the hand of Achilles. But she heard shrieks and
groans from the battlements, and her limbs reeled, and the shuttle
fell from her hands to earth. Then again among her goodly-haired
maids she spake: "Come two of ye this way with me that I may
see what deeds are done. It was the voice of my husband's noble
mother that I heard, and in my own breast my heart leapeth to my
mouth and my knees are numbed beneath me: surely some evil
thing is at hand against the children of Priam. Would that such
word might never reach my ear! yet terribly I dread lest noble
Achilles have cut off bold Hector from the city by himself and
chased him to the plain and ere this ended his perilous pride that
possessed him, for never would he tarry among the throng of men
but ran out before them far, yielding place to no man in his hardihood."

Thus saying she sped through the chamber like one mad, with
beating heart, and with her went her handmaidens. But when
she came to the battlements and the throng of men, she stood still
upon the wall and gazed, and beheld him dragged before the city:
— swift horses dragged him recklessly toward the hollow ships of
the Achaians. Then dark night came on her eyes and shrouded
her, and she fell backward and gasped forth her spirit. From off
her head she shook the bright attiring thereof, frontlet and net and
woven band, and veil, the veil that golden Aphrodite gave her on
the day when Hector of the glancing helm led her forth of the
house of Eëtion, having given bride-gifts untold. And around her
thronged her husband's sisters and his brothers' wives, who held her
up among them, distraught even to death. But when at last she
came to herself and her soul returned into her breast, then wailing
with deep sobs she spake among the women of Troy: "O Hector,
woe is me! to one fate then were we both born, thou in Troy in
the house of Priam, and I in Thebe under woody Plakos, in the
house of Eëtion, who reared me from a little one — ill-fated sire
of cruel-fated child. Ah, would he had begotten me not. Now
thou to the house of Hades beneath the secret places of the earth
departest, and me in bitter mourning thou leavest a widow in thy
halls: and thy son is but an infant child — son of unhappy parents,
thee and me — nor shalt thou profit him, Hector, since thou art
dead, neither he thee. For even if he escape the Achaians' woful
war, yet shall labour and sorrow cleave unto him hereafter, for other
men shall seize his lands. The day of orphanage sundereth a child
from his fellows, and his head is bowed down ever, and his cheeks
are wet with tears. And in his need the child seeketh his father's
friends, plucking this one by cloak and that by coat, and one of
them that pity him holdeth his cup a little to his mouth, and

moisteneth his lips, but his palate he moisteneth not. And some
child unorphaned thrusteth him from the feast with blows and
taunting words, 'Out with thee! no father of thine is at our board.'
Then weeping to his widowed mother shall he return, even Astyanax, who erst upon his father's knee ate only marrow and fat
flesh of sheep; and when sleep fell on him and he ceased from
childish play, then in bed in his nurse's arms he would slumber
softly nested, having satisfied his heart with good things; but now
that he hath lost his father he will suffer many ills, Astyanax —
that name the Trojans gave him, because thou only wert the defence of their gates and their long walls. But now by the beaked
ships, far from thy parents, shall coiling worms devour thee when
the dogs have had their fill, as thou liest naked; yet in these halls
lieth raiment of thine, delicate and fair, wrought by the hands of
women. But verily all these will I consume with burning fire —
to thee no profit, since thou wilt never lie therein, yet that this be
honour to thee from the men and the women of Troy."

Thus spake she wailing, and the women joined their moan.

[tr. Lang, Leaf, Myers]

[The next two days are filled with the funeral of Patroklos and with
funeral games in his honour.]

BOOK XXIV

How the body of Hector was ransomed, and of his funeral.

Then the assembly was broken up, and the tribes were scattered
to betake them each to their own swift ships. The rest bethought
them of supper and sweet sleep to have joy thereof; but Achilles
wept, remembering his dear comrade, nor did sleep that conquereth
all take hold on him, but he kept turning him to this side and to
that, yearning for Patroklos' manhood and excellent valour, and all
the toils he achieved with him and the woes he bare, cleaving the
battles of men and the grievous waves. As he thought thereon he
shed big tears, now lying on his side, now on his back, now on his
face; and then anon he would arise upon his feet and roam wildly
beside the beach of the salt sea. Nor would he be unaware of the
Dawn when she arose over the sea and shores. But when he had
yoked the swift steeds to his car he would bind Hector behind his
chariot to drag him withal; and having thrice drawn him round
the barrow of the dead son of Menoitios he rested again in his hut,
and left Hector lying stretched on his face in the dust. But Apollo
kept away all defacement from his flesh, for he had pity on him
even in death, and covered him all with his golden aegis, that
Achilles might not tear him when he dragged him.

Thus Achilles in his anger entreated noble Hector shamefully;
but the blessed gods when they beheld him pitied him, and urged
the clear-sighted slayer of Argus to steal the corpse away. So to all
the others seemed it good, yet not to Hera or Poseidon or the bright-

eyed Maiden, but they continued as when at the beginning sacred
Ilios became hateful to them, and Priam and his people, by reason
of the sin of Alexandros in that he contemned those goddesses when
they came to his steading, and preferred her who brought him
deadly lustfulness. But when the twelfth morn from that day
arose, then spake among the Immortals Phoebus Apollo: "Hard of
heart are ye, O gods, and cruel. Hath Hector never burnt for you
thigh-bones of unblemished bulls and goats? Now have ye not
taken heart to rescue even his corpse for his wife to look upon and
his mother and his child and his father Priam and his people, who
speedily would burn him in the fire and make his funeral. But fell
Achilles, O gods, ye are fain to abet, whose mind is nowise just nor
the purpose in his breast to be turned away, but he is cruelly minded
as a lion that in great strength and at the bidding of his proud
heart goeth forth against men's flocks to make his meal; even thus
Achilles hath cast out pity, neither hath he shame, that doth both
harm and profit men greatly. It must be that many a man lose
even some dearer one than was this, a brother of the same womb
born or perchance a son; yet bringeth he his wailing and lamentation to an end, for an enduring soul have the Fates given unto men.
But Achilles after bereaving noble Hector of his life bindeth him
behind his horses and draggeth him around the tomb of his dear
comrade: not, verily, is that more honourable or better for him.
Let him take heed lest we wax wroth with him, good man though he
be, for in his fury he is entreating shamefully the senseless clay."

Then in anger spake unto him white-armed Hera: "Even thus
mightest thou speak, O Lord of the silver bow, if ye are to give equal
honour to Achilles and to Hector. Hector is but a mortal and was
suckled at a woman's breast, but Achilles is child of a goddess whom
I myself bred up and reared and gave to a man to be his wife,
even to Peleus who was dearest of all men to the Immortals' heart.
And all ye gods came to her bridal, and thou among them wert
feasting with thy lyre, O lover of ill company, faithless ever."

Then to her in answer spake Zeus who gathereth the clouds:
"Hera, be not wroth utterly with the gods: for these men's honour
is not to be the same, yet Hector also was dearest to the gods of all
mortals that are in Ilios. So was he to me at least, for nowise
failed he in the gifts I loved. Never did my altar lack seemly
feast, drink-offering and the steam of sacrifice, even the honour that
falleth to our due. But verily we will say no more of stealing
away brave Hector, for it cannot be hidden from Achilles, for his
mother abideth ever nigh to him night and day. But I were fain
that some one of the gods would call Thetis to come near to me,
that I may speak unto her a wise word, so that Achilles may take
gifts from Priam and give Hector back."

Thus spake he, and airy-footed Iris sped forth upon the errand
and between Samothrace and rocky Imbros leapt into the black sea,
and the waters closed above her with a noise. And she sped to the
bottom like a weight of lead that mounted on horn of a field-ox

goeth down bearing death to ravenous fishes. And she found
Thetis in a hollow cave; about her sat gathered other goddesses of
the sea, and she in their midst was wailing for the fate of her
noble son who must perish in deep-soiled Troy, far from his native
land. And standing near, fleet-footed Iris spake to her: "Rise,
Thetis; Zeus of immortal counsels calleth thee."

And to her made answer Thetis the silver-footed goddess:
"Wherefore biddeth me that mighty god? I shrink from mingling
among the Immortals, for I have countless woes at heart. Yet go I,
nor shall his word be in vain, whatsoever he saith."

Thus having said the noble goddess took to her a dark-hued robe,
no blacker raiment was there found than that. Then she went
forth, and wind-footed swift Iris led the way before her, and around
them the surge of the sea was sundered. And when they had come
forth upon the shore they sped up to heaven, and found the far-
seeing son of Kronos, and round him sat gathered all the other
blessed gods that are for ever. Then she sat down beside father
Zeus, and Athene gave her place. And Hera set a fair golden cup
in her hand and cheered her with words, and Thetis drank, and
gave back the cup. Then began speech to them the father of gods
and men: "Thou art come to Olympus, divine Thetis, in thy sorrow, with violent grief at thy heart; I know it of myself. Nevertheless will I tell thee wherefore I called thee hither. Nine days
hath dispute arisen among the Immortals concerning the corpse of
Hector and Achilles waster of cities. Fain are they to send clear-
sighted Argeïphontes to steal the body away, but now hear what
glory I accord herein to Achilles, that I may keep through times
to come thy honour and good will. Go with all speed to the host
and bear to thy son my bidding. Say to him that the gods are displeased at him, and that I above all Immortals am wroth, because
with furious heart he holdeth Hector at the beaked ships and hath
not given him back, if haply he may fear me and give Hector back.
But I will send Iris to great-hearted Priam to bid him go to the
ships of the Achaians to ransom his dear son, and carry gifts to
Achilles that may gladden his heart."

Thus spake he, and Thetis the silver-footed goddess was not disobedient to his word, and sped darting upon her way down from
the peaks of Olympus. And she came to her son's hut; there found
she him making grievous moan, and his dear comrades round were
swiftly making ready and furnishing their early meal, and a sheep
great and fleecy was being sacrificed in the hut. Then his lady
mother sate her down close beside him, and stroked him with her
hand and spake to him by his name: "My child, how long with
lamentation and woe wilt thou devour thine heart, taking thought
of neither food nor rest? good were even a woman's embrace, for
not long shalt thou be left alive to me; already death and forceful
fate are standing nigh thee. But hearken forthwith unto me, for
I am the messenger of Zeus to thee. He saith that the gods are
displeased at thee, and that himself above all Immortals is wroth,

because with furious heart thou holdest Hector at the beaked ships and hast not given him back. But come restore him, and take ransom for the dead."

Then to her in answer spake fleet-footed Achilles: "So be it: whoso bringeth ransom let him take back the dead, if verily with heart's intent the Olympian biddeth it himself."

So they in the assembly of the ships, mother and son, spake to each other many winged words. But the son of Kronos thus bade Iris go to holy Ilios: "Go forth, fleet Iris, leave the abode of Olympus and bear my message within Ilios to great-hearted Priam that he go to the ships of the Achaians and ransom his dear son and carry gifts to Achilles that may gladden his heart; let him go alone, and no other man of the Trojans go with him. Only let some elder herald attend on him to guide the mules and smooth-wheeled waggon and carry back to the city the dead man whom noble Achilles slew. Let not death be in his thought nor any fear; such guide will we give unto him, even the slayer of Argus, who shall lead him until his leading bring him to Achilles. And when he shall have led him within the hut, neither shall Achilles himself slay him nor suffer any other herein, for not senseless is he or unforeseeing or wicked, but with all courtesy he will spare a suppliant man."

Thus spake he, and airy-footed Iris sped forth upon the errand. And she came to the house of Priam, and found therein crying and moan. His children sitting around their father within the court were bedewing their raiment with their tears, and the old man in their midst was close wrapped all over in his cloak; and on his head and neck was much mire that he had gathered in his hands as he grovelled upon the earth. And his daughters and his sons' wives were wailing throughout the house, bethinking them of all those valiant men who had lost their lives at the hands of the Argives and were lying low. And the messenger of Zeus stood beside Priam and spake softly unto him, and trembling came upon his limbs: "Be of good cheer in thy heart, O Priam son of Dardanos, and be not dismayed for anything, for no evil come I hither to forebode to thee, but with good will. I am the messenger of Zeus to thee, who, though he be afar off, hath great care and pity for thee. The Olympian biddeth thee ransom noble Hector and carry gifts to Achilles that may gladden his heart: go thou alone, let none other of the Trojans go with thee. Only let some elder herald attend on thee to guide the mules and the smooth-wheeled waggon to carry back to the city the dead man whom noble Achilles slew. Let not death be in thy thought, nor any fear; such guide shall go with thee, even the slayer of Argus, who shall lead thee until his leading bring thee to Achilles. And when he shall have led thee into the hut, neither shall Achilles himself slay thee nor suffer any other herein, for not senseless is he or unforeseeing or wicked, but with all courtesy he will spare a suppliant man."

Thus having spoken fleet Iris departed from him; and he bade

his sons make ready the smooth-wheeled mule waggon, and bind
the wicker carriage thereon. And himself he went down to his
fragrant chamber, of cedar wood, high-roofed, that held full many
jewels: and to Hekabe his wife he called and spake: "Lady, from
Zeus hath an Olympian messenger come to me, that I go to the
ships of the Achaians and ransom my dear son, and carry gifts to
Achilles that may gladden his heart. Come tell me how seemeth
it to thy mind, for of myself at least my desire and heart bid me
mightily to go thither to the ships and enter the wide camp of the
Achaians."

Thus spake he, but his wife lamented aloud and made answer
unto him: "Woe is me, whither is gone thy mind whereby aforetime thou wert famous among stranger men and among them thou
rulest? How art thou fain to go alone to the ships of the Achaians,
to meet the eyes of the man who hath slain full many of thy
brave sons? of iron verily is thy heart. For if he light on thee
and behold thee with his eyes, a savage and ill-trusted man is this,
and he will not pity thee, neither reverence thee at all. Nay, now
let us sit in the hall and make lament afar off. Even thus did
forceful Fate erst spin for Hector with her thread at his beginning,
when I bare him, even I that he should glut fleet-footed dogs, far
from his parents, in the dwelling of a violent man whose inmost
vitals I were fain to fasten and feed upon; then would his deeds
against my son be paid again to him, for not playing the coward
was he slain of him, but championing the men and deep-bosomed
women of Troy, neither bethought he him of shelter or of flight."

Then to her in answer spake the old man godlike Priam: "Stay
me not, for I am fain to go, neither be thyself a bird of ill boding
in my halls, for thou wilt not change my mind. Were it some
other and a child of earth that bade me this, whether some seer
or of the priests that divine from sacrifice, then would we declare
it false and have no part therein; but now, since I have heard the
voice of the goddess myself and looked upon her face, I will go
forth, and her word shall not be void. And if it be my fate to
die by the ships of the mail-clad Achaians, so would I have it; let
Achilles slay me with all speed, when once I have taken in my
arms my son, and have satisfied my desire with moan."

He spake, and opened fair lids of chests wherefrom he chose
twelve very goodly women's robes and twelve cloaks of single fold
and of coverlets a like number and of fair sheets, and of doublets
thereupon. And he weighed and brought forth talents of gold ten
in all, and two shining tripods and four caldrons, and a goblet exceeding fair that men of Thrace had given him when he went
thither on an embassy, a chattel of great price, yet not that even did
the old man grudge from his halls, for he was exceeding fain at
heart to ransom his dear son. Then he drave out all the Trojans
from the colonnade, chiding them with words of rebuke: "Begone,
ye that dishonour and do me shame! Have ye no mourning of
your own at home that ye come to vex me here? Think ye it a

small thing that Zeus Kronos' son hath given me this sorrow, to lose him that was the best man of my sons? Nay, but ye too shall feel it, for easier far shall ye be to the Achaians to slay now he is dead. But for me, ere I behold with mine eyes the city sacked and wasted, let me go down into the house of Hades."

He said, and with his staff chased forth the men, and they went forth before the old man in his haste. Then he called unto his sons, chiding Helenos and Paris and noble Agathon and Pammon and Antiphonos, and Polites of the loud war-cry, and Deiphobos and Hippothoos and proud Dios; nine were they whom the old man called and bade unto him: "Haste ye, ill sons, my shame; would that ye all in Hector's stead had been slain at the swift ships! Woe is me all unblest, since I begat sons the best men in wide Troy-land, but none of them is left for me to claim, neither godlike Mestor, nor Troilos with his chariot of war, nor Hector who was a god among men, neither seemed he as the son of a mortal man but of a god: — all these hath Ares slain, and here are my shames all left to me, false-tongued, light-heeled, the heroes of the dance, plunderers of your own people's sheep and kids. Will ye not make me ready a wain with all speed, and lay all these thereon, that we get us forward on our way?"

Thus spake he, and they fearing their father's voice brought forth the smooth-running mule chariot, fair and new, and bound the body thereof on the frame; and from its peg they took down the mule yoke, a boxwood yoke with knob well fitted with guiding-rings; and they brought forth the yoke-band of nine cubits with the yoke. The yoke they set firmly on the polished pole on the rest at the end thereof, and slipped the ring over the upright pin, which with three turns of the band they lashed to the knob, and then belayed it close round the pole and turned the tongue thereunder. Then they brought from the chamber and heaped on the polished wain the countless ransom of Hector's head, and yoked strong-hooved harness mules, which on a time the Mysians gave to Priam, a splendid gift. But to Priam's car they yoked the horses that the old man kept for his use and reared at the polished crib.

Thus in the high palace were Priam and the herald letting yoke their cars, with wise thoughts at their hearts, when nigh them came Hekabe sore at heart, with honey-sweet wine in her right hand in a golden cup that they might make libation ere they went. And she stood before the horses and spake a word to Priam by name: "Lo now make libation to father Zeus and pray that thou mayest come back home from among the enemy, since thy heart speedeth thee forth to the ships, though fain were I thou wentest not. And next pray to Kronion of the Storm-cloud, the god of Ida, that beholdeth all Troy-land beneath, and ask of him a bird of omen, even the swift messenger that is dearest of all birds to him and of mightiest strength, to appear upon thy right, that seeing the sign with thine own eyes thou mayest go in trust thereto unto the ships of the fleet-horsed Danaans. But if far-seeing Zeus shall not grant unto

thee his messenger, I at least shall not bid thee on to go among
the ships of the Achaians how fain soever thou mayest be."

Then answered and spake unto her godlike Priam: "Lady, I will
not disregard this hest of thine, for good it is to lift up hands to
Zeus, if haply he will have pity."

Thus spake the old man, and bade a house-dame that served him
pour pure water on his hands; and she came near to serve him
with water in a ewer to wash withal. And when he had washed
his hands he took a goblet from his wife: then he stood in the midst
of the court and prayed and poured forth wine as he looked up to
heaven, and spake a word aloud: "Father Zeus that bearest sway
from Ida, most glorious and most great, grant that I find welcome
and pity under Achilles' roof, and send a bird of omen, even the
swift messenger that is dearest of all birds to thee and of mightiest
strength, to appear upon the right, that seeing this sign with mine
own eyes I may go trusting therein unto the ships of the fleet-
horsed Danaans."

Thus spake he praying, and Zeus of wise counsels hearkened
unto him, and straightway sent forth an eagle, surest omen of
winged birds, the dusky hunter called of men the Black Eagle.
Wide as the door, well locking, fitted close, of some rich man's
high-roofed hall, so wide were his wings either way; and he appeared to them speeding on the right hand above the city. And
when they saw the eagle they rejoiced and all their hearts were glad
within their breasts.

Then the old man made haste to go up into his car, and drave
forth from the doorway and the echoing portico. In front the
mules drew the four-wheeled wain, and wise Idaios drave them; behind came the horses which the old man urged with the lash at
speed along the city: and his friends all followed lamenting loud
as though he were faring to his death. And when they were come
down from the city and were now on the plain, then went back
again to Ilios his sons and marriage kin. But the two coming forth
upon the plain were not unbeheld of far-seeing Zeus. But he looked
upon the old man and had compassion on him, and straightway
spake unto Hermes his dear son: "Hermes, since unto thee especially is it dear to companion men, and thou hearest whomsoever
thou wilt, go forth and so guide Priam to the hollow ships of the
Achaians that no man behold or be aware of him, among all the
Danaans' host, until he come to the son of Peleus."

Thus spake he, and the Messenger, the slayer of Argus, was not
disobedient unto his word. Straightway beneath his feet he bound
on his fair sandals, golden, divine, that bare him over the wet sea
and over the boundless land with the breathings of the wind. And
he took up his wand wherewith he entranceth the eyes of such men
as he will, and others he likewise waketh out of sleep: this did the
strong slayer of Argus take in his hand, and flew. And quickly
came he to Troy-land and the Hellespont, and went on his way in

semblance as a young man that is a prince, with the new down on his chin, as when the youth of men is the comeliest.

Now the others, when they had driven beyond the great barrow of Ilios, halted the mules and horses at the river to drink; for darkness was come down over the earth. Then the herald beheld Hermes from hard by, and marked him, and spake and said to Priam: "Consider, son of Dardanos; this is matter of prudent thought. I see a man, methinks we shall full soon be rent in pieces. Come, let us flee in our chariot, or else at least touch his knees and entreat him that he have mercy on us."

Thus spake he, and the old man was confounded, and he was dismayed exceedingly, and the hair on his pliant limbs stood up, and he stood still amazed. But the Helper came nigh of himself and took the old man's hand, and spake and questioned him: "Whither, father, dost thou thus guide these horses and mules through the divine night, when other mortals are asleep? Hadst thou no fear of the fierce-breathing Achaians, thy bitter foes that are hard anigh thee? If one of them should espy thee carrying such treasures through the swift black night, what then would be thy thought? Neither art thou young thyself, and thy companion here is old, that ye should make defence against a man that should assail thee first. But I will nowise harm thee, yea I will keep any other from thy hurt: for the similitude of my dear father I see in thee."

And to him in answer spake the old man, godlike Priam: "Even so, kind son, are all these things as thou sayest. Nevertheless hath some god stretched forth his hand even over me in that he hath sent a wayfarer such as thou to meet me, a bearer of good luck, by the nobleness of thy form and semblance; and thou art wise of heart and of blessed parents art thou sprung."

And to him again spake the Messenger, the slayer of Argus: "All this, old sire, hast thou verily spoken aright. But come say this and tell me truly whether thou art taking forth a great and goodly treasure unto alien men, where it may abide for thee in safety, or whether by this ye are all forsaking holy Ilios in fear; so far the best man among you hath perished, even thy son; for of battle with the Achaians abated he never a jot."

And to him in answer spake the old man, godlike Priam: "Who art thou, noble sir, and of whom art born? For meetly hast thou spoken of the fate of my hapless son."

And to him again spake the Messenger, the slayer of Argus: "Thou art proving me, old sire, in asking me of noble Hector. Him have I full oft seen with mine eyes in glorious battle, and when at the ships he was slaying the Argives he drave thither, piercing them with the keen bronze, and we stood still and marvelled thereat, for Achilles suffered us not to fight, being wroth against Atreus' son. His squire am I, and came in the same well-wrought ship. From the Myrmidons I come, and my father is Polyktor. Wealthy is he, and an old man even as thou, and six other sons

hath he, and I am his seventh. With the others I cast lots, and it
fell to me to fare hither with the host. And now am I come from
the ships to the plain, for at day-break the glancing-eyed Achaians
will set the battle in array around the town. For it chafeth them
to be sitting here, nor can the Achaian lords hold in their fury for
the fray."

And the old man, godlike Priam, answered him, saying: "If
verily thou art a squire of Achilles Peleus' son, come tell me all
the truth, whether still my son is by the ships, or whether ere now
Achilles hath riven him limb from limb and cast him to the dogs."

Then to him again spake the Messenger the slayer of Argus: "Old
sire, not yet have dogs or birds devoured him, but there lieth he
still by Achilles' ship, even as he fell, among the huts, and the
twelfth morn now hath risen upon him, nor doth his flesh corrupt
at all, neither worms consume it, such as devour men slain in war.
Truly Achilles draggeth him recklessly around the barrow of his
dear comrade so oft as divine day dawneth, yet marreth he him
not; thou wouldst marvel if thou couldst go see thyself how dewy
fresh he lieth, and is washed clean of blood, nor anywhere defiled;
and all his wounds wherewith he was stricken are closed; howbeit
many plunged their points in him. So careful are the blessed gods
of thy son, though he be but a dead corpse, for they held him dear
at heart."

Thus spake he, and the old man rejoiced, and answered him
saying: "My son, it is verily a good thing to give due offerings
withal to the Immortals, for never did my child — if that child indeed I had — forget in our halls the gods who inhabit Olympus.
Therefore have they remembered this for him, albeit his portion is
death. But come now take from me this goodly goblet, and guard
me myself and guide me, under Heaven, that I may come unto the
hut of Peleus' son."

Then spake unto him again the Messenger the slayer of Argus:
"Thou art proving me, old sire, who am younger than thou, but
thou wilt not prevail upon me, in that thou biddest me take gifts
from thee without Achilles' privity. I were afraid and shamed at
heart to defraud him, lest some evil come to pass on me hereafter.
But as thy guide I would go even unto famous Argos, accompanying thee courteously in swift ship or on foot. Not from scorn of
thy guide would any assail thee then."

Thus spake the Helper, and leaping on the chariot behind the
horses he swiftly took lash and reins into his hands, and breathed
brave spirit into horses and mules. But when they were come to
the towers and trench of the ships, there were the sentinels just
busying them about their supper. Then the Messenger, the slayer
of Argus, shed sleep upon them all, and straightway opened the
gates and thrust back the bars, and brought within Priam and the
splendid gifts upon his wain. And they came to the lofty hut of
the son of Peleus, which the Myrmidons made for their king and
hewed therefor timber of the pine, and thatched it with downy

thatching-rush that they mowed in the meadows, and around it made for him their lord a great court with close-set palisades; and the door was barred by a single bolt of pine that three Achaians wont to drive home, and three drew back that mighty bar — three of the rest, but Achilles by himself would drive it home. Then opened the Helper Hermes the door for the old man, and brought in the splendid gifts for Peleus' fleet-footed son, and descended from the chariot to the earth and spake aloud: "Old sire, I that have come to thee am an immortal god, even Hermes, for my father sent me to companion thee on thy way. But now will I depart from thee nor come within Achilles' sight; it were cause of wrath that an immortal god should thus show favour openly unto mortals. But thou go in and clasp the knees of Peleus' son and entreat him for his father's sake and his mother's of the lovely hair and for his child's sake that thou mayest move his soul."

Thus Hermes spake, and departed unto high Olympus. But Priam leapt from the car to the earth, and left Idaios in his place; he stayed to mind the horses and mules; but the old man made straight for the house where Achilles dear to Zeus was wont to sit. And therein he found the man himself, and his comrades sate apart: two only, the hero Automedon and Alkimos, of the stock of Ares, were busy in attendance; and he was lately ceased from meat, even from eating and drinking: and still the table stood beside him. But they were unaware of great Priam as he came in, and so stood he anigh and clasped in his hands the knees of Achilles, and kissed his hands, terrible, man-slaying, that slew many of Priam's sons. And as when a grievous curse cometh upon a man who in his own country hath slain another and escapeth to a land of strangers, to the house of some rich man, and wonder possesseth them that look on him — so Achilles wondered when he saw godlike Priam, and the rest wondered likewise, and looked upon one another. Then Priam spake and entreated him, saying: "Bethink thee, O Achilles like to gods, of thy father that is of like years with me, on the grievous pathway of old age. Him haply are the dwellers round about entreating evilly, nor is there any to ward from him ruin and bane. Nevertheless while he heareth of thee as yet alive he rejoiceth in his heart, and hopeth withal day after day that he shall see his dear son returning from Troy-land. But I, I am utterly unblest, since I begat sons the best men in wide Troy-land, but declare unto thee that none of them is left. Fifty I had, when the sons of the Achaians came; nineteen were born to me of one mother, and concubines bare the rest within my halls. Now of the more part had impetuous Ares unstrung the knees, and he who was yet left and guarded city and men, him slewest thou but now as he fought for his country, even Hector. For his sake come I unto the ships of the Achaians that I may win him back from thee, and I bring with me untold ransom. Yea, fear thou the gods, Achilles, and have compassion on me, even me, bethinking thee of thy father. Lo, I am yet more piteous than he, and have braved what none other man on earth hath braved before, to stretch forth my hand toward the face of the slayer of my sons."

Thus spake he, and stirred within Achilles desire to make lament for his father. And he touched the old man's hand and gently moved him back. And as they both bethought them of their dead, so Priam for man-slaying Hector wept sore as he was fallen before Achilles' feet, and Achilles wept for his own father, and now again for Patroklos, and their moan went up throughout the house. But when noble Achilles had satisfied him with lament, and the desire thereof departed from his heart and limbs, straightway he sprang from his seat and raised the old man by his hand, pitying his hoary head and hoary beard, and spake unto him winged words and said: "Ah hapless! many ill things verily thou hast endured in thy heart. How durst thou come alone to the ships of the Achaians and to meet the eyes of the man who hath slain full many of thy brave sons? of iron verily is thy heart. But come then set thee on a seat, and we will let our sorrows lie quiet in our hearts, for all our pain, for no avail cometh of chill lament. This is the lot the gods have spun for miserable men, that they should live in pain; yet themselves are sorrowless. For two urns stand upon the floor of Zeus filled with his evil gifts, and one with blessings. To whomsoever Zeus whose joy is in the lightning dealeth a mingled lot, that man chanceth now upon ill and now again on good, but to whom he giveth but of the bad kind him he bringeth to scorn, and evil famine chaseth him over the goodly earth, and he is a wanderer honoured of neither gods nor men. Even thus to Peleus gave the gods splendid gifts from his birth, for he excelled all men in good fortune and wealth, and was king of the Myrmidons, and mortal though he was the gods gave him a goddess to be his bride. Yet even on him God brought evil, seeing that there arose to him no offspring of princely sons in his halls, save that he begat one son to an untimely death. Neither may I tend him as he groweth old, since very far from my country I am dwelling in Troy-land, to vex thee and thy children. And of thee, old sire, we have heard how of old time thou wert happy, even how of all that Lesbos, seat of Makar, boundeth to the north thereof and Phrygia farther up and the vast Hellespont — of all these folk, men say, thou wert the richest in wealth and in sons, but after that the Powers of Heaven brought this bane on thee, ever are battles and man-slayings around thy city. Keep courage, and lament not unabatingly in thy heart. For nothing wilt thou avail by grieving for thy son, neither shalt thou bring him back to life or ever some new evil come upon thee."

Then made answer unto him the old man, godlike Priam: "Bid me not to a seat, O fosterling of Zeus, so long as Hector lieth uncared for at the huts, but straightway give him back that I may behold him with mine eyes; and accept thou the great ransom that we bring. So mayest thou have pleasure thereof, and come unto thy native land, since thou hast spared me from the first."

Then fleet-footed Achilles looked sternly upon him and said: "No longer chafe me, old sire; of myself am I minded to give Hector back to thee, for there came to me a messenger from Zeus, even my mother who bare me, daughter of the Ancient One of the Sea. And I know, O Priam, in my mind, nor am unaware that some god it is that hath guided thee to the swift ships of the Achaians. For no mortal man, even though in prime of youth, would dare to come among the host, for neither could he escape the watch, nor easily thrust back the bolt of our doors. Therefore now stir my heart no more amid my troubles, lest I leave not even thee in peace, old sire, within my hut, albeit thou art my suppliant, and lest I transgress the commandment of Zeus."

Thus spake he, and the old man feared, and obeyed his word. And the son of Peleus leapt like a lion through the door of the house, not alone, for with him went two squires, the hero Automedon and Alkimos, they whom above all his comrades Achilles honoured, save only Patroklos that was dead. They then loosed from under the yoke the horses and mules, and led in the old man's crier-herald and set him on a chair, and from the wain of goodly felloes they took the countless ransom set on Hector's head. But they left two robes and a well-spun doublet, that Achilles might wrap the dead therein when he gave him to be carried home. And he called forth handmaids and bade them wash and anoint him when they had borne him apart, so that Priam should not look upon his son, lest he should not refrain the wrath at his sorrowing heart when he should look upon his son, and lest Achilles' heart be vexed thereat and he slay him and transgress the commandment of Zeus. So when the handmaids had washed the body and anointed it with oil, and had thrown over it a fair robe and a doublet, then Achilles himself lifted it and laid it on a bier, and his comrades with him lifted it onto the polished waggon. Then he groaned aloud and called on his dear comrade by his name: "Patroklos, be not vexed with me if thou hear even in the house of Hades that I have given back noble Hector unto his dear father, for not unworthy is the ransom he hath given me, whereof I will deal to thee again thy rightful share."

Thus spake noble Achilles, and went back into the hut, and sate him down on the cunningly-wrought couch whence he had arisen by the opposite wall, and spake a word to Priam: "Thy son, old sire, is given back as thou wouldest and lieth on a bier, and with the break of day thou shalt see him thyself as thou carriest him. But now bethink we us of supper. For even faired-haired Niobe bethought her of meat, she whose twelve children perished in her halls, six daughters and six lusty sons. The sons Apollo, in his anger against Niobe, slew with arrows from his silver bow, and the daughters archer Artemis, for that Niobe matched herself against fair-cheeked Leto, saying that the goddess bare but twain but herself many children: so they though they were but twain destroyed the others all. Nine days they lay in their blood, nor was there any to bury them, for Kronion turned the folk to stones. Yet on the tenth day the gods of heaven buried them, and she then bethought her of meat, when she was wearied out with weeping tears. And somewhere now among the cliffs, on the lonely mountains, even on Sipylos, where they say are the couching-places of nymphs that dance around Acheloös, there she, albeit a stone, broodeth still over her troubles from the gods. But come let us too, noble father, take thought of meat, and afterward thou shalt mourn over thy dear son as thou carriest him to Ilios; and many tears shall be his due."

Thus spake fleet Achilles, and sprang up, and slew a pure white sheep, and his comrades skinned and made it ready in seemly fashion, and divided it cunningly and pierced it with spits, and roasted it carefully and drew all off. And Automedon took bread and served it on a table in fair baskets, while Achilles dealt out the flesh. And they stretched forth their hands to the good cheer lying ready before them. But when they had put off the desire of meat and drink, then Priam son of Dardanos marvelled at Achilles to see how great he was and how goodly, for he was like a god to look upon. And Achilles marvelled at Priam son of Dardanos, beholding his noble aspect and hearkening to his words. But when they had gazed their fill upon one another, then first spake the old man, godlike Priam, to Achilles: "Now presently give me whereon to lie, fosterling of Zeus, that of sweet sleep also we may now take our fill at rest: for never yet have mine eyes closed beneath their lids since at thy hands my son lost his life, but I continually mourn and brood over countless griefs, grovelling in the courtyard-close amid the mire. Now at last have I tasted bread and poured bright wine down my throat, but till now I had tasted nought."

He said, and Achilles bade his comrades and handmaids to set a bedstead beneath the portico, and to cast thereon fair shining rugs and spread coverlets above and thereon to lay thick mantles to be a clothing over all. And the maids went forth from the inner hall with torches in their hands, and quickly spread two beds in haste. Then with bitter meaning said fleet-footed Achilles unto Priam: "Lie thou without, dear sire, lest there come hither one of the counsellors of the Achaians, such as ever take counsel with me by my side, as custom is. If any of such should behold thee through the swift black night, forthwith he might haply tell it to Agamemnon shepherd of the host, and thus would there be delay in giving back the dead. But come say this to me and tell it true, how many days' space thou art fain to make funeral for noble Hector, so that for so long I may myself abide and may keep back the host."

And the old man, godlike Priam, answered him saying: "If thou art verily willing that I accomplish noble Hector's funeral, by doing as thou sayest, O Achilles, thou wilt do me grace. For thou knowest how we are pent within the city, and wood from the mountain is far to fetch, and the Trojans are much in fear. Nine days will we make moan for him in our halls, and on the tenth we will hold funeral and the folk shall feast, and on the eleventh we will make a barrow over him, and on the twelfth we will do battle if need be."

Then again spake the fleet noble Achilles unto him saying: "All this, O ancient Priam, shall be as thou biddest; for I will hold back the battle even so long a time as thou tellest me."

Thus speaking he clasped the old man's right hand at the wrist, lest he should be anywise afraid at heart. So they in the forepart of the house laid them down, Priam and the herald, with wise thoughts at their hearts, but Achilles slept in a recess of the firm-wrought hut, and beside him lay fair-cheeked Briseis.

Now all other gods and warriors lords of chariots slumbered all night, by soft sleep overcome. But not on the Helper Hermes did sleep take hold as he sought within his heart how he should guide forth king Priam from the ships unespied of the trusty sentinels. And he stood above his head and spake a word to him: "Old sire, no thought then hast thou of any evil, seeing thou yet sleepest among men that are thine enemies, for that Achilles spared thee. Truly now hast thou won back thy dear son, and at great price. But for thy life will thy sons thou hast left behind be offering threefold ransom, if but Agamemnon Atreus' son be aware of thee, and aware be all the Achaians."

Thus spake he, and the old man feared, and roused the herald. And Hermes yoked the horses and mules for them, and himself drave them lightly through the camp, and none was aware of them.

But when they came to the ford of the fair-flowing river, [even eddying Xanthos, begotten of immortal Zeus,] then Hermes departed up to high Olympus, and Morning of the saffron robe spread over all the earth. And they with wail and moan drave the horses to the city, and the mules drew the dead. Nor marked them any man or fair-girdled woman until Kassandra, peer of golden Aphrodite, having gone up upon Pergamos, was aware of her dear father as he stood in the car, and the herald that was crier to the town. Then beheld she him that lay upon the bier behind the mules, and thereat she wailed and cried aloud throughout all the town: "O men and women of Troy, come ye hither and look upon Hector, if ever while he was alive ye rejoiced when he came back from battle, since great joy was he to the city and all the folk."

Thus spake she, nor was man or woman left within the city, for upon all came unendurable grief. And near the gates they met Priam bringing home the dead. First bewailed him his dear wife and lady mother, as they cast them on the fair-wheeled wain and touched his head; and around them stood the throng and wept. So all day long unto the setting of the sun they had lamented Hector in tears without the gate, had not the old man spoken from the car among the folk: "Give me place for the mules to pass through; hereafter ye shall have your fill of wailing, when I have brought him unto his home."

Thus spake he, and they parted asunder and gave place to the wain. And the others when they had brought him to the famous house, laid him on a fretted bed, and set beside him minstrels leaders of the dirge, who wailed a mournful lay, while the women made moan with them. And among the women white-armed Andromache led the lamentation, while in her hands she held the head of Hector slayer of men: "Husband, thou art gone young from life, and leavest me a widow in thy halls. And the child is yet but a little one, child of ill-fated parents, thee and me; nor methinks shall he grow up to manhood, for ere then shall this city be utterly destroyed. For thou art verily perished who didst watch over it, who guardedst it and keptest safe its noble wives and infant little ones. These soon shall be voyaging in the hollow ships, yea and I too with them, and thou, my child, shalt either go with me unto a place where thou shalt toil at unseemly tasks, labouring before the face of some harsh lord, or else some Achaian will take thee by the arm and hurl thee from the battlement, a grievous death, for that he is wroth because Hector slew his brother or father or son, since full many of the Achaians at Hector's hands have bitten the firm earth. For no light hand had thy father in the grievous fray. Therefore the folk lament him throughout the city, and woe unspeakable and mourning hast thou left to thy parents, Hector, but with me chiefliest shall grievous pain abide. For neither didst thou stretch thy hands to me from a bed in thy death, neither didst speak to me some memorable word that I might have thought on evermore as my tears fall night and day."

Thus spake she wailing, and the women joined their moan. And among them Hekabe again led the loud lament: "Hector, of all my children far dearest to my heart, verily while thou wert alive dear wert thou to the gods, and even in thy doom of death have they had care for thee. For other sons of mine whom he took captive would fleet Achilles sell beyond the unvintaged sea unto Samos and Imbros and smoking Lemnos, but when with keen-edged bronze he had bereft thee of thy life he was fain to drag thee oft around the tomb of his comrade, even Patroklos whom thou slewest, yet might he not raise him up thereby. But now all dewy and fresh thou liest in our halls, like one on whom Apollo, lord of the silver bow, hath descended and slain him with his gentle darts."

Thus spake she wailing, and stirred unending moan. Then thirdly Helen led their sore lament: "Hector, of all my brethren of Troy far dearest to my heart! Truly my lord is godlike Alexandros who brought me to Troy-land — would I had died ere then. For this is now the twentieth year since I went thence and am gone from my own native land, but never yet heard I evil or despiteful word from thee; nay, if any other haply upbraided me in the palace-halls, whether brother or sister of thine or brother's fair-robed wife, or thy mother — but thy father is ever kind to me as he were my own — then wouldst thou soothe such with words and refrain them, by the gentleness of thy spirit and by thy gentle words. Therefore bewail I thee with pain at heart, and my hapless self with thee, for no more is any left in wide Troy-land to be my friend and kind to me, but all men shudder at me."

Thus spake she wailing, and therewith the great multitude of the people groaned. But the old man Priam spake a word among the folk: "Bring wood, men of Troy, unto the city, and be not any-wise afraid at heart of a crafty ambush of the Achaians; for this message Achilles gave me when he sent me from the black ships, that they should do us no hurt until the twelfth morn arise."

Thus spake he, and they yoked oxen and mules to wains, and quickly then they flocked before the city. So nine days they gath-ered great store of wood. But when the tenth morn rose with light for men, then bare they forth brave Hector, weeping tears, and on a lofty pyre they laid the dead man, and thereon cast fire.

But when the daughter of Dawn, rosy-fingered Morning, shone forth, then gathered the folk around glorious Hector's pyre. First quenched they with bright wine all the burning, so far as the fire's strength went, and then his brethren and comrades gathered his white bones lamenting, and big tears flowed down their cheeks. And the bones they took and laid in a golden urn, shrouding them in soft purple robes, and straightway laid the urn in a hollow grave and piled thereon great close-set stones, and heaped with speed a barrow, while watchers were set everywhere around, lest the well-greaved Achaians should make onset before the time. And when they had heaped the barrow they went back, and gathered them together and feasted right well in noble feast at the palace of Priam, Zeus-fostered king.

Thus held they funeral for Hector tamer of horses.

[tr. Lang, Leaf, Myers]

THE ODYSSEY

BOOK I

In a Council of the Gods, Poseidon absent, Pallas procureth an order for the restitution of Odysseus; and appearing to his son Telemachus, in human shape, adviseth him to complain of the Wooers before the Council of the people, and then go to Pylos and Sparta to inquire about his father.

Tell me, Muse, of that man, so ready at need, who wandered far and wide, after he had sacked the sacred citadel of Troy, and many were the men whose towns he saw and whose mind he learnt, yea, and many the woes he suffered in his heart upon the deep, striv-ing to win his own life and the return of his company. Nay, but even so he saved not his company, though he desired it sore. For through the blindness of their own hearts they perished, fools, who devoured the oxen of Helios Hyperion: but the god took from them their day of returning. Of these things, goddess, daughter of Zeus, whencesoever thou hast heard thereof, declare thou even unto us.

Now all the rest, as many as fled from sheer destruction, were at home, and had escaped both war and sea, but Odysseus only, craving for his wife and for his homeward path, the lady nymph Calypso held, that fair goddess, in her hollow caves, longing to have him for her lord. But when now the year had come in the courses of the seasons, wherein the gods had ordained that he should return home to Ithaca, not even there was he quit of labours, not even among his own; but all the gods had pity on him save Poseidon, who raged continually against godlike Odysseus, till he came to his own country. Howbeit Poseidon had now departed for the distant Ethiopians, the Ethiopians that are sundered in twain, the uttermost of men, abiding some where Hyperion sinks and some where he rises. There he looked to receive his hecatomb of bulls and dams, there he made merry sitting at the feast, but the other gods were gathered in the halls of Olympian Zeus. Then among them the father of gods and men began to speak, for he bethought him in his heart of noble Aegisthus, whom the son of Agamemnon, far-famed Orestes, slew. Thinking upon him he spake out among the Immortals:

"Lo you now, how vainly mortal men do blame the gods! For of us they say comes evil, whereas they even of themselves, through the blindness of their own hearts, have sorrows beyond that which is ordained. Even as of late Aegisthus, beyond that which was ordained, took to him the wedded wife of the son of Atreus and killed her lord on his return, and that with sheer doom before his eyes, since we had warned him by the embassy of Hermes the keensighted, the slayer of Argos, that he should neither kill the man, nor woo his wife. For the son of Atreus shall be avenged at the hand of Orestes, so soon as he shall come to man's estate and long for his own country. So spake Hermes, yet he prevailed not on the heart of Aegisthus, for all his good will; but now hath he paid one price for all."

And the goddess, grey-eyed Athene, answered him, saying: "O father, our father Cronides, throned in the highest, that man assuredly lies in a death that is his due; so perish likewise all who work such deeds! But my heart is rent for wise Odysseus, the hapless one, who far from his friends this long while suffereth affliction in a seagirt isle, where is the navel of the sea, a woodland isle, and therein a goddess hath her habitation, the daughter of the wizard Atlas, who knows the depths of every sea, and himself upholds the tall pillars which keep earth and sky asunder. His daughter it is that holds the hapless man in sorrow: and ever with soft and guileful tales she is wooing him to forgetfulness of Ithaca. But Odysseus yearning to see if it were but the smoke leap upwards from his own land, hath a desire to die. As for thee, thine heart regardeth it not at all, Olympian! What! did not Odysseus by the ships of the Argives make thee free offering of sacrifice in the wide Trojan land? Wherefore wast thou then so wroth with him, O Zeus?"

And Zeus the cloud-gatherer answered her, and said: "My child, what word hath escaped the door of thy lips? Yea, how should I forget divine Odysseus, who in understanding is beyond mortals and beyond all men hath done sacrifice to the deathless gods, who keep the wide heaven? Nay, but it is Poseidon, the girdler of the earth, that hath been wroth continually with quenchless anger for the Cyclops' sake whom he blinded of his eye, even godlike Polyphemus whose power is mightiest amongst all the Cyclôpes. His mother was the nymph Thoösa, daughter of Phorcys, lord of the unharvested sea, and in the hollow caves she lay with Poseidon. From that day forth Poseidon the earth-shaker doth not indeed slay Odysseus, but driveth him wandering from his own country. But come, let us here one and all take good counsel as touching his returning, that he may be got home; so shall Poseidon let go his displeasure, for he will in no wise be able to strive alone against all, in despite of all the deathless gods."

Then the goddess, grey-eyed Athene, answered him, and said: "O father, our father Cronides, throned in the highest, if indeed this thing is now well pleasing to the blessed gods, that wise Odysseus should return to his own home, let us then speed Hermes the Messenger, the slayer of Argos, to the island of Ogygia. There with all speed let him declare to the lady of the braided tresses our unerring counsel, even the return of the patient Odysseus, that so he may come to his home. But as for me I will go to Ithaca that I may rouse his son yet the more, planting might in his heart, to call an assembly of the long-haired Achaeans and speak out to all the wooers who slaughter continually the sheep of his thronging flocks, and his kine with trailing feet and shambling gait. And I will guide him to Sparta and to sandy Pylos to seek tidings of his dear father's return, if peradventure he may hear thereof and that so he may be had in good report among men."

She spake and bound beneath her feet her lovely golden sandals, that wax not old, and bare her alike over the wet sea and over the limitless land, swift as the breath of the wind. And she seized her doughty spear, shod with sharp bronze, weighty and huge and strong, wherewith she quells the ranks of heroes with whomsoever she is wroth, the daughter of the mighty sire. Then from the heights of Olympus she came glancing down, and she stood in the land of Ithaca, at the entry of the gate of Odysseus, on the threshold of the courtyard, holding in her hand the spear of bronze, in the semblance of a stranger, Mentes the captain of the Taphians. And there she found the lordly wooers: now they were taking their pleasure at draughts in front of the doors, sitting on hides of oxen, which themselves had slain. And of the henchmen and the ready squires, some were mixing for them wine and water in bowls, and some again were washing the tables with porous sponges and were setting them forth, and others were carving flesh in plenty.

And godlike Telemachus was far the first to descry her, for he was sitting with a heavy heart among the wooers dreaming on his good father, if haply he might come somewhence, and make a scattering of the wooers there throughout the palace, and himself get honour and bear rule among his own possessions. Thinking thereupon, as he sat among wooers, he saw Athene — and he went straight to the outer porch, for he thought it blame in his heart that a stranger should stand long at the gates: and halting nigh her he clasped her right hand and took from her the spear of bronze, and uttered his voice and spake unto her winged words:

"Hail, stranger, with us thou shalt be kindly entreated, and thereafter, when thou hast tasted meat, thou shalt tell us that whereof thou hast need."

Therewith he led the way, and Pallas Athene followed.

[1–125, tr. BUTCHER & LANG]

[Athene advises Telemachus to go to Pylos and Sparta to seek news of his father. The next day Telemachus convenes the assembly of the Ithacans and makes a public complaint against the wooers; in reply the wooers accuse Penelope of leading them on, and they refuse to leave the house of Odysseus until Penelope shall choose a husband. Telemachus then secretly leaves Ithaca and goes to Pylos, where he meets Nestor; Nestor sends him on to see Menelaus and Helen in Sparta. Menelaus relates his wanderings and tells him how he learned from the sea-god Proteus that Odysseus was still alive. While Telemachus prolongs his visit in Sparta, the wooers fit out a ship and prepare an ambush to kill him on his way home to Ithaca.]

BOOK V

The Gods in council command Calypso by Hermes to send away Odysseus on a raft of trees; and Poseidon, returning from Ethiopia and seeing him on the coast of Phaeacia, scattered his raft; and how by the help of Ino he was thrown ashore, and slept on a heap of dry leaves till the next day.

Now the Dawn arose from her couch, from the side of the lordly Tithonus, to bear light to the immortals and to mortal men. And lo, the gods were gathering to session, and among them Zeus, that thunders on high, whose might is above all. And Athene told them the tale of the many woes of Odysseus, recalling them to mind; for near her heart was he that then abode in the dwelling of the nymph:

"Father Zeus, and all ye other blessed gods that live for ever, henceforth let not any sceptred king be kind and gentle with all his heart, nor minded to do righteously, but let him always be a hard man and work unrighteousness, for behold, there is none that remembereth divine Odysseus of the people whose lord he was, and was gentle as a father. Howbeit, as for him he lieth in an island suffering strong pains, in the halls of the nymph Calypso, who holdeth him perforce; so he may not reach his own country, for he hath no ships by him with oars, and no companions to send him on his way over the broad back of the sea. And now, again, they are set on slaying his beloved son on his homeward way, for he is gone to fair Pylos and to goodly Lacedaemon, to seek tidings of his father."

And Zeus, gatherer of the clouds, answered and spake unto her: "My child, what word hath escaped the door of thy lips? Nay, didst thou not thyself plan this device, that Odysseus may assuredly take vengeance on those men at his coming? As for Telemachus, do thou guide him by thine art, as well thou mayest, that so he may come to his own country all unharmed, and the wooers may return in their ship with their labour all in vain."

Therewith he spake to Hermes, his dear son: "Hermes, forasmuch as even in all else thou art our herald, tell unto the nymph of the braided tresses my unerring counsel, even the return of the patient Odysseus, how he is to come to his home, with no furtherance of gods or of mortal men. Nay, he shall sail on a well-bound raft, in sore distress, and on the twentieth day arrive at fertile Scheria, even at the land of the Phaeacians, who are near of kin to the gods. And they shall give him all worship heartily as to a god, and send him on his way in a ship to his own dear country, with gifts of bronze and gold, and raiment in plenty, much store, such as never would Odysseus have won for himself out of Troy, yea, though he had returned unhurt with the share of the spoil that fell to him. On such wise is he fated to see his friends, and come to his high-roofed home and his own country."

So spake he, nor heedless was the messenger, the slayer of Argos. Straightway he bound beneath his feet his lovely golden sandals, that wax not old, that bare him alike over the wet sea and over the limitless land, swift as the breath of the wind. And he took the wand wherewith he lulls the eyes of whomso he will, while others again he even wakes from out of sleep. With this rod in his hand flew the strong slayer of Argos. Above Pieria he passed and leapt from the upper air into the deep. Then he sped along the wave like the cormorant, that chaseth the fishes through the perilous gulfs of the unharvested sea, and wetteth his thick plumage in the brine. Such like did Hermes ride upon the press of the waves. But when he had now reached that far-off isle, he went forth from the sea of violet blue to get him up into the land, till he came to a great cave, wherein dwelt the nymph of the braided tresses: and he found her within. And on the hearth there was a great fire burning, and from afar through the isle was smelt the fragrance of cleft cedar blazing, and of sandal wood. And the nymph within was singing with a sweet voice as she fared to and fro before the loom, and wove with a shuttle of gold. And round about the cave there was a wood blossoming, alder and poplar and sweet-smelling cypress. And therein roosted birds long of wing, owls and falcons and chattering sea-crows, which have their business in the waters. And lo, there about the hollow cave trailed a gadding garden vine, all rich with clusters. And fountains four set orderly were running with clear water, hard by one another, turned each to his own course. And all around soft meadows

bloomed of violets and parsley, yea, even a deathless god who came
thither might wonder at the sight and be glad at heart. There the
messenger, the slayer of Argos, stood and wondered. Now when
he had gazed at all with wonder, anon he went into the wide cave;
nor did Calypso, that fair goddess, fail to know him, when she saw
him face to face; for the gods use not to be strange one to another,
the immortals, not though one have his habitation far away. But
he found not Odysseus, the great-hearted, within the cave, who sat
weeping on the shore even as aforetime, straining his soul with
tears and groans and griefs, and as he wept he looked wistfully
over the unharvested deep. And Calypso, that fair goddess, questioned Hermes, when she had made him sit on a bright shining
seat:

"Wherefore, I pray thee, Hermes, of the golden wand, hast thou
come hither, worshipful and welcome, whereas as of old thou wert
not wont to visit me? Tell me all thy thought; my heart is set on
fulfilling it, if fulfil it I may, and if it hath been fulfilled in the
counsel of fate. But now follow me further, that I may set before
thee the entertainment of strangers."

Therewith the goddess spread a table with ambrosia and set it by
him, and mixed the ruddy nectar. So the messenger, the slayer of
Argos, did eat and drink. Now after he had supped and comforted his soul with food, at the last he answered, and spake to her
on this wise:

"Thou makest question of me on my coming, a goddess of a
god, and I will tell thee this my saying truly, at thy command.
'Twas Zeus that bade me come hither, by no will of mine; nay,
who of his free will would speed over such a wondrous space of
brine, whereby is no city of mortals that do sacrifice to the gods, and
offer choice hecatombs? But surely it is in no wise possible for
another god to go beyond or to make void the purpose of Zeus,
lord of the aegis. He saith that thou hast with thee a man most
wretched beyond his fellows, beyond those men that round the
burg of Priam for nine years fought, and in the tenth year sacked
the city and departed homeward. Yet on the way they sinned
against Athene, and she raised upon them an evil blast and long
waves of the sea. Then all the rest of his good company was lost,
but it came to pass that the wind bare and the wave brought him
hither. And now Zeus biddeth thee send him hence with what
speed thou mayest, for it is not ordained that he die away from his
friends, but rather it is his fate to look on them even yet, and to
come to his high-roofed home and his own country."

So spake he, and Calypso, that fair goddess, shuddered and uttered her voice, and spake unto him winged words: "Hard are ye
gods and jealous exceeding, who ever grudge goddesses openly to
mate with men, if any make a mortal her dear bed-fellow. Even
so when rosy-fingered Dawn took Orion for her lover, ye gods
that live at ease were jealous thereof, till chaste Artemis, of the
golden throne, slew him in Ortygia with the visitation of her gentle

shafts. So too when fair-tressed Demeter yielded to her love, and lay with Iasion in the thrice-ploughed fallow field, Zeus was not long without tidings thereof, and cast at him with his white bolt and slew him. So again ye gods now grudge that a mortal man should dwell with me. Him I saved as he went all alone bestriding the keel of a bark, for that Zeus had crushed and cleft his swift ship with a white bolt in the midst of the wine-dark deep. There all the rest of his good company was lost, but it came to pass that the wind bare and the wave brought him hither. And him have I loved and cherished, and I said that I would make him to know not death and age for ever. Yet forasmuch as it is in no wise possible for another god to go beyond, or make void the purpose of Zeus, lord of the aegis, let him away over the unharvested seas, if the summons and the bidding be of Zeus. But I will give him no despatch, not I, for I have no ships by me with oars, nor company to bear him on his way over the broad back of the sea. Yet will I be forward to put this in his mind, and will hide nought, that all unharmed he may come to his own country."

Then the messenger, the slayer of Argos, answered her: "Yea, speed him now upon his path and have regard unto the wrath of Zeus, lest haply he be angered and bear hard on thee hereafter."

Therewith the great slayer of Argos departed, but the lady nymph went on her way to the great-hearted Odysseus, when she had heard the message of Zeus. And there she found him sitting on the shore, and his eyes were never dry of tears, and his sweet life was ebbing away as he mourned for his return; for the nymph no more found favour in his sight. Howsoever by night he would sleep by her, as needs he must, in the hollow caves, unwilling lover by a willing lady. And in the day-time he would sit on the rocks and on the beach, straining his soul with tears, and groans, and griefs, and through his tears he would look wistfully over the unharvested deep. So standing near him that fair goddess spake to him:

"Hapless man, sorrow no more I pray thee in this isle, nor let thy good life waste away, for even now will I send thee hence with all my heart. Nay, arise and cut long beams, and fashion a wide raft with the axe, and lay deckings high thereupon, that it may bear thee over the misty deep. And I will place therein bread and water, and red wine to thy heart's desire, to keep hunger far away. And I will put raiment upon thee, and send a fair gale in thy wake, that so thou mayest come all unharmed to thine own country, if indeed it be the good pleasure of the gods who hold wide heaven, who are stronger than I am both to will and to do."

So she spake, and the steadfast goodly Odysseus shuddered, and uttering his voice spake to her winged words: "Herein, goddess, thou hast plainly some other thought, and in no wise my further-ance, for that thou biddest me to cross in a raft the great gulf of the sea so dread and difficult, which not even the swift gallant ships pass over rejoicing in the breeze of Zeus. Nor would I go aboard a raft to displeasure thee, unless thou wilt deign, O goddess, to swear a great oath not to plan any hidden guile to mine own hurt."

So spake he, and Calypso, the fair goddess, smiled and caressed him with her hand, and spake and hailed him:

"Knavish thou art, and no weakling in wit, thou that hast conceived and spoken such a word. Let earth be now witness hereto, and the wide heaven above, and that falling water of the Styx, the greatest oath and the most terrible to the blessed gods, that I will not plan any hidden guile to thine own hurt. Nay, but my thoughts are such, and such will be my counsel, as I would devise for myself, if ever so sore a need came over me. For I too have a righteous mind, and my heart within me is not of iron, but pitiful even as thine."

Therewith the fair goddess led the way quickly, and he followed hard in the steps of the goddess. And they reached the hollow cave, the goddess and the man; so he sat him down upon the chair whence Hermes had arisen, and the nymph placed by him all manner of food to eat and drink, such as is meat for men. As for her she sat over against divine Odysseus, and the handmaids placed by her ambrosia and nectar. So they put forth their hands upon the good cheer set before them. But after they had taken their fill of meat and drink, Calypso, the fair goddess, spake first and said:

"Son of Laertes, of the seed of Zeus, Odysseus of many devices, so it is indeed thy wish to get thee home to thine own dear country even in this hour? Good fortune go with thee even so! Yet didst thou know in thine heart what a measure of suffering thou art ordained to fulfil, or ever thou reach thine own country, here, even here, thou wouldst abide with me and keep this house, and wouldst never taste of death, though thou longest to see thy wife, for whom thou hast ever a desire day by day. Not in sooth that I avow me to be less noble than she in form or fashion, for it is in no wise meet that mortal woman should match them with immortals, in shape and comeliness."

And Odysseus of many counsels answered, and spake unto her: "Be not wroth with me hereat, goddess and queen. Myself I know it well, how wise Penelope is meaner to look upon than thou, in comeliness and stature. But she is mortal and thou knowest not age nor death. Yet even so, I wish and long day by day to fare homeward and see the day of my returning. Yea, and if some god shall wreck me in the wine-dark deep, even so I will endure, with a heart within me patient of affliction. For already have I suffered full much, and much have I toiled in perils of waves and war; let this be added to the tale of those."

So spake he, and the sun sank and darkness came on. Then they twain went into the chamber of the hollow rock, and had their delight of love, abiding each by other.

So soon as early Dawn shone forth, the rosy-fingered, anon Odysseus put on him a mantle and doublet, and the nymph clad her in a great shining robe, light of woof and gracious, and about her waist she cast a fair golden girdle, and a veil withal upon her head. Then she considered of the sending of Odysseus, the great-hearted. She gave him a great axe, fitted to his grasp, an axe of bronze double-edged, and with a goodly handle of olive wood fastened well. Next she gave him a polished adze, and she led the way to the border of the isle where tall trees grew, alder and poplar, and pine that reacheth unto heaven, seasoned long since and sere, that might lightly float for him. Now after she had shown him where the tall trees grew, Calypso, the fair goddess, departed homeward. And he set to cutting timber, and his work went busily. Twenty trees in all he felled, and then trimmed them with the axe of bronze, and deftly smoothed them, and over them made straight the line. Meanwhile Calypso, the fair goddess, brought him augers, so he bored each piece and jointed them together, and then made all fast with trenails and dowels. Wide as is the floor of a broad ship of burden, which some man well skilled in carpentry may trace him out, of such beam did Odysseus fashion his broad raft. And thereat he wrought, and set up the deckings, fitting them to the close-set uprights, and finished them off with long gunwales, and therein he set a mast, and a yard-arm fitted thereto, and moreover he made him a rudder to guide the craft. And he fenced it with wattled osier withies from stem to stern, to be a bulwark against the wave, and piled up wood to back them. Meanwhile Calypso, the fair goddess, brought him web of cloth to make his sails; and these too he fashioned very skilfully. And he made fast therein braces and halyards and sheets, and at last he pushed the raft with levers down to the fair salt sea.

It was the fourth day when he had accomplished all. And, lo, on the fifth, the fair Calypso sent him on his way from the island, when she had bathed him and clad him in fragrant attire. Moreover, the goddess placed on board the ship two skins, one of dark wine, and another, a great one, of water, and corn too in a wallet, and she set therein a store of dainties to his heart's desire, and sent forth a warm and gentle wind to blow. And goodly Odysseus rejoiced as he set his sails to the breeze. So he sate and cunningly guided the craft with the helm, nor did sleep fall upon his eyelids, as he viewed the Pleiads and Boötes, that setteth late, and the Bear, which they likewise call the Wain, which turneth ever in one place, and keepeth watch upon Orion, and alone hath no part in the baths of Ocean. This star, Calypso, the fair goddess, bade him to keep ever on the left as he traversed the deep. Ten days and seven he sailed traversing the deep, and on the eighteenth day appeared the shadowy hills of the land of the Phaeacians, at the point where it lay nearest to him; and it showed like a shield in the misty deep.

Now the lord, the Shaker of the Earth, on his way from the Ethiopians espied him afar off from the mountains of the Solymi: even thence he saw Odysseus as he sailed over the deep; and he was mightily angered in spirit, and shaking his head he communed with his own heart. "Lo now, it must be that the gods at the last have changed their purposes concerning Odysseus, while I was away among the Ethiopians. And now he is nigh to the Phaeacian land, where it is ordained that he escape the great issues of the woe which hath come upon him. But methinks that even yet I will drive him far enough in the path of suffering."

With that he gathered the clouds and troubled the waters of the deep, grasping his trident in his hands; and he roused all storms of all manner of winds, and shrouded in clouds the land and sea: and down sped night from heaven. The East Wind and the South Wind clashed, and the stormy West, and the North, that is born in the bright air, rolling onward a great wave. Then were the knees of Odysseus loosened and his heart melted, and heavily he spake to his own great spirit:

"Oh, wretched man that I am! what is to befall me at the last? I fear that indeed the goddess spake all things truly, who said that I should fill up the measure of sorrow on the deep, or ever I came to mine own country; and lo, all these things have an end. In such wise doth Zeus crown the wide heaven with clouds, and hath troubled the deep, and the blasts rush on of all the winds; yea, now is utter doom assured me. Thrice blessed those Danaans, yea, four times blessed, who perished on a time in wide Troy-land, doing a pleasure to the sons of Atreus! Would to God that I too had died, and met my fate on that day when the press of Trojans cast their bronze-shod spears upon me, fighting for the body of the son of Peleus! So should I have gotten my dues of burial, and the Achaeans would have spread my fame; but now it is my fate to be overtaken by a pitiful death."

Even as he spake, the great wave smote down upon him, driving on in terrible wise, that the raft reeled again. And far therefrom he fell, and lost the helm from his hand; and the fierce blast of the jostling winds came and brake his mast in the midst, and sail and yard-arm fell afar into the deep. Long time the water kept him under, nor could he speedily rise from beneath the rush of the mighty wave: for the garments hung heavy which fair Calypso gave him. But late and at length he came up, and spat forth from his mouth the bitter salt water, which ran down in streams from his head. Yet even so forgat he not his raft, for all his wretched plight, but made a spring after it in the waves, and clutched it to him, and sat in the midst thereof, avoiding the issues of death; and the great wave swept it hither and thither along the stream. And as the North Wind in the harvest tide sweeps the thistledown along the plain, and close the tufts cling each to other, even so the winds bare the raft hither and thither along the main. Now the South would toss it to the North to carry, and now again the East would yield it to the West to chase.

But the daughter of Cadmus marked him, Ino of the fair ankles, Leucothea, who in time past was a maiden of mortal speech, but now in the depths of the salt sea she had gotten her share of worship from the gods. She took pity on Odysseus in his wandering and travail, and she rose, like a sea-gull on the wing, from the depth of the mere, and sat upon the well-bound raft and spake saying:

"Hapless one, wherefore was Poseidon, shaker of the earth, so wondrous wroth with thee, seeing that he soweth for thee the seeds

of many evils? Yet shall he not make a full end of thee, for all his
desire. But do even as I tell thee, and methinks thou art not witless.
Cast off these garments, and leave the raft to drift before the winds,
but do thou swim with thine hands and strive to win a footing on
the coast of the Phaeacians, where it is decreed that thou escape.
Here, take this veil imperishable and wind it about thy breast; so
is there no fear that thou suffer aught or perish. But when thou hast
laid hold of the mainland with thy hands, loose it from off thee and
cast it into the wine-dark deep far from the land, and thyself turn
away.'

With that the goddess gave the veil, and for her part dived back
into the heaving deep, like a sea-gull: and the dark wave closed over
her. But the steadfast goodly Odysseus pondered, and heavily he
spake to his own brave spirit:

"Ah, woe is me! Can it be that some one of the immortals is
weaving a new snare for me, that she bids me quit my raft? Nay
verily, I will not yet obey, for I had sight of the shore yet a long way
off, where she told me that I might escape. I am resolved what I
will do;—and methinks on this wise it is best. So long as the timbers abide in the dowels, so long will I endure steadfast in affliction,
but so soon as the wave hath shattered my raft asunder, I will swim,
for meanwhile no better counsel may be.'

While yet he pondered these things in his heart and soul, Poseidon,
shaker of the earth, stirred against him a great wave, terrible and
grievous, and vaulted from the crest, and therewith smote him. And
as when a great tempestuous wind tosseth a heap of parched husks,
and scatters them this way and that, even so did the wave scatter the
long beams of the raft. But Odysseus bestrode a single beam, as
one rideth on a courser, and stript him of the garments which fair
Calypso gave him. And presently he wound the veil beneath his
breast, and fell prone into the sea, outstretching his hands as one eager
to swim. And the lord, the shaker of the earth, saw him and shook
his head, and communed with his own soul. "Even so, after all thy
sufferings, go wandering over the deep, till thou shalt come among
a people, the fosterlings of Zeus. Yet for all that I deem not that
thou shalt think thyself too lightly afflicted." Therewith he lashed
his steeds of the flowing manes, and came to Aegae, where is his
lordly home.

But Athene, daughter of Zeus, turned to new thoughts. Behold,
she bound up the courses of the other winds, and charged them all
to cease and be still; but she roused the swift North and brake the
waves before him, that so Odysseus, of the seed of Zeus, might mingle
with the Phaeacians, lovers of the oar, avoiding death and the fates.

So for two nights and two days he was wandering in the swell of
the sea, and much his heart boded of death. But when at last the
fair-tressed Dawn brought the full light of the third day, thereafter
the breeze fell, and lo, there was a breathless calm, and with a quick
glance ahead (he being upborne on a great wave) he saw the land
very near. And even as when most welcome to his children is the

sight of a father's life, who lies in sickness and strong pains long wasting away, some angry god assailing him; and to their delight the gods have loosed him from his trouble; so welcome to Odysseus showed land and wood; and he swam onward, being eager to set foot on the strand. But when he was within earshot of the shore, and heard now the thunder of the sea against the reefs — for the great wave crashed against the dry land belching in terrible wise, and all was covered with foam of the sea, — for there were no harbours for ships nor shelters, but jutting headlands and reefs and cliffs; then at last the knees of Odysseus were loosened and his heart melted, and in heaviness he spake to his own brave spirit:

"Ah me! now that beyond all hope Zeus hath given me sight of land, and withal I have cloven my way through this gulf of the sea, here there is no place to land on from out of the grey water. For without are sharp crags, and round them the wave roars surging, and sheer the smooth rock rises, and the sea is deep thereby, so that in no wise may I find firm foothold and escape my bane, for as I fain would go ashore, the great wave may haply snatch and dash me on the jagged rock — and a wretched endeavour that would be. But if I swim yet further along the coast to find, if I may, spits that take the waves aslant and havens of the sea, I fear lest the storm-winds catch me again and bear me over the teeming deep, making heavy moan; or else some god may even send forth against me a monster from out of the shore water; and many such pastureth the renowned Amphitrite. For I know how wroth against me hath been the great Shaker of the Earth."

Whilst yet he pondered these things in his heart and mind, a great wave bore him to the rugged shore. There would he have been stript of his skin and all his bones been broken, but that the goddess, grey-eyed Athene, put a thought into his heart. He rushed in, and with both his hands clutched the rock, whereto he clung till the great wave went by. So he escaped that peril, but again with backward wash it leapt on him and smote him and cast him forth into the deep. And as when the cuttlefish is dragged forth from his chamber, the many pebbles clinging to his suckers, even so was the skin stript from his strong hand against the rocks, and the great wave closed over him. There of a truth would luckless Odysseus have perished beyond that which was ordained, had not grey-eyed Athene given him sure counsel. He rose from the line of the breakers that belch upon the shore, and swam outside, ever looking landwards, to find, if he might, spits that take the waves aslant, and havens of the sea. But when he came in his swimming over against the mouth of a fair-flowing river, whereby the place seemed best in his eyes, smooth of rocks, and withal there was a covert from the wind, Odysseus felt the river running, and prayed to him in his heart:

"Hear me, O king, whosoever thou art; unto thee am I come, as to one to whom prayer is made, while I flee the rebukes of Poseidon from the deep. Yea, reverend even to the deathless gods is that man who comes as a wanderer, even as I now have come to thy stream and to thy knees after much travail. Nay pity me, O king; for I avow myself thy suppliant."

So spake he, and the god straightway stayed his stream and withheld his waves, and made the water smooth before him, and brought him safely to the mouths of the river. And his knees bowed and his stout hands fell, for his heart was broken by the brine. And his flesh was all swollen and a great stream of sea water gushed up through his mouth and nostrils. So he lay without breath or speech, swooning, such terrible weariness came upon him. But when now his breath returned and his spirit came to him again, he loosed from off him the veil of the goddess, and let it fall into the salt-flowing river. And the great wave bare it back down the stream, and lightly Ino caught it in her hands. Then Odysseus turned from the river, and fell back in the reeds, and kissed earth, the grain-giver, and heavily he spake unto his own brave spirit:

"Ah, woe is me! what is to betide me? what shall happen unto me at the last? If I watch in the river bed all through the careful night, I fear that the bitter frost and fresh dew may overcome me, as I breathe forth my life for faintness, for the river breeze blows cold betimes in the morning. But if I climb the hill-side up to the shady wood, and there take rest in the thickets, though perchance the cold and weariness leave hold of me, and sweet sleep may come over me, I fear lest of wild beasts I become the spoil and prey."

So as he thought thereon this seemed to him the better way. He went up to the wood, and found it nigh the water in a place of wide prospect. So he crept beneath twin bushes that grew from one stem, both olive trees, one of them wild olive. Through these the force of the wet winds blew never, neither did the bright sun light on it with his rays, nor could the rain pierce through, so close were they twined either to other; and thereunder crept Odysseus, and anon he heaped together with his hands a broad couch; for of fallen leaves there was great plenty, enough to cover two or three men in winter time, however hard the weather. And the steadfast goodly Odysseus beheld it and rejoiced, and he laid him in the midst thereof and flung over him the fallen leaves. And as when a man hath hidden away a brand in the black embers at an upland farm, one that hath no neighbours nigh, and so saveth the seed of fire, that he may not have to seek a light otherwhere, even so did Odysseus cover him with the leaves. And Athene shed sleep upon his eyes, that so it might soon release him from his weary travail, overshadowing his eyelids.

BOOK VI

Nausicaa, going to a river near that place to wash the clothes of her father, mother, and brethren, while the clothes were drying played with her maids at ball; and Odysseus coming forth is fed and clothed, and led on his way to the house of her father, King Alcinous.

So there he lay asleep, the steadfast goodly Odysseus, fordone with toil and drowsiness.   Meanwhile Athene went to the land and the city of the Phaeacians, who of old, upon a time, dwelt in spacious Hypereia; near the Cyclôpes they dwelt, men exceeding proud, who harried them continually, being mightier than they.   Thence the godlike Nausithous made them depart, and he carried them away, and planted them in Scheria, far off from men that live by bread. And he drew a wall around the town, and builded houses and made temples for the gods and meted out the fields.   Howbeit ere this had he been stricken by fate, and had gone down to the house of Hades, and now Alcinous was reigning, with wisdom granted by the gods. To his house went the goddess, grey-eyed Athene, devising a return for the great-hearted Odysseus.   She betook her to the rich-wrought bower, wherein was sleeping a maiden like to the gods in form and comeliness, Nausicaa, the daughter of Alcinous, high of heart.   Beside her on either hand of the pillars of the door were two handmaids, dowered with beauty from the Graces, and the shining doors were shut.

But the goddess, fleet as the breath of the wind, swept towards the couch of the maiden, and stood above her head, and spake to her in the semblance of the daughter of a famous seafarer, Dymas, a girl of like age with Nausicaa, who had found grace in her sight.   In her shape the grey-eyed Athene spake to the princess, saying:

"Nausicaa, how hath thy mother so heedless a maiden to her daughter?   Lo, thou hast shining raiment that lies by thee uncared for, and thy marriage-day is near at hand, when thou thyself must needs go beautifully clad, and have garments to give to them who shall lead thee to the house of the bridegroom!   And, behold, these are the things whence a good report goes abroad among men, wherein a father and lady mother take delight.   But come, let us arise and go a-washing with the breaking of the day, and I will follow with thee to be thy mate in the toil, that without delay thou mayst get thee ready, since truly thou art not long to be a maiden.   Lo, already they are wooing thee, the noblest youths of all the Phaeacians, among that people whence thou thyself dost draw thy lineage.   So come, beseech thy noble father betimes in the morning to furnish thee with mules and a wain to carry the men's raiment, and the robes, and the shining coverlets.   Yea and for thyself it is seemlier far to go thus than on foot, for the places where we must wash are a great way off the town."

So spake the grey-eyed Athene, and departed to Olympus, where, as they say, is the seat of the gods that standeth fast for ever.   Not by winds is it shaken, nor ever wet with rain, nor doth the snow come nigh thereto, but most clear air is spread about it cloudless, and the white light floats over it.   Therein the blessed gods are glad for all their days, and thither Athene went when she had shown forth all to the maiden.

Anon came the throned Dawn, and awakened Nausicaa of the fair robes, who straightway marvelled on the dream, and went through the halls to tell her parents, her father dear and her mother. And she found them within, her mother sitting by the hearth with the women her handmaids, spinning yarn of sea-purple stain, but her father she met as he was going forth to the renowned kings in their council, whither the noble Phaeacians called him. Standing close by her dear father she spake, saying: "Father, dear, couldst thou not lend me a high waggon with strong wheels, that I may take the goodly raiment to the river to wash, so much as I have lying soiled? Yea and it is seemly that thou thyself, when thou art with the princes in council, shouldest have fresh raiment to wear. Also, there are five dear sons of thine in the halls, two married, but three are lusty bachelors, and these are always eager for new-washen garments wherein to go to the dances: for all these things have I taken thought."

This she said, because she was ashamed to speak of glad marriage to her father; but he saw all and answered, saying:

"Neither the mules nor aught else do I grudge thee, my child. Go thy ways, and the thralls shall get thee ready a high waggon with good wheels, and fitted with an upper frame."

Therewith he called to his men, and they gave ear, and without the palace they made ready the smooth-running mule-wain, and led the mules beneath the yoke, and harnessed them under the car, while the maiden brought forth from her bower the shining raiment. This she stored in the polished car, and her mother filled a basket with all manner of food to the heart's desire, dainties too she set therein, and she poured wine into a goat-skin bottle, while Nausicaa climbed into the wain. And her mother gave her soft olive oil also in a golden cruse, that she and her maidens might anoint themselves after the bath. Then Nausicaa took the whip and the shining reins, and touched the mules to start them; then there was a clatter of hoofs, and on they strained without flagging, with their load of the raiment and the maiden. Not alone did she go, for her attendants followed with her.

Now when they were come to the beautiful stream of the river, where truly were the unfailing cisterns, and bright water welled up free from beneath, and flowed past, enough to wash the foulest garments clean, there the girls unharnessed the mules from under the chariot, and turning them loose they drove them along the banks of the eddying river to graze on the honey-sweet clover. Then they took the garments from the wain, in their hands, and bore them to the black water, and briskly trod them down in the trenches, in busy rivalry. Now when they had washed and cleansed all the stains, they spread all out in order along the shore of the deep, even where the sea, in beating on the coast, washed the pebbles clean. Then having bathed and anointed them well with olive oil, they took their midday meal on the river's banks, waiting till the clothes should dry in the brightness of the sun. Anon, when they were satisfied with food, the maidens and the princess, they fell to playing at ball, casting away their tires, and among them Nausicaa of the white arms began the song. And even as Artemis, the archer, moveth down the mountain,

either along the ridges of lofty Taygetus or Erymanthus, taking her
pastime in the chase of boars and swift deer, and with her the wild
wood-nymphs disport them, the daughters of Zeus, lord of the aegis,
and Leto is glad at heart, while high over all she rears her head and
brows, and easily may she be known, — but all are fair; even so the
girl unwed outshone her maiden company.

But when now she was about going homewards, after yoking the
mules and folding up the goodly raiment, then grey-eyed Athene
turned to other thoughts, that so Odysseus might awake, and see the
lovely maiden, who should be his guide to the city of the Phaeacian
men. So then the princess threw the ball at one of her company; she
missed the girl, and cast the ball into the deep eddying current,
whereat they all raised a piercing cry. Then the goodly Odysseus
awoke and sat up, pondering in his heart and spirit:

"Woe is me! to what men's land am I come now? say, are they
froward, and wild, and unjust, or are they hospitable, and of God-
fearing mind? How shrill a cry of maidens rings round me, of the
nymphs that hold the steep hill-tops, and the river-springs, and the
grassy water-meadows! It must be, methinks, that I am near men
of human speech. Go to, I myself will make trial and see."

Therewith the goodly Odysseus crept out from under the coppice,
having broken with his strong hand a leafy bough from the thick
wood, to hold athwart his body, that it might hide his nakedness
withal. And forth he sallied like a lion mountain-bred, trusting in
his strength, who fares out blown and rained upon, with flaming eyes;
amid the kine he goes or amid the sheep or in the track of the wild
deer; yea, his belly bids him go even to the good homestead to make
assay upon the flocks. Even so Odysseus was fain to draw nigh to
the fair-tressed maidens, all naked as he was, such need had come
upon him. But he was terrible in their eyes, being marred with the
salt sea foam, and they fled cowering here and there about the jutting
spits of shore. And the daughter of Alcinous alone stood firm, for
Athene gave her courage of heart, and took all trembling from her
limbs. So she halted and stood over against him, and Odysseus considered whether he should clasp the knees of the lovely maiden, and
so make his prayer, or should stand as he was, apart, and beseech
her with smooth words, if haply she might show him the town, and
give him raiment. And as he thought within himself, it seemed better to stand apart, and beseech her with smooth words, lest the maiden
should be angered with him if he touched her knees: so straightway
he spake a sweet and cunning word:

"I supplicate thee, O queen, whether thou art a goddess or a mortal! If indeed thou art a goddess of them that keep the wide heaven;
to Artemis, then, the daughter of great Zeus, I mainly liken thee, for
beauty and stature and shapeliness. But if thou art one of the daughters of men who dwell on earth, thrice blessed are thy father and thy
lady mother, and thrice blessed thy brethren. Surely their souls ever
glow with gladness for thy sake, each time they see thee entering the
dance, so fair a flower of maidens. But he is of heart the most blessed

beyond all other who shall prevail with gifts of wooing, and lead thee to his home. Never have mine eyes beheld such an one among mortals, neither man nor woman; great awe comes upon me as I look on thee. Yet in Delos once I saw as goodly a thing: a young sapling of a palm tree springing by the altar of Apollo. For thither too I went, and much people with me, on that path where my sore troubles were to be. Yea, and when I looked thereupon, long time I marvelled in spirit, — for never grew there yet so goodly a shoot from ground, — even in such wise as I wonder at thee, lady, and am astonied and do greatly fear to touch thy knees, though grievous sorrow is upon me. Yesterday, on the twentieth day, I escaped from the wine-dark deep, but all that time continually the wave bare me, and the vehement winds drave, from the isle Ogygia. And now some god has cast me on this shore, that here too, methinks, some evil may betide me; for I trow not that trouble will cease; the gods ere that time will yet bring many a thing to pass. But, queen, have pity on me, for after many trials and sore to thee first of all am I come, and of the other folk, who hold this city and land, I know no man. Nay show me the town, give me an old garment to cast about me, if thou hadst, when thou camest here, any wrap for the linen. And may the gods grant thee all thy heart's desire: a husband and a home, and a mind at one with his may they give — a good gift, for there is nothing mightier and nobler than when man and wife are of one heart and mind in a house, a grief to their foes, and to their friends great joy, but their own hearts know it best."

Then Nausicaa of the white arms answered him, and said: "Stranger, forasmuch as thou seemest no evil man nor foolish — and it is Olympian Zeus himself that giveth weal to men, to the good and to the evil, to each one as he will, and this thy lot doubtless is of him, and so thou must in anywise endure it: — and now, since thou hast come to our city and our land, thou shalt not lack raiment, nor aught else that is the due of a hapless suppliant, when he has met them who can befriend him. And I will show thee the town, and name the name of the people. The Phaeacians hold this city and land, and I am the daughter of Alcinous, great of heart, on whom all the might and force of the Phaeacians depend."

Thus she spake, and called to her maidens of the fair tresses: "Halt, my maidens, whither flee ye at the sight of a man? Ye surely do not take him for an enemy? That mortal breathes not, and never will be born, who shall come with war to the land of the Phaeacians, for they are very dear to the gods. Far apart we live in the wash of the waves, the outermost of men, and no other mortals are conversant with us. Nay, but this man is some helpless one come hither in his wanderings, whom now we must kindly entreat, for all strangers and beggars are from Zeus, and a little gift is dear. So, my maidens, give the stranger meat and drink, and bathe him in the river, where withal is a shelter from the winds."

So she spake, but they had halted and called each to the other, and they brought Odysseus to the sheltered place, and made him sit down, as Nausicaa bade them, the daughter of Alcinous, high of heart. Beside them they laid a mantle, and a doublet for raiment, and gave him soft olive oil in the golden cruse, and bade him wash in the streams of the river. Then goodly Odysseus spake among the maidens, saying: "I pray you stand thus apart, while I myself wash the brine from my shoulders, and anoint me with olive oil, for truly oil is long a stranger to my skin. But in your sight I will not bathe, for I am ashamed to make me naked in the company of fair-tressed maidens."

Then they went apart and told all to their lady. But with the river water the goodly Odysseus washed from his skin the salt scurf that covered his back and broad shoulders, and from his head he wiped the crusted brine of the barren sea. But when he had washed his whole body, and anointed him with olive oil, and had clad himself in the raiment that the unwedded maiden gave him, then Athene, the daughter of Zeus, made him greater and more mighty to behold, and from his head caused deep curling locks to flow, like the hyacinth flower. And as when some skilful man overlays gold upon silver — one that Hephaestus and Pallas Athene have taught all manner of craft, and full of grace is his handiwork — even so did Athene shed grace about his head and shoulders.

Then to the shore of the sea went Odysseus apart, and sat down, glowing in beauty and grace, and the princess marvelled at him, and spake among her fair-tressed maidens, saying:

"Listen, my white-armed maidens, and I will say somewhat. Not without the will of all the gods who hold Olympus hath this man come among the godlike Phaeacians. Erewhile he seemed to me uncomely, but now he is like the gods that keep the wide heaven. Would that such an one might be called my husband, dwelling here, and that it might please him here to abide! But come, my maidens, give the stranger meat and drink."

Thus she spake, and they gave ready ear and hearkened, and set beside Odysseus meat and drink, and the steadfast goodly Odysseus did eat and drink eagerly, for it was long since he had tasted food.

Now Nausicaa of the white arms had another thought. She folded the raiment and stored it in the goodly wain, and yoked the mules strong of hoof, and herself climbed into the car. Then she called on Odysseus, and spake and hailed him: "Up now, stranger, and rouse thee to go to the city, that I may convey thee to the house of my wise father, where, I promise thee, thou shalt get knowledge of all the noblest of the Phaeacians. But do thou even as I tell thee, and thou seemest a discreet man enough. So long as we are passing along the fields and farms of men, do thou fare quickly with the maidens behind the mules and the chariot, and I will lead the way. But when we set foot within the city, — whereby goes a high wall with towers, and there is a fair haven on either side of the town, and narrow is the entrance, and curved ships are drawn up on either hand of the mole, for all the folk have stations for their vessels, each man one for himself. And there is the place of assembly about the goodly temple of

Poseidon, furnished with heavy stones, deep bedded in the earth. There men look to the gear of the black ships, hawsers and sails, and there they fine down the oars. For the Phaeacians care not for bow nor quiver, but for masts, and oars of ships, and gallant barques, wherein rejoicing they cross the grey sea. Their ungracious speech it is that I would avoid, lest some man afterward rebuke me, and there are but too many insolent folk among the people. And some one of the baser sort might meet me and say: 'Who is this that goes with Nausicaa, this tall and goodly stranger? Where found she him? Her husband he will be, her very own. Either she has taken in some shipwrecked wanderer of strange men, — for no men dwell near us; or some god has come in answer to her instant prayer; from heaven has he descended, and will have her to wife for evermore. Better so, if herself she has ranged abroad and found a lord from a strange land, for verily she holds in no regard the Phaeacians here in this country, the many men and noble who are her wooers.' So will they speak, and this would turn to my reproach. Yea, and I myself would think it blame of another maiden who did such things in despite of her friends, her father and mother being still alive, and was conversant with men before the day of open wedlock. But, stranger, heed well what I say, that as soon as may be thou mayest gain at my father's hands an escort and a safe return. Thou shalt find a fair grove of Athene, a poplar grove near the road, and a spring wells forth therein, and a meadow lies all around. There is my father's demesne, and his fruitful close, within the sound of a man's shout from the city. Sit thee down there and wait until such time as we may have come into the city, and reached the house of my father. But when thou deemest that we are got to the palace, then go up to the city of the Phaeacians, and ask for the house of my father Alcinous, high of heart. It is easily known, and a young child could be thy guide, for nowise like it are builded the houses of the Phaeacians, so goodly is the palace of the hero Alcinous. But when thou art within the shadow of the halls and the court, pass quickly through the great chamber, till thou comest to my mother, who sits at the hearth in the light of the fire, weaving yarn of sea-purple stain, a wonder to behold. Her chair is leaned against a pillar, and her maidens sit behind her. And there my father's throne leans close to hers, wherein he sits and drinks his wine, like an immortal. Pass thou by him, and cast thy hands about my mother's knees, that thou mayest see quickly and with joy the day of thy returning, even if thou art from a very far country. If but her heart be kindly disposed toward thee, then is there hope that thou shalt see thy friends, and come to thy well-built house, and to thine own country."

She spake, and smote the mules with the shining whip, and quickly they left behind them the streams of the river. And well they trotted and well they paced, and she took heed to drive in such wise that the maidens and Odysseus might follow on foot, and cunningly she plied the lash. Then the sun set, and they came to the famous grove, the sacred place of Athene; so there the goodly Odysseus sat him down. Then straightway he prayed to the daughter of mighty Zeus: "Listen to me, child of Zeus, lord of the aegis, unwearied maiden; hear me even now, since before thou heardest not when I was smitten on the sea, when the renowned Earth-shaker smote me. Grant me to come to the Phaeacians as one dear, and worthy of pity."

So he spake in prayer, and Pallas Athene heard him; but she did not yet appear to him face to face, for she had regard unto her father's brother, who furiously raged against the godlike Odysseus, till he should come to his own country.

[tr. BUTCHER & LANG]

[Odysseus is graciously received by Alcinous and his wife. The next day the Phaeacians give athletic contests and feasts to entertain Odysseus; during the feast the bard Demodocus sings of the Trojan War, at which Odysseus is so overcome with emotion that he breaks into weeping. Alcinous asks him his name and his adventures, and why he weeps at the songs of the minstrel.]

BOOK IX

Odysseus relates, first, what befell him amongst the Cicones at Ismarus; secondly, amongst the Lotophagi; thirdly, how he was used by the Cyclops Polyphemus.

And Odysseus of many counsels answered him saying: King Alcinous, most notable of all the people, verily it is a good thing to list to a minstrel such as this one, like to the gods in voice. Nay, as for me, I say that there is no more gracious or perfect delight than when a whole people makes merry, and the men sit orderly at feast in the halls and listen to the singer, and the tables by them are laden with bread and flesh, and a wine-bearer drawing the wine serves it round and pours it into the cups. This seems to me well-nigh the fairest thing in the world. But now thy heart was inclined to ask of my grievous troubles, that I may mourn for more exceeding sorrow. What then shall I tell of first, what last, for the gods of heaven have given me woes in plenty? Now, first, will I tell my name, that ye too may know it, and that I, when I have escaped the pitiless day, may yet be your host, though my home is in a far country. I am ODYSSEUS, SON OF LAERTES, who am in men's minds for all manner of wiles, and my fame reaches unto heaven. And I dwell in clear-seen Ithaca, wherein is a mountain Neriton, with trembling forest leaves, standing manifest to view, and many islands lie around, very near one to the other, Dulichium and Same, and wooded Zacynthus. Now Ithaca lies low, furthest up the sea-line toward the darkness, but those others face the dawning and the sun; a rugged isle, but a good nurse of noble youths; and for myself I can see nought beside sweeter than a man's own country. Verily Calypso, the fair goddess, would fain have kept me with her in her hollow caves, longing to have me for her lord; and likewise too, guileful Circé of Aia, would have stayed me in her halls, longing to have me for her lord. But never did they prevail upon my heart within my breast. So surely is there nought sweeter than a man's own country and his parents, even though he dwell far off in a rich home, in a strange land, away from them that begat him. But come, let me tell thee too of the troubles of my journeying, which Zeus laid on me as I came from Troy.

The wind that bare me from Ilios brought me nigh to the Cicones, even to Ismarus, whereupon I sacked their city and slew the people. And from out the city we took their wives and much substance, and divided them amongst us, that none through me might go lacking his proper share. Howbeit, thereafter I commanded that we should flee with a swift foot, but my men in their great folly hearkened not. There was much wine still a drinking, and still they slew many flocks of sheep by the seashore and kine with trailing feet and shambling gait. Meanwhile the Cicones went and raised a cry to other Cicones their neighbours, dwelling inland, who were more in number than they and braver withal: skilled they were to fight with men from chariots, and when need was on foot. So they gathered in the early morning as thick as leaves and flowers that spring in their season — yea and in that hour an evil doom of Zeus stood by us, ill-fated men, that so we might be sore afflicted. They set their battle in array by the swift ships, and the hosts cast at one another with their bronze-shod spears. So long as it was morn and the sacred day waxed stronger, so long we abode their assault and beat them off, albeit they outnumbered us. But when the sun was wending to the time of the loosing of cattle, then at last the Cicones drave in the Achaeans and overcame them, and six of my goodly-greaved company perished from each ship: but the remnant of us escaped death and destiny.

Thence we sailed onward stricken at heart, yet glad as men saved from death, albeit we had lost our dear companions. Nor did my curved ships move onward ere we had called thrice on each of those our hapless fellows, who died at the hands of the Cicones on the plain. Now Zeus, gatherer of the clouds, aroused the North Wind against our ships with a terrible tempest, and covered land and sea alike with clouds, and down sped night from heaven. Thus the ships were driven headlong, and their sails were torn to shreds by the might of the wind. So we lowered the sails into the hold, in fear of death, but rowed the ships landward apace. There for two nights and two days we lay continually, consuming our hearts with weariness and sorrow. But when the fair-tressed Dawn had at last brought the full light of the third day, we set up the masts and hoisted the white sails and sat us down, while the wind and the helmsman guided the ships. And now I should have come to mine own country all unhurt, but the wave and the stream of the sea and the North Wind swept me from my course as I was doubling Malea, and drave me wandering past Cythera.

Thence for nine whole days was I borne by ruinous winds over the teeming deep; but on the tenth day we set foot on the land of the lotus-eaters, who eat a flowery food. So we stepped ashore and drew water, and straightway my company took their midday meal

by the swift ships. Now when we had tasted meat and drink I sent
forth certain of my company to go and make search what manner of
men they were who here live upon the earth by bread, and I chose
out two of my fellows, and sent a third with them as herald. Then
straightway they went and mixed with the men of the lotus-eaters,
and so it was that the lotus-eaters devised not death for our fellows,
but gave them of the lotus to taste. Now whosoever of them did eat
the honey-sweet fruit of the lotus, had no more wish to bring tidings
nor to come back, but there he chose to abide with the lotus-eating
men, ever feeding on the lotus, and forgetful of his homeward way.
Therefore I led them back to the ships weeping, and sore against
their will, and dragged them beneath the benches, and bound them
in the hollow barques. But I commanded the rest of my well-loved
company to make speed and go on board the swift ships, lest haply
any should eat of the lotus and be forgetful of returning. Right soon
they embarked and sat upon the benches, and sitting orderly they
smote the grey sea water with their oars.

Thence we sailed onward stricken at heart. And we came to the
land of the Cyclôpes, a froward and lawless folk, who trusting to
the deathless gods plant not aught with their hands, neither plough:
but, behold, all these things spring for them in plenty, unsown and
untilled, wheat, and barley, and vines, which bear great clusters of the
juice of the grape, and the rain of Zeus gives them increase. These
have neither gatherings for council nor oracles of law, but they dwell
in hollow caves on the crests of the high hills, and each one utters the
law to his children and his wives, and they reck not one of another.

Now there is a waste isle stretching without the harbour of the land
of the Cyclôpes, neither nigh at hand nor yet afar off, a woodland isle,
wherein are wild goats unnumbered, for no path of men scares them,
nor do hunters resort thither who suffer hardships in the wood, as
they range the mountain crests. Moreover it is possessed neither by
flocks nor by ploughed lands, but the soil lies unsown evermore and
untilled, desolate of men, and feeds the bleating goats. For the Cyclôpes have by them no ships with vermilion cheek, not yet are there
shipwrights in the island, who might fashion decked barques, which
should accomplish all their desire, voyaging to the towns of men
(as ofttimes men cross the sea to one another in ships), who might
likewise have made of their isle a goodly settlement. Yea, it is in no
wise a sorry land, but would bear all things in their season; for therein
are soft water-meadows by the shores of the grey salt sea, and there
the vines know no decay, and the land is level to plough; thence
might they reap a crop exceeding deep in due season, for verily there
is fatness beneath the soil. Also there is a fair haven, where is no
need of moorings, either to cast anchor or to fasten hawsers, but men
may run the ship on the beach, and tarry until such time as the sailors
are minded to be gone, and favourable breezes blow. Now at the
head of the harbour is a well of bright water issuing from a cave, and
round it are poplars growing. Thither we sailed, and some god
guided us through the night, for it was dark and there was no light

to see, a mist lying deep about the ships, nor did the moon show her light from heaven, but was shut in with clouds. No man then beheld that island, neither saw we the long waves rolling to the beach, till we had run our decked ships ashore. And when our ships were beached, we took down all their sails, and ourselves too stept forth upon the strand of the sea, and there we fell into sound sleep and waited for the bright Dawn.

So soon as early Dawn shone forth, the rosy-fingered, in wonder at the island we roamed over the length thereof: and the Nymphs, the daughters of Zeus, lord of the aegis, started the wild goats of the hills, that my company might have wherewith to sup. Anon we took to us our curved bows from out the ships and long spears, and arrayed in three bands we began shooting at the goats; and the god soon gave us game in plenty. Now twelve ships bare me company, and to each ship fell nine goats for a portion, but for me alone they set ten apart.

Thus we sat there the livelong day until the going down of the sun, feasting on abundant flesh and on sweet wine. For the red wine was not yet spent from out the ships, but somewhat was yet therein, for we had each one drawn off large store thereof in jars, when we took the sacred citadel of the Cicones. And we looked across to the land of the Cyclôpes who dwell nigh, and to the smoke, and to the voice of the men, and of the sheep and of the goats. And when the sun had sunk and darkness had come on, then we laid us to rest upon the sea-beach. So soon as early Dawn shone forth, the rosy-fingered, then I called a gathering of my men, and spake among them all:

"Abide here all the rest of you, my dear companions; but I will go with mine own ship and my ship's company, and make proof of these men, what manner of folk they are, whether froward, and wild, and unjust, or hospitable and of god-fearing mind."

So I spake, and I climbed the ship's side, and bade my company themselves to mount, and to loose the hawsers. So they soon embarked and sat upon the benches, and sitting orderly smote the grey sea water with their oars. Now when we had come to the land that lies hard by, we saw a cave on the border near to the sea, lofty and roofed over with laurels, and there many flocks of sheep and goats were used to rest. And about it a high outer court was built with stones, deep bedded, and with tall pines and oaks with their high crown of leaves. And a man was wont to sleep therein, of monstrous size, who shepherded his flocks alone and afar, and was not conversant with others, but dwelt apart in lawlessness of mind. Yea, for he was a monstrous thing and fashioned marvellously, nor was he like to any man that lives by bread, but like a wooded peak of the towering hills, which stands out apart and alone from others.

Then I commanded the rest of my well-loved company to tarry there by the ship, and to guard the ship, but I chose out twelve men, the best of my company, and sallied forth. Now I had with me a goat-skin of the dark wine and sweet, which Maron, son of Euanthes, had given me, the priest of Apollo, the god that watched over Ismarus. And he gave it, for that we had protected him with his wife and child reverently; for he dwelt in a thick grove of Phoebus Apollo. And he made me splendid gifts; he gave me seven talents of gold well wrought, and he gave me a mixing bowl of pure silver, and furthermore wine which he drew off in twelve jars in all, sweet wine unmingled, a draught divine; nor did any of his servants or of his handmaids in the house know thereof, but himself and his dear wife and one house-dame only. And as often as they drank that red wine honey sweet, he would fill one cup and pour it into twenty measures of water, and a marvellous sweet smell went up from the mixing bowl; then truly it was no pleasure to refrain.

With this wine I filled a great skin, and bare it with me, and corn too I put in a wallet, for my lordly spirit straightway had a boding that a man would come to me, a strange man, clothed in mighty strength, one that knew not judgment and justice.

Soon we came to the cave, but we found him not within; he was shepherding his fat flocks in the pastures. So we went into the cave, and gazed on all that was therein. The baskets were well laden with cheeses, and the folds were thronged with lambs and kids; each kind was penned by itself, the firstlings apart, and the summer lambs apart, apart too the younglings of the flock. Now all the vessels swam with whey, the milk-pails and the bowls, the well-wrought vessels whereinto he milked. My company then spake and besought me first of all to take of the cheeses and to return, and afterwards to make haste and drive off the kids and lambs to the swift ships from out the pens, and to sail over the salt sea water. Howbeit I hearkened not (and far better would it have been), but waited to see the giant himself, and whether he would give me gifts as a stranger's due. Yet was not his coming to be with joy to my company.

Then we kindled a fire, and made burnt-offering, and ourselves likewise took of the cheeses, and did eat, and sat waiting for him within till he came back, shepherding his flocks. And he bore a grievous weight of dry wood, against supper time. This log he cast down with a din inside the cave, and in fear we fled to the secret place of the rock. As for him, he drave his fat flocks into the wide cavern, even all that he was wont to milk; but the males both of the sheep and of the goats he left without in the deep yard. Thereafter he lifted a huge doorstone and weighty, and set it in the mouth of the cave, such an one as two and twenty good four-wheeled wains could not raise from the ground, so mighty a sheer rock did he set against the doorway. Then he sat down and milked the ewes and bleating goats all orderly, and beneath each ewe he placed her young. And anon he curdled one half of the white milk, and massed it together, and stored it in wicker-baskets, and the other half he let stand in pails, that he might have it to take and drink against supper time. Now when he had done all his work busily then he kindled the fire anew, and espied us, and made question:

"Strangers, who are ye? Whence sail ye over the wet ways? On some trading enterprise or at adventure do ye rove, even as sea-robbers over the brine, for at hazard of their own lives they wander, bringing bale to alien men."

So spake he, but as for us our heart within us was broken for terror of the deep voice and his own monstrous shape; yet despite all I answered and spake unto him, saying:

"Lo, we are Achaeans, driven wandering from Troy, by all manner of winds over the great gulf of the sea; seeking our homes we fare, but another path have we come, by other ways: even such, methinks, was the will and the counsel of Zeus. And we avow us to be the men of Agamemnon, son of Atreus, whose fame is even now the mightiest under heaven, so great a city did he sack, and destroyed many people; but as for us we have lighted here, and come to these thy knees, if perchance thou wilt give us a stranger's gift, or make any present, as is the due of strangers. Nay, lord, have regard to the gods, for we are thy suppliants; and Zeus is the avenger of suppliants and sojourners, Zeus, the god of the stranger, who fareth in the company of reverend strangers."

So I spake, and anon he answered out of his pitiless heart: "Thou art witless, my stranger, or thou hast come from afar, who biddest me either to fear or shun the gods. For the Cyclôpes pay no heed to Zeus, lord of the aegis, nor to the blessed gods, for verily we are better men than they. Nor would I, to shun the enmity of Zeus, spare either thee or thy company, unless my spirit bade me. But tell me where thou didst stay thy well-wrought ship on thy coming? Was it perchance at the far end of the island, or hard by, that I may know?"

So he spake tempting me, but he cheated me not, who knew full much, and I answered him again with words of guile:

"As for my ship, Poseidon, the shaker of the earth, brake it to pieces, for he cast it upon the rocks at the border of your country, and brought it nigh the headland, and a wind bare it thither from the sea. But I with these my men escaped from utter doom."

So I spake, and out of his pitiless heart he answered me not a word, but sprang up, and laid his hands upon my fellows, and clutching two together dashed them, as they had been whelps, to the earth, and the brain flowed forth upon the ground and the earth was wet. Then cut he them up piecemeal, and made ready his supper. So he ate even as a mountain-bred lion, and ceased not, devouring entrails and flesh and bones with their marrow. And we wept and raised our hands to Zeus, beholding the cruel deeds; and we were at our wits' end. And after the Cyclops had filled his huge maw with human flesh and the milk he drank thereafter, he lay within the cave, stretched out among his sheep.

So I took counsel in my great heart, whether I should draw near, and pluck my sharp sword from my thigh, and stab him in the breast, where the midriff holds the liver, feeling for the place with my hand. But my second thought withheld me, for so should we too have perished even there with utter doom. For we should not have prevailed to roll away with our hands from the lofty door the heavy stone which he set there. So for that time we made moan, awaiting the bright Dawn.

Now when early Dawn shone forth, the rosy-fingered, again he kindled the fire and milked his goodly flocks all orderly, and beneath each ewe set her lamb. Anon when he had done all his work busily, again he seized yet other two men and made ready his midday meal. And after the meal, lightly he moved away the great door-stone, and drave his fat flocks forth from the cave, and afterwards he set it in his place again, as one might set the lid on a quiver. Then with a loud whoop, the Cyclops turned his fat flocks towards the hills; but I was left devising evil in the deep of my heart, if in any wise I might avenge me, and Athene grant me renown.

And this was the counsel that showed best in my sight. There lay by a sheep-fold a great club of the Cyclops, a club of olive wood, yet green, which he had cut to carry with him when it should be seasoned. Now when we saw it we likened it in size to the mast of a black ship of twenty oars, a wide merchant vessel that traverses the great sea gulf, so huge it was to view in bulk and length. I stood thereby and cut off from it a portion as it were a fathom's length, and set it by my fellows, and bade them fine it down, and they made it even, while I stood by and sharpened it to a point, and straightway I took it and hardened it in the bright fire. Then I laid it well away, and hid it beneath the dung, which was scattered in great heaps in the depths of the cave. And I bade my company cast lots among them, which of them should risk the adventure with me, and lift the bar and turn it about in his eye, when sweet sleep came upon him. And the lot fell upon those four whom I myself would have been fain to choose, and I appointed myself to be the fifth among them. In the evening he came shepherding his flocks of goodly fleece, and presently he drave his fat flocks into the cave each and all, nor left he any without in the deep court-yard, whether through some foreboding, or perchance that the god so bade him do. Thereafter he lifted the huge door-stone and set it in the mouth of the cave, and sitting down he milked the ewes and bleating goats, all orderly, and beneath each ewe he placed her young. Now when he had done all his work busily, again he seized yet other two and made ready his supper. Then I stood by the Cyclops and spake to him, holding in my hands an ivy bowl of the dark wine:

"Cyclops, take and drink wine after thy feast of man's meat, that thou mayest know what manner of drink this was that our ship held. And lo, I was bringing it thee as a drink offering, if haply thou may-est take pity and send me on my way home, but thy mad rage is past all sufferance. O hard of heart, how may another of the many men there be come ever to thee again, seeing that thy deeds have been lawless?"

So I spake, and he took the cup and drank it off, and found great delight in drinking the sweet draught, and asked me for it yet a second time:

"Give it me again of thy grace, and tell me thy name straightway, that I may give thee a stranger's gift, wherein thou mayest be glad. Yea for the earth, the grain-giver, bears for the Cyclôpes the mighty clusters of the juice of the grape, and the rain of Zeus gives them increase, but this is a rill of very nectar and ambrosia."

So he spake, and again I handed him the dark wine. Thrice I bare and gave it him, and thrice in his folly he drank it to the lees. Now when the wine had got about the wits of the Cyclops, then did I speak to him with soft words:

"Cyclops, thou askest me my renowned name, and I will declare it unto thee, and do thou grant me a stranger's gift, as thou didst promise. Noman is my name, and Noman they call me, my father and my mother and all my fellows."

So I spake, and straightway he answered me out of his pitiless heart:

"Noman will I eat last in the number of his fellows, and the others before him: that shall be thy gift."

Therewith he sank backwards and fell with face upturned, and there he lay with his great neck bent round, and sleep, that conquers all men, overcame him. And the wine and the fragments of men's flesh issued forth from his mouth, and he vomited, being heavy with wine. Then I thrust in that stake under the deep ashes, until it should grow hot, and I spake to my companions comfortable words, lest any should hang back from me in fear. But when that bar of olive wood was just about to catch fire in the flame, green though it was, and began to glow terribly, even then I came nigh, and drew it from the coals, and my fellows gathered about me, and some god breathed great courage into us. For their part they seized the bar of olive wood, that was sharpened at the point, and thrust it into his eye, while I from my place aloft turned it about, as when a man bores a ship's beam with a drill while his fellows below spin it with a strap, which they hold at either end, and the auger runs round continually. Even so did we seize the fiery-pointed brand and whirled it round in his eye, and the blood flowed about the heated bar. And the breath of the flame singed his eyelids and brows all about, as the ball of the eye burnt away, and the roots thereof crackled in the flame. And as when a smith dips an axe or adze in chill water with a great hissing, when he would temper it — for hereby anon comes the strength of iron — even so did his eye hiss round the stake of olive. And he raised a great and terrible cry, that the rock rang around, and we fled away in fear, while he plucked forth from his eye the brand bedabbled in much blood. Then maddened with pain he cast it from him with his hands, and called with a loud voice on the Cyclôpes, who dwelt about him in the caves along the windy heights. And they heard the cry and flocked together from every side, and gathering round the cave asked him what ailed him:

"What hath so distressed thee, Polyphemus, that thou criest thus aloud through the immortal night, and makest us sleepless? Surely no mortal driveth off thy flocks against thy will: surely none slayeth thyself by force or craft?"

And the strong Polyphemus spake to them again from out the cave:
"My friends, Noman is slaying me by guile, nor at all by force."

And they answered and spake winged words: "If then no man is
violently handling thee in thy solitude, it can in no wise be that thou
shouldest escape the sickness sent by mighty Zeus. Nay, pray thou
to thy father, the lord Poseidon."

On this wise they spake and departed; and my heart within me
laughed to see how my name and cunning counsel had beguiled them.
But the Cyclops, groaning and travailing in pain, groped with his
hands, and lifted away the stone from the door of the cave, and
himself sat in the entry, with arms outstretched to catch, if he might,
any one that was going forth with his sheep, so witless, methinks,
did he hope to find me. But I advised me how all might be for the
very best, if perchance I might find a way of escape from death for
my companions and myself, and I wove all manner of craft and
counsel, as a man will for his life, seeing that great mischief was
nigh. And this was the counsel that showed best in my sight. The
rams of the flock were well nurtured and thick of fleece, great and
goodly, with wool dark as the violet. Quietly I lashed them together
with twisted withies, whereon the Cyclops slept, that lawless monster.
Three together I took: now the middle one of the three would bear
each a man, but the other twain went on either side, saving my fellows. Thus every three sheep bare their man. But as for me I laid
hold of the back of a young ram who was far the best and the goodliest of all the flock, and curled beneath his shaggy belly there I lay,
and so clung face upward, grasping the wondrous fleece with a steadfast heart. So for that time making moan we awaited the bright
Dawn.

So soon as early Dawn shone forth, the rosy-fingered, then did the
rams of the flock hasten forth to pasture, but the ewes bleated un-
milked about the pens, for their udders were swollen to bursting.
Then their lord, sore stricken with pain, felt along the backs of all
the sheep as they stood up before him, and guessed not in his folly
how that my men were bound beneath the breasts of his thick-fleeced
flocks. Last of all the sheep came forth the ram, cumbered with
his wool, and the weight of me and my cunning. And the strong
Polyphemus laid his hands on him and spake to him, saying:

"Dear ram, wherefore, I pray thee, art thou the last of all the flocks
to go forth from the cave, who of old wast not wont to lag behind
the sheep, but wert ever the foremost to pluck the tender blossom of
the pasture, faring with long strides, and wert still the first to come to
the streams of the rivers, and first didst long to return to the homestead in the evening. But now art thou the very last. Surely thou
art sorrowing for the eye of thy lord, which an evil man blinded,
with his accursed fellows, when he had subdued my wits with wine,
even Noman, whom I say hath not yet escaped destruction. Ah, if
thou couldst feel as I, and be endued with speech, to tell me where he
shifts about to shun my wrath; then should he be smitten, and his
brains be dashed against the floor here and there about the cave, and

my heart be lightened of the sorrows which Noman, nothing worth, hath brought me!"

Therewith he sent the ram forth from him, and when we had gone but a little way from the cave and from the yard, first I loosed myself from under the ram and then I set my fellows free. And swiftly we drave on those stiff-shanked sheep, so rich in fat, and often turned to look about, till we came to the ship. And a glad sight to our fellows were we that had fled from death, but the others they would have bemoaned with tears; howbeit I suffered it not, but with frowning brows forbade each man to weep. Rather I bade them to cast on board the many sheep with goodly fleece, and to sail over the salt sea water. So they embarked forthwith, and sate upon the benches, and sitting orderly smote the grey sea water with their oars. But when I had not gone so far, but that a man's shout might be heard, then I spoke unto the Cyclops taunting him:

"Cyclops, so thou wert not to eat the company of a weakling by main might in thy hollow cave! Thine evil deeds were very sure to find thee out, thou cruel man, who hadst no shame to eat thy guests within thy gates, wherefore Zeus hath requited thee, and the other gods."

So I spake, and he was mightily angered at heart, and he brake off the peak of a great hill and threw it at us, and it fell in front of the dark-prowed ship. And the sea heaved beneath the fall of the rock, and the backward flow of the wave bare the ship quickly to the dry land, with the wash from the deep sea, and drave it to the shore. Then I caught up a long pole in my hands, and thrust the ship from off the land, and roused my company, and with a motion of the head bade them dash in with their oars, that so we might escape our evil plight. So they bent to their oars and rowed on. But when we had now made twice the distance over the brine, I would fain have spoken to the Cyclops, but my company stayed me on every side with soft words, saying:

"Foolhardy that thou art, why wouldst thou rouse a wild man to wrath, who even now hath cast so mighty a throw towards the deep and brought our ship back to land, yea and we thought that we had perished even there? If he had heard any of us utter sound or speech he would have crushed our heads and our ship timbers with a cast of a rugged stone, so mightily he hurls."

So spake they, but they prevailed not on my lordly spirit, and I answered him again from out an angry heart:

"Cyclops, if any one of mortal men shall ask thee of the unsightly blinding of thine eye, say that it was Odysseus that blinded it, the waster of cities, son of Laertes, whose dwelling is in Ithaca."

So I spake, and with a moan he answered me, saying:

"Lo now, in very truth the ancient oracles have come upon me. There lived here a soothsayer, a noble man and a mighty, Telemus, son of Eurymus, who surpassed all men in soothsaying, and waxed old as a seer among the Cyclôpes. He told me that all these things should come to pass in the aftertime, even that I should lose my eyesight at the hand of Odysseus. But I ever looked for some tall and goodly man to come hither, clad in great might, but behold now one that is a dwarf, a man of no worth and a weakling, hath blinded me of my eye after subduing me with wine. Nay come hither, Odysseus, that I may set by thee a stranger's cheer, and speed thy parting hence, that so the Earth-shaker may vouchsafe it thee, for his son am I, and he avows him for my father. And he himself will heal me, if it be his will; and none other of the blessed gods or of mortal men."

Even so he spake, but I answered him, and said: "Would god that I were as sure to rob thee of soul and life, and send thee within the house of Hades, as I am that not even the Earth-shaker will heal thine eye!"

So I spake, and then he prayed to the lord Poseidon stretching forth his hands to the starry heaven: "Hear me, Poseidon, girdler of the earth, god of the dark hair, if indeed I be thine, and thou avowest thee my sire, — grant that he may never come to his home, even Odysseus, waster of cities, the son of Laertes, whose dwelling is in Ithaca; yet if he is ordained to see his friends and come unto his well-builded house, and his own country, late may he come in evil case, with the loss of all his company, in the ship of strangers, and find sorrows in his house."

So he spake in prayer, and the god of the dark locks heard him. And once again he lifted a stone, far greater than the first, and with one swing he hurled it, and he put forth a measureless strength, and cast it but a little space behind the dark-prowed ship, and all but struck the end of the rudder. And the sea heaved beneath the fall of the rock, but the wave bare on the ship and drave it to the further shore.

But when we had now reached that island, where all our other decked ships abode together, and our company were gathered sorrowing, expecting us nevermore, on our coming thither we ran our ship ashore upon the sand, and ourselves too stept forth upon the sea-beach. Next we took forth the sheep of the Cyclops from out the hollow ship, and divided them, that none through me might go lacking his proper share. But the ram for me alone my goodly-greaved company chose out, in the dividing of the sheep, and on the shore I offered him up to Zeus, even to the son of Cronos, who dwells in the dark clouds, and is lord of all, and I burnt the slices of the thighs. But he heeded not the sacrifice, but was devising how my decked ships and my dear company might perish utterly. Thus for that time we sat the livelong day, until the going down of the sun, feasting on abundant flesh and sweet wine. And when the sun had sunk and darkness had come on, then we laid us to rest upon the sea-beach. So soon as early Dawn shone forth, the rosy-fingered, I called to my company, and commanded them that they should themselves climb the ship and loose the hawsers. So they soon embarked and sat upon the benches, and sitting orderly smote the grey sea water with their oars.

Thence we sailed onward stricken at heart, yet glad as men saved from death, albeit we had lost our dear companions.

BOOK X

Odysseus, his entertainment by Aeolus, of whom he received a fair wind for the present, and all the rest of the winds tied up in a bag; which his men untying, flew out, and carried him back to Aeolus, who refused to receive him. His adventure at Laestrygonia with Antiphates, where of twelve ships he lost eleven, men and all. How he went thence to the Isle of Aia, where half of his men were turned by Circé into swine, and how he went himself, and by the help of Hermes recovered them and stayed with Circé a year.

Then we came to the isle Aeolian, where dwelt Aeolus, son of Hippotas, dear to the deathless gods, in a floating island, and all about it is a wall of bronze unbroken, and the cliff runs up sheer from the sea. His twelve children too abide there in his halls, six daughters and six lusty sons; and, behold, he gave his daughters to his sons to wife. And they feast evermore by their dear father and their kind mother, and dainties innumerable lie ready to their hands. And the house is full of the savour of feasting, and the noise thereof rings round, yea in the courtyard, by day, and in the night they sleep each one by his chaste wife in coverlets and on jointed bedsteads. So then we came to their city and their goodly dwelling, and the king entreated me kindly for a whole month, and sought out each thing, Ilios and the ships of the Argives, and the return of the Achaeans. So I told him all the tale in order duly. But when I in turn took the word and asked of my journey, and bade him send me on my way, he too denied me not, but furnished an escort. He gave me a wallet, made of the hide of an ox of nine seasons old, which he let flay, and therein he bound the ways of all the noisy winds; for him the son of Cronos made keeper of the winds, either to lull or to rouse what blasts he will. And he made it fast in the hold of the ship with a shining silver thong, that not the faintest breath might escape. Then he sent forth the blast of the West Wind to blow for me, to bear our ships and ourselves upon our way; but this he was never to bring to pass, for we were undone through our own heedlessness.

For nine whole days we sailed by night and day continually, and now on the tenth day my native land came in sight, and already we were so near that we beheld the folk tending the beacon fires. Then over me there came sweet slumber in my weariness, for all the time I was holding the sheet, nor gave it to any of my company, that so we might come quicker to our own country. Meanwhile my company held converse together, and said that I was bringing home for myself gold and silver, gifts from Aeolus the high-hearted son of Hippotas. And thus would they speak looking each man to his neighbour:

"Lo now, how beloved he is and highly esteemed among all men, to the city and land of whomsoever he may come. Many are the goodly treasures he taketh with him out of the spoil from Troy, while we who have fulfilled like journeying with him return homeward bringing with us but empty hands. And now Aeolus hath given unto him these things freely in his love. Nay come, let us quickly see what they are, even what wealth of gold and silver is in the wallet."

So they spake, and the evil counsel of my company prevailed. They loosed the wallet, and all the winds brake forth. And the violent blast seized my men, and bare them towards the high seas weeping, away from their own country; but as for me, I awoke and communed with my great heart, whether I should cast myself from the ship and perish in the deep, or endure in silence and abide yet among the living. Howbeit I hardened my heart to endure, and muffling my head I lay still in the ship. But the vessels were driven by the evil storm-wind back to the isle Aeolian, and my company made moan.

There we stepped ashore and drew water, and my company presently took their midday meal by the swift ships. Now when we had tasted bread and wine, I took with me a herald and one of my company, and went to the famous dwelling of Aeolus: and I found him feasting with his wife and children. So we went in and sat by the pillars of the door on the threshold, and they all marvelled and asked us:

"How hast thou come hither, Odysseus? What evil god assailed thee? Surely we sent thee on thy way with all diligence, that thou mightest get thee to thine own country and thy home, and whithersoever thou wouldest."

Even so they said, but I spake among them heavy at heart: "My evil company hath been my bane, and sleep thereto remorseless. Come, my friends, do ye heal the harm, for yours is the power."

So I spake, beseeching them in soft words, but they held their peace. And the father answered, saying: "Get thee forth from the island straightway, thou that art the most reprobate of living men. Far be it from me to help or to further that man whom the blessed gods abhor! Get thee forth, for lo, thy coming marks thee hated by the deathless gods."

Therewith he sent me forth from the house making heavy moan. Thence we sailed onwards stricken at heart. And the spirit of the men was spent beneath the grievous rowing by reason of our vain endeavour, for there was no more any sign of a wafting wind. So for the space of six days we sailed by night and day continually, and on the seventh we came to the steep stronghold of Lamos, Telepylos of the Laestrygons, where herdsman hails herdsman as he drives in his flock, and the other who drives forth answers the call. There might a sleepless man have earned a double wage, the one as neatherd, the other shepherding white flocks: so near are the outgoings of the night and of the day. Thither when we had come to the fair haven, whereabout on both sides goes one steep cliff unbroken, and jutting headlands over against each other stretch forth at the mouth of the harbour, and strait is the entrance; thereinto all the others steered their curved ships. Now the vessels were bound within the hollow harbour each hard by other, for no wave ever swelled within it, great or small, but there was a bright calm all around. But I alone moored my dark ship without the harbour, at the uttermost point thereof, and made fast the hawser to a rock. And I went up a craggy hill, a place of outlook, and stood thereon: thence there was no sign of the labour of men or oxen, only we saw the smoke curling upward from the land. Then I sent forth certain of my company to go and search out what manner of men they were who here live upon the earth by bread, choosing out two of my company and sending a third with them as herald. Now when they had gone ashore, they went along a level road whereby wains were wont to draw down wood from the high hills to the town. And without the town they fell in with a damsel drawing water, the noble daughter of Laestrygonian Antiphates. She had come down to the clear-flowing spring Artacia, for thence it was custom to draw water to the town. So they stood by her and spake unto her, and asked who was king of that land, and who they were he ruled over. Then at once she showed them the high-roofed hall of her father. Now when they had entered the renowned house, they found his wife therein: she was huge of bulk as a mountain peak and was loathly in their sight. Straightway she called the renowned Antiphates, her lord, from the assembly-place, and he contrived a pitiful destruction for my men. Forthwith he clutched up one of my company and made ready his midday meal, but the other twain sprang up and came in flight to the ships. Then he raised the war-cry through the town, and the valiant Laestrygonians at the sound thereof, flocked together from every side, a host past number, not like men but like the Giants. They cast at us from the cliffs with great rocks, each of them a man's burden, and anon there arose from the fleet an evil din of men dying and ships shattered withal. And like folk spearing fishes they bare home their hideous meal. While as yet they were slaying my friends within the deep harbour, I drew my sharp sword from my thigh, and with it cut the hawsers of my dark-prowed ship. Quickly then I called to my company, and bade them dash in with the oars, that we might clean escape this evil plight. And all with one accord they tossed the sea water with the oar-blade, in dread of death, and to my delight my barque flew forth to the high seas away from the beetling rocks, but those other ships were lost there, one and all.

Thence we sailed onward stricken at heart, yet glad as men saved from death, albeit we had lost our dear companions. And we came to the isle Aeaean, where dwelt Circé of the braided tresses, an awful goddess of mortal speech, own sister to the wizard Aeëtes. Both were begotten of Helios, who gives light to all men, and their mother was Perse, daughter of Oceanus. There on the shore we put in with our ship into the sheltering haven silently, and some god was our guide. Then we stept ashore, and for two days and two nights lay there, consuming our own hearts for weariness and pain. But when now the fair-tressed Dawn had brought the full light of the third day, then did I seize my spear and my sharp sword, and quickly departing from the ship I went up unto a place of wide prospect, if haply I might see any sign of the labour of men and hear the sound of their speech. So I went up a craggy hill, a place of out-look, and I saw the smoke rising from the broad-wayed earth in the halls of Circé, through the thick coppice and the woodland. Then I mused in my mind and heart whether I should go and make discovery, for that I had seen the smoke and flame. And as I thought thereon this seemed to me the better counsel, to go first to the swift ship and to the sea-banks, and give my company their midday meal, and then send them to make search. But as I came and drew nigh to the curved ship, some god even then took pity on me in my loneliness, and sent a tall antlered stag across my very path. He was coming down from his pasture in the woodland to the river to drink, for verily the might of the sun was sore upon him. And as he came up from out of the stream, I smote him on the spine in the middle of the back, and the brazen shaft went clean through him, and with a moan he fell in the dust, and his life passed from him. Then I set my foot on him and drew forth the brazen shaft from the wound, and laid it hard by upon the ground and let it lie. Next I broke withies and willow twigs, and wove me a rope a fathom in length, well twisted from end to end, and bound together the feet of the huge beast, and went to the black ship bearing him across my neck, and leaning on a spear, for it was in no wise possible to carry him on my shoulder with the one hand, for he was a mighty quarry. And I threw him down before the ship and roused my company with soft words, standing by each man in turn:

"Friends, for all our sorrows we shall not yet a while go down to the house of Hades, ere the coming of the day of destiny; go to then, while as yet there is meat and drink in the swift ship, let us take thought thereof, that we be not famished for hunger."

Even so I spake, and they speedily hearkened to my words. They unmuffled their heads, and there on the shore of the unharvested sea gazed at the stag, for he was a mighty quarry. But after they had delighted their eyes with the sight of him, they washed their hands and got ready the glorious feast. So for that time we sat the live-long day till the going down of the sun, feasting on abundant flesh and sweet wine. But when the sun sank and darkness had come on, then we laid us to rest upon the sea beach. So soon as early Dawn shone forth, the rosy-fingered, I called a gathering of my men and spake in the ears of them all:

"Hear my words, my fellows, despite your evil case. My friends, lo, now we know not where is the place of darkness or of dawning, nor where the Sun, that gives light to men, goes beneath the earth, nor where he rises; therefore let us advise us speedily if any counsel yet may be: as for me, I deem there is none. For I went up a craggy hill, a place of out-look, and saw the island crowned about with the circle of the endless sea, the isle itself lying low; and in the midst thereof mine eyes beheld the smoke through the thick coppice and the woodland."

Even so I spake, but their spirit within them was broken, as they remembered the deeds of Antiphates the Laestrygonian, and all the evil violence of the haughty Cyclops, the man-eater. So they wept aloud shedding big tears. Howbeit no avail came of their weeping.

Then I numbered my goodly-greaved company in two bands, and appointed a leader for each, and I myself took the command of the one part, and godlike Eurylochus of the other. And anon we shook the lots in a brazen-fitted helmet, and out leapt the lot of proud Eurylochus. So he went on his way, and with him two and twenty of my fellowship all weeping; and we were left behind making lament. In the forest glades they found the halls of Circé builded, of polished stone, in a place with wide prospect. And all around the palace mountain-bred wolves and lions were roaming, whom she herself had bewitched with evil drugs that she gave them. Yet the beasts did not set on my men, but lo, they ramped about them and fawned on them, wagging their long tails. And as when dogs fawn about their lord when he comes from the feast, for he always brings them the fragments that soothe their mood, even so the strong-clawed wolves and the lions fawned around them; but they were affrighted when they saw the strange and terrible creatures. So they stood at the outer gate of the fair-tressed goddess, and within they heard Circé singing in a sweet voice, as she fared to and fro before the great web imperishable, such as is the handiwork of goddesses, fine of woof and full of grace and splendour. Then Polites, a leader of men, the dearest to me and the trustiest of all my company, first spake to them:

"Friends, forasmuch as there is one within that fares to and fro before a mighty web singing a sweet song, so that all the floor of the hall makes echo, a goddess she is or a woman; come quickly and cry aloud to her."

He spake the word and they cried aloud and called to her. And straightway she came forth and opened the shining doors and bade them in, and all went with her in their heedlessness. But Eurylochus tarried behind, for he guessed that there was some treason. So she led them in and set them upon the chairs and high seats, and made them a mess of cheese and barley-meal and yellow honey with Pramnian wine, and mixed harmful drugs with the food to make them utterly forget their own country. Now when she had given them the cup and they had drunk it off, presently she smote them with a wand, and in the styes of the swine she penned them. So they had the head and voice, the bristles and the shape of swine, but their mind abode even as of old. Thus were they penned there weeping, and Circé flung them acorns and mast and fruit of the cornel tree to eat, whereon wallowing swine do always batten.

Now Eurylochus came back to the swift black ship to bring tidings of his fellows, and of their unseemly doom. Not a word could he utter, for all his desire, so deeply smitten was he to the heart with grief, and his eyes were filled with tears and his soul was fain of lamentation. But when we all had pressed him with our questions in amazement, even then he told the fate of the remnant of our company.

"We went, as thou didst command, through the coppice, noble Odysseus: we found within the forest glades the fair halls, builded of polished stone, in a place with wide prospect. And there was one that fared before a mighty web and sang a clear song, a goddess she was or a woman, and they cried aloud and called to her. And straightway she came forth, and opened the shining doors and bade them in, and they all went with her in their heedlessness. But I tarried behind, for I guessed that there was some treason. Then they vanished away one and all, nor did any of them appear again, though I sat long time watching."

So spake he, whereon I cast about my shoulder my silver-studded sword, a great blade of bronze, and slung my bow about me and bade him lead me again by the way that he came. But he caught me with both hands, and by my knees he besought me, and bewailing him spake to me winged words:

"Lead me not thither against my will, oh fosterling of Zeus, but leave me here! For well I know thou shalt thyself return no more, nor bring any one of all thy fellowship; nay, let us flee the swifter with those that be here, for even yet may we escape the evil day."

On this wise he spake, but I answered him, saying: "Eurylochus, abide for thy part here in this place, eating and drinking by the black hollow ship: but I will go forth, for a strong constraint is laid on me."

With that I went up from the ship and the sea-shore. But lo, when in my faring through the sacred glades I was now drawing near to the great hall of the enchantress Circé, then did Hermes, of the golden wand, meet me as I approached the house, in the likeness of a young man with the first down on his lip, the time when youth is most gracious. So he clasped my hand and spake and hailed me:

"Ah, hapless man, whither away again, all alone through the wolds, thou that knowest not this country? And thy company yonder in the hall of Circé are penned in the guise of swine, in their deep lairs abiding. Is it in hope to free them that thou art come hither? Nay, methinks, thou thyself shalt never return but remain there with the others. Come then, I will redeem thee from thy distress, and bring deliverance. Lo, take this herb of virtue, and go to the dwelling of Circé, that it may keep from thy head the evil day. And I will tell thee all the magic sleight of Circé. She will mix thee a potion and cast drugs into the mess; but not even so shall she be able to enchant thee; so helpful is this charmed herb that I shall give thee, and I will tell thee all. When it shall be that Circé smites thee with her long wand, even then draw thou thy sharp sword from thy thigh, and spring on her, as one eager to slay her. And she will shrink away and be instant with thee to lie with her. Thenceforth disdain not thou the bed of the goddess, that she may deliver thy company and kindly entertain thee. But command her to swear a mighty oath by the blessed gods, that she will plan nought else of mischief to thine own hurt, lest she make thee a dastard and unmanned, when she hath thee naked."

Therewith the slayer of Argos gave me the plant that he had

plucked from the ground, and he showed me the growth thereof. It was black at the root, but the flower was like to milk. Moly the gods call it, but it is hard for mortal men to dig; howbeit with the gods all things are possible.

Then Hermes departed toward high Olympus, up through the woodland isle, but as for me I held on my way to the house of Circé, and my heart was darkly troubled as I went. So I halted in the portals of the fair-tressed goddess; there I stood and called aloud and the goddess heard my voice, who presently came forth and opened the shining doors and bade me in, and I went with her heavy at heart. So she led me in and set me on a chair with studs of silver, a goodly carven chair, and beneath was a footstool for the feet. And she made me a potion in a golden cup, that I might drink, and she also put a charm therein, in the evil counsel of her heart. Now when she had given it and I had drunk it off and was not bewitched, she smote me with her wand and spake and hailed me:

"Go thy way now to the stye, couch thee there with the rest of thy company."

So spake she, but I drew my sharp sword from my thigh and sprang upon Circé, as one eager to slay her. But with a great cry she slipped under, and clasped my knees, and bewailing herself spake to me winged words:

"Who art thou of the sons of men, and whence? Where is thy city? Where are they that begat thee? I marvel to see how thou hast drunk of this charm, and wast nowise subdued. Nay, for there lives no man else that is proof against this charm, whoso hath drunk thereof, and once it hath passed his lips. But thou hast, methinks, a mind within thee that may not be enchanted. Verily thou art Odysseus, ready at need, whom he of the golden wand, the slayer of Argos, full often told me was to come hither, on his way from Troy with his swift black ship. Nay come, put thy sword into the sheath, and thereafter let us go up into my bed, that meeting in love and sleep we may trust each the other."

So spake she, but I answered her, saying: "Nay, Circé, how canst thou bid me be gentle to thee, who hast turned my company into swine within thy halls, and holding me here with a guileful heart requirest me to pass within thy chamber and go up into thy bed, that so thou mayest make me a dastard and unmanned when thou hast me naked? Nay, never will I consent to go up into thy bed, except thou wilt deign, goddess, to swear a mighty oath, that thou wilt plan nought else of mischief to mine own hurt."

So I spake, and she straightway swore the oath not to harm me, as I bade her. But when she had sworn and had done that oath, then at last I went up into the beautiful bed of Circé.

Now all this while her handmaids busied them in the halls, four maidens that are her serving women in the house. They are born of the wells and of the woods and of the holy rivers, that flow forward into the salt sea. Of these one cast upon the chairs goodly coverlets of purple above, and spread a linen cloth thereunder. And lo, another drew up silver tables to the chairs, and thereon set for them golden baskets. And a third mixed sweet honey-hearted wine in a silver bowl, and set out cups of gold. And a fourth bare water, and kindled a great fire beneath the mighty cauldron. So the water waxed warm; but when it boiled in the bright brazen vessel, she set me in a bath and bathed me with water from out a great cauldron, pouring it over head and shoulders, when she had mixed it to a pleasant warmth, till from my limbs she took away the consuming weariness. Now after she had bathed me and anointed me well with olive oil, and cast about me a fair mantle and a doublet, she led me into the halls and set me on a chair with studs of silver, a goodly carven chair, and beneath was a footstool for the feet. And a handmaid bare water for the hands in a goodly golden ewer, and poured it forth over a silver basin to wash withal; and to my side she drew a polished table, and a grave dame bare wheaten bread and set it by me, and laid on the board many dainties, giving freely of such things as she had by her. And she bade me eat, but my soul found no pleasure therein. I sat with other thoughts, and my heart had a boding of ill.

Now when Circé saw that I sat thus, and that I put not forth my hands to the meat, and that I was mightily afflicted, she drew near to me and spake to me winged words:

"Wherefore thus, Odysseus, dost thou sit there like a speechless man, consuming thine own soul, and dost not touch meat nor drink? Dost thou indeed deem there is some further guile? Nay, thou hast no cause to fear, for already I have sworn thee a strong oath not to harm thee."

So spake she, but I answered her, saying: "Oh, Circé, what righteous man would have the heart to taste meat and drink ere he had redeemed his company, and beheld them face to face? But if in good faith thou biddest me eat and drink, then let them go free, that mine eyes may behold my dear companions."

So I spake, and Circé passed out through the hall with the wand in her hand, and opened the doors of the stye, and drave them forth in the shape of swine of nine seasons old. There they stood before her, and she went through their midst, and anointed each one of them with another charm. And lo, from their limbs the bristles dropped away, wherewith the venom had erewhile clothed them, that lady Circé gave them. And they became men again, younger than before they were, and goodlier far, and taller to behold. And they all knew me again and each one took my hands, and wistful was the lament that sank into their souls, and the roof around rang wondrously. And even the goddess herself was moved with compassion.

Then standing nigh me the fair goddess spake unto me: "Son of Laertes, of the seed of Zeus, Odysseus of many devices, depart now to thy swift ship and the sea-banks. And first of all, draw ye up the ship ashore, and bestow the goods in the caves and all the gear. And thyself return again, and bring with thee thy dear companions."

So spake she, and my lordly spirit consented thereto. So I went on my way to the swift ship and the sea-banks, and there I found my dear company on the swift ship lamenting piteously, shedding big tears. And as when calves of the homestead gather round the droves of kine that have returned to the yard, when they have had their fill of pasture, and all with one accord frisk before them, and the folds may no more contain them, but with a ceaseless lowing they skip about their dams, so flocked they all about me weeping, when their eyes beheld me. Yea, and to their spirit it was as though they had got to their dear country, and the very city of rugged Ithaca, where they were born and reared.

Then making lament they spake to me winged words: "O fosterling of Zeus, we were none otherwise glad at thy returning, than if we had come to Ithaca, our own country. Nay come, of our other companions tell us the tale of their ruin."

So spake they, but I answered them with soft words: "Behold, let us first of all draw up the ship ashore, and bestow our goods in the caves and all our gear. And do ye bestir you, one and all, to go with me, that ye may see your fellows in the sacred dwelling of Circé, eating and drinking, for they have continual store."

So spake I, and at once they hearkened to my words, but Eurylochus alone would have holden all my companions, and uttering his voice he spake to them winged words:

"Wretched men that we are! whither are we going? Why are your hearts so set on sorrow that ye should go down to the hall of Circé, who will surely change us all to swine, or wolves, or lions, to guard her great house perforce, according to the deeds that the Cyclops wrought, when certain of our company went to his inmost fold, and with them went Odysseus, ever hardy, for through the blindness of his heart did they too perish?"

So spake he, but I mused in my heart whether to draw my long hanger from my stout thigh, and therewith smite off his head and bring it to the dust, albeit he was very near of kin to me; but the men of my company stayed me on every side with soothing words:

"Prince of the seed of Zeus, as for this man, we will suffer him, if thou wilt have it so, to abide here by the ship and guard the ship; but as for us, be our guide to the sacred house of Circé."

So they spake and went up from the ship and the sea. Nay, nor yet was Eurylochus left by the hollow ship, but he went with us, for he feared my terrible rebuke.

Meanwhile Circé bathed the rest of my company in her halls with all care, and anointed them well with olive oil; and cast thick mantles and doublets about them. And we found them all feasting nobly in the halls. And when they saw and knew each other face to face, they wept and mourned, and the house rang around. Then she stood near me, that fair goddess, and spake saying:

"Son of Laertes, of the seed of Zeus, Odysseus of many devices, no more now wake this plenteous weeping: myself I know of all the pains ye endured upon the teeming deep, and the great despite done you by unkindly men upon the land. Nay come, eat ye meat and drink wine, till your spirit shall return to you again, as it was when first ye left your own country of rugged Ithaca; but now are ye wasted and wanting heart, mindful evermore of your sore wandering, nor has your heart ever been merry, for very grievous hath been your trial."

So spake she, and our lordly spirit consented thereto. So there we sat day by day for the full circle of a year, feasting on abundant flesh and sweet wine. But when now a year had gone, and the seasons returned as the months waned, and the long days came in their course, then did my dear company call me forth, and say:

"Good sir, now is it high time to mind thee of thy native land, if it is ordained that thou shalt be saved, and come to thy lofty house and thine own country."

So spake they and my lordly spirit consented thereto. So for that time we sat the livelong day till the going down of the sun, feasting on abundant flesh and sweet wine. But when the sun sank and darkness came on, they laid them to rest throughout the shadowy halls.

But when I had gone up into the fair bed of Circé, I besought her by her knees, and the goddess heard my speech, and uttering my voice I spake to her winged words: "Circé, fulfil for me the promise which thou madest me to send me on my homeward way. Now is my spirit eager to be gone, and the spirit of my company, that wear away my heart as they mourn around me, when haply thou art gone from us."

So spake I, and the fair goddess answered me anon: "Son of Laertes, of the seed of Zeus, Odysseus of many devices, tarry ye now no longer in my house against your will; but first must ye perform another journey, and reach the dwelling of Hades and of dread Persephone to seek to the spirit of Theban Teiresias, the blind soothsayer, whose wits abide steadfast. To him Persephone hath given judgment, even in death, that he alone should have understanding; but the other souls sweep shadow-like around."

Thus spake she, but as for me, my heart was broken, and I wept as I sat upon the bed, and my soul had no more care to live and to see the sunlight. But when I had my fill of weeping and grovelling, then at the last I answered and spake unto her saying: "And who, Circé, will guide us on this way? for no man ever yet sailed to hell in a black ship."

So spake I, and the fair goddess answered me anon: "Son of Laertes, of the seed of Zeus, Odysseus of many devices, nay, trouble not thyself for want of a guide, by thy ship abiding, but set up the mast and spread abroad the white sails and sit thee down; and the breeze of the North Wind will bear thy vessel on her way. But when thou hast now sailed in thy ship across the stream Oceanus, where is a waste shore and the groves of Persephone, even tall poplar trees and willows that shed their fruit before the season, there beach thy ship by deep eddying Oceanus, but go thyself to the dank house of Hades. Thereby into Acheron flows Pyriphlegethon, and Cocytus, a branch of the water of the Styx, and there is a rock, and the meeting of the two roaring waters. So, hero, draw nigh thereto, as I command thee, and dig a trench as it were a cubit in length and breadth, and about it pour a drink-offering to all the dead, first with mead and thereafter with sweet wine, and for the third time with water, and sprinkle white meal thereon; and entreat with many prayers the strengthless heads of the dead, and promise that on thy return to Ithaca thou wilt offer in thy halls a barren heifer, the best thou hast, and wilt fill the pyre with treasure, and wilt sacrifice apart, to Teiresias alone, a black ram without spot, the fairest of your flock. But when thou hast with prayers made supplication to the lordly races of the dead, then offer up a ram and a black ewe, bending their heads towards Erebus and thyself turn thy back, with thy face set for the shore of the river. Then will many spirits come to thee of the dead that be departed. Thereafter thou shalt call to thy company and command them to flay the sheep which even now lie slain by the pitiless sword, and to consume them with fire, and to make prayer to the gods, to mighty Hades and to dread Persephone. And thyself draw the sharp sword from thy thigh and sit there, suffering not the strengthless heads of the dead to draw nigh to the blood, ere thou hast word of Teiresias. Then the seer will come to thee quickly, leader of the people; he will surely declare to thee the way and the measure of thy path, and as touching thy returning, how thou mayst go over the teeming deep."

So spake she, and anon came the golden throned Dawn. Then she put on me a mantle and a doublet for raiment, and the nymph clad herself in a great shining robe, light of woof and gracious, and about her waist she cast a fair golden girdle, and put a veil upon her head. But I passed through the halls and roused my men with smooth words, standing by each one in turn:

"Sleep ye now no more nor breathe the sweet slumber; but let us go on our way, for surely she hath shown me all, the lady Circé."

So spake I, and their lordly soul consented thereto. Yet even thence I led not my company safe away. There was one, Elpenor, the youngest of us all, not very valiant in war neither steadfast in mind. He was lying apart from the rest of my men on the housetop of Circé's sacred dwelling, very fain of the cool air, as one heavy with wine. Now when he heard the noise of the voices and of the feet of my fellows as they moved to and fro, he leaped up of a sudden and minded him not to descend again by the way of the tall ladder, but fell right down from the roof, and his neck was broken from the bones of the spine, and his spirit went down to the house of Hades.

Then I spake among my men as they went on their way, saying: "Ye deem now, I see, that ye are going to your own dear country; but Circé hath showed us another way, even to the dwelling of Hades and of dread Persephone, to seek to the spirit of Theban Teiresias."

Even so I spake, but their heart within them was broken, and they sat them down even where they were, and made lament and tore their hair. Howbeit no help came of their weeping.

But as we were now wending sorrowful to the swift ship and the sea-banks, shedding big tears, Circé meanwhile had gone her ways and made fast a ram and a black ewe by the dark ship, lightly passing

us by: who may behold a god against his will, whether going to or
fro?

BOOK XI

Odysseus, his descent into hell, and discourses with the ghosts of the
deceased heroes.

Now when we had gone down to the ship and to the sea, first of all
we drew the ship unto the fair salt water, and placed the mast and sails
in the black ship, and took those sheep and put them therein, and ourselves too climbed on board, sorrowing, and shedding big tears. And
in the wake of our dark-prowed ship she sent a favouring wind that
filled the sails, a kindly escort, — even Circé of the braided tresses, a
dread goddess of human speech. And we set in order all the gear
throughout the ship and sat us down; and the wind and the helmsman guided our barque. And all day long her sails were stretched in
her seafaring; and the sun sank and all the ways were darkened.

She came to the limits of the world, to the deep flowing Oceanus.
There is the land and the city of the Cimmerians, shrouded in mist
and cloud, and never does the shining sun look down on them with
his rays, neither when he climbs up the starry heavens, nor when
again he turns earthward from the firmament, but deadly night is
outspread over miserable mortals. Thither we came and ran the
ship ashore and took out the sheep; but for our part we held on our
way along the stream of Oceanus, till we came to the place which
Circé had declared to us.

There Perimedes and Eurylochus held the victims, but I drew my
sharp sword from my thigh, and dug a pit, as it were a cubit in length
and breadth, and about it poured a drink-offering to all the dead, first
with mead and thereafter with sweet wine, and for the third time
with water. And I sprinkled white meal thereon, and entreated with
many prayers the strengthless heads of the dead, and promised that
on my return to Ithaca I would offer in my halls a barren heifer, the
best I had, and fill the pyre with treasure, and apart unto Teiresias
alone sacrifice a black ram without spot, the fairest of my flock. But
when I had besought the tribes of the dead with vows and prayers,
I took the sheep and cut their throats over the trench, and the dark
blood flowed forth, and lo, the spirits of the dead that be departed
gathered them from out of Erebus. Brides and youths unwed, and
old men of many and evil days, and tender maidens with grief yet
fresh at heart; and many there were, wounded with bronze-shod
spears, men slain in fight with their bloody mail about them. And
these many ghosts flocked together from every side about the trench
with a wondrous cry, and pale fear gat hold on me. Then did I
speak to my company and command them to flay the sheep that lay
slain by the pitiless sword, and to consume them with fire, and to
make prayer to the gods, to mighty Hades and to dread Persephone,
and myself I drew the sharp sword from my thigh and sat there, suf-

fering not the strengthless heads of the dead to draw nigh to the blood, ere I had word of Teiresias.

And first came the soul of Elpenor, my companion, that had not yet been buried beneath the wide-wayed earth; for we left the corpse behind us in the hall of Circé, unwept and unburied, seeing that another task was instant on us. At the sight of him I wept and had compassion on him, and uttering my voice spake to him winged words: "Elpenor, how hast thou come beneath the darkness and the shadow? Thou hast come fleeter on foot than I in my black ship."

So spake I, and with a moan he answered me, saying: "Son of Laertes, of the seed of Zeus, Odysseus of many devices, an evil doom of some god was my bane and wine out of measure. When I laid me down on the house-top of Circé I minded me not to descend again by the way of the tall ladder, but fell right down from the roof, and my neck was broken off from the bones of the spine, and my spirit went down to the house of Hades. And now I pray thee in the name of those whom we left, who are no more with us, thy wife, and thy sire who cherished thee when as yet thou wert a little one, and Telemachus, whom thou didst leave in thy halls alone; forasmuch as I know that on thy way hence from out the dwelling of Hades, thou wilt stay thy well-wrought ship at the isle Aeaean, even then, my lord, I charge thee to think on me. Leave me not unwept and unburied as thou goest hence, nor turn thy back upon me, lest haply I bring on thee the anger of the gods. Nay, burn me there with mine armour, all that is mine, and pile me a barrow on the shore of the grey sea, the grave of a luckless man, that even men unborn may hear my story. Fulfil me this and plant upon the barrow mine oar, wherewith I rowed in the days of my life, while yet I was among my fellows."

Even so he spake, and I answered him saying: "All this, luckless man, will I perform for thee and do."

Even so we twain were sitting holding sad discourse, I on the one side, stretching forth my sword over the blood, while on the other side the ghost of my friend told all his tale.

Anon came up the soul of my mother dead, Anticleia, the daughter of Autolycus the great-hearted, whom I left alive when I departed for sacred Ilios. At the sight of her I wept, and was moved with compassion, yet even so, for all my sore grief, I suffered her not to draw nigh to the blood, ere I had word of Teiresias.

Anon came the soul of Theban Teiresias, with a golden sceptre in his hand, and he knew me and spake unto me: "Son of Laertes, of the seed of Zeus, Odysseus of many devices, what seekest thou *now*, wretched man, wherefore hast thou left the sunlight and come hither to behold the dead and a land desolate of joy? Nay, hold off from the ditch and draw back thy sharp sword, that I may drink of the blood and tell thee sooth."

So spake he and I put up my silver-studded sword into the sheath, and when he had drunk the dark blood, even then did the noble seer speak unto me, saying: "Thou art asking of thy sweet returning,

great Odysseus, but that will the god make hard for thee; for methinks thou shalt not pass unheeded by the Shaker of the Earth, who
hath laid up wrath in his heart against thee, for rage at the blinding
of his dear son.   Yet even so, through many troubles, ye may come
home, if thou wilt restrain thy spirit and the spirit of thy men so soon
as thou shalt bring thy well-wrought ship nigh to the isle Thrinacia,
fleeing the sea of violet blue, when ye find the herds of Helios grazing
and his brave flocks, of Helios who overseeth all and overheareth all
things.   If thou doest these no hurt, being heedful of thy return, so
may ye yet reach Ithaca, albeit in evil case.   But if thou hurtest them,
I foreshow ruin for thy ship and for thy men, and even though thou
shalt thyself escape, late shalt thou return in evil plight, with the loss
of all thy company, on board the ship of strangers, and thou shalt find
sorrows in thy house, even proud men that devour thy living, while
they woo thy godlike wife and offer the gifts of wooing.   Yet I tell
thee, on thy coming thou shalt avenge their violence.   But when thou
hast slain the wooers in thy halls, whether by guile, or openly with
the edge of the sword, thereafter go thy way, taking with thee a
shapen oar, till thou shalt come to such men as know not the sea,
neither eat meat savoured with salt; yea, nor have they knowledge of
ships of purple cheek, nor shapen oars which serve for wings to ships.
And I will give thee a most manifest token, which cannot escape thee.
In the day when another wayfarer shall meet thee and say that thou
hast a winnowing fan on thy stout shoulder, even then make fast thy
shapen oar in the earth and do goodly sacrifice to the lord Poseidon,
even with a ram and a bull and a boar, the mate of swine, and depart
for home and offer holy hecatombs to the deathless gods that keep the
wide heaven, to each in order due.   And from the sea shall thine own
death come, the gentlest death that may be, which shall end thee foredone with smooth old age, and the folk shall dwell happily around
thee.   This that I say is sooth."

So spake he, and I answered him, saying: "Teiresias, all these
threads, methinks, the gods themselves have spun.   But come, declare me this and plainly tell me all.   I see here the spirit of my
mother dead; lo, she sits in silence near the blood, nor deigns to look
her son in the face nor speak to him!   Tell me, prince, how may she
know me again that I am he?"

So spake I, and anon he answered me, and said: "I will tell thee
an easy saying, and will put it in thy heart.   Whomsoever of the dead
that be departed thou shalt suffer to draw nigh to the blood, he shall
tell thee sooth; but if thou shalt grudge any, that one shall go to his
own place again."   Therewith the spirit of the prince Teiresias went
back within the house of Hades, when he had told all his oracles.
But I abode there steadfastly, till my mother drew nigh and drank the
dark blood; and at once she knew me, and bewailing herself spake
to me winged words:

"Dear child, how didst thou come beneath the darkness and the
shadow, thou that art a living man?   Grievous is the sight of these

things to the living, for between us and you are great rivers and dreadful streams; first, Oceanus, which can no wise be crossed on foot, but only if one have a well-wrought ship. Art thou but now come hither with thy ship and thy company in thy long wanderings from Troy? and hast thou not yet reached Ithaca, nor seen thy wife in thy halls?"

Even so she spake, and I answered her, and said: "O my mother, necessity was on me to come down to the house of Hades to seek to the spirit of Theban Teiresias. For not yet have I drawn near to the Achaean shore, nor yet have I set foot on mine own country, but have been wandering evermore in affliction, from the day that first I went with goodly Agamemnon to Ilios of the fair steeds, to do battle with the Trojans. But come, declare me this and plainly tell it all. What doom overcame thee of death that lays men at their length? Was it a slow disease, or did Artemis the archer slay thee with the visitation of her gentle shafts? And tell me of my father and my son, that I left behind me; doth my honour yet abide with them, or hath another already taken it, while they say that I shall come home no more? And tell me of my wedded wife, of her counsel and her purpose, doth she abide with her son and keep all secure, or hath she already wedded the best of the Achaeans?"

Even so I spake, and anon my lady mother answered me: "Yea verily, she abideth with steadfast spirit in thy halls; and wearily for her the nights wane always and the days in shedding of tears. But the fair honour that is thine no man hath yet taken; but Telemachus sits at peace on his demesne, and feasts at equal banquets, whereof it is meet that a judge partake, for all men bid him to their house. And thy father abides there in the field, and goes not down to the town, nor lies he on bedding or rugs or shining blankets, but all the winter he sleeps, where sleep the thralls in the house, in the ashes by the fire, and is clad in sorry raiment. But when the summer comes and the rich harvest-tide, his beds of fallen leaves are strewn lowly all about the knoll of his vineyard plot. There he lies sorrowing and nurses his mighty grief, for long desire of thy return, and old age withal comes heavy upon him. Yea and even so did I too perish and meet my doom. It was not the archer goddess of the keen sight, who slew me in my halls with the visitation of her gentle shafts, nor did any sickness come upon me, such as chiefly with a sad wasting draws the spirit from the limbs; nay, it was my sore longing for thee, and for thy counsels, great Odysseus, and for thy loving-kindness, that reft me of sweet life."

So spake she, and I mused in my heart and would fain have embraced the spirit of my mother dead. Thrice I sprang towards her, and was minded to embrace her; thrice she flitted from my hands as a shadow or even as a dream, and sharp grief arose ever at my heart. And uttering my voice I spake to her winged words:

"Mother mine, wherefore dost thou not abide me who am eager to clasp thee, that even in Hades we twain may cast our arms each about the other, and have our fill of chill lament? Is this but a phantom that the high goddess Persephone hath sent me, to the end that I may groan for more exceeding sorrow?"

So spake I, and my lady mother answered me anon: "Ah me, my child, of all men most ill-fated, Persephone, the daughter of Zeus, doth in no wise deceive thee, but even on this wise it is with mortals when they die. For the sinews no more bind together the flesh and the bones, but the great force of burning fire abolishes these, so soon as the life hath left the white bones, and the spirit like a dream flies forth and hovers near. But haste with all thine heart toward the sunlight, and mark all this, that even hereafter thou mayest tell it to thy wife."

Thus we twain held discourse together; and lo, the women came up, for the high goddess Persephone sent them forth, all they that had been the wives and daughters of mighty men. And they gathered and flocked about the black blood, and I took counsel how I might question them each one. And this was the counsel that showed best in my sight. I drew my long hanger from my stalwart thigh, and suffered them not all at one time to drink of the dark blood. So they drew nigh one by one, and each declared her lineage, and I made question of all.

Then verily did I first see Tyro, sprung of a noble sire, who said that she was the child of noble Salmoneus, and declared herself the wife of Cretheus, son of Aeolus. She loved a river, the divine Enipeus, far the fairest of the floods that run upon the earth, and she would resort to the fair streams of Enipeus. And it came to pass that the girdler of the world, the Earth-shaker, put on the shape of the god, and lay by the lady at the mouths of the whirling stream. Then the dark wave stood around them like a hill-side bowed, and hid the god and the mortal woman. And he undid her maiden girdle, and shed a slumber over her. Now when the god had done the work of love, he clasped her hand and spake and hailed her.

"Woman, be glad in our love, and when the year comes round thou shalt give birth to glorious children, — for not weak are the embraces of the gods, — and do thou keep and cherish them. And now go home and hold thy peace, and tell it not: but behold, I am Poseidon, Shaker of the Earth."

Therewith he plunged beneath the heaving deep. And she conceived and bare Pelias and Neleus, who both grew to be mighty men, servants of Zeus. Pelias dwelt in wide Iolcos, and was rich in flocks; and that other abode in sandy Pylos. And the queen of women bare yet other sons to Cretheus, even Aeson and Pheres and Amythaon, whose joy was in chariots.

And after her I saw Antiope, daughter of Asôpus, and her boast was that she had slept even in the arms of Zeus, and she bare two sons, Amphion and Zethus, who founded first the place of seven-gated Thebes, and they made of it a fenced city, for they might not dwell in spacious Thebes unfenced, for all their valiancy.

Next to her I saw Alcmene, wife of Amphitryon, who lay in the arms of mighty Zeus, and bare Heracles of the lion-heart, steadfast in the fight. And I saw Megara, daughter of Creon, haughty of heart, whom the strong and tireless son of Amphitryon had to wife.

And I saw the mother of Oedipodes, fair Epicaste, who wrought a dread deed unwittingly, being wedded to her own son, and he that had slain his own father wedded her, and straightway the gods made these things known to men. Yet he abode in pain in pleasant Thebes, ruling the Cadmaeans, by reason of the deadly counsels of the gods. But she went down to the house of Hades, the mighty warder; yea, she tied a noose from the high beam aloft, being fast holden in sorrow; while for him she left pains behind full many, even all that the Avengers of a mother bring to pass.

And I saw lovely Chloris, whom Neleus wedded on a time for her beauty, and brought gifts of wooing past number. She was the youngest daughter of Amphion, son of Iasus, who once ruled mightily in Minyan Orchomenus. And she was queen of Pylos, and bare glorious children to her lord, Nestor and Chromius, and princely Periclymenus, and stately Pero too, the wonder of all men. All that dwelt around were her wooers; but Neleus would not give her, save to him who should drive off from Phylace the kine of mighty Iphicles, with shambling gait and broad of brow, hard cattle to drive. And none but the noble seer took in hand to drive them; but a grievous fate from the gods fettered him, even hard bonds and the herdsmen of the wild. But when at length the months and days were being fulfilled, as the year returned upon his course, and the seasons came round, then did mighty Iphicles set him free, when he had spoken out all the oracles; and herein was the counsel of Zeus being accomplished.

And I saw Lede, the famous bed-fellow of Tyndareus, who bare to Tyndareus two sons, hardy of heart, Castor tamer of steeds, and Polydeuces the boxer. These twain yet live, but the quickening earth is over them; and even in the nether world they have honour at the hand of Zeus. And they possess their life in turn, living one day and dying the next, and they have gotten worship even as the gods.

And after her I beheld Iphimedeia, bed-fellow of Aloeus, who said that she had lain with Poseidon, and she bare children twain, but short of life were they, godlike Otus and far-famed Ephialtes. Now these were the tallest men that earth, the grain-giver, ever reared, and far the goodliest after the renowned Orion. At nine seasons old they were of breadth nine cubits, and nine fathoms in height. They it was who threatened to raise even against the immortals in Olympus the din of stormy war. They strove to pile Ossa on Olympus, and on Ossa Pelion with the trembling forest leaves, that there might be a pathway to the sky. Yea, and they would have accomplished it, had they reached the full measure of manhood. But the son of Zeus, whom Leto of the fair locks bare, destroyed the twain, ere the down had bloomed beneath their temples, and darkened their chins with the blossom of youth.

And Phaedra and Procris I saw, and fair Ariadne, the daughter of

wizard Minos, whom Theseus on a time was bearing from Crete to
the hill of sacred Athens, yet had he no joy of her; for Artemis slew
her ere that in seagirt Dia, by reason of the witness of Dionysus.

And Maera and Clymene I saw, and hateful Eriphyle, who took
fine gold for the price of her dear lord's life. But I cannot tell or
name all the wives and daughters of the heroes that I saw; ere that,
the immortal night would wane. Nay, it is even now time to sleep,
whether I go to the swift ship to my company or abide here: and for
my convoy you and the gods will care.

So spake he, and dead silence fell on all, and they were spell-bound
throughout the shadowy halls. Then Arete of the white arms first
spake among them: "Phaeacians, what think you of this man for
comeliness and stature, and within for wisdom of heart? Moreover
he is my guest, though every one of you hath his share in this honour.
Wherefore haste not to send him hence, and stint not these your gifts
for one that stands in such sore need of them; for ye have much
treasure stored in your halls by the grace of the gods."

Then too spake among them the old man, lord Echeneus, that was
an elder among the Phaeacians: "Friends, behold, the speech of our
wise queen is not wide of the mark, nor far from our deeming, so
hearken ye thereto. But on Alcinous here both word and work depend."

Then Alcinous made answer, and spake unto him: "Yea, the word
that she hath spoken shall hold, if indeed I am yet to live and bear
rule among the Phaeacians, masters of the oar. Howbeit let the
stranger, for all his craving to return, nevertheless endure to abide
until the morrow, till I make up the full measure of the gift; and men
shall care for his convoy, all men, but I in chief, for mine is the lordship in the land."

And Odysseus of many counsels answered him, saying: "My lord
Alcinous, most notable of all the people, if ye bade me tarry here even
for a year, and would speed my convoy and give me splendid gifts,
even that I would choose; and better would it be for me to come with
a fuller hand to mine own dear country, so should I get more love
and worship in the eyes of all men, whoso should see me after I was
returned to Ithaca."

And Alcinous answered him, saying: "Odysseus, in no wise do we
deem thee, we that look on thee, to be a knave or a cheat, even as the
dark earth rears many such broadcast, fashioning lies whence none can
even see his way therein. But beauty crowns thy words, and wisdom
is within thee; and thy tale, as when a minstrel sings, thou hast told
with skill, the weary woes of all the Argives and of thine own self.
But come, declare me this and plainly tell it all. Didst thou see any of
thy godlike company who went up at the same time with thee to Ilios
and there met their doom? Behold, the night is of great length, unspeakable, and the time for sleep in the hall is not yet; tell me therefore of those wondrous deeds. I could abide even till the bright

dawn, so long as thou couldst endure to rehearse me these woes of
thine in the hall."

   And Odysseus of many counsels answered him, saying: My lord
Alcinous, most notable of all the people, there is a time for many
words and there is a time for sleep. But if thou art eager still to listen, I would not for my part grudge to tell thee of other things more
pitiful still, even the woes of my comrades, those that perished afterward, for they had escaped with their lives from the dread war-cry
of the Trojans, but perished in returning by the will of an evil woman.
   Now when holy Persephone had scattered this way and that the
spirits of the women folk, thereafter came the soul of Agamemnon,
son of Atreus, sorrowing; and round him others were gathered, the
ghosts of them who had died with him in the house of Aegisthus and
met their doom. And he knew me straightway when he had drunk
the dark blood, yea, and he wept aloud, and shed big tears as he
stretched forth his hands in his longing to reach me. But it might
not be, for he had now no steadfast strength nor power at all in moving, such as was aforetime in his supple limbs.
   At the sight of him I wept and was moved with compassion, and
uttering my voice, spake to him winged words: "Most renowned son
of Atreus, Agamemnon, king of men, say what doom overcame thee
of death that lays men at their length? Did Poseidon smite thee in
thy ships, raising the dolorous blast of contrary winds, or did unfriendly men do thee hurt upon the land, whilst thou wert cutting off
their oxen and fair flocks of sheep, or fighting to win a city and the
women thereof?"
   So spake I, and straightway he answered, and said unto me: "Son
of Laertes, of the seed of Zeus, Odysseus of many devices, it was not
Poseidon that smote me in my ships, and raised the dolorous blast of
contrary winds, nor did unfriendly men do me hurt upon the land,
but Aegisthus it was that wrought me death and doom and slew me,
with the aid of my accursed wife, as one slays an ox at the stall, after
he had bidden me to his house, and entertained me at a feast. Even
so I died by a death most pitiful, and round me my company likewise were slain without ceasing, like swine with glittering tusks
which are slaughtered in the house of a rich and mighty man,
whether at a wedding banquet or a joint-feast or a rich clan-drinking.
Ere now hast thou been at the slaying of many a man, killed in single
fight or in strong battle, yet thou wouldst have sorrowed the most at
this sight, how we lay in the hall round the mixing-bowl and the
laden boards, and the floor all ran with blood. And most pitiful of
all that I heard was the voice of the daughter of Priam, of Cassandra,
whom hard by me the crafty Clytemnestra slew. Then I strove to
raise my hands as I was dying upon the sword, but to earth they fell.
And that shameless one turned her back upon me, and had not the
heart to draw down my eyelids with her fingers nor to close my
mouth. So surely is there nought more terrible and shameless than

a woman who imagines such evil in her heart, even as she too planned a foul deed, fashioning death for her wedded lord. Verily I had thought to come home most welcome to my children and my thralls; but she, out of the depth of her evil knowledge, hath shed shame on herself and on all womankind, which shall be for ever, even on the upright."

Even so he spake, but I answered him, saying: "Lo now, in very sooth, hath Zeus of the far-borne voice wreaked wondrous hatred on the seed of Atreus through the counsels of woman from of old. For Helen's sake so many of us perished, and now Clytemnestra hath practised treason against thee, while yet thou wast afar off."

Even so I spake, and anon he answered me, saying: "Wherefore do thou too, never henceforth be soft even to thy wife, neither show her all the counsel that thou knowest, but a part declare and let part be hid. Yet shalt not thou, Odysseus, find death at the hand of thy wife, for she is very discreet and prudent in all her ways, the wise Penelope, daughter of Icarius. Verily we left her a bride new wed when we went to the war, and a child was at her breast, who now, methinks, sits in the ranks of men, happy in his lot, for his dear father shall behold him on his company, and he shall embrace his sire as is meet. But as for my wife, she suffered me not so much as to have my fill of gazing on my son; ere that she slew me, even her lord. And yet another thing will I tell thee, and do thou ponder it in thy heart. Put thy ship to land in secret, and not openly, on the shore of thy dear country; for there is no more faith in woman. But come, declare me this and plainly tell it all, if haply ye hear of my son as yet living, either, it may be, in Orchomenus or in sandy Pylos, or perchance with Menelaus in wide Sparta, for goodly Orestes hath not yet perished on the earth."

Even so he spake, but I answered him, saying: "Son of Atreus, wherefore dost thou ask me straitly of these things? Nay I know not at all, whether he be alive or dead; it is ill to speak words light as wind."

Thus we twain stood sorrowing, holding sad discourse, while the big tears fell fast: and therewithal came the soul of Achilles, son of Peleus, and of Patroclus and of noble Antilochus and of Aias, who in face and form was goodliest of all the Danaans, after the noble son of Peleus. And the spirit of the son of Aeacus, fleet of foot, knew me again, and making lament spake to me winged words:

"Son of Laertes, of the seed of Zeus, Odysseus of many devices, man overbold, what new deed and hardier than this wilt thou devise in thy heart? How durst thou come down to the house of Hades, where dwell the senseless dead, the phantoms of men outworn?"

So he spake, but I answered him: "Achilles, son of Peleus, mightiest far of the Achaeans, I am come hither to seek to Teiresias, if he may tell me any counsel, how I may come to rugged Ithaca. For not yet have I come nigh the Achaean land, nor set foot on mine own soil, but am still in evil case; while as for thee, Achilles, none other than thou wast heretofore the most blessed of men, nor shall any be hereafter. For of old, in the days of thy life, we Argives gave thee one honour with the gods, and now thou art a great prince here among the dead. Wherefore let not thy death be any grief to thee, Achilles."

Even so I spake, and he straightway answered me, and said: "Nay, speak not comfortably to me of death, oh great Odysseus. Rather would I live on ground as the hireling of another, with a landless man who had no great livelihood, than bear sway among all the dead that be departed. But come, tell me tidings of that lordly son of mine — did he follow to the war to be a leader or not? And tell me of noble Peleus, if thou hast heard aught, — is he yet held in worship among the Myrmidons, or do they dishonour him from Hellas to Phthia, for that old age binds him hand and foot? For I am no longer his champion under the sun, so mighty a man as once I was, when in wide Troy I slew the best of the host, and succoured the Argives. Ah! could I but come for an hour to my father's house as then I was, so would I make my might and hands invincible, to be hateful to many an one of those who do him despite and keep him from his honour."

Even so he spake, but I answered him saying: "As for noble Peleus, verily I have heard nought of him; but concerning thy dear son Neoptolemus, I will tell thee all the truth, according to thy word. It was I that led him up out of Scyros in my good hollow ship, in the wake of the goodly-greaved Achaeans. Now oft as we took counsel around Troy town, he was ever the first to speak, and no word missed the mark; the godlike Nestor and I alone surpassed him. But whensoever we Achaeans did battle on the plain of Troy, he never tarried behind in the throng or the press of men, but ran out far before us all, yielding to none in that might of his. And many men he slew in warfare dread; but I could not tell of all or name their names, even all the host he slew in succouring the Argives; but, ah, how he smote with the sword that son of Telephus, the hero Eurypylus, and many Ceteians of his company were slain around him, by reason of a woman's bribe. He truly was the comeliest man that ever I saw, next to goodly Memnon. And again when we, the best of the Argives, were about to go down into the horse which Epeus wrought, and the charge of all was laid on me, both to open the door of our good ambush and to shut the same, then did the other princes and counsellors of the Danaans wipe away the tears, and the limbs of each one trembled beneath him, but never once did I see thy son's fair face wax pale, nor did he wipe the tears from his cheeks: but he besought me often to let him go forth from the horse, and kept handling his sword-hilt, and his heavy bronze-shod spear, and he was set on mischief against the Trojans. But after we had sacked the steep city of Priam, he embarked unscathed with his share of the spoil, and with a noble prize; he was not smitten with the sharp spear, and got no wound in close fight: and many such chances there be in war, for Ares rageth confusedly."

So I spake, and the spirit of the son of Aeacus, fleet of foot, passed with great strides along the mead of asphodel, rejoicing in that I had told him of his son's renown.

But lo, other spirits of the dead that be departed stood sorrowing, and each one asked of those that were dear to them. The soul of Aias son of Telamon, alone stood apart being still angry for the victory wherein I prevailed against him, in the suit by the ships concerning the arms of Achilles, that his lady mother had set for a prize; and the sons of the Trojans made award and Pallas Athene. Would that I had never prevailed and won such a prize! So goodly a head hath the earth closed over, for the sake of those arms, even over Aias, who in beauty and in feats of war was of a mould above all the other Danaans, next to the noble son of Peleus. To him then I spake softly, saying:

"Aias, son of noble Telamon, so art thou not even in death to forget thy wrath against me, by reason of those arms accursed, which the gods set to be the bane of the Argives? What a tower of strength fell in thy fall, and we Achaeans cease not to sorrow for thee, even as for the life of Achilles, son of Peleus! Nay, there is none other to blame, but Zeus, who hath borne wondrous hate to the army of the Danaan spearsmen, and laid on thee thy doom. Nay, come hither, my lord, that thou mayest hear my word and my speech; master thy wrath and thy proud spirit."

So I spake, but he answered me not a word and passed to Erebus after the other spirits of the dead that be departed. Even then, despite his anger, would he have spoken to me or I to him, but my heart within me was minded to see the spirits of those others that were departed.

There then I saw Minos, glorious son of Zeus, wielding a golden sceptre, giving sentence from his throne to the dead, while they sat and stood around the prince, asking his dooms through the wide-gated house of Hades.

And after him I marked the mighty Orion driving the wild beasts together over the mead of asphodel, the very beasts that himself had slain on the lonely hills, with a strong mace all of bronze in his hands, that is ever unbroken.

And I saw Tityos, son of renowned Earth, lying on a levelled ground, and he covered nine roods as he lay, and vultures twain beset him one on either side, and gnawed at his liver, piercing even to the caul, but he drave them not away with his hands. For he had dealt violently with Leto, the famous bed-fellow of Zeus, as she went up to Pytho through the fair lawns of Paponeus.

Moreover I beheld Tantalus in grievous torment, standing in a mere and the water came nigh unto his chin. And he stood straining as one athirst, but he might not attain to the water to drink of it. For often as that old man stooped down in his eagerness to drink, so often the water was swallowed up and it vanished away, and the black earth still showed at his feet, for some god parched it evermore. And tall trees flowering shed their fruit overhead, pears and pomegranates and apple trees with bright fruit, and sweet figs and olives in their bloom, whereat when that old man reached out his hands to clutch them, the wind would toss them to the shadowy clouds.

Yea and I beheld Sisyphus in strong torment, grasping a monstrous stone with both his hands. He was pressing thereat with hands and feet, and trying to roll the stone upward toward the brow of the hill. But oft as he was about to hurl it over the top, the weight would drive him back, so once again to the plain rolled the stone, the shameless thing. And he once more kept heaving and straining, and the sweat the while was pouring down his limbs, and the dust rose upwards from his head.

And after him I descried the mighty Heracles, his phantom, I say; but as for himself he hath joy at the banquet among the deathless gods, and hath to wife Hebe of the fair ankles, child of great Zeus, and of Here of the golden sandals. And all about him there was a clamour of the dead, as it were fowls flying every way in fear, and he like black Night, with bow uncased, and shaft upon the string, fiercely glancing around, like one in the act to shoot. And about his breast was an awful belt, a baldric of gold, whereon wondrous things were wrought, bears and wild boars and lions with flashing eyes, and strife and battles and slaughters and murders of men. Nay, now that he hath fashioned this, never another may he fashion, whoso stored in his craft the device of that belt! And anon he knew me when his eyes beheld me, and making lament he spake unto me winged words:

"Son of Laertes, of the seed of Zeus, Odysseus of many devices: ah! wretched one, dost thou too lead such a life of evil doom, as I endured beneath the rays of the sun? I was the son of Zeus Cronion, yet had I trouble beyond measure, for I was subdued unto a man far worse than I. And he enjoined on me hard adventures, yea and on a time he sent me hither to bring back the hound of hell; for he devised no harder task for me than this. I lifted the hound and brought him forth from out of the house of Hades; and Hermes sped me on my way and the grey-eyed Athene."

Therewith he departed again into the house of Hades, but I abode there still, if perchance some one of the hero folk besides might come, who died in old time. Yea and I should have seen the men of old, whom I was fain to look on, Theseus and Peirithous, renowned children of the gods. But ere that might be the myriad tribes of the dead thronged up together with wondrous clamour: and pale fear gat hold of me, lest the high goddess Persephone should send me the head of the Gorgon, that dread monster, from out of Hades.

Straightway then I went to the ship, and bade my men mount the vessel, and loose the hawsers. So speedily they went on board, and sat upon the benches. And the wave of the flood bore the barque down the stream of Oceanus, we rowing first, and afterwards the fair wind was our convoy.

BOOK XII

Odysseus, his passage by the Sirens, and by Scylla and Charybdis. The sacrilege committed by his men in the isle Thrinacia. The destruction of his ships and men. How he swam on a plank nine days together, and came to Ogygia, where he stayed seven years with Calypso.

Now after the ship had left the stream of the river Oceanus, and was come to the wave of the wide sea, and the isle Aeaean, where is the dwelling place of early Dawn and her dancing grounds, and the land of sunrising, upon our coming thither we beached the ship in the sand, and ourselves too stept ashore on the sea-beach. There we fell on sound sleep and awaited the bright Dawn.

So soon as early Dawn shone forth, the rosy-fingered, I sent forth my fellows to the house of Circé to fetch the body of the dead Elpenor. And speedily we cut billets of wood and sadly we buried him, where the furthest headland runs out into the sea, shedding big tears. But when the dead man was burned and the arms of the dead, we piled a barrow and dragged up thereon a pillar, and on the topmost mound we set the shapen oar.

Now all that task we finished, and our coming from out of Hades was not unknown to Circé, but she arrayed herself and speedily drew nigh, and her handmaids with her bare flesh and bread in plenty and dark red wine. And the fair goddess stood in the midst and spake in our ears, saying:

"Men overbold, who have gone alive into the house of Hades, to know death twice, while all men else die once for all. Nay come, eat ye meat and drink wine here all day long; and with the breaking of the day ye shall set sail, and myself I will show you the path and declare each thing, that ye may not suffer pain or hurt through any grievous ill-contrivance by sea or on the land."

So spake she, and our lordly souls consented thereto. Thus for that time we sat the livelong day, until the going down of the sun, feasting on abundant flesh and on sweet wine. Now when the sun sank and darkness came on, my company laid them to rest by the hawsers of the ship. Then she took me by the hand and led me apart from my dear company, and made me to sit down and laid herself at my feet, and asked all my tale. And I told her all in order duly. Then at the last the lady Circé spake unto me, saying:

"Even so, now all these things have an end; do thou then hearken even as I tell thee, and the god himself shall bring it back to thy mind. To the Sirens first shalt thou come, who bewitch all men, whosoever shall come to them. Whoso draws nigh them unwittingly and hears the sound of the Sirens' voice, never doth he see wife or babes stand by him on his return, nor have they joy at his coming; but the Sirens enchant him with their clear song, sitting in the meadow, and all about is a great heap of bones of men, corrupt in death, and round the bones the skin is wasting. But do thou drive thy ship past, and knead honey-sweet wax, and anoint therewith the ears of thy company, lest any of the rest hear the song; but if thou thyself art minded to hear, let them bind thee in the swift ship hand and foot, upright in the mast-stead, and from the mast let rope-ends be tied, that with delight thou mayest hear the voice of the Sirens. And if thou shalt beseech thy company and bid them to loose thee, then let them bind thee with yet more bonds. But when thy friends have driven thy ship past these, I will not tell thee fully which path shall thenceforth be thine, but do thou thyself consider it, and I will speak to thee of either way. On the one side there are beetling rocks, and against them the great wave roars of dark-eyed Amphitrite. These, ye must know, are they the blessed gods call the Rocks Wandering. By this way even winged things may never pass, nay, not even the cowering doves that bear ambrosia to Father Zeus, but the sheer rock evermore takes away one even of these, and the Father sends in another to make up the tale. Thereby no ship of men ever escapes that comes thither, but the planks of ships and the bodies of men confusedly are tossed by the waves of the sea and the storms of ruinous fire. One ship only of all that fare by sea hath passed that way, even Argo, that is in all men's minds, on her voyage from Aeëtes. And even her the wave would lightly have cast there upon the mighty rocks, but Here sent her by for love of Iason.

"On the other part are two rocks, whereof the one reaches with sharp peak to the wide heaven, and a dark cloud encompasses it; this never streams away, and there is no clear air about the peak neither in summer nor in harvest tide. No mortal man may scale it or set foot thereon, not though he had twenty hands and feet. For the rock is smooth, and sheer, as it were polished. And in the midst of the cliff is a dim cave turned to Erebus, towards the place of darkness, whereby ye shall even steer your hollow ship, noble Odysseus. Not with an arrow from a bow might a man in his strength reach from his hollow ship into that deep cave. And therein dwelleth Scylla, yelping terribly. Her voice indeed is no greater than the voice of a new-born whelp, but a dreadful monster is she, nor would any look on her gladly, not if it were a god that met her. Verily she hath twelve feet all dangling down, and six necks exceeding long, and on each a hideous head, and therein three rows of teeth set thick and close, full of black death. Up to her middle is she sunk far down in the hollow cave, but forth she holds her heads from the dreadful gulf, and there she fishes, swooping round the rock, for dolphins or seadogs, or whatso greater beast she may anywhere take, whereof the deep-voiced Amphitrite feeds countless flocks. Thereby no sailors boast that they had fled scatheless ever with their ship, for with each head she carries off a man, whom she hath snatched from out the dark-prowed ship.

"But that other cliff, Odysseus, thou shalt note, lying lower, hard by the first: thou couldest send an arrow across. And thereon is a great fig-tree growing, in fullest leaf, and beneath it mighty Charybdis sucks down black water, for thrice a day she spouts it forth, and thrice a day she sucks it down in terrible wise. Never mayest thou be there when she sucks the water, for none might save thee then from thy bane, not even the Earth-shaker! But take heed and swiftly drawing nigh to Scylla's rock drive the ship past, since of a truth it is far better to mourn six of thy company in the ship, than all in the selfsame hour."

So spake she, but I answered, and said unto her: "Come I pray thee herein, goddess, tell me true, if there be any means whereby I might escape from the deadly Charybdis and avenge me on that other, when she would prey upon my company."

So spake I, and that fair goddess answered me: "Man overbold, lo, now again the deeds of war are in thy mind and the travail thereof. Wilt thou not yield thee even to the deathless gods? As for her, she is no mortal, but an immortal plague, dread, grievous, and fierce, and not to be fought with; and against her there is no defence; flight is the bravest way. For if thou tarry to do on thine armour by the cliff, I fear lest once again she sally forth and catch at thee with so many heads, and seize as many men as before. So drive past with all thy force, and call on Cratais, mother of Scylla, which bore her for a bane to mortals. And she will then let her from darting forth thereafter.

"Then thou shalt come unto the isle Thrinacia; there are the many kine of Helios and his brave flocks feeding, seven herds of kine and as many goodly flocks of sheep, and fifty in each flock. They have no part in birth or in corruption, and there are goddesses to shepherd them, nymphs with fair tresses, Phaethusa and Lampetie whom bright Neaera bare to Helios Hyperion. Now when the lady their mother had borne and nursed them, she carried them to the isle Thrinacia to dwell afar, that they should guard their father's flocks and his kine with shambling gait. If thou doest these no hurt, being heedful of thy return, truly ye may even yet reach Ithaca, albeit in evil case. But if thou hurtest them, I foreshow ruin for thy ship and for thy men, and even though thou shouldest thyself escape, late shalt thou return in evil plight with the loss of all thy company."

So spake she, and anon came the golden-throned Dawn. Then the fair goddess took her way up the island. But I departed to my ship and roused my men themselves to mount the vessel and loose the hawsers. And speedily they went aboard and sat upon the benches, and sitting orderly smote the grey sea water with their oars. And in the wake of our dark-prowed ship she sent a favouring wind that filled the sails, a kindly escort, — even Circé of the braided tresses, a dread goddess of human speech. And straightway we set in order the gear throughout the ship and sat us down, and the wind and the helmsman guided our barque.

Then I spake among my company with a heavy heart: "Friends, forasmuch as it is not well that one or two alone should know of the oracles that Circé, the fair goddess, spake unto me, therefore will I declare them, that with foreknowledge we may die, or haply shunning death and destiny escape. First she bade us avoid the sound of the voice of the wondrous Sirens, and their field of flowers, and me only she bade listen to their voices. So bind ye me in a hard bond, that I may abide unmoved in my place, upright in the mast-stead, and from the mast let rope-ends be tied, and if I beseech and bid you to set me free, then do ye straiten me with yet more bonds."

Thus I rehearsed these things one and all, and declared them to my company. Meanwhile our good ship quickly came to the island of the Sirens twain, for a gentle breeze sped her on her way. Then straightway the wind ceased, and lo, there was a windless calm, and some god lulled the waves. Then my company rose up and drew in the ship's sails, and stowed them in the hold of the ship, while they sat at the oars and whitened the water with their polished pine blades. But I with my sharp sword cleft in pieces a great circle of wax, and with my strong hands kneaded it. And soon the wax grew warm, for that my great might constrained it, and the beam of the lord Helios, son of Hyperion. And I anointed therewith the ears of all my men in their order, and in the ship they bound me hand and foot upright in the mast-stead, and from the mast they fastened rope-ends and themselves sat down, and smote the grey sea water with their oars. But when the ship was within the sound of a man's shout from the land, we fleeing swiftly on our way, the Sirens espied the swift ship speeding toward them, and they raised their clear-toned song:

"Hither, come hither, renowned Odysseus, great glory of the Achaeans, here stay thy barque, that thou mayest listen to the voice of us twain. For none hath ever driven by this way in his black ship, till he hath heard from our lips the voice sweet as the honey-comb, and hath had joy thereof and gone on his way the wiser. For lo, we know all things, all the travail that in wide Troy-land the Argives and Trojans bare by the gods' designs, yea, and we know all that shall hereafter be upon the fruitful earth."

So spake they uttering a sweet voice, and my heart was fain to listen, and I bade my company unbind me, nodding at them with a frown, but they bent to their oars and rowed on. Then straight uprose Perimedes and Eurylochus and bound me with more cords and straitened me yet the more. Now when we had driven past them, nor heard we any longer the sound of the Sirens or their song, forthwith my dear company took away the wax wherewith I had anointed their ears and loosed me from my bonds.

But so soon as we left that isle, thereafter presently I saw smoke and a great wave, and heard the sea roaring. Then for very fear the oars flew from their hands, and down the stream they all splashed, and the ship was holden there, for my company no longer plied with their hands the tapering oars. But I paced the ship and cheered on my men, as I stood by each one and spake smooth words:

"Friends, forasmuch as in sorrow we are not all unlearned, truly this is no greater woe that is upon us, than when the Cyclops penned us by main might in his hollow cave; yet even thence we made escape by my manfulness, even by my counsel and my wit, and some day I think that this adventure too we shall remember. Come now, there-fore, let us all give ear to do according to my word. Do ye smite the

deep surf of the sea with your oars, as ye sit on the benches, if peradventure Zeus may grant us to escape from and shun this death.
And as for thee, helmsman, thus I charge thee, and ponder it in thine
heart seeing that thou wieldest the helm of the hollow ship. Keep the
ship well away from this smoke and from the wave and hug the
rocks, lest the ship, ere thou art aware, start from her course to the
other side, and so thou hurl us into ruin."

So I spake, and quickly they hearkened to my words. But of Scylla
I told them nothing more, a bane none might deal with, lest haply
my company should cease from rowing for fear, and hide them in the
hold. In that same hour I suffered myself to forget the hard behest
of Circé in that she bade me in no wise be armed; but I did on my
glorious harness and caught up two long lances in my hands, and
went on to the decking of the prow, for thence methought that Scylla
of the rock would first be seen, who was to bring woe on my company. Yet could I not spy her anywhere, and my eyes waxed weary
for gazing all about toward the darkness of the rock.

Next we began to sail up the narrow strait lamenting. For on the
one hand lay Scylla, and on the other mighty Charybdis in terrible
wise sucked down the salt sea water. As often as she belched it forth,
like a cauldron on a great fire she would seethe up through all her
troubled deeps, and overhead the spray fell on the tops of either cliff.
But oft as she gulped down the salt sea water, within she was all plain
to see through her troubled deeps, and the rock around roared hor-
ribly and beneath the earth was manifest swart with sand, and pale
fear gat hold on my men. Toward her, then, we looked fearing
destruction; but Scylla meanwhile caught from out my hollow ship
six of my company, the hardiest of their hands and the chief in might.
And looking into the swift ship to find my men, even then I marked
their feet and hands as they were lifted on high, and they cried aloud
in their agony, and called me by my name for that last time of all.
Even as when a fisher on some headland lets down with a long rod
his baits for a snare to the little fishes below, casting into the deep
the horn of an ox of the homestead, and as he catches each flings it
writhing ashore, so writhing were they borne upward to the cliff.
And there she devoured them shrieking in her gates, they stretching
forth their hands to me in the dread death-struggle. And the most
pitiful thing was this that mine eyes have seen of all my travail in
searching out the paths of the sea.

Now when we had escaped the Rocks and dread Charybdis and
Scylla, thereafter we soon came to the fair island of the god; where
were the goodly kine, broad of brow, and the many brave flocks of
Helios Hyperion. Then while as yet I was in my black ship upon
the deep, I heard the lowing of the cattle being stalled and the bleating of the sheep, and on my mind there fell the saying of the blind
seer, Theban Teiresias, and of Circé of Aia, who charged me very
straitly to shun the isle of Helios, the gladdener of the world. Then
I spake out among my company in sorrow of heart:

"Hear my words, my men, albeit in evil plight, that I may declare unto you the oracles of Teiresias and of Circé of Aia, who very straitly charged me to shun the isle of Helios, the gladdener of the world. For there she said the most dreadful mischief would befall us. Nay, drive ye then the black ship beyond and past that isle."

So spake I, and their heart was broken within them. And Eurylochus straightway answered me sadly, saying:

"Hardy art thou, Odysseus, of might beyond measure, and thy limbs are never weary; verily thou art fashioned all of iron, that sufferest not thy fellows, foredone with toil and drowsiness, to set foot on shore, where we might presently prepare us a good supper in this sea-girt island. But even as we are thou biddest us fare blindly through the sudden night, and from the isle go wandering on the misty deep. And strong winds, the bane of ships, are born of the night. How could a man escape from utter doom, if there chanced to come a sudden blast of the South Wind, or of the boisterous West, which mainly wreck ships, beyond the will of the gods, the lords of all? Howbeit for this present let us yield to the black night, and we will make ready our supper abiding by the swift ship, and in the morning we will climb on board, and put out into the broad deep."

So spake Eurylochus, and the rest of my company consented thereto. Then at the last I knew that some god was indeed imagining evil, and I uttered my voice and spake unto him winged words:

"Eurylochus, verily ye put force upon me, being but one among you all. But come, swear me now a mighty oath, one and all, to the intent that if we light on a herd of kine or a great flock of sheep, none in the evil folly of his heart may slay any sheep or ox; but in quiet eat ye the meat which the deathless Circé gave."

So I spake, and straightway they swore to refrain as I commanded them. Now after they had sworn and done that oath, we stayed our well-built ship in the hollow harbour near to a well of sweet water, and my company went forth from out the ship and deftly got ready supper. But when they had put from them the desire of meat and drink, thereafter they fell a weeping as they thought upon their dear companions whom Scylla had snatched from out the hollow ship and so devoured. And deep sleep came upon them amid their weeping. And when it was the third watch of the night, and the stars had crossed the zenith, Zeus the cloud-gatherer roused against them an angry wind with wondrous tempest, and shrouded in clouds land and sea alike, and from heaven sped down the night. Now when the Dawn shone forth, the rosy-fingered, we beached the ship, and dragged it up within a hollow cave, where were the fair dancing grounds of the nymphs and the places of their session. Thereupon I ordered a gathering of my men and spake in their midst, saying:

"Friends, forasmuch as there is yet meat and drink in the swift ship, let us keep our hands off those kine, lest some evil thing befall us. For these are the kine and the brave flocks of a dread god, even of Helios, who overseeth all and overheareth all things."

So I spake, and their lordly spirit hearkened thereto. Then for a whole month the South Wind blew without ceasing, and no other wind arose, save only the East and the South.

Now so long as my company still had corn and red wine, they refrained them from the kine, for they were fain of life. But when the corn was now all spent from out the ship, and they went wandering with barbed hooks in quest of game, as needs they must, fishes and fowls, whatsoever might come to their hand, for hunger gnawed at their belly, then at last I departed up the isle, that I might pray to the gods, if perchance some one of them might show me a way of returning. And now when I had avoided my company on my way through the island, I laved my hands where was a shelter from the wind, and prayed to all the gods that hold Olympus. But they shed sweet sleep upon my eyelids. And Eurylochus the while set forth an evil counsel to my company:

"Hear my words, my friends, though ye be in evil case. Truly every shape of death is hateful to wretched mortals, but to die of hunger and so meet doom is most pitiful of all. Nay come, we will drive off the best of the kine of Helios and will do sacrifice to the deathless gods who keep wide heaven. And if we may yet reach Ithaca, our own country, forthwith will we rear a rich shrine to Helios Hyperion, and therein would we set many a choice offering. But if he be somewhat wroth for his cattle with straight horns, and is fain to wreck our ship, and the other gods follow his desire, rather with one gulp at the wave would I cast my life away, than be slowly straitened to death in a desert isle."

So spake Eurylochus, and the rest of the company consented thereto. Forthwith they drave off the best of the kine of Helios that were nigh at hand, for the fair kine of shambling gait and broad of brow were feeding no great way from the dark-prowed ship. Then they stood around the cattle and prayed to the gods, plucking the fresh leaves from an oak of lofty boughs, for they had no white barley on board the decked ship. Now after they had prayed and cut the throats of the kine and flayed them, they cut out slices of the thighs and wrapped them in the fat, making a double fold, and thereon they laid raw flesh. Yet had they no pure wine to pour over the flaming sacrifices, but they made libation with water and roasted the entrails over the fire. Now after the thighs were quite consumed and they had tasted the inner parts, they cut the rest up small and spitted it on spits. In the same hour deep sleep sped from my eyelids and I sallied forth to the swift ship and the sea-banks. But on my way as I drew near to the curved ship, the sweet savour of the fat came all about me; and I groaned and spake out before the deathless gods:

"Father Zeus, and all ye other blessed gods that live for ever, verily to my undoing ye have lulled me with a ruthless sleep, and my company abiding behind have imagined a monstrous deed."

Then swiftly to Helios Hyperion came Lampetie of the long robes, with the tidings that we had slain his kine. And straight he spake with angry heart amid the Immortals:

"Father Zeus, and all ye other blessed gods that live for ever, take vengeance I pray you on the company of Odysseus, son of Laertes, that have insolently slain my cattle, wherein I was wont to be glad as I went toward the starry heaven, and when I again turned earthward from the firmament. And if they pay me not full atonement for the cattle, I will go down to Hades and shine among the dead."

And Zeus the cloud-gatherer answered him, saying: "Helios, do thou, I say, shine on amidst the deathless gods, and amid mortal men upon the earth, the grain-giver. But as for me, I will soon smite their swift ship with my white bolt, and cleave it in pieces in the midst of the wine-dark deep."

This I heard from Calypso of the fair hair; and she said that she herself had heard it from Hermes the Messenger.

But when I had come down to the ship and to the sea, I went up to my companions and rebuked them one by one; but we could find no remedy, the cattle were dead and gone. And soon thereafter the gods showed forth signs and wonders to my company. The skins were creeping, and the flesh bellowing upon the spits, both the roast and raw, and there was a sound as the voice of kine.

Then for six days my dear company feasted on the best of the kine of Helios which they had driven off. But when Zeus, son of Cronos, had added the seventh day thereto, thereafter the wind ceased to blow with a rushing storm, and at once we climbed the ship and launched into the broad deep, when we had set up the mast and hoisted the white sails.

But now when we left that isle nor any other land appeared, but sky and sea only, even then the son of Cronos stayed a dark cloud above the hollow ship, and beneath it the deep darkened. And the ship ran on her way for no long while, for of a sudden came the shrilling West, with the rushing of a great tempest, and the blast of wind snapped the two forestays of the mast, and the mast fell backward and all the gear dropped into the bilge. And behold, on the hind part of the ship the mast struck the head of the pilot and brake all the bones of his skull together, and like a diver he dropt down from the deck, and his brave spirit left his bones. In that same hour Zeus thundered and cast his bolt upon the ship, and she reeled all over being stricken by the bolt of Zeus, and was filled with sulphur, and lo, my company fell from out the vessel. Like sea-gulls they were borne round the black ship upon the billows, and the god reft them of returning.

But I kept pacing through my ship, till the surge loosened the sides from the keel, and the wave swept her along stript of her tackling, and brake her mast clean off at the keel. Now the backstay fashioned of an oxhide had been flung thereon; therewith I lashed together both keel and mast and sitting thereon I was borne by the ruinous winds.

Then verily the West Wind ceased to blow with a rushing storm, and swiftly withal the South Wind came, bringing sorrow to my soul, that so I might again measure back that space of sea, the way to deadly Charybdis. All the night was I borne, but with the rising of the sun I came to the rock of Scylla, and to dread Charybdis. Now she had sucked down her salt sea water, when I was swung up on high to the tall fig tree whereto I clung like a bat, and could find no sure rest for my feet nor place to stand, for the roots spread far below and the branches hung aloft out of reach, long and large, and overshadowed Charybdis. Steadfast I clung till she should spew forth mast and keel again; and late they came to my desire. At the hour when a man rises up from the assembly and goes to supper, one who judges the many quarrels of the young men that seek to him for law, at that same hour those timbers came forth to view from out Charybdis. And I let myself drop down hands and feet, and plunged heavily in the midst of the waters beyond the long timbers, and sitting on these I rowed hard with my hands. But the father of gods and of men suffered me no more to behold Scylla, else I should never have escaped from utter doom.

Thence for nine days was I borne, and on the tenth night the gods brought me nigh to the isle of Ogygia, where dwells Calypso of the braided tresses, an awful goddess of mortal speech, who took me in and entreated me kindly. But why rehearse all this tale? For even yesterday I told it to thee and to thy noble wife in thy house; and it liketh me not twice to tell a plain-told tale.

[tr. BUTCHER & LANG]

[The next day the Phaeacians send Odysseus to Ithaca in one of their ships and leave him asleep on the shore. There he meets Athene, who informs him of the situation in his home; at her advice he goes disguised as a beggar to the hut of the loyal swineherd, Eumaeus, and spends several days there while Athene brings Telemachus safely back from Sparta.

Telemachus, on his arrival at Ithaca, goes first to the hut of Eumaeus, where Odysseus discovers himself to his son, but cautions him to reveal his identity to no one until they can devise a plan to deal with the wooers. The following day Odysseus, still disguised as a beggar, goes to his home, where he is arrogantly mistreated by the wooers. After the feast he and Telemachus remove all the arms from the great hall of the house. Odysseus then converses with Penelope, without revealing himself, and learns that she is about to make a trial of the suitors: whoever shall most easily string the great bow of Odysseus and shoot an arrow through twelve axes in a line, shall be her new husband.

The next day, at the feasting of the wooers, Penelope brings forth the bow and ordains the contest. None of the wooers can string the bow. Odysseus asks permission to try the bow, Telemachus and Eumaeus give it to him, and the defenseless suitors are locked in the hall, as Odysseus strings the bow and sends an arrow speeding through the line of axes.]

BOOK XXII

The killing of the wooers.

Then Odysseus of many counsels stripped him of his rags and leaped on to the great threshold with his bow and quiver full of

arrows, and poured forth all the swift shafts there before his feet, and
spake among the wooers:

"Lo, now is this terrible trial ended at last; and now will I know of
another mark, which never yet man has smitten, if perchance I may
hit it and Apollo grant me renown."

With that he pointed the bitter arrow at Antinous. Now he was
about raising to his lips a fair twy-eared chalice of gold, and behold,
he was handling it to drink of the wine, and death was far from his
thoughts. For who among men at feast would deem that one man
amongst so many, how hardy soever he were, would bring on him
foul death and black fate? But Odysseus aimed and smote him with
the arrow in the throat, and the point passed clean out through his
delicate neck, and he fell sidelong and the cup dropped from his
hand as he was smitten, and at once through his nostrils there came
up a thick jet of slain man's blood, and quickly he spurned the table
from him with his foot, and spilt the food on the ground, and the
bread and the roast flesh were defiled. Then the wooers raised a
clamour through the halls when they saw the man fallen, and they
leaped from their high seats, as men stirred by fear, all through the
hall, peering everywhere along the well-builded walls, and nowhere
was there a shield or mighty spear to lay hold on. Then they reviled
Odysseus with angry words:

"Stranger, thou shootest at men to thy hurt. Never again shalt
thou enter other lists, now is utter doom assured thee. Yea, for now
hast thou slain the man that was far the best of all the noble youths in
Ithaca; wherefore vultures shall devour thee here."

So each one spake, for indeed they thought that Odysseus had not
slain him wilfully; but they knew not in their folly that on their own
heads, each and all of them, the bands of death had been made fast.
Then Odysseus of many counsels looked fiercely on them, and spake:

"Ye dogs, ye said in your hearts that I should never more come
home from the land of the Trojans, in that ye wasted my house, and
lay with the maidservants by force, and traitorously wooed my wife
while I was yet alive, and ye had no fear of the gods, that hold the
wide heaven, nor of the indignation of men hereafter. But now the
bands of death have been made fast upon you one and all."

Even so he spake, and pale fear gat hold on the limbs of all, and
each man looked about, where he might shun utter doom. And
Eurymachus alone answered him, and spake: "If thou art indeed
Odysseus of Ithaca, come home again, with right thou speakest thus,
of all that the Achaeans have wrought, many infatuate deeds in thy
halls and many in the field. Howbeit, he now lies dead that is to
blame for all, Antinous; for he brought all these things upon us, not
as longing very greatly for the marriage nor needing it sore, but with
another purpose, that Cronion has not fulfilled for him, namely, that
he might himself be king over all the land of stablished Ithaca, and
he was to have lain in wait for thy son and killed him. But now he
is slain after his deserving, and do thou spare thy people, even thine
own; and we will hereafter go about the township and yield thee

amends for all that has been eaten and drunken in thy halls, each for himself bringing atonement of twenty oxen worth, and requiting thee in gold and bronze till thy heart is softened, but till then none may blame thee that thou art angry."

Then Odysseus of many counsels looked fiercely on him, and said: "Eurymachus, not even if ye gave me all your heritage, all that ye now have, and whatsoever else ye might in any wise add thereto, not even so would I henceforth hold my hands from slaying, ere the wooers had paid for all their transgressions. And now the choice lies before you, whether to fight in fair battle or to fly, if any may avoid death and the fates. But there be some, methinks, that shall not escape from utter doom."

He spake, and their knees were straightway loosened and their hearts melted within them. And Eurymachus spake among them yet again:

"Friends, it is plain that this man will not hold his unconquerable hands, but now that he has caught up the polished bow and quiver, he will shoot from the smooth threshold, till he has slain us all; wherefore let us take thought for the delight of battle. Draw your blades, and hold up the tables to ward off the arrows of swift death, and let us all have at him with one accord, and drive him, if it may be, from the threshold and the doorway and then go through the city, and quickly would the cry be raised. Thereby should this man soon have shot his latest bolt."

Therewith he drew his sharp two-edged sword of bronze, and leapt on Odysseus with a terrible cry, but in the same moment goodly Odysseus shot the arrow forth and struck him on the breast by the pap, and drave the swift shaft into his liver. So he let the sword fall from his hand, and grovelling over the table he bowed and fell, and spilt the food and the two-handled cup on the floor. And in his agony he smote the ground with his brow, and spurning with both his feet he overthrew the high seat, and the mist of death was shed upon his eyes.

Then Amphinomus made at renowned Odysseus, setting straight at him, and drew his sharp sword, if perchance he might make him give ground from the door. But Telemachus was beforehand with him, and cast and smote him from behind with a bronze-shod spear between the shoulders, and drave it out through the breast, and he fell with a crash and struck the ground full with his forehead. Then Telemachus sprang away, leaving the long spear fixed in Amphinomus, for he greatly dreaded lest one of the Achaeans might run upon him with his blade, and stab him as he drew forth the spear, or smite him with a down stroke of the sword. So he started and ran and came quickly to his father, and stood by him, and spake winged words:

"Father, lo, now I will bring thee a shield and two spears and a helmet all of bronze, close fitting on the temples, and when I return I will arm myself, and likewise give arms to the swineherd and to the neatherd yonder: for it is better to be clad in full armour."

And Odysseus of many counsels answered him saying: "Run and bring them while I have arrows to defend me, lest they thrust me from the doorway, one man against them all."

So he spake, and Telemachus obeyed his dear father, and went forth to the chamber, where his famous weapons were lying. Thence he took out four shields and eight spears, and four helmets of bronze, with thick plumes of horse hair, and he started to bring them and came quickly to his father. Now he girded the gear of bronze about his own body first, and in like manner the two thralls did on the goodly armour, and stood beside the wise and crafty Odysseus. Now he, so long as he had arrows to defend him, kept aiming and smote the wooers one by one in his house, and they fell thick one upon another. But when the arrows failed the prince in his archery, he leaned his bow against the doorpost of the stablished hall, against the shining faces of the entrance. As for him he girt his fourfold shield about his shoulders and bound on his mighty head a well-wrought helmet, with horse hair crest, and terribly the plume waved aloft. And he grasped two mighty spears tipped with bronze.

Now there was in the well-builded wall a certain postern raised above the floor, and there by the topmost level of the threshold of the stablished hall, was a way into an open passage, closed by well-fitted folding doors. So Odysseus bade the goodly swineherd stand near thereto and watch the way, for thither was there but one approach. Then Agelaus spake among them, and declared his word to all:

"Friends, will not some man climb up to the postern, and give word to the people, and a cry would be raised straightway; so should this man soon have shot his latest bolt?"

Then Melanthius, the goatherd, answered him, saying: "It may in no wise be, prince Agelaus; for the fair gate of the courtyard is terribly nigh, and perilous is the entrance to the passage, and one man, if he were valiant, might keep back a host. But come, let me bring you armour from the inner chamber, that ye may be clad in hauberks, for, methinks, within that room and not elsewhere did Odysseus and his renowned son lay by the arms."

Therewith Melanthius, the goatherd, climbed up by the clerestory of the hall to the inner chambers of Odysseus, whence he took twelve shields and as many spears, and as many helmets of bronze with thick plumes of horse hair, and he came forth and brought them speedily, and gave them to the wooers. Then the knees of Odysseus were loosened and his heart melted within him, when he saw them girding on the armour and brandishing the long spears in their hands, and great, he saw, was the adventure. Quickly he spake to Telemachus winged words:

"Telemachus, sure I am that one of the women in the halls is stirring up an evil battle against us, or perchance it is Melanthius."

Then wise Telemachus answered him: "My father, it is I that have erred herein and none other is to blame, for I left the well-fitted door of the chamber open, and there has been one of them but too quick to spy it.   Go now, goodly Eumaeus, and close the door of the chamber, and mark if it be indeed one of the women that does this mischief, or Melanthius, son of Dolius, as methinks it is."

Even so they spake one to the other.   And Melanthius, the goat-herd, went yet again to the chamber to bring the fair armour.   But the goodly swineherd was ware thereof, and quickly he spake to Odysseus who stood nigh him:

"Son of Laertes, of the seed of Zeus, Odysseus, of many devices, lo, there again is that baleful man, whom we ourselves suspect, going to the chamber; do thou tell me truly, shall I slay him if I prove the better man, or bring him hither to thee, that he may pay for the many transgressions that he has devised in thy house?"

Then Odysseus of many counsels answered saying: "Verily, I and Telemachus will keep the proud wooers within the halls, for all their fury, but do ye twain tie his feet and arms behind his back and cast him into the chamber, and close the doors after you, and make fast to his body a twisted rope, and drag him up the lofty pillar till he be near the roof-beams, that he may hang there and live for long, and suffer grievous torment."

So he spake, and they gave good heed and hearkened.   So they went forth to the chamber, but the goatherd who was within knew not of their coming.   Now he was seeking for the armour in the secret place of the chamber, but they twain stood in waiting on either side the doorposts.   And when Melanthius, the goatherd, was cross-ing the threshold with a goodly helm in one hand, and in the other a wide shield and an old, stained with rust, the shield of the hero Laertes that he bare when he was young — but at that time it was laid by, and the seams of the straps were loosened, — then the twain rushed on him and caught him, and dragged him in by the hair, and cast him on the floor in sorrowful plight, and bound him hand and foot in a bitter bond, tightly winding each limb behind his back, even as the son of Laertes bade them, the steadfast goodly Odysseus.   And they made fast to his body a twisted rope, and dragged him up the lofty pillar till he came near the roof-beams.   Then didst thou speak to him and gird at him, swineherd Eumaeus:

"Now in good truth, Melanthius, shalt thou watch all night, lying in a soft bed as beseems thee, nor shall the early-born Dawn escape thy ken, when she comes forth from the streams of Oceanus, on her golden throne, in the hour when thou art wont to drive the goats to make a meal for the wooers in the halls."

So he was left there, stretched tight in the deadly bond.   But they twain got into their harness, and closed the shining door, and went to Odysseus, wise and crafty chief.   There they stood breathing fury, four men by the threshold, while those others within the halls were many and good warriors.   Then Athene, daughter of Zeus, drew nigh them, like Mentor in fashion and in voice, and Odysseus was glad when he saw her and spake, saying:

"Mentor, ward from us hurt, and remember me thy dear com-panion, that befriended thee often, and thou art of like age with me."

So he spake, deeming the while that it was Athene, summoner of the host. But the wooers on the other side shouted in the halls, and first Agelaus son of Damastor rebuked Athene, saying:

"Mentor, let not the speech of Odysseus beguile thee to fight against the wooers, and to succour him. For methinks that on this wise we shall work our will. When we shall have slain these men, father and son, thereafter shalt thou perish with them, such deeds thou art set on doing in these halls; nay, with thine own head shalt thou pay the price. But when with the sword we shall have overcome your violence, we will mingle all thy possessions, all that thou hast at home or in the field, with the wealth of Odysseus, and we will not suffer thy sons nor thy daughters to dwell in the halls, nor thy good wife to gad about in the town of Ithaca."

So spake he, and Athene was mightily angered at heart, and chid Odysseus in wrathful words: "Odysseus, thou hast no more steadfast might nor any prowess, as when for nine whole years continually thou didst battle with the Trojans for high born Helen, of the white arms, and many men thou slewest in terrible warfare, and by thy device the wide-wayed city of Priam was taken. How then, now that thou art come to thy house and thine own possessions, dost thou bewail thee and art of feeble courage to stand before the wooers? Nay, come hither, friend, and stand by me, and I will show thee a thing, that thou mayest know what manner of man is Mentor, son of Alcimus, to repay good deeds in the ranks of foemen."

She spake, and gave him not yet clear victory in full, but still for a while made trial of the might and prowess of Odysseus and his renowned son. As for her she flew up to the roof timber of the murky hall, in such fashion as a swallow flies, and there sat down.

Now Agelaus, son of Damastor, urged on the wooers, and likewise Eurynomus and Amphimedon and Demoptolemus and Peisandrus son of Polyctor, and wise Polybus, for these were in valiancy far the best men of the wooers, that still lived and fought for their lives; for the rest had fallen already beneath the bow and the thick rain of arrows. Then Agelaus spake among them, and made known his word to all:

"Friends, now at last will this man hold his unconquerable hands. Lo, now has Mentor left him and spoken but vain boasts, and these remain alone at the entrance of the doors. Wherefore now, throw not your long spears all together, but come, do ye six cast first, if perchance Zeus may grant us to smite Odysseus and win renown. Of the rest will we take no heed, so soon as that man shall have fallen."

So he spake and they all cast their javelins, as he bade them, eagerly; but behold, Athene so wrought that they were all in vain. One man smote the doorpost of the stablished hall, and another the well-fastened door, and the ashen spear of yet another wooer, heavy with bronze, stuck fast in the wall. So when they had avoided all the spears of the wooers, the steadfast goodly Odysseus began first to speak among them:

"Friends, now my word is that we too cast and hurl into the press of the wooers, that are mad to slay and strip us beyond the measure of their former iniquities."

So he spake, and they all took good aim and threw their sharp spears, and Odysseus smote Demoptolemus, and Telemachus Euryades, and the swineherd slew Elatus, and the neatherd Peisandrus. Thus they all bit the wide floor with their teeth, and the wooers fell back into the inmost part of the hall. But the others dashed upon them, and drew forth the shafts from the bodies of the dead.

Then once more the wooers threw their sharp spears eagerly; but behold, Athene so wrought that many of them were in vain. One man smote the doorpost of the stablished hall, and another the well-fastened door, and the ashen spear of another wooer, heavy with bronze, stuck in the wall. Yet Amphimedon hit Telemachus on the hand by the wrist lightly, and the shaft of bronze wounded the surface of the skin. And Ctesippus grazed the shoulder of Eumaeus with a long spear high above the shield, and the spear flew over and fell to the ground. Then again Odysseus, the wise and crafty, he and his men cast their swift spears into the press of the wooers, and now once more Odysseus, waster of cities, smote Eurydamas, and Telemachus Amphimedon, and the swineherd slew Polybus, and last, the neatherd struck Ctesippus in the breast and boasted over him, saying:

"O son of Polytherses, thou lover of jeering, never give place at all to folly to speak so big, but leave thy case to the gods, since in truth they are far mightier than thou. This gift is thy recompense for the ox-foot that thou gavest of late to the divine Odysseus, when he went begging through the house."

So spake the keeper of the shambling kine. Next Odysseus wounded the son of Damastor in close fight with his long spear, and Telemachus wounded Leocritus son of Euenor, right in the flank with his lance, and drave the bronze point clean through, that he fell prone and struck the ground full with his forehead. Then Athene held up her destroying aegis on high from the roof, and their minds were scared, and they fled through the hall, like a drove of kine that the flitting gadfly falls upon and scatters hither and thither in spring time, when the long days begin. But the others set on like vultures of crooked claws and curved beak, that come forth from the mountains and dash upon smaller birds, and these scour low in the plain, stooping in terror from the clouds, while the vultures pounce on them and slay them, and there is no help nor way of flight, and men are glad at the sport; even so did the company of Odysseus set upon the wooers and smite them right and left through the hall; and there rose a hideous moaning as their heads were smitten, and the floor all ran with blood.

Now Leiodes took hold of the knees of Odysseus eagerly, and besought him and spake winged words: "I entreat thee by thy knees, Odysseus, and do thou show mercy on me and have pity. For never yet, I say, have I wronged a maiden in thy halls by froward word or

deed, nay I bade the other wooers refrain, whoso of them wrought
thus. But they hearkened not unto me to keep their hands from
evil. Wherefore they have met a shameful death through their
own infatuate deeds. Yet I, the soothsayer among them, that have
wrought no evil, shall fall even as they, for no grace abides for good
deeds done."

Then Odysseus of many counsels looked askance at him, and said:
"If indeed thou dost avow thee to be the soothsayer of these men,
thou art like to have often prayed in the halls that the issue of a glad
return might be far from me, and that my dear wife should follow
thee and bear thee children; wherefore thou shalt not escape the
bitterness of death."

Therewith he caught up a sword in his strong hand, that lay where
Agelaus had let it fall to the ground when he was slain, and drave it
clean through his neck, and as he yet spake his head fell even to the
dust.

But the son of Terpes, the minstrel, still sought how he might shun
black fate, Phemius, who sang among the wooers of necessity. He
stood with the loud lyre in his hand hard by the postern gate, and his
heart was divided within him, whether he should slip forth from the
hall and sit down by the well-wrought altar of great Zeus of the household court, whereon Laertes and Odysseus had burnt many pieces of
the thighs of oxen, or should spring forward and beseech Odysseus
by his knees. And as he thought thereupon this seemed to him the
better way, to embrace the knees of Odysseus, son of Laertes. So he
laid the hollow lyre on the ground between the mixing-bowl and the
high seat inlaid with silver, and himself sprang forward and seized
Odysseus by the knees, and besought him and spake winged words:

"I entreat thee by thy knees, Odysseus, and do thou show mercy on
me and have pity. It will be a sorrow to thyself in the aftertime if
thou slayest me who am a minstrel, and sing before gods and men.
Yea none has taught me but myself, and the god has put into my
heart all manner of lays, and methinks I sing to thee as to a god,
wherefore be not eager to cut off my head. And Telemachus will
testify of this, thine own dear son, that not by mine own will or
desire did I resort to thy house to sing to the wooers at their feasts;
but being so many and stronger than I they led me by constraint."

So he spake, and the mighty prince Telemachus heard him and
quickly spake to his father at his side: "Hold thy hand, and wound
not this blameless man with the sword; and let us save also the
henchman Medon, that ever had charge of me in our house when I
was a child, unless perchance Philoetius or the swineherd have already
slain him, or he hath met thee in thy raging through the house."

So he spake, and Medon, wise of heart, heard him. For he lay
crouching beneath a high seat, clad about in the new-flayed hide of
an ox and shunned black fate. So he rose up quickly from under
the seat, and cast off the ox-hide, and sprang forth and caught Telemachus by the knees, and besought him and spake winged words:

"Friend, here am I; prithee stay thy hand and speak to thy father, lest he harm me with the sharp sword in the greatness of his strength, out of his anger for the wooers that wasted his possessions in the halls, and in their folly held thee in no honour."

And Odysseus of many counsels smiled on him and said: "Take courage, for lo, he has saved thee and delivered thee, that thou mayst know in thy heart, and tell it even to another, how far more excellent are good deeds than evil. But go forth from the halls and sit down in the court apart from the slaughter, thou and the full-voiced minstrel, till I have accomplished all that I must needs do in the house."

Therewith the two went forth and gat them from the hall. So they sat down by the altar of great Zeus, peering about on every side, still expecting death. And Odysseus peered all through the house, to see if any man was yet alive and hiding away to shun black fate. But he found all the sort of them fallen in their blood in the dust, like fishes that the fishermen have drawn forth in the meshes of the net into a hollow of the beach from out the grey sea, and all the fish, sore longing for the salt sea waves, are heaped upon the sand, and the sun shines forth and takes their life away; so now the wooers lay heaped upon each other. Then Odysseus of many counsels spake to Telemachus:

"Telemachus, go, call me the nurse Eurycleia, that I may tell her a word that is on my mind."

So he spake, and Telemachus obeyed his dear father, and smote at the door, and spake to the nurse Eurycleia: "Up now, aged wife, that overlookest all the women servants in our halls, come hither, my father calls thee and has somewhat to say to thee."

Even so he spake, and wingless her speech remained, and she opened the doors of the fair-lying halls, and came forth, and Telemachus led the way before her. So she found Odysseus among the bodies of the dead, stained with blood and soil of battle, like a lion that has eaten of an ox of the homestead and goes on his way, and all his breast and his cheeks on either side are flecked with blood, and he is terrible to behold; even so was Odysseus stained, both hands and feet. Now the nurse, when she saw the bodies of the dead and the great gore of blood, made ready to cry aloud for joy, beholding so great an adventure. But Odysseus checked and held her in her eagerness, and uttering his voice spake to her winged words:

"Within thine own heart rejoice, old nurse, and be still, and cry not aloud; for it is an unholy thing to boast over slain men. Now these hath the destiny of the gods overcome, and their own cruel deeds, for they honoured none of earthly men, neither the bad nor yet the good, that came among them. Wherefore they have met a shameful death through their own infatuate deeds. But come, tell me the tale of the women in my halls, which of them dishonour me, and which be guiltless."

Then the good nurse Eurycleia answered him: "Yea now, my child, I will tell thee all the truth. Thou hast fifty women-servants in thy halls, that we have taught the ways of housewifery, how to card wool and to bear bondage. Of these twelve in all have gone the way of shame, and honour not me, nor their lady Penelope. And Telemachus hath but newly come to his strength, and his mother suffered him not to take command over the women in this house. But now, let me go aloft to the shining upper chamber, and tell all to thy wife, on whom some god hath sent a sleep."

And Odysseus of many counsels answered her, saying: "Wake her not yet, but bid the women come hither, who in time past behaved themselves unseemly."

So he spake, and the old wife passed through the hall, to tell the women and to hasten their coming. Then Odysseus called to him Telemachus, and the neatherd, and the swineherd, and spake to them winged words:

"Begin ye now to carry out the dead, and bid the women help you, and thereafter cleanse the fair high seats and the tables with water and porous sponges. And when ye have set all the house in order, lead the maidens without the stablished hall, between the vaulted room and the goodly fence of the court, and there slay them with your long blades, till they shall have all given up the ghost and forgotten the love that of old they had at the bidding of the wooers, in secret dalliance."

Even so he spake, and the women came all in a crowd together, making a terrible lament and shedding big tears. So first they carried forth the bodies of the slain, and set them beneath the gallery of the fenced court, and propped them one on another; and Odysseus himself hasted the women and directed them, and they carried forth the dead perforce. Thereafter they cleansed the fair high seats and the tables with water and porous sponges. And Telemachus, and the neatherd, and the swineherd, scraped with spades the floor of the well-builded house, and, behold, the maidens carried all forth and laid it without the doors.

Now when they had made an end of setting the hall in order, they led the maidens forth from the stablished hall, and drove them up in a narrow space between the vaulted room and the goodly fence of the court, whence none might avoid; and wise Telemachus began to speak to his fellows, saying:

"God forbid that I should take these women's lives by a clean death, these that have poured dishonour on my head and on my mother, and have lain with the wooers."

With that word he tied the cable of a dark-prowed ship to a great pillar and flung it round the vaulted room, and fastened it aloft, that none might touch the ground with her feet. And even as when thrushes, long of wing, or doves fall into a net that is set in a thicket, as they seek to their roosting-place, and a loathly bed harbours them, even so the women held their heads all in a row, and about all their necks nooses were cast, that they might die by the most pitiful death. And they writhed with their feet for a little space, but for no long while.

Then they led out Melanthius through the doorway and the court, and cut off his nostrils and his ears with the pitiless sword, and drew forth his vitals for the dogs to devour raw, and cut off his hands and feet in their cruel anger.

Thereafter they washed their hands and feet, and went into the house to Odysseus, and all the adventure was over. So Odysseus called to the good nurse Eurycleia: "Bring sulphur, old nurse, that cleanses all pollution and bring me fire, that I may purify the house with sulphur, and do thou bid Penelope come here with her handmaidens, and tell all the women to hasten into the hall."

Then the good nurse Eurycleia made answer: "Yea, my child, herein thou hast spoken aright. But go to, let me bring thee a mantle and a doublet for raiment, and stand not thus in the halls with thy broad shoulders wrapped in rags; it were blame in thee so to do."

And Odysseus of many counsels answered her saying: "First let a fire now be made me in the hall."

So he spake, and the good nurse Eurycleia was not slow to obey, but brought fire and brimstone; and Odysseus thoroughly purged the women's chamber and the great hall and the court.

Then the old wife went through the fair halls of Odysseus to tell the women, and to hasten their coming. So they came forth from their chamber with torches in their hands, and fell about Odysseus, and embraced him and kissed and clasped his head and shoulders and his hands lovingly, and a sweet longing came on him to weep and moan, for he remembered them every one.

[tr. BUTCHER & LANG]

[Odysseus reveals himself to Penelope and briefly recounts his adventures to her. The next day he goes out to the country to see his father, Laertes. The kinsmen of the slain wooers plan revenge on Odysseus and set out in force to attack him; a pitched battle between the kinsmen of the wooers and the loyal adherents of Odysseus is just starting when Athene intervenes and ends the struggle.]

TRAGEDY

Investigations of the origin of Greek tragedy have brought to light two important points which every reader must continually bear in mind. In the first place, tragedy was always associated with a chorus which sang and danced. The choral odes, so important in the plays of Aeschylus though less significant in Euripides, are ultimately adaptations and modifications of early choral poetry. In the second place, tragedy was always closely integrated with religious ritual. This fact in some measure explains the fundamentally serious and impressive character of the plays themselves. Furthermore their presentation at religious festivals such as the celebration in honour of Dionysus during the fifth and fourth centuries bespeaks their continued close relations to religion.

The plays were presented in open air theatres with a curved bank of seats resembling the closed end of a modern horseshoe stadium, and accommodating as many as 17,000 persons. On the level in front of the seats was a circular area called the orchestra and opposite the seats was a stage building which usually represented the façade of a temple or palace. The action of the plays usually took place in front of the scene building, whereas normally the dances of the chorus were performed in the orchestra. The dramas were divided into a regular number of parts. A normal tragedy opens with a prologue followed by a *parodos* in which the chorus enters and sings its opening song. Then there follow alternating episodes or dramatic acts and choral passages which are called *stasima*. The play then concludes with the *exodos* or the finale when the chorus leaves the orchestra.

The reader should bear in mind that the plays, at least at Athens, were given only on two occasions during the year, at the Lenaea, the festival of the Wine-Press held in January/February, or at the so-called Greater Dionysia, held in March/April in honour of the god Dionysus. On each occasion there was a competition, with a tragic poet normally submitting a group of four plays in the contest. Three of these plays were either on separate themes, or constituted a trilogy bearing on the same theme. The poet likewise had to submit a fourth and lighter after-piece called a satyr-play, which was supposed to relieve in some measure the stress of the preceding tragedies. Three poets competed normally in one contest and their combined productions filled the program for three days of the festival. The poet himself usually supervised the productions and from time to time even acted in them himself. He probably also helped to choose his cast which was filled entirely by male actors, as well as to train the chorus. Part of the civic responsibility of wealthy citizens was to sustain the expense of producing these elaborate compositions.

AESCHYLUS, the first of the three great Greek tragedians, was born in 525 B.C. and died in 455 B.C. Thus his life extends from the period before Athens had achieved any power, through the decade of the

Persian Wars down to her rise to supremacy. The poet started competing in the dramatic contests in 499 B.C., but did not win a first prize until 484. Thereafter he was the most popular playwright in Athens, writing, so far as we know, about ninety plays of which only seven now survive. Fortunately the seven are the result of a careful and intelligent selection. Among his thirteen victorious dramas is his last trilogy and masterpiece, the *Oresteia*, the first and third plays of which are the *Agamemnon* and the *Eumenides*.

Aeschylus' greatest achievement in the drama is his expression of a lofty and elevated theology. Even in his earliest plays we find the poet beginning to develop his conception of Zeus as a godhead purified from the taints of anthropomorphism. The trilogy on Prometheus, of which the *Prometheus Bound* is the first and sole surviving play, focuses upon the nature of god. It seems to ask: What is the divine power which lies behind the universe and if that power is benevolent, why is it that man suffers; why is there evil in the world? There is a strong temptation in interpreting this play to view Prometheus as a typical Aristotelian tragic hero who is suffering as a result of his flaw of rebelliousness. But actually the play is not concerned specifically with the character of Prometheus, but rather it deals with evil and its relation to the godhead. Still there is a difficult problem in the play, because the Zeus of the *Prometheus Bound* represents brute power as it is posed against Prometheus who represents beneficence and wisdom. Critics are handicapped since we do not possess the last two-thirds of the trilogy but it seems to be a fair assumption that Zeus and Prometheus function throughout the whole as powerful symbols, each representing one important aspect of deity. We might conjecture that at the end of the trilogy these two forces, power and wisdom, which separately are in conflict, were presented as mystically fused into a single divine nature, both all-wise and all-powerful. Aeschylus may have been attempting to show that god conceived of either as sheer wisdom without power or as sheer power without wisdom is hopelessly inadequate as an object of man's faith when man has to face the brute fact of evil in the world.

If we interpret the *Prometheus Bound* in this way we can see in it an earlier attempt of Aeschylus to resolve the theological problem which he interpreted at fuller length in the *Oresteia*. In this trilogy the human story of the curse upon the house of Atreus and the sufferings of Agamemnon, Clytemnestra and Orestes provide material for the poet to illustrate the problem which he sets on a religious level. Throughout in the choral passages Zeus is presented as a benevolent deity, a friend, a refuge, a god who ordained that man through suffering shall learn wisdom. But contrasted with Zeus is the attitude represented symbolically by the Furies in the *Eumenides*. These dread goddesses are symbols of mechanical justice and fate. Their code is strictly an eye for an eye and a tooth for a tooth. According to them, Orestes, no matter what the circumstances of his crime, must suffer for it. Orestes is pardoned in the *Eumenides* for no logically convincing reason, but the play continues in a concluding portion where no human characters are upon the stage. In this closing scene the Furies are transmuted into goddesses of grace and the justice which they symbolize is fused with the mercy which Zeus symbolizes into a single god who can be called an all-comprehending Father.

EURIPIDES, the youngest of the three tragedians, may best be considered next because in many respects he contrasts sharply with Aeschylus. Born in the decade before Salamis and living until 406 B.C. he witnessed the rise to power of his native city, Athens, and her eventual collapse in the Peloponnesian War. He composed approximately ninety-two plays of which seventeen tragedies and one satyr-play survive. Another tragedy, the *Rhesus,* is ascribed to him though its genuineness has been frequently doubted. He won first prize in the dramatic contests only four times, a fact which indicates that he was not popular among his contemporaries. Perhaps he did not gain favour because he expressed bold and unorthodox views for which the comic poets, like the conservative Aristophanes, were ready to attack him. Certainly doubt and skepticism are apparent in his writing. However, the large number of his preserved plays attests to his greater popularity in later generations.

The *Hippolytus* is typical of Euripidean tragedy at its best. Here the poet takes a concrete problem, Phaedra's illegitimate love for her stepson in conflict with Hippolytus' unrelenting chastity. In a sense we have the force of Aphrodite posed against the force of Artemis and these two goddesses appear as quasi-symbols in the play. But Euripides rises above the level of this particular problem by characterizing Hippolytus as a man who is boundlessly convinced of his own virtue and purity, and who never ceases to insist upon it. He is overweeningly proud and from his pride comes the catastrophe. The closing scene where Hippolytus realizes how his father Theseus must suffer because he must continue to live indicates the real stature of Hippolytus' character and his final triumph over his pride.

The *Bacchae,* a play written late in Euripides' life, contains a study of religion. Critics have puzzled long over its interpretation and no satisfactory solution seems to emerge. In it we find some of Euripides' best lyric and emotional poetry. At times we feel that the poet believes religion to be the most important and vital factor in man's life. At other times he seems to hold the conviction that religion is a curse and an abomination to human beings. Euripides' final answer may be that he believes in God or a divine power incomprehensible to man, but whom man must worship and at the same time endure life no matter what it offers.

In contrast to both Aeschylus and Euripides, we find SOPHOCLES as a great mediating figure between them. Sophocles' life, 495 B.C. to 405 B.C. roughly coincides with that of Euripides. He was born of a wealthy Athenian family, served on several occasions in public office with distinction, but otherwise gave himself entirely to activity in the theatre. His tragedies carried off the first prize more than twenty times, a higher score of victories than either Aeschylus or Euripides achieved. More prolific than either of his rivals, he composed one hundred and twenty-five plays, of which only seven are now extant. Although he witnessed the collapse of Athens which brought such despair to Euripides, Sophocles' strength and power seem to increase with the years. We see him always sensitive and sympathetic with human suffering, yet he evinces a greater and greater vision into the essence of human life. His vision plus the unrivaled perfection of his dramatic technique make it difficult to deal with him critically. Even Aristophanes who had a keen sense for the sham never made sport of him in his comedies.

Included in the present collection are two of Sophocles' masterpieces. Both of these deal with the unhappy story of the ruling house of Thebes. In the *Antigone* Sophocles treats the conflict between the law of man and the law of God. Creon, the King of Thebes, has in tyrannical fashion ordered that the rites of burial should not be administered to his nephew, Polyneices, who has fallen in a treasonable attack upon the city. Antigone, Polyneices' sister, feels that it is her duty to follow the law of God as she sees it, which dictates that such rites should be given to the dead. Antigone holds to her faith, even though it brings about her death. Creon, on the other hand, is a man who feels confident that he knows all the answers to the mysteries of life and stubbornly maintains his position. He angrily reacts against criticism and when finally he gives way, it is too late to repair the damage which his action has caused. Hence he, more than Antigone, is the tragic figure in the play. Yet its final meaning appears to be that man must preserve his intellectual and spiritual humility and that he must conform to the law of God which is sovereign in the universe.

Oedipus the King is perhaps the greatest of all the Greek tragedies. From the time of Aristotle, the flawless structure of its plot has been admired. In it we find Sophocles using with greatest effect the device of dramatic irony. The whole play in one sense is devoted to the gradual revelation to Oedipus that he, in ignorance, has killed his father and married his mother. The intensity of the play increases, as Oedipus himself unrelentingly pursues his quest for the truth which the audience has known from the beginning. The dramatic impact is overpowering when the last link in the chain of evidence is forged. However, the feature of the play which makes it a universal tragedy for all mankind appears when Oedipus, once he has discovered the truth, does not plead his ignorance as an excuse; rather he accepts full responsibility for what he has done. As Paul Elmer More has observed, Sophocles has here portrayed simultaneously the intellectual impotence of man and his moral responsibility. Thus Sophocles appears to be the crowning figure in the trio of Greek tragedians. He possesses religious insight and a scope of vision comparable to that of Aeschylus, and at the same time a power of psychological analysis and understanding of human nature comparable to that of Euripides. The contribution of these three poets to dramatic literature has never been rivaled save in the case of Shakespeare.

AESCHYLUS

(*ca.* 525–455 B.C.)

PROMETHEUS BOUND

Translated by PAUL ELMER MORE

Characters in the Play

Power
Force
Hephaestus
Prometheus
Chorus of the Daughters of Oceanus
Oceanus
Io
Hermes

PROMETHEUS BOUND

[SCENE: — *A rocky gorge in Scythia.* POWER *and* FORCE *enter, carrying* PROMETHEUS *as a captive. They are accompanied by* HEPHAESTUS.]

PO.: To this far region of the earth, this pathless wilderness of Scythia, at last we are come. O Hephaestus, thine is the charge, on thee are laid the Father's commands in never-yielding fetters linked of adamant to bind this miscreant to the high-ridged rocks. For this is he who stole the flame of all-working fire, thy own bright flower, and gave to mortal men. Now for the evil done he pays this forfeit to the gods; so haply he shall learn some patience with the reign of Zeus and put away his love for human kind.

HE.: O Power and Force, your share in the command of Zeus is done, and for you nothing remains; but I — some part of courage still is wanting to bind with force a kindred god to this winter-bitten gorge. Yet must I summon daring to my heart, such dread dwells in the Father's word. — [*to* PROMETHEUS] O high magnanimous son of prudent Themis, against thy will and mine with brazen bonds no hand can loose I bind thee to this unvisited lonely rock. No human voice will reach thee here, nor any form of man be seen. Parched by the blazing fires of the sun thy skin shall change its pleasant hue; grateful to thee the starry-kirtled night shall come veiling the day, and grateful again the sun dispelling the morn's white frost. Forever the weariness of unremitting pain shall waste thy strength, for he is not born who can deliver thee. See now the profit of thy human charity: thou, a god not fearing the wrath of the gods, hast given to mortal men honours beyond their due; and therefore on this joyless rock thou must keep vigil, sleepless and weary-clinging, with unbended knees, pouring out thy ceaseless lamentations and unheeded cries; for the mind of Zeus knows no turning, and ever harsh the hand that newly grasps the sway.

PO.: It may be so, yet why seek delay in vainly spent pity? Feel you no hatred for this enemy of the gods, who hath betrayed to mortals your own chief honour?

HE.: Kinship and old fellowship will have their due.

PO.: 'Tis true; but where is strength to disobey the father's words? Fearest thou not rather this?

HE.: Ever merciless thou art, and steeped in cruelty.

PO.: It healeth nothing to weep for him. Take not up an idle burden wherein there is no profit.

HE.: Alas, my cherished craft, thrice hateful now!

PO.: Why hateful? In simple sooth thy art hath no blame for these present ills.

HE.: Yet would it were another's, not mine!

PO.: All toil alike in sorrow, unless one were lord of heaven; none is truly free, save only Zeus.

HE.: This task confirms it; I can nothing deny.

PO.: Make haste then to bind him in fetters, lest the father detect thee loitering.

HE.: Behold the curb; it is ready to hand.

PO.: Strongly with thy hammer, strongly weld it about his hands; make him fast to the rock.

HE.: The work goes on, it is well done.

PO.: Harder strike them, tighter draw the links, leave nothing loose; strange skill he hath to find a way where none appeared.

HE.: One arm is fastened, and none may loose it.

PO.: Fetter the other, make it sure; he shall learn how all his cunning is folly before Zeus.

HE.: Save now my art hath never wrought harm to any.

PO.: Now strongly drive the biting tooth of the adamantine wedge straight through his breast.

HE.: Alas, Prometheus! I groan for thy pangs.

PO.: Dost thou shrink? Wilt thou groan for the foes of Zeus? Take heed, lest thou groan for thyself.

HE.: Thou lookest upon a spectacle grievous to the eye.

PO.: I look upon one suffering as he deserves. — Now about his sides strain tight the girth.

HE.: It must needs be done; yet urge me not overmuch.

PO.: Yet will I urge and harry thee on. — Now lower; with force constrain his legs.

HE.: 'Tis even done; nor was the labour long.

PO.: Weld fast the galling fetters; remember that he who appraises is strict to exact.

HE.: Cruel thy tongue, and like thy cruel face.

PO.: Be thine the tender heart! Rebuke not my bolder mood, nor chide my austerity.

HE.: Let us go; now the clinging web binds all his limbs.

[HEPHAESTUS *departs.*]

PO.: There, wanton in thy insolence! Now for thy creatures of a day filch divine honours. Tell me, will mortal men drain for thee these tortures? Falsely the gods call thee Prometheus, the Contriver, for no cunning contrivance shall help thee to slip from this bondage.

[POWER *and* FORCE *depart.*]

PROMETHEUS [*alone, chanting*]:
O air divine, and O swift-wingèd winds!
Ye river fountains, and thou myriad-twinkling
Laughter of ocean waves! O mother earth!
And thou, O all-discerning orb o' the sun! —
To you, I cry to you; behold what I,
A god, endure of evil from the gods.

Behold, with what dread torments
I through the slow-revolving
Ages of time must wrestle;
Such hideous bonds the new lord

Of heaven hath found for my torture.
Woe! woe! for the present disasters
I groan, and for those that shall come;
Nor know I in what far sky
The dawn of deliverance shall rise.

Yet what is this I say?   All future things
I see unerring, nor shall any chance
Of evil overtake me unaware.
The will of Destiny we should endure
Lightly as may be, knowing still how vain
To take up arms against Necessity.
Silent I cannot keep, I cannot tongue
These strange calamities.   Lo, I am he
Who, darkly hiding in a fennel reed
Fountains of fire, so secretly purloined
And gave to be the teacher of all arts
And giver of all good to mortal men.
And now this forfeit for my sin I pay,
Thus lodged in fetters under the bare sky.

Woe's me!
What murmur hovereth near?
What odour, where visible shape
Is none?   Some god, or a mortal,
Or one of the middle race?
Hath he come to this world's-end
Idly to gloat o'er my toils,
Or what would he have? — Behold me
Fettered, the god ill-fated,
The foeman of Zeus, the detested
Of all who enter his courts,
And only because of my love,
My too-great love for mankind.
Ah me! once more the murmur
I hear as of hovering birds;
And the air is whirring with quick
Beating of wings.   For me
There is fear, whatever approaches.

[*The* CHORUS OF THE DAUGHTERS OF OCEANUS *enters, drawn in a winged
car.*]

strophe 1

CH. [*singing*]: Fear nothing; in friendship and eager
With wingèd contention of speed
Together we draw near thy rock.
Scarce we persuaded our father,
But now at last the swift breezes
Have brought us.   Down in the depth
Of our sea-cave came the loud noise

Of the welding of iron; and wonderment
Banished our maiden shame;
All in haste, unsandalled, hither
We flew in this wingèd car.

PR.: Ah me! ah me!
O all ye children of Tethys,
Daughters of father Oceanus
Who ever with tide unwearied
Revolveth the whole world round, —
Behold now prisoned in chains
On the dizzy verge of this gorge
Forever I keep sad watch.

antistrophe 1

CH.: I see, O Prometheus, thy body
In the toils and torture of bondage
Withering here on this rock;
And a mist as of terror, a cloud
Of tears o'erveils my eyes:
New helmsmen guide in the heavens,
And Zeus unlawfully rules
With new laws, and the might of old
He hath banished to uttermost darkness.

PR.: Would that me too he had hurled,
Bound in these cruel, unyielding
Bonds, down, down under earth,
Beneath wide Hades, where go
The tribe of innumerable dead,
Down to the infinite depths
Of Tartarus! There no god,
No mortal would gloat o'er my ruin.
Now like a toy of the winds
I hang, my anguish a joy
To my foes.

strophe 2

CH.: Who of the gods is so hardened?
To whom is thy sorrow a joy?
Who save only Zeus
But feels the pang of thy torments?
But he, ever savage of soul,
Swayeth the children of heaven;
Nor ever will cease till his heart
Is satiate grown, or another
Snatches the empire by guile.

PR.: Ay, and this Lord of the blessed
Shall call in the fulness of time
Upon me whom he tortures in bondage,
Shall implore me to utter the plot

That will rob him of honour and throne.
No sweet-lipped charm of persuasion
Then shall allure me, and never
In cringing fear of his threats
The knowledge will I impart,
Till first he has loosened these bonds,
And for all my anguish he too
Hath humbled his neck unto judgment.

antistrophe 2

CH.: Bold art thou, and calamity
Softens thee not, but ever
Thy thought is quick on thy tongue.
Terror pierceth my heart,
And fearing I ask what shore,
O wanderer tempest-tost,
Far-off of peace shall receive thee!
Stern is the son of Cronos,
And deaf his heart to beseeching.
PR.: I know of his hardness, I know
That justice he holds in his palm;
Yet his pride shall be humbled, I think;
His hardness made soft, and his wrath
Shall bow to the blows of adversity;
He, too, in milder mood
Shall come, imploring of me
The friendship I willingly grant.

LEADER OF THE CHORUS: Unfold to us the whole story.   For what crime does Zeus so shamefully and bitterly torture you?   Tell us, if there is no harm in telling.
PR.: Painful are these things to relate, painful is silence, and all is wretchedness.   When first the gods knew wrath, and faction raised its head amongst them, and some would tear old Cronos from his throne that Zeus might take his place, and others were determined that Zeus should never reign over the gods, then I with wise counsel sought to guide the Titans, children of Earth and Sky, — but all in vain.   My crafty schemes they disdained, and in their pride of strength thought it were easy to make themselves lords by force. Often to me my mother Themis (or call her Earth, for many names she hath, being one) had foretold in oracles what was to be, with warning that not by might or brutal force should victory come, but by guile alone.   So I counselled them, but they turned their eyes from me in impatience.   Of the courses which then lay open, far the best, it seemed, was to take my mother as my helper and to join my will with the will of Zeus.   By my advice the cavernous gloom of Tartarus now hides in night old Cronos and his peers.   Thus the new tyrant of heaven took profit of me, and thus rewards me with these torments.   'Tis the disease of tyranny, no more, to take

no heed of friendship. You ask why he tortures me; hear now the reason. No sooner was he established on his father's throne than he began to award various offices to the different gods, ordering his government throughout. Yet no care was in his heart for miserable men, and he was fain to blot out the whole race and in their stead create another. None save me opposed his purpose; I only dared; I rescued mankind from the heavy blow that was to cast them into Hades. Therefore I am bowed down by this anguish, painful to endure, pitiable to behold. Mercy I had for mortals, but found no mercy for myself: so piteously I am disciplined, an ignoble spectacle for Zeus.

LE.: Fashioned of rock is he, and iron is his heart, O Prometheus, who feels not indignation at thy disasters. Rather would I not have seen them at all, and seeing them I am sore of heart.

PR.: To my very friends I am a spectacle of pity.

LE.: Yet it may be — did thy transgressions end there?

PR.: Through me mankind ceased to foresee death.

LE.: What remedy could heal that sad disease?

PR.: Blind hopes I made to dwell in them.

LE.: O merciful boon for mortals.

PR.: And more than all I gave them fire.

LE.: And so in their brief life they are lords of flaming fire?

PR.: Through it they will learn many arts.

LE.: And was it for crimes like this Zeus —

PR.: Tortures me, and ceases not nor relents.

LE.: And is there no goal to the struggle before thee?

PR.: There is none, save when it seems to him good.

LE.: When shall it so seem? What hope? Seest thou not thy error? That thou hast erred, I say in sorrow and with sorrow to thee. But enough of that; seek thou some release from the conflict.

PR.: How easy for one who fares in pleasant ways to admonish those in adversity. But all this I knew; with open eyes, with willing mind, I erred; I do not deny it. Mankind I helped, but could not help myself. Yet I dreamed not that here in this savage solitary gorge, on this high rock, I should waste away beneath such torments. Yet care not to bewail these present disasters; but descend to the earth, and hear of the woes to come and all that is to be. I pray you heed my word; have compassion on one who is now caught in the toils; for sorrow flitteth now to one and now to another, and visiteth each in his turn.

> CH. [*singing*]: We list to your words, O Prometheus.—
> Lo, with light foot I step
> From the swift-rushing car; the pure air,
> The highway I leave of the birds;
> And now to the rugged earth
> I descend. I listen, I wait
> For thy story of pain and disaster.
> [OCEANUS *enters, borne on a winged horse.*]

oc.: To thee I come, O Prometheus;
Borne on this swift-wingèd bird
That knoweth the will of his rider
And needeth no curb, from afar
I have flown a wearisome way,
Weary but ended at last.
I am grieved with thy grief; I am drawn
By our kinship, and even without it
Thee more than all others I honour.
I speak simple sooth, and my tongue
Knows not to flatter in idleness.
Nay, tell me what aid I may render;
For never thy lips shall avow
Oceanus failed thee in friendship.

pr.: Ho! What is this I look upon? What then, art thou too come
to stare upon my ruin? What new daring has brought thee from
thy ocean stream and thy rock-roofed unbuilded caverns hither to
our earth, the mother of iron? Art thou come to view my fate with
indignation for my calamities? Behold the spectacle! behold me,
the friend of Zeus, who helped him to a throne, now bowed down
by his torments.

oc.: I see, Prometheus; and, though thou art thyself cunning in device, I would admonish thee to prudence. Learn to know thyself,
put on the habit of new ways, for there is a new tyrant among the
gods. If still thou hurlest forth these harsh and biting words, perchance from afar off, Zeus, sitting above, may hear thee, and thy
present burden of sorrows will seem as the sport of children. But,
O wretched sufferer, put away thy moody wrath, and seek some
respite from thy ills. My advice may sound as the trite sayings of
old, yet thou thyself canst see what are the wages of too bold a
tongue. Thou hast not learned humility, nor to yield to evils, but
rather wouldst add others new to thy present store. Take me for
thy teacher, and kick not against the pricks, for there rules in heaven
an austere monarch who is responsible to none. Now I will go and
make trial to win thy release from this grievous state. Do thou
keep thy peace, and restrain thy blustering speech. Or knowest
thou not in thy wisdom what penalties overtake an idle tongue?

pr.: I give you joy that, having shared and dared with me, you have
still kept yourself free of blame. I bid you trouble not your peace;
his will is immutable and you cannot persuade him. Even beware,
lest by your going you bring sorrow upon yourself.

oc.: Thou art wiser to think for others than for thyself, and this I
infer from the events. But deter me not from going, for I boast,
yes, I may boast, that Zeus will grant me this boon and deliver thee
from these toils.

pr.: I thank you with gratitude that shall never fail, for you lack
nothing in zeal. But trouble not yourself; it is idle, and your care
will avail me nothing, despite your zeal. Hold your peace, and

keep your foot well from these snares. If I suffer, let me suffer alone. Yet not alone, for I am burdened by the fate of Atlas, my brother. He in the far western ways stands bearing on his shoulders the mighty pillar of earth and sky, a weary burden to hold. And I have seen with pity the earth-born dweller of the Cilician caves, the impetuous, the hundred-headed Typho, when he was bent by force. For he withstood the host of the gods, hissing forth terror from his horrid throats, whilst Gorgonian fires flamed from his eyes, as if to take by violence the very throne of Zeus; but the unsleeping weapon of Zeus fell upon him, the down-rushing thunderbolt with breath of flame, and smote him from his loud-vaunted boastings; and stricken to the heart he was scorched to embers, and thunder rent from him his strength. Now a helpless sprawling bulk he lies near the ocean strait, buried beneath the roots of Aetna; whilst above on the utmost summit Hephaestus welds the molten ore. Thence some day, I ween, shall burst forth rivers of fire to devour with savage maw the wide fields of fair-fruited Sicily, — such wrath shall Typho, scorched by the thunder of Zeus, send up, a tempest, terrible, seething, with breath of flame. — But thou art not untried, and needest not me for a teacher. Save thyself, as thou best knowest how; and leave me to drain this flood of calamity, till the mind of Zeus grows light of its anger.

oc.: Knowest thou not, Prometheus, there are words of healing for a mind distempered?

pr.: Ay, if in good time we soothe the heart, nor violently repress its tumid rage.

oc.: In prudent zeal and daring combined, tell me what peril hidden lies.

pr.: Labour in vain and vain simplicity.

oc.: Leave me, I prythee, to my mind's disease; for it is well having wisdom not to appear wise.

pr.: The folly of thy mission will seem mine.

oc.: It is clear your words dismiss me home.

pr.: Your tears for me might win hatred for yourself.

oc.: His hatred you mean, who newly wears the sovereignty?

pr.: Ay, his; beware that you vex not his heart.

oc.: Your calamity, Prometheus, is my teacher.

pr.: Be gone, take yourself off, keep your present mind.

oc.: I am gone even with your urgent words. See, the winged beast flutters the broad path of the air; gladly would he bend the weary knee in his stall at home.

[OCEANUS *departs as the* CHORUS *begins its song.*]

strophe 1

CH.: I mourn, O Prometheus, for thee,
       I wail for thy hapless fate;
       And tears in a melting flood
       Flow down from the fount of my eyes,
       Drenching my cheeks. O insolent

Laws, O sceptre of Zeus,
How over the gods of old
Ye wield despotic might!

antistrophe 1

Lo, all the land groans aloud;
And the people that dwell in the West
Lament for thy time-honoured reign
And the sway of thy kindred, Prometheus;
And they who have builded their homes
In holy Asia to the wail
Of thine anguish lament.

strophe 2

And they
Of the Colchian land, the virgins
Exulting in war; and the Scythians
By the far Maeotian Lake
In the uttermost regions of earth;

antistrophe 2

And the martial flower of Arabia,
Whose battle resounds with the crashing
Of brazen spears, they too
In their citadel reared aloft
Near Caucasus groan for thy fate.

epode

One other, a Titan god,
I have seen in his anguish,
Atlas, the mighty one, bound
In chains adamantine, who still
With groaning upholds on his back
The high-arched vault of the skies.

epode

While ever the surge of the sea
Moans to the sound of his cry,
And the depths of its waters lament;
The fountains of hallowed rivers
Sigh for his anguish in pity;
While from its dark abyss
The unseen world far below
Mutters and rumbles in concert.

PR.: Think not I am silent through pride or insolence; dumb rage
gnaws at my very heart for this outrage upon me. Yet who but
I established these new gods in their honours? But I speak not of
this, for already you are aware of the truth. Rather listen to the

sad story of mankind, who like children lived until I gave them
understanding and a portion of reason; yet not in disparagement
of men I speak, but meaning to set forth the greatness of my charity. For seeing they saw not, and hearing they understood not, but
like as shapes in a dream they wrought all the days of their life in
confusion. No houses of brick raised in the warmth of the sun
they had, nor fabrics of wood, but like the little ants they dwelt
underground in the sunless depth of caverns. No certain sign of
approaching winter they knew, no harbinger of flowering summer;
ever they laboured at random, till I taught them to discern the
seasons by the rising and the obscure setting of the stars. Numbers
I invented for them, the chiefest of all discoveries; I taught them
the grouping of letters, to be a memorial and record of the past, the
mistress of the arts and mother of the Muses. I first brought under
the yoke beasts of burden, who by draft and carrying relieved men
of their hardest labours; I yoked the proud horse to the chariot,
teaching him obedience to the reins, to be the adornment of wealth
and luxury. I too contrived for sailors sea-faring vessels with their
flaxen wings. Alas for me! such inventions I devised for mankind, but for myself I have no cunning to escape disaster.
LE.: Sorrow and humiliation are your portion: you have failed in
    understanding and gone astray; and like a poor physician falling
    into sickness you despond and know not the remedies for your own
    disease.
PR.: Hear but the rest, and you will wonder more at my inventions
    and many arts. If sickness visited them, they had no healing drug,
    no salve or soothing potion, but wasted away for want of remedies,
    and this was my greatest boon; for I revealed to them the mingling
    of bland medicaments for the banishing of all diseases. And many
    modes of divination I appointed: from dreams I first taught them
    to judge what should befall in waking state; I found the subtle in-
    terpretation of words half heard or heard by chance, and of meet-
    ings by the way; and the flight of taloned birds with their promise
    of fortune or failure I clearly denoted, their various modes of life,
    their mutual feuds, their friendships and consortings; I taught men
    to observe the smooth plumpness of entrails, and the colour of the
    gall pleasing to the gods, and the mottled symmetry of liver-lobe.
    Burning the thigh-bones wrapt in fat and the long chine, I guided
    mankind to a hidden art, and read to them the intimations of the
    altar-flames that before were meaningless. So much then for these
    inventions. And the secret treasures of the earth, all benefits to
    men, copper, iron, silver, gold, — who but I could boast their dis-
    covery? No one, I ween, unless in idle vaunting. Nay, hear the
    whole matter in a word, — all human arts are from Prometheus.
LE.: Care not for mortals overmuch, whilst you neglect your own
    profit. Indeed, I am of good hope that yet some day, freed from
    bondage, you shall equal the might of Zeus.
PR.: Not yet hath all-ordaining Destiny decreed my release; but after
    many years, broken by a world of disaster and woe, I shall be de-

livered. The craft of the forger is weaker far than Necessity.

LE.: Who then holds the helm of Necessity?

PR.: The Fates triform and the unforgetting Furies.

LE.: And Zeus, is he less in power than these?

PR.: He may not avoid what is destined.

LE.: What is destined for Zeus but endless rule?

PR.: Ask not, neither set thy heart on knowing.

LE.: Some solemn secret thou wouldst clothe in mystery.

PR.: Speak no more of it; the time is not yet to divulge it, and the
secret must still be deeply shrouded. Harbouring this I shall one
day escape from this outrage and ignominy of bondage.

strophe 1

CH. [*singing*]: May never Zeus, the all-wielder,
    Against my feeble will
    Set his strength; nor ever may I
    By the stanchless flood of my father,
    By the shores of Oceanus, cease
    With hallowed offering of oxen
    To worship the gods. May never
    My tongue give offence, but always
    This purpose abide in my soul.

antistrophe 1

    Ah, sweet to prolong our days
    In the courage of hope, and sweet
    With ever dawning delights
    To nourish the heart. I shudder,
    Prometheus, for thee, for thy weight
    Of myriad-pilèd woe;
    Ay, fearing not Zeus, in self-will
    Too much thou honourest mortals;

strophe 2

    For thankless thy favour, O friend:
    And where is the valour, what help
    From men who appear and are gone?
    Their weakness hast thou not discovered,
    Their feeble blindness wherein
    Like dreaming shadows they move?
    Never their counsels shall break
    Through the harmony ordered of Zeus.

antistrophe 2

    I too have pondered this wisdom,
    Beholding thy terrible ruin,
    Prometheus. Ah me, for the change!
    With what other notes I chanted

Thy bridal song, the shrill
Hymenean strains at the bath
And the couch, on the happy day
When our sister Hesione, won
By thy bounty, entered thy home!

[IO *enters, transformed in part to a heifer, followed by the Spectre of* ARGUS. *She is in a half-frenzied state.*]

IO [*chanting*]: What land have I reached? what people?
     Who is this I behold in chains
     On this storm-riven rock? What crime
     Hath brought thee to perishing thus?
     Ah whither, to what far regions
     Hath misery borne me? Ah me!
     Once more I am stung by the gadfly,
     Pursued by the wraith of dead Argus.
     Save me, O Earth! Once more
     In my terror I see him, the watcher;
     He is there, and his myriad eyes
     Are upon me. Shall earth nevermore
     Conceal her buried dead?
     He hath come from the pit to pursue me,
     He drives me weary and famished
     Over the long sea sands;
     And ever his shrill scrannel pipe,
     Waxen-jointed, is droning forth
     A slumberous strain.

                    Alas!
     To what land far-off have I wandered?
     What error, O Zeus, what crime
     Is mine that thus I am yoked
     Unto misery? Why am I stung
     With frenzy that drives me unresting
     Forever? Let fires consume me;
     Let the deep earth yawning engulf me;
     Or the monstrous brood of the sea
     Devour; but O great King,
     Hark to my pleading for respite!
     I have wandered enough, I am weary,
     And still I discern no repose. —
                         [*To* PROMETHEUS]
     And thou, hast thou heard me, the virgin
     Wearing these horns of a heifer?
PR.: I hear the frenzied child of Inachus,
     The maiden who with love could all inflame
     Great Zeus's heart, and now by Hera's hate
     Forever flees before this stinging pest.
IO [*chanting*]: Thou knowest my father then?

And who, I prythee, art thou
That callest me thus by name,
Oh name most wretched! and tellest
The wasting plague heaven-sent
And the pest with its haunting sting?
Ah me! behold I am come
With leapings of madness, by hunger
And craving impelled, and subdued
By the crafty anger of Hera.
Who in this world of calamity,
Who suffers as I? — But thou,
If thou canst, declare what awaits me
Of sorrow; what healing balm
I may find. Speak thou, I implore thee,
I, the wandering virgin of sorrows.

PR.: Clearly I will set forth all you would learn; speaking not in dark riddles, but in full simplicity, as speech is due between friends. Behold, I whom you see am Prometheus, the giver of fire to mankind.

IO: You who appeared to men with all-sufficient bounty, — tell me why are you, O enduring Prometheus, given over to chastisement?

PR.: But now I have ceased bewailing these calamities.

IO: And will you deny me this simple boon?

PR.: What do you ask?   You may learn all from me.

IO: Declare who chained you to this rocky gorge.

PR.: The will of Zeus, but Hephaestus' hand.

IO: For what crimes are you punished thus?

PR.: I have told you enough; ask no more.

IO: One further boon: what term shall end my wanderings? what time is ordained for my peace?

PR.: Better for you not to know than to know.

IO: Yet hide not what remains for me to endure.

PR.: So much alone I am willing to grant.

IO: Why then do you delay?   I would know all.

PR.: It is not churlishness; I am loth to bruise your heart.

IO: Spare me not further than I myself desire.

PR.: Since you so crave, it is well; hear me then.

LE.: Nay, not yet.   Grant me also a share in your grace. Let us first hear from her the story of her sorrow and the disasters that prey on her life.   Then do you declare to her what struggle still remains.

PR.: 'Tis for thee, Io, to bestow this favour; and fittingly, for these are thy father's sisters. Time is not lost, I deem, in bewailing and mourning our fate when answering tears stand ready in the listener's eye.

IO: Hard would it be to disregard your wish;
And if my words have credit in your ears
The tale is rendered.   Yet as one who speaks
And still laments, my sorrows I recount, —

How wild, perturbing wonders in my soul
Wrought by the will of heaven, and how in shape
This bestial transformation I endured.
For always in the drowsy hours of night
I, sleeping in my virgin chambers, saw
Strange visitations pass, and as they passed
Each smiled and whispered: O sweet-favoured girl,
Why cherish long thy maiden loneliness,
When love celestial calleth? Fair art thou,
And thronèd Zeus, heart-smitten with desire,
Yearns from his heaven to woo thee. Nay, sweet child,
Disdain him not. Now to the meadow land
Of Lerna, where thy father's pastures lie
And the sleek cattle browse, do thou steal forth
Alone, and haply there thy yielding grace
May soothe the passion in the Sovereign's eye.—
Such dreams, filling with fear the hours of sleep,
Drove me at last to tell my father all.
And he was troubled; many times in doubt
To Pythian Delphi and the speaking oaks
Of far Dodona messengers he sent,
Inquiring by what act or pleasing word
The grace of heaven to win. But ever these
With oracles of shifting speech returned,
Inexplicably dark. Yet in the end
Came one clear cruel utterance, oh, too clear!
That bade him drive me forth from home and land,
An exile doomed in solitary ways
To wander to the confines of the world.
With such commands came words of dreadful import,
And threats of flaming thunderbolts from Zeus
With burning wrath to desolate his race,
If he durst disobey. Much doubted he,
But at the last Apollo's warning voice
And Zeus's curb upon his soul prevailed:
He drave me forth, and all my life's young joy
Ended in bitter grief for him and me.
Straightway my form this strange distortion knew,
With horns here on my front; and madly stung
By this insatiate fly, with antic bounds
I sped away to the sweet-flowing fount
Of Cenchreae and the Lernéan well;
While close upon me Argus, born of earth,
Savage and sleepless trailed, his wakeful eyes
Fixed on my track. And though a sudden fate
Him overmastered, yet this stinging fly
Still with his lash pursues from land to land.—
Such is my tale; and now if in thy wit
It lies to prophesy what toils remain,

So say, nor by false pitying speech misguide;
For glozing words I deem the worst disease.

CH. [*singing*]: Oh strange!   Oh, more than incredible!
Never I thought such words
Surpassing the wildest belief
Should enter my ears, such a tale
Of horror and woe and calamity.
I am stung to the soul, and compassion
Benumbs my heart.   O Fate!
Alas, O Fate!   I shudder
Beholding the lot of this maiden.

PR.: You are quick to lament and very prone to fear.   Yet wait a
little till you have heard what remains.

LE.: Speak, tell us all; to the sick it is sweet to know betimes what
awaits them of pain.

PR.: Lightly I granted your former request, for you desired first to
hear from her lips the story of her conflict; hear now the evils that
Hera hath still in store for this maiden; — and do you, O daughter
of Inachus, take my words to your heart that you may know the
goal of your wanderings. — Turn first toward the rising sun, and
thitherward proceeding over unploughed fields you will reach the
nomad Scythians, a people of mighty archers, who in their wicker-
woven houses dwell aloft on smooth-rolling wagons.   Approach
not these, but pass on through the land, keeping ever near to the
surf-beaten shores of the Euxine.   To the left dwell the Chalybes,
famous workers of iron; and of them you must beware, for they are
a savage race and regard not strangers.   Then will you come to the
River of Violence, fierce as its name and treacherous to ford; cross
not over it until you have reached the Caucasus, highest of mountains, where the river pours out its fury over the brows of the cliffs.
Here over the star-neighbouring summits you must toil and turn
to the southern path: so in time you will reach the host of the
Amazons, ever hostile to men, who one day shall inhabit Themi-
scyra on the Thermodon, where Salmydessus opens upon the sea
her ravenous jaws, a terror to strange sailors, a cruel step-dame to
ships.   Gladly the Amazons will guide thee on thy way.   And thou
wilt come to the Cimmerian isthmus by the narrow gateway of the
lake; and leaving this with brave heart thou wilt cross over the
Maeotic strait, which ever after in memorial of thy crossing men
shall call the Bosporus, the fording of the heifer.   Thus thou wilt
abandon the plain of Europe and venture on the continent of Asia.
— Now doth not the tyrant of the gods seem to you altogether
violent?   Behold how this god, desiring to mingle with a mortal
woman, hath imposed on her these wanderings. — Thou hast met,
O maiden, a bitter claimant for thy favour; and the words thou
hast heard are not even the prelude to what must follow.

IO: Alas, for me!

PR.: Once more you cry out and groan; what will you do when you have learned the troubles that remain?

LE.: Nay, have you calamities still to recount?

PR.: As it were a stormy sea of lamentable woe.

IO: What profit have I in life? Why do I not hurl myself out of hand from this rude precipice, that broken on the plain below I may have speedy respite from my troubles? It were better to die once for all than to drag out my lingering days in anguish.

PR.: How hardly would you endure my struggles, for death that would release me from my woes is denied me by Destiny. Now there is no goal before me of my conflict until Zeus is thrown from his supremacy.

IO: And shall Zeus ever fall from power?

PR.: You would rejoice, I think, to see his overthrow.

IO: Why should I not, who am abused by Zeus?

PR.: You may learn from me that your wish is truth.

IO: Who shall despoil him of the tyrant's sceptre?

PR.: He shall himself despoil by his own folly.

IO: How may it be? Speak, if there is no harm.

PR.: An ill-fated espousal shall work him grief.

IO: A spouse divine or human? tell if thou mayst.

PR.: What is it to thee? I may not speak her name.

IO: His bride shall drag him from the throne?

PR.: A son she shall bear, mightier than his father.*

IO: Hath he no refuge from this doom?

PR.: There is none, except I be loosed from my bonds.

IO: Who is to loose thee against the will of Zeus?

PR.: Thy own children's child must do the deed.†

IO: What sayest thou? my son shall end thy evils?

PR.: The third after the tenth generation.

IO: Thy oracle is dark to my understanding.

PR.: Pass it by; thy own ill fate is involved therein.

IO: The boon is offered, and straightway thou withdrawest it.

PR.: I grant thee the knowledge of either of two desires.

IO: Tell me the twain, and let me choose.

PR.: 'Tis done; choose whether I tell thee plainly of thy coming tribulations or of him who is to deliver me.

LE.: Yet rather bestow the one favour on her and the other on me, and be not chary of your words. To her set forth her future wanderings, and to me your deliverer, as I long to hear.

PR.: Your eagerness compels me, and I will relate all you ask. To you first, Io, I will proclaim trials of wandering, and do you record them on the tablets of your brain. — When you have crossed the tide that bounds two continents, then toward the flaming sun-trodden regions of the dawn pass on beyond the surge of the sea till

* The reference is to the son whom Thetis will bear if she consummates her marriage with Zeus. This secret knowledge constitutes Prometheus' only defence against Zeus.
† This refers to Heracles.

you reach the Gorgonean plains of Cisthene, the home of the Graeae, the three daughters of Phorcys, ancient virgins, possessing among them but one eye and one tooth, upon whom neither the sun looks down with his beams, nor ever the moon by night. And near by are the three other sisters, the winged, snake-haired, man-hating Gorgons, upon whom no mortal may look and live. Such wardens guard that land. Yet hear another spectacle of dread: beware the sharp-beaked hounds of Zeus that never bark, the griffins, and beware the one-eyed Arimaspian host of riders who dwell by the gold-washing tide of Pluto's stream; approach them not. And you will come to a far-off land, a swarthy people, who live by the fountain of the sun and Aethiopia's river. Follow its banks until you arrive at the Cataract where from the Bybline hills the Nile pours out its waters sweet and worshipful. This stream will guide you to the great Nilotic delta, where at the last fate bids you and your children, Io, establish your far-off home. Now if my speech seems stammering and hard to understand, still question me and be advised; for there is more leisure to me than I could wish.

ᴄʜ.: If anything remains untold of her life of weary wanderings, now recount it to her, but if all is said, then grant us the favour we beg. You have not forgotten it.

ᴘʀ.: She has heard her journeyings to the end; yet that she may know my words are not spoken in vain, I will relate her toils before coming hither, and this shall be a witness to the truth of my prophecy. I will pass over the greater part of the tale, and come to the end of your wanderings. For thus you came at last to the Molossian plains and Dodona with its lofty ridges, where is the oracle and home of Thesprotian Zeus and that strange portent of the talking oaks which in language clear and void of riddles addressed you as the renowned future spouse of Zeus, and the memory of this must still speak in your breast. From thence, urged on by frenzy, you rushed by the sea-shore path to the great gulf of Rhea, and back returned like a vessel tempest-tost from port. Now no longer the gulf shall be known by its old name, but shall be called the Ionian Sea, as a memorial to all men of your journeying. This knowledge is a sign to you of my understanding, that it discerns more than meets the eye. — The rest I tell to you, daughters of Oceanus, and to her together, returning again to the track of my former tale. There is a city, Canobus, standing on the verge of the land at the very mouth and silted bar of the Nile, where at the last Zeus shall restore you to your mind with but the stroke and gentle touching of his hand. There you shall bear a child to Zeus, the swarthy Epaphus, "Touch-born," who shall gather as lord the fruit of all the valley of the broad-flowing Nile. The fourth generation after him, a band of fifty sisters * shall return perforce to Argos, to flee the courtship of their fifty cousins. And these, like hawks that follow hard upon a flock of doves, shall pursue the maidens, seeking marriage ill to

* The Danaids.

seek, for God shall grudge them the sweet pleasure of that love.
In the Pelasgian land the maidens shall find a home, when in the
watches of the night with deed of murderous revenge they, women
as they are, have slain their suitors, each plunging her deadly blade
into her new lord's throat — so might the Queen of Love appear
to my foes! Yet longing shall soothe one maiden's heart to spare
her fellow, and blunt the edge of her resolve, for of the twain it
will please her rather to be called timid than bloodthirsty. And
from her a royal race shall spring in Argos — time fails to tell the
whole — and a mighty man of valour, renowned with the bow, who
shall deliver me from these toils. All this my ancient mother, the
Titan Themis, foretold to me in an oracle; but how it shall come
to pass needs yet many words to relate, and the hearing would profit
you nothing.

    IO [*chanting*]: Eleleu! eleleu!
            Once more the spasm, the madness
            Smiteth my brain as a fire.
            I am stung by the pest, I am pierced
            With a dart never forged in the fire;
            My seated heart at my ribs
            Doth knock, and my straining eyes
            Revolve in their orbs; I am borne
            As a vessel is lashed by the tempest;
            My tongue hath broke its control,
            And my turbid words beat madly
            In billows of horror and woe.
            [IO *departs, as the* CHORUS *begins its song.*]

                                                strophe

    CH.: Wise among mortals I count him
            Who weighed this truth in his mind
            And divulged it: better the union
            Of equal with equal in wedlock.
            How shall the toiler, the craftsman,
            Be lifted in idle desire
            To mate with the glory of wealth
            Or the honour of noble descent?

                                                antistrophe

            Never, O kindly powers,
            Behold me the partner of Zeus;
            Never may one of the gods
            Descend from the skies for my love.
            Horror sufficient I feel
            For Io, the virgin, the outcast,
            Who hateth her lord and is driven
            By Hera to wander forlorn.

epode

Wedlock if equal I fear not;
But oh! may never a god
With love's irresistible glance
Constrain me!   Hard were the battle,
For who were I to resist him?
What way of escape would remain
From the counsel and purpose of Zeus?

PR.: Yet shall Zeus himself, the stubborn of soul, be humbled, for the union he purposes in his heart shall hurl him to outer darkness from his throne of supremacy.   Then at last the curse of his father Cronos shall be fulfilled to the uttermost, the curse that he swore when thrown from his ancient seat.   All this I know and how the curse shall work, and I only of the gods may point out a refuge from these disasters.   Therefore let him sit boldly now, trusting in his thunders that reverberate through the sky, and wielding fiery darts in his hands; they shall avail him naught nor save him from falling in ruin unendurable.   A mighty wrestler he is preparing against himself, an irresistible champion, who shall search out a fire more terrible than his lightning and a roaring noise to drown his thunder, and who shall break in pieces that sea-scourge and shaker of the earth, the trident-spear of Poseidon.   And Zeus, broken on this rock, shall learn how far apart it is to rule and be a slave.

LE.: Thy bodings against Zeus are but thy own desire.

PR.: I speak what is to be, and that is my desire.

LE.: Must we look for one to reign above Zeus?

PR.: Troubles more grievous to bear shall bow his neck.

LE.: Thou tremblest not to utter such words?

PR.: Why should I tremble whose fate is not to die?

LE.: Yet he might still harder torments inflict.

PR.: So let him; I am prepared for all.

LE.: Yet the wise bow down to Nemesis.

PR.: So worship, flatter, adore the ruler of the day; but I have no thought in my heart for Zeus.   Let him act, let him reign his little while as he will; for he shall not long rule over the gods. — [HERMES *enters.*] But I see here the lackey of Zeus, the servant of the new tyrant.   No doubt he has come with tidings of some new device.

HER.: Thee, the wise, the bitter beyond bitterness, the thief of fire, who hast revolted against the gods and betrayed their honours to thy creatures of a day, — to thee I speak.   The father bids thee declare the chance of wedlock thou vauntest, that shall bereave him of his sceptre; and this thou art to state clearly and not involve thy speech in riddles.   Put me not, O Prometheus, to double my journey; thou seest that Zeus is not appeased by dubious words.

PR.: Haughty thy speech and swollen with pride, as becomes a servant of the gods.   Ye are but young in tyranny, and think to inhabit a citadel unassaulted of grief; yet have I not seen two tyrants fall therefrom? And third I shall behold this present lord cast down in utter ruin. Do I seem to cower and quail before these new gods? Hardly, I think; there is no fear in me. But do you trudge back the road you came; for all your pains of asking are in vain.

HER.: Yet forget not such insolence has brought you to this pass of evil.

PR.: Be assured I would not barter my hard lot for your menial service.

HER.: It is better no doubt to serve this rock than to be the trusted herald of Zeus.

PR.: I but answered insult with insult.

HER.: You seem to glory in your present state.

PR.: What, I? So might I see my enemies glory, — and you among them!

HER.: You blame me too for your calamities?

PR.: In simple sooth I count all the gods my foes, who requited my benefits with injuries.

HER.: Your madness I see is a deep-rooted disease.

PR.: If hatred of foes is madness, I am mad.

HER.: Who could endure you in prosperity!

PR.: Alas, prosperity!

HER.: Zeus has not learned that cry, alas.

PR.: Time, growing ever older, teaches all things.

HER.: It has not taught you wisdom yet.

PR.: Else I should hardly talk with you, a slave.

HER.: It seems you will not answer the father's demands.

PR.: My debt of gratitude I fain would pay.

HER.: You have reviled and scorned me as a child.

PR. [in supreme anger]: And are you not simpler than a child if you hope to learn aught from me? There is no torment or contrivance in the power of Zeus to wring this utterance from me, except these bonds are loosened. Therefore let him hurl upon me the red levin, let him confound the reeling world with tempest of white-feathered snow and subterranean thunders; none of these things shall extort from me the knowledge that may ward off his overthrow.

HER.: Consider if you shall profit by this.

PR.: I have considered long since and formed my plan.

HER.: Yet subdue thyself in time, rash fool, to regard thy present ills in wisdom.

PR.: You vex me to no purpose, as one might waste his words on a wave of the sea. Dream not that ever in fear of Zeus's will I shall grow woman-hearted, and raise my supine hands in supplication to my hated foe for deliverance from these bonds; — it is not in my nature.

HER.: Though I speak much, my words will all be wasted; my appeals have no power to soften and appease your heart, but champing the bit like a new-yoked colt you are restive and struggle against the reins. There is no strength of wisdom in your savage mood, for mere self-will in a foolish man avails nothing. And consider, if thou disregard my words, what a tempest of evils, wave on wave inevitable, shall break upon thee; for first the father will smite this rugged cliff with rending of thunder and hurtling fires, and in its harsh and rock-ribbed embrace enfold thy hidden body. Then after a weary age of years once more thou shalt come forth to the light; and the winged hound of Zeus, the ravening eagle, with savage greed shall tear the mighty ruin of thy limbs, feasting all day an uninvited guest, and glutting his maw on thy black-gnawed liver. Neither look for any respite from this agony, unless some god shall appear as a voluntary successor to thy toils, and of his own free will goeth down to sunless Hades and the dark depths of Tartarus. Therefore take heed; for my words are not vain boasting, but all too truly spoken. The lips of Zeus know not to utter falsehood, but all that he saith he will accomplish. Do thou consider and reflect, and regard not vaunting pride as better than wise counsel.

LE.: To us Hermes seems to utter words not untimely; for he admonishes you to abandon vaunting pride and seek for wise counsel. Obey him; it is shameful for a wise man to go astray.

PR. [*chanting*]: All this ere he uttered his message
            I knew; yet feel no dishonour
            In suffering wrong from a foe.
            Ay, let the lightning be launched
            With curled and forkèd flame
            On my head; let the air confounded
            Shudder with thunderous peals
            And convulsion of raging winds;
            Let tempests beat on the earth
            Till her rooted foundations tremble;
            The boisterous surge of the sea
            Leap up to mingle its crest
            With the stars eclipsed in their orbs;
            Let the whirling blasts of Necessity
            Seize on my body and hurl it
            Down to the darkness of Tartarus, —
            Yet all he shall not destroy me!
HER.: I hear the delirious cries
            Of a mind unhinged; his prayer
            Is frenzy, and all that he doth. —
            But ye who condole with his anguish,
            Be quick, I implore, and depart,
            Ere the deafening roar of the thunder
            Daze and bewilder your senses.
CH.: Waste not thy breath in vain warnings,
            Nor utter a word unendurable;
            For who art thou in the pathway
            Of evil and falsehood to guide me?

Better I deem it to suffer
Whate'er he endures; for traitors
My soul abhorreth, their shame
I spew from my heart as a pest.

HER.: Yet remember my counsel in season,
And blame not your fortune when caught
In the snare of Disaster, nor cry
Unto Zeus that he throws you unwarned
Into sorrow.   Yourselves take the blame;
Foretaught and with eyes unveiled
You walk to be snared in the vast
And implicate net of Disaster.

[HERMES *goes out.   A storm bursts, with thunder and lightning.
The rocks are sundered;* PROMETHEUS *slowly sinks from sight, while
the* CHORUS *scatters to right and left.*]

PR.: Lo, in grim earnest the world
Is shaken, the roar of thunders
Reverberates, gleams the red levin,
And whirlwinds lick up the dust.
All the blasts of the winds leap out
And meet in tumultuous conflict,
Confounding the sea and the heavens.
'Tis Zeus who driveth his furies
To smite me with terror and madness.
O mother Earth all-honoured,
O Air revolving thy light
A common boon unto all,
Behold what wrongs I endure.

AGAMEMNON

Translated by E. D. A. Morshead

AGAMEMNON

[SCENE: — *Before the palace of* AGAMEMNON *in Argos. In front of the palace there are statues of the gods, and altars prepared for sacrifice. It is night. On the roof of the palace can be discerned a* WATCHMAN.]

WA.: I pray the gods to quit me of my toils,
　　To close the watch I keep, this livelong year;
　　For as a watch-dog lying, not at rest,
　　Propped on one arm, upon the palace-roof
　　Of Atreus' race, too long, too well I know
　　The starry conclave of the midnight sky,
　　Too well, the splendours of the firmament,
　　The lords of light, whose kingly aspect shows —
　　What time they set or climb the sky in turn —
　　The year's divisions, bringing frost or fire.

　　And now, as ever, am I set to mark
　　When shall stream up the glow of signal-flame,
　　The bale-fire bright, and tell its Trojan tale —
　　Troy town is ta'en: such issue holds in hope
　　She in whose woman's breast beats heart of man.*

　　Thus upon mine unrestful couch I lie,
　　Bathed with the dews of night, unvisited
　　By dreams — ah me! — for in the place of sleep
　　Stands Fear as my familiar, and repels
　　The soft repose that would mine eyelids seal.

　　And if at whiles, for the lost balm of sleep,
　　I medicine my soul with melody
　　Of trill or song — anon to tears I turn,
　　Wailing the woe that broods upon this home,
　　Not now by honour guided as of old.
　　But now at last fair fall the welcome hour
　　That sets me free, whene'er the thick night glow
　　With beacon-fire of hope deferred no more.
　　All hail!
　　[*A beacon-light is seen reddening the distant sky.*]
　　Fire of the night, that brings my spirit day,
　　Shedding on Argos light, and dance, and song,
　　Greetings to fortune, hail!

　　Let my loud summons ring within the ears
　　Of Agamemnon's queen, that she anon
　　Start from her couch and with a shrill voice cry
　　A joyous welcome to the beacon-blaze,

* Clytemnestra.

165

For Ilion's fall; such fiery message gleams
From yon high flame; and I, before the rest,
Will foot the lightsome measure of our joy;
For I can say, *My master's dice fell fair —*
Behold! the triple sice, the lucky flame!
Now be my lot to clasp, in loyal love,
The hand of him restored, who rules our home:
Home — but I say no more: upon my tongue
Treads hard the ox o' the adage.*

       Had it voice,
The home itself might soothliest tell its tale;
I, of set will, speak words the wise may learn,
To others, nought remember nor discern.

[*He withdraws. The* CHORUS OF ARGIVE ELDERS *enters, each leaning
on a staff. During their song* CLYTEMNESTRA *appears in the background, kindling the altars.*]
  CH. [*singing*]: Ten livelong years have rolled away,
    Since the twin lords of sceptred sway,
    By Zeus endowed with pride of place,
    The doughty chiefs of Atreus' race,
     Went forth of yore,
    To plead with Priam, face to face,
     Before the judgment-seat of War!

    A thousand ships from Argive land
    Put forth to bear the martial band,
    That with a spirit stern and strong
    Went out to right the kingdom's wrong —
    Pealed, as they went, the battle-song,
     Wild as the vultures' cry;
    When o'er the eyrie, soaring high,
    In wild bereavèd agony,
    Around, around, in airy rings,
    They wheel with oarage of their wings,
    But not the eyas-brood behold,
    That called them to the nest of old;
    But let Apollo from the sky,
    Or Pan, or Zeus, but hear the cry,
    The exile cry, the wail forlorn,
    Of birds from whom their home is torn —
    On those who wrought the rapine fell,
    Heaven sends the vengeful fiends of hell.

    Even so doth Zeus, the jealous lord
    And guardian of the hearth and board,
    Speed Atreus' sons, in vengeful ire,
    'Gainst Paris — sends them forth on fire,
    Her to buy back, in war and blood,

* A proverbial expression connoting complete silence.

Whom one did wed but many woo'd!
And many, many, by his will,
The last embrace of foes shall feel,
And many a knee in dust be bowed,
And splintered spears on shields ring loud,
Of Trojan and of Greek, before
That iron bridal-feast be o'er!
But as he willed 'tis ordered all,
And woes, by heaven ordained, must fall —
Unsoothed by tears or spilth of wine
Poured forth too late, the wrath divine
Glares vengeance on the flameless shrine.

And we in grey dishonoured eld,
Feeble of frame, unfit were held
To join the warrior array
That then went forth unto the fray:
And here at home we tarry, fain
Our feeble footsteps to sustain,
Each on his staff — so strength doth wane,
And turns to childishness again.
For while the sap of youth is green,
And, yet unripened, leaps within,
The young are weakly as the old,
And each alike unmeet to hold
The vantage post of war!
And ah! when flower and fruit are o'er,
   And on life's tree the leaves are sere,
   Age wendeth propped its journey drear,
As forceless as a child, as light
And fleeting as a dream of night
Lost in the garish day!
But thou, O child of Tyndareus,
   Queen Clytemnestra, speak! and say
   What messenger of joy to-day
Hath won thine ear? what welcome news,
That thus in sacrificial wise
E'en to the city's boundaries
Thou biddest altar-fires arise?
Each god who doth our city guard,
And keeps o'er Argos watch and ward
   From heaven above, from earth below —
The mighty lords who rule the skies,
The market's lesser deities,
   To each and all the altars glow,
Piled for the sacrifice!
And here and there, anear, afar,
Streams skyward many a beacon-star,
Conjur'd and charm'd and kindled well

By pure oil's soft and guileless spell,
Hid now no more
Within the palace' secret store.

O queen, we pray thee, whatsoe'er,
    Known unto thee, were well revealed,
That thou wilt trust it to our ear,
    And bid our anxious heart be healed!
That waneth now unto despair —
Now, waxing to a presage fair,
Dawns, from the altar, Hope — to scare
From our rent hearts the vulture Care.

strophe 1

List! for the power is mine, to chant on high
    The chiefs' emprise, the strength that omens gave!
List! on my soul breathes yet a harmony,
    From realms of ageless powers, and strong to save!

How brother kings, twin lords of one command,
    Led forth the youth of Hellas in their flower,
Urged on their way, with vengeful spear and brand,
    By warrior-birds, that watched the parting hour.

Go forth to Troy, the eagles seemed to cry —
    And the sea-kings obeyed the sky-kings' word,
When on the right they soared across the sky,
    And one was black, one bore a white tail barred.

High o'er the palace were they seen to soar,
    Then lit in sight of all, and rent and tare,
Far from the fields that she should range no more,
    Big with her unborn brood, a mother-hare.

(Ah woe and well-a-day! but be the issue fair!)

antistrophe 1

And one beheld, the soldier-prophet true,
    And the two chiefs, unlike of soul and will,
In the twy-coloured eagles straight he knew,
    And spake the omen forth, for good and ill.

Go forth, he cried, *and Priam's town shall fall.
    Yet long the time shall be; and flock and herd,
The people's wealth, that roam before the wall,
    Shall force hew down, when Fate shall give the word.*

*But O beware! lest wrath in Heaven abide,
    To dim the glowing battle-forge once more,
And mar the mighty curb of Trojan pride,
    The steel of vengeance, welded as for war!*

For virgin Artemis bears jealous hate
  Against the royal house, the eagle-pair,
Who rend the unborn brood, insatiate —
  Yea, loathes their banquet on the quivering hare.

(Ah woe and well-a-day! but be the issue fair!)

epode

For well she loves — the goddess kind and mild —
  The tender new-born cubs of lions bold,
Too weak to range — and well the sucking child
  Of every beast that roams by wood and wold.

So to the Lord of Heaven she prayeth still,
  "Nay, if it must be, be the omen true!
Yet do the visioned eagles presage ill;
  The end be well, but crossed with evil too!"

Healer Apollo! be her wrath controll'd,
  Nor weave the long delay of thwarting gales,
To war against the Danaans and withhold
  From the free ocean-waves their eager sails!

She craves, alas! to see a second life
  Shed forth, a curst unhallowed sacrifice —
'Twixt wedded souls, artificer of strife,
  And hate that knows not fear, and fell device.

At home there tarries like a lurking snake,
  Biding its time, a wrath unreconciled,
A wily watcher, passionate to slake,
  In blood, resentment for a murdered child.

Such was the mighty warning, pealed of yore —
  Amid good tidings, such the word of fear,
What time the fateful eagles hovered o'er
  The kings, and Calchas read the omen clear.

(In strains like his, once more,
Sing woe and well-a-day! but be the issue fair!)

strophe 2

Zeus — if to The Unknown
  That name of many names seem good —
Zeus, upon Thee I call.
  Thro' the mind's every road
I passed, but vain are all,
Save that which names thee Zeus, the Highest One,
  Were it but mine to cast away the load,
The weary load, that weighs my spirit down.

antistrophe 2

He that was Lord of old,
In full-blown pride of place and valour bold,
   Hath fallen and is gone, even as an old tale told!
   And he that next held sway,
   By stronger grasp o'erthrown
   Hath pass'd away!*
And whoso now shall bid the triumph-chant arise
   To Zeus, and Zeus alone,
He shall be found the truly wise.

strophe 3

'Tis Zeus alone who shows the perfect way
   Of knowledge: He hath ruled,
Men shall learn wisdom, by affliction schooled.

   In visions of the night, like dropping rain,
   Descend the many memories of pain
Before the spirit's sight: through tears and dole
   Comes wisdom o'er the unwilling soul —
   A boon, I wot, of all Divinity,
That holds its sacred throne in strength, above the sky!

antistrophe 3

And then the elder chief, at whose command
   The fleet of Greece was manned,
     Cast on the seer no word of hate,
     But veered before the sudden breath of Fate —

   Ah, weary while! for, ere they put forth sail,
   Did every store, each minish'd vessel, fail,
     While all the Achaean host
     At Aulis anchored lay,
   Looking across to Chalcis and the coast
   Where refluent waters welter, rock, and sway;

strophe 4

   And rife with ill delay
From northern Strymon blew the thwarting blast —
   Mother of famine fell,
   That holds men wand'ring still
Far from the haven where they fain would be! —
   And pitiless did waste
Each ship and cable, rotting on the sea,
   And, doubling with delay each weary hour,
Withered with hope deferred th' Achaeans' warlike flower.

* Uranus and Cronus, predecessors of Zeus on the throne of heaven.

But when, for bitter storm, a deadlier relief,
 And heavier with ill to either chief,
Pleading the ire of Artemis, the seer avowed,
 The two Atreidae smote their sceptres on the plain,
 And, striving hard, could not their tears restrain!

antistrophe 4

And then the elder monarch spake aloud —
 Ill lot were mine, to disobey!
And ill, to smite my child, my household's love and pride!
To stain with virgin blood a father's hands, and slay
 My daughter, by the altar's side!
 'Twixt woe and woe I dwell —
I dare not like a recreant fly,
And leave the league of ships, and fail each true ally;
For rightfully they crave, with eager fiery mind,
The virgin's blood, shed forth to lull the adverse wind —
 God send the deed be well!

strophe 5

 Thus on his neck he took
 Fate's hard compelling yoke;
Then, in the counter-gale of will abhorr'd, accursed,
 To recklessness his shifting spirit veered —
 Alas! that Frenzy, first of ills and worst,
With evil craft men's souls to sin hath ever stirred!

 And so he steeled his heart — ah, well-a-day —
 Aiding a war for one false woman's sake,
  His child to slay,
 And with her spilt blood make
An offering, to speed the ships upon their way!

antistrophe 5

 Lusting for war, the bloody arbiters
Closed heart and ears, and would nor hear nor heed
  The girl-voice plead,
 Pity me, Father! nor her prayers,
  Nor tender, virgin years.

 So, when the chant of sacrifice was done,
 Her father bade the youthful priestly train
Raise her, like some poor kid, above the altar-stone,
 From where amid her robes she lay
  Sunk all in swoon away —
Bade them, as with the bit that mutely tames the steed,
 Her fair lips' speech refrain,
Lest she should speak a curse on Atreus' home and seed,

strophe 6

So, trailing on the earth her robe of saffron dye,
With one last piteous dart from her beseeching eye
  Those that should smite she smote —
Fair, silent, as a pictur'd form, but fain
To plead, *Is all forgot?*
How oft those halls of old,
Wherein my sire high feast did hold,
  Rang to the virginal soft strain,
    When I, a stainless child,
  Sang from pure lips and undefiled,
    Sang of my sire, and all
His honoured life, and how on him should fall
    Heaven's highest gift and gain!

antistrophe 6

And then — but I beheld not, nor can tell,
  What further fate befel:
But this is sure, that Calchas' boding strain
  Can ne'er be void or vain.
This wage from Justice' hand do sufferers earn,
  The future to discern:
And yet — farewell, O secret of To-morrow!
  Fore-knowledge is fore-sorrow.
Clear with the clear beams of the morrow's sun,
  The future presseth on.
Now, let the house's tale, how dark soe'er,
  Find yet an issue fair! —
So prays the loyal, solitary band
  That guards the Apian land.

[*They turn to* CLYTEMNESTRA, *who leaves the altars and comes forward.*]

LEADER OF THE CHORUS:
    O queen, I come in reverence of thy sway —
    For, while the ruler's kingly seat is void,
    The loyal heart before his consort bends.
    Now — be it sure and certain news of good,
    Or the fair tidings of a flatt'ring hope,
    That bids thee spread the light from shrine to shrine,
    I, fain to hear, yet grudge not if thou hide.
CL.: As saith the adage, *From the womb of Night*
    Spring forth, with promise fair, the young child Light.
    Ay — fairer even than all hope my news —
    By Grecian hands is Priam's city ta'en!
LE.: What say'st thou? doubtful heart makes treach'rous ear.
CL.: Hear then again, and plainly — Troy is ours!
LE.: Thrills thro' my heart such joy as wakens tears.
CL.: Ay, thro' those tears thine eye looks loyalty.

LE.: But hast thou proof, to make assurance sure?
CL.: Go to; I have — unless the god has lied.
LE.: Hath some night-vision won thee to belief?
CL.: Out on all presage of a slumb'rous soul!
LE.: But wert thou cheered by Rumour's wingless word?
CL.: Peace — thou dost chide me as a credulous girl.
LE.: Say then, how long ago the city fell?
CL.: Even in this night that now brings forth the dawn.
LE.: Yet who so swift could speed the message here?
CL.: From Ida's top Hephaestus, lord of fire,
Sent forth his sign; and on, and ever on,
Beacon to beacon sped the courier-flame.
From Ida to the crag, that Hermes loves,
Of Lemnos; thence unto the steep sublime
Of Athos, throne of Zeus, the broad blaze flared.
Thence, raised aloft to shoot across the sea,
The moving light, rejoicing in its strength,
Sped from the pyre of pine, and urged its way,
In golden glory, like some strange new sun,
Onward, and reached Macistus' watching heights.
There, with no dull delay nor heedless sleep,
The watcher sped the tidings on in turn,
Until the guard upon Messapius' peak
Saw the far flame gleam on Euripus' tide,
And from the high-piled heap of withered furze
Lit the new sign and bade the message on.
Then the strong light, far-flown and yet undimmed,
Shot thro' the sky above Asopus' plain,
Bright as the moon, and on Cithaeron's crag
Aroused another watch of flying fire.
And there the sentinels no whit disowned,
But sent redoubled on, the hest of flame —
Swift shot the light, above Gorgopis' bay,
To Aegiplanctus' mount, and bade the peak
Fail not the onward ordinance of fire.
And like a long beard streaming in the wind,
Full-fed with fuel, roared and rose the blaze,
And onward flaring, gleamed above the cape,
Beneath which shimmers the Saronic bay,
And thence leapt light unto Arachne's peak,
The mountain watch that looks upon our town.
Thence to th' Atreides' roof — in lineage fair,
A bright posterity of Ida's fire.
So sped from stage to stage, fulfilled in turn,
Flame after flame, along the course ordained,
And lo! the last to speed upon its way
Sights the end first, and glows unto the goal.
And Troy is ta'en, and by this sign my lord
Tells me the tale, and ye have learned my word.

LE.: To heaven, O queen, will I upraise new song:
But, wouldst thou speak once more, I fain would hear
From first to last the marvel of the tale.

CL.: Think you — this very morn — the Greeks in Troy,
And loud therein the voice of utter wail!
Within one cup pour vinegar and oil,
And look! unblent, unreconciled, they war.
So in the twofold issue of the strife
Mingle the victor's shout, the captives' moan.
For all the conquered whom the sword has spared
Cling weeping — some unto a brother slain,
Some childlike to a nursing father's form,
And wail the loved and lost, the while their neck
Bows down already 'neath the captive's chain.
And lo! the victors, now the fight is done,
Goaded by restless hunger, far and wide
Range all disordered thro' the town, to snatch
Such victual and such rest as chance may give
Within the captive halls that once were Troy —
Joyful to rid them of the frost and dew,
Wherein they couched upon the plain of old —
Joyful to sleep the gracious night all through,
Unsummoned of the watching sentinel.
Yet let them reverence well the city's gods,
The lords of Troy, tho' fallen, and her shrines;
So shall the spoilers not in turn be spoiled.
Yea, let no craving for forbidden gain
Bid conquerors yield before the darts of greed.
For we need yet, before the race be won,
Homewards, unharmed, to round the course once more.
For should the host wax wanton ere it come,
Then, tho' the sudden blow of fate be spared,
Yet in the sight of gods shall rise once more
The great wrong of the slain, to claim revenge.
Now, hearing from this woman's mouth of mine,
The tale and eke its warning, pray with me,
Luck sway the scale, with no uncertain poise,
For my fair hopes are changed to fairer joys.

LE.: A gracious word thy woman's lips have told,
Worthy a wise man's utterance, O my queen;
Now with clear trust in thy convincing tale
I set me to salute the gods with song,
Who bring us bliss to counterpoise our pain.
             [CLYTEMNESTRA *goes into the palace.*]

CH. [*singing*]: Zeus, Lord of heaven! and welcome night
Of victory, that hast our might
    With all the glories crowned!
On towers of Ilion, free no more,

Hast flung the mighty mesh of war,
  And closely girt them round,
Till neither warrior may 'scape,
Nor stripling lightly overleap
The trammels as they close, and close,
Till with the grip of doom our foes
  In slavery's coil are bound!

Zeus, Lord of hospitality,
In grateful awe I bend to thee —
  'Tis thou hast struck the blow!
  At Alexander, long ago,
  We marked thee bend thy vengeful bow,
But long and warily withhold
The eager shaft, which, uncontrolled
And loosed too soon or launched too high,
Had wandered bloodless through the sky.

strophe 1

Zeus, the high God! — whate'er be dim in doubt,
  This can our thought track out —
The blow that fells the sinner is of God,
  And as he wills, the rod
Of vengeance smiteth sore. One said of old,
  The gods list not to hold
A reckoning with him whose feet oppress
  The grace of holiness —
An impious word! for whenso'er the sire
  Breathed forth rebellious fire —
What time his household overflowed the measure
  Of bliss and health and treasure —
His children's children read the reckoning plain,
  At last, in tears and pain.
On me let weal that brings no woe be sent,
  And therewithal, content!
Who spurns the shrine of Right, nor wealth nor power
  Shall be to him a tower,
To guard him from the gulf: there lies his lot,
  Where all things are forgot.

antistrophe 1

Lust drives him on — lust, desperate and wild,
  Fate's sin-contriving child —
And cure is none; beyond concealment clear,
  Kindles sin's baleful glare.
As an ill coin beneath the wearing touch
  Betrays by stain and smutch
Its metal false — such is the sinful wight.
  Before, on pinions light,

Fair Pleasure flits, and lures him childlike on,
    While home and kin make moan
Beneath the grinding burden of his crime;
    Till, in the end of time,
Cast down of heaven, he pours forth fruitless prayer
    To powers that will not hear.

    And such did Paris come
    Unto Atreides' home,
And thence, with sin and shame his welcome to repay,
    Ravished the wife away —

strophe 2

And she, unto her country and her kin
Leaving the clash of shields and spears and arming ships,
And bearing unto Troy destruction for a dower,
    And overbold in sin,
 Went fleetly thro' the gates, at midnight hour.
    Oft from the prophets' lips
Moaned out the warning and the wail — Ah woe!
Woe for the home, the home! and for the chieftains, woe!
    Woe for the bride-bed, warm
Yet from the lovely limbs, the impress of the form
    Of her who loved her lord, awhile ago!
        And woe! for him who stands
Shamed, silent, unreproachful, stretching hands
    That find her not, and sees, yet will not see,
        That she is far away!
And his sad fancy, yearning o'er the sea,
        Shall summon and recall
Her wraith, once more to queen it in his hall.
        And sad with many memories,
The fair cold beauty of each sculptured face —
    And all to hatefulness is turned their grace,
Seen blankly by forlorn and hungering eyes!

antistrophe 2

    And when the night is deep,
Come visions, sweet and sad, and bearing pain
    Of hopings vain —
Void, void and vain, for scarce the sleeping sight
    Has seen its old delight,
When thro' the grasps of love that bid it stay
    It vanishes away
On silent wings that roam adown the ways of sleep.

    Such are the sights, the sorrows fell,
About our hearth — and worse, whereof I may not tell.
    But, all the wide town o'er,

Each home that sent its master far away
    From Hellas' shore,
Feels the keen thrill of heart, the pang of loss, to-day.
    For, truth to say,
The touch of bitter death is manifold!
Familiar was each face, and dear as life,
    That went unto the war,
But thither, whence a warrior went of old,
    Doth nought return —
Only a spear and sword, and ashes in an urn!

strophe 3

    For Ares, lord of strife,
Who doth the swaying scales of battle hold,
War's money-changer, giving dust for gold,
    Sends back, to hearts that held them dear,
Scant ash of warriors, wept with many a tear,
Light to the hand, but heavy to the soul;
    Yea, fills the light urn full
    With what survived the flame —
Death's dusty measure of a hero's frame!

Alas! one cries, *and yet alas again!*
Our chief is gone, the hero of the spear,
    And hath not left his peer!
Ah woe! another moans — *my spouse is slain,*
    The death of honour, rolled in dust and blood,
Slain for a woman's sin, a false wife's shame!
    Such muttered words of bitter mood
Rise against those who went forth to reclaim;
    Yea, jealous wrath creeps on against th' Atreides' name.

    And others, far beneath the Ilian wall,
Sleep their last sleep — the goodly chiefs and tall,
    Couched in the foeman's land, whereon they gave
Their breath, and lords of Troy, each in his Trojan grave.

antistrophe 3

    Therefore for each and all the city's breast
    Is heavy with a wrath supprest,
As deeply and deadly as a curse more loud
    Flung by the common crowd:
And, brooding deeply, doth my soul await
    Tidings of coming fate,
Buried as yet in darkness' womb.
For not forgetful is the high gods' doom
    Against the sons of carnage: all too long
Seems the unjust to prosper and be strong,
    Till the dark Furies come,

And smite with stern reversal all his home,
  Down into dim obstruction — he is gone,
And help and hope, among the lost, is none!

O'er him who vaunteth an exceeding fame,
  Impends a woe condign;
The vengeful bolt upon his eyes doth flame,
  Sped from the hand divine.
This bliss be mine, ungrudged of God, to feel —
  To tread no city to the dust,
  Nor see my own life thrust
Down to a slave's estate beneath another's heel!

epode

Behold, throughout the city wide
Have the swift feet of Rumour hied,
  Roused by the joyful flame:
But is the news they scatter, sooth?
Or haply do they give for truth
  Some cheat which heaven doth frame?
A child were he and all unwise,
  Who let his heart with joy be stirred.
To see the beacon-fires arise,
  And then, beneath some thwarting word,
  Sicken anon with hope deferred.
  The edge of woman's insight still
  Good news from true divideth ill;
Light rumours leap within the bound
Then fences female credence round,
But, lightly born, as lightly dies
The tale that springs of her surmise.

[*Several days are assumed to have elapsed.*]

LE.: Soon shall we know whereof the bale-fires tell,
  The beacons, kindled with transmitted flame;
  Whether, as well I deem, their tale is true,
  Or whether like some dream delusive came
  The welcome blaze but to befool our soul.
  For lo! I see a herald from the shore
  Draw hither, shadowed with the olive-wreath —
  And thirsty dust, twin-brother of the clay,
  Speaks plain of travel far and truthful news —
  No dumb surmise, nor tongue of flame in smoke,
  Fitfully kindled from the mountain pyre;
  But plainlier shall his voice say, *All is well,*
  Or — but away, forebodings adverse, now,
  And on fair promise fair fulfilment come!
  And whoso for the state prays otherwise,
  Himself reap harvest of his ill desire!

[*A* HERALD *enters. He is an advance messenger from* AGAMEMNON'S *forces, which have just landed.*]

HE.: O land of Argos, fatherland of mine!
  To thee at last, beneath the tenth year's sun,
  My feet return; the bark of my emprise,
  Tho' one by one hope's anchors broke away,
  Held by the last, and now rides safely here.
  Long, long my soul despaired to win, in death,
  Its longed-for rest within our Argive land:
  And now all hail, O earth, and hail to thee,
  New-risen sun! and hail our country's God,
  High-ruling Zeus, and thou, the Pythian lord,
  Whose arrows smote us once — smite thou no more!
  Was not thy wrath wreaked full upon our heads,
  O king Apollo, by Scamander's side?
  Turn thou, be turned, be saviour, healer, now!
  And hail, all gods who rule the street and mart
  And Hermes hail! my patron and my pride,
  Herald of heaven, and lord of heralds here!
  And Heroes, ye who sped us on our way —
  To one and all I cry, *Receive again*
  With grace such Argives as the spear has spared.

  Ah, home of royalty, belovèd halls,
  And solemn shrines, and gods that front the morn!
  Benign as erst, with sun-flushed aspect greet
  The king returning after many days.
  For as from night flash out the beams of day,
  So out of darkness dawns a light, a king,
  On you, on Argos — Agamemnon comes.
  Then hail and greet him well! such meed befits
  Him whose right hand hewed down the towers of Troy
  With the great axe of Zeus who righteth wrong —
  And smote the plain, smote down to nothingness
  Each altar, every shrine; and far and wide
  Dies from the whole land's face its offspring fair.
  Such mighty yoke of fate he set on Troy —
  Our lord and monarch, Atreus' elder son,
  And comes at last with blissful honour home;
  Highest of all who walk on earth to-day —
  Not Paris nor the city's self that paid
  Sin's price with him, can boast, *Whate'er befall,*
  The guerdon we have won outweighs it all.
  But at Fate's judgment-seat the robber stands
  Condemned of rapine, and his prey is torn
  Forth from his hands, and by his deed is reaped
  A bloody harvest of his home and land
  Gone down to death, and for his guilt and lust
  His father's race pays double in the dust.

LE.: Hail, herald of the Greeks, new-come from war.

HE.: All hail! not death itself can fright me now.

LE.: Was thine heart wrung with longing for thy land?

HE.: So that this joy doth brim mine eyes with tears.

LE.: On you too then this sweet distress did fall —

HE.: How say'st thou? make me master of thy word.

LE.: You longed for us who pined for you again.

HE.: Craved the land us who craved it, love for love?

LE.: Yea, till my brooding heart moaned out with pain.

HE.: Whence thy despair, that mars the army's joy?

LE.: *Sole cure of wrong is silence,* saith the saw.

HE.: Thy kings afar, couldst thou fear other men?

LE.: Death had been sweet, as thou didst say but now.

HE.: 'Tis true; Fate smiles at last.   Throughout our toil,
These many years, some chances issued fair,
And some, I wot, were chequered with a curse.
But who, on earth, hath won the bliss of heaven,
Thro' time's whole tenor an unbroken weal?
I could a tale unfold of toiling oars,
Ill rest, scant landings on a shore rock-strewn,
All pains, all sorrows, for our daily doom.
And worse and hatefuller our woes on land;
For where we couched, close by the foeman's wall,
The river-plain was ever dank with dews,
Dropped from the sky, exuded from the earth,
A curse that clung unto our sodden garb,
And hair as horrent as a wild beast's fell.
Why tell the woes of winter, when the birds
Lay stark and stiff, so stern was Ida's snow?
Or summer's scorch, what time the stirless wave
Sank to its sleep beneath the noon-day sun?
Why mourn old woes? their pain has passed away;
And passed away, from those who fell, all care,
For evermore, to rise and live again.
Why sum the count of death, and render thanks
For life by moaning over fate malign?
Farewell, a long farewell to all our woes!
To us, the remnant of the host of Greece,
Comes weal beyond all counterpoise of woe;
Thus boast we rightfully to yonder sun,
Like him far-fleeted over sea and land.
The Argive host prevailed to conquer Troy,
And in the temples of the gods of Greece
Hung up these spoils, a shining sign of Time.
Let those who learn this legend bless aright
The city and its chieftains, and repay
The meed of gratitude to Zeus who willed
And wrought the deed.   So stands the tale fulfilled.

LE.: Thy words o'erbear my doubt: for news of good,

> The ear of age hath ever youth enow:
> But those within and Clytemnestra's self
> Would fain hear all; glad thou their ears and mine.
>
>   [CLYTEMNESTRA *enters from the palace.*]

CL.: That night, when first the fiery courier came,
In sign that Troy is ta'en and razed to earth,
So wild a cry of joy my lips gave out,
That I was chidden — *Hath the beacon watch*
Made sure unto thy soul the sack of Troy?
A very woman thou, whose heart leaps light
At wandering rumours! — and with words like these
They showed me how I strayed, misled of hope.
Yet on each shrine I set the sacrifice,
And, in the strain they held for feminine,
Went heralds thro' the city, to and fro,
With voice of loud proclaim, announcing joy;
And in each fane they lit and quenched with wine
The spicy perfumes fading in the flame.
All is fulfilled: I spare your longer tale —
The king himself anon shall tell me all.

Remains to think what honour best may greet
My lord, the majesty of Argos, home.
What day beams fairer on a woman's eyes
Than this, wheron she flings the portal wide,
To hail her lord, heaven-shielded, home from war?
This to my husband, that he tarry not,
But turn the city's longing into joy!
Yea, let him come, and coming may he find
A wife no other than he left her, true
And faithful as a watch-dog to his home,
His foemen's foe, in all her duties leal,
Trusty to keep for ten long years unmarred
The store whereon he set his master-seal.
Be steel deep-dyed, before ye look to see
Ill joy, ill fame, from other wight, in me!

HE.: 'Tis fairly said: thus speaks a noble dame,
Nor speaks amiss, when truth informs the boast.

        [CLYTEMNESTRA *withdraws again into the palace.*]

LE.: So has she spoken — be it yours to learn
By clear interpreters her specious word.
Turn to me, herald — tell me if anon
The second well-loved lord of Argos comes?
Hath Menelaus safely sped with you?

HE.: Alas — brief boon unto my friends it were,
To flatter them, for truth, with falsehoods fair!

LE.: Speak joy, if truth be joy, but truth, at worst —
Too plainly, truth and joy are here divorced.

HE.: The hero and his bark were rapt away

    Far from the Grecian fleet; 'tis truth I say.
LE.: Whether in all men's sight from Ilion borne,
    Or from the fleet by stress of weather torn?
HE.: Full on the mark thy shaft of speech doth light,
    And one short word hath told long woes aright.
LE.: But say, what now of him each comrade saith?
    What their forebodings, of his life or death?
HE.: Ask me no more: the truth is known to none,
    Save the earth-fostering, all-surveying Sun.
LE.: Say, by what doom the fleet of Greece was driven?
    How rose, how sank the storm, the wrath of heaven?
HE.: Nay, ill it were to mar with sorrow's tale
    The day of blissful news. The gods demand
    Thanksgiving sundered from solicitude.
    If one as herald came with rueful face
    To say, *The curse has fallen, and the host*
    Gone down to death; and one wide wound has reached
    The city's heart, and out of many homes
    Many are cast and consecrate to death,
    Beneath the double scourge, that Ares loves,
    The bloody pair, the fire and sword of doom —
    If such sore burden weighed upon my tongue,
    'Twere fit to speak such words as gladden fiends.
    But — coming as he comes who bringeth news
    Of safe return from toil, and issues fair,
    To men rejoicing in a weal restored —
    Dare I to dash good words with ill, and say
    How the gods' anger smote the Greeks in storm?
    For fire and sea, that erst held bitter feud,
    Now swore conspiracy and pledged their faith,
    Wasting the Argives worn with toil and war.
    Night and great horror of the rising wave
    Came o'er us, and the blasts that blow from Thrace
    Clashed ship with ship, and some with plunging prow
    Thro' scudding drifts of spray and raving storm
    Vanished, as strays by some ill shepherd driven.
    And when at length the sun rose bright, we saw
    Th' Aegaean sea-field flecked with flowers of death,
    Corpses of Grecian men and shattered hulls.
    For us indeed, some god, as well I deem,
    No human power, laid hand upon our helm,
    Snatched us or prayed us from the powers of air,
    And brought our bark thro' all, unharmed in hull:
    And saving Fortune sat and steered us fair,
    So that no surge should gulf us deep in brine,
    Nor grind our keel upon a rocky shore.
    So 'scaped we death that lurks beneath the sea,
    But, under day's white light, mistrustful all
    Of fortune's smile, we sat and brooded deep,

Shepherds forlorn of thoughts that wandered wild
O'er this new woe; for smitten was our host,
And lost as ashes scattered from the pyre.
Of whom if any draw his life-breath yet,
Be well assured, he deems of us as dead,
As we of him no other fate forebode.
But heaven save all! If Menelaus live,
He will not tarry, but will surely come:
Therefore if anywhere the high sun's ray
Descries him upon earth, preserved by Zeus,
Who wills not yet to wipe his race away,
Hope still there is that homeward he may wend.
Enough — thou hast the truth unto the end.

                          [*The* HERALD *departs.*]

                                             strophe 1

CH. [*singing*]: Say, from whose lips the presage fell?
       Who read the future all too well,
          And named her, in her natal hour,
          Helen, the bride with war for dower?
       'Twas one of the Invisible,
          Guiding his tongue with prescient power.
       On fleet, and host, and citadel,
          War, sprung from her, and death did lour,
       When from the bride-bed's fine-spun veil
       She to the Zephyr spread her sail.
       Strong blew the breeze — the surge closed o'er
       The cloven track of keel and oar,
          But while she fled, there drove along,
          Fast in her wake, a mighty throng —
       Athirst for blood, athirst for war,
          Forward in fell pursuit they sprung,
       Then leapt on Simois' bank ashore,
          The leafy coppices among —
       No rangers, they, of wood and field,
       But huntsmen of the sword and shield.

                                          antistrophe 1

       Heaven's jealousy, that works its will,
       Sped thus on Troy its destined ill,
          Well named, at once, the Bride and Bane;
          And loud rang out the bridal strain;
       But they to whom that song befell
          Did turn anon to tears again;
       Zeus tarries, but avenges still
          The husband's wrong, the household's stain!
       He, the hearth's lord, brooks not to see
       Its outraged hospitality.

Even now, and in far other tone,
Troy chants her dirge of mighty moan,
  Woe upon Paris, woe and hate!
  Who wooed his country's doom for mate —
This is the burthen of the groan,
  Wherewith she wails disconsolate
The blood, so many of her own
  Have poured in vain, to fend her fate;
Troy! thou hast fed and freed to roam
A lion-cub within thy home!

strophe 2

A suckling creature, newly ta'en
From mother's teat, still fully fain
  Of nursing care; and oft caressed,
  Within the arms, upon the breast,
Even as an infant, has it lain;
  Or fawns and licks, by hunger pressed,
The hand that will assuage its pain;
  In life's young dawn, a well-loved guest,
A fondling for the children's play,
A joy unto the old and grey.

antistrophe 2

But waxing time and growth betrays
The blood-thirst of the lion-race,
  And, for the house's fostering care,
  Unbidden all, it revels there,
And bloody recompense repays —
  Rent flesh of kine, its talons tare:
A mighty beast, that slays, and slays,
  And mars with blood the household fair,
A God-sent pest invincible,
A minister of fate and hell.

strophe 3

Even so to Ilion's city came by stealth
  A spirit as of windless seas and skies,
A gentle phantom-form of joy and wealth,
  With love's soft arrows speeding from its eyes —
Love's rose, whose thorn doth pierce the soul in subtle wise.

Ah, well-a-day! the bitter bridal-bed,
  When the fair mischief lay by Paris' side!
What curse on palace and on people sped
  With her, the Fury sent on Priam's pride,
By angered Zeus! what tears of many a widowed bride!

antistrophe 3

Long, long ago to mortals this was told,
  How sweet security and blissful state
Have curses for their children — so men hold —
  And for the man of all-too prosperous fate
Springs from a bitter seed some woe insatiate.

Alone, alone, I deem far otherwise;
  Not bliss nor wealth it is, but impious deed,
From which that after-growth of ill doth rise!
  Woe springs from wrong, the plant is like the seed —
While Right, in honour's house, doth its own likeness breed.

strophe 4

Some past impiety, some grey old crime,
  Breeds the young curse, that wantons in our ill,
Early or late, when haps th' appointed time —
  And out of light brings power of darkness still,
A master-fiend, a foe, unseen, invincible;

A pride accursed, that broods upon the race
  And home in which dark Atè holds her sway —
Sin's child and Woe's, that wears its parents' face;

antistrophe 4

While Right in smoky cribs shines clear as day,
And decks with weal his life, who walks the righteous way.

From gilded halls, that hands polluted raise,
  Right turns away with proud averted eyes,
And of the wealth, men stamp amiss with praise,
  Heedless, to poorer, holier temples hies,
And to Fate's goal guides all, in its appointed wise.

[AGAMEMNON *enters, riding in a chariot and accompanied by a great
procession.* CASSANDRA *follows in another chariot. The* CHORUS *sings
its welcome.*]

                Hail to thee, chief of Atreus' race,
                Returning proud from Troy subdued!
                How shall I greet thy conquering face?
                How nor a fulsome praise obtrude,
                Nor stint the meed of gratitude?
                For mortal men who fall to ill
                Take little heed of open truth,
                But seek unto its semblance still:
                The show of weeping and of ruth
                To the forlorn will all men pay,
                But, of the grief their eyes display,
                Nought to the heart doth pierce its way.

And, with the joyous, they beguile
Their lips unto a feignèd smile,
And force a joy, unfelt the while;
But he who as a shepherd wise
Doth know his flock, can ne'er misread
Truth in the falsehood of his eyes,
Who veils beneath a kindly guise
    A lukewarm love in deed.
And thou, our leader — when of yore
Thou badest Greece go forth to war
For Helen's sake — I dare avow
That then I held thee not as now;
That to my vision thou didst seem
Dyed in the hues of disesteem.
I held thee for a pilot ill,
And reckless, of thy proper will,
Endowing others doomed to die
With vain and forced audacity!
Now from my heart, ungrudgingly,
To those that wrought, this word be said —
Well fall the labour ye have sped —
Let time and search, O king, declare
What men within thy city's bound
Were loyal to the kingdom's care,
    And who were faithless found.

AG. [*still standing in the chariot*]: First, as is meet, a king's All-hail
    be said
To Argos, and the gods that guard the land —
Gods who with me availed to speed us home,
With me availed to wring from Priam's town
The due of justice. In the court of heaven
The gods in conclave sat and judged the cause,
Not from a pleader's tongue, and at the close,
Unanimous into the urn of doom
This sentence gave, *On Ilion and her men,*
Death: and where hope drew nigh to pardon's urn
No hand there was to cast a vote therein.
And still the smoke of fallen Ilion
Rises in sight of all men, and the flame
Of Atè's hecatomb is living yet,
And where the towers in dusty ashes sink,
Rise the rich fumes of pomp and wealth consumed.
For this must all men pay unto the gods
The meed of mindful hearts and gratitude:
For by our hands the meshes of revenge
Closed on the prey, and for one woman's sake
Troy trodden by the Argive monster lies —
The foal, the shielded band that leapt the wall,
What time with autumn sank the Pleiades.

Yea, o'er the fencing wall a lion sprang
Ravening, and lapped his fill of blood of kings.

Such prelude spoken to the gods in full,
To you I turn, and to the hidden thing
Whereof ye spake but now: and in that thought
I am as you, and what ye say, say I.
For few are they who have such inborn grace,
As to look up with love, and envy not,
When stands another on the height of weal.
Deep in his heart, whom jealousy hath seized,
Her poison lurking doth enhance his load;
For now beneath his proper woes he chafes,
And sighs withal to see another's weal.

I speak not idly, but from knowledge sure —
There be who vaunt an utter loyalty,
That is but as the ghost of friendship dead,
A shadow in a glass, of faith gone by.
One only — he who went reluctant forth
Across the seas with me — Odysseus — he
Was loyal unto me with strength and will,
A trusty trace-horse bound unto my car.
Thus — be he yet beneath the light of day,
Or dead, as well I fear — I speak his praise.

Lastly, whate'er be due to men or gods,
With joint debate, in public council held,
We will decide, and warily contrive
That all which now is well may so abide:
For that which haply needs the healer's art,
That will we medicine, discerning well
If cautery or knife befit the time.

Now, to my palace and the shrines of home,
I will pass in, and greet you first and fair,
Ye gods, who bade me forth, and home again —
And long may Victory tarry in my train!

[CLYTEMNESTRA *enters from the palace, followed by maidens bearing crimson robes.*]

CL.: Old men of Argos, lieges of our realm,
Shame shall not bid me shrink lest ye should see
The love I bear my lord.   Such blushing fear
Dies at the last from hearts of human kind.
From mine own soul and from no alien lips,
I know and will reveal the life I bore,
Reluctant, through the lingering livelong years,
The while my lord beleaguered Ilion's wall.

First, that a wife sat sundered from her lord,
In widowed solitude, was utter woe —

And woe, to hear how rumour's many tongues
All boded evil — woe, when he who came
And he who followed spake of ill on ill,
Keening *Lost, lost, all lost!* thro' hall and bower.
Had this my husband met so many wounds,
As by a thousand channels rumour told,
No network e'er was full of holes as he.
Had he been slain, as oft as tidings came
That he was dead, he well might boast him now
A second Geryon of triple frame,
With triple robe of earth above him laid —
For that below, no matter — triply dead,
Dead by one death for every form he bore.
And thus distraught by news of wrath and woe,
Oft for self-slaughter had I slung the noose,
But others wrenched it from my neck away.
Hence haps it that Orestes, thine and mine,
The pledge and symbol of our wedded troth,
Stands not beside us now, as he should stand.
Nor marvel thou at this: he dwells with one
Who guards him loyally; 'tis Phocis' king,
Strophius, who warned me erst, *Bethink thee, queen,*
What woes of doubtful issue well may fall!
Thy lord in daily jeopardy at Troy,
While here a populace uncurbed may cry,
"Down with the council, down!" bethink thee too,
'Tis the world's way to set a harder heel
On fallen power.
                    For thy child's absence then
Such mine excuse, no wily afterthought.
For me, long since the gushing fount of tears
Is wept away; no drop is left to shed.
Dim are the eyes that ever watched till dawn,
Weeping, the bale-fires, piled for thy return,
Night after night unkindled. If I slept,
Each sound — the tiny humming of a gnat,
Roused me again, again, from fitful dreams
Wherein I felt thee smitten, saw thee slain,
Thrice for each moment of mine hour of sleep.

All this I bore, and now, released from woe,
I hail my lord as watch-dog of a fold,
As saving stay-rope of a storm-tossed ship,
As column stout that holds the roof aloft,
As only child unto a sire bereaved,
As land beheld, past hope, by crews forlorn,
As sunshine fair when tempest's wrath is past,
As gushing spring to thirsty wayfarer.
So sweet it is to 'scape the press of pain.

With such salute I bid my husband hail!
Nor heaven be wroth therewith! for long and hard
I bore that ire of old.
              Sweet lord, step forth,
Step from thy car, I pray — nay, not on earth
Plant the proud foot, O king, that trod down Troy!
Women! why tarry ye, whose task it is
To spread your monarch's path with tapestry?
Swift, swift, with purple strew his passage fair,
That justice lead him to a home, at last,
He scarcely looked to see.
[*The attendant women spread the tapestry.*]
              For what remains,
Zeal unsubdued by sleep shall nerve my hand
To work as right and as the gods command.

AG. [*still in the chariot*]: Daughter of Leda, watcher o'er my home,
Thy greeting well befits mine absence long,
For late and hardly has it reached its end.
Know, that the praise which honour bids us crave,
Must come from others' lips, not from our own:
See too that not in fashion feminine
Thou make a warrior's pathway delicate;
Not unto me, as to some Eastern lord,
Bowing thyself to earth, make homage loud.
Strew not this purple that shall make each step
An arrogance; such pomp beseems the gods,
Not me. A mortal man to set his foot
On these rich dyes? I hold such pride in fear,
And bid thee honour me as man, not god.
Fear not — such footcloths and all gauds apart,
Loud from the trump of Fame my name is blown;
Best gift of heaven it is, in glory's hour,
To think thereon with soberness: and thou —
Bethink thee of the adage, *Call none blest
Till peaceful death have crowned a life of weal.*
'Tis said: I fain would fare unvexed by fear.
CL.: Nay, but unsay it — thwart not thou my will!
AG.: Know, I have said, and will not mar my word.
CL.: Was it fear made this meekness to the gods?
AG.: If cause be cause, 'tis mine for this resolve.
CL.: What, think'st thou, in thy place had Priam done?
AG.: He surely would have walked on broidered robes.
CL.: Then fear not thou the voice of human blame.
AG.: Yet mighty is the murmur of a crowd.
CL.: Shrink not from envy, appanage of bliss.
AG.: War is not woman's part, nor war of words.
CL.: Yet happy victors well may yield therein.
AG.: Dost crave for triumph in this petty strife?
CL.: Yield; of thy grace permit me to prevail!

AG.: Then, if thou wilt, let some one stoop to loose
       Swiftly these sandals, slaves beneath my foot;
       And stepping thus upon the sea's rich dye,
       I pray, *Let none among the gods look down*
       With jealous eye on me — reluctant all,
       To trample thus and mar a thing of price,
       Wasting the wealth of garments silver-worth.
       Enough hereof: and, for the stranger maid,
       Lead her within, but gently: God on high
       Looks graciously on him whom triumph's hour
       Has made not pitiless.   None willingly
       Wear the slave's yoke — and she, the prize and flower
       Of all we won, comes hither in my train,
       Gift of the army to its chief and lord.
       — Now, since in this my will bows down to thine,
       I will pass in on purples to my home.
       [*He descends from the chariot, and moves toward the palace.*]
CL.: A Sea there is — and who shall stay its springs?
       And deep within its breast, a mighty store,
       Precious as silver, of the purple dye,
       Whereby the dipped robe doth its tint renew.
       Enough of such, O king, within thy halls
       There lies, a store that cannot fail; but I —
       I would have gladly vowed unto the gods
       Cost of a thousand garments trodden thus,
       (Had once the oracle such gift required)
       Contriving ransom for thy life preserved.
       For while the stock is firm the foliage climbs,
       Spreading a shade, what time the dog-star glows;
       And thou, returning to thine hearth and home,
       Art as a genial warmth in winter hours,
       Or as a coolness, when the lord of heaven
       Mellows the juice within the bitter grape.
       Such boons and more doth bring into a home
       The present footstep of its proper lord.
       Zeus, Zeus, Fulfilment's lord! my vows fulfil,
       And whatsoe'er it be, work forth thy will!
                    [*She follows* AGAMEMNON *into the palace.*]

                                                    strophe 1

CH. [*singing*]: Wherefore for ever on the wings of fear
              Hovers a vision dread
          Before my boding heart? a strain,
          Unbidden and unwelcome, thrills mine ear,
              Oracular of pain.
          Not as of old upon my bosom's throne
              Sits Confidence, to spurn
              Such fears, like dreams we know not to discern.
Old, old and grey long since the time has grown,

Which saw the linkèd cables moor
The fleet, when erst it came to Ilion's sandy shore;

And now mine eyes and not another's see
   Their safe return.

Yet none the less in me
The inner spirit sings a boding song,
   Self-prompted, sings the Furies' strain —
     And seeks, and seeks in vain,
     To hope and to be strong!

Ah! to some end of Fate, unseen, unguessed,
   Are these wild throbbings of my heart and breast —
    Yea, of some doom they tell —
     Each pulse, a knell.
Lief, lief I were, that all
To unfulfilment's hidden realm might fall.

Too far, too far our mortal spirits strive,
   Grasping at utter weal, unsatisfied —
Till the fell curse, that dwelleth hard beside,
Thrust down the sundering wall.   Too fair they blow,
   The gales that waft our bark on Fortune's tide!
   Swiftly we sail, the sooner all to drive
   Upon the hidden rock, the reef of woe.
Then if the hand of caution warily
   Sling forth into the sea
Part of the freight, lest all should sink below,
From the deep death it saves the bark: even so,
   Doom-laden though it be, once more may rise
   His household, who is timely wise.

How oft the famine-stricken field
Is saved by God's large gift, the new year's yield!

But blood of man once spilled,
Once at his feet shed forth, and darkening the plain, —
   Nor chant nor charm can call it back again.

So Zeus hath willed:
Else had he spared the leech Asclepius, skilled
   To bring man from the dead: the hand divine
Did smite himself with death — a warning and a sign —

Ah me! if Fate, ordained of old,
Held not the will of gods constrained, controlled,
   Helpless to us-ward, and apart —

Swifter than speech my heart
Had poured its presage out!
Now, fretting, chafing in the dark of doubt,
    'Tis hopeless to unfold
Truth, from fear's tangled skein; and, yearning to proclaim
    Its thought, my soul is prophecy and flame.

[CLYTEMNESTRA *comes out of the palace and addresses* CASSANDRA, *who has remained motionless in her chariot.*]

CL.: Get thee within thou too, Cassandra, go!
    For Zeus to thee in gracious mercy grants
    To share the sprinklings of the lustral bowl,
    Beside the altar of his guardianship,
    Slave among many slaves. What, haughty still?
    Step from the car; Alcmena's son, 'tis said,
    Was sold perforce and bore the yoke of old.
    Ay, hard it is, but, if such fate befall,
    'Tis a fair chance to serve within a home
    Of ancient wealth and power. An upstart lord,
    To whom wealth's harvest came beyond his hope,
    Is as a lion to his slaves, in all
    Exceeding fierce, immoderate in sway.
    Pass in: thou hearest what our ways will be
LE.: Clear unto thee, O maid, is her command,
    But thou — within the toils of Fate thou art —
    If such thy will, I urge thee to obey;
    Yet I misdoubt thou dost nor hear nor heed.
CL.: I wot — unless like swallows she doth use
    Some strange barbarian tongue from oversea —
    My words must speak persuasion to her soul.
LE.: Obey: there is no gentler way than this.
    Step from the car's high seat and follow her.
CL.: Truce to this bootless waiting here without!
    I will not stay: beside the central shrine
    The victims stand, prepared for knife and fire —
    Offerings from hearts beyond all hope made glad.
    Thou — if thou reckest aught of my command,
    'Twere well done soon: but if thy sense be shut
    From these my words, let thy barbarian hand
    Fulfil by gesture the default of speech.
LE.: No native is she, thus to read thy words
    Unaided: like some wild thing of the wood,
    New-trapped, behold! she shrinks and glares on thee.
CL.: 'Tis madness and the rule of mind distraught,
    Since she beheld her city sink in fire,
    And hither comes, nor brooks the bit, until
    In foam and blood her wrath be champed away.
    See ye to her; unqueenly 'tis for me,
    Unheeded thus to cast away my words.

[CLYTEMNESTRA *enters the palace.*]

LE.: But with me pity sits in anger's place.
  Poor maiden, come thou from the car; no way
  There is but this — take up thy servitude.
CASSANDRA [*chanting*]: Woe, woe, alas! Earth, Mother Earth! and
    thou
  Apollo, Apollo!
LE.: Peace! shriek not to the bright prophetic god,
  Who will not brook the suppliance of woe.
CA. [*chanting*]: Woe, woe, alas! Earth, Mother Earth! and thou
  Apollo, Apollo!
LE.: Hark, with wild curse she calls anew on him,
  Who stands far off and loathes the voice of wail.
CA. [*chanting*]: Apollo, Apollo!
  God of all ways, but only Death's to me,
  Once and again, O thou, Destroyer named,
  Thou hast destroyed me, thou, my love of old!
LE.: She grows presageful of her woes to come,
  Slave tho' she be, instinct with prophecy.
CA. [*chanting*]: Apollo, Apollo!
  God of all ways, but only Death's to me,
  O thou Apollo, thou Destroyer named!
  What way hast led me, to what evil home?
LE.: Know'st thou it not? The home of Atreus' race:
  Take these my words for sooth and ask no more.
CA. [*chanting*]: Home cursed of God! Bear witness unto me,
    Ye visioned woes within —
  The blood-stained hands of them that smite their kin —
  The strangling noose, and, spattered o'er
  With human blood, the reeking floor!
LE.: How like a sleuth-hound questing on the track,
  Keen-scented unto blood and death she hies!
CA. [*chanting*]: Ah! can the ghostly guidance fail,
  Whereby my prophet-soul is onwards led?
  Look! for their flesh the spectre-children wail,
  Their sodden limbs on which their father fed!
LE.: Long since we knew of thy prophetic fame, —
  But for those deeds we seek no prophet's tongue.
CA. [*chanting*]: God! 'tis another crime —
  Worse than the storied woe of olden time,
  Cureless, abhorred, that one is plotting here —
  A shaming death, for those that should be dear!
    Alas! and far away, in foreign land,
    He that should help doth stand!
LE.: I knew th' old tales, the city rings withal —
  But now thy speech is dark, beyond my ken.
CA. [*chanting*]: O wretch, O purpose fell!
  Thou for thy wedded lord
  The cleansing wave hast poured —

A treacherous welcome!
              How the sequel tell?
Too soon 'twill come, too soon, for now, even now,
    She smites him, blow on blow!

LE.: Riddles beyond my rede — I peer in vain
    Thro' the dim films that screen the prophecy.

CA. [*chanting*]: God! a new sight! a net, a snare of hell,
    Set by her hand — herself a snare more fell!
      A wedded wife, she slays her lord,
     Helped by another hand!

              Ye powers, whose hate
    Of Atreus' home no blood can satiate,
Raise the wild cry above the sacrifice abhorred!

CH. [*chanting*]: Why biddest thou some fiend, I know not whom,
    Shriek o'er the house?   Thine is no cheering word.
      Back to my heart in frozen fear I feel
      My wanning life-blood run —
      The blood that round the wounding steel
      Ebbs slow, as sinks life's parting sun —
Swift, swift and sure, some woe comes pressing on!

CA. [*chanting*]: Away, away — keep him away —
    The monarch of the herd, the pasture's pride,
    Far from his mate!   In treach'rous wrath,
    Muffling his swarthy horns, with secret scathe
     She gores his fenceless side!
    Hark! in the brimming bath,
    The heavy plash — the dying cry —
Hark — in the laver — hark, he falls by treachery!

CH. [*chanting*]: I read amiss dark sayings such as thine,
    Yet something warns me that they tell of ill,
        O dark prophetic speech,
        Ill tidings dost thou teach
        Ever, to mortals here below!
        Ever some tale of awe and woe
        Thro' all thy windings manifold
        Do we unriddle and unfold!

CA. [*chanting*]: Ah well-a-day! the cup of agony,
    Whereof I chant, foams with a draught for me.
    Ah lord, ah leader, thou hast led me here —
    Was't but to die with thee whose doom is near?

CH. [*chanting*]: Distraught thou art, divinely stirred,
    And wailest for thyself a tuneless lay,
    As piteous as the ceaseless tale
    Wherewith the brown melodious bird
    Doth ever Itys! Itys! wail,
Deep-bowered in sorrow, all its little life-time's day!

CA. [*chanting*]: Ah for thy fate, O shrill-voiced nightingale!
    Some solace for thy woes did Heaven afford,
    Clothed thee with soft brown plumes, and life apart from wail—

But for my death is edged the double-biting sword!

CH. [*chanting*]: What pangs are these, what fruitless pain,
    Sent on thee from on high?
    Thou chantest terror's frantic strain,
    Yet in shrill measured melody.
    How thus unerring canst thou sweep along
    The prophet's path of boding song?

CA. [*chanting*]: Woe, Paris, woe on thee! thy bridal joy
    Was death and fire upon thy race and Troy!
    And woe for thee, Scamander's flood!
    Beside thy banks, O river fair,
    I grew in tender nursing care
    From childhood unto maidenhood!
Now not by thine, but by Cocytus' stream
And Acheron's banks shall ring my boding scream.

CH. [*chanting*]: Too plain is all, too plain!
A child might read aright thy fateful strain.
    Deep in my heart their piercing fang
    Terror and sorrow set, the while I heard
    That piteous, low, tender word,
Yet to mine ear and heart a crushing pang.

CA. [*chanting*]: Woe for my city, woe for Ilion's fall!
    Father, how oft with sanguine stain
    Streamed on thine altar-stone the blood of cattle, slain
      That heaven might guard our wall!
      But all was shed in vain.
    Low lie the shattered towers whereas they fell,
And I — ah burning heart! — shall soon lie low as well.

CH. [*chanting*]: Of sorrow is thy song, of sorrow still!
    Alas, what power of ill
    Sits heavy on thy heart and bids thee tell
    In tears of perfect moan thy deadly tale?
Some woe — I know not what — must close thy pious wail.

CA. [*more calmly*]: List! for no more the presage of my soul,
    Bride-like, shall peer from its secluding veil;
    But as the morning wind blows clear the east,
    More bright shall blow the wind of prophecy,
    And as against the low bright line of dawn
    Heaves high and higher yet the rolling wave,
    So in the clearing skies of prescience
    Dawns on my soul a further, deadlier woe,
    And I will speak, but in dark speech no more.
    Bear witness, ye, and follow at my side —
    I scent the trail of blood, shed long ago.
    Within this house a choir abidingly
    Chants in harsh unison the chant of ill;
    Yea, and they drink, for more enhardened joy,
    Man's blood for wine, and revel in the halls,

Departing never, Furies of the home.
They sit within, they chant the primal curse,
Each spitting hatred on that crime of old,
The brother's couch, the love incestuous
That brought forth hatred to the ravisher.
Say, is my speech or wild and erring now,
Or doth its arrow cleave the mark indeed?
They called me once, *The prophetess of lies,*
The wandering hag, the pest of every door —
Attest ye now, *She knows in very sooth*
The house's curse, the storied infamy.

LE.: Yet how should oath — how loyally soe'er
I swear it — aught avail thee? In good sooth,
My wonder meets thy claim: I stand amazed
That thou, a maiden born beyond the seas,
Dost as a native know and tell aright
Tales of a city of an alien tongue.

CA.: That is my power — a boon Apollo gave.

LE.: God though he were, yearning for mortal maid?

CA.: Ay! what seemed shame of old is shame no more.

LE.: Such finer sense suits not with slavery.

CA.: He strove to win me, panting for my love.

LE.: Came ye by compact unto bridal joys?

CA.: Nay — for I plighted troth, then foiled the god.

LE.: Wert thou already dowered with prescience?

CA.: Yea — prophetess to Troy of all her doom.

LE.: How left thee then Apollo's wrath unscathed?

CA.: I, false to him, seemed prophet false to all.

LE.: Not so — to us at least thy words seem sooth.

CA.: Woe for me, woe! Again the agony —
Dread pain that sees the future all too well
With ghastly preludes whirls and racks my soul.
Behold ye — yonder on the palace roof
The spectre-children sitting — look, such things
As dreams are made on, phantoms as of babes,
Horrible shadows, that a kinsman's hand
Hath marked with murder, and their arms are full —
A rueful burden — see, they hold them up,
The entrails upon which their father fed!

For this, for this, I say there plots revenge
A coward lion, couching in the lair —
Guarding the gate against my master's foot —
My master — mine — I bear the slave's yoke now,
And he, the lord of ships, who trod down Troy,
Knows not the fawning treachery of tongue
Of this thing false and dog-like — how her speech
Glozes and sleeks her purpose, till she win
By ill fate's favour the desirèd chance,

Moving like Atè to a secret end.
O aweless soul! the woman slays her lord —
Woman? what loathsome monster of the earth
Were fit comparison?   The double snake —
Or Scylla, where she dwells, the seaman's bane,
Girt round about with rocks? some hag of hell,
Raving a truceless curse upon her kin?
Hark — even now she cries exultingly
The vengeful cry that tells of battle turned —
How fain, forsooth, to greet her chief restored!
Nay then, believe me not: what skills belief
Or disbelief?   Fate works its will — and thou
Wilt see and say in ruth, *Her tale was true.*

LE.: Ah — 'tis Thyestes' feast on kindred flesh —
I guess her meaning and with horror thrill,
Hearing no shadow'd hint of th' o'er-true tale,
But its full hatefulness: yet, for the rest,
Far from the track I roam, and know no more.

CA.: 'Tis Agamemnon's doom thou shalt behold.

LE.: Peace, hapless woman, to thy boding words!

CA.: Far from my speech stands he who sains and saves.

LE.: Ay — were such doom at hand — which God forbid!

CA.: Thou prayest idly — these move swift to slay.

LE.: What man prepares a deed of such despite?

CA.: Fool! thus to read amiss mine oracles.

LE.: Deviser and device are dark to me.

CA.: Dark! all too well I speak the Grecian tongue.

LE.: Ay — but in thine, as in Apollo's strains,
Familiar is the tongue, but dark the thought.

CA.: Ah, ah the fire! it waxes, nears me now —
Woe, woe for me, Apollo of the dawn!

Lo, how the woman-thing, the lioness
Couched with the wolf — her noble mate afar —
Will slay me, slave forlorn!   Yea, like some witch,
She drugs the cup of wrath, that slays her lord,
With double death — his recompense for me!
Ay, 'tis for me, the prey he bore from Troy,
That she hath sworn his death, and edged the steel!
Ye wands, ye wreaths that cling around my neck,
Ye showed me prophetess yet scorned of all —
I stamp you into death, or e'er I die —
Down, to destruction!
                    Thus I stand revenged —
Go, crown some other with a prophet's woe.
Look! it is he, it is Apollo's self
Rending from me the prophet-robe he gave.
God! while I wore it yet, thou saw'st me mocked
There at my home by each malicious mouth —

To all and each, an undivided scorn.
The name alike and fate of witch and cheat —
Woe, poverty, and famine — all I bore;
And at this last the god hath brought me here
Into death's toils, and what his love had made,
His hate unmakes me now: and I shall stand
Not now before the altar of my home,
But me a slaughter-house and block of blood
Shall see hewn down, a reeking sacrifice.
Yet shall the gods have heed of me who die,
For by their will shall one requite my doom.
He, to avenge his father's blood outpoured,
Shall smite and slay with matricidal hand.
Ay, he shall come — tho' far away he roam,
A banished wanderer in a stranger's land —
To crown his kindred's edifice of ill,
Called home to vengeance by his father's fall:
Thus have the high gods sworn, and shall fulfil.
And now why mourn I, tarrying on earth,
Since first mine Ilion has found its fate
And I beheld, and those who won the wall
Pass to such issue as the gods ordain?
I too will pass and like them dare to die!
          [*She turns and looks upon the palace door.*]
Portal of Hades, thus I bid thee hail!
Grant me one boon — a swift and mortal stroke,
That all unwrung by pain, with ebbing blood
Shed forth in quiet death, I close mine eyes.

LE.: Maid of mysterious woes, mysterious lore,
      Long was thy prophecy: but if aright
      Thou readest all thy fate, how, thus unscared,
      Dost thou approach the altar of thy doom,
      As fronts the knife some victim, heaven-controlled?

CA.: Friends, there is no avoidance in delay.

LE.: Yet who delays the longest, his the gain.

CA.: The day is come — flight were small gain to me!

LE.: O brave endurance of a soul resolved!

CA.: That were ill praise, for those of happier doom.

LE.: All fame is happy, even famous death.

CA.: Ah sire, ah brethren, famous once were ye!
      [*She moves to enter the house, then starts back.*]

LE.: What fear is this that scares thee from the house?

CA.: Pah!

LE.: What is this cry? some dark despair of soul?

CA.: Pah! the house fumes with stench and spilth of blood.

LE.: How? 'tis the smell of household offerings.

CA.: 'Tis rank as charnel-scent from open graves.

LE.: Thou canst not mean this scented Syrian nard?

CA.: Nay, let me pass within to cry aloud

The monarch's fate and mine — enough of life.
Ah friends!
Bear to me witness, since I fall in death,
That not as birds that shun the bush and scream
I moan in idle terror.   This attest
When for my death's revenge another dies,
A woman for a woman, and a man
Falls, for a man ill-wedded to his curse.
Grant me this boon — the last before I die.

LE.: Brave to the last!   I mourn thy doom foreseen.

CA.: Once more one utterance, but not of wail,
     Though for my death — and then I speak no more.

Sun! thou whose beam I shall not see again,
To thee I cry, Let those whom vengeance calls
To slay their kindred's slayers, quit withal
The death of me, the slave, the fenceless prey.

Ah state of mortal man! in time of weal,
A line, a shadow! and if ill fate fall,
One wet sponge-sweep wipes all our trace away —
And this I deem less piteous, of the twain.

                              [*She enters the palace.*]

CH. [*singing*]: Too true it is! our mortal state
          With bliss is never satiate,
          And none, before the palace high
          And stately of prosperity,
          Cries to us with a voice of fear,
          Away! 'tis ill to enter here!

          Lo! this our lord hath trodden down,
          By grace of heaven, old Priam's town,
               And praised as god he stands once more
               On Argos' shore!
          Yet now — if blood shed long ago
          Cries out that other blood shall flow —
          His life-blood, his, to pay again
          The stern requital of the slain —
          Peace to that braggart's vaunting vain,
               Who, having heard the chieftain's tale,
               Yet boasts of bliss untouched by bale!
                         [*A loud cry is heard from within.*]

VOICE OF AGAMEMNON: O I am sped — a deep, a mortal blow.

LE.: Listen, listen! who is screaming as in mortal agony?

VOICE OF AG.: O! O! again, another, another blow!

LE.: The bloody act is over — I have heard the monarch's cry —
     Let us swiftly take some counsel, lest we too be doomed to die.

ONE OF THE CHORUS: 'Tis best, I judge, aloud for aid to call,
     "Ho! loyal Argives! to the palace, all!"

ANOTHER: Better, I deem, ourselves to bear the aid,
    And drag the deed to light, while drips the blade.
ANOTHER: Such will is mine, and what thou say'st I say:
    Swiftly to act! the time brooks no delay.
ANOTHER: Ay, for 'tis plain, this prelude of their song
    Foretells its close in tyranny and wrong.
ANOTHER: Behold, we tarry — but thy name, Delay,
    They spurn, and press with sleepless hand to slay.
ANOTHER: I know not what 'twere well to counsel now —
    Who wills to act, 'tis his to counsel how.
ANOTHER: Thy doubt is mine: for when a man is slain,
    I have no words to bring his life again.
ANOTHER: What? e'en for life's sake, bow us to obey
    These house-defilers and their tyrant sway?
ANOTHER: Unmanly doom! 'twere better far to die —
    Death is a gentler lord than tyranny.
ANOTHER: Think well — must cry or sign of woe or pain
    Fix our conclusion that the chief is slain?
ANOTHER: Such talk befits us when the deed we see —
    Conjecture dwells afar from certainty.
LE.: I read one will from many a diverse word,
    To know aright, how stands it with our lord!

[*The central doors of the palace open, disclosing* CLYTEMNESTRA, *who
comes forward. She has blood smeared upon her forehead. The
body of* AGAMEMNON *lies, muffled in a long robe, within a silver-sided
laver; the corpse of* CASSANDRA *is laid beside him.*]

CL.: Ho, ye who heard me speak so long and oft
    The glozing word that led me to my will —
    Hear how I shrink not to unsay it all!
    How else should one who willeth to requite
    Evil for evil to an enemy
    Disguised as friend, weave the mesh straitly round him,
    Not to be overleaped, a net of doom?
    This is the sum and issue of old strife,
    Of me deep-pondered and at length fulfilled.
    All is avowed, and as I smote I stand
    With foot set firm upon a finished thing!
    I turn not to denial: thus I wrought
    So that he could nor flee nor ward his doom.
    Even as the trammel hems the scaly shoal,
    I trapped him with inextricable toils,
    The ill abundance of a baffling robe;
    Then smote him, once, again — and at each wound
    He cried aloud, then as in death relaxed
    Each limb and sank to earth; and as he lay,
    Once more I smote him, with the last third blow,
    Sacred to Hades, saviour of the dead.
    And thus he fell, and as he passed away,

Spirit with body chafed; each dying breath
Flung from his breast swift bubbling jets of gore,
And the dark sprinklings of the rain of blood
Fell upon me; and I was fain to feel
That dew — not sweeter is the rain of heaven
To cornland, when the green sheath teems with **grain**.
Elders of Argos — since the thing stands so,
I bid you to rejoice, if such your will:
Rejoice or not, I vaunt and praise the deed,
And well I ween, if seemly it could be,
'Twere not ill done to pour libations here,
Justly — ay, more than justly — on his corpse
Who filled his home with curses as with wine,
And thus returned to drain the cup he filled.

LE.: I marvel at thy tongue's audacity,
To vaunt thus loudly o'er a husband slain.

CL.: Ye hold me as a woman, weak of will,
And strive to sway me: but my heart is stout,
Nor fears to speak its uttermost to you,
Albeit ye know its message.   Praise or blame,
Even as ye list, — I reck not of your words.
Lo! at my feet lies Agamemnon slain,
My husband once — and him this hand of mine,
A right contriver, fashioned for his death.
Behold the deed!

CH. [*chanting*]: Woman, what deadly birth,
What venomed essence of the earth
   Or dark distilment of the wave,
      To thee such passion gave,
   Nerving thine hand
   To set upon thy brow this burning crown,
      The curses of thy land?
      Our king by thee cut off, hewn down!
         Go forth — they cry — accursèd and forlorn,
         To hate and scorn!

CL.: O ye just men, who speak my sentence now,
The city's hate, the ban of all my realm!
Ye had no voice of old to launch such doom
On him, my husband, when he held as light
My daughter's life as that of sheep or goat,
One victim from the thronging fleecy fold!
Yea, slew in sacrifice his child and mine,
The well-loved issue of my travail-pangs,
To lull and lay the gales that blew from Thrace.
That deed of his, I say, that stain and shame,
Had rightly been atoned by banishment;
But ye, who then were dumb, are stern to judge
This deed of mine that doth affront your ears.

Storm out your threats, yet knowing this for sooth,
That I am ready, if your hand prevail
As mine now doth, to bow beneath your sway:
If God say nay, it shall be yours to learn
By chastisement a late humility.

CH. [*chanting*]: Bold is thy craft, and proud
Thy confidence, thy vaunting loud;
Thy soul, that chose a murd'ress' fate,
Is all with blood elate —
Maddened to know
The blood not yet avenged, the damnèd spot
Crimson upon thy brow.
But Fate prepares for thee thy lot —
Smitten as thou didst smite, without a friend,
To meet thine end!

CL.: Hear then the sanction of the oath I swear —
By the great vengeance for my murdered child,
By Atè, by the Fury unto whom
This man lies sacrificed by hand of mine,
I do not look to tread the hall of Fear,
While in this hearth and home of mine there burns
The light of love — Aegisthus — as of old
Loyal, a stalwart shield of confidence —
As true to me as this slain man was false,
Wronging his wife with paramours at Troy,
Fresh from the kiss of each Chryseis there!
Behold him dead — behold his captive prize,
Seeress and harlot — comfort of his bed,
True prophetess, true paramour — I wot
The sea-bench was not closer to the flesh,
Full oft, of every rower, than was she.
See, ill they did, and ill requites them now.
His death ye know: she as a dying swan
Sang her last dirge, and lies, as erst she lay,
Close to his side, and to my couch has left
A sweet new taste of joys that know no fear.

strophe 1

CH. [*singing*]: Ah woe and well-a-day! I would that Fate —
Not bearing agony too great,
Nor stretching me too long on couch of pain —
Would bid mine eyelids keep
The morningless and unawakening sleep!
For life is weary, now my lord is slain,
The gracious among kings!
Hard fate of old he bore and many grievous things,
And for a woman's sake, on Ilian land —
Now is his life hewn down, and by a woman's hand.

refrain 1

O Helen, O infatuate soul,
Who bad'st the tides of battle roll,
O'erwhelming thousands, life on life,
'Neath Ilion's wall!
And now lies dead the lord of all.
The blossom of thy storied sin
Bears blood's inexpiable stain,
O thou that erst, these halls within,
Wert unto all a rock of strife,
A husband's bane!

CL. [*chanting*]: Peace! pray not thou for death as though
Thine heart was whelmed beneath this woe,
Nor turn thy wrath aside to ban
The name of Helen, nor recall
How she, one bane of many a man,
Sent down to death the Danaan lords,
To sleep at Troy the sleep of swords,
And wrought the woe that shattered all.

antistrophe 1

CH.: Fiend of the race! that swoopest fell
Upon the double stock of Tantalus,
Lording it o'er me by a woman's will,
Stern, manful, and imperious —
A bitter sway to me!
Thy very form I see,
Like some grim raven, perched upon the slain,
Exulting o'er the crime, aloud, in tuneless strain!

CL. [*chanting*]: Right was that word — thou namest well
The brooding race-fiend, triply fell!
From him it is that murder's thirst,
Blood-lapping, inwardly is nursed —
Ere time the ancient scar can sain,
New blood comes welling forth again.

strophe 2

CH.: Grim is his wrath and heavy on our home,
That fiend of whom thy voice has cried,
Alas, an omened cry of woe unsatisfied,
An all-devouring doom!

Ah woe, ah Zeus! from Zeus all things befall —
Zeus the high cause and finisher of all! —
Lord of our mortal state, by him are willed
All things, by him fulfilled!

Yet ah my king, my king no more!
What words to say, what tears to pour
  Can tell my love for thee?
The spider-web of treachery
She wove and wound, thy life around,
  And lo! I see thee lie,
And thro' a coward, impious wound
  Pant forth thy life and die!
A death of shame — ah woe on woe!
A treach'rous hand, a cleaving blow!

CL. [*chanting*]: My guilt thou harpest, o'er and o'er!
  I bid thee reckon me no more
    As Agamemnon's spouse.
  The old Avenger, stern of mood
  For Atreus and his feast of blood,
      Hath struck the lord of Atreus' house,
  And in the semblance of his wife
      The king hath slain. —
  Yea, for the murdered children's life,
      A chieftain's in requital ta'en.

antistrophe 2

CH.: Thou guiltless of this murder, thou!
      Who dares such thought avow?
  Yet it may be, wroth for the parent's deed,
  The fiend hath holpen thee to slay the son.
    Dark Ares, god of death, is pressing on
    Thro' streams of blood by kindred shed,
    Exacting the accompt for children dead,
  For clotted blood, for flesh on which their sire did feed.

refrain 2

Yet ah my king, my king no more!
What words to say, what tears to pour
  Can tell my love for thee?
The spider-web of treachery
She wove and wound, thy life around,
  And lo! I see thee lie,
And thro' a coward, impious wound
  Pant forth thy life and die!
A death of shame — ah woe on woe!
A treach'rous hand, a cleaving blow!

CL. [*chanting*]: I deem not that the death he died
      Had overmuch of shame:
    For this was he who did provide

Foul wrong unto his house and name:
His daughter, blossom of my womb,
He gave unto a deadly doom,
Iphigenia, child of tears!
And as he wrought, even so he fares.
Nor be his vaunt too loud in hell;
For by the sword his sin he wrought,
And by the sword himself is brought
    Among the dead to dwell.

strophe 3

CH.:   Ah whither shall I fly?
For all in ruin sinks the kingly hall;
Nor swift device nor shift of thought have I,
    To 'scape its fall.
A little while the gentler rain-drops fail;
I stand distraught — a ghastly interval,
Till on the roof-tree rings the bursting hail
  Of blood and doom.   Even now fate whets the steel
  On whetstone new and deadlier than of old,
    The steel that smites, in Justice' hold,
    Another death to deal.
O Earth! that I had lain at rest
And lapped for ever in thy breast,
Ere I had seen my chieftain fall
Within the laver's silver wall,
Low-lying on dishonoured bier!
And who shall give him sepulchre,
And who the wail of sorrow pour?
Woman, 'tis thine no more!
A graceless gift unto his shade
Such tribute, by his murd'ress paid!
Strive not thus wrongly to atone
The impious deed thy hand hath done.
Ah who above the god-like chief
Shall weep the tears of loyal grief?
Who speak above his lowly grave
The last sad praises of the brave?

CL. [*chanting*]: Peace! for such task is none of thine.
    By me he fell, by me he died,
And now his burial rites be mine!
Yet from these halls no mourners' train
    Shall celebrate his obsequies;
Only by Acheron's rolling tide
His child shall spring unto his side,
    And in a daughter's loving wise
Shall clasp and kiss him once again!

CH.: Lo! sin by sin and sorrow dogg'd by sorrow —
    And who the end can know?
The slayer of to-day shall die to-morrow —
    The wage of wrong is woe.
While Time shall be, while Zeus in heaven is lord,
    His law is fixed and stern;
On him that wrought shall vengeance be outpoured —
    The tides of doom return.
The children of the curse abide within
    These halls of high estate —
And none can wrench from off the home of sin
    The clinging grasp of fate.

CL. [*chanting*]: Now walks thy word aright, to tell
    This ancient truth of oracle;
    But I with vows of sooth will pray
    To him, the power that holdeth sway
      O'er all the race of Pleisthenes —
    Tho' dark the deed and deep the guilt,
    With this last blood, my hands have split,
      I pray thee let thine anger cease!
    I pray thee pass from us away
      To some new race in other lands,
    There, if thou wilt, to wrong and slay
      The lives of men by kindred hands.

    For me 'tis all sufficient meed,
    Tho' little wealth or power were won,
    So I can say, 'Tis past and done.
    The bloody lust and murderous,
    The inborn frenzy of our house,
      Is ended, by my deed!

    [AEGISTHUS *and his armed attendants enter.*]
AE.: Dawn of the day of rightful vengeance, hail!
    I dare at length aver that gods above
    Have care of men and heed of earthly wrongs.
    I, I who stand and thus exult to see
    This man lie wound in robes the Furies wove,
    Slain in the requital of his father's craft.
    Take ye the truth, that Atreus, this man's sire,
    The lord and monarch of this land of old,
    Held with my sire Thyestes deep dispute,
    Brother with brother, for the prize of sway,
    And drave him from his home to banishment.
    Thereafter, the lorn exile homeward stole
    And clung a suppliant to the hearth divine,
    And for himself won this immunity —

Not with his own blood to defile the land
That gave him birth.   But Atreus, godless sire
Of him who here lies dead, this welcome planned —
With zeal that was not love he feigned to hold
In loyal joy a day of festal cheer,
And bade my father to his board, and set
Before him flesh that was his children once.
First, sitting at the upper board alone,
He hid the fingers and the feet, but gave
The rest — and readily Thyestes took
What to his ignorance no semblance wore
Of human flesh, and ate: behold what curse
That eating brought upon our race and name!
For when he knew what all unhallowed thing
He thus had wrought, with horror's bitter cry
Back-starting, spewing forth the fragments foul,
On Pelops' house a deadly curse he spake —
As darkly as I spurn this damnèd food,
So perish all the race of Pleisthenes!
Thus by that curse fell he whom here ye see,
And I — who else? — this murder wove and planned;
For me, an infant yet in swaddling bands,
Of the three children youngest, Atreus sent
To banishment by my sad father's side:
But Justice brought me home once more, grown now
To manhood's years; and stranger tho' I was,
My right hand reached unto the chieftain's life,
Plotting and planning all that malice bade.
And death itself were honour now to me,
Beholding him in Justice' ambush ta'en.

LE.: Aegisthus, for this insolence of thine
That vaunts itself in evil, take my scorn.
Of thine own will, thou sayest, thou hast slain
The chieftain, by thine own unaided plot
Devised the piteous death: I rede thee well,
Think not thy head shall 'scape, when right prevails,
The people's ban, the stones of death and doom.

AE.: This word from thee, this word from one who rows
Low at the oars beneath, what time we rule,
We of the upper tier?   Thou'lt know anon,
'Tis bitter to be taught again in age,
By one so young, submission at the word.
But iron of the chain and hunger's throes
Can minister unto an o'erswoln pride
Marvellous well, ay, even in the old.
Hast eyes, and seest not this?   Peace — kick not thus
Against the pricks, unto thy proper pain!

LE.: Thou womanish man, waiting till war did cease,
Home-watcher and defiler of the couch,

And arch-deviser of the chieftain's doom!

AE.: Bold words again! but they shall end in tears.
The very converse, thine, of Orpheus' tongue:
He roused and led in ecstasy of joy
All things that heard his voice melodious;
But thou as with the futile cry of curs
Wilt draw men wrathfully upon thee.   Peace!
Or strong subjection soon shall tame thy tongue.

LE.: Ay, thou art one to hold an Argive down —
Thou, skilled to plan the murder of the king,
But not with thine own hand to smite the blow!

AE.: That fraudful force was woman's very part,
Not mine, whom deep suspicion from of old
Would have debarred.   Now by his treasure's aid
My purpose holds to rule the citizens.
But whoso will not bear my guiding hand,
Him for his corn-fed mettle I will drive
Not as a trace-horse, light-caparisoned,
But to the shafts with heaviest harness bound.
Famine, the grim mate of the dungeon dark,
Shall look on him and shall behold him tame.

LE.: Thou losel soul, was then thy strength too slight
To deal in murder, while a woman's hand,
Staining and shaming Argos and its gods,
Availed to slay him?   Ho, if anywhere
The light of life smite on Orestes' eyes,
Let him, returning by some guardian fate,
Hew down with force her paramour and her!

AE.: How thy word and act shall issue, thou shalt shortly understand.

LE.: Up to action, O my comrades! for the fight is hard at hand.
Swift, your right hands to the sword hilt! bare the weapon as
    for strife —

AE.: Lo! I too am standing ready, hand on hilt for death or life.

LE.: 'Twas thy word and we accept it: onward to the chance of war!

CL.: Nay, enough, enough, my champion! we will smite and slay no
    more.
Already have we reaped enough the harvest-field of guilt:
Enough of wrong and murder, let no other blood be spilt.
Peace, old men! and pass away unto the homes by Fate decreed,
Lest ill valour meet our vengeance — 'twas a necessary deed.
But enough of toils and troubles — be the end, if ever, now,
Ere thy talon, O Avenger, deal another deadly blow.
'Tis a woman's word of warning, and let who will list thereto.

AE.: But that these should loose and lavish reckless blossoms of the
    tongue,
And in hazard of their fortune cast upon me words of wrong,
And forget the law of subjects, and revile their ruler's word —

LE.: Ruler? but 'tis not for Argives, thus to own a dastard lord!

AE.: I will follow to chastise thee in my coming days of sway.

LE.: Not if Fortune guide Orestes safely on his homeward way.

AE.: Ah, well I know how exiles feed on hopes of their return.

LE.: Fare and batten on pollution of the right, while 'tis thy turn.

AE.: Thou shalt pay, be well assurèd, heavy quittance for thy pride.

LE.: Crow and strut, with her to watch thee, like a cock, his mate beside!

CL.: Heed not thou too highly of them — let the cur-pack growl and yell:
I and thou will rule the palace and will order all things well.

[AEGISTHUS *and* CLYTEMNESTRA *move towards the palace, as the* CHORUS *sullenly withdraws.*]

[In the second play of the trilogy, the *Choephori,* or "The Libation Bearers," Orestes returns secretly to Argos after many years. Apollo at Delphi has ordered him to avenge his father by killing his mother, Clytemnestra, and Aegisthus, under threat of the direst consequences if he should refuse. Orestes accomplishes the deed with the aid of his sister Electra, but immediately after the murder of Clytemnestra he is driven mad by the avenging Furies of his murdered mother and he rushes wildly from the stage; the chorus sadly sums up the situation [1065–1076, tr. MORSHEAD]:
"Behold, the storm of woe divine
That raves and beats on Atreus' line
Its third great blast hath blown.
First was Thyestes' loathly woe —
The rueful feast of long ago,
On children's flesh, unknown.
And next the kingly chief's despite,
When he who led the Greeks to fight
Was in the bath hewn down.
And now the offspring of the race
Stands in the third, the saviour's place,
To save — or to consume?
O whither, ere it be fulfilled,
Ere its fierce blast be hushed and stilled,
Shall blow the wind of doom?"]

THE EUMENIDES

Translated by E. D. A. MORSHEAD

Characters in the Play

The Pythian Priestess
Apollo
Orestes
The Ghost of Clytemnestra
Chorus of Furies
Athena
Attendants of Athena
Twelve Athenian Citizens

THE EUMENIDES

[Scene: — *Before the temple of* APOLLO *at Delphi. The* PYTHIAN PRIESTESS *enters and approaches the doors of the temple.*]

PYTHIAN PRIESTESS: First, in this prayer, of all the gods I name
The prophet-mother Earth; and Themis next,
Second who sat — for so with truth is said —
On this her mother's shrine oracular.
Then by her grace, who unconstrained allowed,
There sat thereon another child of Earth —
Titanian Phoebe.   She, in after time,
Gave o'er the throne, as birthgift to a god,
Phoebus, who in his own bears Phoebe's name.
He from the lake and ridge of Delos' isle
Steered to the port of Pallas' Attic shores,
The home of ships; and thence he passed and came
Unto this land and to Parnassus' shrine.
And at his side, with awe revering him,
There went the children of Hephaestus' seed,
The hewers of the sacred way, who tame
The stubborn tract that erst was wilderness.
   And all this folk, and Delphos, chieftain-king
Of this their land, with honour gave him home;
And in his breast Zeus set a prophet's soul,
And gave to him this throne, whereon he sits,
Fourth prophet of the shrine, and, Loxias hight,
Gives voice to that which Zeus his sire decrees.

Such gods I name in my preluding prayer,
And after them, I call with honour due
On Pallas, wardress of the fane, and Nymphs
Who dwell around the rock Corycian,
Where in the hollow cave, the wild birds' haunt,
Wander the feet of lesser gods; and there,
Right well I know it, Bromian Bacchus dwells,
Since he in godship led his Maenad host,
Devising death for Pentheus, whom they rent
Piecemeal, as hare among the hounds.   And last,
I call on Pleistus' springs, Poseidon's might,
And Zeus most high, the great Accomplisher.
Then as a seeress to the sacred chair
I pass and sit; and may the powers divine
Make this mine entrance fruitful in response
Beyond each former advent, triply blest.
And if there stand without, from Hellas bound,
Men seeking oracles, let each pass in
In order of the lot, as use allows;
For the god guides whate'er my tongue proclaims.

213

[*She goes into the interior of the temple; after a short interval, she returns in great fear.*]

    Things fell to speak of, fell for eyes to see,
    Have sped me forth again from Loxias' shrine,
    With strength unstrung, moving erect no more,
    But aiding with my hands my failing feet,
    Unnerved by fear. A beldame's force is naught —
    Is as a child's, when age and fear combine.
    For as I pace towards the inmost fane
    Bay-filleted by many a suppliant's hand,
    Lo, at the central altar I descry
    One crouching as for refuge — yea, a man
    Abhorred of heaven; and from his hands, wherein
    A sword new-drawn he holds, blood reeked and fell:
    A wand he bears, the olive's topmost bough,
    Twined as of purpose with a deep close tuft
    Of whitest wool. This, that I plainly saw,
    Plainly I tell. But lo, in front of him,
    Crouched on the altar-steps, a grisly band
    Of women slumbers — not like women they,
    But Gorgons rather; nay, that word is weak,
    Nor may I match the Gorgons' shape with theirs!
    Such have I seen in painted semblance erst —
    Winged Harpies, snatching food from Phineus' board, —
    But these are wingless, black, and all their shape
    The eye's abomination to behold.
    Fell is the breath — let none draw nigh to it —
    Wherewith they snort in slumber; from their eyes
    Exude the damnèd drops of poisonous ire:
    And such their garb as none should dare to bring
    To statues of the gods or homes of men.
    I wot not of the tribe wherefrom can come
    So fell a legion, nor in what land Earth
    Could rear, unharmed, such creatures, nor avow
    That she had travailed and had brought forth death.
    But, for the rest, be all these things a care
    Unto the mighty Loxias, the lord
    Of this our shrine: healer and prophet he,
    Discerner he of portents, and the cleanser
    Of other homes — behold, his own to cleanse!

[*She goes out. The central doors open, disclosing the interior of the temple.* ORESTES *clings to the central altar; the* FURIES *lie slumbering at a little distance;* APOLLO *and* HERMES *appear from the innermost shrine.*]

AP. [*to* ORESTES]: Lo, I desert thee never: to the end,
    Hard at thy side as now, or sundered far,
    I am thy guard, and to thine enemies
    Implacably oppose me: look on them,
    These greedy fiends, beneath my craft subdued!

See, they are fallen on sleep, these beldames old,
Unto whose grim and wizened maidenhood
Nor god nor man nor beast can e'er draw near.
Yea, evil were they born, for evil's doom,
Evil the dark abyss of Tartarus
Wherein they dwell, and they themselves the hate
Of men on earth, and of Olmpian gods.
But thou, flee far and with unfaltering speed;
For they shall hunt thee through the mainland wide
Where'er throughout the tract of travelled earth
Thy foot may roam, and o'er and o'er the seas
And island homes of men.   Faint not nor fail,
Too soon and timidly within thy breast
Shepherding thoughts forlorn of this thy toil;
But unto Pallas' city go, and there
Crouch at her shrine, and in thine arms enfold
Her ancient image: there we well shall find
Meet judges for this cause and suasive pleas,
Skilled to contrive for thee deliverance
From all this woe.   Be such my pledge to thee,
For by my hest thou didst thy mother slay.

or.: O king Apollo, since right well thou know'st
What justice bids, have heed, fulfil the same, —
Thy strength is all-sufficient to achieve.

ap.: Have thou too heed, nor let thy fear prevail
Above thy will.   And do thou guard him, Hermes,
Whose blood is brother unto mine, whose sire
The same high God.   Men call thee guide and guard,
Guide therefore thou and guard my suppliant;
For Zeus himself reveres the outlaw's right,
Boon of fair escort, upon man conferred.

[apollo, hermes, *and* orestes *go out. The* ghost of clytemnestra
rises.]

ghost: Sleep on! awake! what skills your sleep to me —
Me, among all the dead by you dishonoured —
Me from whom never, in the world of death,
Dieth this course, *'Tis she who smote and slew,*
And shamed and scorned I roam?   Awake, and hear
My plaint of dead men's hate intolerable.
Me, sternly slain by them that should have loved,
Me doth no god arouse him to avenge,
Hewn down in blood by matricidal hands.
Mark ye these wounds from which the heart's blood ran,
And by whose hand, bethink ye! for the sense
When shut in sleep hath then the spirit-sight,
But in the day the inward eye is blind.
List, ye who drank so oft with lapping tongue
The wineless draught by me outpoured to soothe
Your vengeful ire! how oft on kindled shrine

I laid the feast of darkness, at the hour
Abhorred of every god but you alone!
Lo, all my service trampled down and scorned!
And he hath baulked your chase, as stag the hounds;
Yea, lightly bounding from the circling toils,
Hath wried his face in scorn, and flieth far.
Awake and hear — for mine own soul I cry —
Awake, ye powers of hell! the wandering ghost
That once was Clytemnestra calls — Arise!
[*The* FURIES *mutter grimly, as in a dream.*]
Mutter and murmur! He hath flown afar —
My kin have gods to guard them, I have none!
                    [*The* FURIES *mutter as before.*]
O drowsed in sleep too deep to heed my pain!
Orestes flies, who me, his mother, slew.
                    [*The* FURIES *give a confused cry.*]
Yelping, and drowsed again? Up and be doing
That which alone is yours, the deed of hell!
                    [*The* FURIES *give another cry.*]
Lo, sleep and toil, the sworn confederates,
Have quelled your dragon-anger, once so fell!

THE FURIES [*muttering more fiercely and loudly*]: Seize, seize, seize, seize — mark, yonder!

GHOST: In dreams ye chase a prey, and like some hound,
        That even in sleep doth ply his woodland toil,
        Ye bell and bay. What do ye, sleeping here?
        Be not o'ercome with toil, nor, sleep-subdued,
        Be heedless of my wrong. Up! thrill your heart
        With the just chidings of my tongue, — such words
        Are as a spur to purpose firmly held.
        Blow forth on him the breath of wrath and blood,
        Scorch him with reek of fire that burns in you,
        Waste him with new pursuit — swift, hound him down!
                            [*The* GHOST *sinks.*]

FIRST FURY [*awaking*]: Up! rouse another as I rouse thee; up!
            Sleep'st thou? Rise up, and spurning sleep away,
            See we if false to us this prelude rang.

strophe 1

CHORUS OF FURIES [*singing*]: Alack, alack, O sisters, we have toiled,
            O much and vainly have we toiled and borne!
            Vainly! and all we wrought the gods have foiled,
                And turnèd us to scorn!
        He hath slipped from the net, whom we chased: he hath 'scaped
        us who should be our prey —
        O'ermastered by slumber we sank, and our quarry hath stolen
        away!

antistrophe 1

Thou, child of the high God Zeus, Apollo, hast robbed us and
    wronged;
Thou, a youth, hast down-trodden the right that to godship
    more ancient belonged;
Thou hast cherished thy suppliant man; the slayer, the God-
    forsaken,
The bane of a parent, by craft from out of our grasp thou hast
    taken;
A god, thou hast stolen from us the avengers a matricide son —
And who shall consider thy deed and say, *It is rightfully done?*

strophe 2

    The sound of chiding scorn
      Came from the land of dream;
Deep to mine inmost heart I felt it thrill and burn,
    Thrust as a strong-grasped goad, to urge
      Onward the chariot's team.
    Thrilled, chilled with bitter inward pain
I stand as one beneath the doomsman's scourge.

antistrophe 2

Shame on the younger gods who tread down right,
    Sitting on thrones of might!
Woe on the altar of earth's central fane!
    Clotted on step and shrine,
Behold, the guilt of blood, the ghastly stain!

strophe 3

    Woe upon thee, Apollo! uncontrolled,
      Unbidden, hast thou, prophet-god, imbrued
      The pure prophetic shrine with wrongful blood!
    For thou too heinous a respect didst hold
Of man, too little heed of powers divine!
    And us the Fates, the ancients of the earth,
      Didst deem as nothing worth.

antistrophe 3

Scornful to me thou art, yet shalt not fend
    My wrath from him; though unto hell he flee,
      There too are we!
And he the blood-defiled, should feel and rue,
Though I were not, fiend-wrath that shall not end,
Descending on his head who foully slew.

      [APOLLO *enters from the inner shrine.*]
AP.: Out! I command you.   Out from this my home —
    Haste, tarry not!   Out from the mystic shrine,

Lest thy lot be to take into thy breast
The winged bright dart that from my golden string
Speeds hissing as a snake, — lest, pierced and thrilled
With agony, thou shouldst spew forth again
Black frothy heart's-blood, drawn from mortal men,
Belching the gory clots sucked forth from wounds.
These be no halls where such as you can prowl —
Go where men lay on men the doom of blood,
Heads lopped from necks, eyes from their spheres plucked out,
Hacked flesh, the flower of youthful seed crushed out,
Feet hewn away, and hands, and death beneath
The smiting stone, low moans and piteous
Of men impaled — Hark, hear ye for what feast
Ye hanker ever, and the loathing gods
Do spit upon your craving?   Lo, your shape
Is all too fitted to your greed; the cave
Where lurks some lion, lapping gore, were home
More meet for you.   Avaunt from sacred shrines,
Nor bring pollution by your touch on all
That nears you. Hence! and roam unshepherded —
No god there is to tend such herd as you.
LEADER OF THE CHORUS: O king Apollo, in our turn hear us.
    Thou hast not only part in these ill things,
    But art chief cause and doer of the same.
AP.: How? stretch thy speech to tell this, and have done.
LE.: Thine oracle bade this man slay his mother.
AP.: I bade him quit his sire's death, — wherefore not?
LE.: Then didst thou aid and guard red-handed crime.
AP.: Yea, and I bade him to this temple flee.
LE.: And yet forsooth dost chide us following him!
AP.: Ay — not for you it is, to near this fane.
LE.: Yet is such office ours, imposed by fate.
AP.: What office? vaunt the thing ye deem so fair.
LE.: From home to home we chase the matricide.
AP.: What? to avenge a wife who slays her lord?
LE.: That is not blood outpoured by kindred hands.
AP.: How darkly ye dishonour and annul
    The troth to which the high accomplishers,
    Hera and Zeus, do honour. Yea, and thus
    Is Aphrodite to dishonour cast,
    The queen of rapture unto mortal men.
    Know, that above the marriage-bed ordained
    For man and woman standeth Right as guard,
    Enhancing sanctity of trothplight sworn;
    Therefore, if thou art placable to those
    Who have their consort slain, nor will'st to turn
    On them the eye of wrath, unjust art thou
    In hounding to his doom the man who slew

His mother.   Lo, I know thee full of wrath
Against one deed, but all too placable
Unto the other, minishing the crime.
But in this cause shall Pallas guard the right.

LE.: Deem not my quest shall ever quit that man.

AP.: Follow then, make thee double toil in vain!

LE.: Think not by speech mine office to curtail.

AP.: None hast thou, that I would accept of thee!

LE.: Yea, high thine honour by the throne of Zeus:
But I, drawn on by scent of mother's blood,
Seek vengeance on this man and hound him down.
       [*The* CHORUS *goes in pursuit of* ORESTES.]

AP.: But I will stand beside him; 'tis for me
To guard my suppliant: gods and men alike
Do dread the curse of such an one betrayed,
And in me Fear and Will say *Leave him not.*
[*He goes into the temple.*]

[*The scene changes to Athens.   In the foreground is the Temple of*
ATHENA *on the Acropolis; her statue stands in the centre;* ORESTES *is
seen clinging to it.*]

OR.: Look on me, queen Athena; lo, I come
By Loxias' behest; thou of thy grace
Receive me, driven of avenging powers —
Not now a red-hand slayer unannealed,
But with guilt fading, half-effaced, outworn
On many homes and paths of mortal men.
For to the limit of each land, each sea,
I roamed, obedient to Apollo's hest,
And come at last, O Goddess, to thy fane,
And clinging to thine image, bide my doom.
       [*The* CHORUS OF FURIES *enters, questing like hounds.*]

LE.: Ho! clear is here the trace of him we seek:
Follow the track of blood, the silent sign!
Like to some hound that hunts a wounded fawn,
We snuff along the scent of dripping gore,
And inwardly we pant, for many a day
Toiling in chase that shall fordo the man;
For o'er and o'er the wide land have I ranged,
And o'er the wide sea, flying without wings,
Swift as a sail I pressed upon his track,
Who now hard by is crouching, well I wot,
For scent of mortal blood allures me here.

CH. [*chanting*]: Follow, seek him — round and round
       Scent and snuff and scan the ground,
       Lest unharmed he slip away,
       He who did his mother slay!
   Hist — he is there!   See him his arms entwine

Around the image of the maid divine —
   Thus aided, for the deed he wrought
   Unto the judgment wills he to be brought.

It may not be! a mother's blood, poured forth
   Upon the stainèd earth,
None gathers up: it lies — bear witness, Hell! —
   For aye indelible!
And thou who sheddest it shalt give thine own
   That shedding to atone!
Yea, from thy living limbs I suck it out,
   Red, clotted, gout by gout, —
A draught abhorred of men and gods; but I
   Will drain it, suck thee dry;
Yea, I will waste thee living, nerve and vein;
   Yea, for thy mother slain,
Will drag thee downward, there where thou shalt dree
   The weird of agony!
And thou and whosoe'er of men hath sinned —
   Hath wronged or God, or friend,
Or parent, — learn ye how to all and each
   The arm of doom can reach!
Sternly requiteth, in the world beneath,
   The judgment-seat of Death;
Yea, Death, beholding every man's endeavour,
   Recordeth it for ever.

OR.: I, schooled in many miseries, have learnt
How many refuges of cleansing shrines
There be; I know when law alloweth speech
And when imposeth silence. Lo, I stand
Fixed now to speak, for he whose word is wise
Commands the same. Look, how the stain of blood
Is dull upon mine hand and wastes away,
And laved and lost therewith is the deep curse
Of matricide; for while the guilt was new,
'Twas banished from me at Apollo's hearth,
Atoned and purified by death of swine.
Long were my word if I should sum the tale,
How oft since then among my fellow-men
I stood and brought no curse. Time cleanses all —
Time, the coeval of all things that are.
   Now from pure lips, in words of omen fair,
I call Athena, lady of this land,
To come, my champion: so, in aftertime,
She shall not fail of love and service leal,
Not won by war, from me and from my land
And all the folk of Argos, vowed to her.
   Now, be she far away in Libyan land

Where flows from Triton's lake her natal wave, —
Stand she with planted feet, or in some hour
Of rest conceal them, champion of her friends
Where'er she be, — or whether o'er the plain
Phlegraean she look forth, as warrior bold —
I cry to her to come, where'er she be,
(And she, as goddess, from afar can hear)
And aid and free me, set among my foes.

LE.: Thee not Apollo nor Athena's strength
Can save from perishing, a castaway
Amid the Lost, where no delight shall meet
Thy soul — a bloodless prey of nether powers,
A shadow among shadows. Answerest thou
Nothing? dost cast away my words with scorn,
Thou, prey prepared and dedicate to me?
Not as a victim slain upon the shrine,
But living shalt thou see thy flesh my food.
Hear now the binding chant that makes thee mine.

CH. [*chanting*]: Weave the weird dance, — behold the hour
            To utter forth the chant of hell,
            Our sway among mankind to tell,
          The guidance of our power.
          Of Justice are we ministers,
            And whoso'er of men may stand
            Lifting a pure unsullied hand,
          That man no doom of ours incurs,
            And walks thro' all his mortal path
            Untouched by woe, unharmed by wrath.
            But if, as yonder man, he hath
            Blood on the hands he strives to hide,
            We stand avengers at his side,
          Decreeing, *Thou hast wronged the dead:*
            We are doom's witnesses to thee.
          The price of blood, his hands have shed,
          We wring from him; in life, in death,
            Hard at his side are we!

                                              strophe 1

Night, Mother Night, who brought me forth, a torment
            To living men and dead,
Hear me, O hear! by Leto's stripling son
            I am dishonourèd:
He hath ta'en from me him who cowers in refuge,
            To me made consecrate, —
A rightful victim, him who slew his mother.
            Given o'er to me and fate.

refrain 1

Hear the hymn of hell,
  O'er the victim sounding, —
Chant of frenzy, chant of ill,
  Sense and will confounding!
Round the soul entwining
  Without lute or lyre —
Soul in madness pining,
  Wasting as with fire!

antistrophe 1

Fate, all-pervading Fate, this service spun, commanding
  That I should bide therein:
Whosoe'er of mortals, made perverse and lawless,
  Is stained with blood of kin,
By his side are we, and hunt him ever onward,
  Till to the Silent Land,
The realm of death, he cometh; neither yonder
  In freedom shall he stand.

refrain 1

Hear the hymn of hell,
  O'er the victim sounding, —
Chant of frenzy, chant of ill,
  Sense and will confounding!
Round the soul entwining
  Without lute or lyre —
Soul in madness pining,
  Wasting as with fire!

strophe 2

When from womb of Night we sprang, on us this labour
  Was laid and shall abide.
Gods immortal are ye, yet beware ye touch not
  That which is our pride!
None may come beside us gathered round the blood-feast —
  For us no garments white
Gleam on a feastal day; for us a darker fate is,
  Another darker rite.

refrain 2

That is mine hour when falls an ancient line —
  When in the household's heart
The God of blood doth slay by kindred hands, —
  Then do we bear our part:
On him who slays we sweep with chasing cry:
  Though he be triply strong,

We wear and waste him; blood atones for blood,
    New pain for ancient wrong.

antistrophe 2

I hold this task — 'tis mine, and not another's.
    The very gods on high,
Though they can silence and annul the prayers
    Of those who on us cry,
They may not strive with us who stand apart,
    A race by Zeus abhorred,
Blood-boltered, held unworthy of the council
    And converse of Heaven's lord.

strophe 3

Therefore the more I leap upon my prey;
    Upon their head I bound;
My foot is hard; as one that trips a runner
    I cast them to the ground;
Yea, to the depth of doom intolerable;
    And they who erst were great,
And upon earth held high their pride and glory,
    Are brought to low estate.
In underworld they waste and are diminished,
    The while around them fleet
Dark wavings of my robes, and, subtly woven,
    The paces of my feet.

antistrophe 3

Who falls infatuate, he sees not neither knows he
    That we are at his side;
So closely round about him, darkly flitting,
    The cloud of guilt doth glide.
Heavily 'tis uttered, how around his hearthstone
    The mirk of hell doth rise.

strophe 4

Stern and fixed the law is; we have hands t' achieve it,
    Cunning to devise.
Queens are we and mindful of our solemn vengeance.
    Not by tear or prayer
Shall a man avert it.   In unhonoured darkness,
    Far from gods, we fare,
Lit unto our task with torch of sunless regions,
    And o'er a deadly way —
Deadly to the living as to those who see not
    Life and light of day —
Hunt we and press onward.

antistrophe 4

Who of mortals hearing
 Doth not quake for awe,
Hearing all that Fate thro' hand of God hath given us
 For ordinance and law?
Yea, this right to us, in dark abysm and backward
 Of ages it befel:
None shall wrong mine office, tho' in nether regions
 And sunless dark I dwell.

        [ATHENA *enters.*]

ATH.: Far off I heard the clamour of your cry,
As by Scamander's side I set my foot
Asserting right upon the land given o'er
To me by those who o'er Achaea's host
Held sway and leadership: no scanty part
Of all they won by spear and sword, to me
They gave it, land and all that grew thereon,
As chosen heirloom for my Theseus' clan.
Thence summoned, sped I with a tireless foot, —
Hummed on the wind, instead of wings, the fold
Of this mine aegis, by my feet propelled,
As, linked to mettled horses, speeds a car.
And now, beholding here Earth's nether brood,
I fear it nought, yet are mine eyes amazed
With wonder. Who are ye? of all I ask,
And of this stranger to my statue clinging.
But ye — your shape is like no human form,
Like to no goddess whom the gods behold,
Like to no shape which mortal women wear.
Yet to stand by and chide a monstrous form
Is all unjust — from such words Right revolts.

LE.: O child of Zeus, one word shall tell thee all.
We are the children of eternal Night,
And Furies in the underworld are called.

ATH.: I know your lineage now and eke your name.

LE.: Yea, and eftsoons indeed my rights shalt know.

ATH.: Fain would I learn them; speak them clearly forth.

LE.: We chase from home the murderers of men.

ATH.: And where at last can he that slew make pause?

LE.: Where this is law — *All joy abandon here.*

ATH.: Say, do ye bay this man to such a flight?

LE.: Yea, for of choice he did his mother slay.

ATH.: Urged by no fear of other wrath and doom?

LE.: What spur can rightly goad to matricide?

ATH.: Two stand to plead — one only have I heard.

LE.: He will not swear nor challenge us to oath.

ATH.: The form of justice, not its deed, thou willest.

LE.: Prove thou that word; thou art not scant of skill.
ATH.: I say that oaths shall not enforce the wrong.
LE.: Then test the cause, judge and award the right.
ATH.: Will ye to me then this decision trust?
LE.: Yea, reverencing true child of worthy sire.
ATH. [*to* ORESTES]: O man unknown, make thou thy plea in turn.
    Speak forth thy land, thy lineage, and thy woes;
    Then, if thou canst, avert this bitter blame —
    If, as I deem, in confidence of right
    Thou sittest hard beside my holy place,
    Clasping this statue, as Ixion sat,
    A sacred suppliant for Zeus to cleanse, —
    To all this answer me in words made plain.
OR.: O queen Athena, first from thy last words
    Will I a great solicitude remove.
    Not one blood-guilty am I; no foul stain
    Clings to thine image from my clinging hand;
    Whereof one potent proof I have to tell.
    Lo, the law stands — *The slayer shall not plead,*
    Till by the hand of him who cleanses blood
    A suckling creature's blood besprinkle him.
    Long since have I this expiation done, —
    In many a home, slain beasts and running streams
    Have cleansed me.   Thus I speak away that fear.
    Next, of my lineage quickly thou shalt learn:
    An Argive am I, and right well thou know'st
    My sire, that Agamemnon who arrayed
    The fleet and them that went therein to war —
    That chief with whom thy hand combined to crush
    To an uncitied heap what once was Troy;
    That Agamemnon, when he homeward came,
    Was brought unto no honourable death,
    Slain by the dark-souled wife who brought me forth
    To him, — enwound and slain in wily nets,
    Blazoned with blood that in the laver ran.
    And I, returning from an exiled youth,
    Slew her, my mother — lo, it stands avowed!
    With blood for blood avenging my loved sire;
    And in this deed doth Loxias bear part,
    Decreeing agonies, to goad my will,
    Unless by me the guilty found their doom.
    Do thou decide if right or wrong were done —
    Thy dooming, whatsoe'er it be, contents me.
ATH.: Too mighty is this matter, whosoe'er
    Of mortals claims to judge hereof aright.
    Yea, me, even me, eternal Right forbids
    To judge the issues of blood-guilt, and wrath
    That follows swift behind.   This too gives pause,

That thou as one with all due rites performed
Dost come, unsinning, pure, unto my shrine.
Whate'er thou art, in this my city's name,
As uncondemned, I take thee to my side. —
Yet have these foes of thine such dues by fate,
I may not banish them: and if they fail,
O'erthrown in judgment of the cause, forthwith
Their anger's poison shall infect the land —
A dropping plague-spot of eternal ill.
Thus stand we with a woe on either hand:
Stay they, or go at my commandment forth,
Perplexity or pain must needs befall.
Yet, as on me Fate hath imposed the cause,
I choose unto me judges that shall be
An ordinance for ever, set to rule
The dues of blood-guilt, upon oath declared.
But ye, call forth your witness and your proof,
Words strong for justice, fortified by oath;
And I, whoe'er are truest in my town,
Them will I choose and bring, and straitly charge,
Look on this cause, discriminating well,
And pledge your oath to utter nought of wrong.
                              [ATHENA *withdraws*.]

strophe 1

CH. [*singing*]: Now are they all undone, the ancient laws,
        If here the slayer's cause
Prevail; new wrong for ancient right shall be
        If matricide go free.
Henceforth a deed like his by all shall stand,
        Too ready to the hand:
Too oft shall parents in the aftertime
        Rue and lament this crime, —
Taught, not in false imagining, to feel
        Their children's thrusting steel:
No more the wrath, that erst on murder fell
        From us, the queens of Hell,
Shall fall, no more our watching gaze impend —
        Death shall smite unrestrained.

antistrophe 1

Henceforth shall one unto another cry
Lo, they are stricken, lo, they fall and die
Around me! and that other answers him,
        O thou that lookest that thy woes should cease,
            Behold, with dark increase
        They throng and press upon thee; yea, and dim
        Is all the cure, and every comfort vain!

Let none henceforth cry out, when falls the blow
    Of sudden-smiting woe,
Cry out in sad reiterated strain
O Justice, aid! aid, O ye thrones of Hell!
   So though a father or a mother wail
  New-smitten by a son, it shall no more avail,
Since, overthrown by wrong, the fane of Justice fell!

Know, that a throne there is that may not pass away,
   And one that sitteth on it — even Fear,
Searching with steadfast eyes man's inner soul:
Wisdom is child of pain, and born with many a tear;
     But who henceforth,
What man of mortal men, what nation upon earth,
  That holdeth nought in awe nor in the light
  Of inner reverence, shall worship Right
      As in the older day?

Praise not O Man, the life beyond control,
Nor that which bows unto a tyrant's sway.
    Know that the middle way
Is dearest unto God, and they thereon who wend,
    They shall achieve the end;
But they who wander or to left or right
    Are sinners in his sight.
  Take to thy heart this one, this soothfast word —
   Of wantonness impiety is sire;
  Only from calm control and sanity unstirred
Cometh true weal, the goal of every man's desire.

Yea, whatsoe'er befall, hold thou this word of mine:
    Bow down at Justice' shrine,
  Turn thou thine eyes away from earthly lure,
 Nor with a godless foot that altar spurn.
For as thou dost shall Fate do in return,
    And the great doom is sure.
Therefore let each adore a parent's trust,
  And each with loyalty revere the guest
    That in his halls doth rest.

For whoso uncompelled doth follow what is just,
    He ne'er shall be unblest;
  Yea, never to the gulf of doom
    That man shall come.

But he whose will is set against the gods,
  Who treads beyond the law with foot impure,
Till o'er the wreck of Right confusion broods, —
  Know that for him, though now he sail secure,
The day of storm shall be; then shall he strive and fail
Down from the shivered yard to furl the sail,

antistrophe 4

And call on Powers, that heed him nought, to save,
  And vainly wrestle with the whirling wave.
    Hot was his heart with pride —
    I shall not fall, he cried.
    But him with watching scorn
    The god beholds, forlorn,
  Tangled in toils of Fate beyond escape,
  Hopeless of haven safe beyond the cape —
Till all his wealth and bliss of bygone day
  Upon the reef of Rightful Doom is hurled,
    And he is rapt away
Unwept, for ever, to the dead forgotten world.

[ATHENA *enters, with* TWELVE ATHENIAN CITIZENS. *A large crowd follows.*]

ATH.: O herald, make proclaim, bid all men come.
  Then let the shrill blast of the Tyrrhene trump,
  Fulfilled with mortal breath, thro' the wide air
  Peal a loud summons, bidding all men heed.
  For, till my judges fill this judgment-seat,
  Silence behoves, — that this whole city learn,
  What for all time mine ordinance commands,
  And these men, that the cause be judged aright.
                  [APOLLO *enters.*]

LE.: O king Apollo, rule what is thine own,
  But in this thing what share pertains to thee?

AP.: First, as a witness come I, for this man
  Is suppliant of mine by sacred right,
  Guest of my holy hearth and cleansed by me
  Of blood-guilt: then, to set me at his side
  And in his cause bear part, as part I bore
  Erst in his deed, whereby his mother fell.
  Let whoso knoweth now announce the cause.

ATH. [*to the* CHORUS]: 'Tis I announce the cause — first speech be
    yours;
  For rightfully shall they whose plaint is tried
  Tell the tale first and set the matter clear.

LE.: Though we be many, brief shall be our tale.
                  [*To* ORESTES]
  Answer thou, setting word to match with word;
  And first avow — hast thou thy mother slain?

OR.: I slew her. I deny no word hereof.

LE.: Three falls decide the wrestle — this is one.

OR.: Thou vauntest thee — but o'er no final fall.

LE.: Yet must thou tell the manner of thy deed.

OR.: Drawn sword in hand, I gashed her neck. 'Tis told.

LE.: But by whose word, whose craft, wert thou impelled?

OR.: By oracles of him who here attests me.

LE.: The prophet-god bade thee thy mother slay?

OR.: Yea, and thro' him less ill I fared, till now.

LE.: If the vote grip thee, thou shalt change that word.

OR.: Strong is my hope; my buried sire shall aid.

LE.: Go to now, trust the dead, a matricide!

OR.: Yea, for in her combined two stains of sin.

LE.: How? speak this clearly to the judges' mind.

OR.: Slaying her husband, she did slay my sire.

LE.: Therefore thou livest; death assoils her deed.

OR.: Then while she lived why didst thou hunt her not?

LE.: She was not kin by blood to him she slew.

OR.: And I, am I by blood my mother's kin?

LE.: O cursed with murder's guilt, how else wert thou
The burden of her womb? Dost thou forswear
Thy mother's kinship, closest bond of love?

OR.: It is thine hour, Apollo — speak the law,
Averring if this deed were justly done;
For done it is, and clear and undenied.
But if to thee this murder's cause seem right
Or wrongful, speak — that I to these may tell.

AP.: To you, Athena's mighty council-court,
Justly for justice will I plead, even I,
The prophet-god, nor cheat you by one word.
For never spake I from my prophet-seat
One word, of man, of woman, or of state,
Save what the Father of Olympian gods
Commanded unto me. I rede you then,
Bethink you of my plea, how strong it stands,
And follow the decree of Zeus our sire, —
For oaths prevail not over Zeus' command.

LE.: Go to; thou sayest that from Zeus befell
The oracle that this Orestes bade
With vengeance quit the slaying of his sire,
And hold as nought his mother's right of kin!

AP.: Yea, for it stands not with a common death,
That he should die, a chieftain and a king
Decked with the sceptre which high heaven confers —
Die, and by female hands, not smitten down
By a far-shooting bow, held stalwartly
By some strong Amazon. Another doom
Was his: O Pallas, hear, and ye who sit
In judgment, to discern this thing aright! —

She with a specious voice of welcome true
Hailed him, returning from the mighty mart
Where war for life gives fame, triumphant home;
Then o'er the laver, as he bathed himself,
She spread from head to foot a covering net,
And in the endless mesh of cunning robes
Enwound and trapped her lord, and smote him down.
Lo, ye have heard what doom this chieftain met,
The majesty of Greece, the fleet's high lord:
Such as I tell it, let it gall your ears,
Who stand as judges to decide this cause.

LE.: Zeus, as thou sayest, holds a father's death
As first of crimes, — yet he of his own act
Cast into chains his father, Cronus old:
How suits that deed with that which now ye tell?
O ye who judge, I bid ye mark my words!

AP.: O monsters loathed of all, O scorn of gods,
He that hath bound may loose: a cure there is,
Yea, many a plan that can unbind the chain.
But when the thirsty dust sucks up man's blood
Once shed in death, he shall arise no more.
No chant nor charm for this my Sire hath wrought.
All else there is, he moulds and shifts at will,
Not scant of strength nor breath, whate'er he do.

LE.: Think yet, for what acquittal thou dost plead:
He who hath shed a mother's kindred blood,
Shall he in Argos dwell, where dwelt his sire?
How shall he stand before the city's shrines,
How share the clansmen's holy lustral bowl?

AP.: This too I answer; mark a soothfast word.
Not the true parent is the woman's womb
That bears the child; she doth but nurse the seed
New-sown: the male is parent; she for him,
As stranger for a stranger, hoards the germ
Of life, unless the god its promise blight.
And proof hereof before you will I set.
Birth may from fathers, without mothers, be:
See at your side a witness of the same,
Athena, daughter of Olympian Zeus,
Never within the darkness of the womb
Fostered nor fashioned, but a bud more bright
Than any goddess in her breast might bear.
And I, O Pallas, howsoe'er I may,
Henceforth will glorify thy town, thy clan,
And for this end have sent my suppliant here
Unto thy shrine; that he from this time forth
Be loyal unto thee for evermore,
O goddess-queen, and thou unto thy side

Mayst win and hold him faithful, and his line,
And that for aye this pledge and troth remain
To children's children of Athenian seed.

ATH.: Enough is said; I bid the judges now
With pure intent deliver just award.

LE.: We too have shot our every shaft of speech,
And now abide to hear the doom of law.

ATH. [*to* APOLLO *and* ORESTES]: Say, how ordaining shall I 'scape your
          blame?

AP.: I spake, ye heard; enough.   O stranger men,
Heed well your oath as ye decide the cause.

ATH.: O men of Athens, ye who first do judge
The law of bloodshed, hear me now ordain.
Here to all time for Aegeus' Attic host
Shall stand this council-court of judges sworn,
Here the tribunal, set on Ares' Hill
Where camped of old the tented Amazons,
What time in hate of Theseus they assailed
Athens, and set against her citadel
A counterwork of new sky-pointing towers,
And there to Ares held their sacrifice,
Where now the rock hath name, even Ares' Hill.
And hence shall Reverence and her kinsman Fear
Pass to each free man's heart, by day and night
Enjoining, *Thou shalt do no unjust thing,*
So long as law stands as it stood of old
Unmarred by civic change.   Look you, the spring
Is pure; but foul it once with influx vile
And muddy clay, and none can drink thereof.
Therefore, O citizens, I bid ye bow
In awe to this command, *Let no man live
Uncurbed by law nor curbed by tyranny;*
Nor banish ye the monarchy of Awe
Beyond the walls; untouched by fear divine,
No man doth justice in the world of men.
Therefore in purity and holy dread
Stand and revere; so shall ye have and hold
A saving bulwark of the state and land,
Such as no man hath ever elsewhere known,
Nor in far Scythia, nor in Pelops' realm.
Thus I ordain it now, a council-court
Pure and unsullied by the lust of gain,
Sacred and swift to vengeance, wakeful ever
To champion men who sleep, the country's guard.
Thus have I spoken, thus to mine own clan
Commended it for ever.   Ye who judge,
Arise, take each his vote, mete out the right,
Your oath revering.   Lo, my word is said.

[The twelve judges come forward, one by one, to the urns of decision; the first votes; as each of the others follows, the LEADER *and* APOLLO *speak alternately.]*

LE.: I rede ye well, beware! nor put to shame,
    In aught, this grievous company of hell.

AP.: I too would warn you, fear mine oracles —
    From Zeus they are, — nor make them void of fruit.

LE.: Presumptuous is thy claim, blood-guilt to judge,
    And false henceforth thine oracles shall be.

AP.: Failed then the counsels of my sire, when turned
    Ixion, first of slayers, to his side?

LE.: These are but words; but I, if justice fail me,
    Will haunt this land in grim and deadly deed.

AP.: Scorn of the younger and the elder gods
    Art thou: 'tis I that shall prevail anon.

LE.: Thus didst thou too of old in Pheres' halls,
    O'erreaching Fate to make a mortal deathless.*

AP.: Was it not well, my worshipper to aid,
    Then most of all when hardest was the need?

LE.: I say thou didst annul the lots of life,
    Cheating with wine the deities of eld.

AP.: I say thou shalt anon, thy pleadings foiled,
    Spit venom vainly on thine enemies.

LE.: Since this young god o'errides mine ancient right,
    I tarry but to claim your law, not knowing
    If wrath of mine shall blast your state or spare.

ATH.: Mine is the right to add the final vote,
    And I award it to Orestes' cause.
    For me no mother bore within her womb,
    And, save for wedlock evermore eschewed,
    I vouch myself the champion of the man,
    Not of the woman, yea, with all my soul, —
    In heart, as birth, a father's child alone.
    Thus will I not too heinously regard
    A woman's death who did her husband slay,
    The guardian of her home; and if the votes
    Equal do fall, Orestes shall prevail.

    Ye of the judges who are named thereto,
    Swiftly shake forth the lots from either urn.
        [Two judges come forward, one to each urn.]

OR.: O bright Apollo, what shall be the end?

LE.: O Night, dark mother mine, dost mark these things?

OR.: Now shall my doom be life, or strangling cords.

LE.: And mine, lost honour or a wider sway.

AP.: O stranger judges, sum aright the count
    Of votes cast forth, and, parting them, take heed

* Apollo had agreed to spare the life of Admetus, son of Pheres, provided that he could get someone to die in his stead.

Ye err not in decision. The default
Of one vote only bringeth ruin deep,
One, cast aright, doth stablish house and home.
ATH.: Behold, this man is free from guilt of blood,
    For half the votes condemn him, half set free!
OR.: O Pallas, light and safety of my home,
    Thou, thou hast given me back to dwell once more
    In that my fatherland, amerced of which
    I wandered; now shall Grecian lips say this,
    The man is Argive once again, and dwells
    Again within his father's wealthy hall,
    By Pallas saved, by Loxias, and by Him,
    The great third saviour, Zeus omnipotent —
    Who thus in pity for my father's fate
    Doth pluck me from my doom, beholding these,
    Confederates of my mother. Lo, I pass
    To mine own home, but proffering this vow
    Unto thy land and people: *Nevermore,*
    Thro' all the manifold years of Time to be,
    Shall any chieftain of mine Argive land
    Bear hitherward his spears for fight arrayed.
    For we, though lapped in earth we then shall lie,
    By thwart adversities will work our will
    On them who shall transgress this oath of mine,
    Paths of despair and journeyings ill-starred
    For them ordaining, till their task they rue.
    But if this oath be rightly kept, to them
    Will we the dead be full of grace, the while
    With loyal league they honour Pallas' town.
    And now farewell, thou and thy city's folk —
    Firm be thine arms' grasp, closing with thy foes,
    And, strong to save, bring victory to thy spear.

        [ORESTES *and* APOLLO *depart.*]

CH. [*chanting*]: Woe on you, younger gods! the ancient right
        Ye have o'erridden, rent it from my hands.

    I am dishonoured of you, thrust to scorn!
            But heavily my wrath
Shall on this land fling forth the drops that blast and burn,
    Venom of vengeance, that shall work such scathe
    As I have suffered; where that dew shall fall,
            Shall leafless blight arise,
    Wasting Earth's offspring, — Justice, hear my call! —
    And thorough all the land in deadly wise
    Shall scatter venom, to exude again
            In pestilence on men.
    What cry avails me now, what deed of blood,
    Unto this land what dark despite?
            Alack, alack, forlorn

                  Are we, a bitter injury have borne!
                  Alack, O sisters, O dishonoured brood
                          Of mother Night!
\TH.: Nay, bow ye to my words, chafe not nor moan:
      Ye are not worsted nor disgraced; behold,
      With balanced vote the cause had issue fair,
      Nor in the end did aught dishonour thee.
      But thus the will of Zeus shone clearly forth,
      And his own prophet-god avouched the same,
      Orestes slew: his slaying is atoned.
      Therefore I pray you, not upon this land
      Shoot forth the dart of vengeance; be appeased,
      Nor blast the land with blight, nor loose thereon
      Drops of eternal venom, direful darts
      Wasting and marring nature's seed of growth.
      For I, the queen of Athens' sacred right,
      Do pledge to you a holy sanctuary
      Deep in the heart of this my land, made just
      By your indwelling presence, while ye sit
      Hard by your sacred shrines that gleam with oil
      Of sacrifice, and by this folk adored.
CH. [*chanting*]: Woe on you, younger gods! the ancient right
                  Ye have o'erridden, rent it from my hands.

              I am dishonoured of you, thrust to scorn!
                      But heavily my wrath
      Shall on this land fling forth the drops that blast and burn,
              Venom of vengeance, that shall work such scathe
              As I have suffered; where that dew shall fall,
                      Shall leafless blight arise,
              Wasting Earth's offspring, — Justice, hear my call! —
      And thorough all the land in deadly wise
      Shall scatter venom, to exude again
                  In pestilence on men.
      What cry avails me now, what deed of blood,
      Unto this land what dark despite?
                  Alack, alack, forlorn
              Are we, a bitter injury have borne!
              Alack, O sisters, O dishonoured brood
                      Of mother Night!
ATH.: Dishonoured are ye not; turn not, I pray,
      As goddesses your swelling wrath on men,
      Nor make the friendly earth despiteful to them.
      I too have Zeus for champion — 'tis enough —
      I only of all goddesses do know
      To ope the chamber where his thunderbolts
      Lie stored and sealed; but here is no such need.
      Nay, be appeased, nor cast upon the ground
      The malice of thy tongue, to blast the world;

Calm thou thy bitter wrath's black inward surge,
For high shall be thine honour, set beside me
For ever in this land, whose fertile lap
Shall pour its teeming firstfruits unto you,
Gifts for fair childbirth and for wedlock's crown:
Thus honoured, praise my spoken pledge for aye.

CH. [*chanting*]: I, I dishonoured in this earth to dwell, —
Ancient of days and wisdom! I breathe forth
Poison and breath of frenzied ire. O Earth,
        Woe, woe for thee, for me!
From side to side what pains be these that thrill?
Hearken, O mother Night, my wrath, mine agony!
Whom from mine ancient rights the gods have thrust,
        And brought me to the dust —
Woe, woe is me! — with craft invincible.

ATH.: Older art thou than I, and I will bear
With this thy fury. Know, although thou be
More wise in ancient wisdom, yet have I
From Zeus no scanted measure of the same,
Wherefore take heed unto this prophecy —
If to another land of alien men
Ye go, too late shall ye feel longing deep
For mine. The rolling tides of time bring round
A day of brighter glory for this town;
And thou, enshrined in honour by the halls
Where dwelt Erechtheus, shalt a worship win
From men and from the train of womankind,
Greater than any tribe elsewhere shall pay.
Cast thou not therefore on this soil of mine
Whetstones that sharpen souls to bloodshedding,
The burning goads of youthful hearts, made hot
With frenzy of the spirit, not of wine.
Nor pluck as 'twere the heart from cocks that strive,
To set it in the breast of citizens
Of mine, a war-god's spirit, keen for fight,
Made stern against their country and their kin.
The man who grievously doth lust for fame,
War, full, immitigable, let him wage
Against the stranger; but of kindred birds
I hold the challenge hateful. Such the boon
I proffer thee — within this land of lands,
Most loved of gods, with me to show and share
Fair mercy, gratitude and grace as fair.

CH. [*chanting*]: I, I dishonoured in this earth to dwell, —
Ancient of days and wisdom! I breathe forth
Poison and breath of frenzied ire. O Earth,
        Woe, woe for thee, for me!
From side to side what pains be these that thrill?
Hearken, O mother Night, my wrath, mine agony!

    Whom from mine ancient rights the gods have thrust
        And brought me to the dust —
   Woe, woe is me! — with craft invincible.
ATH.: I will not weary of soft words to thee,
   That never mayst thou say, *Behold me spurned,*
   An elder by a younger deity,
   And from this land rejected and forlorn,
   Unhonoured by the men who dwell therein.
   But, if Persuasion's grace be sacred to thee,
   Soft in the soothing accents of my tongue,
   Tarry, I pray thee; yet, if go thou wilt,
   Not rightfully wilt thou on this my town
   Sway down the scale that beareth wrath and teen
   Or wasting plague upon this folk.   'Tis thine,
   If so thou wilt, inheritress to be
   Of this my land, its utmost grace to win.
LE.: O queen, what refuge dost thou promise me?
ATH.: Refuge untouched by bale: take thou my boon.
LE.: What, if I take it, shall mine honour be?
ATH.: No house shall prosper without grace of thine.
LE.: Canst thou achieve and grant such power to me?
ATH.: Yea, for my hand shall bless thy worshippers.
LE.: And wilt thou pledge me this for time eterne?
ATH.: Yea: none can bid me pledge beyond my power.
LE.: Lo, I desist from wrath, appeased by thee.
ATH.: Then in the land's heart shalt thou win thee friends.
LE.: What chant dost bid me raise, to greet the land?
ATH.: Such as aspires towards a victory
   Unrued by any: chants from breast of earth,
   From wave, from sky; and let the wild winds' breath
   Pass with soft sunlight o'er the lap of land, —
   Strong wax the fruits of earth, fair teem the kine,
   Unfailing, for my town's prosperity,
   And constant be the growth of mortal seed.
   But more and more root out the impious,
   For as a gardener fosters what he sows,
   So foster I this race, whom righteousness
   Doth fend from sorrow.   Such the proffered boon.
   But I, if wars must be, and their loud clash
   And carnage, for my town, will ne'er endure
   That aught but victory shall crown her fame.
CH. [*chanting*]: Lo, I accept it; at her very side
       Doth Pallas bid me dwell:
   I will not wrong the city of her pride,
   Which even Almighty Zeus and Ares hold
       Heaven's earthly citadel,
   Loved home of Grecian gods, the young, the old,
       The sanctuary divine,
       The shield of every shrine!

For Athens I say forth a gracious prophecy, —
The glory of the sunlight and the skies
Shall bid from earth arise
Warm wavelets of new life and glad prosperity.

ATH. [*chanting*]: Behold, with gracious heart well pleased
I for my citizens do grant
Fulfilment of this covenant:
And here, their wrath at length appeased,
These mighty deities shall stay.
For theirs it is by right to sway
The lot that rules our mortal day,
And he who hath not inly felt
Their stern decree, ere long on him,
Not knowing why and whence, the grim
Life-crushing blow is dealt.
The father's sin upon the child
Descends, and sin is silent death,
And leads him on the downward path,
By stealth beguiled,
Unto the Furies: though his state
On earth were high, and loud his boast,
Victim of silent ire and hate
He dwells among the Lost.

CH [*chanting*]: To my blessing now give ear. —
Scorching blight nor singèd air
Never blast thine olives fair!
Drouth, that wasteth bud and plant,
Keep to thine own place. Avaunt,
Famine fell, and come not hither
Stealthily to waste and wither!
Let the land, in season due,
Twice her waxing fruits renew;
Teem the kine in double measure;
Rich in new god-given treasure;
Here let men the powers adore
For sudden gifts unhoped before!

ATH. [*chanting*]: O hearken, warders of the wall
That guards mine Athens, what a dower
Is unto her ordained and given!
For mighty is the Furies' power,
And deep-revered in courts of heaven
And realms of hell; and clear to all
They weave thy doom, mortality!
And some in joy and peace shall sing;
But unto other some they bring
Sad life and tear-dimmed eye.

CH. [*chanting*]: And far away I ban thee and remove,
Untimely death of youths too soon brought low!
And to each maid, O gods, when time is come for love,

Grant ye a warrior's heart, a wedded life to know.
Ye too, O Fates, children of mother Night,
    Whose children too are we, O goddesses
Of just award, of all by sacred right
    Queens, who in time and in eternity
Do rule, a present power for righteousness,
    Honoured beyond all Gods, hear ye and grant my cry!

ATH. [*chanting*]: And I too, I with joy am fain,
              Hearing your voice this gift ordain
              Unto my land.   High thanks be thine,
              Persuasion, who with eyes divine
              Into my tongue didst look thy strength,
              To bend and to appease at length
                Those who would not be comforted.
              Zeus, king of parley, doth prevail,
              And ye and I will strive nor fail,
                That good may stand in evil's stead,
              And lasting bliss for bale.

CH. [*chanting*]: And nevermore these walls within
              Shall echo fierce sedition's din,
                Unslaked with blood and crime;
              The thirsty dust shall nevermore
              Suck up the darkly streaming gore
              Of civic broils, shed out in wrath
              And vengeance, crying death for death!
              But man with man and state with state
              Shall vow *The pledge of common hate*
              And common friendship, that for man
              Hath oft made blessing out of ban,
                Be ours unto all time.

ATH. [*chanting*]: Skill they, or not, the path to find
              Of favouring speech and presage kind?
              Yea, even from these, who, grim and stern,
                Glared anger upon you of old,
              O citizens, ye now shall earn
                A recompense right manifold.
              Deck them aright, extol them high,
              Be loyal to their loyalty,
                And ye shall make your town and land
                Sure, propped on Justice' saving hand,
                  And Fame's eternity.

CH. [*chanting*]: Hail ye, all hail! and yet again, all hail,
              O Athens, happy in a weal secured!
              O ye who sit by Zeus' right hand, nor fail
              Of wisdom set among you and assured,
              Loved of the well-loved Goddess-Maid! the King
              Of gods doth reverence you, beneath her guarding wing.

ATH. [*chanting*]: All hail unto each honoured guest!
              Whom to the chambers of your rest

'Tis mine to lead, and to provide
The hallowed torch, the guard and guide.
Pass down, the while these altars glow
With sacred fire, to earth below
        And your appointed shrine.
There dwelling, from the land restrain
The force of fate, the breath of bane,
But waft on us the gift and gain
        Of Victory divine!
And ye, the men of Cranaos' seed,
I bid you now with reverence lead
These alien Powers that thus are made
Athenian evermore.   To you
Fair be their will henceforth, to do
        Whate'er may bless and aid!

CH. [*chanting*]: Hail to you all! hail yet again,
        All who love Athens, gods and men,
            Adoring her as Pallas' home!
        And while ye reverence what ye grant —
        My sacred shrine and hidden haunt —
            Blameless and blissful be your doom!

ATH.: Once more I praise the promise of your vows,
        And now I bid the golden torches' glow
        Pass down before you to the hidden depth
        Of earth, by mine own sacred servants borne,
        My loyal guards of statue and of shrine.
        Come forth, O flower of Theseus' Attic land,
        O glorious band of children and of wives,
        And ye, O train of matrons crowned with eld!
        Deck you with festal robes of scarlet dye
        In honour of this day: O gleaming torch,
        Lead onward, that these gracious powers of earth
        Henceforth be seen to bless the life of men.

[ATHENA *leads the procession downwards into the Cave of the* FURIES,
*now Eumenides, under the Areopagus: as they go, the escort of
women and children chant aloud.*]

CHANT: With loyalty we lead you; proudly go,
        Night's childless children, to your home below!
            (*O citizens, awhile from words forbear!*)
        To darkness' deep primeval lair,
        Far in Earth's bosom, downward fare,
            Adored with prayer and sacrifice.
            (*O citizens, forbear your cries!*)
        Pass hitherward, ye powers of Dread,
        With all your former wrath allayed,
            Into the heart of this loved land;
        With joy unto your temple wend,
        The while upon your steps attend

The flames that feed upon the brand —
(*Now, now ring out your chant, your joy's acclaim!*)
   Behind them, as they downward fare,
   Let holy hands libations bear,
      And torches' sacred flame.
   All-seeing Zeus and Fate come down
   To battle fair for Pallas' town!
Ring out your chant, ring out your joy's acclaim!

SOPHOCLES

(ca. 495–405 B.C.)

OEDIPUS THE KING

Translated by R. C. JEBB

CHARACTERS IN THE PLAY

OEDIPUS, *King of Thebes*
PRIEST OF ZEUS
CREON, *brother of* JOCASTA
TEIRESIAS, *the blind prophet*
JOCASTA
FIRST MESSENGER, *a shepherd from Corinth*
A SHEPHERD, *formerly in the service of Laius*
SECOND MESSENGER, *from the house*
CHORUS OF THEBAN ELDERS

Mute Persons
A train of Suppliants (old men, youths, and children).
The children ANTIGONE *and* ISMENE, *daughters of*
OEDIPUS *and* JOCASTA

OEDIPUS THE KING

[SCENE: — *Before the royal palace of Oedipus at Thebes. In front of the large central doors there is an altar; a smaller altar stands also near each of the two side-doors. Suppliants — old men, youths, and young children — are seated on the steps of the altars. They are dressed in white tunics and cloaks, — their hair bound with white fillets. On the altars they have laid down olive-branches wreathed with fillets of wool. The PRIEST OF ZEUS, a venerable man, is alone standing, facing the central doors of the palace. These are now thrown open. Followed by two attendants, who place themselves on either side of the doors, OEDIPUS enters, in the robes of a king. For a moment he gazes silently on the groups at the altars, and then speaks.*]

OE.: My children, latest-born to Cadmus who was of old, why are ye set before me thus with wreathed branches of suppliants, while the city reeks with incense, rings with prayers for health and cries of woe? I deemed it unmeet, my children, to hear these things at the mouth of others, and have come hither myself, I, Oedipus renowned of all.

Tell me, then, thou venerable man — since it is thy natural part to speak for these — in what mood are ye placed here, with what dread or what desire? Be sure that I would gladly give all aid; hard of heart were I, did I not pity such suppliants as these.

PRIEST: Nay, Oedipus, ruler of my land, thou seest of what years we are who beset thy altars, — some, nestlings still too tender for far flights, — some, bowed with age, priests, as I of Zeus, — and these, the chosen youth; while the rest of the folk sit with wreathed branches in the market-places, ard before the two shrines of Pallas, and where Ismenus gives answer by fire.

For the city, as thou thyself seest, is now too sorely vexed, and can no more lift her head from beneath the angry waves of death; a blight is on her in the fruitful blossoms of the land, in the herds among the pastures, in the barren pangs of women; and withal the flaming god, the malign plague, hath swooped on us, and ravages the town; by whom the house of Cadmus is made waste, but dark Hades rich in groans and tears.

It is not as deeming thee ranked with gods that I and these children are suppliants at thy hearth, but as deeming thee first of men, both in life's common chances, and when mortals have to do with more than man: seeing that thou camest to the town of Cadmus, and didst quit us of the tax that we rendered to the hard songstress; and this, though thou knewest nothing from us that could avail thee, nor hadst been schooled; no, by a god's aid, 'tis said and believed, didst thou uplift our life.

And now, Oedipus, king glorious in all eyes, we beseech thee, all we suppliants, to find for us some succour, whether by the whisper of a god thou knowest it, or haply as in the power of man; for I see that, when men have been proved in deeds past, the issues of their counsels, too, most often have effect.

On, best of mortals, again uplift our State! On, guard thy fame, — since now this land calls thee saviour for thy former zeal; and never be it our memory of thy reign that we were first restored and afterward cast down: nay, lift up this State in such wise that it fall no more!

With good omen didst thou give us that past happiness; now also show thyself the same. For if thou art to rule this land, even as thou art now its lord, 'tis better to be lord of men than of a waste: since neither walled town nor ship is anything, if it is void and no men dwell with thee therein.

OE.: Oh my piteous children, known, well known to me are the desires wherewith ye have come: well wot I that ye suffer all; yet, sufferers as ye are, there is not one of you whose suffering is as mine. Your pain comes on each one of you for himself alone, and for no other; but my soul mourns at once for the city, and for myself, and for thee.

So that ye rouse me not, truly, as one sunk in sleep: no, be sure that I have wept full many tears, gone many ways in wanderings of thought. And the sole remedy which, well pondering, I could find, this I have put into act. I have sent the son of Menoeceus, Creon, mine own wife's brother, to the Pythian house of Phoebus, to learn by what deed or word I might deliver this town. And already, when the lapse of days is reckoned, it troubles me what he doth; for he tarries strangely, beyond the fitting space. But when he comes, then shall I be no true man if I do not all that the god shows.

PR.: Nay, in season hast thou spoken; at this moment these sign to me that Creon draws near.

OE.: O king Apollo, may he come to us in the brightness of saving fortune, even as his face is bright!

PR.: Nay, to all seeming, he brings comfort; else would he not be coming crowned thus thickly with berry-laden bay.

OE.: We shall know soon: he is at range to hear. — [Enter CREON] Prince, my kinsman, son of Menoeceus, what news hast thou brought us from the god?

CR.: Good news: I tell thee that even troubles hard to bear, — if haply they find the right issue, — will end in perfect peace.

OE.: But what is the oracle? So far, thy words make me neither bold nor yet afraid.

CR.: If thou wouldest hear while these are nigh, I am ready to speak; or else to go within.

OE.: Speak before all: the sorrow which I bear is for these more than for mine own life.

CR.: With thy leave, I will tell what I heard from the god. Phoebus our lord bids us plainly to drive out a defiling thing, which (he saith) hath been harboured in this land, and not to harbour it, so that it cannot be healed.

OE.: By what rite shall we cleanse us? What is the manner of the misfortune?

CR.: By banishing a man, or by bloodshed in quittance of bloodshed, since it is that blood which brings the tempest on our city.

OE.: And who is the man whose fate he thus reveals?

CR.: Laius, king, was lord of our land before thou wast pilot of this State.

OE.: I know it well — by hearsay, for I saw him never.

CR.: He was slain; and the god now bids us plainly to wreak vengeance on his murderers — whosoever they be.

OE.: And where are they upon the earth? Where shall the dim track of this old crime be found?

CR.: In this land, — said the god. What is sought for can be caught; only that which is not watched escapes.

OE.: And was it in the house, or in the field, or on strange soil that Laius met this bloody end?

CR.: 'Twas on a visit to Delphi, as he said, that he had left our land; and he came home no more, after he had once set forth.

OE.: And was there none to tell? Was there no comrade of his journey who saw the deed, from whom tidings might have been gained, and used?

CR.: All perished, save one who fled in fear, and could tell for certain but one thing of all that he saw.

OE.: And what was that? One thing might show the clue to many, could we get but a small beginning for hope.

CR.: He said that robbers met and fell on them, not in one man's might, but with full many hands.

OE.: How, then, unless there was some trafficking in bribes from here, should the robber have dared thus far?

CR.: Such things were surmised; but, Laius once slain, amid our troubles no avenger arose.

OE.: But, when royalty had fallen thus, what trouble in your path can have hindered a full search?

CR.: The riddling Sphinx had made us let dark things go, and was inviting us to think of what lay at our doors.

OE.: Nay, I will start afresh, and once more make dark things plain. Right worthily hath Phoebus, and worthily hast thou, bestowed this care on the cause of the dead; and so, as is meet, ye shall find me too leagued with you in seeking vengeance for this land, and for the god besides. On behalf of no far-off friend, no, but in mine own cause, shall I dispel this taint. For whoever was the slayer of Laius might wish to take vengeance on me also with a hand as fierce. Therefore, in doing right to Laius, I serve myself.

Come, haste ye, my children, rise from the altar-steps, and lift these suppliant boughs; and let some other summon hither the folk of Cadmus, warned that I mean to leave nought untried; for our health (with the god's help) shall be made certain — or our ruin.

PR.: My children, let us rise; we came at first to seek what this man promises of himself. And may Phoebus, who sent these oracles, come to us therewith, our saviour and deliverer from the pest.

[*Exeunt* OEDIPUS *and* PRIEST. *Enter* CHORUS OF THEBAN ELDERS.]

strophe 1

CH. [*singing*]: O sweetly-speaking message of Zeus, in what spirit hast thou come from golden Pytho unto glorious Thebes? I am on the rack, terror shakes my soul, O thou Delian healer to whom wild cries rise, in holy fear of thee, what thing thou wilt work for me, perchance unknown before, perchance renewed with the revolving years: tell me, thou immortal Voice, born of Golden Hope!

antistrophe 1

First call I on thee, daughter of Zeus, divine Athena, and on thy sister, guardian of our land, Artemis, who sits on her throne of fame, above the circle of our Agora, and on Phoebus the far-darter: O shine forth on me, my three-fold help against death! If ever aforetime, in arrest of ruin hurrying on the city, ye drove a fiery pest beyond our borders, come now also!

strophe 2

Woe is me, countless are the sorrows that I bear; a plague is on all our host, and thought can find no weapon for defence. The fruits of the glorious earth grow not; by no birth of children do women surmount the pangs in which they shriek; and life on life mayest thou see sped, like bird on nimble wing, aye, swifter than resistless fire, to the shore of the western god.

antistrophe 2

By such deaths, past numbering, the city perishes: unpitied, her children lie on the ground, spreading pestilence, with none to mourn: and meanwhile young wives, and grey-haired mothers with them, uplift a wail at the steps of the altars, some here, some there, entreating for their weary woes. The prayer of the Healer rings clear, and, blent therewith, the voice of lamentation: for these things, golden daughter of Zeus, send us the bright face of comfort.

strophe 3

And grant that the fierce god of death, who now with no brazen shields, yet amid cries as of battle, wraps me in the flame of his onset, may turn his back in speedy flight from our land, borne by a fair wind to the great deep of Amphitrite, or to those waters in which none find haven, even to the Thracian wave; for if night leave aught undone, day follows to accomplish this. O thou who wieldest the powers of the fire-fraught lightning, O Zeus our father, slay him beneath thy thunderbolt!

antistrophe 3

Lycean King, fain were I that thy shafts also, from thy bent bow's string of woven gold, should go abroad in their might, our champions in the face of the foe; yea, and the flashing fires of Artemis wherewith she glances through the Lycian hills. And I call him whose locks are bound with gold, who is named with the name of this land, ruddy Bacchus to whom Bacchants cry, the comrade of the Maenads, to draw near with the blaze of his blithe torch, our ally against the god unhonoured among gods.

[OEDIPUS *enters during the closing strains of the choral song.*]

OE.: Thou prayest: and in answer to thy prayer, — if thou wilt give a loyal welcome to my words and minister to thine own disease, — thou mayest hope to find succour and relief from woes. These words will I speak publicly, as one who has been a stranger to this report, a stranger to the deed; for I should not be far on the track, if I were tracing it alone, without a clue. But as it is, — since it was only after the time of the deed that I was numbered a Theban among Thebans, — to you, the Cadmeans all, I do thus proclaim.

Whosoever of you knows by whom Laius son of Labdacus was slain, I bid him to declare all to me. And if he is afraid, I tell him to remove the danger of the charge from his path by denouncing himself; for he shall suffer nothing else unlovely, but only leave the land, unhurt. Or if any one knows an alien, from another land, as the assassin, let him not keep silence; for I will pay his guerdon, and my thanks shall rest with him besides.

But if ye keep silence — if any one, through fear, shall seek to screen friend or self from my behest — hear ye what I then shall do. I charge you that no one of this land, whereof I hold the empire and the throne, give shelter or speak word unto that murderer, whosoever he be, — make him partner of his prayer or sacrifice, or serve him with the lustral rite; but that all ban him their homes, knowing that *this* is our defiling thing, as the oracle of the Pythian god hath newly shown me. I then am on this wise the ally of the god and of the slain. And I pray solemnly that the slayer, whoso he be, whether his hidden guilt is lonely or hath partners, evilly, as he is evil, may wear out his unblest life. And for myself I pray that if, with my privity, he should become an inmate of my house, I may suffer the same things which even now I called down upon others. And on you I lay it to make all these words good, for my sake, and for the sake of the god, and for our land's, thus blasted with barrenness by angry heaven.

For even if the matter had not been urged on us by a god, it was not meet that ye should leave the guilt thus unpurged, when one so noble, and he your king, had perished; rather were ye bound to search it out. And now, since 'tis I who hold the powers which once he held, who possess his bed and the wife who bare seed to him; and since, had his hope of issue not been frustrate, children born of one mother would have made ties betwixt him and me —

but, as it was, fate swooped upon his head; by reason of these things will I uphold this cause, even as the cause of mine own sire, and will leave nought untried in seeking to find him whose hand shed that blood, for the honour of the son of Labdacus and of Polydorus and elder Cadmus and Agenor who was of old.

And for those who obey me not, I pray that the gods send them neither harvest of the earth nor fruit of the womb, but that they be wasted by their lot that now is, or by one yet more dire. But for all you, the loyal folk of Cadmus to whom these things seem good, may Justice, our ally, and all the gods be with you graciously for ever.

LEADER OF THE CHORUS: As thou hast put me on my oath, on my oath, O king, I will speak. I am not the slayer, nor can I point to him who slew. As for the question, it was for Phoebus, who sent it, to tell us this thing — who can have wrought the deed.

OE.: Justly said; but no man on the earth can force the gods to what they will not.

LE.: I would fain say what seems to me next best after this.

OE.: If there is yet a third course, spare not to show it.

LE.: I know that our lord Teiresias is the seer most like to our lord Phoebus; from whom, O king, a searcher of these things might learn them most clearly.

OE.: Not even this have I left out of my cares. On the hint of Creon, I have twice sent a man to bring him; and this long while I marvel why he is not here.

LE.: Indeed (his skill apart) the rumours are but faint and old.

OE.: What rumours are they? I look to every story.

LE.: Certain wayfarers were said to have killed him.

OE.: I, too, have heard it, but none sees him who saw it.

LE.: Nay, if he knows what fear is, he will not stay when he hears thy curses, so dire as they are.

OE.: When a man shrinks not from a deed, neither is he scared by a word.

LE.: But there is one to convict him. For here they bring at last the godlike prophet, in whom alone of men doth live the truth.

[*Enter* TEIRESIAS, *led by a boy.*]

OE.: Teiresias, whose soul grasps all things, the lore that may be told and the unspeakable, the secrets of heaven and the low things of earth, — thou feelest, though thou canst not see, what a plague doth haunt our State, — from which, great prophet, we find in thee our protector and only saviour. Now, Phoebus — if indeed thou knowest it not from the messengers — sent answer to our question that the only riddance from this pest which could come was if we should learn aright the slayers of Laius, and slay them, or send them into exile from our land. Do thou, then, grudge neither voice of birds nor any other way of seer-lore that thou hast, but rescue thyself and the State, rescue me, rescue all that is defiled by the dead. For we are in thy hand; and man's noblest task is to help others by his best means and powers.

TE.: Alas, how dreadful to have wisdom where it profits not the wise! Aye, I knew this well, but let it slip out of mind; else would I never have come here.

OE.: What now? How sad thou hast come in!

TE.: Let me go home; most easily wilt thou bear thine own burden to the end, and I mine, if thou wilt consent.

OE.: Thy words are strange, nor kindly to this State which nurtured thee, when thou withholdest this response.

TE.: Nay, I see that thou, on thy part, openest not thy lips in season: therefore I speak not, that neither may I have thy mishap.

OE.: For the love of the gods, turn not away, if thou hast knowledge: all we suppliants implore thee on our knees.

TE.: Aye, for ye are all without knowledge; but never will I reveal my griefs — that I say not thine.

OE.: How sayest thou? Thou knowest the secret, and wilt not tell it, but art minded to betray us and to destroy the State?

TE.: I will pain neither myself nor thee. Why vainly ask these things? Thou wilt not learn them from me.

OE.: What, basest of the base, — for thou wouldest anger a very stone, — wilt thou never speak out? Can nothing touch thee? Wilt thou never make an end?

TE.: Thou blamest my temper, but seest not that to which thou thyself art wedded: no, thou findest fault with me.

OE.: And who would not be angry to hear the words with which thou now dost slight this city?

TE.: The future will come of itself, though I shroud it in silence.

OE.: Then, seeing that it must come, thou on thy part shouldst tell me thereof.

TE.: I will speak no further; rage, then, if thou wilt, with the fiercest wrath thy heart doth know.

OE.: Aye, verily, I will not spare — so wroth I am — to speak all my thought. Know that thou seemest to me e'en to have helped in plotting the deed, and to have done it, short of slaying with thy hands. Hadst thou eyesight, I would have said that the doing, also, of this thing was thine alone.

TE.: In sooth? — I charge thee that thou abide by the decree of thine own mouth, and from this day speak neither to these nor to me: *thou* art the accursed defiler of this land.

OE.: So brazen with thy blustering taunt? And wherein dost thou trust to escape thy due?

TE.: I have escaped: in my truth is my strength.

OE.: Who taught thee this? It was not, at least, thine art.

TE.: Thou: for thou didst spur me into speech against my will.

OE.: What speech? Speak again that I may learn it better.

TE.: Didst thou not take my sense before? Or art thou tempting me in talk?

OE.: No, I took it not so that I can call it known: — speak again.

TE.: I say that thou art the slayer of the man whose slayer thou seekest.

OE.: Now thou shalt rue that thou hast twice said words so dire.

TE.: Wouldst thou have me say more, that thou mayest be more wroth?

OE.: What thou wilt; it will be said in vain.

TE.: I say that thou hast been living in unguessed shame with thy nearest kin, and seest not to what woe thou hast come.

OE.: Dost thou indeed think that thou shalt always speak thus without smarting?

TE.: Yes, if there is any strength in truth.

OE.: Nay, there is, — for all save thee; for thee that strength is not, since thou art maimed in ear, and in wit, and in eye.

TE.: Aye, and thou art a poor wretch to utter taunts which every man here will soon hurl at thee.

OE.: Night, endless night hath thee in her keeping, so that thou canst never hurt me, or any man who sees the sun.

TE.: No, thy doom is not to fall by *me*: Apollo is enough, whose care it is to work that out.

OE.: Are these Creon's devices, or thine?

TE.: Nay, Creon is no plague to thee; thou art thine own.

OE.: O wealth, and empire, and skill surpassing skill in life's keen rivalries, how great is the envy that cleaves to you, if for the sake, yea, of this power which the city hath put into my hands, a gift unsought, Creon the trusty, Creon mine old friend, hath crept on me by stealth, yearning to thrust me out of it, and hath suborned such a scheming juggler as this, a tricky quack, who hath eyes only for his gains, but in his art is blind!

Come, now, tell me, where hast thou proved thyself a seer? Why, when the Watcher was here who wove dark song, didst thou say nothing that could free this folk? Yet the riddle, at least, was not for the first comer to read; there was need of a seer's skill; and none such thou wast found to have, either by help of birds, or as known from any god: no, I came, I, Oedipus the ignorant, and made her mute, when I had seized the answer by my wit, untaught of birds. And it is I whom thou art trying to oust, thinking to stand close to Creon's throne. Methinks thou and the plotter of these things will rue your zeal to purge the land. Nay, didst thou not seem to be an old man, thou shouldst have learned to thy cost how bold thou art.

LE.: To our thinking, both this man's words and thine, Oedipus, have been said in anger. Not for such words is our need, but to seek how we shall best discharge the mandates of the god.

TE.: King though thou art, the right of reply, at least, must be deemed the same for both; of that I too am lord. Not to thee do I live servant, but to Loxias; and so I shall not stand enrolled under Creon for my patron. And I tell thee — since thou hast taunted me even with blindness — that thou hast sight, yet seest not in what misery thou art, nor where thou dwellest, nor with whom. Dost thou know of what stock thou art? And thou hast been an unwitting foe to thine own kin, in the shades, and on the earth above; and the double lash of thy mother's and thy father's curse shall one day drive thee from this land in dreadful haste, with darkness then on the eyes that now see true.

And what place shall not be harbour to thy shriek, what of all Cithaeron shall not ring with it soon, when thou hast learnt the meaning of the nuptials in which, within that house, thou didst find a fatal haven, after a voyage so fair? And a throng of other ills thou guessest not, which shall make thee level with thy true self and with thine own brood.

Therefore heap thy scorns on Creon and on my message: for no one among men shall ever be crushed more miserably than thou.

oe.: Are these taunts to be indeed borne from *him*? — Hence, ruin take thee! Hence, this instant! Back! — away! — avaunt thee from these doors!

te.: I had never come, not I, hadst thou not called me.

oe.: I knew not that thou wast about to speak folly, or it had been long ere I had sent for thee to my house.

te.: Such am I, — as thou thinkest, a fool; but for the parents who begat thee, sane.

oe.: What parents? Stay . . . and who of men is my sire?

te.: This day shall show thy birth and shall bring thy ruin.

oe.: What riddles, what dark words thou always speakest!

te.: Nay, art not thou most skilled to unravel dark speech?

oe.: Make that my reproach in which thou shalt find me great.

te.: Yet 'twas just that fortune that undid thee.

oe.: Nay, if I delivered this town, I care not.

te.: Then I will go: so do thou, boy, take me hence.

oe.: Aye, let him take thee: while here, thou art a hindrance, thou, a trouble: when thou hast vanished, thou wilt not vex me more.

te.: I will go when I have done mine errand, fearless of thy frown: for thou canst never destroy me. And I tell thee — the man of whom thou hast this long while been in quest, uttering threats, and proclaiming a search into the murder of Laius — that man is here, — in seeming, an alien sojourner, but anon he shall be found a native Theban, and shall not be glad of his fortune. A blind man, he who now hath sight, a beggar, who now is rich, he shall make his way to a strange land, feeling the ground before him with his staff. And he shall be found at once brother and father of the children with whom he consorts; son and husband of the woman who bore him; heir to his father's bed, shedder of his father's blood.

So go thou in and think on that; and if thou find that I have been at fault, say thenceforth that I have no wit in prophecy.

[TEIRESIAS *is led out by the boy.* OEDIPUS *enters the palace.*]

strophe 1

ch. [*singing*]: Who is he of whom the divine voice from the Delphian rock hath spoken, as having wrought with red hands horrors that no tongue can tell?

It is time that he ply in flight a foot stronger than the feet of storm-swift steeds: for the son of Zeus is springing on him, all

armed with fiery lightnings, and with him come the dread, unerring Fates.

antistrophe 1

Yea, newly given from snowy Parnassus, the message hath flashed
forth to make all search for the unknown man. Into the wild
wood's covert, among caves and rocks he is roaming, fierce as a
bull, wretched and forlorn on his joyless path, still seeking to put
from him the doom spoken at Earth's central shrine: but that doom
ever lives, ever flits around him.

strophe 2

Dreadly, in sooth, dreadly doth the wise augur move me, who
approve not, nor am able to deny. How to speak, I know not; I
am fluttered with forebodings; neither in the present have I clear
vision, nor of the future. Never in past days, nor in these, have I
heard how the house of Labdacus or the son of Polybus had, either
against other, any grief that I could bring as proof in assailing the
public fame of Oedipus, and seeking to avenge the line of Labdacus
for the undiscovered murder.

antistrophe 2

Nay, Zeus indeed and Apollo are keen of thought, and know
the things of earth; but that mortal seer wins knowledge above
mine, of this there can be no sure test; though man may surpass
man in lore. Yet, until I see the word made good, never will I assent when men blame Oedipus. Before all eyes, the winged maiden
came against him of old, and he was seen to be wise; he bore the
test, in welcome service to our State; never, therefore, by the verdict
of my heart shall he be adjudged guilty of crime.

[*Enter* CREON]

CR.: Fellow-citizens, having learned that Oedipus the king lays dire
charges against me, I am here, indignant. If, in the present troubles, he thinks that he has suffered from *me*, by word or deed, aught
that tends to harm, in truth I crave not my full term of years, when
I must bear such blame as this. The wrong of this rumour touches
me not in one point alone, but has the largest scope, if I am to be
called a traitor in the city, a traitor too by thee and by my friends.

LE.: Nay, but this taunt came under stress, perchance, of anger, rather
than from the purpose of the heart.

CR.: And the saying was uttered, that *my* counsels won the seer to
utter his falsehoods?

LE.: Such things were said — I know not with what meaning.

CR.: And was this charge laid against me with steady eyes and steady
mind?

LE.: I know not; I see not what my masters do: but here comes our
lord forth from the house.

[*Enter* OEDIPUS]

OE.: Sirrah, how camest thou here? Hast thou a front so bold that thou hast come to my house, who art the proved assassin of its master, — the palpable robber of my crown? Come, tell me, in the name of the gods, was it cowardice or folly that thou sawest in me, that thou didst plot to do this thing? Didst thou think that I would not note this deed of thine creeping on me by stealth, or, aware, would not ward it off? Now is not thine attempt foolish, — to seek, without followers or friends, a throne, — a prize which followers and wealth must win?

CR.: Mark me now, — in answer to thy words, hear a fair reply, and then judge for thyself on knowledge.

OE.: Thou art apt in speech, but I have a poor wit for thy lessons, since I have found thee my malignant foe.

CR.: Now first hear how I will explain this very thing —

OE.: Explain me not one thing — that thou art not false.

CR.: If thou deemest that stubbornness without sense is a good gift, thou art not wise.

OE.: If thou deemest that thou canst wrong a kinsman and escape the penalty, thou art not sane.

CR.: Justly said, I grant thee: but tell me what is the wrong that thou sayest thou hast suffered from me.

OE.: Didst thou advise, or didst thou not, that I should send for that reverend seer?

CR.: And now I am still of the same mind.

OE.: How long is it, then, since Laius —

CR.: Since Laius . . . ? I take not thy drift . . .

OE.: — was swept from men's sight by a deadly violence?

CR.: The count of years would run far into the past.

OE.: Was this seer, then, of the craft in those days?

CR.: Yea, skilled as now, and in equal honour.

OE.: Made he, then, any mention of me at that time?

CR.: Never, certainly, when I was within hearing.

OE.: But held ye not a search touching the murder?

CR.: Due search we held, of course — and learned nothing.

OE.: And how was it that this sage did not tell his story *then*?

CR.: I know not; where I lack light, 'tis my wont to be silent.

OE.: Thus much, at least, thou knowest, and couldst declare with light enough.

CR.: What is that? If I know it, I will not deny.

OE.: That, if he had not conferred with thee, he would never have named *my* slaying of Laius.

CR.: If so he speaks, thou best knowest; but I claim to learn from thee as much as thou hast now from me.

OE.: Learn thy fill: I shall never be found guilty of the blood.

CR.: Say, then — thou hast married my sister?

OE.: The question allows not of denial.

CR.: And thou rulest the land as she doth, with like sway?

OE.: She obtains from me all her desire.

CR.: And rank not I as a third peer of you twain?

OE.: Aye, 'tis just therein that thou art seen a false friend.

CR.: Not so, if thou wouldst reason with thine own heart as I with mine. And first weigh this, — whether thou thinkest that any one would choose to rule amid terrors rather than in unruffled peace, — granting that he is to have the same powers. Now I, for one, have no yearning in my nature to be a king rather than to do kingly deeds, no, nor hath any man who knows how to keep a sober mind. For now I win all boons from thee without fear; but, were I ruler myself, I should be doing much e'en against mine own pleasure.

How, then, could royalty be sweeter for me to have than painless rule and influence? Not yet am I so misguided as to desire other honours than those which profit. Now, all wish me joy; now, every man has a greeting for me; now, those who have a suit to thee crave speech with me, since therein is all their hope of success. Then why should I resign these things, and take those? No mind will become false, while it is wise. Nay, I am no lover of such policy, and, if another put it into deed, never could I bear to act with him.

And, in proof of this, first, go to Pytho, and ask if I brought thee true word of the oracle; then next, if thou find that I have planned aught in concert with the soothsayer, take and slay me, by the sentence not of one mouth, but of twain — by mine own, no less than thine. But make me not guilty in a corner, on unproved surmise. It is not right to adjudge bad men good at random, or good men bad. I count it a like thing for a man to cast off a true friend as to cast away the life in his own bosom, which most he loves. Nay, thou wilt learn these things with sureness in time, for time alone shows a just man; but thou couldst discern a knave even in one day.

LE.: Well hath he spoken, O king, for one who giveth heed not to fall: the quick in counsel are not sure.

OE.: When the stealthy plotter is moving on me in quick sort, I, too, must be quick with my counterplot. If I await him in repose, his ends will have been gained, and mine missed.

CR.: What wouldst thou, then? Cast me out of the land?

OE.: Not so: I desire thy death — not thy banishment — that thou mayest show forth what manner of thing is envy.

CR.: Thou speakest as resolved not to yield or to believe?

OE.: No; for thou persuadest me not that thou art worthy of belief.

CR.: No, for I find thee not sane.

OE.: Sane, at least, in mine own interest.

CR.: Nay, thou shouldst be so in mine also.

OE.: Nay, thou art false.

CR.: But if thou understandest nought?

OE.: Yet must I rule.

CR.: Not if thou rule ill.

OE.: Hear him, O Thebes!

CR.: Thebes is for me also — not for thee alone.

[JOCASTA *enters from the palace.*]

LE.: Cease, princes; and in good time for you I see Jocasta coming
yonder from the house, with whose help ye should compose your
present feud.

JO.: Misguided men, why have ye raised such foolish strife of
tongues? Are ye not ashamed, while the land is thus sick, to stir
up troubles of your own? Come, go thou into the house, — and
thou, Creon, to thy home, — and forbear to make much of a petty
grief.

CR.: Kinswoman, Oedipus thy lord claims to do dread things unto
me, even one or other of two ills, — to thrust me from the land of
my fathers, or to slay me amain.

OE.: Yea; for I have caught him, lady, working evil, by ill arts, against
my person.

CR.: Now may I see no good, but perish accursed, if I have done
aught to thee of that wherewith thou chargest me!

JO.: O, for the gods' love, believe it, Oedipus — first, for the awful
sake of this oath unto the gods, — then for my sake and for theirs
who stand before thee!

[*The following lines between the* CHORUS *and* OEDIPUS *and between
the* CHORUS, JOCASTA, *and* OEDIPUS *are chanted responsively.*]

strophe 1

CH.: Consent, reflect, hearken, O my king, I pray thee!

OE.: What grace, then wouldest thou have me grant thee?

CH.: Respect him who aforetime was not foolish, and who now is
strong in his oath.

OE.: Now dost thou know what thou cravest?

CH.: Yea.

OE.: Declare, then, what thou meanest.

CH.: That thou shouldest never use an unproved rumour to cast a
dishonouring charge on the friend who has bound himself with a
curse.

OE.: Then be very sure that, when thou seekest this, for me thou art
seeking destruction, or exile from this land.

strophe 2

CH.: No, by him who stands in the front of all the heavenly host, no,
by the Sun! Unblest, unfriended, may I die by the uttermost
doom, if I have that thought! But my unhappy soul is worn by
the withering of the land, and again by the thought that our old
sorrows should be crowned by sorrows springing from you twain.

OE.: Then let him go, though I am surely doomed to death, or to be
thrust dishonoured from the land. Thy lips, not his, move my
compassion by their plaint; but he, where'er he be, shall be hated.

CR.: Sullen in yielding art thou seen, even as vehement in the excesses
of thy wrath; but such natures are justly sorest for themselves to
bear.

OE.: Then wilt thou not leave me in peace, and get thee gone?

CR.: I will go my way; I have found thee undiscerning, but in the sight of these I am just.

[*Exit* CREON]

antistrophe 1

CH.: Lady, why dost thou delay to take yon man into the house?

JO.: I will do so, when I have learned what hath chanced.

CH.: Blind suspicion, bred of talk, arose; and, on the other part, injustice wounds.

JO.: It was on both sides?

CH.: Aye.

JO.: And what was the story?

CH.: Enough, methinks, enough — when our land is already vexed — that the matter should rest where it ceased.

OE.: Seest thou to what thou hast come, for all thy honest purpose, in seeking to slack and blunt my zeal?

antistrophe 2

CH.: King, I have said it not once alone — be sure that I should have been shown a madman, bankrupt in sane counsel, if I put thee away — thee, who gavest a true course to my beloved country when distraught by troubles — thee, who now also art like to prove our prospering guide.

JO.: In the name of the gods, tell me also, O king, on what account thou hast conceived this steadfast wrath.

OE.: That will I; for I honour thee, lady, above yonder men: — the cause is Creon, and the plots that he hath laid against me.

JO.: Speak on — if thou canst tell clearly how the feud began.

OE.: He says that I stand guilty of the blood of Laius.

JO.: As on his own knowledge? Or on hearsay from another?

OE.: Nay, he hath made a rascal seer his mouthpiece; as for himself, he keeps his lips wholly pure.

JO.: Then absolve thyself of the things whereof thou speakest; hearken to me, and learn for thy comfort that nought of mortal birth is a sharer in the science of the seer. I will give thee pithy proof of that.

An oracle came to Laius once — I will not say from Phoebus himself, but from his ministers — that the doom should overtake him to die by the hand of his child, who should spring from him and me.

Now Laius, — as, at least, the rumour saith, — was murdered one day by foreign robbers at a place where three highways meet. And the child's birth was not three days past, when Laius pinned its ankles together, and had it thrown, by others' hands, on a trackless mountain.

So, in that case, Apollo brought it not to pass that the babe should become the slayer of his sire, or that Laius should die — the dread thing which he feared — by his child's hand. Thus did the messages of seer-craft map out the future. Regard them, thou, not at all. Whatsoever needful things the god seeks, he himself will easily bring to light.

OE.: What restlessness of soul, lady, what tumult of the mind hath just come upon me since I heard thee speak!

JO.: What anxiety hath startled thee, that thou sayest this?

OE.: Methought I heard this from thee, — that Laius was slain where three highways meet.

JO.: Yea, that was the story; nor hath it ceased yet.

OE.: And where is the place where this befell?

JO.: The land is called Phocis; and branching roads lead to the same spot from Delphi and from Daulia.

OE.: And what is the time that hath passed since these things were?

JO.: The news was published to the town shortly before thou wast first seen in power over this land.

OE.: O Zeus, what hast thou decreed to do unto me?

JO.: And wherefore, Oedipus, doth this thing weigh upon thy soul?

OE.: Ask me not yet; but say what was the stature of Laius, and how ripe his manhood.

JO.: He was tall, — the silver just lightly strewn among his hair; and his form was not greatly unlike to thine.

OE.: Unhappy that I am! Methinks I have been laying myself even now under a dread curse, and knew it not.

JO.: How sayest thou? I tremble when I look on thee, my king.

OE.: Dread misgivings have I that the seer can see. But thou wilt show better if thou wilt tell me one thing more.

JO.: Indeed — though I tremble — I will answer all thou askest, when I hear it.

OE.: Went he in small force, or with many armed followers, like a chieftain?

JO.: Five they were in all, — a herald one of them; and there was one carriage, which bore Laius.

OE.: Alas! 'Tis now clear indeed. — Who was he who gave you these tidings, lady?

JO.: A servant — the sole survivor who came home.

OE.: Is he haply at hand in the house now?

JO.: No, truly; so soon as he came thence, and found thee reigning in the stead of Laius, he supplicated me, with hand laid on mine, that I would send him to the fields, to the pastures of the flocks, that he might be far from the sight of this town. And I sent him; he was worthy, for a slave, to win e'en a larger boon than that.

OE.: Would, then, that he could return to us without delay!

JO.: It is easy: but wherefore dost thou enjoin this?

OE.: I fear, lady, that mine own lips have been unguarded; and therefore am I fain to behold him.

JO.: Nay, he shall come. But I too, methinks, have a claim to learn what lies heavy on thy heart, my king.

OE.: Yea, and it shall not be kept from thee, now that my forebodings have advanced so far. Who, indeed, is more to me than thou, to whom I should speak in passing through such a fortune as this?

My father was Polybus of Corinth, — my mother, the Dorian Merope; and I was held the first of all the folk in that town, until a chance befell me, worthy, indeed, of wonder, though not worthy of mine own heat concerning it. At a banquet, a man full of wine cast it at me in his cups that I was not the true son of my sire. And I, vexed, restrained myself for that day as best I might; but on the next I went to my mother and father, and questioned them; and they were wroth for the taunt with him who had let that word fly. So on their part I had comfort; yet was this thing ever rankling in my heart; for it still crept abroad with strong rumour. And, unknown to mother or father, I went to Delphi; and Phoebus sent me forth disappointed of that knowledge for which I came, but in his response set forth other things, full of sorrow and terror and woe; even that I was fated to defile my mother's bed; and that I should show unto men a brood which they could not endure to behold; and that I should be the slayer of the sire who begat me.

And I, when I had listened to this, turned to flight from the land of Corinth, thenceforth wotting of its region by the stars alone, to some spot where I should never see fulfilment of the infamies fore-told in mine evil doom. And on my way I came to the regions in which thou sayest that this prince perished. Now, lady, I will tell thee the truth. When in my journey I was near to those three roads, there met me a herald, and a man seated in a carriage drawn by colts, as thou hast described; and he who was in front, and the old man himself, were for thrusting me rudely from the path. Then, in anger, I struck him who pushed me aside — the driver; and the old man, seeing it, watched the moment when I was pass-ing, and, from the carriage, brought his goad with two teeth down full upon my head. Yet was he paid with interest; by one swift blow from the staff in this hand he was rolled right out of the car-riage, on his back; and I slew every man of them.

But if this stranger had any tie of kinship with Laius, who is now more wretched than the man before thee? What mortal could prove more hated of heaven? Whom no stranger, no citizen, is allowed to receive in his house; whom it is unlawful that any one accost; whom all must repel from their homes! And this — this curse — was laid on me by no mouth but mine own! And I pol-lute the bed of the slain man with the hands by which he perished. Say, am I vile? Oh, am I not utterly unclean? — seeing that I must be banished, and in banishment see not mine own people, nor set foot in mine own land, or else be joined in wedlock to my mother, and slay my sire, even Polybus, who begat and reared me.

Then would not he speak aright of Oedipus, who judged these things sent by some cruel power above man? Forbid, forbid, ye pure and awful gods, that I should see that day! No, may I be swept from among men, ere I behold myself visited with the brand of such a doom!

LE.: To us, indeed, these things, O king, are fraught with fear; yet
    have hope, until at least thou hast gained full knowledge from
    him who saw the deed.

OE.: Hope, in truth, rests with me thus far alone; I can await the man
    summoned from the pastures.

JO.: And when he has appeared — what wouldst thou have of him?

OE.: I will tell thee. If his story be found to tally with thine, I, at
    least, shall stand clear of disaster.

JO.: And what of special note didst thou hear from me?

OE.: Thou wast saying that he spoke of Laius as slain by robbers. If,
    then, he still speaks, as before, of several, I was not the slayer: a
    solitary man could not be held the same with that band. But if he
    names one lonely wayfarer, then beyond doubt this guilt leans to
    me.

JO.: Nay, be assured that thus, at least, the tale was first told; he
    cannot revoke that, for the city heard it, not I alone. But even if he
    should diverge somewhat from his former story, never, king, can
    he show that the murder of Laius, at least, is truly square to
    prophecy; of whom Loxias plainly said that he must die by the
    hand of my child. Howbeit that poor innocent never slew him,
    but perished first itself. So henceforth, for what touches divina-
    tion, I would not look to my right hand or my left.

OE.: Thou judgest well. But nevertheless send some one to fetch
    the peasant, and neglect not this matter.

JO.: I will send without delay. But let us come into the house: noth-
    ing will I do save at thy good pleasure.

[OEDIPUS and JOCASTA go into the palace.]

strophe 1

CH. [*singing*]: May destiny still find me winning the praise of rever-
    ent purity in all words and deeds sanctioned by those laws of range
    sublime, called into life throughout the high clear heaven, whose
    father is Olympus alone; their parent was no race of mortal men,
    no, nor shall oblivion ever lay them to sleep; the god is mighty in
    them, and he grows not old.

antistrophe 1

Insolence breeds the tyrant; Insolence, once vainly surfeited on
wealth that is not meet nor good for it, when it hath scaled the topmost ramparts, is hurled to a dire doom, wherein no service of the
feet can serve. But I pray that the god never quell such rivalry as
benefits the State; the god will I ever hold for our protector.

strophe 2

But if any man walks haughtily in deed or word, with no fear of
Justice, no reverence for the images of gods, may an evil doom
seize him for his ill-starred pride, if he will not win his vantage
fairly, nor keep him from unholy deeds, but must lay profaning
hands on sanctities.

Where such things are, what mortal shall boast any more that he can ward the arrows of the gods from his life? Nay, if such deeds are in honour, wherefore should we join in the sacred dance?

No more will I go reverently to earth's central and inviolate shrine, no more to Abae's temple or Olympia, if these oracles fit not the issue, so that all men shall point at them with the finger. Nay, king, — if thou art rightly called, — Zeus all-ruling, may it not escape thee and thine ever-deathless power!

The old prophecies concerning Laius are fading; already men are setting them at nought, and nowhere is Apollo glorified with honours; the worship of the gods is perishing.

[JOCASTA *comes forth, bearing a branch, wreathed with festoons of wool, which, as a suppliant, she is about to lay on the altar of the household god, Lycean Apollo, in front of the palace.*]

JO.: Princes of the land, the thought has come to me to visit the shrines of the gods, with this wreathed branch in my hands, and these gifts of incense. For Oedipus excites his soul overmuch with all manner of alarms, nor, like a man of sense, judges the new things by the old, but is at the will of the speaker, if he speak terrors.

Since, then, by counsel I can do no good, to thee, Lycean Apollo, for thou art nearest, I have come, a suppliant with these symbols of prayer, that thou mayest find us some riddance from uncleanness. For now we are all afraid, seeing *him* affrighted, even as they who see fear in the helmsman of their ship.

[*While* JOCASTA *is offering her prayers to the god, a* MESSENGER, *evidently a stranger, enters and addresses the Elders of the* CHORUS.]

ME.: Might I learn from you, strangers, where is the house of the king Oedipus? Or, better still, tell me where he himself is — if ye know.

LE.: This is his dwelling, and he himself, stranger, is within; and this lady is the mother of his children.

ME.: Then may she be ever happy in a happy home, since she is his heaven-blest queen.

JO.: Happiness to thee also, stranger! 'tis the due of thy fair greeting. — But say what thou hast come to seek or to tell.

ME.: Good tidings, lady, for thy house and for thy husband.

JO.: What are they? And from whom hast thou come?

ME.: From Corinth: and at the message which I will speak anon thou wilt rejoice — doubtless; yet haply grieve.

JO.: And what is it? How hath it thus a double potency?

ME.: The people will make him king of the Isthmian land, as 'twas said there.

JO.: How then? Is the aged Polybus no more in power?

ME.: No, verily: for death holds him in the tomb.

JO.: How sayest thou? Is Polybus dead, old man?

ME.: If I speak not the truth, I am content to die.

JO.: O handmaid, away with all speed, and tell this to thy master!
O ye oracles of the gods, where stand ye now! This is the man
whom Oedipus long feared and shunned, lest he should slay him;
and now this man hath died in the course of destiny, not by his
hand.

[OEDIPUS *enters from the palace.*]

OE.: Jocasta, dearest wife, why hast thou summoned me forth from
these doors?

JO.: Hear this man, and judge, as thou listenest, to what the awful
oracles of the gods have come.

OE.: And he — who may he be, and what news hath he for me?

JO.: He is from Corinth, to tell that thy father Polybus lives no
longer, but hath perished.

OE.: How, stranger? Let me have it from thine own mouth.

ME.: If I must first make these tidings plain, know indeed that he is
dead and gone.

OE.: By treachery, or by visit of disease?

ME.: A light thing in the scale brings the aged to their rest.

OE.: Ah, he died, it seems, of sickness?

ME.: Yea, and of the long years that he had told.

OE.: Alas, alas! Why, indeed, my wife, should one look to the
hearth of the Pythian seer, or to the birds that scream above our
heads, on whose showing I was doomed to slay my sire? But he is
dead, and hid already beneath the earth; and here am I, who have
not put hand to spear. — Unless, perchance, he was killed by longing for me: thus, indeed, I should be the cause of his death. But
the oracles as they stand, at least, Polybus hath swept with him to
his rest in Hades: they are worth nought.

JO.: Nay, did I not so foretell to thee long since?

OE.: Thou didst: but I was misled by my fear.

JO.: Now no more lay aught of those things to heart.

OE.: But surely I must needs fear my mother's bed?

JO.: Nay, what should mortal fear, for whom the decrees of Fortune
are supreme, and who hath clear foresight of nothing? 'Tis best
to live at random, as one may. But fear not thou touching wedlock
with thy mother. Many men ere now have so fared in dreams also:
but he to whom these things are as nought bears his life most easily.

OE.: All these bold words of thine would have been well, were not
my mother living; but as it is, since she lives, I must needs fear —
though thou sayest well.

JO.: Howbeit thy father's death is a great sign to cheer us.

OE.: Great, I know; but my fear is of her who lives.

ME.: And who is the woman about whom ye fear?

OE.: Merope, old man, the consort of Polybus.

ME.: And what is it in her that moves your fear?

OE.: A heaven-sent oracle of dread import, stranger.

ME.: Lawful, or unlawful, for another to know?

OE.: Lawful, surely. Loxias once said that I was doomed to espouse mine own mother, and to shed with mine own hands my father's blood. Wherefore my home in Corinth was long kept by me afar; with happy event, indeed, — yet still 'tis sweet to see the face of parents.

ME.: Was it indeed for fear of this that thou wast an exile from that city?

OE.: And because I wished not, old man, to be the slayer of my sire.

ME.: Then why have I not freed thee, king, from this fear, seeing that I came with friendly purpose?

OE.: Indeed thou shouldst have guerdon due from me.

ME.: Indeed 'twas chiefly for this that I came — that, on thy return home, I might reap some good.

OE.: Nay, I will never go near my parents.

ME.: Ah my son, 'tis plain enough that thou knowest not what thou doest.

OE.: How, old man? For the gods' love, tell me.

ME.: If for these reasons thou shrinkest from going home.

OE.: Aye, I dread lest Phoebus prove himself true for me.

ME.: Thou dreadest to be stained with guilt through thy parents?

OE.: Even so, old man — this it is that ever affrights me.

ME.: Dost thou know, then, that thy fears are wholly vain?

OE.: How so, if I was born of those parents?

ME.: Because Polybus was nothing to thee in blood.

OE.: What sayest thou? Was Polybus not my sire?

ME.: No more than he who speaks to thee, but just so much.

OE.: And how can my sire be level with him who is as nought to me?

ME.: Nay, he begat thee not, any more than I.

OE.: Nay, wherefore, then, called he me his son?

ME.: Know that he had received thee as a gift from my hands of yore.

OE.: And yet he loved me so dearly, who came from another's hand?

ME.: Yea, his former childlessness won him thereto.

OE.: And thou — hadst thou bought me or found me by chance, when thou gavest me to him?

ME.: Found thee in Cithaeron's winding glens.

OE.: And wherefore wast thou roaming in those regions?

ME.: I was there in charge of mountain flocks.

OE.: What, thou wast a shepherd — a vagrant hireling?

ME.: But thy preserver, my son, in that hour.

OE.: And what pain was mine when thou didst take me in thine arms?

ME.: The ankles of thy feet might witness.

OE.: Ah me, why dost thou speak of that old trouble?

ME.: I freed thee when thou hadst thine ankles pinned together.

OE.: Aye, 'twas a dread brand of shame that I took from my cradle.

ME.: Such, that from that fortune thou wast called by the name which still is thine.

OE.: Oh, for the gods' love — was the deed my mother's or father's? Speak!

ME.: I know not; he who gave thee to me wots better of that than I.

OE.: What, thou hadst me from another? Thou didst not light on me thyself?

ME.: No: another shepherd gave thee up to me.

OE.: Who was he? Art thou in case to tell clearly?

ME.: I think he was called one of the household of Laius.

OE.: The king who ruled this country long ago?

ME.: The same: 'twas in his service that the man was a herd.

OE.: Is he still alive, that I might see him?

ME.: Nay, ye folk of the country should know best.

OE.: Is there any of you here present that knows the herd of whom he speaks — that hath seen him in the pastures or the town? Answer! The hour hath come that these things should be finally revealed.

LE.: Methinks he speaks of no other than the peasant whom thou wast already fain to see; but our lady Jocasta might best tell that.

OE.: Lady, wottest thou of him whom we lately summoned? Is it of him that this man speaks?

JO.: Why ask of whom he spoke? Regard it not . . . waste not a thought on what he said . . . 'twere idle.

OE.: It must not be that, with such clues in my grasp, I should fail to bring my birth to light.

JO.: For the gods' sake, if thou hast any care for thine own life, forbear this search! My anguish is enough.

OE.: Be of good courage; though I be found the son of servile mother, — aye, a slave by three descents, — *thou* wilt not be proved baseborn.

JO.: Yet hear me, I implore thee: do not thus.

OE.: I must not hear of not discovering the whole truth.

JO.: Yet I wish thee well — I counsel thee for the best.

OE.: These best counsels, then, vex my patience.

JO.: Ill-fated one! Mayst thou never come to know who thou art!

OE.: Go, some one, fetch me the herdsman hither, — and leave yon woman to glory in her princely stock.

JO.: Alas, alas, miserable! — that word alone can I say unto thee, and no other word henceforth for ever.

[*She rushes into the palace.*]

LE.: Why hath the lady gone, Oedipus, in a transport of wild grief? I misdoubt, a storm of sorrow will break forth from this silence.

OE.: Break forth what will! Be my race never so lowly, I must crave to learn it. Yon woman, perchance, — for she is proud with more than a woman's pride — thinks shame of my base source. But I, who hold myself son of Fortune that gives good, will not be dishonoured. She is the mother from whom I spring; and the months, my kinsmen, have marked me sometimes lowly, sometimes great. Such being my lineage, never more can I prove false to it, or spare to search out the secret of my birth.

strophe

CH. [*singing*]: If I am a seer or wise of heart, O Cithaeron, thou shalt not fail — by yon heaven, thou shalt not! — to know at to-morrow's full moon that Oedipus honours thee as native to him, as his nurse, and his mother, and that thou art celebrated in our dance and song, because thou art well-pleasing to our prince. O Phoebus to whom we cry, may these things find favour in thy sight!

antistrophe

Who was it, my son, who of the race whose years are many that bore thee in wedlock with Pan, the mountain-roaming father? Or was it a bride of Loxias that bore thee? For dear to him are all the upland pastures. Or perchance 'twas Cyllene's lord,* or the Bacchants' god, dweller on the hill-tops, that received thee, a new-born joy, from one of the Nymphs of Helicon, with whom he most doth sport.

OE.: Elders, if 'tis for me to guess, who have never met with him, I think I see the herdsman of whom we have long been in quest; for in his venerable age he tallies with yon stranger's years, and withal I know those who bring him, methinks, as servants of mine own. But perchance thou mayest have the advantage of me in knowledge, if thou hast seen the herdsman before.

LE.: Aye, I know him, be sure; he was in the service of Laius — trusty as any man, in his shepherd's place.

[*The* HERDSMAN *is brought in.*]

OE.: I ask thee first, Corinthian stranger, is this he whom thou meanest?

ME.: This man whom thou beholdest.

OE.: Ho thou, old man — I would have thee look this way, and answer all that I ask thee. Thou wast once in the service of Laius?

HERDSMAN: I was — a slave not bought, but reared in his house.

OE.: Employed in what labour, or what way of life?

HER.: For the best part of my life I tended flocks.

OE.: And what the regions that thou didst chiefly haunt?

HER.: Sometimes it was Cithaeron, sometimes the neighbouring ground.

OE.: Then wottest thou of having noted yon man in these parts —

HER.: Doing what? . . . What man dost thou mean? . . .

OE.: This man here — or of having ever met him before?

HER.: Not so that I could speak at once from memory.

ME.: And no wonder, master. But I will bring clear recollection to his ignorance. I am sure that he well wots of the time when we abode in the region of Cithaeron, — he with two flocks, I, his comrade, with one, — three full half-years, from spring to Arcturus; and then for the winter I used to drive my flock to mine own fold, and he took his to the fold of Laius. Did aught of this happen as I tell, or did it not?

* Hermes

HER.: Thou speakest the truth — though 'tis long ago.

ME.: Come, tell me now — wottest thou of having given me a boy in those days, to be reared as mine own foster-son?

HER.: What now? Why dost thou ask the question?

ME.: Yonder man, my friend, is he who then was young.

HER.: Plague seize thee — be silent once for all!

OE.: Ha! chide him not, old man — thy words need chiding more than his.

HER.: And wherein, most noble master, do I offend?

OE.: In not telling of the boy concerning whom he asks.

HER.: He speaks without knowledge — he is busy to no purpose.

OE.: Thou wilt not speak with a good grace, but thou shalt on pain.

HER.: Nay, for the gods' love, misuse not an old man!

OE.: Ho, some one — pinion him this instant!

HER.: Alas, wherefore? what more wouldst thou learn?

OE.: Didst thou give this man the child of whom he asks?

HER.: I did, — and would I had perished that day!

OE.: Well, thou wilt come to that, unless thou tell the honest truth.

HER.: Nay, much more am I lost, if I speak.

OE.: The fellow is bent, methinks, on more delays . . .

HER.: No, no! — I said before that I gave it to him.

OE.: Whence hadst thou got it? In thine own house, or from another?

HER.: Mine own it was not — I had received it from a man.

OE.: From whom of the citizens here? from what home?

HER.: Forbear, for the gods' love, master, forbear to ask more!

OE.: Thou art lost if I have to question thee again.

HER.: It was a child, then, of the house of Laius.

OE.: A slave? or one born of his own race?

HER.: Ah me — I am on the dreaded brink of speech.

OE.: And I of hearing; yet must I hear.

HER.: Thou must know, then, that 'twas said to be his own child — but thy lady within could best say how these things are.

OE.: How? She gave it to thee?

HER.: Yea, O king.

OE.: For what end?

HER.: That I should make away with it.

OE.: Her own child, the wretch?

HER.: Aye, from fear of evil prophecies.

OE.: What were they?

HER.: The tale ran that he must slay his sire.

OE.: Why, then, didst thou give him up to this old man?

HER.: Through pity, master, as deeming that he would bear him away to another land, whence he himself came; but he saved him for the direst woe. For if thou art what this man saith, know that thou wast born to misery.

OE.: Oh, oh! All brought to pass — all true! Thou light, may I now look my last on thee — I who have been found accursed in

birth, accursed in wedlock, accursed in the shedding of blood!
[*He rushes into the palace.*]

strophe 1

CH. [*singing*]: Alas, ye generations of men, how mere a shadow do I count your life! Where, where is the mortal who wins more of happiness than just the seeming, and, after the semblance, a falling away? Thine is a fate that warns me, — thine, thine, unhappy Oedipus — to call no earthly creature blest.

antistrophe 1

For he, O Zeus, sped his shaft with peerless skill, and won the prize of an all-prosperous fortune; he slew the maiden with crooked talons who sang darkly; he arose for our land as a tower against death. And from that time, Oedipus, thou hast been called our king, and hast been honoured supremely, bearing sway in great Thebes.

strophe 2

But now whose story is more grievous in men's ears? Who is a more wretched captive to fierce plagues and troubles, with all his life reversed?

Alas, renowned Oedipus! The same bounteous place of rest sufficed thee, as child and as sire also, that thou shouldst make thereon thy nuptial couch. Oh, how can the soil wherein thy father sowed, unhappy one, have suffered thee in silence so long?

antistrophe 2

Time the all-seeing hath found thee out in thy despite: he judgeth the monstrous marriage wherein begetter and begotten have long been one.

Alas, thou child of Laius, would, would that I had never seen thee! I wail as one who pours a dirge from his lips; sooth to speak, 'twas thou that gavest me new life, and through thee darkness hath fallen upon mine eyes.

[*Enter* SECOND MESSENGER *from the palace.*]

ME.: Ye who are ever most honoured in this land, what deeds shall ye hear, what deeds behold, what burden of sorrow shall be yours, if, true to your race, ye still care for the house of Labdacus! For I ween that not Ister nor Phasis could wash this house clean, so many are the ills that it shrouds, or will soon bring to light, — ills wrought not unwittingly, but of purpose. And those griefs smart most which are seen to be of our own choice.

LE.: Indeed those which we knew before fall not short of claiming sore lamentation: besides them, what dost thou announce?

ME.: This is the shortest tale to tell and to hear: our royal lady Jocasta is dead.

LE.: Alas, hapless one! From what cause?

 me.: By her own hand. The worst pain in what hath chanced is not
for you, for yours it is not to behold. Nevertheless, so far as mine
own memory serves, ye shall learn that unhappy woman's fate.

When, frantic, she had passed within the vestibule, she rushed
straight towards her nuptial couch, clutching her hair with the fingers of both hands; once within the chamber, she dashed the doors
together at her back; then called on the name of Laius, long since
a corpse, mindful of that son, begotten long ago, by whom the
sire was slain, leaving the mother to breed accursed offspring with
his own.

And she bewailed the wedlock wherein, wretched, she had borne
a two-fold brood, husband by husband, children by her child. And
how thereafter she perished, is more than I know. For with a
shriek Oedipus burst in, and suffered us not to watch her woe unto
the end; on him, as he rushed around, our eyes were set. To and
fro he went, asking us to give him a sword, — asking where he
should find the wife who was no wife, but a mother whose womb
had borne alike himself and his children. And, in his frenzy, a
power above man was his guide; for 'twas none of us mortals who
were nigh. And with a dread shriek, as though some one beckoned
him on, he sprang at the double doors, and from their sockets
forced the bending bolts, and rushed into the room.

There beheld we the woman hanging by the neck in a twisted
noose of swinging cords. But he, when he saw her, with a dread,
deep cry of misery, loosed the halter whereby she hung. And when
the hapless woman was stretched upon the ground, then was the
sequel dread to see. For he tore from her raiment the golden
brooches wherewith she was decked, and lifted them, and smote
full on his own eye-balls, uttering words like these: 'No more shall
ye behold such horrors as I was suffering and working! long
enough have ye looked on those whom ye ought never to have
seen, failed in knowledge of those whom I yearned to know —
henceforth ye shall be dark!'

To such dire refrain, not once alone but oft struck he his eyes
with lifted hand; and at each blow the ensanguined eye-balls be-
dewed his beard, nor sent forth sluggish drops of gore, but all at
once a dark shower of blood came down like hail.

From the deeds of twain such ills have broken forth, not on one
alone, but with mingled woe for man and wife. The old happiness
of their ancestral fortune was aforetime happiness indeed; but to-
day — lamentation, ruin, death, shame, all earthly ills that can be
named — all, all are theirs.

le.: And hath the sufferer now any respite from pain?

me.: He cries for some one to unbar the gates and show to all the
Cadmeans his father's slayer, his mother's — the unholy word must
not pass my lips, — as purposing to cast himself out of the land,
and abide no more, to make the house accursed under his own
curse. Howbeit he lacks strength, and one to guide his steps; for
the anguish is more than man may bear. And he will show this

to thee also; for lo, the bars of the gates are withdrawn, and soon thou shalt behold a sight which even he who abhors it must pity.

[*The central door of the palace is now opened.* OEDIPUS *comes forth, leaning on attendants; the bloody stains are still upon his face. The following lines between* OEDIPUS *and the* CHORUS *are chanted responsively.*]

CH.: O dread fate for men to see, O most dreadful of all that have met mine eyes! Unhappy one, what madness hath come on thee? Who is the unearthly foe that, with a bound of more than mortal range, hath made thine ill-starred life his prey?

Alas, alas, thou hapless one! Nay, I cannot e'en look on thee, though there is much that I would fain ask, fain learn, much that draws my wistful gaze, — with such a shuddering dost thou fill me!

OE.: Woe is me! Alas, alas, wretched that I am! Whither, whither am I borne in my misery? How is my voice swept abroad on the wings of the air? Oh my Fate, how far hast thou sprung!

CH.: To a dread place, dire in men's ears, dire in their sight.

strophe 1

OE.: O thou horror of darkness that enfoldest me, visitant unspeakable, resistless, sped by a wind too fair!

Ay me! and once again, ay me!

How is my soul pierced by the stab of these goads, and withal by the memory of sorrows!

CH.: Yea, amid woes so many a twofold pain may well be thine to mourn and to bear.

antistrophe 1

OE.: Ah, friend, thou still art steadfast in thy tendance of me, — thou still hast patience to care for the blind man! Ah me! Thy presence is not hid from me — no, dark though I am, yet know I thy voice full well.

CH.: Man of dread deeds, how couldst thou in such wise quench thy vision? What more than human power urged thee?

strophe 2

OE.: Apollo, friends, Apollo was he that brought these my woes to pass, these my sore, sore woes: but the hand that struck the eyes was none save mine, wretched that I am! Why was I to see, when sight could show me nothing sweet?

CH.: These things were even as thou sayest.

OE.: Say, friends, what can I more behold, what can I love, what greeting can touch mine ear with joy? Haste, lead me from the land, friends, lead me hence, the utterly lost, the thrice accursed, yea, the mortal most abhorred of heaven!

CH.: Wretched alike for thy fortune and for thy sense thereof, would that I had never so much as known thee!

oe.: Perish the man, whoe'er he was, that freed me in the pastures from the cruel shackle on my feet, and saved me from death, and gave me back to life, — a thankless deed! Had I died then, to my friends and to thine own soul I had not been so sore a grief.

ch.: I also would have had it thus.

oe.: So had I not come to shed my father's blood, nor been called among men the spouse of her from whom I sprang: but now am I forsaken of the gods, son of a defiled mother, successor to his bed who gave me mine own wretched being: and if there be yet a woe surpassing woes, it hath become the portion of Oedipus.

ch.: I know not how I can say that thou hast counselled well: for thou wert better dead than living and blind.

oe.: Show me not at large that these things are not best done thus: give me counsel no more. For, had I sight, I know not with what eyes I could e'en have looked on my father, when I came to the place of the dead, aye, or on my miserable mother, since against both I have sinned such sins as strangling could not punish. But deem ye that the sight of children, born as mine were born, was lovely for me to look upon? No, no, not lovely to mine eyes for ever! No, nor was this town with its towered walls, nor the sacred statues of the gods, since I, thrice wretched that I am, — I, noblest of the sons of Thebes, — have doomed myself to know these no more, by mine own command that all should thrust away the impious one, — even him whom gods have shown to be unholy — and of the race of Laius!

After bearing such a stain upon me, was I to look with steady eyes on this folk? No, verily: no, were there yet a way to choke the fount of hearing, I had not spared to make a fast prison of this wretched frame, that so I should have known nor sight nor sound; for 'tis sweet that our thought should dwell beyond the sphere of griefs.

Alas, Cithaeron, why hadst thou a shelter for me? When I was given to thee, why didst thou not slay me straightway, that so I might never have revealed my source to men? Ah, Polybus, — ah, Corinth, and thou that wast called the ancient house of my fathers, how seeming-fair was I your nursling, and what ills were festering beneath! For now I am found evil, and of evil birth. O ye three roads, and thou secret glen, — thou coppice, and narrow way where three paths met — ye who drank from my hands that father's blood which was mine own, — remember ye, perchance, what deeds I wrought for you to see, — and then, when I came hither, what fresh deeds I went on to do?

O marriage-rites, ye gave me birth, and when ye had brought me forth, again ye bore children to your child, ye created an incestuous kinship of fathers, brothers, sons, — brides, wives, mothers, — yea, all the foulest shame that is wrought among men! Nay, but 'tis unmeet to name what 'tis unmeet to do: — haste ye, for the gods'

love, hide me somewhere beyond the land, or slay me, or cast me
into the sea, where ye shall never behold me more! Approach, —
deign to lay your hands on a wretched man; — hearken, fear not, —
my plague can rest on no mortal beside.

[*Enter* CREON]

LE.: Nay, here is Creon, in meet season for thy requests, crave they
act or counsel; for he alone is left to guard the land in thy stead.

OE.: Ah me, how indeed shall I accost him? What claim to credence
can be shown on my part? For in the past I have been found
wholly false to him.

CR.: I have not come in mockery, Oedipus, nor to reproach thee with
any bygone fault. [*To the attendants*] But ye, if ye respect the children of men no more, revere at least the all-nurturing flame of
our lord the Sun, — spare to show thus nakedly a pollution such as
this, — one which neither earth can welcome, nor the holy rain, nor
the light. Nay, take him into the house as quickly as ye may; for
it best accords with piety that kinsfolk alone should see and hear a
kinsman's woes.

OE.: For the gods' love — since thou hast done a gentle violence to
my presage, who hast come in a spirit so noble to me, a man most
vile — grant me a boon: — for thy good I will speak, not for mine
own.

CR.: And what wish art thou so fain to have of me?

OE.: Cast me out of this land with all speed, to a place where no mortal
shall be found to greet me more.

CR.: This would I have done, be thou sure, but that I craved first to
learn all my duty from the god.

OE.: Nay, his behest hath been set forth in full, — to let me perish, the
parricide, the unholy one, that I am.

CR.: Such was the purport; yet, seeing to what a pass we have come,
'tis better to learn clearly what should be done.

OE.: Will ye, then, seek a response on behalf of such a wretch as I am?

CR.: Aye, for thou thyself wilt now surely put faith in the god.

OE.: Yea; and on thee lay I this charge, to thee will I make this entreaty: — give to her who is within such burial as thou thyself
wouldest; for thou wilt meetly render the last rites to thine own.
But for me — never let this city of my sire be condemned to have
me dwelling therein, while I live: no, suffer me to abide on the
hills, where yonder is Cithaeron, famed as mine, — which my
mother and sire, while they lived, set for my appointed tomb, —
that so I may die by their decree who sought to slay me. Howbeit
of thus much am I sure, — that neither sickness nor aught else can
destroy me; for never had I been snatched from death, but in reserve
for some strange doom.

Nay, let *my* fate go whither it will: but as touching my children,
— I pray thee, Creon, take no care on thee for my sons; they are
men, so that, be they where they may, they can never lack the
means to live. But my two girls, poor hapless ones, — who never
knew my table spread apart, or lacked their father's presence, but

ever in all things shared my daily bread, — I pray thee, care for *them*; and — if thou canst — suffer me to touch them with my hands, and to indulge my grief. Grant it, prince, grant it, thou noble heart! Ah, could I but once touch them with my hands, I should think that they were with me, even as when I had sight. . .

[CREON's *attendants lead in the children* ANTIGONE *and* ISMENE.]

Ha? O ye gods, can it be my loved ones that I hear sobbing, — can Creon have taken pity on me and sent me my children — my darlings? Am I right?

CR.: Yea: 'tis of my contriving, for I knew thy joy in them of old, — the joy that now is thine.

OE.: Then blessed be thou, and, for guerdon of this errand, may heaven prove to thee a kinder guardian than it hath to me! My children, where are ye? Come hither, — hither to the hands of him whose mother was your own, the hands whose offices have wrought that your sire's once bright eyes should be such orbs as these, — his, who seeing nought, knowing nought, became your father by her from whom he sprang! For you also do I weep — behold you I cannot — when I think of the bitter life in days to come which men will make you live. To what company of the citizens will ye go, to what festival, from which ye shall not return home in tears, instead of sharing in the holiday? But when ye are now come to years ripe for marriage, who shall he be, who shall be the man, my daughters, that will hazard taking unto him such reproaches as must be baneful alike to my offspring and to yours? For what misery is wanting? Your sire slew his sire, he had seed of her who bare him, and begat you at the sources of his own being! Such are the taunts that will be cast at you; and who then will wed? The man lives not, no, it cannot be, my children, but ye must wither in barren maidenhood.

Ah, son of Menoeceus, hear me — since thou art the only father left to them, for we, their parents, are lost, both of us, — allow them not to wander poor and unwed, who are thy kinswomen, nor abase them to the level of my woes. Nay, pity them, when thou seest them at this tender age so utterly forlorn, save for thee. Signify thy promise, generous man, by the touch of thy hand! To you, my children, I would have given much counsel, were your minds mature; but now I would have this to be your prayer — that ye live where occasion suffers, and that the life which is your portion may be happier than your sire's.

CR.: Thy grief hath had large scope enough: nay, pass into the house.

OE.: I must obey, though 'tis in no wise sweet.

CR.: Yea: for it is in season that all things are good.

OE.: Knowest thou, then, on what conditions I will go?

CR.: Thou shalt name them; so shall I know them when I hear.

OE.: See that thou send me to dwell beyond this land.

CR.: Thou askest me for what the god must give.

OE.: Nay, to the gods I have become most hateful.

CR.: Then shalt thou have thy wish anon.

OE.: So thou consentest?

CR.: 'Tis not my wont to speak idly what I do not mean.

OE.: Then 'tis time to lead me hence.

CR.: Come, then, — but let thy children go.

OE.: Nay, take not these from me!

CR.: Crave not to be master in all things: for the mastery which thou didst win hath not followed thee through life.

CH. [*singing*]: Dwellers in our native Thebes, behold, this is Oedipus, who knew the famed riddle, and was a man most mighty; on whose fortunes what citizen did not gaze with envy? Behold into what a stormy sea of dread trouble he hath come!

Therefore, while our eyes wait to see the destined final day, we must call no one happy who is of mortal race, until he hath crossed life's border, free from pain.*

* These last lines derive from the maxim attributed to Solon; see p. 979.

ANTIGONE

Translated by R. C. JEBB

CHARACTERS IN THE PLAY

ANTIGONE
ISMENE } *daughters of Oedipus*

CREON, *King of Thebes*

EURYDICE, *his wife*

HAEMON, *his son*

TEIRESIAS, *the blind prophet*

GUARD, *set to watch the corpse of Polyneices*

FIRST MESSENGER

SECOND MESSENGER, *from the house*

CHORUS OF THEBAN ELDERS

ANTIGONE

[SCENE: — *The same as in the* Oedipus the King, *an open space before the royal palace, once that of Oedipus, at Thebes. The back-scene represents the front of the palace, with three doors, of which the central and largest is the principal entrance into the house. The time is at daybreak on the morning after the fall of the two brothers, Eteocles and Polyneices, and the flight of the defeated Argives.* ANTIGONE *calls* ISMENE *forth from the palace, in order to speak to her alone.*]

AN.: Ismene, sister, mine own dear sister, knowest thou what ill there is, of all bequeathed by Oedipus, that Zeus fulfils not for us twain while we live? Nothing painful is there, nothing fraught with ruin, no shame, no dishonour, that I have not seen in thy woes and mine.

And now what new edict is this of which they tell, that our Captain hath just published to all Thebes? Knowest thou aught? Hast thou heard? Or is it hidden from thee that our friends are threatened with the doom of our foes?

IS.: No word of friends, Antigone, gladsome or painful, hath come to me, since we two sisters were bereft of brothers twain, killed in one day by a twofold blow; and since in this last night the Argive host hath fled, I know no more, whether my fortune be brighter, or more grievous.

AN.: I knew it well, and therefore sought to bring thee beyond the gates of the court, that thou mightest hear alone.

IS.: What is it? 'Tis plain that thou art brooding on some dark tidings.

AN.: What, hath not Creon destined our brothers, the one to honoured burial, the other to unburied shame? Eteocles, they say, with due observance of right and custom, he hath laid in the earth, for his honour among the dead below. But the hapless corpse of Polyneices — as rumour saith, it hath been published to the town that none shall entomb him or mourn, but leave unwept, unsepulchred, a welcome store for the birds, as they espy him, to feast on at will.

Such, 'tis said, is the edict that the good Creon hath set forth for thee and for me, — yes, for *me*, — and is coming hither to proclaim it clearly to those who know it not; nor counts the matter light, but, whoso disobeys in aught, his doom is death by stoning before all the folk. Thou knowest it now; and thou wilt soon show whether thou art nobly bred, or the base daughter of a noble line.

IS.: Poor sister, — and if things stand thus, what could I help to do or undo?

AN.: Consider if thou wilt share the toil and the deed.

IS.: In what venture? What can be thy meaning?

AN.: Wilt thou aid this hand to lift the dead?

IS.: Thou wouldst bury him, — when 'tis forbidden to Thebes?

AN.: I will do my part, — and thine, if thou wilt not, — to a brother. False to him will I never be found.

IS.: Ah, over-bold! when Creon hath forbidden?

AN.: Nay, he hath no right to keep me from mine own.

IS.: Ah me! think, sister, how our father perished, amid hate and scorn, when sins bared by his own search had moved him to strike both eyes with self-blinding hand; then the mother wife, two names in one, with twisted noose did despite unto her life; and last, our two brothers in one day, — each shedding, hapless one, a kinsman's blood, — wrought out with mutual hands their common doom. And now *we* in turn — we two left all alone — think how we shall perish, more miserably than all the rest, if, in defiance of the law, we brave a king's decree or his powers. Nay, we must remember, first, that we were born women, as who should not strive with men; next, that we are ruled of the stronger, so that we must obey in these things, and in things yet sorer. I, therefore, asking the Spirits Infernal to pardon, seeing that force is put on me herein, will hearken to our rulers; for 'tis witless to be over busy.

AN.: I will not urge thee, — no, nor, if thou yet shouldst have the mind, wouldst thou be welcome as a worker with *me*. Nay, be what thou wilt; but I will bury him: well for me to die in doing that. I shall rest, a loved one with him whom I have loved, sinless in my crime; for I owe a longer allegiance to the dead than to the living: in that world I shall abide for ever. But if *thou* wilt, be guilty of dishonouring laws which the gods have stablished in honour.

IS.: I do them no dishonour; but to defy the State, — I have no strength for that.

AN.: Such be thy plea: — I, then, will go to heap the earth above the brother whom I love.

IS.: Alas, unhappy one! How I fear for thee!

AN.: Fear not for me: guide thine own fate aright.

IS.: At least, then, disclose this plan to none, but hide it closely, — and so, too, will I.

AN.: Oh, denounce it! Thou wilt be far more hateful for thy silence, if thou proclaim not these things to all.

IS.: Thou hast a hot heart for chilling deeds.

AN.: I know that I please where I am most bound to please.

IS.: Aye, if thou canst; but thou wouldst what thou canst not.

AN.: Why, then, when my strength fails, I shall have done.

IS.: A hopeless quest should not be made at all.

AN.: If thus thou speakest, thou wilt have hatred from me, and will justly be subject to the lasting hatred of the dead. But leave me, and the folly that is mine alone, to suffer this dread thing; for I shall not suffer aught so dreadful as an ignoble death.

IS.: Go, then, if thou must; and of this be sure, — that, though thine errand is foolish, to thy dear ones thou art truly dear.

[*Exit* ANTIGONE *on the spectators' left.* ISMENE *retires into the palace*

by one of the two side-doors. When they have departed, the
CHORUS OF THEBAN ELDERS *enters.*]

strophe 1

CH. [*singing*]: Beam of the sun, fairest light that ever dawned on
Thebe of the seven gates, thou hast shone forth at last, eye of golden
day, arisen above Dirce's streams! The warrior of the white shield,
who came from Argos in his panoply, hath been stirred by thee to
headlong flight, in swifter career;

systema 1

LEADER OF THE CHORUS: who set forth against our land by reason of
the vexed claims of Polyneices; and, like shrill-screaming eagle, he
flew over into our land, in snow-white pinion sheathed, with an
armèd throng, and with plumage of helms.

antistrophe 1

CH.: He paused above our dwellings; he ravened around our seven-
fold portals with spears athirst for blood; but he went hence, or
ever his jaws were glutted with our gore, or the Fire-god's pine-fed
flame had seized our crown of towers. So fierce was the noise of
battle raised behind him, a thing too hard for him to conquer, as
he wrestled with his dragon foe.

systema 2

LE.: For Zeus utterly abhors the boasts of a proud tongue; and when
he beheld them coming on in a great stream, in the haughty pride
of clanging gold, he smote with brandished fire one who was now
hasting to shout victory at his goal upon our ramparts.

strophe 2

CH.: Swung down, he fell on the earth with a crash, torch in hand,
he who so lately, in the frenzy of the mad onset, was raging against
us with the blasts of his tempestuous hate. But those threats fared
not as he hoped; and to other foes the mighty War-god dispensed
their several dooms, dealing havoc around, a mighty helper at our
need.

systema 3

LE.: For seven captains at seven gates, matched against seven, left the
tribute of their panoplies to Zeus who turns the battle; save those
two of cruel fate, who, born of one sire and one mother, set against
each other their twain conquering spears, and are sharers in a common death.

antistrophe 2

CH.: But since Victory of glorious name hath come to us, with joy
responsive to the joy of Thebe whose chariots are many, let us

enjoy forgetfulness after the late wars, and visit all the temples of the gods with night-long dance and song; and may Bacchus be our leader, whose dancing shakes the land of Thebe.

systema 4

LE.: But lo, the king of the land comes yonder, Creon, son of Menoeceus, our new ruler by the new fortunes that the gods have given; what counsel is he pondering, that he hath proposed this special conference of elders, summoned by his general mandate?

[*Enter* CREON, *from the central doors of the palace, in the garb of king, with two attendants.*]

CR.: Sirs, the vessel of our State, after being tossed on wild waves, hath once more been safely steadied by the gods: and ye, out of all the folk, have been called apart by my summons, because I knew, first of all, how true and constant was your reverence for the royal power of Laius; how, again, when Oedipus was ruler of our land, and when he had perished, your steadfast loyalty still upheld their children. Since, then, his sons have fallen in one day by a twofold doom, — each smitten by the other, each stained with a brother's blood, — I now possess the throne and all its powers, by nearness of kinship to the dead.

No man can be fully known, in soul and spirit and mind, until he hath been seen versed in rule and law-giving. For if any, being supreme guide of the State, cleaves not to the best counsels, but, through some fear, keeps his lips locked, I hold, and have ever held, him most base; and if any makes a friend of more account than his fatherland, that man hath no place in my regard. For I — be Zeus my witness, who sees all things always — would not be silent if I saw ruin, instead of safety, coming to the citizens; nor would I ever deem the country's foe a friend to myself; remembering this, that our country is the ship that bears us safe, and that only while she prospers in our voyage can we make true friends.

Such are the rules by which I guard this city's greatness. And in accord with them is the edict which I have now published to the folk touching the sons of Oedipus; — that Eteocles, who hath fallen fighting for our city, in all renown of arms, shall be entombed, and crowned with every rite that follows the noblest dead to their rest. But for his brother, Polyneices, — who came back from exile, and sought to consume utterly with fire the city of his fathers and the shrines of his fathers' gods, — sought to taste of kindred blood, and to lead the remnant into slavery; — touching this man, it hath been proclaimed to our people that none shall grace him with sepulture or lament, but leave him unburied, a corpse for birds and dogs to eat, a ghastly sight of shame.

Such the spirit of my dealing; and never, by deed of mine, shall the wicked stand in honour before the just; but whoso hath good will to Thebes, he shall be honoured of me, in his life and in his death.

LE.: Such is thy pleasure, Creon, son of Menoeceus, touching this city's foe, and its friend; and thou hast power, I ween, to take what order thou wilt, both for the dead, and for all us who live.

CR.: See, then, that ye be guardians of the mandate.

LE.: Lay the burden of this task on some younger man.

CR.: Nay, watchers of the corpse have been found.

LE.: What, then, is this further charge that thou wouldst give?

CR.: That ye side not with the breakers of these commands.

LE.: No man is so foolish that he is enamoured of death.

CR.: In sooth, that is the meed; yet lucre hath oft ruined men through their hopes.

[*A* GUARD *enters from the spectators' left.*]

GU.: My liege, I will not say that I come breathless from speed, or that I have plied a nimble foot; for often did my thoughts make me pause, and wheel round in my path, to return. My mind was holding large discourse with me; 'Fool, why goest thou to thy certain doom?' 'Wretch, tarrying again? And if Creon hears this from another, must not thou smart for it?' So debating, I went on my way with lagging steps, and thus a short road was made long. At last, however, it carried the day that I should come hither — to thee; and, though my tale be nought, yet will I tell it; for I come with a good grip on one hope, — that I can suffer nothing but what is my fate.

CR.: And what is it that disquiets thee thus?

GU.: I wish to tell thee first about myself — I did not do the deed — I did not see the doer — it were not right that I should come to any harm.

CR.: Thou hast a shrewd eye for thy mark; well dost thou fence thyself round against the blame; clearly thou hast some strange thing to tell.

GU.: Aye, truly; dread news makes one pause long.

CR.: Then tell it, wilt thou, and so get thee gone?

GU.: Well, this is it. — The corpse — some one hath just given it burial, and gone away, — after sprinkling thirsty dust on the flesh, with such other rites as piety enjoins.

CR.: What sayest thou? What living man hath dared this deed?

GU.: I know not; no stroke of pickaxe was seen there, no earth thrown up by mattock; the ground was hard and dry, unbroken, without track of wheels; the doer was one who had left no trace. And when the first day-watchman showed it to us, sore wonder fell on all. The dead man was veiled from us; not shut within a tomb, but lightly strewn with dust, as by the hand of one who shunned a curse. And no sign met the eye as though any beast of prey or any dog had come nigh to him, or torn him.

Then evil words flew fast and loud among us, guard accusing guard; and it would e'en have come to blows at last, nor was there any to hinder. Every man was the culprit, and no one was convicted, but all disclaimed knowledge of the deed. And we were ready to take red-hot iron in our hands; — to walk through fire; —

to make oath by the gods that we had not done the deed, — that we were not privy to the planning or the doing.

At last, when all our searching was fruitless, one spake, who made us all bend our faces on the earth in fear; for we saw not how we could gainsay him, or escape mischance if we obeyed. His counsel was that this deed must be reported to thee, and not hidden. And this seemed best; and the lot doomed my hapless self to win this prize. So here I stand, — as unwelcome as unwilling, well I wot; for no man delights in the bearer of bad news.

LE.: O king, my thoughts have long been whispering, can this deed, perchance, be e'en the work of gods?

CR.: Cease, ere thy words fill me utterly with wrath, lest thou be found at once an old man and foolish. For thou sayest what is not to be borne, in saying that the gods have care for this corpse. Was it for high reward of trusty service that they sought to hide his nakedness, who came to burn their pillared shrines and sacred treasures, to burn their land, and scatter its laws to the winds? Or dost thou behold the gods honouring the wicked? It cannot be. No! From the first there were certain in the town that muttered against me, chafing at this edict, wagging their heads in secret; and kept not their necks duly under the yoke, like men contented with my sway.

'Tis by them, well I know, that these have been beguiled and bribed to do this deed. Nothing so evil as money ever grew to be current among men. This lays cities low, this drives men from their homes, this trains and warps honest souls till they set themselves to works of shame; this still teaches folk to practise villainies, and to know every godless deed.

But all the men who wrought this thing for hire have made it sure that, soon or late, they shall pay the price. Now, as Zeus still hath my reverence, know this — I tell it thee on my oath: — If ye find not the very author of this burial, and produce him before mine eyes, death alone shall not be enough for you, till first, hung up alive, ye have revealed this outrage, — that henceforth ye may thieve with better knowledge whence lucre should be won, and learn that it is not well to love gain from every source. For thou wilt find that ill-gotten pelf brings more men to ruin than to weal.

GU.: May I speak? Or shall I just turn and go?

CR.: Knowest thou not that even now thy voice offends?

GU.: Is thy smart in the ears, or in the soul?

CR.: And why wouldst thou define the seat of my pain?

GU.: The doer vexes thy mind, but I, thine ears.

CR.: Ah, thou art a born babbler, 'tis well seen.

GU.: May be, but never the doer of this deed.

CR.: Yea, and more, — the seller of thy life for silver.

GU.: Alas! 'Tis sad, truly, that he who judges should misjudge.

CR.: Let thy fancy play with 'judgment' as it will; — but, if ye show me not the doers of these things, ye shall avow that dastardly gains work sorrows. [CREON *goes into the palace.*]

GU.: Well, may he be found! so 'twere best. But, be he caught or be he not — fortune must settle that — truly thou wilt not see me here again. Saved, even now, beyond hope and thought, I owe the gods great thanks. [*The* GUARD *goes out on the spectators' left.*]

strophe 1

CH. [*singing*]: Wonders are many, and none is more wonderful than man; the power that crosses the white sea, driven by the stormy south-wind, making a path under surges that threaten to engulf him; and Earth, the eldest of the gods, the immortal, the unwearied, doth he wear, turning the soil with the offspring of horses, as the ploughs go to and fro from year to year.

antistrophe 1

And the light-hearted race of birds, and the tribes of savage beasts, and the sea-brood of the deep, he snares in the meshes of his woven toils, he leads captive, man excellent in wit. And he masters by his arts the beast whose lair is in the wilds, who roams the hills; he tames the horse of shaggy mane, he puts the yoke upon its neck, he tames the tireless mountain bull.

strophe 2

And speech, and wind-swift thought, and all the moods that mould a state, hath he taught himself; and how to flee the arrows of the frost, when 'tis hard lodging under the clear sky, and the arrows of the rushing rain; yea, he hath resource for all; without resource he meets nothing that must come: only against Death shall he call for aid in vain; but from baffling maladies he hath devised escapes.

antistrophe 2

Cunning beyond fancy's dream is the fertile skill which brings him, now to evil, now to good. When he honours the laws of the land, and that justice which he hath sworn by the gods to uphold, proudly stands his city: no city hath he who, for his rashness, dwells with sin. Never may he share my hearth, never think my thoughts, who doth these things!

[*Enter the* GUARD *on the spectators' left, leading in* ANTIGONE.]

LE.: What portent from the gods is this? — my soul is amazed. I know her — how can I deny that yon maiden is Antigone?

O hapless, and child of hapless sire, — of Oedipus! What means this? Thou brought a prisoner? — thou, disloyal to the king's laws, and taken in folly?

GU.: Here she is, the doer of the deed: — we caught this girl burying him: — but where is Creon?

[CREON *enters hurriedly from the palace.*]

LE.: Lo, he comes forth again from the house, at our need.

CR.: What is it? What hath chanced, that makes my coming timely?

GU.: O king, against nothing should men pledge their word; for the afterthought belies the first intent. I could have vowed that I should not soon be here again, — scared by thy threats, with which I had just been lashed: but, — since the joy that surprises and transcends our hopes is like in fulness to no other pleasure, — I have come, though 'tis in breach of my sworn oath, bringing this maid; who was taken showing grace to the dead. This time there was no casting of lots; no, this luck hath fallen to me, and to none else. And now, sire, take her thyself, question her, examine her, as thou wilt; but I have a right to free and final quittance of this trouble.

CR.: And thy prisoner here — how and whence hast thou taken her?

GU.: She was burying the man; thou knowest all.

CR.: Dost thou mean what thou sayest? Dost thou speak aright?

GU.: I saw her burying the corpse that thou hadst forbidden to bury. Is that plain and clear?

CR.: And how was she seen? how taken in the act?

GU.: It befell on this wise. When we had come to the place, — with those dread menaces of thine upon us, — we swept away all the dust that covered the corpse, and bared the dank body well; and then sat us down on the brow of the hill, to windward, heedful that the smell from him should not strike us; every man was wide awake, and kept his neighbour alert with torrents of threats, if anyone should be careless of this task.

So went it, until the sun's bright orb stood in mid heaven, and the heat began to burn: and then suddenly a whirlwind lifted from the earth a storm of dust, a trouble in the sky, and filled the plain, marring all the leafage of its woods; and the wide air was choked therewith: we closed our eyes, and bore the plague from the gods.

And when, after a long while, this storm had passed, the maid was seen; and she cried aloud with the sharp cry of a bird in its bitterness, — even as when, within the empty nest, it sees the bed stripped of its nestlings. So she also, when she saw the corpse bare, lifted up a voice of wailing, and called down curses on the doers of that deed. And straightway she brought thirsty dust in her hands; and from a shapely ewer of bronze, held high, with thrice-poured drink-offering she crowned the dead.

We rushed forward when we saw it, and at once closed upon our quarry, who was in no wise dismayed. Then we taxed her with her past and present doings; and she stood not on denial of aught, — at once to my joy and to my pain. To have escaped from ills one's self is a great joy; but 'tis painful to bring friends to ill. Howbeit, all such things are of less account to me than mine own safety.

CR.: Thou — thou whose face is bent to earth — dost thou avow, or disavow, this deed?

AN.: I avow it; I make no denial.

CR. [to GUARD]: Thou canst betake thee wither thou wilt, free and clear of a grave charge. [Exit GUARD. To ANTIGONE] Now, tell me thou — not in many words, but briefly — knewest thou that an edict had forbidden this?

AN.: I knew it: could I help it? It was public.

cr.: And thou didst indeed dare to transgress that law?

an.: Yes; for it was not Zeus that had published me that edict; not
such are the laws set among men by the Justice who dwells with
the gods below; nor deemed I that thy decrees were of such force,
that a mortal could override the unwritten and unfailing statutes of
heaven. For their life is not of to-day or yesterday, but from all
time, and no man knows when they were first put forth.

Not through dread of any human pride could I answer to the
gods for breaking *these*. Die I must, — I knew that well (how
should I not?) — even without thy edicts. But if I am to die before
my time, I count that a gain: for when any one lives, as I do, compassed about with evils, can such an one find aught but gain in
death?

So for me to meet this doom is trifling grief; but if I had suffered
my mother's son to lie in death an unburied corpse, that would have
grieved me; for this, I am not grieved. And if my present deeds
are foolish in thy sight, it may be that a foolish judge arraigns my
folly.

le.: The maid shows herself passionate child of passionate sire, and
knows not how to bend before troubles.

cr.: Yet I would have thee know that o'er-stubborn spirits are most
often humbled; 'tis the stiffest iron, baked to hardness in the fire,
that thou shalt oftenest see snapped and shivered; and I have known
horses that show temper brought to order by a little curb; there is
no room for pride, when thou art thy neighbour's slave. — This girl
was already versed in insolence when she transgressed the laws that
had been set forth; and, that done, lo, a second insult, — to vaunt
of this, and exult in her deed.

Now verily I am no man, she is the man, if this victory shall rest
with her, and bring no penalty. No! be she sister's child, or nearer
to me in blood than any that worships Zeus at the altar of our house,
— she and her kinsfolk shall not avoid a doom most dire; for indeed
I charge that other with a like share in the plotting of this burial.

And summon her — for I saw her e'en now within, — raving,
and not mistress of her wits. So oft, before the deed, the mind
stands self-convicted in its treason, when folks are plotting mischief
in the dark. But verily this, too, is hateful, — when one who hath
been caught in wickedness then seeks to make the crime a glory.

an.: Wouldst thou do more than take and slay me?

cr.: No more, indeed; having that, I have all.

an.: Why then dost thou delay? In thy discourse there is nought
that pleases me, — never may there be! — and so my words must
needs be unpleasing to thee. And yet, for glory — whence could
I have won a nobler, than by giving burial to mine own brother?
All here would own that they thought it well, were not their lips
sealed by fear. But royalty, blest in so much besides, hath the
power to do and say what it will.

cr.: Thou differest from all these Thebans in that view.

an.: These also share it; but they curb their tongues for thee.

cr.: And art thou not ashamed to act apart from them?

an.: No; there is nothing shameful in piety to a brother.

cr.: Was it not a brother, too, that died in the opposite cause?

an.: Brother by the same mother and the same sire.

cr.: Why, then, dost thou render a grace that is impious in his sight?

an.: The dead man will not say that he so deems it.

cr.: Yea, if thou makest him but equal in honour with the wicked.

an.: It was his brother, not his slave, that perished.

cr.: Wasting this land; while *he* fell as its champion.

an.: Nevertheless, Hades desires these rites.

cr.: But the good desires not a like portion with the evil.

an.: Who knows but this seems blameless in the world below?

cr.: A foe is never a friend — not even in death.

an.: 'Tis not my nature to join in hating, but in loving.

cr.: Pass, then, to the world of the dead, and, if thou must needs love, love them.   While I live, no woman shall rule me.

[*Enter* ISMENE *from the house, led in by two attendants.*]

ch. [*chanting*]: Lo, yonder Ismene comes forth, shedding such tears as fond sisters weep; a cloud upon her brow casts its shadow over her darkly-flushing face, and breaks in rain on her fair cheek.

cr.: And thou, who, lurking like a viper in my house, wast secretly draining my life-blood, while I knew not that I was nurturing two pests, to rise against my throne — come, tell me now, wilt thou also confess thy part in this burial, or wilt thou forswear all knowledge of it?

is.: I have done the deed, — if she allows my claim, — and share the burden of the charge.

an.: Nay, justice will not suffer thee to do that: thou didst not consent to the deed, nor did I give thee part in it.

is.: But, now that ills beset thee, I am not ashamed to sail the sea of trouble at thy side.

an.: Whose was the deed, Hades and the dead are witnesses: a friend in words is not the friend that I love.

is.: Nay, sister, reject me not, but let me die with thee, and duly honour the dead.

an.: Share not thou my death, nor claim deeds to which thou hast not put thy hand: my death will suffice.

is.: And what life is dear to me, bereft of thee?

an.: Ask Creon; all thy care is for him.

is.: Why vex me thus, when it avails thee nought?

an.: Indeed, if I mock, 'tis with pain that I mock thee.

is.: Tell me, — how can I serve thee, even now?

an.: Save thyself: I grudge not thy escape.

is.: Ah, woe is me! And shall I have no share in thy fate?

an.: Thy choice was to live; mine, to die.

is.: At least thy choice was not made without my protest.

an.: One world approved thy wisdom; another, mine.

is.: Howbeit, the offence is the same for both of us.

AN.: Be of good cheer; thou livest; but my life hath long been given to death, that so I might serve the dead.

CR.: Lo, one of these maidens hath newly shown herself foolish, as the other hath been since her life began.

IS.: Yea, O king, such reason as nature may have given abides not with the unfortunate, but goes astray.

CR.: Thine did, when thou chosest vile deeds with the vile.

IS.: What life could I endure, without her presence?

CR.: Nay, speak not of her 'presence'; she lives no more.

IS.: But wilt thou slay the betrothed of thine own son?

CR.: Nay, there are other fields for him to plough.

IS.: But there can never be such love as bound him to her.

CR.: I like not an evil wife for my son.

AN.: Haemon, beloved! How thy father wrongs thee!

CR.: Enough, enough of thee and of thy marriage!

LE.: Wilt thou indeed rob thy son of this maiden?

CR.: 'Tis Death that shall stay these bridals for me.

LE.: 'Tis determined, it seems, that she shall die.

CR.: Determined, yes, for thee and for me.— [To the two attendants] No more delay — servants, take them within! Henceforth they must be women, and not range at large; for verily even the bold seek to fly, when they see Death now closing on their life.

[Exeunt attendants, guarding ANTIGONE and ISMENE. — CREON remains.]

strophe 1

CH. [singing]: Blest are they whose days have not tasted of evil. For when a house hath once been shaken from heaven, there the curse fails nevermore, passing from life to life of the race; even as, when the surge is driven over the darkness of the deep by the fierce breath of Thracian seawinds, it rolls up the black sand from the depths, and there is a sullen roar from wind-vexed headlands that front the blows of the storm.

antistrophe 1

I see that from olden time the sorrows in the house of the Labdacidae are heaped upon the sorrows of the dead; and generation is not freed by generation, but some god strikes them down, and the race hath no deliverance.

For now that hope of which the light had been spread above the last root of the house of Oedipus — that hope, in turn, is brought low — by the blood-stained dust due to the gods infernal, and by folly in speech, and frenzy at the heart.

strophe 2

Thy power, O Zeus, what human trespass can limit? That power which neither Sleep, the all-ensnaring, nor the untiring months of the gods can master; but thou, a ruler to whom time brings not old age, dwellest in the dazzling splendour of Olympus.

And through the future, near and far, as through the past, shall this law hold good: Nothing that is vast enters into the life of mortals without a curse.

antistrophe 2

For that hope whose wanderings are so wide is to many men a comfort, but to many a false lure of giddy desires; and the disappointment comes on one who knoweth nought till he burn his foot against the hot fire.

For with wisdom hath some one given forth the famous saying, that evil seems good, soon or late, to him whose mind the god draws to mischief; and but for the briefest space doth he fare free of woe.

LE.: But lo, Haemon, the last of thy sons; — comes he grieving for the doom of his promised bride, Antigone, and bitter for the baffled hope of his marriage?

[*Enter* HAEMON]

CR.: We shall know soon, better than seers could tell us. — My son, hearing the fixed doom of thy betrothed, art thou come in rage against thy father? Or have I thy good will, act how I may?

HA.: Father, I am thine; and thou, in thy wisdom, tracest for me rules which I shall follow. No marriage shall be deemed by me a greater gain than thy good guidance.

CR.: Yea, this, my son, should be thy heart's fixed law, — in all things to obey thy father's will. 'Tis for this that men pray to see dutiful children grow up around them in their homes, — that such may requite their father's foe with evil, and honour, as their father doth, his friend. But he who begets unprofitable children — what shall we say that he hath sown, but troubles for himself, and much triumph for his foes? Then do not thou, my son, at pleasure's beck, dethrone thy reason for a woman's sake; knowing that this is a joy that soon grows cold in clasping arms, — an evil woman to share thy bed and thy home. For what wound could strike deeper than a false friend? Nay, with loathing, and as if she were thine enemy, let this girl go to find a husband in the house of Hades. For since I have taken her, alone of all the city, in open disobedience, I will not make myself a liar to my people — I will slay her.

So let her appeal as she will to the majesty of kindred blood. If I am to nurture mine own kindred in naughtiness, needs must I bear with it in aliens. He who does his duty in his own household will be found righteous in the State also. But if any one transgresses, and does violence to the laws, or thinks to dictate to his rulers, such an one can win no praise from me. No, whomsoever the city may appoint, that man must be obeyed, in little things and great, in just things and unjust; and I should feel sure that one who thus obeys would be a good ruler no less than a good subject, and in the storm of spears would stand his ground where he was set, loyal and dauntless at his comrade's side.

But disobedience is the worst of evils. This it is that ruins cities;

this makes homes desolate; by this, the ranks of allies are broken into headlong rout; but, of the lives whose course is fair, the greater part owes safety to obedience. Therefore we must support the cause of order, and in no wise suffer a woman to worst us. Better to fall from power, if we must, by a man's hand; then we should not be called weaker than a woman.

LE.: To us, unless our years have stolen our wit, thou seemest to say wisely what thou sayest.

HA.: Father, the gods implant reason in men, the highest of all things that we call our own. Not mine the skill — far from me be the quest! — to say wherein thou speakest not aright; and yet another man, too, might have some useful thought. At least, it is my natural office to watch, on thy behalf, all that men say, or do, or find to blame. For the dread of thy frown forbids the citizen to speak such words as would offend thine ear; but I can hear these murmurs in the dark, these moanings of the city for this maiden; 'no woman,' they say, 'ever merited her doom less, — none ever was to die so shamefully for deeds so glorious as hers; who, when her own brother had fallen in bloody strife, would not leave him unburied, to be devoured by carrion dogs, or by any bird: — deserves not *she* the meed of golden honour?'

Such is the darkling rumour that spreads in secret. For me, my father, no treasure is so precious as thy welfare. What, indeed, is a nobler ornament for children than a prospering sire's fair fame, or for sire than son's? Wear not, then, one mood only in thyself; think not that thy word, and thine alone, must be right. For if any man thinks that he alone is wise, — that in speech, or in mind, he hath no peer, — such a soul, when laid open, is ever found empty.

No, though a man be wise, 'tis no shame for him to learn many things, and to bend in season. Seest thou, beside the wintry torrent's course, how the trees that yield to it save every twig, while the stiff-necked perish root and branch? And even thus he who keeps the sheet of his sail taut, and never slackens it, upsets his boat, and finishes his voyage with keel uppermost.

Nay, forego thy wrath; permit thyself to change. For if I, a younger man, may offer my thought, it were far best, I ween, that men should be all-wise by nature; but, otherwise — and oft the scale inclines not so — 'tis good also to learn from those who speak aright.

LE.: Sire, 'tis meet that thou shouldst profit by his words, if he speaks aught in season, and thou, Haemon, by thy father's; for on both parts there hath been wise speech.

CR.: Men of my age — are we indeed to be schooled, then, by men of his?

HA.: In nothing that is not right; but if I am young, thou shouldst look to my merits, not to my years.

CR.: Is it a merit to honour the unruly?

HA.: I could wish no one to show respect for evil-doers.

CR.: Then is not she tainted with that malady?

HA.: Our Theban folk, with one voice, denies it.

CR.: Shall Thebes prescribe to me how I must rule?

HA.: See, there thou hast spoken like a youth indeed.

CR.: Am I to rule this land by other judgment than mine own?

HA.: That is no city which belongs to one man.

CR.: Is not the city held to be the ruler's?

HA.: Thou wouldst make a good monarch of a desert.

CR.: This boy, it seems, is the woman's champion.

HA.: If thou art a woman; indeed, my care is for thee.

CR.: Shameless, at open feud with thy father!

HA.: Nay, I see thee offending against justice.

CR.: Do I offend, when I respect mine own prerogatives?

HA.: Thou dost not respect them, when thou tramplest on the gods' honours.

CR.: O dastard nature, yielding place to woman!

HA.: Thou wilt never find me yield to baseness.

CR.: All thy words, at least, plead for that girl.

HA.: And for thee, and for me, and for the gods below.

CR.: Thou canst never marry her, on this side the grave.

HA.: Then she must die, and in death destroy another.

CR.: How! doth thy boldness run to open threats?

HA.: What threat is it, to combat vain resolves?

CR.: Thou shalt rue thy witless teaching of wisdom.

HA.: Wert thou not my father, I would have called thee unwise.

CR.: Thou woman's slave, use not wheedling speech with me.

HA.: Thou wouldst speak, and then hear no reply?

CR.: Sayest thou so? Now, by the heaven above us — be sure of it — thou shalt smart for taunting me in this opprobrious strain. Bring forth that hated thing, that she may die forthwith in his presence — before his eyes — at her bridegroom's side!

HA.: No, not at my side — never think it — shall she perish; nor shalt thou ever set eyes more upon my face: — rave, then, with such friends as can endure thee. [*Exit* HAEMON]

LE.: The man is gone, O king, in angry haste; a youthful mind, when stung, is fierce.

CR.: Let him do, or dream, more than man — good speed to him! — But he shall not save these two girls from their doom.

LE.: Dost thou indeed purpose to slay both?

CR.: Not her whose hands are pure: thou sayest well.

LE.: And by what doom mean'st thou to slay the other?

CR.: I will take her where the path is loneliest, and hide her, living, in a rocky vault, with so much food set forth as piety prescribes, that the city may avoid a public stain. And there, praying to Hades, the only god whom she worships, perchance she will obtain release from death; or else will learn, at last, though late, that it is lost labour to revere the dead. [CREON *goes into the palace.*]

strophe

CH. [*singing*]: Love, unconquered in the fight, Love, who makest havoc of wealth, who keepest thy vigil on the soft cheek of a maiden;

thou roamest over the sea, and among the homes of dwellers in the wilds; no immortal can escape thee, nor any among men whose life is for a day; and he to whom thou hast come is mad.

antistrophe

The just themselves have their minds warped by thee to wrong, for their ruin: 'tis thou that hast stirred up this present strife of kinsmen; victorious is the love-kindling light from the eyes of the fair bride; it is a power enthroned in sway beside the eternal laws; for there the goddess Aphrodite is working her unconquerable will.

[ANTIGONE *is led out of the palace by two of* CREON's *attendants who are about to conduct her to her doom.*]

But now I also am carried beyond the bounds of loyalty, and can no more keep back the streaming tears, when I see Antigone thus passing to the bridal chamber where all are laid to rest.

[*The following lines between* ANTIGONE *and the* CHORUS *are chanted responsively.*]

strophe 1

AN.: See me, citizens of my fatherland, setting forth on my last way, looking my last on the sunlight that is for me no more; no, Hades who gives sleep to all leads me living to Acheron's shore; who have had no portion in the chant that brings the bride, nor hath any song been mine for the crowning of bridals; whom the lord of the Dark Lake shall wed.

systema 1

CH.: Glorious, therefore, and with praise, thou departest to that deep place of the dead: wasting sickness hath not smitten thee; thou hast not found the wages of the sword; no, mistress of thine own fate, and still alive, thou shalt pass to Hades, as no other of mortal kind hath passed.

antistrophe 1

AN.: I have heard in other days how dread a doom befell our Phrygian guest, the daughter of Tantalus, on the Sipylian heights; * how, like clinging ivy, the growth of stone subdued her; and the rains fail not, as men tell, from her wasting form, nor fails the snow, while beneath her weeping lids the tears bedew her bosom; and most like to hers is the fate that brings me to my rest.

systema 2

CH.: Yet she was a goddess, thou knowest, and born of gods; we are mortals, and of mortal race. But 'tis great renown for a woman who hath perished that she should have shared the doom of the godlike, in her life, and afterward in death.

* A reference to the story of Niobe.

strophe 2

AN.: Ah, I am mocked!   In the name of our fathers' gods, can ye not wait till I am gone, — must ye taunt me to my face, O my city, and ye, her wealthy sons?   Ah, fount of Dirce, and thou holy ground of Thebe whose chariots are many; ye, at least, will bear me witness, in what sort, unwept of friends, and by what laws I pass to the rock-closed prison of my strange tomb, ah me unhappy! who have no home on the earth or in the shades, no home with the living or with the dead.

strophe 3

CH.: Thou hast rushed forward to the utmost verge of daring; and against that throne where Justice sits on high thou hast fallen, my daughter, with a grievous fall.   But in this ordeal thou art paying, haply, for thy father's sin.

antistrophe 2

AN.: Thou hast touched on my bitterest thought, — awaking the ever-new lament for my sire and for all the doom given to us, the famed house of Labdacus.   Alas for the horrors of the mother's bed! alas for the wretched mother's slumber at the side of her own son, — and my sire!   From what manner of parents did I take my miserable being!   And to them I go thus, accursed, unwed, to share their home.   Alas, my brother, ill-starred in thy marriage, in thy death thou hast undone my life!

antistrophe 3

CH.: Reverent action claims a certain praise for reverence; but an offence against power cannot be brooked by him who hath power in his keeping.   Thy self-willed temper hath wrought thy ruin.

epode

AN.: Unwept, unfriended, without marriage-song, I am led forth in my sorrow on this journey that can be delayed no more.   No longer, hapless one, may I behold yon day-star's sacred eye; but for my fate no tear is shed, no friend makes moan.

[CREON *enters from the palace.*]

CR.: Know ye not that songs and wailings before death would never cease, if it profited to utter them?   Away with her — away!   And when ye have enclosed her, according to my word, in her vaulted grave, leave her alone, forlorn — whether she wishes to die, or to live a buried life in such a home.   Our hands are clean as touching this maiden.   But this is certain — she shall be deprived of her sojourn in the light.

AN.: Tomb, bridal-chamber, eternal prison in the caverned rock, whither I go to find mine own, those many who have perished, and whom Persephone hath received among the dead!   Last of all shall I pass thither, and far most miserably of all, before the term of my life is spent. But I cherish good hope that my coming will be welcome to my father, and pleasant to thee, my mother, and welcome, brother, to thee; for, when ye died, with mine own hands I washed and dressed you, and poured drink-offerings at your graves; and now, Polyneices, 'tis for tending thy corpse that I win such recompense as this.

And yet I honoured thee, as the wise will deem, rightly. Never, had I been a mother of children, or if a husband had been mouldering in death, would I have taken this task upon me in the city's despite. What law, ye ask, is my warrant for that word? The husband lost, another might have been found, and child from another, to replace the first-born; but, father and mother hidden with Hades, no brother's life could ever bloom for me again. Such was the law whereby I held thee first in honour; but Creon deemed me guilty of error therein, and of outrage, ah brother mine! And now he leads me thus, a captive in his hands; no bridal bed, no bridal song hath been mine, no joy of marriage, no portion in the nurture of children; but thus, forlorn of friends, unhappy one, I go living to the vaults of death.*

And what law of heaven have I transgressed? Why, hapless one, should I look to the gods any more, — what ally should I invoke, — when by piety I have earned the name of impious? Nay, then, if these things are pleasing to the gods, when I have suffered my doom, I shall come to know my sin; but if the sin is with my judges, I could wish them no fuller measure of evil than they, on their part, mete wrongfully to me.

CH.: Still the same tempest of the soul vexes this maiden with the same fierce gusts.

CR.: Then for this shall her guards have cause to rue their slowness.

AN.: Ah me! that word hath come very near to death.

CR.: I can cheer thee with no hope that this doom is not thus to be fulfilled.

AN.: O city of my fathers in the land of Thebe! O ye gods, eldest of our race! — they lead me hence — now, now — they tarry not! Behold me, princes of Thebes, the last daughter of the house of your kings, — see what I suffer, and from whom, because I feared to cast away the fear of Heaven! [ANTIGONE *is led away by the guards.*]

strophe 1

CH. [*singing*]: Even thus endured Danae in her beauty to change the light of day for brass-bound walls; and in that chamber, secret as the grave, she was held close prisoner; yet was she of a proud lineage, O my daughter, and charged with the keeping of the seed of Zeus, that fell in the golden rain.

But dreadful is the mysterious power of fate; there is no deliverance from it by wealth or by war, by fenced city, or dark, sea-beaten ships.

* Lines 904–920, rendered in this paragraph, are rejected as spurious by Jebb.

antistrophe 1

And bonds tamed the son of Dryas, swift to wrath, that king of the Edonians; so paid he for his frenzied taunts, when, by the will of Dionysus, he was pent in a rocky prison. There the fierce exuberance of his madness slowly passed away. That man learned to know the god, whom in his frenzy he had provoked with mockeries; for he had sought to quell the god-possessed women, and the Bacchanalian fire; and he angered the Muses that love the flute.

strophe 2

And by the waters of the Dark Rocks, the waters of the twofold sea, are the shores of Bosporus, and Thracian Salmydessus; where Ares, neighbour to the city, saw the accurst, blinding wound dealt to the two sons of Phineus by his fierce wife, — the wound that brought darkness to those vengeance-craving orbs, smitten with her bloody hands, smitten with her shuttle for a dagger.

antistrophe 2

Pining in their misery, they bewailed their cruel doom, those sons of a mother hapless in her marriage; but she traced her descent from the ancient line of the Erechtheidae; and in far-distant caves she was nursed amid her father's storms, that child of Boreas, swift as a steed over the steep hills, a daughter of gods; yet upon her also the gray Fates bore hard, my daughter.

[*Enter* TEIRESIAS, *led by a Boy, on the spectators' right.*]

TE.: Princes of Thebes, we have come with linked steps, both served by the eyes of one; for thus, by a guide's help, the blind must walk.

CR.: And what, aged Teiresias, are thy tidings?

TE.: I will tell thee; and do thou hearken to the seer.

CR.: Indeed, it has not been my wont to slight thy counsel.

TE.: Therefore didst thou steer our city's course aright.

CR.: I have felt, and can attest, thy benefits.

TE.: Mark that now, once more, thou standest on fate's fine edge.

CR.: What means this? How I shudder at thy message!

TE.: Thou wilt learn, when thou hearest the warnings of mine art. As I took my place on mine old seat of augury, where all birds have been wont to gather within my ken, I heard a strange voice among them; they were screaming with dire, feverish rage, that drowned their language in a jargon; and I knew that they were rending each other with their talons, murderously; the whirr of wings told no doubtful tale.

Forthwith, in fear, I essayed burnt-sacrifice on a duly kindled altar: but from my offerings the Fire-god showed no flame; a dank moisture, oozing from the thigh-flesh, trickled forth upon the embers, and smoked, and sputtered; the gall was scattered to the air; and the streaming thighs lay bared of the fat that had been wrapped round them.

Such was the failure of the rites by which I vainly asked a sign, as from this boy I learned; for he is my guide, as I am guide to others.   And 'tis thy counsel that hath brought this sickness on our State.   For the altars of our city and of our hearths have been tainted, one and all, by birds and dogs, with carrion from the hapless corpse, the son of Oedipus: and therefore the gods no more accept prayer and sacrifice at our hands, or the flame of meat-offering; nor doth any bird give a clear sign by its shrill cry, for they have tasted the fatness of a slain man's blood.

Think, then, on these things, my son.   All men are liable to err; but when an error hath been made, that man is no longer witless or unblest who heals the ill into which he hath fallen, and remains not stubborn.

Self-will, we know, incurs the charge of folly.   Nay, allow the claim of the dead; stab not the fallen; what prowess is it to slay the slain anew?   I have sought thy good, and for thy good I speak: and never is it sweeter to learn from a good counsellor than when he counsels for thine own gain.

CR.: Old man, ye all shoot your shafts at me, as archers at the butts; — ye must needs practise on me with seer-craft also; — aye, the seer-tribe hath long trafficked in me, and made me their merchandise.   Gain your gains, drive your trade, if ye list, in the silver-gold of Sardis and the gold of India; but ye shall not hide that man in the grave, — no, though the eagles of Zeus should bear the carrion morsels to their Master's throne — no, not for dread of that defilement will I suffer his burial: — for well I know that no mortal can defile the gods. — But, aged Teiresias, the wisest fall with a shameful fall, when they clothe shameful thoughts in fair words, for lucre's sake.

TE.: Alas!   Doth any man know, doth any consider . . .
CR.: Whereof?   What general truth dost thou announce?
TE.: How precious, above all wealth, is good counsel.
CR.: As folly, I think, is the worst mischief.
TE.: Yet thou art tainted with that distemper.
CR.: I would not answer the seer with a taunt.
TE.: But thou dost, in saying that I prophesy falsely.
CR.: Well, the prophet-tribe was ever fond of money.
TE.: And the race bred of tyrants loves base gain.
CR.: Knowest thou that thy speech is spoken of thy king?
TE.: I know it; for through me thou hast saved Thebes.
CR.: Thou art a wise seer; but thou lovest evil deeds.
TE.: Thou wilt rouse me to utter the dread secret in my soul.
CR.: Out with it! — Only speak it not for gain.
TE.: Indeed, methinks, I shall not, — as touching thee.
CR.: Know that thou shalt not trade on my resolve.
TE.: Then know thou — aye, know it well — that thou shalt not live through many more courses of the sun's swift chariot, ere one begotten of thine own loins shall have been given by thee, a corpse for corpses; because thou hast thrust children of the sunlight to the

shades, and ruthlessly lodged a living soul in the grave; but keepest in this world one who belongs to the gods infernal, a corpse un-buried, unhonoured, all unhallowed. In such thou hast no part, nor have the gods above, but this is a violence done to them by thee. Therefore the avenging destroyers lie in wait for thee, the Furies of Hades and of the gods, that thou mayest be taken in these same ills.

And mark well if I speak these things as a hireling. A time not long to be delayed shall awaken the wailing of men and of women in thy house. And a tumult of hatred against thee stirs all the cities whose mangled sons had the burial-rite from dogs, or from wild beasts, or from some winged bird that bore a polluting breath to each city that contains the hearths of the dead.

Such arrows for thy heart — since thou provokest me — have I launched at thee, archer-like, in my anger, — sure arrows, of which thou shalt not escape the smart. — Boy, lead me home, that he may spend his rage on younger men, and learn to keep a tongue more temperate, and to bear within his breast a better mind than now he bears.

[*The Boy leads* TEIRESIAS *out.*]

LE.: The man hath gone, O King, with dread prophecies. And, since the hair on this head, once dark, hath been white, I know that he hath never been a false prophet to our city.

CR.: I, too, know it well, and am troubled in soul. 'Tis dire to yield; but, by resistance, to smite my pride with ruin — this, too, is a dire choice.

LE.: Son of Menoeceus, it behoves thee to take wise counsel.

CR.: What should I do, then? Speak, and I will obey.

LE.: Go thou, and free the maiden from her rocky chamber, and make a tomb for the unburied dead.

CR.: And this is thy counsel? Thou wouldst have me yield?

LE.: Yea, King, and with all speed; for swift harms from the gods cut short the folly of men.

CR.: Ah me, 'tis hard, but I resign my cherished resolve, — I obey. We must not wage a vain war with destiny.

LE.: Go, thou, and do these things; leave them not to others.

CR.: Even as I am I'll go: — on, on, my servants, each and all of you, — take axes in your hands, and hasten to the ground that ye see yonder! Since our judgment hath taken this turn, I will be present to unloose her, as I myself bound her. My heart misgives me, 'tis best to keep the established laws, even to life's end.

[CREON *and his servants hasten out on the spectators' left.*]

strophe 1

CH. [*singing*]: O thou of many names, glory of the Cadmeian bride, offspring of loud-thundering Zeus! thou who watchest over famed Italia, and reignest, where all guests are welcomed, in the sheltered plain of Eleusinian Deo! O Bacchus, dweller in Thebe, mother-city of Bacchants, by the softly-gliding stream of Ismenus, on the soil where the fierce dragon's teeth were sown!

antistrophe 1

Thou hast been seen where torch-flames glare through smoke, above the crests of the twin peaks, where move the Corycian nymphs, thy votaries, hard by Castalia's stream.

Thou comest from the ivy-mantled slopes of Nysa's hills, and from the shore green with many-clustered vines, while thy name is lifted up on strains of more than mortal power, as thou visitest the ways of Thebe:

strophe 2

Thebe, of all cities, thou holdest first in honour, thou, and thy mother whom the lightning smote; and now, when all our people is captive to a violent plague, come thou with healing feet over the Parnassian height, or over the moaning strait!

antistrophe 2

O thou with whom the stars rejoice as they move, the stars whose breath is fire; O master of the voices of the night; son begotten of Zeus; appear, O king, with thine attendant Thyiads, who in night-long frenzy dance before thee, the giver of good gifts, Iacchus!

[*Enter* MESSENGER, *on the spectators' left.*]

ME.: Dwellers by the house of Cadmus and of Amphion, there is no estate of mortal life that I would ever praise or blame as settled. Fortune raises and Fortune humbles the lucky or unlucky from day to day, and no one can prophesy to men concerning those things which are established. For Creon was blest once, as I count bliss; he had saved this land of Cadmus from its foes; he was clothed with sole dominion in the land; he reigned, the glorious sire of princely children. And now all hath been lost. For when a man hath forfeited his pleasures, I count him not as living, — I hold him but a breathing corpse. Heap up riches in thy house, if thou wilt; live in kingly state; yet, if there be no gladness therewith, I would not give the shadow of a vapour for all the rest, compared with joy.

LE.: And what is this new grief that thou hast to tell for our princes?

ME.: Death; and the living are guilty for the dead.

LE.: And who is the slayer? Who the stricken? Speak.

ME.: Haemon hath perished; his blood hath been shed by no stranger.

LE.: By his father's hand, or by his own?

ME.: By his own, in wrath with his sire for the murder.

LE.: O prophet, how true, then, hast thou proved thy word!

ME.: These things stand thus; ye must consider of the rest.

LE.: Lo, I see the hapless Eurydice, Creon's wife, approaching; she comes from the house by chance, haply, — or because she knows the tidings of her son.

[*Enter* EURYDICE *from the palace.*]

EU.: People of Thebes, I heard your words as I was going forth, to salute the goddess Pallas with my prayers. Even as I was loosing the fastenings of the gate, to open it, the message of a household woe smote on mine ear: I sank back, terror-stricken, into the arms of my handmaids, and my senses fled. But say again what the tidings were; I shall hear them as one who is no stranger to sorrow.

ME.: Dear lady, I will witness of what I saw, and will leave no word of the truth untold. Why, indeed, should I soothe thee with words in which I must presently be found false? Truth is ever best. — I attended thy lord as his guide to the furthest part of the plain, where the body of Polyneices, torn by dogs, still lay unpitied. We prayed the goddess of the roads, and Pluto, in mercy to restrain their wrath; we washed the dead with holy washing; and with freshly-plucked boughs we solemnly burned such relics as there were. We raised a high mound of his native earth; and then we turned away to enter the maiden's nuptial chamber with rocky couch, the caverned mansion of the bride of Death. And, from afar off, one of us heard a voice of loud wailing at that bride's unhallowed bower; and came to tell our master Creon.

And as the king drew nearer, doubtful sounds of a bitter cry floated around him; he groaned, and said in accents of anguish, 'Wretched that I am, can my foreboding be true? Am I going on the wofullest way that ever I went? My son's voice greets me. — Go, my servants, — haste ye nearer, and when ye have reached the tomb, pass through the gap, where the stones have been wrenched away, to the cell's very mouth, — and look, and see if 'tis Haemon's voice that I know, or if mine ear is cheated by the gods.'

This search, at our despairing master's word, we went to make; and in the furthest part of the tomb we descried *her* hanging by the neck, slung by a thread-wrought halter of fine linen; while *he* was embracing her with arms thrown around her waist, — bewailing the loss of his bride who is with the dead, and his father's deeds, and his own ill-starred love.

But his father, when he saw him, cried aloud with a dread cry and went in, and called to him with a voice of wailing: — 'Unhappy, what a deed hast thou done! What thought hath come to thee? What manner of mischance hath marred thy reason? Come forth, my child! I pray thee — I implore!' But the boy glared at him with fierce eyes, spat in his face, and, without a word of answer, drew his cross-hilted sword: — as his father rushed forth in flight, he missed his aim; — then, hapless one, wroth with himself, he straightway leaned with all his weight against his sword, and drove it, half its length, into his side; and, while sense lingered, he clasped the maiden to his faint embrace, and, as he gasped, sent forth on her pale cheek the swift stream of the oozing blood.

Corpse enfolding corpse he lies; he hath won his nuptial rites, poor youth, not here, yet in the halls of Death; and he hath witnessed to mankind that, of all curses which cleave to man, ill counsel is the sovereign curse.

[EURYDICE *retires into the house.*]

LE.: What wouldst thou augur from this? The lady hath turned back, and is gone, without a word, good or evil.

ME.: I, too, am startled; yet I nourish the hope that, at these sore tidings of her son, she cannot deign to give her sorrow public vent, but in the privacy of the house will set her handmaids to mourn the household grief. For she is not untaught of discretion, that she should err.

LE.: I know not; but to me, at least, a strained silence seems to portend peril, no less than vain abundance of lament.

ME.: Well, I will enter the house, and learn whether indeed she is not hiding some repressed purpose in the depths of a passionate heart. Yea, thou sayest well: excess of silence, too, may have a perilous meaning.

[*The* MESSENGER *goes into the palace. Enter* CREON, *on the spectators' left, with attendants, carrying the shrouded body of* HAEMON *on a bier. The following lines between* CREON *and the* CHORUS *are chanted responsively.*]

CH.: Lo, yonder the king himself draws near, bearing that which tells too clear a tale, — the work of no stranger's madness, — if we may say it, — but of his own misdeeds.

strophe 1

CR.: Woe for the sins of a darkened soul, stubborn sins, fraught with death! Ah, ye behold us, the sire who hath slain, the son who hath perished! Woe is me, for the wretched blindness of my counsels! Alas, my son, thou hast died in thy youth, by a timeless doom, woe is me! — thy spirit hath fled, — not by thy folly, but by mine own!

strophe 2

CH.: Ah me, how all too late thou seemest to see the right!

CR.: Ah me, I have learned the bitter lesson! But then, methinks, oh then, some god smote me from above with crushing weight, and hurled me into ways of cruelty, woe is me, — overthrowing and trampling on my joy! Woe, woe, for the troublous toils of men!

[*Enter* MESSENGER *from the house.*]

ME.: Sire, thou hast come, methinks, as one whose hands are not empty, but who hath store laid up besides; thou bearest yonder burden with thee; and thou art soon to look upon the woes within thy house.

CR.: And what worse ill is yet to follow upon ills?

ME.: Thy queen hath died, true mother of yon corpse — ah, hapless lady! — by blows newly dealt.

antistrophe 1

CR.: Oh Hades, all-receiving, whom no sacrifice can appease! Hast thou, then, no mercy for me? O thou herald of evil, bitter tidings, what word dost thou utter? Alas, I was already as dead, and thou hast smitten me anew! What sayest thou, my son? What is this new message that thou bringest — woe, woe is me! — of a wife's doom, — of slaughter heaped on slaughter?

CH.: Thou canst behold: 'tis no longer hidden within.

[*The doors of the palace are opened, and the corpse of* EURYDICE *is disclosed.*]

antistrophe 2

CR.: Ah me, — yonder I behold a new, a second woe! What destiny, ah what, can yet await me? I have but now raised my son in my arms, — and there, again, I see a corpse before me! Alas, alas, unhappy mother! Alas, my child!

ME.: There, at the altar, self-stabbed with a keen knife, she suffered her darkening eyes to close, when she had wailed for the noble fate of Megareus who died before, and then for his fate who lies there, — and when, with her last breath, she had invoked evil fortunes upon thee, the slayer of thy sons.

strophe 3

CR.: Woe, woe! I thrill with dread. Is there none to strike me to the heart with two-edged sword? — O miserable that I am, and steeped in miserable anguish!

ME.: Yea, both this son's doom, and that other's, were laid to thy charge by her whose corpse thou seest.

CR.: And what was the manner of the violent deed by which she passed away?

ME.: Her own hand struck her to the heart, when she had learned her son's sorely lamented fate.

strophe 4

CR.: Ah me, this guilt can never be fixed on any other of mortal kind, for my acquittal! I, even I, was thy slayer, wretched that I am — I own the truth. Lead me away, O my servants, lead me hence with all speed, whose life is but as death!

CH.: Thy counsels are good, if there can be good with ills; briefest is best, when trouble is in our path.

antistrophe 3

CR.: Oh, let it come, let it appear, that fairest of fates for me, that brings my last day, — aye, best fate of all! Oh, let it come, that I may never look upon to-morrow's light.

CH.: These things are in the future; present tasks claim our care: the ordering of the future rests where it should rest.

CR.: All my desires, at least, were summed in that prayer.

CH.: Pray thou no more; for mortals have no escape from destined woe.

antistrophe 4

CR.: Lead me away, I pray you; a rash, foolish man; who have slain thee, ah my son, unwittingly, and thee, too, my wife — unhappy that I am! I know not which way I should bend my gaze, or where I should seek support; for all is amiss with that which is in my hands, — and yonder, again, a crushing fate hath leapt upon my head.

[*As* CREON *is being conducted into the palace, the* LEADER OF THE CHORUS *speaks the closing verses.*]

LE.: Wisdom is the supreme part of happiness; and reverence towards the gods must be inviolate. Great words of prideful men are ever punished with great blows, and, in old age, teach the chastened to be wise.

EURIPIDES

(*ca.* 484–406 B.C.)

HIPPOLYTUS

Translated by GILBERT MURRAY

THE GODDESS APHRODITE.

THE GODDESS ARTEMIS.

THESEUS, *King of Athens and Trozên.*

PHAEDRA, *daughter of Minos, King of Crete, wife to Theseus.*

HIPPOLYTUS, *bastard son of Theseus and the Amazon Hippolytê.*

THE NURSE OF PHAEDRA.

AN OLD HUNTSMAN.

A HENCHMAN OF HIPPOLYTUS.

A CHORUS OF HUNTSMEN.

A CHORUS OF TROZENIAN WOMEN, WITH THEIR LEADER.

ATTENDANTS ON THE THREE ROYAL PERSONS.

"The scene is laid in Trozên. The play was first acted when Epameinon was Archon, Olympiad 87, year 4 (B.C. 429). Euripides was first, Iophon second, Ion third."

HIPPOLYTUS

[*The scene represents the front of the royal castle of Trozên, the chief door being in the centre, facing the audience. Two statues are visible, that of* ARTEMIS *on the right, that of* APHRODITE *or* CYPRIS *on the left. The goddess* APHRODITE *is discovered alone.*]

APH.: Great among men, and not unnamed am I,
　　The Cyprian, in God's inmost halls on high.
　　And wheresoe'er from Pontus to the far
　　Red West men dwell, and see the glad day-star,
　　And worship Me, the pious heart I bless,
　　And wreck that life that lives in stubbornness.
　　For that there is, even in a great God's mind,
　　That hungereth for the praise of human kind.
　　　So runs my word; and soon the very deed
　　Shall follow. For this Prince of Theseus' seed,
　　Hippolytus, child of that dead Amazon,
　　And reared by saintly Pittheus in his own
　　Strait ways, hath dared, alone of all Trozên,
　　To hold me least of spirits and most mean,
　　And spurns my spell and seeks no woman's kiss.
　　But great Apollo's sister, Artemis,
　　He holds of all most high, gives love and praise,
　　And through the wild dark woods for ever strays,
　　He and the Maid together, with swift hounds
　　To slay all angry beasts from out these bounds,
　　To more than mortal friendship consecrate!
　　　I grudge it not. No grudge know I, nor hate;
　　Yet, seeing he hath offended, I this day
　　Shall smite Hippolytus. Long since my way
　　Was opened, nor needs now much labour more.
　　　For once from Pittheus' castle to the shore
　　Of Athens came Hippolytus over-seas
　　Seeking the vision of the Mysteries.
　　And Phaedra there, his father's Queen high-born,
　　Saw him, and, as she saw, her heart was torn
　　With great love, by the working of my will.
　　And for his sake, long since, on Pallas' hill,
　　Deep in the rock, that Love no more might roam,
　　She built a shrine, and named it *Love-at-home*:
　　And the rock held it, but its face alway
　　Seeks Trozên o'er the seas. Then came the day
　　When Theseus, for the blood of kinsmen shed,
　　Spake doom of exile on himself, and fled,
　　Phaedra beside him, even to this Trozên.
　　And here that grievous and amazèd Queen,
　　Wounded and wondering, with ne'er a word,

Wastes slowly; and her secret none hath heard
Nor dreamed.
                     But never thus this love shall end!
To Theseus' ear some whisper will I send,
And all be bare!   And that proud Prince, my foe,
His sire shall slay with curses.   Even so
Endeth that boon the great Lord of the Main
To Theseus gave, the Three Prayers not in vain.
    And she, not in dishonour, yet shall die.
I would not rate this woman's pain so high
As not to pay mine haters in full fee
That vengeance that shall make all well with me.

    But soft, here comes he, striding from the chase,
Our prince Hippolytus! — I will go my ways. —
And hunters at his heels: and a loud throng
Glorying Artemis with praise and song!
Little he knows that Hell's gates opened are,
And this his last look on the great Day-star!

[APHRODITE *withdraws, unseen by* HIPPOLYTUS *and a band of* HUNTS-
MEN, *who enter from the left, singing. They pass the Statue of*
APHRODITE *without notice.*]

         HIP. [*singing*]: Follow, O follow me,
                  Singing on your ways
                Her in whose hand are we,
                Her whose own flock we be,
                The Zeus-Child, the Heavenly;
                  To Artemis be praise!
    HUNTSMEN [*singing*]: Hail to thee, Maiden blest,
                Proudest and holiest:
                God's Daughter, great in bliss,
                Leto-born, Artemis!
                Hail to thee, Maiden, far
                Fairest of all that are,
                  Yea, and most high thine home,
                Child of the Father's hall;
                Hear, O most virginal,
                Hear, O most fair of all,
                  In high God's golden dome.

[*The* HUNTSMEN *have gathered about the altar of* ARTEMIS.   HIPPOLY-
TUS *now advances from them, and approaches the Statue with a
wreath in his hand.*]

HIP.: To thee this wreathèd garland, from a green
         And virgin meadow bear I, O my Queen,
         Where never shepherd leads his grazing ewes
         Nor scythe has touched.   Only the river dews
         Gleam, and the spring bee sings, and in the glade
         Hath Solitude her mystic garden made.

No evil hand may cull it: only he
Whose heart hath known the heart of Purity,
Unlearned of man, and true whate'er befall.
Take therefore from pure hands this coronal,
O mistress loved, thy golden hair to twine.
For, sole of living men, this grace is mine,
To dwell with thee, and speak, and hear replies
Of voice divine, though none may see thine eyes.
　　Oh, keep me to the end in this same road!

[*An* OLD HUNTSMAN, *who has stood apart from the rest, here comes up
to* HIPPOLYTUS.]

HUN.: My Prince — for 'Master' name I none but God —
　　Gave I good counsel, wouldst thou welcome it?
HIP.: Right gladly, friend; else were I poor of wit.
HUN.: Knowest thou one law, that through the world has won?
HIP.: What wouldst thou?　And how runs thy law?　Say on.
HUN.: It hates that Pride that speaks not all men fair!
HIP.: And rightly.　Pride breeds hatred everywhere.
HUN.: And good words love, and grace in all men's sight?
HIP.: Aye, and much gain withal, for trouble slight.
HUN.: How deem'st thou of the Gods?　Are they the same?
HIP.: Surely: we are but fashioned on their frame.
HUN.: Why then wilt thou be proud, and worship not . . .
HIP.: Whom?　If the name be speakable, speak out!
HUN.: She stands here at thy gate: the Cyprian Queen!
HIP.: I greet her from afar: my life is clean.
HUN.: Clean?　Nay, proud, proud; a mark for all to scan!
HIP.: Each mind hath its own bent, for God or man.
HUN.: God grant thee happiness . . . and wiser thought!
HIP.: These Spirits that reign in darkness like me not.
HUN.: What the Gods ask, O Son, that man must pay!
HIP. [*turning from him to the others*]:
　　On, huntsmen, to the Castle!　Make your way
　　Straight to the feast room; 'tis a merry thing
　　After the chase, a board of banqueting.
　　And see the steeds be groomed, and in array
　　The chariot dight.　I drive them forth to-day.

[*He pauses, and makes a slight gesture of reverence to the Statue on
the left.　Then to the* OLD HUNTSMAN.]

　　That for thy Cyprian, friend, and nought beside!

[HIPPOLYTUS *follows the* HUNTSMEN, *who stream off by the central door
into the Castle.　The* OLD HUNTSMAN *remains.*]

HUN. [*approaching the Statue and kneeling*]:
　　O Cyprian — for a young man in his pride
　　I will not follow! — here before thee, meek,
　　In that one language that a slave may speak,
　　I pray thee; Oh, if some wild heart in froth
　　Of youth surges against thee, be not wroth

For ever! Nay, be far and hear not then:
Gods should be gentler and more wise than men!
[*He rises and follows the others into the Castle.*]

[*The Orchestra is empty for a moment, then there enter from right
and left several Trozenian women, young and old. Their number
eventually amounts to fifteen.*]

strophe 1

CHORUS [*singing*]: There riseth a rock-born river,
          Of Ocean's tribe, men say;
     The crags of it gleam and quiver,
          And pitchers dip in the spray:
     A woman was there with raiment white
     To bathe and spread in the warm sunlight,
          And she told a tale to me there by the river,
               The tale of the Queen and her evil day:

antistrophe 1

          How, ailing beyond allayment,
               Within she hath bowed her head,
          And with shadow of silken raiment
               The bright brown hair bespread.
     For three long days she hath lain forlorn,
     Her lips untainted of flesh or corn,
          For that secret sorrow beyond allayment
               That steers to the far sad shore of the dead.

strophe 2

Some Women: Is this some Spirit, O child of man?
          Doth Hecat hold thee perchance, or Pan?
          Doth She of the Mountains work her ban,
               Or the dread Corybantes bind thee?
Others: Nay, is it sin that upon thee lies,
          Sin of forgotten sacrifice,
          In thine own Dictynna's sea-wild eyes?
               Who in Limna here can find thee;
          For the Deep's dry floor is her easy way,
          And she moves in the salt wet whirl of the spray.

antistrophe 2

Others: Or doth the Lord of Erechtheus' race,
          Thy Theseus, watch for a fairer face,
          For secret arms in a silent place,
               Far from thy love or chiding?
Others: Or hath there landed, amid the loud
          Hum of Piraeus' sailor-crowd,
          Some Cretan venturer, weary-browed,
               Who bears to the Queen some tiding;

Some far home-grief, that hath bowed her low,
And chained her soul to a bed of woe?

epode

An Older Woman: Nay — know ye not? — this burden hath alway
      lain
On the devious being of woman; yea, burdens twain,
The burden of Wild Will and the burden of Pain.
Through my heart once that wind of terror sped;
      But I, in fear confessèd,
Cried from the dark to Her in heavenly bliss,
The Helper of Pain, the Bow-Maid Artemis:
Whose feet I praise for ever, where they tread
      Far off among the blessèd!

LEADER: But see, the Queen's grey nurse at the door,
      Sad-eyed and sterner, methinks, than of yore,
         With the Queen.   Doth she lead her hither,
      To the wind and sun? — Ah, fain would I know
      What strange betiding hath blanched that brow,
         And made that young life wither.

[*The* NURSE *comes out from the central door, followed by* PHAEDRA, *who is supported by two handmaids. They make ready a couch for* PHAEDRA *to lie upon.*]

NURSE [*chanting*]: O sick and sore are the days of men!
      What wouldst thou?   What shall I change again?
      Here is the Sun for thee; here is the sky;
      And thy weary pillows wind-swept lie,
         By the castle door.
      But the cloud of thy brow is dark, I ween;
      And soon thou wilt back to thy bower within:
      So swift to change is the path of thy feet,
      And near things hateful, and far things sweet;
         So was it before!

      Oh, pain were better than tending pain!
      For that were single, and this is twain,
      With grief of heart and labour of limb.
      Yet all man's life is but ailing and dim,
         And rest upon earth comes never.
      But if any far-off state there be,
      Dearer than life to mortality;
      The hand of the Dark hath hold thereof,
      And mist is under and mist above.
      And so we are sick for life, and cling
      On earth to this nameless and shining thing.
      For other life is a fountain sealed,
      And the deeps below us are unrevealed,
         And we drift on legends for ever!

[PHAEDRA *during this has been laid on her couch; she speaks to the handmaids. The following lines are chanted responsively between* PHAEDRA *and the* NURSE.]

PH.: Yes; lift me: not my head so low.
 There, hold my arms. — Fair arms they seem! —
 My poor limbs scarce obey me now!
 Take off that hood that weighs my brow,
  And let my long hair stream.

NU.: Nay, toss not, Child, so feveredly.
 The sickness best will win relief
 By quiet rest and constancy.
  All men have grief.

PH. [*not noticing her*]: Oh for a deep and dewy spring,
 With runlets cold to draw and drink!
 And a great meadow blossoming,
 Long-grassed, and poplars in a ring,
  To rest me by the brink!

NU.: Nay, Child! Shall strangers hear this tone
 So wild, and thoughts so fever-flown?

PH.: Oh, take me to the Mountain! Oh,
 Past the great pines and through the wood,
 Up where the lean hounds softly go,
  A-whine for wild things' blood,
 And madly flies the dappled roe.
 O God, to shout and speed them there,
 An arrow by my chestnut hair
 Drawn tight, and one keen glimmering spear —
  Ah! if I could!

NU.: What wouldst thou with them — fancies all! —
 Thy hunting and thy fountain brink?
 What wouldst thou? By the city wall
 Canst hear our own brook plash and fall
  Downhill, if thou wouldst drink.

PH.: O Mistress of the Sea-lorn Mere
 Where horse-hoofs beat the sand and sing,
 O Artemis, that I were there
 To tame Enetian steeds and steer
  Swift chariots in the ring!

NU.: Nay, mountainward but now thy hands
 Yearned out, with craving for the chase;
 And now toward the unseaswept sands
  Thou roamest, where the coursers pace!
 O wild young steed, what prophet knows
 The power that holds thy curb, and throws
  Thy swift heart from its race?

[*At these words* PHAEDRA *gradually recovers herself and pays attention.*]

PH.: What have I said? Woe's me! And where
 Gone straying from my wholesome mind?
 What? Did I fall in some god's snare?

— Nurse, veil my head again, and blind
Mine eyes. — There is a tear behind
That lash. — Oh, I am sick with shame!
  Aye, but it hath a sting,
To come to reason; yet the name
Of madness is an awful thing. —
Could I but die in one swift flame
Unthinking, unknowing!

NU.: I veil thy face, Child. — Would that so
Mine own were veiled for evermore,
  So sore I love thee! . . . Though the lore
Of long life mocks me, and I know
How love should be a lightsome thing
  Not rooted in the deep o' the heart;
  With gentle ties, to twine apart
If need so call, or closer cling. —
Why do I love thee so? O fool,
  O fool, the heart that bleeds for twain,
  And builds, men tell us, walls of pain,
To walk by love's unswerving rule,
The same for ever, stern and true!
  For 'Thorough' is no word of peace:
  'Tis 'Naught-too-much' makes trouble cease,
And many a wise man bows thereto.

[*The* LEADER OF THE CHORUS *here approaches the* NURSE.]

LE.: Nurse of our Queen, thou watcher old and true,
  We see her great affliction, but no clue
  Have we to learn the sickness. Wouldst thou tell
  The name and sort thereof, 'twould like us well.

NU.: Small leechcraft have I, and she tells no man.

LE.: Thou know'st no cause? Nor when the unrest began?

NU.: It all comes to the same. She will not speak.

LE.: How she is changed and wasted! And how weak!

NU.: 'Tis the third day she hath fasted utterly.

LE.: What, is she mad? Or doth she seek to die?

NU.: I know not. But to death it sure must lead.

LE.: 'Tis strange that Theseus takes hereof no heed.

NU.: She hides her wound, and vows it is not so.

LE.: Can he not look into her face and know?

NU.: Nay, he is on a journey these last days.

LE.: Canst thou not force her, then? Or think of ways
  To trap the secret of the sick heart's pain?

NU.: Have I not tried all ways, and all in vain?
  Yet will I cease not now, and thou shalt tell
  If in her grief I serve my mistress well!

[*She goes across to where* PHAEDRA *lies; and presently, while speaking, kneels by her.*]

Dear daughter mine, all that before was said
Let both of us forget; and thou instead
Be kindlier, and unlock that prisoned brow.
And I, who followed then the wrong road, now
Will leave it and be wiser. If thou fear
Some secret sickness, there be women here
To give thee comfort.   [PHAEDRA *shakes her head.*]
                    No; not secret? Then
Is it a sickness meet for aid of men?
Speak, that a leech may tend thee.
                            Silent still?
Nay, Child, what profits silence? If 'tis ill
This that I counsel, make me see the wrong:
If well, then yield to me.
                    Nay, Child, I long
For one kind word, one look!
          [PHAEDRA *lies motionless. The* NURSE *rises.*]
                    Oh, woe is me!
Women, we labour here all fruitlessly,
All as far off as ever from her heart!
She ever scorned me, and now hears no part
Of all my prayers!   [*Turning to* PHAEDRA *again*]
                    Nay, hear thou shalt, and be,
If so thou will, more wild than the wild sea;
But know, thou art thy little ones' betrayer!
If thou die now, shall child of thine be heir
To Theseus' castle? Nay, not thine, I ween,
But hers! That barbèd Amazonian Queen
Hath left a child to bend thy children low,
A bastard royal-hearted—sayst not so?—
Hippolytus . . .

PH.:   Ah!
          [*She starts up, sitting, and throws the veil off.*]
NU.:   That stings thee?
PH.:   Nurse, most sore
Thou hast hurt me! In God's name, speak that name no more.
NU.: Thou seest? Thy mind is clear; but with thy mind
    Thou wilt not save thy children, nor be kind
    To thine own life.
PH.:   My children? Nay, most dear
I love them. — Far, far other grief is here.
NU. [*after a pause, wondering*]: Thy hand is clean, O Child, from
    stain of blood?
PH.: My hand is clean; but is my heart, O God?
NU.: Some enemy's spell hath made thy spirit dim?
PH.: He hates me not that slays me, nor I him.
NU.: Theseus, the King, hath wronged thee in man's wise?
PH.: Ah, could but I stand guiltless in his eyes!
NU.: O speak! What is this death-fraught mystery?

PH.: Nay, leave me to my wrong. I wrong not thee.

NU: [*suddenly throwing herself in supplication at* PHAEDRA'S *feet*]:
    Not wrong me, whom thou wouldst all desolate leave!

PH. [*rising and trying to move away*]: What wouldst thou? Force
    me? Clinging to my sleeve?

NU.: Yea, to thy knees; and weep; and let not go!

PH.: Woe to thee, Woman, if thou learn it, woe!

NU.: I know no bitterer woe than losing thee.

PH.: I am lost! Yet the deed shall honour me.

NU.: Why hide what honours thee? 'Tis all I claim!

PH.: Why, so I build up honour out of shame!

NU.: Then speak, and higher still thy fame shall stand.

PH.: Go, in God's name! — Nay, leave me; loose my hand!

NU.: Never, until thou grant me what I pray.

PH. [*yielding, after a pause*]: So be it. I dare not tear that hand away.

NU. [*rising and releasing* PHAEDRA]: Tell all thou wilt, Daughter. I
    speak no more.

PH. [*after a long pause*]: Mother, poor Mother, that didst love so sore!

NU.: What mean'st thou, Child? The Wild Bull of the Tide?

PH.: And thou, sad sister, Dionysus' bride! *

NU.: Child! wouldst thou shame the house where thou wast born?

PH.: And I the third, sinking most all-forlorn!

NU. [*to herself*]: I am all lost and feared. What will she say?

PH.: From there my grief comes, not from yesterday.

NU.: I come no nearer to thy parable.

PH.: Oh, would that thou couldst tell what I must tell!

NU.: I am no seer in things I wot not of.

PH. [*again hesitating*]: What is it that they mean, who say men . . .
    love?

NU.: A thing most sweet, my Child, yet dolorous.

PH.: Only the half, belike, hath fallen on us!

NU.: On thee? Love? — Oh, what sayst thou? What man's son?

PH.: What man's? There was a Queen, an Amazon . . .

NU.: Hippolytus, sayst thou?

PH. [*again wrapping her face in the veil*]: Nay, 'twas thou, not I!
[PHAEDRA *sinks back on the couch and covers her face again. The*
NURSE *starts violently from her and walks up and down.*]

NU.: O God! What wilt thou say, Child? Wouldst thou try
    To kill me? — Oh, 'tis more than I can bear;
    Women, I will no more of it, this glare
    Of hated day, this shining of the sky.
    I will fling down my body, and let it lie
    Till life be gone!
                    Women, God rest with you,
    My works are over! For the pure and true
    Are forced to evil, against their own heart's vow,
    And love it!

* See Minotaur and Ariadne in the Glossary.

[*She suddenly sees the Statue of* CYPRIS, *and stands with her eyes riveted upon it.*]

Ah, Cyprian! No god art thou,
But more than god, and greater, that hath thrust
Me and my queen and all our house to dust!
[*She throws herself on the ground close to the statue.*]

CHORUS [*singing*]:

Some Women: O Women, have ye heard? Nay, dare ye hear
    The desolate cry of the young Queen's misery?
A Woman: My Queen, I love thee dear,
    Yet liefer were I dead than framed like thee.
Others: Woe, woe to me for this thy bitter bane,
    Surely the food man feeds upon is pain!
Others: How wilt thou bear thee through this livelong day,
    Lost, and thine evil naked to the light?
    Strange things are close upon us — who shall say
      How strange? — save one thing that is plain to sight,
    The stroke of the Cyprian and the fall thereof
    On thee, thou child of the Isle of fearful Love! *

[PHAEDRA *during this has risen from the couch and comes forward collectedly. As she speaks the* NURSE *gradually rouses herself, and listens more calmly.*]

PH.: O Women, dwellers in this portal-seat
    Of Pelops' land, gazing towards my Crete,
    How oft, in other days than these, have I
    Through night's long hours thought of man's misery,
    And how this life is wrecked! And, to mine eyes,
    Not in man's knowledge, not in wisdom, lies
    The lack that makes for sorrow. Nay, we scan
    And know the right — for wit hath many a man —
    But will not to the last end strive and serve.
    For some grow too soon weary, and some swerve
    To other paths, setting before the Right
    The diverse far-off image of Delight;
    And many are delights beneath the sun!
    Long hours of converse; and to sit alone
    Musing — a deadly happiness! — and Shame:
    Though two things there be hidden in one name,
    And Shame can be slow poison if it will!
      This is the truth I saw then, and see still;
    Nor is there any magic that can stain
    That white truth for me, or make me blind again.
    Come, I will show thee how my spirit hath moved.
    When the first stab came, and I knew I loved,
    I cast about how best to face mine ill.
    And the first thought that came, was to be still

* Crete.

And hide my sickness. — For no trust there is
In man's tongue, that so well admonishes
And counsels and betrays, and waxes fat
With griefs of its own gathering! — After that
I would my madness bravely bear, and try
To conquer by mine own heart's purity.
    My third mind, when these two availed me naught
To quell love, was to die —

                          [*Motion of protest among the Women.*]
                          the best, best thought —
— Gainsay me not — of all that man can say!
I would not have mine honour hidden away;
Why should I have my shame before men's eyes
Kept living?   And I knew, in deadly wise,
Shame was the deed and shame the suffering;
And I a woman, too, to face the thing,
Despised of all!
                    Oh, utterly accurst
Be she of women, whoso dared the first
To cast her honour out to a strange man!
'Twas in some great house, surely, that began
This plague upon us; then the baser kind,
When the good led towards evil, followed blind
And joyous!   Cursed be they whose lips are clean
And wise and seemly, but their hearts within
Rank with bad daring!   How can they, O Thou
That walkest on the waves, great Cyprian, how
Smile in their husbands' faces, and not fall,
Not cower before the Darkness that knows all,
Aye, dread the dead still chambers, lest one day
The stones find voice, and all be finished!
                                      Nay,
Friends, 'tis for this I die; lest I stand there
Having shamed my husband and the babes I bare.
In ancient Athens they shall some day dwell,
My babes, free men, free-spoken, honourable,
And when one asks their mother, proud of me!
For, oh, it cows a man, though bold he be,
To know a mother's or a father's sin.
    'Tis written, one way is there, one, to win
This life's race, could man keep it from his birth,
A true clean spirit.   And through all this earth
To every false man, that hour comes apace
When Time holds up a mirror to his face,
And girl-like, marvelling, there he stares to see
How foul his heart!   Be it not so with me!

LE.: Ah God, how sweet is virtue, and how wise,
       And honour its due meed in all men's eyes!

NU. [*who has now risen and recovered herself*]:
　　Mistress, a sharp swift terror struck me low
　　A moment since, hearing of this thy woe.
　　But now — I was a coward!　And men say
　　Our second thought the wiser is alway.
　　　This is no monstrous thing; no grief too dire
　　To meet with quiet thinking.　In her ire
　　A most strong goddess hath swept down on thee.
　　Thou lovest.　Is that so strange?　Many there be
　　Beside thee! . . . And because thou lovest, wilt fall
　　And die!　And must all lovers die, then?　All
　　That are or shall be?　A blithe law for them!
　　Nay, when in might she swoops, no strength can stem
　　Cypris; and if man yields him, she is sweet;
　　But is he proud and stubborn?　From his feet
　　She lifts him, and — how think you? — flings to scorn!
　　　She ranges with the stars of eve and morn,
　　She wanders in the heaving of the sea,
　　And all life lives from her. — Aye, this is she
　　That sows Love's seed and brings Love's fruit to birth;
　　And great Love's brethren are all we on earth!
　　　Nay, they who con grey books of ancient days
　　Or dwell among the Muses, tell — and praise —
　　How Zeus himself once yearned for Semelê;
　　How maiden Eôs in her radiancy
　　Swept Kephalos to heaven away, away,
　　For sore love's sake.　And there they dwell, men say,
　　And fear not, fret not; for a thing too stern
　　Hath met and crushed them!　And must thou, then, turn
　　And struggle?　Sprang there from thy father's blood
　　Thy little soul all lonely?　Or the god
　　That rules thee, is he other than our gods?
　　　Nay, yield thee to men's ways, and kiss their rods!
　　How many, deem'st thou, of men good and wise,
　　Know their own home's blot, and avert their eyes?
　　How many fathers, when a son has strayed
　　And toiled beneath the Cyprian, bring him aid,
　　Not chiding?　And man's wisdom e'er hath been
　　To keep what is not good to see, unseen!
　　　A straight and perfect life is not for man;
　　Nay, in a shut house, let him, if he can,
　　'Mid sheltered rooms, make all lines true.　But here,
　　Out in the wide sea fallen, and full of fear,
　　Hopest thou so easily to swim to land?
　　　Canst thou but set thine ill days on one hand
　　And more good days on the other, verily,
　　O child of woman, life is well with thee!
　　Nay, dear my daughter, cease thine evil mind,
　　Cease thy fierce pride!　For pride it is, and blind,

To seek to outpass gods! — Love on and dare:
A god hath willed it! And, since pain is there,
Make the pain sleep! Songs are there to bring calm,
And magic words. And I shall find the balm,
Be sure, to heal thee. Else in sore dismay
Were men, could not we women find our way!

LE.: Help is there, Queen, in all this woman says,
To ease thy suffering. But 'tis thee I praise;
Albeit that praise is harder to thine ear
Than all her chiding was, and bitterer!

PH.: Oh, this it is hath flung to dogs and birds
Men's lives and homes and cities — fair false words!
Oh, why speak things to please our ears? We crave
Not that. 'Tis honour, honour, we must save!

NU.: Why prate so proud? 'Tis no words, brave nor base,
Thou cravest; 'tis a man's arms! [PHAEDRA *moves indignantly.*]
                          Up and face
The truth of what thou art, and name it straight!
Were not thy life thrown open here for Fate
To beat on; hadst thou been a woman pure
Or wise or strong; never had I for lure
Of joy nor heartache led thee on to this!
But when a whole life one great battle is,
To win or lose — no man can blame me then.

PH.: Shame on thee! Lock those lips, and ne'er again
Let word nor thought so foul have harbour there!

NU.: Foul, if thou wilt: but better than the fair
For thee and me. And better, too, the deed
Behind them, if it save thee in thy need,
Than that word Honour thou wilt die to win!

PH.: Nay, in God's name, — such wisdom and such sin
Are all about thy lips! — urge me no more.
For all the soul within me is wrought o'er
By Love; and if thou speak and speak, I may
Be spent, and drift where now I shrink away.

NU.: Well, if thou wilt! — 'Twere best never to err,
But, having erred, to take a counsellor
Is second. — Mark me now. I have within
Love-philtres, to make peace where storm hath been,
That, with no shame, no scathe of mind, shall save
Thy life from anguish; wilt but thou be brave!
                          [*To herself, reflecting*]
Ah, but from him, the well-beloved, some sign
We need, or word, or raiment's hem, to twine
Amid the charm, and one spell knit from twain.

PH.: Is it a potion or a salve? Be plain.

NU.: Who knows? Seek to be helped, Child, not to know.

PH.: Why art thou ever subtle? I dread thee, so.

NU.: Thou wouldst dread everything! — What dost thou dread?

PH.: Lest to his ear some word be whisperèd.
NU.: Let be, Child!   I will make all well with thee!
         — Only do thou, O Cyprian of the Sea,
         Be with me!   And mine own heart, come what may,
         Shall know what ear to seek, what word to say!
[*The* NURSE, *having spoken these last words in prayer apart to the
Statue of* CYPRIS, *turns back and goes into the house.* PHAEDRA *sits
pensive again on her couch till towards the end of the following
Song, when she rises and bends close to the door.*]

strophe 1

CH. [*singing*]: Erôs, Erôs, who blindest, tear by tear,
         Men's eyes with hunger; thou swift Foe, that pliest
Deep in our hearts joy like an edgèd spear;
Come not to me with Evil haunting near,
Wrath on the wind, nor jarring of the clear
         Wing's music as thou fliest!
There is no shaft that burneth, not in fire,
Not in wild stars, far off and flinging fear,
As in thine hands the shaft of All Desire,
         Erôs, Child of the Highest!

antistrophe 1

In vain, in vain, by old Alpheüs' shore
         The blood of many bulls doth stain the river,
And all Greece bows on Phœbus' Pythian floor;
Yet bring we to the Master of Man no store,
The Keybearer, who standeth at the door
         Close-barred, where hideth ever
The heart of the shrine.   Yea, though he sack man's life
         Like a sacked city, and moveth evermore
Girt with calamity and strange ways of strife,
         Him have we worshipped never!

strophe 2

There roamed a Steed in Oechalia's wild,
         A Maid without yoke, without Master,
And Love she knew not, that far King's child:
But he came, he came, with a song in the night,
With fire, with blood; and she strove in flight,
A Torrent Spirit, a Maenad white,
         Faster and vainly faster,
Sealed unto Heracles by the Cyprian's Might.
         Alas, thou Bride of Disaster!

antistrophe 2

O Mouth of Dirce, O god-built wall,
         That Dirce's wells run under,
Ye know the Cyprian's fleet footfall!

Ye saw the heaven's around her flare,
When she lulled to her sleep that Mother fair
Of Twy-born Bacchus, and decked her there
    The Bride of the bladed Thunder.
For her breath is on all that hath life, and she floats in the air,
    Bee-like, death-like, a wonder.

[*During the last lines* PHAEDRA *has approached the door and is listening.*]
PH.: Silence, ye Women! Something is amiss.
LE.: How? In the house? — Phaedra, what fear is this?
PH.: Let me but listen! There are voices. Hark!
LE.: I hold my peace: yet is thy presage dark.
PH.:   Oh, misery!
    O God, that such a thing should fall on me!
LE. [*chanting*]: What sound, what word,
    O Woman, Friend, makes that sharp terror start
    Out at thy lips? What ominous cry half-heard
        Hath leapt upon thine heart?
PH.: I am undone! — Bend to the door and hark,
    Hark what a tone sounds there, and sinks away!
LE. [*chanting*]: Thou art beside the bars. 'Tis thine to mark
    The castle's floating message. Say, Oh, say
        What thing hath come to thee?
PH.: Why, what thing should it be?
    The son of that proud Amazon speaks again
    In bitter wrath: speaks to my handmaiden!
LE. [*chanting*]: I hear a noise of voices, nothing clear.
    For thee the din hath words, as through barred locks
        Floating, at thy heart it knocks.
PH.: "Pander of Sin" it says. — Now canst thou hear? —
    And there: "Betrayer of a master's bed."
LE. [*chanting*]: Ah me, betrayed! Betrayed!
    Sweet Princess, thou art ill bested,
    Thy secret brought to light, and ruin near,
        By her thou heldest dear,
    By her that should have loved thee and obeyed!
PH.: Aye, I am slain. She thought to help my fall
    With love instead of honour, and wrecked all.
LE.: Where wilt thou turn thee, where?
    And what help seek, O wounded to despair?
PH.: I know not, save one thing, to die right soon.
    For such as me God keeps no other boon.
[*The door in the centre bursts open, and* HIPPOLYTUS *comes forth, closely followed by the* NURSE. PHAEDRA *cowers aside.*]
HIP.: O Mother Earth, O Sun that makest clean,
    What poison have I heard, what speechless sin!
NU.: Hush, O my Prince, lest others mark, and guess . . .
HIP.: I have heard horrors! Shall I hold my peace?

NU.: Yea, by this fair right arm, Son, by thy pledge . . .
HIP.: Down with that hand!   Touch not my garment's edge!
NU.: Oh, by thy knees, be silent or I die!
HIP.: Why, when thy speech was all so guiltless?   Why?
NU.: It is not meet, fair Son, for every ear!
HIP.: Good words can bravely forth, and have no fear.
NU.: Thine oath, thine oath!   I took thine oath before!
HIP.: 'Twas but my tongue, 'twas not my soul that swore.*
NU.: O Son, what wilt thou?   Wilt thou slay thy kin?
HIP.: I own no kindred with the spawn of sin!

> [*He flings her from him.*]

NU.: Nay, spare me!   Man was born to err; oh, spare!
HIP.: O God, why hast Thou made this gleaming snare,
Woman, to dog us on the happy earth?
Was it Thy will to make Man, why his birth
Through Love and Woman?   Could we not have rolled
Our store of prayer and offering, royal gold,
Silver and weight of bronze before Thy feet,
And bought of God new child-souls, as were meet
For each man's sacrifice, and dwelt in homes
Free, where nor Love nor Woman goes and comes?
   How, is that daughter not a bane confessed,
Whom her own sire sends forth — (He knows her best!) —
And, will some man but take her, pays a dower!
And he, poor fool, takes home the poison-flower;
Laughs to hang jewels on the deadly thing
He joys in; labours for her robe-wearing,
Till wealth and peace are dead.   He smarts the less
In whose high seat is set a Nothingness,
A woman naught availing.   Worst of all
The wise deep-thoughted!   Never in my hall
May she sit throned who thinks and waits and sighs!
For Cypris breeds most evil in the wise,
And least in her whose heart has naught within;
For puny wit can work but puny sin.
   Why do we let their handmaids pass the gate?
Wild beasts were best, voiceless and fanged, to wait
About their rooms, that they might speak with none,
Nor ever hear one answering human tone!
But now dark women in still chambers lay
Plans that creep out into the light of day
On handmaids' lips —   [*Turning to the* NURSE]
               As thine accursèd head
Braved the high honour of my Father's bed,
And came to traffic. . . Our white torrent's spray
Shall drench mine ears to wash those words away!
And couldst thou dream that *I* . . . ?   I feel impure
Still at the very hearing!   Know for sure,

* A famous line constantly parodied and misrepresented by the comic poets.

Woman, naught but mine honour saves ye both.
Hadst thou not trapped me with that guileful oath,
No power had held me secret till the King
Knew all! But now, while he is journeying,
I too will go my ways and make no sound.
And when he comes again, I shall be found
Beside him, silent, watching with what grace
Thou and thy mistress greet him face to face!
Then shall I have the taste of it, and know
What woman's guile is. — Woe upon you, woe!
How can I too much hate you, while the ill
Ye work upon the world grows deadlier still?
Too much? Make woman pure, and wild Love tame,
Or let me cry for ever on their shame!

[*He goes off in fury to the left.* PHAEDRA *still cowering in her place
begins to sob.*]

PH. [*singing*]: Sad, sad and evil-starred
            Is Woman's state.
       What shelter now is left or guard?
    What spell to loose the iron knot of fate?
          And this thing, O my God,
     O thou sweet Sunlight, is but my desert!
    I cannot fly before the avenging rod
          Falls, cannot hide my hurt.
   What help, O ye who love me, can come near,
          What god or man appear,
    To aid a thing so evil and so lost?
   Lost, for this anguish presses, soon or late,
    To that swift river that no life hath crossed.
    No woman ever lived so desolate!

LE.: Ah me, the time for deeds is gone; the boast
     Proved vain that spake thine handmaid; and all lost!

[*At these words* PHAEDRA *suddenly remembers the* NURSE, *who is
cowering silently where* HIPPOLYTUS *had thrown her from him.
She turns upon her.*]

PH.: O wicked, wicked, wicked! Murderess heart
     To them that loved thee! Hast thou played thy part?
     Am I enough trod down?
                          May Zeus, my sire,
     Blast and uproot thee! Stab thee dead with fire!
     Said I not — Knew I not thine heart? — to name
     To no one soul this that is now my shame?
     And thou couldst not be silent! So no more
     I die in honour. But enough; a store
     Of new words must be spoke and new things thought.
     This man's whole being to one blade is wrought
     Of rage against me. Even now he speeds
     To abase me to the King with thy misdeeds;
     Tell Pittheus; fill the land with talk of sin!

Cursèd be thou, and whoso else leaps in
To bring bad aid to friends that want it not.

[*The* NURSE *has raised herself, and faces* PHAEDRA, *downcast but calm.*]

NU.: Mistress, thou blamest me; and all thy lot
So bitter sore is, and the sting so wild,
I bear with all. Yet, if I would, my Child,
I have mine answer, couldst thou hearken aught.
  I nursed thee, and I love thee; and I sought
Only some balm to heal thy deep despair,
And found — not what I sought for. Else I were
Wise, and thy friend, and good, had all sped right.
So fares it with us all in the world's sight.

PH.: First stab me to the heart, then humour me
With words! 'Tis fair; 'tis all as it should be!

NU.: We talk too long, Child. I did ill; but, oh,
There is a way to save thee, even so!

PH.: A way? No more ways! One way hast thou trod
Already, foul and false and loathed of god!
Begone out of my sight; and ponder how
Thine own life stands! I need no helpers now.

[*She turns from the* NURSE, *who creeps abashed away into the Castle.*]

Only do ye, high Daughters of Trozên,
Let all ye hear be as it had not been;
Know naught, and speak of naught! 'Tis my last prayer.

LE.: By God's pure daughter, Artemis, I swear,
No word will I of these thy griefs reveal!

PH.: 'Tis well. But now, yea, even while I reel
And falter, one poor hope, as hope now is,
I clutch at in this coil of miseries;
To save some honour for my children's sake;
Yea, for myself some fragment, though things break
In ruin around me. Nay, I will not shame
The old proud Cretan castle whence I came,
I will not cower before King Theseus' eyes,
Abased, for want of one life's sacrifice!

LE.: What wilt thou? Some dire deed beyond recall?

PH. [*musing*]: Die; but how die?

LE.:   Let not such wild words fall!

PH.: Give thou not such light counsel! Let me be
To sate the Cyprian that is murdering me!
To-day shall be her day; and, all strife past,
Her bitter Love shall quell me at the last.
  Yet, dying, shall I die another's bane!
He shall not stand so proud where I have lain
Bent in the dust! Oh, he shall stoop to share
The life I live in, and learn mercy there!

[*She goes off wildly into the Castle.*]

CH. [*singing*]: Could I take me to some cavern for mine hiding,
   In the hill-tops where the Sun scarce hath trod;
Or a cloud make the home of mine abiding,
   As a bird among the bird-droves of God!
     Could I wing me to my rest amid the roar
     Of the deep Adriatic on the shore,
Where the waters of Eridanus are clear,
   And Phaëthon's sad sisters by his grave
Weep into the river, and each tear
     Gleams, a drop of amber, in the wave.

To the strand of the Daughters of the Sunset,
   The Apple-tree, the singing and the gold;
Where the mariner must stay him from his onset,
   And the red wave is tranquil as of old;
     Yea, beyond that Pillar of the End
     That Atlas guardeth, would I wend;
Where a voice of living waters never ceaseth
   In God's quiet garden by the sea,
And Earth, the ancient life-giver, increaseth
     Joy among the meadows, like a tree.

   O shallop of Crete, whose milk-white wing
   Through the swell and the storm-beating,
   Bore us thy Prince's daughter,
Was it well she came from a joyous home
To a far King's bridal across the foam?
   What joy hath her bridal brought her?
Sure some spell upon either hand
Flew with thee from the Cretan strand,
Seeking Athena's tower divine;
And there, where Munychus fronts the brine,
Crept by the shore-flung cables' line,
   The curse from the Cretan water!

And, for that dark spell that about her clings,
Sick desires of forbidden things
   The soul of her rend and sever;
The bitter tide of calamity
Hath risen above her lips; and she,
   Where bends she her last endeavour?
She will hie her alone to her bridal room,
And a rope swing slow in the rafters' gloom;
And a fair white neck shall creep to the noose,

A-shudder with dread, yet firm to choose
The one strait way for fame, and lose
The Love and the pain for ever.

[*The Voice of the* NURSE *is heard from within, crying, at first in-
articulately, then clearly.*]

VOICE: Help ho! The Queen! Help, whoso hearkeneth!
    Help! Theseus' spouse caught in a noose of death!

A WOMAN: God, is it so soon finished? That bright head
    Swinging beneath the rafters! Phaedra dead!

VOICE: O haste! This knot about her throat is made
    So fast! Will no one bring me a swift blade?

A WOMAN: Say, friends, what think ye? Should we haste within,
    And from her own hand's knotting loose the Queen?

ANOTHER: Nay, are there not men there? 'Tis an ill road
    In life, to finger at another's load.

VOICE: Let it lie straight! Alas! the cold white thing
    That guards his empty castle for the King!

A WOMAN: Ah! "Let it lie straight!" Heard ye what she said?
    No need for helpers now; the Queen is dead!

[*The* WOMEN, *intent upon the voices from the Castle, have not noticed the approach of* THESEUS. *He enters from the left; his dress
and the garland on his head show that he has returned from some
oracle or special abode of a God. He stands for a moment perplexed.*]

TH.: Ho, Women, and what means this loud acclaim
    Within the house? The vassals' outcry came
    To smite mine ears far off. It were more meet
    To fling out wide the Castle gates, and greet
    With joy a herald from God's Presence!

[*The confusion and horror of the* WOMEN'S *faces gradually affects
him. A dirge-cry comes from the Castle.*]
                                        How?
Not Pittheus? Hath Time struck that hoary brow?
Old is he, old, I know. But sore it were,
Returning thus, to find his empty chair!

        [*The* WOMEN *hesitate; then the Leader comes forward.*]

LE.: O Theseus, not on any old man's head
    This stroke falls. Young and tender is the dead.

TH.: Ye Gods! One of my children torn from me?

LE.: Thy motherless children live, most grievously.

TH.: How sayst thou? What? My wife? . . .
                                    Say how she died.

LE.: In a high death-knot that her own hands tied.

TH.: A fit of the old cold anguish — Tell me all —
    That held her? Or did some fresh thing befall?

LE.: We know no more. But now arrived we be,
    Theseus, to mourn for thy calamity.

[THESEUS *stays for a moment silent, and puts his hand to his brow
He notices the wreath.*]

TH.: What?   And all garlanded I come to her
      With flowers, most evil-starred God's-messenger!
         Ho, varlets, loose the portal bars; undo
      The bolts; and let me see the bitter view
      Of her whose death hath brought me to mine own.

[*The great central door of the Castle is thrown open wide, and the
body of* PHAEDRA *is seen lying on a bier, surrounded by a group of*
HANDMAIDS, *wailing.*]

HANDMAIDS [*chanting*]: Ah me, what thou hast suffered and hast
                        done:
      A deed to wrap this roof in flame!
   Why was thine hand so strong, thine heart so bold?
   Wherefore, O dead in anger, dead in shame,
   The long, long wrestling ere thy breath was cold?
            O ill-starred Wife,
   What brought this blackness over all thy life?

         [*A throng of* MEN *and* WOMEN *has gradually collected.*]

TH. [*chanting*]: Ah me, this is the last
   — Hear, O my countrymen! — and bitterest
   Of Theseus' labours!   Fortune all unblest,
   How hath thine heavy heel across me passed!
   Is it the stain of sins done long ago,
            Some fell God still remembereth,
   That must so dim and fret my life with death?
   I cannot win to shore; and the waves flow
   Above mine eyes, to be surmounted not.
            Ah wife, sweet wife, what name
            Can fit thine heavy lot?
   Gone like a wild bird, like a blowing flame,
   In one swift gust, where all things are forgot!
            Alas! this misery!
   Sure 'tis some stroke of God's great anger rolled
            From age to age on me,
   For some dire sin wrought by dim kings of old.

LE.: Sire, this great grief hath come to many an one,
      A true wife lost.   Thou art not all alone.

TH. [*chanting*]: Deep, deep beneath the Earth,
                  Dark may my dwelling be,
   And Night my heart's one comrade, in the dearth,
   O Love, of thy most sweet society.
   This is my death, O Phaedra, more than thine.

                  [*He turns suddenly on the Attendants.*]
   Speak who speak can?   What was it?   What malign
   Swift stroke, O heart discounselled, leapt on thee?
   What, will ye speak?   Or are they dumb as death,

This herd of thralls, my high house harboureth?
Ah me, why shouldst thou die?
A wide and royal grief I here behold,
Not to be borne in peace, not to be told.
       As a lost man am I,
My children motherless and my house undone,
      Since thou art vanished quite,
Purest of hearts that e'er the wandering Sun
Touched, or the star-eyed splendour of the Night.
             [*He throws himself beside the body.*]

CH. [*chanting*]: Unhappy one, O most unhappy one;
     With what strange evil is this Castle vexed!
Mine eyes are molten with the tears that run
     For thee and thine; but what thing follows next?
       I tremble when I think thereon!

[*They have noticed that there is a tablet with writing fastened to
the dead woman's wrist.* THESEUS *also sees it.*]

TH.: Ha, what is this that hangs from her dear hand?
A tablet! It would make me understand
Some dying wish, some charge about her bed
And children. 'Twas the last prayer, ere her head
Was bowed for ever.   [*Taking the tablet*]
          Fear not, my lost bride,
No woman born shall lie at Theseus' side,
Nor rule in Theseus' house!
               A seal! Ah, see
How her gold signet here looks up at me,
Trustfully. Let me tear this thread away,
And read what tale the tablet seeks to say.

[*He proceeds to undo and read the tablet. The* CHORUS *breaks into
horrified groups.*]

SOME WOMEN [*chanting*]: Woe, woe! God brings to birth
    A new grief here, close on the other's tread!
       My life hath lost its worth.
May all go now with what is finishèd!
The castle of my King is overthrown,
A house no more, a house vanished and gone!

OTHER WOMEN [*chanting*]: O God, if it may be in any way,
    Let not this house be wrecked! Help us who pray!
    I know not what is here: some unseen thing
    That shows the Bird of Evil on the wing.

[THESEUS *has read the tablet and breaks out in uncontrollable emotion.*]

TH.: Oh, horror piled on horror! — Here is writ . . .
Nay, who could bear it, who could speak of it?

LE.: What, O my King? If I may hear it, speak!

TH.: Doth not the tablet cry aloud, yea, shriek,
Things not to be forgotten? — Oh, to fly
And hide mine head! No more a man am I.

Ah, God, what ghastly music echoes here!

LE.: How wild thy voice! Some terrible thing is near.

TH.: No; my lips' gates will hold it back no more;
  This deadly word,
That struggles on the brink and will not o'er,
  Yet will not stay unheard.
  [*He raises his hand, to make proclamation to all present.*]
  Ho, hearken all this land!
    [*The people gather expectantly about him.*]
Hippolytus by violence hath laid hand
On this my wife, forgetting God's great eye.

[*Murmurs of amazement and horror;* THESEUS, *apparently calm,
raises both arms to heaven.*]

Therefore, O Thou my Father, hear my cry,
Poseidon! Thou didst grant me for mine own
Three prayers; for one of these, slay now my son,
Hippolytus; let him not outlive this day,
If true thy promise was! Lo, thus I pray.

LE.: Oh, call that wild prayer back! O King, take heed!
I know that thou wilt live to rue this deed.

TH.: It may not be. — And more, I cast him out
From all my realms. He shall be held about
By two great dooms. Or by Poseidon's breath
He shall fall swiftly to the house of Death;
Or wandering, outcast, o'er strange land and sea
Shall live and drain the cup of misery.

LE.: Ah, see! here comes he at the point of need.
Shake off that evil mood, O King: have heed
For all thine house and folk. — Great Theseus, hear!

[THESEUS *stands silent in fierce gloom.* HIPPOLYTUS *comes in from
the right.*]

HIP.: Father, I heard thy cry, and sped in fear
To help thee. — But I see not yet the cause
That racked thee so. — Say, Father, what it was.

[*The murmurs in the crowd, the silent gloom of his Father, and the
horror of the* CHORUS-WOMEN *gradually work on* HIPPOLYTUS *and be-
wilder him. He catches sight of the bier.*]

Ah, what is that! Nay, Father, not the Queen
Dead! [*Murmurs in the crowd.*]
  'Tis most strange. 'Tis passing strange, I ween.
'Twas here I left her. Scarce an hour hath run
Since here she stood and looked on this same sun.
What is it with her? Wherefore did she die?
    [THESEUS *remains silent. The murmurs increase.*]
Father, to thee I speak. Oh, tell me, why,
Why art thou silent? What doth silence know
Of skill to stem the bitter flood of woe?
And human hearts in sorrow crave the more
For knowledge, though the knowledge grieve them sore.

It is not love, to veil thy sorrows in
From one most near to thee, and more than kin.
TH. [*to himself*]: Fond race of men, so striving and so blind,
Ten thousand arts and wisdoms can ye find,
Desiring all and all imagining:
But ne'er have reached nor understood one thing,
To make a true heart there where no heart is!
HIP.: That were indeed beyond man's mysteries,
To make a false heart true against his will.
But why this subtle talk? It likes me ill,
Father; thy speech runs wild beneath this blow.
TH. [*as before*]: O would that God had given us here below
Some test of love, some sifting of the soul,
To tell the false and true! Or through the whole
Of men two voices ran, one true and right,
The other as chance willed it; that we might
Convict the liar by the true man's tone,
And not live duped forever, every one!
HIP.: What? Hath some friend proved false?
                                        Or in thine ear
Whispered some slander? Stand I tainted here,
Though utterly innocent?   [*Murmurs from the crowd.*]
                        Yea, dazed am I;
'Tis thy words daze me, falling all awry,
Away from reason, by fell fancies vexed!
TH.: O heart of man, what height wilt venture next?
What end comes to thy daring and thy crime?
For if with each man's life 'twill higher climb,
And every age break out in blood and lies
Beyond its fathers, must not God devise
Some new world far from ours, to hold therein
Such brood of all unfaithfulness and sin?
    Look, all, upon this man, my son, his life
Sprung forth from mine! He hath defiled my wife;
And standeth here convicted by the dead,
A most black villain!
[HIPPOLYTUS *falls back with a cry and covers his face with his robe.*]
                        Nay, hide not thine head!
Pollution, is it? Thee it will not stain.
Look up, and face thy Father's eyes again!
    Thou friend of Gods, of all mankind elect;
Thou the pure heart, by thoughts of ill unflecked!
I care not for thy boasts. I am not mad,
To deem that Gods love best the base and bad.
    Now is thy day! Now vaunt thee; thou so pure,
No flesh of life may pass thy lips! Now lure
Fools after thee; call Orpheus King and Lord; *
Make ecstasies and wonders! Thumb thine hoard

* Theseus is taunting Hippolytus for being associated with the Orphic mysteries.

Of ancient scrolls and ghostly mysteries —
Now thou art caught and known!

                           Shun men like these,
I charge ye all!   With solemn words they chase
Their prey, and in their hearts plot foul disgrace.
   My wife is dead. — "Ha, so that saves thee now?"
That is what grips thee worst, thou caitiff, thou!
What oaths, what subtle words, shall stronger be
Than this dead hand, to clear the guilt from thee?
   "She hated thee," thou sayest; "the bastard born
Is ever sore and bitter as a thorn
To the true brood." — A sorry bargainer
In the ills and goods of life thou makest her,
If all her best-beloved she cast away
To wreak blind hate on thee! — What, wilt thou say,
"Through every woman's nature one blind strand
Of passion winds, that men scarce understand?" —
Are we so different?   Know I not the fire
And perilous flood of a young man's desire,
Desperate as any woman, and as blind,
When Cypris stings?   Save that the man behind
Has all men's strength to aid him.   Nay, 'twas thou . . .
   But what avail to wrangle with thee now,
When the dead speaks for all to understand,
A perfect witness!

                  Hie thee from this land
To exile with all speed.   Come never more
To god-built Athens, not to the utmost shore
Of any realm where Theseus' arm is strong!
What?   Shall I bow my head beneath this wrong,
And cower to thee?   Not Isthmian Sinis so
Will bear men witness that I laid him low,
Nor Sciron's rocks, that share the salt sea's prey,
Grant that my hand hath weight vile things to slay!

LE.: Alas! whom shall I call of mortal men
   Happy?   The highest are cast down again.

HIP.: Father, the hot strained fury of thy heart
   Is terrible.   Yet, albeit so swift thou art
   Of speech, if all this matter were laid bare,
   Speech were not then so swift; nay, nor so fair. . .
                 [*Murmurs again in the crowd.*]
   I have no skill before a crowd to tell
   My thoughts.   'Twere best with few, that know me well. —
   Nay, that is natural; tongues that sound but rude
   In wise men's ears, speak to the multitude
   With music.

           None the less, since there is come
   This stroke upon me, I must not be dumb,
   But speak perforce. . . And there will I begin

Where thou beganst, as though to strip my sin
Naked, and I not speak a word!

                     Dost see
This sunlight and this earth? I swear to thee
There dwelleth not in these one man — deny
All that thou wilt! — more pure of sin than I.
   Two things I know on earth: God's worship first;
Next to win friends about me, few, that thirst
To hold them clean of all unrighteousness.
Our rule doth curse the tempters, and no less
Who yieldeth to the tempters. — How, thou say'st,
"Dupes that I jest at?" Nay; I make a jest
Of no man. I am honest to the end,
Near or far off, with him I call my friend.
And most in that one thing, where now thy mesh
Would grip me, stainless quite! No woman's flesh
Hath e'er this body touched. Of all such deed
Naught wot I, save what things a man may read
In pictures or hear spoke; nor am I fain,
Being virgin-souled, to read or hear again.
   My life of innocence moves thee not; so be it.
Show then what hath seduced me; let me see it.
Was that poor flesh so passing fair, beyond
All women's loveliness?

                  Was I some fond
False plotter, that I schemed to win through her
Thy castle's heirdom? Fond indeed I were!
Nay, a stark madman! "But a crown," thou sayst,
"Usurped, is sweet." Nay, rather most unblest
To all wise-hearted; sweet to fools and them
Whose eyes are blinded by the diadem.
In contests of all valour fain would I
Lead Hellas; but in rank and majesty
Not lead, but be at ease, with good men near
To love me, free to work and not to fear.
That brings more joy than any crown or throne.

[*He sees from the demeanour of* THESEUS *and of the crowd that his
words are not winning them, but rather making them bitterer than
before. It comes to his lips to speak the whole truth.*]

   I have said my say; save one thing . . . one alone.
     O had I here some witness in my need,
As I was witness! Could she hear me plead,
Face me and face the sunlight; well I know,
Our deeds would search us out for thee, and show
Who lies!
           But now, I swear — so hear me both,
The Earth beneath and Zeus who Guards the Oath —
I never touched this woman that was thine!

No words could win me to it, nor incline
My heart to dream it. May God strike me down,
Nameless and fameless, without home or town,
An outcast and a wanderer of the world;
May my dead bones rest never, but be hurled
From sea to land, from land to angry sea,
If evil is my heart and false to thee!

[*He waits a moment; but sees that his Father is unmoved. The
truth again comes to his lips.*]

If 'twas some fear that made her cast away
Her life . . . I know not. More I must not say.
Right hath she done when in her was no right;
And Right I follow to mine own despite!

LE.: It is enough! God's name is witness large,
And thy great oath, to assoil thee of this charge.

TH.: Is not the man a juggler and a mage,
Cool wits and one right oath — what more? — to assuage
Sin and the wrath of injured fatherhood!

HIP.: Am I so cool? Nay, Father, 'tis thy mood
That makes me marvel! By my faith, wert thou
The son, and I the sire; and deemed I now
In very truth thou hadst my wife assailed,
I had not exiled thee, nor stood and railed,
But lifted once mine arm, and struck thee dead!

TH.: Thou gentle judge! Thou shalt not so be sped
To simple death, nor by thine own decree.
Swift death is bliss to men in misery.
Far off, friendless forever, thou shalt drain
Amid strange cities the last dregs of pain!

HIP.: Wilt verily cast me now beyond thy pale,
Not wait for Time, the lifter of the veil?

TH.: Aye, if I could, past Pontus, and the red
Atlantic marge! So do I hate thine head.

HIP.: Wilt weigh nor oath nor faith nor prophet's word
To prove me? Drive me from thy sight unheard?

TH.: This tablet here, that needs no prophet's lot
To speak from, tells me all. I ponder not
Thy fowls that fly above us! Let them fly.

HIP.: O ye great Gods, wherefore unlock not I
My lips, ere yet ye have slain me utterly,
Ye whom I love most? No. It may not be!
The one heart that I need I ne'er should gain
To trust me. I should break mine oath in vain.

TH.: Death! but he chokes me with his saintly tone! —
Up, get thee from this land! Begone! Begone!

HIP.: Where shall I turn me? Think. To what friend's door
Betake me, banished on a charge so sore?

TH.: Whoso delights to welcome to his hall

Vile ravishers . . . to guard his hearth withal!

HIP.: Thou seekst my heart, my tears?   Aye, let it be
Thus!   I am vile to all men, and to thee!

TH.: There was a time for tears and thought; the time
Ere thou didst up and gird thee to thy crime.

HIP.: Ye stones, will ye not speak?   Ye castle walls!
Bear witness if I be so vile, so false!

TH.: Aye, fly to voiceless witnesses!   Yet here
A dumb deed speaks against thee, and speaks clear!

HIP.: Alas!
Would I could stand and watch this thing, and see
My face, and weep for very pity of me!

TH.: Full of thyself, as ever!   Not a thought
For them that gave thee birth; nay, they are naught!

HIP.: O my wronged Mother!   O my birth of shame!
May none I love e'er bear a bastard's name!

TH. [*in a sudden blaze of rage*]: Up, thralls, and drag him from my
presence!   What?
'Tis but a foreign felon!   Heard ye not?
[*The thralls still hesitate in spite of his fury.*]

HIP.: They touch me at their peril!   Thine own hand
Lift, if thou canst, to drive me from the land.

TH.: That will I straight, unless my will be done!
[HIPPOLYTUS *comes close to him and kneels.*]
Nay!   Not for thee my pity!   Get thee gone!

[HIPPOLYTUS *rises, makes a sign of submission, and slowly moves
away.* THESEUS, *as soon as he sees him going, turns rapidly and
enters the Castle. The door is closed again.* HIPPOLYTUS *has stopped
for a moment before the Statue of* ARTEMIS, *and, as* THESEUS *departs,
breaks out in prayer.*]

HIP.: So; it is done!   O dark and miserable!
I see it all, but see not how to tell
The tale. — O thou belovèd, Leto's Maid,
Chase-comrade, fellow-rester in the glade,
Lo, I am driven with a caitiff's brand
Forth from great Athens!   Fare ye well, O land
And city of old Erechtheus!   Thou, Trozên,
What riches of glad youth mine eyes have seen
In thy broad plain!   Farewell!   This is the end;
The last word, the last look!
Come, every friend
And fellow of my youth that still may stay,
Give me god-speed and cheer me on my way.
Ne'er shall ye see a man more pure of spot
Than me, though mine own Father loves me not!

[HIPPOLYTUS *goes away to the right, followed by many* HUNTSMEN
*and other young men. The rest of the crowd has by this time dis-
persed, except the Women of the* CHORUS *and some Men of the*
CHORUS OF HUNTSMEN.]

CHORUS [*singing*]:

strophe 1

Men: Surely the thought of the Gods hath balm in it alway, to win me
　　　Far from my griefs; and a thought, deep in the dark of my mind,
　　Clings to a great Understanding.　Yet all the spirit within me
　　Faints, when I watch men's deeds matched with the guerdon they find.
　　　　　For Good comes in Evil's traces,
　　　　　And the Evil the Good replaces;
　　　　　And Life, 'mid the changing faces,
　　　　　　Wandereth weak and blind.

antistrophe 1

Women: What wilt thou grant me, O God?　Lo, this is the prayer of my travail —
　　　Some well-being; and chance not very bitter thereby;
　　A Spirit uncrippled by pain; and a mind not deep to unravel
　　Truth unseen, nor yet dark with the brand of a lie.
　　　　　With a veering mood to borrow
　　　　　Its light from every morrow,
　　　　　Fair friends and no deep sorrow,
　　　　　　Well could man live and die!

strophe 2

Men: Yet my spirit is no more clean,
　　　And the weft of my hope is torn,
　　For the deed of wrong that mine eyes have seen,
　　　The lie and the rage and the scorn;
　　A Star among men, yea, a Star
　　　That in Hellas was bright,
　　By a Father's wrath driven far
　　　To the wilds and the night.
　　Oh, alas for the sands of the shore!
　　　Alas for the brakes of the hill,
　　Where the wolves shall fear thee no more,
　　　And thy cry to Dictynna is still!

antistrophe 2

Women: No more in the yoke of thy car
　　　Shall the colts of Enetia fleet;
　　Nor Limna's echoes quiver afar
　　　To the clatter of galloping feet.
　　The sleepless music of old,
　　　That leaped in the lyre,
　　Ceaseth now, and is cold,
　　　In the halls of thy sire.

The bowers are discrowned and unladen
  Where Artemis lay on the lea;
And the love-dream of many a maiden
  Lost, in the losing of thee.

epode

A Maiden: And I, even I,
  For thy fall, O Friend,
    Amid tears and tears,
  Endure to the end
    Of the empty years,
Of a life run dry.
  In vain didst thou bear him,
    Thou Mother forlorn!
  Ye Gods that did snare him,
  Lo, I cast in your faces
    My hate and my scorn!
  Ye love-linkèd Graces,
    (Alas for the day!)
      Was he naught, then, to you,
  That ye cast him away,
    The stainless and true,
From the old happy places?

LE.: Look yonder! Surely from the Prince 'tis one
  That cometh, full of haste and woe-begone.
[A HENCHMAN enters in haste.]
HE.: Ye women, whither shall I go to seek
  King Theseus? Is he in this dwelling? Speak!
LE.: Lo, where he cometh through the Castle gate!
[THESEUS comes out from the Castle.]
HE.: O King, I bear thee tidings of dire weight
  To thee, aye, and to every man, I ween,
  From Athens to the marches of Trozên.
TH.: What? Some new stroke hath touched, unknown to me,
  The sister cities of my sovranty?
HE.: Hippolytus is . . . Nay, not dead; but stark
  Outstretched, a hairsbreadth this side of the dark.
TH. [*as though unmoved*]: How slain? Was there some other man,
    whose wife
  He had like mine defiled, that sought his life?
HE.: His own wild team destroyed him, and the dire
  Curse of thy lips.
           The boon of thy great Sire
  Is granted thee, O King, and thy son slain.
TH.: Ye Gods! And thou, Poseidon! Not in vain
  I called thee Father; thou hast heard my prayer!
    How did he die? Speak on. How closed the snare
  Of Heaven to slay the shamer of my blood?

HE.: 'Twas by the bank of beating sea we stood,
       We thralls, and decked the steeds, and combed each mane,
       Weeping; for word had come that ne'er again
       The foot of our Hippolytus should roam
       This land, but waste in exile by thy doom.
         So stood we till he came, and in his tone
       No music now save sorrow's, like our own,
       And in his train a concourse without end
       Of many a chase-fellow and many a friend.
       At last he brushed his sobs away, and spake:
       "Why this fond loitering? I would not break
       My Father's law. — Ho, there! My coursers four
       And chariot, quick! This land is mine no more."
         Thereat, be sure, each man of us made speed.
       Swifter than speech we brought them up, each steed
       Well dight and shining, at our Prince's side.
       He grasped the reins upon the rail: one stride
       And there he stood, a perfect charioteer,
       Each foot in its own station set. Then clear
       His voice rose, and his arms to heaven were spread:
       "O Zeus, if I be false, strike thou me dead!
       But, dead or living, let my Father see
       One day, how falsely he hath hated me!"
         Even as he spake, he lifted up the goad
       And smote; and the steeds sprang. And down the road
       We henchmen followed, hard beside the rein,
       Each hand, to speed him, toward the Argive plain
       And Epidaurus.
                           So we made our way
       Up toward the desert region, where the bay
       Curls to a promontory near the verge
       Of our Trozên, facing the southward surge
       Of Saron's gulf. Just there an angry sound,
       Slow-swelling, like God's thunder underground,
       Broke on us, and we trembled. And the steeds
       Pricked their ears skyward, and threw back their heads.
       And wonder came on all men, and affright,
       Whence rose that awful voice. And swift our sight
       Turned seaward, down the salt and roaring sand.
         And there, above the horizon, seemed to stand
       A wave unearthly, crested in the sky;
       Till Sciron's Cape first vanished from mine eye,
       Then sank the Isthmus hidden, then the rock
       Of Epidaurus. Then it broke, one shock
       And roar of gasping sea and spray flung far,
       And shoreward swept, where stood the Prince's car.
         Three lines of wave together raced, and, full
       In the white crest of them, a wild Sea-Bull
       Flung to the shore, a fell and marvellous Thing.

The whole land held his voice, and answering
Roared in each echo. And all we, gazing there,
Gazed seeing not; 'twas more than eyes could bear.
　　Then straight upon the team wild terror fell.
Howbeit, the Prince, cool-eyed and knowing well
Each changing mood a horse has, gripped the reins
Hard in both hands; then as an oarsman strains
Up from his bench, so strained he on the thong,
Back in the chariot swinging. But the young
Wild steeds bit hard the curb, and fled afar;
Nor rein nor guiding hand nor morticed car
Stayed them at all. For when he veered them round,
And aimed their flying feet to grassy ground,
In front uprose that Thing, and turned again
The four great coursers, terror-mad. But when
Their blind rage drove them toward the rocky places,
Silent, and ever nearer to the traces,
It followed, rockward, till one wheel-edge grazed.
　　The chariot tript and flew, and all was mazed
In turmoil. Up went wheel-box with a din,
Where the rock jagged, and nave and axle-pin.
And there — the long reins round him — there was he
Dragging, entangled irretrievably.
A dear head battering at the chariot side,
Sharp rocks, and ripped flesh, and a voice that cried:
"Stay, stay, O ye who fattened at my stalls,
Dash me not into nothing! — O thou false
Curse of my Father! — Help! Help, whoso can,
An innocent, innocent and stainless man!"
　　Many there were that laboured then, I wot,
To bear him succour, but could reach him not,
Till — who knows how? — at last the tangled rein
Unclasped him, and he fell, some little vein
Of life still pulsing in him.
　　　　　　　　　　　All beside,
The steeds, the hornèd Horror of the Tide,
Had vanished — who knows where? — in that wild land.
　　O King, I am a bondsman of thine hand;
Yet love nor fear nor duty me shall win
To say thine innocent son hath died in sin.
All women born may hang themselves, for me,
And swing their dying words from every tree
On Ida! For I know that he was true!

LE.: O God, so cometh new disaster, new
　　Despair! And no escape from what must be!
TH.: Hate of the man thus stricken lifted me
　　At first to joy at hearing of thy tale;
　　But now, some shame before the Gods, some pale
　　Pity for mine own blood, hath o'er me come.

I laugh not, neither weep, at this fell doom.
HE.: How then? Behoves it bear him here, or how
Best do thy pleasure? — Speak, Lord. Yet if thou
Wilt mark at all my word, thou wilt not be
Fierce-hearted to thy child in misery.
TH.: Aye, bring him hither. Let me see the face
Of him who durst deny my deep disgrace
And his own sin; yea, speak with him, and prove
His clear guilt by God's judgments from above.

[*The* HENCHMAN *departs to fetch* HIPPOLYTUS; THESEUS *sits waiting in stern gloom, while the* CHORUS *sing. At the close of their song a Divine Figure is seen approaching on a cloud in the air and the voice of* ARTEMIS *speaks.*]

CH. [*singing*]: Thou comest to bend the pride
                Of the hearts of God and man,
            Cypris; and by thy side,
                In earth-encircling span,
            He of the changing plumes,
            The Wing that the world illumes,
        As over the leagues of land flies he,
        Over the salt and sounding sea.

            For mad is the heart of Love,
                And gold the gleam of his wing;
            And all to the spell thereof
                Bend, when he makes his spring;
            All life that is wild and young
                In mountain and wave and stream,
            All that of earth is sprung,
                Or breathes in the red sunbeam;
        Yea, and Mankind. O'er all a royal throne,
        Cyprian, Cyprian, is thine alone!

A VOICE FROM THE CLOUD:
            O thou that rulest in Aegeus' Hall,
            I charge thee, hearken!
                                Yea, it is I,
            Artemis, Virgin of God most High.
            Thou bitter King, art thou glad withal
                For thy murdered son?
            For thine ear bent low to a lying Queen,
            For thine heart so swift amid things unseen?
            Lo, all may see what end thou hast won!
            Go, sink thine head in the waste abyss;
            Or aloft to another world than this,
                Birdwise with wings,
                Fly far to thine hiding,
            Far over this blood that clots and clings;
            For in righteous men and in holy things

No rest is thine nor abiding!

[*The cloud has become stationary in the air.*]

Hear, Theseus, all the story of thy grief!
Verily, I bring but anguish, not relief;
Yet, 'twas for this I came, to show how high
And clean was thy son's heart, that he may die
Honoured of men; aye, and to tell no less
The frenzy, or in some sort the nobleness,
Of thy dead wife. One Spirit there is, whom we
That know the joy of white virginity,
Most hate in heaven. She sent her fire to run
In Phaedra's veins, so that she loved thy son.
Yet strove she long with love, and in the stress
Fell not, till by her Nurse's craftiness
Betrayed, who stole, with oaths of secrecy,
To entreat thy son. And he, most righteously,
Nor did her will, nor, when thy railing scorn
Beat on him, broke the oath that he had sworn,
For God's sake. And thy Phaedra, panic-eyed,
Wrote a false writ, and slew thy son, and died,
Lying; but thou wast nimble to believe!

[THESEUS, *at first bewildered, then dumbfounded, now utters a
deep groan.*]

It stings thee, Theseus? — Nay, hear on, and grieve
Yet sorer. Wottest thou three prayers were thine
Of sure fulfilment, from thy Sire divine?
Hast thou no foes about thee, then, that one —
Thou vile King! — must be turned against thy son?
The deed was thine. Thy Sea-born Sire but heard
The call of prayer, and bowed him to his word.
But thou in his eyes and in mine art found
Evil, who wouldst not think, nor probe, nor sound
The deeps of prophet's lore, nor day by day
Leave Time to search; but, swifter than man may,
Let loose the curse to slay thine innocent son!

TH.: O Goddess, let me die!

ARTEMIS: Nay; thou hast done
A heavy wrong; yet even beyond this ill
Abides for thee forgiveness. 'Twas the will
Of Cypris that these evil things should be,
Sating her wrath. And this immutably
Hath Zeus ordained in heaven: no God may thwart
A God's fixed will; we grieve but stand apart.
Else, but for fear of the Great Father's blame,
Never had I to such extreme of shame
Bowed me, be sure, as here to stand and see
Slain him I loved best of mortality!
Thy fault, O King, its ignorance sunders wide
From very wickedness; and she who died

By death the more disarmed thee, making dumb
The voice of question. And the storm has come
Most bitterly of all on thee! Yet I
Have mine own sorrow, too. When good men die,
There is no joy in heaven, albeit our ire
On child and house of the evil falls like fire.

[*A throng is seen approaching;* HIPPOLYTUS *enters, supported by his attendants.*]

CH. [*chanting*]: Lo, it is he! The bright young head
    Yet upright there!
 Ah, the torn flesh and the blood-stained hair;
  Alas for the kindred's trouble!
It falls as fire from a God's hand sped,
  Two deaths, and mourning double.

HIP. [*chanting*]: Ah, pain, pain, pain!
 O unrighteous curse! O unrighteous sire!
No hope. — My head is stabbed with fire,
And a leaping spasm about my brain.
 Stay, let me rest. I can no more.
O fell, fell steeds that my own hand fed,
Have ye maimed me and slain, that loved me of yore?
— Soft there, ye thralls! No trembling hands
As ye lift me, now! — Who is that that stands
At the right? — Now firm, and with measured tread,
Lift one accursèd and stricken sore
  By a father's sinning.

Thou, Zeus, dost see me? Yea, it is I;
The proud and pure, the server of God,
The white and shining in sanctity!
To a visible death, to an open sod,
  I walk my ways;
And all the labour of saintly days
  Lost, lost, without meaning!

  Ah God, it crawls
   This agony, over me!
  Let be, ye thralls!
   Come, Death, and cover me;
  Come, O thou Healer blest!

  But a little more,
   And my soul is clear,
  And the anguish o'er
   Oh, a spear, a spear!
  To rend my soul to its rest!

Oh, strange, false Curse! Was there some bloodstained head,
Some father of my line, unpunishèd
  Whose guilt lived in his kin.

And passed, and slept, till after this long day
It lights. . . Oh, why on me? Me, far away
   And innocent of sin?

     O words that cannot save!
When will this breathing end in that last deep
Pain that is painlessness? 'Tis sleep I crave.
   When wilt thou bring me sleep,
Thou dark and midnight magic of the grave!
AR.: Sore-stricken man, bethink thee in this stress,
   Thou dost but die for thine own nobleness.
HIP.: Ah!
   O breath of heavenly fragrance! Though my pain
Burns, I can feel thee and find rest again.
   The Goddess Artemis is with me here.
AR.: With thee and loving thee, poor sufferer!
HIP.: Dost see me, Mistress, nearing my last sleep?
AR.: Aye, and would weep for thee, if Gods could weep.
HIP.: Who now shall hunt with thee or hold thy quiver?
AR.: He dies; but my love cleaves to him for ever.
HIP.: Who guide thy chariot, keep thy shrine-flowers fresh?
AR.: The accursèd Cyprian caught him in her mesh!
HIP.: The Cyprian? Now I see it! — Aye, 'twas she.
AR.: She missed her worship, loathed thy chastity!
HIP.: Three lives by her one hand! 'Tis all clear now.
AR.: Yea, three; thy father and his Queen and thou.
HIP.: My father; yea, he too is pitiable!
AR.: A plotting Goddess tripped him, and he fell.
HIP.: Father, where art thou? . . . Oh, thou sufferest sore!
TH.: Even unto death, child. There is joy no more.
HIP.: I pity thee in this coil; aye, more than me.
TH.: Would I could lie there dead instead of thee!
HIP.: Oh, bitter bounty of Poseidon's love!
TH.: Would God my lips had never breathed thereof!
HIP. [gently]: Nay, thine own rage had slain me then, some wise!
TH.: A lying spirit had made blind mine eyes!
HIP.: Ah me!
   Would that a mortal's curse could reach to God!
AR.: Let be! For not, though deep beneath the sod
   Thou liest, not unrequited nor unsung
   Shall this fell stroke, from Cypris' rancour sprung,
   Quell thee, mine own, the saintly and the true!
    My hand shall win its vengeance, through and through
   Piercing with flawless shaft what heart soe'er
   Of all men living is most dear to Her.*
   Yea, and to thee, for this sore travail's sake,
   Honours most high in Trozên will I make;
   For yokeless maids before their bridal night

* This refers to Adonis.

Shall shear for thee their tresses; and a rite
Of honouring tears be thine in ceaseless store;
And virgins' thoughts in music evermore
Turn toward thee, and praise thee in the Song
Of Phaedra's far-famed love and thy great wrong.
  O seed of ancient Aegeus, bend thee now
And clasp thy son. Aye, hold and fear not thou!
Not knowingly hast thou slain him; and man's way,
When Gods send error, needs must fall astray.
  And thou, Hippolytus, shrink not from the King,
Thy father. Thou wast born to bear this thing.
  Farewell! I may not watch man's fleeting breath,
Nor stain mine eyes with the effluence of death.
And sure that Terror now is very near.
                    [*The cloud slowly rises and floats away.*]

HIP.: Farewell, farewell, most Blessèd! Lift thee clear
  Of soiling men! Thou wilt not grieve in heaven
  For my long love! . . . Father, thou art forgiven.
  It was Her will. I am not wroth with thee. . .
  I have obeyed Her all my days! . . .
                                        Ah me,
  The dark is drawing down upon mine eyes;
  It hath me! . . . Father! . . . Hold me! Help me rise!
TH. [*supporting him in his arms*]: Ah, woe! How dost thou tor-
      ture me, my son!
HIP.: I see the Great Gates opening. I am gone.
TH.: Gone? And my hand red-reeking from this thing!
HIP.: Nay, nay; thou art assoiled of manslaying.
TH.: Thou leav'st me clear of murder? Sayst thou so?
HIP.: Yea, by the Virgin of the Stainless Bow!
TH.: Dear Son! Ah, now I see thy nobleness!
HIP.: Pray that a true-born child may fill my place.
TH.: Ah me, thy righteous and godfearing heart!
HIP.: Farewell;
  A long farewell, dear Father, ere we part!
          [THESEUS *bends down and embraces him passionately.*]
TH.: Not yet! — O hope and bear while thou hast breath!
HIP.: Lo, I have borne my burden. This is death. . .
  Quick, Father; lay the mantle on my face.
          [THESEUS *covers his face with a mantle and rises.*]
TH.: Ye bounds of Pallas and of Pelops' race,
  What greatness have ye lost!
                              Woe, woe is me!
  Thou Cyprian, long shall I remember thee!

CH. [*chanting*]: On all this folk, both low and high,
  A grief hath fallen beyond men's fears.
  There cometh a throbbing of many tears,
    A sound as of waters falling.

For when great men die,
A mighty name and a bitter cry
Rise up from a nation calling.

[*They move into the Castle, carrying the body of* HIPPOLYTUS.]

THE BACCHAE

Translated by GILBERT MURRAY

CHARACTERS IN THE PLAY

DIONYSUS, THE GOD; *son of Zeus and of the Theban princess Semele*
CADMUS, *formerly King of Thebes, father of Semele*
PENTHEUS, *King of Thebes, grandson of Cadmus*
AGAVE, *daughter of Cadmus, mother of Pentheus*
TEIRESIAS, *an aged Theban prophet*
A SOLDIER OF PENTHEUS' GUARD
TWO MESSENGERS
A CHORUS OF INSPIRED DAMSELS, *following Dionysus from the East*

THE BACCHAE

[SCENE: — *The background represents the front of the Castle of* PEN-
THEUS, *King of Thebes. At one side is visible the sacred Tomb of
Semele, a little enclosure overgrown with wild vines, with a cleft
in the rocky floor of it from which there issues at times steam or
smoke. The God* DIONYSUS *is discovered alone.*]

DI.: Behold, God's Son is come unto this land
　　Of Thebes, even I, Dionysus, whom the brand
　　Of heaven's hot splendour lit to life, when she
　　Who bore me, Cadmus' daughter Semele,
　　Died here. So, changed in shape from God to man,
　　I walk again by Dirce's streams and scan
　　Ismenus' shore. There by the castle side
　　I see her place, the Tomb of the Lightning's Bride,
　　The wreck of smouldering chambers, and the great
　　Faint wreaths of fire undying — as the hate
　　Dies not, that Hera held for Semele.
　　　　Aye, Cadmus hath done well; in purity
　　He keeps this place apart, inviolate,
　　His daughter's sanctuary; and I have set
　　My green and clustered vines to robe it round.
　　　　Far now behind me lies the golden ground
　　Of Lydian and of Phrygian; far away
　　The wide hot plains where Persian sunbeams play,
　　The Bactrian war-holds, and the storm-oppressed
　　Clime of the Mede, and Araby the Blest,
　　And Asia all, that by the salt sea lies
　　In proud embattled cities, motley-wise
　　Of Hellene and Barbarian interwrought;
　　And now I come to Hellas — having taught
　　All the world else my dances and my rite
　　Of mysteries, to show me in men's sight
　　Manifest God.
　　　　　　　　And first of Hellene lands
　　I cry this Thebes to waken; set her hands
　　To clasp my wand, mine ivied javelin,
　　And round her shoulders hang my wild fawn-skin.
　　For they have scorned me whom it least beseemed,
　　Semele's sisters; mocked my birth, nor deemed
　　That Dionysus sprang from Dian* seed.
　　My mother sinned, said they; and in her need,
　　With Cadmus plotting, cloaked her human shame
　　With the dread name of Zeus; for that the flame
　　From heaven consumed her, seeing she lied to God.
　　　　Thus must they vaunt; and therefore hath my rod

---

* *i.e.*, belonging to Zeus.

343

On them first fallen, and stung them forth wild-eyed
From empty chambers; the bare mountain side
Is made their home, and all their hearts are flame.
Yea, I have bound upon the necks of them
The harness of my rites. And with them all
The seed of womankind from hut and hall
Of Thebes, hath this my magic goaded out.
And there, with the old King's daughters, in a rout
Confused, they make their dwelling-place between
The roofless rocks and shadowy pine trees green.
Thus shall this Thebes, how sore soe'er it smart,
Learn and forget not, till she crave her part
In mine adoring; thus must I speak clear
To save my mother's fame, and crown me here
As true God, born by Semele to Zeus.

Now Cadmus yieldeth up his throne and use
Of royal honour to his daughter's son
Pentheus; who on my body hath begun
A war with God. He thrusteth me away
From due drink-offering, and, when men pray,
My name entreats not. Therefore on his own
Head and his people's shall my power be shown.
Then to another land, when all things here
Are well, must I fare onward, making clear
My godhead's might. But should this Theban town
Essay with wrath and battle to drag down
My maids, lo, in their path myself shall be,
And maniac armies battled after me!
For this I veil my godhead with the wan
Form of the things that die, and walk as Man.

O Brood of Tmolus o'er the wide world flown,
O Lydian band, my chosen and mine own,
Damsels uplifted o'er the orient deep
To wander where I wander, and to sleep
Where I sleep; up, and wake the old sweet sound,
The clang that I and mystic Rhea found,
The Timbrel of the Mountain! Gather all
Thebes to your song round Pentheus' royal hall.
I seek my new-made worshippers, to guide
Their dances up Cithaeron's pine-clad side.

[*As he departs, there comes stealing in from the left a band of fifteen
Eastern Women, the light of the sunrise streaming upon their long
white robes and ivy-bound hair. They wear fawn-skins over the
robes, and carry some of them timbrels, some pipes and other instruments. Many bear the thyrsus, or sacred Wand, made of reed
ringed with ivy. They enter stealthily till they see that the place
is empty, and then begin their mystic song of worship.*]

CHORUS [*singing*]:

A Maiden: From Asia, from the dayspring that uprises,
  To Bromios ever glorying we came.
  We laboured for our Lord in many guises;
  We toiled, but the toil is as the prize is;
    Thou Mystery, we hail thee by thy name!
Another: Who lingers in the road?   Who espies us?
  He shall hide him in his house nor be bold.
  Let the heart keep silence that defies us;
  For I sing this day to Dionysus
    The song that is appointed from of old.

strophe 1

All: Oh, blessèd he in all wise,
    Who hath drunk the Living Fountain,
      Whose life no folly staineth,
        And his soul is near to God;
    Whose sins are lifted, pall-wise
      As he worships on the Mountain,
        And where Cybele ordaineth,
          Our Mother, he has trod:

      His head with ivy laden
        And his thyrsus tossing high,
          For our God he lifts his cry;
      "Up, O Bacchae, wife and maiden,
          Come, O ye Bacchae, come;
      Oh, bring the Joy-bestower,
      God-seed of God the Sower,
      Bring Bromios in his power
          From Phrygia's mountain dome;
        To street and town and tower,
          Oh, bring ye Bromios home!"

antistrophe 1

    Whom erst in anguish lying
      For an unborn life's desire,
        As a dead thing in the Thunder
          His mother cast to earth;
    For her heart was dying, dying,
      In the white heart of the fire;
        Till Zeus, the Lord of Wonder,
          Devised new lairs of birth;

        Yea, his own flesh tore to hide him,
          And with clasps of bitter gold
          Did a secret son enfold,
      And the Queen knew not beside him,
          Till the perfect hour was there;

Then a hornèd God was found,
And a God with serpents crowned;
And for that are serpents wound
   In the wands his maidens bear,
And the songs of serpents sound
   In the mazes of their hair.

strophe 2

Some Maidens: All hail, O Thebes, thou nurse of Semele!
  With Semele's wild ivy crown thy towers;
Oh, burst in bloom of wreathing bryony,
   Berries and leaves and flowers;
  Uplift the dark divine wand,
  The oak-wand and the pine-wand,
And don thy fawn-skin, fringed in purity
   With fleecy white, like ours.

Oh, cleanse thee in the wands' waving pride!
  Yea, all men shall dance with us and pray,
When Bromios his companies shall guide
  Hillward, ever hillward, where they stay,
   The flock of the Believing,
   The maids from loom and weaving
By the magic of his breath borne away.

antistrophe 2

Others: Hail thou, O Nurse of Zeus, O Caverned Haunt
  Where fierce arms clanged to guard God's cradle rare,
For thee of old some crested Corybant
   First woke in Cretan air
  The wild orb of our orgies,
  Our Timbrel; and thy gorges
Rang with this strain; and blended Phrygian chant
  And sweet keen pipes were there.

But the Timbrel, the Timbrel was another's,
  And away to Mother Rhea it must wend;
And to our holy singing from the Mother's
  The mad Satyrs carried it, to blend
   In the dancing and the cheer
   Of our third and perfect Year;
And it serves Dionysus in the end!

epode

A Maiden: O glad, glad on the mountains
  To swoon in the race outworn,
   When the holy fawn-skin clings,
   And all else sweeps away,
  To the joy of the red quick fountains,

The blood of the hill-goat torn,
  The glory of wild-beast ravenings,
    Where the hill-tops catch the day;
  To the Phrygian, Lydian, mountains!
    'Tis Bromios leads the way.
Another: Then streams the earth with milk, yea, streams
  With wines and nectar of the bee,
  And through the air dim perfume steams
  Of Syrian frankincense; and He,
  Our leader, from his thyrsus spray
  A torchlight tosses high and higher,
  A torchlight like a beacon-fire,
  To waken all that faint and stray;
  And sets them leaping as he sings,
  His tresses rippling to the sky,
  And deep beneath the Maenad cry
    His proud voice rings:
      "Come, O ye Bacchae, come!"
All: Hither, O fragrant of Tmolus the Golden,
  Come with the voice of timbrel and drum;
  Let the cry of your joyance uplift and embolden
    The God of the joy-cry; O Bacchanals, come!
  With pealing of pipes and with Phrygian clamour,
    On, where the vision of holiness thrills,
  And the music climbs and the maddening glamour,
    With the wild White Maids, to the hills, to the hills!
  Oh, then, like a colt as he runs by a river,
    A colt by his dam, when the heart of him sings,
  With the keen limbs drawn and the fleet foot a-quiver,
    Away the Bacchanal springs!

[*Enter* TEIRESIAS. *He is an old man and blind, leaning upon a staff and moving with slow stateliness, though wearing the Ivy and the Bacchic fawn-skin.*]

TE.: Ho, there, who keeps the gate? —Go, summon me
  Cadmus, Agenor's son, who crossed the sea
  From Sidon and upreared this Theban hold.
  Go, whosoe'er thou art. See he be told
  Teiresias seeketh him. Himself will gauge
  Mine errand, and the compact, age with age,
  I vowed with him, grey hair with snow-white hair,
  To deck the new God's thyrsus, and to wear
  His fawn-skin, and with ivy crown our brows.

[*Enter* CADMUS *from the Castle. He is even older than* TEIRESIAS, *and wears the same attire.*]

CA.: True friend! I knew that voice of thine, that flows
  Like mellow wisdom from a fountain wise.
  And, lo, I come prepared, in all the guise
  And harness of this God. Are we not told

His is the soul of that dead life of old
That sprang from mine own daughter? Surely then
Must thou and I with all the strength of men
Exalt him.
             Where then shall I stand, where tread
The dance and toss this bowed and hoary head?
O friend, in thee is wisdom; guide my grey
And eld-worn steps, eld-worn Teiresias. — Nay;
I am not weak.

[*At the first movement of worship his manner begins to change,
a mysterious strength and exaltation enter into him.*]
             Surely this arm could smite
The wild earth with its thyrsus, day and night,
And faint not! Sweetly and forgetfully
The dim years fall from off me!

TE.:   As with thee,
With me 'tis likewise. Light am I and young,
And will essay the dancing and the song.

CA.: Quick, then, our chariots to the mountain road.

TE.: Nay; to take steeds were to mistrust the God.

CA.: So be it. Mine old arms shall guide thee there.

TE.: The God himself shall guide! Have thou no care.

CA.: And in all Thebes shall no man dance but we?

TE.: Aye, Thebes is blinded. Thou and I can see.

CA.: 'Tis weary waiting; hold my hand, friend; so.

TE.: Lo, there is mine. So linkèd let us go.

CA.: Shall things of dust the Gods' dark ways despise?

TE.: Or prove our wit on Heaven's high mysteries?
Not thou and I! That heritage sublime
Our sires have left us, wisdom old as time,
No word of man, how deep soe'er his thought
And won of subtlest toil, may bring to naught.
   Aye, men will rail that I forget my years,
To dance and wreathe with ivy these white hairs;
What recks it? Seeing the God no line hath told
To mark what man shall dance, or young or old;
But craves his honours from mortality
All, no man marked apart; and great shall be!

CA. [*after looking away toward the Mountain*]: Teiresias, since this
          light thou canst not read,
I must be seer for thee. Here comes in speed
Pentheus, Echion's son, whom I have raised
To rule my people in my stead. — Amazed
He seems. Stand close, and mark what we shall hear.

[*The two stand back, partially concealed, while there enters in hot
haste* PENTHEUS, *followed by a bodyguard. He is speaking to the*
SOLDIER *in command.*]

PEN.: Scarce had I crossed our borders, when mine ear
    Was caught by this strange rumour, that our own

Wives, our own sisters, from their hearths are flown
To wild and secret rites; and cluster there
High on the shadowy hills, with dance and prayer
To adore this new-made God, this Dionyse,
Whate'er he be! — And in their companies
Deep wine-jars stand, and ever and anon
Away into the loneliness now one
Steals forth, and now a second, maid or dame,
Where love lies waiting, not of God!   The flame,
They say, of Bacchios wraps them. Bacchios! Nay,
'Tis more to Aphrodite that they pray.
    Howbeit, all that I have found, my men
Hold bound and shackled in our dungeon den;
The rest, I will go hunt them! Aye, and snare
My birds with nets of iron, to quell their prayer
And mountain song and rites of rascaldom!
    They tell me, too, there is a stranger come,
A man of charm and spell, from Lydian seas,
A head all gold and cloudy fragrancies,
A wine-red cheek, and eyes that hold the light
Of the very Cyprian. Day and livelong night
He haunts amid the damsels, o'er each lip
Dangling his cup of joyance! — Let me grip
Him once, but once, within these walls, right swift
That wand shall cease its music, and that drift
Of tossing curls lie still — when my rude sword
Falls between neck and trunk! 'Tis all his word,
This tale of Dionysus; how that same
Babe that was blasted by the lightning flame
With his dead mother, for that mother's lie,
Was re-conceived, born perfect from the thigh
Of Zeus, and now is God! What call ye these?
Dreams? Gibes of the unknown wanderer? Blasphemies
That crave the very gibbet?
                            Stay! God wot,
Here is another marvel! See I not
In motley fawn-skins robed the vision-seer
Teiresias? And my mother's father here —
O depth of scorn! — adoring with the wand
Of Bacchios? — Father! — Nay, mine eyes are fond;
It is not your white heads so fancy-flown!
It cannot be! Cast off that ivy crown,
O mine own mother's sire! Set free that hand
That cowers about its staff.
                            'Tis thou hast planned
This work, Teiresias! 'Tis thou must set
Another altar and another yet
Amongst us, watch new birds, and win more hire
Of gold, interpreting new signs of fire!

But for thy silver hairs, I tell thee true,
Thou now wert sitting chained amid thy crew
Of raving damsels, for this evil dream
Thou hast brought us, of new Gods!   When once the gleam
Of grapes hath lit a Woman's Festival,
In all their prayers is no more health at all!

LEADER OF THE CHORUS [*the words are not heard by* PENTHEUS]: In-
  jurious King, hast thou no care for God,
Nor Cadmus, sower of the Giants' Sod,*
Life-spring to great Echion and to thee?

TE.: Good words, my son, come easily, when he
That speaks is wise, and speaks but for the right.
Else come they never!   Swift are thine, and bright
As though with thought, yet have no thought at all.
  Lo, this new God, whom thou dost flout withal,
I cannot speak the greatness wherewith He
In Hellas shall be great!   Two spirits there be,
Young Prince, that in man's world are first of worth.
Demeter one is named; she is the Earth —
Call her which name thou wilt! — who feeds man's frame
With sustenance of things dry.   And that which came
Her work to perfect, second, is the Power
From Semele born.   He found the liquid shower
Hid in the grape.   He rests man's spirit dim
From grieving, when the vine exalteth him.
He giveth sleep to sink the fretful day
In cool forgetting.   Is there any way
With man's sore heart, save only to forget?
  Yea, being God, the blood of him is set
Before the Gods in sacrifice, that we
For his sake may be blest. — And so, to thee,
That fable shames him, how this God was knit
Into God's flesh?   Nay, learn the truth of it,
Cleared from the false. — When from that deadly light
Zeus saved the babe, and up to Olympus' height
Raised him, and Hera's wrath would cast him thence,
Then Zeus devised him a divine defence.
A fragment of the world-encircling fire †
He rent apart, and wrought to his desire
Of shape and hue, in the image of the child,
And gave to Hera's rage.   And so, beguiled
By change and passing time, this tale was born,
How the babe-god was hidden in the torn
Flesh of his sire.   He hath no shame thereby.
  A prophet is he likewise.   Prophecy
Cleaves to all frenzy, but beyond all else
To frenzy of prayer.   Then in us verily dwells

* See ECHION in the Glossary.
† *i.e.*, the ether, out of which phantoms were made.

The God himself, and speaks the thing to be.
Yea, and of Ares' realm a part hath he.
When mortal armies, mailèd and arrayed,
Have in strange fear, or ever blade met blade,
Fled maddened, 'tis this God hath palsied them.
Aye, over Delphi's rock-built diadem
Thou yet shalt see him leaping with his train
Of fire across the twin-peaked mountain-plain,
Flaming the darkness with his mystic wand,
And great in Hellas. — List and understand,
King Pentheus! Dream not thou that force is power;
Nor, if thou hast a thought, and that thought sour
And sick, oh, dream not thought is wisdom! — Up,
Receive this God to Thebes; pour forth the cup
Of sacrifice, and pray, and wreathe thy brow.

   Thou fearest for the damsels? Think thee now;
How toucheth this the part of Dionyse
To hold maids pure perforce? In them it lies,
And their own hearts; and in the wildest rite
Cometh no stain to her whose heart is white.

   Nay, mark me! Thou hast thy joy, when the Gate
Stands thronged, and Pentheus' name is lifted great
And high by Thebes in clamour; shall not He
Rejoice in his due meed of majesty?

   Howbeit, this Cadmus whom thou scorn'st and I
Will wear His crown, and tread His dances! Aye,
Our hairs are white, yet shall that dance be trod!
I will not lift mine arm to war with God
For thee nor all thy words. Madness most fell
Is on thee, madness wrought by some dread spell,
But not by spell nor leechcraft to be cured!

CH.: Grey prophet, worthy of Phoebus is thy word,
   And wise in honouring Bromios, our great God.

CA.: My son, right well Teiresias points thy road.
   Oh, make thine habitation here with us,
   Not lonely, against men's uses. Hazardous
   Is this quick bird-like beating of thy thought
   Where no thought dwells. — Grant that this God be naught,
   Yet let that Naught be Somewhat in thy mouth;
   Lie boldly, and say He Is! So north and south
   Shall marvel, how there sprang a thing divine
   From Semele's flesh, and honour all our line.

                 [*Drawing nearer to* PENTHEUS]
   Is there not blood before thine eyes even now?
   Our lost Actaeon's blood, whom long ago
   His own red hounds through yonder forest dim
   Tore unto death, because he vaunted him
   Against most holy Artemis? Oh, beware,
   And let me wreathe thy temples. Make thy prayer

With us, and walk thee humbly in God's sight.

      [He makes as if to set the wreath on PENTHEUS' *head.]*

PEN.: Down with that hand! Aroint thee to thy rite,

    Nor smear on me thy foul contagion!

                              [Turning upon TEIRESIAS*]*

                        This

    Thy folly's head and prompter shall not miss

    The justice that he needs! — Go, half my guard,

    Forth to the rock-seat where he dwells in ward

    O'er birds and wonders; rend the stone with crow

    And trident; make one wreck of high and low,

    And toss his bands to all the winds of air!

      Ha, have I found the way to sting thee, there?

    The rest, forth through the town! And seek amain

    This girl-faced stranger, that hath wrought such bane

    To all Thebes, preying on our maids and wives.

    Seek till ye find; and lead him here in gyves,

    Till he be judged and stoned, and weep in blood

    The day he troubled Pentheus with his God!

[The guards set forth in two bodies; PENTHEUS *goes into the Castle.]*

TE.: Hard heart, how little dost thou know what seed

    Thou sowest! Blind before, and now indeed

    Most mad! — Come, Cadmus, let us go our way,

    And pray for this our persecutor, pray

    For this poor city, that the righteous God

    Move not in anger. — Take thine ivy rod

    And help my steps, as I help thine. 'Twere ill,

    If two old men should fall by the roadway. Still,

    Come what come may, our service shall be done

    To Bacchios, the All-Father's mystic son.

      O Pentheus, named of sorrow! Shall he claim

    From all thy house fulfilment of his name,

    Old Cadmus? — Nay, I speak not from mine art,

    But as I see — blind words and a blind heart!

        [The two Old Men go off towards the Mountain.]

            CHORUS [*singing*]:

                              strophe 1

Some Maidens: Thou Immaculate on high;

          Thou Recording Purity;

          Thou that stoopest, Golden Wing,

          Earthward, manward, pitying,

          Hearest thou this angry King?

          Hearest thou the rage and scorn

           'Gainst the Lord of Many Voices,

          Him of mortal mother born,

           Him in whom man's heart rejoices,

          Girt with garlands and with glee,

First in Heaven's sovranty?
  For his kingdom, it is there,
    In the dancing and the prayer,
  In the music and the laughter,
    In the vanishing of care,
And of all before and after;
In the Gods' high banquet, when
  Gleams the grape-blood, flashed to heaven;
Yea, and in the feasts of men
Comes his crownèd slumber; then
  Pain is dead and hate forgiven!

antistrophe 1

Others: Loose thy lips from out the rein;
    Lift thy wisdom to disdain;
    Whatso law thou canst not see,
    Scorning; so the end shall be
    Uttermost calamity!
    'Tis the life of quiet breath,
     'Tis the simple and the true,
    Storm nor earthquake shattereth,
     Nor shall aught the house undo
    Where they dwell. For, far away,
    Hidden from the eyes of day,
     Watchers are there in the skies,
     That can see man's life, and prize
    Deeds well done by things of clay.
     But the world's Wise are not wise,
    Claiming more than mortal may.
    Life is such a little thing;
     Lo, their present is departed,
    And the dreams to which they cling
    Come not. Mad imagining
     Theirs, I ween, and empty-hearted!

strophe 2

Divers Maidens: Where is the Home for me?
    O Cyprus, set in the sea,
  Aphrodite's home in the soft sea-foam,
    Would I could wend to thee;
  Where the wings of the Loves are furled,
  And faint the heart of the world.
    Aye, unto Paphos' isle,
    Where the rainless meadows smile
  With riches rolled from the hundred-fold
    Mouths of the far-off Nile,
  Streaming beneath the waves
  To the roots of the seaward caves.

But a better land is there
Where Olympus cleaves the air,
The high still dell where the Muses dwell,
Fairest of all things fair!
O there is Grace, and there is the Heart's Desire,
And peace to adore thee, thou Spirit of Guiding Fire!

antistrophe 2

A God of Heaven is he,
And born in majesty;
Yet hath he mirth in the joy of the Earth,
And he loveth constantly
Her who brings increase,
The Feeder of Children, Peace.
No grudge hath he of the great;
No scorn of the mean estate;
But to all that liveth His wine he giveth,
Griefless, immaculate;
Only on them that spurn
Joy, may his anger burn.

Love thou the Day and the Night;
Be glad of the Dark and the Light;
And avert thine eyes from the lore of the wise,
That have honour in proud men's sight.
The simple nameless herd of Humanity
Hath deeds and faith that art truth enough for me!

[*As the* CHORUS *ceases, a party of the guards return, leading in the midst of them* DIONYSUS, *bound. The* SOLDIER *in command stands forth, as* PENTHEUS, *hearing the tramp of feet, comes out from the Castle.*]

SOLDIER: Our quest is finished, and thy prey, O King,
Caught; for the chase was swift, and this wild thing
Most tame; yet never flinched, nor thought to flee,
But held both hands out unresistingly —
No change, no blanching of the wine-red cheek.
He waited while we came, and bade us wreak
All thy decree; yea, laughed, and made my hest
Easy, till I for very shame confessed
And said: "O stranger, not of mine own will
I bind thee, but his bidding to fulfil
Who sent me."
                 And those prisoned Maids withal
Whom thou didst seize and bind within the wall
Of thy great dungeon, they are fled, O King,
Free in the woods, a-dance and glorying
To Bromios. Of their own impulse fell
To earth, men say, fetter and manacle,
And bars slid back untouched of mortal hand.

Yea, full of many wonders to thy land
Is this man come. . . Howbeit, it lies with thee!

PEN.: Ye are mad! — Unhand him. Howso swift he be,
My toils are round him and he shall not fly.

[*The guards loose the arms of* DIONYSUS; PENTHEUS *studies him for a while in silence, then speaks jeeringly.* DIONYSUS *remains gentle and unafraid.*]

Marry, a fair shape for a woman's eye,
Sir stranger! And thou seek'st no more, I ween!
Long curls, withal! That shows thou ne'er hast been
A wrestler! — down both cheeks so softly tossed
And winsome! And a white skin! It hath cost
Thee pains, to please thy damsels with this white
And red of cheeks that never face the light!

[DIONYSUS *is silent.*]

Speak, sirrah; tell me first thy name and race.

DI.: No glory is therein, nor yet disgrace.
Thou hast heard of Tmolus, the bright hill of flowers?

PEN.: Surely; the ridge that winds by Sardis' towers.

DI.: Thence am I; Lydia was my fatherland.

PEN.: And whence these revelations, that thy band
Spreadeth in Hellas?

DI.:   Their intent and use
Dionysus oped to me, the Child of Zeus.

PEN. [*brutally*]: Is there a Zeus there, that can still beget
Young Gods?

DI.:   Nay, only He whose seal was set
Here in thy Thebes on Semele.

PEN.:   What way
Descended he upon thee? In full day
Or vision of night?

DI.:   Most clear he stood, and scanned
My soul, and gave his emblems to mine hand.

PEN.: What like be they, these emblems?

DI.:   That may none
Reveal, nor know, save his Elect alone.

PEN.: And what good bring they to the worshipper?

DI.: Good beyond price, but not for thee to hear.

PEN.: Thou trickster! Thou wouldst prick me on the more
To seek them out!

DI.:   His mysteries abhor
The touch of sin-lovers.

PEN.:   And so thine eyes
Saw this God plain; what guise had he?

DI.:   What guise
It liked him. 'Twas not I ordained his shape.

PEN.: Aye, deftly turned again. An idle jape,
And nothing answered!

DI.:   Wise words being brought

    To blinded eyes will seem as things of nought.
PEN.: And comest thou first to Thebes, to have thy God
    Established?
DI.:   Nay; all Barbary hath trod
    His dance ere this.
PEN.:   A low blind folk, I ween,
    Beside our Hellenes!
DI.:   Higher and more keen
    In this thing, though their ways are not thy way.
PEN.: How is thy worship held, by night or day?
DI.: Most oft by night; 'tis a majestic thing,
    The darkness.
PEN.:   Ha! with women worshipping?
    'Tis craft and rottenness!
DI.:   By day no less,
    Whoso will seek may find unholiness.
PEN.: Enough! Thy doom is fixed, for false pretence
    Corrupting Thebes.
DI.:   Not mine; but thine, for dense
    Blindness of heart, and for blaspheming God!
PEN.: A ready knave it is, and brazen-browed.
    This mystery-priest!
DI.:   Come, say what it shall be,
    My doom; what dire thing wilt thou do to me?
PEN.: First, shear that delicate curl that dangles there.
    [He beckons to the soldiers, who approach DIONYSUS.]
DI.: I have vowed it to my God; 'tis holy hair.
    [The soldiers cut off the tress.]
PEN.: Next, yield me up thy staff!
DI.:   Raise thine own hand
    To take it. This is Dionysus' wand.
    [PENTHEUS takes the staff.]
PEN.: Last, I will hold thee prisoned here.
DI.:   My Lord
    God will unloose me, when I speak the word.
PEN.: He may, if e'er again amid his bands
    Of saints he hears thy voice!
DI.:   Even now he stands
    Close here, and sees all that I suffer.
PEN.:   What?
    Where is he? For mine eyes discern him not.
DI.: Where I am! 'Tis thine own impurity
    That veils him from thee.
PEN.:   The dog jeers at me!
    At me and Thebes! Bind him!
    [The soldiers begin to bind him.]
DI.:   I charge ye, bind
    Me not! I having vision and ye blind!
PEN.: And I, with better right, say bind the more!

[*The soldiers obey.*]

DI.: Thou knowest not what end thou seekest, nor
    What deed thou doest, nor what man thou art!

PEN. [*mocking*]: Agave's son, and on the father's part
    Echion's, hight Pentheus!

DI.:   So let it be,
    A name fore-written to calamity!

PEN.: Away, and tie him where the steeds are tied;
    Aye, let him lie in the manger! — There abide
    And stare into the darkness! — And this rout
    Of womankind that clusters thee about,
    Thy ministers of worship, are my slaves!
    It may be I will sell them o'er the waves,
    Hither and thither; else they shall be set
    To labour at my distaffs, and forget
    Their timbrel and their songs of dawning day!

DI.: I go; for that which may not be, I may
    Not suffer! Yet for this thy sin, lo, He
    Whom thou deniest cometh after thee
    For recompense. Yea, in thy wrong to us,
    Thou hast cast Him into thy prison-house!

[DIONYSUS, *without his wand, his hair shorn, and his arms tightly
bound, is led off by the guards to his dungeon.* PENTHEUS *returns
into the Palace.*]

CHORUS [*singing*]:

strophe

Some Maidens: Achelous' roaming daughter,
    Holy Dirce, virgin water,
    Bathed he not of old in thee,
    The Babe of God, the Mystery?
    When from out the fire immortal
        To himself his God did take him,
        To his own flesh, and bespake him:
    "Enter now life's second portal,
    Motherless Mystery; lo, I break
    Mine own body for thy sake,
        Thou of the Twofold Door, and seal thee
    Mine, O Bromios," — thus he spake —
        "And to this thy land reveal thee."

All: Still my prayer towards thee quivers,
                Dirce, still to thee I hie me;
            Why, O Blessèd among Rivers,
                Wilt thou fly me and deny me?
                By his own joy I vow,
                By the grape upon the bough,
    Thou shalt seek Him in the midnight, thou shalt love Him,
        even now!

Others:

Dark and of the dark impassioned
Is this Pentheus' blood; yea, fashioned
Of the Dragon, and his birth
From Echion, child of Earth.
He is no man, but a wonder;
　　Did the Earth-Child not beget him,
　　As a red Giant, to set him
Against God, against the Thunder?
He will bind me for his prize,
Me, the Bride of Dionyse;
　　And my priest, my friend, is taken
Even now, and buried lies;
　　In the dark he lies forsaken!

All:

Lo, we race with death, we perish,
　　Dionysus, here before thee!
Dost thou mark us not, nor cherish,
　　Who implore thee, and adore thee?
　　　　Hither down Olympus' side,
　　　　Come, O Holy One defied,
Be thy golden wand uplifted o'er the tyrant in his pride!

epode

A Maiden:

Oh, where art thou?　In thine own
Nysa, thou our help alone?
O'er fierce beasts in orient lands
　　Doth thy thronging thyrsus wave,
　　By the high Corycian Cave,
Or where stern Olympus stands;
In the elm-woods and the oaken,
　　There where Orpheus harped of old,
　　And the trees awoke and knew him,
　　And the wild things gathered to him,
As he sang amid the broken
　　Glens his music manifold?
Blessed Land of Pierie,
Dionysus loveth thee;
　　He will come to thee with dancing,
Come with joy and mystery;
With the Maenads at his hest
Winding, winding to the West;
　　Cross the flood of swiftly glancing
Axios in majesty;
Cross the Lydias, the giver
　　Of good gifts and waving green;
Cross that Father-Stream of story,
Through a land of steeds and glory

Rolling, bravest, fairest River
　　E'er of mortals seen!

A VOICE WITHIN: Io! Io!
　　Awake, ye damsels; hear my cry,
　　　Calling my Chosen; hearken ye!
A MAIDEN: Who speaketh? Oh, what echoes thus?
ANOTHER: A Voice, a Voice, that calleth us!
VOICE: Be of good cheer! Lo, it is I,
　　　The Child of Zeus and Semele.
A MAIDEN: O Master, Master, it is Thou!
ANOTHER: O Holy Voice, be with us now!
VOICE: Spirit of the Chained Earthquake,
　　Hear my word; awake, awake!
　　　[*An Earthquake suddenly shakes the pillars of the Castle.*]
A MAIDEN: Ha! what is coming? Shall the hall
　　Of Pentheus racked in ruin fall?
LEADER: Our God is in the house! Ye maids adore Him!
CH.:　　　　　　　　　　　　　　　　　We adore Him all!
VOICE: Unveil the Lightning's eye; arouse
　　The fire that sleeps, against this house!
　　　　　[*Fire leaps up on the Tomb of Semele.*]
A MAIDEN: Ah, saw ye, marked ye there the flame
　　From Semele's enhallowed sod
　　Awakened? Yea, the Death that came
　　Ablaze from heaven of old, the same
　　Hot splendour of the shaft of God?
LE.: Oh, cast ye, cast ye, to the earth! The Lord
　　Cometh against this house! Oh, cast ye down,
　　Ye trembling damsels; He, our own adored,
　　God's Child hath come, and all is overthrown!
[*The* MAIDENS *cast themselves upon the ground, their eyes earth-ward.* DIONYSUS, *alone and unbound, enters from the Castle.*]
DI.: Ye Damsels of the Morning Hills, why lie ye thus dismayed?
　　Ye marked him, then, our Master, and the mighty hand he laid
　　On tower and rock, shaking the house of Pentheus? — But
　　　　arise,
　　And cast the trembling from your flesh, and lift untroubled
　　　　eyes.
LE.: O Light in Darkness, is it thou? O Priest, is this thy face?
　　My heart leaps out to greet thee from the deep of loneliness.
DI.: Fell ye so quick despairing, when beneath the Gate I passed?
　　Should the gates of Pentheus quell me, or his darkness make
　　　　me fast?
LE.: Oh, what was left if thou wert gone? What could I but de-
　　　　spair?
　　How hast thou 'scaped the man of sin? Who freed thee from
　　　　the snare?

DI.: I had no pain nor peril; 'twas mine own hand set me free.

LE.: Thine arms were gyvèd!

DI.:   Nay, no gyve, no touch, was laid on me!
'Twas there I mocked him, in his gyves, and gave him dreams
    for food.
For when he led me down, behold, before the stall there stood
A Bull of Offering. And this King, he bit his lips, and straight
Fell on and bound it, hoof and limb, with gasping wrath and
    sweat.
And I sat watching! — Then a Voice; and lo, our Lord was
    come,
And the house shook, and a great flame stood o'er his mother's
    tomb.
And Pentheus hied this way and that, and called his thralls
    amain
For water, lest his roof-tree burn; and all toiled, all in vain.
Then deemed a-sudden I was gone; and left his fire, and sped
Back to the prison portals, and his lifted sword shone red.
But there, methinks, the God had wrought — I speak but as
    I guess —
Some dream-shape in mine image; for he smote at emptiness,
Stabbed in the air, and strove in wrath, as though 'twere me
    he slew.
Then 'mid his dreams God smote him yet again! He over-
    threw
All that high house. And there in wreck for evermore it lies,
That the day of this my bondage may be sore in Pentheus'
    eyes!
    And now his sword is fallen, and he lies outworn and wan
Who dared to rise against his God in wrath, being but man.
And I uprose and left him, and in all peace took my path
Forth to my Chosen, recking light of Pentheus and his wrath.
    But soft, methinks a footstep sounds even now within the
    hall;
'Tis he; how think ye he will stand, and what words speak
    withal?
I will endure him gently, though he come in fury hot.
For still are the ways of Wisdom, and her temper trembleth
    not!
                        [*Enter* PENTHEUS *in fury.*]

PEN.: It is too much! This Eastern knave hath slipped
His prison, whom I held but now, hard gripped
In bondage. — Ha! 'Tis he! — What, sirrah, how
Show'st thou before my portals?
                        [*He advances furiously upon him.*]

DI.:   Softly thou!
And set a quiet carriage to thy rage.

PEN.: How comest thou here? How didst thou break thy cage?
Speak!

DI.:   Said I not, or didst thou mark not me,
            There was One living that should set me free?
PEN.: Who? Ever wilder are these tales of thine.
DI.: He who first made for man the clustered vine.
PEN.: I scorn him and his vines!
DI.:   For Dionyse
            'Tis well; for in thy scorn his glory lies.
PEN. [*to his guard*]: Go swift to all the towers, and bar withal
            Each gate!
DI.:   What, cannot God o'erleap a wall?
PEN.: Oh, wit thou hast, save where thou needest it!
DI.: Whereso it most imports, there is my wit! —
            Nay, peace! Abide till he who hasteth from
            The mountain side with news for thee, be come.
            We will not fly, but wait on thy command.
            [*Enter suddenly and in haste a* MESSENGER *from the Mountain.*]
ME.: Great Pentheus, Lord of all this Theban land,
            I come from high Cithaeron, where the frore
            Snow spangles gleam and cease not evermore. . .
PEN.: And what of import may thy coming bring?
ME.: I have seen the Wild White Women there, O King,
            Whose fleet limbs darted arrow-like but now
            From Thebes away, and come to tell thee how
            They work strange deeds and passing marvel. Yet
            I first would learn thy pleasure. Shall I set
            My whole tale forth, or veil the stranger part?
            Yea, Lord, I fear the swiftness of thy heart,
            Thine edgèd wrath and more than royal soul.
PEN.: Thy tale shall nothing scathe thee. — Tell the whole.
            It skills not to be wroth with honesty.
            Nay, if thy news of them be dark, 'tis he
            Shall pay it, who bewitched and led them on.
ME.: Our herded kine were moving in the dawn
            Up to the peaks, the greyest, coldest time,
            When the first rays steal earthward, and the rime
            Yields, when I saw three bands of them. The one
            Autonoe led, one Ino, one thine own
            Mother, Agave. There beneath the trees
            Sleeping they lay, like wild things flung at ease
            In the forest; one half sinking on a bed
            Of deep pine greenery; one with careless head
            Amid the fallen oak leaves; all most cold
            In purity — not as thy tale was told
            Of wine-cups and wild music and the chase
            For love amid the forest's loneliness.
            Then rose the Queen Agave suddenly
            Amid her band, and gave the God's wild cry,
            "Awake, ye Bacchanals! I hear the sound
            Of hornèd kine. Awake ye!" — Then, all round,

Alert, the warm sleep fallen from their eyes,
A marvel of swift ranks I saw them rise,
Dames young and old, and gentle maids unwed
Among them. O'er their shoulders first they shed
Their tresses, and caught up the fallen fold
Of mantles where some clasp had loosened hold,
And girt the dappled fawn-skins in with long
Quick snakes that hissed and writhed with quivering tongue.
And one a young fawn held, and one a wild
Wolf cub, and fed them with white milk, and smiled
In love, young mothers with a mother's breast
And babes at home forgotten! Then they pressed
Wreathed ivy round their brows, and oaken sprays
And flowering bryony. And one would raise
Her wand and smite the rock, and straight a jet
Of quick bright water came. Another set
Her thyrsus in the bosomed earth, and there
Was red wine that the God sent up to her,
A darkling fountain. And if any lips
Sought whiter draughts, with dipping finger-tips
They pressed the sod, and gushing from the ground
Came springs of milk. And reed-wands ivy-crowned
Ran with sweet honey, drop by drop. — O King,
Hadst thou been there, as I, and seen this thing,
With prayer and most high wonder hadst thou gone
To adore this God whom now thou rail'st upon!
　　Howbeit, the kine-wardens and shepherds straight
Came to one place, amazed, and held debate;
And one being there who walked the streets and scanned
The ways of speech, took lead of them whose hand
Knew but the slow soil and the solemn hill,
And flattering spoke, and asked: "Is it your will,
Masters, we stay the mother of the King,
Agave, from her lawless worshipping,
And win us royal thanks?" — And this seemed good
To all; and through the branching underwood
We hid us, cowering in the leaves. And there
Through the appointed hour they made their prayer
And worship of the Wand, with one accord
Of heart and cry — "Iacchos, Bromios, Lord,
God of God born!" — And all the mountain felt,
And worshipped with them; and the wild things knelt
And ramped and gloried, and the wilderness
Was filled with moving voices and dim stress.
　　Soon, as it chanced, beside my thicket-close
The Queen herself passed dancing, and I rose
And sprang to seize her. But she turned her face
Upon me: "Ho, my rovers of the chase,
My wild White Hounds, we are hunted! Up, each rod

And follow, follow, for our Lord and God!"
Thereat, for fear they tear us, all we fled
Amazed; and on, with hand unweaponèd
They swept towards our herds that browsed the green
Hill grass. Great uddered kine then hadst thou seen
Bellowing in sword-like hands that cleave and tear,
A live steer riven asunder, and the air
Tossed with rent ribs or limbs of cloven tread,
And flesh upon the branches, and a red
Rain from the deep green pines. Yea, bulls of pride,
Horns swift to rage, were fronted and aside
Flung stumbling, by those multitudinous hands
Dragged pitilessly. And swifter were the bands
Of garbèd flesh and bone unbound withal
Than on thy royal eyes the lids may fall.

   Then on like birds, by their own speed upborne,
They swept towards the plains of waving corn
That lie beside Asopus' banks, and bring
To Thebes the rich fruit of her harvesting.
On Hysiae and Erythrae that lie nursed
Amid Cithaeron's bowering rocks, they burst
Destroying, as a foeman's army comes.
They caught up little children from their homes,
High on their shoulders, babes unheld, that swayed
And laughed and fell not; all a wreck they made;
Yea, bronze and iron did shatter, and in play
Struck hither and thither, yet no wound had they;
Caught fire from out the hearths, yea, carried hot
Flames in their tresses and were scorchèd not!
   The village folk in wrath took spear and sword,
And turned upon the Bacchae. Then, dread Lord,
The wonder was. For spear nor barbèd brand
Could scathe nor touch the damsels; but the Wand,
The soft and wreathèd wand their white hands sped,
Blasted those men and quelled them, and they fled
Dizzily. Sure some God was in these things!
   And the holy women back to those strange springs
Returned, that God had sent them when the day
Dawned, on the upper heights; and washed away
The stain of battle. And those girdling snakes
Hissed out to lap the waterdrops from cheeks
And hair and breast.
                    Therefore I counsel thee,
O King, receive this Spirit, whoe'er he be,
To Thebes in glory. Greatness manifold
Is all about him; and the tale is told
That this is he who first to man did give
The grief-assuaging vine. Oh, let him live;
For if he die, then Love herself is slain,

And nothing joyous in the world again!

LE.: Albeit I tremble, and scarce may speak my thought
 To a king's face, yet will I hide it not.
 Dionyse is God, no God more true nor higher!

PEN.: It bursts hard by us, like a smothered fire,
 This frenzy of Bacchic women! All my land
 Is made their mock. — This needs an iron hand!
  Ho, Captain! Quick to the Electran Gate;
 Bid gather all my men-at-arms thereat;
 Call all that spur the charger, all who know
 To wield the orbèd targe or bend the bow;
 We march to war! — 'Fore God, shall women dare
 Such deeds against us? 'Tis too much to bear!

DI.: Thou mark'st me not, O King, and holdest light
 My solemn words; yet, in thine own despite,
 I warn thee still. Lift thou not up thy spear
 Against a God, but hold thy peace, and fear
 His wrath! He will not brook it, if thou fright
 His Chosen from the hills of their delight.

PEN.: Peace, thou! And if for once thou hast slipped thy chain,
 Give thanks! — Or shall I knot thine arms again?

DI.: Better to yield him prayer and sacrifice
 Than kick against the pricks, since Dionyse
 Is God, and thou but mortal.

PEN.: That will I!
 Yea, sacrifice of women's blood, to cry
 His name through all Cithaeron!

DI.: Ye shall fly,
 All, and abase your shields of bronzen rim
 Before their wands.

PEN.: There is no way with him,
 This stranger that so dogs us! Well or ill
 I may entreat him, he must babble still!

DI.: Wait, good my friend! These crooked matters may
 Even yet be straightened.

 [PENTHEUS *has started as though to seek his army at the gate.*]

PEN.: Aye, if I obey
 Mine own slaves' will; how else?

DI.: Myself will lead
 The damsels hither, without sword or steed.

PEN.: How now? — This is some plot against me!

DI.: What
 Dost fear? Only to save thee do I plot.

PEN.: It is some compact ye have made, whereby
 To dance these hills for ever!

DI.: Verily,
 That is my compact, plighted with my Lord!

PEN. [*turning from him*]: Ho, armourers! Bring forth my shield
 and sword! —

And thou, be silent!

DI. [*after regarding him fixedly, speaks with resignation*]:
>   Ah! — Have then thy will!

[*He fixes his eyes upon* PENTHEUS *again, while the armourers bring out his armour; then speaks in a tone of command.*]
>   Man, thou wouldst fain behold them on the hill
>   Praying!

PEN. [*who during the rest of this scene, with a few exceptions, simply speaks the thoughts that* DIONYSUS *puts into him, losing power over his own mind*]:
>   That would I, though it cost me all
>   The gold of Thebes!

DI: So much?   Thou art quick to fall
>   To such great longing.

PEN. [*somewhat bewildered at what he has said*]:
>   Aye; 'twould grieve me much
>   To see them flown with wine.

DI.:   Yet cravest thou such
>   A sight as would much grieve thee?

PEN.:   Yes; I fain
>   Would watch, ambushed among the pines.

DI.:   'Twere vain
>   To hide.   They soon will track thee out.

PEN.:   Well said!
>   'Twere best done openly.

DI.:   Wilt thou be led
>   By me, and try the venture?

PEN.:   Aye, indeed!
>   Lead on.   Why should we tarry?

DI.:   First we need
>   A rich and trailing robe of fine linen
>   To gird thee.

PEN.:   Nay; am I a woman, then,
>   And no man more?

DI.:   Wouldst have them slay thee dead?
>   No man may see their mysteries.

PEN.:   Well said! —
>   I marked thy subtle temper long ere now.

DI.: 'Tis Dionyse that prompteth me.

PEN.:   And how
>   Mean'st thou the further plan?

DI.:   First take thy way
>   Within.   I will array thee.

PEN.:   What array?
>   The woman's?   Nay, I will not.

DI.:   Doth it change
>   So soon, all thy desire to see this strange
>   Adoring?

PEN.:   Wait! What garb wilt thou bestow
     About me?
DI.:   First a long tress dangling low
     Beneath thy shoulders.
PEN.:   Aye, and next?
DI.:   The said
     Robe, falling to thy feet; and on thine head
     A snood.
PEN.:   And after? Hast thou aught beyond?
DI.: Surely; the dappled fawn-skin and the wand.
PEN. [*after a struggle with himself*]:
     Enough! I cannot wear a robe and snood.
DI.: Wouldst liefer draw the sword and spill men's blood?
PEN. [*again doubting*]: True, that were evil. — Aye; 'tis best to go
     First to some place of watch.
DI.:   Far wiser so,
     Than seek by wrath wrath's bitter recompense.
PEN.: What of the city streets? Canst lead me hence
     Unseen of any?
DI.:   Lonely and untried
     Thy path from hence shall be, and I thy guide!
PEN.: I care for nothing, so these Bacchanals
     Triumph not against me! . . . Forward to my halls
     Within! — I will ordain what seemeth best.
DI.: So be it, O King! 'Tis mine to obey thine hest,
     Whate'er it be.
PEN. [*after hesitating once more and waiting*]:
                    Well, I will go — perchance
     To march and scatter them with serried lance,
     Perchance to take thy plan. . . I know not yet.
                         [*Exit* PENTHEUS *into the Castle.*]
DI.: Damsels, the lion walketh to the net!
     He finds his Bacchae now, and sees and dies,
     And pays for all his sin! — O Dionyse,
     This is thine hour and thou not far away.
     Grant us our vengeance! — First, O Master, stay
     The course of reason in him, and instil
     A foam of madness. Let his seeing will,
     Which ne'er had stooped to put thy vesture on,
     Be darkened, till the deed is lightly done.
     Grant likewise that he find through all his streets
     Loud scorn, this man of wrath and bitter threats
     That made Thebes tremble, led in woman's guise.
        I go to fold that robe of sacrifice
     On Pentheus, that shall deck him to the dark,
     His mother's gift! — So shall he learn and mark
     God's true Son, Dionyse, in fulness God,
     Most fearful, yet to man most soft of mood.
            [*Exit* DIONYSUS, *following* PENTHEUS *into the Castle.*]

CHORUS [*singing*]:

strophe

Some Maidens: Will they ever come to me, ever again
              The long long dances,
          On through the dark till the dim stars wane?
          Shall I feel the dew on my throat, and the stream
          Of wind in my hair? Shall our white feet gleam
              In the dim expanses?
          Oh, feet of a fawn to the greenwood fled,
            Alone in the grass and the loveliness;
          Leap of the hunted, no more in dread,
            Beyond the snares and the deadly press:
          Yet a voice still in the distance sounds,
          A voice and a fear and a haste of hounds;
          O wildly labouring, fiercely fleet,
              Onward yet by river and glen . . .
          Is it joy or terror, ye storm-swift feet? . . .
          To the dear lone lands untroubled of men,
      Where no voice sounds, and amid the shadowy green
      The little things of the woodland live unseen.

      What else is Wisdom? * What of man's endeavour
        Or God's high grace, so lovely and so great?
        To stand from fear set free, to breathe and wait;
        To hold a hand uplifted over Hate;
      And shall not Loveliness be loved for ever?

antistrophe

Others: O Strength of God, slow art thou and still,
              Yet failest never!
          On them that worship the Ruthless Will,
          On them that dream, doth His judgment wait.
          Dreams of the proud man, making great
              And greater ever,
          Things which are not of God. In wide
            And devious coverts, hunter-wise,
          He coucheth Time's unhasting stride,
            Following, following, him whose eyes
          Look not to Heaven. For all is vain,
          The pulse of the heart, the plot of the brain,
          That striveth beyond the laws that live.
          And is thy Faith so much to give,
          Is it so hard a thing to see,
          That the Spirit of God, whate'er it be,

* For an interpretation of this passage see Murray's note in the original edition
of this translation (*Euripides,* trans. by Gilbert Murray, Longmans, Green and Co.,
1902).

The Law that abides and changes not, ages long,
The Eternal and Nature-born — these things be strong?

What else is Wisdom?   What of man's endeavour
 Or God's high grace so lovely and so great?
 To stand from fear set free, to breathe and wait:
 To hold a hand uplifted over Hate;
And shall not Loveliness be loved for ever?

epode

LE.:   Happy he, on the weary sea
Who hath fled the tempest and won the haven.
 Happy whoso hath risen, free,
Above his striving.   For strangely graven
 Is the orb of life, that one and another
 In gold and power may outpass his brother.
 And men in their millions float and flow
And seethe with a million hopes as leaven;
 And they win their Will, or they miss their Will,
 And the hopes are dead or are pined for still;
 But whoe'er can know,
 As the long days go,
That To Live is happy, hath found his Heaven!

[*Re-enter* DIONYSUS *from the Castle.*]

DI.: O eye that cravest sights thou must not see,
 O heart athirst for that which slakes not!   Thee,
 Pentheus, I call; forth and be seen, in guise
 Of woman, Maenad, saint of Dionyse,
 To spy upon His Chosen and thine own
 Mother!

[*Enter* PENTHEUS, *clad like a Bacchanal, and strangely excited, a spirit of Bacchic madness overshadowing him.*]

     Thy shape, methinks, is like to one
 Of Cadmus' royal maids!

PEN.:   Yea; and mine eye
Is bright!   Yon sun shines twofold in the sky,
Thebes twofold and the Wall of Seven Gates. . .
And is it a Wild Bull this, that walks and waits
Before me?   There are horns upon thy brow!
What art thou, man or beast?   For surely now
The Bull is on thee!

DI.:   He who erst was wrath,
Goes with us now in gentleness.   He hath
Unsealed thine eyes to see what thou shouldst see.

PEN.: Say; stand I not as Ino stands, or she
Who bore me?

DI.:   When I look on thee, it seems
I see their very selves! — But stay; why streams

That lock abroad, not where I laid it, crossed
Under the coif?

PEN.:   I did it, as I tossed
My head in dancing, to and fro, and cried
His holy music!

DI. [*tending him*]:   It shall soon be tied
Aright. 'Tis mine to tend thee. . . Nay, but stand
With head straight.

PEN.:   In the hollow of thy hand
I lay me. Deck me as thou wilt.

DI.:   Thy zone
Is loosened likewise; and the folded gown
Not evenly falling to the feet.

PEN.:   'Tis so,
By the right foot. But here, methinks, they flow
In one straight line to the heel.

DI. [*while tending him*]:   And if thou prove
Their madness true, aye, more than true, what love
And thanks hast thou for me?

PEN. [*not listening to him*]:   In my right hand
Is it, or thus, that I should bear the wand,
To be most like to them?

DI.:   Up let it swing
In the right hand, timed with the right foot's spring. . .
'Tis well thy heart is changed!

PEN. [*more wildly*]:   What strength is this!
Cithaeron's steeps and all that in them is —
How say'st thou? — Could my shoulders lift the whole?

DI.: Surely thou canst, and if thou wilt! Thy soul,
Being once so sick, now stands as it should stand.

PEN.: Shall it be bars of iron? Or this bare hand
And shoulder to the crags, to wrench them down?

DI.: Wouldst wreck the Nymphs' wild temples, and the brown
Rocks, where Pan pipes at noonday?

PEN.:   Nay; not I!
Force is not well with women. I will lie
Hid in the pine-brake.

DI.:   Even as fits a spy
On holy and fearful things, so shalt thou lie!

PEN. [*with a laugh*]: They lie there now, methinks — the wild birds, caught
By love among the leaves, and fluttering not!

DI.: It may be. That is what thou goest to see,
Aye, and to trap them — so they trap not thee!

PEN.: Forth through the Thebans' town! I am their king,
Aye, their one Man, seeing I dare this thing!

DI.: Yea, thou shalt bear their burden, thou alone;
Therefore thy trial awaiteth thee! — But on;
With me into thine ambush shalt thou come

Unscathed; then let another bear thee home!
PEN.: The Queen, my mother.
DI.:   Marked of every eye.
PEN.: For that I go!
DI.:   Thou shalt be borne on high!
PEN.: That were like pride!
DI.:   Thy mother's hands shall share
Thy carrying.
PEN.:   Nay; I need not such soft care!
DI.: So soft?
PEN.:   Whate'er it be, I have earned it well!
                    [*Exit* PENTHEUS *towards the Mountain.*]
DI.: Fell, fell art thou; and to a doom so fell
Thou walkest, that thy name from South to North
Shall shine, a sign for ever! — Reach thou forth
Thine arms, Agave, now, and ye dark-browed
Cadmeian sisters! Greet this prince so proud
To the high ordeal, where save God and me,
None walks unscathed! — The rest this day shall see.
                    [*Exit* DIONYSUS *following* PENTHEUS.]

CHORUS [*singing*]:

                                        strophe

Some Maidens: O hounds raging and blind,
                        Up by the mountain road,
                    Sprites of the maddened mind,
                        To the wild Maids of God;
                    Fill with your rage their eyes,
                        Rage at the rage unblest,
                    Watching in woman's guise,
                        The spy upon God's Possessed.

A Bacchanal: Who shall be first, to mark
                        Eyes in the rock that spy,
                    Eyes in the pine-tree dark —
                        Is it his mother? — and cry:
                    "Lo, what is this that comes,
                        Haunting, troubling still,
                    Even in our heights, our homes,
                        The wild Maids of the Hill?
                    What flesh bare this child?
                        Never on woman's breast
                    Changeling so evil smiled;
                        Man is he not, but Beast!
                    Lion-shape of the wild,
                        Gorgon-breed of the waste!"

All: Hither, for doom and deed!
                        Hither with lifted sword,

Justice, Wrath of the Lord,
Come in our visible need!
Smite till the throat shall bleed,
Smite till the heart shall bleed,
Him the tyrannous, lawless, Godless, Echion's earth-born seed!

antistrophe

Others: Tyrannously hath he trod;
  Marched him, in Law's despite,
Against thy Light, O God,
  Yea, and thy Mother's Light;
Girded him, falsely bold,
  Blinded in craft, to quell
And by man's violence hold
  Things unconquerable.

A Bacchanal: A strait pitiless mind
  Is death unto godliness;
And to feel in human kind
  Life, and a pain the less.
Knowledge, we are not foes!
  I seek thee diligently;
But the world with a great wind blows,
  Shining, and not from thee;
Blowing to beautiful things,
  On, amid dark and light,
Till Life, through the trammellings
  Of Laws that are not the Right,
Breaks, clean and pure, and sings
  Glorying to God in the height!

All: Hither for doom and deed!
  Hither with lifted sword,
Justice, Wrath of the Lord,
  Come in our visible need!
Smite till the throat shall bleed,
Smite till the heart shall bleed,
Him the tyrannous, lawless, Godless, Echion's earth-born seed!

epode

LE.: Appear, appear, whatso thy shape or name
  O Mountain Bull, Snake of the Hundred Heads,
   Lion of Burning Flame!
 O God, Beast, Mystery, come!   Thy mystic maids
 Are hunted! — Blast their hunter with thy breath,
   Cast o'er his head thy snare;
 And laugh aloud and drag him to his death,
  Who stalks thy herded madness in its lair!

[*Enter hastily a* MESSENGER *from the Mountain, pale and distraught.*]
ME.: Woe to the house once blest in Hellas!   Woe

To thee, old King Sidonian, who didst sow
The dragon-seed on Ares' bloody lea!
Alas, even thy slaves must weep for thee!

LE.: News from the mountain? — Speak! How hath it sped?

ME.: Pentheus, my king, Echion's son, is dead!

LE.:   All hail, God of the Voice,
                  Manifest ever more!

ME.: What say'st thou? — And how strange thy tone, as though
In joy at this my master's overthrow!

LE.:   With fierce joy I rejoice,
                  Child of a savage shore;
For the chains of my prison are broken, and the dread where
    I cowered of yore!

ME.: And deem'st thou Thebes so beggared, so forlorn
Of manhood, as to sit beneath thy scorn?

LE.:   Thebes hath o'er me no sway!
                  None save Him I obey,
Dionysus, Child of the Highest, Him I obey and adore!

ME.: One can forgive thee! — Yet 'tis no fair thing,
Maids, to rejoice in a man's suffering.

LE.:   Speak of the mountain side!
                  Tell us the doom he died,
The sinner smitten to death, even where sin was sore!

ME.: We climbed beyond the utmost habitings
Of Theban shepherds, passed Asopus' springs,
And struck into the land of rock on dim
Cithaeron — Pentheus, and, attending him,
I, and the Stranger who should guide our way.
Then first in a green dell we stopped, and lay,
Lips dumb and feet unmoving, warily
Watching, to be unseen and yet to see.
    A narrow glen it was, by crags o'ertowered,
Torn through by tossing waters, and there lowered
A shadow of great pines over it. And there
The Maenad maidens sate; in toil they were,
Busily glad. Some with an ivy chain
Tricked a worn wand to toss its locks again;
Some, wild in joyance, like young steeds set free,
Made answering songs of mystic melody.
    But my poor master saw not the great band
Before him. "Stranger," cried he, "where we stand
Mine eyes can reach not these false saints of thine.
Mount we the bank, or some high-shouldered pine,
And I shall see their follies clear!" At that
There came a marvel. For the Stranger straight
Touched a great pine-tree's high and heavenward crown,
And lower, lower, lower, urged it down
To the herbless floor. Round like a bending bow,
Or slow wheel's rim a joiner forces to,

So in those hands that tough and mountain stem
Bowed slow — oh, strength not mortal dwelt in them! —
To the very earth.   And there he sat the King,
And slowly, lest it cast him in its spring,
Let back the young and straining tree, till high
It towered again amid the towering sky;
And Pentheus in the branches!   Well, I ween,
He saw the Maenads then, and well was seen!
For scarce was he aloft, when suddenly
There was no Stranger any more with me,
But out of Heaven a Voice — oh, what voice else? —
'Twas He that called!   "Behold, O damosels,
I bring ye him who turneth to despite
Both me and ye, and darkeneth my great Light.
'Tis yours to avenge!"   So spake he, and there came
'Twixt earth and sky a pillar of high flame.
And silence took the air, and no leaf stirred
In all the forest dell.   Thou hadst not heard
In that vast silence any wild thing's cry.
And up they sprang; but with bewildered eye,
Agaze and listening, scarce yet hearing true.
Then came the Voice again.   And when they knew
Their God's clear call, old Cadmus' royal brood,
Up, like wild pigeons startled in a wood,
On flying feet they came, his mother blind,
Agave, and her sisters, and behind
All the wild crowd, more deeply maddened then.
Through the angry rocks and torrent-tossing glen,
Until they spied him in the dark pine-tree:
Then climbed a crag hard by and furiously
Some sought to stone him, some their wands would fling
Lance-wise aloft, in cruel targeting.
But none could strike.   The height o'ertopped their rage,
And there he clung, unscathed, as in a cage
Caught.   And of all their strife no end was found.
Then, "Hither," cried Agave; "stand we round
And grip the stem, my Wild Ones, till we take
This climbing cat-o'-the-mount!   He shall not make
A tale of God's high dances!"   Out then shone
Arm upon arm, past count, and closed upon
The pine, and gripped; and the ground gave, and down
It reeled.   And that high sitter from the crown
Of the green pine-top, with a shrieking cry
Fell, as his mind grew clear, and there hard by
Was horror visible.   'Twas his mother stood
O'er him, first priestess of those rites of blood.
He tore the coif, and from his head away
Flung it, that she might know him, and not slay
To her own misery.   He touched the wild

Cheek, crying: "Mother, it is I, thy child,
Thy Pentheus, born thee in Echion's hall!
Have mercy, Mother!   Let it not befall
Through sin of mine, that thou shouldst slay thy son!"
   But she, with lips a-foam and eyes that run
Like leaping fire, with thoughts that ne'er should be
On earth, possessed by Bacchios utterly,
Stays not nor hears.   Round his left arm she put
Both hands, set hard against his side her foot,
Drew . . . and the shoulder severed! — Not by might
Of arm, but easily, as the God made light
Her hand's essay.   And at the other side
Was Ino rending; and the torn flesh cried,
And on Autonoe pressed, and all the crowd
Of ravening arms.   Yea, all the air was loud
With groans that faded into sobbing breath,
Dim shrieks, and joy, and triumph-cries of death.
And here was borne a severed arm, and there
A hunter's booted foot; white bones lay bare
With rending; and swift hands ensanguinèd
Tossed as in sport the flesh of Pentheus dead.
   His body lies afar.   The precipice
Hath part, and parts in many an interstice
Lurk of the tangled woodland — no light quest
To find.   And, ah, the head!   Of all the rest,
His mother hath it, pierced upon a wand,
As one might pierce a lion's, and through the land,
Leaving her sisters in their dancing place,
Bears it on high!   Yea, to these walls her face
Was set, exulting in her deed of blood,
Calling upon her Bromios, her God,
Her Comrade, Fellow-Render of the Prey,
Her All-Victorious, to whom this day
She bears in triumph . . . her own broken heart!
   For me, after that sight, I will depart
Before Agave comes. — Oh, to fulfil
God's laws, and have no thought beyond His will,
Is man's best treasure.   Aye, and wisdom true,
Methinks, for things of dust to cleave unto!

                    [*The* MESSENGER *departs into the Castle.*]

                    CHORUS [*singing*]:
Some Maidens: Weave ye the dance, and call
                         Praise to God!
                    Bless ye the Tyrant's fall!
                         Down is trod
                    Pentheus, the Dragon's Seed!
                    Wore he the woman's weed?
                    Clasped he his death indeed,

Clasped the rod?
A Bacchanal: Yea, the wild ivy lapt him, and the doomed
   Wild Bull of Sacrifice before him loomed!
Others: Ye who did Bromios scorn,
              Praise Him the more,
         Bacchanals, Cadmus-born;
              Praise with sore
        Agony, yea, with tears!
        Great are the gifts he bears!
        Hands that a mother rears
              Red with gore!

LE.: But stay, Agave cometh!   And her eyes
   Make fire around her, reeling!   Ho, the prize
   Cometh!   All hail, O Rout of Dionyse!
[*Enter from the Mountain* AGAVE, *mad, and to all seeming won-
drously happy, bearing the head of* PENTHEUS *in her hand. The*
CHORUS MAIDENS *stand horror-struck at the sight; the* LEADER, *also
horror-struck, strives to accept it and rejoice in it as the God's deed.*]
AGAVE: Ye from the lands of Morn!
LE.: Call me not; I give praise!
AG.: Lo, from the trunk new-shorn
   Hither a Mountain Thorn
   Bear we!   O Asia-born
   Bacchanals, bless this chase!
LE.: I see. Yea; I see.
   Have I not welcomed thee?
AG.: [*very calmly and peacefully*]:
   He was young in the wildwood:
     Without nets I caught him!
     Nay; look without fear on
       The Lion; I have ta'en him!
LE.: Where in the wildwood?
   Whence have ye brought him?
AG.: Cithaeron. . .
LE.:   Cithaeron?
AG.: The Mountain hath slain him!
LE.: Who first came nigh him?
AG.: I, I, 'tis confessèd!
   And they named me there by him
     Agave the Blessèd!
LE.: Who was next in the band on him?
AG.: The daughters. . .
LE.:   The daughters?
AG.: Of Cadmus laid hand on him.
   But the swift hand that slaughters
   Is mine; mine is the praise!
   Bless ye this day of days!

[*The* LEADER *tries to speak, but is not able;* AGAVE *begins gently stroking the head.*]

AG.: Gather ye now to the feast!

LE.: Feast! — O miserable!

AG.: See, it falls to his breast,
Curling and gently tressed,
The hair of the Wild Bull's crest —
The young steer of the fell!

LE.: Most like a beast of the wild
That head, those locks defiled.

AG. [*lifting up the head, more excitedly*]:
He wakened his Mad Ones,
A Chase-God, a wise God!
He sprang them to seize this!
He preys where his band preys.

LE. [*brooding, with horror*]:
In the trail of thy Mad Ones
Thou tearest thy prize, God!

AG.: Dost praise it?

LE.:   I praise this?

AG.:   Ah, soon shall the land praise!

LE.: And Pentheus, O Mother,
Thy child?

AG.:   He shall cry on
My name as none other,
Bless the spoils of the Lion!

LE.: Aye, strange is thy treasure!

AG.: And strange was the taking!

LE.: Thou art glad?

AG.:   Beyond measure;
Yea, glad in the breaking
Of dawn upon all this land,
By the prize, the prize of my hand!

LE.: Show then to all the land, unhappy one,
The trophy of this deed that thou hast done!

AG.: Ho, all ye men that round the citadel
And shining towers of ancient Thebe dwell,
Come! Look upon this prize, this lion's spoil,
That we have taken — yea, with our own toil,
We, Cadmus' daughters! Not with leathern-set
Thessalian javelins, not with hunter's net,
Only white arms and swift hands' bladed fall.
Why make ye much ado, and boast withal
Your armourers' engines? See, these palms were bare
That caught the angry beast, and held, and tare
The limbs of him! . . . Father! . . . Go, bring to me
My father! . . . Aye, and Pentheus, where is he,
My son? He shall set up a ladder-stair
Against this house, and in the triglyphs there

Nail me this lion's head, that gloriously
I bring ye, having slain him — I, even I!
[*She goes through the crowd towards the Castle, showing the head
and looking for a place to hang it. Enter from the Mountain* CAD-
MUS, *with attendants, bearing the body of* PENTHEUS *on a bier.*]

CA.: On, with your awful burden. Follow me,
   Thralls, to his house, whose body grievously
   With many a weary search at last in dim
   Cithaeron's glens I found, torn limb from limb,
   And through the interweaving forest weed
   Scattered. — Men told me of my daughter's deed,
   When I was just returned within these walls,
   With grey Teiresias, from the Bacchanals.
   And back I hied me to the hills again
   To seek my murdered son. There saw I plain
   Actaeon's mother, ranging where he died,
   Autonoe; and Ino by her side,
   Wandering ghastly in the pine-copses.
      Agave was not there. The rumour is
   She cometh fleet-foot hither. — Ah! 'Tis true;
   A sight I scarce can bend mine eyes unto.

AG. [*turning from the Palace and seeing him*]:
   My father, a great boast is thine this hour.
   Thou hast begotten daughters, high in power
   And valiant above all mankind — yea, all
   Valiant, though none like me! I have let fall
   The shuttle by the loom, and raised my hand
   For higher things, to slay from out thy land
   Wild beasts! See, in mine arms I bear the prize,
   That nailed above these portals it may rise
   To show what things thy daughters did! Do thou
   Take it, and call a feast. Proud art thou now
   And highly favoured in our valiancy!

CA.: O depth of grief, how can I fathom thee
   Or look upon thee! — Poor, poor, bloodstained hand!
   Poor sisters! — A fair sacrifice to stand
   Before God's altars, daughter; yea, and call
   Me and my citizens to feast withal!
      Nay, let me weep — for thine affliction most,
   Then for mine own. All, all of us are lost,
   Not wrongfully, yet is it hard, from one
   Who might have loved — our Bromios, our own!

AG.: How crabbèd and how scowling in the eyes
   Is man's old age! — Would that my son likewise
   Were happy of his hunting, in my way,
   When with his warrior bands he will essay
   The wild beast! — Nay, his violence is to fight
   With God's will! Father, thou shouldst set him right. . .
   Will no one bring him hither, that mine eyes

May look on his, and show him this my prize!

CA.: Alas, if ever ye can know again
 The truth of what ye did, what pain of pain
 That truth shall bring! Or were it best to wait
 Darkened for evermore, and deem your state
 Not misery, though ye know no happiness?

AG.: What seest thou here to chide, or not to bless?

CA. [*after hesitation, resolving himself*]:
 Raise me thine eyes to yon blue dome of air!

AG.: 'Tis done. What dost thou bid me seek for there?

CA.: Is it the same, or changèd in thy sight?

AG.: More shining than before, more heavenly bright!

CA.: And that wild tremor, is it with thee still?

AG. [*troubled*]: I know not what thou sayest; but my will
 Clears, and some change cometh, I know not how.

CA.: Canst hearken then, being changed, and answer, now?

AG.: I have forgotten something; else I could.

CA.: What husband led thee of old from mine abode?

AG.: Echion, whom men named the Child of Earth.

CA.: And what child in Echion's house had birth?

AG.: Pentheus, of my love and his father's bred.

CA.: Thou bearest in thine arms an head — what head?

AG. [*beginning to tremble, and not looking at what she carries*]:
 A lion's — so they all said in the chase.

CA.: Turn to it now — 'tis no long toil — and gaze.

AG.: Ah! But what is it? What am I carrying here?

CA.: Look once upon it full, till all be clear!

AG.: I see . . . most deadly pain! Oh, woe is me!

CA.: Wears it the likeness of a lion to thee?

AG.: No; 'tis the head — O God! — of Pentheus, this!

CA.: Blood-drenched ere thou wouldst know him! Aye, 'tis his.

AG.: Who slew him? — How came I to hold this thing?

CA.: O cruel Truth, is this thine home-coming?

AG.: Answer! My heart is hanging on thy breath!

CA.: 'Twas thou. — Thou and thy sisters wrought his death.

AG.: In what place was it? His own house, or where?

CA.: Where the dogs tore Actaeon, even there.

AG.: Why went he to Cithaeron? What sought he?

CA.: To mock the God and thine own ecstasy.

AG.: But how should we be on the hills this day?

CA.: Being mad! A spirit drove all the land that way.

AG.: 'Tis Dionyse hath done it! Now I see.

CA. [*earnestly*]: Ye wronged Him! Ye denied his deity!

AG. [*turning from him*]: Show me the body of the son I love!

CA. [*leading her to the bier*]: 'Tis here, my child. Hard was the
 quest thereof.

AG.: Laid in due state?

 [*As there is no answer, she lifts the veil of the bier, and sees.*]

                              Oh, if I wrought a sin,
          'Twas mine!   What portion had my child therein?
CA.: He made him like to you, adoring not
          The God; who therefore to one bane hath brought
          You and his body, wrecking all our line,
          And me. Aye, no man-child was ever mine;
          And now this first-fruit of the flesh of thee,
          Sad woman, foully here and frightfully
          Lies murdered!   Whom the house looked up unto,
                                    [*kneeling by the body*]
          O Child, my daughter's child! who heldest true
          My castle walls; and to the folk a name
          Of fear thou wast; and no man sought to shame
          My grey beard, when they knew that thou wast there,
          Else had they swift reward! — And now I fare
          Forth in dishonour, outcast, I, the great
          Cadmus, who sowed the seed-rows of this state
          Of Thebes, and reaped the harvest wonderful.
          O my belovèd, though thy heart is dull
          In death, O still belovèd, and alway
          Belovèd!   Never more, then, shalt thou lay
          Thine hand to this white beard, and speak to me
          Thy "Mother's Father"; ask "Who wrongeth thee?
          Who stints thine honour, or with malice stirs
          Thine heart?   Speak, and I smite thine injurers!"
          But now — woe, woe, to me and thee also,
          Woe to thy mother and her sisters, woe
          Alway! Oh, whoso walketh not in dread
          Of Gods, let him but look on this man dead!
LE.: Lo, I weep with thee. 'Twas but due reward
          God sent on Pentheus; but for thee . . . 'Tis hard.
AG.: My father, thou canst see the change in me,

               *   *   *   *   *
               *   *   *   *   *

[*A page or more has here been torn out of the MS. from which
all our copies of "The Bacchae" are derived. It evidently contained
a speech of Agave (followed presumably by some words of the*
CHORUS*), and an appearance of* DIONYSUS *upon a cloud. He must
have pronounced judgment upon the Thebans in general, and especially upon the daughters of* CADMUS, *have justified his own action,
and declared his determination to establish his godhead. Where
the MS. begins again, we find him addressing* CADMUS.]

               *   *   *   *   *

DI.:

               *   *   *   *   *
               *   *   *   *   *

          And tell of Time, what gifts for thee he bears,
          What griefs and wonders in the winding years.

For thou must change and be a Serpent Thing *
Strange, and beside thee she whom thou didst bring
Of old to be thy bride from Heaven afar,
Harmonia, daughter of the Lord of War.
Yea, and a chariot of kine — so spake
The word of Zeus — thee and thy Queen shall take
Through many lands, Lord of a wild array
Of orient spears. And many towns shall they
Destroy beneath thee, that vast horde, until
They touch Apollo's dwelling, and fulfil
Their doom, back driven on stormy ways and steep.
Thee only and thy spouse shall Ares keep,
And save alive to the Islands of the Blest.
　　Thus speaketh Dionysus, Son confessed
Of no man but of Zeus! — Ah, had ye seen
Truth in the hour ye would not, all had been
Well with ye, and the Child of God your friend!

AG.: Dionysus, we beseech thee! We have sinned!
DI.: Too late! When there was time, ye knew me not!
AG.: We have confessed. Yet is thine hand too hot.
DI.: Ye mocked me, being God; this is your wage.
AG.: Should God be like a proud man in his rage?
DI.: 'Tis as my sire, Zeus, willed it long ago.
AG. [turning from him almost with disdain]:
　　Old Man, the word is spoken; we must go.
DI.: And seeing ye must, what is it that ye wait?
CA.: Child, we are come into a deadly strait,
　　All; thou, poor sufferer, and thy sisters twain,
　　And my sad self. Far off to barbarous men,
　　A grey-haired wanderer, I must take my road.
　　And then the oracle, the doom of God,
　　That I must lead a raging horde far-flown
　　To prey on Hellas; lead my spouse, mine own
　　Harmonia, Ares' child, discorporate
　　And haunting forms, dragon and dragon-mate,
　　Against the tombs and altar-stones of Greece,
　　Lance upon lance behind us; and not cease
　　From toils, like other men, nor dream, nor past
　　The foam of Acheron find my peace at last.
AG.: Father! And I must wander far from thee!
CA.: O Child, why wilt thou reach thine arms to me,
　　As yearns the milk-white swan, when old swans die?
AG.: Where shall I turn me else? No home have I.
　　CA.: I know not; I can help thee not.
　　AG.: Farewell, O home, O ancient tower!
　　　　Lo, I am outcast from my bower,

* Cadmus and Harmonia were to be changed into serpents; they were to lead
a barbarian invasion into Greece, which should prosper until the treasures of Delphi
were touched.

And leave ye for a worser lot.
CA.: Go forth, go forth to misery,
The way Actaeon's father went!
AG.: Father, for thee my tears are spent.
CA.: Nay, Child, 'tis I must weep for thee;
For thee and for thy sisters twain!
AG.: On all this house, in bitter wise,
Our Lord and Master, Dionyse,
Hath poured the utter dregs of pain!
DI.: In bitter wise, for bitter was the shame
Ye did me, when Thebes honoured not my name.
AG.: Then lead me where my sisters be;
Together let our tears be shed,
Our ways be wandered; where no red
Cithaeron waits to gaze on me;
Nor I gaze back; no thyrsus stem,
Nor song, nor memory in the air.
Oh, other Bacchanals be there,
Not I, not I, to dream of them!

[AGAVE *with her group of attendants goes out on the side away from the Mountain.* DIONYSUS *rises upon the Cloud and disappears.*]

CH. [*singing*]: There be many shapes of mystery.
And many things God makes to be,
Past hope or fear.
And the end men looked for cometh not,
And a path is there where no man thought.
So hath it fallen here.

[*Exeunt*]

COMEDY

Comedy was presented at the same festivals and under the same general conditions as was tragedy, and the theatre was the same as that described in the previous introduction. The origins of the form are the subject of an endless debate; but whether the immediate predecessor of comedy was the phallic song (as Aristotle says) or a "beast-comos" with a chorus of revelers disguised as animals is a question which need not be argued here. For our purposes it is sufficient to note two facts which are important in explaining the nature of the earliest Greek comedies which have come down to us. The first of these is that the ultimate ancestor of comedy was undoubtedly some sort of fertility rite; the second is that comedy, as we know it, developed in fifth-century Athens with the encouragement of the growing democracy.

The first statement serves to explain the presence of the constant and startling indecency in early comedy. Primitive man, in his attempts to control nature, often makes use of "sympathetic magic," in which acts performed on or by one object are supposed to affect some other object which the first object symbolizes. Representations of the reproductive organs, the most obvious symbols of fertility, are constantly used in such rites; and the ceremony often includes ribald jests and obscene remarks, as if to stimulate nature to do her utmost. The connection of comedy at Athens with the festival of Dionysus, the god of fertility and wine, helped to preserve the tradition of indecency in comic productions.

Comedy was officially recognized by the state and admitted to the City Dionysia at Athens in 487 B.C., and there is little doubt that it was recognized and encouraged as a democratic measure. Early comedy is filled with outspoken abuse and satire of prominent individuals; it is, of course, characteristic of comedy in all ages to ridicule those who deviate from accepted social standards or who unjustifiably exalt themselves above their fellows, but early Athenian comedy is unrivaled in its freedom of abuse and mockery of real, living persons. Such attacks were, perhaps, found useful in the leveling process which took place in ancient democracies; at any rate, early comedy always tended to represent the views of the average citizen — the "little fellow" — against all abnormal and outstanding individuals, most of whom are presented by the comic poet as charlatans and imposters. Besides this liberty of personal abuse, early comedy assumed for itself the right to discuss and comment on all aspects of civic life, including politics, education, and art. Here the reader should remember that the audience which listened to these comic discussions was the same group of citizens who had, perhaps a day or two before, seriously debated these same questions in the popular assembly, and nothing delighted them more than a witty burlesque of one of the leading issues of the day.

Aristophanes is the only poet of this early comedy whose works have been preserved. We know very little about his life; he was born about 447 B.C., produced his first play in 427 and his last in 386. He thus lived through one of the most critical periods of Athenian history, for which his plays provide a wonderful store of information and a somewhat biased, partisan commentary. The best known of his comedies are the *Clouds,* an attack on the educational theories of the Sophists with a not too unpleasant caricature of Socrates; the *Birds,* a charming fantasy of a Utopia established in the clouds by two nimble-witted Athenians; the *Lysistrata;* and the *Frogs,* a burlesque descent to Hades where we find Aeschylus and Euripides debating over the merits of their tragedies. The comedies of Aristophanes reveal to us a man of tremendous creative powers with a facility in comic invention which is unapproached in literature, a dramatist careless or impatient of dramatic consistency and probability, a poet of great lyric gifts, and a buffoon with an unbounded delight in horseplay and ribald jests.

The *Lysistrata,* one of the best comedies in respect to dramatic structure, was produced in 411 B.C. at a moment when Athens' fortunes were at their lowest point: the disaster of the Sicilian Expedition in 413 had stripped the city of a large part of its manpower, many of the strongest allies had revolted, the Spartans were striving for control of the Aegean Sea with Persian support, and internally the city was on the verge of a revolution. In the midst of this situation Aristophanes produced his last and best plea for peace. The plot of the comedy is extremely simple: the women of Greece, led by the Athenian Lysistrata, unite and agree on a sexstrike to force their husbands to make a just and reasonable peace; despite the frailty of some of the women, the plan succeeds admirably: the strike has the desired effect on the men, as we see in a scene that leaves nothing to the imagination, and the play ends in general rejoicing. The Rabelaisian nature of the plot scarcely conceals the earnestness and anxiety which Aristophanes must have felt; although peace with honour was impossible for Athens at this time, and therefore the play can hardly be considered as a serious piece of political reasoning, none the less the *Lysistrata* reveals a sincere belief that the Greeks must come to terms somehow or be completely ruined. It is important to observe that at the very outset Lysistrata says that her purpose is "to save all Greece," and this note of Panhellenism is splendidly developed at the end of the comedy. The *Lysistrata* is an excellent play with which to begin one's reading of Aristophanes, since its theme and broad humour are readily comprehended by the modern reader without any detailed commentary on the situation which inspired the comedy; a highly successful production which ran in New York for several months in 1930 demonstrated that Aristophanes can speak to moderns as directly as any contemporary playwright.

The various changes which comedy underwent in the fourth century can be summarized briefly: the chorus, whose stately songs and elaborate dances had formed such a large part of the earlier comedies, was gradually reduced in importance until it became a mere interlude between scenes. At the same time the old, out-spoken political criticism disappeared, partly because Athens had lost her place as the dominating power in Greek affairs and politics no longer played so vital a part in the lives of the Athenians, but even more because prose developed as the recognized medium for the discussion of important ideas. Comedy turned for its subjects to mythological burlesques and broad social themes. Late in the century the so-called New Comedy appeared, a comedy of manners reflecting the life of the Athenian *bourgeoisie*. These new plays were more refined and better constructed than the older comedies, but lacked the comic verve and high spirits of Aristophanes. Most of them deal with the difficulties of young love, and the intricate complications of the plot are often solved by a conventional recognition-scene at the end. Until a generation ago we knew these Greek comedies only through the adaptations and translations made by the Roman dramatists, Plautus and Terence; but we now possess several large portions of the Greek text of some of Menander's plays, which were found on papyrus rolls in Egypt. Menander was probably the best of these Greek writers of New Comedy; in later ages he was certainly the most widely read. He was an Athenian of the upper classes, whose life fell in the period of the Macedonian domination of Athens. He was noted for his well-constructed and elaborately complicated plots, his fine delineation of character (although most of his characters are not individuals but the types which New Comedy regularly portrayed), and the excellence and purity of his diction. His interest in ethical situations — that is, in situations which reveal character — combined with his ability to express proverbial wisdom in perfect and memorable phrases made him one of the most often quoted of Greek authors.

The Arbitration, which is printed here, is the most nearly complete of his surviving comedies and gives an excellent picture of his dramatic qualities. Since about half the play is lost and the plot is quite complicated, a summary of the antecedent facts is given here. About ten months before the beginning of the play Pamphila, a respectable Athenian girl, had been assaulted by a drunken youth at a festival; she was subsequently married to Charisius, a decent and likeable young man. Five months after the marriage, during her husband's absence, Pamphila gave birth to a son; the baby was exposed in the fields, but Charisius learned the facts from his officious slave, Onesimus. The young husband, who was really fond of his wife, did not repudiate her; instead when the play opens, he has left his home and entered into a life of extravagant self-indulgence, devoting his attention to Habrotonon, a music-girl whom he had known before his marriage. His actions bring Smicrines, the parsimonious old father of Pamphila, into the picture; he tries without success to get Pamphila to leave her husband. In the meantime, the baby has been discovered by a goatherd and given to a charcoal-burner, Syriscus, and their argument over the trinkets, or "birth-tokens," which were exposed with the baby eventually leads to the only possible happy solution: Charisius will be found to be the father of the baby. The working-out of this somewhat conventional solution can easily be comprehended from the extant portions of the play. While we find nothing uproariously funny in all this, there is plenty of excellent material for high comedy, particularly in the part of Smicrines, whose apoplectic rage becomes increasingly ridiculous as the audience becomes aware of the true state of affairs. It would be extremely one-sided to refuse to see anything funny in Menander because he is not like Aristophanes; the sensible reader will be able to enjoy both poets if he does not demand of one the traits of the other.

ARISTOPHANES

(*ca.* 447–385 B.C.)

LYSISTRATA

Translated into English prose and verse
by CHARLES T. MURPHY

CHARACTERS IN THE PLAY

LYSISTRATA ⎫
CALONICE ⎬ *Athenian women*
MYRRHINE ⎭
LAMPITO, *a Spartan woman*
LEADER OF THE CHORUS OF OLD MEN
CHORUS OF OLD MEN
LEADER OF THE CHORUS OF OLD WOMEN
CHORUS OF OLD WOMEN
ATHENIAN MAGISTRATE
THREE ATHENIAN WOMEN
CINESIAS, *an Athenian, husband of* MYRRHINE
SPARTAN HERALD
SPARTAN AMBASSADORS
ATHENIAN AMBASSADORS
TWO ATHENIAN CITIZENS
CHORUS OF ATHENIANS
CHORUS OF SPARTANS

(As is usual in ancient comedy, the leading characters have significant names. LYSISTRATA is "She who disbands the armies"; MYRRHINE's name is chosen to suggest *myrton,* a Greek word meaning *pudenda muliebria;* LAMPITO is a celebrated Spartan name; CINESIAS, although a real name in Athens, is chosen to suggest a Greek verb *kinein, to move,* then *to make love, to have intercourse,* and the name of his deme, Paionidai, suggests the verb *paiein,* which has about the same significance.)

Structure of the Comedy

1–253, Prologue
254–386, Parodos, or Entrance of the Chorus
387–475, Scene (or Pro-agon)
476–613, Agon,* or Debate
614–705, Parabasis of the Chorus *
706–780, Episode I *
781–828, Stasimon I *
829–1013, Episode II (954–979, Kommos *)
1014–1071, Stasimon II
1072–1188, Episode III
1189–1215, Stasimon III
1216–1321, Exodos *

Produced in 411 B.C.

* See Glossary.

LYSISTRATA

[SCENE: *in Athens, beneath the Acropolis. In the center of the stage is the Propylaea, or gate-way to the Acropolis; to one side is a small grotto, sacred to Pan. The Orchestra represents a slope leading up to the gate-way.*
It is early in the morning. LYSISTRATA *is pacing impatiently up and down.*]

LYS.: If they'd been summoned to worship the God of Wine, or Pan, or to visit the Queen of Love, why, you couldn't have pushed your way through the streets for all the timbrels. But now there's not a single woman here — except my neighbour; here she comes. [*Enter* CALONICE] Good day to you, Calonice.

CAL.: And to you, Lysistrata. [*noticing* LYSISTRATA's *impatient air*] But what ails you? Don't scowl, my dear; it's not becoming to you to knit your brows like that.

LYS. [*sadly*]: Ah, Calonice, my heart aches; I'm so annoyed at us women. For among men we have a reputation for sly trickery —

CAL.: And rightly too, on my word!

LYS.: — but when they were told to meet here to consider a matter of no small importance, they lie abed and don't come.

CAL.: Oh, they'll come all right, my dear. It's not easy for a woman to get out, you know. One is working on her husband, another is getting up the maid, another has to put the baby to bed, or wash and feed it.

LYS.: But after all, there are other matters more important than all that.

CAL.: My dear Lysistrata, just what is this matter you've summoned us women to consider? What's up? Something big?

LYS.: Very big.

CAL. [*interested*]: Is it stout, too?

LYS. [*smiling*]: Yes indeed — both big and stout.

CAL.: What? And the women still haven't come?

LYS.: It's not what you suppose; they'd have come soon enough for *that*. But I've worked up something, and for many a sleepless night I've turned it this way and that.

CAL. [*in mock disappointment*]: Oh, I guess it's pretty fine and slender, if you've turned it this way and that.

LYS.: So fine that the safety of the whole of Greece lies in us women.

CAL.: In us women? It depends on a very slender reed then.

LYS.: Our country's fortunes are in our hands; and whether the Spartans shall perish —

CAL.: Good! Let them perish, by all means.

LYS.: — and the Boeotians shall be completely annihilated.

CAL.: Not completely! Please spare the eels.

LYS.: As for Athens, I won't use any such unpleasant words. But you understand what I mean. But if the women will meet here

— the Spartans, the Boeotians, and we Athenians — then all together we will save Greece.

CAL.: But what could women do that's clever or distinguished? We
just sit around all dolled up in silk robes, looking pretty in our
sheer gowns and evening slippers.

LYS.: These are just the things I hope will save us: these silk robes,
perfumes, evening slippers, rouge, and our chiffon blouses.

CAL.: How so?

LYS.: So never a man alive will lift a spear against the foe —

CAL.: I'll get a silk gown at once.

LYS.: — or take up his shield —

CAL.: I'll put on my sheerest gown!

LYS.: — or sword.

CAL.: I'll buy a pair of evening slippers.

LYS.: Well then, shouldn't the women have come?

CAL.: Come? Why, they should have *flown* here.

LYS.: Well, my dear, just watch: they'll act in true Athenian fashion
— everything too late! And now there's not a woman here from
the shore or from Salamis.

CAL.: They're coming, I'm sure; at daybreak they were laying —
to their oars to cross the straits.

LYS.: And those I expected would be the first to come — the women
of Acharnae — they haven't arrived.

CAL.: Yet the wife of Theagenes means to come: she consulted
Hecate about it. [*seeing a group of women approaching*] But
look! Here come a few. And there are some more over here.
Hurrah! Where do they come from?

LYS.: From Anagyra.

CAL.: Yes indeed! We've raised up quite a stink from Anagyra
anyway.

[*Enter* MYRRHINE *in haste, followed by several other women.*]

MYR. [*breathlessly*]: Have we come in time, Lysistrata? What do
you say? Why so quiet?

LYS.: I can't say much for you, Myrrhine, coming at this hour on
such important business.

MYR.: Why, I had trouble finding my girdle in the dark. But if
it's so important, we're here now; tell us.

LYS.: No. Let's wait a little for the women from Boeotia and the
Peloponnesus.

MYR.: That's a much better suggestion. Look! Here comes Lampito now.

[*Enter* LAMPITO *with two other women.*]

LYS.: Greetings, my dear Spartan friend. How pretty you look, my
dear. What a smooth complexion and well-developed figure!
You could throttle an ox.

LAM.: Faith, yes, I think I could. I take exercises and kick my
heels against my bum. [*She demonstrates with a few steps of the
Spartan "bottom-kicking" dance.*]

LYS.: And what splendid breasts you have.

LAM.: La! You handle me like a prize steer.

LYS.: And who is this young lady with you?

LAM.: Faith, she's an Ambassadress from Boeotia.

LYS.: Oh yes, a Boeotian, and blooming like a garden too.

CAL. [lifting up her skirt]: My word! How neatly her garden's weeded!

LYS.: And who is the other girl?

LAM.: Oh, she's a Corinthian swell.

MYR. [after a rapid examination]: Yes indeed. She swells very nicely [pointing] here and here.

LAM.: Who has gathered together this company of women?

LYS.: I have.

LAM.: Speak up, then. What do you want?

MYR.: Yes, my dear, do tell us what this important matter is.

LYS.: Very well, I'll tell you. But before I speak, let me ask you a little question.

MYR.: Anything you like.

LYS. [earnestly]: Tell me: don't you yearn for the fathers of your children, who are away at the wars? I know you all have husbands abroad.

CAL.: Why, yes; mercy me! my husband's been away for five months in Thrace keeping guard on — Eucrates.

MYR.: And mine for seven whole months in Pylus.

LAM.: And mine, as soon as ever he returns from the fray, readjusts his shield and flies out of the house again.

LYS.: And as for lovers, there's not even a ghost of one left. Since the Milesians revolted from us, I've not even seen an eight-inch dingus * to be a leather consolation for us widows. Are you willing, if I can find a way, to help me end the war?

MYR.: Goodness, yes! I'd do it, even if I had to pawn my dress and — get drunk on the spot!

CAL.: And I, even if I had to let myself be split in two like a flounder.

LAM.: I'd climb up Mt. Taygetus if I could catch a glimpse of peace.

LYS.: I'll tell you, then, in plain and simple words. My friends, if we are going to force our men to make peace, we must do without —

MYR.: Without what? Tell us.

LYS.: Will you do it?

MYR.: We'll do it, if it kills us.

LYS.: Well then, we must do without sex altogether. [general consternation] Why do you turn away? Where go you? Why turn so pale? Why those tears? Will you do it or not? What means this hesitation?

MYR.: I won't do it! Let the war go on.

* Cf. Herodas, A Private Chat, p. 829.

CAL.: Nor I! Let the war go on.

LYS.: So, my little flounder? Didn't you say just now you'd split yourself in half?

CAL.: Anything else you like. I'm willing, even if I have to walk through fire. Anything rather than sex. There's nothing like it, my dear.

LYS. [*to* MYRRHINE]: What about you?

MYR. [*sullenly*]: I'm willing to walk through fire, too.

LYS.: Oh vile and cursed breed! No wonder they make tragedies about us: we're naught but "love-affairs and bassinets." But you, my dear Spartan friend, if you alone are with me, our enterprise might yet succeed. Will you vote with me?

LAM.: 'Tis cruel hard, by my faith, for a woman to sleep alone without her nooky; but for all that, we certainly do need peace.

LYS.: O my dearest friend! You're the only real woman here.

CAL. [*wavering*]: Well, if we do refrain from — [*shuddering*] what you say (God forbid!), would that bring peace?

LYS.: My goodness, yes! If we sit at home all rouged and powdered, dressed in our sheerest gowns, and neatly depilated, our men will get excited and want to take us; but if you don't come to them and keep away, they'll soon make a truce.

LAM.: Aye; Menelaus caught sight of Helen's naked breast and dropped his sword, they say.

CAL.: What if the men give us up?

LYS.: "Flay a skinned dog," as Pherecrates says.

CAL.: Rubbish! These make-shifts are no good. But suppose they grab us and drag us into the bedroom?

LYS.: Hold on to the door.

CAL.: And if they beat us?

LYS.: Give in with a bad grace. There's no pleasure in it for them when they have to use violence. And you must torment them in every possible way. They'll give up soon enough; a man gets no joy if he doesn't get along with his wife.

MYR.: If this is your opinion, we agree.

LAM.: As for our own men, we can persuade them to make a just and fair peace; but what about the Athenian rabble? Who will persuade them not to start any more monkey-shines?

LYS.: Don't worry. We guarantee to convince them.

LAM.: Not while their ships are rigged so well and they have that mighty treasure in the temple of Athene.

LYS.: We've taken good care for that too: we shall seize the Acropolis today. The older women have orders to do this, and while we are making our arrangements, they are to pretend to make a sacrifice and occupy the Acropolis.

LAM.: All will be well then. That's a very fine idea.

LYS.: Let's ratify this, Lampito, with the most solemn oath.

LAM.: Tell us what oath we shall swear.

LYS.: All right. Where's our Policewoman? [*to a Scythian slave*]

What are you gaping at? Set a shield upside-down here in front
of me, and give me the sacred meats.

CAL.: Lysistrata, what sort of an oath are we to take?

LYS.: What oath? I'm going to slaughter a sheep over the shield,
as they do in Aeschylus.*

CAL.: Don't, Lysistrata! No oaths about peace over a shield.

LYS.: What shall the oath be, then?

CAL.: How about getting a white horse somewhere and cutting
out its entrails for the sacrifice?

LYS.: White horse indeed!

CAL.: Well then, how shall we swear?

MYR.: I'll tell you: let's place a large black bowl upside-down and
then slaughter — a flask of Thasian wine. And then let's swear
— not to pour in a single drop of water.

LAM.: Lord! How I like that oath!

LYS.: Someone bring out a bowl and a flask.
[A slave brings the utensils for the sacrifice.]

CAL.: Look, my friends! What a big jar! Here's a cup that
'twould give me joy to handle. [She picks up the bowl.]

LYS.: Set it down and put your hands on our victim. [as CALONICE
places her hands on the flask] O Lady of Persuasion and dear
Loving Cup, graciously vouchsafe to receive this sacrifice from
us women. [She pours the wine into the bowl.]

CAL.: The blood has a good colour and spurts out nicely.

LAM.: Faith, it has a pleasant smell, too.

MYR.: Oh, let me be the first to swear, ladies!

CAL.: No, by our Lady! Not unless you're alloted the first turn.

LYS.: Place all your hands on the cup, and one of you repeat on
behalf of all what I say. Then all will swear and ratify the oath.
I will suffer no man, be he husband or lover,

CAL.: I will suffer no man, be he husband or lover,

LYS.: To approach me all hot and horny. [as CALONICE hesitates]
Say it!

CAL. [slowly and painfully]: To approach me all hot and horny.
O Lysistrata, I feel so weak in the knees!

LYS.: I will remain at home unmated,

CAL.: I will remain at home unmated,

LYS.: Wearing my sheerest gown and carefully adorned,

CAL.: Wearing my sheerest gown and carefully adorned,

LYS.: That my husband may burn with desire for me.

CAL.: That my husband may burn with desire for me.

LYS.: And if he takes me by force against my will,

CAL.: And if he takes me by force against my will,

LYS.: I shall do it badly and keep from moving.

CAL.: I shall do it badly and keep from moving.

LYS.: I will not stretch my slippers toward the ceiling,

CAL.: I will not stretch my slippers toward the ceiling,

LYS.: Nor will I take the posture of the lioness on the knife-handle.

* In the Seven against Thebes.

CAL.: *Nor will I take the posture of the lioness on the knife-handle.*
LYS.: *If I keep this oath, may I be permitted to drink from this cup,*
CAL.: *If I keep this oath, may I be permitted to drink from this cup,*
LYS.: *But if I break it, may the cup be filled with water.*
CAL.: *But if I break it, may the cup be filled with water.*
LYS.: Do you all swear to this?
ALL: I do, so help me!
LYS.: Come then, I'll just consummate this offering. [*She takes a long drink from the cup.*]
CAL. [*snatching the cup away*]: Shares, my dear! Let's drink to our continued friendship.
[*A shout is heard from off-stage.*]
LAM.: What's that shouting?
LYS.: That's what I was telling you: the women have just seized the Acropolis. Now, Lampito, go home and arrange matters in Sparta; and leave these two ladies here as hostages. We'll enter the Acropolis to join our friends and help them lock the gates.
CAL.: Don't you suppose the men will come to attack us?
LYS.: Don't worry about them. Neither threats nor fire will suffice to open the gates, except on the terms we've stated.
CAL.: I should say not! Else we'd belie our reputation as unmanageable pests.
[LAMPITO *leaves the stage. The other women retire and enter the Acropolis through the Propylaea.*]

[*Enter the* CHORUS OF OLD MEN, *carrying fire-pots and a load of heavy sticks.*]
LEADER OF MEN: Onward, Draces, step by step, though your shoulder's aching.
      Cursèd logs of olive-wood, what a load you're making!
FIRST SEMI-CHORUS OF OLD MEN [*singing*]:
      Aye, many surprises await a man who lives to a ripe old age;
      For who could suppose, Strymodorus my lad, that the women
            we've nourished (alas!),
        Who sat at home to vex our days,
        Would seize the holy image here,
        And occupy this sacred shrine,
        With bolts and bars, with fell design,
        To lock the Propylaea?
LEADER: Come with speed, Philourgus, come! to the temple hast'ning.
      There we'll heap these logs about in a circle round them,
      And whoever has conspired, raising this rebellion,
      Shall be roasted, scorched, and burnt, all without exception,
      Doomed by one unanimous vote — but first the wife of Lycon.
SECOND SEMI-CHORUS [*singing*]:
      No, no! by Demeter, while I'm alive, no woman shall mock
           at me.
      Not even the Spartan Cleomenes, our citadel first to seize,

Got off unscathed; for all his pride
And haughty Spartan arrogance,
He left his arms and sneaked away,
Stripped to his shirt, unkempt, unshav'd,
With six years' filth still on him.

LEADER: I besieged that hero bold, sleeping at my station,
Marshalled at these holy gates sixteen deep against him.
Shall I not these cursèd pests punish for their daring,
Burning these Euripides-and-God-detested women?
Aye! or else may Marathon overturn my trophy.

FIRST SEMI-CHORUS [*singing*]:
There remains of my road
Just this brow of the hill;
There I speed on my way.
Drag the logs up the hill, though we've got no ass to help.
(God! my shoulder's bruised and sore!)
Onward still must we go.
Blow the fire! Don't let it go out
Now we're near the end of our road.

ALL [*blowing on the fire-pots*]:
Whew! Whew! Drat the smoke!

SECOND SEMI-CHORUS [*singing*]:
Lord, what smoke rushing forth
From the pot, like a dog
Running mad, bites my eyes!
This must be Lemnos-fire. What a sharp and stinging smoke!
Rushing onward to the shrine
Aid the gods. Once for all
Show your mettle, Laches my boy!
To the rescue hastening all!

ALL [*blowing on the fire-pots*]:
Whew! Whew! Drat the smoke!

[*The chorus has now reached the edge of the orchestra nearest the stage, in front of the Propylaea. They begin laying their logs and fire-pots on the ground.*]

LEADER: Thank heaven, this fire is still alive. Now let's first put down these logs here and place our torches in the pots to catch; then let's make a rush for the gates with a battering-ram. If the women don't unbar the gate at our summons, we'll have to smoke them out.

Let me put down my load. Ouch! That hurts! [*to the audience*] Would any of the generals in Samos like to lend a hand with this log? [*throwing down a log*] Well, *that* won't break my back any more, at any rate. [*turning to his fire-pot*] Your job, my little pot, is to keep those coals alive and furnish me shortly with a red-hot torch.

O mistress Victory, be my ally and grant me to rout these audacious women in the Acropolis.

[*While the men are busy with their logs and fires, the* CHORUS OF OLD WOMEN *enters, carrying pitchers of water.*]

LEADER OF WOMEN: What's this I see? Smoke and flames? Is that a fire ablazing?

Let's rush upon them. Hurry up! They'll find us women ready.

FIRST SEMI-CHORUS OF OLD WOMEN [*singing*]:

With wingèd foot onward I fly,
Ere the flames consume Neodice;
Lest Critylla be overwhelmed
By a lawless, accurst herd of old men.
I shudder with fear. Am I too late to aid them?
At break of the day filled we our jars with water
Fresh from the spring, pushing our way straight through the crowds. Oh, what a din!
Mid crockery crashing, jostled by slave-girls,
Sped we to save them, aiding our neighbours,
Bearing this water to put out the flames.

SECOND SEMI-CHORUS OF OLD WOMEN [*singing*]:

Such news I've heard: doddering fools
Come with logs, like furnace-attendants,
Loaded down with three hundred pounds,
Breathing many a vain, blustering threat,
That all these abhorred sluts will be burnt to charcoal.
O goddess, I pray never may they be kindled;
Grant them to save Greece and our men; madness and war help them to end.
With this as our purpose, golden-plumed Maiden,
Guardian of Athens, seized we thy precinct.
Be my ally, Warrior-maiden,
'Gainst these old men, bearing water with me.

[*The women have now reached their position in the orchestra, and their* LEADER *advances toward the* LEADER OF THE MEN.]

L. WOM.: Hold on there! What's this, you utter scoundrels? No decent, God-fearing citizens would act like this.

L. MEN: Oho! Here's something unexpected: a swarm of women have come out to attack us.

L. WOM.: What, do we frighten you? Surely you don't think we're too many for you. And yet there are ten thousand times more of us whom you haven't even seen.

L. MEN: What say, Phaedria? Shall we let these women wag their tongues? Shan't we take our sticks and break them over their backs?

L. WOM.: Let's set our pitchers on the ground; then if anyone lays a hand on us, they won't get in our way.

L. MEN: By God! If someone gave them two or three smacks on the jaw, like Bupalus, they wouldn't talk so much!

L. WOM.: Go on, hit me, somebody! Here's my jaw! But no other bitch will bite a piece out of you before me.

L. MEN: Silence! or I'll knock out your — senility!

L. WOM.: Just lay one finger on Stratyllis, I dare you!

L. MEN: Suppose I dust you off with this fist? What will you do?

L. WOM.: I'll tear the living guts out of you with my teeth.

L. MEN: No poet is more clever than Euripides: "There is no beast so shameless as a woman."

L. WOM.: Let's pick up our jars of water, Rhodippe.

L. MEN: Why have you come here with water, you detestable slut?

L. WOM.: And why have you come with fire, you funeral vault? To cremate yourself?

L. MEN: To light a fire and singe your friends.

L. WOM.: And I've brought water to put out your fire.

L. MEN: What? You'll put out my fire?

L. WOM.: Just try and see!

L. MEN: I wonder: shall I scorch you with this torch of mine?

L. WOM.: If you've got any soap, I'll give you a bath.

L. MEN: Give *me* a bath, you stinking hag?

L. WOM.: Yes — a bridal bath!

L. MEN: Just listen to her! What crust!

L. WOM.: Well, I'm a free citizen.

L. MEN: I'll put an end to your bawling. [*The men pick up their torches.*]

L. WOM.: You'll never do jury-duty again. [*The women pick up their pitchers.*]

L. MEN: Singe her hair for her!

L. WOM.: Do your duty, water! [*The women empty their pitchers on the men.*]

L. MEN: Ow! Ow! For heaven's sake!

L. WOM.: Is it too hot?

L. MEN: What do you mean "hot"? Stop! What are you doing?

L. WOM.: I'm watering you, so you'll be fresh and green.

L. MEN: But I'm all withered up with shaking.

L. WOM.: Well, you've got a fire; why don't you dry yourself?

[*Enter an Athenian* MAGISTRATE, *accompanied by four Scythian policemen.*]

MAG.: Have these wanton women flared up again with their timbrels and their continual worship of Sabazius? Is this another Adonis-dirge upon the roof-tops — which we heard not long ago in the Assembly? That confounded Demostratus was urging us to sail to Sicily, and the whirling women shouted, "Woe for Adonis!" And then Demostratus said we'd best enroll the infantry from Zacynthus, and a tipsy woman on the roof shrieked, "Beat your breasts for Adonis!" And that vile and filthy lunatic forced his measure through. Such license do our women take.

L. MEN: What if you heard of the insolence of these women here? Besides their other violent acts, they threw water all over us, and we have to shake out our clothes just as if we'd leaked in them.

MAG.: And rightly, too, by God! For we ourselves lead the women astray and teach them to play the wanton; from these roots such notions blossom forth. A man goes into the jeweler's shop and says, "About that necklace you made for my wife, goldsmith: last night, while she was dancing, the fastening-bolt slipped out of the hole. I have to sail over to Salamis today; if you're free, do come around tonight and fit in a new bolt for her." Another goes to the shoe-maker, a strapping young fellow with manly parts, and says, "See here, cobbler, the sandal-strap chafes my wife's little — toe; it's so tender. Come around during the siesta and stretch it a little, so she'll be more comfortable." Now we see the results of such treatment: here I'm a special Councillor and need money to procure oars for the galleys; and I'm locked out of the Treasury by these women.

But this is no time to stand around. Bring up crow-bars there! I'll put an end to their insolence. [*to one of the policemen*] What are you gaping at, you wretch? What are you staring at? Got an eye out for a tavern, eh? Set your crow-bars here to the gates and force them open. [*retiring to a safe distance*] I'll help from over here.

[*The gates are thrown open and* LYSISTRATA *comes out followed by several other women.*]

LYS.: Don't force the gates; I'm coming out of my own accord. We don't need crow-bars here; what we need is good sound common-sense.

MAG.: Is that so, you strumpet? Where's my policeman? Officer, arrest her and tie her arms behind her back.

LYS.: By Artemis, if he lays a finger on me, he'll pay for it, even if he is a public servant.

[*The policeman retires in terror.*]

MAG.: You there, are you afraid? Seize her round the waist — and you, too. Tie her up, both of you!

FIRST WOMAN [*as the second policeman approaches* LYSISTRATA]: By Pandrosus, if you but touch her with your hand, I'll kick the stuffings out of you.

[*The second policeman retires in terror.*]

MAG.: Just listen to that: "kick the stuffings out." Where's another policeman? Tie *her* up first, for her chatter.

SECOND WOMAN: By the Goddess of the Light, if you lay the tip of your finger on her, you'll soon need a doctor.

[*The third policeman retires in terror.*]

MAG.: What's this? Where's my policeman? Seize *her* too. I'll soon stop your sallies.

THIRD WOMAN: By the Goddess of Tauros, if you go near her, I'll tear out your hair until it shrieks with pain.

[*The fourth policeman retires in terror.*]

MAG.: Oh, damn it all! I've run out of policemen. But women must never defeat us. Officers, let's charge them all together. Close up your ranks!

[*The policemen rally for a mass attack.*]

LYS.: By heaven, you'll soon find out that we have four companies of warrior-women, all fully equipped within!

MAG. [*advancing*]: Twist their arms off, men!

LYS. [*shouting*]: To the rescue, my valiant women!
O sellers-of-barley-green-stuffs-and-eggs,
O sellers-of-garlic, ye keepers-of-taverns, and vendors-of-bread,
Grapple! Smite! Smash!
Won't you heap filth on them? Give them a tongue-lashing!
[*The women beat off the policemen.*]
Halt! Withdraw! No looting on the field.

MAG.: Damn it! My police-force has put up a very poor show.

LYS.: What did you expect? Did you think you were attacking slaves? Didn't you know that women are filled with passion?

MAG.: Aye, passion enough — for a good strong drink!

L. MEN: O chief and leader of this land, why spend your words in vain?
Don't argue with these shameless beasts. You know not how we've fared:
A soapless bath they've given us; our clothes are soundly soaked.

L. WOM.: Poor fool! You never should attack or strike a peaceful girl.
But if you do, your eyes must swell. For I am quite content
To sit unmoved, like modest maids, in peace and cause no pain;
But let a man stir up my hive, he'll find me like a wasp.

CHORUS OF MEN [*singing*]:
O God, whatever shall we do with creatures like Womankind?
This can't be endured by any man alive. Question them!
Let us try to find out what this means.
To what end have they seized on this shrine,
This steep and rugged, high and holy,
Undefiled Acropolis?

L. MEN.: Come, put your questions; don't give in, and probe her every statement.
For base and shameful it would be to leave this plot untested.

MAG.: Well then, first of all I wish to ask her this: for what purpose have you barred us from the Acropolis?

LYS.: To keep the treasure safe, so you won't make war on account of it.

MAG.: What? Do we make war on account of the treasure?

LYS.: Yes, and you cause all our other troubles for it, too. Peisander and those greedy office-seekers keep things stirred up so they can find occasions to steal. Now let them do what they like: they'll never again make off with any of this money.

MAG.: What will you do?

LYS.: What a question! We'll administer it ourselves.

MAG.: *You* will administer the treasure?

LYS.: What's so strange in that? Don't we administer the household money for you?

MAG.: That's different.

LYS.: How is it different?

MAG.: We've got to make war with this money.

LYS.: But that's the very first thing: you mustn't make war.

MAG.: How else can we be saved?

LYS.: We'll save you.

MAG.: *You?*

LYS.: Yes, we!

MAG.: God forbid!

LYS.: We'll save you, whether you want it or not.

MAG.: Oh! This is terrible!

LYS.: You don't like it, but we're going to do it none the less.

MAG.: Good God! it's illegal!

LYS.: We *will* save you, my little man!

MAG.: Suppose I don't want you to?

LYS.: That's all the more reason.

MAG.: What business have you with war and peace?

LYS.: I'll explain.

MAG. [*shaking his fist*]: Speak up, or you'll smart for it.

LYS.: Just listen, and try to keep your hands still.

MAG.: I can't. I'm so mad I can't stop them.

FIRST WOMAN: Then you'll be the one to smart for it.

MAG.: Croak to yourself, old hag! [*to* LYSISTRATA] Now then, speak up.

LYS.: Very well. Formerly we endured the war for a good long time with our usual restraint, no matter what you men did. You wouldn't let us say "boo," although nothing you did suited us. But we watched you well, and though we stayed at home we'd often hear of some terribly stupid measure you'd proposed. Then, though grieving at heart, we'd smile sweetly and say, "What was passed in the Assembly today about writing on the treaty-stone?" "What's that to you?" my husband would say. "Hold your tongue!" And I held my tongue.

FIRST WOM.: But I wouldn't have — not I!

MAG.: You'd have been soundly smacked, if you hadn't kept still.

LYS.: So I kept still at home. Then we'd hear of some plan still worse than the first; we'd say, "Husband, how could you pass such a stupid proposal?" He'd scowl at me and say, "If you don't mind your spinning, your head will be sore for weeks. *War shall be the concern of Men.*" *

MAG.: And he was right, upon my word!

LYS.: Why right, you confounded fool, when your proposals were so stupid and we weren't allowed to make suggestions?
"There's not a *man* left in the country," says one. "No, not

* Homer, *Iliad* vi. 492.

one," says another. Therefore all we women have decided in council to make a common effort to save Greece. How long should we have waited? Now, if you're willing to listen to our excellent proposals and keep silence for us in your turn, we still may save you.

MAG.: We men keep silence for you? That's terrible; I won't endure it!

LYS.: Silence!

MAG.: Silence for *you,* you wench, when you're wearing a snood? I'd rather die!

LYS.: Well, if that's all that bothers you — here! take my snood and tie it round your head. [*During the following words the women dress up the* MAGISTRATE *in women's garments.*] And *now* keep quiet! Here, take this spinning-basket, too, and card your wool with robes tucked up, munching on beans. *War shall be the concern of Women!*

L. WOM.: Arise and leave your pitchers, girls; no time is this to falter. We too must aid our loyal friends; our turn has come for action.

CHORUS OF WOMEN [*singing*]:
I'll never tire of aiding them with song and dance; never may
Faintness keep my legs from moving to and fro endlessly.
For I yearn to do all for my friends;
They have charm, they have wit, they have grace,
With courage, brains, and best of virtues —
Patriotic sapience.

L. WOM.: Come, child of manliest ancient dames, offspring of stinging nettles,
Advance with rage unsoftened; for fair breezes speed you onward.

LYS.: If only sweet Eros and the Cyprian Queen of Love shed charm over our breasts and limbs and inspire our men with amorous longing and priapic spasms, I think we may soon be called Peacemakers among the Greeks.

MAG.: What will you do?

LYS.: First of all, we'll stop those fellows who run madly about the Marketplace in arms.

FIRST WOM.: Indeed we shall, by the Queen of Paphos.

LYS.: For now they roam about the market, amid the pots and greenstuffs, armed to the teeth like Corybantes.

MAG.: That's what manly fellows ought to do!

LYS.: But it's so silly: a chap with a Gorgon-emblazoned shield buying pickled herring.

FIRST WOM.: Why, just the other day I saw one of those long-haired dandies who command our cavalry ride up on horseback and pour into his bronze helmet the egg-broth he'd bought from an old dame. And there was a Thracian slinger too, shaking his lance like Tereus; he'd scared the life out of the poor fig-peddler and was gulping down all her ripest fruit.

MAG.: How can you stop all the confusion in the various states and bring them together?

LYS.: Very easily.

MAG.: Tell me how.

LYS.: Just like a ball of wool, when it's confused and snarled: we take it thus, and draw out a thread here and a thread there with our spindles; thus we'll unsnarl this war, if no one prevents us, and draw together the various states with embassies here and embassies there.

MAG.: Do you suppose you can stop this dreadful business with balls of wool and spindles, you nit-wits?

LYS.: Why, if *you* had any wits, you'd manage all affairs of state like our wool-working.

MAG.: How so?

LYS.: First you ought to treat the city as we do when we wash the dirt out of a fleece: stretch it out and pluck and thrash out of the city all those prickly scoundrels; aye, and card out those who conspire and stick together to gain office, pulling off their heads. Then card the wool, all of it, into one fair basket of goodwill, mingling in the aliens residing here, any loyal foreigners, and anyone who's in debt to the Treasury; and consider that all our colonies lie scattered round about like remnants; from all of these collect the wool and gather it together here, wind up a great ball, and then weave a good stout cloak for the democracy.

MAG.: Dreadful! Talking about thrashing and winding balls of wool, when you haven't the slightest share in the war!

LYS.: Why, you dirty scoundrel, we bear more than twice as much as you. First, we bear children and send off our sons as soldiers.

MAG.: Hush! Let bygones be bygones!

LYS.: Then, when we ought to be happy and enjoy our youth, we sleep alone because of your expeditions abroad. But never mind us married women: I grieve most for the maids who grow old at home unwed.

MAG.: Don't men grow old, too?

LYS.: For heaven's sake! That's not the same thing. When a man comes home, no matter how grey he is, he soon finds a girl to marry. But woman's bloom is short and fleeting; if she doesn't grasp her chance, no man is willing to marry her and she sits at home a prey to every fortune-teller.

MAG. [*coarsely*]: But if a man can still get it up —

LYS.: See here, you: what's the matter? Aren't you dead yet? There's plenty of room for you. Buy yourself a shroud and I'll bake you a honey-cake. [*handing him a copper coin for his passage across the Styx*] Here's your fare! Now get yourself a wreath. [*During the following dialogue the women dress up the* MAGISTRATE *as a corpse.*]

FIRST WOM.: Here, take these fillets.

SECOND WOM.: Here, take this wreath.

LYS.: What do you want? What's lacking? Get moving; off to

the ferry! Charon is calling you; don't keep him from sailing.

MAG.: Am I to endure these insults? By God! I'm going straight
to the magistrates to show them how I've been treated.

LYS.: Are you grumbling that you haven't been properly laid out?
Well, the day after tomorrow we'll send around all the usual offerings early in the morning.

[*The* MAGISTRATE *goes out still wearing his funeral decorations.*
LYSISTRATA *and the women retire into the Acropolis.*]

L. MEN.: Wake, ye sons of freedom, wake! 'Tis no time for sleeping.
        Up and at them, like a man! Let us strip for action.

[*The* CHORUS OF MEN *remove their outer cloaks.*]

CHORUS OF MEN [*singing*]:
        Surely there is something here greater than meets the eye;
        For without a doubt I smell Hippias' tyranny.
        Dreadful fear assails me lest certain bands of Spartan men,
        Meeting here with Cleisthenes, have inspired through treachery
        All these god-detested women secretly to seize
        Athens' treasure in the temple, and to stop that pay
                Whence I live at my ease.

L. MEN.: Now isn't it terrible for them to advise the state and chatter
about shields, being mere women?
        And they think to reconcile us with the Spartans — men who
hold nothing sacred any more than hungry wolves. Surely this is
a web of deceit, my friends, to conceal an attempt at tyranny. But
they'll never lord it over me; I'll be on my guard and from now on,
        "The blade I bear   A myrtle spray shall wear." *
I'll occupy the market under arms and stand next to Aristogeiton.
        Thus I'll stand beside him. [*He strikes the pose of the famous
statue of the tyrannicides, with one arm raised.*] And here's my
chance to take this accurst old hag and — [*striking the* LEADER OF
WOMEN] smack her on the jaw!

L. WOM.: You'll go home in such a state your Ma won't recognize
        you!
        Ladies all, upon the ground let us place these garments.

[*The* CHORUS OF WOMEN *remove their outer garments.*]

CHORUS OF WOM. [*singing*]:
        Citizens of Athens, hear useful words for the state.
        Rightly; for it nurtured me in my youth royally.
        As a child of seven years carried I the sacred box;
        Then I was a Miller-maid, grinding at Athene's shrine;
        Next I wore the saffron robe and played Brauronia's Bear;
        And I walked as Basket-bearer, wearing chains of figs,
                As a sweet maiden fair.

L. WOM.: Therefore, am I not bound to give good advice to the city?
        Don't take it ill that I was born a woman, if I contribute some-
thing better than our present troubles. I pay my share; for I con-

* The scolion in honour of Harmodius and Aristogeiton; see p. 998.

tribute MEN. But you miserable old fools contribute nothing, and after squandering our ancestral treasure, the fruit of the Persian Wars, you make no contribution in return. And now, all on account of you, we're facing ruin.

What, muttering, are you? If you annoy me, I'll take this hard, rough slipper and — [*striking the* LEADER OF MEN] smack you on the jaw!

CHORUS OF MEN [*singing*]:
> This is outright insolence! Things go from bad to worse.
> If you're men with any guts, prepare to meet the foe.
> Let us strip our tunics off! We need the smell of male
> Vigour. And we cannot fight all swaddled up in clothes.

[*They strip off their tunics.*]
> Come then, my comrades, on to the battle, ye who once to
>   Leipsydrion came;
> Then ye were MEN. Now call back your youthful vigour.
>   With light, wingèd footstep advance,
>   Shaking old age from your frame.

L. MEN: If any of us give these wenches the slightest hold, they'll stop at nothing: such is their cunning.

They will even build ships and sail against us, like Artemisia. Or if they turn to mounting, I count our Knights as done for: a woman's such a tricky jockey when she gets astraddle, with a good firm seat for trotting. Just look at those Amazons that Micon painted, fighting on horseback against men!

But we must throw them all in the pillory — [*seizing and choking the* LEADER OF WOMEN] grabbing hold of yonder neck!

CHORUS OF WOM. [*singing*]:
> 'Ware my anger! Like a boar 'twill rush upon you men.
> Soon you'll bawl aloud for help, you'll be so soundly trimmed!
> Come, my friends, let's strip with speed, and lay aside these
>   robes;
> Catch the scent of women's rage. Attack with tooth and nail!

[*They strip off their tunics.*]
> Now then, come near me, you miserable man! you'll never eat
>   garlic or black beans again.
> And if you utter a single hard word, in rage I will "nurse" you
>   as once
>   The beetle requited her foe.*

L. WOM.: For you don't worry me; no, not so long as my Lampito lives and our Theban friend, the noble Ismenia.

You can't do anything, not even if you pass a dozen — decrees! You miserable fool, all our neighbours hate you. Why, just the other day when I was holding a festival for Hecate, I invited as a playmate from our neighbours the Boeotians a charming, well-bred Copaic — eel. But they refused to send me one on account of your decrees.

* Aesop's fable (no. 223), *The Eagle and the Beetle*.

And you'll never stop passing decrees until I grab your foot
and — [*tripping up the* LEADER OF MEN] toss you down and break
your neck!

[*Here an interval of five days is supposed to elapse.* LYSISTRATA *comes
out from the Acropolis.*]

L. WOM. [*dramatically*]: Empress of this great emprise and undertaking,
Why come you forth, I pray, with frowning brow?

LYS.: Ah, these cursèd women! Their deeds and female notions
make me pace up and down in utter despair.

L. WOM.: Ah, what sayest thou?

LYS.: The truth, alas! the truth.

L. WOM.: What dreadful tale hast thou to tell thy friends?

LYS.: 'Tis shame to speak, and not to speak is hard.

L. WOM.: Hide not from me whatever woes we suffer.

LYS.: Well then, to put it briefly, we want — laying!

L. WOM.: O Zeus, Zeus!

LYS.: Why call on Zeus? That's the way things are. I can no
longer keep them away from the men, and they're all deserting. I
caught one wriggling through a hole near the grotto of Pan, an-
another sliding down a rope, another deserting her post; and yesterday I found one getting on a sparrow's back to fly off to Orsi-
lochus, and had to pull her back by the hair. They're digging up
all sorts of excuses to get home. Look, here comes one of them
now. [*A woman comes hastily out of the Acropolis.*] Here you!
Where are you off to in such a hurry?

FIRST WOM.: I want to go home. My very best wool is being devoured by moths.

LYS.: Moths? Nonsense! Go back inside.

FIRST WOM.: I'll come right back; I swear it. I just want to lay it out
on the bed.

LYS.: Well, you won't lay it out, and you won't go home, either.

FIRST WOM.: Shall I let my wool be ruined?

LYS.: If necessary, yes. [*Another woman comes out.*]

SECOND WOM.: Oh dear! Oh dear! My precious flax! I left it at
home all unpeeled.

LYS.: Here's another one, going home for her "flax." Come back
here!

SECOND WOM.: But I just want to work it up a little and then I'll be
right back.

LYS.: No indeed! If you start this, all the other women will want
to do the same. [*A third woman comes out.*]

THIRD WOM.: O Eilithyia, goddess of travail, stop my labour till I
come to a lawful spot!

LYS.: What's this nonsense?

THIRD WOM.: I'm going to have a baby — right now!

LYS.: But you weren't even pregnant yesterday.

THIRD WOM.: Well, I am today. O Lysistrata, do send me home to see a midwife, right away.

LYS.: What are you talking about? [*putting her hand on her stomach*] What's this hard lump here?

THIRD WOM.: A little boy.

LYS.: My goodness, what have you got there? It seems hollow; I'll just find out. [*pulling aside her robe*] Why, you silly goose, you've got Athene's sacred helmet there. And you said you were having a baby!

THIRD WOM.: Well, I *am* having one, I swear!

LYS.: Then what's this helmet for?

THIRD WOM.: If the baby starts coming while I'm still in the Acropolis, I'll creep into this like a pigeon and give birth to it there.

LYS.: Stuff and nonsense! It's plain enough what you're up to. You just wait here for the christening of this — helmet.

THIRD WOM.: But I can't sleep in the Acropolis since I saw the sacred snake.

FIRST WOM.: And I'm dying for lack of sleep: the hooting of the owls keeps me awake.

LYS.: Enough of these shams, you wretched creatures. You want your husbands, I suppose. Well, don't you think they want us? I'm sure they're spending miserable nights. Hold out, my friends, and endure for just a little while. There's an oracle that we shall conquer, if we don't split up. [*producing a roll of paper*] Here it is.

FIRST WOM.: Tell us what it says.

LYS.: Listen.
"When in the length of time the Swallows shall gather together,
Fleeing the Hoopoe's amorous flight and the Cockatoo shunning,
Then shall your woes be ended and Zeus who thunders in
    heaven
Set what's below on top — "

FIRST WOM.: What? Are we going to be on top?

LYS.: "But if the Swallows rebel and flutter away from the temple,
Never a bird in the world shall seem more wanton and worth-
    less."

FIRST WOM.: That's clear enough, upon my word!

LYS.: By all that's holy, let's not give up the struggle now. Let's go back inside. It would be a shame, my dear friends, to disobey the oracle.

[*The women all retire to the Acropolis again.*]

CHORUS OF MEN [*singing*]:
    I have a tale to tell,
    Which I know full well.
        It was told me
        In the nursery.

    Once there was a likely lad,
        Melanion they name him;

The thought of marriage made him mad,
   For which I cannot blame him.

So off he went to mountains fair;
   (No women to upbraid him!)
A mighty hunter of the hare,
   He had a dog to aid him.

He never came back home to see
   Detested women's faces.
He showed a shrewd mentality.
   With him I'd fain change places!

ONE OF THE MEN [*to one of the women*]:
   Come here, old dame; give me a kiss.
WOM.: You'll ne'er eat garlic, if you dare!
MAN: I want to kick you — just like this!
WOM.: Oh, there's a leg with bushy hair!
MAN: Myronides and Phormio
   Were hairy — and they thrashed the foe.

   CHORUS OF WOMEN [*singing*]:
   I have another tale,
   With which to assail
     Your contention
     'Bout Melanion.

Once upon a time a man
   Named Timon left our city,
To live in some deserted land.
   (We thought him rather witty.)

He dwelt alone amidst the thorn;
   In solitude he brooded.
From some grim Fury he was born:
   Such hatred he exuded.

He cursed you men, as scoundrels through
   And through, till life he ended.
He couldn't stand the sight of you!
   But women he befriended.

WOM. [*to one of the men*]: I'll smash your face in, if you like.
MAN: Oh no, please don't!   You frighten me.
WOM.: I'll lift my foot — and thus I'll strike.
MAN: Aha!   Look there!   What's that I see?
WOM.: Whate'er you see, you cannot say
   That I'm not neatly trimmed today.

[LYSISTRATA *appears on the wall of the Acropolis.*]
LYS.: Hello!   Hello!   Girls, come here quick!
[*Several women appear beside her.*]
WOM.: What is it?   Why are you calling?

LYS.: I see a man coming: he's in a dreadful state. He's mad with passion. O Queen of Cyprus, Cythera, and Paphos, just keep on this way!

WOM.: Where is the fellow?

LYS.: There, beside the shrine of Demeter.

WOM.: Oh yes, so he is. Who is he?

LYS.: Let's see. Do any of you know him?

MYR.: Yes indeed. That's my husband, Cinesias.

LYS.: It's up to you, now: roast him, rack him, fool him, love him — and leave him! Do everything, except what our oath forbids.

MYR.: Don't worry; I'll do it.

LYS.: I'll stay here to tease him and warm him up a bit. Off with you.

[*The other women retire from the wall. Enter* CINESIAS *followed by a slave carrying a baby.* CINESIAS *is obviously in great pain and distress.*]

CIN. [*groaning*]: Oh-h! Oh-h-h! This is killing me! O God, what tortures I'm suffering!

LYS. [*from the wall*]: Who's that within our lines?

CIN.: Me.

LYS.: A *man*?

CIN. [*pointing*]: A *man*, indeed!

LYS.: Well, go away!

CIN.: Who are you to send me away?

LYS.: The captain of the guard.

CIN.: Oh, for heaven's sake, call out Myrrhine for me.

LYS.: Call Myrrhine? Nonsense! Who are you?

CIN.: Her husband, Cinesias of Paionidai.

LYS. [*appearing much impressed*]: Oh, greetings, friend. Your name is not without honour here among us. Your wife is always talking about you, and whenever she takes an egg or an apple, she says, "Here's to my dear Cinesias!"

CIN. [*quivering with excitement*]: Oh, ye gods in heaven!

LYS.: Indeed she does! And whenever our conversations turn to men, your wife immediately says, "All others are mere rubbish compared with Cinesias."

CIN. [*groaning*]: Oh! Do call her for me.

LYS.: Why should I? What will you give me?

CIN.: Whatever you want. All I have is yours — and you see what I've got!

LYS.: Well then, I'll go down and call her. [*She descends.*]

CIN.: And hurry up! I've had no joy of life ever since she left home. When I go in the house, I feel awful: everything seems so empty and I can't enjoy my dinner. I'm in such a state all the time!

MYR. [*from behind the wall*]: I *do* love him so. But he won't let me love him. No, no! Don't ask me to see him!

CIN.: O my darling, O Myrrhine honey, why do you do this to me? [MYRRHINE *appears on the wall.*] Come down here!

MYR.: No, I won't come down.

CIN.: Won't you come, Myrrhine, when *I* call you?

MYR.: No; you don't want me.

CIN.: *Don't want you?* I'm in agony!

MYR.: I'm going now.

CIN.: Please don't! At least, listen to your baby. [*to the baby*] Here you, call your mamma! [*pinching the baby*]

BABY: Ma-ma! Ma-ma! Ma-ma!

CIN. [*to* MYRRHINE]: What's the matter with you? Have you no pity for your child, who hasn't been washed or fed for five whole days?

MYR.: Oh, poor child; your father pays no attention to you.

CIN.: Come down then, you heartless wretch, for the baby's sake.

MYR.: Oh, what it is to be a mother! I've got to come down, I suppose. [*She leaves the wall and shortly reappears at the gate.*]

CIN. [*to himself*]: She seems much younger, and she has such a sweet look about her. Oh, the way she teases me! And her pretty, provoking ways make me burn with longing.

MYR. [*coming out of the gate and taking the baby*]: O my sweet little angel. Naughty papa! Here, let Mummy kiss you, Mamma's little sweetheart! [*She fondles the baby lovingly.*]

CIN. [*in despair*]: You heartless creature, why do you do this? Why follow these other women and make both of us suffer so? [*He tries to embrace her.*]

MYR.: Don't touch me!

CIN.: You're letting all our things at home go to wrack and ruin.

MYR.: I don't care.

CIN.: You don't care that your wool is being plucked to pieces by the chickens?

MYR.: Not in the least.

CIN.: And you haven't celebrated the rites of Aphrodite for ever so long. Won't you come home?

MYR.: Not on your life, unless you men make a truce and stop the war.

CIN.: Well then, if that pleases you, we'll do it.

MYR.: Well then, if that pleases *you,* I'll come home — afterwards! Right now I'm on oath not to.

CIN.: Then just lie down here with me for a moment.

MYR.: No — [*in a teasing voice*] and yet, I won't say I don't love you.

CIN.: You love me? Oh, do lie down here, Myrrhine dear!

MYR.: What, you silly fool! in front of the baby?

CIN. [*hastily thrusting the baby at the slave*]: Of course not. Here — home! Take him, Manes! [*The slave goes off with the baby.*] See, the baby's out of the way. Now won't you lie down?

MYR.: But where, my dear?

CIN.: Where? The grotto of Pan's a lovely spot.

MYR.: How could I purify myself before returning to the shrine?

CIN.: Easily: just wash here in the Clepsydra.

MYR.: And then, shall I go back on my oath?

CIN.: On my head be it! Don't worry about the oath.

MYR.: All right, then. Just let me bring out a bed.

CIN.: No, don't. The ground's all right.

MYR.: Heavens, no! Bad as you are, I won't let you lie on the bare ground. [*She goes into the Acropolis.*]

CIN.: Why, she really loves me; it's plain to see.

MYR. [*returning with a bed*]: There! Now hurry up and lie down. I'll just slip off this dress. But — let's see: oh yes, I must fetch a mattress.

CIN.: Nonsense! No mattress for me.

MYR.: Yes indeed! It's not nice on the bare springs.

CIN.: Give me a kiss.

MYR. [*giving him a hasty kiss*]: There! [*She goes.*]

CIN. [*in mingled distress and delight*]: Oh-h! Hurry back!

MYR. [*returning with a mattress*]: Here's the mattress; lie down on it. I'm taking my things off now — but — let's see: you have no pillow.

CIN.: I don't *want* a pillow!

MYR.: But I do. [*She goes.*]

CIN.: Cheated again, just like Heracles and his dinner!

MYR. [*returning with a pillow*]: Here, lift your head. [*to herself, wondering how else to tease him*] Is that all?

CIN.: Surely that's all! Do come here, precious!

MYR.: I'm taking off my girdle. But remember: don't go back on your promise about the truce.

CIN.: Hope to die, if I do.

MYR.: You don't have a blanket.

CIN. [*shouting in exasperation*]: *I don't want one!* I WANT TO —

MYR.: Sh-h! There, there, I'll be back in a minute. [*She goes.*]

CIN.: She'll be the death of me with these bed-clothes.

MYR. [*returning with a blanket*]: Here, get up.

CIN.: I've got *this* up!

MYR.: Would you like some perfume?

CIN.: Good heavens, no! I won't have it!

MYR.: Yes, you shall, whether you want it or not. [*She goes.*]

CIN.: O lord! Confound all perfumes anyway!

MYR. [*returning with a flask*]: Stretch out your hand and put some on.

CIN. [*suspiciously*]: By God, I don't much like this perfume. It smacks of shilly-shallying, and has no scent of the marriage-bed.

MYR.: Oh dear! This is Rhodian perfume I've brought.

CIN.: It's quite all right, dear. Never mind.

MYR.: Don't be silly! [*She goes out with the flask.*]

CIN.: Damn the man who first concocted perfumes!

MYR. [*returning with another flask*]: Here, try this flask.

CIN.: I've got another one all ready for you. Come, you wretch, lie down and stop bringing me things.

MYR.: All right; I'm taking off my shoes. But, my dear, see that you vote for peace.

CIN. [*absently*]: I'll consider it. [MYRRHINE *runs away to the Acrop-*

olis.] I'm ruined! The wench has skinned me and run away!
[*chanting, in tragic style*] Alas! Alas! Deceived, deserted by this
fairest of women, whom shall I — lay? Ah, my poor little child,
how shall I nurture thee? Where's Cynalopex? I needs must
hire a nurse!

L. MEN [*chanting*]: Ah, wretched man, in dreadful wise beguiled,
bewrayed, thy soul is sore distressed. I pity thee, alas! alas! What
soul, what loins, what liver could stand this strain? How firm and
unyielding he stands, with naught to aid him of a morning.

CIN.: O lord! O Zeus! What tortures I endure!

L. MEN: This is the way she's treated you, that vile and cursèd wanton.

L. WOM.: Nay, not vile and cursèd, but sweet and dear.

L. MEN: Sweet, you say? Nay, hateful, hateful!

CIN.: Hateful indeed! O Zeus, Zeus!
Seize her and snatch her away,
Like a handful of dust, in a mighty,
Fiery tempest! Whirl her aloft, then let her drop
Down to the earth, with a crash, as she falls —
On the point of this waiting
Thingummybob! [*He goes out.*]

[*Enter a Spartan* HERALD, *in an obvious state of excitement, which he
is doing his best to conceal.*]

HER.: Where can I find the Senate or the Prytanes? I've got an important message. [*The Athenian* MAGISTRATE *enters.*]

MAG.: Say there, are you a man or Priapus?

HER. [*in annoyance*]: I'm a herald, you lout! I've come from Sparta
about the truce.

MAG.: Is that a spear you've got under your cloak?

HER.: No, of course not!

MAG.: Why do you twist and turn so? Why hold your cloak in
front of you? Did you rupture yourself on the trip?

HER.: By gum, the fellow's an old fool.

MAG. [*pointing*]: Why, you dirty rascal, you're all excited.

HER.: Not at all. Stop this tom-foolery.

MAG.: Well, what's that I see?

HER.: A Spartan message-staff.

MAG.: Oh, certainly! That's just the kind of message-staff I've got.
But tell me the honest truth: how are things going in Sparta?

HER.: All the land of Sparta is up in arms — and our allies are up,
too. We need Pellene.

MAG.: What brought this trouble on you? A sudden Panic?

HER.: No, Lampito started it and then all the other women in Sparta
with one accord chased their husbands out of their beds.

MAG.: How do you feel?

HER.: Terrible. We walk around the city bent over like men lighting matches in a wind. For our women won't let us touch them
until we all agree and make peace throughout Greece.

MAG.: This is a general conspiracy of the women; I see it now. Well, hurry back and tell the Spartans to send ambassadors here with full powers to arrange a truce. And I'll go tell the Council to choose ambassadors from here; I've got a little something here that will soon persuade them!

HER.: I'll fly there; for you've made an excellent suggestion.

[*The* HERALD *and the* MAGISTRATE *depart on opposite sides of the stage.*]

L. MEN: No beast or fire is harder than womankind to tame,
   Nor is the spotted leopard so devoid of shame.

L. WOM.: Knowing this, you dare provoke us to attack?
   I'd be your steady friend, if you'd but take us back.

L. MEN: I'll never cease my hatred keen of womankind.

L. WOM.: Just as you will. But now just let me help you find
   That cloak you threw aside. You look so silly there
   Without your clothes. Here, put it on and don't go bare.

L. MEN: That's very kind, and shows you're not entirely bad.
   But I threw off my things when I was good and mad.

L. WOM.: At last you seem a man, and won't be mocked, my lad.
   If you'd been nice to me, I'd take this little gnat
   That's in your eye and pluck it out for you, like that.

L. MEN: So that's what's bothered me and bit my eye so long!
   Please dig it out for me. I own that I've been wrong.

L. WOM.: I'll do so, though you've been a most ill-natured brat.
   Ye gods! See here! A huge and monstrous little gnat!

L. MEN: Oh, how that helps! For it was digging wells in me.
   And now it's out, my tears are flowing fast and free.

L. WOM.: Here, let me wipe them off, although you're such a knave,
   And kiss me.

L. MEN: No!

L. WOM.:   Whate'er you say, a kiss I'll have. [*She kisses him.*]

L. MEN: Oh, confound these women! They've a coaxing way about
   them.
   He was wise and never spoke a truer word, who said,
   "We can't live with women, but we cannot live without them."
   Now I'll make a truce with you. We'll fight no more; instead,
   I will not injure you if you do me no wrong.
   And now let's join our ranks and then begin a song.

COMBINED CHORUS [*singing*]:
   Athenians, we're not prepared,
   To say a single ugly word
   About our fellow-citizens.
  Quite the contrary: we desire but to say and to do
  Naught but good. Quite enough are the ills now on hand.

   Men and women, be advised:
    If anyone requires
   Money — minae two or three —,
    We've got what he desires.

My purse is yours, on easy terms:
  When Peace shall reappear,
Whate'er you've borrowed will be due.
  So speak up without fear.

You needn't pay me back, you see,
  If you can get a cent from me!

We're about to entertain
  Some foreign gentlemen;
We've soup and tender, fresh-killed pork.
  Come round to dine at ten.

Come early; wash and dress with care,
  And bring the children, too.
Then step right in, no "by your leave."
  We'll be expecting you.

Walk in as if you owned the place.
You'll find the door — shut in your face!

[*Enter a group of Spartan Ambassadors; they are in the same desperate condition as the Herald in the previous scene.*]

LEADER OF CHORUS: Here come the envoys from Sparta, sprouting long beards and looking for all the world as if they were carrying pig-pens in front of them.
    Greetings, gentlemen of Sparta. Tell me, in what state have you come?

SPARTAN: Why waste words? You can plainly see what state we've come in!

L. CHO.: Wow! You're in a pretty high-strung condition, and it seems to be getting worse.

SPA.: It's indescribable. Won't someone please arrange a peace for us — in any way you like.

L. CHO.: Here come our own, native ambassadors, crouching like wrestlers and holding their clothes in front of them; this seems an athletic kind of malady.

[*Enter several Athenian Ambassadors.*]

ATH.: Can anyone tell us where Lysistrata is? You see our condition.

L. CHO.: Here's another case of the same complaint. Tell me, are the attacks worse in the morning?

ATH.: No, we're always afflicted this way. If someone doesn't soon arrange this truce, you'd better not let me get my hands on — Cleisthenes!

L. CHO.: If you're smart, you'll arrange your cloaks so none of the fellows who smashed the Hermae can see you.

ATH.: Right you are; a very good suggestion.

SPA.: Aye, by all means. Here, let's hitch up our clothes.

ATH.: Greetings, Spartan. We've suffered dreadful things.

SPA.: My dear fellow, we'd have suffered still worse if one of those fellows had seen us in this condition.

ATH.: Well, gentlemen, we must get down to business. What's your errand here?

SPA.: We're ambassadors about peace.

ATH.: Excellent; so are we. Only Lysistrata can arrange things for us; shall we summon her?

SPA.: Aye, and Lysistratus too, if you like.

L. CHO.: No need to summon her, it seems. She's coming out of her own accord.

[*Enter* LYSISTRATA *accompanied by a statue of a nude female figure, which represents Reconciliation.*]

> Hail, noblest of women; now must thou be
> A judge shrewd and subtle, mild and severe,
> Be sweet yet majestic: all manners employ.
> The leaders of Hellas, caught by thy love-charms,
> Have come to thy judgment, their charges submitting.

LYS.: This is no difficult task, if one catch them still in amorous passion, before they've resorted to each other. But I'll soon find out. Where's Reconciliation? Go, first bring the Spartans here, and don't seize them rudely and violently, as our tactless husbands used to do, but as befits a woman, like an old, familiar friend; if they won't give you their hands, take them however you can. Then go fetch these Athenians here, taking hold of whatever they offer you. Now then, men of Sparta, stand here beside me, and you Athenians on the other side, and listen to my words.

I am a woman, it is true, but I have a mind; I'm not badly off in native wit, and by listening to my father and my elders, I've had a decent schooling.

Now I intend to give you a scolding which you both deserve. With one common font you worship at the same altars, just like brothers, at Olympia, at Thermopylae, at Delphi — how many more might I name, if time permitted; — and the Barbarians stand by waiting with their armies; yet you are destroying the men and towns of Greece.

ATH.: Oh, this tension is killing me!

LYS.: And now, men of Sparta, — to turn to you — don't you remember how the Spartan Pericleidas came here once as a suppliant, and sitting at our altar, all pale with fear in his crimson cloak, begged us for an army? For all Messene had attacked you and the god sent an earthquake too? Then Cimon went forth with four thousand hoplites and saved all Lacedaemon. Such was the aid you received from Athens, and now you lay waste the country which once treated you so well.

ATH. [*hotly*]: They're in the wrong, Lysistrata, upon my word, they are!

SPA. [*absently, looking at the statue of Reconciliation*]: We're in the wrong. What hips! How lovely they are!

LYS.: Don't think I'm going to let you Athenians off. Don't you remember how the Spartans came in arms when you were wearing the rough, sheepskin cloak of slaves and slew the host of Thessalians, the comrades and allies of Hippias? Fighting with you on that day, alone of all the Greeks, they set you free and instead of a sheepskin gave your folk a handsome robe to wear.

SPA. [*looking at* LYSISTRATA]: I've never seen a more distinguished woman.

ATH. [*looking at Reconciliation*]: I've never seen a more voluptuous body!

LYS.: Why then, with these many noble deeds to think of, do you fight each other? Why don't you stop this villainy? Why not make peace? Tell me, what prevents it?

SPA. [*waving vaguely at Reconciliation*]: We're willing, if you're willing to give up your position on yonder flank.

LYS.: What position, my good man?

SPA.: Pylus; we've been panting for it for ever so long.

ATH.: No, by God! You shan't have it!

LYS.: Let them have it, my friend.

ATH.: Then what shall we have to rouse things up?

LYS.: Ask for another place in exchange.

ATH.: Well, let's see: first of all [*pointing to various parts of Reconciliation's anatomy*] give us Echinus here, this Maliac Inlet in back there, and these two Megarian legs.

SPA.: No, by heavens! You can't have *everything,* you crazy fool!

LYS.: Let it go. Don't fight over a pair of legs.

ATH. [*taking off his cloak*]: I think I'll strip and do a little planting now.

SPA. [*following suit*]: And I'll just do a little fertilizing, by gosh!

LYS.: Wait until the truce is concluded. Now if you've decided on this course, hold a conference and discuss the matter with your allies.

ATH.: Allies? Don't be ridiculous! They're in the same state we are. Won't all our allies want the same thing we do — to jump in bed with their women?

SPA.: Ours will, I know.

ATH.: Especially the Carystians, by God!

LYS.: Very well. Now purify yourselves, that your wives may feast and entertain you in the Acropolis; we've provisions by the basketfull. Exchange your oaths and pledges there, and then each of you may take his wife and go home.

ATH.: Let's go at once.

SPA.: Come on, where you will.

ATH.: For God's sake, let's hurry!

[*They all go into the Acropolis.*]

CHO. [*singing*]:
> Whate'er I have of coverlets
> And robes of varied hue

And golden trinkets, — without stint
  I offer them to you.

Take what you will and bear it home,
  Your children to delight,
Or if your girl's a Basket-maid;
  Just choose whate'er's in sight.

There's naught within so well secured
  You cannot break the seal
And bear it off; just help yourselves;
  No hesitation feel.

But you'll see nothing, though you try,
Unless you've sharper eyes than I!

If anyone needs bread to feed
  A growing family,
I've lots of wheat and full-grown loaves;
  So just apply to me.

Let every poor man who desires
  Come round and bring a sack
To fetch the grain; my slave is there
  To load it on his back.

But don't come near my door, I say:
Beware the dog, and stay away!

[*An* ATHENIAN *enters carrying a torch; he knocks at the gate.*]

ATH.: Open the door! [*to the* CHORUS, *which is clustered around the gate*] Make way, won't you! What are you hanging around for? Want me to singe you with this torch? [*to himself*] No; it's a stale trick, I won't do it! [*to the audience*] Still, if I've got to do it to please *you,* I suppose I'll have to take the trouble.

[*A* SECOND ATHENIAN *comes out of the gate.*]

SEC. ATH.: And I'll help you.

FIR. ATH. [*waving his torch at the* CHORUS]: Get out! Go bawl your heads off! Move on there, so the Spartans can leave in peace when the banquet's over.

[*They brandish their torches until the* CHORUS *leaves the Orchestra.*]

SEC. ATH.: I've never seen such a pleasant banquet: the Spartans are charming fellows, indeed they are! And we Athenians are very witty in our cups.

FIR. ATH.: Naturally: for when we're sober we're never at our best. If the Athenians would listen to me, we'd always get a little tipsy on our embassies. As things are now, we go to Sparta when we're sober and look around to stir up trouble. And then we don't hear what they say — and as for what they *don't* say, we have all sorts of suspicions. And then we bring back varying reports about the mission. But this time everything is pleasant; even if a man should

sing the Telamon-song when he ought to sing "Cleitagoras," we'd
praise him and swear it was excellent.

[*The two* CHORUSES *return, as a* CHORUS OF ATHENIANS *and a* CHORUS
OF SPARTANS.]

Here they come back again.   Go to the devil, you scoundrels!

SEC. ATH.: Get out, I say!   They're coming out from the feast.

[*Enter the Spartan and Athenian envoys, followed by* LYSISTRATA *and
all the women.*]

SPA. [*to one of his fellow-envoys*]: My good fellow, take up your
pipes; I want to do a fancy two-step and sing a jolly song for the
Athenians.

ATH.: Yes, do take your pipes, by all means.   I'd love to see you
dance.

SPA. [*singing and dancing with the* CHORUS OF SPARTANS]:
These youths inspire
To song and dance, O Memory;
Stir up my Muse, to tell how we
And Athens' men, in our galleys clashing
At Artemisium, 'gainst foemen dashing
    In godlike ire,
Conquered the Persian and set Greece free.

Leonidas
Led on his valiant warriors
Whetting their teeth like angry boars.
Abundant foam on their lips was flow'ring,
A stream of sweat from their limbs was show'ring.
    The Persian was
Numberless as the sand on the shores.

O Huntress who slayest the beasts in the glade,
O Virgin divine, hither come to our truce,
Unite us in bonds which all time will not loose.
Grant us to find in this treaty, we pray,
An unfailing source of true friendship today,
And all of our days, helping us to refrain
From weaseling tricks which bring war in their train.
    Then hither, come hither!   O huntress maid.

LYS.: Come then, since all is fairly done, men of Sparta, lead away
your wives, and you, Athenians, take yours.   Let every man stand
beside his wife, and every wife beside her man, and then, to celebrate our fortune, let's dance.   And in the future, let's take care
to avoid these misunderstandings.

CHORUS OF ATHENIANS [*singing and dancing*]:
Lead on the dances, your graces revealing.
Call Artemis hither, call Artemis' twin,
Leader of dances, Apollo the Healing,
Kindly God — hither! let's summon him in!

Nysian Bacchus call,
Who with his Maenads, his eyes flashing fire,
Dances, and last of all
Zeus of the thunderbolt flaming, the Sire,
And Hera in majesty,
Queen of prosperity.

Come, ye Powers who dwell above
Unforgetting, our witnesses be
Of Peace with bonds of harmonious love —
The Peace which Cypris has wrought for me.
Alleluia! Io Paean!
Leap in joy — hurrah! hurrah!
'Tis victory — hurrah! hurrah!
Euoi! Euoi! Euai! Euai!

LYS. [to the Spartans]: Come now, sing a new song to cap ours.

CHORUS OF SPARTANS [singing and dancing]:
Leaving Taygetus fair and renown'd,
Muse of Laconia, hither come:
Amyclae's god in hymns resound,
Athene of the Brazen Home,
And Castor and Pollux, Tyndareus' sons,
Who sport where Eurotas murmuring runs.

On with the dance! Heia! Ho!
All leaping along,
Mantles a-swinging as we go!
Of Sparta our song.
There the holy chorus ever gladdens,
There the beat of stamping feet,
As our winsome fillies, lovely maidens,
Dance, beside Eurotas' banks a-skipping, —
Nimbly go to and fro
Hast'ning, leaping feet in measures tripping,
Like the Bacchae's revels, hair a-streaming.
Leda's child, divine and mild,
Leads the holy dance, her fair face beaming.
On with the dance! as your hand
Presses the hair
Streaming away unconfined.
Leap in the air
Light as the deer; footsteps resound
Aiding our dance, beating the ground.
Praise Athene, Maid divine, unrivalled in her might,
Dweller in the Brazen Home, unconquered in the fight.
[All go out singing and dancing.]

MENANDER

(343/2–292/1 B.C.)

THE ARBITRATION

Translated by L. A. POST

CHARACTERS IN THE PLAY

SYRISCUS, *a charcoal-burner*
DAVUS, *a goatherd*
SMICRINES, *an Athenian business man*
ONESIMUS, *slave of* CHARISIUS
HABROTONON, *harp-girl of* CHARISIUS
PAMPHILA, *daughter of* SMICRINES *and wife of* CHARISIUS
CHARISIUS, *a young Athenian, son-in-law of* SMICRINES
SOPHRONA, *the old nurse of* PAMPHILA
CHAERESTRATUS, *neighbour of* CHARISIUS
SIMIAS, *a friend of* CHARISIUS
CARIO, *a cook*

THE ARBITRATION

ACT I

Of the first act of the play we possess very little. We can, how-ever, guess at the general course of the action. There was prob-ably a prologue which explained the facts that have already been mentioned. There was a good deal of jesting on the part of the cook. He is a loud-mouthed drunken railer. He knows all the back-stairs gossip of Athens and retails it boisterously with the embroidery of a crude imagination. He insists on knowing why Charisius, who has recently married, is away from home with the harp-girl Habrotonon, and Onesimus finds his companion's free and easy ways rather trying. He is too discreet to tell all he knows. Finally Chaerestratus comes from his house and orders the cook to go inside and prepare lunch. Onesimus also departs, but Chaerestratus remains to observe a new arrival. This is Smicrines, the father of Pamphila. He is as unattractive as she is charming. He is the strict old man, who has no patience with weakness or extravagance, and insists always on the letter of the bond. On the present occasion he is in a state of great excite-ment, because he has heard in the city of Charisius' extravagant expenditures on cooks and harp-girls. "Twelve drachmas a day to a slave dealer for a girl! Why, a man could live on that for a month and six days besides!" "Yes," says Chaerestratus in a sarcastic aside, "it would keep him alive on poor-house soup." Smicrines finally goes into Charisius' house to see what Pamphila has to say about her husband's conduct. Thereupon Chaeres-tratus retires into his own house to inform Charisius that his father-in-law has arrived and is likely to make trouble.

ACT II

At the beginning of the second act Smicrines reappears. Knowing nothing of Pamphila's baby, he is indignant at Chari-sius' behaviour and sees no justification for it. He is not quite sure what to do, but is determined to do something. He is about to set out for the city to ask advice, when he is confronted with a strange situation. Two slaves, rudely clad in skins, are in-volved in a dispute. They come on the stage arguing. Syriscus, the charcoal-burner, is accompanied by his wife, who carries a baby. He is eloquently expostulating with the sullen Davus, a goatherd, who maintains his case with equal heat.

SY.: You're afraid of a fair trial.

DA.: It's a put-up game of yours, curse you.

SY.: You've no right to keep what's not yours. We must get some-one to arbitrate.

DA.: I'm willing; let's argue it out.

SY.: Who's to decide it?

DA.: Anyone will do for me. It serves me right though. Why did I give you anything?

SY. [*indicating* SMICRINES]: How about that man? Does he suit you as a judge?

DA.: Yes, good luck to it.

SY. [*to* SMICRINES]: If you please, sir, could you spare us a minute?

SM. [*testily*]: You? What for?

SY.: We have a disagreement about something.

SM.: Well, what's that to me?

SY.: We are looking for someone to decide it impartially. So if nothing prevents, do settle our dispute.

SM.: Confound the rascals. Do you mean to say that you go about arguing cases, you fellows in goatskins?

SY.: Suppose we do. It won't take long and it's no trouble to understand the case. Grant the favour, sir. Don't be contemptuous, please. Justice should rule at every moment, everywhere. Whoever happens to come along should make this cause his own concern, for it's a common interest that touches all men's lives.

DA. [*alarmed at this burst of eloquence*]: I've got quite an orator on my hands. Why did I give him anything?

SM.: Well, tell me. Will you abide by my decision?

SY.: Absolutely.

SM.: I'll hear the case. Why shouldn't I? [*Turning to the sullen* DAVUS] You speak first, you that aren't saying anything.

DA. [*sure of his case but not very sure of his words, which come slowly enough to leave room for frequent pauses*]: I'll go back a bit first — not just my dealings with this fellow — so you'll understand the transaction. In the scrubland not far from here I was watching my flocks, sir, perhaps a month ago to-day, all by myself, when I found a baby left deserted there with a necklace and some such trinkets as these.

[*He shows some trinkets.*]

SY.: The dispute is about them.

DA.: He won't let me speak.

SM. [*to* SYRISCUS]: If you interrupt, I'll take my stick to you.

DA.: And serve him right too.

SM.: Go on.

DA.: I will. I picked it up and went back home with it and was going to raise it. That's what I intended then. In the night, though, like every one else, I thought it over to myself and argued it out: "Why should I bring up a baby and have all that trouble? Where am I to get all that money to spend? What do I want with all that worry?" That's the state I was in. Early next morning I was tending my flock again, when along came this fellow, he's a charcoal-burner, to this same spot to get out stumps there. He had made friends with me before that. So we got talking together and he saw that I was gloomy and said: "Why so thoughtful, Davus?"

"Why indeed," said I, "I meddle with what doesn't concern me."
So I tell him what had happened, how I found the baby and how
I picked it up. And he broke in at once, before I had finished my
story, and began entreating me: "As you hope for luck, Davus," he
kept saying every other thing, "do give me the baby, as you hope
for fortune, as you hope for freedom. I've a wife, you see," says he,
"and she had a baby, but it died." Meaning this woman who is
here now with the child. Did you entreat me, Syriscus?

Y.: I admit it.

A.: He spent the whole day at it. Finally I yielded to his coaxing
and teasing and promised him the child and he went off wishing me
a million blessings. When he took it too, he kissed my hands.
Didn't you?

Y.: Yes, I did.

A.: He took himself off. Just now he and his wife happened on me
and all of a sudden he claims the objects that I found with the child
— it was some small matters, tomfoolery, nothing really — and says
he's cheated because I don't consent and lay claim to them myself.
I say, though, that he ought to be thankful for the share he did get
by his entreaties. Though I don't give him all of it, that's no reason
why I should have to stand examination. Even if he had found it
while we were going about together and it had been a case of share-
your-luck, why he would have got part and I the rest. But I was
alone when I found it and you weren't even there and yet you think
you ought to have all and I nothing.

To conclude, I have given you something of mine. If you are
satisfied with it, you may still keep it; but if you aren't satisfied and
have changed your mind, then give it back again to me and take
neither more nor less than your due. But for you to have the whole
business, part with my consent, the rest forced from me, is not fair.
That's all I have to say.

Y. [keeping a respectful eye on the stick]: Is that all?

M.: Didn't you hear what he said? He has finished.

Y. [His words come fast enough but his flights of eloquence have a
tendency to sink unexpectedly. However, his quick turns and lively
gestures supply any deficiencies and DAVUS is left stranded just
where he thought himself most secure.]: Good. Then I'll take my
turn. He was alone when he found the baby. He is right about
everything that he has mentioned. The facts are as stated, sir. I
dispute nothing. I got the child from him by entreating and imploring him. For his story is true.

Information came to me from a certain shepherd that he had been
talking to, one of his fellow-workmen, to the effect that he had also
found at the same time some trinkets. [With a dramatic gesture
toward the infant] To claim these has come, sir, in person, my client
here. Give me the child, wife. [Taking the baby from his wife's
arms] This infant claims from you his necklace and his tokens,
Davus. He says that they were placed with him for his adornment,
not for your bread and butter. I too support his claim, since I have

been made his guardian. You made me so yourself, when you gave him to me. [*Appealing to* SMICRINES] It is now your part, sir, it seems to me, to decide whether the trinkets, gold or whatever they are, are to be kept for the child as his mother, whoever she was, intended them, until he grows up, or whether the very man who robbed him is to keep another's property, just because he found it first. But why then didn't I claim them when I got the baby? Because I wasn't entitled yet to speak for him. Nor have I come now to claim anything for myself. Share your luck indeed! Never call it finding where there's a party wronged. Here is no find appropriated, but a fund misappropriated.

Think of this too, sir. Perhaps this babe is better born than we. He may, though brought up among labourers, look down on our condition, seek his own native level, have pluck to ply some noble occupation, hunt lions, bear arms, take part in races at the games. You have seen actors, I am sure, and all these things are familiar to you. A certain Neleus and Pelias, the famous ones, were found by an aged goatherd clad in a goatskin just like mine. When he saw that they were nobler born than he, he told them all, how he found and picked them up, and he gave them a wallet full of tokens and from that they found out everything about themselves for certain and now became kings, who once were goatherds. Yes, but if some Davus had stolen and sold these tokens to get twelve shillings for himself, they would have passed their lives in ignorance of their great and noble birth. Surely, sir, it is not right for me to sustain his body, while Davus seizes and destroys his hope of preserving his identity. Men have been kept by means of tokens from marrying their sisters, have found and rescued a mother, have saved a brother's life. Life is full of pitfalls for us all, sir. We must use foresight to avoid them, must look a long way ahead to find the means.

But give him back, says he, if you're not satisfied. There he thinks he has something solid to fall back on. He's wrong. It's not right for you, when you are required to restore something that belongs to the child, to claim him as well to boot — so that you can do your thieving more undisturbed another time, now that chance has preserved something that belongs to him. I have finished. Give your decision, whatever you believe to be right.

SM.: Why, it's easily decided. Everything that was left with the child belongs to him. That's my verdict.

DA. [*expectantly*]: Good. But the child?

SM.: By Zeus, I'll not assign him to you, who have been trying to wrong him, but rather to the one who came to his aid and prosecuted you when you would have defrauded him.

SY.: Heaven bless you, sir.

DA. [*disappointed and furious*]: The verdict's scandalous, so help me Zeus. I alone found all of it and I've been stripped of all of it, and the man that didn't find anything has it. Am I to hand it over?

SM.: Yes.

DA.: The verdict's scandalous, curse me if it isn't!

SY.: Hurry up with it.

DA.: Heracles, what treatment!

SY.: Undo your wallet, and let me see. That's where you carry it. [*Appealing to* SMICRINES *who is leaving*] Wait a minute, please, to see that he hands it over.

DA.: Why did I ever let *him* judge the case?

SY.: Hand it over, you scum.

DA.: Disgraceful, the way I've been treated!

SM. [*to* SYRISCUS]: Have you everything?

SY.: I really think so. Unless he swallowed something while I was pleading, when it was going against him.

DA.: I wouldn't have believed it.

[SMICRINES *departs.*]

SY.: Good-bye, sir. It's high time all judges were like that.

DA.: Heracles, what a skin game! There never was a more scandalous verdict.

SY.: You were a thief.

DA.: Thief yourself, see to it now that you keep them for him safe and sound. Don't you fear, I'll have my eye on you the whole time.

SY.: Clear out and be hanged. [DAVUS *goes.*] Now wife, take these things and carry them inside to the master. We'll wait here for Chaerestratus just now and set off for our work to-morrow when we have paid the rent. But first we must check these things off one at a time. Have you a box? Well, put them in your dress fold [*As* SYRISCUS *tells over the objects and tosses them to his wife,* ONESIMUS *comes from the house and squints at the sun to note the time. He is responsible for the entertainment provided by his master* CHARISIUS *in the house of* CHAERESTRATUS.]

ON.: A slower cook was never seen. By this time yesterday they had been at the wine for a long while.

SY. [*examining the trinkets*]: This looks like a fowl or something and a very plump one too. Here is something set with stones. Here is a toy axe.

ON. [*true to his ruling passion*]: What's this?

SY.: Here is an iron ring with gold trimmings. The seal is a bull or a goat, I can't tell which, done by Cleostratus, it says.

ON. [*recognizing the ring*]: Here, let me see it.

SY. [*handing him the ring*]: There. But who are *you?*

ON.: The very same.

SY.: Who's the same?

ON.: The ring.

SY.: What ring? I don't understand.

ON.: My master Charisius'.

SY.: You're crazy.

ON.: He lost it.

SY.: Put down the ring, plague take you.

ON.: Put down our ring for you? How came it to be in your possession?

SY.: O Apollo and the gods, what a frightful plague! What a job it is to protect an orphan's property! Every one who comes up is suddenly all agog for plunder. Put down the ring, I say.

ON.: Are you trying to be funny with me? It belongs to the master, by Apollo and the gods.

SY.: Without a doubt I'd sooner have my throat cut than sacrifice anything to him. It's settled. I'll go to law with them all one after another. They're the babe's, not mine. Here is a necklace or something. Take it, wife. And a bit of red cloth. Go on in. [*To* ONESIMUS] Now what have you to say?

ON.: I? This belongs to Charisius. He lost it once when he had been drinking, so he said.

SY.: Well, Chaerestratus is my master. Either keep it safe or give it back to me, so that I may produce it intact for you.

ON.: I prefer to look after it myself.

SY.: It makes no difference to me either way, for I believe we both turn in here at the same house. [*Both turn to enter* CHAERESTRATUS' *house where* CHARISIUS *is temporarily established with his party.*]

ON.: Just now, though, the party is under way, and it isn't perhaps a good time to tell him about it. But to-morrow I will.

SY.: I'll wait for you and to-morrow I'll be ready to leave the decision to anyone you please. I've not come off badly this time either, but apparently I've got to neglect everything else and devote my time to lawsuits. That's the only way to keep things nowadays.

[*They go in and a chorus of revellers enter and entertain the audience.*]

ACT III

[ONESIMUS *comes from the house in great perplexity and soliloquizes.*]

ON.: At least half a dozen times I've started to go to the master and show him the ring. I get up close to him, right by his side, and then duck. In fact I'm sorry for what I told him the last time. [*Thoughtfully*] You see he keeps saying pretty frequently: "Perdition take the rascal that told me of this." Really I'm afraid he'll come to terms with his wife, then take me and put me out of the way, because I told him her secret and because I have knowledge of it. It's just as well that I refrained from adding another complication. This too might get me into pretty hot water.

[*Here he is interrupted by sounds of a struggle.* CHARISIUS' *harp-girl*, HABROTONON, *is trying to escape from the importunities of his guests, who have noticed how little attention she gets from their host. She finally breaks away.*]

HA.: Let me go, please, and don't bother me. Apparently I've been unintentionally making a fool of my unfortunate self. I thought I had a lover, but the fellow's hatred for me is something diabolical. He has got so now that he won't even let me, mercy on us, have a place at the same table with him, but puts me at a distance.

ON. [*to himself*]: Then shall I give it back to the man I just had it of? Nonsense.

HA. [*puzzled as she reflects on* CHARISIUS' *strange conduct*]: My goodness, what ails the man to throw away all that money?   As far as
he is concerned I'm qualified to carry the basket for the goddess, for
pity's sake.   Holy and pure from marriage rites, as they say, I've
sat since day before yesterday.

ON. [*wondering what excuse he is to make to* SYRISCUS]: But then how,
ye gods, how, I entreat you . . .

[*At this moment* SYRISCUS *comes from the house in search of* ONESIMUS,
whom he suspects of appropriating the ring under false pretences.]

SY.: Where can he be?   I've looked for him everywhere inside.
Here you.   Give me back the ring, my friend, or show it to the
man you're finally going to.   Let's get the case settled.   I've to go
somewhere.

ON. [*embarrassed, but superior*]: This is the way it is, fellow.   This
ring really does belong to my master Charisius, I'm absolutely certain of that, but I'm afraid to bring it to his attention.   It just about
means making him father of the child it was found with, if I deliver
it to him.

SY.: How's that, you simpleton?

ON.: He lost it one time at the Tauropolia when there was a night
celebration with women taking part.   The natural inference is that
he assaulted a girl; she had a baby and of course abandoned it, the
one in question.   Now if the girl could be found first, then one
might produce the ring and it would be definite evidence of something.   Otherwise it means suspicion and disturbance.

SY. [*still suspicious*]: Just look to that yourself.   But if you're trying
to frighten me off, meaning me to take back the ring and give you
a little present, you're out of your head.   I'm not the man to compromise.

ON.: I don't ask you to either.

SY.: I'll be back when I have done an errand, for I'm going to town
just now.   I'll see then what's to be done about it.

[*As* SYRISCUS *leaves,* HABROTONON *approaches* ONESIMUS.   *It has occurred to her that she may still win* CHARISIUS' *favour by a new
method.*]

HA.: Is it the baby that the woman is nursing now inside that this
charcoal-burner found?

ON.: So he says.

HA.: Isn't that great!   For pity's sake!

ON.: And with it was this ring of my master's.

HA. [*impressively indignant*]: Oh! you wretch!   If he really is your
young master, and you look on and see him brought up as a slave,
wouldn't you deserve to be put to death?

ON. [*surrounded by pitfalls*]: But there's this to be said, no one knows
who his mother is.

HA.: But he lost it, you say, at the Tauropolia?

ON.: Yes, when he was carousing, so the boy that attended him said.

HA.: Evidently he attacked the women who were celebrating the revels by themselves. In fact I was there when just such a thing occurred.

ON.: You were there?

HA.: Yes, last year at the Tauropolia. I was playing the lute for some young ladies and she was with them. I wasn't a performer myself, for at that time I hadn't — I mean I didn't yet know what a man is. [ONESIMUS *smiles knowingly*.] Indeed I didn't, by Aphrodite.

ON.: Yes, but do you know who the girl was?

HA.: I could ask. She was a friend of the women that I was with.

ON.: Did you hear who her father was?

HA.: I don't know anything about her except that I should recognize her if I saw her. A good-looking girl, goodness, yes, and rich too, they said.

ON.: Perhaps it's the same one.

HA.: I don't know about that. Well, while she was with us there, she strayed off and then suddenly comes running up alone, crying and tearing her hair. She had utterly ruined a very fine Tarantine shawl, and delicate, my goodness! Why, it was all in tatters!

ON.: And she had this ring?

HA.: Perhaps she did, but she didn't show it to me. I'm going to stick to the truth, you see.

ON.: What am I to do now?

HA.: You look to that. But, if you're sensible and take my advice, you'll let your master know of this. If the child's mother is free born, why shouldn't he know of what's occurred?

ON.: Let's find out first who she is, Habrotonon. Will you help me to do that now?

HA.: I really can't until I am sure who the man in question is. I'm afraid I might give information to the ladies I spoke of with no result. For all anyone knows someone else may have lost it after receiving the ring from him as a pledge. Perhaps he was dicing and gave it as security for an agreement, or he bound himself to something, found himself in a tight place and handed over the ring. Any number of other things of the sort regularly happen at drinking-bouts. Until I know the man responsible I'll neither look for her nor report anything of the sort.

ON.: Indeed you're quite right. What is to be done, though?

HA.: See here, Onesimus. See if you approve of my idea. I'll pretend it all happened to me. I'll take this ring and go in to him.

ON.: Go on and explain, I see it at once.

HA.: When he notices that I have the ring he'll ask me where I got it. I'll say: "At the Tauropolia when I was still a maid," taking on myself all that happened to her. Most of it I know.

ON.: Magnificent!

HA.: If the escapade comes home to him, he'll immediately dash straight into the trap. He's been drinking and he'll tell everything first without stopping to think. Whatever he says I'll agree to, for safety's sake mentioning nothing before he does.

ON.: Superfine, by Helius!

HA.: I'll be cunning and use vague language, to keep from going wrong, like: "How reckless you were, what a savage!"

ON.: Fine!

HA.: "How roughly you handled me and the clothes you ruined, alas!" I'll say. But first I want to go inside and get the baby, cry over and hug him and ask the woman where she got him.

ON.: Lord save us! [*His fears are aroused by a certain touch of genius in* HABROTONON's *technique.*]

HA.: And to cap it all I'll say: "So now, take note, you've a baby born," and I'll produce our foundling here.

ON.: *There's* brass and trickiness, Habrotonon!

HA.: And if this test works and he proves to be the child's father, we'll look for the girl at our leisure.

ON.: You don't mention the fact that you'll get your freedom. For as soon as he supposes you to be the child's mother, he'll obviously buy your liberty at once.

HA.: I don't know. I hope so.

ON.: So you don't know? But, Habrotonon, do I get any thanks for my part?

HA.: Goodness, yes! I shall consider you responsible for everything I get.

ON.: But if after that you purposely forget to look for the mother and play me false, how about that?

HA.: For pity's sake, why do you think I want children? Liberty is all I pray for. [*Fervently*] Ye gods, may that be my reward for what I'm doing.

ON.: I hope it will be.

HA.: So you approve?

ON.: I approve most heartily, for if you play any tricks, I'll attack you then. There'll be a way. For the present, though, let's see if it's so.

HA. [*looking pointedly at the ring*]: So you agree?

ON. [*loath to relinquish the ring*]: By all means.

HA.: Go ahead and give me my ring.

ON.: Go ahead and take it.

HA. [*as she receives the ring*]: Dear Lady *Eloquence,* be with me to help and give the words I speak success.

[*She goes in to play her part while* ONESIMUS *soliloquizes.*]

ON.: Intuitional, the female. When she sees that love won't lead her to liberty, and that she's not getting anywhere that way, she takes the other route. As for me, though, I shall be a slave all my days, moonstruck driveller that I am with no foresight at all about such things. But perhaps I shall get something from her if she has any luck. In fact I deserve to . . . How I waste my time counting on anything! I think I'm possessed, expecting gratitude from a woman! I only hope I shan't be worse off than I am. My mistress' case is pretty shaky now, for it only needs the discovery of a girl of citizen birth as mother of this baby to make him take her and dismiss the other [*i.e., Habrotonon*]. Of course his wife at home will jump at the chance to leave for good. [*He means that, finding herself now the injured party, she could get a divorce with no loss of reputation and would be glad to choose that solution.*] And this time I think I've rather neatly avoided the charge that I have a finger in the pie. I've sworn off being too helpful. If anyone discovers that I haven't minded my own business or haven't held my tongue about anything another time, he may take my teeth and pull them. [*Clenched teeth are a symbol of obstinate silence in Greek.*] [*He sees* SMICRINES *approaching from the city.*] But who's this coming? Smicrines, coming back from town in no mood of philosophic calm. Perhaps he has learned the truth from someone. I'll take myself off out of his way to avoid trouble.

Onesimus retires to the house as Smicrines appears and delivers a tirade of which we can guess the drift. Just enough of the manuscript is preserved to indicate the development of the plot. Here and there a brief phrase can be reconstructed. Smicrines has accumulated in town further evidence of his son-in-law's extravagance. As he puts it, "The whole city buzzes with the scandal." He knows for how many days Charisius has been living with the harp-girl, how much he spends on cooks, guesses that he gambles, and is so thoroughly alarmed for his ducats and his daughter that he is resolved to rescue them both from Charisius' hands without delay. He soon has new evidence of Charisius' misdeeds.

For Habrotonon has been playing her part within so successfully that Charisius has acknowledged as his the baby with which she confronted him. The resulting confusion completely breaks up the party. The cook emerges with his slaves and outfit, leaving the house in high dudgeon because of the interruption which has spoiled the feast that he was providing. He is violently berating the household as he leaves. "A high time they're having with their lunch," comments Smicrines, and the cook continues: "Bad luck for me, bad luck and plenty of it. This time I've been caught somehow off my guard, but if ever again you happen to want a cook, you may go to the devil." Smicrines questions the cook and gets a good deal more than the truth. He hears not only that Charisius has a son by Habrotonon, but that he intends to purchase her freedom at a ruinous cost and keep her in violation of the terms of his marriage contract, which no doubt forbade him to raise children except Pamphila's or to establish another woman as her rival. The cook departs hastily, as Simias and other guests come from the house. They comment freely on Charisius' predicament. The comrade who had been so high and mighty about self-indulgence was now involved in a public scandal. Smicrines accosts them and gets confirmation of what the cook had told him. "But perhaps," he says, "I'm being indiscreet and meddling where I'm not concerned, since apparently

I have grounds for taking my daughter and leaving. I'll do just that. I've practically made up my mind. I call you to witness that my daughter's rights have been infringed." Simias and Chaerestratus fail to mollify the old man. When someone asserts that Charisius hates the so-called life of pleasure, Smicrines retorts with a list of his recent outings, and expresses indignation at his treatment of his connections by marriage, to whom doubtless he had originally been recommended by his frugality. "This Sir Touch-me-not won't have everything his own way. He *will* waste his substance in a tavern, will he, live with the beauty that he's adopting into the household, while he completely cuts the acquaintance of his legal wife and her father?" No, no, Smicrines will see to that. Here the act ends.

ACT IV

At the beginning of the fourth act Smicrines is talking to Pamphila, whom he has summoned from the house in order to take her away. He is astounded to find that she does not at once agree to leave her husband when she hears how he is behaving. We have two or three scraps of the long argument that ensued between them. Pamphila remonstrates in ladylike tones: "Necessary for my own good perhaps, but that's what you must make me see. Otherwise you'd be, not a father dealing with his daughter, but a master with his slave." Smicrines retorts: "Is there room here for argument and demonstration? Isn't it as plain as day? The case cries to heaven, Pamphila. If, however, you insist on my explaining, I'm prepared. I will put before you three possibilities. He'd be ruined for evermore and so would you." He then points out how impossible she would find the situation, if she were to attempt to live in the house with Charisius, supposing him to bring home a mistress and her child. "It's hard," he said, "Pamphila, for a free woman to hold her own against a bought mistress, who schemes more, knows more, has no shame, humours the man better." Neither can Charisius afford to keep up two households. "Look at the expense. Double for Thesmophoria and Scirophoria. Realize how ruinous it will be for his capital. Mustn't we agree that his case is desperate? Consider your position again. He says he has to go off to the Piraeus. He'll go there and stay a while. You'll be miserable about it, I'm sure. You'll wait a long while without your dinner, while he of course is drinking with his mistress." The third possibility, that Charisius might spend all his time with the harp-girl and desert Pamphila altogether, must have been presented by Smicrines in even darker colours.

Pamphila, however, held her own against her father's eloquence and even against the despair in her own heart. When he pointed out her distress she agreed: "Indeed my eyes are all swollen with weeping." But marriage was for her a life-partnership. No matter how much she might suffer, no matter

to what straits she might be brought, she would not of her own
accord leave her husband. Charisius meanwhile was listening
to this conversation. His feelings are described later. The effect on Smicrines of his daughter's determination to face ruin
and misery rather than forsake her husband can be imagined.
He goes off in a towering rage. Pamphila is left alone. She is
desperately unhappy and sees no hope for herself, now that she
has a rival, who has presented Charisius with a son. As she
stands dejected by her door, the supposed rival, Habrotonon,
comes out with the baby, still playing the part of anxious mother.
Pamphila naturally desires at first to avoid the woman, not guessing with what dramatic suddenness her sorrow is to be turned to
joy.

HA. [*coming out*]: I am going out with him. He's been wailing,
my goodness, ever so long. There's something wrong with my
baby.

PA. [*seeing her rival*]: Will no god take pity on me in my misery?

HA.: Darling baby, when will you see your mother? [*Noticing*
PAMPHILA] But who is this next door?

PA.: I will go.

HA. [*recognizing her*]: Wait a minute, ma'am.

PA.: Are you speaking to me?

HA.: Yes. Look and see if you recognize me. [*As* PAMPHILA *turns,*
HABROTONON *scans her face.*] She's the very one I saw. How do
you do, my dear?

PA.: But who are you?

HA.: Just give me your hand. Tell me, my dear, didn't you attend
a celebration for girls at last year's Tauropolia?

[*But* PAMPHILA's *eye is caught by the trinkets that the babe is wearing
She exclaims at the sight.*]

PA.: Woman, where, tell me, did you get that child?

HA.: Do you see something you recognize that he's wearing? Have
no fear of me, ma'am.

PA.: Isn't he your own?

HA.: I pretended he was, not to wrong his real mother, but to find her
when I had time. And now I have found her, for you are the one
I saw that other time.

PA.: But who is his father?

HA.: Charisius.

PA.: Are you certain, my dear?

HA.: Indeed I am. But aren't you the young wife that lives here?

PA.: Yes indeed.

HA.: Happy woman, some god has taken pity on you. But someone
is coming out next door. I heard a noise. Take me in with you,
so that I can go on and tell you all the rest of the story just as it
happened.

[*While* HABROTONON *is giving the overjoyed* PAMPHILA *a full account
of the adventures of the baby that had brought sorrow but was now*

bringing greater joy, we learn of the crisis CHARISIUS *has passed through. He had by chance overheard* PAMPHILA's *conversation with her father. As she steadfastly refused to let anything induce her to desert her husband, not even his disloyalty to her,* CHARISIUS, *long torn between love and pride, has been completely humbled.* ONESIMUS, *eavesdropping as usual, grew more and more alarmed as he saw* CHARISIUS *become furious with rage, rage against himself and against anyone who might seem to have injured the gentle* PAMPHILA. *Not feeling safe in the same house with his master,* ONESIMUS *slips out and gives vent to his feelings.*]

ON.: He's not quite sane. By Apollo, he's mad. He's really gone mad. By the gods he *is* mad. My master I mean, Charisius. He's had an atrabilious stroke or some such thing. How else can you explain it? He spent a long time by the door inside just now craning his neck and listening. His wife's father was having a talk with her about the business, I suppose. The way he kept changing colour, gentlemen, I don't care even to mention. Then he cried out: "Oh darling! what a wonderful thing to say!" and beat his head violently. Then again after a while: "What a wife I had and now have lost, alas!" And to cap it all, when he had heard them to the end and had gone in at last, inside there was groaning, tearing of hair, continual frenzy. Over and over again he'd repeat: "Criminal that I am, when I had myself done a thing like that, when I had myself got an illegitimate child, to be so unfeeling, so utterly unforgiving to her in the same unhappy situation. No humanity; no mercy." He calls himself names as hard as he can, his eyes are bloodshot with fury. I'm shaking in my shoes; I'm all wilted with terror. If he catches sight of me, who told on her, anywhere, while he's in this state, he'll maybe kill me. That's why I've quietly slipped out here. Where am I to turn though? What can I think of? It's all over. I'm done for. He's at the door coming out. O Zeus Saviour, help me if you can. [*As* ONESIMUS *hides,* CHARISIUS *comes out in a state of complete abasement and soliloquizes.*]

CH.: Oh, wasn't I a paragon, thinking always of my reputation, trying to discover what honour and dishonour really are, without spot or flaw in my own life! Heaven has used me well, just as I deserve. Precisely there I showed that I was only human. You poor, poor fool, swollen with conceit and loud in your preaching, intolerant of your wife's misfortune that she couldn't help, I will exhibit the same fault in you yourself, and then she will treat you gently, though you are bringing shame on her. You shall be revealed as having neither luck, nor skill, nor heart. How different from your intentions at that minute were her words to her father: "She had come to her husband to share his life, she had no right to run away from the misfortune that had come." But you with your mighty superiority are behaving like a savage. Where is your wisdom now? What will happen to her if you go on? Her father is going to show no consideration for her. What care I

for her father? I'll tell him plainly: "You stop making trouble,
Smicrines. My wife is not going to leave me. What do you mean
by upsetting and brow-beating Pamphila?"

[*No sooner has* CHARISIUS *made up his mind to make his wife's cause
his own than he reaps his just reward, for* HABROTONON *comes to
bring him the good news about the baby. Naturally she is not a
welcome sight to* CHARISIUS, *who almost at the same moment espies
the unlucky* ONESIMUS. *In vain* ONESIMUS *affirms his innocence
of eavesdropping.* HABROTONON *confesses that she is not after all
the mother of* CHARISIUS' *child. Still more furious at the thought
of the fraud that has been practised on him,* CHARISIUS *drives the ab-
ject* ONESIMUS *to throw all the blame on* HABROTONON, *who at last
makes* CHARISIUS *listen.*]

HA.: Stop attacking us, you foolish man. The child is your own lawful wife's, no other.

CH.: Would he were!

HA.: By Demeter I swear it.

CH.: What sort of a story is that?

HA.: Absolutely true.

CH.: Is the child really Pamphila's? It was mine before.

HA.: And yours as well, to be sure.

CH.: Pamphila's! Habrotonon, I beg you, you mustn't excite me!

[*The fourth act ends when* CHARISIUS *is finally convinced and goes to*
PAMPHILA. *Husband and wife are reunited.*]

ACT V

The fifth act rounds out the story. Unfortunately we cannot
be certain what happened to Habrotonon. Of course she gets her
freedom. So in all probability does Onesimus. Simias and
Chaerestratus are involved in the explanations, but we do not
know just how their relations with Charisius and Habrotonon
had been complicated by her temporary appearance in the rôle
of mother of his son. At any rate all is set right. Habrotonon is
complimented on her wit and courage and is perhaps placed in
charge of Simias, who remarks, as the stage is cleared: "A girl
like this couldn't have escaped his attentions (*i.e.* Chaerestratus'),
but I will treat her with respect."

Smicrines remains to be dealt with. At this moment he reappears. Pamphila had sent the old nurse to get him so that he
might hear the news. Not guessing what has happened, he is
angered by the nurse's suggestion of a coming reconciliation and
makes himself ridiculous by a violent outburst.

SM. [*berating and shaking* SOPHRONA]: If I don't smash your head,
Sophrona, I hope to be hanged. You'll admonish me too, will
you? I'm too hasty about carrying off my daughter, you cursed
hag? Am I to wait for her good husband to consume my dowry;
and then make speeches about my own property? You too urge
that, do you? Isn't it better to take the bull by the horns? You'll

be good and sorry if you say another word. My dispute is with
Pamphila. Just you urge her to change her mind when you see
her. For, Sophrona, as I hope for salvation, when I'm on the way
home — did you see the pond as you passed? That's where I'm
going to spend the night ducking the life out of you and I'll force
you to agree with me instead of taking sides against me. [*He approaches* CHARISIUS' *house where he expects to find* PAMPHILA *alone
and unprotected.*] The door is shut, so I must knock. Boys!
Boys! Open the door, someone. Boys! Don't you hear me?

ON. [*Opening the door but not admitting* SMICRINES, *for his newly-
gained freedom has made him suddenly bold*]: Who's that knocking? Ha, Smicrines, that strict accountant, come for his dowry
and his daughter.

SM. [*surprised*]: Himself, curse you.

ON.: And sure, he's right. His haste befits a man of calculation and
great wisdom. [*He notices* SOPHRONA, *helpless in the grip of* SMI-
CRINES, *and is struck by her humorous resemblance to Persephoné
or to any other beauty in the hands of a ravisher.*] And his prize,
Lord save us, what a stunner!

SM.: By all the gods and spirits . . .

ON.: Do you believe, Smicrines, that the gods can spare the time to
mete out daily to every individual his share of good or evil?

SM.: What's that?

ON.: I'll make it quite plain. The total number of cities in the world
is approximately a thousand. Each has thirty thousand inhabitants.
Are the gods busy damning or saving each of them one by one?
Surely not, for so you make them lead a life of toil. Then are they
not at all concerned for us, you'll say. In each man they have
placed his character as commander. This ever present guardian
it is that ruins one man, if he fails to use it aright, and saves
another. [*Indicating himself*] This is our god, this the cause of
each man's good or evil fortune. Propitiate this by doing nothing
absurd or foolish, that good fortune may attend you.

SM.: So my character, you scurvy knave, is doing something foolish
now, is it?

ON.: It's wrecking you.

SM.: What impudence!

ON.: But do you really think it right, Smicrines, to separate a daughter
from her husband?

SM.: Who says it is right? In this case though it's necessary.

ON.: You see? Wrong is necessary by his reasoning. It's not his
character but something else that is ruining him. [*He taps his
forehead significantly.*] Now this once, when you were bent on
evil action, pure luck has delivered you. You arrive to find what
was amiss all settled and atonement made. But another time,
Smicrines, I warn you, don't let me catch you getting headstrong.
But now I release you from these charges. Go find inside your
grandson and salute him.

SM.: My grandson, you carrion!

ON.: So you too were a blockhead for all you thought you were so wise. Is this the way you kept your eye on a young girl ripe for marriage? That's the reason we have these miraculous five-month infants to bring up.

SM.: I don't know what you mean.

ON.: Yes, but the old woman knows, I fancy. That time at the Tauropolia it was my master, Sophrona, who found her separated from the dancers. Do you see?

SO.: Yes.

ON.: And now they've recognized each other and all's well.

SM. [*to* SOPHRONA]: What's this he's saying, you cursed hag?

SO. [*quoting Euripides*]:
    'Twas Nature's will who recketh naught of laws,
    And Nature made her woman for this very cause.

SM.: What, have you lost your senses?

SO.: I'll quote you a whole passage from the *Auge* of Euripides, complete, if you won't see at last.

SM.: Your tragic airs drive me wild. Are you fully aware of what he is saying?

SO.: I'm well aware.

ON.: You may be sure that the nurse knew before.

SM.: But it's a frightful thing.

SO.: There never was anything more fortunate. If what you say is true, the child belongs to both, and all is well.

[*The rest is missing.* SMICRINES, ONESIMUS, *and* SOPHRONA *will be ready to go in after a few more lines, and with their disappearance the play will end.*]

PHILOSOPHY

PLATO

(ca. 427–ca. 347 B.C.)

The indisputable facts which we possess concerning the life of Plato are very few. His dates, from *ca.* 427 B.C. to *ca.* 347 B.C. include the period from the early years of the Peloponnesian War down to about a decade before the Battle of Chaeronea which finally established Macedonian supremacy in the Greek World. Plato was a member of an aristocratic Athenian family and consequently it is easy to imagine the general lines which his boyhood and youth must have followed. We do know that, before meeting Socrates, Plato was a pupil of a Heraclitean philosopher named Cratylus whose position was marked by a thorough-going skepticism. At the age of twenty the young philosopher first came in contact with Socrates and remained the devoted pupil and associate of the Athenian sage until the execution of Socrates in 399 B.C. Tradition has it that Plato then withdrew from Athens until about 386 B.C. when he returned to establish his school, the Academy, which is rightly termed the first university of Europe, organized specifically for the free and open pursuit of truth.

The remaining forty years of Plato's life were spent in Athens except for two visits to Sicily which he made in an abortive effort to put into practice some of his political theories for the ruling tyrant of Syracuse, Dionysius II. Presumably a large number of the earlier tentative dialogues such as the *Euthyphro* as well as those dealing with the trial and death of Socrates had been written prior to the founding of the Academy. Shortly thereafter the *Republic* appeared, the masterpiece of Plato's maturity. In the following years his activity included teaching, lecturing, and the composition of the later more technical dialogues. The *Laws,* the final work of his old age, marks the close of a long and brilliant career.

Socrates is the leading figure in the dialogues, particularly those which best realize the dramatic potentialities of the dialogue form. In the later pieces, when the form had tended to become externalized, Socrates is a less important figure, and finally disappears entirely. For example, he does not appear in the *dramatis personae* of the *Laws.* One of the standing problems of interpretation, therefore, in the dialogues which feature Socrates, lies in distinguishing between Socrates the dramatic character and the so-called "historical" Socrates. Or, to put it another way, we must answer the question to what extent does Socrates function as merely the mouthpiece for Plato's own ideas. Scholarly opinion is of course divided. Some say that the Platonic Socrates is completely non-historical. Others say that in the dialogues up through the *Republic* (and these would include all our selections in the volume except those from the *Phaedrus* and the

Laws) Socrates is almost completely historical. According to this theory the *Apology* is taken to be the actual speech delivered by Socrates when he was on trial for his life.

Whatever may be the merits of this argument, some few assertions can be made with confidence. In the first place, the Socrates of history can safely be designated as the thinker who was largely responsible for the whole new orientation of philosophy in the later years of the fifth century. Prior to his time philosophers in the main had been preoccupied with the external world, with the problems of the nature of matter, of the order and arrangement of the universe, of being and existence; in other words, the characteristic questions of cosmology and ontology. Socrates, by focusing attention upon the inner nature of man, brought to the fore-ground the problems of ethics and epistemology. One might say that he took the old Delphic maxim, "Know thyself" and put it to use philosophically. Henceforward, philosophy always has operated in a context whose limits were extended and fixed by Socrates.

In the second place, the "historical" Socrates must have been a man who by his characteristic method of healthy doubt and continual question and answer established the foundation of dialectic, the systematic analysis of presuppositions. This "historical" Socrates must have been uppermost in Plato's mind as he was composing his dialogues, and one cannot underestimate the debt which the younger philosopher owes to his master. Yet the fact still remains that the Socrates whom we know best is the Socrates of Plato, a literary and dramatic characterization which has the historical figure at its core. Though we may never be able to isolate the strictly historical elements in the Platonic portrait, still we do have in this literary portrait a person whom we know intimately and love and understand as we do every great characterization which emerges from the creative imagination of a literary artist. Thus Plato's Socrates is more real than any Socrates produced by pure historical research.

As has already been implied, one must remember that Plato was not embarking on a purely untried field when he undertook to expound his philosophy. In one sense it may be said that he found in the Pre-Socratic thinkers, in the drama, history, poets and Sophists at least the germs of practically all of his own philosophical notions. We have already mentioned those two preceding centuries of self-conscious effort to determine the nature of the external physical world as well as the contribution of Socrates. But for the adequate understanding of Plato it is important to review more specifically certain salient features of his heritage, some of which he incorporated into his thought and enlarged, whereas others he sought to isolate and refute.

Let us consider the significant elements of the more strictly philosophical aspect in the Greek tradition prior to Plato. First of all, thinkers such as Thales, Anaximander and Anaximenes had sought to identify the fundamental element or substratum underlying matter. As time went on a vast advance from practical and utilitarian mathematics to a pure science of number was achieved most notably by the Pythagoreans. Before Plato both dynamic and mechanical theories of the universe had been advanced, *i.e.,* that the universe was a machine or that it was created and guided by some force or power or intelligence or God. Already Leucippus and Democritus had promulgated a full-fledged atomic theory, a position basic to a mechanistic view of the universe. The Pythagoreans had developed both mystically and philosophically the religious conception of immortality. The idea of evolution, however inchoate the form, had already been born. Heraclitus had argued that all is change, that impermanence is the rule of the world, that there is no abiding unity, that all is many and in motion. The Eleatics, such as Zeno and Parmenides, had urged, *per contra,* that the senses deceive, that motion is illusory, that all is rest, and all that exists is Being. In addition they made the all-important distinction between knowledge and opinion, *i.e.,* between the truth and what men believed to be true. And last, Plato's predecessors had become aware of the principle of contradiction, the ultimate foundation of all logical thought.

Such in brief are some of the more important notions which Plato could find in the Pre-Socratics alone. In addition in poetry and tragedy there were innumerable moral, ethical, and religious ideas. Such a trilogy as the *Oresteia* of Aeschylus expressed the deepest of religious insights. The lyric poets were filled with many a moral and ethical conception. The many-sided influence of Homer should not be overlooked. Further, Herodotus had written his history around the informing idea of Nemesis, that the gods are jealous of those men who have become too powerful. Thus, if we look at the rich treasures of thought and feeling which Plato received from his past, he becomes great not because he himself originated a large number of philosophical conceptions, but rather because of his unrivaled power of synthesis. How he used, by development, emphasis, and opposition, the conceptions which were more or less ready to hand gives him his distinction. So vast was his achievement that the twentieth-century philosopher, Professor Alfred North Whitehead of Harvard, can insist that all subsequent philosophy is by way of being foot-notes to Plato.

The selections from Plato's works which follow have been chosen so that the reader may be introduced thoroughly to the most significant aspects of Platonic philosophy. The *Euthyphro* provides the best beginning, since in this crisp and lively dialogue can be found in embryo almost all of Plato's characteristic tenets. Here we are presented with Socrates as he deals with piety as a value. Plato's Theory of Ideas is promulgated and the discussion is carried on in Plato's best dialectic manner. Furthermore the dialogue gives a clue to Plato's consistent attitude towards the relation of metaphysics to religion. For example, when Socrates demonstrates that the gods love holiness because it is holy and that holiness is not holy because the gods love it, Plato is making the same distinction as he will draw more explicitly in the late dialogue, the *Timaeus.* There in mythical terms Plato says that the maker of the universe undertook the task of creation because he was good and proceeded in this activity by keeping his eye fixed on the eternal Ideas as patterns or models for him as he worked. This conception that God or the gods and the Ideas, that is, the ultimates in the realm of religion and of metaphysics, are distinct is clearly adumbrated in the *Euthyphro*.

The dramatic setting of the *Euthyphro* reveals Socrates as he is waiting outside the court-room to answer the indictment of impiety that had been laid against him. The *Apology* carries the chronicle further by giving us Plato's version of Socrates' speech in his own defense. The *Crito* presents the next episode where Socrates refuses the plea of his friends to escape from prison to avoid paying the death penalty. The most notable feature of the *Crito* is the imaginary dialogue which Socrates carries on with the personified Laws of his country to show that there is an implied contract involving mutual obligations between each citizen and his state. The last pages of the *Phaedo* complete the sequence on the trial and death of Socrates.

The *Ion* has been included not only because it contains some of Plato's most suggestive thoughts on the philosophy of art and literary criticism but also because it has captured the imaginations of so many men of creative genius in later ages. The passages from the *Phaedrus* and the *Symposium* are important for the distinctive ways in which they complement Plato's full length delineation of his Theory of Ideas in Books V, VI, and VII of the *Republic*. This section appears here in its entirety and beyond question contains the best statement of the very core of Platonism, particularly in the famous images, the Divided Line and the Allegory of the Cave. The tenth book of the *Laws* brings the group of selections to a fitting conclusion, since it reflects so clearly the increasing emphasis which Plato put upon religion in the later years of his philosophical activity. Thus it balances and puts into a fuller perspective the presentation of the Theory of Ideas in the *Republic*. The reader, if he masters all these passages of Plato, should be able to extend his knowledge of Platonism with a minimum of difficulty.

EUTHYPHRO

PERSONS OF THE DIALOGUE

SOCRATES   EUTHYPHRO

SCENE: — *The Porch of the King Archon*

Euthyphro. Why have you left the Lyceum, Socrates? and what are you doing in the Porch of the King Archon? Surely you cannot be concerned in a suit before the King, like myself?

Socrates. Not in a suit, Euthyphro; impeachment is the word which the Athenians use.

Euth. What! I suppose that some one has been prosecuting you, for I cannot believe that you are the prosecutor of another.

Soc. Certainly not.

Euth. Then some one else has been prosecuting you?

Soc. Yes.

Euth. And who is he?

Soc. A young man who is little known, Euthyphro; and I hardly know him: his name is Meletus, and he is of the deme of Pitthis. Perhaps you may remember his appearance; he has a beak, and long straight hair, and a beard which is ill grown.

Euth. No, I do not remember him, Socrates. But what is the charge which he brings against you?

Soc. What is the charge? Well, a very serious charge, which shows a good deal of character in the young man, and for which he is certainly not to be despised. He says he knows how the youth are corrupted and who are their corruptors. I fancy that he must be a wise man, and seeing that I am the reverse of a wise man, he has found me out, and is going to accuse me of corrupting his young friends. And of this our mother the state is to be the judge. Of all our political men he is the only one who seems to me to begin in the right way, with the cultivation of virtue in youth; like a good husbandman, he makes the young shoots his first care, and clears away us who are the destroyers of them. This is only the first step; he will afterwards attend to the elder branches; and if he goes on as he has begun, he will be a very great public benefactor.

Euth. I hope that he may; but I rather fear, Socrates, that the opposite will turn out to be the truth. My opinion is that in attacking you he is simply aiming a blow at the foundation of the state. But in what way does he say that you corrupt the young?

Soc. He brings a wonderful accusation against me, which at first hearing excites surprise: he says that I am a poet or maker of gods, and that I invent new gods and deny the existence of old ones; this is the ground of his indictment.

Euth. I understand, Socrates; he means to attack you about the familiar sign which occasionally, as you say, comes to you. He thinks that you are a neologian, and he is going to have you up before the

441

court for this. He knows that such a charge is readily received by
the world, as I myself know too well; for when I speak in the assembly about divine things, and foretell the future to them, they
laugh at me and think me a madman. Yet every word that I say
is true. But they are jealous of us all; and we must be brave and
go at them.

Soc. Their laughter, friend Euthyphro, is not a matter of much
consequence. For a man may be thought wise; but the Athenians, I
suspect, do not much trouble themselves about him until he begins to
impart his wisdom to others; and then for some reason or other,
perhaps, as you say, from jealousy, they are angry.

Euth, I am never likely to try their temper in this way.

Soc. I dare say not, for you are reserved in your behaviour, and
seldom impart your wisdom. But I have a benevolent habit of pouring out myself to everybody, and would even pay for a listener, and
I am afraid that the Athenians may think me too talkative. Now if,
as I was saying, they would only laugh at me, as you say that they
laugh at you, the time might pass gaily enough in the court; but
perhaps they may be in earnest, and then what the end will be you
soothsayers only can predict.

Euth. I dare say that the affair will end in nothing, Socrates, and
that you will win your cause; and I think that I shall win my own.

Soc. And what is your suit, Euthyphro? are you the pursuer or
the defendant?

Euth. I am the pursuer.

Soc. Of whom?

Euth. You will think me mad when I tell you.

Soc. Why, has the fugitive wings?

Euth. Nay, he is not very volatile at his time of life.

Soc. Who is he?

Euth. My father.

Soc. Your father! my good man?

Euth. Yes.

Soc. And of what is he accused?

Euth. Of murder, Socrates.

Soc. By the powers, Euthyphro! how little does the common herd
know of the nature of right and truth. A man must be an extraordinary man, and have made great strides in wisdom, before he could
have seen his way to bring such an action.

Euth. Indeed, Socrates, he must.

Soc. I suppose that the man whom your father murdered was one
of your relatives — clearly he was; for if he had been a stranger you
would never have thought of prosecuting him.

Euth. I am amused, Socrates, at your making a distinction between one who is a relation and one who is not a relation; for surely
the pollution is the same in either case, if you knowingly associate
with the murderer when you ought to clear yourself and him by
proceeding against him. The real question is whether the murdered
man has been justly slain. If justly, then your duty is to let the mat-

ter alone; but if unjustly, then even if the murderer lives under the same roof with you and eats at the same table, proceed against him. Now the man who is dead was a poor dependant of mine who worked for us as a field labourer on our farm in Naxos, and one day in a fit of drunken passion he got into a quarrel with one of our domestic servants and slew him. My father bound him hand and foot and threw him into a ditch, and then sent to Athens to ask of a diviner what he should do with him. Meanwhile he never attended to him and took no care about him, for he regarded him as a murderer; and thought that no great harm would be done even if he did die. Now this was just what happened. For such was the effect of cold and hunger and chains upon him, that before the messenger returned from the diviner, he was dead. And my father and family are angry with me for taking the part of the murderer and prosecuting my father. They say that he did not kill him, and that if he did, the dead man was but a murderer, and I ought not to take any notice, for that a son is impious who prosecutes a father. Which shows, Socrates, how little they know what the gods think about piety and impiety.

Soc. Good heavens, Euthyphro! and is your knowledge of religion and of things pious and impious so very exact, that, supposing the circumstances to be as you state them, you are not afraid lest you too may be doing an impious thing in bringing an action against your father?

Euth. The best of Euthyphro, and that which distinguishes him, Socrates, from other men, is his exact knowledge of all such matters. What should I be good for without it?

Soc. Rare friend! I think that I cannot do better than be your disciple. Then before the trial with Meletus comes on I shall challenge him, and say that I have always had a great interest in religious questions, and now, as he charges me with rash imaginations and innovations in religion, I have become your disciple. You, Meletus, as I shall say to him, acknowledge Euthyphro to be a great theologian, and sound in his opinions; and if you approve of him you ought to approve of me, and not have me into court; but if you disapprove, you should begin by indicting him who is my teacher, and who will be the ruin, not of the young, but of the old; that is to say, of myself whom he instructs, and of his old father whom he admonishes and chastises. And if Meletus refuses to listen to me, but will go on, and will not shift the indictment from me to you, I cannot do better than repeat this challenge in the court.

Euth. Yes, indeed, Socrates; and if he attempts to indict me I am mistaken if I do not find a flaw in him; the court shall have a great deal more to say to him than to me.

Soc. And I, my dear friend, knowing this, am desirous of becoming your disciple. For I observe that no one appears to notice you — not even this Meletus; but his sharp eyes have found me out at once, and he has indicted me for impiety. And therefore, I adjure you to tell me the nature of piety and impiety, which you said that you knew so well, and of murder, and of other offences against the gods. What are they? Is not piety in every action always the same? and impiety, again — is it not always the opposite of piety, and also the same with itself, having, as impiety, one notion which includes whatever is impious?

Euth. To be sure, Socrates.

Soc. And what is piety, and what is impiety?

Euth. Piety is doing as I am doing; that is to say, prosecuting any one who is guilty of murder, sacrilege, or of any similar crime — whether he be your father or mother, or whoever he may be — that makes no difference; and not to prosecute them is impiety. And please to consider, Socrates, what a notable proof I will give you of the truth of my words, a proof which I have already given to others: — of the principle, I mean, that the impious, whoever he may be, ought not to go unpunished. For do not men regard Zeus as the best and most righteous of the gods? — and yet they admit that he bound his father (Cronos) because he wickedly devoured his sons, and that he too had punished his own father (Uranus) for a similar reason, in a nameless manner. And yet when I proceed against my father, they are angry with me. So inconsistent are they in their way of talking when the gods are concerned, and when I am concerned.

Soc. May not this be the reason, Euthyphro, why I am charged with impiety — that I cannot away with these stories about the gods? and therefore I suppose that people think me wrong. But, as you who are well informed about them approve of them, I cannot do better than assent to your superior wisdom. What else can I say, confessing as I do, that I know nothing about them? Tell me, for the love of Zeus, whether you really believe that they are true.

Euth. Yes, Socrates; and things more wonderful still, of which the world is in ignorance.

Soc. And do you really believe that the gods fought with one another, and had dire quarrels, battles, and the like, as the poets say, and as you may see represented in the works of great artists? The temples are full of them; and notably the robe of Athene, which is carried up to the Acropolis at the great Panathenaea, is embroidered with them. Are all these tales of the gods true, Euthyphro?

Euth. Yes, Socrates; and, as I was saying, I can tell you, if you would like to hear them, many other things about the gods which would quite amaze you.

Soc. I dare say; and you shall tell me them at some other time when I have leisure. But just at present I would rather hear from you a more precise answer, which you have not as yet given, my friend, to the question, What is 'piety'? When asked, you only replied, Doing as you do, charging your father with murder.

Euth. And what I said was true, Socrates.

Soc. No doubt, Euthyphro; but you would admit that there are many other pious acts?

Euth. There are.

Soc. Remember that I did not ask you to give me two or three examples of piety, but to explain the general idea which makes all pious things to be pious. Do you not recollect that there was one idea * which made the impious impious, and the pious pious?

Euth. I remember.

Soc. Tell me what is the nature of this idea, and then I shall have a standard to which I may look, and by which I may measure actions, whether yours or those of any one else, and then I shall be able to say that such and such an action is pious, such another impious.

Euth. I will tell you, if you like.

Soc. I should very much like.

Euth. Piety, then, is that which is dear to the gods, and impiety is that which is not dear to them.

Soc. Very good, Euthyphro; you have now given me the sort of answer which I wanted. But whether what you say is true or not I cannot as yet tell, although I make no doubt that you will prove the truth of your words.

Euth. Of course.

Soc. Come, then, and let us examine what we are saying. That thing or person which is dear to the gods is pious, and that thing or person which is hateful to the gods is impious, these two being the extreme opposites of one another. Was not that said?

Euth. It was.

Soc. And well said?

Euth. Yes, Socrates, I thought so; it was certainly said.

Soc. And further, Euthyphro, the gods were admitted to have enmities and hatreds and differences?

Euth. Yes, that was also said.

Soc. And what sort of difference creates enmity and anger? Suppose for example that you and I, my good friend, differ about a number; do differences of this sort make us enemies and set us at variance with one another? Do we not go at once to arithmetic, and put an end to them by a sum?

Euth. True.

Soc. Or suppose that we differ about magnitudes, do we not quickly end the differences by measuring?

Euth. Very true.

Soc. And we end a controversy about heavy and light by resorting to a weighing machine?

Euth. To be sure.

Soc. But what differences are there which cannot be thus decided, and which therefore make us angry and set us at enmity with one another? I dare say the answer does not occur to you at the moment, and therefore I will suggest that these enmities arise when the matters of difference are the just and unjust, good and evil, honourable and dishonourable. Are not these the points about which men differ, and about which when we are unable satisfactorily to

---

* Plato in this sentence makes clear that he is presupposing in the argument his Theory of Ideas.

decide our differences, you and I and all of us quarrel, when we do quarrel?

Euth. Yes, Socrates, the nature of the differences about which we quarrel is such as you describe.

Soc. And the quarrels of the gods, noble Euthyphro, when they occur, are of a like nature?

Euth. Certainly they are.

Soc. They have differences of opinion, as you say, about good and evil, just and unjust, honourable and dishonourable: there would have been no quarrels among them, if there had been no such differences — would there now?

Euth. You are quite right.

Soc. Does not every man love that which he deems noble and just and good, and hate the opposite of them?

Euth. Very true.

Soc. But, as you say, people regard the same things, some as just and others as unjust, — about these they dispute; and so there arise wars and fightings among them.

Euth. Very true.

Soc. Then the same things are hated by the gods and loved by the gods, and are both hateful and dear to them?

Euth. True.

Soc. And upon this view the same things, Euthyphro, will be pious and also impious?

Euth. So I should suppose.

Soc. Then, my friend, I remark with surprise that you have not answered the question which I asked. For I certainly did not ask you to tell me what action is both pious and impious: but now it would seem that what is loved by the gods is also hated by them. And therefore, Euthyphro, in thus chastising your father you may very likely be doing what is agreeable to Zeus but disagreeable to Cronos or Uranus, and what is acceptable to Hephaestus but unacceptable to Hera, and there may be other gods who have similar differences of opinion.

Euth. But I believe, Socrates, that all the gods would be agreed as to the propriety of punishing a murderer: there would be no difference of opinion about that.

Soc. Well, but speaking of men, Euthyphro, did you ever hear any one arguing that a murderer or any sort of evil-doer ought to be let off?

Euth. I should rather say that these are the questions which they are always arguing, especially in courts of law: they commit all sorts of crimes, and there is nothing which they will not do or say in their own defence.

Soc. But do they admit their guilt, Euthyphro, and yet say that they ought not to be punished?

Euth. No; they do not.

Soc. Then there are some things which they do not venture to

say and do: for they do not venture to argue that the guilty are to
be unpunished, but they deny their guilt, do they not?

Euth. Yes.

Soc. Then they do not argue that the evil-doer should not be
punished, but they argue about the fact of who the evil-doer is, and
what he did and when?

Euth. True.

Soc. And the gods are in the same case, if as you assert they quarrel
about just and unjust, and some of them say while others deny that
injustice is done among them. For surely neither God nor man
will ever venture to say that the doer of injustice is not to be punished?

Euth. That is true, Socrates, in the main.

Soc. But they join issue about the particulars — gods and men
alike; and, if they dispute at all, they dispute about some act which
is called in question, and which by some is affirmed to be just, by
others to be unjust. Is not that true?

Euth. Quite true.

Soc. Well then, my dear friend Euthyphro, do tell me, for my
better instruction and information, what proof have you that in the
opinion of all the gods a servant who is guilty of murder, and is put
in chains by the master of the dead man, and dies because he is put
in chains before he who bound him can learn from the interpreters
of the gods what he ought to do with him, dies unjustly; and that
on behalf of such an one a son ought to proceed against his father
and accuse him of murder. How would you show that all the gods
absolutely agree in approving of his act? Prove to me that they do,
and I will applaud your wisdom as long as I live.

Euth. It will be a difficult task; but I could make the matter very
clear indeed to you.

Soc. I understand; you mean to say that I am not so quick of apprehension as the judges: for to them you will be sure to prove that
the act is unjust, and hateful to the gods.

Euth. Yes indeed, Socrates; at least if they will listen to me.

Soc. But they will be sure to listen if they find that you are a good
speaker. There was a notion that came into my mind while you
were speaking; I said to myself: 'Well, and what if Euthyphro does
prove to me that all the gods regarded the death of the serf as unjust,
how do I know anything more of the nature of piety and impiety?
for granting that this action may be hateful to the gods, still piety and
impiety are not adequately defined by these distinctions, for that
which is hateful to the gods has been shown to be also pleasing and
dear to them.' And therefore, Euthyphro, I do not ask you to prove
this; I will suppose, if you like, that all the gods condemn and abomi-
nate such an action. But I will amend the definition so far as to say
that what all the gods hate is impious, and what they love pious or
holy; and what some of them love and others hate is both or neither.
Shall this be our definition of piety and impiety?

Euth. Why not, Socrates?

Soc. Why not! certainly, as far as I am concerned, Euthyphro, there is no reason why not. But whether this admission will greatly assist you in the task of instructing me as you promised, is a matter for you to consider.

Euth. Yes, I should say that what all the gods love is pious and holy, and the opposite which they all hate, impious.

Soc. Ought we to enquire into the truth of this, Euthyphro, or simply to accept the mere statement on our own authority and that of others? What do you say?

Euth. We should enquire; and I believe that the statement will stand the test of enquiry.

Soc. We shall know better, my good friend, in a little while. The point which I should first wish to understand is whether the pious or holy is beloved by the gods because it is holy, or holy because it is beloved of the gods.

Euth. I do not understand your meaning, Socrates.

Soc. I will endeavour to explain: we speak of carrying and we speak of being carried, of leading and being led, seeing and being seen. You know that in all such cases there is a difference, and you know also in what the difference lies?

Euth. I think that I understand.

Soc. And is not that which is beloved distinct from that which loves?

Euth. Certainly.

Soc. Well; and now tell me, is that which is carried in this state of carrying because it is carried, or for some other reason?

Euth. No; that is the reason.

Soc. And the same is true of what is led and of what is seen?

Euth. True.

Soc. And a thing is not seen because it is visible, but conversely, visible because it is seen; nor is a thing led because it is in the state of being led, or carried because it is in the state of being carried, but the converse of this. And now I think, Euthyphro, that my meaning will be intelligible; and my meaning is, that any state of action or passion implies previous action or passion. It does not become because it is becoming, but it is in a state of becoming because it becomes; neither does it suffer because it is in a state of suffering, but it is in a state of suffering because it suffers. Do you not agree?

Euth. Yes.

Soc. Is not that which is loved in some state either of becoming or suffering?

Euth. Yes.

Soc. And the same holds as in the previous instances; the state of being loved follows the act of being loved, and not the act the state.

Euth. Certainly.

Soc. And what do you say of piety, Euthyphro: is not piety, according to your definition, loved by all the gods?

Euth. Yes.

Soc. Because it is pious or holy, or for some other reason?

Euth. No, that is the reason.

Soc. It is loved because it is holy, not holy because it is loved?

Euth. Yes.

Soc. And that which is dear to the gods is loved by them, and is in a state to be loved of them because it is loved of them?

Euth. Certainly.

Soc. Then that which is dear to the gods, Euthyphro, is not holy, nor is that which is holy loved of God, as you affirm; but they are two different things.

Euth. How do you mean, Socrates?

Soc. I mean to say that the holy has been acknowledged by us to be loved by God because it is holy, not to be holy because it is loved.

Euth. Yes.

Soc. But that which is dear to the gods is dear to them because it is loved by them, not loved by them because it is dear to them.

Euth. True.

Soc. But, friend Euthyphro, if that which is holy is the same with that which is dear to God, and is loved because it is holy, then that which is dear to God would have been loved as being dear to God; but if that which is dear to God is dear to him because loved by him, then that which is holy would have been holy because loved by him. But now you see that the reverse is the case, and that they are quite different from one another. For one (θεοφιλές) is of a kind to be loved because it is loved, and the other (ὅσιον) is loved because it is of a kind to be loved. Thus you appear to me, Euthyphro, when I ask you what is the essence of holiness, to offer an attribute only, and not the essence — the attribute of being loved by all the gods. But you still refuse to explain to me the nature of holiness. And therefore, if you please, I will ask you not to hide your treasure, but to tell me once more what holiness or piety really is, whether dear to the gods or not (for that is a matter about which we will not quarrel); and what is impiety?

Euth. I really do not know, Socrates, how to express what I mean. For somehow or other our arguments, on whatever ground we rest them, seem to turn round and walk away from us.

Soc. Your words, Euthyphro, are like the handiwork of my ancestor Daedalus; and if I were the sayer or propounder of them, you might say that my arguments walk away and will not remain fixed where they are placed because I am a descendant of his. But now, since these notions are your own, you must find some other gibe, for they certainly, as you yourself allow, show an inclination to be on the move.

Euth. Nay, Socrates, I shall still say that you are the Daedalus who sets arguments in motion; not I, certainly, but you make them move or go round, for they would never have stirred, as far as I am concerned.

Soc. Then I must be a greater than Daedalus: for whereas he only made his own inventions to move, I move those of other people as well. And the beauty of it is, that I would rather not. For I would give the wisdom of Daedalus, and the wealth of Tantalus, to be able to detain them and keep them fixed. But enough of this. As I perceive that you are lazy, I will myself endeavour to show you how you might instruct me in the nature of piety; and I hope that you will not grudge your labour. Tell me, then, — Is not that which is pious necessarily just?

Euth. Yes.

Soc. And is, then, all which is just pious? or, is that which is pious all just, but that which is just, only in part and not all, pious?

Euth. I do not understand you, Socrates.

Soc. And yet I know that you are as much wiser than I am, as you are younger. But, as I was saying, revered friend, the abundance of your wisdom makes you lazy. Please to exert yourself, for there is no real difficulty in understanding me. What I mean I may explain by an illustration of what I do not mean. The poet (Stasinus) sings —

> Of Zeus, the author and creator of all these things,
> You will not tell: for where there is fear there is also reverence.

Now I disagree with this poet. Shall I tell you in what respect?

Euth. By all means.

Soc. I should not say that where there is fear there is also reverence; for I am sure that many persons fear poverty and disease, and the like evils, but I do not perceive that they reverence the objects of their fear.

Euth. Very true.

Soc. But where reverence is, there is fear; for he who has a feeling of reverence and shame about the commission of any action, fears and is afraid of an ill reputation.

Euth. No doubt.

Soc. Then we are wrong in saying that where there is fear there is also reverence; and we should say, where there is reverence there is also fear. But there is not always reverence where there is fear; for fear is a more extended notion, and reverence is a part of fear, just as the odd is a part of number, and number is a more extended notion than the odd. I suppose that you follow me now?

Euth. Quite well.

Soc. That was the sort of question which I meant to raise when I asked whether the just is always the pious, or the pious always the just; and whether there may not be justice where there is not piety; for justice is the more extended notion of which piety is only a part. Do you dissent?

Euth. No, I think that you are quite right.

Soc. Then, if piety is a part of justice, I suppose that we should enquire what part? If you had pursued the enquiry in the previous cases; for instance, if you had asked me what is an even number, and what part of number the even is, I should have had no difficulty in replying, a number which represents a figure having two equal sides. Do you not agree?

Euth. Yes, I quite agree.

Soc. In like manner, I want you to tell me what part of justice is piety or holiness, that I may be able to tell Meletus not to do me injustice, or indict me for impiety, as I am now adequately instructed by you in the nature of piety or holiness, and their opposites.

Euth. Piety or holiness, Socrates, appears to me to be that part of justice which attends to the gods, as there is the other part of justice which attends to men.

Soc. That is good, Euthyphro; yet still there is a little point about which I should like to have further information, What is the meaning of 'attention'? For attention can hardly be used in the same sense when applied to the gods as when applied to other things. For instance, horses are said to require attention, and not every person is able to attend to them, but only a person skilled in horsemanship. Is it not so?

Euth. Certainly.

Soc. I should suppose that the art of horsemanship is the art of attending to horses?

Euth. Yes.

Soc. Nor is every one qualified to attend to dogs, but only the huntsman?

Euth. True.

Soc. And I should also conceive that the art of the huntsman is the art of attending to dogs?

Euth. Yes.

Soc. As the art of the oxherd is the art of attending to oxen?

Euth. Very true.

Soc. In like manner holiness or piety is the art of attending to the gods? — that would be your meaning, Euthyphro?

Euth. Yes.

Soc. And is not attention always designed for the good or benefit of that to which the attention is given? As in the case of horses, you may observe that when attended to by the horseman's art they are benefited and improved, are they not?

Euth. True.

Soc. As the dogs are benefited by the huntsman's art, and the oxen by the art of the oxherd, and all other things are tended or attended for their good and not for their hurt?

Euth. Certainly, not for their hurt.

Soc. But for their good?

Euth. Of course.

Soc. And does piety or holiness, which has been defined to be the art of attending to the gods, benefit or improve them? Would you say that when you do a holy act you make any of the gods better?

Euth. No, no; that was certainly not what I meant.

Soc. And I, Euthyphro, never supposed that you did. I asked you the question about the nature of the attention, because I thought that you did not.

Euth. You do me justice, Socrates; that is not the sort of attention which I mean.

Soc. Good: but I must still ask what is this attention to the gods which is called piety?

Euth. It is such, Socrates, as servants show to their masters.

Soc. I understand — a sort of ministration to the gods.

Euth. Exactly.

Soc. Medicine is also a sort of ministration or service, having in view the attainment of some object — would you not say of health?

Euth. I should.

Soc. Again, there is an art which ministers to the ship-builder with a view to the attainment of some result?

Euth. Yes, Socrates, with a view to the building of a ship.

Soc. As there is an art which ministers to the housebuilder with a view to the building of a house?

Euth. Yes.

Soc. And now tell me, my good friend, about the art which ministers to the gods: what work does that help to accomplish? For you must surely know if, as you say, you are of all men living the one who is best instructed in religion.

Euth. And I speak the truth, Socrates.

Soc. Tell me then, oh tell me — what is that fair work which the gods do by the help of our ministrations?

Euth. Many and fair, Socrates, are the works which they do.

Soc. Why, my friend, and so are those of a general. But the chief of them is easily told. Would you not say that victory in war is the chief of them?

Euth. Certainly.

Soc. Many and fair, too, are the works of the husbandman, if I am not mistaken; but his chief work is the production of food from the earth?

Euth. Exactly.

Soc. And of the many and fair things done by the gods, which is the chief or principal one?

Euth. I have told you already, Socrates, that to learn all these things accurately will be very tiresome. Let me simply say that piety or holiness is learning how to please the gods in word and deed, by prayers and sacrifices. Such piety is the salvation of families and states, just as the impious, which is unpleasing to the gods, is their ruin and destruction.

Soc. I think that you could have answered in much fewer words the chief question which I asked, Euthyphro, if you had chosen. But I see plainly that you are not disposed to instruct me — clearly not: else why, when we reached the point, did you turn aside? Had you only answered me I should have truly learned of you by this time the nature of piety. Now, as the asker of a question is necessarily dependent on the answerer, whither he leads I must follow; and can only ask again, what is the pious, and what is piety? Do you mean that they are a sort of science of praying and sacrificing?

Euth. Yes, I do.

Soc. And sacrificing is giving to the gods, and prayer is asking of the gods?

Euth. Yes, Socrates.

Soc. Upon this view, then, piety is a science of asking and giving?

Euth. You understand me capitally, Socrates.

Soc. Yes, my friend; the reason is that I am a votary of your science, and give my mind to it, and therefore nothing which you say will be thrown away upon me. Please then to tell me, what is the nature of this service to the gods? Do you mean that we prefer requests and give gifts to them?

Euth. Yes, I do.

Soc. Is not the right way of asking to ask of them what we want?

Euth. Certainly.

Soc. And the right way of giving is to give to them in return what they want of us. There would be no meaning in an art which gives to any one that which he does not want.

Euth. Very true, Socrates.

Soc. Then piety, Euthyphro, is an art which gods and men have of doing business with one another?

Euth. That is an expression which you may use, if you like.

Soc. But I have no particular liking for anything but the truth. I wish, however, that you would tell me what benefit accrues to the gods from our gifts. There is no doubt about what they give to us; for there is no good thing which they do not give; but how we can give any good thing to them in return is far from being equally clear. If they give everything and we give nothing, that must be an affair of business in which we have very greatly the advantage of them.

Euth. And do you imagine, Socrates, that any benefit accrues to the gods from our gifts?

Soc. But if not, Euthyphro, what is the meaning of gifts which are conferred by us upon the gods?

Euth. What else, but tributes of honour; and, as I was just now saying, what pleases them?

Soc. Piety, then, is pleasing to the gods, but not beneficial or dear to them?

Euth. I should say that nothing could be dearer.

Soc. Then once more the assertion is repeated that piety is dear to the gods?

Euth. Certainly.

Soc. And when you say this, can you wonder at your words not standing firm, but walking away? Will you accuse me of being the Daedalus who makes them walk away, not perceiving that there is another and far greater artist than Daedalus who makes them go round in a circle, and he is yourself; for the argument, as you will perceive, comes round to the same point. Were we not saying that the holy or pious was not the same with that which is loved of the gods? Have you forgotten?

Euth. I quite remember.

Soc. And are you not saying that what is loved of the gods is holy; and is not this the same as what is dear to them — do you see?

Euth. True.

Soc. Then either we were wrong in our former assertion; or, if we were right then, we are wrong now.

Euth. One of the two must be true.

Soc. Then we must begin again and ask, What is piety? That is an enquiry which I shall never be weary of pursuing as far as in me lies; and I entreat you not to scorn me, but to apply your mind to the utmost, and tell me the truth. For, if any man knows, you are he; and therefore I must detain you, like Proteus, until you tell. If you had not certainly known the nature of piety and impiety, I am confident that you would never, on behalf of a serf, have charged your aged father with murder. You would not have run such a risk of doing wrong in the sight of the gods, and you would have had too much respect for the opinions of men. I am sure, therefore, that you know the nature of piety and impiety. Speak out then, my dear Euthyphro, and do not hide your knowledge.

Euth. Another time, Socrates; for I am in a hurry, and must go now.

Soc. Alas! my companion, and will you leave me in despair? I was hoping that you would instruct me in the nature of piety and impiety; and then I might have cleared myself of Meletus and his indictment. I would have told him that I had been enlightened by Euthyphro, and had given up rash innovations and speculations, in which I indulged only through ignorance, and that now I am about to lead a better life.

[tr. B. Jowett]

APOLOGY

How you, O Athenians, have been affected by my accusers, I cannot tell; but I know that they almost made me forget who I was — so persuasively did they speak; and yet they have hardly uttered a word of truth. But of the many falsehoods told by them, there was one which quite amazed me; — I mean when they said that you should be upon your guard and not allow yourselves to be deceived by the force of my eloquence. To say this, when they were certain to be detected as soon as I opened my lips and proved myself to be anything but a great speaker, did indeed appear to me most shameless — unless by the force of eloquence they mean the force of truth; for if such is their meaning, I admit that I am eloquent. But in how different a way from theirs! Well, as I was saying, they have scarcely spoken the truth at all; but from me you shall hear the whole truth: not, however, delivered after their manner in a set oration duly ornamented with words and phrases. No, by heaven! but I shall use the words and arguments which occur to me at the moment; for I am confident in the justice of my cause:* at my time of life I ought not to be appearing before you, O men of Athens, in the character of a juvenile orator — let no one expect it of me. And I must beg of you to grant me a favour: — If I defend myself in my accustomed manner, and you hear me using the words which I have been in the habit of using in the agora, at the tables of the money-changers, or anywhere else, I would ask you not to be surprised, and not to interrupt me on this account. For I am more than seventy years of age, and appearing now for the first time in a court of law, I am quite a stranger to the language of the place; and therefore I would have you regard me as if I were really a stranger, whom you would excuse if he spoke in his native tongue, and after the fashion of his country: — Am I making an unfair request of you? Never mind the manner, which may or may not be good; but think only of the truth of my words, and give heed to that: let the speaker speak truly and the judge decide justly.

And first, I have to reply to the older charges and to my first accusers, and then I will go on to the later ones. For of old I have had many accusers, who have accused me falsely to you during many years; and I am more afraid of them than of Anytus and his associates, who are dangerous, too, in their own way. But far more dangerous are the others, who began when you were children, and took possession of your minds with their falsehoods, telling of one Socrates, a wise man, who speculated about the heaven above, and searched into the earth beneath, and made the worse appear the better cause. The disseminators of this tale are the accusers whom I dread; for their hearers are apt to fancy that such enquirers do not believe in the existence of the gods. And they are many, and their charges against me are of ancient date, and they were made by them in the days when you were more impressible than you are now — in childhood, or it may have been in youth — and the cause when heard went by default, for there was none to answer. And hardest of all, I do not know and cannot tell the names of my accusers; unless in the chance case of a comic poet. All who from envy and malice have persuaded you — some of them having first convinced themselves — all this class of men are most difficult to deal with; for I cannot have them up here, and cross-examine them, and therefore I must simply fight with shadows in my own defence, and argue when there is no one who answers. I will ask you then to assume with me, as I was saying, that my opponents are of two kinds; one recent, the other ancient: and I hope that you will see the propriety of my answering the latter first, for these accusations you heard long before the others, and much oftener.

Well, then, I must make my defence, and endeavour to clear away in a short time, a slander which has lasted a long time. May I succeed, if to succeed be for my good and yours, or likely to avail me

---

* Or, I am certain that I am right in taking this course.

in my cause! The task is not an easy one; I quite understand the nature of it. And so leaving the event with God, in obedience to the law I will now make my defence.

I will begin at the beginning, and ask what is the accusation which has given rise to the slander of me, and in fact has encouraged Meletus to prefer this charge against me. Well, what do the slanderers say? They shall be my prosecutors, and I will sum up their words in an affidavit: 'Socrates is an evil-doer, and a curious person, who searches into things under the earth and in heaven, and he makes the worse appear the better cause; and he teaches the aforesaid doctrines to others.' Such is the nature of the accusation: it is just what you have yourselves seen in the comedy of Aristophanes,* who has in-troduced a man whom he calls Socrates, going about and saying that he walks in air, and talking a deal of nonsense concerning matters of which I do not pretend to know either much or little — not that I mean to speak disparagingly of any one who is a student of natural philosophy. I should be very sorry if Meletus could bring so grave a charge against me. But the simple truth is, O Athenians, that I have nothing to do with physical speculations. Very many of those here present are witnesses to the truth of this, and to them I appeal. Speak then, you who have heard me, and tell your neighbours whether any of you have ever known me hold forth in few words or in many upon such matters. . . You hear their answer. And from what they say of this part of the charge you will be able to judge of the truth of the rest.

As little foundation is there for the report that I am a teacher, and take money; this accusation has no more truth in it than the other. Although, if a man were really able to instruct mankind, to receive money for giving instruction would, in my opinion, be an honour to him. There is Gorgias of Leontium, and Prodicus of Ceos, and Hip-pias of Elis, who go the round of the cities, and are able to persuade the young men to leave their own citizens by whom they might be taught for nothing, and come to them whom they not only pay, but are thankful if they may be allowed to pay them. There is at this time a Parian philosopher residing in Athens, of whom I have heard; and I came to hear of him in this way: — I came across a man who has spent a world of money on the Sophists, Callias, the son of Hip-ponicus, and knowing that he had sons, I asked him: 'Callias,' I said, 'if your two sons were foals or calves, there would be no difficulty in finding some one to put over them; we should hire a trainer of horses, or a farmer probably, who would improve and perfect them in their own proper virtue and excellence; but as they are human beings, whom are you thinking of placing over them? Is there any one who understands human and political virtue? You must have thought about the matter, for you have sons; is there any one?' 'There is,' he said. 'Who is he?' said I; 'and of what country? and what does he charge?' 'Evenus the Parian,' he replied; 'he is the man, and his charge is five minae.' Happy is Evenus, I said to myself, if he really

* *Clouds, 225 ff.*

has this wisdom, and teaches at such a moderate charge. Had I the
same, I should have been very proud and conceited; but the truth is
that I have no knowledge of the kind.

I dare say, Athenians, that some one among you will reply, 'Yes,
Socrates, but what is the origin of these accusations which are brought
against you; there must have been something strange which you have
been doing?   All these rumours and this talk about you would never
have arisen if you had been like other men: tell us, then, what is
the cause of them, for we should be sorry to judge hastily of you.'
Now I regard this as a fair challenge, and I will endeavour to explain
to you the reason why I am called wise and have such an evil fame.
Please to attend them.   And although some of you may think that I
am joking, I declare that I will tell you the entire truth.   Men of
Athens, this reputation of mine has come of a certain sort of wisdom
which I possess. If you ask me what kind of wisdom, I reply, wisdom
such as may perhaps be attained by man, for to that extent I am inclined to believe that I am wise; whereas the persons of whom I was
speaking have a superhuman wisdom, which I may fail to describe,
because I have it not myself; and he who says that I have, speaks
falsely, and is taking away my character   And here, O men of Athens,
I must beg you not to interrupt me, even if I seem to say something extravagant.   For the word which I will speak is not mine.   I will refer
you to a witness who is worthy of credit; that witness shall be the God
of Delphi — he will tell you about my wisdom, if I have any, and of
what sort it is.   You must have known Chaerephon; he was early a
friend of mine, and also a friend of yours, for he shared in the recent
exile of the people, and returned with you.   Well, Chaerephon, as
you know, was very impetuous in all his doings, and he went to
Delphi and boldly asked the oracle to tell him whether — as I was
saying, I must beg you not to interrupt — he asked the oracle to tell
him whether any one was wiser than I was, and the Pythian prophetess answered, that there was no man wiser.   Chaerephon is dead
himself; but his brother, who is in court, will confirm the truth of
what I am saying.

Why do I mention this?   Because I am going to explain to you
why I have such an evil name.   When I heard the answer, I said to
myself, What can the god mean? and what is the interpretation of
his riddle? for I know that I have no wisdom, small or great.   What
then can he mean when he says that I am the wisest of men?   And
yet he is a god, and cannot lie; that would be against his nature.
After long consideration, I thought of a method of trying the question.   I reflected that if I could only find a man wiser than myself,
then I might go to the god with a refutation in my hand.   I should
say to him, 'Here is a man who is wiser than I am; but you said
that I was the wisest.'   Accordingly I went to one who had the reputation of wisdom, and observed him — his name I need not mention; he was a politician whom I selected for examination — and the
result was as follows: When I began to talk with him, I could not
help thinking that he was not really wise, although he was thought

wise by many, and still wiser by himself; and thereupon I tried to explain to him that he thought himself wise, but was not really wise; and the consequence was that he hated me, and his enmity was shared by several who were present and heard me. So I left him, saying to myself, as I went away: Well, although I do not suppose that either of us knows anything really beautiful and good, I am better off than he is, — for he knows nothing, and thinks that he knows; I neither know nor think that I know. In this latter particular, then, I seem to have slightly the advantage of him. Then I went to another who had still higher pretensions to wisdom, and my conclusion was exactly the same. Whereupon I made another enemy of him, and of many others besides him.

Then I went to one man after another, being not unconscious of the enmity which I provoked, and I lamented and feared this: But necessity was laid upon me, — the word of God, I thought, ought to be considered first. And I said to myself, Go I must to all who appear to know, and find out the meaning of the oracle. And I swear to you, Athenians, by the dog I swear! — for I must tell you the truth — the result of my mission was just this: I found that the men most in repute were all but the most foolish; and that others less esteemed were really wiser and better. I will tell you the tale of my wanderings and of the 'Herculean' labours, as I may call them, which I endured only to find at last the oracle irrefutable. After the politicians, I went to the poets; tragic, dithyrambic, and all sorts. And there, I said to myself, you will be instantly detected; now you will find out that you are more ignorant than they are. Accordingly, I took them some of the most elaborate passages in their own writings, and asked what was the meaning of them — thinking that they would teach me something. Will you believe me? I am almost ashamed to confess the truth, but I must say that there is hardly a person present who would not have talked better about their poetry than they did themselves. Then I knew that not by wisdom do poets write poetry, but by a sort of genius and inspiration; they are like diviners or soothsayers who also say many fine things, but do not understand the meaning of them. The poets appeared to me to be much in the same case; and I further observed that upon the strength of their poetry they believed themselves to be the wisest of men in other things in which they were not wise. So I departed, conceiving myself to be superior to them for the same reason that I was superior to the politicians.

At last I went to the artisans, for I was conscious that I knew nothing at all, as I may say, and I was sure that they knew many fine things; and here I was not mistaken, for they did know many things of which I was ignorant, and in this they certainly were wiser than I was. But I observed that even the good artisans fell into the same error as the poets; — because they were good workmen they thought that they also knew all sorts of high matters, and this defect in them overshadowed their wisdom; and therefore I asked myself on behalf of the oracle, whether I would like to be as

I was, neither having their knowledge nor their ignorance, or like them in both; and I made answer to myself and to the oracle that I was better off as I was.

This inquisition has led to my having many enemies of the worst and most dangerous kind, and has given occasion also to many calumnies. And I am called wise, for my hearers always imagine that I myself possess the wisdom which I find wanting in others: but the truth is, O men of Athens, that God only is wise; and by his answer he intends to show that the wisdom of men is worth little or nothing; he is not speaking of Socrates, he is only using my name by way of illustration, as if he said, He, O men, is the wisest, who, like Socrates, knows that his wisdom is in truth worth nothing. And so I go about the world, obedient to the god, and search and make enquiry into the wisdom of any one, whether citizen or stranger, who appears to be wise; and if he is not wise, then in vindication of the oracle I show him that he is not wise; and my occupation quite absorbs me, and I have no time to give either to any public matter of interest or to any concern of my own, but I am in utter poverty by reason of my devotion to the god.

There is another thing: — young men of the richer classes, who have not much to do, come about me of their own accord; they like to hear the pretenders examined, and they often imitate me, and proceed to examine others; there are plenty of persons, as they quickly discover, who think that they know something, but really know little or nothing; and then those who are examined by them instead of being angry with themselves are angry with me: This confounded Socrates, they say; this villainous misleader of youth! — and then if somebody asks them, Why, what evil does he practise or teach? they do not know, and cannot tell; but in order that they may not appear to be at a loss, they repeat the ready-made charges which are used against all philosophers about teaching things up in the clouds and under the earth, and having no gods, and making the worse appear the better cause; for they do not like to confess that their pretence of knowledge has been detected — which is the truth; and as they are numerous and ambitious and energetic, and are drawn up in battle array and have persuasive tongues, they have filled your ears with their loud and inveterate calumnies. And this is the reason why my three accusers, Meletus and Anytus and Lycon, have set upon me; Meletus, who has a quarrel with me on behalf of the poets; Anytus, on behalf of the craftsmen and politicians; Lycon, on behalf of the rhetoricians: and as I said at the beginning, I cannot expect to get rid of such a mass of calumny all in a moment. And this, O men of Athens, is the truth and the whole truth; I have concealed nothing, I have dissembled nothing. And yet, I know that my plainness of speech makes them hate me, and what is their hatred but a proof that I am speaking the truth? — Hence has arisen the prejudice against me; and this is the reason of it, as you will find out either in this or in any future enquiry.

I have said enough in my defence against the first class of my accusers; I turn to the second class. They are headed by Meletus, that good man and true lover of his country, as he calls himself. Against these, too, I must try to make a defence:—Let their affidavit be read: it contains something of this kind: It says that Socrates is a doer of evil, who corrupts the youth; and who does not believe in the gods of the state, but has other new divinities of his own. Such is the charge; and now let us examine the particular counts. He says that I am a doer of evil, and corrupt the youth; but I say, O men of Athens, that Meletus is a doer of evil, in that he pretends to be in earnest when he is only in jest, and is so eager to bring men to trial from a pretended zeal and interest about matters in which he really never had the smallest interest. And the truth of this I will endeavour to prove to you.

Come hither, Meletus, and let me ask a question of you. You think a great deal about the improvement of youth?

Yes, I do.

Tell the judges, then, who is their improver; for you must know, as you have taken the pains to discover their corrupter, and are citing and accusing me before them. Speak, then, and tell the judges who their improver is.—Observe, Meletus, that you are silent, and have nothing to say. But is not this rather disgraceful, and a very considerable proof of what I was saying, that you have no interest in the matter? Speak up, friend, and tell us who their improver is.

The laws.

But that, my good sir, is not my meaning. I want to know who the person is, who, in the first place, knows the laws.

The judges, Socrates, who are present in court.

What, do you mean to say, Meletus, that they are able to instruct and improve youth?

Certainly they are.

What, all of them, or some only and not others?

All of them.

By the goddess Hera, that is good news! There are plenty of improvers, then. And what do you say of the audience,—do they improve them?

Yes, they do.

And the senators?

Yes, the senators improve them.

But perhaps the members of the assembly corrupt them?—or do they too improve them?

They improve them.

Then every Athenian improves and elevates them; all with the exception of myself; and I alone am their corrupter? Is that what you affirm?

That is what I stoutly affirm.

I am very unfortunate if you are right. But suppose I ask you a question: How about horses? Does one man do them harm and all the world good? Is not the exact opposite the truth? One man is able to do them good, or at least not many; — the trainer of horses, that is to say, does them good, and others who have to do with them rather injure them? Is not that true, Meletus, of horses, or of any other animals? Most assuredly it is; whether you and Anytus say yes or no. Happy indeed would be the condition of youth if they had one corrupter only, and all the rest of the world were their improvers. But you, Meletus, have sufficiently shown that you never had a thought about the young: your carelessness is seen in your not caring about the very things which you bring against me.

And now, Meletus, I will ask you another question — by Zeus I will: Which is better, to live among bad citizens, or among good ones? Answer, friend, I say; the question is one which may be easily answered. Do not the good do their neighbours good, and the bad do them evil?

Certainly.

And is there any one who would rather be injured than benefited by those who live with him? Answer, my good friend, the law requires you to answer — does any one like to be injured?

Certainly not.

And when you accuse me of corrupting and deteriorating the youth, do you allege that I corrupt them intentionally or unintentionally?

Intentionally, I say.

But you have just admitted that the good do their neighbours good, and evil do them evil. Now, is that a truth which your superior wisdom has recognized thus early in life, and am I, at my age, in such darkness and ignorance as not to know that if a man with whom I have to live is corrupted by me, I am very likely to be harmed by him; and yet I corrupt him, and intentionally, too, — so you say, although neither I nor any other human being is ever likely to be convinced by you. But either I do not corrupt them, or I corrupt them unintentionally; and on either view of the case you lie. If my offence is unintentional, the law has no cognizance of unintentional offences: you ought to have taken me privately, and warned and admonished me; for if I had been better advised, I should have left off doing what I only did unintentionally — no doubt I should; but you would have nothing to say to me and refused to teach me. And now you bring me up in this court, which is a place not of instruction, but of punishment.

It will be very clear to you, Athenians, as I was saying, that Meletus has no care at all, great or small, about the matter. But still I should like to know, Meletus, in what I am affirmed to corrupt the young. I suppose you mean, as I infer from your indictment, that I teach them not to acknowledge the gods which the state acknowledges, but some other new divinities or spiritual agencies in their stead. These are the lessons by which I corrupt the youth, as you say.

Yes, that I say emphatically.

Then, by the gods, Meletus, of whom we are speaking, tell me and the court, in somewhat plainer terms, what you mean! for I do not as yet understand whether you affirm that I teach other men to acknowledge some gods, and therefore that I do believe in gods, and am not an entire atheist — this you do not lay to my charge, — but only you say that they are not the same gods which the city recognizes — the charge is that they are different gods. Or, do you mean that I am an atheist simply, and a teacher of atheism?

I mean the latter — that you are a complete atheist.

What an extraordinary statement! Why do you think so, Meletus? Do you mean that I do not believe in the godhead of the sun or moon, like other men?

I assure you, judges, that he does not: for he says that the sun is stone, and the moon earth.

Friend Meletus, you think that you are accusing Anaxagoras: and you have but a bad opinion of the judges, if you fancy them illiterate to such a degree as not to know that these doctrines are found in the books of Anaxagoras the Clazomenian, which are full of them. And so, forsooth, the youth are said to be taught them by Socrates, when there are not unfrequently exhibitions of them at the theatre * (price of admission one drachma at the most); and they might pay their money, and laugh at Socrates if he pretends to father these extraordinary views. And so, Meletus, you really think that I do not believe in any god?

I swear by Zeus that you believe absolutely in none at all.

Nobody will believe you, Meletus, and I am pretty sure that you do not believe yourself. I cannot help thinking, men of Athens, that Meletus is reckless and impudent, and that he has written this indictment in a spirit of mere wantonness and youthful bravado. Has he not compounded a riddle, thinking to try me? He said to himself: — I shall see whether the wise Socrates will discover my facetious contradiction, or whether I shall be able to deceive him and the rest of them. For he certainly does appear to me to contradict himself in the indictment as much as if he said that Socrates is guilty of not believing in the gods, and yet of believing in them — but this is not like a person who is in earnest.

I should like you, O men of Athens, to join me in examining what I conceive to be his inconsistency; and do you, Meletus, answer. And I must remind the audience of my request that they would not make a disturbance if I speak in my accustomed manner:

Did ever man, Meletus, believe in the existence of human things, and not of human beings? . . . I wish, men of Athens, that he would answer, and not be always trying to get up an interruption. Did ever any man believe in horsemanship, and not in horses? or in flute-playing, and not in flute-players? No, my friend; I will answer to you and to the court, as you refuse to answer for yourself. There is no man who ever did. But now please to answer the next question: Can a man believe in spiritual and divine agencies, and not in spirits or demigods?

He cannot.

* Probably an allusion to Aristophanes who caricatured, and to Euripides who borrowed the notions of Anaxagoras, as well as to other dramatic poets.

How lucky I am to have extracted that answer, by the assistance of the court! But then you swear in the indictment that I teach and believe in divine or spiritual agencies (new or old, no matter for that); at any rate, I believe in spiritual agencies, — so you say and swear in the affidavit; and yet if I believe in divine beings, how can I help believing in spirits or demigods; — must I not? To be sure I must; and therefore I may assume that your silence gives consent. Now what are spirits or demigods? are they not either gods or the sons of gods?

Certainly they are.

But this is what I call the facetious riddle invented by you: the demigods or spirits are gods, and you say first that I do not believe in gods, and then again that I do believe in gods; that is, if I believe in demigods. For if the demigods are the illegitimate sons of gods, whether by the nymphs or by any other mothers, of whom they are said to be the sons — what human being will ever believe that there are no gods if they are the sons of gods? You might as well affirm the existence of mules, and deny that of horses and asses. Such non-sense, Meletus, could only have been intended by you to make trial of me. You have put this into the indictment because you had nothing real of which to accuse me. But no one who has a particle of under-standing will ever be convinced by you that the same men can be-lieve in divine and superhuman things, and yet not believe that there are gods and demigods and heroes.

I have said enough in answer to the charge of Meletus: any elaborate defence is unnecessary; but I know only too well how many are the enmities which I have incurred, and this is what will be my destruction if I am destroyed; — not Meletus, nor yet Anytus, but the envy and detraction of the world, which has been the death of many good men, and will probably be the death of many more; there is no danger of my being the last of them.

Some one will say: And are you not ashamed, Socrates, of a course of life which is likely to bring you to an untimely end? To him I may fairly answer: There you are mistaken: a man who is good for anything ought not to calculate the chance of living or dying; he ought only to consider whether in doing anything he is doing right or wrong — acting the part of a good man or of a bad. Whereas, upon your view, the heroes who fell at Troy were not good for much, and the son of Thetis above all, who altogether despised danger in comparison with disgrace; and when he was so eager to slay Hector, his goddess mother said to him, that if he avenged his companion Patroclus, and slew Hector, he would die himself — 'Fate,' she said, in these or the like words, 'waits for you next after Hector;' he, receiving this warning, utterly despised danger and death, and instead of fearing them, feared rather to live in dishonour, and not to avenge his friend. 'Let me die forthwith,' he replies, 'and be avenged of my enemy, rather than abide here by the beaked ships, a laughing-stock and a burden of the earth.' Had Achilles any thought of death and danger? For wherever a man's place is, whether the place which he has chosen or that in which he has been placed by a commander, there he ought to remain in the hour of danger; he should not think of death or of anything but of disgrace. And this, O men of Athens, is a true saying.

Strange, indeed, would be my conduct, O men of Athens, if I who, when I was ordered by the generals whom you chose to command me at Potidaea and Amphipolis and Delium, remained where they placed me, like any other man, facing death — if now, when, as I conceive and imagine, God orders me to fulfil the philosopher's mission of searching into myself and other men, I were to desert my post through fear of death, or any other fear; that would indeed be strange, and I might justly be arraigned in court for denying the existence of the gods, if I disobeyed the oracle because I was afraid of death, fancying that I was wise when I was not wise. For the fear of death is indeed the pretence of wisdom, and not real wisdom, being a pretence of knowing the unknown; and no one knows whether death, which men in their fear apprehend to be the greatest evil, may not be the greatest good. Is not this ignorance of a disgraceful sort, the ignorance which is the conceit that man knows what he does not know? And in this respect only I believe myself to differ from men in general, and may perhaps claim to be wiser than they are: — that whereas I know but little of the world below, I do not suppose that I know: but I do know that injustice and disobedience to a better, whether God or man, is evil and dishonourable, and I will never fear or avoid a possible good rather than a certain evil. And therefore if you let me go now, and are not convinced by Anytus, who said that since I had been prosecuted I must be put to death (or if not that I ought never to have been prosecuted at all); and that if I escape now, your sons will all be utterly ruined by listening to my words — if you say to me, Socrates, this time we will not mind Anytus, and you shall be let off, but upon one condition, that you are not to enquire and speculate in this way any more, and that if you are caught doing so again you shall die; — if this was the condition on which you let me go, I should reply: Men of Athens, I honour and love you; but I shall obey God rather than you, and while I have life and strength I shall never cease from the practice and teaching of philosophy, exhorting any one whom I meet and saying to him after my manner: You, my friend, — a citizen of the great and mighty and wise city of Athens, — are you not ashamed of heaping up the greatest amount of money and honour and reputation, and caring so little about wisdom and truth and the greatest improvement of the soul, which you never regard or heed at all? And if the person with whom I am arguing, says: Yes, but I do care; then I do not leave him or let him go at once; but I proceed to interrogate and examine and cross-examine him, and if I think that he has no virtue in him, but only says that he has, I reproach him with undervaluing the greater, and overvaluing the less. And I shall repeat the same words to every one whom I meet, young and old, citizen and alien, but especially to the citizens, inasmuch as they are my brethren. For know that this is the command of God; and I believe that no greater good has ever happened in the state than my service to the God.   For I do nothing but go about persuading you all, old and young alike, not to take thought for your persons or your properties, but first and chiefly to care about the greatest improvement of the soul.   I tell you that virtue is not given by money, but that from virtue comes money and every other good of man, public as well as private.   This is my teaching, and if this is the doctrine which corrupts the youth, I am a mischievous person.   But if any one says that this is not my teaching, he is speaking an untruth.   Wherefore, O men of Athens, I say to you, do as Anytus bids or not as Anytus bids, and either acquit me or not; but whichever you do, understand that I shall never alter my ways, not even if I have to die many times.

Men of Athens, do not interrupt, but hear me; there was an understanding between us that you should hear me to the end: I have something more to say, at which you may be inclined to cry out; but I believe that to hear me will be good for you, and therefore I beg that you will not cry out.   I would have you know, that if you kill such an one as I am, you will injure yourselves more than you will injure me.   Nothing will injure me, not Meletus nor yet Anytus — they cannot, for a bad man is not permitted to injure a better than himself.   I do not deny that Anytus may, perhaps, kill him, or drive him into exile, or deprive him of civil rights; and he may imagine, and others may imagine, that he is inflicting a great injury upon him: but there I do not agree.   For the evil of doing as he is doing — the evil of unjustly taking away the life of another — is greater far.

And now, Athenians, I am not going to argue for my own sake, as you may think, but for yours, that you may not sin against the God by condemning me, who am his gift to you.   For if you kill me you will not easily find a successor to me, who, if I may use such a ludicrous figure of speech, am a sort of gadfly, given to the state by God; and the state is a great and noble steed who is tardy in his motions owing to his very size, and requires to be stirred into life. I am that gadfly which God has attached to the state, and all day long and in all places am always fastening upon you, arousing and persuading and reproaching you.   You will not easily find another like me, and therefore I would advise you to spare me.   I dare say that you may feel out of temper (like a person who is suddenly awakened from sleep), and you think that you might easily strike me dead as Anytus advises, and then you would sleep on for the remainder of your lives, unless God in his care of you sent you another gadfly.   When I say that I am given to you by God, the proof of my mission is this: — if I had been like other men, I should not have neglected all my own concerns or patiently seen the neglect of them during all these years, and have been doing yours, coming to you individually like a father or elder brother, exhorting you to regard virtue; such conduct, I say, would be unlike human nature.   If I had gained anything, or if my exhortations had been paid, there would have been some sense in my doing so; but now, as you will perceive, not even the impudence of my accusers dares to say that I have ever exacted or sought pay of any one; of that they have no witness. And I have a sufficient witness to the truth of what I say — my poverty.

Some one may wonder why I go about in private giving advice and busying myself with the concerns of others, but do not venture to come forward in public and advise the state. I will tell you why. You have heard me speak at sundry times and in divers places of an oracle or sign which comes to me, and is the divinity which Meletus ridicules in the indictment. This sign, which is a kind of voice, first began to come to me when I was a child; it always forbids but never commands me to do anything which I am going to do. This is what deters me from being a politician. And rightly, as I think. For I am certain, O men of Athens, that if I had engaged in politics, I should have perished long ago, and done no good either to you or to myself. And do not be offended at my telling you the truth: for the truth is, that no man who goes to war with you or any other multitude, honestly striving against the many lawless and unrighteous deeds which are done in a state, will save his life; he who will fight for the right, if he would live even for a brief space, must have a private station and not a public one.

I can give you convincing evidence of what I say, not words only, but what you value far more — actions. Let me relate to you a passage of my own life which will prove to you that I should never have yielded to injustice from any fear of death, and that 'as I should have refused to yield' I must have died at once. I will tell you a tale of the courts, not very interesting perhaps, but nevertheless true. The only office of state which I ever held, O men of Athens, was that of senator: the tribe Antiochis, which is my tribe, had the presidency at the trial of the generals who had not taken up the bodies of the slain after the battle of Arginusae; and you proposed to try them in a body, contrary to law, as you all thought afterwards; but at the time I was the only one of the Prytanes who was opposed to the illegality, and I gave my vote against you; and when the orators threatened to impeach and arrest me, and you called and shouted, I made up my mind that I would run the risk, having law and justice with me, rather than take part in your injustice because I feared imprisonment and death. This happened in the days of the democracy. But when the oligarchy of the Thirty was in power, they sent for me and four others into the rotunda, and bade us bring Leon the Salaminian from Salamis, as they wanted to put him to death. This was a specimen of the sort of commands which they were always giving with the view of implicating as many as possible in their crimes; and then I showed, not in word only but in deed, that, if I may be allowed to use such an expression, I cared not a straw for death, and that my great and only care was lest I should do an unrighteous or unholy thing. For the strong arm of that oppressive power did not frighten me into doing wrong; and when we came out of the rotunda the other four went to Salamis and fetched Leon, but I went quietly home. For which I might have lost my life, had not the power of the Thirty shortly afterwards come to an end. And many will witness to my words.

Now do you really imagine that I could have survived all these years, if I had led a public life, supposing that like a good man I had always maintained the right and had made justice, as I ought, the first thing? No indeed, men of Athens, neither I nor any other man. But I have been always the same in all my actions, public as well as private, and never have I yielded any base compliance to those who are slanderously termed my disciples, or to any other. Not that I have any regular disciples. But if any one likes to come and hear me while I am pursuing my mission, whether he be young or old, he is not excluded. Nor do I converse only with those who pay; but any one, whether he be rich or poor, may ask and answer me and listen to my words; and whether he turns out to be a bad man or a good one, neither result can be justly imputed to me; for I never taught or professed to teach him anything. And if any one says that he has ever learned or heard anything from me in private which all the world has not heard, let me tell you that he is lying.

But I shall be asked, Why do people delight in continually conversing with you? I have told you already, Athenians, the whole truth about this matter: they like to hear the cross-examination of the pretenders to wisdom; there is amusement in it. Now this duty of cross-examining other men has been imposed upon me by God; and has been signified to me by oracles, visions, and in every way in which the will of divine power was ever intimated to any one. This is true, O Athenians; or, if not true, would be soon refuted. If I am or have been corrupting the youth, those of them who are now grown up and become sensible that I gave them bad advice in the days of their youth should come forward as accusers, and take their revenge; or if they do not like to come themselves, some of their relatives, fathers, brothers, or other kinsmen, should say what evil their families have suffered at my hands. Now is their time. Many of them I see in the court. There is Crito, who is of the same age and of the same deme with myself, and there is Critobulus his son, whom I also see. Then again there is Lysanias of Sphettus, who is the father of Aeschines — he is present; and also there is Antiphon of Cephisus, who is the father of Epigenes; and there are the brothers of several who have associated with me. There is Nicostratus the son of Theosdotides, and the brother of Theodotus (now Theodotus himself is dead, and therefore he, at any rate, will not seek to stop him); and there is Paralus the son of Demodocus, who had a brother Theages; and Adeimantus the son of Ariston, whose brother Plato is present; and Aeantodorus, who is the brother of Apollodorus, whom I also see. I might mention a great many others, some of whom Meletus should have produced as witnesses in the course of his speech; and let him still produce them, if he has forgotten — I will make way for him. And let him say, if he has any testimony of the sort which he can produce. Nay, Athenians, the very opposite is the truth. For all these are ready to witness on behalf of the corrupter, of the injurer of their kindred, as Meletus and Anytus call me; not the corrupted youth only — there might have been a motive for that — but their uncorrupted elder relatives. Why should they too support me with their testimony? Why, indeed, except for the sake of truth and justice, and because they know that I am speaking the truth, and that Meletus is a liar.

Well, Athenians, this and the like of this is all the defence which I have to offer. Yet a word more. Perhaps there may be some one who is offended at me, when he calls to mind how he himself on a similar, or even a less serious occasion, prayed and entreated the judges with many tears, and how he produced his children in court, which was a moving spectacle, together with a host of relations and friends; whereas I, who am probably in danger of my life, will do none of these things. The contrast may occur to his mind, and he may be set against me, and vote in anger because he is displeased at me on this account. Now if there be such a person among you, — mind, I do not say that there is, — to him I may fairly reply: My friend, I am a man, and like other men, a creature of flesh and blood, and not 'of wood or stone,' as Homer says; and I have a family, yes, and sons, O Athenians, three in number, one almost a man, and two others who are still young; and yet I will not bring any of them hither in order to petition you for an acquittal. And why not? Not from any self-assertion or want of respect for you. Whether I am or am not afraid of death is another question, of which I will not now speak. But, having regard to public opinion, I feel that such conduct would be discreditable to myself, and to you, and to the whole state. One who has reached my years, and who has a name for wisdom, ought not to demean himself. Whether this opinion of me be deserved or not, at any rate the world has decided that Socrates is in some way superior to other men. And if those among you who are said to be superior in wisdom and courage, and any other virtue, demean themselves in this way, how shameful is their conduct! I have seen men of reputation, when they have been condemned, behaving in the strangest manner: they seemed to fancy that they were going to suffer something dreadful if they died, and that they could be immortal if you only allowed them to live; and I think that such are a dishonour to the state, and that any stranger coming in would have said of them that the most eminent men of Athens, to whom the Athenians themselves give honour and command, are no better than women. And I say that these things ought not to be done by those of us who have a reputation; and if they are done, you ought not to permit them; you ought rather to show that you are far more disposed to condemn the man who gets up a doleful scene and makes the city ridiculous, than him who holds his peace.

But, setting aside the question of public opinion, there seems to be something wrong in asking a favour of a judge, and thus procuring an acquittal, instead of informing and convincing him. For his duty is, not to make a present of justice, but to give judgment; and he has sworn that he will judge according to the laws, and not according to his own good pleasure; and we ought not to encourage you, nor should you allow yourself to be encouraged, in this habit of perjury — there can be no piety in that.   Do not then require me to do what I consider dishonourable and impious and wrong, especially now, when I am being tried for impiety on the indictment of Meletus.   For if, O men of Athens, by force of persuasion and entreaty I could over-power your oaths, then I should be teaching you to believe that there are no gods, and in defending should simply convict myself of the charge of not believing in them.   But that is not so — far otherwise. For I do believe that there are gods, and in a sense higher than that in which any of my accusers believe in them.   And to you and to God I commit my cause, to be determined by you as is best for you and me.

There are many reasons why I am not grieved, O men of Athens, at the vote of condemnation.   I expected it, and am only surprised that the votes are so nearly equal; for I had thought that the majority against me would have been far larger; but now, had thirty votes gone over to the other side, I should have been acquitted.   And I may say, I think, that I have escaped Meletus.   I may say more; for without the assistance of Anytus and Lycon, any one may see that he would not have had a fifth part of the votes, as the law requires, in which case he would have incurred a fine of a thousand drachmae.

And so he proposes death as the penalty.   And what shall I pro-pose on my part, O men of Athens?   Clearly that which is my due. And what is my due?   What return shall be made to the man who has never had the wit to be idle during his whole life; but has been careless of what the many care for — wealth, and family interests, and military offices, and speaking in the assembly, and magistracies, and plots, and parties.   Reflecting that I was really too honest a man to be a politician and live, I did not go where I could do no good to you or to myself; but where I could do the greatest good privately to every one of you, thither I went, and sought to persuade every man among you that he must look to himself, and seek virtue and wisdom before he looks to his private interests, and look to the state before he looks to the interests of the state; and that this should be the order which he observes in all his actions.   What shall be done to such an one? Doubtless some good thing, O men of Athens, if he has his reward; and the good should be of a kind suitable to him.   What would be a reward suitable to a poor man who is your benefactor, and who desires leisure that he may instruct you?   There can be no reward so fitting as maintenance in the Prytaneum, O men of Athens, a reward which he deserves far more than the citizen who has won the prize at Olympia in the horse or chariot race, whether the chariots were drawn by two horses or by many.   For I am in want, and he has enough; and he only gives you the appearance of happiness, and I give you the reality. And if I am to estimate the penalty fairly, I should say that maintenance in the Prytaneum is the just return.

Perhaps you think that I am braving you in what I am saying now, as in what I said before about the tears and prayers. But this is not so. I speak rather because I am convinced that I never intentionally wronged any one, although I cannot convince you — the time has been too short; if there were a law at Athens, as there is in other cities, that a capital cause should not be decided in one day, then I believe that I should have convinced you. But I cannot in a moment refute great slanders; and, as I am convinced that I never wronged another, I will assuredly not wrong myself. I will not say of myself that I deserve any evil, or propose any penalty. Why should I? Because I am afraid of the penalty of death which Meletus proposes? When I do not know whether death is a good or an evil, why should I propose a penalty which would certainly be an evil? Shall I say imprisonment? And why should I live in prison, and be the slave of the magistrates of the year — of the Eleven? Or shall the penalty be a fine, and imprisonment until the fine is paid? There is the same objection. I should have to lie in prison, for money I have none, and cannot pay. And if I say exile (and this may possibly be the penalty which you will affix), I must indeed be blinded by the love of life, if I am so irrational as to expect that when you, who are my own citizens, cannot endure my discourses and words, and have found them so grievous and odious that you will have no more of them, others are likely to endure me. No indeed, men of Athens, that is not very likely. And what a life should I lead, at my age, wandering from city to city, ever changing my place of exile, and always being driven out! For I am quite sure that wherever I go, there, as here, the young men will flock to me; and if I drive them away, their elders will drive me out at their request; and if I let them come, their fathers and friends will drive me out for their sakes.

Some one will say: Yes, Socrates, but cannot you hold your tongue, and then you may go into a foreign city, and no one will interfere with you? Now I have great difficulty in making you understand my answer to this. For if I tell you that to do as you say would be a disobedience to the God, and therefore that I cannot hold my tongue, you will not believe that I am serious; and if I say again that daily to discourse about virtue, and of those other things about which you hear me examining myself and others, is the greatest good of man, and that the unexamined life is not worth living,* you are still less likely to believe me. Yet I say what is true, although a thing of which it is hard for me to persuade you. Also, I have never been accustomed to think that I deserve to suffer any harm. Had I money I might have estimated the offence at what I was able to pay, and not have been much the worse. But I have none, and therefore I must ask you to proportion the fine to my means. Well, perhaps I could afford a mina, and therefore I propose that penalty: Plato, Crito, Critobulus, and Apollodorus, my friends here, bid me say thirty minae, and they

---

* This is one of the most famous sayings in Plato.

will be the sureties.   Let thirty minae be the penalty; for which sum
they will be ample security to you.

Not much time will be gained, O Athenians, in return for the evil
name which you will get from the detractors of the city, who will say
that you killed Socrates, a wise man; for they will call me wise, even
although I am not wise, when they want to reproach you.   If you had
waited a little while, your desire would have been fulfilled in the
course of nature.   For I am far advanced in years, as you may perceive, and not far from death.   I am speaking now not to all of you,
but only to those who have condemned me to death.   And I have
another thing to say to them: You think that I was convicted because
I had no words of the sort which would have procured my acquittal
— I mean, if I had thought fit to leave nothing undone or unsaid.
Not so; the deficiency which led to my conviction was not of words
— certainly not.   But I had not the boldness or impudence or inclination to address you as you would have liked me to do, weeping and
wailing and lamenting, and saying and doing many things which you
have been accustomed to hear from others, and which, as I maintain,
are unworthy of me.   I thought at the time that I ought not to do
anything common or mean when in danger: nor do I now repent of
the style of my defence; I would rather die having spoken after my
manner, than speak in your manner and live.   For neither in war nor
yet at law ought I or any man to use every way of escaping death.
Often in battle there can be no doubt that if a man will throw away
his arms, and fall on his knees before his pursuers, he may escape
death; and in other dangers there are other ways of escaping death,
if a man is willing to say and do anything.   The difficulty, my friends,
is not to avoid death, but to avoid unrighteousness; for that runs
faster than death.   I am old and move slowly, and the slower runner
has overtaken me, and my accusers are keen and quick, and the faster
runner, who is unrighteousness, has overtaken them.   And now I
depart hence condemned by you to suffer the penalty of death, — they
too go their ways condemned by the truth to suffer the penalty of
villainy and wrong; and I must abide by my award — let them abide
by theirs.   I suppose that these things may be regarded as fated, — and
I think that they are well.
     And now, O men who have condemned me, I would fain prophesy
to you; for I am about to die, and in the hour of death men are gifted
with prophetic power.   And I prophesy to you who are my murderers, that immediately after my departure punishment far heavier
than you have inflicted on me will surely await you.   Me you have
killed because you wanted to escape the accuser, and not to give an
account of your lives.   But that will not be as you suppose: far otherwise.   For I say that there will be more accusers of you than there are
now; accusers whom hitherto I have restrained: and as they are
younger they will be more inconsiderate with you, and you will be
more offended at them.   If you think that by killing men you can

prevent some one from censuring your evil lives, you are mistaken; that is not a way of escape which is either possible or honourable; the easiest and the noblest way is not to be disabling others, but to be improving yourselves. This is the prophecy which I utter before my departure to the judges who have condemned me.

Friends, who would have acquitted me, I would like also to talk with you about the thing which has come to pass, while the magistrates are busy, and before I go to the place at which I must die. Stay then a little, for we may as well talk with one another while there is time. You are my friends, and I should like to show you the meaning of this event which has happened to me. O my judges — for you I may truly call judges — I should like to tell you of a wonderful circumstance. Hitherto the divine faculty of which the internal oracle is the source has constantly been in the habit of opposing me even about trifles, if I was going to make a slip or error in any matter; and now as you see there has come upon me that which may be thought, and is generally believed to be, the last and worst evil. But the oracle made no sign of opposition, either when I was leaving my house in the morning, or when I was on my way to the court, or while I was speaking, at anything which I was going to say; and yet I have often been stopped in the middle of a speech, but now in nothing I either said or did touching the matter in hand has the oracle opposed me. What do I take to be the explanation of this silence? I will tell you. It is an intimation that what has happened to me is a good, and that those of us who think that death is an evil are in error. For the customary sign would surely have opposed me had I been going to evil and not to good.

Let us reflect in another way, and we shall see that there is great reason to hope that death is a good; for one of two things — either death is a state of nothingness and utter unconsciousness, or, as men say, there is a change and migration of the soul from this world to another. Now if you suppose that there is no consciousness, but a sleep like the sleep of him who is undisturbed even by dreams, death will be an unspeakable gain. For if a person were to select the night in which his sleep was undisturbed even by dreams, and were to compare with this the other days and nights of his life, and then were to tell us how many days and nights he had passed in the course of his life better and more pleasantly than this one, I think that any man, I will not say a private man, but even the great king will not find many such days or nights, when compared with the others. Now if death be of such a nature, I say that to die is gain; for eternity is then only a single night. But if death is the journey to another place, and there, as men say, all the dead abide, what good, O my friends and judges, can be greater than this? If indeed when the pilgrim arrives in the world below, he is delivered from the professors of justice in this world, and finds the true judges who are said to give judgment there, Minos and Rhadamanthus and Aeacus and Triptolemus, and other sons of God who were righteous in their own life, that pilgrimage will be worth making. What would not a man give if he might converse with Orpheus and Musaeus and Hesiod and Homer? Nay, if this be true, let me die again and again. I myself, too, shall have a wonderful interest in there meeting and conversing with Palamedes, and Ajax the son of Telamon, and any other ancient hero who has suffered death through an unjust judgment; and there will be no small pleasure, as I think, in comparing my own sufferings with theirs. Above all, I shall then be able to continue my search into true and false knowledge; as in this world, so also in the next; and I shall find out who is wise, and who pretends to be wise, and is not. What would not a man give, O judges, to be able to examine the leader of the great Trojan expedition; or Odysseus or Sisyphus, or numberless others, men and women too! What infinite delight would there be in conversing with them and asking them questions! In another world they do not put a man to death for asking questions: assuredly not. For besides being happier than we are, they will be immortal, if what is said is true.

Wherefore, O judges, be of good cheer about death, and know of a certainty, that no evil can happen to a good man, either in life or after death. He and his are not neglected by the gods; nor has my own approaching end happened by mere chance. But I see clearly that the time had arrived when it was better for me to die and be released from trouble; wherefore the oracle gave no sign. For which reason, also, I am not angry with my condemners, or with my accusers; they have done me no harm, although they did not mean to do me any good; and for this I may gently blame them.

Still I have a favour to ask of them. When my sons are grown up, I would ask you, O my friends, to punish them; and I would have you trouble them, as I have troubled you, if they seem to care about riches, or anything, more than about virtue; or if they pretend to be something when they are really nothing, — then reprove them, as I have reproved you, for not caring about that for which they ought to care, and thinking that they are something when they are really nothing. And if you do this, both I and my sons will have received justice at your hands.

The hour of departure has arrived, and we go our ways — I to die, and you to live. Which is better God only knows.

[tr. B. Jowett]

CRITO

PERSONS OF THE DIALOGUE

SOCRATES   CRITO

Scene: — The Prison of Socrates

Socrates. Why have you come at this hour, Crito? it must be quite early?

Crito. Yes, certainly.

Soc. What is the exact time?

Cr. The dawn is breaking.

Soc. I wonder that the keeper of the prison would let you in.

Cr. He knows me, because I often come, Socrates; moreover, I have done him a kindness.

Soc. And are you only just arrived?

Cr. No, I came some time ago.

Soc. Then why did you sit and say nothing, instead of at once awakening me?

Cr. I should not have liked myself, Socrates, to be in such great trouble and unrest as you are — indeed I should not: I have been watching with amazement your peaceful slumbers; and for that reason I did not awake you, because I wished to minimize the pain. I have always thought you to be of a happy disposition; but never did I see anything like the easy, tranquil manner in which you bear this calamity.

Soc. Why, Crito, when a man has reached my age he ought not to be repining at the approach of death.

Cr. And yet other old men find themselves in similar misfortunes, and age does not prevent them from repining.

Soc. That is true. But you have not told me why you come at this early hour.

Cr. I come to bring you a message which is sad and painful; not, as I believe, to yourself, but to all of us who are your friends, and saddest of all to me.

Soc. What? Has the ship come from Delos, on the arrival of which I am to die?

Cr. No, the ship has not actually arrived, but she will probably be here to-day, as persons who have come from Sunium tell me that they left her there; and therefore to-morrow, Socrates, will be the last day of your life.

Soc. Very well, Crito; if such is the will of God, I am willing; but my belief is that there will be a delay of a day.

Cr. Why do you think so?

Soc. I will tell you. I am to die on the day after the arrival of the ship.

Cr. Yes; that is what the authorities say.

Soc. But I do not think that the ship will be here until to-morrow; this I infer from a vision which I had last night, or rather only just now, when you fortunately allowed me to sleep.

Cr. And what was the nature of the vision?

Soc. There appeared to me the likeness of a woman, fair and comely, clothed in bright raiment, who called to me and said: O Socrates,

'The third day hence to fertile Phthia shalt thou go.' *

Cr. What a singular dream, Socrates!

Soc. There can be no doubt about the meaning, Crito, I think.

* Homer, *Iliad*, ix. 363.

Cr. Yes; the meaning is only too clear. But, oh! my beloved Socrates, let me entreat you once more to take my advice and escape.
For if you die I shall not only lose a friend who can never be replaced, but there is another evil: people who do not know you and
me will believe that I might have saved you if I had been willing to
give money, but that I did not care. Now, can there be a worse disgrace than this — that I should be thought to value money more than
the life of a friend? For the many will not be persuaded that I
wanted you to escape, and that you refused.

Soc. But why, my dear Crito, should we care about the opinion
of the many? Good men, and they are the only persons who are
worth considering, will think of these things truly as they occurred.

Cr. But you see, Socrates, that the opinion of the many must be
regarded, for what is now happening shows that they can do the
greatest evil to any one who has lost their good opinion.

Soc. I only wish it were so, Crito; and that the many could do
the greatest evil; for then they would also be able to do the greatest
good — and what a fine thing this would be! But in reality they
can do neither; for they cannot make a man either wise or foolish;
and whatever they do is the result of chance.

Cr. Well, I will not dispute with you; but please to tell me, Socrates, whether you are not acting out of regard to me and your other
friends: are you not afraid that if you escape from prison we may
get into trouble with the informers for having stolen you away, and
lose either the whole or a great part of our property; or that even a
worse evil may happen to us? Now, if you fear on our account, be
at ease; for in order to save you, we ought surely to run this, or even
a greater risk; be persuaded, then, and do as I say.

Soc. Yes, Crito, that is one fear which you mention, but by no
means the only one.

Cr. Fear not — there are persons who are willing to get you out of
prison at no great cost; and as for the informers, they are far from
being exorbitant in their demands — a little money will satisfy them.
My means, which are certainly ample, are at your service, and if you
have a scruple about spending all mine, here are strangers who will
give you the use of theirs; and one of them, Simmias the Theban, has
brought a large sum of money for this very purpose; and Cebes and
many others are prepared to spend their money in helping you to
escape. I say, therefore, do not hesitate on our account, and do not
say, as you did in the court,* that you will have a difficulty in knowing what to do with yourself anywhere else. For men will love you
in other places to which you may go, and not in Athens only; there
are friends of mine in Thessaly, if you like to go to them, who will
value and protect you, and no Thessalian will give you any trouble.
Nor can I think that you are at all justified, Socrates, in betraying
your own life when you might be saved; in acting thus you are playing into the hands of your enemies, who are hurrying on your destruction. And further I should say that you are deserting your own

* Cf. *Apol.* 37 C, D.

children; for you might bring them up and educate them; instead of which you go away and leave them, and they will have to take their chance; and if they do not meet with the usual fate of orphans, there will be small thanks to you. No man should bring children into the world who is unwilling to persevere to the end in their nurture and education. But you appear to be choosing the easier part, not the better and manlier, which would have been more becoming in one who professes to care for virtue in all his actions, like yourself. And indeed, I am ashamed not only of you, but of us who are your friends, when I reflect that the whole business will be attributed entirely to our want of courage. The trial need never have come on, or might have been managed differently; and this last act, or crowning folly, will seem to have occurred through our negligence and cowardice, who might have saved you, if we had been good for anything; and you might have saved yourself, for there was no difficulty at all. See now, Socrates, how sad and discreditable are the consequences, both to us and you. Make up your mind then, or rather have your mind already made up, for the time of deliberation is over, and there is only one thing to be done, which must be done this very night, and if we delay at all will be no longer practicable or possible; I beseech you therefore, Socrates, be persuaded by me, and do as I say.

Soc. Dear Crito, your zeal is invaluable, if a right one; but if wrong, the greater the zeal the greater the danger; and therefore we ought to consider whether I shall or shall not do as you say. For I am and always have been one of those natures who must be guided by reason, whatever the reason may be which upon reflection appears to me to be the best; and now that this chance has befallen me, I cannot repudiate my own words: the principles which I have hitherto honoured and revered I still honour, and unless we can at once find other and better principles, I am certain not to agree with you; no. not even if the power of the multitude could inflict many more imprisonments, confiscations, deaths, frightening us like children with hobgoblin terrors. What will be the fairest way of considering the question? Shall I return to your old argument about the opinions of men? — we were saying that some of them are to be regarded, and others not. Now were we right in maintaining this before I was condemned? And has the argument which was once good now proved to be talk for the sake of talking — mere childish nonsense? That is what I want to consider with your help, Crito: — whether, under my present circumstances, the argument appears to be in any way different or not; and is to be allowed by me or disallowed. That argument, which, as I believe, is maintained by many persons of authority, was to the effect, as I was saying, that the opinions of some men are to be regarded, and of other men not to be regarded. Now you, Crito, are not going to die to-morrow — at least, there is no human probability of this — and therefore you are disinterested and not liable to be deceived by the circumstances in which you are placed. Tell me then, whether I am right in saying that some opinions, and the opinions of some men only, are to be valued, and that other opinions, and the opinions of other men, are not to be valued. I ask you whether I was right in maintaining this?

Cr. Certainly.

Soc. The good are to be regarded, and not the bad?

Cr. Yes.

Soc. And the opinions of the wise are good, and the opinions of the unwise are evil?

Cr. Certainly.

Soc. And what was said about another matter? Is the pupil who devotes himself to the practice of gymnastics supposed to attend to the praise and blame and opinion of every man, or of one man only — his physician or trainer, whoever he may be?

Cr. Of one man only.

Soc. And he ought to fear the censure and welcome the praise of that one only, and not of the many?

Cr. Clearly so.

Soc. And he ought to act and train, and eat and drink in the way which seems good to his single master who has understanding, rather than according to the opinion of all other men put together?

Cr. True.

Soc. And if he disobeys and disregards the opinion and approval of the one, and regards the opinion of the many who have no understanding, will he not suffer evil?

Cr. Certainly he will.

Soc. And what will the evil be, whither tending and what affecting, in the disobedient person?

Cr. Clearly, affecting the body; that is what is destroyed by the evil.

Soc. Very good; and is not this true, Crito, of other things which we need not separately enumerate? In questions of just and unjust, fair and foul, good and evil, which are the subjects of our present consultation, ought we to follow the opinion of the many and to fear them; or the opinion of the one man who has understanding? ought we not to fear and reverence him more than all the rest of the world: and if we desert him shall we not destroy and injure that principle in us which may be assumed to be improved by justice and deteriorated by injustice; — there is such a principle?

Cr. Certainly there is, Socrates.

Soc. Take a parallel instance: — if, acting under the advice of those who have no understanding, we destroy that which is improved by health and is deteriorated by disease, would life be worth having? And that which has been destroyed is — the body?

Cr. Yes.

Soc. Could we live, having an evil and corrupted body?

Cr. Certainly not.

Soc. And will life be worth having, if that higher part of man be destroyed, which is improved by justice and depraved by injustice? Do we suppose that principle, whatever it may be in man, which has to do with justice and injustice, to be inferior to the body?

Cr. Certainly not.

Soc. More honourable than the body?

Cr. Far more.

Soc. Then, my friend, we must not regard what the many say of us: but what he, the one man who has understanding of just and unjust, will say, and what the truth will say. And therefore you begin in error when you advise that we should regard the opinion of the many about just and unjust, good and evil, honourable and dishonourable. — 'Well,' some one will say, 'but the many can kill us.'

Cr. Yes, Socrates; that will clearly be the answer.

Soc. And it is true: but still I find with surprise that the old argument is unshaken as ever. And I should like to know whether I may say the same of another proposition — that not life, but a good life, is to be chiefly valued?

Cr. Yes, that also remains unshaken.

Soc. And a good life is equivalent to a just and honourable one — that holds also?

Cr. Yes, it does.

Soc. From these premisses I proceed to argue the question whether I ought or ought not to try and escape without the consent of the Athenians: and if I am clearly right in escaping, then I will make the attempt; but if not, I will abstain. The other considerations which you mention, of money and loss of character and the duty of educating one's children, are, I fear, only the doctrines of the multitude, who would be as ready to restore people to life, if they were able, as they are to put them to death — and with as little reason. But now, since the argument has thus far prevailed, the only question which remains to be considered is, whether we shall do rightly either in escaping or in suffering others to aid in our escape and paying them in money and thanks, or whether in reality we shall not do rightly; and if the latter, then death or any other calamity which may ensue on my remaining here must not be allowed to enter into the calculation.

Cr. I think that you are right, Socrates; how then shall we proceed?

Soc. Let us consider the matter together, and do you either refute me if you can, and I will be convinced; or else cease, my dear friend, from repeating to me that I ought to escape against the wishes of the Athenians: for I highly value your attempts to persuade me to do so, but I may not be persuaded against my own better judgment. And now please to consider my first position, and try how you can best answer me.

Cr. I will.

Soc. Are we to say that we are never intentionally to do wrong, or that in one way we ought and in another we ought not to do wrong, or is doing wrong always evil and dishonourable, as I was just now saying, and as has been already acknowledged by us? Are all our former admissions which were made within a few days to be thrown away? And have we, at our age, been earnestly discoursing with one another all our life long only to discover that we are no better than children? Or, in spite of the opinion of the many, and in spite of consequences whether better or worse, shall we insist on the truth of what was then said, that injustice is always an evil and dishonour to him who acts unjustly? Shall we say so or not?

Cr. Yes.

Soc. Then we must do no wrong?

Cr. Certainly not.

Soc. Nor when injured injure in return, as the many imagine; for we must injure no one at all?

Cr. Clearly not.

Soc. Again, Crito, may we do evil?

Cr. Surely not, Socrates.

Soc. And what of doing evil in return for evil, which is the morality of the many — is that just or not?

Cr. Not just.

Soc. For doing evil to another is the same as injuring him?

Cr. Very true.

Soc. Then we ought not to retaliate or render evil for evil to any one, whatever evil we may have suffered from him. But I would have you consider, Crito, whether you really mean what you are saying. For this opinion has never been held, and never will be held, by any considerable number of persons; and those who are agreed and those who are not agreed upon this point have no common ground, and can only despise one another when they see how widely they differ. Tell me, then, whether you agree with and assent to my first principle, that neither injury nor retaliation nor warding off evil by evil is ever right. And shall that be the premiss of our argument? Or do you decline and dissent from this? For so I have ever thought, and continue to think; but, if you are of another opinion, let me hear what you have to say. If, however, you remain of the same mind as formerly, I will proceed to the next step.

Cr. You may proceed, for I have not changed my mind.

Soc. Then I will go on to the next point, which may be put in the form of a question: — Ought a man do what he admits to be right, or ought he to betray the right?

Cr. He ought to do what he thinks right.

Soc. But if this is true, what is the application? In leaving the prison against the will of the Athenians, do I wrong any? or rather do I not wrong those whom I ought least to wrong? Do I not desert the principles which were acknowledged by us to be just — what do you say?

Cr. I cannot tell, Socrates; for I do not know.

Soc. Then consider the matter in this way: — Imagine that I am about to play truant (you may call the proceeding by any name which you like), and the laws and the government come and interrogate me: * 'Tell us, Socrates,' they say; 'what are you about? are you not

* In this passage it is interesting to note that Plato advances the theory of citizenship as involving a contract between the individual and the state.

going by an act of yours to overturn us — the laws, and the whole
state, as far as in you lies? Do you imagine that a state can subsist
and not be overthrown, in which the decisions of law have no power,
but are set aside and trampled upon by individuals?' What will be
our answer, Crito, to these and the like words? Any one, and especially a rhetorician, will have a good deal to say on behalf of the law
which requires a sentence to be carried out. He will argue that this
law should not be set aside; and shall we reply, 'Yes; but the state
has injured us and given an unjust sentence.' Suppose I say that?

Cr. Very good, Socrates.

Soc. 'And was that our agreement with you?' the law would answer; 'or were you to abide by the sentence of the state?' And if I
were to express my astonishment at their words, the law would
probably add: 'Answer, Socrates, instead of opening your eyes — you
are in the habit of asking and answering questions. Tell us, —
What complaint have you to make against us which justifies you in
attempting to destroy us and the state? In the first place did we not
bring you into existence? Your father married your mother by our
aid and begat you. Say whether you have any objection to urge
against those of us who regulate marriage?' None, I should reply.
'Or against those of us who after birth regulate the nurture and
education of children, in which you also were trained? Were not
the laws, which have the charge of education, right in commanding
your father to train you in music and gymnastic?' Right, I should
reply. 'Well then, since you were brought into the world and nurtured and educated by us, can you deny in the first place that you
are our child and slave, as your fathers were before you? And if
this is true you are not on equal terms with us; nor can you think
that you have a right to do to us what we are doing to you. Would
you have any right to strike or revile or do any other evil to your
father or your master, if you had one, because you have been struck
or reviled by him, or received some other evil at his hands? — you
would not say this? And because we think right to destroy you, do
you think that you have any right to destroy us in return, and your
country as far as in you lies? Will you, O professor of true virtue,
pretend that you are justified in this? Has a philosopher like you
failed to discover that our country is more to be valued and higher
and holier far than mother or father or any ancestor, and more to be
regarded in the eyes of the gods and of men of understanding? also
to be soothed, and gently and reverently entreated when angry, even
more than a father, and either to be persuaded, or if not persuaded,
to be obeyed? And when we are punished by her, whether with imprisonment or stripes, the punishment is to be endured in silence; and
if she leads us to wounds or death in battle, thither we follow as is
right; neither may any one yield or retreat or leave his rank, but
whether in battle or in a court of law, or in any other place, he must
do what his city and his country order him; or he must change their
view of what is just: and if he may do no violence to his father or
mother, much less may he do violence to his country.' What answer

shall we make to this, Crito? Do the laws speak truly, or do they not?

Cr. I think that they do.

Soc. Then the laws will say, 'Consider, Socrates, if we are speaking truly that in your present attempt you are going to do us an injury. For, having brought you into the world, and nurtured and educated you, and given you and every other citizen a share in every good which we had to give, we further proclaim to any Athenian by the liberty which we allow him, that if he does not like us when he has become of age and has seen the ways of the city, and made our acquaintance, he may go where he pleases and take his goods with him. None of us laws will forbid him or interfere with him. Any one who does not like us and the city, and who wants to emigrate to a colony or to any other city, may go where he likes, retaining his property. But he who has experience of the manner in which we order justice and administer the state, and still remains, has entered into an implied contract that he will do as we command him. And he who disobeys us is, as we maintain, thrice wrong; first, because in disobeying us he is disobeying his parents; secondly, because we are the authors of his education; thirdly, because he has made an agreement with us that he will duly obey our commands; and he neither obeys them nor convinces us that our commands are unjust; and we do not rudely impose them, but give him the alternative of obeying or convincing us; — that is what we offer, and he does neither.

'These are the sort of accusations to which, as we were saying, you, Socrates, will be exposed if you accomplish your intentions; you, above all other Athenians.' Suppose now I ask, why I rather than anybody else? they will justly retort upon me that I above all other men have acknowledged the agreement. 'There is clear proof,' they will say, 'Socrates, that we and the city were not displeasing to you. Of all Athenians you have been the most constant resident in the city, which, as you never leave, you may be supposed to love. For you never went out of the city either to see the games, except once when you went to the Isthmus, or to any other place unless when you were on military service; nor did you travel as other men do. Nor had you any curiosity to know other states or their laws: your affections did not go beyond us and our state; we were your special favourites, and you acquiesced in our government of you; and here in this city you begat your children, which is a proof of your satisfaction. Moreover, you might in the course of the trial, if you had liked, have fixed the penalty at banishment; the state which refuses to let you go now would have let you go then. But you pretended that you preferred death to exile, and that you were not unwilling to die. And now you have forgotten these fine sentiments, and pay no respect to us the laws, of whom you are the destroyer; and are doing what only a miserable slave would do, running away and turning your back upon the compacts and agreements which you made as a citizen. And first of all answer this very question: Are we right in saying that you agreed to be governed according to us in deed, and not in word only? Is that true or not?' How shall we answer, Crito? Must we not assent?

Cr. We cannot help it, Socrates.

Soc. Then will they not say: 'You, Socrates, are breaking the covenants and agreements which you made with us at your leisure, not in any haste or under any compulsion or deception, but after you have had seventy years to think of them, during which time you were at liberty to leave the city, if we were not to your mind, or if our covenants appeared to you to be unfair. You had your choice, and might have gone either to Lacedaemon or Crete, both which states are often praised by you for their good government, or to some other Hellenic or foreign state. Whereas you, above all other Athenians, seemed to be so fond of the state, or, in other words, of us her laws (and who would care about a state which has no laws?), that you never stirred out of her; the halt, the blind, the maimed were not more stationary in her than you were. And now you run away and forsake your agreements. Not so, Socrates, if you will take our advice; do not make yourself ridiculous by escaping out of the city.

'For just consider, if you transgress and err in this sort of way, what good will you do either to yourself or to your friends? That your friends will be driven into exile and deprived of citizenship, or will lose their property, is tolerably certain; and you yourself, if you fly to one of the neighbouring cities, as, for example, Thebes or Megara, both of which are well governed, will come to them as an enemy, Socrates, and their government will be against you, and all patriotic citizens will cast an evil eye upon you as a subverter of the laws, and you will confirm in the minds of the judges the justice of their own condemnation of you. For he who is a corrupter of the laws is more than likely to be a corrupter of the young and foolish portion of mankind. Will you then flee from well-ordered cities and virtuous men? and is existence worth having on these terms? Or will you go to them without shame, and talk to them, Socrates? And what will you say to them? What you say here about virtue and justice and institutions and laws being the best things among men? Would that be decent of you? Surely not. But if you go away from well-governed states to Crito's friends in Thessaly, where there is great disorder and licence, they will be charmed to hear the tale of your escape from prison, set off with ludicrous particulars of the manner in which you were wrapped in a goatskin or some other disguise, and metamorphosed as the manner is of runaways; but will there be no one to remind you that in your old age you were not ashamed to violate the most sacred laws from a miserable desire of a little more life? Perhaps not, if you keep them in a good temper; but if they are out of temper you will hear many degrading things; you will live, but how? — as the flatterer of all men, and the servant of all men; and doing what? — eating and drinking in Thessaly, having gone abroad in order that you may get a dinner. And where will be your fine sentiments about justice and virtue? Say that you wish to live

for the sake of your children — you want to bring them up and educate them — will you take them into Thessaly and deprive them of
Athenian citizenship?   Is this the benefit which you will confer upon
them?   Or are you under the impression that they will be better
cared for and educated here if you are still alive, although absent
from them; for your friends will take care of them?   Do you fancy
that if you are an inhabitant of Thessaly they will take care of them,
and if you are an inhabitant of the other world that they will not take
care of them?   Nay; but if they who call themselves friends are good
for anything, they will — to be sure they will.

'Listen, then, Socrates, to us who have brought you up.   Think not
of life and children first, and of justice afterwards, but of justice first,
that you may be justified before the princes of the world below.   For
neither will you nor any that belong to you be happier or holier or
juster in this life, or happier in another, if you do as Crito bids.   Now
you depart in innocence, a sufferer and not a doer of evil; a victim,
not of the laws but of men.   But if you go forth, returning evil for
evil, and injury for injury, breaking the covenants and agreements
which you have made with us, and wronging those whom you ought
least of all to wrong, that is to say, yourself, your friends, your country, and us, we shall be angry with you while you live, and our
brethren, the laws in the world below, will receive you as an enemy;
for they will know that you have done your best to destroy us.   Listen, then, to us and not to Crito.'

This, dear Crito, is the voice which I seem to hear murmuring in
my ears, like the sound of the flute in the ears of the mystic; that
voice, I say, is humming in my ears, and prevents me from hearing
any other.   And I know that anything more which you may say will
be vain.   Yet speak, if you have anything to say.

Cr. I have nothing to say, Socrates.

Soc. Leave me then, Crito, to fulfil the will of God, and to follow
whither he leads.

[tr. B. JOWETT]

PHAEDO

PERSONS OF THE DIALOGUE

PHAEDO, *the narrator*   SIMMIAS
SOCRATES   CEBES
ATTENDANT OF THE PRISON   CRITO
APOLLODORUS

SCENE: — *The Prison of Socrates*

[The *Phaedo* follows directly after the *Crito* in the series of four dialogues
which give us the story of the trial and death of Socrates   It contains the
full length report of the conversation which Socrates is supposed to have
held on the last day of his life, as he waited in his cell with his friends for
the executioner to bring him the hemlock cup.   Very few dialogues of

Plato are so rich in dramatic power as well as highly technical metaphysi-
cal inquiry as the *Phaedo*. After an opening section which tells of the incidents of the early morning and Socrates' awakening from a deep and peaceful sleep, the group considers at length the validity of belief in the immortality of the soul. Socrates advances several powerful arguments in favour
of such a belief, adducing evidence drawn from a wide variety of sources.
It is noteworthy that in these sections of the *Phaedo* Plato propounds his favourite Theory of Ideas in full detail. At the close of the great dialectical
passage, Plato, as is his wont, becomes the poet, and he puts in the mouth
of Socrates a majestic imaginative myth presenting a panorama of the
varied existences which constitute total Reality. Throughout the myth
he never ceases to emphasize the moral responsibility of the individual
human being. Then follow the immortal pages of this selection which
reveal Plato at his narrative and dramatic best.]

Those too who have been pre-eminent for holiness of life are released from this earthly prison, and go to their pure home which is
above, and dwell in the purer earth; and of these, such as have duly
purified themselves with philosophy live henceforth altogether without the body, in mansions fairer still, which may not be described,
and of which the time would fail me to tell.

Wherefore, Simmias, seeing all these things, what ought not we
to do that we may obtain virtue and wisdom in this life? Fair is the
prize, and the hope great!

A man of sense ought not to say, nor will I be very confident, that
the description which I have given of the soul and her mansions is
exactly true. But I do say that, inasmuch as the soul is shown to be
immortal, he may venture to think, not improperly or unworthily,
that something of the kind is true. The venture is a glorious one,
and he ought to comfort himself with words like these, which is the
reason why I lengthen out the tale. Wherefore, I say, let a man be
of good cheer about his soul, who having cast away the pleasures and
ornaments of the body as alien to him and working harm rather than
good, has sought after the pleasures of knowledge; and has arrayed
the soul, not in some foreign attire, but in her own proper jewels,
temperance, and justice, and courage, and nobility, and truth — in
these adorned she is ready to go on her journey to the world below,
when her hour comes. You, Simmias and Cebes, and all other men,
will depart at some time or other. Me already, as a tragic poet would
say, the voice of fate calls. Soon I must drink the poison; and I think
that I had better repair to the bath first, in order that the women
may not have the trouble of washing my body after I am dead.

When he had done speaking, Crito said: And have you any commands for us, Socrates — anything to say about your children, or any
other matter in which we can serve you?

Nothing particular, Crito, he replied: only, as I have always told
you, take care of yourselves; that is a service which you may be ever
rendering to me and mine and to all of us, whether you promise to
do so or not. But if you have no thought for yourselves, and care not
to walk according to the rule which I have prescribed for you, not

now for the first time, however much you may profess or promise at the moment, it will be of no avail.

We will do our best, said Crito: And in what way shall we bury you?

In any way that you like; but you must get hold of me, and take care that I do not run away from you. Then he turned to us, and added with a smile: — I cannot make Crito believe that I am the same Socrates who have been talking and conducting the argument; he fancies that I am the other Socrates whom he will soon see, a dead body — and he asks, How shall he bury me? And though I have spoken many words in the endeavour to show that when I have drunk the poison I shall leave you and go to the joys of the blessed, — these words of mine, with which I was comforting you and myself, have had, as I perceive, no effect upon Crito. And therefore I want you to be surety for me to him now, as at the trial he was surety to the judges for me: but let the promise be of another sort; for he was surety for me to the judges that I would remain, and you must be my surety to him that I shall not remain, but go away and depart; and then he will suffer less at my death, and not be grieved when he sees my body being burned or buried. I would not have him sorrow at my hard lot, or say at the burial, Thus we lay out Socrates, or, Thus we follow him to the grave or bury him; for false words are not only evil in themselves, but they infect the soul with evil. Be of good cheer then, my dear Crito, and say that you are burying my body only, and do with that whatever is usual, and what you think best.

When he had spoken these words, he arose and went into a chamber to bathe; Crito followed him and told us to wait. So we remained behind, talking and thinking of the subject of discourse, and also of the greatness of our sorrow; he was like a father of whom we were being bereaved, and we were about to pass the rest of our lives as orphans. When he had taken the bath his children were brought to him — (he had two young sons and an elder one); and the women of his family also came, and he talked to them and gave them a few directions in the presence of Crito; then he dismissed them and returned to us.

Now the hour of sunset was near, for a good deal of time had passed while he was within. When he came out, he sat down with us again after his bath, but not much was said. Soon the jailer, who was the servant of the Eleven, entered and stood by him, saying: — To you, Socrates, whom I know to be the noblest and gentlest and best of all who ever came to this place, I will not impute the angry feelings of other men, who rage and swear at me, when, in obedience to the authorities, I bid them drink the poison — indeed, I am sure that you will not be angry with me; for others, as you are aware, and not I, are to blame. And so fare you well, and try to bear lightly what must needs be — you know my errand. Then bursting into tears he turned away and went out.

Socrates looked at him and said: I return your good wishes, and will do as you bid. Then turning to us, he said, How charming the man is: since I have been in prison he has always been coming to see me, and at times he would talk to me, and was as good to me as could be, and now see how generously he sorrows on my account. We must do as he says, Crito; and therefore let the cup be brought, if the poison is prepared: if not, let the attendant prepare some.

Yet, said Crito, the sun is still upon the hill-tops, and I know that many a one has taken the draught late, and after the announcement has been made to him, he has eaten and drunk, and enjoyed the society of his beloved; do not hurry — there is time enough.

Socrates said: Yes, Crito, and they of whom you speak are right in so acting, for they think that they will be gainers by the delay; but I am right in not following their example, for I do not think that I should gain anything by drinking the poison a little later; I should only be ridiculous in my own eyes for sparing and saving a life which is already forfeit. Please then to do as I say, and not to refuse me.

Crito made a sign to the servant, who was standing by; and he went out, and having been absent for some time, returned with the jailer carrying the cup of poison. Socrates said: You, my good friend, who are experienced in these matters, shall give me directions how I am to proceed. The man answered: You have only to walk about until your legs are heavy, and then to lie down, and the poison will act. At the same time he handed the cup to Socrates, who in the easiest and gentlest manner, without the least fear or change of colour or feature, looking at the man with all his eyes, Echecrates, as his manner was, took the cup and said: What do you say about making a libation out of this cup to any god? May I, or not? The man answered: We only prepare, Socrates, just so much as we deem enough. I understand, he said: but I may and must ask the gods to prosper my journey from this to the other world — even so — and so be it according to my prayer. Then raising the cup to his lips, quite readily and cheerfully he drank off the poison. And hitherto most of us had been able to control our sorrow; but now when we saw him drinking, and saw too that he had finished the draught, we could no longer forbear, and in spite of myself my own tears were flowing fast; so that I covered my face and wept, not for him, but at the thought of my own calamity in having to part from such a friend. Nor was I the first; for Crito, when he found himself unable to restrain his tears, had got up, and I followed; and at that moment, Apollodorus, who had been weeping all the time, broke out in a loud and passionate cry which made cowards of us all. Socrates alone retained his calmness: What is this strange outcry? he said. I sent away the women mainly in order that they might not misbehave in this way, for I have been told that a man should die in peace. Be quiet then, and have patience. When we heard his words we were ashamed, and refrained our tears; and he walked about until, as he said, his legs began to fail, and then he lay on his back, according to the directions, and the man who gave him the poison now and then looked at his feet and legs; and after a while he pressed his foot hard, and asked him if he could feel; and he said, No; and then his leg, and so upwards and upwards, and showed us that he was cold and stiff.   And he felt them himself, and said: When the poison reaches the heart, that will be the end.   He was beginning to grow cold about the groin, when he uncovered his face, for he had covered himself up, and said — they were his last words — he said: Crito, I owe a cock to Asclepius; will you remember to pay the debt?   The debt shall be paid, said Crito; is there anything else?   There was no answer to this question; but in a minute or two a movement was heard, and the attendants uncovered him; his eyes were set, and Crito closed his eyes and mouth.

Such was the end, Echecrates, of our friend; concerning whom I may truly say, that of all the men of his time whom I have known, he was the wisest and justest and best.

[114b–118, tr. B. Jowett]

ION

PERSONS OF THE DIALOGUE

SOCRATES   ION

Socrates. Welcome, Ion.   Are you from your native city of Ephesus?

Ion. No, Socrates; but from Epidaurus, where I attended the festival of Asclepius.

Soc. And do the Epidaurians have contests of rhapsodes at the festival?

Ion. O yes; and of all sorts of musical performers.

Soc. And were you one of the competitors — and did you succeed?

Ion. I obtained the first prize of all, Socrates.

Soc. Well done; and I hope that you will do the same for us at the Panathenaea.

Ion. And I will, please heaven.

Soc. I often envy the profession of a rhapsode, Ion; for you have always to wear fine clothes, and to look as beautiful as you can is a part of your art.   Then, again, you are obliged to be continually in the company of many good poets; and especially of Homer, who is the best and most divine of them; and to understand him, and not merely learn his words by rote, is a thing greatly to be envied.   And no man can be a rhapsode who does not understand the meaning of the poet.   For the rhapsode ought to interpret the mind of the poet to his hearers, but how can he interpret him well unless he knows what he means?   All this is greatly to be envied.

Ion. Very true, Socrates; interpretation has certainly been the most laborious part of my art; and I believe myself able to speak about Homer better than any man; and that neither Metrodorus of Lampsacus, nor Stesimbrotus of Thasos, nor Glaucon, nor any one else who ever was, had as good ideas about Homer as I have, or as many.

Soc. I am glad to hear you say so, Ion; I see that you will not refuse to acquaint me with them.

Ion. Certainly, Socrates; and you really ought to hear how exquisitely I render Homer. I think that the Homeridae should give me a golden crown.

Soc. I shall take an opportunity of hearing your embellishments of him at some other time. But just now I should like to ask you a question: Does your art extend to Hesiod and Archilochus, or to Homer only?

Ion. To Homer only; he is in himself quite enough.

Soc. Are there any things about which Homer and Hesiod agree?

Ion. Yes; in my opinion there are a good many.

Soc. And can you interpret better what Homer says, or what Hesiod says, about these matters in which they agree?

Ion. I can interpret them equally well, Socrates, where they agree.

Soc. But what about matters in which they do not agree? — for example, about divination, of which both Homer and Hesiod have something to say, —

Ion. Very true:

Soc. Would you or a good prophet be a better interpreter of what these two poets say about divination, not only when they agree, but when they disagree?

Ion. A prophet.

Soc. And if you were a prophet, would you be able to interpret them when they disagree as well as when they agree?

Ion. Clearly.

Soc. But how did you come to have this skill about Homer only, and not about Hesiod or the other poets? Does not Homer speak of the same themes which all other poets handle? Is not war his great argument? and does he not speak of human society and of intercourse of men, good and bad, skilled and unskilled, and of the gods conversing with one another and with mankind, and about what happens in heaven and in the world below, and the generations of gods and heroes? Are not these the themes of which Homer sings?

Ion. Very true, Socrates.

Soc. And do not the other poets sing of the same?

Ion. Yes, Socrates; but not in the same way as Homer.

Soc. What, in a worse way?

Ion. Yes, in a far worse.

Soc. And Homer in a better way?

Ion. He is incomparably better.

Soc. And yet surely, my dear friend Ion, in a discussion about arithmetic, where many people are speaking, and one speaks better than the rest, there is somebody who can judge which of them is the good speaker?

Ion. Yes.

Soc. And he who judges of the good will be the same as he who judges of the bad speakers?

Ion. The same.

Soc. And he will be the arithmetician?

Ion. Yes.

Soc. Well, and in discussions about the wholesomeness of food, when many persons are speaking, and one speaks better than the rest, will he who recognizes the better speaker be a different person from him who recognizes the worse, or the same?

Ion. Clearly the same.

Soc. And who is he, and what is his name?

Ion. The physician.

Soc. And speaking generally, in all discussions in which the subject is the same and many men are speaking, will not he who knows the good know the bad speaker also? For if he does not know the bad, neither will he know the good when the same topic is being discussed.

Ion. True.

Soc. Is not the same person skilful in both?

Ion. Yes.

Soc. And you say that Homer and the other poets, such as Hesiod and Archilochus, speak of the same things, although not in the same way; but the one speaks well and the other not so well?

Ion. Yes; and I am right in saying so.

Soc. And if you knew the good speaker, you would also know the inferior speakers to be inferior?

Ion. That is true.

Soc. Then, my dear friend, can I be mistaken in saying that Ion is equally skilled in Homer and in other poets, since he himself acknowledges that the same person will be a good judge of all those who speak of the same things; and that almost all poets do speak of the same things?

Ion. Why then, Socrates, do I lose attention and go to sleep and have absolutely no ideas of the least value, when any one speaks of any other poet; but when Homer is mentioned, I wake up at once and am all attention and have plenty to say?

Soc. The reason, my friend, is obvious. No one can fail to see that you speak of Homer without any art or knowledge. If you were able to speak of him by rules of art, you would have been able to speak of all other poets; for poetry is a whole.

Ion. Yes.

Soc. And when any one acquires any other art as a whole, the same may be said of them. Would you like me to explain my meaning, Ion?

Ion. Yes, indeed, Socrates; I very much wish that you would: for I love to hear you wise men talk.

Soc. O that we were wise, Ion, and that you could truly call us so; but you rhapsodes and actors, and the poets whose verses you sing, are wise; whereas I am a common man, who only speak the truth. For consider what a very commonplace and trivial thing is this which I have said — a thing which any man might say: that when a man has acquired a knowledge of a whole art, the enquiry into good and bad is one and the same. Let us consider this matter; is not the art of painting a whole?

Ion. Yes.

Soc. And there are and have been many painters good and bad?

Ion. Yes.

Soc. And did you ever know any one who was skilful in pointing out the excellences and defects of Polygnotus the son of Aglaophon, but incapable of criticizing other painters; and when the work of any other painter was produced, went to sleep and was at a loss, and had no ideas; but when he had to give his opinion about Polygnotus, or whoever the painter might be, and about him only, woke up and was attentive and had plenty to say?

Ion. No indeed, I have never known such a person.

Soc. Or did you ever know of any one in sculpture, who was skilful in expounding the merits of Daedalus the son of Metion, or of Epeius the son of Panopeus, or of Theodorus the Samian, or of any individual sculptor; but when the works of sculptors in general were produced, was at a loss and went to sleep and had nothing to say?

Ion. No indeed; no more than the other.

Soc. And if I am not mistaken, you never met with any one among flute-players or harp-players or singers to the harp or rhapsodes who was able to discourse of Olympus or Thamyras or Orpheus, or Phemius the rhapsode of Ithaca, but was at a loss when he came to speak of Ion of Ephesus, and had no notion of his merits or defects?

Ion. I cannot deny what you say, Socrates. Nevertheless I am conscious in my own self, and the world agrees with me in thinking that I do speak better and have more to say about Homer than any other man. But I do not speak equally well about others — tell me the reason of this.

Soc. I perceive, Ion; and I will proceed to explain to you what I imagine to be the reason of this. The gift which you possess of speaking excellently about Homer is not an art, but, as I was just saying, an inspiration; there is a divinity moving you, like that contained in the stone which Euripides calls a magnet, but which is commonly known as the stone of Heraclea. This stone not only attracts iron rings, but also imparts to them a similar power of attracting other rings; and sometimes you may see a number of pieces of iron and rings suspended from one another so as to form quite a long chain: and all of them derive their power of suspension from the original stone. In like manner the Muse first of all inspires men herself; and from these inspired persons a chain of other persons is suspended, who take the inspiration. For all good poets, epic as well as lyric, compose their beautiful poems not by art, but because they are inspired and possessed. And as the Corybantian revellers when they dance are not in their right mind, so the lyric poets are not in their right mind when they are composing their beautiful strains: but when falling under the power of music and metre they are inspired and possessed; like Bacchic maidens who draw milk and honey from the rivers when they are under the influence of Dionysus but not when they are in their right mind. And the soul of the lyric poet does the same, as they themselves say; for they tell us that they bring songs from honeyed fountains, culling them out of the gardens and dells of the Muses; they, like the bees, winging their way from flower to flower. And this is true. For the poet is a light and winged and holy thing, and there is no invention in him until he has been inspired and is out of his senses, and the mind is no longer in him: when he has not attained to this state, he is powerless and is unable to utter his oracles. Many are the noble words in which poets speak concerning the actions of men; but like yourself when speaking about Homer, they do not speak of them by any rules of art: they are simply inspired to utter that to which the Muse impels them, and that only; and when inspired, one of them will make dithyrambs, another hymns of praise, another choral strains, another epic or iambic verses — and he who is good at one is not good at any other kind of verse: for not by art does the poet sing, but by power divine. Had he learned by rules of art, he would have known how to speak not of one theme only, but of all; and therefore God takes away the minds of poets, and uses them as his ministers, as he also uses diviners and holy prophets, in order that we who hear them may know them to be speaking not of themselves who utter these priceless words in a state of unconsciousness, but that God himself is the speaker, and that through them he is conversing with us. And Tynnichus the Chalcidian affords a striking instance of what I am saying: he wrote nothing that any one would care to remember but the famous paean which is in every one's mouth, one of the finest poems ever written, simply an invention of the Muses, as he himself says. For in this way the God would seem to indicate to us and not allow us to doubt that these beautiful poems are not human, or the work of man, but divine and the work of God; and that the poets are only the interpreters of the gods by whom they are severally possessed. Was not this the lesson which the God intended to teach when by the mouth of the worst of poets he sang the best of songs? Am I not right, Ion?

Ion. Yes, indeed, Socrates, I feel that you are; for your words touch my soul, and I am persuaded that good poets by a divine inspiration interpret the things of the gods to us.

Soc. And you rhapsodists are the interpreters of the poets?

Ion. There again you are right.

Soc. Then you are the interpreters of interpreters?

Ion. Precisely.

Soc. I wish you would frankly tell me, Ion, what I am going to ask of you: When you produce the greatest effect upon the audience in the recitation of some striking passage, such as the apparition of Odysseus leaping forth on the floor, recognized by the suitors and casting his arrows at his feet, or the description of Achilles rushing at Hector, or the sorrows of Andromache, Hecuba, or Priam, — are you in your right mind? Are you not carried out of yourself, and does not your soul in an ecstasy seem to be among the persons or places of which you are speaking, whether they are in Ithaca or in Troy or whatever may be the scene of the poem?

Ion. That proof strikes home to me, Socrates. For I must frankly confess that at the tale of pity my eyes are filled with tears, and when I speak of horrors, my hair stands on end and my heart throbs.

Soc. Well, Ion, and what are we to say of a man who at a sacrifice or festival, when he is dressed in holiday attire, and has golden crowns upon his head, of which nobody has robbed him, appears weeping or panic-stricken in the presence of more than twenty thousand friendly faces, when there is no one despoiling or wronging him; — is he in his right mind or is he not?

Ion. No indeed, Socrates, I must say that, strictly speaking, he is not in his right mind.

Soc. And are you aware that you produce similar effects on most spectators?

Ion. Only too well; for I look down upon them from the stage, and behold the various emotions of pity, wonder, sternness, stamped upon their countenances when I am speaking: and I am obliged to give my very best attention to them; for if I make them cry I myself shall laugh, and if I make them laugh I myself shall cry when the time of payment arrives.

Soc. Do you know that the spectator is the last of the rings which, as I am saying, receive the power of the original magnet from one another? The rhapsode like yourself and the actor are intermediate links, and the poet himself is the first of them. Through all these the God sways the souls of men in any direction which he pleases, and makes one man hang down from another. Thus there is a vast chain of dancers and masters and undermasters of choruses, who are suspended, as if from the stone, at the side of the rings which hang down from the Muse. And every poet has some Muse from whom he is suspended, and by whom he is said to be possessed, which is nearly the same thing; for he is taken hold of. And from these first rings, which are the poets, depend others, some deriving their inspiration from Orpheus, others from Musaeus; but the greater number are possessed and held by Homer. Of whom, Ion, you are one, and are possessed by Homer; and when any one repeats the words of another poet you go to sleep, and know not what to say; but when any one recites a strain of Homer you wake up in a moment, and your soul leaps within you, and you have plenty to say; for not by art or knowledge about Homer do you say what you say, but by divine inspiration and by possession; just as the Corybantian revellers too have a quick perception of that strain only which is appropriated to the God by whom they are possessed, and have plenty of dances and words for that, but take no heed of any other. And you, Ion, when the name of Homer is mentioned have plenty to say, and have nothing to say of others. You ask, 'Why is this?' The answer is that you praise Homer not by art but by divine inspiration.

Ion. That is good, Socrates; and yet I doubt whether you will ever have eloquence enough to persuade me that I praise Homer only when I am mad and possessed; and if you could hear me speak of him I am sure you would never think this to be the case.

Soc. I should like very much to hear you, but not until you have answered a question which I have to ask. On what part of Homer do you speak well? — not surely about every part.

Ion. There is no part, Socrates, about which I do not speak well: of that I can assure you.

Soc. Surely not about things in Homer of which you have no knowledge?

Ion. And what is there in Homer of which I have no knowledge?

Soc. Why, does not Homer speak in many passages about arts? For example, about driving; if I can only remember the lines I will repeat them.

Ion. I remember, and will repeat them.

Soc. Tell me then, what Nestor says to Antilochus, his son, where he bids him be careful of the turn at the horse-race in honour of Patroclus.

Ion. 'Bend gently,' he says, 'in the polished chariot to the left of them, and urge the horse on the right hand with whip and voice; and slacken the rein. And when you are at the goal, let the left horse draw near, yet so that the nave of the well-wrought wheel may not even seem to touch the extremity; and avoid catching the stone.' *

Soc. Enough. Now, Ion, will the charioteer or the physician be the better judge of the propriety of these lines?

Ion. The charioteer, clearly.

Soc. And will the reason be that this is his art, or will there be any other reason?

Ion. No, that will be the reason.

Soc. And every art is appointed by God to have knowledge of a certain work; for that which we know by the art of the pilot we do not know by the art of medicine?

Ion. Certainly not.

Soc. Nor do we know by the art of the carpenter that which we know by the art of medicine?

Ion. Certainly not.

Soc. And this is true of all the arts; — that which we know with one art we do not know with the other? But let me ask a prior question: You admit that there are differences of arts?

Ion. Yes.

Soc. You would argue, as I should, that when one art is of one kind of knowledge and another of another, they are different?

Ion. Yes.

Soc. Yes, surely; for if the subject of knowledge were the same, there would be no meaning in saying that the arts were different, — if they both gave the same knowledge. For example, I know that here are five fingers, and you know the same. And if I were to ask whether I and you became acquainted with this fact by the help of the same art of arithmetic, you would acknowledge that we did?

Ion. Yes.

Soc. Tell me, than, what I was intending to ask you, — whether

* *Iliad*, xxiii. 335.

this holds universally? Must the same art have the same subject of knowledge, and different arts other subjects of knowledge?

Ion. That is my opinion, Socrates.

Soc. Then he who has no knowledge of a particular art will have no right judgment of the sayings and doings of that art?

Ion. Very true.

Soc. Then which will be a better judge of the lines which you were reciting from Homer, you or the charioteer?

Ion. The charioteer.

Soc. Why, yes, because you are a rhapsode and not a charioteer.

Ion. Yes.

Soc. And the art of the rhapsode is different from that of the charioteer?

Ion. Yes.

Soc. And if a different knowledge, then a knowledge of different matters?

Ion. True.

Soc. You know the passage in which Hecamede, the concubine of Nestor, is described as giving to the wounded Machaon a posset, as he says,

'Made with Pramnian wine; and she grated cheese of goat's milk with a grater of bronze, and at his side placed an onion which gives a relish to drink.' *

Now would you say that the art of the rhapsode or the art of medicine was better able to judge of the propriety of these lines?

Ion. The art of medicine.

Soc. And when Homer says,

'And she descended into the deep like a leaden plummet, which, set in the horn of ox that ranges in the fields, rushes along carrying death among the ravenous fishes,' — †

will the art of the fisherman or of the rhapsode be better able to judge whether these lines are rightly expressed or not?

Ion. Clearly, Socrates, the art of the fisherman.

Soc. Come now, suppose that you were to say to me: 'Since you, Socrates, are able to assign different passages in Homer to their corresponding arts, I wish that you would tell me what are the passages of which the excellence ought to be judged by the prophet and prophetic art'; and you will see how readily and truly I shall answer you. For there are many such passages, particularly in the Odyssey; as, for example, the passage in which Theoclymenus the prophet of the house of Melampus says to the suitors: —

'Wretched men! what is happening to you? Your heads and your faces and your limbs underneath are shrouded in night; and the voice of lamentation bursts forth, and your cheeks are wet with tears. And the vestibule is full, and the court is full, of ghosts descending into the darkness of Erebus, and the sun has perished out of heaven, and an evil mist is spread abroad.' ‡

* *Iliad*, xi. 638, 630.　　† *Iliad*, xxiv. 80.　　‡ *Odyssey*, xx. 351.

And there are many such passages in the Iliad also; as for example in the description of the battle near the rampart, where he says: —

'As they were eager to pass the ditch, there came to them an omen: a soaring eagle, holding back the people on the left, bore a huge bloody dragon in his talons, still living and panting; nor had he yet resigned the strife, for he bent back and smote the bird which carried him on the breast by the neck, and he in pain let him fall from him to the ground into the midst of the multitude. And the eagle, with a cry, was borne afar on the wings of the wind.' *

These are the sort of things which I should say that the prophet ought to consider and determine.

Ion. And you are quite right, Socrates, in saying so.

Soc. Yes, Ion, and you are right also. And as I have selected from the Iliad and Odyssey for you passages which describe the office of the prophet and the physician and the fisherman, do you, who know Homer so much better than I do, Ion, select for me passages which relate to the rhapsode and the rhapsode's art, and which the rhapsode ought to examine and judge of better than other men.

Ion. All passages, I should say, Socrates.

Soc. Not all, Ion, surely. Have you already forgotten what you were saying? A rhapsode ought to have a better memory.

Ion. Why, what am I forgetting?

Soc. Do you not remember that you declared the art of the rhapsode to be different from the art of the charioteer?

Ion. Yes, I remember.

Soc. And you admitted that being different they would have different subjects of knowledge?

Ion. Yes.

Soc. Then upon your own showing the rhapsode, and the art of the rhapsode, will not know everything?

Ion. I should exclude certain things, Socrates.

Soc. You mean to say that you would exclude pretty much the subjects of the other arts. As he does not know all of them, which of them will he know?

Ion. He will know what a man and what a woman ought to say, and what a freeman and what a slave ought to say, and what a ruler and what a subject.

Soc. Do you mean that a rhapsode will know better than the pilot what the ruler of a sea-tossed vessel ought to say?

Ion. No; the pilot will know best.

Soc. Or will the rhapsode know better than the physician what the ruler of a sick man ought to say?

Ion. He will not.

Soc. But he will know what a slave ought to say?

Ion. Yes.

Soc. Suppose the slave to be a cowherd; the rhapsode will know

* *Iliad,* xii. 200.

better than the cowherd what he ought to say in order to soothe the infuriated cows?

Ion. No, he will not.

Soc. But he will know what a spinning-woman ought to say about the working of wool?

Ion. No.

Soc. At any rate he will know what a general ought to say when exhorting his soldiers?

Ion. Yes, that is the sort of thing which the rhapsode will be sure to know.

Soc. Well, but is the art of the rhapsode the art of the general?

Ion. I am sure that I should know what a general ought to say.

Soc. Why, yes, Ion, because you may possibly have a knowledge of the art of the general as well as of the rhapsode; and you may also have a knowledge of horsemanship as well as of the lyre: and then you would know when horses were well or ill managed. But suppose I were to ask you: By the help of which art, Ion, do you know whether horses are well managed, by your skill as a horseman or as a performer on the lyre — what would you answer?

Ion. I should reply, by my skill as a horseman.

Soc. And if you judged of performers on the lyre, you would admit that you judged of them as a performer on the lyre, and not as a horseman?

Ion. Yes.

Soc. And in judging of the general's art, do you judge of it as a general or a rhapsode?

Ion. To me there appears to be no difference between them.

Soc. What do you mean? Do you mean to say that the art of the rhapsode and of the general is the same?

Ion. Yes, one and the same.

Soc. Then he who is a good rhapsode is also a good general?

Ion. Certainly, Socrates.

Soc. And he who is a good general is also a good rhapsode?

Ion. No; I do not say that.

Soc. But you do say that he who is a good rhapsode is also a good general.

Ion. Certainly.

Soc. And you are the best of Hellenic rhapsodes?

Ion. Far the best, Socrates.

Soc. And are you the best general, Ion?

Ion. To be sure, Socrates; and Homer was my master.

Soc. But then, Ion, what in the name of goodness can be the reason why you, who are the best of generals as well as the best of rhapsodes in all Hellas, go about as a rhapsode when you might be a general? Do you think that the Hellenes want a rhapsode with his golden crown, and do not want a general?

Ion. Why, Socrates, the reason is, that my countrymen, the Ephesians, are the servants and soldiers of Athens, and do not need a general; and you and Sparta are not likely to have me, for you think that you have enough generals of your own.

Soc. My good Ion, did you never hear of Apollodorus of Cyzicus?

Ion. Who may he be?

Soc. One who, though a foreigner, has often been chosen their general by the Athenians: and there is Phanosthenes of Andros, and Heraclides of Clazomenae, whom they have also appointed to the command of their armies and to other offices, although aliens, after they had shown their merit. And will they not choose Ion the Ephesian to be their general, and honour him, if he prove himself worthy? Were not the Ephesians originally Athenians, and Ephesus is no mean city? But, indeed, Ion, if you are correct in saying that by art and knowledge you are able to praise Homer, you do not deal fairly with me, and after all your professions of knowing many glorious things about Homer, and promises that you would exhibit them, you are only a deceiver, and so far from exhibiting the art of which you are a master, will not, even after my repeated entreaties, explain to me the nature of it. You have literally as many forms as Proteus; and now you go all manner of ways, twisting and turning, and, like Proteus, become all manner of people at once, and at last slip away from me in the disguise of a general, in order that you may escape exhibiting your Homeric lore. And if you have art, then, as I was saying, in falsifying your promise that you would exhibit Homer, you are not dealing fairly with me. But if, as I believe, you have no art, but speak all these beautiful words about Homer unconsciously under his inspiring influence, then I acquit you of dishonesty, and shall only say that you are inspired. Which do you prefer to be thought, dishonest or inspired?

Ion. There is a great difference, Socrates, between the two alternatives; and inspiration is by far the nobler.

Soc. Then, Ion, I shall assume the nobler alternative; and attribute to you in your praises of Homer inspiration, and not art.

[tr. B. Jowett]

PHAEDRUS

PERSONS OF THE DIALOGUE

SOCRATES

PHAEDRUS

Scene: — *Under a plane-tree, by the banks of the Ilissus.*

[Professor Shorey in his book, *What Plato Said*, has contrasted the "classic architecture" of the *Symposium* with the "Gothic architecture" of the *Phaedrus*. The comparison in these terms is most suggestive. At the opening of this somewhat baffling dialogue Socrates and his young friend Phaedrus walk into the country near Athens along the banks of the river Ilissus. Presently they recline under the shade of a plane tree to discuss a speech of the orator Lysias which has recently captured the fancy of Phaedrus. The young man reads the speech which attempts to defend the claims of the non-lover over the lover in any erotic relationship. Phaedrus obviously marvels at the speech because of its rhetorical virtuosity but Socrates half-seriously insists that he himself can improve upon Lysias. Socrates then extemporizes a speech which takes the same side of the argument, but he suddenly stops, saying that he can go no further, for he is doing an impiety to Eros, the great god of love. So Socrates begins again on his so-called second speech which is printed here in its entirety. It is in reality a myth, and one of the most famous which Plato ever composed. Certainly the image of the soul as a charioteer driving an ill-matched team of horses, one a noble, white animal, the other a black, ugly, ill-tempered beast, has never ceased to inspire thinkers, artists and men of letters from Plato's day to this. In the remainder of the dialogue Socrates and Phaedrus discuss the three speeches. They take up in turn rhetoric, the art of writing and various other questions that are crucial for literary criticism. Students of rhetoric and the philosophy of art can find here the origin of many of Aristotle's ideas on these subjects as well as the necessary completion of Plato's own aesthetic theory which is only partially sketched in the *Republic*.]

Soc. Know then, fair youth, that the former discourse was the word of Phaedrus, the son of Vain Man, who dwells in the city of Myrrhina (Myrrhinusius). And this which I am about to utter is the recantation of Stesichorus the son of Godly Man (Euphemus), who comes from the town of Desire (Himera), and is to the following effect: 'I told a lie when I said' that the beloved ought to accept the non-lover when he might have the lover, because the one is sane, and the other mad. It might be so if madness were simply an evil; but there is also a madness which is a divine gift, and the source of the chiefest blessings granted to men. For prophecy is a madness, and the prophetess at Delphi and the priestesses at Dodona when out of their senses have conferred great benefits on Hellas, both in public and private life, but when in their senses few or none. And I might also tell you how the Sibyl and other inspired persons have given to many an one many an intimation of the future which has saved them from falling. But it would be tedious to speak of what every one knows.

There will be more reason in appealing to the ancient inventors of names, who would never have connected prophecy (μαντική), which foretells the future and is the noblest of arts, with madness (μανική), or called them both by the same name, if they had deemed madness to be a disgrace or dishonour; — they must have thought that there was an inspired madness which was a noble thing; for the two words, μαντική and μανική, are really the same, and the letter τ is only a modern and tasteless insertion. And this is confirmed by the name which was given by them to the rational investigation of futurity, whether made by the help of birds or of other signs — this, for as much as it is an art which supplies from the reasoning faculty mind (νοῦς) and information (ἱστορία) to human thought (οἴησις), they originally termed οἰονοιστική, but the word has been lately altered and made sonorous by the modern introduction of the letter omega (οἰονοιστική and οἰωνιστική), and in proportion as prophecy (μαντική) is more perfect and august than augury, both in name and fact, in the same proportion, as the ancients testify, is madness superior to a sane mind (σωφροσύνη), for the one is only of human, but the other of divine origin. Again, where plagues and mightiest woes have bred in certain families, owing to some ancient blood-guiltiness, there madness has entered with holy prayers and rites, and by inspired utterances found a way of deliverance for those who are in need; and he who has part in this gift, and is truly possessed and duly out of his mind, is by the use of purifications and mysteries made whole and exempt from evil, future as well as present, and has a release from the calamity which was afflicting him. The third kind is the madness of those who are possessed by the Muses; which taking hold of a delicate and virgin soul, and there inspiring frenzy, awakens lyrical and all other numbers; with these adorning the myriad actions of ancient heroes for the instruction of posterity. But he who, having no touch of the Muses' madness in his soul, comes to the door and thinks that he will get into the temple by the help of art — he, I say, and his poetry are not admitted; the sane man disappears and is nowhere when he enters into rivalry with the madman.

I might tell of many other noble deeds which have sprung from inspired madness. And therefore, let no one frighten or flutter us by saying that the temperate friend is to be chosen rather than the inspired, but let him further show that love is not sent by the gods for any good to lover or beloved; if he can do so we will allow him to carry off the palm. And we, on our part, will prove in answer to him that the madness of love is the greatest of heaven's blessings, and the proof shall be one which the wise will receive, and the witling disbelieve. But first of all, let us view the affections and actions of the soul divine and human, and try to ascertain the truth about them. The beginning of our proof is as follows: —

The soul through all her being is immortal, for that which is ever in motion is immortal; but that which moves another and is moved by another, in ceasing to move ceases also to live. Only the self-moving, never leaving self, never ceases to move, and is the fountain and beginning of motion to all that moves besides. Now, the beginning is unbegotten, for that which is begotten has a beginning; but the beginning is begotten of nothing, for if it were begotten of something, then the begotten would not come from a beginning. But if unbegotten, it must also be indestructible; for if beginning were destroyed, there could be no beginning out of anything, nor anything out of a beginning; and all things must have a beginning. And therefore the self-moving is the beginning of motion; and this can neither be destroyed nor begotten, else the whole heavens and all creation would collapse and stand still, and never again have motion or birth. But if the self-moving is proved to be immortal, he who affirms that self-motion is the very idea and essence of the soul will not be put to confusion. For the body which is moved from without is soulless; but that which is moved from within has a soul, for such is the nature of the soul. But if this be true, must not the soul be the self-moving, and therefore of necessity unbegotten and immortal? Enough of the soul's immortality.

Of the nature of the soul, though her true form be ever a theme of large and more than mortal discourse, let me speak briefly, and in a figure. And let the figure be composite — a pair of winged horses and a charioteer. Now the winged horses and the charioteers of the gods are all of them noble and of noble descent, but those of other races are mixed; the human charioteer drives his in a pair; and one of them is noble and of noble breed, and the other is ignoble and of ignoble breed; and the driving of them of necessity gives a great deal of trouble to him. I will endeavour to explain to you in what way the mortal differs from the immortal creature. The soul in her totality has the care of inanimate being everywhere, and traverses the whole heaven in divers forms appearing: — when perfect and fully winged she soars upward, and orders the whole world; whereas the imperfect soul, losing her wings and drooping in her flight at last settles on the solid ground — there, finding a home, she receives an earthly frame which appears to be self-moved, but is really moved by her power; and this composition of soul and body is called a living and mortal creature. For immortal no such union can be reasonably believed to be; although fancy, not having seen nor surely known the nature of God, may imagine an immortal creature having both a body and also a soul which are united throughout all time. Let that, however, be as God wills, and be spoken of acceptably to him. And now let us ask the reason why the soul loses her wings!

The wing is the corporeal element which is most akin to the divine, and which by nature tends to soar aloft and carry that which gravitates downwards into the upper region, which is the habitation of the gods. The divine is beauty, wisdom, goodness, and the like; and by these the wing of the soul is nourished, and grows apace; but when fed upon evil and foulness and the opposite of good, wastes and falls away. Zeus, the mighty lord, holding the reins of a winged chariot, leads the way in heaven, ordering all and taking care of all; and there follows him the array of gods and demi-gods, marshalled in eleven bands; Hestia alone abides at home in the house of heaven; of the rest they who are reckoned among the princely twelve march in their appointed order. They see many blessed sights in the inner heaven, and there are many ways to and fro, along which the blessed gods are passing, every one doing his own work; he may follow who will and can, for jealousy has no place in the celestial choir. But when they go to banquet and festival, then they move up the steep to the top of the vault of heaven. The chariots of the gods in even poise, obeying the rein, glide rapidly; but the others labour, for the vicious steed goes heavily, weighing down the charioteer to the earth when his steed has not been thoroughly trained: — and this is the hour of agony and extremest conflict for the soul. For the immortals, when they are at the end of their course, go forth and stand upon the outside of heaven, and the revolution of the spheres carries them round, and they behold the things beyond. But of the heaven which is above the heavens, what earthly poet ever did or ever will sing worthily? It is such as I will describe; for I must dare to speak the truth, when truth is my theme. There abides the very being with which true knowledge is concerned; the colourless, formless, intangible essence, visible only to mind, the pilot of the soul. The divine intelligence, being nurtured upon mind and pure knowledge, and the intelligence of every soul which is capable of receiving the food proper to it, rejoices at beholding reality, and once more gazing upon truth, is replenished and made glad, until the revolution of the worlds brings her round again to the same place. In the revolution she beholds justice, and temperance, and knowledge absolute, not in the form of generation or of relation, which men call existence, but knowledge absolute in existence absolute; and beholding the other true existences in like manner, and feasting upon them, she passes down into the interior of the heavens and returns home; and there the charioteer putting up his horses at the stall, gives them ambrosia to eat and nectar to drink.

Such is the life of the gods; but of other souls, that which follows God best and is likest to him lifts the head of the charioteer into the outer world, and is carried round in the revolution, troubled indeed by the steeds, and with difficulty beholding true being; while another only rises and falls, and sees, and again fails to see by reason of the unruliness of the steeds. The rest of the souls are also longing after the upper world and they all follow, but not being strong enough they are carried round below the surface, plunging, treading on one another, each striving to be first; and there is confusion and perspiration and the extremity of effort; and many of them are lamed or have their wings broken through the ill-driving of the charioteers; and all of them after a fruitless toil, not having attained to the mysteries of true being, go away, and feed upon opinion. The reason why the souls exhibit this exceeding eagerness to behold the plain of truth is that pasturage is found there, which is suited to the highest part of the soul; and the wing on which the soul soars is nourished with this. And there is a law of Destiny, that the soul which attains any vision of truth in company with a god is preserved from harm until the next period, and if attaining always is always unharmed. But when she is unable to follow, and fails to behold the truth, and through some ill-hap sinks beneath the double load of forgetfulness and vice, and her wings fall from her and she drops to the ground, then the law ordains that this soul shall at her first birth pass, not into any other animal, but only into man; and the soul which has seen most of truth shall come to the birth as a philosopher, or artist, or some musical and loving nature; that which has seen truth in the second degree shall be some righteous king or warrior chief; the soul which is of the third class shall be a politician, or economist, or trader; the fourth shall be a lover of gymnastic toils, or a physician; the fifth shall lead the life of a prophet or hierophant; to the sixth the character of a poet or some other imitative artist will be assigned; to

the seventh the life of an artisan or husbandman; to the eighth that
of a sophist or demagogue; to the ninth that of a tyrant; — all these
are states of probation, in which he who does righteously improves,
and he who does unrighteously, deteriorates his lot.

Ten thousand years must elapse before the soul of each one can
return to the place from whence she came, for she cannot grow her
wings in less; only the soul of a philosopher, guileless and true, or
the soul of a lover, who is not devoid of philosophy, may acquire
wings in the third of the recurring periods of a thousand years; he is
distinguished from the ordinary good man who gains wings in three
thousand years: — and they who choose this life three times in succession have wings given them, and go away at the end of three thousand years. But the others receive judgment when they have completed their first life, and after the judgment they go, some of them to
the houses of correction which are under the earth, and are punished;
others to some place in heaven whither they are lightly borne by justice, and there they live in a manner worthy of the life which they
led here when in the form of men. And at the end of the first thousand years the good souls and also the evil souls both come to draw
lots and choose their second life, and they may take any which they
please. The soul of a man may pass into the life of a beast, or from
the beast return again into the man. But the soul which has never
seen the truth will not pass into the human form. For a man must
have intelligence of universals, and be able to proceed from the many
particulars of sense to one conception of reason; — this is the recollection of those things which our soul once saw while following God
— when regardless of that which we now call being she raised her
head up towards the true being. And therefore the mind of the
philosopher alone has wings; and this is just, for he is always, according to the measure of his abilities, clinging in recollection to those
things in which God abides, and in beholding which He is what He
is. And he who employs aright these memories is ever being initiated
into perfect mysteries and alone becomes truly perfect. But, as he
forgets earthly interests and is rapt in the divine, the vulgar deem
him mad, and rebuke him; they do not see that he is inspired.

Thus far I have been speaking of the fourth and last kind of madness, which is imputed to him who, when he sees the beauty of earth,
is transported with the recollection of the true beauty; he would like
to fly away, but he cannot; he is like a bird fluttering and looking
upward and careless of the world below; and he is therefore thought
to be mad. And I have shown this of all inspirations to be the noblest and highest and the offspring of the highest to him who has or
shares in it, and that he who loves the beautiful is called a lover because he partakes of it. For, as has been already said, every soul of
man has in the way of nature beheld true being; this was the condition of her passing into the form of man. But all souls do not easily
recall the things of the other world; they may have seen them for a
short time only, or they may have been unfortunate in their earthly
lot, and, having had their hearts turned to unrighteousness through

some corrupting influence, they may have lost the memory of the holy things which once they saw. Few only retain an adequate remembrance of them; and they, when they behold here any image of that other world, are rapt in amazement; but they are ignorant of what this rapture means, because they do not clearly perceive. For there is no light of justice or temperance or any of the higher ideas which are precious to souls in the earthly copies of them: they are seen through a glass dimly; and there are few who, going to the images, behold in them the realities, and these only with difficulty. There was a time when with the rest of the happy band they saw beauty shining in brightness, — we philosophers following in the train of Zeus, others in company with other gods; and then we beheld the beatific vision and were initiated into a mystery which may be truly called most blessed, celebrated by us in our state of innocence, before we had any experience of evils to come, when we were admitted to the sight of apparitions innocent and simple and calm and happy, which we beheld shining in pure light, pure ourselves and not yet enshrined in that living tomb which we carry about, now that we are imprisoned in the body, like an oyster in his shell. Let me linger over the memory of scenes which have passed away.

But of beauty, I repeat again that we saw her there shining in company with the celestial forms; and coming to earth we find her here too, shining in clearness through the clearest aperture of sense. For sight is the most piercing of our bodily senses; though not by that is wisdom seen; her loveliness would have been transporting if there had been a visible image of her, and the other ideas, if they had visible counterparts, would be equally lovely. But this is the privilege of beauty, that being the loveliest she is also the most palpable to sight. Now he who is not newly initiated or who has become corrupted, does not easily rise out of this world to the sight of true beauty in the other; he looks only at her earthly namesake, and instead of being awed at the sight of her, he is given over to pleasure, and like a brutish beast he rushes on to enjoy and beget; he consorts with wantonness, and is not afraid or ashamed of pursuing pleasure in violation of nature. But he whose initiation is recent, and who has been the spectator of many glories in the other world, is amazed when he sees any one having a godlike face or form, which is the expression of divine beauty; and at first a shudder runs through him, and again the old awe steals over him; then looking upon the face of his beloved as of a god he reverences him, and if he were not afraid of being thought a downright madman, he would sacrifice to his beloved as to the image of a god; then while he gazes on him there is a sort of reaction, and the shudder passes into an unusual heat and perspiration; for, as he receives the effluence of beauty through the eyes, the wing moistens and he warms. And as he warms, the parts out of which the wing grew, and which had been hitherto closed and rigid, and had prevented the wing from shooting forth, are melted, and as nourishment streams upon him, the lower end of the wings begins to swell and grow from the root upwards; and the growth extends under the whole soul — for once the whole was winged. During this process the whole soul is all in a state of ebullition and effervescence, — which may be compared to the irritation and uneasiness in the gums at the time of cutting teeth, — bubbles up, and has a feeling of uneasiness and tickling; but when in like manner the soul is beginning to grow wings, the beauty of the beloved meets her eye and she receives the sensible warm motion of particles which flow towards her, therefore called emotion (ἵμερος), and is refreshed and warmed by them, and then she ceases from her pain with joy. But when she is parted from her beloved and her moisture fails, then the orifices of the passage out of which the wing shoots dry up and close, and intercept the germ of the wing; which, being shut up with the emotion, throbbing as with the pulsations of an artery, pricks the aperture which is nearest, until at length the entire soul is pierced and maddened and pained, and at the recollection of beauty is again delighted. And from both of them together the soul is oppressed at the strangeness of her condition, and is in a great strait and excitement, and in her madness can neither sleep by night nor abide in her place by day. And wherever she thinks that she will behold the beautiful one, thither in her desire she runs. And when she has seen him, and bathed herself in the waters of beauty, her constraint is loosened, and she is refreshed, and has no more pangs and pains; and this is the sweetest of all pleasures at the time, and is the reason why the soul of the lover will never forsake his beautiful one, whom he esteems above all; he has forgotten mother and brethren and companions, and he thinks nothing of the neglect and loss of his property; the rules and proprieties of life, on which he formerly prided himself, he now despises, and is ready to sleep like a servant, wherever he is allowed, as near as he can to his desired one, who is the object of his worship, and the physician who can alone assuage the greatness of his pain. And this state, my dear imaginary youth to whom I am talking, is by men called love, and among the gods has a name at which you, in your simplicity, may be inclined to mock; there are two lines in the apocryphal writings of Homer in which the name occurs. One of them is rather outrageous, and not altogether metrical. They are as follows: —

> Mortals call him fluttering love,
> But the immortals call him winged one,
> Because the growing of wings is a necessity to him.

You may believe this, but not unless you like. At any rate the loves of lovers and their causes are such as I have described.

Now the lover who is taken to be the attendant of Zeus is better able to bear the winged god, and can endure a heavier burden; but the attendants and companions of Ares, when under the influence of love, if they fancy that they have been at all wronged, are ready to kill and put an end to themselves and their beloved. And he who follows in the train of any other god, while he is unspoiled and the impression lasts, honours and imitates him, as far as he is able; and after the manner of his god he behaves in his intercourse with his beloved and with the rest of the world during the first period of his earthly existence. Every one chooses his love from the ranks of beauty according to his character, and this he makes his god, and fashions and adorns as a sort of image which he is to fall down and worship. The followers of Zeus desire that their beloved should have a soul like him; and therefore they seek out some one of a philosophical and imperial nature, and when they have found him and loved him, they do all they can to confirm such a nature in him, and if they have no experience of such a disposition hitherto, they learn of any one who can teach them, and themselves follow in the same way. And they have the less difficulty in finding the nature of their own god in themselves, because they have been compelled to gaze intensely on him; their recollection clings to him, and they become possessed of him, and receive from him their character and disposition, so far as man can participate in God. The qualities of their god they attribute to the beloved, wherefore they love him all the more, and if, like the Bacchic Nymphs, they draw inspiration from Zeus, they pour out their own fountain upon him, wanting to make him as like as possible to their own god. But those who are the followers of Hera seek a royal love, and when they have found him they do just the same with him; and in like manner the followers of Apollo, and of every other god walking in the ways of their god, seek a love who is to be made like him whom they serve, and when they have found him, they themselves imitate their god, and persuade their love to do the same, and educate him into the manner and nature of the god as far as they each can; for no feelings of envy or jealousy are entertained by them towards their beloved, but they do their utmost to create in him the greatest likeness of themselves and of the god whom they honour. Thus fair and blissful to the beloved is the desire of the inspired lover, and the imitation of which I speak into the mysteries of true love, if he be captured by the lover and their purpose is effected. Now the beloved is taken captive in the following manner: —

As I said at the beginning of this tale, I divided each soul into three — two horses and a charioteer; and one of the horses was good and the other bad: the division may remain, but I have not yet explained in what the goodness or badness of either consists, and to that I will proceed. The right-hand horse is upright and cleanly made; he has a lofty neck and an aquiline nose; his colour is white, and his eyes dark; he is a lover of honour and modesty and temperance, and the follower of true glory; he needs no touch of the whip, but is guided by word and admonition only. The other is a crooked lumbering animal, put together anyhow; he has a short thick neck; he is flat-faced and of a dark colour, with grey eyes and blood-red complexion; * the mate of insolence and pride, shag-eared and deaf, hardly yielding to whip and spur. Now when the charioteer beholds the vision of love, and has his whole soul warmed through sense, and

* Or with grey and blood-shot eyes.

is full of the prickings and ticklings of desire, the obedient steed, then as always under the government of shame, refrains from leaping on the beloved; but the other, heedless of the pricks and of the blows of the whip, plunges and runs away, giving all manner of trouble to his companion and the charioteer, whom he forces to approach the beloved and to remember the joys of love. They at first indignantly oppose him and will not be urged on to do terrible and unlawful deeds; but at last, when he persists in plaguing them, they yield and agree to do as he bids them. And now they are at the spot and behold the flashing beauty of the beloved; which when the charioteer sees, his memory is carried to the true beauty, whom he beholds in company with Modesty like an image placed upon a holy pedestal. He sees her, but he is afraid and falls backwards in adoration, and by his fall is compelled to pull back the reins with such violence as to bring both the steeds on their haunches, the one willing and unresisting, the unruly one very unwilling; and when they have gone back a little, the one is overcome with shame and wonder, and his whole soul is bathed in perspiration; the other, when the pain is over which the bridle and the fall had given him, having with difficulty taken breath, is full of wrath and reproaches, which he heaps upon the charioteer and his fellow-steed, for want of courage and manhood, declaring that they have been false to their agreement and guilty of desertion. Again they refuse, and again he urges them on, and will scarce yield to their prayer that he would wait until another time. When the appointed hour comes, they make as if they had forgotten, and he reminds them, fighting and neighing and dragging them on, until at length he, on the same thoughts intent, forces them to draw near again. And when they are near he stoops his head and puts up his tail, and takes the bit in his teeth and pulls shamelessly. Then the charioteer is worse off than ever; he falls back like a racer at the barrier, and with a still more violent wrench drags the bit out of the teeth of the wild steed and covers his abusive tongue and jaws with blood, and forces his legs and haunches to the ground and punishes him sorely. And when this has happened several times and the villain has ceased from his wanton way, he is tamed and humbled, and follows the will of the charioteer, and when he sees the beautiful one he is ready to die of fear. And from that time forward the soul of the lover follows the beloved in modesty and holy fear.

And so the beloved who, like a god, has received every true and loyal service from his lover, not in pretence but in reality, being also himself of a nature friendly to his admirer, if in former days he has blushed to own his passion and turned away his lover, because his youthful companions or others slanderously told him that he would be disgraced, now as years advance, at the appointed age and time, is led to receive him into communion. For fate which has ordained that there shall be no friendship among the evil has also ordained that there shall ever be friendship among the good. And the beloved when he has received him into communion and intimacy, is quite amazed at the good-will of the lover; he recognises that the

inspired friend is worth all other friends or kinsmen; they have nothing of friendship in them worthy to be compared with his. And
when his feeling continues and he is nearer to him and embraces
him, in gymnastic exercises and at other times of meeting, then the
fountain of that stream, which Zeus when he was in love with Ganymede named Desire, overflows upon the lover, and some enters into
his soul, and some when he is filled flows out again; and as a breeze
or an echo rebounds from the smooth rocks and returns whence it
came, so does the stream of beauty, passing through the eyes which
are the windows of the soul, come back to the beautiful one; there
arriving and quickening the passages of the wings, watering them
and inclining them to grow, and filling the soul of the beloved also
with love. And thus he loves, but he knows not what; he does not
understand and cannot explain his own state; he appears to have
caught the infection of blindness from another; the lover is his mirror in whom he is beholding himself, but he is not aware of this.
When he is with the lover, both cease from their pain, but when
he is away then he longs as he is longed for, and has love's image,
love for love (Anteros) lodging in his breast, which he calls and believes to be not love but friendship only, and his desire is as the desire
of the other, but weaker; he wants to see him, touch him, kiss, embrace him, and probably not long afterwards his desire is accomplished. When they meet, the wanton steed of the lover has a word
to say to the charioteer; he would like to have a little pleasure in return for many pains, but the wanton steed of the beloved says not a
word, for he is bursting with passion which he understands not; —
he throws his arms round the lover and embraces him as his dearest
friend; and, when they are side by side, he is not in a state in which
he can refuse the lover anything, if he ask him; although his fellow-
steed and the charioteer oppose him with the arguments of shame
and reason. After this their happiness depends upon their self-control; if the better elements of the mind which lead to order and
philosophy prevail, then they pass their life here in happiness and
harmony — masters of themselves and orderly — enslaving the vicious
and emancipating the virtuous elements of the soul; and when the
end comes, they are light and winged for flight, having conquered in
one of the three heavenly or truly Olympian victories; nor can human
discipline or divine inspiration confer any greater blessing on man
than this. If, on the other hand, they leave philosophy and lead the
lower life of ambition, then probably, after wine or in some other
careless hour, the two wanton animals take the two souls when off
their guard and bring them together, and they accomplish that desire of their hearts which to the many is bliss; and this having once
enjoyed they continue to enjoy, yet rarely because they have not the
approval of the whole soul. They too are dear, but not so dear to
one another as the others, either at the time of their love or afterwards. They consider that they have given and taken from each
other the most sacred pledges, and they may not break them and fall
into enmity. At last they pass out of the body, unwinged, but eager

to soar, and thus obtain no mean reward of love and madness. For those who have once begun the heavenward pilgrimage may not go down again to darkness and the journey beneath the earth, but they live in light always; happy companions in their pilgrimage, and when the time comes at which they receive their wings they have the same plumage because of their love.

Thus great are the heavenly blessings which the friendship of a lover will confer upon you, my youth. Whereas the attachment of the non-lover, which is alloyed with a worldly prudence and has worldly and niggardly ways of doling out benefits, will breed in your soul those vulgar qualities which the populace applaud, will send you bowling round the earth during a period of nine thousand years, and leave you a fool in the world below.

And thus, dear Eros, I have made and paid my recantation, as well and as fairly as I could; more especially in the matter of the poetical figures which I was compelled to use, because Phaedrus would have them. And now forgive the past and accept the present, and be gracious and merciful to me, and do not in thine anger deprive me of sight, or take from me the art of love which thou hast given me, but grant that I may be yet more esteemed in the eyes of the fair. And if Phaedrus or I myself said anything rude in our first speeches, blame Lysias, who is the father of the brat, and let us have no more of his progeny; bid him study philosophy, like his brother Polemarchus; and then his lover Phaedrus will no longer halt between two opinions, but will dedicate himself wholly to love and to philosophical discourses.

Phaedr. I join in the prayer, Socrates, and say with you, if this be for my good, may your words come to pass.

[243e–257b, tr. B. JOWETT]

SYMPOSIUM

THE SPEECHES OF ARISTOPHANES AND SOCRATES

SCENE: — *The House of Agathon*

[Plato in the *Symposium* tells of the conversation which took place at a banquet given at the house of the poet Agathon in celebration of his first victory in the contest for tragedians. The guests include representatives of various aspects of the cultivated life of Athens in the latter part of the fifth century B.C. Phaedrus, the young companion of Socrates is there. Eryximachus, a noted physician of the time, and the great comic poet Aristophanes are also numbered among the company. At the suggestion of Phaedrus the group decides to pass the evening by having each person in turn give a speech in praise of Eros, the god of love. Phaedrus and another guest named Pausanias open the series of encomia and succeed in establishing the distinction between physical and spiritual love. The doctor Eryximachus delivers himself of a rather pedantic utterance filled with many allusions to contemporary medical theory and practice. The following selection is the next speech which Plato puts in the mouth of Aristophanes, a thoroughly humorous and Rabelaisian discourse which

purports to account for the origin of sexuality. Nowhere does Plato exhibit his power of literary parody to greater advantage than in this
speech.]

Aristophanes professed to open another vein of discourse; he had
a mind to praise Love in another way, unlike that either of Pausanias
or Eryximachus. Mankind, he said, judging by their neglect of him,
have never, as I think, at all understood the power of Love. For if
they had understood him they would surely have built noble temples
and altars, and offered solemn sacrifices in his honour; but this is
not done, and most certainly ought to be done: since of all the gods
he is the best friend of men, the helper and the healer of the ills which
are the great impediment to the happiness of the race. I will try
to describe his power to you, and you shall teach the rest of the world
what I am teaching you. In the first place, let me treat of the nature
of man and what has happened to it; for the original human nature
was not like the present, but different. The sexes were not two as
they are now, but originally three in number; there was man, woman,
and the union of the two, having a name corresponding to this double
nature, which had once a real existence, but is now lost, and the
word 'Androgynous' is only preserved as a term of reproach. In the
second place, the primeval man was round, his back and sides forming a circle; and he had four hands and four feet, one head with two
faces, looking opposite ways, set on a round neck and precisely alike;
also four ears, two privy members, and the remainder to correspond.
He could walk upright as men now do, backwards or forwards as he
pleased, and he could also roll over and over at a great pace, turning
on his four hands and four feet, eight in all, like tumblers going over
and over with their legs in the air; this was when he wanted to run
fast. Now the sexes were three, and such as I have described them;
because the sun, moon, and earth are three; and the man was originally
the child of the sun, woman of the earth, and the man-woman
of the moon, which is made up of sun and earth, and they were all
round and moved round and round like their parents. Terrible was
their might and strength, and the thoughts of their hearts were great,
and they made an attack upon the gods; of them is told the tale of
Otys and Ephialtes who, as Homer says, dared to scale heaven, and
would have laid hands upon the gods. Doubt reigned in the celestial
councils. Should they kill them and annihilate the race with thunderbolts, as they had done the giants, then there would be an end of
the sacrifices and worship which men offered to them; but, on the
other hand, the gods could not suffer their insolence to be unre-
strained. At last, after a good deal of reflection, Zeus discovered a
way. He said: 'Methinks I have a plan which will humble their
pride and improve their manners; men shall continue to exist, but I
will cut them in two and then they will be diminished in strength and
increased in numbers; this will have the advantage of making them
more profitable to us. They shall walk upright on two legs, and if
they continue insolent and will not be quiet, I will split them again

and they shall hop about on a single leg.' He spoke and cut men in
two, like a sorb-apple which is halved for pickling, or as you might
divide an egg with a hair; and as he cut them one after another, he
bade Apollo give the face and the half of the neck a turn in order
that the man might contemplate the section of himself: he would
thus learn a lesson of humility.   Apollo was also bidden to heal their
wounds and compose their forms.   So he gave a turn to the face and
pulled the skin from the sides all over that which in our language is
called the belly, like the purses which draw in, and he made one
mouth at the centre, which he fastened in a knot (the same which is
called the navel); he also moulded the breast and took out most of
the wrinkles, much as a shoemaker might smooth leather upon a
last; he left a few, however, in the region of the belly and navel, as
a memorial of the primeval state.   After the division the two parts
of man, each desiring his other half, came together, and throwing
their arms about one another, entwined in mutual embraces, longing
to grow into one, they were on the point of dying from hunger and
self-neglect, because they did not like to do anything apart; and when
one of the halves died and the other survived, the survivor sought another mate, man or woman as we call them, — being the sections of
entire men or women, — and clung to that.   They were being destroyed, when Zeus in pity of them invented a new plan: he turned
the parts of generation round to the front, for this had not been always their position, and they sowed the seed no longer as hitherto
like grasshoppers in the ground, but in one another; and after the
transposition the male generated in the female in order that by the
mutual embraces of man and woman they might breed, and the race
might continue; or if man came to man they might be satisfied, and
rest, and go their ways to the business of life: so ancient is the desire
of one another which is implanted in us, reuniting our original nature,
making one of two, and healing the state of man.   Each of us when
separated, having one side only, like a flat fish, is but the inden-
ture of a man, and he is always looking for his other half.   Men who
are a section of that double nature which was once called Androgynous are lovers of women; adulterers are generally of this breed, and
also adulterous women who lust after men: the women who are a
section of the woman do not care for men, but have female attach-
ments; the female companions are of this sort.   But they who are a
section of the male follow the male, and while they are young, being
slices of the original man, they hang about men and embrace them,
and they are themselves the best of boys and youths, because they
have the most manly nature.   Some indeed assert that they are shameless, but this is not true; for they do not act thus from any want of
shame, but because they are valiant and manly, and have a manly
countenance, and they embrace that which is like them.   And these
when they grow up become our statesmen, and these only, which is
a great proof of the truth of what I am saying.   When they reach
manhood they are lovers of youth, and are not naturally inclined to
marry or beget children, — if at all, they do so only in obedience to

the law; but they are satisfied if they may be allowed to live with one
another unwedded; and such a nature is prone to love and ready to
return love, always embracing that which is akin to him.   And when
one of them meets with his other half, the actual half of himself,
whether he be a lover of youth or a lover of another sort, the pair are
lost in an amazement of love and friendship and intimacy, and will
not be out of the other's sight, as I may say, even for a moment: these
are the people who pass their whole lives together; yet they could not
explain what they desire of one another.   For the intense yearning
which each of them has towards the other does not appear to be the
desire of lover's intercourse, but of something else which the soul of
either evidently desires and cannot tell, and of which she has only a
dark and doubtful presentiment.   Suppose Hephaestus, with his instruments, to come to the pair who are lying side by side and to say
to them, 'What do you people want of one another?' they would be
unable to explain.   And suppose further, that when he saw their
perplexity he said: 'Do you desire to be wholly one; always day and
night to be in one another's company? for if this is what you desire,
I am ready to melt you into one and let you grow together, so that
being two you shall become one, and while you live live a common
life as if you were a single man, and after your death in the world
below still be one departed soul instead of two — I ask whether this
is what you lovingly desire, and whether you are satisfied to attain
this?' — there is not a man of them who when he heard the proposal
would deny or would not acknowledge that this meeting and melting
into one another, this becoming one instead of two, was the very expression of his ancient need.   And the reason is that human nature
was originally one and we were a whole, and the desire and pursuit
of the whole is called love.   There was a time, I say, when we were
one, but now because of the wickedness of mankind God has dispersed us, as the Arcadians were dispersed into villages by the Lacedaemonians.   And if we are not obedient to the gods, there is a
danger that we shall be split up again and go about in basso-relievo,
like the profile figures having only half a nose which are sculptured
on monuments, and that we shall be like tallies.   Wherefore let us
exhort all men to piety, that we may avoid evil, and obtain the good,
of which Love is to us the lord and minister; and let no one oppose
him — he is the enemy of the gods who oppose him.   For if we are
friends of the God and at peace with him we shall find our own true
loves, which rarely happens in this world at present.   I am serious,
and therefore I must beg Eryximachus not to make fun or to find any
allusion in what I am saying to Pausanias and Agathon, who, as I
suspect, are both of the manly nature, and belong to the class which
I have been describing.   But my words have a wider application —
they include men and women everywhere; and I believe that if our
loves were perfectly accomplished, and each one returning to his
primeval nature had his original true love, then our race would be
happy.   And if this would be best of all, the best in the next degree
and under present circumstances must be the nearest approach to such

an union; and that will be the attainment of a congenial love. Wherefore, if we would praise him who has given to us the benefit, we must praise the god Love, who is our greatest benefactor, both leading us in this life back to our own nature, and giving us high hopes for the future, for he promises that if we are pious, he will restore us to our original state, and heal us and make us happy and blessed. This, Eryximachus, is my discourse of love, which, although different to yours, I must beg you to leave unassailed by the shafts of your ridicule, in order that each may have his turn; each, or rather either, for Agathon and Socrates are the only ones left.

[189c–193e, tr. B. Jowett]

[Agathon's turn comes next and he chooses to praise Eros in language that is flowery, euphuistic, and brilliantly rhetorical. It ends with a great flow of words which are carefully selected for their rhythm and sound. The host's verbal pyrotechnics bring down the house. Socrates' speech which follows contains the philosophical core of the dialogue.]

And now, taking my leave of you, I will rehearse a tale of love which I heard from Diotima of Mantineia, a woman wise in this and in many other kinds of knowledge, who in the days of old, when the Athenians offered sacrifice before the coming of the plague, delayed the disease ten years. She was my instructress in the art of love, and I shall repeat to you what she said to me, beginning with the admissions made by Agathon, which are nearly if not quite the same which I made to the wise woman when she questioned me: I think that this will be the easiest way, and I shall take both parts myself as well as I can. As you, Agathon, suggested, I must speak first of the being and nature of Love, and then of his works. First I said to her in nearly the same words which he used to me, that Love was a mighty god, and likewise fair; and she proved to me as I proved to him that, by my own showing, Love was neither fair nor good. 'What do you mean, Diotima,' I said, 'is love then evil and foul?' 'Hush,' she cried; 'must that be foul which is not fair?' 'Certainly,' I said. 'And is that which is not wise, ignorant? do you not see that there is a mean between wisdom and ignorance?' 'And what may that be?' I said. 'Right opinion,' she replied; 'which, as you know, being incapable of giving a reason, is not knowledge (for how can knowledge be devoid of reason? nor again, ignorance, for neither can ignorance attain the truth), but is clearly something which is a means between ignorance and wisdom.' 'Quite true,' I replied. 'Do not then insist,' she said, 'that what is not fair is of necessity foul, or what is not good evil; or infer that because love is not fair and good he is therefore foul and evil; for he is in a mean between them.' 'Well,' I said, 'Love is surely admitted by all to be a great god.' 'By those who know or by those who do not know?' 'By all.' 'And how, Socrates,' she said with a smile, 'can Love be acknowledged to be a great god by those who say that he is not a god at all?' 'And who are they?' I said. 'You and I are two of them,' she replied. 'How can that be?' I said. 'It is quite intelligible,' she replied; 'for you yourself would acknowledge that the gods are happy and fair — of course you would — would you dare to say that any god was not?' 'Certainly not,' I replied. 'And you mean by the happy, those who are the possessors of things good or fair?' 'Yes.' 'And you admitted that Love, because he was in want, desires those good and fair things of which he is in want?' 'Yes, I did.' 'But how can he be a god who has no portion in what is either good or fair?' 'Impossible.' 'Then you see that you also deny the divinity of Love.'

'What then is Love?' I asked; 'Is he mortal?' 'No.' 'What then?' 'As in the former instance, he is neither mortal nor immortal, but in a mean between the two.' 'What is he, Diotima?' 'He is a great spirit (δαίμων), and like all spirits he is intermediate between the divine and the mortal.' 'And what,' I said, 'is his power?' 'He interprets,' she replied, 'between gods and men, conveying and taking across to the gods the prayers and sacrifices of men, and to men the commands and replies of the gods; he is the mediator who spans the chasm which divides them, and therefore in him all is bound together, and through him the arts of the prophet and the priest, their sacrifices and mysteries and charms, and all prophecy and incantation, find their way. For God mingles not with man; but through Love all the intercourse and converse of god with man, whether awake or asleep, is carried on. The wisdom which understands this is spiritual; all other wisdom, such as that of arts and handicrafts, is mean and vulgar. Now these spirits or intermediate powers are many and diverse, and one of them is Love.' 'And who,' I said, 'was his father, and who his mother?' 'The tale,' she said, 'will take time; nevertheless I will tell you. On the birthday of Aphrodite there was a feast of the gods, at which the god Poros or Plenty, who is the son of Metis or Discretion, was one of the guests. When the feast was over, Penia or Poverty, as the manner is on such occasions, came about the doors to beg. Now Plenty, who was the worse for nectar (there was no wine in those days), went into the garden of Zeus and fell into a heavy sleep; and Poverty considering her own straitened circumstances, plotted to have a child by him, and accordingly she lay down at his side and conceived Love, who partly because he is naturally a lover of the beautiful, and because Aphrodite is herself beautiful, and also because he was born on her birthday, is her follower and attendant. And as his parentage is, so also are his fortunes. In the first place he is always poor, and anything but tender and fair, as the many imagine him; and he is rough and squalid, and has no shoes, nor a house to dwell in; on the bare earth exposed he lies under the open heaven, in the streets, or at the doors of houses, taking his rest; and like his mother he is always in distress. Like his father too, whom he also partly resembles, he is always plotting against the fair and good; he is bold, enterprising, strong, a mighty hunter, always weaving some intrigue or other, keen in the pursuit of wisdom, fertile in resources; a philosopher at all times, terrible as an enchanter, sorcerer, sophist. He is by nature neither mortal nor immortal, but alive and flourishing at one moment when he is in plenty, and dead at another moment, and again alive by reason of his father's nature. But that which is always flowing in is always flowing out, and so he is never in want and never in wealth; and, further, he is in a mean between ignorance and knowledge. The truth of the matter is this: No god is a philosopher or seeker after wisdom, for he is wise already; nor does any man who is wise seek after wisdom. Neither do the ignorant seek after wisdom. For herein is the evil of ignorance, that he who is neither good nor wise is nevertheless satisfied with himself: he has no desire for that of which he feels no want.' 'But who then, Diotima,' I said, 'are the lovers of wisdom, if they are neither the wise nor the foolish?' 'A child may answer that question,' she replied; 'they are those who are in a mean between the two; Love is one of them. For wisdom is a most beautiful thing, and Love is of the beautiful; and therefore Love is also a philosopher or lover of wisdom, and being a lover of wisdom is in a mean between the wise and the ignorant. And of this too his birth is the cause; for his father is wealthy and wise, and his mother poor and foolish. Such, my dear Socrates, is the nature of the spirit Love. The error in your conception of him was very natural, and as I imagine from what you say, has arisen out of a confusion of love and the beloved, which made you think that love was all beautiful. For the beloved is the truly beautiful, and delicate, and perfect, and blessed; but the principle of love is of another nature, and is such as I have described.'

I said: 'O thou stranger woman, thou sayest well; but, assuming Love to be such as you say, what is the use of him to men?' 'That, Socrates,' she replied, 'I will attempt to unfold: of his nature and birth I have already spoken; and you acknowledge that love is of the beautiful. But some one will say: Of the beautiful in what, Socrates and Diotima? — or rather let me put the question more clearly, and ask: When a man loves the beautiful, what does he desire?' I answered her 'That the beautiful may be his.' 'Still,' she said, 'the answer suggests a further question: What is given by the possession of beauty?' 'To what you have asked,' I replied, 'I have no answer ready.' 'Then,' she said, 'let me put the word "good" in the place of the beautiful, and repeat the question once more: If he who loves loves the good, what is it then that he loves?' 'The possession of the good,' I said. 'And what does he gain who possesses the good?' 'Happiness,' I replied; 'there is less difficulty in answering that question.' 'Yes,' she said, 'the happy are made happy by the acquisition of good things. Nor is there any need to ask why a man desires happiness; the answer is already final.' 'You are right,' I said. 'And is this wish and this desire common to all? and do all men always desire their own good, or only some men? — what say you?' 'All men,' I replied; 'the desire is common to all.' 'Why, then,' she rejoined, 'are not all men, Socrates, said to love, but only some of them? whereas you say that all men are always loving the same things.' 'I myself wonder,' I said, 'why this is.' 'There is nothing to wonder at,' she replied; 'the reason is that one part of love is separated off and receives the name of the whole, but the other parts have other names.' 'Give an illustration,' I said. She answered me as follows: 'There is poetry, which, as you know, is complex and manifold. All creation or passage of non-being into being is poetry or making, and the processes of all art are creative; and the masters of arts are all poets or makers.' 'Very true.' 'Still,' she said, 'you know that they are not called poets, but have other names; only that portion of the art which is separated off from the rest, and is concerned with music and metre, is termed poetry, and they who possess poetry in this sense of the word are called poets.' 'Very true,' I said. 'And the same holds of love. For you may say generally that all desire of good and happiness is only the great and subtle power of love; but they who are drawn towards him by any other path, whether the path of money-making or gymnastics or philosophy, are not called lovers — the name of the whole is appropriated to those whose affection takes one form only — they alone are said to love, or to be lovers.' 'I dare say,' I replied, 'that you are right.' 'Yes,' she added, 'and you hear people say that lovers are seeking for their other half; but I say that they are seeking neither for the half of themselves, nor for the whole, unless the half or the whole be also a good. And they will cut off their own hands and feet and cast them away, if they are evil; for they love not what is their own, unless perchance there be some one who calls what belongs to him the good, and what belongs to another the evil. For there is nothing which men love but the good. Is there anything?' 'Certainly, I should say, that there is nothing. 'Then,' she said, 'the simple truth is, that men love the good.' 'Yes,' I said. 'To which must be added that they love the possession of the good?' 'Yes, that must be added.' 'And not only the possession, but the everlasting possession of the good?' 'That must be added too.' 'Then love,' she said, 'may be described generally as the love of the everlasting possession of the good?' 'That is most true.'

'Then if this be the nature of love, can you tell me further,' she said, 'what is the manner of the pursuit? what are they doing who show all this eagerness and heat which is called love? and what is the object which they have in view? Answer me.' 'Nay, Diotima,' I replied, 'if I had known, I should not have wondered at your wisdom, neither should I have come to learn from you about this very matter.' 'Well,' she said, 'I will teach you: — The object which they have in view is birth in beauty, whether of body or soul.' 'I do not understand you,' I said; 'the oracle requires an explanation.' 'I will make my meaning clearer,' she replied. 'I mean to say, that all men are bringing to the birth in their bodies and in their souls. There is a certain age at which human nature is desirous of procreation — procreation which must be in beauty and not in deformity; and this procreation is the union of man and woman, and is a divine thing; for conception and generation are an immortal principle in the mortal creature, and in the inharmonious they can never be. But the deformed is always inharmonious with the divine, and the beautiful harmonious.

Beauty, then, is the destiny or goddess of parturition who presides
at birth, and therefore, when approaching beauty, the conceiving
power is propitious, and diffusive, and benign, and begets and bears
fruit: at the sight of ugliness she frowns and contracts and has a
sense of pain, and turns away, and shrivels up, and not without a
pang refrains from conception. And this is the reason why, when
the hour of conception arrives, and the teeming nature is full, there
is such a flutter and ecstasy about beauty whose approach is the
alleviation of the pain of travail. For love, Socrates, is not, as you
imagine, the love of the beautiful only.' 'What then?' 'The love
of generation and of birth in beauty.' 'Yes,' I said. 'Yes, indeed,'
she replied. 'But why of generation?' 'Because to the mortal creature, generation is a sort of eternity and immortality,' she replied;
'and if, as has been already admitted, love is of the everlasting possession of the good, all men will necessarily desire immortality together
with good: Wherefore love is of immortality.'

    All this she taught me at various times when she spoke of love.
And I remember her once saying to me, 'What is the cause, Socrates,
of love, and the attendant desire? See you not how all animals, birds,
as well as beasts, in their desire of procreation, are in agony when
they take the infection of love, which begins with the desire of union;
whereto is added the care of offspring, on whose behalf the weakest
are ready to battle against the strongest even to the uttermost, and to
die for them, and will let themselves be tormented with hunger or
suffer anything in order to maintain their young. Man may be supposed to act thus from reason; but why should animals have these
passionate feelings? Can you tell me why?' Again I replied that
I did not know. She said to me: 'And do you expect ever to become a master in the art of love, if you do not know this?' 'But I
have told you already, Diotima, that my ignorance is the reason why
I come to you; for I am conscious that I want a teacher; tell me then
the cause of this and of the other mysteries of love.' 'Marvel not,'
she said, 'if you believe that love is of the immortal, as we have several
times acknowledged; for here again, and on the same principle too,
the mortal nature is seeking as far as is possible to be everlasting and
immortal: and this is only to be attained by generation, because generation always leaves behind a new existence in the place of the old.
Nay even in the life of the same individual there is succession and
not absolute unity: a man is called the same, and yet in the short interval which elapses between youth and age, and in which every
animal is said to have life and identity, he is undergoing a perpetual
process of loss and reparation — hair, flesh, bones, blood, and the
whole body are always changing. Which is true not only of the
body, but also of the soul, whose habits, tempers, opinions, desires,
pleasures, pains, fears, never remain the same in any one of us, but
are always coming and going; and equally true of knowledge, and
what is still more surprising to us mortals, not only do the sciences
in general spring up and decay, so that in respect of them we are
never the same; but each of them individually experiences a like

change. For what is implied in the word "recollection," but the departure of knowledge, which is ever being forgotten, and is renewed and preserved by recollection, and appears to be the same although in reality new, according to that law of succession by which all mortal things are preserved, not absolutely the same, but by substitution, the old worn-out mortality leaving another new and similar existence behind — unlike the divine, which is always the same and not another? And in this way, Socrates, the mortal body, or mortal anything, partakes of immortality; but the immortal in another way. Marvel not then at the love which all men have of their offspring; for that universal love and interest is for the sake of immortality.'

I was astonished at her words, and said: 'Is this really true, O thou wise Diotima?' And she answered with all the authority of an accomplished sophist: 'Of that, Socrates, you may be assured; — think only of the ambition of men, and you will wonder at the senselessness of their ways, unless you consider how they are stirred by the love of an immortality of fame. They are ready to run all risks greater far than they would have run for their children, and to spend money and undergo any sort of toil, and even to die, for the sake of leaving behind them a name which shall be eternal. Do you imagine that Alcestis would have died to save Admetus, or Achilles to avenge Patroclus, or your own Codrus in order to preserve the kingdom for his sons, if they had not imagined that the memory of their virtues, which still survives among us, would be immortal? Nay,' she said, 'I am persuaded that all men do all things, and the better they are the more they do them, in hope of the glorious fame of immortal virtue; for they desire the immortal.

'Those who are pregnant in the body only, betake themselves to women and beget children — this is the character of their love; their offspring, as they hope, will preserve their memory and give them the blessedness and immortality which they desire in the future. But souls which are pregnant — for there certainly are men who are more creative in their souls than in their bodies — conceive that which is proper for the soul to conceive or contain. And what are these conceptions? — wisdom and virtue in general. And such creators are poets and all artists who are deserving of the name inventor. But the greatest and fairest sort of wisdom by far is that which is concerned with the ordering of states and families, and which is called temperance and justice. And he who in youth has the seed of those implanted in him and is himself inspired, when he comes to maturity desires to beget and generate. He wanders about seeking beauty that he may beget offspring — for in deformity he will beget nothing — and naturally embraces the beautiful rather than the deformed body; above all when he finds a fair and noble and well-nurtured soul, he embraces the two in one person, and to such an one he is full of speech about virtue and the nature and pursuits of a good man; and he tries to educate him; and at the touch of the beautiful which is ever present to his memory, even when absent, he brings forth that which he had conceived long before, and in com-

pany with him tends that which he brings forth; and they are married by a far nearer tie and have a closer friendship than those who
beget mortal children, for the children who are their common offspring are fairer and more immortal. Who, when he thinks of
Homer and Hesiod and other great poets, would not rather have
their children than ordinary human ones? Who would not emulate
them in the creation of children such as theirs, which have preserved
their memory and given them everlasting glory? Or who would
not have such children as Lycurgus left behind him to be the saviours,
not only of Lacedaemon, but of Hellas, as one may say? There is
Solon, too, who is the revered father of Athenian laws; and many
others there are in many other places, both among Hellenes and
barbarians, who have given to the world many noble works, and
have been the parents of virtue of every kind; and many temples
have been raised in their honour for the sake of children such as
theirs; which were never raised in honour of any one, for the sake
of his mortal children.

'These are the lesser mysteries of love, into which even you, Socrates, may enter; to the greater and more hidden ones which are the
crown of these, and to which, if you pursue them in a right spirit,
they will lead, I know not whether you will be able to attain. But I
will do my utmost to inform you, and do you follow if you can. For
he who would proceed aright in this matter should begin in youth to
visit beautiful forms; and first, if he be guided by his instructor aright,
to love one such form only — out of that he should create fair
thoughts; and soon he will of himself perceive that the beauty of one
form is akin to the beauty of another; and then if beauty of form in
general is his pursuit, how foolish would he be not to recognize that
the beauty in every form is one and the same! And when he perceives this he will abate his violent love of the one, which he will
despise and deem a small thing, and will become a lover of all
beautiful forms; in the next stage he will consider that the beauty of
the mind is more honourable than the beauty of the outward form.
So that if a virtuous soul have but a little comeliness, he will be content
to love and tend him, and will search out and bring to the birth
thoughts which may improve the young, until he is compelled to
contemplate and see the beauty of institutions and laws, and to understand that the beauty of them all is of one family, and that personal
beauty is a trifle; and after laws and institutions he will go on to the
sciences, that he may see their beauty, being not like a servant in love
with the beauty of one youth or man or institution, himself a slave
mean and narrow-minded, but drawing towards and contemplating
the vast sea of beauty, he will create many fair and noble thoughts and
notions in boundless love of wisdom; until on that shore he grows and
waxes strong, and at last the vision is revealed to him of a single
science, which is the science of beauty everywhere. To this I will
proceed; please to give me your very best attention:

'He who has been instructed thus far in the things of love, and who
has learned to see the beautiful in due order and succession, when he

comes toward the end will suddenly perceive a nature of wondrous beauty (and this, Socrates, is the final cause of all our former toils) —a nature which in the first place is everlasting, not growing and decaying, or waxing and waning; secondly, not fair in one point of view and foul in another, or at one time or in one relation or at one place fair, at another time or in another relation or at another place foul, as if fair to some and foul to others, or in the likeness of a face or hands or any other part of the bodily frame, or in any form of speech or knowledge, or existing in any other being, as for example, in an animal, or in heaven, or in earth, or in any other place; but beauty absolute, separate, simple, and everlasting, which without diminution and without increase, or any change, is imparted to the ever-growing and perishing beauties of all other things. He who from these ascending under the influence of true love, begins to perceive that beauty, is not far from the end. And the true order of going, or being led by another, to the things of love, is to begin from the beauties of earth and mount upwards for the sake of that other beauty, using these as steps only, and from one going on to two, and from two to all fair forms, and from fair forms to fair practices, and from fair practices to fair notions, until from fair notions he arrives at the notion of absolute beauty, and at last knows what the essence of beauty is. This, my dear Socrates,' said the stranger of Mantineia, 'is that life above all others which man should live, in the contemplation of beauty absolute; a beauty which if you once beheld, you would see not to be after the measure of gold, and garments, and fair boys and youths, whose presence now entrances you; and you and many a one would be content to live seeing them only and conversing with them without meat or drink, if that were possible — you only want to look at them and to be with them. But what if man had eyes to see the true beauty — the divine beauty, I mean, pure and clear and unalloyed, not clogged with the pollutions of mortality and all the colours and vanities of human life — thither looking, and holding converse with the true beauty simple and divine? Remember how in that communion only, beholding beauty with the eye of the mind, he will be enabled to bring forth, not images of beauty, but realities (for he has hold not of an image but of a reality), and bringing forth and nourishing true virtue to become the friend of God and be immortal, if mortal man may. Would that be an ignoble life?'

Such, Phaedrus — and I speak not only to you, but to all of you — were the words of Diotima; and I am persuaded of their truth. And being persuaded of them, I try to persuade others, that in the attainment of this end human nature will not easily find a helper better than love. And therefore, also, I say that every man ought to honour him as I myself honour him, and walk in his ways, and exhort others to do the same, and praise the power and spirit of love according to the measure of my ability now and ever.

The words which I have spoken, you, Phaedrus, may call an encomium of love, or anything else which you please.

[201d–212c, tr. B. JOWETT]

[As Socrates concludes, suddenly Alcibiades, who is thoroughly in his cups, bursts in and the orderly procedure of the speeches is brought to a close. Instead, Alcibiades takes the floor, to speak not in praise of Eros but of Socrates himself. The portrait of the sage which follows gains in power by coming from the lips of the brilliant and fatally unstable Athenian leader to whom Socrates was devoted and yet who never possessed the moral stamina to practise the precept and counsel which Socrates tried to give him. Plato closes the dialogue by reporting how more revelers came, how the feebler drinkers departed, and how at the very end Socrates alone is left trying to persuade a drowsy Aristophanes and Agathon that the same man can be both a comic and a tragic poet.]

THE REPUBLIC

PERSONS OF THE DIALOGUE

SOCRATES, *who is the narrator*
GLAUCON   Others who are mute auditors
ADEIMANTUS

SCENE: — *The House of Cephalus in the Piraeus.*

[The dramatic setting for the conversation of the *Republic* is in the house of Cephalus, a wealthy resident-alien in the Piraeus. The participants in the discussion include, besides Cephalus, his son Polemarchus, the Sophist Thrasymachus, and the older brothers of Plato, Glaucon and Adeimantus. The dialogue opens with a quest for the nature of justice, a theme which had already received lengthy treatment in the *Gorgias*. Various tentative definitions are framed and subsequently refuted. Socrates has some difficulty in overcoming the Nietzschean "might-makes-right" theory of Thrasymachus, whose final capitulation brings the first book to a conclusion.

The second book opens with a direct challenge to Socrates by Glaucon and Adeimantus. They ask, "Who is the happier? The man who is most completely just and yet seems to be the most completely unjust, and hence is deprived of all the honours and rewards of this world; or the man who is most completely unjust and yet seems to be the most completely just, and therefore receives all the honours and rewards of this world." Socrates accepts the challenge by insisting that the man who is most completely just is the happier, no matter what may happen to him during his life. In a sense the remainder of the *Republic* is Socrates' attempt to substantiate his position. His first step is to introduce the famous analogy between the individual and the state. As the individual soul has three parts, the rational, the spirited, and the concupiscent, so the state has three corresponding elements, the rulers, the military guardians, and the mass of the population. In terms of this analysis Socrates advances his working definition of justice as the proper performance by each element of its own function, and the harmonious working together of the elements for the good of the whole.

In the third, fourth and fifth books Socrates develops in detail his theory of the education which should be given to the guardian class. Here Plato presents his famous notions on the censorship of poetry, on the elimination of private property, on eugenics and the community of wives and children. The stage is finally set for Socrates' paradoxical statement with which the present selection opens, that until philosophers are kings or kings philosophers states "will never have rest from their evils."]

BOOK V

But still I must say, Socrates, that if you are allowed to go on in this way you will entirely forget the other question which at the commencement of this discussion you thrust aside: — Is such an order of things possible, and how, if at all? For I am quite ready to acknowledge that the plan which you propose, if only feasible, would do all sorts of good to the State. I will add, what you have omitted, that your citizens will be the bravest of warriors, and will never leave their ranks, for they will all know one another, and each will call the other father, brother, son; and if you suppose the women to join their armies, whether in the same rank or in the rear, either as a terror to the enemy, or as auxiliaries in case of need, I know that they will then be absolutely invincible; and there are many domestic advantages which might also be mentioned and which I also fully acknowledge: but, as I admit all these advantages and as many more as you please, if only this State of yours were to come into existence, we need say no more about them; assuming then the existence of the State, let us now turn to the question of possibility and ways and means — the rest may be left.

If I loiter for a moment, you instantly make a raid upon me, I said, and have no mercy; I have hardly escaped the first and second waves,* and you seem not to be aware that you are now bringing upon me the third, which is the greatest and heaviest. When you have seen and heard the third wave, I think you will be more considerate and will acknowledge that some fear and hesitation was natural respecting a proposal so extraordinary as that which I have now to state and investigate.

The more appeals of this sort which you make, he said, the more determined are we that you shall tell us how such a State is possible: speak out and at once.

Let me begin by reminding you that we found our way hither in the search after justice and injustice.

True, he replied; but what of that?

I was only going to ask whether, if we have discovered them, we are to require that the just man should in nothing fail of absolute justice; or may we be satisfied with an approximation, and the attainment in him of a higher degree of justice than is to be found in other men?

The approximation will be enough.

We are enquiring into the nature of absolute justice and into the character of the perfectly just, and into injustice and the perfectly unjust, that we might have an ideal. We were to look at these in order that we might judge of our own happiness and unhappiness according to the standard which they exhibited and the degree in which we resembled them, but not with any view of showing that they could exist in fact.

---

* *i.e.*, "waves of paradox" which, Socrates has said, bid fair to overwhelm him.

True, he said.

Would a painter be any the worse because, after having delineated
with consummate art an ideal of a perfectly beautiful man, he was
unable to show that any such man could ever have existed?

He would be none the worse.

Well, and were we not creating an ideal of a perfect State?

To be sure.

And is our theory a worse theory because we are unable to prove
the possibility of a city being ordered in the manner described?

Surely not, he replied.

That is the truth, I said. But if, at your request, I am to try and
show how and under what conditions the possibility is highest, I must
ask you, having this in view, to repeat your former admissions.

What admissions?

I want to know whether ideals are ever fully realized in language?
Does not the word express more than the fact, and must not the actual,
whatever a man may think, always, in the nature of things, fall short
of the truth? What do you say?

I agree.

Then you must not insist on my proving that the actual State will
in every respect coincide with the ideal: if we are only able to discover how a city may be governed nearly as we proposed, you will
admit that we have discovered the possibility which you demand; and
will be contented. I am sure that I should be contented — will not
you?

Yes, I will.

Let me next endeavour to show what is that fault in States which is
the cause of their present maladministration, and what is the least
change which will enable a State to pass into the truer form; and let
the change, if possible, be of one thing only, or, if not, of two; at any
rate, let the changes be as few and slight as possible.

Certainly, he replied.

I think, I said, that there might be a reform of the State if only one
change were made, which is not a slight or easy though still a possible
one.

What is it? he said.

Now then, I said, I go to meet that which I liken to the greatest of
the waves; yet shall the word be spoken, even though the wave break
and drown me in laughter and dishonour; and do you mark my
words.

Proceed.

I said: *Until philosophers are kings, or the kings and princes of this
world have the spirit and power of philosophy, and political greatness
and wisdom meet in one, and those commoner natures who pursue
either to the exclusion of the other are compelled to stand aside, cities
will never have rest from their evils, — no, nor the human race, as I
believe, — and then only will this our State have a possibility of life
and behold the light of day.** Such was the thought, my dear

* This is the most famous single statement in Plato's writings.

Glaucon, which I would fain have uttered if it had not seemed too extravagant; for to be convinced that in no other State can there be happiness private or public is indeed a hard thing.

Socrates, what do you mean? I would have you consider that the word which you have uttered is one at which numerous persons, and very respectable persons too, in a figure pulling off their coats all in a moment, and seizing any weapon that comes to hand, will run at you might and main, before you know where you are, intending to do heaven knows what; and if you don't prepare an answer, and put yourself in motion, you will be 'pared by their fine wits,' and no mistake.

You got me into the scrape, I said.

And I was quite right; however, I will do all I can to get you out of it; but I can only give you good-will and good advice, and perhaps, I may be able to fit answers to your questions better than another — that is all. And now, having such an auxiliary, you must do your best to show the unbelievers that you are right.

I ought to try, I said, since you offer me such invaluable assistance. And I think that, if there is to be a chance of our escaping, we must explain to them whom we mean when we say that philosophers are to rule in the State; then we shall be able to defend ourselves: There will be discovered to be some natures who ought to study philosophy and to be leaders in the State; and others who are not born to be philosophers, and are meant to be followers rather than leaders.

Then now for a definition, he said.

Follow me, I said, and I hope that I may in some way or other be able to give you a satisfactory explanation.

Proceed.

I dare say that you remember, and therefore I need not remind you, that a lover, if he is worthy of the name, ought to show his love, not to some one part of that which he loves, but to the whole.

I really do not understand, and therefore beg of you to assist my memory.

Another person, I said, might fairly reply as you do; but a man of pleasure like yourself ought to know that all who are in the flower of youth do somehow or other raise a pang or emotion in a lover's breast, and are thought by him to be worthy of his affectionate regards. Is not this a way which you have with the fair: one has a snub nose, and you praise his charming face; the hook-nose of another has, you say, a royal look; while he who is neither snub nor hooked has the grace of regularity: the dark visage is manly, the fair are children of the gods; and as to the sweet 'honey pale,' as they are called, what is the very name but the invention of a lover who talks in diminutives, and is not adverse to paleness if appearing on the cheek of youth? In a word, there is no excuse which you will not make, and nothing which you will not say, in order not to lose a single flower that blooms in the spring-time of youth.

If you make me an authority in matters of love, for the sake of the argument, I assent.

And what do you say of lovers of wine? Do you not see them doing the same? They are glad of any pretext of drinking any wine.

Very good.

And the same is true of ambitious men; if they cannot command an army, they are willing to command a file; and if they cannot be honoured by really great and important persons, they are glad to be honoured by lesser and meaner people, — but honour of some kind they must have.

Exactly.

Once more let me ask: Does he who desires any class of goods, desire the whole class or a part only?

The whole.

And may we not say of the philosopher that he is a lover, not of a part of wisdom only, but of the whole?

Yes, of the whole.

And he who dislikes learning, especially in youth, when he has no power of judging what is good and what is not, such an one we maintain not to be a philosopher or a lover of knowledge, just as he who refuses his food is not hungry, and may be said to have a bad appetite and not a good one?

Very true, he said.

Whereas he who has a taste for every sort of knowledge and who is curious to learn and is never satisfied, may be justly termed a philosopher? Am I not right?

Glaucon said: If curiosity makes a philosopher, you will find many a strange being will have a title to the name. All the lovers of sights have a delight in learning, and must therefore be included. Musical amateurs, too, are a folk strangely out of place among philosophers, for they are the last persons in the world who would come to anything like a philosophical discussion, if they could help, while they run about at the Dionysiac festivals as if they had let out their ears to hear every chorus; whether the performance is in town or country — that makes no difference — they are there. Now are we to maintain that all these and any who have similar tastes, as well as the professors of quite minor arts, are philosophers?

Certainly not, I replied; they are only an imitation.

He said: Who then are the true philosophers?

Those, I said, who are lovers of the vision of truth.

That is also good, he said; but I should like to know what you mean?

To another, I replied, I might have a difficulty in explaining; but I am sure that you will admit a proposition which I am about to make.

What is the proposition?

That since beauty is the opposite of ugliness, they are two?

Certainly.

And inasmuch as they are two, each of them is one?

True again.

And of just and unjust, good and evil, and of every other class, the same remark holds: taken singly, each of them is one; but from the various combinations of them with actions and things and with one another, they are seen in all sorts of lights and appear many?

Very true.

And this is the distinction which I draw between the sight-loving, art-loving, practical class and those of whom I am speaking, and who are alone worthy of the name of philosophers.

How do you distinguish them? he said.

The lovers of sounds and sights, I replied, are, as I conceive, fond of fine tones and colours and forms and all the artificial products that are made out of them, but their mind is incapable of seeing or loving absolute beauty.

True, he replied.

Few are they who are able to attain to the sight of this.

Very true.

And he who, having a sense of beautiful things has no sense of absolute beauty, or who, if another lead him to a knowledge of that beauty is unable to follow — of such an one I ask, Is he awake or in a dream only? Reflect: is not the dreamer, sleeping or waking, one who likens dissimilar things, who puts the copy in the place of the real object?

I should certainly say that such an one was dreaming.

But take the case of the other, who recognises the existence of abso-lute beauty and is able to distinguish the idea from the objects which participate in the idea, neither putting the objects in the place of the idea nor the idea in the place of the objects — is he a dreamer, or is he awake?

He is wide awake.

And may we not say that the mind of the one who knows has knowledge, and that the mind of the other, who opines only, has opinion?

Certainly.

But suppose that the latter should quarrel with us and dispute our statement, can we administer any soothing cordial or advice to him, without revealing to him that there is sad disorder in his wits?

We must certainly offer him some good advice, he replied.

Come, then, and let us think of something to say to him. Shall we begin by assuring him that he is welcome to any knowledge which he may have, and that we are rejoiced at his having it? But we should like to ask him a question: Does he who has knowledge know something or nothing? (You must answer for him.)

I answer that he knows something.

Something that is or is not?

Something that is; for how can that which is not ever be known?

And are we assured, after looking at the matter from many points of view, that absolute being is or may be absolutely known, but that the utterly non-existent is utterly unknown?

Nothing can be more certain.

Good. But if there be anything which is of such a nature as to be and not to be, that will have a place intermediate between pure being and the absolute negation of being?

Yes, between them.

And, as knowledge corresponded to being and ignorance of necessity to not-being, for that intermediate between being and not-being there has to be discovered a corresponding intermediate between ignorance and knowledge, if there be such?

Certainly.

Do we admit the existence of opinion?

Undoubtedly.

As being the same with knowledge, or another faculty?

Another faculty.

Then opinion and knowledge have to do with different kinds of matter corresponding to this difference of faculties?

Yes.

And knowledge is relative to being and knows being. But before I proceed further I will make a division.

What division?

I will begin by placing faculties in a class by themselves: they are powers in us, and in all other things, by which we do as we do. Sight and hearing, for example, I should call faculties. Have I clearly explained the class which I mean?

Yes, I quite understand.

Then let me tell you my view about them. I do not see them, and therefore the distinctions of figure, colour, and the like, which enable me to discern the differences of some things, do not apply to them. In speaking of a faculty I think only of its sphere and its result; and that which has the same sphere and the same result I call the same faculty, but that which has another sphere and another result I call different. Would that be your way of speaking?

Yes.

And will you be so very good as to answer one more question? Would you say that knowledge is a faculty, or in what class would you place it?

Certainly knowledge is a faculty, and the mightiest of all faculties.

And is opinion also a faculty?

Certainly, he said; for opinion is that with which we are able to form an opinion.

And yet you were acknowledging a little while ago that knowledge is not the same as opinion?

Why, yes, he said: how can any reasonable being ever identify that which is infallible with that which errs?

An excellent answer, proving, I said, that we are quite conscious of a distinction between them.

Yes.

Then knowledge and opinion having distinct powers have also distinct spheres or subject-matters?

That is certain.

Being is the sphere or subject-matter of knowledge, and knowledge is to know the nature of being?

Yes.

And opinion is to have an opinion?

Yes.

And do we know what we opine? or is the subject-matter of opinion the same as the subject-matter of knowledge?

Nay, he replied, that has been already disproven; if difference in faculty implies difference in the sphere or subject-matter, and if, as we were saying, opinion and knowledge are distinct faculties, then the sphere of knowledge and of opinion cannot be the same.

Then if being is the subject-matter of knowledge, something else must be the subject-matter of opinion?

Yes, something else.

Well then, is not-being the subject-matter of opinion? or, rather, how can there be an opinion at all about not-being? Reflect: when a man has an opinion, has he not an opinion about something? Can he have an opinion which is an opinion about nothing?

Impossible.

He who has an opinion has an opinion about some one thing?

Yes.

And not-being is not one thing but, properly speaking, nothing?

True.

Of not-being, ignorance was assumed to be the necessary correlative; of being, knowledge?

True, he said.

Then opinion is not concerned either with being or with not-being?

Not with either.

And can therefore neither be ignorance nor knowledge?

That seems to be true.

But is opinion to be sought without and beyond either of them, in a greater clearness than knowledge, or in a greater darkness than ignorance?

In neither.

Then I suppose that opinion appears to you to be darker than knowledge, but lighter than ignorance?

Both; and in no small degree.

And also to be within and between them?

Yes.

Then you would infer that opinion is intermediate?

No question.

But were we not saying before, that if anything appeared to be of a sort which is and is not at the same time, that sort of thing would appear also to lie in the interval between pure being and absolute not-being; and that the corresponding faculty is neither knowledge nor ignorance, but will be found in the interval between them?

True.

And in that interval there has now been discovered something which we call opinion?

There has.

Then what remains to be discovered is the object which partakes equally of the nature of being and not-being, and cannot rightly be termed either, pure and simple; this unknown term, when discovered, we may truly call the subject of opinion, and assign each to their proper faculty, — the extremes to the faculties of the extremes and the mean to the faculty of the mean.

True.

This being premised, I would ask the gentleman who is of opinion that there is no absolute or unchangeable idea of beauty — in whose opinion the beautiful is the manifold — he, I say, your lover of beautiful sights, who cannot bear to be told that the beautiful is one, and the just is one, or that anything is one — to him I would appeal, saying, Will you be so very kind, sir, as to tell us whether, of all these beautiful things, there is one which will not be found ugly; or of the just, which will not be found unjust; or of the holy, which will not also be unholy?

No, he replied; the beautiful will in some point of view be found ugly; and the same is true of the rest.

And may not the many which are doubles be also halves? — doubles, that is, of one thing, and halves of another?

Quite true.

And things great and small, heavy and light, as they are termed, will not be denoted by these any more than by the opposite names?

True; both these and the opposite names will always attach to all of them.

And can any one of those many things which are called by particular names be said to be this rather than not to be this?

He replied: They are like the punning riddles which are asked at feasts or the children's puzzle about the eunuch aiming at the bat, with what he hit him, as they say in the puzzle, and upon what the bat was sitting.* The individual objects of which I am speaking are also a riddle, and have a double sense: nor can you fix them in your mind, either as being or not-being, or both, or neither.

Then what will you do with them? I said. Can they have a better place than between being and not-being? For they are clearly not in greater darkness or negation than not-being, or more full of light and existence than being.

That is quite true, he said.

Thus then we seem to have discovered that the many ideas which the multitude entertain about the beautiful and about all other things are tossing about in some region which is half-way between pure being and pure not-being?

* Cf. P. Shorey, *Republic,* Loeb Library, 1930, note *ad loc.*
"[The riddle] might run in English,
A tale there is, a man yet not a man,
Seeing, saw not, a bird and not a bird,
Perching upon a bough and not a bough,
And hit it — not, with a stone and not a stone.
The key words of the answer are eunuch, bat, reed, pumice-stone."

We have.

Yes; and we had before agreed that anything of this kind which we might find was to be described as matter of opinion, and not as matter of knowledge; being the intermediate flux which is caught and detained by the intermediate faculty.

Quite true.

Then those who see the many beautiful, and who yet neither see absolute beauty, nor can follow any guide who points the way thither; who see the many just, and not absolute justice, and the like, — such persons may be said to have opinion but not knowledge?

That is certain.

But those who see the absolute and eternal and immutable may be said to know, and not to have opinion only?

Neither can that be denied.

The one love and embrace the subjects of knowledge, the other those of opinion? The latter are the same, as I dare say you will remember, who listened to sweet sounds and gazed upon fair colours, but would not tolerate the existence of absolute beauty.

Yes, I remember.

Shall we then be guilty of any impropriety in calling them lovers of opinion rather than lovers of wisdom, and will they be very angry with us for thus describing them?

I shall tell them not to be angry; no man should be angry at what is true.

But those who love the truth in each thing are to be called lovers of wisdom and not lovers of opinion.

Assuredly.

[471c–480]

BOOK VI

And thus, Glaucon, after the argument has gone a weary way, the true and the false philosophers have at length appeared in view.

I do not think, he said, that the way could have been shortened.

I suppose not, I said; and yet I believe that we might have had a better view of both of them if the discussion could have been confined to this one subject and if there were not many other questions awaiting us, which he who desires to see in what respect the life of the just differs from that of the unjust must consider.

And what is the next question? he asked.

Surely, I said, the one which follows next in order. Inasmuch as philosophers only are able to grasp the eternal and unchangeable, and those who wander in the region of the many and variable are not philosophers, I must ask you which of the two classes should be the rulers of our State?

And how can we rightly answer that question?

Which ever of the two are best able to guard the laws and institutions of our State — let them be our guardians.

Very good.

Neither, I said, can there be any question that the guardian who is to keep anything should have eyes rather than no eyes?

There can be no question of that.

And are not those who are verily and indeed wanting in the knowledge of the true being of each thing, and who have in their souls no clear pattern, and are unable as with a painter's eye to look at the absolute truth and to that original to repair, and having perfect vision of the other world to order the laws about beauty, goodness, justice in this, if not already ordered, and to guard and preserve the order of them — are not such persons, I ask, simply blind?

Truly, he replied, they are much in that condition.

And shall they be our guardians when there are others who, besides being their equals in experience and falling short of them in no particular of virtue, also know the very truth of each thing?

There can be no reason, he said, for rejecting those who have this greatest of all great qualities; they must always have the first place unless they fail in some other respect.

Suppose then, I said, that we determine how far they can unite this and the other excellences.

By all means.

In the first place, as we began by observing, the nature of the philosopher has to be ascertained. We must come to an understanding about him, and, when we have done so, then, if I am not mistaken, we shall also acknowledge that such an union of qualities is possible, and that those in whom they are united, and those only, should be rulers in the State.

What do you mean?

Let us suppose that philosophical minds always love knowledge of a sort which shows them the eternal nature not varying from generation and corruption.

Agreed.

And further, I said, let us agree that they are lovers of all true being; there is no part whether greater or less, or more or less honourable, which they are willing to renounce; as we said before of the lover and the man of ambition.

True.

And if they are to be what we were describing, is there not another quality which they should also possess?

What quality?

Truthfulness: they will never intentionally receive into their mind falsehood, which is their detestation, and they will love the truth.

Yes, that may be safely affirmed of them.

'May be,' my friend, I replied, is not the word; say rather 'must be affirmed': for he whose nature is amorous of anything cannot help loving all that belongs or is akin to the object of his affections.

Right, he said.

And is there anything more akin to wisdom than truth?

How can there be?

Can the same nature be a lover of wisdom and a lover of falsehood?

Never.

The true lover of learning then must from his earliest youth, as far as in him lies, desire all truth?

Assuredly.

But then again, as we know by experience, he whose desires are strong in one direction will have them weaker in others; they will be like a stream which has been drawn off into another channel.

True.

He whose desires are drawn towards knowledge in every form will be absorbed in the pleasures of the soul, and will hardly feel bodily pleasure — I mean, if he be a true philosopher and not a sham one.

That is most certain.

Such an one is sure to be temperate and the reverse of covetous; for the motives which make another man desirous of having and spending, have no place in his character.

Very true.

Another criterion of the philosophical nature has also to be considered.

What is that?

There should be no secret corner of illiberality; nothing can be more antagonistic than meanness to a soul which is ever longing after the whole of things both divine and human.

Most true, he replied.

Then how can he who has magnificence of mind and is the spectator of all time and all existence, think much of human life?

He cannot.

Or can such an one account death fearful?

No indeed.

Then the cowardly and mean nature has no part in true philosophy?

Certainly not.

Or again: can he who is harmoniously constituted, who is not covetous or mean, or a boaster, or a coward — can he, I say, ever be unjust or hard in his dealings?

Impossible.

Then you will soon observe whether a man is just and gentle, or rude and unsociable; these are the signs which distinguish even in youth the philosophical nature from the unphilosophical.

True.

There is another point which should be remarked.

What point?

Whether he has or has not a pleasure in learning; for no one will love that which gives him pain, and in which after much toil he makes little progress.

Certainly not.

And again, if he is forgetful and retains nothing of what he learns, will he not be an empty vessel?

That is certain.

Labouring in vain, he must end in hating himself and his fruitless occupation?

Yes.

Then a soul which forgets cannot be ranked among genuine philosophic natures; we must insist that the philosopher should have a good memory?

Certainly.

And once more, the inharmonious and unseemly nature can only tend to disproportion?

Undoubtedly.

And do you consider truth to be akin to proportion or to disproportion?

To proportion.

Then, besides other qualities, we must try to find a naturally well-proportioned and gracious mind, which will move spontaneously towards the true being of everything.

Certainly.

Well, and do not all these qualities, which we have been enumerating, go together, and are they not, in a manner, necessary to a soul, which is to have a full and perfect participation of being?

They are absolutely necessary, he replied.

And must not that be a blameless study which he only can pursue who has the gift of a good memory, and is quick to learn, — noble, gracious, the friend of truth, justice, courage, temperance, who are his kindred?

The god of jealousy himself, he said, could find no fault with such a study.

And to men like him, I said, when perfected by years and education, and to these only you will entrust the State.

Here Adeimantus interposed and said: To these statements, Socrates, no one can offer a reply; but when you talk in this way, a strange feeling passes over the minds of your hearers: They fancy that they are led astray a little at each step in the argument, owing to their own want of skill in asking and answering questions; these littles accumulate, and at the end of the discussion they are found to have sustained a mighty overthrow and all their former notions appear to be turned upside down. And as unskilful players of draughts are at last shut up by their more skilful adversaries and have no piece to move, so they too find themselves shut up at last; for they have nothing to say in this new game of which words are the counters; and yet all the time they are in the right. The observation is suggested to me by what is now occurring. For any one of us might say, that although in words he is not able to meet you at each step of the argument, he sees as a fact that the votaries of philosophy, when they carry on the study, not only in youth as a part of education, but as the pursuit of their maturer years, most of them become strange monsters, not to say utter rogues, and that those who may be considered the best of them are made useless to the world by the very study which you extol.

Well, and do you think that those who say so are wrong?

I cannot tell, he replied; but I should like to know what is your opinion.

Hear my answer; I am of opinion that they are quite right.

Then how can you be justified in saying that cities will not cease from evil until philosophers rule in them, when philosophers are acknowledged by us to be of no use to them?

You ask a question, I said, to which a reply can only be given in a parable.

Yes, Socrates; and that is a way of speaking to which you are not at all accustomed, I suppose.

I perceive, I said, that you are vastly amused at having plunged me into such a hopeless discussion; but now hear the parable, and then you will be still more amused at the meagreness of my imagination: for the manner in which the best men are treated in their own States is so grievous that no single thing on earth is comparable to it; and therefore, if I am to plead their cause, I must have recourse to fiction, and put together a figure made up of many things, like the fabulous unions of goats and stags which are found in pictures. Imagine then a fleet or a ship in which there is a captain who is taller and stronger than any of the crew, but he is a little deaf and has a similar infirmity in sight, and his knowledge of navigation is not much better. The sailors are quarrelling with one another about the steering — every one is of opinion that he has a right to steer, though he has never learned the art of navigation and cannot tell who taught him or when he learned, and will further assert that it cannot be taught, and they are ready to cut in pieces any one who says the contrary. They throng about the captain, begging and praying him to commit the helm to them; and if at any time they do not prevail, but others are preferred to them, they kill the others or throw them overboard, and having first chained up the noble captain's senses with drink or some narcotic drug, they mutiny and take possession of the ship and make free with the stores; thus, eating and drinking, they proceed on their voyage in such a manner as might be expected of them. Him who is their partisan and cleverly aids them in their plot for getting the ship out of the captain's hands into their own whether by force or persuasion, they compliment with the name of sailor, pilot, able seaman, and abuse the other sort of man, whom they call a good-for-nothing; but that the true pilot must pay attention to the year and seasons and sky and stars and winds, and whatever else belongs to his art, if he intends to be really qualified for the command of a ship, and that he must and will be the steerer, whether other people like or not — the possibility of this union of authority with the steerer's art has never seriously entered into their thoughts or been made part of their calling. Now in vessels which are in a state of mutiny and by sailors who are mutineers, how will the true pilot be regarded? Will he not be called by them a prater, a star-gazer, a good-for-nothing?

Of course, said Adeimantus.

Then you will hardly need, I said, to hear the interpretation of the figure, which describes the true philosopher in his relation to the State; for you understand already.

Certainly.

Then suppose you now take this parable to the gentleman who is surprised at finding that philosophers have no honour in their cities; explain it to him and try to convince him that their having honour would be far more extraordinary.

I will.

Say to him, that, in deeming the best votaries of philosophy to be useless to the rest of the world, he is right; but also tell him to attribute their uselessness to the fault of those who will not use them, and not to themselves. The pilot should not humbly beg the sailors to be commanded by him — that is not the order of nature; neither are 'the wise to go to the doors of the rich' — the ingenious author of this saying told a lie — but the truth is, that, when a man is ill, whether he be rich or poor, to the physician he must go, and he who wants to be governed, to him who is able to govern. The ruler who is good for anything ought not to beg his subjects to be ruled by him; although the present governors of mankind are of a different stamp; they may be justly compared to the mutinous sailors, and the true helmsmen to those who are called by them good-for-nothings and star-gazers.

Precisely so, he said.

For these reasons, and among men like these, philosophy, the noblest pursuit of all, is not likely to be much esteemed by those of the opposite faction; not that the greatest and most lasting injury is done to her by her opponents, but by her own professing followers, the same of whom you suppose the accuser to say, that the greater number of them are arrant rogues, and the best are useless; in which opinion I agreed.

Yes.

And the reason why the good are useless has now been explained?

True.

Then shall we proceed to show that the corruption of the majority is also unavoidable, and that this is not to be laid to the charge of philosophy any more than the other?

By all means.

And let us ask and answer in turn, first going back to the description of the gentle and noble nature. Truth, as you will remember, was his leader, whom he followed always and in all things; failing in this, he was an impostor, and had no part or lot in true philosophy.

Yes, that was said.

Well, and is not this one quality, to mention no others, greatly at variance with present notions of him?

Certainly, he said.

And have we not a right to say in his defence, that the true lover of knowledge is always striving after being — that is his nature; he will not rest in the multiplicity of individuals which is an appearance only, but will go on — the keen edge will not be blunted, nor the force of his desire abate until he have attained the knowledge of the true nature of every essence by a sympathetic and kindred power in the soul, and by that power drawing near and mingling and becoming incorporate with very being, having begotten mind and truth, he will have knowledge and will live and grow truly, and then, and not till then, will he cease from his travail.

Nothing, he said, can be more just than such a description of him.

And will the love of a lie be any part of a philosopher's nature? Will he not utterly hate a lie?

He will.

And when truth is the captain, we cannot suspect any evil of the band which he leads?

Impossible.

Justice and health of mind will be of the company, and temperance will follow after?

True, he replied.

Neither is there any reason why I should again set in array the philosopher's virtues, as you will doubtless remember that courage, magnificence, apprehension, memory, were his natural gifts. And you objected that, although no one could deny what I then said, still, if you leave words and look at facts, the persons who are thus described are some of them manifestly useless, and the greater number utterly depraved; we were then led to enquire into the grounds of these accusations, and have now arrived at the point of asking why are the majority bad, which question of necessity brought us back to the examination and definition of the true philosopher.

Exactly.

And we have next to consider the corruptions of the philosophic nature, why so many are spoiled and so few escape spoiling — I am speaking of those who were said to be useless but not wicked — and, when we have done with them, we will speak of the imitators of philosophy, what manner of men are they who aspire after a profession which is above them and of which they are unworthy, and then, by their manifold inconsistencies, bring upon philosophy, and upon all philosophers, that universal reprobation of which we speak.

What are these corruptions? he said.

I will see if I can explain them to you. Every one will admit that a nature having in perfection all the qualities which we required in a philosopher, is a rare plant which is seldom seen among men.

Rare indeed.

And what numberless and powerful causes tend to destroy these rare natures!

What causes?

In the first place there are their own virtues, their courage, temperance, and the rest of them, every one of which praiseworthy qualities (and this is a most singular circumstance) destroys and distracts from philosophy the soul which is the possessor of them.

That is very singular, he replied.

Then there are all the ordinary goods of life — beauty, wealth, strength, rank, and great connections in the State — you understand the sort of things — these also have a corrupting and distracting effect.

I understand; but I should like to know more precisely what you mean about them.

Grasp the truth as a whole, I said, and in the right way; you will then have no difficulty in apprehending the preceding remarks, and they will no longer appear strange to you.

And how am I to do so? he asked.

Why, I said, we know that all germs or seeds, whether vegetable or animal, when they fail to meet with proper nutriment or climate or soil, in proportion to their vigour, are all the more sensitive to the want of a suitable environment, for evil is a greater enemy to what is good than what is not.

Very true.

There is reason in supposing that the finest natures, when under alien conditions, receive more injury than the inferior, because the contrast is greater.

Certainly.

And may we not say, Adeimantus, that the most gifted minds, when they are ill-educated, become pre-eminently bad? Do not great crimes and the spirit of pure evil spring out of a fulness of nature ruined by education rather than from any inferiority, whereas weak natures are scarcely capable of any very great good or very great evil?

There I think that you are right.

And our philosopher follows the same analogy — he is like a plant which, having proper nurture, must necessarily grow and mature into all virtue, but, if sown and planted in an alien soil, becomes the most noxious of all weeds, unless he be preserved by some divine power. Do you really think, as people so often say, that our youth are corrupted by Sophists, or that private teachers of the art corrupt them in any degree worth speaking of? Are not the public who say these things the greatest of all Sophists? And do they not educate to perfection young and old, men and women alike, and fashion them after their own hearts?

When is this accomplished? he said.

When they meet together, and the world sits down at an assembly, or in a court of law, or a theatre, or a camp, or in any other popular resort, and there is a great uproar, and they praise some things which are being said or done, and blame other things, equally exaggerating both, shouting and clapping their hands, and the echo of the rocks and the place in which they are assembled redoubles the sound of the praise or blame — at such a time will not a young man's heart, as they say, leap within him? Will any private training enable him to stand firm against the overwhelming flood of popular opinion? or will he be carried away by the stream? Will he not have the notions of good and evil which the public in general have — he will do as they do, and as they are, such will he be?

Yes, Socrates; necessity will compel him.

And yet, I said, there is a still greater necessity, which has not been mentioned.

What is that?

The gentle force of attainder or confiscation or death, which, as you are aware, these new Sophists and educators, who are the public, apply when their words are powerless.

Indeed they do; and in right good earnest.

Now what opinion of any other Sophist, or of any private person, can be expected to overcome in such an unequal contest?

None, he replied.

No, indeed, I said, even to make the attempt is a great piece of folly; there neither is, nor has been, nor is ever likely to be, any different type of character which has had no other training in virtue but that which is supplied by public opinion — I speak, my friend, of human virtue only; what is more than human, as the proverb says, is not included: for I would not have you ignorant that, in the present evil state of governments, whatever is saved and comes to good is saved by the power of God, as we may truly say.

I quite assent, he replied.

Then let me crave your assent also to a further observation.

What are you going to say?

Why, that all those mercenary individuals, whom the many call Sophists and whom they deem to be their adversaries, do, in fact, teach nothing but the opinion of the many, that is to say, the opinions of their assemblies; and this is their wisdom. I might compare them to a man who should study the tempers and desires of a mighty strong beast who is fed by him — he would learn how to approach and handle him, also at what times and from what causes he is dangerous or the reverse, and what is the meaning of his several cries, and by what sounds, when another utters them, he is soothed or infuriated; and you may suppose further, that when, by continually attending upon him, he has become perfect in all this, he calls his knowledge wisdom, and makes of it a system or art, which he proceeds to teach, although he has no real notion of what he means by the principles or passions of which he is speaking, but calls this honourable and that dishonourable, or good or evil, or just or unjust, all in accordance with the tastes and tempers of the great brute. Good he pronounces to be that in which the beast delights and evil to be that which he dislikes; and he can give no other account of them except that the just and noble are the necessary, having never himself seen, and having no power of explaining to others the nature of either, or the difference between them, which is immense. By heaven, would not such an one be a rare educator?

Indeed he would.

And in what way does he who thinks that wisdom is the discernment of the tempers and tastes of the motley multitude, whether in painting or music, or, finally, in politics, differ from him whom I have been describing? For when a man consorts with the many,

and exhibits to them his poem or other work of art or the service
which he has done the State, making them his judges when he is not
obliged, the so-called necessity of Diomede * will oblige him to produce whatever they praise.   And yet the reasons are utterly ludicrous
which they give in confirmation of their own notions about the honourable and good.   Did you ever hear any of them which were not?

No, nor am I likely to hear.

You recognise the truth of what I have been saying?   Then let
me ask you to consider further whether the world will ever be induced to believe in the existence of absolute beauty rather than of
the many beautiful, or of the absolute in each kind rather than
of the many in each kind?

Certainly not.

Then the world cannot possibly be a philosopher?

Impossible.

And therefore philosophers must inevitably fall under the censure
of the world?

They must.

And of individuals who consort with the mob and seek to please
them?

That is evident.

Then, do you see any way in which the philosopher can be preserved in his calling to the end? and remember what we were saying
of him, that he was to have quickness and memory and courage and
magnificence — these were admitted by us to be the true philosopher's
gifts.

Yes.

Will not such an one from his early childhood be in all things
first among all, especially if his bodily endowments are like his mental ones?

Certainly, he said.

And his friends and fellow-citizens will want to use him as he gets
older for their own purposes?

No question.

Falling at his feet, they will make requests to him and do him
honour and flatter him, because they want to get into their hands
now, the power which he will one day possess.

That often happens, he said.

And what will a man such as he is be likely to do under such circumstances, especially if he be a citizen of a great city, rich and noble,
and a tall proper youth? †   Will he not be full of boundless aspira-
tions, and fancy himself able to manage the affairs of Hellenes and of
barbarians, and having got such notions into his head will he not
dilate and elevate himself in the fulness of vain pomp and senseless
pride?

To be sure he will.

* An ancient scholar says this refers to the time when Diomedes bound Odysseus
and drove him back to camp after Odysseus had unsuccessfully attempted to murder
him.
† In this whole passage there is an obvious allusion to Alcibiades.

Now, when he is in this state of mind, if some one gently comes to him and tells him that he is a fool and must get understanding, which can only be got by slaving for it, do you think that, under such adverse circumstances, he will be easily induced to listen?

Far otherwise.

And even if there be some one who through inherent goodness or natural reasonableness has had his eyes opened a little and is humbled and taken captive by philosophy, how will his friends behave when they think that they are likely to lose the advantage which they were hoping to reap from his companionship? Will they not do and say anything to prevent him from yielding to his better nature and to render his teacher powerless, using to this end private intrigues as well as public prosecutions?

There can be no doubt of it.

And how can one who is thus circumstanced ever become a philosopher?

Impossible.

Then were we not right in saying that even the very qualities which make a man a philosopher may, if he be ill-educated, divert him from philosophy, no less than riches and their accompaniments and the other so-called goods of life?

We were quite right.

Thus, my excellent friend, is brought about all that ruin and failure which I have been describing of the natures best adapted to the best of all pursuits; they are natures which we maintain to be rare at any time; this being the class out of which come the men who are the authors of the greatest evil to States and individuals; and also of the greatest good when the tide carries them in that direction; but a small man never was the doer of any great thing either to individuals or to States.

That is most true, he said.

And so philosophy is left desolate, with her marriage rite incomplete: for her own have fallen away and forsaken her, and while they are leading a false and unbecoming life, other unworthy persons, seeing that she has no kinsmen to be her protectors, enter in and dishonour her; and fasten upon her the reproaches which, as you say, her reprovers utter, who affirm of her votaries that some are good for nothing, and that the greater number deserve the severest punishment.

That is certainly what people say.

Yes; and what else would you expect, I said, when you think of the puny creatures who, seeing this land open to them — a land well stocked with fair names and showy titles — like prisoners running out of prison into a sanctuary, take a leap out of their trades into philosophy; those who do so being probably the cleverest hands at their own miserable crafts? For, although philosophy be in this evil case, still there remains a dignity about her which is not to be found in the arts. And many are thus attracted by her whose natures are imperfect and whose souls are maimed and disfigured by their meannesses, as their bodies are by their trades and crafts. Is not this unavoidable?

Yes.

Are they not exactly like a bald little tinker who has just got out of durance and come into a fortune; he takes a bath and puts on a new coat, and is decked out as a bridegroom going to marry his master's daughter, who is left poor and desolate?

A most exact parallel.

What will be the issue of such marriages? Will they not be vile and bastard?

There can be no question of it.

And when persons who are unworthy of education approach philosophy and make an alliance with her who is a rank above them what sort of ideas and opinions are likely to be generated? Will they not deserve to be called sophisms, having nothing in them genuine, or worthy of or akin to true wisdom?

No doubt, he said.

Then, Adeimantus, I said, the worthy disciples of philosophy will be but a small remnant: perchance some noble and well-educated person, detained by exile in her service, who in the absence of corrupting influences remains devoted to her; or some lofty soul born in a mean city, the politics of which he contemns and neglects; and there may be a gifted few who leave the arts, which they justly despise, and come to her; — or peradventure there are some who are restrained by our friend Theages' bridle; for everything in the life of Theages conspired to divert him from philosophy; but ill-health kept him away from politics. My own case of the internal sign is hardly worth mentioning, for rarely, if ever, has such a monitor been given to any other man. Those who belong to this small class have tasted how sweet and blessed a possession philosophy is, and have also seen enough of the madness of the multitude; and they know that no politician is honest, nor is there any champion of justice at whose side they may fight and be saved. Such an one may be compared to a man who has fallen among wild beasts — he will not join in the wickedness of his fellows, but neither is he able singly to resist all their fierce natures, and therefore seeing that he would be of no use to the State or to his friends, and reflecting that he would have to throw away his life without doing any good either to himself or others, he holds his peace, and goes his own way. He is like one who, in the storm of dust and sleet which the driving wind hurries along, retires under the shelter of a wall; and seeing the rest of mankind full of wickedness, he is content, if only he can live his own life and be pure from evil or unrighteousness, and depart in peace and good-will, with bright hopes.

Yes, he said, and he will have done a great work before he departs.

A great work — yes; but not the greatest, unless he find a State suitable to him; for in a State which is suitable to him, he will have a larger growth and be the saviour of his country, as well as of himself.

The causes why philosophy is in such an evil name have now been sufficiently explained: the injustice of the charges against her has been shown — is there anything more which you wish to say?

Nothing more on that subject, he replied; but I should like to know which of the governments now existing is in your opinion the one adapted to her.

Not any of them, I said; and that is precisely the accusation which I bring against them — not one of them is worthy of the philosophic nature, and hence that nature is warped and estranged; — as the exotic seed which is sown in a foreign land becomes denaturalized, and is wont to be overpowered and to lose itself in the new soil, even so this growth of philosophy, instead of persisting, degenerates and receives another character. But if philosophy ever finds in the State that perfection which she herself is, then will be seen that she is in truth divine, and that all other things, whether natures of men or institutions, are but human; — and now, I know, that you are going to ask, What that State is.

No, he said; there you are wrong, for I was going to ask another question — whether it is the State of which we are the founders and inventors, or some other?

Yes, I replied, ours in most respects; but you may remember my saying before, that some living authority would always be required in the State having the same idea of the constitution which guided you when as legislator you were laying down the laws.

That was said, he replied.

Yes, but not in a satisfactory manner; you frightened us by interposing objections, which certainly showed that the discussion would be long and difficult; and what still remains is the reverse of easy.

What is there remaining?

The question how the study of philosophy may be so ordered as not to be the ruin of the State: All great attempts are attended with risk; 'hard is the good,' as men say.

Still, he said, let the point be cleared up, and the enquiry will then be complete.

I shall not be hindered, I said, by any want of will, but, if at all, by a want of power: my zeal you may see for yourselves; and please to remark in what I am about to say how boldly and unhesitatingly I declare that States should pursue philosophy, not as they do now, but in a different spirit.

In what manner?

At present, I said, the students of philosophy are quite young; beginning when they are hardly past childhood, they devote only the time saved from moneymaking and housekeeping to such pursuits; and even those of them who are reputed to have most of the philosophic spirit, when they come within sight of the great difficulty of the subject, I mean dialectic, take themselves off. In after life when invited by some one else, they may, perhaps, go and hear a lecture, and about this they make much ado, for philosophy is not considered by them to be their proper business: at last, when they grow old, in most cases they are extinguished more truly than Heracleitus' sun, inasmuch as they never light up again.*

But what ought to be their course?

Just the opposite. In childhood and youth their study, and what philosophy they learn, should be suited to their tender years: during this period while they are growing up towards manhood, the chief and special care should be given to their bodies that they may have them to use in the service of philosophy; as life advances and the intellect begins to mature, let them increase the gymnastics of the soul; but when the strength of our citizens fails and is past civil and military duties, then let them range at will and engage in no serious labour, as we intend them to live happily here, and to crown this life with a similar happiness in another.

How truly in earnest you are, Socrates! he said; I am sure of that; and yet most of your hearers, if I am not mistaken, are likely to be still more earnest in their opposition to you, and will never be convinced; Thrasymachus least of all.

Do not make a quarrel, I said, between Thrasymachus and me, who have recently become friends, although, indeed, we were never enemies; for I shall go on striving to the utmost until I either convert him and other men, or do something which may profit them against the day when they live again, and hold the like discourse in another state of existence.

You are speaking of a time which is not very near.

Rather, I replied, of a time which is as nothing in comparison with eternity. Nevertheless, I do not wonder that the many refuse to believe; for they have never seen that of which we are now speaking realized; they have seen only a conventional imitation of philosophy, consisting of words artificially brought together, not like these of ours having a natural unity. But a human being who in word and work is perfectly moulded, as far as he can be, into the proportion and likeness of virtue — such a man ruling in a city which bears the same image, they have never yet seen, neither one nor many of them — do you think that they ever did?

No indeed.

No, my friend, and they have seldom, if ever, heard free and noble sentiments; such as men utter when they are earnestly and by every means in their power seeking after truth for the sake of knowledge, while they look coldly on the subtleties of controversy, of which the end is opinion and strife, whether they meet with them in the courts of law or in society.

They are strangers, he said, to the words of which you speak.

And this was what we foresaw, and this was the reason why truth forced us to admit, not without fear and hesitation, that neither cities nor States nor individuals will ever attain perfection until the small class of philosophers whom we termed useless but not corrupt are

* Heracleitus said that the sun was extinguished every evening and relighted every morning.

providentially compelled, whether they will or not, to take care of
the State, and until a like necessity be laid on the State to obey them;
or until kings, or if not kings, the sons of kings or princes, are divinely
inspired with a true love of true philosophy. That either or both of
these alternatives are impossible, I see no reason to affirm: if they
were so, we might indeed be justly ridiculed as dreamers and vision-
aries. Am I not right?

Quite right.

If then, in the countless ages of the past, or at the present hour in
some foreign clime which is far away and beyond our ken, the perfected philosopher is or has been or hereafter shall be compelled by
a superior power to have the charge of the State, we are ready to assert to the death, that this our constitution has been, and is — yea,
and will be whenever the Muse of Philosophy is queen. There is no
impossibility in all this; that there is a difficulty, we acknowledge
ourselves.

My opinion agrees with yours, he said.

But do you mean to say that this is not the opinion of the multitude?

I should imagine not, he replied.

O my friend, I said, do not attack the multitude: they will change
their minds, if, not in an aggressive spirit, but gently and with the
view of soothing them and removing their dislike of over-education,
you show them your philosophers as they really are and describe as
you were just now doing their character and profession, and then
mankind will see that he of whom you are speaking is not such as
they supposed — if they view him in this new light, they will surely
change their notion of him, and answer in another strain. Who
can be at enmity with one who loves them, who that is himself gentle
and free from envy will be jealous of one in whom there is no
jealousy? Nay, let me answer for you, that in a few this harsh temper
may be found but not in the majority of mankind.

I quite agree with you, he said.

And do you not also think, as I do, that the harsh feeling which the
many entertain towards philosophy originates in the pretenders, who
rush in uninvited, and are always abusing them, and finding fault
with them, who make persons instead of things the theme of their
conversation? and nothing can be more unbecoming in philosophers
than this.

It is most unbecoming.

For he, Adeimantus, whose mind is fixed upon true being, has
surely no time to look down upon the affairs of earth, or to be filled
with malice and envy, contending against men; his eye is ever directed towards things fixed and immutable, which he sees neither injuring nor injured by one another, but all in order moving according
to reason; these he imitates, and to these he will, as far as he can,
conform himself. Can a man help imitating that with which he
holds reverential converse?

Impossible.

And the philosopher holding converse with the divine order, becomes orderly and divine, as far as the nature of man allows; but like every one else, he will suffer from detraction.

Of course.

And if a necessity be laid upon him of fashioning, not only himself, but human nature generally, whether in States or individuals, into that which he beholds elsewhere, will he, think you, be an unskilful artificer of justice, temperance, and every civil virtue?

Anything but unskilful.

And if the world perceives that what we are saying about him is the truth, will they be angry with philosophy? Will they disbelieve us, when we tell them that no State can be happy which is not designed by artists who imitate the heavenly pattern?

They will not be angry if they understand, he said. But how will they draw out the plan of which you are speaking?

They will begin by taking the State and the manners of men, from which, as from a tablet, they will rub out the picture, and leave a clean surface. This is no easy task. But whether easy or not, herein will lie the difference between them and every other legislator, — they will have nothing to do either with individual or State, and will inscribe no laws, until they have either found, or themselves made, a clean surface.

They will be very right, he said.

Having effected this, they will proceed to trace an outline of the constitution?

No doubt.

And when they are filling in the work, as I conceive, they will often turn their eyes upwards and downwards: I mean that they will first look at absolute justice and beauty and temperance, and again at the human copy; and will mingle and temper the various elements of life into the image of a man; and thus they will conceive according to that other image, which, when existing among men, Homer calls the form and likeness of God.

Very true, he said.

And one feature they will erase, and another they will put in, until they have made the ways of men, as far as possible, agreeable to the ways of God?

Indeed, he said, in no way could they make a fairer picture.

And now, I said, are we beginning to persuade those whom you described as rushing at us with might and main, that the painter of constitutions is such an one as we are praising; at whom they were so very indignant because to his hands we committed the State; and are they growing a little calmer at what they have just heard?

Much calmer, if there is any sense in them.

Why, where can they still find any ground for objection? Will they doubt that the philosopher is a lover of truth and being?

They would not be so unreasonable.

Or that his nature, being such as we have delineated, is akin to the highest good?

Neither can they doubt this.

But again, will they tell us that such a nature, placed under favourable circumstances, will not be perfectly good and wise if any ever was? Or will they prefer those whom we have rejected?

Surely not.

Then will they still be angry at our saying, that, until philosophers bear rule, States and individuals will have no rest from evil, nor will this our imaginary State ever be realized?

I think that they will be less angry.

Shall we assume that they are not only less angry but quite gentle, and that they have been converted and for very shame, if for no other reason, cannot refuse to come to terms?

By all means, he said.

Then let us suppose that the reconciliation has been effected. Will any one deny the other point, that there may be sons of kings or princes who are by nature philosophers?

Surely no man, he said.

And when they have come into being will any one say that they must of necessity be destroyed; that they can hardly be saved is not denied even by us; but that in the whole course of ages no single one of them can escape — who will venture to affirm this?

Who indeed!

But, said I, one is enough; let there be one man who has a city obedient to his will, and he might bring into existence the ideal polity about which the world is so incredulous.

Yes, one is enough.

The ruler may impose the laws and institutions which we have been describing, and the citizens may possibly be willing to obey them?

Certainly.

And that others should approve, of what we approve, is no miracle or impossibility?

I think not.

But we have sufficiently shown, in what has preceded, that all this, if only possible, is assuredly for the best.

We have.

And now we say not only that our laws, if they could be enacted, would be for the best, but also that the enactment of them, though difficult, is not impossible.

Very good.

And so with pain and toil we have reached the end of one subject, but more remains to be discussed; — how and by what studies and pursuits will the saviours of the constitution be created, and at what ages are they to apply themselves to their several studies?

Certainly.

I omitted the troublesome business of the possession of women, and the procreation of children, and the appointment of the rulers, because I knew that the perfect State would be eyed with jealousy and was difficult of attainment; but that piece of cleverness was not of much service to me, for I had to discuss them all the same. The women and children are now disposed of, but the other question of the rulers must be investigated from the very beginning. We were saying, as you will remember, that they were to be lovers of their country, tried by the test of pleasures and pains, and neither in hardships, nor in dangers, nor at any other critical moment were to lose their patriotism — he was to be rejected who failed, but he who always came forth pure, like gold tried in the refiner's fire, was to be made a ruler, and to receive honours and rewards in life and after death. This was the sort of thing which was being said, and then the argument turned aside and veiled her face; not liking to stir the question which has now arisen.

I perfectly remember, he said.

Yes, my friend, I said, and I then shrank from hazarding the bold word; but now let me dare to say — that the perfect guardian must be a philosopher.

Yes, he said, let that be affirmed.

And do not suppose that there will be many of them; for the gifts which were deemed by us to be essential rarely grow together; they are mostly found in shreds and patches.

What do you mean? he said.

You are aware, I replied, that quick intelligence, memory, sagacity, cleverness, and similar qualities, do not often grow together, and that persons who possess them and are at the same time high-spirited and magnanimous are not so constituted by nature as to live orderly and in a peaceful and settled manner; they are driven any way by their impulses, and all solid principle goes out of them.

Very true, he said.

On the other hand, those steadfast natures which can better be depended upon, which in a battle are impregnable to fear and immovable, are equally immovable when there is anything to be learned; they are always in a torpid state, and are apt to yawn and go to sleep over any intellectual toil.

Quite true.

And yet we were saying that both qualities were necessary in those to whom the higher education is to be imparted, and who are to share in any office or command.

Certainly, he said.

And will they be a class which is rarely found?

Yes, indeed.

Then the aspirant must not only be tested in those labours and dangers and pleasures which we mentioned before, but there is another kind of probation which we did not mention — he must be exercised also in many kinds of knowledge, to see whether the soul will be able to endure the highest of all, or will faint under them, as in any other studies and exercises.

Yes, he said, you are quite right in testing him. But what do you mean by the highest of all knowledge?

You may remember, I said, that we divided the soul into three parts;

and distinguished the several natures of justice, temperance, courage, and wisdom?

Indeed, he said, if I had forgotten, I should not deserve to hear more.

And do you remember the word of caution which preceded the discussion of them?

To what do you refer?

We were saying, if I am not mistaken, that he who wanted to see them in their perfect beauty must take a longer and more circuitous way, at the end of which they would appear; but that we could add on a popular exposition of them on a level with the discussion which had preceded. And you replied that such an exposition would be enough for you, and so the enquiry was continued in what to me seemed to be a very inaccurate manner; whether you were satisfied or not, it is for you to say.

Yes, he said, I thought and the others thought that you gave us a fair measure of truth.

But, my friend, I said, a measure of such things which in any degree falls short of the whole truth is not fair measure; for nothing imperfect is the measure of anything, although persons are too apt to be contented and think that they need search no further.

Not an uncommon case when people are indolent.

Yes, I said; and there cannot be any worse fault in a guardian of the State and of the laws.

True.

The guardian then, I said, must be required to take the longer circuit, and toil at learning as well as at gymnastics, or he will never reach the highest knowledge of all which, as we were just now saying, is his proper calling.

What, he said, is there a knowledge still higher than this — higher than justice and the other virtues?

Yes, I said, there is. And of the virtues too we must behold not the outline merely, as at present — nothing short of the most finished picture should satisfy us. When little things are elaborated with an infinity of pains, in order that they may appear in their full beauty and utmost clearness, how ridiculous that we should not think the highest truths worthy of attaining the highest accuracy!

A right noble thought; but do you suppose that we shall refrain from asking you what is this highest knowledge?

Nay, I said, ask if you will; but I am certain that you have heard the answer many times, and now you either do not understand me or, as I rather think, you are disposed to be troublesome; for you have often been told that the idea of good is the highest knowledge, and that all other things become useful and advantageous only by their use of this. You can hardly be ignorant that of this I was about to speak, concerning which, as you have often heard me say, we know so little; and, without which, any other knowledge or possession of any kind will profit us nothing. Do you think that the possession of all other things is of any value if we do not possess the good? or the knowledge of all other things if we have no knowledge of beauty and goodness?

Assuredly not.

You are further aware that most people affirm pleasure to be the good, but the finer sort of wits say it is knowledge?

Yes.

And you are aware too that the latter cannot explain what they mean by knowledge, but are obliged after all to say knowledge of the good?

How ridiculous!

Yes, I said, that they should begin by reproaching us with our ignorance of the good, and then presume our knowledge of it — for the good they define to be knowledge of the good, just as if we understood them when they use the term 'good' — this is of course ridiculous.

Most true, he said.

And those who make pleasure their good are in equal perplexity; for they are compelled to admit that there are bad pleasures as well as good.

Certainly.

And therefore to acknowledge that bad and good are the same?

True.

There can be no doubt about the numerous difficulties in which this question is involved.

There can be none.

Further, do we not see that many are willing to do or to have or to seem to be what is just and honourable without the reality; but no one is satisfied with the appearance of good — the reality is what they seek; in the case of the good, appearance is despised by every one.

Very true, he said.

Of this then, which every soul of man pursues and makes the end of all his actions, having a presentiment that there is such an end, and yet hesitating because neither knowing the nature nor having the same assurance of this as of other things, and therefore losing whatever good there is in other things, — of a principle such and so great as this ought the best men in our State, to whom everything is entrusted, to be in the darkness of ignorance?

Certainly not, he said.

I am sure, I said, that he who does not know how the beautiful and the just are likewise good will be but a sorry guardian of them; and I suspect that no one who is ignorant of the good will have a true knowledge of them.

That, he said, is a shrewd suspicion of yours.

And if we only have a guardian who has this knowledge our State will be perfectly ordered?

Of course, he replied; but I wish that you would tell me whether you conceive this supreme principle of the good to be knowledge or pleasure, or different from either?

Aye, I said, I knew all along that a fastidious gentleman like you would not be contented with the thoughts of other people about these matters.

True, Socrates; but I must say that one who like you has passed a lifetime in the study of philosophy should not be always repeating the opinions of others, and never telling his own.

Well, but has any one a right to say positively what he does not know?

Not, he said, with the assurance of positive certainty; he has no right to do that: but he may say what he thinks, as a matter of opinion.

And do you not know, I said, that all mere opinions are bad, and the best of them blind? You would not deny that those who have any true notion without intelligence are only like blind men who feel their way along the road?

Very true.

And do you wish to behold what is blind and crooked and base, when others will tell you of brightness and beauty?

Still, I must implore you, Socrates, said Glaucon, not to turn away just as you are reaching the goal; if you will only give such an explanation of the good as you have already given of justice and temperance and the other virtues, we shall be satisfied.

Yes, my friend, and I shall be at least equally satisfied, but I cannot help fearing that I shall fail, and that my indiscreet zeal will bring ridicule upon me. No, sweet sirs, let us not at present ask what is the actual nature of the good, for to reach what is now in my thoughts would be an effort too great for me. But of the child of the good who is likest him, I would fain speak, if I could be sure that you wished to hear — otherwise, not.

By all means, he said, tell us about the child, and you shall remain in our debt for the account of the parent.

I do indeed wish, I replied, that I could pay, and you receive, the account of the parent, and not, as now, of the offspring only; take, however, this latter by way of interest,* and at the same time have a care that I do not render a false account, although I have no intention of deceiving you.

Yes, we will take all the care that we can: proceed.

Yes, I said, but I must first come to an understanding with you, and remind you of what I have mentioned in the course of this discussion, and at many other times.

What?

The old story, that there is a many beautiful and a many good, and so of other things which we describe and define; to all of them 'many' is applied.

True, he said.

And there is an absolute beauty and an absolute good, and of other things to which the term 'many' is applied there is an absolute; for

* A play upon τόκος, which means both 'offspring' and 'interest.'

they may be brought under a single idea, which is called the essence of each.

Very true.

The many, as we say, are seen but not known, and the ideas are known but not seen.

Exactly.

And what is the organ with which we see the visible things?

The sight, he said.

And with the hearing, I said, we hear, and with the other senses perceive the other objects of sense?

True.

But have you remarked that sight is by far the most costly and complex piece of workmanship which the artificer of the senses ever contrived?

No, I never have, he said.

Then reflect: has the ear or voice need of any third or additional nature in order that the one may be able to hear and the other to be heard?

Nothing of the sort.

No, indeed, I replied; and the same is true of most, if not all, the other senses — you would not say that any of them requires such an addition?

Certainly not.

But you see that without the addition of some other nature there is no seeing or being seen?

How do you mean?

Sight being, as I conceive, in the eyes, and he who has eyes wanting to see; colour being also present in them, still unless there be a third nature specially adapted to the purpose, the owner of the eyes will see nothing and the colours will be invisible.

Of what nature are you speaking?

Of that which you term light, I replied.

True, he said.

Noble, then, is the bond which links together sight and visibility, and great beyond other bonds by no small difference of nature; for light is their bond, and light is no ignoble thing?

Nay, he said, the reverse of ignoble.

And which, I said, of the gods in heaven would you say was the lord of this element? Whose is that light which makes the eye to see perfectly and the visible to appear?

You mean the sun, as you and all mankind say.

May not the relation of sight to this deity be described as follows?

How?

Neither sight nor the eye in which sight resides is the sun?

No.

Yet of all the organs of sense the eye is the most like the sun?

By far the most like.

And the power which the eye possesses is a sort of effluence which is dispensed from the sun?

Exactly.

Then the sun is not sight, but the author of sight who is recognised by sight.

True, he said.

And this is he whom I call the child of the good, whom the good begat in his own likeness, to be in the visible world, in relation to sight and the things of sight, what the good is in the intellectual world in relation to mind and the things of mind.

Will you be a little more explicit? he said.

Why, you know, I said, that the eyes, when a person directs them towards objects on which the light of day is no longer shining, but the moon and stars only, see dimly, and are nearly blind; they seem to have no clearness of vision in them?

Very true.

But when they are directed towards objects on which the sun shines, they see clearly and there is sight in them?

Certainly.

And the soul is like the eye: when resting upon that on which truth and being shine, the soul perceives and understands and is radiant with intelligence; but when turned towards the twilight of becoming and perishing, then she has opinion only, and goes blinking about, and is first of one opinion and then of another, and seems to have no intelligence?

Just so.

Now, that which imparts truth to the known and the power of knowing to the knower is what I would have you term the idea of good, and this you will deem to be the cause of science, and of truth in so far as the latter becomes the subject of knowledge; beautiful too, as are both truth and knowledge, you will be right in esteeming this other nature as more beautiful than either; and, as in the previous instance, light and sight may be truly said to be like the sun, and yet not to be the sun, so in this other sphere, science and truth may be deemed to be like the good, but not the good; the good has a place of honour yet higher.

What a wonder of beauty that must be, he said, which is the author of science and truth, and yet surpasses them in beauty; for you surely cannot mean to say that pleasure is the good?

God forbid, I replied; but may I ask you to consider the image in another point of view?

In what point of view?

You would say, would you not, that the sun is not only the author of visibility in all visible things, but of generation and nourishment and growth, though he himself is not generation?

Certainly.

In like manner the good may be said to be not only the author of knowledge to all things known, but of their being and essence, and yet the good is not essence, but far exceeds essence in dignity and power.

Glaucon said, with a ludicrous earnestness: By the light of heaven, how amazing!

Yes, I said, and the exaggeration may be set down to you; for you made me utter my fancies.

And pray continue to utter them; at any rate let us hear if there is anything more to be said about the similitude of the sun.

Yes, I said, there is a great deal more.

Then omit nothing, however slight.

I will do my best, I said; but I should think that a great deal will have to be omitted.

You have to imagine, then, that there are two ruling powers, and that one of them is set over the intellectual world, the other over the visible. I do not say heaven, lest you should fancy that I am playing upon the name (οὐρανός, ὁρατός), May I suppose that you have this distinction of the visible and intelligible fixed in your mind?

I have.

Now take a line which has been cut into two unequal parts, and divide each of them again in the same proportion, and suppose the two main divisions to answer, one to the visible and the other to the intelligible, and then compare the subdivisions in respect of their clearness and want of clearness, and you will find that the first section in the sphere of the visible consists of images. And by images I mean, in the first place, shadows, and in the second place, reflections in water and in solid, smooth and polished bodies and the like: Do you understand?

Yes, I understand.

Imagine, now, the other section, of which this is only the resemblance, to include the animals which we see, and everything that grows or is made.

Very good.

Would you not admit that both the sections of this division have different degrees of truth, and that the copy is to the original as the sphere of opinion is to the sphere of knowledge?

Most undoubtedly.

Next proceed to consider the manner in which the sphere of the intellectual is to be divided.

In what manner?

Thus:— There are two subdivisions, in the lower of which the soul uses the figures given by the former division as images; the enquiry can only be hypothetical, and instead of going upwards to a principle descends to the other end; in the higher of the two, the soul passes out of hypotheses, and goes up to a principle which is above hypotheses, making no use of images as in the former case, but proceeding only in and through the ideas themselves.

I do not quite understand your meaning, he said.

Then I will try again; you will understand me better when I have made some preliminary remarks. You are aware that students of geometry, arithmetic, and the kindred sciences assume the odd and the even and the figures and three kinds of angles and the like in their several branches of science; these are their hypotheses, which they and every body are supposed to know, and therefore they do not deign to give any account of them either to themselves or others; but they begin with them, and go on until they arrive at last, and in a consistent manner, at their conclusion?

Yes, he said, I know.

And do you not know also that although they make use of the visible forms and reason about them, they are thinking not of these, but of the ideals which they resemble; not of the figures which they draw, but of the absolute square and the absolute diameter, and so on — the forms which they draw or make, and which have shadows and reflections in water of their own, are converted by them into images, but they are really seeking to behold the things themselves, which can only be seen with the eye of the mind?

That is true.

And of this kind I spoke as the intelligible, although in the search after it the soul is compelled to use hypotheses; not ascending to a first principle, because she is unable to rise above the region of hypothesis, but employing the objects of which the shadows below are resemblances in their turn as images, they having in relation to the shadows and reflections of them a greater distinctness, and therefore a higher value.

I understand, he said, that you are speaking of the province of geometry and the sister arts.

And when I speak of the other division of the intelligible, you will understand me to speak of that other sort of knowledge which reason herself attains by the power of dialectic, using the hypotheses not as first principles, but only as hypotheses — that is to say, as steps and points of departure into a world which is above hypotheses, in order that she may soar beyond them to the first principle of the whole; and clinging to this and then to that which depends on this, by successive steps she descends again without the aid of any sensible object, from ideas, through ideas, and in ideas she ends.

I understand you, he replied; not perfectly, for you seem to me to be describing a task which is really tremendous; but, at any rate, I understand you to say that knowledge and being, which the science of dialectic contemplates, are clearer than the notions of the arts, as they are termed, which proceed from hypotheses only: these are also contemplated by the understanding, and not by the senses: yet, because they start from hypotheses and do not ascend to a principle, those who contemplate them appear to you not to exercise the higher reason upon them, although when a first principle is added to them they are cognizable by the higher reason. And the habit which is concerned with geometry and the cognate sciences I suppose that you would term understanding and not reason, as being intermediate between opinion and reason.

You have quite conceived my meaning, I said; and now, corresponding to these four divisions, let there be four faculties in the soul — reason answering to the highest, understanding to the second, faith to the third, and perception of shadows to the last — and let there be a scale of them, and let us suppose that the several faculties have clearness in the same degree that their objects have truth.

I understand, he replied, and give my assent, and accept your arrangement.*

BOOK VII

And now, I said, let me show in a figure how far our nature is enlightened or unenlightened: — Behold! human beings living in an underground den, which has a mouth open towards the light and reaching all along the den; here they have been from their childhood, and have their legs and necks chained so that they cannot move, and can only see before them, being prevented by the chains from turning round their heads. Above and behind them a fire is blazing at a distance, and between the fire and the prisoners there is a raised way; and you will see, if you look, a low wall built along the way, like the screen which marionette players have in front of them, over which they show the puppets.

I see.

And do you see, I said, men passing along the wall carrying all sorts of vessels, and statues and figures of animals made of wood and stone and various materials, which appear over the wall? Some of them are talking, others silent.

You have shown me a strange image, and they are strange prisoners.

Like ourselves, I replied; and they see only their own shadows, or the shadows of one another, which the fire throws on the opposite wall of the cave?

True, he said; how could they see anything but the shadows if they were never allowed to move their heads?

And of the objects which are being carried in like manner they would only see the shadows?

Yes, he said.

And if they were able to converse with one another, would they not suppose that they were naming what was actually before them?

Very true.

And suppose further that the prison had an echo which came from

* This whole passage may be understood better if studied with the aid of the accompanying diagram.

	The Sun			The Idea of the Good	
	The Realm of Opinion			The Realm of Knowledge or "Science"	
	A	D	C	E	B
Objective:	Images	Natural Objects, Artefacta	The Objects of Mathematics	Ideas	
Subjective:	Conjecture	Belief	Understanding	The Higher Reason	

the other side, would they not be sure to fancy when one of the passers-by spoke that the voice which they heard came from the passing shadow?

No question, he replied.

To them, I said, the truth would be literally nothing but the shadows of the images.

That is certain.

And now look again, and see what will naturally follow if the prisoners are released and disabused of their error. At first, when any of them is liberated and compelled suddenly to stand up and turn his neck round and walk and look towards the light, he will suffer sharp pains; the glare will distress him, and he will be unable to see the realities of which in his former state he had seen the shadows; and then conceive some one saying to him, that what he saw before was an illusion, but that now, when he is approaching nearer to being and his eye is turned towards more real existence, he has a clearer vision, — what will be his reply? And you may further imagine that his instructor is pointing to the objects as they pass and requiring him to name them, — will he not be perplexed? Will he not fancy that the shadows which he formerly saw are truer than the objects which are now shown to him?

Far truer.

And if he is compelled to look straight at the light, will he not have a pain in his eyes which will make him turn away to take refuge in the objects of vision which he can see, and which he will conceive to be in reality clearer than the things which are now being shown to him?

True, he said.

And suppose once more, that he is reluctantly dragged up a steep and rugged ascent, and held fast until he is forced into the presence of the sun himself, is he not likely to be pained and irritated? When he approaches the light his eyes will be dazzled, and he will not be able to see anything at all of what are now called realities.

Not all in a moment, he said.

He will require to grow accustomed to the sight of the upper world. And first he will see the shadows best, next the reflections of men and other objects in the water, and then the objects themselves; then he will gaze upon the light of the moon and the stars and the spangled heaven; and he will see the sky and the stars by night better than the sun or the light of the sun by day?

Certainly.

Last of all he will be able to see the sun, and not mere reflections of him in the water, but he will see him in his own proper place, and not in another; and he will contemplate him as he is.

Certainly.

He will then proceed to argue that this is he who gives the season and the years, and is the guardian of all that is in the visible world, and in a certain way the cause of all things which he and his fellows have been accustomed to behold?

Clearly, he said, he would first see the sun and then reason about him.

And when he remembered his old habitation, and the wisdom of the den and his fellow-prisoners, do you not suppose that he would felicitate himself on the change, and pity them?

Certainly, he would.

And if they were in the habit of conferring honours among themselves on those who were quickest to observe the passing shadows and to remark which of them went before, and which followed after, and which were together; and who were therefore best able to draw conclusions as to the future, do you think that he would care for such honours and glories, or envy the possessors of them? Would he not say with Homer,

'Better to be the poor servant of a poor master,'

and to endure anything, rather than think as they do and live after their manner?

Yes, he said, I think that he would rather suffer anything than entertain these false notions and live in this miserable manner.

Imagine once more, I said, such an one coming suddenly out of the sun to be replaced in his old situation; would he not be certain to have his eyes full of darkness?

To be sure, he said.

And if there were a contest, and he had to compete in measuring the shadows with the prisoners who had never moved out of the den, while his sight was still weak, and before his eyes had become steady (and the time which would be needed to acquire this new habit of sight might be very considerable), would he not be ridiculous? Men would say of him that up he went and down he came without his eyes; and that it was better not even to think of ascending; and if any one tried to loose another and lead him up to the light, let them only catch the offender, and they would put him to death.

No question, he said.

This entire allegory, I said, you may now append, dear Glaucon, to the previous argument; the prison-house is the world of sight, the light of the fire is the sun, and you will not misapprehend me if you interpret the journey upwards to be the ascent of the soul into the intellectual world according to my poor belief, which, at your desire, I have expressed — whether rightly or wrongly God knows. But, whether true or false, my opinion is that in the world of knowledge the idea of good appears last of all, and is seen only with an effort; and, when seen, is also inferred to be the universal author of all things beautiful and right, parent of light and of the lord of light in this visible world, and the immediate source of reason and truth in the intellectual; and that this is the power upon which he who would act rationally either in public or private life must have his eye fixed.

I agree, he said, as far as I am able to understand you.

Moreover, I said, you must not wonder that those who attain to this beatific vision are unwilling to descend to human affairs; for their souls are ever hastening into the upper world where they desire to dwell; which desire of theirs is very natural, if our allegory may be trusted.

Yes, very natural.

And is there anything surprising in one who passes from divine contemplations to the evil state of man, misbehaving himself in a ridiculous manner; if, while his eyes are blinking and before he has become accustomed to the surrounding darkness, he is compelled to fight in courts of law, or in other places, about the images or the shadows of images of justice, and is endeavouring to meet the conceptions of those who have never yet seen absolute justice?

Anything but surprising, he replied.

Any one who has common sense will remember that the bewilderments of the eyes are of two kinds, and arise from two causes, either from coming out of the light or from going into the light, which is true of the mind's eye, quite as much as of the bodily eye; and he who remembers this when he sees any one whose vision is perplexed and weak, will not be too ready to laugh; he will first ask whether that soul of man has come out of the brighter life, and is unable to see because unaccustomed to the dark, or having turned from darkness to the day is dazzled by excess of light. And he will count the one happy in his condition and state of being, and he will pity the other; or, if he have a mind to laugh at the soul which comes from below into the light, there will be more reason in this than in the laugh which greets him who returns from above out of the light into the den.

That, he said, is a very just distinction.

But then, if I am right, certain professors of education must be wrong when they say that they can put a knowledge into the soul which was not there before, like sight into blind eyes.

They undoubtedly say this, he replied.

Whereas, our argument shows that the power and capacity of learning exists in the soul already; and that just as the eye was unable to turn from darkness to light without the whole body, so too the instrument of knowledge can only by the movement of the whole soul be turned from the world of becoming into that of being, and learn by degrees to endure the sight of being, and of the brightest and best of being, or in other words, of the good.

Very true.

And must there not be some art which will effect conversion in the easiest and quickest manner; not implanting the faculty of sight, for that exists already, but has been turned in the wrong direction, and is looking away from the truth?

Yes, he said, such an art may be presumed.

And whereas the other so-called virtues of the soul seem to be akin to bodily qualities, for even when they are not originally innate they can be implanted later by habit and exercise, the virtue of wisdom more than anything else contains a divine element which always remains, and by this conversion is rendered useful and profitable; or, on the other hand, hurtful and useless. Did you never observe the narrow intelligence flashing from the keen eye of a clever rogue — how eager he is, how clearly his paltry soul sees the way to his end; he is the reverse of blind, but his keen eye-sight is forced into the service of evil, and he is mischievous in proportion to his cleverness?

Very true, he said.

But what if there had been a circumcision of such natures in the days of their youth; and they had been severed from those sensual pleasures, such as eating and drinking, which, like leaden weights, were attached to them at their birth, and which drag them down and turn the vision of their souls upon the things that are below — if, I say, they had been released from these impediments and turned in the opposite direction, the very same faculty in them would have seen the truth as keenly as they see what their eyes are turned to now.

Very likely.

Yes, I said; and there is another thing which is likely, or rather a necessary inference from what has preceded, that neither the uneducated and uninformed of the truth, nor yet those who never make an end of their education, will be able ministers of State; not the former, because they have no single aim of duty which is the rule of all their actions, private as well as public; nor the latter, because they will not act at all except upon compulsion, fancying that they are already dwelling apart in the islands of the blest.

Very true, he replied.

Then, I said, the business of us who are the founders of the State will be to compel the best minds to attain that knowledge which we have already shown to be the greatest of all — they must continue to ascend until they arrive at the good; but when they have ascended and seen enough we must not allow them to do as they do now.

What do you mean?

I mean that they remain in the upper world: but this must not be allowed; they must be made to descend again among the prisoners in the den, and partake of their labours and honours, whether they are worth having or not.

But is not this unjust? he said; ought we to give them a worse life, when they might have a better?

You have again forgotten, my friend, I said, the intention of the legislator, who did not aim at making any one class in the State happy above the rest; the happiness was to be in the whole State, and he held the citizens together by persuasion and necessity, making them benefactors of the State, and therefore benefactors of one another; to this end he created them, not to please themselves, but to be his instruments in binding up the State.

True, he said, I had forgotten.

Observe, Glaucon, that there will be no injustice in compelling our philosophers to have a care and providence of others; we shall explain to them that in other States, men of their class are not obliged to share in the toils of politics: and this is reasonable, for they grow up at their own sweet will, and the government would rather not have them.

Being self-taught, they cannot be expected to show any gratitude for a culture which they have never received. But we have brought you into the world to be rulers of the hive, kings of yourselves and of the other citizens, and have educated you far better and more perfectly than they have been educated, and you are better able to share in the double duty. Wherefore each of you, when his turn comes, must go down to the general underground abode, and get the habit of seeing in the dark. When you have acquired the habit, you will see ten thousand times better than the inhabitants of the den, and you will know what the several images are, and what they represent, because you have seen the beautiful and just and good in their truth. And thus our State which is also yours will be a reality, and not a dream only, and will be administered in a spirit unlike that of other States, in which men fight with one another about shadows only and are distracted in the struggle for power, which in their eyes is a great good. Whereas the truth is that the State in which the rulers are most reluctant to govern is always the best and most quietly governed, and the State in which they are most eager, the worst.

Quite true, he replied.

And will our pupils, when they hear this, refuse to take their turn at the toils of State, when they are allowed to spend the greater part of their time with one another in the heavenly light?

Impossible, he answered; for they are just men, and the commands which we impose upon them are just; there can be no doubt that every one of them will take office as a stern necessity, and not after the fashion of our present rulers of State.

Yes, my friend, I said; and there lies the point. You must contrive for your future rulers another and a better life than that of a ruler, and then you may have a well-ordered State; for only in the State which offers this, will they rule who are truly rich, not in silver and gold, but in virtue and wisdom, which are the true blessings of life. Whereas if they go to the administration of public affairs, poor and hungering after their own private advantage, thinking that hence they are to snatch the chief good, order there can never be; for they will be fighting about office, and the civil and domestic broils which thus arise will be the ruin of the rulers themselves and of the whole State.

Most true, he replied.

And the only life which looks down upon the life of political ambition is that of true philosophy. Do you know of any other?

Indeed, I do not, he said.

And those who govern ought not to be lovers of the task? For, if they are, there will be rival lovers, and they will fight.

No question.

Who then are those whom we shall compel to be guardians? Surely they will be the men who are wisest about affairs of State, and by whom the State is best administered, and who at the same time have other honours and another and a better life than that of politics?

They are the men, and I will choose them, he replied.

And now shall we consider in what way such guardians will be produced, and how they are to be brought from darkness to light, —as some are said to have ascended from the world below to the gods?

By all means, he replied.

The process, I said, is not the turning over of an oyster-shell,* but the turning round of a soul passing from a day which is little better than night to the true day of being, that is, the ascent from below, which we affirm to be true philosophy?

Quite so.

And should we not enquire what sort of knowledge has the power of effecting such a change?

Certainly.

What sort of knowledge is there which would draw the soul from becoming to being? And another consideration has just occurred to me: You will remember that our young men are to be warrior athletes?

Yes, that was said.

Then this new kind of knowledge must have an additional quality?

What quality?

Usefulness in war.

Yes, if possible.

There were two parts in our former scheme of education, were there not?

Just so.

There was gymnastic which presided over the growth and decay of the body, and may therefore be regarded as having to do with generation and corruption?

True.

Then that is not the knowledge which we are seeking to discover?

No.

But what do you say of music, what also entered to a certain extent into our former scheme?

Music, he said, as you will remember, was the counterpart of gymnastic, and trained the guardians by the influences of habit, by harmony making them harmonious, by rhythm rhythmical, but not giving them science; and the words, whether fabulous or possibly true, had kindred elements of rhythm and harmony in them. But in music there was nothing which tended to that good which you are now seeking.

You are most accurate, I said, in your recollection; in music there certainly was nothing of the kind. But what branch of knowledge is there, my dear Glaucon, which is of the desired nature; since all the useful arts were reckoned mean by us?

Undoubtedly; and yet if music and gymnastic are excluded, and the arts are also excluded, what remains?

Well, I said, there may be nothing left of our special subjects; and

---

* In allusion to a game in which two parties fled or pursued according as an oyster-shell which was thrown into the air fell with the dark or light side uppermost.

then we shall have to take something which is not special, but of universal application.

What may that be?

A something which all arts and sciences and intelligences use in common, and which every one first has to learn among the elements of education.

What is that?

The little matter of distinguishing one, two, and three — in a word, number and calculation: — do not all arts and sciences necessarily partake of them?

Yes.

Then the art of war partakes of them?

To be sure.

Then Palamedes, whenever he appears in tragedy, proves Agamemnon ridiculously unfit to be a general. Did you never remark how he declares that he had invented number, and had numbered the ships and set in array the ranks of the army at Troy; which implies that they had never been numbered before, and Agamemnon must be supposed literally to have been incapable of counting his own feet — how could he if he was ignorant of number? And if that is true, what sort of general must he have been?

I should say a very strange one, if this was as you say.

Can we deny that a warrior should have a knowledge of arithmetic?

Certainly he should, if he is to have the smallest understanding of military tactics, or indeed, I should rather say, if he is to be a man at all.

I should like to know whether you have the same notion which I have of this study?

What is your notion?

It appears to me to be a study of the kind which we are seeking, and which leads naturally to reflection, but never to have been rightly used; for the true use of it is simply to draw the soul towards being.

Will you explain your meaning? he said.

I will try, I said; and I wish you would share the enquiry with me, and say 'yes' or 'no' when I attempt to distinguish in my own mind what branches of knowledge have this attracting power, in order that we may have clearer proof that arithmetic is, as I suspect, one of them.

Explain, he said.

I mean to say that objects of sense are of two kinds; some of them do not invite thought because the sense is an adequate judge of them; while in the case of other objects sense is so untrustworthy that further enquiry is imperatively demanded.

You are clearly referring, he said, to the manner in which the senses are imposed upon by distance, and by painting in light and shade.

No, I said, that is not at all my meaning.

Then what is your meaning?

When speaking of uninviting objects, I mean those which do not pass from one sensation to the opposite; inviting objects are those which do; in this latter case the sense coming upon the object, whether at a distance or near, gives no more vivid idea of anything in particular than of its opposite. An illustration will make my meaning clearer: — here are three fingers — a little finger, a second finger, and a middle finger.

Very good.

You may suppose that they are seen quite close: And here comes the point.

What is it?

Each of them equally appears a finger, whether seen in the middle or at the extremity, whether white or black, or thick or thin — it makes no difference; a finger is a finger all the same. In these cases a man is not compelled to ask of thought the question what is a finger? for the sight never intimates to the mind that a finger is other than a finger.

True.

And therefore, I said, as we might expect, there is nothing here which invites or excites intelligence.

There is not, he said.

But is this equally true of the greatness and smallness of the fingers? Can sight adequately perceive them? and is no difference made by the circumstance that one of the fingers is in the middle and another at the extremity? And in like manner does the touch adequately perceive the qualities of thickness or thinness, of softness or hardness? And so of the other senses; do they give perfect intimations of such matters? Is not their mode of operation on this wise — the sense which is concerned with the quality of hardness is necessarily concerned also with the quality of softness, and only intimates to the soul that the same thing is felt to be both hard and soft?

You are quite right, he said.

And must not the soul be perplexed at this intimation which the sense gives of a hard which is also soft? What, again, is the meaning of light and heavy, if that which is light is also heavy, and that which is heavy, light?

Yes, he said, these intimations which the soul receives are very curious and require to be explained.

Yes, I said, and in these perplexities the soul naturally summons to her aid calculation and intelligence, that she may see whether the several objects announced to her are one or two.

True.

And if they turn out to be two, is not each of them one and different?

Certainly.

And if each is one, and both are two, she will conceive the two as in a state of division, for if they were undivided they could only be conceived of as one?

True.

The eye certainly did see both small and great, but only in a confused manner; they were not distinguished.

Yes.

Whereas the thinking mind, intending to light up the chaos, was compelled to reverse the process, and look at small and great as separate and not confused.

Very true.

Was not this the beginning of the enquiry 'What is great?' and 'What is small?'

Exactly so.

And thus arose the distinction of the visible and the intelligible.

Most true.

This was what I meant when I spoke of impressions which invited the intellect, or the reverse — those which are simultaneous with opposite impressions, invite thought; those which are not simultaneous do not.

I understand, he said, and agree with you.

And to which class do unity and number belong?

I do not know, he replied.

Think a little and you will see that what has preceded will supply the answer; for if simple unity could be adequately perceived by the sight or by any other sense, then, as we were saying in the case of the finger, there would be nothing to attract towards being; but when there is some contradiction always present, and one is the reverse of one and involves the conception of plurality, then thought begins to be aroused within us, and the soul perplexed and wanting to arrive at a decision asks 'What is absolute unity?' This is the way in which the study of the one has a power of drawing and converting the mind to the contemplation of true being.

And surely, he said, this occurs notably in the case of one; for we see the same thing to be both one and infinite in multitude?

Yes, I said; and this being true of one must be equally true of all number?

Certainly.

And all arithmetic and calculation have to do with number?

Yes.

And they appear to lead the mind towards truth?

Yes, in a very remarkable manner.

Then this is knowledge of the kind for which we are seeking, having a double use, military and philosophical; for the man of war must learn the art of number or he will not know how to array his troops, and the philosopher also, because he has to rise out of the sea of change and lay hold of true being, and therefore he must be an arithmetician.

That is true.

And our guardian is both warrior and philosopher?

Certainly.

Then this is a kind of knowledge which legislation may fitly prescribe; and we must endeavour to persuade those who are to be the principal men of our State to go and learn arithmetic, not as amateurs, but they must carry on the study until they see the nature of numbers with the mind only; nor again, like merchants or retail-traders, with a view to buying or selling, but for the sake of their military use, and of the soul herself; and because this will be the easiest way for her to pass from becoming to truth and being.

That is excellent, he said.

Yes, I said, and now having spoken of it, I must add how charming the science is! and in how many ways it conduces to our desired end, if pursued in the spirit of a philosopher, and not of a shopkeeper!

How do you mean?

I mean, as I was saying, that arithmetic has a very great and elevating effect, compelling the soul to reason about abstract number, and rebelling against the introduction of visible or tangible objects into the argument. You know how steadily the masters of the art repel and ridicule any one who attempts to divide absolute unity when he is calculating, and if you divide, they multiply, taking care that one shall continue one and not become lost in fractions.

That is very true.

Now, suppose a person were to say to them: O my friends, what are these wonderful numbers about which you are reasoning, in which, as you say, there is a unity such as you demand, and each unit is equal, invariable, indivisible, — what would they answer?

They would answer, as I should conceive, that they were speaking of those numbers which can only be realized in thought.

Then you see that this knowledge may be truly called necessary, necessitating as it clearly does the use of the pure intelligence in the attainment of pure truth?

Yes; that is a marked characteristic of it.

And have you further observed, that those who have a natural talent for calculation are generally quick at every other kind of knowledge; and even the dull, if they have had an arithmetical training, although they may derive no other advantage from it, always become much quicker than they would otherwise have been.

Very true, he said.

And indeed, you will not easily find a more difficult study, and not many as difficult.

You will not.

And, for all these reasons, arithmetic is a kind of knowledge in which the best natures should be trained, and which must not be given up.

I agree.

Let this then be made one of our subjects of education. And next, shall we enquire whether the kindred science also concerns us?

You mean geometry?

Exactly so.

Clearly, he said, we are concerned with that part of geometry which relates to war; for in pitching a camp, or taking up a position, or closing or extending the lines of an army, or any other military manoeuvre, whether in actual battle or on a march, it will make all the difference whether a general is or is not a geometrician.

Yes, I said, but for that purpose a very little of either geometry or calculation will be enough; the question relates rather to the greater and more advanced part of geometry — whether that tends in any degree to make more easy the vision of the idea of good; and thither, as I was saying, all things tend which compel the soul to turn her gaze towards that place, where is the full perfection of being, which she ought, by all means, to behold.

True, he said.

Then if geometry compels us to view being, it concerns us; if becoming only, it does not concern us?

Yes, that is what we assert.

Yet anybody who has the least acquaintance with geometry will not deny that such a conception of the science is in flat contradiction to the ordinary language of geometricians.

How so?

They have in view practice only, and are always speaking, in a narrow and ridiculous manner, of squaring and extending and applying and the like — they confuse the necessities of geometry with those of daily life; whereas knowledge is the real object of the whole science.

Certainly, he said.

Then must not a further admission be made?

What admission?

That the knowledge at which geometry aims is knowledge of the eternal, and not of aught perishing and transient.

That, he replied, may be readily allowed, and is true.

Then, my noble friend, geometry will draw the soul towards truth, and create the spirit of philosophy, and raise up that which is now unhappily allowed to fall down.

Nothing will be more likely to have such an effect.

Then nothing should be more sternly laid down than that the inhabitants of your fair city should by all means learn geometry. Moreover the science has indirect effects, which are not small.

Of what kind? he said.

There are the military advantages of which you spoke, I said; and in all departments of knowledge, as experience proves, any one who has studied geometry is infinitely quicker of apprehension than one who has not.

Yes indeed, he said, there is an infinite difference between them.

Then shall we propose this as a second branch of knowledge which our youth will study?

Let us do so, he replied.

And suppose we make astronomy the third — what do you say?

I am strongly inclined to it, he said; the observation of the seasons and of months and years is as essential to the general as it is to the farmer or sailor.

I am amused, I said, at your fear of the world, which makes you guard against the appearance of insisting upon useless studies; and I quite admit the difficulty of believing that in every man there is an eye of the soul which, when by other pursuits lost and dimmed, is by these purified and re-illumined; and is more precious far than ten thousand bodily eyes, for by it alone is truth seen. Now there are two classes of persons: one class of those who will agree with you and will take your words as a revelation; another class to whom they will be utterly unmeaning, and who will naturally deem them to be idle tales, for they see no sort of profit which is to be obtained from them. And therefore you had better decide at once with which of the two you are proposing to argue. You will very likely say with neither, and that your chief aim in carrying on the argument is your own improvement; at the same time you do not grudge to others any benefit which they may receive.

I think that I should prefer to carry on the argument mainly on my own behalf.

Then take a step backward, for we have gone wrong in the order of the sciences.

What was the mistake? he said.

After plane geometry, I said, we proceeded at once to solids in revolution, instead of taking solids in themselves; whereas after the second dimension the third, which is concerned with cubes and dimensions of depth, ought to have followed.

That is true, Socrates; but so little seems to be known as yet about these subjects.

Why, yes, I said, and for two reasons:—in the first place, no government patronises them; this leads to a want of energy in the pursuit of them, and they are difficult; in the second place, students cannot learn them unless they have a director. But then a director can hardly be found, and even if he could, as matters now stand, the students, who are very conceited, would not attend to him. That, however, would be otherwise if the whole State became the director of these studies and gave honour to them; then disciples would want to come, and there would be continuous and earnest search, and discoveries would be made; since even now, disregarded as they are by the world, and maimed of their fair proportions, and although none of their votaries can tell the use of them, still these studies force their way by their natural charm, and very likely, if they had the help of the State, they would some day emerge into light.

Yes, he said, there is a remarkable charm in them. But I do not clearly understand the change in the order. First you began with a geometry of plane surfaces?

Yes, I said.

And you placed astronomy next, and then you made a step backward?

Yes, and I have delayed you by my hurry; the ludicrous state of solid geometry, which, in natural order, should have followed, made me pass over this branch and go on to astronomy, or motion of solids.

True, he said.

Then assuming that the science now omitted would come into existence if encouraged by the State, let us go on to astronomy, which will be fourth.

The right order, he replied. And now, Socrates, as you rebuked the vulgar manner in which I praised astronomy before, my praise shall be given in your own spirit. For every one, as I think, must see that astronomy compels the soul to look upwards and leads us from this world to another.

Every one but myself, I said; to every one else this may be clear, but not to me.

And what then would you say?

I should rather say that those who elevate astronomy into philosophy appear to me to make us look downwards and not upwards.

What do you mean? he asked.

You, I replied, have in your mind a truly sublime conception of our knowledge of the things above. And I dare say that if a person were to throw his head back and study the fretted ceiling, you would still think that his mind was the percipient, and not his eyes. And you are very likely right, and I may be a simpleton: but, in my opinion, that knowledge only which is of being and of the unseen can make the soul look upwards, and whether a man gapes at the heavens or blinks on the ground, seeking to learn some particular of sense, I would deny that he can learn, for nothing of that sort is matter of science; his soul is looking downwards, not upwards, whether his way to knowledge is by water or by land, whether he floats, or only lies on his back.

I acknowledge, he said, the justice of your rebuke. Still, I should like to ascertain how astronomy can be learned in any manner more conducive to that knowledge of which we are speaking?

I will tell you, I said: The starry heaven which we behold is wrought upon a visible ground, and therefore, although the fairest and most perfect of visible things, must necessarily be deemed inferior far to the true motions of absolute swiftness and absolute slowness, which are relative to each other, and carry with them that which is contained in them, in the true number and in every true figure. Now, these are to be apprehended by reason and intelligence, but not by sight.

True, he replied.

The spangled heavens should be used as a pattern and with a view to that higher knowledge; their beauty is like the beauty of figures or pictures excellently wrought by the hand of Daedalus, or some other great artist, which we may chance to behold; any geometrician who saw them would appreciate the exquisiteness of their workmanship, but he would never dream of thinking that in them he could find the true equal or the true double, or the truth of any other proportion.

No, he replied, such an idea would be ridiculous.

And will not a true astronomer have the same feeling when he looks at the movements of the stars? Will he not think that heaven and the things in heaven are framed by the Creator of them in the most perfect manner? But he will never imagine that the proportions of night and day, or of both to the month, or of the month to the year, or of the stars to these and to one another, and any other things that are material and visible can also be eternal and subject to no deviation —

that would be absurd; and it is equally absurd to take so much pains in investigating their exact truth.

I quite agree, though I never thought of this before.

Then, I said, in astronomy, as in geometry, we should employ problems, and let the heavens alone if we would approach the subject in the right way and so make the natural gift of reason to be of any real use.

That, he said, is a work infinitely beyond our present astronomers.

Yes, I said; and there are many other things which must also have a similar extension given to them, if our legislation is to be of any value. But can you tell me of any other suitable study?

No, he said, not without thinking.

Motion, I said, has many forms, and not one only; two of them are obvious enough even to wits no better than ours; and there are others, as I imagine, which may be left to wiser persons.

But where are the two?

There is a second, I said, which is the counterpart of the one already named.

And what may that be?

The second, I said, would seem relatively to the ears to be what the first is to the eyes; for I conceive that as the eyes are designed to look up at the stars, so are the ears to hear harmonious motions; and these are sister sciences — as the Pythagoreans say, and we, Glaucon, agree with them?

Yes, he replied.

But this, I said, is a laborious study, and therefore we had better go and learn of them; and they will tell us whether there are any other applications of these sciences. At the same time, we must not lose sight of our own higher object.

What is that?

There is a perfection which all knowledge ought to reach, and which our pupils ought also to attain, and not to fall short of, as I was saying that they did in astronomy. For in the science of harmony, as you probably know, the same thing happens. The teachers of harmony compare the sounds and consonances which are heard only, and their labour, like that of the astronomers, is in vain.

Yes, by heaven! he said; and 'tis as good as a play to hear them talking about their condensed notes, as they call them; they put their ears close alongside of the strings like persons catching a sound from their neighbour's wall — one set of them declaring that they distinguish an intermediate note and have found the least interval which should be the unit of measurement; the others insisting that the two sounds have passed into the same — either party setting their ears before their understanding.

You mean, I said, those gentlemen who tease and torture the strings and rack them on the pegs of the instrument: I might carry on the metaphor and speak after their manner of the blows which the plectrum gives, and make accusations against the strings, both of backwardness and forwardness to sound; but this would be tedious, and therefore I will only say that these are not the men, and that I am referring to the Pythagoreans, of whom I was just now proposing to enquire about harmony. For they too are in error, like the astronomers; they investigate the numbers of the harmonies which are heard, but they never attain to problems — that is to say, they never reach the natural harmonies of number, or reflect why some numbers are harmonious and others not.

That, he said, is a thing of more than mortal knowledge.

A thing, I replied, which I would rather call useful; that is, if sought after with a view to the beautiful and good; but if pursued in any other spirit, useless.

Very true, he said.

Now, when all these studies reach the point of inter-communion and connection with one another, and come to be considered in their mutual affinities, then, I think, but not till then, will the pursuit of them have a value for our objects; otherwise there is no profit in them.

I suspect so; but you are speaking, Socrates, of a vast work.

What do you mean? I said; the prelude or what? Do you not know that all this is but the prelude to the actual strain which we have to learn? For you surely would not regard the skilled mathematician as a dialectician?

Assuredly not, he said; I have hardly ever known a mathematician who was capable of reasoning.

But do you imagine that men who are unable to give and take a reason will have the knowledge which we require of them?

Neither can this be supposed.

And so, Glaucon, I said, we have at last arrived at the hymn of dialectic. This is that strain which is of the intellect only, but which the faculty of sight will nevertheless be found to imitate; for sight, as you may remember, was imagined by us after a while to behold the real animals and stars, and last of all the sun himself. And so with dialectic; when a person starts on the discovery of the absolute by the light of reason only, and without any assistance of sense, and perseveres until by pure intelligence he arrives at the perception of the absolute good, he at last finds himself at the end of the intellectual world, as in the case of sight at the end of the visible.

Exactly, he said.

Then this is the progress which you call dialectic?

True.

But the release of the prisoners from chains, and their translation from the shadows to the images and to the light, and the ascent from the underground den to the sun, while in his presence they are vainly trying to look on animals and plants and the light of the sun, but are able to perceive even with their weak eyes the images in the water [which are divine], and are the shadows of true existence (not shadows of images cast by a light of fire, which compared with the sun is only an image) — this power of elevating the highest principle in the soul to the contemplation of that which is best in existence,

with which we may compare the raising of that faculty which is the
very light of the body to the sight of that which is brightest in the
material and visible world — this power is given, as I was saying, by
all that study and pursuit of the arts which has been described.

I agree in what you are saying, he replied, which may be hard to
believe, yet, from another point of view, is harder still to deny. This
however is not a theme to be treated of in passing only, but will have
to be discussed again and again. And so, whether our conclusion be
true or false, let us assume all this, and proceed at once from the
prelude or preamble to the chief strain, and describe that in like
manner. Say, then, what is the nature and what are the divisions
of dialectic, and what are the paths which lead thither; for these paths
will also lead to our final rest.

Dear Glaucon, I said, you will not be able to follow me here, though
I would do my best, and you should behold not an image only but
the absolute truth, according to my notion. Whether what I told
you would or would not have been a reality I cannot venture to say;
but you would have seen something like reality; of that I am confident.

Doubtless, he replied.

But I must also remind you, that the power of dialectic alone can
reveal this, and only to one who is a disciple of the previous sciences.

Of that assertion you may be as confident as of the last.

And assuredly no one will argue that there is any other method of
comprehending by any regular process all true existence or of ascertaining what each thing is in its own nature; for the arts in general
are concerned with the desires or opinions of men, or are cultivated with a view to production and construction, or for the preservation of such productions and constructions; and as to the mathematical sciences which, as we were saying, have some apprehension
of true being — geometry and the like — they only dream about being, but never can they behold the waking reality so long as they leave
the hypotheses which they use unexamined, and are unable to give
an account of them. For when a man knows not his own first principle, and when the conclusion and intermediate steps are also constructed out of he knows not what, how can he imagine that such
a fabric of convention can ever become science?

Impossible, he said.

Then dialectic, and dialectic alone, goes directly to the first principle and is the only science which does away with hypotheses in order
to make her ground secure; the eye of the soul, which is literally
buried in an outlandish slough, is by her gentle aid lifted upwards;
and she uses as handmaids and helpers in the work of conversion,
the sciences which we have been discussing. Custom terms them
sciences, but they ought to have some other name, implying greater
clearness than opinion and less clearness than science: and this, in
our previous sketch, was called understanding. But why should
we dispute about names when we have realities of such importance
to consider?

Why indeed, he said, when any name will do which expresses the thought of the mind with clearness?

At any rate, we are satisfied, as before, to have four divisions; two for intellect and two for opinion, and to call the first division science, the second understanding, the third belief, and the fourth perception of shadows, opinion being concerned with becoming, and intellect with being; and so to make a proportion: —

As being is to becoming, so is pure intellect to opinion.
And as intellect is to opinion, so is science to belief, and understanding to the perception of shadows.

But let us defer the further correlation and subdivision of the subjects of opinion and of intellect, for it will be a long enquiry, many times longer than this has been.

As far as I understand, he said, I agree.

And do you also agree, I said, in describing the dialectician as one who attains a conception of the essence of each thing? And he who does not possess and is therefore unable to impart this conception, in whatever degree he fails, may in that degree also be said to fail in intelligence? Will you admit so much?

Yes, he said; how can I deny it?

And you would say the same of the conception of the good? Until the person is able to abstract and define rationally the idea of good, and unless he can run the gauntlet of all objections, and is ready to disprove them, not by appeals to opinion, but to absolute truth, never faltering at any step of the argument — unless he can do all this, you would say that he knows neither the idea of good nor any other good; he apprehends only a shadow, if anything at all, which is given by opinion and not by science; — dreaming and slumbering in this life, before he is well awake here, he arrives at the world below, and has his final quietus.

In all that I should most certainly agree with you.

And surely you would not have the children of your ideal State, whom you are nurturing and educating — if the ideal ever becomes a reality — you would not allow the future rulers to be like posts, having no reason in them, and yet to be set in authority over the highest matters?

Certainly not.

Then you will make a law that they shall have such an education as will enable them to attain the greatest skill in asking and answering questions?

Yes, he said, you and I together will make it.

Dialectic, then, as you will agree, is the coping-stone of the sciences, and is set over them; no other science can be placed higher — the nature of knowledge can no further go?

I agree, he said.

[514a–535a, tr. B. JOWETT]

[The seventh book concludes with a recapitulation of the qualities necessary in a philosopher-ruler, followed by a precise outline of the course his education should take until he is finally prepared to assume responsible office.　In the eighth and ninth books Plato describes in detail various types of degenerate states and their corresponding individuals.　The series ends with a presentation of the utter misery of the tyrant and tyranny. The argument of the *Republic* virtually closes here and Socrates maintains that he has now answered adequately the challenge of Glaucon and Adeimantus in the second book.　In the first half of the tenth book Plato seeks to confirm and strengthen the argument for banishing the poets from his "ideal" state.　He then proceeds to reaffirm his belief in the immortality of the soul, and thus he is ready to introduce the concluding myth, the *Vision of Er,* in which he develops fully the implications of this doctrine for the human individual.]

BOOK X

THE VISION OF ER

These, then, are the prizes and rewards and gifts which are bestowed upon the just by gods and men in this present life, in addition to the other good things which justice of herself provides.

Yes, he said; and they are fair and lasting.

And yet, I said, all these are as nothing, either in number or greatness in comparison with those other recompenses which await both just and unjust after death.　And you ought to hear them, and then both just and unjust will have received from us a full payment of the debt which the argument owes to them.

Speak, he said; there are few things which I would more gladly hear.

Well, I said, I will tell you a tale; not one of the tales which Odysseus tells to the hero Alcinous, yet this too is a tale of a hero, Er the son of Armenius, a Pamphylian by birth.　He was slain in battle, and ten days afterwards, when the bodies of the dead were taken up already in a state of corruption, his body was found unaffected by decay, and carried away home to be buried.　And on the twelfth day, as he was lying on the funeral pile, he returned to life and told them what he had seen in the other world.　He said that when his soul left the body he went on a journey with a great company, and that they came to a mysterious place at which there were two openings in the earth; they were near together, and over against them were two other openings in the heaven above.　In the intermediate space there were judges seated, who commanded the just, after they had given judgment on them and had bound their sentences in front of them, to ascend by the heavenly way on the right hand; and in like manner the unjust were bidden by them to descend by the lower way on the left hand; these also bore the symbols of their deeds, but fastened on their backs.　He drew near, and they told him that he was to be the messenger who would carry the report of the other world to men, and they bade him hear and see all that was to be heard and seen in that place.　Then he beheld and saw on one side the souls departing at either opening of heaven and earth when sentence had been given on them; and at the two other openings other souls, some ascending out of the earth dusty and worn with travel, some descending out of heaven clean and bright. And arriving ever and anon they seemed to have come from a long journey, and they went forth with gladness into the meadow, where they encamped as at a festival; and those who knew one another embraced and conversed, the souls which came from earth curiously enquiring about the things above, and the souls which came from heaven about the things beneath. And they told one another of what had happened by the way, those from below weeping and sorrowing at the remembrance of the things which they had endured and seen in their journey beneath the earth (now the journey lasted a thousand years), while those from above were describing heavenly delights and visions of inconceivable beauty. The story, Glaucon, would take too long to tell; but the sum was this: — He said that for every wrong which they had done to any one they suffered tenfold; or once in a hundred years — such being reckoned to be the length of man's life, and the penalty being thus paid ten times in a thousand years. If, for example, there were any who had been the cause of many deaths, or had betrayed or enslaved cities or armies, or been guilty of any other evil behaviour, for each and all of their offences they received punishment ten times over, and the rewards of beneficence and justice and holiness were in the same proportion. I need hardly repeat what he said concerning young children dying almost as soon as they were born. Of piety and impiety to gods and parents, and of murderers, there were retributions other and greater far which he described. He mentioned that he was present when one of the spirits asked another, 'Where is Ardiaeus the Great?' (Now this Ardiaeus lived a thousand years before the time of Er: he had been the tyrant of some city of Pamphylia, and had murdered his aged father and his elder brother, and was said to have committed many other abominable crimes.) The answer of the other spirit was: 'He comes not hither and will never come. And this,' said he, 'was one of the dreadful sights which we ourselves witnessed. We were at the mouth of the cavern, and, having completed all our experiences, were about to reascend, when of a sudden Ardiaeus appeared and several others, most of whom were tyrants; and there were also besides the tyrants private individuals who had been great criminals: they were just, as they fancied, about to return into the upper world, but the mouth, instead of admitting them, gave a roar, whenever any of these incurable sinners or some one who had not been sufficiently punished tried to ascend; and then wild men of fiery aspect, who were standing by and heard the sound, seized and carried them off; and Ardiaeus and others they bound head and foot and hand, and threw them down and flayed them with scourges, and dragged them along the road at the side, carding them on thorns like wool, and declaring to the passers-by what were their crimes, and that they were being taken away to be cast into hell.' And of all the many terrors which they had endured, he said that there was none like the terror which each of them felt at that moment, lest they should hear the voice; and

when there was silence, one by one they ascended with exceeding joy.
These, said Er, were the penalties and retributions, and there were
blessings as great.

Now when the spirits which were in the meadow had tarried seven
days, on the eighth they were obliged to proceed on their journey,
and, on the fourth day after, he said that they came to a place where
they could see from above a line of light, straight as a column, extending right through the whole heaven and through the earth, in
colour resembling the rainbow, only brighter and purer; another
day's journey brought them to the place, and there, in the midst of
the light, they saw the ends of the chains of heaven let down from
above: for this light is the belt of heaven, and holds together the
circle of the universe, like the under-girders of a trireme. From these
ends is extended the spindle of Necessity, on which all the revolutions
turn. The shaft and hook of this spindle are made of steel, and the
whorl is made partly of steel and also partly of other materials.
Now the whorl is in form like the whorl used on earth; and the
description of it implied that there is one large hollow whorl which
is quite scooped out, and into this is fitted another lesser one, and
another, and another, and four others, making eight in all, like vessels
which fit into one another; the whorls show their edges on the upper
side, and on their lower side all together form one continuous whorl.
This is pierced by the spindle, which is driven home through the
centre of the eighth. The first and outermost whorl has the rim
broadest, and the seven inner whorls are narrower, in the following
proportions — the sixth is next to the first in size, the fourth next to
the sixth; then comes the eighth; the seventh is fifth, the fifth is
sixth, the third is seventh, last and eighth comes the second. The
largest [or fixed stars] is spangled, and the seventh [or sun] is
brightest; the eighth [or moon] coloured by the reflected light of
the seventh; the second and fifth [Saturn and Mercury] are in colour
like one another, and yellower than the preceding; the third [Venus]
has the whitest light; the fourth [Mars] is reddish; the sixth [Jupi-
ter] is in whiteness second. Now the whole spindle has the same
motion; but, as the whole revolves in one direction, the seven inner
circles move slowly in the other, and of these the swiftest is the eighth;
next in swiftness are the seventh, sixth, and fifth, which move together; third in swiftness appeared to move according to the law of
this reversed motion the fourth; the third appeared fourth and the
second fifth. The spindle turns on the knees of Necessity; and on
the upper surface of each circle is a siren, who goes round with them,
hymning a single tone or note. The eight together form one harmony; and round about, at equal intervals, there is another band,
three in number, each sitting upon her throne: these are the Fates,
daughters of Necessity, who are clothed in white robes and have chap-
lets upon their heads, Lachesis and Clotho and Atropos, who accompany with their voices the harmony of the sirens — Lachesis singing
of the past, Clotho of the present, Atropos of the future; Clotho from
time to time assisting with a touch of her right hand the revolution

of the outer circle of the whorl or spindle, and Atropos with her left hand touching and guiding the inner ones, and Lachesis laying hold of either in turn, first with one hand and then with the other.

When Er and the spirits arrived, their duty was to go at once to Lachesis; but first of all there came a prophet who arranged them in order; then he took from the knees of Lachesis lots and samples of lives, and having mounted a high pulpit, spoke as follows: 'Hear the word of Lachesis, the daughter of Necessity. Mortal souls, behold a new cycle of life and mortality. Your genius will not be allotted to you, but you will choose your genius; and let him who draws the first lot have the first choice, and the life which he chooses shall be his destiny. Virtue is free, and as a man honours or dishonours her he will have more or less of her; the responsibility is with the chooser — God is justified.' When the Interpreter had thus spoken he scattered lots indifferently among them all, and each of them took up the lot which fell near him, all but Er himself (he was not allowed), and each as he took his lot perceived the number which he had obtained. Then the Interpreter placed on the ground before them the samples of lives; and there were many more lives than the souls present, and they were of all sorts. There were lives of every animal and of man in every condition. And there were tyrannies among them, some lasting out the tyrant's life, others which broke off in the middle and came to an end in poverty and exile and beggary; and there were lives of famous men, some who were famous for their form and beauty as well as for their strength and success in games, or, again, for their birth and the qualities of their ancestors; and some who were the reverse of famous for the opposite qualities. And of women likewise; there was not, however, any definite character in them, because the soul, when choosing a new life, must of necessity become different. But there was every other quality, and they all mingled with one another, and also with elements of wealth and poverty, and disease and health; and there were mean states also. And here, my dear Glaucon, is the supreme peril of our human state; and therefore the utmost care should be taken. Let each one of us leave every other kind of knowledge and seek and follow one thing only, if peradventure he may be able to learn and may find some one who will make him able to learn and discern between good and evil, and so to choose always and everywhere the better life as he has opportunity. He should consider the bearing of all these things which have been mentioned severally and collectively upon virtue; he should know what the effect of beauty is when combined with poverty or wealth in a particular soul, and what are the good and evil consequences of noble and humble birth, of private and public station, of strength and weakness, of cleverness and dullness, and of all the natural and acquired gifts of the soul, and the operation of them when conjoined; he will then look at the nature of the soul, and from the consideration of all these qualities he will be able to determine which is the better and which is the worse; and so he will choose, giving the name of evil to the life which will make his soul more unjust, and good to the life which will make his soul more just; all else he will disregard. For we have seen and know that this is the best choice both in life and after death. A man must take with him into the world below an adamantine faith in truth and right, that there too he may be undazzled by the desire of wealth or the other allurements of evil, lest, coming upon tyrannies and similar villainies, he do irremediable wrongs to others and suffer yet worse himself; but let him know how to choose the mean and avoid the extremes on either side, as far as possible, not only in this life but in all that which is to come. For this is the way of happiness.

And according to the report of the messenger from the other world this was what the prophet said at the time: 'Even for the last comer, if he chooses wisely and will live diligently, there is appointed a happy and not undesirable existence. Let not him who chooses first be careless, and let not the last despair.' And when he had spoken, he who had the first choice came forward and in a moment chose the greatest tyranny; his mind having been darkened by folly and sensuality, he had not thought out the whole matter before he chose, and did not at first sight perceive that he was fated, among other evils, to devour his own children. But when he had time to reflect, and saw what was in the lot, he began to beat his breast and lament over his choice, forgetting the proclamation of the prophet; for, instead of throwing the blame of his misfortune on himself, he accused chance and the gods, and everything rather than himself. Now he was one of those who came from heaven, and in a former life had dwelt in a well-ordered State, but his virtue was a matter of habit only, and he had no philosophy. And it was true of others who were similarly overtaken, that the greater number of them came from heaven and therefore they had never been schooled by trial, whereas the pilgrims who came from earth having themselves suffered and seen others suffer were not in a hurry to choose. And owing to this inexperience of theirs, and also because the lot was a chance, many of the souls exchanged a good destiny for an evil or an evil for a good. For if a man had always on his arrival in this world dedicated himself from the first to sound philosophy, and had been moderately fortunate in the number of the lot, he might, as the messenger reported, be happy here, and also his journey to another life and return to this, instead of being rough and underground, would be smooth and heavenly. Most curious, he said, was the spectacle — sad and laughable and strange; for the choice of the souls was in most cases based on their experience of a previous life. There he saw the soul which had once been Orpheus choosing the life of a swan out of enmity to the race of women, hating to be born of a woman because they had been his murderers; he beheld also the soul of Thamyras choosing the life of a nightingale; birds, on the other hand, like the swan and other musicians, wanting to be men. The soul which obtained the twentieth lot chose the life of a lion, and this was the soul of Ajax the son of Telamon, who would not be a man, remembering the injustice which was done him in the judgment about the arms. The next was

Agamemnon, who took the life of an eagle, because, like Ajax, he hated human nature by reason of his sufferings. About the middle came the lot of Atalanta; she, seeing the great fame of an athlete, was unable to resist the temptation: and after her there followed the soul of Epeus the son of Panopeus passing into the nature of a woman cunning in the arts; and far away among the last who chose, the soul of the jester Thersites was putting on the form of a monkey. There came also the soul of Odysseus having yet to make a choice, and his lot happened to be the last of them all. Now the recollection of former toils had disenchanted him of ambition, and he went about for a considerable time in search of the life of a private man who had no cares; he had some difficulty in finding this, which was lying about and had been neglected by everybody else; and when he saw it, he said that he would have done the same had his lot been first instead of last, and that he was delighted to have it. And not only did men pass into animals, but I must also mention that there were animals tame and wild who changed into one another and into corresponding human natures — the good into the gentle and the evil into the savage, in all sorts of combinations.

All the souls had now chosen their lives, and they went in the order of their choice to Lachesis, who sent with them the genius whom they had severally chosen, to be the guardian of their lives and the fulfiller of the choice: this genius led the souls first to Clotho, and drew them within the revolution of the spindle impelled by her hand, thus ratifying the destiny of each; and then, when they were fastened to this, carried them to Atropos, who spun the threads and made them irreversible, whence without turning round they passed beneath the throne of Necessity; and when they had all passed, they marched on in a scorching heat to the plain of Forgetfulness, which was a barren waste destitute of trees and verdure; and then towards evening they encamped by the river of Unmindfulness, whose water no vessel can hold; of this they were all obliged to drink a certain quantity, and those who were not saved by wisdom drank more than was necessary; and each one as he drank forgot all things. Now after they had gone to rest, about the middle of the night there was a thunderstorm and earthquake, and then in an instant they were driven upwards in all manner of ways to their birth, like stars shooting. He himself was hindered from drinking the water. But in what manner or by what means he returned to the body he could not say; only, in the morning, awaking suddenly, he found himself lying on the pyre.

And thus, Glaucon, the tale has been saved and has not perished, and will save us if we are obedient to the word spoken; and we shall pass safely over the river of Forgetfulness and our soul will not be defiled. Wherefore my counsel is that we hold fast ever to the heavenly way and follow after justice and virtue always, considering that the soul is immortal and able to endure every sort of good and every sort of evil. Thus shall we live dear to one another and to the gods, both while remaining here and when, like conquerors in the games who go round to gather gifts, we receive our reward. And it shall be well with us both in this life and in the pilgrimage of a thousand years which we have been describing.

[614a–621d, tr. B. JOWETT]

THE LAWS

BOOK X

PERSONS OF THE DIALOGUE

An ATHENIAN STRANGER   CLEINIAS, *a Cretan*
MEGILLUS, *a Lacedaemonian*

[The crowning masterpiece of Plato's old age is the *Laws,* a dialogue which is not as well known as it should be. Only three speakers share in the discussion. They are Cleinias, a Cretan, Megillus, a Lacedemonian, and a stranger from Athens, who proves to be the mouthpiece for Plato's own ideas in the argument. These three elder statesmen set themselves the task of drawing up a code of laws for a new colony, which, according to the fiction of the dialogue, is about to be founded in Crete. Almost every aspect of legislation and constitution building is exhaustively treated in the *Laws.* As the dialogue progresses, Plato develops the fundamental principle that the state must be a theocracy. The entire structure of the government, he argues, all its regulations, its whole conception of justice must depend upon a right belief in God and upon the conviction that God is the ultimate power in the universe. The tenth book, which is reprinted here virtually in its entirety, is therefore climactic since it deals directly with religion and with the justification of the ways of God to man. As Professor Shorey maintains in his book, *What Plato Said,* "The tenth book of the *Laws* is the earliest, the most influential, and, a Platonist would say, still the best extant theodicy or treatise on natural religion."]

Ath. No one who in obedience to the laws believed that there were Gods, ever intentionally did any unholy act, or uttered any unlawful word; but he who did must have supposed one of three things, — either that they did not exist, — which is the first possibility, or secondly, that, if they did, they took no care of man, or thirdly, that they were easily appeased and turned aside from their purpose by sacrifices and prayers.

Cle. What shall we say or do to these persons?

Ath. My good friend, let us first hear the jests which I suspect that they in their superiority will utter against us.

Cle. What jests?

Ath. They will make some irreverent speech of this sort: — 'O inhabitants of Athens, and Sparta, and Cnosus,' they will reply, 'in that you speak truly; for some of us deny the very existence of the Gods, while others, as you say, are of opinion that they do not care about us; and others that they are turned from their course by gifts. Now we have a right to claim, as you yourself allowed, in the matter of laws, that before you are hard upon us and threaten us, you should argue with us and convince us — you should first attempt to teach and persuade us that there are Gods by reasonable evidences, and also that they are too good to be unrighteous, or to be propitiated, or turned from their course by gifts. For when we hear such things said of them by those who are esteemed to be the best of poets, and orators, and prophets, and priests, and by innumerable others, the thoughts of most of us are not set upon abstaining from unrighteous acts, but upon doing them and atoning for them. When lawgivers profess that they are gentle and not stern, we think that they should first of all use persuasion to us, and show us the existence of Gods, if not in a better manner than other men, at any rate in a truer; and who knows but that we shall hearken to you? If then our request is a fair one, please to accept our challenge.'

Cle. But is there any difficulty in proving the existence of the Gods?

Ath. How would you prove it?

Cle. How? In the first place, the earth and the sun, and the stars and the universe, and the fair order of the seasons, and the division of them into years and months, furnish proofs of their existence; and also there is the fact that all Hellenes and barbarians believe in them.

Ath. I fear, my sweet friend, though I will not say that I much regard, the contempt with which the profane will be likely to assail us. For you do not understand the nature of their complaint, and you fancy that they rush into impiety only from a love of sensual pleasure.

Cle. Why, Stranger, what other reason is there?

Ath. One which you who live in a different atmosphere would never guess.

Cle. What is it?

Ath. A very grievous sort of ignorance which is imagined to be the greatest wisdom.

Cle. What do you mean?

Ath. At Athens there are tales preserved in writing which the virtue of your state, as I am informed, refuses to admit. They speak of the Gods in prose as well as verse, and the oldest of them tell of the origin of the heavens and of the world, and not far from the beginning of their story they proceed to narrate the birth of the Gods, and how after they were born they behaved to one another. Whether these stories have in other ways a good or a bad influence, I should not like to be severe upon them, because they are ancient; but, looking at them with reference to the duties of children to their parents, I cannot praise them, or think that they are useful, or at all true. Of the words of the ancients I have nothing more to say; and I should wish to say of them only what is pleasing to the Gods. But as to our younger generation and their wisdom, I cannot let them off when they do mischief. For do but mark the effect of their words: when you and I argue for the existence of the Gods, and produce the sun, moon, stars, and earth, claiming for them a divine being, if we would listen to the aforesaid philosophers we should say that they are earth and stones only, which can have no care at all of human affairs, and that all religion is a cooking up of words and a make-believe.

Cle. One such teacher, O Stranger, would be bad enough, and you imply that there are many of them, which is worse.

Ath. Well, then; what shall we say or do? — Shall we assume that some one is accusing us among unholy men, who are trying to escape from the effect of our legislation; and that they say of us — How dreadful that you should legislate on the supposition that there are Gods! Shall we make a defence of ourselves? or shall we leave them and return to our laws, lest the prelude should become longer than the law? For the discourse will certainly extend to great length, if we are to treat the impiously disposed as they desire, partly demonstrating to them at some length the things of which they demand an explanation, partly making them afraid or dissatisfied, and then proceed to the requisite enactments.

Cle. Yes, Stranger; but then how often have we repeated already that on the present occasion there is no reason why brevity should be preferred to length; for who is 'at our heels?' — as the saying goes, and it would be paltry and ridiculous to prefer the shorter to the better. It is a matter of no small consequence, in some way or other to prove that there are Gods, and that they are good, and regard justice more than men do. The demonstration of this would be the best and noblest prelude of all our laws. And therefore, without impatience, and without hurry, let us unreservedly consider the whole matter, summoning up all the power of persuasion which we possess.

Ath. Seeing you thus in earnest, I would fain offer up a prayer that I may succeed: — but I must proceed at once. Who can be calm when he is called upon to prove the existence of the Gods? Who can avoid hating and abhorring the men who are and have been the cause of this argument; I speak of those who will not believe the tales which they have heard as babes and sucklings from their mothers and nurses, repeated by them both in jest and earnest, like charms, who have also heard them in the sacrificial prayers, and seen sights accompanying them, — sights and sounds delightful to children, — and their parents during the sacrifices showing an intense earnestness on behalf of their children and of themselves, and with eager interest talking to the Gods, and beseeching them, as though they were firmly convinced of their existence; who likewise see and hear the prostrations and invocations which are made by Hellenes and barbarians at the rising and setting of the sun and moon, in all the vicissitudes of life, not as if they thought that there were no Gods, but as if there could be no doubt of their existence, and no suspicion of their non-existence; when men, knowing all these things, despise them on no real grounds, as would be admitted by all who have any particle of intelligence, and when they force us to say what we are now saying, how can any one in gentle terms remonstrate with the like of them, when he has to begin by proving to them the very

existence of the Gods? Yet the attempt must be made; for it would
be unseemly that one half of mankind should go mad in their lust
of pleasure, and the other half in their indignation at such persons.
Our address to these lost and perverted natures should not be spoken
in passion; let us suppose ourselves to select some one of them, and
gently reason with him, smothering our anger: — O my son, we will
say to him, you are young, and the advance of time will make you
reverse many of the opinions which you now hold. Wait awhile,
and do not attempt to judge at present of the highest things; and
that is the highest of which you now think nothing — to know the
Gods rightly and to live accordingly. And in the first place let me
indicate to you one point which is of great importance, and about
which I cannot be deceived: — You and your friends are not the first
who have held this opinion about the Gods. There have always
been persons more or less numerous who have had the same disorder.
I have known many of them, and can tell you, that no one who had
taken up in youth this opinion, that the Gods do not exist, ever continued in the same until he was old; the two other notions certainly
do continue in some cases, but not in many; the notion, I mean, that
the Gods exist, but take no heed of human things, and the other notion that they do take heed of them, but are easily propitiated with
sacrifices and prayers. As to the opinion about the Gods which may
some day become clear to you, I advise you go wait and consider if
it be true or not; ask of others, and above all of the legislator. In
the meantime take care that you do not offend against the Gods.
For the duty of the legislator is and always will be to teach you the
truth of these matters.

Cle. Our address, Stranger, thus far, is excellent.

Ath. Quite true, Megillus and Cleinias, but I am afraid that we
have unconsciously lighted on a strange doctrine.

Cle. What doctrine do you mean?

Ath. The wisest of all doctrines, in the opinion of many.

Cle. I wish that you would speak plainer.

Ath. The doctrine that all things do become, have become, and
will become, some by nature, some by art, and some by chance.

Cle. Is not that true?

Ath. Well, philosophers are probably right; at any rate we may
as well follow in their track, and examine what is the meaning of
them and their disciples.

Cle. By all means.

Ath. They say that the greatest and fairest things are the work of
nature and of chance, the lesser of art, which, receiving from nature
the greater and primeval creations, moulds and fashions all those
lesser works which are generally termed artificial.

Cle. How is that?

Ath. I will explain my meaning still more clearly. They say that
fire and water, and earth and air, all exist by nature and chance, and
none of them by art, and that as to the bodies which come next in
order, — earth, and sun, and moon, and stars, — they have been

created by means of these absolutely inanimate existences. The elements are severally moved by chance and some inherent force according to certain affinities among them — of hot with cold, or of dry with moist, or of soft with hard, and according to all the other accidental admixtures of opposites which have been formed by necessity. After this fashion and in this manner the whole heaven has been created, and all that is in the heaven, as well as animals and all plants, and all the seasons come from these elements, not by the action of mind, as they say, or of any God, or from art, but as I was saying, by nature and chance only. Art sprang up afterwards and out of these, mortal and of mortal birth, and produced in play certain images and very partial imitations of the truth, having an affinity to one another, such as music and painting create and their companion arts. And there are other arts which have a serious purpose, and these co-operate with nature, such, for example, as medicine, and husbandry, and gymnastic. And they say that politics co-operate with nature, but in a less degree, and have more of art; also that legislation is entirely a work of art, and is based on assumptions which are not true.

Cle. How do you mean?

Ath. In the first place, my dear friend, these people would say that the Gods exist not by nature, but by art, and by the laws of states, which are different in different places, according to the agreement of those who make them; and that the honourable is one thing by nature and another thing by law, and that the principles of justice have no existence at all in nature, but that mankind are always disputing about them and altering them; and that the alterations which are made by art and by law have no basis in nature, but are of authority for the moment and at the time at which they are made. — These, my friends, are the sayings of wise men, poets and prose writers, which find a way into the minds of youth. They are told by them that the highest right is might, and in this way the young fall into impieties, under the idea that the Gods are not such as the law bids them imagine; and hence arise factions, these philosophers inviting them to lead a true life according to nature, that is, to live in real dominion over others, and not in legal subjection to them.

Cle. What a dreadful picture, Stranger, have you given, and how great is the injury which is thus inflicted on young men to the ruin both of states and families!

Ath. True, Cleinias; but then what should the lawgiver do when this evil is of long standing? should he only rise up in the state and threaten all mankind, proclaiming that if they will not say and think that the Gods are such as the law ordains (and this may be extended generally to the honourable, the just, and to all the highest things, and to all that relates to virtue and vice), and if they will not make their actions conform to the copy which the law gives them, then he who refuses to obey the law shall die, or suffer stripes and bonds, or privation of citizenship, or in some cases be punished by loss of property and exile? Should he not rather, when he is making laws for men, at the same time infuse the spirit of persuasion into his words, and mitigate the severity of them as far as he can?

Cle. Why, Stranger, if such persuasion be at all possible, then a legislator who has anything in him ought never to weary of persuading men; he ought to leave nothing unsaid in support of the ancient opinion that there are Gods, and of all those other truths which you were just now mentioning; he ought to support the law and also art, and acknowledge that both alike exist by nature, and no less than nature, if they are the creations of mind in accordance with right reason, as you appear to me to maintain, and I am disposed to agree with you in thinking.

Ath. Yes, my enthusiastic Cleinias; but are not these things when spoken to a multitude hard to be understood, not to mention that they take up a dismal length of time?

Cle. Why, Stranger, shall we, whose patience failed not when drinking or music were the themes of discourse, weary now of discoursing about the Gods, and about divine things? And the greatest help to rational legislation is that the laws when once written down are always at rest; they can be put to the test at any future time, and therefore, if on first hearing they seem difficult, there is no reason for apprehension about them, because any man however dull can go over them and consider them again and again; nor if they are tedious but useful, is there any reason or religion, as it seems to me, in any man refusing to maintain the principles of them to the utmost of his power.

Meg. Stranger, I like what Cleinias is saying.

Ath. Yes, Megillus, and we should do as he proposes; for if impious discourses were not scattered, as I may say, throughout the world, there would have been no need for any vindication of the existence of the Gods — but seeing that they are spread far and wide, such arguments are needed; and who should come to the rescue of the greatest laws, when they are being undermined by bad men, but the legislator himself?

Meg. There is no more proper champion of them.

Ath. Well, then, tell me, Cleinias, — for I must ask you to be my partner, — does not he who talks in this way conceive fire and water and earth and air to be the first elements of all things? these he calls nature, and out of these he supposes the soul to be formed afterwards; and this is not a mere conjecture of ours about his meaning, but is what he really means.

Cle. Very true.

Ath. Then, by Heaven, we have discovered the source of this vain opinion of all those physical investigators; and I would have you examine their arguments with the utmost care, for their impiety is a very serious matter; they not only make a bad and mistaken use of argument, but they lead away the minds of others: that is my opinion of them.

Cle. You are right; but I should like to know how this happens.

Ath. I fear that the argument may seem singular.

Cle. Do not hesitate, Stranger; I see that you are afraid of such a discussion carrying you beyond the limits of legislation. But if there be no other way of showing our agreement in the belief that there are Gods, of whom the law is said now to approve, let us take this way, my good sir.

Ath. Then I suppose that I must repeat the singular argument of those who manufacture the soul according to their own impious notions; they affirm that which is the first cause of the generation and destruction of all things, to be not first, but last, and that which is last to be first, and hence they have fallen into error about the true nature of the Gods.

Cle. Still I do not understand you.

Ath. Nearly all of them, my friends, seem to be ignorant of the nature and power of the soul, especially in what relates to her origin: they do not know that she is among the first of things, and before all bodies, and is the chief author of their changes and transpositions. And if this is true, and if the soul is older than the body, must not the things which are of the soul's kindred be of necessity prior to those which appertain to the body?

Cle. Certainly.

Ath. Then thought and attention and mind and art and law will be prior to that which is hard and soft and heavy and light; and the great and primitive works and actions will be works of art; they will be the first, and after them will come nature and works of nature, which however is a wrong term for men to apply to them; these will follow, and will be under the government of art and mind.

Cle. But why is the word 'nature' wrong?

Ath. Because those who use the term mean to say that nature is the first creative power; but if the soul turn out to be the primeval element, and not fire or air, then in the truest sense and beyond other things the soul may be said to exist by nature; and this would be true if you proved that the soul is older than the body, but not otherwise.

Cle. You are quite right.

Ath. Shall we, then, take this as the next point to which our attention should be directed?

Cle. By all means.

Ath. Let us be on our guard lest this most deceptive argument with its youthful looks, beguiling us old men, give us the slip and make a laughing-stock of us. Who knows but we may be aiming at the greater, and fail of attaining the lesser? Suppose that we three have to pass a rapid river, and I, being the youngest of the three and experienced in rivers, take upon me the duty of making the attempt first by myself; leaving you in safety on the bank, I am to examine whether the river is passable by older men like yourselves, and if such appears to be the case then I shall invite you to follow, and my experience will help to convey you across; but if the river is impassable by you, then there will have been no danger to anybody but myself, — would not that seem to be a very fair proposal? I mean to say that the argument in prospect is likely to be too much for you, out of your depth and beyond your strength, and I should be afraid that the stream of my questions might create in you who are not in the habit of answering, giddiness and confusion of mind, and hence a feeling of unpleasantness and unsuitableness might arise. I think therefore that I had better first ask the questions and then answer them myself while you listen in safety; in that way I can carry on the argument until I have completed the proof that the soul is prior to the body.

Cle. Excellent, Stranger, and I hope that you will do as you propose.

Ath. Come, then, and if ever we are to call upon the Gods, let us call upon them now in all seriousness to come to the demonstration of their own existence. And so holding fast to the rope we will venture upon the depths of the argument. When questions of this sort are asked of me, my safest answer would appear to be as follows: — Some one says to me, 'O Stranger, are all things at rest and nothing in motion, or is the exact opposite of this true, or are some things in motion and others at rest?' — To this I shall reply that some things are in motion and others at rest. 'And do not things which move move in a place, and are not the things which are at rest at rest in a place?' Certainly. 'And some move or rest in one place and some in more places than one?' You mean to say, we shall rejoin, that those things which rest at the centre move in one place, just as the circumference goes round of globes which are said to be at rest? 'Yes.' And we observe that, in the revolution, the motion which carries round the larger and the lesser circle at the same time is proportionally distributed to greater and smaller, and is greater and smaller in a certain proportion. Here is a wonder which might be thought an impossibility, that the same motion should impart swiftness and slowness in due proportion to larger and lesser circles. 'Very true.' And when you speak of bodies moving in many places, you seem to me to mean those which move from one place to another, and sometimes have one centre of motion and sometimes more than one because they turn upon their axis; and whenever they meet anything, if it be stationary, they are divided by it; but if they get in the midst between bodies which are approaching and moving towards the same spot from opposite directions, they unite with them. 'I admit the truth of what you are saying.' Also when they unite they grow, and when they are divided they waste away, — that is, supposing the constitution of each to remain, or if that fails, then there is a second reason of their dissolution. 'And when are all things created and how?' Clearly, they are created when the first principle receives increase and attains to the second dimension, and from this arrives at the one which is neighbour to this, and after reaching the third becomes perceptible to sense. Everything which is thus changing and moving is in process of generation; only when at rest has it real existence, but when passing into another state it is destroyed utterly. Have we not mentioned all motions that there are, and comprehended them under their kinds and numbered them with the exception, my friends, of two?

Cle. Which are they?

Ath. Just the two, with which our present enquiry is concerned.

Cle. Speak plainer.

Ath. I suppose that our enquiry has reference to the soul?

Cle. Very true.

Ath. Let us assume that there is a motion able to move other things, but not to move itself; — that is one kind; and there is another kind which can move itself as well as other things, working in composition and decomposition, by increase and diminution and generation and destruction, — that is also one of the many kinds of motion.

Cle. Granted.

Ath. And we will assume that which moves other, and is changed by other, to be the ninth, and that which changes itself and others, and is co-incident with every action and every passion, and is the true principle of change and motion in all that is, — that we shall be inclined to call the tenth.

Cle. Certainly.

Ath. And which of these ten motions ought we to prefer as being the mightiest and most efficient?

Cle. I must say that the motion which is able to move itself is ten thousand times superior to all the others.

Ath. Very good; but may I make one or two corrections in what I have been saying?

Cle. What are they?

Ath. When I spoke of the tenth sort of motion, that was not quite correct.

Cle. What was the error?

Ath. According to the true order, the tenth was really the first in generation and power; then follows the second, which was strangely enough termed the ninth by us.

Cle. What do you mean?

Ath. I mean this: when one thing changes another, and that another, of such will there be any primary changing element? How can a thing which is moved by another ever be the beginning of change? Impossible. But when the self-moved changes other, and that again other, and thus thousands upon tens of thousands of bodies are set in motion, must not the beginning of all this motion be the change of the self-moving principle?

Cle. Very true, and I quite agree.

Ath. Or, to put the question in another way, making answer to ourselves: — If, as most of these philosophers have the audacity to affirm, all things were at rest in one mass, which of the above-mentioned principles of motion would first spring up among them?

Cle. Clearly the self-moving; for there could be no change in them arising out of any external cause; the change must first take place in themselves.

Ath. Then we must say that self-motion being the origin of all motions, and the first which arises among things at rest as well as among things in motion, is the eldest and mightiest principle of change, and that which is changed by another and yet moves other is second.

Cle. Quite true.

Ath. At this stage of the argument let us put a question.

Cle. What question?

Ath. If we were to see this power existing in any earthy, watery, or fiery substance, simple or compound — how should we describe it?

Cle. We mean to ask whether we should call such a self-moving power life?

Ath. I do.

Cle. Certainly we should.

Ath. And when we see soul in anything, must we not do the same — must we not admit that this is life?

Cle. We must.

Ath. And now, I beseech you, reflect; — you would admit that we have a threefold knowledge of things?

Cle. What do you mean?

Ath. I mean that we know the essence, and that we know the definition of the essence, and the name, — these are the three; and there are two questions which may be raised about anything.

Cle. How two?

Ath. Sometimes a person may give the name and ask the definition; or he may give the definition and ask the name. I may illustrate what I mean in this way.

Cle. How?

Ath. Number like some other things is capable of being divided into equal parts; when thus divided, number is named 'even,' and the definition of the name 'even' is 'number divisible into two equal parts'?

Cle. True.

Ath. I mean, that when we are asked about the definition and give the name, or when we are asked about the name and give the definition — in either case, whether we give name or definition, we speak of the same thing, calling 'even' the number which is divided into two equal parts.

Cle. Quite true.

Ath. And what is the definition of that which is named 'soul'? Can we conceive of any other than that which has been already given — the motion which can move itself?

Cle. You mean to say that the essence which is defined as the self-moved is the same with that which has the name soul?

Ath. Yes; and if this is true, do we still maintain that there is anything wanting in the proof that the soul is the first origin and moving power of all that is, or has become, or will be, and their contraries, when she has been clearly shown to be the source of change and motion in all things?

Cle. Certainly not; the soul as being the source of motion, has been most satisfactorily shown to be the oldest of all things.

Ath. And is not that motion which is produced in another, by reason of another, but never has any self-moving power at all, being in truth the change of an inanimate body, to be reckoned second, or by any lower number which you may prefer?

Cle. Exactly.

Ath. Then we are right, and speak the most perfect and absolute truth, when we say that the soul is prior to the body, and that the body is second and comes afterwards, and is born to obey the soul, which is the ruler?

Cle. Nothing can be more true.

Ath. Do you remember our old admission, that if the soul was prior to the body the things of the soul were also prior to those of the body?

Cle. Certainly.

Ath. Then characters and manners, and wishes and reasonings, and true opinions, and reflections, and recollections are prior to length and breadth and depth and strength of bodies, if the soul is prior to the body.

Cle. To be sure.

Ath. In the next place, must we not of necessity admit that the soul is the cause of good and evil, base and honourable, just and unjust, and of all other opposites, if we suppose her to be the cause of all things?

Cle. We must.

Ath. And as the soul orders and inhabits all things that move, however moving, must we not say that she orders also the heavens?

Cle. Of course.

Ath. One soul or more?   More than one — I will answer for you; at any rate, we must not suppose that there are less than two — one the author of good, and the other of evil.

Cle. Very true.

Ath. Yes, very true; the soul then directs all things in heaven, and earth, and sea by her movements, and these are described by the terms — will, consideration, attention, deliberation, opinion true and false, joy and sorrow, confidence, fear, hatred, love, and other primary notions akin to these; which again receive the secondary motions of corporeal substances, and guide all things to growth and decay, to composition and decomposition, and to the qualities which accompany them, such as heat and cold, heaviness and lightness, hardness and softness, blackness and whiteness, bitterness and sweetness, and all those other qualities which the soul uses, herself a goddess, when truly receiving the divine mind she disciplines all things rightly to their happiness; but when she is the companion of folly, she does the very contrary of all this.   Shall we assume so much, or do we still entertain doubts?

Cle. There is no room at all for doubt.

Ath. Shall we say then that it is the soul which controls heaven and earth, and the whole world? — that it is a principle of wisdom and virtue, or a principle which has neither wisdom nor virtue?   Suppose that we make answer as follows: —

Cle. How would you answer?

Ath. If, my friend, we say that the whole path and movement of heaven, and of all that is therein, is by nature akin to the movement and revolution and calculation of mind, and proceeds by kindred laws, then, as is plain, we must say that the best soul takes care of the world and guides it along the good path.

Cle. True.

Ath. But if the world moves wildly and irregularly, then the evil soul guides it.

Cle. True again.

Ath. Of what nature is the movement of mind? — To this question it is not easy to give an intelligent answer; and therefore I ought to assist you in framing one.

Cle. Very good.

Ath. Then let us not answer as if we would look straight at the sun, making ourselves darkness at midday, — I mean as if we were under the impression that we could see with mortal eyes, or know adequately the nature of mind; — it will be safer to look at the image only.

Cle. What do you mean?

Ath. Let us select of the ten motions the one which mind chiefly resembles; this I will bring to your recollection, and will then make the answer on behalf of us all.

Cle. That will be excellent.

Ath. You will surely remember our saying that all things were either at rest or in motion?

Cle. I do.

Ath. And that of things in motion some were moving in one place, and others in more than one?

Cle. Yes.

Ath. Of these two kinds of motion, that which moves in one place must move about a centre like globes made in a lathe, and is most entirely akin and similar to the circular movement of mind.

Cle. What do you mean?

Ath. In saying that both mind and the motion which is in one place move in the same and like manner, in and about the same, and in relation to the same, and according to one proportion and order, and are like the motion of a globe, we invented a fair image, which does no discredit to our ingenuity.

Cle. It does us great credit.

Ath. And the motion of the other sort which is not after the same manner, nor in the same, nor about the same, nor in relation to the same, nor in one place, nor in order, nor according to any rule or proportion, may be said to be akin to senselessness and folly?

Cle. That is most true.

Ath. Then, after what has been said, there is no difficulty in distinctly stating, that since soul carries all things round, either the best soul or the contrary must of necessity carry round and order and arrange the revolution of the heaven.

Cle. And judging from what has been said, Stranger, there would be impiety in asserting that any but the most perfect soul or souls carries round the heavens.

Ath. You have understood my meaning right well, Cleinias, and now let me ask you another question.

Cle. What are you going to ask?

Ath. If the soul carries round the sun and moon, and the other stars, does she not carry round each individual of them?

Cle. Certainly.

Ath. Then of one of them let us speak, and the same argument will apply to all.

Cle. Which will you take?

Ath. Every one sees the body of the sun, but no one sees his soul, nor the soul of any other body living or dead; and yet there is great reason to believe that this nature, unperceived by any of our senses, is circumfused around them all, but is perceived by mind; and therefore by mind and reflection only let us apprehend the following point.

Cle. What is that?

Ath. If the soul carries round the sun, we shall not be far wrong in supposing one of three alternatives.

Cle. What are they?

Ath. Either the soul which moves the sun this way and that, resides within the circular and visible body, like the soul which carries us about every way; or the soul provides herself with an external body of fire or air, as some affirm, and violently propels body by body; or thirdly, she is without such a body, but guides the sun by some extraordinary and wonderful power.

Cle. Yes, certainly; the soul can only order all things in one of these three ways.

Ath. And this soul of the sun, which is therefore better than the sun, whether taking the sun about in a chariot to give light to men, or acting from without, or in whatever way, ought by every man to be deemed a God.

Cle. Yes, by every man who has the least particle of sense.

Ath. And of the stars too, and of the moon, and of the years and months and seasons, must we not say in like manner, that since a soul or souls having every sort of excellence are the causes of all of them, those souls are Gods, whether they are living beings and reside in bodies, and in this way order the whole heaven, or whatever be the place and mode of their existence; — and will any one who admits all this venture to deny that all things are full of Gods?

Cle. No one, Stranger, would be such a madman.

Ath. And now, Megillus and Cleinias, let us offer terms to him who has hitherto denied the existence of the Gods, and leave him.

Cle. What terms?

Ath. Either he shall teach us that we were wrong in saying that the soul is the original of all things, and arguing accordingly; or, if he be not able to say anything better, then he must yield to us and live for the remainder of his life in the belief that there are Gods. — Let us see, then, whether we have said enough or not enough to those who deny that there are Gods.

Cle. Certainly, — quite enough, Stranger.

Ath. Then to them we will say no more. And now we are to address him who, believing that there are Gods, believes also that they take no heed of human affairs: To him we say, — O thou best of men, in believing that there are Gods you are led by some affinity to them, which attracts you towards your kindred and makes you honour and believe in them. But the fortunes of evil and unrighteous men in private as well as public life, which, though not really happy, are wrongly counted happy in the judgment of men, and are celebrated both by poets and prose writers — these draw you aside from your natural piety. Perhaps you have seen impious men growing old and leaving their children's children in high offices, and their prosperity shakes your faith — you have known or heard or been yourself an eyewitness of many monstrous impieties, and have beheld men by such criminal means from small beginnings attaining to sovereignty and the pinnacle of greatness; and considering all these things you do not like to accuse the Gods of them, because they are your relatives; and so from some want of reasoning power, and also from an unwillingness to find fault with them, you have come to believe that they exist indeed, but have no thought or care of human things. Now, that your present evil opinion may not grow to still greater impiety, and that we may if possible use arguments which may conjure away the evil before it arrives, we will add another argument to that originally addressed to him who utterly denied the existence of the Gods. And do you, Megillus and Cleinias, answer for the young man as you did before; and if any impediment comes in our way, I will take the word out of your mouths, and carry you over the river as I did just now.

Cle. Very good; do as you say, and we will help you as well as we can.

Ath. There will probably be no difficulty in proving to him that the Gods care about the small as well as about the great. For he was present and heard what was said, that they are perfectly good, and that the care of all things is most entirely natural to them.

Cle. No doubt he heard that.

Ath. Let us consider together in the next place what we mean by this virtue which we ascribe to them. Surely we should say that to be temperate and to possess mind belongs to virtue, and the contrary to vice?

Cle. Certainly.

Ath. Yes; and courage is a part of virtue, and cowardice of vice?

Cle. True.

Ath. And the one is honourable, and the other dishonourable?

Cle. To be sure.

Ath. And the one, like other meaner things, is a human quality, but the Gods have no part in anything of the sort?

Cle. That again is what everybody will admit.

Ath. But do we imagine carelessness and idleness and luxury to be virtues? What do you think?

Cle. Decidedly not.

Ath. They rank under the opposite class?

Cle. Yes.

Ath. And their opposites, therefore, would fall under the opposite class?

Cle. Yes.

Ath. But are we to suppose that one who possesses all these good qualities will be luxurious and heedless and idle, like those whom the poet compares to stingless drones?

Cle. And the comparison is a most just one.

Ath. Surely God must not be supposed to have a nature which He Himself hates? — he who dares to say this sort of thing must not be tolerated for a moment.

Cle. Of course not. How could He have?

Ath. Should we not on any principle be entirely mistaken in praising any one who has some special business entrusted to him, if he have a mind which takes care of great matters and no care of small ones? Reflect; he who acts in this way, whether he be God or man, must act from one of two principles.

Cle. What are they?

Ath. Either he must think that the neglect of the small matters is of no consequence to the whole, or if he knows that they are of consequence, and he neglects them, his neglect must be attributed to carelessness and indolence. Is there any other way in which his neglect can be explained? For surely, when it is impossible for him to take care of all, he is not negligent if he fails to attend to these things great or small, which a God or some inferior being might be wanting in strength or capacity to manage?

Cle. Certainly not.

Ath. Now, then, let us examine the offenders, who both alike confess that there are Gods, but with a difference, — the one saying that they may be appeased, and the other that they have no care of small matters: there are three of us and two of them, and we will say to them, — In the first place, you both acknowledge that the Gods hear and see and know all things, and that nothing can escape them which is matter of sense and knowledge: — do you admit this?

Cle. Yes.

Ath. And do you admit also that they have all power which mortals and immortals can have?

Cle. They will, of course, admit this also.

Ath. And surely we three and they two — five in all — have acknowledged that they are good and perfect?

Cle. Assuredly.

Ath. But, if they are such as we conceive them to be, can we possibly suppose that they ever act in the spirit of carelessness and indolence? For in us inactivity is the child of cowardice, and carelessness of inactivity and indolence.

Cle. Most true.

Ath. Then not from inactivity and carelessness is any God ever negligent; for there is no cowardice in them.

Cle. That is very true.

Ath. Then the alternative which remains is, that if the Gods neglect the lighter and lesser concerns of the universe, they neglect them because they know that they ought not to care about such matters — what other alternative is there but the opposite of their knowing?

Cle. There is none.

Ath. And, O most excellent and best of men, do I understand you to mean that they are careless because they are ignorant, and do not know that they ought to take care, or that they know, and yet like the meanest sort of men, knowing the better, choose the worse because they are overcome by pleasures and pains?

Cle. Impossible.

Ath. Do not all human things partake of the nature of soul? And is not man the most religious of all animals?

Cle. That is not to be denied.

Ath. And we acknowledge that all mortal creatures are the property of the Gods, to whom also the whole of heaven belongs?

Cle. Certainly.

Ath. And, therefore, whether a person says that these things are to the Gods great or small — in either case it would not be natural for the Gods who own us, and who are the most careful and the best of owners, to neglect us. — There is also a further consideration.

Cle. What is it?

Ath. Sensation and power are in an inverse ratio to each other in respect to their ease and difficulty.

Cle. What do you mean?

Ath. I mean that there is greater difficulty in seeing and hearing the small than the great, but more facility in moving and controlling and taking care of small and unimportant things than of their opposites.

Cle. Far more.

Ath. Suppose the case of a physician who is willing and able to cure some living thing as a whole, — how will the whole fare at his hands if he takes care only of the greater and neglects the parts which are lesser?

Cle. Decidedly not well.

Ath. No better would be the result with pilots or generals, or householders or statesmen, or any other such class, if they neglected the small and regarded only the great; — as the builders say, the larger stones do not lie well without the lesser.

Cle. Of course not.

Ath. Let us not, then, deem God inferior to human workmen, who, in proportion to their skill, finish and perfect their works, small as well as great, by one and the same art; or that God, the wisest of beings, who is both willing and able to take care, is like a lazy good-for-nothing, or a coward, who turns his back upon labour and gives no thought to smaller and easier matters, but to the greater only.

Cle. Never, Stranger, let us admit a supposition about the Gods which is both impious and false.

Ath. I think that we have now argued enough with him who delights to accuse the Gods of neglect.

Cle. Yes.

Ath. He has been forced to acknowledge that he is in error, but he still seems to me to need some words of consolation.

Cle. What consolation will you offer him?

Ath. Let us say to the youth: — The ruler of the universe has ordered all things with a view to the excellence and preservation of the whole, and each part, as far as may be, has an action and passion appropriate to it. Over these, down to the least fraction of them, ministers have been appointed to preside, who have wrought out their perfection with infinitesimal exactness. And one of these portions of the universe is thine own, unhappy man, which, however little, contributes to the whole; and you do not seem to be aware that this and every other creation is for the sake of the whole, and in order that the life of the whole may be blessed; and that you are created for the sake of the whole, and not the whole for the sake of you. For every physician and every skilled artist does all things for the sake of the whole, directing his effort towards the common good, executing the part for the sake of the whole, and not the whole for the sake of the part. And you are annoyed because you are ignorant how what is best for you happens to you and to the universe, as far as the laws of the common creation admit. Now, as the soul combining first with one body and then with another undergoes all sorts of changes, either of herself, or through the influence of another soul, all that remains to the player of the game is that he should shift the pieces; sending the better nature to the better place, and the worse to the worse, and so assigning to them their proper portion.

Cle. In what way do you mean?

Ath. In a way which may be supposed to make the care of all things easy to the Gods. If any one were to form or fashion all things without any regard to the whole, — if, for example, he formed a living element of water out of fire, instead of forming many things out of one or one out of many in regular order attaining to a first or second or third birth, the transmutation would have been infinite; but now the ruler of the world has a wonderfully easy task.

Cle. How so?

Ath. I will explain: — When the king saw that our actions had life, and that there was much virtue in them and much vice, and that the soul and body, although not, like the Gods of popular opinion, eternal, yet having once come into existence, were indestructible (for if either of them had been destroyed, there would have been no generation of living beings); and when he observed that the good of the soul was ever by nature designed to profit men, and the evil to harm them — he, seeing all this, contrived so to place each of the parts that their position might in the easiest and best manner procure the victory of good and the defeat of evil in the whole. And he contrived a general plan by which a thing of a certain nature found a certain seat and room. But the formation of qualities he left to the wills of individuals. For every one of us is made pretty much what he is by the bent of his desires and the nature of his soul.

Cle. Yes, that is probably true.

Ath. Then all things which have a soul change, and possess in themselves a principle of change, and in changing move according to law and to the order of destiny: natures which have undergone a lesser change move less and on the earth's surface, but those which have suffered more change and have become more criminal sink into the abyss, that is to say, into Hades and other places in the world below, of which the very names terrify men, and which they picture to themselves as in a dream, both while alive and when released from the body. And whenever the soul receives more of good or evil from her own energy and the strong influence of others — when she has communion with divine virtue and becomes divine, she is carried into another and better place, which is perfect in holiness; but when she has communion with evil, then she also changes the place of her life.

'This is the justice of the Gods who inhabit Olympus.' *

O youth or young man, who fancy that you are neglected by the Gods, know that if you become worse you shall go to the worse souls, or if better to the better, and in every succession of life and death you will do and suffer what like may fitly suffer at the hands of like. This is the justice of heaven, which neither you nor any other unfortunate will ever glory in escaping, and which the ordaining powers have specially ordained; take good heed thereof, for it will be sure to take heed of you. If you say: — I am small and will creep into the depths of the earth, or I am high and will fly up to heaven, you are not so small or so high but that you shall pay the fitting penalty, either here or in the world below or in some still more savage place whither you shall be conveyed. This is also the explanation of the fate of those whom you saw, who had done unholy and evil deeds, and from small beginnings had grown great, and you fancied that from being miserable they had become happy; and in their actions, as in a mirror, you seemed to see the universal neglect of the Gods, not knowing how they make all things work together and contribute to the great whole. And thinkest thou, bold man, that thou needest not to know this? — he who knows it not can never form any true idea of the happiness or unhappiness of life or hold any rational discourse respecting either. If Cleinias and this our reverend company succeed in proving to you that you know not what you say of the Gods, then will God help you; but should you desire to hear more, listen to what we say to the third opponent, if you have any understanding whatsoever. For I think that we have sufficiently proved the existence of the Gods, and that they care

* *Odyssey,* xix. 43.

for men: — The other notion that they are appeased by the wicked, and take gifts, is what we must not concede to any one, and what every man should disprove to the utmost of his power.

Cle. Very good; let us do as you say.

Ath. Well, then, by the Gods themselves I conjure you to tell me, — if they are to be propitiated, how are they to be propitiated? Who are they, and what is their nature? Must they not be at least rulers who have to order unceasingly the whole heaven?

Cle. True.

Ath. And to what earthly rulers can they be compared, or who to them? How in the less can we find an image of the greater? Are they charioteers of contending pairs of steeds, or pilots of vessels? Perhaps they might be compared to the generals of armies, or they might be likened to physicians providing against the diseases which make war upon the body, or to husbandmen observing anxiously the effects of the seasons on the growth of plants; or perhaps to shepherds of flocks. For as we acknowledge the world to be full of many goods and also of evils, and of more evils than goods, there is, as we affirm, an immortal conflict going on among us, which requires marvellous watchfulness; and in that conflict the Gods and demigods are our allies, and we are their property. Injustice and insolence and folly are the destruction of us, and justice and temperance and wisdom are our salvation; and the place of these latter is in the life of the Gods, although some vestige of them may occasionally be discerned among mankind. But upon this earth we know that there dwell souls possessing an unjust spirit, who may be compared to brute animals, which fawn upon their keepers, whether dogs or shepherds, or the best and most perfect masters; for they in like manner, as the voices of the wicked declare, prevail by flattery and prayers and incantations, and are allowed to make their gains with impunity. And this sin, which is termed dishonesty, is an evil of the same kind as what is termed disease in living bodies or pestilence in years or seasons of the year, and in cities and governments has another name, which is injustice.

Cle. Quite true.

Ath. What else can he say who declares that the Gods are always lenient to the doers of unjust acts, if they divide the spoil with them? As if wolves were to toss a portion of their prey to the dogs, and they, mollified by the gift, suffered them to tear the flocks. Must not he who maintains that the Gods can be propitiated argue thus?

Cle. Precisely so.

Ath. And to which of the above-mentioned classes of guardians would any man compare the Gods without absurdity? Will he say that they are like pilots, who are themselves turned away from their duty by 'libations of wine and the savour of fat,' and at last overturn both ship and sailors?

Cle. Assuredly not.

Ath. And surely they are not like charioteers who are bribed to give up the victory to other chariots?

Cle. That would be a fearful image of the Gods.

Ath. Nor are they like generals, or physicians, or husbandmen, or shepherds; and no one would compare them to dogs who have been silenced by wolves.

Cle. A thing not to be spoken of.

Ath. And are not all the Gods the chiefest of all guardians, and do they not guard our highest interests?

Cle. Yes; the chiefest.

Ath. And shall we say that those who guard our noblest interests, and are the best of guardians, are inferior in virtue to dogs, and to men even of moderate excellence, who would never betray justice for the sake of gifts which unjust men impiously offer them?

Cle. Certainly not; nor is such a notion to be endured, and he who holds this opinion may be fairly singled out and characterized as of all impious men the wickedest and most impious.

Ath. Then are the three assertions — that the Gods exist, and that they take care of men, and that they can never be persuaded to do injustice, now sufficiently demonstrated? May we say that they are?

Cle. You have our entire assent to your words.

[885b–907b, tr. B. Jowett]

ARISTOTLE

(384–322 B.C.)

When we approach the writings of Aristotle after having studied Plato, we should bear in mind that there is a fundamental and radical opposition between these two philosophers. This opposition is certainly not to be viewed in an antiquarian light; rather it is a difference which has perpetuated itself from their day to ours and will undoubtedly continue until the end of time. The reality of the issue appears clearly in the history of Christianity and the institution of the Christian Church. St. Augustine, for example, sympathized strongly with Plato and appealed to him often in his writings; but in the thirteenth century when St. Thomas Aquinas set himself the stupendous task of fashioning a philosophy for Christianity, he adapted in practically all its features the system of Aristotle to the Christian position. From time to time, however, there have been Platonic reactions among Christian thinkers and theologians. Similar phenomena in the course of European history in its secular aspects can be noted; for example, there are periods when Plato's influence is strong, as in the Renaissance, or in the Romantic age in English literature, with such poets as Shelley. Or, on the other hand, there have been periodic revivals of Aristotelianism, as can be seen in England and America in recent years. All these facts justify Coleridge in having said that all men are either Platonists or Aristotelians.

Aristotle was born in Stageira, a small town in Thrace, in 384 B.C., just two years after Plato had founded the Academy. He came to Athens at the age of seventeen and immediately entered Plato's school where he remained for the next twenty years, until the death of the elder philosopher. This period is unique, for here we find two of the greatest minds in all European history in intimate and close contact with one another for a long space of time, and out of it have emerged ideas, concepts, and principles which have contributed deeply to the core of the civilization in which we now live. On Plato's death, Aristotle left Athens, perhaps because the new head of the Academy, Speusippus, seemed to be too preoccupied with mathematics, a tendency to which Aristotle objected. At all events, he went to Assos, a small town in the Troad, and lectured there for two or three years. He was subsequently called by Philip of Macedon to become the tutor of the young Alexander. At about the time of Philip's death Aristotle returned to Athens, founded his school, the Lyceum, and taught there for the next eleven years. We are told that in the morning he delivered esoteric discourses for his special students which dealt with more difficult material such as logic, physics, biology, astronomy, psychology and metaphysics. In the afternoon he delivered his so-called exoteric lectures which were public and were somewhat more popular. His subjects here were ethics, politics, rhetoric and literary criticism. On Alexander's death in 323 B.C. the enemies of Macedon in Athens trumped up false charges against Aristotle and he left the city, so the story goes, thinking on the death of Socrates and determined not to allow the Athenians, as he remarked, "to sin twice against philosophy." He retired to Chalcis in Euboea, where he died in the following year.

Aristotle left an enormous amount of material. Although much of this is now lost, still the preserved works fill eleven good-sized volumes. The style is very uneven; and many passages are brief, cryptic, choppy and repetitious. Some scholars have held the theory that this corpus is a collection of lecture notes taken by Aristotle's students. This hypothesis is generally rejected, for the writings are far too coherent and self-consistent to be the lecture notes of any students. Consequently the theory that these are the lecture notes of Aristotle himself is much more plausible, and explains why some pages are carefully worked out and others not. The writings are elaborately cross-referenced, a fact which suggests their nature as lecture notes. Furthermore, alternate treatments of the same topics appear and hence it is logical to suppose that Aristotle kept his notes in a fluid condition, making frequent revision and alteration as time went on.

Paul Elmer More, in his book, *The Skeptical Approach to Religion,* has compared a passage in Plato's *Republic* with a passage in Aristotle's *Nicomachean Ethics* in order to give a sharp contrast between the attitudes of the two thinkers. In the *Republic* when Socrates is asked which man is the happier, the just man who seems to be most completely unjust or the unjust man who seems to be most completely just, one of his questioners affirms that the former who seems to be unjust "will be scourged, racked, fettered, will have his eyes burned out, and at last, after suffering every kind of torture, will be crucified." The question put to Socrates is "Will such a man, who is really just, be happier, even though he endures those sufferings?" Socrates' answer is "yes," and in one sense the remainder of the *Republic* is an effort to validate this reply. With this passage Mr. More contrasts a section from Aristotle where he is talking about the necessaries for happiness. Aristotle says (and he may have the particular passage of the *Republic* in mind) "Therefore the happy man needs the goods of the body, external goods, and the goods of fortune so that these (or the lack of these) may not stand in the way of his being happy. Those who maintain that the man who is being broken on the wheel, or the man who is beset with great misfortunes, is happy, whether they mean to or not, are talking nonsense." One can note the different temper of Plato and Aristotle. Aristotle calls Plato's position nonsense on the face of it. Plato, however, believes in it, attempts to demonstrate its truth, never quite succeeds in doing so, and yet maintains it with all his powers of moral and spiritual eloquence.

In studying the works of Aristotle which follow here one must have in mind some conception of Aristotle's basic philosophical position. The most fundamental principle which should be associated with Aristotle is his profound and deep conviction that the individual thing is that which is ultimately real; that is, the individual desk, chair, tree, animal, or man. It is the particular in all its complexity that is real for Aristotle. Here we have the sharp distinction with Plato who maintained that the non-spatial, non-temporal Idea was the real and the "thing" in Aristotle's sense was that which is subject to change, transient, and impermanent, and therefore relatively unreal. Plato, as a result, is not preoccupied with these "things" in and for themselves, but Aristotle on the other hand definitely is, and hence provides a healthy and thoroughgoing complement and corrective to the over-enthusiastic Platonizer.

Aristotle's thinking begins by analyzing the individual "things" which he believes to be real. Thus we find him, so to speak, burrowing into these objects, scrutinizing them in an attempt to arrive at their inner essence, and then to apprehend their relation with other objects. So, to take the example of a desk, when it is subjected to analysis it appears to be a composite of some kind of matter or material, wood, which has had some kind of form imposed upon it. Hence two concepts immediately emerge which are very important for Aristotle, *viz.,* matter and form. As he continues he burrows further into the object and differentiates between what he calls "essence," that which really makes a thing to be precisely what it is, and "accidents," qualities which may vary or change, or may accidentally be attached to an object. For example, that a desk is brown, is in Aristotle's sense an "accident." Its essence or essential nature as a desk would not change if it were painted black. Or to take the illustration of a man, — a man's weight or height, or the color of his hair or of his eyes would be an "accident," and would have nothing to do with his inner essence, his essential nature as a human being.

Thus far we have been considering Aristotle as he examines things or objects from a static point of view. When he approaches them from a dynamic point of view, as they change and develop, he advances his famous doctrine of causality. This doctrine maintains that each thing has four causes — material, formal, efficient and final. If we take the illustration of a house, according to Aristotle's analysis, the material cause is the wood, plaster, etc., out of which the house is constructed. The formal cause would be the architect's plans, the efficient cause, the builder, and the final cause, the purpose of the house, to be a living place to provide shelter for human beings. From the dynamic approach also arises the distinction between potentiality and actuality. The familiar illustration of the acorn and the oak may serve us here. The acorn has the capacity in it of becoming an oak tree, or as Aristotle would put it, the acorn *is* a potential oak tree. Similarly a boy is potentially a man. Manhood is his end or aim, and he continually moves toward that state of actuality. Further Aristotle would insist that we should not look at this actualization of man merely from the physical point of view. He insists that the complete actualization of a man lies in the moral sphere and he believes that each individual should become as close to the most complete actualization of man as possible. In summary, then, we have these basic Aristotelian conceptions: the individual thing is ultimately real; and it, when analyzed from static and dynamic points of view, reveals the fundamental notions of matter, form, essence, accidents, causality, potentiality and actuality.

It should not take much imagination to guess what Aristotle thought specifically of Plato's Theory of Ideas. Anyone who believes in the ultimate reality of individual things will have little sympathy for a person who maintains that ultimate reality lies in an abstract realm of non-spatial, non-temporal ideas. So Aristotle objects vigorously to Plato's theory, in the main, on two grounds. First, he is dissatisfied with Plato's account of the relation between a particular and an idea. When Plato says that the particular "participates in" or "imitates" the idea, Aristotle dismisses this explanation as mere empty verbiage. It is obvious that here Aristotle is pointing to a real difficulty in the Platonic system although it should be noted in passing that Plato himself was perfectly aware of this problem. Secondly, Aristotle raises the difficulty of the efficiency of the ideas. In effect, he asks why talk of ideas if they can't be shown to *do* anything. All they do, he avers, is to complicate the picture. He would insist that there is plenty enough in the world of space and time to puzzle us; why create a whole other realm of ideas quite gratuitously, so he would argue, which only doubles the number of things that have to be explained. The upshot of the whole argument is that in Aristotle's view the ideas do not exist. It should be remembered, however, that when Aristotle develops his theory of logical universals as inhering in particular things, he is preserving one aspect of Plato's Theory of Ideas, its logical function. Also we should note that Aristotle in distinction to Plato never deviates from a thoroughgoing reliance upon the reason as such. Implicit in all his writings is the conviction that the reason or the approach of rationalism is in itself sufficient to resolve the problems of philosophy.

The foregoing analysis should provide a skeleton background against which the present selections from the *Metaphysics,* the *Ethics* and the *Poetics* should be read.* The first book of the *Metaphysics* is here included because it is the major source of our information concerning the pre-Socratic philosophers, and indeed it in itself is the first history of philosophy. Certain critics, most notably Professor Cherniss, have argued convincingly that Aristotle is by no means to be trusted completely in his interpretation of the thinkers who preceded him. His whole treatment is dominated by the assumption that he himself is the end and final completion of a whole trend of philosophical development. Thus all his predecessors are appraised according to the degree to which they approximate or anticipate Aristotle's own position.

* Further study of these documents and the other Aristotelian writings will inevitably raise questions concerning the development of Aristotle's thought. For a consideration of this problem the reader is referred to Werner Jaeger's exhaustive treatment in his book *Aristotle* (Oxford University Press, 1934).

The second book of *Nicomachean Ethics* is important because it contains Aristotle's full analysis of the doctrine of the mean which is obviously the key concept of his whole ethical theory. The passage from the tenth book reveals Aristotle in one of the rare moments when he writes with eloquence and fervour. When he urges man in the living of his life to make himself as immortal as is possible for him, we find Aristotle writing under a Platonic influence. Certainly this section of the tenth book should indicate that although Plato and Aristotle were radically opposed, still there is scarcely a page in the works of the later philosopher which does not bespeak great indebtedness to his master.

The *Poetics,* which is one of Aristotle's less technical treatises, reveals that he has studied poetry with the same analytical powers which he had brought to bear in the various other fields of thought. The treament of poetry in many ways is very systematic and complete and yet there are certain curious gaps. Aristotle devotes his attention almost completely to a discussion of tragedy. To be sure, there is a section on poetic diction and a section on epic poetry, but nothing is said concerning lyric poetry. The profound influence of the *Poetics* on subsequent criticism results from the great number of shrewd insights into the nature of poetry and drama, rather than because Aristotle presents in the treatise a fully synthesized philosophy of art or theory of literary criticism. His more notable remarks include his definition of tragedy, his conception of the tragic hero, his analysis of the constituent elements of tragedy, his notion of imitation and his opinion that the end of tragedy is to provide a catharsis of pity and fear and similar emotions. Perhaps the most profound remark in the *Poetics* is Aristotle's statement that poetry is more philosophic and of graver import than history since its statements are of the nature rather of universals whereas those of history are singulars. Aristotle here insists that that which the artist "imitates" in the objects of his imitation is the universal or the universals. Thus when Aristotle tells us that the objects of imitation for a tragic poet are men in action, he means the "universals" of these men in action, not what they do by chance or luck or accident. In this connection, Aristotle's word "action" should be related closely to his conception of actuality and activity.

Even from this brief summary we can easily see why the *Poetics* can be read and re-read with profit as an inexhaustible source of critical stimulation. Perhaps its greatest value lies in Aristotle's convincing argument that art is serious and philosophical, and it is in this Aristotelian context that all the great achievements in the creation and criticism of art have been viewed in the history of Western culture.

METAPHYSICS

1. All men by nature desire to know. An indication of this is the delight we take in our senses; for even apart from their usefulness they are loved for themselves; and above all others the sense of sight. For not only with a view to action, but even when we are not going to do anything, we prefer seeing (one might say) to everything else. The reason is that this, most of all the senses, makes us know and brings to light many differences between things.

By nature animals are born with the faculty of sensation, and from sensation memory is produced in some of them, though not in others. And therefore the former are more intelligent and apt at learning than those which cannot remember; those which are incapable of hearing sounds are intelligent though they cannot be taught, e. g. the bee, and any other race of animals that may be like it; and those which besides memory have this sense of hearing can be taught.

The animals other than man live by appearances and memories, and have but little of connected experience; but the human race lives also by art and reasonings. Now from memory experience is produced in men; for the several memories of the same thing produce finally the capacity for a single experience. And experience seems pretty much like science and art, but really science and art come to men *through* experience; for 'experience made art,' as Polus says, 'but inexperience luck.' Now art arises when from many notions gained by experience one universal judgment about a class of objects is produced. For to have a judgment that when Callias was ill of this disease this did him good, and similarly in the case of Socrates and in many individual cases, is a matter of experience; but to judge that it has done good to all persons of a certain constitution, marked off in one class, when they were ill of this disease, e. g. to phlegmatic or bilious people when burning with fever — this is a matter of art.

With a view to action experience seems in no respect inferior to art, and men of experience succeed even better than those who have theory without experience. (The reason is that experience is knowledge of individuals, art of universals, and actions and productions are all concerned with the individual; for the physician does not cure *man,* except in an incidental way, but Callias or Socrates or some other called by some such individual name, who happens to be a man. If, then, a man has the theory without the experience, and recognizes the universal but does not know the individual included in this, he will often fail to cure; for it is the individual that is to be cured.) But yet we think that *knowledge* and *understanding* belong to art rather than to experience, and we suppose artists to be wiser than men of experience (which implies that Wisdom depends in all cases rather on knowledge); and this because the former know the cause, but the latter do not. For men of experience know that the thing is so, but do not know why, while the others know the 'why' and the cause. Hence we think also that the master-workers in each craft are more honourable and know in a truer sense and are wiser than the manual workers, because they know the causes of the things that are done (we think the manual workers are like certain lifeless things which act indeed, but act without knowing what they do, as fire burns — but while the lifeless things perform each of their functions by a natural tendency, the labourers perform them through habit); thus we view them as being wiser not in virtue of being able to act, but of having the theory for themselves and knowing the causes. And in general it is a sign of the man who knows and of the man who does not know, that the former can teach, and therefore we think art more truly knowledge than experience is; for artists can teach, and men of mere experience cannot.

Again, we do not regard any of the senses as Wisdom; yet surely these give the most authoritative knowledge of particulars. But they do not tell us the 'why' of anything — e. g. why fire is hot; they only say *that* it is hot.

At first he who invented any art whatever that went beyond the common perceptions of man was naturally admired by men, not only because there was something useful in the inventions, but because he was thought wise and superior to the rest. But as more arts were invented, and some were directed to the necessities of life, others to recreation, the inventors of the latter were naturally always regarded as wiser than the inventors of the former, because their branches of knowledge did not aim at utility. Hence when all such inventions were already established, the sciences which do not aim at giving pleasure or at the necessities of life were discovered, and first in the places where men first began to have leisure. This is why the mathematical arts were founded in Egypt; for there the priestly caste was allowed to be at leisure.

We have said in the *Ethics* * what the difference is between art and science and the other kindred faculties; but the point of our present discussion is this, that all men suppose what is called Wisdom to deal with the first causes and the principles of things; so that, as has been said before, the man of experience is thought to be wiser than the possessors of any sense-perception whatever, the artist wiser than the men of experience, the master-worker than the mechanic, and the theoretical kinds of knowledge to be more of the nature of Wisdom than the productive. Clearly then Wisdom is knowledge about certain principles and causes.

2. Since we are seeking this knowledge, we must inquire of what kind are the causes and the principles, the knowledge of which is Wisdom. If one were to take the notions we have about the wise man, this might perhaps make the answer more evident. We suppose first, then, that the wise man knows all things, as far as possible,

* 1139^b 14-1141^b 8.

although he has not knowledge of each of them in detail; secondly, that he who can learn things that are difficult, and not easy for man to know, is wise (sense-perception is common to all, and therefore easy and no mark of Wisdom); again, that he who is more exact and more capable of teaching the causes is wiser, in every branch of knowledge; and that of the sciences, also, that which is desirable on its own account and for the sake of knowing it is more of the nature of Wisdom than that which is desirable on account of its results, and the superior science is more of the nature of Wisdom than the ancillary; for the wise man must not be ordered but must order, and he must not obey another, but the less wise must obey *him*.

Such and so many are the notions, then, which we have about Wisdom and the wise. Now of these characteristics that of knowing all things must belong to him who has in the highest degree universal knowledge; for he knows in a sense all the instances that fall under the universal. And these things, the most universal, are on the whole the hardest for men to know; for they are farthest from the senses. And the most exact of the sciences are those which deal most with first principles; for those which involve fewer principles are more exact than those which involve additional principles, e. g. arithmetic than geometry. But the science which investigates causes is also *instructive,* in a higher degree, for the people who instruct us are those who tell the causes of each thing. And understanding and knowledge pursued for their own sake are found most in the knowledge of that which is most knowable (for he who chooses to know for the sake of knowing will choose most readily that which is most truly knowledge, and such is the knowledge of that which is most knowable); and the first principles and the causes are most knowable; for by reason of these, and from these, all other things come to be known, and not these by means of the things subordinate to them. And the science which knows to what end each thing must be done is the most authoritative of the sciences, and more authoritative than any ancillary science; and this end is the good of that thing, and in general the supreme good in the whole of nature. Judged by all the tests we have mentioned, then, the name in question falls to the same science; this must be a science that investigates the first principles and causes; for the good, i. e. the end, is one of the causes.

That it is not a science of production is clear even from the history of the earliest philosophers. For it is owing to their wonder that men both now begin and at first began to philosophize; they wondered originally at the obvious difficulties, then advanced little by little and stated difficulties about the greater matters, e. g. about the phenomena of the moon and those of the sun and of the stars, and about the genesis of the universe. And a man who is puzzled and wonders thinks himself ignorant (whence even the lover of myth is in a sense a lover of Wisdom, for the myth is composed of wonders); therefore since they philosophized in order to escape from ignorance, evidently they were pursuing science in order to know, and not for any utilitarian end. And this is confirmed by the facts; for it was when almost all the necessities of life and the things that make for comfort and recreation had been secured, that such knowledge began to be sought. Evidently then we do not seek it for the sake of any other advantage; but as the man is free, we say, who exists for his own sake and not for another's, so we pursue this as the only free science, for it alone exists for its own sake.

Hence also the possession of it might be justly regarded as beyond human power; for in many ways human nature is in bondage, so that according to Simonides 'God alone can have this privilege,' and it is unfitting that man should not be content to seek the knowledge that is suited to him. If, then, there is something in what the poets say, and jealousy is natural to the divine power, it would probably occur in this case above all, and all who excelled in this knowledge would be unfortunate. But the divine power cannot be jealous (nay, according to the proverb, 'bards tell many a lie'), nor should any other science be thought more honourable than one of this sort. For the most divine science is also most honourable; and this science alone must be, in two ways, most divine. For the science which it would be most meet for God to have is a divine science, and so is any science that deals with divine objects; and this science alone has both these qualities; for (1) God is thought to be among the causes of all things and to be a first principle, and (2) such a science either God alone can have, or God above all others. All the sciences, indeed, are more necessary than this, but none is better.

Yet the acquisition of it must in a sense end in something which is the opposite of our original inquiries. For all men begin, as we said, by wondering that things are as they are, as they do about self-moving marionettes, or about the solstices or the incommensurability of the diagonal of a square with the side; for it seems wonderful to all who have not yet seen the reason, that there is a thing which cannot be measured even by the smallest unit. But we must end in the contrary and, according to the proverb, the better state, as is the case in these instances too when men learn the cause; for there is nothing which would surprise a geometer so much as if the diagonal turned out to be commensurable.

We have stated, then, what is the nature of the science we are searching for, and what is the mark which our search and our whole investigation must reach.

3. Evidently we have to acquire knowledge of the original causes (for we say we know each thing only when we think we recognize its first cause), and causes are spoken of in four senses. In one of these we mean the substance, i. e. the essence (for the 'why' is reducible finally to the definition, and the ultimate 'why' is a cause and principle); in another the matter or substratum, in a third the source of the change, and in a fourth the cause opposed to this, the purpose and the good (for this is the end of all generation and change). We have studied these causes sufficiently in our work on nature, but yet let us call to our aid those who have attacked the investigation of

being and philosophized about reality before us. For obviously they too speak of certain principles and causes; to go over their views, then, will be of profit to the present inquiry, for we shall either find another kind of cause, or be more convinced of the correctness of those which we now maintain.

Of the first philosophers, then, most thought the principles which were of the nature of matter were the only principles of all things. That of which all things that are consist, the first from which they come to be, the last into which they are resolved (the substance remaining, but changing in its modifications), this they say is the element and this the principle of things, and therefore they think nothing is either generated or destroyed, since this sort of entity is always conserved, as we say Socrates neither comes to be absolutely when he comes to be beautiful or musical, nor ceases to be when he loses these characteristics, because the substratum, Socrates himself, remains. Just so they say nothing else comes to be or ceases to be; for there must be some entity — either one or more than one — from which all other things come to be, it being conserved.

Yet they do not all agree as to the number and the nature of these principles. Thales, the founder of this type of philosophy, says the principle is water (for which reason he declared that the earth rests on water), getting the notion perhaps from seeing that the nutriment of all things is moist, and that heat itself is generated from the moist and kept alive by it (and that from which they come to be is a principle of all things). He got his notion from this fact, and from the fact that the seeds of all things have a moist nature, and that water is the origin of the nature of moist things.

Some think that even the ancients who lived long before the present generation, and first framed accounts of the gods, had a similar view of nature; for they made Ocean and Tethys the parents of creation, and described the oath of the gods as being by water, to which they give the name of Styx; for what is oldest is most honourable, and the most honourable thing is that by which one swears. It may perhaps be uncertain whether this opinion about nature is primitive and ancient, but Thales at any rate is said to have declared himself thus about the first cause. Hippo no one would think fit to include among these thinkers, because of the paltriness of his thought.

Anaximenes and Diogenes make air prior to water, and the most primary of the simple bodies, while Hippasus of Metapontium and Heraclitus of Ephesus say this of fire, and Empedocles says it of the four elements (adding a fourth — earth — to those which have been named); for these, he says, always remain and do not come to be, except that they come to be more or fewer, being aggregated into one and segregated out of one.

Anaxagoras of Clazomenae, who, though older than Empedocles, was later in his philosophical activity, says the principles are infinite in number; for he says almost all the things that are made of parts like themselves, in the manner of water or fire, are generated and destroyed in this way, only by aggregation and segregation, and are not in any other sense generated or destroyed, but remain eternally.

From these facts one might think that the only cause is the so-called material cause; but as men thus advanced, the very facts opened the way for them and joined in forcing them to investigate the subject. However true it may be that all generation and destruction proceed from some one or (for that matter) from more elements, why does this happen and what is the cause? For at least the substratum itself does not make itself change; e. g. neither the wood nor the bronze causes the change of either of them, nor does the wood manufacture a bed and the bronze a statue, but something else is the cause of the change. And to seek this is to seek the second cause, as *we* should say — that from which comes the beginning of the movement. Now those who at the very beginning set themselves to this kind of inquiry, and said the substratum was one,* were not at all dissatisfied with themselves; but some at least of those who maintain it to be one † — as though defeated by this search for the second cause — say the one and nature as a whole is unchangeable not only in respect of generation and destruction (for this is a primitive belief, and all agreed in it), but also of all other change; and this view is peculiar to them. Of those who said the universe was one, then, none succeeded in discovering a cause of this sort, except perhaps Parmenides, and he only inasmuch as he supposes that there is not only one but also in some sense two causes. But for those who make more elements ‡ it is more possible to state the second cause, e. g. for those who make hot and cold, or fire and earth, the elements; for they treat fire as having a nature which fits it to move things, and water and earth and such things they treat in the contrary way.

When these men and the principles of this kind had had their day, as the latter were found inadequate to generate the nature of things men were again forced by the truth itself, as we said, to inquire into the next kind of cause. For it is not likely either that fire or earth or any such element should be the reason why things manifest goodness and beauty both in their being and in their coming to be, or that those thinkers should have supposed it was; nor again could it be right to entrust so great a matter to spontaneity and chance. When one man § said, then, that reason was present — as in animals, so throughout nature — as the cause of order and of all arrangement, he seemed like a sober man in contrast with the random talk of his predecessors. We know that Anaxagoras certainly adopted these views, but Hermotimus of Clazomenae is credited with expressing them earlier. Those who thought thus stated that there is a principle of things which is at the same time the cause of beauty, and that sort of cause from which things acquire movement.

4. One might suspect that Hesiod was the first to look for such a thing — or some one else who put love or desire among existing things as a principle, as Parmenides, too, does; for he, in constructing the genesis of the universe, says: —

---

* Thales, Anaximenes, and Heraclitus.　　† The Eleatics.
‡ The reference is probably to Empedocles.　　§ Anaxagoras.

> Love first of all the Gods she planned.

And Hesiod says: —

> First of all things was chaos made, and then
> Broad-breasted earth, . . .
> And love, 'mid all the gods pre-eminent,

which implies that among existing things there must be from the first a cause which will move things and bring them together. How these thinkers should be arranged with regard to priority of discovery let us be allowed to decide later; but since the contraries of the various forms of good were also perceived to be present in nature — not only order and the beautiful, but also disorder and the ugly, and bad things in greater number than good, and ignoble things than beautiful — therefore another thinker introduced friendship and strife, each of the two the cause of one of these two sets of qualities. For if we were to follow out the view of Empedocles, and interpret it according to its meaning and not to its lisping expression, we should find that friendship is the cause of good things, and strife of bad. Therefore, if we said that Empedocles in a sense both mentions, and is the first to mention, the bad and the good as principles, we should perhaps be right, since the cause of all goods is the good itself.

These thinkers, as we say, evidently grasped, and to this extent, two of the causes which we distinguished in our work on nature — the matter and the source of the movement — vaguely, however, and with no clearness, but as untrained men behave in fights; for they go round their opponents and often strike fine blows, but they do not fight on scientific principles, and so too these thinkers do not seem to know what they say; for it is evident that, as a rule, they make no use of their causes except to a small extent. For Anaxagoras uses reason as a *deus ex machina* for the making of the world, and when he is at a loss to tell from what cause something necessarily is, then he drags reason in, but in all other cases ascribes events to anything rather than to reason. And Empedocles, though he uses the causes to a greater extent than this, neither does so sufficiently nor attains consistency in their use. At least, in many cases he makes love segregate things, and strife aggregate them. For whenever the universe is dissolved into its elements by strife, fire is aggregated into one, and so is each of the other elements; but whenever again under the influence of love they come together into one, the parts must again be segregated out of each element.

Empedocles, then, in contrast with his predecessors, was the first to introduce the dividing of this cause, not positing one source of movement, but different and contrary sources. Again, he was the first to speak of four material elements; yet he does not *use* four, but treats them as two only; he treats fire by itself, and its opposites — earth, air, and water — as one kind of thing. We may learn this by study of his verses.

This philosopher then, as we say, has spoken of the principles in this way, and made them of this number. Leucippus and his associate Democritus say that the full and the empty are the elements, calling the one being and the other non-being — the full and solid being being, the empty non-being (whence they say being no more is than non-being, because the solid no more is than the empty); and they make these the material causes of things.   And as those who make the underlying substance one generate all other things by its modifications, supposing the rare and the dense to be the sources of the modifications, in the same way these philosophers say the differences in the elements are the causes of all other qualities.   These differences, they say, are three — shape and order and position.   For they say the real is differentiated only by 'rhythm' and 'inter-contact' and 'turning'; and of these rhythm is shape, inter-contact is order, and turning is position; for A differs from N in shape, AN from NA in order, ☲ from H in position.   The question of movement — whence or how it is to belong to things — these thinkers, like the others, lazily neglected.

Regarding the two causes, then, as we say, the inquiry seems to have been pushed thus far by the early philosophers.

5. Contemporaneously with these philosophers and before them, the so-called Pythagoreans, who were the first to take up mathematics, not only advanced this study, but also having been brought up in it they thought its principles were the principles of all things.   Since of these principles numbers are by nature the first, and in numbers they seemed to see many resemblances to the things that exist and come into being — more than in fire and earth and water (such and such a modification of numbers being justice, another being soul and reason, another being opportunity — and similarly almost all other things being numerically expressible); since, again, they saw that the modifications and the ratios of the musical scales were expressible in numbers; — since, then, all other things seemed in their whole nature to be modelled on numbers, and numbers seemed to be the first things in the whole of nature, they supposed the elements of numbers to be the elements of all things, and the whole heaven to be a musical scale and a number.   And all the properties of numbers and scales which they could show to agree with the attributes and parts and the whole arrangement of the heavens, they collected and fitted into their scheme; and if there was a gap anywhere, they readily made additions so as to make their whole theory coherent.   E. g. as the number 10 is thought to be perfect and to comprise the whole nature of numbers, they say that the bodies which move through the heavens are ten, but as the visible bodies are only nine, to meet this they invent a tenth — the 'counter-earth.'   We have discussed these matters more exactly elsewhere.

But the object of our review is that we may learn from these philosophers also what they suppose to be the principles and how these fall under the causes we have named.   Evidently, then, these thinkers also consider that number is the principle both as matter for things and as forming both their modifications and their permanent states.

and hold that the elements of number are the even and the odd, and that of these the latter is limited, and the former unlimited; and that the One proceeds from both of these (for it is both even and odd), and number from the One; and that the whole heaven, as has been said, is numbers.

Other members of this same school say there are ten principles, which they arrange in two columns of cognates — limit and unlimited, odd and even, one and plurality, right and left, male and female, resting and moving, straight and curved, light and darkness, good and bad, square and oblong.   In this way Alcmaeon of Croton seems also to have conceived the matter, and either he got this view from them or they got it from him; for he expressed himself similarly to them.   For he says most human affairs go in pairs, meaning not definite contrarieties such as the Pythagoreans speak of, but any chance contrarieties, e. g. white and black, sweet and bitter, good and bad, great and small.   He threw out indefinite suggestions about the other contrarieties, but the Pythagoreans declared both how many and which their contrarieties are.

From both these schools, then, we can learn this much, that the contraries are the principles of things; and how many these principles are and which they are, we can learn from one of the two schools.   But how these principles can be brought together under the causes we have named has not been clearly and articulately stated by them; they seem, however, to range the elements under the head of matter; for out of these as immanent parts they say substance is composed and moulded.

From these facts we may sufficiently perceive the meaning of the ancients who said the elements of nature were more than one; but there are some who spoke of the universe as if it were one entity, though they were not all alike either in the excellence of their statement or in its conformity to the facts of nature.   The discussion of them is in no way appropriate to our present investigation of causes, for they do not, like some of the natural philosophers, assume being to be one and yet generate it out of the one as out of matter, but they speak in another way; those others add change, since they generate the universe, but these thinkers say the universe is unchangeable.   Yet *this* much is germane to the present inquiry: Parmenides seems to fasten on that which is one in definition, Melissus on that which is one in matter, for which reason the former says that it is limited, the latter that it is unlimited; while Xenophanes, the first of these partisans of the One (for Parmenides is said to have been his pupil), gave no clear statement, nor does he seem to have grasped the nature of either of these causes, but with reference to the whole material universe he says the One is God.   Now these thinkers, as we said, must be neglected for the purposes of the present inquiry — two of them entirely, as being a little too naïve, viz. Xenophanes and Melissus; but Parmenides seems in places to speak with more insight. For, claiming that, besides the existent, nothing non-existent exists, he thinks that of necessity one thing exists, viz. the existent and nothing else (on this we have spoken more clearly in our work on nature), but being forced to follow the observed facts, and supposing the existence of that which is one in definition, but more than one according to our sensations, he now posits two causes and two principles, calling them hot and cold, i. e. fire and earth; and of these he ranges the hot with the existent, and the other with the non-existent.

From what has been said, then, and from the wise men who have now sat in council with us, we have got thus much — on the one hand from the earliest philosophers, who regard the first principle as corporeal (for water and fire and such things are bodies), and of whom some suppose that there is one corporeal principle, others that there are more than one, but both put these under the head of matter; and on the other hand from some who posit both this cause and besides this the source of movement, which we have got from some as single and from others as twofold.

Down to the Italian school, then, and apart from it, philosophers have treated these subjects rather obscurely, except that, as we said, they have in fact used two kinds of cause, and one of these — the source of movement — some treat as one and others as two. But the Pythagoreans have said in the same way that there are two principles, but added this much, which is peculiar to them, that they thought that finitude and infinity were not attributes of certain other things, e. g. of fire or earth or anything else of this kind, but that infinity itself and unity itself were the substance of the things of which they are predicated. This is why number was the substance of all things. On this subject, then, they expressed themselves thus; and regarding the question of essence they began to make statements and definitions, but treated the matter too simply. For they both defined superficially and thought that the first subject of which a given definition was predicable was the substance of the thing defined, as if one supposed that 'double' and '2' were the same, because 2 is the first thing of which 'double' is predicable. But surely to be double and to be 2 are not the same; if they are, one thing will be many — a consequence which they actually drew. From the earlier philosophers, then, and from their successors we can learn thus much.

6. After the systems we have named came the philosophy of Plato, which in most respects followed these thinkers, but had peculiarities that distinguished it from the philosophy of the Italians. For, having in his youth first become familiar with Cratylus and with the Heraclitean doctrines (that all sensible things are ever in a state of flux and there is no knowledge about them), these views he held even in later years. Socrates, however, was busying himself about ethical matters and neglecting the world of nature as a whole but seeking the universal in these ethical matters, and fixed thought for the first time on definitions; Plato accepted his teaching, but held that the problem applied not to sensible things but to entities of another kind — for this

reason, that the common definition could not be a definition of any sensible thing, as they were always changing. Things of this other sort, then, he called Ideas, and sensible things, he said, were all named after these, and in virtue of a relation to these; for the many existed by participation in the Ideas that have the same name as they. Only the name 'participation' was new; for the Pythagoreans say that things exist by 'imitation' of numbers, and Plato says they exist by participation, changing the name. But what the participation or the imitation of the Forms could be they left an open question.

Further, besides sensible things and Forms he says there are the objects of mathematics, which occupy an intermediate position, differing from sensible things in being eternal and unchangeable, from Forms in that there are many alike, while the Form itself is in each case unique.

Since the Forms were the causes of all other things, he thought their elements were the elements of all things. As matter, the great and the small were principles; as essential reality, the One; for from the great and the small, by participation in the One, come the Numbers.

But he agreed with the Pythagoreans in saying that the One is substance and not a predicate of something else; and in saying that the Numbers are the causes of the reality of other things he agreed with them; but positing a dyad and constructing the infinite out of great and small, instead of treating the infinite as one, is peculiar to him; and so is his view that the Numbers exist apart from sensible things, while *they* say that the things themselves are Numbers, and do not place the objects of mathematics between Forms and sensible things. His divergence from the Pythagoreans in making the One and the Numbers separate from things, and his introduction of the Forms, were due to his inquiries in the region of definitions (for the earlier thinkers had no tincture of dialectic), and his making the other entity besides the One a dyad was due to the belief that the numbers, except those which were prime, could be neatly produced out of the dyad as out of some plastic material.

Yet what *happens* is the contrary; the theory is not a reasonable one. For they make many things out of the matter, and the form generates only once, but what we observe is that one table is made from one matter, while the man who applies the form, though he is one, makes many tables. And the relation of the male to the female is similar; for the latter is impregnated by one copulation, but the male impregnates many females; yet these are analogues of those first principles.

Plato, then, declared himself thus on the points in question; it is evident from what has been said that he has used only two causes, that of the essence and the material cause (for the Forms are the causes of the essence of all other things, and the One is the cause of the essence of the Forms); and it is evident what the underlying matter is, of which the Forms are predicated in the case of sensible things, and the One in the case of Forms, viz. that this is a dyad, the great and the small. Further, he has assigned the cause of good and that of evil to the elements, one to each of the two, as we say some of his predecessors sought to do, e. g. Empedocles and Anaxagoras.

7. Our review of those who have spoken about first principles and reality and of the way in which they have spoken, has been concise and summary; but yet we have learnt *this* much from them, that of those who speak about 'principle' and 'cause' no one has mentioned any principle except those which have been distinguished in our work on nature, but all evidently have some inkling of *them,* though only vaguely. For some speak of the first principle as matter, whether they suppose one or more first principles, and whether they suppose this to be a body or to be incorporeal; e. g. Plato spoke of the great and the small, the Italians of the infinite, Empedocles of fire, earth, water, and air, Anaxagoras of the infinity of things composed of similar parts. These, then, have all had a notion of this kind of cause, and so have all who speak of air or fire or water, or something denser than fire and rarer than air; for some have said the prime element is of this kind.

These thinkers grasped this cause only; but certain others have mentioned the source of movement, e. g. those who make friendship and strife, or reason, or love, a principle.

The essence, i. e. the substantial reality, no one has expressed distinctly. It is hinted at chiefly by those who believe in the Forms; for they do not suppose either that the Forms are the matter of sensible things, and the One the matter of the Forms, or that they are the source of movement (for they say these are causes rather of immobility and of being at rest), but they furnish the Forms as the essence of every other thing, and the One as the essence of the Forms.

That for whose sake actions and changes and movements take place, they assert to be a cause in a way, but not in this way, i. e. not in the way in which it is its *nature* to be a cause. For those who speak of reason or friendship class these causes as goods; they do not speak, however, as if anything that exists either existed or came into being for the sake of these, but as if movements started from these. In the same way those who say the One or the existent is the good, say that it is the cause of substance, but not that substance either is or comes to be for the sake of this. Therefore it turns out that in a sense they both say and do not say the good is a cause; for they do not call it a cause *qua* good but only incidentally.

All these thinkers, then, as they cannot pitch on another cause, seem to testify that we have determined rightly both how many and of what sort the causes are. Besides this it is plain that when the causes are being looked for, either all four must be sought thus or they must be sought in one of these four ways. Let us next discuss the possible difficulties with regard to the way in which each of these thinkers has spoken, and with regard to his situation relatively to the first principles.

8. Those, then, who say the universe is one and posit one kind of thing as matter, and as corporeal matter which has spatial magnitude, evidently go astray in many ways. For they posit the elements of bodies only, not of incorporeal things, though there are also incorporeal things. And in trying to state the causes of generation and destruction, and in giving a physical account of all things, they do away with the cause of movement. Further, they err in not positing the substance, i. e. the essence, as the cause of anything, and besides this in lightly calling any of the simple bodies except earth the first principle, without inquiring how they are produced out of one another, — I mean fire, water, earth, and air. For some things are produced out of each other by combination, others by separation, and this makes the greatest difference to their priority and posteriority. For (1) in a way the property of being most elementary of all would seem to belong to the first thing from which they are produced by combination, and *this* property would belong to the most fine-grained and subtle of bodies. For this reason those who make fire the principle would be most in agreement with this argument. But each of the other thinkers agrees that the element of corporeal things is of this sort. At least none of those who named one element claimed that earth was the element, evidently because of the coarseness of its grain. (Of the other three elements each has found some judge on its side; for some maintain that fire, others that water, others that air is the element. Yet why, after all, do they not name earth also, as most men do? For people say all things are earth. And Hesiod says earth was produced first of corporeal things; so primitive and popular has the opinion been.) According to this argument, then, no one would be right who either says the first principle is any of the elements other than fire, or supposes it to be denser than air but rarer than water. But (2) if that which is later in generation is prior in nature, and that which is concocted and compounded is later in generation, the contrary of what we have been saying must be true — water must be prior to air, and earth to water.

So much, then, for those who posit one cause such as we mentioned; but the same is true if one supposes more of these, as Empedocles says the matter of things is four bodies. For he too is confronted by consequences some of which are the same as have been mentioned, while others are peculiar to him. For we see these bodies produced from one another, which implies that the same body does not always remain fire or earth (we have spoken about this in our works on nature); and regarding the cause of movement and the question whether we must posit one or two, he must be thought to have spoken neither correctly nor altogether plausibly. And in general, change of quality is necessarily done away with for those who speak thus, for on their view cold will not come from hot nor hot from cold. For if it did there would be something that accepted the contraries themselves, and there would be some one entity that became fire and water, which Empedocles denies.

As regards Anaxagoras, if one were to suppose that he said there were two elements, the supposition would accord thoroughly with an argument which Anaxagoras himself did not state articulately, but which he must have accepted if any one had led him on to it.   True, to say that in the beginning all things were mixed is absurd both on other grounds and because it follows that they must have existed before in an unmixed form, and because nature does not allow any chance thing to be mixed with any chance thing, and also because on this view modifications and accidents could be separated from substances (for the same things which are mixed can be separated); yet if one were to follow him up, piecing together what he means, he would perhaps be seen to be somewhat modern in his views.   For when nothing was separated out, evidently nothing could be truly asserted of the substance that then existed.   I mean, e. g., that it was neither white nor black, nor grey nor any other colour, but of necessity colourless; for if it had been coloured, it would have had one of these colours.   And similarly, by this same argument, it was flavourless, nor had it any similar attribute; for it could not be either of any quality or of any size, nor could it be any definite kind of thing.   For if it were, one of the particular forms would have belonged to it, and this is impossible, since all were mixed together; for the particular form would necessarily have been already separated out, but he says all were mixed except reason, and this alone was unmixed and pure.   From this it follows, then, that he must say the principles are the One (for this is simple and unmixed) and the Other, which is of such a nature as we suppose the indefinite to be before it is defined and partakes of some form.   Therefore, while expressing himself neither rightly nor clearly, he means something like what the later thinkers say and what is now more clearly seen to be the case.

But these thinkers are, after all, at home only in arguments about generation and destruction and movement; for it is practically only of this sort of substance that they seek the principles and the causes. But those who extend their vision to all things that exist, and of existing things suppose some to be perceptible and others not perceptible evidently study both classes, which is all the more reason why one should devote some time to seeing what is good in their views and what bad from the standpoint of the inquiry we have now before us.

The 'Pythagoreans' treat of principles and elements stranger than those of the physical philosophers (the reason is that they got the principles from non-sensible things, for the objects of mathematics, except those of astronomy, are of the class of things without movement); yet their discussions and investigations are all about nature; for they generate the heavens, and with regard to their parts and attributes and functions they observe the phenomena, and use up the principles and the causes in explaining these, which implies that they agree with the others, the physical philosophers, that the *real* is just all that which is perceptible and contained by the so-called 'heavens.' But the causes and the principles which they mention are, as we said, sufficient to act as steps even up to the higher realms of reality, and are more suited to these than to theories about nature. They do not tell us at all, however, how there can be movement if limit and unlimited and odd and even are the only things assumed, or how without movement and change there can be generation and destruction, or the bodies that move through the heavens can do what they do.

Further, if one either granted them that spatial magnitude consists of these elements, or this were proved, still how would some bodies be light and others have weight? To judge from what they assume and maintain they are speaking no more of mathematical bodies than of perceptible; hence they have said nothing whatever about fire or earth or the other bodies of this sort, I suppose because they have nothing to say which applies *peculiarly* to perceptible things.

Further, how are we to combine the beliefs that the attributes of number, and number itself, are causes of what exists and happens in the heavens both from the beginning and now, and that there is no other number than this number out of which the world is composed? When in one particular region they place opinion and opportunity, and, a little above or below, injustice and decision or mixture, and allege, as proof, that each of these is a number, and that there happens to be already in this place a plurality of the extended bodies composed of numbers, because these attributes of number attach to the various places — this being so, is this number, which we must suppose each of these abstractions to be, the same number which is exhibited in the material universe, or is it another than this? Plato says it is different; yet even he thinks that both these bodies and their causes are numbers, but that the *intelligible* numbers are causes, while the others are *sensible*.

9. Let us leave the Pythagoreans for the present; for it is enough to have touched on them as much as we have done. But as for those who posit the Ideas as causes, firstly, in seeking to grasp the causes of the things around us, they introduced others equal in number to these, as if a man who wanted to count things thought he would not be able to do it while they were few, but tried to count them when he had added to their number. For the Forms are practically equal to — or not fewer than — the things, in trying to explain which these thinkers proceeded from them to the Forms. For to each thing there answers an entity which has the same name and exists apart from the substances, and so also in the case of all other groups there is a one over many, whether the many are in this world or are eternal.

Further, of the ways in which we prove that the Forms exist, none is convincing; for from some no inference necessarily follows, and from some arise Forms even of things of which we think there are no Forms. For according to the arguments from the existence of the sciences there will be Forms of all things of which there are sciences, and according to the 'one over many' argument there will be Forms even of negations, and according to the argument that there is an object for thought even when the thing has perished, there will be Forms of perishable things; for we have an image of these. Further, of the more accurate arguments, some lead to Ideas of relations, of which we say there is no independent class, and others introduce the 'third man.'

And in general the arguments for the Forms destroy the things for whose existence we are more zealous than for the existence of the Ideas; for it follows that not the dyad but number is first, i. e. that the relative is prior to the absolute — besides all the other points on which certain people by following out the opinions held about the Ideas have come into conflict with the principles of the theory.

Further, according to the assumption on which our belief in the Ideas rests, there will be Forms not only of substances but also of many other things (for the concept is single not only in the case of substances but also in the other cases, and there are sciences not only of substance but also of other things, and a thousand other such difficulties confront them). But according to the necessities of the case and the opinions held about the Forms, if Forms can be shared in there must be Ideas of substances only. For they are not shared in incidentally, but a thing must share in its Forms as in something not predicated of a subject (by 'being shared in incidentally' I mean that e. g. if a thing shares in 'double itself,' it shares also in 'eternal,' but incidentally; for 'eternal' happens to be predicable of the 'double'). Therefore the Forms will be substance; but the same terms indicate substance in this and in the ideal world (or what will be the meaning of saying that there is something apart from the particulars — the one over many?). And if the Ideas and the particulars that share in them have the same form, there will be something common to these; for why should '2' be one and the same in the perishable 2's or in those which are many but eternal, and not the same in the '2 itself' as in the particular 2? But if they have not the same form, they must have only the name in common, and it is as if one were to call both Callias and a wooden image a 'man,' without observing any community between them.

Above all one might discuss the question what on earth the Forms contribute to sensible things, either to those that are eternal or to those that come into being and cease to be. For they cause neither movement nor any change in them. But again they help in no wise either towards the knowledge of the other things (for they are not even the substance of these, else they would have been in them), or towards their being, if they are not *in* the particulars which share in them; though if they were, they might be thought to be causes, as white causes whiteness in a white object by entering into its composition. But this argument, which first Anaxagoras and later Eudoxus and certain others used, is very easily upset; for it is not difficult to collect many insuperable objections to such a view.

But, further, all other things cannot come from the Forms in any of the usual senses of 'from.' And to say that they are patterns and the other things share in them is to use empty words and poetical metaphors. For what is it that works, looking to the Ideas? And anything can either be, or become, like another without being copied from it, so that whether Socrates exists or not a man like Socrates might come to be; and evidently this might be so even if Socrates were eternal. And there will be several patterns of the same thing, and therefore several Forms; e. g. 'animal' and 'two-footed' and also 'man himself' will be Forms of man. Again, the Forms are patterns not only of sensible things, but of Forms themselves also; i. e. the genus, as genus of various species, will be so; therefore the same thing will be pattern and copy.

Again, it would seem impossible that the substance and that of which it is the substance should exist apart; how, therefore, could the Ideas, being the substances of things, exist apart? In the *Phaedo* the case is stated in this way—that the Forms are causes both of being and of becoming; yet when the Forms exist, still the things that share in them do not come into being, unless there is something to originate movement; and many other things come into being (e. g. a house or a ring) of which we say there are no Forms. Clearly, therefore, even the other things can both be and come into being owing to such causes as produce the things just mentioned.

Again, if the Forms are numbers, how can they be causes? Is it because existing things are other numbers, e. g. one number is man, another is Socrates, another Callias? Why then are the one set of numbers causes of the other set? It will not make any difference even if the former are eternal and the latter are not. But if it is because things in this sensible world (e. g. harmony) are ratios of numbers, evidently the things between which they are ratios are some one class of things. If, then, this—the matter—is some definite thing, evidently the numbers themselves too will be ratios of something to something else. E. g. if Callias is a numerical ratio between fire and earth and water and air, his Idea also will be a number of certain other underlying things; and man-himself, whether it is a number in a sense or not, will still be a numerical ratio of certain things and not a number proper, nor will it be a kind of number merely because it is a numerical ratio.

Again, from many numbers one number is produced, but how can one Form come from many Forms? And if the number comes not from the many numbers themselves but from the units in them, e. g. in 10,000, how is it with the units? If they are specifically alike, numerous absurdities will follow, and also if they are not alike (neither the units in one number being themselves like one another nor those in other numbers being all like to all); for in what will they differ, as they are without quality? This is not a plausible view, nor is it consistent with our thought on the matter.

Further, they must set up a second kind of number (with which arithmetic deals), and all the objects which are called 'intermediate' by some thinkers; and how do these exist or from what principles do they proceed? Or why must they be intermediate between the things in this sensible world and the things-themselves?

Further, the units in 2 must each come from a prior 2; but this is impossible.

Further, why is a number, when taken all together, one?

Again, besides what has been said, if the units are *diverse* the Platonists should have spoken like those who say there are four, or two, elements; for each of these thinkers gives the name of element not to that which is common, e. g. to body, but to fire and earth, whether there is something common to them, viz. body, or not. But in fact the Platonists speak as if the One were *homogeneous* like fire or water; and if this is so, the numbers will not be substances. Evidently, if there is a One-itself and this is a first principle, 'one' is being used in more than one sense; for otherwise the theory is impossible.

When we wish to reduce substances to their principles, we state that lines come from the short and long (i. e. from a kind of small and great), and the plane from the broad and narrow, and body from the deep and shallow. Yet how then can either the plane contain a line or the solid a line or a plane? For the broad and narrow is a different class from the deep and shallow. Therefore, just as number is not present in these, because the many and few are different from these, evidently no other of the higher classes will be present in the lower. But again the broad is not a genus which includes the deep, for then the solid would have been a species of plane. Further, from what principle will the presence of the *points* in the line be derived? Plato even used to object to this class of things as being a geometrical fiction. He gave the name of principle of the line — and this he often posited — to the indivisible lines. Yet these must have a limit; therefore the argument from which the existence of the line follows proves also the existence of the point.

In general, though philosophy seeks the cause of perceptible things, we have given this up (for we say nothing of the cause from which change takes its start), but while we fancy we are stating the substance of perceptible things, we assert the existence of a second class of substances, while our account of the way in which they are the substances of perceptible things is empty talk; for 'sharing,' as we said before, means nothing.

Nor have the Forms any connexion with what we see to be the cause in the case of the arts, that for whose sake both all mind and the whole of nature are operative * — with this cause which we assert to be one of the first principles; but mathematics has come to be identical with philosophy for modern thinkers, though they say that it should be studied for the sake of other things.

Further, one might suppose that the substance which according to them underlies as matter is too mathematical, and is a predicate and differentia of the substance, i. e. of the matter, rather than matter itself; i. e. the great and the small are like the rare and the dense which the physical philosophers speak of, calling these the primary differentiae of the substratum; for these are a kind of excess and defect. And regarding movement, if the great and the small are to

* *sc.* the final cause.

be movement, evidently the Forms will be moved; but if they are not to be movement, whence did movement come? The whole study of nature has been annihilated.

And what is thought to be easy — to show that all things are one — is not done; for what is proved by the method of setting out instances is not that all things are one but that there is a One-itself, — if we grant all the assumptions. And not even this follows, if we do not grant that the universal is a genus; and this in some cases it cannot be.

Nor can it be explained either how the lines and planes and solids that come after the numbers exist or can exist, or what significance they have; for these can neither be Forms (for they are not numbers), nor the intermediates (for those are the objects of mathematics), nor the perishable things. This is evidently a distinct fourth class.

In general, if we search for the elements of existing things without distinguishing the many senses in which things are said to exist, we cannot find them, especially if the search for the elements of which things are made is conducted in this manner. For it is surely impossible to discover what 'acting' or 'being acted on,' or 'the straight,' is made of, but if elements can be discovered at all, it is only the elements of substances; therefore either to seek the elements of all existing things or to think one has them is incorrect.

And how could we *learn* the elements of all things? Evidently we cannot start by knowing anything before. For as he who is learning geometry, though he may know other things before, knows none of the things with which the science deals and about which he is to learn, so is it in all other cases. Therefore if there is a science of all things, such as some assert to exist, he who is learning this will know nothing before. Yet all learning is by means of premises which are (either all or some of them) known before — whether the learning be by demonstration or by definitions; for the elements of the definition must be known before and be familiar; and learning by induction proceeds similarly. But again, if the science were actually innate, it were strange that we are unaware of our possession of the greatest of sciences.

Again, how is one to *come to know* what all things are made of, and how is this to be made *evident?* This also affords a difficulty; for there might be a conflict of opinion, as there is about certain syllables; some say *za* is made out of *s* and *d* and *a,* while others say it is a distinct sound and none of those that are familiar.

Further, how could we know the objects of sense without having the sense in question? Yet we ought to, if the elements of which all things consist, as complex sounds consist of the elements proper to sound, are the same.

10. It is evident, then, even from what we have said before, that all men seem to seek the causes named in the *Physics,* and that we cannot name any beyond these; but they seek these vaguely; and though in a sense they have all been described before, in a sense they have

not been described at all. For the earliest philosophy is, on all subjects, like one who lisps, since it is young and in its beginnings. For even Empedocles says bone exists by virtue of the ratio in it. Now this is the essence and the substance of the thing. But it is similarly necessary that flesh and each of the other tissues should be the ratio of its elements, or that not one of them should; for it is on account of this that both flesh and bone and everything else will exist, and not on account of the matter, which *he* names — fire and earth and water and air. But while he would necessarily have agreed if another had said this, he has not said it clearly.

On these questions our views have been expressed before; but let us return to enumerate the difficulties that might be raised on these same points; for perhaps we may get from them some help towards our later difficulties.

[tr. W. D. Ross]

NICOMACHEAN ETHICS

BOOK II

1. Virtue, then, being of two kinds, intellectual and moral, intellectual virtue in the main owes both its birth and its growth to teaching (for which reason it requires experience and time), while moral virtue comes about as a result of habit, whence also its name *ethike* is one that is formed by a slight variation from the word *ethos* (habit). From this it is also plain that none of the moral virtues arises in us by nature; for nothing that exists by nature can form a habit contrary to its nature. For instance the stone which by nature moves downwards cannot be habituated to move upwards, not even if one tries to train it by throwing it up ten thousand times; nor can fire be habituated to move downwards, nor can anything else that by nature behaves in one way be trained to behave in another. Neither by nature, then, nor contrary to nature do the virtues arise in us; rather we are adapted by nature to receive them, and are made perfect by habit.

Again, of all the things that come to us by nature we first acquire the potentiality and later exhibit the activity (this is plain in the case of the senses; for it was not by often seeing or often hearing that we got these senses, but on the contrary we had them before we used them, and did not come to have them by using them); but the virtues we get by first exercising them, as also happens in the case of the arts as well. For the things we have to learn before we can do them, we learn by doing them, e. g. men become builders by building and lyre-players by playing the lyre; so too we become just by doing just acts, temperate by doing temperate acts, brave by doing brave acts.

This is confirmed by what happens in states; for legislators make the citizens good by forming habits in them, and this is the wish of every legislator, and those who do not effect it miss their mark, and it is in this that a good constitution differs from a bad one.

Again, it is from the same causes and by the same means that every virtue is both produced and destroyed, and similarly every art; for it is from playing the lyre that both good and bad lyre-players are produced. And the corresponding statement is true of builders and of all the rest; men will be good or bad builders as a result of building well or badly. For if this were not so, there would have been no need of a teacher, but all men would have been born good or bad at their craft. This, then, is the case with the virtues also; by doing the acts that we do in our transactions with other men we become just or unjust, and by doing the acts that we do in the presence of danger, and being habituated to feel fear or confidence, we become brave or cowardly. The same is true of appetites and feelings of anger; some men become temperate and good-tempered, others self-indulgent and irascible, by behaving in one way or the other in the appropriate circumstances Thus, in one word, states of character arise out of like activities. This is why the activities we exhibit must be of a certain kind; it is because the states of character correspond to the differences between these. It makes no small difference, then, whether we form habits of one kind or of another from our very youth; it makes a very great difference, or rather *all* the difference.

2. Since, then, the present inquiry does not aim at theoretical knowledge like the others (for we are inquiring not in order to know what virtue is, but in order to become good, since otherwise our inquiry would have been of no use), we must examine the nature of actions, namely how we ought to do them; for these determine also the nature of the states of character that are produced, as we have said. Now, that we must act according to the right rule is a common principle and must be assumed — it will be discussed later, i. e. both what the right rule is, and how it is related to the other virtues. But this must be agreed upon beforehand, that the whole account of matters of conduct must be given in outline and not precisely, as we said at the very beginning that the accounts we demand must be in accordance with the subject-matter; matters concerned with conduct and questions of what is good for us have no fixity, any more than matters of health. The general account being of this nature, the account of particular cases is yet more lacking in exactness; for they do not fall under any art or precept but the agents themselves must in each case consider what is appropriate to the occasion, as happens also in the art of medicine or of navigation.

But though our present account is of this nature we must give what help we can. First, then, let us consider this, that it is the nature of such things to be destroyed by defect and excess, as we see in the case of strength and of health (for to gain light on things imperceptible we must use the evidence of sensible things); both excessive and defective exercise destroys the strength, and similarly drink or food which is above or below a certain amount destroys the health, while that which is proportionate both produces and increases and preserves it. So too is it, then, in the case of temperance and courage and the other virtues. For the man who flies from and fears everything and does not stand his ground against anything becomes a coward, and the man who fears nothing at all but goes to meet every danger becomes rash; and similarly the man who indulges in every pleasure and abstains from none becomes self-indulgent, while the man who shuns every pleasure, as boors do, becomes in a way insensible; temperance and courage, then, are destroyed by excess and defect, and preserved by the mean.

But not only are the sources and causes of their origination and growth the same as those of their destruction, but also the sphere of their actualization will be the same; for this is also true of the things which are more evident to sense, e. g. of strength; it is produced by taking much food and undergoing much exertion, and it is the strong man that will be most able to do these things. So too is it with the virtues; by abstaining from pleasures we become temperate, and it is when we have become so that we are most able to abstain from them; and similarly too in the case of courage; for by being habituated to despise things that are terrible and to stand our ground against them we become brave, and it is when we have become so that we shall be most able to stand our ground against them.

3. We must take as a sign of states of character the pleasure or pain that ensues on acts; for the man who abstains from bodily pleasures and delights in this very fact is temperate, while the man who is annoyed at it is self-indulgent, and he who stands his ground against things that are terrible and delights in this or at least is not pained is brave, while the man who is pained is a coward. For moral excellence is concerned with pleasures and pains; it is on account of the pleasure that we do bad things, and on account of the pain that we abstain from noble ones. Hence we ought to have been brought up in a particular way from our very youth, as Plato says, so as both to delight in and to be pained by the things that we ought; for this is the right education.

Again, if the virtues are concerned with actions and passions, and every passion and every action is accompanied by pleasure and pain, for this reason also virtue will be concerned with pleasures and pains. This is indicated also by the fact that punishment is inflicted by these means; for it is a kind of cure, and it is the nature of cures to be effected by contraries.

Again, as we said but lately, every state of soul has a nature relative to and concerned with the kind of things by which it tends to be made worse or better; but it is by reason of pleasures and pains that men become bad, by pursuing and avoiding these — either the pleasures and pains they ought not or when they ought not or as they ought not, or by going wrong in one of the other similar ways that may be distinguished. Hence men even define the virtues as certain states of impassivity and rest; not well, however, because they speak absolutely, and do not say 'as one ought' and 'as one ought not' and 'when one ought or ought not,' and the other things that may be added. We assume, then, that this kind of excellence tends to do what is best with regard to pleasures and pains, and vice does the contrary.

The following facts also may show us that virtue and vice are concerned with these same things. There being three objects of choice and three of avoidance, the noble, the advantageous, the pleasant, and their contraries, the base, the injurious, the painful, about all of these the good man tends to go right and the bad man to go wrong, and especially about pleasure; for this is common to the animals, and also it accompanies all objects of choice; for even the noble and the advantageous appear pleasant.

Again, it has grown up with us all from our infancy; this is why it is difficult to rub off this passion, engrained as it is in our life. And we measure even our actions, some of us more and others less, by the rule of pleasure and pain. For this reason, then, our whole inquiry must be about these; for to feel delight and pain rightly or wrongly has no small effect on our actions.

Again, it is harder to fight with pleasure than with anger, to use Heraclitus' phrase, but both art and virtue are always concerned with what is harder; for even the good is better when it is harder. Therefore for this reason also the whole concern both of virtue and of political science is with pleasures and pains; for the man who uses these well will be good, he who uses them badly bad.

That virtue, then, is concerned with pleasures and pains, and that by the acts from which it arises it is both increased and, if they are done differently, destroyed, and that the acts from which it arose are those in which it actualizes itself — let this be taken as said.

4. The question might be asked, what we mean by saying that we must become just by doing just acts, and temperate by doing temperate acts; for if men do just and temperate acts, they are already just and temperate, exactly as, if they do what is in accordance with the laws of grammar and of music, they are grammarians and musicians.

Or is this not true even of the arts? It is possible to do something that is in accordance with the laws of grammar, either by chance or at the suggestion of another. A man will be a grammarian, then, only when he has both done something grammatical and done it grammatically; and this means doing it in accordance with the grammatical knowledge in himself.

Again, the case of the arts and that of the virtues are not similar; for the products of the arts have their goodness in themselves, so that it is enough that they should have a certain character, but if the acts that are in accordance with the virtues have themselves a certain character it does not follow that they are done justly or temperately. The agent also must be in a certain condition when he does them; in the first place he must have knowledge, secondly he must choose the acts, and choose them for their own sakes, and thirdly his action must proceed from a firm and unchangeable character. These are not reckoned in as conditions of the possession of the arts, except the bare knowledge; but as a condition of the possession of the virtues knowledge has little or no weight, while the other conditions count not for a little but for everything, i. e. the very conditions which result from often doing just and temperate acts.

Actions, then, are called just and temperate when they are such as the just or the temperate man would do; but it is not the man who does these that is just and temperate, but the man who also does them *as* just and temperate men do them. It is well said, then, that it is by doing just acts that the just man is produced, and by doing temperate acts the temperate man; without doing these no one would have even a prospect of becoming good.

But most people do not do these, but take refuge in theory and think they are being philosophers and will become good in this way, behaving somewhat like patients who listen attentively to their doctors, but do none of the things they are ordered to do. As the latter will not be made well in body by such a course of treatment, the former will not be made well in soul by such a course of philosophy.

5. Next we must consider what virtue is. Since things that are found in the soul are of three kinds — passions, faculties, states of character, virtue must be one of these. By passions I mean appetite, anger, fear, confidence, envy, joy, friendly feeling, hatred, longing, emulation, pity, and in general the feelings that are accompanied by pleasure or pain; by faculties the things in virtue of which we are said to be capable of feeling these, e. g. of becoming angry or being pained or feeling pity; by states of character the things in virtue of which we stand well or badly with reference to the passions, e. g. with reference to anger we stand badly if we feel it violently or too weakly, and well if we feel it moderately; and similarly with reference to the other passions.

Now neither the virtues nor the vices are *passions,* because we are not called good or bad on the ground of our passions, but are so called on the ground of our virtues and our vices, and because we are neither praised nor blamed for our passions (for the man who feels fear or anger is not praised, nor is the man who simply feels anger blamed, but the man who feels it in a certain way), but for our virtues and our vices we *are* praised or blamed.

Again, we feel anger and fear without choice, but the virtues are modes of choice or involve choice. Further, in respect of the passions we are said to be moved, but in respect of the virtues and the vices we are said not to be moved but to be disposed in a particular way.

For these reasons also they are not *faculties*; for we are neither called good nor bad, nor praised nor blamed, for the simple capacity of feeling the passions; again, we have the faculties by nature, but we are not made good or bad by nature; we have spoken of this before.

If, then, the virtues are neither passions nor faculties, all that remains is that they should be *states of character*.

Thus we have stated what virtue is in respect of its genus.

6. We must, however, not only describe virtue as a state of character, but also say what sort of state it is. We may remark, then, that every virtue or excellence both brings into good condition the thing of which it is the excellence and makes the work of that thing be done well; e. g. the excellence of the eye makes both the eye and its work good; for it is by the excellence of the eye that we see well. Similarly the excellence of the horse makes a horse both good in itself and good at running and at carrying its rider and at awaiting the attack of the enemy. Therefore, if this is true in every case, the virtue of man also will be the state of character which makes a man good and which makes him do his own work well.

How this is to happen we have stated already, but it will be made plain also by the following consideration of the specific nature of virtue. In everything that is continuous and divisible it is possible to take more, less, or an equal amount, and that either in terms of the thing itself or relatively to us; and the equal is an intermediate between excess and defect. By the intermediate in the object I mean that which is equidistant from each of the extremes, which is one and the same for all men; by the intermediate relatively to us that which is neither too much nor too little — and this is not one, nor the same for all. For instance, if ten is many and two is few, six is the intermediate, taken in terms of the object; for it exceeds and is exceeded by an equal amount; this is intermediate according to arithmetical proportion. But the intermediate relatively to us is not to be taken so; if ten pounds are too much for a particular person to eat and two too little, it does not follow that the trainer will order six pounds; for this also is perhaps too much for the person who is to take it, or too little — too little for Milo, too much for the beginner in athletic exercises. The same is true of running and wrestling. Thus a master of any art avoids excess and defect, but seeks the intermediate and chooses this — the intermediate not in the object but relatively to us.

If it is thus, then, that every art does its work well — by looking to the intermediate and judging its works by this standard (so that we often say of good works of art that it is not possible either to take away or to add anything, implying that excess and defect destroy the goodness of works of art, while the mean preserves it; and good artists, as we say, look to this in their work), and if, further, virtue is more exact and better than any art, as nature also is, then virtue must have the quality of aiming at the intermediate. I mean moral virtue; for it is this that is concerned with passions and actions, and in these there is excess, defect, and the intermediate. For instance, both fear and confidence and appetite and anger and pity and in general pleasure and pain may be felt both too much and too little, and in both cases not well; but to feel them at the right times, with reference to the right objects, towards the right people, with the right motive, and in the right way, is what is both intermediate and best, and this is characteristic of virtue. Similarly with regard to actions also there is excess, defect, and the intermediate. Now virtue is concerned with passions and actions, in which excess is a form of failure, and so is defect, while the intermediate is praised and is a form of success; and being praised and being successful are both characteristics of virtue. Therefore virtue is a kind of mean, since, as we have seen, it aims at what is intermediate.

Again, it is possible to fail in many ways (for evil belongs to the class of the unlimited, as the Pythagoreans conjectured, and good to that of the limited), while to succeed is possible only in one way (for which reason also one is easy and the other difficult — to miss the mark easy, to hit it difficult); for these reasons also, then, excess and defect are characteristic of vice, and the mean of virtue;

For men are good in but one way, but bad in many.

Virtue, then, is a state of character concerned with choice, lying in a mean, i. e. the mean relative to us, this being determined by a rational principle, and by that principle by which the man of practical wisdom would determine it. Now it is a mean between two vices, that which depends on excess and that which depends on defect; and again it is a mean because the vices respectively fall short of or exceed what is right in both passions and actions, while virtue both finds and chooses that which is intermediate. Hence in respect of its substance and the definition which states its essence virtue is a mean, with regard to what is best and right an extreme.

But not every action nor every passion admits of a mean; for some have names that already imply badness, e. g. spite, shamelessness, envy, and in the case of actions adultery, theft, murder; for all of these and suchlike things imply by their names that they are themselves bad, and not the excesses or deficiencies of them. It is not possible, then, ever to be right with regard to them; one must always be wrong. Nor does goodness or badness with regard to such things depend on committing adultery with the right woman, at the right time, and in the right way, but simply to do any of them is to go wrong. It would be equally absurd, then, to expect that in unjust, cowardly, and voluptuous action there should be a mean, an excess, and a deficiency; for at that rate there would be a mean of excess and of deficiency, an excess of excess, and a deficiency of deficiency. But as there is no excess and deficiency of temperance and courage because what is intermediate is in a sense an extreme, so too of the actions we have mentioned there is no mean nor any excess and deficiency, but however they are done they are wrong; for in general there is neither a mean of excess and deficiency, nor excess and deficiency of a mean.

7. We must, however, not only make this general statement, but also apply it to the individual facts. For among statements about conduct those which are general apply more widely, but those which are particular are more genuine, since conduct has to do with individual

cases, and our statements must harmonize with the facts in these cases. We may take these cases from our table. With regard to feelings of fear and confidence courage is the mean; of the people who exceed, he who exceeds in fearlessness has no name (many of the states have no name), while the man who exceeds in confidence is rash, and he who exceeds in fear and falls short in confidence is a coward. With regard to pleasures and pains — not all of them, and not so much with regard to the pains — the mean is temperance, the excess self-indulgence. Persons deficient with regard to the pleasures are not often found; hence such persons also have received no name. But let us call them 'insensible.'

With regard to giving and taking of money the mean is liberality, the excess and the defect prodigality and meanness. In these actions people exceed and fall short in contrary ways; the prodigal exceeds in spending and falls short in taking, while the mean man exceeds in taking and falls short in spending. (At present we are giving a mere outline or summary, and are satisfied with this; later these states will be more exactly determined.) With regard to money there are also other dispositions — a mean, magnificence (for the magnificent man differs from the liberal man; the former deals with large sums, the latter with small ones), an excess, tastelessness and vulgarity, and a deficiency, niggardliness; these differ from the states opposed to liberality, and the mode of their difference will be stated later.

With regard to honour and dishonour the mean is proper pride, the excess is known as a sort of 'empty vanity,' and the deficiency is undue humility; and as we said liberality was related to magnificence, differing from it by dealing with small sums, so there is a state similarly related to proper pride, being concerned with small honours while that is concerned with great. For it is possible to desire honour as one ought, and more than one ought, and less, and the man who exceeds in his desires is called ambitious, the man who falls short unambitious, while the intermediate person has no name. The dispositions also are nameless, except that that of the ambitious man is called ambition. Hence the people who are at the extremes lay claim to the middle place; and we ourselves sometimes call the intermediate person ambitious and sometimes unambitious, and sometimes praise the ambitious man and sometimes the unambitious. The reason of our doing this will be stated in what follows; but now let us speak of the remaining states according to the method which has been indicated.

With regard to anger also there is an excess, a deficiency, and a mean. Although they can scarcely be said to have names, yet since we call the intermediate person good-tempered let us call the mean good temper; of the persons at the extremes let the one who exceeds be called irascible, and his vice irascibility, and the man who falls short an inirascible sort of person, and the deficiency inirascibility.

There are also three other means, which have a certain likeness to one another, but differ from one another: for they are all concerned with intercourse in words and actions, but differ in that one is concerned with truth in this sphere, the other two with pleasantness; and of this one kind is exhibited in giving amusement, the other in all the circumstances of life. We must therefore speak of these too, that we may the better see that in all things the mean is praiseworthy, and the extremes neither praiseworthy nor right, but worthy of blame. Now most of these states also have no names, but we must try, as in the other cases, to invent names ourselves so that we may be clear and easy to follow. With regard to truth, then, the intermediate is a truthful sort of person and the mean may be called truthfulness, while the pretence which exaggerates is boastfulness and the person characterized by it a boaster, and that which understates is mock modesty and the person characterized by it mock-modest. With regard to pleasantness in the giving of amusement the intermediate person is ready-witted and the disposition ready wit, the excess is buffoonery and the person characterized by it a buffoon, while the man who falls short is a sort of boor and his state is boorishness. With regard to the remaining kind of pleasantness, that which is exhibited in life in general, the man who is pleasant in the right way is friendly and the mean is friendliness, while the man who exceeds is an obsequious person if he has no end in view, a flatterer if he is aiming at his own advantage, and the man who falls short and is unpleasant in all circumstances is a quarrelsome and surly sort of person.

There are also means in the passions and concerned with the passions; since shame is not a virtue, and yet praise is extended to the modest man. For even in these matters one man is said to be intermediate, and another to exceed, as for instance the bashful man who is ashamed of everything; while he who falls short or is not ashamed of anything at all is shameless, and the intermediate person is modest. Righteous indignation is a mean between envy and spite, and these states are concerned with the pain and pleasures that are felt at the fortunes of our neighbours; the man who is characterized by righteous indignation is pained at undeserved good fortune, the envious man, going beyond him, is pained at all good fortune, and the spiteful man falls so far short of being pained that he even rejoices. But these states there will be an opportunity of describing elsewhere; with regard to justice, since it has not one simple meaning, we shall, after describing the other states, distinguish its two kinds and say how each of them is a mean; and similarly we shall treat also of the rational virtues.

8. There are three kinds of disposition, then, two of them vices, involving excess and deficiency respectively, and one a virtue, viz. the mean, and all are in a sense opposed to all; for the extreme states are contrary both to the intermediate state and to each other, and the intermediate to the extremes; as the equal is greater relatively to the less, less relatively to the greater, so the middle states are excessive relatively to the deficiencies, deficient relatively to the excesses, both in passions and in actions. For the brave man appears rash relatively

to the coward, and cowardly relatively to the rash man; and similarly the temperate man appears self-indulgent relatively to the insensible man, insensible relatively to the self-indulgent, and the liberal man prodigal relatively to the mean man, mean relatively to the prodigal. Hence also the people at the extremes push the intermediate man each over to the other, and the brave man is called rash by the coward, cowardly by the rash man, and correspondingly in the other cases.

These states being thus opposed to one another, the greatest contrariety is that of the extremes to each other, rather than to the intermediate; for these are further from each other than from the intermediate, as the great is further from the small and the small from the great than both are from the equal. Again, to the intermediate some extremes show a certain likeness, as that of rashness to courage and that of prodigality to liberality; but the extremes show the greatest unlikeness to each other; now contraries are defined as the things that are furthest from each other, so that things that are further apart are more contrary.

To the mean in some cases the deficiency, in some the excess is more opposed; e.g. it is not rashness, which is an excess, but cowardice, which is a deficiency, that is more opposed to courage, and not insensibility, which is a deficiency, but self-indulgence, which is an excess, that is more opposed to temperance. This happens from two reasons, one being drawn from the thing itself; for because one extreme is nearer and liker to the intermediate, we oppose not this but rather its contrary to the intermediate. E. g., since rashness is thought liker and nearer to courage, and cowardice more unlike, we oppose rather the latter to courage; for things that are further from the intermediate are thought more contrary to it. This, then, is one cause, drawn from the thing itself; another is drawn from ourselves; for the things to which we ourselves more naturally tend seem more contrary to the intermediate. For instance, we ourselves tend more naturally to pleasures, and hence are more easily carried away towards self-indulgence than towards propriety. We describe as contrary to the mean, then, rather the directions in which we more often go to great lengths; and therefore self-indulgence, which is an excess, is the more contrary to temperance.

9. That moral virtue is a mean, then, and in what sense it is so, and that it is a mean between two vices, the one involving excess, the other deficiency, and that it is such because its character is to aim at what is intermediate in passions and in actions, has been sufficiently stated. Hence also it is no easy task to be good. For in everything it is no easy task to find the middle, e. g. to find the middle of a circle is not for every one but for him who knows; so, too, any one can get angry — that is easy — or give or spend money; but to do this to the right person, to the right extent, at the right time, with the right motive, and in the right way, *that* is not for every one, nor is it easy; wherefore goodness is both rare and laudable and noble.

Hence he who aims at the intermediate must first depart from what is the more contrary to it, as Calypso advises —

Hold the ship out beyond that surf and spray.*

For of the extremes one is more erroneous, one less so; therefore, since to hit the mean is hard in the extreme, we must as a second best, as people say, take the least of the evils; and this will be done best in the way we describe.

But we must consider the things towards which we ourselves also are easily carried away; for some of us tend to one thing, some to another; and this will be recognizable from the pleasure and the pain we feel. We must drag ourselves away to the contrary extreme; for we shall get into the intermediate state by drawing well away from error, as people do in straightening sticks that are bent.

Now in everything the pleasant or pleasure is most to be guarded against; for we do not judge it impartially. We ought, then, to feel towards pleasure as the elders of the people felt towards Helen, and in all circumstances repeat their saying; for if we dismiss pleasure thus we are less likely to go astray. It is by doing this, then, (to sum the matter up) that we shall best be able to hit the mean.

But this is no doubt difficult, and especially in individual cases; for it is not easy to determine both how and with whom and on what provocation and how long one should be angry; for we too sometimes praise those who fall short and call them good-tempered, but sometimes we praise those who get angry and call them manly. The man, however, who deviates little from goodness is not blamed, whether he do so in the direction of the more or of the less, but only the man who deviates more widely; for *he* does not fail to be noticed. But up to what point and to what extent a man must deviate before he becomes blameworthy it is not easy to determine by reasoning, any more than anything else that is perceived by the senses; such things depend on particular facts, and the decision rests with perception. So much, then, is plain, that the intermediate state is in all things to be praised, but that we must incline sometimes towards the excess, sometimes towards the deficiency; for so shall we most easily hit the mean and what is right.

[tr. W. D. Ross]

BOOK X

6. Now that we have spoken of the virtues, the forms of friendship, and the varieties of pleasure, what remains is to discuss in outline the nature of happiness, since this is what we state the end of human nature to be. Our discussion will be the more concise if we first sum up what we have said already. We said, then, that it is not a disposition; for if it were it might belong to some one who was asleep throughout his life, living the life of a plant, or, again, to some one who was suffering the greatest misfortunes. If these implications are

* *Odyssey*, xii. 219 f. (Mackail's trans.). But it was Circe who gave the advice (xii. 108), and the actual quotation is from Odysseus' orders to his steersman.

unacceptable, and we must rather class happiness as an activity, as we have said before, and if some activities are necessary, and desirable for the sake of something else, while others are so in themselves, evidently happiness must be placed among those desirable in themselves, not among those desirable for the sake of something else; for happiness does not lack anything, but is self-sufficient.   Now those activities are desirable in themselves from which nothing is sought beyond the activity.   And of this nature virtuous actions are thought to be; for to do noble and good deeds is a thing desirable for its own sake.

Pleasant amusements also are thought to be of this nature; we choose them not for the sake of other things; for we are injured rather than benefited by them, since we are led to neglect our bodies and our property.   But most of the people who are deemed happy take refuge in such pastimes, which is the reason why those who are ready-witted at them are highly esteemed at the courts of tyrants; they make themselves pleasant companions in the tyrants' favourite pursuits, and that is the sort of man they want.   Now these things are thought to be of the nature of happiness because people in despotic positions spend their leisure in them, but perhaps such people prove nothing; for virtue and reason, from which good activities flow, do not depend on despotic position; nor, if these people, who have never tasted pure and generous pleasure, take refuge in the bodily pleasures, should these for that reason be thought more desirable; for boys, too, think the things that are valued among themselves are the best.   It is to be expected, then, that, as different things seem valuable to boys and to men, so they should to bad men and to good.   Now, as we have often maintained, those things are both valuable and pleasant which are such to the good man; and to each man the activity in accordance with his own disposition is most desirable, and, therefore, to the good man that which is in accordance with virtue.   Happiness, therefore, does not lie in amusement; it would, indeed, be strange if the end were amusement, and one were to take trouble and suffer hardship all one's life in order to amuse oneself.   For, in a word, everything that we choose we choose for the sake of something else — except happiness, which is an end.   Now to exert oneself and work for the sake of amusement seems silly and utterly childish.   But to amuse oneself in order that one may exert oneself, as Anacharsis puts it, seems right; for amusement is a sort of relaxation, and we need relaxation because we cannot work continuously.   Relaxation, then, is not an end; for it is taken for the sake of activity.

The happy life is thought to be virtuous; now a virtuous life requires exertion, and does not consist in amusement.   And we say that serious things are better than laughable things and those connected with amusement, and that the activity of the better of any two things — whether it be two elements of our being or two men — is the more serious; but the activity of the better is *ipso facto* superior and more of the nature of happiness.   And any chance person — even a slave — can enjoy the bodily pleasures no less than the best man; but no one assigns to a slave a share in happiness — unless he assigns to him also a share in human life. For happiness does not lie in such occupations, but, as we have said before, in virtuous activities.

7. If happiness is activity in accordance with virtue, it is reasonable that it should be in accordance with the highest virtue; and this will be that of the best thing in us. Whether it be reason or something else that is this element which is thought to be our natural ruler and guide and to take thought of things noble and divine, whether it be itself also divine or only the most divine element in us, the activity of this in accordance with its proper virtue will be perfect happiness. That this activity is contemplative we have already said.

Now this would seem to be in agreement both with what we said before and with the truth. For, firstly, this activity is the best (since not only is reason the best thing in us, but the objects of reason are the best of knowable objects); and, secondly, it is the most continuous, since we can contemplate truth more continuously than we can *do* anything. And we think happiness has pleasure mingled with it, but the activity of philosophic wisdom is admittedly the pleasantest of virtuous activities; at all events the pursuit of it is thought to offer pleasures marvellous for their purity and their enduringness, and it is to be expected that those who know will pass their time more pleasantly than those who inquire. And the self-sufficiency that is spoken of must belong most to the contemplative activity. For while a philosopher, as well as a just man or one possessing any other virtue, needs the necessaries of life, when they are sufficiently equipped with things of that sort the just man needs people towards whom and with whom he shall act justly, and the temperate man, the brave man, and each of the others is in the same case, but the philosopher, even when by himself, can contemplate truth, and the better the wiser he is; he can perhaps do so better if he has fellow-workers, but still he is the most self-sufficient. And this activity alone would seem to be loved for its own sake; for nothing arises from it apart from the contemplating, while from practical activities we gain more or less apart from the action. And happiness is thought to depend on leisure; for we are busy that we may have leisure, and make war that we may live in peace. Now the activity of the practical virtues is exhibited in political or military affairs, but the actions concerned with these seem to be unleisurely. Warlike actions are completely so (for no one chooses to be at war, or provokes war, for the sake of being at war; any one would seem absolutely murderous if he were to make enemies of his friends in order to bring about battle and slaughter); but the action of the statesman is also unleisurely, and — apart from the political action itself — aims at despotic power and honours, or at all events happiness, for him and his fellow citizens — a happiness different from political action, and evidently sought as being different. So if among virtuous actions political and military actions are distinguished by nobility and greatness, and these are unleisurely and aim at an end and are not desirable for their own sake, but the activity of reason, which is contemplative, seems both to be superior in serious worth and to aim at no end beyond itself, and to have its pleasure proper to itself (and this augments the activity), and the self-sufficiency, leisureliness, unweariedness (so far as this is possible for man), and all the other attributes ascribed to the supremely happy man are evidently those connected with this activity, it follows that this will be the complete happiness of man, if it be allowed a complete term of life (for none of the attributes of happiness is *in*complete).

But such a life would be too high for man; for it is not in so far as he is man that he will live so, but in so far as something divine is present in him; and by so much as this is superior to our composite nature is its activity superior to that which is the exercise of the other kind of virtue. If reason is divine, then, in comparison with man, the life according to it is divine in comparison with human life. But we must not follow those who advise us, being men, to think of human things, and, being mortal, of mortal things, but must, so far as we can, make ourselves immortal, and strain every nerve to live in accordance with the best thing in us; for even if it be small in bulk, much more does it in power and worth surpass everything. This would seem, too, to be each man himself, since it is the authoritative and better part of him. It would be strange, then, if he were to choose not the life of his self but that of something else. And what we said before will apply now; that which is proper to each thing is by nature best and most pleasant for each thing; for man, therefore, the life according to reason is best and pleasantest, since reason more than anything else *is* man. This life therefore is also the happiest.

8. But in a secondary degree the life in accordance with the other kind of virtue is happy; for the activities in accordance with this befit our human estate. Just and brave acts, and other virtuous acts, we do in relation to each other, observing our respective duties with regard to contracts and services and all manner of actions and with regard to passions; and all of these seem to be typically human. Some of them seem even to arise from the body, and virtue of character to be in many ways bound up with the passions. Practical wisdom, too, is linked to virtue of character, and this to practical wisdom, since the principles of practical wisdom are in accordance with the moral virtues and rightness in morals is in accordance with practical wisdom. Being connected with the passions also, the moral virtues must belong to our composite nature; and the virtues of our composite nature are human; so, therefore, are the life and the happiness which correspond to these. The excellence of the reason is a thing apart; we must be content to say this much about it, for to describe it precisely is a task greater than our purpose requires. It would seem, however, also to need external equipment but little, or less than moral virtue does. Grant that both need the necessaries, and do so equally, even if the statesman's work is the more concerned with the body and things of that sort; for there will be little difference there; but in what they need for the exercise of their activities there will be much difference.

The liberal man will need money for the doing of his liberal deeds, and the just man too will need it for the returning of services (for wishes are hard to discern, and even people who are not just pretend to wish to act justly); and the brave man will need power if he is to accomplish any of the acts that correspond to his virtue, and the temperate man will need opportunity; for how else is either he or any of the others to be recognized? It is debated, too, whether the will or the deed is more essential to virtue, which is assumed to involve both; it is surely clear that its perfection involves both; but for deeds many things are needed, and more, the greater and nobler the deeds are. But the man who is contemplating the truth needs no such thing, at least with a view to the exercise of his activity; indeed they are, one may say, even hindrances, at all events to his contemplation; but in so far as he is a man and lives with a number of people, he chooses to do virtuous acts; he will therefore need such aids to living a human life.

But that perfect happiness is a contemplative activity will appear from the following consideration as well. We assume the gods to be above all other beings blessed and happy; but what sort of actions must we assign to them? Acts of justice? Will not the gods seem absurd if they make contracts and return deposits, and so on? Acts of a brave man, then, confronting dangers and running risks because it is noble to do so? Or liberal acts? To whom will they give? It will be strange if they are really to have money or anything of the kind. And what would their temperate acts be? Is not such praise tasteless, since they have no bad appetites? If we were to run through them all, the circumstances of action would be found trivial and unworthy of gods. Still, every one supposes that they *live* and therefore that they are active; we cannot suppose them to sleep like Endymion. Now if you take away from a living being action, and still more production, what is left but contemplation? Therefore the activity of God, which surpasses all others in blessedness, must be contemplative; and of human activities, therefore, that which is most akin to this must be most of the nature of happiness.

This is indicated, too, by the fact that the other animals have no share in happiness, being completely deprived of such activity. For while the whole life of the gods is blessed, and that of men too in so far as some likeness of such activity belongs to them, none of the other animals is happy, since they in no way share in contemplation. Happiness extends, then, just so far as contemplation does, and those to whom contemplation more fully belongs are more truly happy, not as a mere concomitant but in virtue of the contemplation; for this is in itself precious. Happiness, therefore, must be some form of contemplation.

But, being a man, one will also need external prosperity; for our nature is not self-sufficient for the purpose of contemplation, but our body also must be healthy and must have food and other attention. Still, we must not think that the man who is to be happy will need many things or great things, merely because he cannot be supremely happy without external goods; for self-sufficiency and action do not involve excess, and we can do noble acts without ruling earth and sea; for even with moderate advantages one can act virtuously (this is manifest enough; for private persons are thought to do worthy acts no less than despots — indeed even more); and it is enough that we should have so much as that; for the life of the man who is active in accordance with virtue will be happy.   Solon, too, was perhaps sketching well the happy man when he described him as moderately furnished with externals but as having done (as Solon thought) the noblest acts, and lived temperately; for one can with but moderate possessions do what one ought.   Anaxagoras also seems to have supposed the happy man not to be rich nor a despot, when he said that he would not be surprised if the happy man were to seem to most people a strange person; for they judge by externals, since these are all they perceive.   The opinions of the wise seem, then, to harmonize with our arguments.   But while even such things carry some conviction, the truth in practical matters is discerned from the facts of life; for these are the decisive factor.   We must therefore survey what we have already said, bringing it to the test of the facts of life, and if it harmonizes with the facts we must accept it, but if it clashes with them we must suppose it to be mere theory.   Now he who exercises his reason and cultivates it seems to be both in the best state of mind and most dear to the gods.   For if the gods have any care for human affairs, as they are thought to have, it would be reasonable both that they should delight in that which was best and most akin to them (i. e. reason) and that they should reward those who love and honour this most, as caring for the things that are dear to them and acting both rightly and nobly.   And that all these attributes belong most of all to the philosopher is manifest.   He, therefore, is the dearest to the gods.   And he who is that will presumably be also the happiest; so that in this way too the philosopher will more than any other be happy.

9. If these matters and the virtues, and also friendship and pleasure, have been dealt with sufficiently in outline, are we to suppose that our programme has reached its end?   Surely, as the saying goes, where there are things to be done the end is not to survey and recognize the various things, but rather to do them; with regard to virtue, then, it is not enough to know, but we must try to have and use it, or try any other way there may be of becoming good.   Now if arguments were in themselves enough to make men good, they would justly, as Theognis says, have won very great rewards, and such rewards should have been provided; but as things are, while they seem to have power to encourage and stimulate the generous-minded among our youth, and to make a character which is gently born, and a true lover of what is noble, ready to be possessed by virtue, they are not able to encourage the many to nobility and goodness. For these do not by nature obey the sense of shame, but only fear, and do not abstain from bad acts because of their baseness but through

fear of punishment; living by passion they pursue their own pleasures and the means to them, and avoid the opposite pains, and have not even a conception of what is noble and truly pleasant, since they have never tasted it. What argument would remould such people? It is hard, if not impossible, to remove by argument the traits that have long since been incorporated in the character; and perhaps we must be content if, when all the influences by which we are thought to become good are present, we get some tincture of virtue.

Now some think that we are made good by nature, others by habituation, others by teaching. Nature's part evidently does not depend on us, but as a result of some divine causes is present in those who are truly fortunate; while argument and teaching, we may suspect, are not powerful with all men, but the soul of the student must first have been cultivated by means of habits for noble joy and noble hatred, like earth which is to nourish the seed. For he who lives as passion directs will not hear argument that dissuades him, nor understand it if he does; and how can we persuade one in such a state to change his ways? And in general passion seems to yield not to argument but to force. The character, then, must somehow be there already with a kinship to virtue, loving what is noble and hating what is base.

But it is difficult to get from youth up a right training for virtue if one has not been brought up under right laws; for to live temperately and hardily is not pleasant to most people, especially when they are young. For this reason their nurture and occupations should be fixed by law; for they will not be painful when they have become customary. But it is surely not enough that when they are young they should get the right nurture and attention; since they must, even when they are grown up, practise and be habituated to them, we shall need laws for this as well, and generally speaking to cover the whole of life; for most people obey necessity rather than argument, and punishments rather than the sense of what is noble.

This is why some think that legislators ought to stimulate men to virtue and urge them forward by the motive of the noble, on the assumption that those who have been well advanced by the formation of habits will attend to such influences; and that punishments and penalties should be imposed on those who disobey and are of inferior nature, while the incurably bad should be completely banished. A good man (they think), since he lives with his mind fixed on what is noble, will submit to argument, while a bad man, whose desire is for pleasure, is corrected by pain like a beast of burden. This is, too, why they say the pains inflicted should be those that are most opposed to the pleasures such men love.

However that may be, if (as we have said) the man who is to be good must be well trained and habituated, and go on to spend his time in worthy occupations and neither willingly nor unwillingly do bad actions, and if this can be brought about if men live in accordance with a sort of reason and right order, provided this has force — if this be so, the paternal command indeed has not the required force or compulsive power (nor in general has the command of one man, unless he be a king or something similar), but the law *has* compulsive power, while it is at the same time a rule proceeding from a sort of practical wisdom and reason. And while people hate *men* who oppose their impulses, even if they oppose them rightly, the law in its ordaining of what is good is not burdensome.

In the Spartan state alone, or almost alone, the legislator seems to have paid attention to questions of nurture and occupations; in most states such matters have been neglected, and each man lives as he pleases, Cyclops-fashion, 'to his own wife and children dealing law.' * Now it is best that there should be a public and proper care for such matters; but if they are neglected by the community it would seem right for each man to help his children and friends towards virtue, and that they should have the power, or at least the will, to do this.

It would seem from what has been said that he can do this better if he makes himself capable of legislating. For public control is plainly effected by laws, and good control by good laws; whether written or unwritten would seem to make no difference, nor whether they are laws providing for the education of individuals or of groups — any more than it does in the case of music or gymnastics and other such pursuits. For as in cities laws and prevailing types of character have force, so in households do the injunctions and the habits of the father, and these have even more because of the tie of blood and the benefits he confers; for the children start with a natural affection and disposition to obey. Further, private education has an advantage over public, as private medical treatment has; for while in general rest and abstinence from food are good for a man in a fever, for a particular man they may not be; and a boxer presumably does not prescribe the same style of fighting to all his pupils. It would seem, then, that the detail is worked out with more precision if the control is private; for each person is more likely to get what suits his case.

But the details can be best looked after, one by one, by a doctor or gymnastic instructor or any one else who has the general knowledge of what is good for every one or for people of a certain kind (for the sciences both are said to be, and are, concerned with what is universal); not but what some particular detail may perhaps be well looked after by an unscientific person, if he has studied accurately in the light of experience what happens in each case, just as some people seem to be their own best doctors, though they could give no help to any one else. None the less, it will perhaps be agreed that if a man does wish to become master of an art or science he must go to the universal, and come to know it as well as possible; for, as we have said, it is with this that the sciences are concerned.

And surely he who wants to make men, whether many or few, better by his care must try to become capable of legislating, if it is through laws that we can become good. For to get any one whatever

* *Odyssey,* IX. 114 f.

— any one who is put before us — into the right condition is not for the first chance comer; if any one can do it, it is the man who knows, just as in medicine and all other matters which give scope for care and prudence.

Must we not, then, next examine whence or how one can learn how to legislate? Is it, as in all other cases, from statesmen? Certainly it was thought to be a part of statesmanship. Or is a difference apparent between statesmanship and the other sciences and arts? In the others the same people are found offering to teach the arts and practising them, e. g. doctors or painters; but while the sophists profess to teach politics, it is practised not by any of them but by the politicians, who would seem to do so by dint of a certain skill and experience rather than of thought; for they are not found either writing or speaking about such matters (though it were a nobler occupation perhaps than composing speeches for the law-courts and the assembly), nor again are they found to have made statesmen of their own sons or any other of their friends. But it was to be expected that they should if they could; for there is nothing better than such a skill that they could have left to their cities, or could prefer to have for themselves, or, therefore, for those dearest to them. Still, experience seems to contribute not a little; else they could not have become politicians by familiarity with politics; and so it seems that those who aim at knowing about the art of politics need experience as well.

But those of the sophists who profess the art seem to be very far from teaching it. For, to put the matter generally, they do not even know what kind of thing it is nor what kinds of things it is about; otherwise they would not have classed it as identical with rhetoric or even inferior to it, nor have thought it easy to legislate by collecting the laws that are thought well of; they say it is possible to select the best laws, as though even the selection did not demand intelligence and as though right judgment were not the greatest thing, as in matters of music. For while people experienced in any department judge rightly the works produced in it, and understand by what means or how they are achieved, and what harmonizes with what, the inexperienced must be content if they do not fail to see whether the work has been well or ill made — as in the case of painting. Now laws are as it were the 'works' of the political art; how then can one learn from them to be a legislator, or judge which are best? Even medical men do not seem to be made by a study of text-books. Yet people try, at any rate, to state not only the treatments, but also how particular classes of people can be cured and should be treated — distinguishing the various habits of body; but while this seems useful to experienced people, to the inexperienced it is valueless. Surely, then, while collections of laws, and of constitutions also, may be serviceable to those who can study them and judge what is good or bad and what enactments suit what circumstances, those who go through such collections without a practised faculty will not have right judgment (unless it be as a spontaneous gift of nature), though they may perhaps become more intelligent in such matters.

Now our predecessors have left the subject of legislation to us unexamined; it is perhaps best, therefore, that we should ourselves study
it, and in general study the question of the constitution, in order to
complete to the best of our ability our philosophy of human nature.
First, then, if anything has been said well in detail by earlier thinkers,
let us try to review it; then in the light of the constitutions we have
collected let us study what sorts of influence preserve and destroy
states, and what sorts preserve or destroy the particular kinds of constitution, and to what causes it is due that some are well and others
ill administered.   When these have been studied we shall perhaps be
more likely to see with a comprehensive view, which constitution is
best, and how each must be ordered, and what laws and customs it
must use, if it is to be at its best.*   Let us make a beginning of our
discussion.

[1176a30–1181b24. tr. W. D. Ross]

POETICS

1. Our subject being poetry, I propose to speak not only of the art in
general, but also of its species and their respective capacities, of the
structure of plot required for a good poem, of the number and nature
of the constituent parts of a poem, and likewise of any other matters
in the same line of inquiry.   Let us follow the natural order and begin
with the primary facts.

Epic poetry and tragedy, as also comedy, dithyrambic poetry, and
most flute-playing and lyre-playing, are all, viewed as a whole, modes
of imitation.   But at the same time they differ from one another in
three ways, either by a difference of kind in their means, or by differences in the objects, or in the manner of their imitations.

Just as form and colour are used as means by some, who (whether
by art or constant practice) imitate and portray many things by their
aid, and the voice is used by others, so also in the above-mentioned
group of arts, the means with them as a whole are rhythm, language,
and harmony — used, however, either singly or in certain combinations.   A combination of rhythm and harmony alone is the means
in flute-playing and lyre-playing, and any other arts there may be of
the same description, e.g., imitative piping.   Rhythm alone, without
harmony, is the means in the dancer's imitations; for even he, by the
rhythms of his attitudes, may represent men's characters, as well as
what they do and suffer.   There is further an art which imitates by
language alone, without harmony, in prose or in verse, and if in
verse, either in some one or in a plurality of metres.   This form of
imitation is to this day without a name.   We have no common name
for a mime of Sophron or Xenarchus and a Socratic conversation;
and we should still be without one even if the imitation in the two
instances were in trimeters or elegiacs or some other kind of verse —
though it is the way with people to tack on 'poet' to the name of a

* This paragraph is a programme for the *Politics*, agreeing to a large extent with
the existing contents of that work.

metre, and talk of elegiac-poets and epic-poets, thinking that they call them poets not by reason of the imitative nature of their work, but indiscriminately by reason of the metre they write in. Even if a theory of medicine or physical philosophy be put forth in a metrical form, it is usual to describe the writer in this way. Homer and Empedocles, however, have really nothing in common apart from their metre; so that, if the one is to be called a poet, the other should be termed a physicist rather than a poet. We should be in the same position also, if the imitation in these instances were in all the metres, like the *Centaur* (a rhapsody in a medley of all metres) of Chaeremon; and Chaeremon one has to recognize as a poet. So much, then, as to these arts. There are lastly certain other arts which combine all the means enumerated, rhythm, melody, and verse, *e.g.,* dithyrambic and nomic poetry, tragedy and comedy; with this difference, however, that the three kinds of means are in some of them all employed together, and in others brought in separately, one after the other. These elements of difference in the above arts I term the means of their imitation.

2. The objects the imitator represents are actions, with agents who are necessarily either good men or bad — the diversities of human character being nearly always derivative from this primary distinction, since the line between virtue and vice is one dividing the whole of mankind. It follows, therefore, that the agents represented must be either above our own level of goodness, or beneath it, or just such as we are; in the same way as, with the painters, the personages of Polygnotus are better than we are, those of Pauson worse, and those of Dionysius just like ourselves. It is clear that each of the above-mentioned arts will admit of these differences, and that it will become a separate art by representing objects with this point of difference. Even in dancing, flute-playing, and lyre-playing such diversities are possible; and they are also possible in the nameless art that uses language, prose or verse without harmony, as its means. Homer's personages, for instance, are better than we are; Cleophon's are on our own level; and those of Hegemon of Thasos, the first writer of parodies, and Nicochares, the author of the *Diliad,* are beneath it. The same is true of the dithyramb and the nome; the personages may be presented in them with the difference exemplified in the . . . of . . . and Argas, and in the Cyclopses of Timotheus and Philoxenus. This difference it is that distinguishes tragedy and comedy also; the one would make its personages worse, and the other better, than the men of the present day.

3. A third difference in these arts is in the manner in which each kind of object is represented. Given both the same means and the same kind of object for imitation, one may either (1) speak at one moment in narrative and at another in an assumed character, as Homer does; or (2) one may remain the same throughout, without any such change; or (3) the imitators may represent the whole story dramatically, as though they were actually doing the things described.

As we said at the beginning, therefore, the differences in the imitation of these arts come under three heads: their means, their objects, and their manner. So that as an imitator Sophocles will be on one side akin to Homer, both portraying good men; and on another to Aristophanes, since both present their personages as acting and doing. This in fact, according to some, is the reason for plays being termed dramas, because in a play the personages act the story. Hence too both tragedy and comedy are claimed by the Dorians as their discoveries; comedy by the Megarians, by those in Greece as having arisen when Megara became a democracy, and by the Sicilian Megarians on the ground that the poet Epicharmus was of their country, and a good deal earlier than Chionides and Magnes. Even tragedy also is claimed by certain of the Peloponnesian Dorians. In support of this claim they point to the words 'comedy' and 'drama.' . . . So much, then, as to the number and nature of the points of difference in the imitation of these arts.

4. It is clear that the general origin of poetry was due to two causes, each of them part of human nature. Imitation is natural to man from childhood, one of his advantages over the lower animals being this, that he is the most imitative creature in the world, and learns at first by imitation. And it is also natural for all to delight in works of imitation. The truth of this second point is shown by experience. Though the objects themselves may be painful to see, we delight to view the most realistic representations of them in art, the forms for example of the lowest animals and of dead bodies. The explanation is to be found in a further fact. To be learning something is the greatest of pleasures not only to the philosopher, but also to the rest of mankind, however small their capacity for it. The reason of the delight in seeing the picture is that one is at the same time learning, gathering the meaning of things, e.g., that the man there is so-and-so; for if one has not seen the thing before, one's pleasure will not be in the picture as an imitation of it, but will be due to the execution or colouring or some similar cause. Imitation, then, being natural to us — as also the sense of harmony and rhythm, the metres being obviously species of rhythms — it was through their original aptitude, and by a series of improvements for the most part gradual on their first efforts, that they created poetry out of their improvisations.

Poetry, however, soon broke up into two kinds according to the differences of character in the individual poets; for the graver among them would represent noble actions, and those of noble personages, and the meaner sort the actions of the ignoble. The latter class produced invectives at first, just as others did hymns and panegyrics. We know of no such poem by any of the pre-Homeric poets, though there were probably many such writers among them. Instances, however, may be found from Homer downwards, e.g., his *Margites,* and the similar poems of others. In this poetry of invective its natural fitness brought an iambic metre into use; hence our present term 'iambic,' because it was the metre of their 'iambs' or invectives against one another. The result was that the old poets became some of them writers of heroic and others of iambic verse. Homer's position, however, is peculiar. Just as he was in the serious style the poet of poets, standing alone not only through the literary excellence, but also through the dramatic character of his imitations, so too he was the first to outline for us the general forms of comedy by producing not a dramatic invective, but a dramatic picture of the ridiculous. His *Margites* in fact stands in the same relation to our comedies as the *Iliad* and *Odyssey* to our tragedies. As soon, however, as tragedy and comedy appeared in the field, those naturally drawn to the one line of poetry became writers of comedies instead of iambs, and those naturally drawn to the other, writers of tragedies instead of epics, because these new modes of art were grander and of more esteem than the old.

If it be asked whether tragedy is now all that it need be in its formative elements, to consider that, and decide it theoretically and in relation to the theatres, is a matter for another inquiry. It certainly began in improvisations, as did also comedy; the one originating with the authors of the dithyramb, the other with those of the phallic songs, which still survive as institutions in many of our cities. And its advance after that was little by little, through their improving on whatever they had before them at each stage. It was in fact only after a long series of changes that the movement of tragedy stopped on its attaining to its natural form. (1) The number of actors was first increased to two by Aeschylus, who curtailed the business of the chorus, and made the dialogue, or spoken portion, take the leading part in the play. (2) A third actor and scenery were due to Sophocles. (3) Tragedy acquired also its magnitude. Discarding short stories and a ludicrous diction, through its passing out of its satyric stage, it assumed, though only at a late point in its progress, a tone of dignity; and its metre changed then from trochaic to iambic. The reason for their original use of the trochaic tetrameter was that their poetry was satyric and more connected with dancing than it now is. As soon, however, as a spoken part came in, nature herself found the appropriate metre. The iambic, we know, is the most speakable of metres, as is shown by the fact that we very often fall into it in conversation, whereas we rarely talk hexameters, and only when we depart from the speaking tone of voice. (4) Another change was a plurality of episodes or acts. As for the remaining matters, the superadded embellishments and the account of their introduction, these must be taken as said, as it would probably be a long piece of work to go through the details.

5. As for comedy, it is (as has been observed) an imitation of men worse than the average — worse, however, not as regards any and every sort of fault, but only as regards one particular kind, the ridiculous, which is a species of the ugly. The ridiculous may be defined as a mistake or deformity not productive of pain or harm to others. The mask, for instance, that excites laughter, is something ugly and distorted without causing pain.

Though the successive changes in tragedy and their authors are not unknown, we cannot say the same of comedy. Its early stages passed unnoticed, because it was not as yet taken up in a serious way. It was only at a late point in its progress that a chorus of comedians was officially granted by the archon; they used to be mere volunteers. It had also already certain definite forms at the time when the record of those termed comic poets begins. Who it was who supplied it with masks, or prologues, or a plurality of actors and the like, has remained unknown. The invented fable, or plot, however, originated in Sicily with Epicharmus and Phormis. Of Athenian poets Crates was the first to drop the comedy of invective and frame stories of a general and non-personal nature, in other words, fables or plots.

Epic poetry, then, has been seen to agree with tragedy to this extent, that of being an imitation of serious subjects in a grand kind of verse. It differs from it, however, (1) in that it is in one kind of verse and in narrative form; and (2) in its length, which is due to its action having no fixed limit of time, whereas tragedy endeavours to keep as far as possible within a single circuit of the sun, or something near that. This, I say, is another point of difference between them, though at first the practice in this respect was just the same in tragedies as in epic poems. They differ also (3) in their constituents, some being common to both and others peculiar to tragedy. Hence a judge of good and bad in tragedy is a judge of that in epic poetry also. All the parts of an epic are included in tragedy; but those of tragedy are not all of them to be found in the epic.

6. Reserving hexameter poetry and comedy for consideration hereafter, let us proceed now to the discussion of tragedy. Before doing so, however, we must gather up the definition resulting from what has been said. A tragedy, then, is the imitation of an action that is serious and also, as having magnitude, complete in itself; in language with pleasurable accessories, each kind brought in separately in the parts of the work; in a dramatic, not in a narrative form; with incidents arousing pity and fear, wherewith to accomplish its catharsis of such emotions. Here by 'language with pleasurable accessories' I mean that with rhythm and harmony or song superadded; and by 'the kinds separately' I mean that some portions are worked out with verse only, and others in turn with song.

As they act the stories, it follows that in the first place the spectacle (or stage-appearance of the actors) must be some part of the whole; and in the second melody and diction, these two being the means of their imitation. Here by 'diction' I mean merely this, the composition of the verses; and by 'melody,' what is too completely understood to require explanation. But further, the subject represented also is an action; and the action involves agents, who must necessarily have their distinctive qualities both of character and thought, since it is from these that we ascribe certain qualities to their actions. There are in the natural order of things, therefore, two causes, character and thought, of their actions, and consequently of their success or failure in their lives. Now the action (that which was done) is represented in the play by the fable or plot. The fable, in our present sense of the term, is simply this, the combination of the incidents or things done in the story; whereas character is what makes us ascribe certain moral qualities to the agents; and thought is shown in all they say when proving a particular point or, it may be, enunciating a general truth. There are six parts consequently of every tragedy, as a whole, that is, of such or such quality, *viz.,* a fable or plot, characters, diction, thought, spectacle and melody; two of them arising from the means, one from the manner, and three from the objects of the dramatic imitation; and there is nothing else besides these six. Of these, its formative elements, then, not a few of the dramatists have made due use, as every play, one may say, admits of spectacle, character, fable, diction, melody, and thought.

The most important of the six is the combination of the incidents of the story. Tragedy is essentially an imitation not of persons, but of action and life, of happiness and misery. All human happiness or misery takes the form of action; the end for which we live is a certain kind of activity, not a quality. Character gives us qualities, but it is in our actions — what we do — that we are happy or the reverse. In a play accordingly they do not act in order to portray the characters; they include the characters for the sake of the action. So that it is the action in it, *i.e.,* its fable or plot, that is the end and purpose of the tragedy; and the end is everywhere the chief thing. Besides this, a tragedy is impossible without action, but there may be one without character. The tragedies of most of the moderns are characterless — a defect common among poets of all kinds, and with its counterpart in painting in Zeuxis as compared with Polygnotus; for whereas the latter is strong in character, the work of Zeuxis is devoid of it. And again, one may string together a series of characteristic speeches of the utmost finish as regards diction and thought, and yet fail to produce the true tragic effect; but one will have much better success with a tragedy which, however inferior in these respects, has a plot, a combination of incidents, in it. And again, the most powerful elements of attraction in tragedy, the peripeties and discoveries, are parts of the plot. A further proof is in the fact that beginners succeed earlier with the diction and characters than with the construction of a story; and the same may be said of nearly all the early dramatists. We maintain, therefore, that the first essential, the life and soul, so to speak, of tragedy is the plot; and that the characters come second. Compare the parallel in painting, where the most beautiful colours laid on without order will not give one the same pleasure as a simple black-and-white sketch of a portrait. We maintain that tragedy is primarily an imitation of action, and that it is mainly for the sake of the action that it imitates the personal agents. Third comes the element of thought, *i.e.,* the power of saying whatever can be said or what is appropriate to the occasion. This is what, in the speeches in tragedy, falls under the arts of politics and rhetoric; for the older poets make their personages discourse like statesmen, and the moderns like rhetoricians. One must not confuse it with character. Character in a play is that which reveals the moral purpose of the agents, *i.e.,* the sort of thing they seek or avoid, where that is not obvious. Hence there is no room for character in a speech on a purely indifferent subject. Thought, on the other hand, is shown in all they say when proving or disproving some particular point, or enunciating some universal proposition. Fourth among the literary elements is the diction of the personages, *i.e.,* as before explained, the expression of their thoughts in words, which is practically the same thing with verse as with prose. As for the two remaining parts, the melody is the greatest of the pleasurable accessories of tragedy. The spectacle, though an attraction, is the least artistic of all the parts, and has least to do with the art of poetry. The tragic effect is quite possible without a public performance and actors; and besides, the getting-up of the spectacle is more a matter for the costumer than the poet.

7. Having thus distinguished the parts, let us now consider the proper construction of the fable or plot, as that is at once the first and the most important thing in tragedy. We have laid it down that a tragedy is an imitation of an action that is complete in itself, as a whole of some magnitude; for a whole may be of no magnitude to speak of. Now a whole is that which has beginning, middle, and end. A beginning is that which is not itself necessarily after anything else, and which has naturally something else after it; an end is that which is naturally after something itself, either as its necessary or usual consequent, and with nothing else after it; and a middle, that which is by nature after one thing and has also another after it. A well-constructed plot, therefore, cannot either begin or end at any point one likes; beginning and end in it must be of the forms just described. Again to be beautiful, a living creature, and every whole made up of parts, must not only present a certain order in its arrangement of parts, but also be of a certain definite magnitude. Beauty is a matter of size and order, and therefore impossible either (1) in a very minute creature, since our perception becomes indistinct as it approaches instantaneity; or (2) in a creature of vast size — one, say, 1000 miles long — as in that case, instead of the object being seen all at once, the unity and wholeness of it is lost to the beholder. Just in the same way, then, as a beautiful whole made up of parts, or a beautiful living creature, must be of some size, a size to be taken in by the eye, so a story or plot must be of some length, but of a length to be taken in by the memory. As for the limit of its length, so far as that is relative to public performances and spectators, it does not fall within the theory of poetry. If they had to perform a hundred tragedies, they would be timed by water-clocks, as they are said to have been at one period. The limit, however, set by the actual nature of the thing is this; the longer the story, consistently with its being comprehensible as a whole, the finer it is by reason of its magnitude. As a rough general formula, 'a length which allows of the hero passing by a series of probable or necessary stages from misfortune to happiness, or from happiness to misfortune,' may suffice as a limit for the magnitude of the story.

8. The unity of a plot does not consist, as some suppose, in its having one man as its subject. An infinity of things befall that one man, some of which it is impossible to reduce to unity; and in like manner there are many actions of one man which cannot be made to form one action. One sees, therefore, the mistake of all the poets who have written a *Heracleid*, a *Theseid*, or similar poems. They suppose that because Heracles was one man, the story also of Heracles must be one story. Homer, however, evidently understood this point quite well, whether by art or instinct, just in the same way as he excels the rest in every other respect. In writing an *Odyssey* he did not make the poem cover all that ever befell his hero. It befell him, for instance, to get wounded on Parnassus and also to feign madness at the time of the call to arms; but the two incidents had no probable or necessary connexion with one another. Instead of doing that, he took an action with a unity of the kind we are describing as the subject of the *Odyssey*, as also of the *Iliad*. The truth is that, just as in the other imitative arts one imitation is always of one thing, so in poetry the story, as an imitation of action, must represent one action, a complete whole, with its several incidents so closely connected that the transposal or withdrawal of any one of them will disjoin and dislocate the whole. For that which makes no perceptible difference by its presence or absence is no real part of the whole.

9. From what we have said it will be seen that the poet's function is to describe not the thing that has happened, but a kind of thing that might happen, *i.e.*, what is possible as being probable or necessary. The distinction between historian and poet is not in the one writing prose and the other verse. You might put the work of Herodotus into verse, and it would still be a species of history. It consists really in this, that the one describes the thing that has been, and the other a kind of thing that might be. Hence poetry is something more philosophic and of graver import than history, since its statements are of the nature rather of universals, whereas those of history are singulars. By a universal statement I mean one as to what such or such a kind of man will probably or necessarily say or do, which is the aim of poetry, though it affixes proper names to the characters; by a singular statement, one as to what, say, Alcibiades did or had done to him. In comedy, this has become clear by this time; it is only when their plot is already made up of probable incidents that they give it a basis of proper names, choosing for the purpose any names that may occur to them, instead of writing like the old iambic poets about particular persons. In tragedy, however, they still adhere to the historic names, and for this reason; what convinces is the possible. Now whereas we are not yet sure as to the possibility of that which has not happened, that which has happened is manifestly possible; else it would not have come to pass. Nevertheless even in tragedy there are some plays with but one or two known names in them, the rest being inventions; and there are some without a single known name, *e.g.*, Agathon's *Antheus*, in which both incidents and names are of the poet's invention; and it is no less de-

lightful on that account. So that one must not aim at a rigid adherence to the traditional stories on which tragedies are based. It would be absurd, in fact, to do so, as even the known stories are only known to a few, though they are a delight none the less to all. It is evident from the above that the poet must be more the poet of his stories or plots than of his verses, inasmuch as he is a poet by virtue of the imitative element in his work, and it is actions that he imitates. And if he should come to take a subject from actual history, he is none the less a poet for that, since some historic occurrences may very well be in the probable and possible order of things, and it is in that aspect of them that he is their poet.

Of simple plots and actions the episodic are the worst. I call a plot episodic when there is neither probability nor necessity in the sequence of its episodes. Actions of this sort bad poets construct through their own fault, and good ones on account of the players. His work being for public performance, a good poet often stretches out a plot beyond its capabilities, and is thus obliged to twist the sequence of incident.

Tragedy, however, is an imitation not only of a complete action, but also of incidents arousing pity and fear. Such incidents have the very greatest effect on the mind when they occur unexpectedly and at the same time in consequence of one another. There is more of the marvellous in them then than if they happened of themselves or by mere chance. Even matters of chance seem most marvellous if there is an appearance of design as it were in them; as for instance the statue of Mitys at Argos killed the author of Mitys' death by falling down on him when a looker-on at a public spectacle; for incidents like that we think to be not without a meaning. A plot, therefore, of this sort is necessarily finer than others.

10. Plots are either simple or complex, since the actions they represent are naturally of this twofold description. The action proceeding in the way defined as one continuous whole I call simple when the change in the hero's fortunes takes place without peripety or discovery; and complex, when it involves one or the other, or both. These should each of them arise out of the structure of the plot itself, so as to be the consequence, necessary or probable, of the antecedents. There is a great difference between a thing happening *propter hoc* and *post hoc*.

11. A peripety is the change from one state of things within the play to its opposite of the kind described, and that too in the way we are saying, in the probable or necessary sequence of events; as it is for instance in *Oedipus*. Here the opposite state of things is produced by the messenger, who, coming to gladden Oedipus and to remove his fears as to his mother, reveals the secret of his birth. And in *Lynceus*, just as he is being led off for execution, with Danaus at his side to put him to death, the incidents preceding this bring it about that he is saved and Danaus put to death. A discovery is, as the very word implies, a change from ignorance to knowledge, and thus to either love or hate, in the personages marked for good or evil

fortune. The finest form of discovery is one attended by peripeties, like that which goes with the discovery in *Oedipus*. There are no doubt other forms of it; what we have said may happen in a way in reference to inanimate things, even things of a very casual kind; and it is also possible to discover whether some one has done or not done something. But the form most directly connected with the plot and the action of the piece is the first-mentioned. This, with a peripety, will arouse either pity or fear, actions of that nature being what tragedy is assumed to represent; and it will also serve to bring about the happy or unhappy ending. The discovery, then, being of persons, it may be that of one party only to the other, the latter being already known; or both the parties may have to discover themselves. Iphigenia, for instance, was discovered to Orestes by sending the letter; and another discovery was required to reveal him to Iphigenia.

Two parts of the plot, then, peripety and discovery, are on matters of this sort. A third part is suffering, which we may define as an action of a destructive or painful nature, such as murders on the stage, tortures, woundings, and the like. The other two have been already explained.

12. The parts of tragedy to be treated as formative elements in the whole were mentioned in a previous chapter. From the point of view, however, of its quantity, *i.e.,* the separate sections into which it is divided, a tragedy has the following parts: prologue, episode, exode, and a choral portion, distinguished into parode and stasimon; these two are common to all tragedies, whereas songs from the stage and *commoe* are only found in some. The prologue is all that precedes the parode of the chorus; an episode, all that comes in between two whole choral songs; the exode, all that follows after the last choral song. In the choral portion the parode is the whole first statement of the chorus; a stasimon, a song of the chorus without anapaests or trochees; a *commos,* a lamentation sung by chorus and actor in concert. The parts of tragedy to be used as formative elements in the whole we have already mentioned. The above are its parts from the point of view of its quantity, or the separate sections into which it is divided.

13. The next points after what we have said above will be these: (1) what is the poet to aim at, and what is he to avoid, in constructing his plots? and (2) what are the conditions on which the tragic effect depends? We assume that for the finest form of tragedy the plot must be not simple but complex, and further that it must imitate actions arousing pity and fear, since that is the distinctive function of this kind of imitation. It follows, therefore, that there are three forms of plot to be avoided. (1) A good man must not be seen passing from happiness to misery, or (2) a bad man from misery to happiness. The first situation is not fear-inspiring or piteous, but simply odious to us. The second is the most untragic that can be; it has no one of the requisites of tragedy; it does not appeal either to the human feeling in us, or to our pity, or to our fears. Nor on the other hand should (3) an extremely bad man be seen falling from

happiness into misery. Such a story may arouse the human feeling in us, but it will not move us to either pity or fear. Pity is occasioned by undeserved misfortune, and fear by that of one like ourselves; so that there will be nothing either piteous or fear-inspiring in the situation. There remains, then, the intermediate kind of personage, a man not pre-eminently virtuous and just, whose misfortune, however, is brought upon him not by vice and depravity, but by some error of judgment, of the number of those in the enjoyment of great reputation and prosperity; *e.g.,* Oedipus, Thyestes, and the men of note of similar families. The perfect plot, accordingly, must have a single, and not (as some tell us) a double issue; the change in the hero's fortunes must be not from misery to happiness, but on the contrary from happiness to misery; and the cause of it must lie not in any depravity, but in some great error on his part; the man himself being either such as we have described, or better, not worse, than that. Fact also confirms our theory. Though the poets began by accepting any tragic story that came to hand, in these days the finest tragedies are always on the story of some few houses, on that of Alcmeon, Oedipus, Orestes, Meleager, Thyestes, Telephus, or any others that may have been involved, as either agents or sufferers, in some deed of horror. The theoretically best tragedy, then, has a plot of this description. The critics, therefore, are wrong, who blame Euripides for taking this line in his tragedies, and giving many of them an unhappy ending. It is, as we have said, the right line to take. The best proof is this: on the stage, and in the public performances, such plays, properly worked out, are seen to be the most truly tragic; and Euripides, even if his execution be faulty in every other point, is seen to be nevertheless the most tragic certainly of the dramatists. After this comes the construction of plot which some rank first, one with a double story (like the *Odyssey*) and an opposite issue for the good and the bad personages. It is ranked as first only through the weakness of the audiences. The poets merely follow their public, writing as its wishes dictate. But the pleasure here is not that of tragedy. It belongs rather to comedy, where the bitterest enemies in the piece (*e.g.,* Orestes and Aegisthus) walk off good friends at the end, with no slaying of any one by any one.

14. The tragic fear and pity may be aroused by the spectacle; but they may also be aroused by the very structure and incidents of the play; which is the better way and shows the better poet. The plot in fact should be so framed that, even without seeing the things take place, he who simply hears the account of them shall be filled with horror and pity at the incidents; which is just the effect that the mere recital of the story in *Oedipus* would have on one. To produce this same effect by means of the spectacle is less artistic, and requires extraneous aid. Those, however, who make use of the spectacle to put before us that which is merely monstrous and not productive of fear are wholly out of touch with tragedy. Not every kind of pleasure should be required of a tragedy, but only its own proper pleasure.

The tragic pleasure is that of pity and fear, and the poet has to produce it by a work of imitation; it is clear, therefore, that the causes should be included in the incidents of his story. Let us see, then, what kinds of incident strike one as horrible, or rather as piteous. In a deed of this description the parties must necessarily be either friends, or enemies, or indifferent to one another. Now when enemy does it on enemy, there is nothing to move us to pity either in his doing or in his meditating the deed, except so far as the actual pain of the sufferer is concerned; and the same is true when the parties are indifferent to one another. Whenever the tragic deed, however, is done within the family, when murder or the like is done or meditated by brother on brother, by son on father, by mother on son, or son on mother, these are the situations the poet should seek after. The traditional stories, accordingly, must be kept as they are, *e.g.*, the murder of Clytaemnestra by Orestes and of Eriphyle by Alcmeon.

At the same time even with these there is something left to the poet himself; it is for him to devise the right way of treating them. Let us explain more clearly what we mean by 'the right way.' The deed of horror may be done by the doer knowingly and consciously, as in the old poets, and in Medea's murder of her children in Euripides. Or he may do it, but in ignorance of his relationship, and discover that afterwards, as does the Oedipus in Sophocles. Here the deed is outside the play; but it may be within it, like the act of the Alcmeon in Astydamas, or that of the Telegonus in *Ulysses Wounded.* A third possibility is for one meditating some deadly injury to another, in ignorance of his relationship, to make the discovery in time to draw back. These exhaust the possibilities, since the deed must necessarily be either done or not done, and either knowingly or unknowingly.

The worst situation is when the personage is with full knowledge on the point of doing the deed, and leaves it undone. It is odious and also, through the absence of suffering, untragic. Hence it is that no one is made to act thus except in some few instances, *e.g.,* Haemon and Creon in *Antigone.* Next after this comes the actual perpetration of the deed meditated. A better situation than that, however, is for the deed to be done in ignorance, and the relationship discovered afterwards, since there is nothing odious in it, and the discovery will serve to astound us. But the best of all is the last; what we have in *Cresphontes,* for example, where Merope, on the point of slaying her son, recognizes him in time; in *Iphigenia,* where sister and brother are in a like position; and in *Helle,* where the son recognizes his mother, when on the point of giving her up to her enemy. This will explain why our tragedies are restricted, as we said just now, to such a small number of families. It was accident rather than art that led the poets in quest of subjects to embody this kind of incident in their plots. They are still obliged, accordingly, to have recourse to the families in which such horrors have occurred. On the construction of the plot, and the kind of plot required for tragedy, enough has now been said.

15. In the characters there are four points to aim at. First and fore-

most, that they shall be good.   There will be an element of character in the play, if, as has been observed, what a personage says or does reveals a certain moral purpose, and a good element of character if the purpose so revealed is good.   Such goodness is possible in every type of personage, even in a woman or a slave, though the one is perhaps an inferior, and the other a wholly worthless being.   The second point is to make them appropriate.   The character before us may be, say, manly; but it is not appropriate in a female character to be manly, or clever.   The third is to make them like the reality, which is not the same as their being good and appropriate, in our sense of the term.   The fourth is to make them consistent and the same throughout.   Even if inconsistency be part of the man before one for imitation as presenting that form of character, he should still be consistently inconsistent.   We have an instance of baseness of character, not required for the story, in the Menelaus in *Orestes*; of the incongruous and inappropriate in the lamentation of Ulysses in *Scylla,* and in the (clever) speech of Melanippe; and of inconsistency in *Iphigenia at Aulis,* where Iphigenia the suppliant is utterly unlike the later Iphigenia.   The right thing, however, is in the characters just as in the incidents of the play to endeavour always after the necessary or the probable; so that whenever such-and-such a personage says or does such-and-such a thing, it shall be the probable or necessary outcome of his character; and whenever this incident follows on that, it shall be either the necessary or the probable consequence of it.   From this one sees (to digress for a moment) that the denouement also should arise out of the plot itself, and not depend on a stage-artifice, as in *Medea,* or in the story of the (arrested) departure of the Greeks in the *Iliad.*   The artifice must be reserved for matters outside the play: for past events beyond human knowledge, or events yet to come, which require to be foretold or announced, since it is the privilege of the gods to know everything.   There should be nothing improbable among the actual incidents.   If it be unavoidable, however, it should be outside the tragedy, like the improbability in the *Oedipus* of Sophocles.   But to return to the characters, as tragedy is an imitation of personages better than the ordinary man, we in our way should follow the example of good portrait-painters, who reproduce the distinctive features of a man, and at the same time, without losing the likeness, make him handsomer than he is. The poet in like manner, in portraying men quick or slow to anger, or with similar infirmities of character, must know how to represent them as such, and at the same time as good men, as Homer has represented Achilles as good.   All these rules one must keep in mind throughout, and further, those also for such points of stage-effect as directly depend on the art of the poet, since in these too one may often make mistakes.   Enough, however, has been said on the subject in one of our published writings.

16. Discovery in general has been explained already.   As for the species of discovery, the first to be noted is (1) the least artistic form of it, of which the poets make most use through mere lack of inven-

tion, discovery by signs or marks. Of these signs some are congenital, like the 'lance-head which the Earth-born have on them,' or 'stars,' such as Carcinus brings in in his *Thyestes;* others acquired after birth, these latter being either marks on the body, *e.g.,* scars, or external tokens, like necklaces, or to take another sort of instance, the ark in the discovery in *Tyro.* Even these, however, admit of two uses, a better and a worse. The scar of Ulysses is an instance. The discovery of him through it is made in one way by the nurse and in another by the swineherds. A discovery using signs as a means of assurance is less artistic, as indeed are all such as imply reflexion; whereas one bringing them in all of a sudden, as in the *Bath Story,* is of a better order. Next after these are (2) discoveries made directly by the poet, which are inartistic for that very reason; *e.g.,* Orestes' discovery of himself in *Iphigenia.* Whereas his sister reveals who she is by the letter, Orestes is made to say himself what the poet rather than the story demands. This, therefore, is not far removed from the first-mentioned fault, since he might have presented certain tokens as well. Another instance is the 'shuttle's voice' in the *Tereus* of Sophocles. (3) A third species is discovery through memory, from a man's consciousness being awakened by something seen or heard. Thus in *The Cyprioe* of Dicaeogenes, the sight of the picture makes the man burst into tears; and in the *Tale of Alcinous,* hearing the harper, Ulysses is reminded of the past and weeps, the discovery of them being the result. (4) A fourth kind is Discovery through reasoning; *e.g.,* in *The Choephoroe:* 'One like me is here; there is no one like me but Orestes; he, therefore, must be here.' Or that which Polyidus the Sophist suggested for *Iphigenia,* since it was natural for Orestes to reflect: 'My sister was sacrificed, and I am to be sacrificed like her.' Or that in the *Tydeus* of Theodectes: 'I came to find a son, and am to die myself.' Or that in *The Phinidae:* on seeing the place the women inferred their fate, that they were to die there, since they had also been exposed there. (5) There is, too, a composite discovery arising from bad reasoning on the side of the other party. An instance of it is in *Ulysses the False Messenger:* he said he should know the bow, which he had not seen; but to suppose from that he would know it again (as though he had once seen it) was bad reasoning. (6) The best of all discoveries, however, is that arising from the incidents themselves, when the great surprise comes about through a probable incident, like that in the *Oedipus* of Sophocles, and also in *Iphigenia,* for it was not improbable that she should wish to have a letter taken home. These last are the only discoveries independent of the artifice of signs and necklaces. Next after them come discoveries through reasoning.

17. At the time when he is constructing his plots and engaged on the diction in which they are worked out, the poet should remember (1) to put the actual scenes as far as possible before his eyes. In this way, seeing everything with the vividness of an eye-witness as it were, he will devise what is appropriate, and be least likely to overlook incongruities. This is shown by what was censured in Carcinus,

the return of Amphiaraus from the sanctuary. It would have passed
unnoticed if it had not been actually seen by the audience; but on the
stage his play failed, the incongruity of the incident offending the
spectators. (2) As far as may be, too, the poet should even act his
story with the very gestures of his personages. Given the same natural qualifications, he who feels the emotions to be described will be
the most convincing. Distress and anger, for instance, are portrayed
most truthfully by one who is feeling them at the moment. Hence
it is that poetry demands a man with a special gift for it, or else one
with a touch of madness in him. The former can easily assume the
required mood, and the latter may be actually beside himself with
emotion. (3) His story, again, whether already made or of his
own making, he should first simplify and reduce to a universal form,
before proceeding to lengthen it out by the insertion of episodes.
The following will show how the universal element in *Iphigenia,*
for instance, may be viewed. A certain maiden having been offered
in sacrifice, and spirited away from her sacrificers into another land,
where the custom was to sacrifice all strangers to the Goddess, she
was made there the priestess of this rite. Long after that the brother
of the priestess happened to come. The fact, however, of the oracle
having for a certain reason bidden him go thither, and his object in
going, are outside the plot of the play. On his coming he was arrested, and about to be sacrificed, when he revealed who he was, either
as Euripides puts it, or (as suggested by Polyidus) by the not improbable exclamation, 'So I too am doomed to be sacrificed, as my
sister was'; and the disclosure led to his salvation. This done, the
next thing, after the proper names have been fixed as a basis for the
story, is to work in episodes or accessory incidents. One must mind,
however, that the episodes are appropriate, like the fit of madness in
Orestes, which led to his arrest, and the purifying, which brought
about his salvation. In plays, then, the episodes are short; in epic
poetry they serve to lengthen out the poem. The argument of the
Odyssey is not a long one. A certain man has been abroad many
years. Poseidon is ever on the watch for him, and he is all alone.
Matters at home too have come to this, that his substance is being
wasted and his son's death plotted by suitors to his wife. Then he
arrives there himself after his grievous sufferings; reveals himself,
and falls on his enemies; and the end is his salvation and their death.
This being all that is proper to the *Odyssey,* everything else in it is
episode.
18. (4) There is a further point to be borne in mind. Every tragedy
is in part complication and in part denouement; the incidents before
the opening scene, and often certain also of those within the play,
forming the complication; and the rest the denouement. By complication I mean all from the beginning of the story to the point just
before the change in the hero's fortunes; by denouement, all from
the beginning of the change to the end. In the *Lynceus* of Theodectes, for instance, the complication includes, together with the pre-
supposed incidents, the seizure of the child and that in turn of the

parents; and the denouement all from the indictment for the murder to the end. Now it is right, when one speaks of a tragedy as the same or not the same as another, to do so on the ground before all else of their plot, *i.e.,* as having the same or not the same complication and denouement. Yet there are many dramatists who, after a good complication, fail in the denouement. But it is necessary for both points of construction to be always duly mastered. (5) There are four distinct species of tragedy, that being the number of the constituents also that have been mentioned: first, the complex tragedy, which is all peripety and discovery; second, the tragedy of suffering, *e.g.,* the *Ajaxes* and *Ixions*; third, the tragedy of character, *e.g., The Phthiotides* and *Peleus.* The fourth constituent is that of 'spectacle,' exemplified in *The Phorcides,* in *Prometheus,* and in all plays with the scene laid in the nether world. The poet's aim, then, should be to combine every element of interest, if possible, or else the more important and the major part of them. This is now especially necessary owing to the unfair criticism to which the poet is subjected in these days. Just because there have been poets before him strong in the several species of tragedy, the critics now expect the one man to surpass that which was the strong point of each one of his predecessors.

(6) One should also remember what has been said more than once, and not write a tragedy on an epic body of incident (*i.e.,* one with a plurality of stories in it), by attempting to dramatize, for instance, the entire story of the *Iliad.* In the epic, owing to its scale, every part is treated at proper length; with a drama, however, on the same story the result is very disappointing. This is shown by the fact that all who have dramatized the fall of Ilium in its entirety, and not part by part, like Euripides, or the whole of the Niobe story, instead of a portion, like Aeschylus, either fail utterly or have but ill success on the stage; for that and that alone was enough to ruin even a play by Agathon. Yet in their peripeties, as also in their simple plots, the poets I mean show wonderful skill in aiming at the kind of effect they desire, a tragic situation that arouses the human feeling in one, like the clever villain (*e.g.,* Sisyphus) deceived, or the brave wrongdoer worsted. This is probable, however, only in Agathon's sense, when he speaks of the probability of even improbabilities coming to pass. (7) The chorus too should be regarded as one of the actors; it should be an integral part of the whole, and take a share in the action, that which it has in Sophocles rather than in Euripides. With the later poets, however, the songs in a play of theirs have no more to do with the plot of that than of any other tragedy. Hence it is that they are now singing intercalary pieces, a practice first introduced by Agathon. And yet what real difference is there between singing such intercalary pieces, and attempting to fit in a speech, or even a whole act, from one play into another?

19. The plot and characters having been discussed, it remains to consider the diction and thought. As for the thought, we may assume what is said of it in our art of rhetoric, as it belongs more properly to that department of inquiry. The thought of the person-

ages is shown in everything to be effected by their language: in every effort to prove or disprove, to arouse emotion (pity, fear, anger, and the like), or to maximize or minimize things.   It is clear, also, that their mental procedure must be on the same lines in their actions likewise, whenever they wish them to arouse pity or horror, or have a look of importance or probability.   The only difference is that with the act the impression has to be made without explanation, whereas with the spoken word it has to be produced by the speaker and result from his language.   What, indeed would be the good of the speaker, if things appeared in the required light even apart from anything he says?

As regards the diction, one subject for inquiry under this head is the turns given to the language when spoken; *e.g.,* the difference between command and prayer, simple statement and threat, question and answer, and so forth.   The theory of such matters, however, belongs to elocution and the professors of that art.   Whether the poet knows these things or not, his art as a poet is never seriously criticized on that account.   What fault can one see in Homer's 'Sing of the wrath, Goddess'? — which Protagoras has criticized as being a command where a prayer was meant, since to bid one do or not do, he tells us, is a command.   Let us pass over this, then, as appertaining to another art, and not to that of poetry.

20. The diction viewed as a whole is made up of the following parts: the letter (or ultimate element), the syllable, the conjunction, the article, the noun, the verb, the case, and the speech. . .*

21. Nouns are of two kinds, either (1) simple, *i.e.,* made up of non-significant parts, like the word γῆ, or (2) double.   In the latter case the word may be made up either of a significant and a non-significant part (a distinction which disappears in the compound), or of two significant parts.   It is possible also to have triple, quadruple or higher compounds, like most of our amplified names; *e.g.,* 'Hermocaïcoxanthus' and the like.   Whatever its structure, a noun must always be either (1) the ordinary word for the thing, or (2) a strange word, or (3) a metaphor, or (4) an ornamental word, or (5) a coined word, or (6) a word lengthened out, or (7) curtailed, or (8) altered in form. By the ordinary word I mean that in general use in a country; and by a strange word, one in use elsewhere. . .

Metaphor consists in giving the thing a name that belongs to something else, the transference being either from genus to species, or from species to genus, or from species to species, or on grounds of analogy. That from genus to species is exemplified in 'Here stands my ship,' for lying at anchor is the 'standing' of a particular kind of thing; that from species to genus in 'Truly ten thousand good deeds has Ulysses wrought,' where 'ten thousand,' which is a particular large number, is put in place of the generic 'a large number'; that from species to species in 'Drawing the life with the bronze,' and in 'Severing with the enduring bronze,' where the poet uses 'draw' in the sense of 'sever' and 'sever' in that of 'draw,' both words meaning to 'take away' something.   That from analogy is possible whenever there are four terms so

---

* The rest of this chapter dealing with technical grammar has been omitted.

related that the second (B) is to the first (A), as the fourth (D) to the
third (C); for one may then metaphorically put B in lieu of D, and D
in lieu of B. Now and then, too, they qualify the metaphor by adding
on to it that to which the word it supplants is relative. Thus a cup
(B) is in relation to Dionysus (A) what a shield (D) is to Ares (C).
The cup accordingly will be metaphorically described as the 'shield *of*
Dionysus' (D+A), and the shield as the 'cup *of* Ares' (B+C). Or,
to take another instance, as old age (D) is to life (C), so is evening
(B) to day (A). One will accordingly describe evening (B) as the
'old age of the day' (D+A), or by the Empedoclean equivalent, and
old age (D) as the 'evening' or 'sunset of life' (B+C). It may be
that some of the terms thus related have no special name of their own,
but for all that they will be metaphorically described in just the same
way. Thus to cast forth seed-corn is called 'sowing'; but to cast forth
its flame, as said of the sun, has no special name. This nameless act
(B), however, stands in just the same relation to its object, sunlight
(A), as sowing (D) to the seed-corn (C). Hence the expression in
the poet, 'sowing around a god-created *flame*' (D+A). There is also
another form of qualified metaphor. Having given the thing the
alien name, one may by a negative addition deny of it one of the
attributes naturally associated with its new name. An instance of
this would be to call the shield not the 'cup *of* Ares,' as in the former
case, but a 'cup that holds no wine.' . . . A coined word is a name
which, being quite unknown among a people, is given by the poet
himself; *e.g.,* (for there are some words that seem to be of this origin)
horns, and priest. . .

22. The perfection of diction is for it to be at once clear and not mean.
The clearest indeed is that made up of the ordinary words for things;
but it is mean, as is shown by the poetry of Cleophon and Sthenelus.
On the other hand the diction becomes distinguished and non-prosaic
by the use of unfamiliar terms, *i.e.,* strange words, metaphors, lengthened forms, and everything that deviates from the ordinary modes of
speech. But a whole statement in such terms will be either a riddle
or a barbarism, a riddle if made up of metaphors, a barbarism if made
up of strange words. The very nature indeed of a riddle is this, to
describe a fact in an impossible combination of words (which cannot
be done with the real names for things, but can be with their meta-
phorical substitutes); *e.g.,* 'I saw a man glue brass on another with
fire,' and the like. The corresponding use of strange words results in
a barbarism. A certain admixture, accordingly, of unfamiliar terms
is necessary. These, the strange word, the metaphor, the ornamental
equivalent, etc., will save the language from seeming mean and prosaic, while the ordinary words in it will secure the requisite clearness.
What helps most, however, to render the diction at once clear and
non-prosaic is the use of the lengthened, curtailed, and altered forms
of words. Their deviation from the ordinary words will, by
making the language unlike that in general use, give it a non-
prosaic appearance; and their having much in common with the
words in general use will give it the quality of clearness. It is

not right, then, to condemn these modes of speech, and ridicule
the poet for using them, as some have done; *e.g.,* the elder Euclid,
who said it was easy to make poetry if one were to be allowed to
lengthen the words in the statement itself as much as one likes, a procedure he caricatured. . . A too apparent use of these licences has
certainly a ludicrous effect, but they are not alone in that; the rule of
moderation applies to all the constituents of the poetic vocabulary;
even with metaphors, strange words, and the rest, the effect will be the
same, if one uses them improperly and with a view to provoking
laughter. The proper use of them is a very different thing. To
realize the difference, one should take an epic verse and see how it
reads when the normal words are introduced. The same should be
done too with the strange word, the metaphor, and the rest; for one
has only to put the ordinary words in their place to see the truth of
what we are saying. The same iambic, for instance, is found in
Aeschylus and Euripides, and as it stands in the former it is a poor
line; whereas Euripides, by the change of a single word, the substitution of a strange for what is by usage the ordinary word, has made it
seem a fine one. . . Add to this that Ariphrades used to ridicule the
tragedians for introducing expressions unknown in the language of
common life. . . The mere fact of their not being in ordinary speech
gives the diction a non-prosaic character; but Ariphrades was unaware
of that. It is a great thing, indeed, to make a proper use of these
poetical forms, as also of compounds and strange words. But the
greatest thing by far is to be a master of metaphor. It is the one thing
that cannot be learnt from others; and it is also a sign of genius, since
a good metaphor implies an intuitive perception of the similarity in
dissimilars.

Of the kinds of words we have enumerated it may be observed that
compounds are most in place in the dithyramb, strange words in
heroic, and metaphors in iambic poetry. Heroic poetry, indeed, may
avail itself of them all. But in iambic verse, which models itself as
far as possible on the spoken language, only those kinds of words
are in place which are allowable also in an oration, *i.e.,* the ordinary
word, the metaphor, and the ornamental equivalent.

23. Let this, then, suffice as an account of tragedy, the art imitating
by means of action on the stage. As for the poetry which merely
narrates, or imitates by means of versified language (without action),
it is evident that it has several points in common with tragedy.

The construction of its stories should clearly be like that in a drama;
they should be based on a single action, one that is a complete whole in
itself, with a beginning, middle, and end, so as to enable the work to
produce its own proper pleasure with all the organic unity of a living
creature. Nor should one suppose that there is anything like them in
our usual histories. A history has to deal not with one action, but
with one period and all that happened in that to one or more persons,
however disconnected the several events may have been. Just as two
events may take place at the same time, *e.g.,* the sea-fight off Salamis
and the battle with the Carthaginians in Sicily, without converging to

the same end, so too of two consecutive events one may sometimes come after the other with no one end as their common issue. Nevertheless most of our epic poets, one may say, ignore the distinction. Herein, then, to repeat what we have said before, we have a further proof of Homer's marvellous superiority to the rest. He did not attempt to deal even with the Trojan war in its entirety, though it was a whole with a definite beginning and end, through a feeling apparently that it was too long a story to be taken in in one view, or if not that, too complicated from the variety of incident in it. As it is, he has singled out one section of the whole. Many of the other incidents, however, he brings in as episodes, using the catalogue of the ships, for instance, and other episodes to relieve the uniformity of his narrative. As for the other epic poets, they treat of one man, or one period, or else of an action which, although one, has a multiplicity of parts in it. This last is what the authors of the *Cypria* and *Little Iliad* have done. And the result is that, whereas the *Iliad* or *Odyssey* supplies materials for only one, or at most two tragedies, the *Cypria* does that for several, and the *Little Iliad* for more than eight: for an *Adjudgment of Arms*, a *Philoctetes*, a *Neoptolemus*, a *Eurypylus*, a *Ulysses as Beggar*, a *Laconian Women*, a *Fall of Ilium*, and a *Departure of the Fleet*, as also a *Sinon*, and a *Women of Troy*.

24. Besides this, epic poetry must divide into the same species as tragedy; it must be either simple or complex, a story of character or one of suffering. Its parts, too, with the exception of song and spectacle, must be the same, as it requires peripeties, discoveries, and scenes of suffering just like tragedy. Lastly, the thought and diction in it must be good in their way. All these elements appear in Homer first; and he has made due use of them. His two poems are each examples of construction, the *Iliad* simple and a story of suffering, the *Odyssey* complex (there is discovery throughout it) and a story of character. And they are more than this, since in diction and thought too they surpass all other poems.

There is, however, a difference in the epic as compared with tragedy, (1) in its length, and (2) in its metre. (1) As to its length, the limit already suggested will suffice; it must be possible for the beginning and end of the work to be taken in in one view — a condition which will be fulfilled if the poem be shorter than the old epics, and about as long as the series of tragedies offered for one hearing. For the extension of its length epic poetry has a special advantage, of which it makes large use. In a play one cannot represent an action with a number of parts going on simultaneously; one is limited to the part on the stage and connected with the actors. Whereas in epic poetry the narrative form makes it possible for one to describe a number of simultaneous incidents; and these, if germane to the subject, increase the body of the poem. This then is a gain to the epic, tending to give it grandeur and also variety of interest and room for episodes of diverse kinds. Uniformity of incident by the satiety it soon creates is apt to ruin tragedies on the stage. (2) As for its metre, the heroic has been assigned it from experience. Were any one to attempt a narrative poem in some one, or in several, of the other metres, the incongruity of the thing would be apparent. The heroic in fact is the gravest and weightiest of metres, which is what makes it more tolerant than the rest of strange words and metaphors, that also being a point in which the narrative form of poetry goes beyond all others. The iambic and trochaic, on the other hand, are metres of movement, the one representing that of life and action, the other that of the dance. Still more unnatural would it appear, if one were to write an epic in a medley of metres, as Chaeremon did. Hence it is that no one has ever written a long story in any but heroic verse. Nature herself, as we have said, teaches us to select the metre appropriate to such a story.

Homer, admirable as he is in every other respect, is especially so in this, that he alone among epic poets is not unaware of the part to be played by the poet himself in the poem. The poet should say very little *in propria persona,* as he is no imitator when doing that. Whereas the other poets are perpetually coming forward in person, and say but little, and that only here and there, as imitators, Homer after a brief preface brings in forthwith a man, a woman, or some other character, no one of them characterless, but each with distinctive characteristics.

The marvellous is certainly required in tragedy. The epic, however, affords more opening for the improbable, the chief factor in the marvellous, because in it the agents are not visibly before one. The scene of the pursuit of Hector would be ridiculous on the stage — the Greeks halting instead of pursuing him, and Achilles shaking his head to stop them; but in the poem the absurdity is overlooked. The marvellous, however, is a cause of pleasure, as is shown by the fact that we all tell a story with additions, in the belief that we are doing our hearers a pleasure. Homer more than any other has taught the rest of us the art of framing lies in the right way. I mean the use of paralogism. Whenever, if A is or happens, a consequent, B, is or happens, men's notion is that, if the B is, the A also is; but that is a false conclusion. Accordingly, if A is untrue, but there is something else, B, that on the assumption of its truth follows as its consequent, the right thing then is to add on the B. Just because we know the truth of the consequent, we are in our own minds led on to the erroneous inference of the truth of the antecedent. Here is an instance, from the *Bath Story* in the *Odyssey.*

A likely impossibility is always preferable to an unconvincing possibility. The story should never be made up of improbable incidents; there should be nothing of the sort in it. If, however, such incidents are unavoidable, they should be outside the piece, like the hero's ignorance in *Oedipus* of the circumstances of Laius' death; not within it, like the report of the Pythian games in *Electra,* or the man's having come to Mysia from Tegea without uttering a word on the way, in *The Mysians.* So that it is ridiculous to say that one's plot would have been spoilt without them, since it is fundamentally wrong to make up such plots. If the poet has taken such a plot, however, and one sees that he might have put it in a more probable form, he is guilty of absurdity as well as a fault of art. Even in the *Odyssey* the improbabilities in the setting ashore of Ulysses would be clearly intolerable in the hands of an inferior poet. As it is, the poet conceals them, his other excellences veiling their absurdity. Elaborate diction, however, is required only in places where there is no action, and no character or thought to be revealed. Where there is character or thought, on the other hand, an over-ornate diction tends to obscure them.

25. As regards problems and their solutions, one may see the number and nature of the assumptions on which they proceed by viewing the matter in the following way. (1) The poet being an imitator just like the painter or other maker of likenesses, he must necessarily in all instances represent things in one or other of three aspects, either as they were or are, or as they are said or thought to be or to have been, or as they ought to be. (2) All this he does in language, with an admixture, it may be, of strange words and metaphors, as also of the various modified forms of words, since the use of these is conceded in poetry. (3) It is to be remembered, too, that there is not the same kind of correctness in poetry as in politics, or indeed any other art. There is, however, within the limits of poetry itself a possibility of two kinds of error, the one directly, the other only accidentally connected with the art. If the poet meant to describe the thing correctly, and failed through lack of power of expression, his art itself is at fault. But if it was through his having meant to describe it in some incorrect way (*e.g.,* to make the horse in movement have both right legs thrown forward) that the technical error (one in a matter of, say, medicine or some other special science), or impossibilities of whatever kind they may be, have got into his description, his error in that case is not in the essentials of the poetic art. These, therefore, must be the premisses of the solutions in answer to the criticisms involved in the problems.

As to the criticisms relating to the poet's art itself, any impossibilities there may be in his descriptions of things are faults. But from another point of view they are justifiable, if they serve the end of poetry itself, if (to assume what we have said of that end) they make the effect of some portion of the work more astounding. The pursuit of Hector is an instance in point. If, however, the poetic end might have been as well or better attained without sacrifice of technical correctness in such matters, the impossibility is not to be justified, since the description should be, if it can, entirely free from error. One may ask, too, whether the error is in a matter directly or only accidentally connected with the poetic art, since it is a lesser error in an artist not to know, for instance, that the hind has no horns, than to produce an unrecognizable picture of one.

If the poet's description be criticized as not true to fact, one may urge perhaps that the object ought to be as described — an answer like that of Sophocles, who said that he drew men as they ought to be, and Euripides as they were. If the description, however, be neither true nor of the thing as it ought to be, the answer must be then, that it is in accordance with opinion. The tales about gods, for instance, may be as wrong as Xenophanes thinks, neither true nor the better thing to say; but they are certainly in accordance with opinion. Of other statements in poetry one may perhaps say, not that they are better than the truth, but that the fact was so at the time; e.g., the description of the arms, 'their spears stood upright, butt-end upon the ground'; for that was the usual way of fixing them then, as it is still with the Illyrians. As for the question whether something said or done in a poem is morally right or not, in dealing with that one should consider not only the intrinsic quality of the actual word or deed, but also the person who says or does it, the person to whom he says or does it, the time, the means, and the motive of the agent, whether he does it to attain a greater good, or to avoid a greater evil.

Other criticisms one must meet by considering the language of the poet: (1) by the assumption of a strange word . . . as where Homer may perhaps mean not mules, but sentinels; . . . or mean perhaps, not that Dolon's body was deformed, but that his face was ugly. . . A worker in iron we call a 'brazier'; and it is on the same principle that Ganymede is described as the 'wine-server' of Zeus, though the gods do not drink wine. This latter, however, may be an instance of metaphor. But whenever also a word seems to imply some contradiction, it is necessary to reflect how many ways there may be of understanding it in the passage in question . . . whether by taking it in this sense or in that one will best avoid the fault of which Glaucon speaks: 'They start with some improbable presumption; and having so decreed it themselves, proceed to draw inferences, and censure the poet as though he had actually said whatever they happen to believe, if his statement conflicts with their own notion of things.' This is how Homer's silence about Icarius has been treated. Starting with the notion of his having been a Lacedaemonian, the critics think it strange for Telemachus not to have met him when he went to Lacedaemon; whereas the fact may have been as the Cephallenians say, that the wife of Ulysses was of a Cephallenian family, and that her father's name was Icadius, not Icarius. So that it is probably a mistake of the critics that has given rise to the problem.

Speaking generally, one has to justify (1) the impossible by reference to the requirements of poetry, or to the better, or to opinion. For the purposes of poetry a convincing impossibility is preferable to an unconvincing possibility; and if men such as Zeuxis depicted be impossible, the answer is that it is better they should be like that, as the artist ought to improve on his model. (2) The improbable one has to justify either by showing it to be in accordance with opinion, or by urging that at times it is not improbable; for there is a probability of things happening also against probability. (3) The contradictions found in the poet's language one should first test as one does an opponent's confutation in a dialectical argument, so as to see whether he means the same thing, in the same relation, and in the same sense, before admitting that he has contradicted either something he has said himself or what a man of sound sense assumes as true. But there is no possible apology for improbability of plot or depravity of character when they are not necessary and no use is made of them, like the improbability in the appearance of Aegeus in *Medea* and the baseness of Menelaus in *Orestes*. The objections, then, of critics start with faults of five kinds: the allegation is always that something is either (1) impossible, (2) improbable, (3) corrupting, (4) contradictory, or (5) against technical correctness. The answers to these objections must be sought under one or other of the above-mentioned heads, which are twelve in number.

26. The question may be raised whether the epic or the tragic is the higher form of imitation. It may be argued that, if the less vulgar is the higher, and the less vulgar is always that which addresses the better public, an art addressing any and every one is of a very vulgar order. It is a belief that their public cannot see the meaning, unless they add something themselves, that causes the perpetual movements of the performers — bad flute-players, for instance, rolling about, if quoit-throwing is to be represented, and pulling at the conductor, if Scylla is the subject of the piece. Tragedy, then, is said to be an art of this order, to be in fact just what the later actors were in the eyes of their predecessors; for Mynniscus used to call Callippides 'the ape,' because he thought he so overacted his parts; and a similar view was taken of Pindarus also. All tragedy, however, is said to stand to the epic as the newer to the older school of actors. The one, accordingly, is said to address a cultivated audience, which does not need the accompaniment of gesture; the other, an uncultivated one. If, therefore, tragedy is a vulgar art, it must clearly be lower than the epic.

The answer to this is twofold. In the first place, one may urge (1) that the censure does not touch the art of the dramatic poet, but only that of his interpreter; for it is quite possible to overdo the gesturing even in an epic recital, as did Sosistratus, and in a singing contest, as did Mnasitheus of Opus; (2) that one should not condemn all movement, unless one means to condemn even the dance, but only that of ignoble people, which is the point of the criticism passed on Callippides and in the present day on others, that their women are not like gentlewomen; (3) that tragedy may produce its effect even without movement or action in just the same way as epic poetry, for from the mere reading of a play its quality may be seen, so that, if it be superior in all other respects, this element of inferiority is no necessary part of it.

In the second place, one must remember (1) that tragedy has everything that the epic has (even the epic metre being admissible), together with a not inconsiderable addition in the shape of the music (a very real factor in the pleasure of the drama) and the spectacle; (2) that its reality of presentation is felt in the play as read, as well as in the play as acted; (3) that the tragic imitation requires less space for the attainment of its end, which is a great advantage, since the more concentrated effect is more pleasurable than one with a large admixture of time to dilute it (consider the *Oedipus* of Sophocles, for instance, and the effect of expanding it into the number of lines of the *Iliad*); (4) that there is less unity in the imitation of the epic poets, as is proved by the fact that any one work of theirs supplies matter for several tragedies, the result being that, if they take what is really a single story, it seems curt when briefly told, and thin and waterish when on the scale of length usual with their verse. In saying that there is less unity in an epic I mean an epic made up of a plurality of actions, in the same way as the *Iliad* and *Odyssey* have many such parts, each one of them in itself of some magnitude; yet the structure of the two Homeric poems is as perfect as can be, and the action in them is as nearly as possible one action. If, then, tragedy is superior in these respects, and also besides these, in its poetic effect (since the two forms of poetry should give us, not any or every pleasure, but the very special kind we have mentioned), it is clear that, as attaining the poetic effect better than the epic, it will be the higher form of art.

So much for tragedy and epic poetry, for these two arts in general and their species, the number and nature of their constituent parts, the causes of success and failure in them, the objections of the critics, and the solutions in answer to them. . .

[tr. I. Bywater]

THE STOICS AND EPICUREANS

Stoicism and Epicureanism represent two developments in the history of Greek philosophy which owe much to Platonism and yet fundamentally react against its radical dualism. Plato had postulated two modes of being, one in the realm of Ideas, and the other in the realm of phenomena. Since a dualism of this sort is not satisfying to the demands of reason, which by its very nature strives to reduce things to a monistic first principle, it is not surprising to find in the post-Platonic and post-Aristotelian schools of Stoicism and Epicureanism two monisms which are ultimately rationalistic.

Stoicism was founded by Zeno of Citium who was born in 336 B.C. He taught his students at Athens in the famous *Stoa Poikile* or Painted Porch from which the school derives its name. Zeno and his early associates took the Platonic moral values of endurance and self-sufficiency and made them the basis for their ethic. With this he combined an essentially Aristotelian logic and a physics formulated by Heracleitus, the fifth century philosopher who believed fire to be the ultimate principle in things. At bottom Stoicism is a mechanistic materialism. All things are a result of an evolution from fire, and with deadly inevitability all things will be reduced again to fire after which the process will repeat itself in never ending succession. Thus the Stoics conceived the cosmos to be a great machine all of whose parts are intimately connected with one another. They further believed that it must be self-sufficient and if self-sufficient therefore good. As a result we have the Stoic theory that evil does not exist. Men erroneously think things are evil because they have misused their impressions, have not employed reason with dexterity, have not, in short, lived "in accordance with nature" which is intrinsically good.

With all its ethical power, the Stoic philosophy was always beset with distressing paradoxes. These in the main occur because the sect attempted to overlay their materialistic monism with a pantheism, a combination of two basically incompatible views. Apparently the Stoic felt that the very inevitability with which the cosmic machine operates is evidence of the divine element in it, and hence Stoic writers are continually referring to Fate, Destiny, Providence, Zeus, God, all names for the same divine constituent in things. The human individual for the Stoic was valued because in some sense he had in his soul some part of the divine. The consequent Stoic individualism set as its goal inner peace and contentment which could be achieved by discriminating always beween what is and what is not in an individual's power and by preserving steadfastly the view that evil does not exist. But because a radical paradox emerges from the impossible union of mechanism and pantheism, the Stoic never could clarify the relation between the individual and God, or between individual and individual. The theoretical denial of evil can never eliminate its brutal factuality, and hence Stoic optimism tends to breed a practical frustrating pessimism. Likewise it was difficult for the Stoic to reconcile his own individual concern for inner peace with the doctrine of the universal brotherhood of man, which he held because he believed that all elements of the cosmos are deeply interconnected with one another.

Despite all these difficulties, the Stoic position inspired many penetrating ethical and religious insights. The *Hymn to Zeus* by Cleanthes, Zeno's successor, is notable for its eloquent delineation of God's nature. The *Manual* of Epictetus, dating from the first century after Christ, contains in compact form the main lines of Stoic ethical doctrine. The short selection from the *Meditations* of Marcus Aurelius (A.D. 121–180) reflects the reactions of that sensitive ruler who did his best to appraise the disintegration of the Roman Empire, and its attendant evils of war, plague and poverty, with the firmness of a Stoic sage.

Epicureanism is represented by a letter from the founder of the school to one of his disciples. Epicurus (341 B.C.–270 B.C.) in his system combined part of the Platonic attitude towards pleasure with the atomic physics of Democritus, and produced a hedonistic materialism. In several respects this system is similar to Stoicism. Both philosophies are individualistic and set the highest value upon inner calm and contentment. Both make much of the principle of moderation. Both exalt the power of reason and insist that its proper use will relieve man of his most persistent cares and anxieties. At this point, however, the similarities cease. Epicurus, as will be seen in his *Letter to Herodotus,* follows Democritean atomism to insist that only atoms and void exist. All things, the human soul included, are thus merely the result of combinations of atoms and void. The claim of immortality for the soul cannot be upheld for it is only a concatenation of atoms and hence like the body is subject to dissolution. Epicurus postulates a refined pleasure as the highest human good, and recommends that men withdraw themselves from society in order to pursue that good with the maximum possible success. In this doctrine of withdrawal from life, the Epicurean denies society and political order, and hence was never able to approach man's political and social problems with the power of Stoicism and its cardinal belief in universal brotherhood. Epicurus' value rather is found in his insistence upon scientific empiricism, and in his belief that the right use of reason could give light to man where before there had only been darkness.

Stoicism and Epicureanism round out our picture of Greek philosophy. In these two schools and in the works of Plato and Aristotle we find all the major positions which Greek thought has contributed to our own western European civilization. In their fusion with the Hebraic and Christian tradition we have inherited the central ideals for human life which western culture at its best strives to follow.

CLEANTHES

(*ca.* 300–220 B.C.)

HYMN TO ZEUS

O God most glorious, called by many a name,
Nature's great King, through endless years the same;
Omnipotence, who by thy just decree
Controllest all, hail, Zeus, for unto thee
Behoves thy creatures in all lands to call.
We are thy children, we alone, of all
On earth's broad ways that wander to and fro,
Bearing thine image wheresoe'er we go.
Wherefore with songs of praise thy power I will forth show.
Lo! yonder Heaven, that round the earth is wheeled,
Follows thy guidance, still to thee doth yield
Glad homage; thine unconquerable hand
Such flaming minister, the levin brand,
Wieldeth, a sword two-edged, whose deathless might
Pulsates through all that Nature brings to light;
Vehicle of the universal Word, that flows
Through all, and in the light celestial glows
Of stars both great and small.   A King of Kings
Through ceaseless ages, God, whose purpose brings
To birth, whate'er on land or in the sea
Is wrought, or in high heaven's immensity;
Save what the sinner works infatuate.
Nay, but thou knowest to make crooked straight:
Chaos to thee is order: in thine eyes
The unloved is lovely, who didst harmonize
Things evil with things good, that there should be
One Word through all things everlastingly.
One Word — whose voice alas! the wicked spurn;
Insatiate for the good their spirits yearn:
Yet seeing see not, neither hearing hear
God's universal law, which those revere,
By reason guided, happiness who win.
The rest, unreasoning, diverse shapes of sin
Self-prompted follow: for an idle name
Vainly they wrestle in the lists of fame:
Others inordinately riches woo,
Or dissolute, the joys of flesh pursue.
Now here, now there they wander, fruitless still,
For ever seeking good and finding ill.
Zeus the all-bountiful, whom darkness shrouds,
Whose lightning lightens in the thunder-clouds;
Thy children save from error's deadly sway:

whereby we may judge both the problem of sense-perception and the unseen.

Having made these points clear, we must now consider things imperceptible to the senses. First of all, that nothing is created out of that which does not exist: for if it were, everything would be created out of everything with no need of seeds. And again, if that which disappears were destroyed into that which did not exist, all things would have perished, since that into which they were dissolved would not exist. Furthermore, the universe always was such as it is now, and always will be the same. For there is nothing into which it changes: for outside the universe there is nothing which could come into it and bring about the change.

Moreover, the universe is bodies and space: for that bodies exist, sense itself witnesses in the experience of all men, and in accordance with the evidence of sense we must of necessity judge of the imperceptible by reasoning, as I have already said. And if there were not that which we term void and place and intangible existence, bodies would have nowhere to exist and nothing through which to move, as they are seen to move. And besides these two nothing can even be thought of either by conception or on the analogy of things conceivable such as could be grasped as whole existences and not spoken of as the accidents or properties of such existences. Furthermore, among bodies some are compounds, and others those of which compounds are formed. And these latter are indivisible and unalterable (if, that is, all things are not to be destroyed into the non-existent, but something permanent is to remain behind at the dissolution of compounds): they are completely solid in nature, and can by no means be dissolved in any part. So it must needs be that the first-beginnings are indivisible corporeal existences.

Moreover, the universe is boundless. For that which is bounded has an extreme point: and the extreme point is seen against something else. So that as it has no extreme point, it has no limit; and as it has no limit, it must be boundless and not bounded. Furthermore, the infinite is boundless both in the number of the bodies and in the extent of the void. For if on the one hand the void were boundless, and the bodies limited in number, the bodies could not stay anywhere, but would be carried about and scattered through the infinite void, not having other bodies to support them and keep them in place by means of collisions. But if, on the other hand, the void were limited, the infinite bodies would not have room wherein to take their place.

Besides this the indivisible and solid bodies, out of which too the compounds are created and into which they are dissolved, have an incomprehensible number of varieties in shape: for it is not possible that such great varieties of things should arise from the same atomic shapes, if they are limited in number. And so in each shape the atoms are quite infinite in number, but their differences of shape are not quite infinite, but only incomprehensible in number.

And the atoms move continuously for all time, some of them falling straight down, others swerving, and others recoiling from their collisions. And of the latter, some are borne on, separating to a long distance from one another, while others again recoil and recoil, whenever they chance to be checked by the interlacing with others, or else shut in by atoms interlaced around them. For on the one hand the nature of the void which separates each atom by itself brings this about, as it is not able to afford resistance, and on the other hand the hardness which belongs to the atoms makes them recoil after collision to as great a distance as the interlacing permits separation after the collision. And these motions have no beginning, since the atoms and the void are the cause.

These brief sayings, if all these points are borne in mind, afford a sufficient outline for our understanding of the nature of existing things.

Furthermore, there are infinite worlds both like and unlike this world of ours. For the atoms being infinite in number, as was proved already, are borne on far out into space. For those atoms, which are of such nature that a world could be created out of them or made by them, have not been used up either on one world or on a limited number of worlds, nor again on all the worlds which are alike, or on those which are different from these. So that there nowhere exists an obstacle to the infinite number of the worlds.

Moreover, there are images like in shape to the solid bodies, far surpassing perceptible things in their subtlety of texture. For it is not impossible that such emanations should be formed in that which surrounds the objects, nor that there should be opportunities for the formation of such hollow and thin frames, nor that there should be effluences which preserve the respective position and order which they had before in the solid bodies: these images we call idols.

Next, nothing among perceptible things contradicts the belief that the images have unsurpassable fineness of texture. And for this reason they have also unsurpassable speed of motion, since the movement of all their atoms is uniform, and besides nothing or very few things hinder their emission by collisions, whereas a body composed of many or infinite atoms is at once hindered by collisions. Besides this, nothing contradicts the belief that the creation of the idols takes place as quick as thought. For the flow of atoms from the surface of bodies is continuous, yet it cannot be detected by any lessening in the size of the object because of the constant filling up of what is lost. The flow of images preserves for a long time the position and order of the atoms in the solid body, though it is occasionally confused. Moreover, compound idols are quickly formed in the air around, because it is not necessary for their substance to be filled in deep inside: and besides there are certain other methods in which existences of this sort are produced. For not one of these beliefs is contradicted by our sensations, if one looks to see in what way sensation will bring us the clear visions from external objects, and in what way again the corresponding sequences of qualities and movements.

Now we must suppose too that it is when something enters us

from external objects that we not only see but think of their shapes. For external objects could not make on us an impression of the nature of their own colour and shape by means of the air which lies between us and them, nor again by means of the rays or effluences of any sort which pass from us to them — nearly so well as if models, similar in colour and shape, leave the objects and enter according to their respective size either into our sight or into our mind; moving along swiftly, and so by this means reproducing the image of a single continuous thing and preserving the corresponding sequence of qualities and movements from the original object as the result of their uniform contact with us, kept up by the vibration of the atoms deep in the interior of the concrete body.

And every image which we obtain by an act of apprehension on the part of the mind or of the sense-organs, whether of shape or of properties, this image is the shape or the properties of the concrete object, and is produced by the constant repetition of the image or the impression it has left. Now falsehood and error always lie in the addition of opinion with regard to what is waiting to be confirmed or not contradicted, and then is not confirmed or is contradicted. For the similarity between the things which exist, which we call real and the images received as a likeness of things and produced either in sleep or through some other acts of apprehension on the part of the mind or the other instruments of judgment, could never be, unless there were some effluences of this nature actually brought into contact with our senses. And error would not exist unless another kind of movement too were produced inside ourselves, closely linked to the apprehension of images, but differing from it; and it is owing to this, supposing it is not confirmed, or is contradicted, that falsehood arises; but if it is confirmed or not contradicted, it is true. Therefore we must do our best to keep this doctrine in mind, in order that on the one hand the standards of judgment dependent on the clear visions may not be undermined, and on the other error may not be as firmly established as truth and so throw all into confusion.

Moreover, hearing, too, results when a current is carried off from the object speaking or sounding or making a noise, or causing in any other way a sensation of hearing. Now this current is split up into particles, each like the whole, which at the same time preserve a correspondence of qualities with one another and a unity of character which stretches right back to the object which emitted the sound: this unity it is which in most cases produces comprehension in the recipient, or, if not, merely makes manifest the presence of the external object. For without the transference from the object of some correspondence of qualities, comprehension of this nature could not result. We must not then suppose that the actual air is moulded into shape by the voice which is emitted or by other similar sounds — for it will be very far from being so acted upon by it — but that the blow which takes place inside us, when we emit our voice, causes at once a squeezing out of certain particles, which produce a stream of breath, of such a character as to afford us the sensation of hearing.

Furthermore, we must suppose that smell too, just like hearing, could never bring about any sensation, unless there were certain particles carried off from the object of suitable size to stir this sense-organ, some of them in a manner disorderly and alien to it, others in a regular manner and akin in nature.

Moreover, we must suppose that the atoms do not possess any of the qualities belonging to perceptible things, except shape, weight, and size, and all that necessarily goes with shape. For every quality changes; but the atoms do not change at all, since there must needs be something which remains solid and indissoluble at the dissolution of compounds, which can cause changes; not changes into the non-existent or from the non-existent, but changes effected by the shifting of position of some particles, and by the addition or departure of others. For this reason it is essential that the bodies which shift their position should be imperishable and should not possess the nature of what changes, but parts and configuration of their own. For thus much must needs remain constant. For even in things perceptible to us which change their shape by the withdrawal of matter it is seen that shape remains to them, whereas the qualities do not remain in the changing object, in the way in which shape is left behind, but are lost from the entire body. Now these particles which are left behind are sufficient to cause the differences in compound bodies, since it is essential that some things should be left behind and not be destroyed into the non-existent.

Moreover, we must not either suppose that every size exists among the atoms, in order that the evidence of phenomena may not contradict us, but we must suppose that there are some variations of size. For if this be the case, we can give a better account of what occurs in our feelings and sensations. But the existence of atoms of every size is not required to explain the differences of qualities in things, and at the same time some atoms would be bound to come within our ken and be visible; but this is never seen to be the case, nor is it possible to imagine how an atom could become visible.

Besides this we must not suppose that in a limited body there can be infinite parts or parts of every degree of smallness. Therefore, we must not only do away with division into smaller and smaller parts to infinity, in order that we may not make all things weak, and so in the composition of aggregate bodies be compelled to crush and squander the things that exist into the non-existent, but we must not either suppose that in limited bodies there is a possibility of continuing to infinity in passing even to smaller and smaller parts. For if once one says that there are infinite parts in a body or parts of any degree of smallness, it is not possible to conceive how this should be, and indeed how could the body any longer be limited in size? (For it is obvious that these infinite particles must be of some size or other; and however small they may be, the size of the body too would be infinite.) And again, since the limited body has an extreme point, which is distinguishable, even though not perceptible by itself, you cannot conceive that the succeeding point to it is not similar in character, or that if you go on in this way from one point to another, it should be possible for you to proceed to infinity marking such points in your mind. We must notice also that the least thing in sensation is neither exactly like that which admits of progression from one part to another, nor again is it in every respect wholly unlike it, but it has a certain affinity with such bodies, yet cannot be divided into parts. But when on the analogy of this resemblance we think to divide off parts of it, one on the one side and another on the other, it must needs be that another point like the first meets our view. And we look at these points in succession starting from the first, not within the limits of the same point nor in contact part with part, but yet by means of their own proper characteristics measuring the size of bodies, more in a greater body and fewer in a smaller. Now we must suppose that the least part in the atom too bears the same relation to the whole; for though in smallness it is obvious that it exceeds that which is seen by sensation, yet it has the same relations. For indeed we have already declared on the ground of its relation to sensible bodies that the atom has size, only we placed it far below them in smallness. Further, we must consider these least indivisible points as boundary-marks, providing in themselves as primary units the measure of size for the atoms, both for the smaller and the greater, in our contemplation of these unseen bodies by means of thought. For the affinity which the least parts of the atom have to the homogeneous parts of sensible things is sufficient to justify our conclusion to this extent: but that they should ever come together as bodies with motion is quite impossible.

Furthermore, in the infinite we must not speak of 'up' or 'down,' as though with reference to an absolute highest or lowest — and indeed we must say that, though it is possible to proceed to infinity in the direction above our heads from wherever we take our stand, the absolute highest point will never appear to us — nor yet can that which passes beneath the point thought of to infinity be at the same time both up and down in reference to the same thing: for it is impossible to think this. So that it is possible to consider as one single motion that which is thought of as the upward motion to infinity and as another the downward motion, even though that which passes from us into the regions above our heads arrives countless times at the feet of beings above and that which passes downwards from us at the head of beings below; for none the less the whole motions are thought of as opposed, the one to the other, to infinity.

Moreover, the atoms must move with equal speed, when they are borne onwards through the void, nothing colliding with them. For neither will the heavy move more quickly than the small and light, when, that is, nothing meets them: nor again the small more quickly than the great, having their whole course uniform, when nothing collides with them either: nor is the motion upwards or sideways owing to blows quicker, nor again that downwards owing to their own weight. For as long as either of the two motions prevails, so long will it have a course as quick as thought, until something checks it either from outside or from its own weight counteracting the force of that which dealt the blow. Moreover, their passage through the void, when it takes place without meeting any bodies which might collide, accomplishes every comprehensible distance in an inconceivably short time. For it is collision and its absence which take the outward appearance of slowness and quickness. Moreover, it will be said that in compound bodies too one atom is faster than another, though as a matter of fact all are equal in speed: this will be said because even in the least period of continuous time all the atoms in aggregate bodies move towards one place, even though in moments of time perceptible only by thought they do not move towards one place but are constantly jostling one against another, until the continuity of their movement comes under the ken of sensation. For the addition of opinion with regard to the unseen, that the moments perceptible only by thought will also contain continuity of motion, is not true in such cases; for we must remember that it is what we observe with the senses or grasp with the mind by an apprehension that is true. Nor must it either be supposed that in moments perceptible only by thought the moving body too passes to the several places to which its component atoms move (for this too is unthinkable, and in that case, when it arrives all together in a sensible period of time from any point that may be in the infinite void, it would not be taking its departure from the place from which we apprehend its motion); for the motion of the whole body will be the outward expression of its internal collisions, even though up to the limits of perception we suppose the speed of its motion not to be retarded by collision. It is of advantage to grasp this first principle as well.

Next, referring always to the sensations and the feelings, for in this way you will obtain the most trustworthy ground of belief, you must consider that the soul is a body of fine particles distributed throughout the whole structure, and most resembling wind with a certain admixture of heat, and in some respects like to one of these and in some to the other. There is also the part which is many degrees more advanced even than these in fineness of composition, and for this reason is more capable of feeling in harmony with the rest of the structure as well. Now all this is made manifest by the activities of the soul and the feelings and the readiness of its movements and its processes of thought and by what we lose at the moment of death. Further, you must grasp that the soul possesses the chief cause of sensation: yet it could not have acquired sensation, unless it were in some way enclosed by the rest of the structure. And this in its turn having afforded the soul this cause of sensation acquires itself too a share in this contingent capacity from the soul. Yet it does not acquire all the capacities which the soul possesses: and therefore when the soul is released from the body, the body no longer has sensation. For it never possessed this power in itself, but used to afford opportunity for it to another existence, brought into being at the same time with itself: and this existence, owing to the power now consummated within itself as a result of motion, used spontaneously to produce for itself the capacity of sensation and then to communicate it to the body as well, in virtue of its contact and correspondence of movement, as I have already said. Therefore, so long as the soul remains in the body, even though some other part of the body be lost, it will never lose sensation; nay more, whatever portions of the soul may perish too, when that which enclosed it is removed either in whole or in part, if the soul continues to exist at all, it will retain sensation. On the other hand the rest of the structure, though it continues to exist either as a whole or in part, does not retain sensation, if it has once lost that sum of atoms, however small it be, which together goes to produce the nature of the soul. Moreover, if the whole structure is dissolved, the soul is dispersed and no longer has the same powers nor performs its movements, so that it does not possess sensation either. For it is impossible to imagine it with sensation, if it is not in this organism and cannot effect these movements, when what encloses and surrounds it is no longer the same as the surroundings in which it now exists and performs these movements. Furthermore, we must clearly comprehend as well, that the incorporeal in the general acceptation of the term is applied to that which could be thought of as such as an independent existence. Now it is impossible to conceive the incorporeal as a separate existence, except the void: and the void can neither act nor be acted upon, but only provides opportunity of motion through itself to bodies. So that those who say that the soul is incorporeal are talking idly. For it would not be able to act or be acted on in any respect, if it were of this nature. But as it is, both these occurrences are clearly distinguished in respect of the soul. Now if one refers all these reasonings about the soul to the standards of feeling and sensation and remembers what was said at the outset, he will see that they are sufficiently embraced in these general formulae to enable him to work out with certainty on this basis the details of the system as well.

Moreover, as regards shape and colour and size and weight and all other things that are predicated of body, as though they were concomitant properties either of all things or of things visible or recognizable through the sensation of these qualities, we must not suppose that they are either independent existences (for it is impossible to imagine that), nor that they absolutely do not exist, nor that they are some other kind of incorporeal existence accompanying body, nor that they are material parts of body: rather we should suppose that the whole body in its totality owes its own permanent existence to all these, yet not in the sense that it is composed of properties brought together to form it (as when, for instance, a larger structure is put together out of the parts which compose it, whether the first units of size or other parts smaller than itself, whatever it is), but only, as I say, that it owes its own permanent existence to all of them. All these properties have their own peculiar means of being perceived and distinguished, provided always that the aggregate body goes along with them and is never wrested from them, but in virtue of its comprehension as an aggregate of qualities acquires the predicate of body.

Furthermore, there often happen to bodies and yet do not permanently accompany them accidents, of which we must suppose neither that they do not exist at all nor that they have the nature of a whole body, nor that they can be classed among unseen things nor as incorporeal. So that when according to the most general usage we employ this name, we make it clear that accidents have neither the nature of the whole, which we comprehend in its aggregate and call body, nor that of the qualities which permanently accompany it, without which a given body cannot be conceived. But as the result of certain acts of apprehension, provided the aggregate body goes along with them, they might each be given this name, but only on occasions when each one of them is seen to occur, since accidents are not permanent accompaniments. And we must not banish this clear vision from the realm of existence, because it does not possess the nature of the whole to which it is joined nor that of the permanent accompaniments, nor must we suppose that such contingencies exist independently (for this is inconceivable both with regard to them and to the permanent properties), but, just as it appears in sensation, we must think of them all as accidents occurring to bodies, and that not as permanent accompaniments, or again as having in themselves a place in the ranks of material existence; rather they are seen to be just what our actual sensation shows their proper character to be.

Moreover, you must firmly grasp this point as well; we must not look for time, as we do for all other things which we look for in an object, by referring them to the general conceptions which we perceive in our own minds, but we must take the direct intuition, in accordance with which we speak of 'a long time' or 'a short time,' and examine it, applying our intuition to time as we do to other things. Neither must we search for expressions as likely to be better, but employ just those which are in common use about it. Nor again must we predicate of time anything else as having the same essential nature as this special perception, as some people do, but we must turn our thoughts particularly to that only with which we associate this peculiar perception and by which we measure it. For indeed this requires no demonstration, but only reflection, to show that it is with days and nights and their divisions that we associate it, and likewise also with internal feelings or absence of feeling, and with movements and states of rest; in connexion with these last again we think of this very perception as a peculiar kind of accident, and in virtue of this we call it time.

And in addition to what we have already said we must believe that worlds, and indeed every limited compound body which continuously exhibits a similar appearance to the things we see, were created from the infinite, and that all such things, greater and less alike, were separated off from individual agglomerations of matter; and that all are again dissolved, some more quickly, some more slowly, some suffering from one set of causes, others from another. And further we must believe that these worlds were neither created all of necessity with one configuration nor yet with every kind of shape. Furthermore, we must believe that in all worlds there are living creatures and plants and other things we see in this world; for indeed no one could prove that in a world of one kind there might or might not have been included the kinds of seeds from which living things and plants and all the rest of the things we see are composed, and that in a world of another kind they could not have been.

Moreover, we must suppose that human nature too was taught and constrained to do many things of every kind merely by circumstances; and that later on reasoning elaborated what had been suggested by nature and made further inventions, in some matters quickly, in others slowly, at some epochs and times making great advances, and lesser again at others.   And so names too were not at first deliberately given to things, but men's natures according to their different nationalities had their own peculiar feelings and received their peculiar impressions, and so each in their own way emitted air formed into shape by each of these feelings and impressions, according to the differences made in the different nations by the places of their abode as well.   And then later on by common consent in each nationality special names were deliberately given in order to make their meanings less ambiguous to one another and more briefly demonstrated. And sometimes those who were acquainted with them brought in things hitherto unknown and introduced sounds for them, on some occasions being naturally constrained to utter them, and on others choosing them by reasoning in accordance with the prevailing mode of formation, and thus making their meaning clear.

Furthermore, the motions of the heavenly bodies and their turnings and eclipses and risings and settings, and kindred phenomena to these, must not be thought to be due to any being who controls and ordains or has ordained them and at the same time enjoys perfect bliss together with immortality (for trouble and care and anger and kindness are not consistent with a life of blessedness, but these things come to pass where there is weakness and fear and dependence on neighbours).   Nor again must we believe that they, which are but fire agglomerated in a mass, possess blessedness, and voluntarily take upon themselves these movements.   But we must preserve their full majestic significance in all expressions which we apply to such conceptions, in order that there may not arise out of them opinions contrary to this notion of majesty.   Otherwise this very contradiction will cause the greatest disturbance in men's souls.   Therefore we must believe that it is due to the original inclusion of matter in such agglomerations during the birth-process of the world that this law of regular succession is also brought about.

Furthermore, we must believe that to discover accurately the cause of the most essential facts is the function of the science of nature, and that blessedness for us in the knowledge of celestial phenomena lies in this and in the understanding of the nature of the existences seen in these celestial phenomena, and of all else that is akin to the exact knowledge requisite for our happiness: in knowing too that what occurs in several ways or is capable of being otherwise has no place here, but that nothing which suggests doubt or alarm can be included at all in that which is naturally immortal and blessed. Now this we can ascertain by our mind is absolutely the case. But what falls within the investigation of risings and settings and turnings and eclipses, and all that is akin to this, is no longer of any value for the happiness which knowledge brings, but persons who have perceived all this, but yet do not know what are the natures of these things and what are the essential causes, are still in fear, just as if they did not know these things at all: indeed, their fear may be even greater, since the wonder which arises out of the observation of these things cannot discover any solution or realize the regulation of the essentials. And for this very reason, even if we discover several causes for turnings and settings and risings and eclipses and the like, as has been the case already in our investigation of detail, we must not suppose that our inquiry into these things has not reached sufficient accuracy to contribute to our peace of mind and happiness. So we must carefully consider in how many ways a similar phenomenon is produced on earth, when we reason about the causes of celestial phenomena and all that is imperceptible to the senses; and we must despise those persons who do not recognize either what exists or comes into being in one way only, or that which may occur in several ways in the case of things which can only be seen by us from a distance, and further are not aware under what conditions it is impossible to have peace of mind. If, therefore, we think that a phenomenon probably occurs in some such particular way, and that in circumstances under which it is equally possible for us to be at peace, when we realize that it may occur in several ways, we shall be just as little disturbed as if we know that it occurs in some particular way.

And besides all these matters in general we must grasp this point, that the principal disturbance in the minds of men arises because they think that these celestial bodies are blessed and immortal, and yet have wills and actions and motives inconsistent, with these attributes; and because they are always expecting or imagining some everlasting misery, such as is depicted in legends, or even fear the loss of feeling in death as though it would concern them themselves; and, again, because they are brought to this pass not by reasoned opinion, but rather by some irrational presentiment, and therefore, as they do not know the limits of pain, they suffer a disturbance equally great or even more extensive than if they had reached this belief by opinion. But peace of mind is being delivered from all this, and having a constant memory of the general and most essential principles.

Wherefore we must pay attention to internal feelings and to external sensations in general and in particular, according as the subject is general or particular, and to every immediate intuition in accordance with each of the standards of judgment. For if we pay attention to these, we shall rightly trace the causes whence arose our mental disturbance and fear, and, by learning the true causes of celestial phenomena and all other occurrences that come to pass from time to time, we shall free ourselves from all which produces the utmost fear in other men.

Here, Herodotus, is my treatise on the chief points concerning the nature of the general principles, abridged so that my account would be easy to grasp with accuracy. I think that, even if one were unable to proceed to all the detailed particulars of the system, he would from this obtain an unrivalled strength compared with other men. For indeed he will clear up for himself many of the detailed points by reference to our general system, and these very principles, if he stores them in his mind, will constantly aid him. For such is their character that even those who are at present engaged in working out the details to a considerable degree, or even completely, will be able to carry out the greater part of their investigations into the nature of the whole by conducting their analysis in reference to such a survey as this. And as for all who are not fully among those on the way to being perfected, some of them can from this summary obtain a hasty view of the most important matters without oral instruction so as to secure peace of mind.

[tr. C. Bailey]

EPICTETUS

(*ca.* 50–*ca.* 125 A.D.)

THE MANUAL

1

Of all existing things some are in our power, and others are not in our power. In our power are thought, impulse, will to get and will to avoid, and, in a word, everything which is our own doing. Things not in our power include the body, property, reputation, office, and, in a word, everything which is not our own doing. Things in our power are by nature free, unhindered, untrammelled; things not in our power are weak, servile, subject to hindrance, dependent on others. Remember then that if you imagine that what is naturally slavish is free, and what is naturally another's is your own, you will be hampered, you will mourn, you will be put to confusion, you will blame gods and men; but if you think that only your own belongs to you, and that what is another's is indeed another's, no one will ever put compulsion or hindrance on you, you will blame none, you will accuse none, you will do nothing against your will, no one will harm you, you will have no enemy, for no harm can touch you.

Aiming then at these high matters, you must remember that to attain them requires more than ordinary effort; you will have to give up some things entirely, and put off others for the moment. And if you would have these also — office and wealth — it may be that you will fail to get them, just because your desire is set on the former, and you will certainly fail to attain those things which alone bring freedom and happiness.

Make it your study then to confront every harsh impression with the words, 'You are but an impression, and not at all what you seem to be.' Then test it by those rules that you possess; and first by this — the chief test of all — 'Is it concerned with what is in our power or with what is not in our power?' And if it is concerned with what is not in our power, be ready with the answer that it is nothing to you.

2

Remember that the will to get promises attainment of what you will, and the will to avoid promises escape from what you avoid; and he who fails to get what he wills is unfortunate, and he who does not escape what he wills to avoid is miserable. If then you try to avoid only what is unnatural in the region within your control, you will escape from all that you avoid; but if you try to avoid disease or death or poverty you will be miserable.

Therefore let your will to avoid have no concern with what is not in man's power; direct it only to things in man's power that are contrary to nature. But for the moment you must utterly remove the will to get; for if you will to get something not in man's power you

682

are bound to be unfortunate; while none of the things in man's power
that you could honourably will to get is yet within your reach. Impulse to act and not to act, these are your concern; yet exercise them
gently and without strain, and provisionally.

3

When anything, from the meanest thing upwards, is attractive or
serviceable or an object of affection, remember always to say to yourself, 'What is its nature?' If you are fond of a jug, say you are fond
of a jug; then you will not be disturbed if it be broken. If you kiss
your child or your wife, say to yourself that you are kissing a human
being, for then if death strikes it you will not be disturbed.

4

When you are about to take something in hand, remind yourself
what manner of thing it is. If you are going to bathe put before
your mind what happens in the bath — water pouring over some,
others being jostled, some reviling, others stealing; and you will set
to work more securely if you say to yourself at once: 'I want to bathe,
and I want to keep my will in harmony with nature,' and so in each
thing you do; for in this way, if anything turns up to hinder you in
your bathing, you will be ready to say, 'I did not want only to bathe,
but to keep my will in harmony with nature, and I shall not so keep
it, if I lose my temper at what happens.'

5

What disturbs men's minds is not events but their judgments on
events. For instance, death is nothing dreadful, or else Socrates
would have thought it so. No, the only dreadful thing about it is
men's judgment that it is dreadful. And so when we are hindered,
or disturbed, or distressed, let us never lay the blame on others, but
on ourselves, that is, on our own judgments. To accuse others for
one's own misfortunes is a sign of want of education; to accuse oneself shows that one's education has begun; to accuse neither oneself
nor others shows that one's education is complete.

6

Be not elated at an excellence which is not your own. If the horse
in his pride were to say, 'I am handsome,' we could bear with it.
But when you say with pride, 'I have a handsome horse,' know that
the good horse is the ground of your pride. You ask then what you
can call your own. The answer is — the way you deal with your
impressions. Therefore when you deal with your impressions in
accord with nature, then you may be proud indeed, for your pride
will be in a good which is your own.

7

When you are on a voyage, and your ship is at anchorage, and
you disembark to get fresh water, you may pick up a small shellfish or a truffle by the way, but you must keep your attention fixed on
the ship, and keep looking towards it constantly, to see if the Helmsman calls you; and if he does, you have to leave everything, or be
bundled on board with your legs tied like a sheep. So it is in life.
If you have a dear wife or child given you, they are like the shellfish

or the truffle, they are very well in their way. Only, if the Helmsman call, run back to your ship, leave all else, and do not look behind you. And if you are old, never go far from the ship, so that when you are called you may not fail to appear.

8

Ask not that events should happen as you will, but let your will be that events should happen as they do, and you shall have peace.

9

Sickness is a hindrance to the body, but not to the will, unless the will consent. Lameness is a hindrance to the leg, but not to the will. Say this to yourself at each event that happens, for you shall find that though it hinders something else it will not hinder you.

10

When anything happens to you, always remember to turn to yourself and ask what faculty you have to deal with it. If you see a beautiful boy or a beautiful woman, you will find continence the faculty to exercise there; if trouble is laid on you, you will find endurance; if ribaldry, you will find patience. And if you train yourself in this habit your impressions will not carry you away.

11

Never say of anything, 'I lost it,' but say, 'I gave it back.' Has your child died? It was given back. Has your wife died? She was given back. Has your estate been taken from you? Was not this also given back? But you say, 'He who took it from me is wicked.' What does it matter to you through whom the Giver asked it back? As long as He gives it you, take care of it, but not as your own; treat it as passers-by treat an inn.

12

If you wish to make progress, abandon reasonings of this sort: 'If I neglect my affairs I shall have nothing to live on'; 'If I do not punish my son, he will be wicked.' For it is better to die of hunger, so that you be free from pain and free from fear, than to live in plenty and be troubled in mind. It is better for your son to be wicked than for you to be miserable. Wherefore begin with little things. Is your drop of oil spilt? Is your sup of wine stolen? Say to yourself, 'This is the price paid for freedom from passion, this is the price of a quiet mind.' Nothing can be had without a price. When you call your slave-boy, reflect that he may not be able to hear you, and if he hears you, he may not be able to do anything you want. But he is not so well off that it rests with him to give you peace of mind.

13

If you wish to make progress, you must be content in external matters to seem a fool and a simpleton; do not wish men to think you know anything, and if any should think you to be somebody, distrust yourself. For know that it is not easy to keep your will in accord with nature and at the same time keep outward things; if you attend to one you must needs neglect the other.

14

It is silly to want your children and your wife and your friends to live for ever, for that means that you want what is not in your control to be in your control, and what is not your own to be yours. In the same way if you want your servant to make no mistakes, you are a fool, for you want vice not to be vice but something different. But if you want not to be disappointed in your will to get, you can attain to that.

Exercise yourself then in what lies in your power. Each man's master is the man who has authority over what he wishes or does not wish, to secure the one or to take away the other. Let him then who wishes to be free not wish for anything or avoid anything that depends on others; or else he is bound to be a slave.

15

Remember that you must behave in life as you would at a banquet. A dish is handed round and comes to you; put out your hand and take it politely. It passes you; do not stop it. It has not reached you; do not be impatient to get it, but wait till your turn comes. Bear yourself thus towards children, wife, office, wealth, and one day you will be worthy to banquet with the gods. But if when they are set before you, you do not take them but despise them, then you shall not only share the gods' banquet, but shall share their rule. For by so doing Diogenes and Heraclitus and men like them were called divine and deserved the name.

16

When you see a man shedding tears in sorrow for a child abroad or dead, or for loss of property, beware that you are not carried away by the impression that it is outward ills that make him miserable. Keep this thought by you: 'What distresses him is not the event, for that does not distress another, but his judgment on the event.' Therefore do not hesitate to sympathize with him so far as words go, and if it so chance, even to groan with him; but take heed that you do not also groan in your inner being.

17

Remember that you are an actor in a play, and the Playwright chooses the manner of it: if he wants it short, it is short; if long, it is long. If he wants you to act a poor man you must act the part with all your powers; and so if your part be a cripple or a magistrate or a plain man. For your business is to act the character that is given you and act it well; the choice of the cast is Another's.

18

When a raven croaks with evil omen, let not the impression carry you away, but straightway distinguish in your own mind and say, 'These portents mean nothing to me; but only to my bit of a body or my bit of property or name, or my children or my wife. But for me all omens are favourable if I will, for, whatever the issue may be, it is in my power to get benefit therefrom.'

19

You can be invincible, if you never enter on a contest where victory is not in your power. Beware then that when you see a man raised to honour or great power or high repute you do not let your impression carry you away. For if the reality of good lies in what is in our power, there is no room for envy or jealousy. And you will not wish to be praetor, or prefect or consul, but to be free; and there is but one way to freedom — to despise what is not in our power.

20

Remember that foul words or blows in themselves are no outrage, but your judgment that they are so. So when any one makes you angry, know that it is your own thought that has angered you. Wherefore make it your first endeavour not to let your impressions carry you away. For if once you gain time and delay, you will find it easier to control yourself.

21

Keep before your eyes from day to day death and exile and all things that seem terrible, but death most of all, and then you will never set your thoughts on what is low and will never desire anything beyond measure.

22

If you set your desire on philosophy you must at once prepare to meet with ridicule and the jeers of many who will say, 'Here he is again, turned philosopher. Where has he got these proud looks?' Nay, put on no proud looks, but hold fast to what seems best to you, in confidence that God has set you at this post. And remember that if you abide where you are, those who first laugh at you will one day admire you, and that if you give way to them, you will get doubly laughed at.

23

If it ever happen to you to be diverted to things outside, so that you desire to please another, know that you have lost your life's plan. Be content then always to be a philosopher; if you wish to be regarded as one too, show yourself that you are one and you will be able to achieve it.

24

Let not reflections such as these afflict you: 'I shall live without honour, and never be of any account'; for if lack of honour is an evil, no one but yourself can involve you in evil any more than in shame. Is it your business to get office or to be invited to an entertainment? Certainly not.

Where then is the dishonour you talk of? How can you be 'of no account anywhere,' when you ought to count for something in those matters only which are in your power, where you may achieve the highest worth?

'But my friends,' you say, 'will lack assistance.'

What do you mean by 'lack assistance'? They will not have cash from you and you will not make them Roman citizens. Who told you that to do these things is in our power, and not dependent upon others? Who can give to another what is not his to give?

'Get them then,' says he, 'that we may have them.'

If I can get them and keep my self-respect, honour, magnanimity,

show the way and I will get them. But if you call on me to lose the
good things that are mine, in order that you may win things that are
not good, look how unfair and thoughtless you are. And which do
you really prefer? Money, or a faithful, modest friend? Therefore
help me rather to keep these qualities, and do not expect from me
actions which will make me lose them.

'But my country,' says he, 'will lack assistance, so far as lies in me.'

Once more I ask, What assistance do you mean? It will not owe
colonnades or baths to you. What of that? It does not owe shoes
to the blacksmith or arms to the shoemaker; it is sufficient if each man
fulfils his own function. Would you do it no good if you secured
to it another faithful and modest citizen?

'Yes.'

Well, then, you would not be useless to it.

'What place then shall I have in the city?'

Whatever place you can hold while you keep your character for
honour and self-respect. But if you are going to lose these qualities
in trying to benefit your city, what benefit, I ask, would you have
done her when you attain to the perfection of being lost to shame and
honour?

25

Has some one had precedence of you at an entertainment or a levée
or been called in before you to give advice? If these things are good
you ought to be glad that he got them; if they are evil, do not be angry
that you did not get them yourself. Remember that if you want to
get what is not in your power, you cannot earn the same reward as
others unless you act as they do. How is it possible for one who does
not haunt the great man's door to have equal shares with one who
does, or one who does not go in his train equality with one who does;
or one who does not praise him with one who does? You will be
unjust then and insatiable if you wish to get these privileges for
nothing, without paying their price. What is the price of a lettuce?
An obol perhaps. If then a man pays his obol and gets his lettuces,
and you do not pay and do not get them, do not think you are defrauded. For as he has the lettuces so you have the obol you did not
give. The same principle holds good too in conduct. You were not
invited to some one's entertainment? Because you did not give the
host the price for which he sells his dinner. He sells it for compliments, he sells it for attentions. Pay him the price then, if it is to
your profit. But if you wish to get the one and yet not give up the
other, nothing can satisfy you in your folly.

What! you say, you have nothing instead of the dinner?

Nay, you have this, you have not praised the man you did not want
to praise, you have not had to bear with the insults of his doorstep.

26

It is in our power to discover the will of Nature from those matters
on which we have no difference of opinion. For instance, when another man's slave has broken the wine-cup we are very ready to say
at once, 'Such things must happen.' Know then that when your own

cup is broken, you ought to behave in the same way as when your neighbour's was broken. Apply the same principle to higher matters. Is another's child or wife dead? Not one of us but would say, 'Such is the lot of man'; but when one's own dies, straightway one cries, 'Alas! miserable am I.' But we ought to remember what our feelings are when we hear it of another.

27
As a mark is not set up for men to miss it, so there is nothing intrinsically evil in the world.

28
If any one trusted your body to the first man he met, you would be indignant, but yet you trust your mind to the chance comer, and allow it to be disturbed and confounded if he revile you; are you not ashamed to do so?

29
In everything you do consider what comes first and what follows, and so approach it. Otherwise you will come to it with a good heart at first because you have not reflected on any of the consequences, and afterwards, when difficulties have appeared, you will desist to your shame. Do you wish to win at Olympia? So do I, by the gods, for it is a fine thing. But consider the first steps to it, and the consequences, and so lay your hand to the work. You must submit to discipline, eat to order, touch no sweets, train under compulsion, at a fixed hour, in heat and cold, drink no cold water, nor wine, except by order; you must hand yourself over completely to your trainer as you would to a physician, and then when the contest comes you must risk getting hacked, and sometimes dislocate your hand, twist your ankle, swallow plenty of sand, sometimes get a flogging, and with all this suffer defeat. When you have considered all this well, then enter on the athlete's course, if you still wish it. If you act without thought you will be behaving like children, who one day play at wrestlers, another day at gladiators, now sound the trumpet, and next strut the stage. Like them you will be now an athlete, now a gladiator, then orator, then philosopher, but nothing with all your soul. Like an ape, you imitate every sight you see, and one thing after another takes your fancy. When you undertake a thing you do it casually and half-heartedly, instead of considering it and looking at it all round. In the same way some people, when they see a philosopher and hear a man speaking like Euphrates (and indeed who can speak as he can?), wish to be philosophers themselves.

Man, consider first what it is you are undertaking; then look at your own powers and see if you can bear it. Do you want to compete in the pentathlon or in wrestling? Look to your arms, your thighs, see what your loins are like. For different men are born for different tasks. Do you suppose that if you do this you can live as you do now — eat and drink as you do now, indulge desire and discontent just as before? Nay, you must sit up late, work hard, abandon your own people, be looked down on by a mere slave, be ridiculed by those who meet you, get the worst of it in everything — in honour, in office,

in justice, in every possible thing.   This is what you have to consider:
whether you are willing to pay this price for peace of mind, freedom,
tranquillity.   If not, do not come near; do not be, like the children,
first a philosopher, then a tax-collector, then an orator, then one of
Caesar's procurators.   These callings do not agree.   You must be one
man, good or bad; you must develop either your Governing Principle,
or your outward endowments; you must study either your inner man,
or outward things — in a word, you must choose between the position
of a philosopher and that of a mere outsider.

30

Appropriate acts are in general measured by the relations they are
concerned with.   'He is your father.'   This means you are called on
to take care of him, give way to him in all things, bear with him if he
reviles or strikes you.

'But he is a bad father.'

Well, have you any natural claim to a good father?   No, only to a
father.

'My brother wrongs me.'

Be careful then to maintain the relation you hold to him, and do
not consider what he does, but what you must do if your purpose is
to keep in accord with nature.   For no one shall harm you, without
your consent; you will only be harmed, when you think you are
harmed.   You will only discover what is proper to expect from neighbour, citizen, or praetor, if you get into the habit of looking at the
relations implied by each.

31

For piety towards the gods know that the most important thing is
this: to have right opinions about them — that they exist, and that
they govern the universe well and justly — and to have set yourself
to obey them, and to give way to all that happens, following events
with a free will, in the belief that they are fulfilled by the highest
mind.   For thus you will never blame the gods, nor accuse them of
neglecting you.   But this you cannot achieve, unless you apply your
conception of good and evil to those things only which are in our
power, and not to those which are out of our power.   For if you apply
your notion of good or evil to the latter, then, as soon as you fail to
get what you will to get or fail to avoid what you will to avoid, you
will be bound to blame and hate those you hold responsible.   For
every living creature has a natural tendency to avoid and shun what
seems harmful and all that causes it, and to pursue and admire what
is helpful and all that causes it.   It is not possible then for one who
thinks he is harmed to take pleasure in what he thinks is the author
of the harm, any more than to take pleasure in the harm itself.   That
is why a father is reviled by his son, when he does not give his son a
share of what the son regards as good things; thus Polynices and
Eteocles were set at enmity with one another by thinking that a king's
throne was a good thing.   That is why the farmer, and the sailor, and
the merchant, and those who lose wife or children revile the gods.
For men's religion is bound up with their interest.   Therefore he

who makes it his concern rightly to direct his will to get and his will to avoid, is thereby making piety his concern. But it is proper on each occasion to make libation and sacrifice and to offer first-fruits according to the custom of our fathers, with purity and not in slovenly or careless fashion, without meanness and without extravagance.

32

When you make use of prophecy remember that while you know not what the issue will be, but are come to learn it from the prophet, you do know before you come what manner of thing it is, if you are really a philosopher. For if the event is not in our control, it cannot be either good or evil. Therefore do not bring with you to the prophet the will to get or the will to avoid, and do not approach him with trembling, but with your mind made up, that the whole issue is indifferent and does not affect you and that, whatever it be, it will be in your power to make good use of it, and no one shall hinder this. With confidence then approach the gods as counsellors, and further, when the counsel is given you, remember whose counsel it is, and whom you will be disregarding if you disobey. And consult the oracle, as Socrates thought men should, only when the whole question turns upon the issue of events, and neither reason nor any art of man provides opportunities for discovering what lies before you. Therefore, when it is your duty to risk your life with friend or country, do not ask the oracle whether you should risk your life. For if the prophet warns you that the sacrifice is unfavourable, though it is plain that this means death or exile or injury to some part of your body, yet reason requires that even at this cost you must stand by your friend and share your country's danger. Wherefore pay heed to the greater prophet, Pythian Apollo, who cast out of his temple the man who did not help his friend when he was being killed.

33

Lay down for yourself from the first a definite stamp and style of conduct, which you will maintain when you are alone and also in the society of men. Be silent for the most part, or, if you speak, say only what is necessary and in a few words. Talk, but rarely, if occasion calls you, but do not talk of ordinary things — of gladiators, or horse-races, or athletes, or of meats or drinks — these are topics that arise everywhere — but above all do not talk about men in blame or compliment or comparison. If you can, turn the conversation of your company by your talk to some fitting subject; but if you should chance to be isolated among strangers, be silent. Do not laugh much, nor at many things, nor without restraint.

Refuse to take oaths, altogether if that be possible, but if not, as far as circumstances allow.

Refuse the entertainments of strangers and the vulgar. But if occasion arise to accept them, then strain every nerve to avoid lapsing into the state of the vulgar. For know that, if your comrade have a stain on him, he that associates with him must needs share the stain, even though he be clean in himself.

For your body take just so much as your bare need requires, such as food, drink, clothing, house, servants, but cut down all that tends to luxury and outward show.

Avoid impurity to the utmost of your power before marriage, and if you indulge your passion, let it be done lawfully. But do not be offensive or censorious to those who indulge it, and do not be always bringing up your own chastity. If some one tells you that so and so speaks ill of you, do not defend yourself against what he says, but answer, 'He did not know my other faults, or he would not have mentioned these alone.'

It is not necessary for the most part to go to the games; but if you should have occasion to go, show that your first concern is for yourself; that is, wish that only to happen which does happen, and him only to win who does win, for so you will suffer no hindrance. But refrain entirely from applause, or ridicule, or prolonged excitement. And when you go away do not talk much of what happened there, except so far as it tends to your improvement. For to talk about it implies that the spectacle excited your wonder.

Do not go lightly or casually to hear lectures; but if you do go, maintain your gravity and dignity and do not make yourself offensive. When you are going to meet any one, and particularly some man of reputed eminence, set before your mind the thought, 'What would Socrates or Zeno have done?' and you will not fail to make proper use of the occasion.

When you go to visit some great man, prepare your mind by thinking that you will not find him in, that you will be shut out; that the doors will be slammed in your face, that he will pay no heed to you. And if in spite of all this you find it fitting for you to go, go and bear what happens and never say to yourself, 'It was not worth all this'; for that shows a vulgar mind and one at odds with outward things.

In your conversation avoid frequent and disproportionate mention of your own doings or adventures; for other people do not take the same pleasure in hearing what has happened to you as you take in recounting your adventures.

Avoid raising men's laughter; for it is a habit that easily slips into vulgarity, and it may well suffice to lessen your neighbour's respect.

It is dangerous too to lapse into foul language; when anything of the kind occurs, rebuke the offender, if the occasion allow, and if not, make it plain to him by your silence, or a blush or a frown, that you are angry at his words.

34

When you imagine some pleasure, beware that it does not carry you away, like other imaginations. Wait a while, and give yourself pause. Next remember two things: how long you will enjoy the pleasure, and also how long you will afterwards repent and revile yourself. And set on the other side the joy and self-satisfaction you will feel if you refrain. And if the moment seems come to realize it, take heed that you be not overcome by the winning sweetness and attraction of it; set in the other scale the thought how much better is the consciousness of having vanquished it.

35

When you do a thing because you have determined that it ought to be done, never avoid being seen doing it, even if the opinion of the multitude is going to condemn you. For if your action is wrong, then avoid doing it altogether, but if it is right, why do you fear those who will rebuke you wrongly?

36

The phrases, 'It is day' and 'It is night,' mean a great deal if taken separately, but have no meaning if combined. In the same way, to choose the larger portion at a banquet may be worth while for your body, but if you want to maintain social decencies it is worthless. Therefore, when you are at meat with another, remember not only to consider the value of what is set before you for the body, but also to maintain your self-respect before your host.

37

If you try to act a part beyond your powers, you not only disgrace yourself in it, but you neglect the part which you could have filled with success.

38

As in walking you take care not to tread on a nail or to twist your foot, so take care that you do not harm your Governing Principle. And if we guard this in everything we do, we shall set to work more securely.

39

Every man's body is a measure for his property, as the foot is the measure for his shoe. If you stick to this limit, you will keep the right measure; if you go beyond it, you are bound to be carried away down a precipice in the end; just as with the shoe, if you once go beyond the foot, your shoe puts on gilding, and soon purple and embroidery. For when once you go beyond the measure there is no limit.

40

Women from fourteen years upwards are called 'madam' by men. Wherefore, when they see that the only advantage they have got is to be marriageable, they begin to make themselves smart and to set all their hopes on this. We must take pains then to make them understand that they are really honoured for nothing but a modest and decorous life.

41

It is a sign of a dull mind to dwell upon the cares of the body, to prolong exercise, eating, drinking, and other bodily functions. These things are to be done by the way; all your attention must be given to the mind.

42

When a man speaks evil or does evil to you, remember that he does or says it because he thinks it is fitting for him. It is not possible for him to follow what seems good to you, but only what seems good to him, so that, if his opinion is wrong, he suffers, in that he is the victim of deception. In the same way, if a composite judgment which is true is thought to be false, it is not the judgment that suffers, but the man who is deluded about it.   If you act on this principle you will be gentle to him who reviles you, saying to yourself on each occasion, 'He thought it right.'

43

Everything has two handles, one by which you can carry it, the other by which you cannot.   If your brother wrongs you, do not take it by that handle, the handle of his wrong, for you cannot carry it by that, but rather by the other handle — that he is a brother, brought up with you, and then you will take it by the handle that you can carry by.

44

It is illogical to reason thus, 'I am richer than you, therefore I am superior to you,' 'I am more eloquent than you, therefore I am superior to you.'   It is more logical to reason, 'I am richer than you, therefore my property is superior to yours,' 'I am more eloquent than you, therefore my speech is superior to yours.'   You are something more than property or speech.

45

If a man wash quickly, do not say that he washes badly, but that he washes quickly.   If a man drink much wine, do not say that he drinks badly, but that he drinks much.   For till you have decided what judgment prompts him, how do you know that he acts badly?   If you do as I say, you will assent to your apprehensive impressions and to none other.

46

On no occasion call yourself a philosopher, nor talk at large of your principles among the multitude, but act on your principles.   For instance, at a banquet do not say how one ought to eat, but eat as you ought.   Remember that Socrates had so completely got rid of the thought of display that when men came and wanted an introduction to philosophers he took them to be introduced; so patient of neglect was he.   And if a discussion arise among the multitude on some principle, keep silent for the most part; for you are in great danger of blurting out some undigested thought.   And when some one says to you, 'You know nothing,' and you do not let it provoke you, then know that you are really on the right road.   For sheep do not bring grass to their shepherds and show them how much they have eaten, but they digest their fodder and then produce it in the form of wool and milk.   Do the same yourself; instead of displaying your principles to the multitude, show them the results of the principles you have digested.

47

When you have adopted the simple life, do not pride yourself upon it, and if you are a water-drinker do not say on every occasion, 'I am a water-drinker.'   And if you ever want to train laboriously, keep it to yourself and do not make a show of it.   Do not embrace statues.   If you are very thirsty take a good draught of cold water, and rinse your mouth and tell no one.

48

The ignorant man's position and character is this: he never looks to himself for benefit or harm, but to the world outside him. The philosopher's position and character is that he always looks to himself for benefit and harm.

The signs of one who is making progress are: he blames none, praises none, complains of none, accuses none, never speaks of himself as if he were somebody, or as if he knew anything. And if any one compliments him he laughs in himself at his compliment; and if one blames him, he makes no defence. He goes about like a convalescent, careful not to disturb his constitution on its road to recovery, until it has got firm hold. He has got rid of the will to get, and his will to avoid is directed no longer to what is beyond our power but only to what is in our power and contrary to nature. In all things he exercises his will without strain. If men regard him as foolish or ignorant he pays no heed. In one word, he keeps watch and guard on himself as his own enemy, lying in wait for him.

49

When a man prides himself on being able to understand and interpret the books of Chrysippus, say to yourself, 'If Chrysippus had not written obscurely this man would have had nothing on which to pride himself.'

What is my object? To understand Nature and follow her. I look then for some one who interprets her, and having heard that Chrysippus does I come to him. But I do not understand his writings, so I seek an interpreter. So far there is nothing to be proud of. But when I have found the interpreter it remains for me to act on his precepts; that and that alone is a thing to be proud of. But if I admire the mere power of exposition, it comes to this — that I am turned into a grammarian instead of a philosopher, except that I interpret Chrysippus in place of Homer. Therefore, when some one says to me, 'Read me Chrysippus,' when I cannot point to actions which are in harmony and correspondence with his teaching, I am rather inclined to blush.

50

Whatever principles you put before you, hold fast to them as laws which it will be impious to transgress. But pay no heed to what any one says of you; for this is something beyond your own control.

51

How long will you wait to think yourself worthy of the highest and transgress in nothing the clear pronouncement of reason? You have received the precepts which you ought to accept, and you have accepted them. Why then do you still wait for a master, that you may delay the amendment of yourself till he comes? You are a youth no longer, you are now a full-grown man. If now you are careless and indolent and are always putting off, fixing one day after another as the limit when you mean to begin attending to yourself, then, living or dying, you will make no progress but will continue unawares in ignorance. Therefore make up your mind before it is too late to live

as one who is mature and proficient, and let all that seems best to you
be a law that you cannot transgress.   And if you encounter anything
troublesome or pleasant or glorious or inglorious, remember that the
hour of struggle is come, the Olympic contest is here and you may
put off no longer, and that one day and one action determines whether
the progress you have achieved is lost or maintained.

This was how Socrates attained perfection, paying heed to nothing
but reason, in all that he encountered.   And if you are not yet Socrates, yet ought you to live as one who would wish to be a Socrates.

52

The first and most necessary department of philosophy deals with
the application of principles; for instance, 'not to lie'.   The second
deals with demonstrations; for instance, 'How comes it that one ought
not to lie?'   The third is concerned with establishing and analysing
these processes; for instance, 'How comes it that this is a demonstration?   What is demonstration, what is consequence, what is contradiction, what is true, what is false?'   It follows then that the third
department is necessary because of the second, and the second because
of the first.   The first is the most necessary part, and that in which
we must rest.   But we reverse the order: we occupy ourselves with
the third, and make that our whole concern, and the first we completely neglect.   Wherefore we lie, but are ready enough with the
demonstration that lying is wrong.

53

On every occasion we must have these thoughts at hand,
   'Lead me, O Zeus, and lead me, Destiny,
   Whither ordainèd is by your decree.
   I'll follow, doubting not, or if with will
   Recreant I falter, I shall follow still.'

[Cleanthes]

   'Who rightly with necessity complies
   In things divine we count him skilled and wise.'

[Euripides, Fragment 965]

   'Well, Crito, if this be the gods' will, so be it.'

[Plato, *Crito*, 43d]

   'Anytus and Meletus have power to put me to death,
   but not to harm me.'

[Plato, *Apology*, 30c]

[tr. P. E. MATHESON]

MARCUS AURELIUS

(121–180 A.D)

MEDITATIONS

BOOK III

We ought to consider not only that our life is daily wasting away and a smaller part of it is left, but another thing also must be taken into the account, that if a man should live longer, it is quite uncertain whether the understanding will still continue sufficient for the comprehension of things, and retain the power of contemplation which strives to acquire the knowledge of the divine and the human. For if he shall begin to fall into dotage, perspiration and nutrition and imagination and appetite, and whatever else there is of the kind, will not fail; but the power of making use of ourselves, and filling up the measure of our duty, and clearly separating all appearances, and considering whether a man should now depart from life, and whatever else of the kind absolutely requires a disciplined reason, all this is already extinguished. We must make haste then, not only because we are daily nearer to death, but also because the conception of things and the understanding of them cease first.

We ought to observe also that even the things which follow after the things which are produced according to nature contain something pleasing and attractive. For instance, when bread is baked some parts are split at the surface, and these parts which thus open, and have a certain fashion contrary to the purpose of the baker's art, are beautiful in a manner, and in a peculiar way excite a desire for eating. And again, figs, when they are quite ripe, gape open; and in the ripe olives the very circumstance of their being near to rottenness adds a peculiar beauty to the fruit. And the ears of corn bending down, and the lion's eyebrows, and the foam which flows from the mouth of wild boars, and many other things — though they are far from being beautiful, if a man should examine them severally, — still, because they are consequent upon the things which are formed by nature, help to adorn them, and they please the mind; so that if a man should have a feeling and deeper insight with respect to the things which are produced in the universe, there is hardly one of those which follow by way of consequence which will not seem to him to be in a manner disposed so as to give pleasure. And so he will see even the real gaping jaws of wild beasts with no less pleasure than those which painters and sculptors show by imitation; and in an old woman and an old man he will be able to see a certain maturity and comeliness; and the attractive loveliness of young persons he will be able to look on with chaste eyes; and many such things will present themselves, not pleasing to every man, but to him only who has become truly familiar with nature and her works.

Hippocrates after curing many diseases himself fell sick and died.

The Chaldaei foretold the deaths of many, and then fate caught them too. Alexander, and Pompeius, and Gaius Caesar, after so often completely destroying whole cities, and in battle cutting to pieces many ten thousands of cavalry and infantry, themselves too at last departed from life. Heraclitus, after so many speculations on the conflagration of the universe, was filled with water internally and died smeared all over with mud. And lice destroyed Democritus; and other lice killed Socrates. What means all this? Thou hast embarked, thou hast made the voyage, thou art come to shore; get out. If indeed to another life, there is no want of gods, not even there. But if to a state without sensation, thou wilt cease to be held by pains and pleasures, and to be a slave to the vessel, which is as much inferior as that which serves it is superior: for the one is intelligence and deity; the other is earth and corruption.

Do not waste the remainder of thy life in thoughts about others, when thou dost not refer thy thoughts to some object of common utility. For thou losest the opportunity of doing something else when thou hast such thoughts as these, What is such a person doing, and why, and what is he saying, and what is he thinking of, and what is he contriving, and whatever else of the kind makes us wander away from the observation of our own ruling power. We ought then to check in the series of our thoughts everything that is without a purpose and useless, but most of all the overcurious feeling and the malignant; and a man should use himself to think of those things only about which if one should suddenly ask, What hast thou now in thy thoughts? with perfect openness thou mightest immediately answer, This or That; so that from thy words it should be plain that everything in thee is simple and benevolent, and such as befits a social animal, and one that cares not for thoughts about pleasure or sensual enjoyments at all, nor has any rivalry or envy and suspicion, or anything else for which thou wouldst blush if thou shouldst say that thou hadst it in thy mind. For the man who is such and no longer delays being among the number of the best, is like a priest and minister of the gods, using too the deity which is planted within him, which makes the man uncontaminated by pleasure, unharmed by any pain, untouched by any insult, feeling no wrong, a fighter in the noblest fight, one who cannot be overpowered by any passion, dyed deep with justice, accepting with all his soul everything which happens and is assigned to him as his portion; and not often, nor yet without great necessity and for the general interest, imagining what another says, or does, or thinks. For it is only what belongs to himself that he makes the matter for his activity; and he constantly thinks of that which is allotted to himself out of the sum total of things, and he makes his own acts fair, and he is persuaded that his own portion is good. For the lot which is assigned to each man is carried along with him and carries him along with it. And he remembers also that every rational animal is his kinsman, and that to care for all men is according to man's nature; and a man should hold on to the opinion not of all, but of those only who confessedly live according to nature. But as to those who live not so, he always bears in mind what kind of men they are both at home and from home, both by night and by day, and what they are, and with what men they live an impure life. Accordingly, he does not value at all the praise which comes from such men, since they are not even satisfied with themselves.

Labour not unwillingly, not without regard to the common interest, nor without due consideration nor with distraction; nor let studied ornament set off thy thoughts, and be not either a man of many words, or busy about too many things. And further, let the deity which is in thee be the guardian of a living being, manly and of ripe age, and engaged in matter political, and a Roman, and a ruler, who has taken his post like a man waiting for the signal which summons him from life, and ready to go, having need neither of oath nor of any man's testimony. Be cheerful also, and seek not external help nor the tranquillity which others give. A man then must stand erect, not be kept erect by others.

[1-5, tr. G. Long]

HISTORY

The Greeks were not the first to chronicle the events of the past, but they invented history in the sense in which we use the word to-day. The Greek word *historia* means an investigation or inquiry into the alleged facts, in order to determine what the *true* facts are; in achieving this purpose the investigator is bound to apply the tests of logic and common sense to the mass of material he collects, and such a process gives rise to critical and "scientific" history. Among the Greeks this process apparently began with Hecataeus of Miletus (*fl.* 495 B.C.), whose lost work entitled *Genealogies* began with the words: "What I write here is the account which I considered to be true. For the stories of the Greeks are numerous and, in my opinion, ridiculous." The earlier Greek historians, to be sure, fell far short of modern standards for historical criticism: their information was often insufficient, they lacked the aids of archaeological evidence and exact chronological data, and they were incurably credulous. None the less, we must not underestimate their achievement: they were the first to apply any sort of critical tests to the confused and contradictory record of the past.

The second great achievement of the Greeks in historical writing was the creation of "philosophical" history. They sought not for a record of isolated and unrelated events, but for the causes of things and the inner meaning of human events, so that history might become an approach to reality and a meaningful interpretation of life. As far as we can judge, an essentially philosophic approach to history, despite its shortcomings, first appeared in Herodotus, who saw in the constant flux of human fortunes the divine hand of Nemesis, or Retribution. He shared with many Greek thinkers a belief that cities and men were ill adapted to stand prosperity: wealth and power lead to arrogance, which is punished by an envious divinity, who does not permit men to entertain great thoughts about themselves. No doubt, such preconceptions lead to error and misinterpretations of historical material; yet the fact is that no historian can deal adequately with human events without some universal concepts to which he may refer the scattered and apparently unrelated events of the past. Thucydides is, in this respect, much more "scientific" than Herodotus; for he rejects the superhuman element in history altogether and seeks the underlying explanation of historical events in the human spheres of mass psychology and political principles. The course of human events depends not on the arbitrary actions of an unpredictable deity, but on the political institutions, the character and emotions of the men involved — factors which can be weighed and calculated in advance; it is for this reason that Thucydides proclaims his work "an everlasting possession." For him, and for Polybius, history is a school for the statesman and an educative force in the community, although Polybius, when he started writing history, seems to have had a conception of Fortune, or Tyché, as a superhuman power which exercises a direct and unpredictable control over human affairs, much like Herodotus' divine Nemesis.

Finally, the Greeks developed the presentation of historical material in artistic form. In part, the literary value of the Greek historians depends on the universal and philosophic aspects of history which have already been mentioned; but it also stems from a conscious attempt to cast history in a literary form, with the aid of a careful arrangement of material and the use of the various rhetorical devices which contribute to an artistic prose style. Considered as a work of art, Herodotus' history, with its broad scope, its variety of incidents and interludes, and its flowing narrative style, has been aptly compared to the epic. Thucydides is akin rather to the dramatists: his work is concentrated on a strictly delimited theme, and admits few digressions; the Sicilian Expedition forms a sort of *peripety,* or reversal of fortune, for the Athenians; and the speeches which interrupt the narrative perform, in part, the function of the choral odes in a tragedy. Thucydides attains the ideal balance between artistic form and accurate presentation of facts; after his time history steadily degenerated into a form of rhetorical exercise. Polybius is the one striking exception to this tendency: he treats history with a minimum of unnecessary rhetoric and, as far as he is able, with scientific accuracy.

In conclusion, a few words on each of the historians represented here must be added; for additional material the reader is referred to the handbooks listed in the Bibliography, particularly to Bury's, *The Ancient Greek Historians.*

Herodotus was a native of Halicarnassus, a Greek city in Asia Minor, from which he was banished about 454 B.C.; he traveled widely, spent some time in Athens, and went as a colonist to the city of Thurii in Italy, which was founded in 444 B.C. The date of his death is unknown, but he refers to events as late as 429 B.C. His history covers the period from the founding of the Persian Empire by Cyrus to the events of the year 478 B.C.; whether or not he meant to end his work at this date is an unsettled question. It is filled with digressions, and, besides history in our sense, includes investigations and speculations on geography, ethnology, religion, and various other topics. To its variety of contents the work owes much of its attraction for readers in all ages. But its greatest charm lies in the many engaging anecdotes which Herodotus inserts; no author, save perhaps Plutarch, delights so much in a good story for its own sake. Since many of these stories are incredible, not to say absurd, Herodotus has earned a reputation for naive credulity; it is, however, important to note his remark: "I am bound to relate what is told me, but I am not bound to believe it all alike — and let this remark apply to all my history." (VII. 152) Within the limits possible in his age, Herodotus was indeed a skeptic. Finally, a large portion of his appeal to moderns lies in his inspiring theme; Herodotus has succeeded in recapturing and conveying to his readers the heroic quality of the Greek resistance which turned back the invasion of Eastern despotism on the very threshold of Western Europe.

Thucydides the Athenian, the greatest historian of antiquity, was about a generation younger than Herodotus. He tells us that when the Peloponnesian War broke out (431 B.C.), he was of mature years and started taking notes on the war, judging that it would be long and important. He was elected one of the Athenian generals in 424, and was in command in Thrace when the Athenians lost Amphipolis, their most important stronghold in that district; for his failure to hold the city he was banished and lived in exile for twenty years; after the fall of Athens in 404 B.C., he returned to his native city and lived there until his death shortly after 400. His history of the war was left incomplete, for his account breaks off in the events of the year 411. Thucydides' principles of historical investigation are carefully set forth and illustrated in the opening chapters of his first book, to which the reader is referred for a statement of his aims and ideals (pp. 739–748); in the words of a competent modern historian: "This sketch remains a shining example of sheer historical insight and grasp." * The reader should also note Thucydides' objective presentation of his material (he allows his characters to speak for themselves and seldom gives an explicit moral judgment), his use of speeches to illuminate events and to place them in their proper setting, and his keen interest in political principles, from which he largely eliminated conventional morality and sentiment.

Xenophon was an Athenian of wholly respectable and conventional mentality. As a young man he listened to the discussions of Socrates (whom he comprehended only in part), and then left Athens to serve under Cyrus the Younger in the expedition described in the *Anabasis*. He was later exiled from Athens for fighting on the Spartan side at the battle of Coronea (394 B.C.), and spent most of the rest of his life on a country estate in Elis. His chief historical works are the *Hellenica*, a history of Greece from 411 to 361 B.C., and the *Anabasis*. He was a somewhat prosaic man, with the gifts of a first-rate journalist; what he himself has seen, he reports clearly and often vividly, and when he is dealing with a fascinating subject, like the march of the Ten Thousand in the *Anabasis*, he is at his best. But he lacks the penetrating mind of the true historian and fails to grasp the underlying significance of the events he relates. He was a hero-worshipper and a monarchist by instinct; this trait is shown both in his *Agesilaus*, a eulogizing biography of the Spartan king under whom he had served, and in the sketch of Cyrus, which is given below; the latter passage was later elaborated by Xenophon into a full-scale, moralizing biography, the *Education of Cyrus*, a romanticized portrait of Cyrus the Great, which was doubtless intended as a "Mirror of the Prince" for future rulers.

Polybius, the last great Greek historian, lived in the second century B.C.; he was an Arcadian, the son of a leading statesman of the Achaean League. In 167 B.C. he was taken to Rome as a hostage,

* Bury, *Ancient Greek Historians*, p. 102.

along with two thousand other prominent members of the League. Polybius had the good fortune to become intimate with some of the most important Roman statesmen, especially the younger Scipio, and he spent sixteen years in Rome. His situation gave him an unparalleled insight into the history of his own times, and he conceived the idea of his great work, which seeks to explain how in a short period of fifty-three years (220–167 B.C.) the Romans conquered the civilized world; he later expanded the work to include events down to 146 B.C. Of all later historians, Polybius most closely approaches Thucydides: both believed that the first duty of an historian is to discover and set forth the facts as they actually occurred; and they agree that the purpose of their work is to instruct, not to entertain. But Thucydides is an artist, Polybius, a preacher: he constantly draws the moral for his readers, and his diffuse explanations of the obvious become wearisome. He insists, even more than Thucydides, on the importance of political considerations in history, and the most famous portion of his work is the section which he devoted to his theory of constitutional cycles and the analysis of the Roman constitution — a passage which had a notable influence on the authors of our own Constitution,* thereby fulfilling Polybius' hope that his work might serve as a handbook for future statesmen.

* Cf. Gilbert Chinard, "Polybius and the American Constitution," *Journal of the History of Ideas* I (1940) 38–58.

HERODOTUS

(*ca.* 490–*ca.* 425 B.C.)

THE PERSIAN WARS

SOLON AND CROESUS

[According to Herodotus, Croesus, King of Lydia, *ca.* 560–546 B.C., was the first to commence aggression against the Greeks; he brought under his sway almost all the nations in Asia Minor west of the Halys River and subdued, one by one, all the Greek cities in the same area, forcing them to pay him tribute.

The famous conversation of Solon and Croesus, which is reported in the following chapters, has been unanimously condemned as fabulous by historians, both ancient and modern, on chronological grounds, although Plutarch thought such grounds insufficient for rejecting so good a story (see p. 860 below). The interview should be considered, however, not from the point of view of its historicity but of its function in Herodotus' narrative. At the very beginning of his account of the struggle between East and West, the historian tries to set forth in this conversation the contrasting ideals and manners of the two antagonists, Europe and Asia. Also, in Solon's words Herodotus expresses his own views on the transitory nature of human fortunes and on the divine law of Nemesis, the chief features of his philosophy of history.]

When all these conquests had been added to the Lydian empire, and the prosperity of Sardis was now at its height, there came thither, one after another, all the sages of Greece living at the time, and among them Solon, the Athenian. He was on his travels, having left Athens to be absent ten years, under the pretence of wishing to see the world, but really to avoid being forced to repeal any of the laws which, at the request of the Athenians, he had made for them. Without his sanction the Athenians could not repeal them, as they had bound themselves under a heavy curse to be governed for ten years by the laws which should be imposed on them by Solon.

On this account, as well as to see the world, Solon set out upon his travels, in the course of which he went to Egypt to the court of Amasis, and also came on a visit to Croesus at Sardis. Croesus received him as his guest, and lodged him in the royal palace. On the third or fourth day after, he bade his servants conduct Solon over his treasuries, and show him all their greatness and magnificence. When he had seen them all, and, so far as time allowed, inspected them, Croesus addressed this question to him, "Stranger of Athens, we have heard much of your wisdom and of your travels through many lands, from love of knowledge and a wish to see the world. I am curious therefore to inquire of you, whom, of all the men that you have seen, you consider the most happy?" This he asked because he thought himself the happiest of mortals: but Solon answered him without flattery, according to his true sentiments, "Tellus of Athens, sire." Full of astonishment at what he heard, Croesus demanded sharply,

"And wherefore do you deem Tellus happiest?" To which the other replied, "First, because his country was flourishing in his days, and he himself had sons both beautiful and good, and he lived to see children born to each of them, and these children all grew up; and further because, after a life spent in what our people look upon as comfort, his end was surpassingly glorious. In a battle between the Athenians and their neighbours near Eleusis, he came to the assistance of his countrymen, routed the foe, and died upon the field most gallantly. The Athenians gave him a public funeral on the spot where he fell, and paid him the highest honours."

Thus did Solon admonish Croesus by the example of Tellus, enumerating the manifold particulars of his happiness. When he had ended, Croesus inquired a second time, who after Tellus seemed to him the happiest, expecting that, at any rate, he would be given the second place. "Cleobis and Bito," Solon answered, "they were of Argive race: their fortune was enough for their wants, and they were besides endowed with so much bodily strength that they had both gained prizes at the Games. Also this tale is told of them: There was a great festival in honour of the goddess Hera at Argos, to which their mother must needs be taken in a car. Now the oxen did not come home from the field in time: so the youths, fearful of being too late, put the yoke on their own necks, and themselves drew the car in which their mother rode. Five miles they drew her, and stopped before the temple. This deed of theirs was witnessed by the whole assembly of worshippers, and then their life closed in the best possible way. Herein, too, God showed forth most evidently, how much better a thing for man death is than life. For the Argive men stood thick around the car and extolled the vast strength of the youths; and the Argive women extolled the mother who was blessed with such a pair of sons; and the mother herself, overjoyed at the deed and at the praises it had won, standing straight before the image, besought the goddess to bestow on Cleobis and Bito, the sons who had so mightily honoured her, the highest blessing to which mortals can attain. Her prayer ended, they offered sacrifice, and partook of the holy banquet, after which the two youths fell asleep in the temple. They never woke more, but so passed from the earth. The Argives, looking on them as among the best of men, caused statues of them to be made, which they gave to the shrine at Delphi."

When Solon had thus assigned these youths the second place, Croesus broke in angrily, "What, stranger of Athens, is my happiness, then, valued so little by you, that you do not even put me on a level with private men?"

"Croesus," replied the other, "you asked a question concerning the condition of man, of one who knows that the power above us is full of jealousy, and fond of troubling our lot. A long life gives one to witness much, and experience much oneself, that one would not choose. Seventy years I regard as the limit of the life of man. In these seventy years are contained, without reckoning intercalary months, 25,200 days. Add an intercalary month to every other year, that the seasons may come round at the right time, and there will be, besides the seventy years, thirty-five such months, making an addition of 1,050 days. The whole number of the days contained in the seventy years will thus be 26,250, whereof not one but will produce events unlike the rest. Hence man is wholly accident. For yourself, Croesus, I see that you are wonderfully rich, and the lord of many nations; but with respect to your question, I have no answer to give, until I hear that you have closed your life happily. For assuredly he who possesses great store of riches is no nearer happiness than he who has what suffices for his daily needs, unless luck attend upon him, and so he continue in the enjoyment of all his good things to the end of life. For many of the wealthiest men have been unfavoured of fortune, and many whose means were moderate, have had excellent luck. Men of the former class excel those of the latter but in two respects; these last excel the former in many. The wealthy man is better able to content his desires, and to bear up against a sudden buffet of calamity. The other has less ability to withstand these evils (from which, however, his good luck keeps him clear), but he enjoys all these following blessings: he is whole of limb, a stranger to disease, free from misfortune, happy in his children, and comely to look upon. If, in addition to all this, he end his life well, he is of a truth the man of whom you are in search, the man who may rightly be termed happy. Call him, however, until he die, not happy but fortunate. Scarcely, indeed, can any man unite all these advantages: as there is no country which contains within it all that it needs, but each, while it possesses some things, lacks others, and the best country is that which contains the most; so no single human being is complete in every respect — something is always lacking. He who unites the greatest number of advantages, and retaining them to the day of his death, then dies peaceably, that man alone, sire, is, in my judgment, entitled to bear the name of 'happy.' But in every matter we must mark well the end; for oftentimes God gives men a gleam of happiness, and then plunges them into ruin."

Such was the speech which Solon addressed to Croesus, a speech which brought him neither largess nor honour. The king saw him depart with much indifference, since he thought that a man must be an arrant fool who made no account of present good, but bade men always wait and mark the end.

[I. 29–33, tr. G. Rawlinson]

[The kingdom of Croesus was later overthrown by Cyrus the Great, the founder of the Persian Empire, who thus became the overlord of all the Greek cities in Asia.

After the death of Cyrus, his son and successor, Cambyses, undertook the conquest of Egypt. At this point Herodotus interrupts his narrative of the growth of the Persian power to describe at great length the geography, customs, wonders, and history of Egypt — a digression that fills the entire second book of his history. A short, but typical selection follows.]

THE EGYPTIANS

Concerning Egypt itself I shall extend my remarks to a great length, because there is no country that possesses so many wonders, nor any that has such a number of works which defy description. Not only is the climate different from that of the rest of the world, and the rivers unlike any other rivers, but the people also, in most of their manners and customs, exactly reverse the common practice of mankind. The women attend the markets and trade, while the men sit at home at the loom; and here, while the rest of the world works the woof up the warp, the Egyptians work it down; the women likewise carry burdens upon their shoulders, while the men carry them upon their heads. Women stand up to urinate, men sit down. They eat their food out of doors in the streets, but relieve themselves in their houses, giving as a reason that what is unseemly, but necessary, ought to be done in secret, but what has nothing unseemly about it, should be done openly. A woman cannot serve the priestly office, either for god or goddess, but men are priests to both; sons need not support their parents unless they choose, but daughters must, whether they choose or no.

In other countries the priests have long hair, in Egypt their heads are shaven; elsewhere it is customary, in mourning, for near relations to cut their hair close; the Egyptians, who wear no hair at any other time, when they lose a relative, let their beards and the hair of their heads grow long. All other men pass their lives separate from animals, the Egyptians have animals always living with them; others make barley and wheat their food, it is a disgrace to do so in Egypt, where the grain they live on is spelt, which some call zea. Dough they knead with their feet, but they mix mud, and even take up dung with their hands. They are the only people in the world — they at least, and such as have learnt the practice from them — who use circumcision. Their men wear two garments apiece, their women but one. They put on the rings and fasten the ropes to sails inside, others put them outside. When they write or calculate, instead of going, like the Greeks, from left to right, they move their hand from right to left; and they insist, notwithstanding, that it is they who go to the right, and the Greeks who go to the left. They have two quite different kinds of writing, one of which is called sacred, the other common.

They are religious to excess, far beyond any other race of men, and use the following ceremonies: They drink out of brazen cups, which they scour every day: there is no exception to this practice. They wear linen garments, which they are specially careful to have always fresh washed. They practise circumcision for the sake of cleanliness, considering it better to be cleanly than comely. The priests shave their whole body every other day, that no lice or other impure thing may adhere to them when they are engaged in the service of the gods. Their dress is entirely of linen, and their shoes of the papyrus plant: it is not lawful for them to wear either dress or shoes of any other material. They bathe twice every day in cold water, and twice each night. Besides which they observe, so to speak, thousands of ceremonies. They enjoy, however, not a few advantages. They consume none of their own property, and are at no expense for anything; but every day bread is baked for them of the sacred corn, and a plentiful supply of beef and of goose's flesh is assigned to each, and also a portion of wine made from the grape. Fish they are not allowed to eat; and beans, which none of the Egyptians ever sow, or eat, if they come up of their own accord, either raw or boiled, the priests will not even endure to look on, since they consider it an unclean kind of pulse. Instead of a single priest, each god has the attendance of a college, at the head of which is a chief priest; when one of these dies, his son is appointed in his room.

Male kine are reckoned to belong to Epaphus, and are therefore tested in the following manner: One of the priests appointed for the purpose searches to see if there is a single black hair on the whole body, since in that case the beast is unclean. He examines him all over, standing on his legs, and again laid upon his back; after which he takes the tongue out of his mouth, to see if it be clean in respect of the prescribed marks (what they are I will mention elsewhere); he also inspects the hairs of the tail, to observe if they grow naturally. If the animal is pronounced clean in all these various points, the priest marks him by twisting a piece of papyrus round his horns, and attaching thereto some sealing-clay, which he then stamps with his own signet-ring. After this the beast is led away; and it is forbidden, under the penalty of death, to sacrifice an animal which has not been marked in this way.

The following is their manner of sacrifice: They lead the victim, marked with their signet, to the altar where they are about to offer it, and setting the wood alight, pour a libation of wine upon the altar in front of the victim, and at the same time invoke the god. Then they slay the animal, and cutting off his head, proceed to flay the body. Next they take the head, and heaping imprecations on it, if there is a market-place and a body of Greek traders in the city, they carry it there and sell it instantly; if, however, there are no Greeks among them, they throw the head into the river. The imprecation is to this effect: They pray that if any evil is impending either over those who sacrifice, or over universal Egypt, it may be made to fall upon that head. These practices, the imprecations upon the heads, and the libation of wine, prevail all over Egypt, and extend to victims of all sorts; and hence the Egyptians will never eat the head of any animal.

The disembowelling and burning are however different in different sacrifices. I will mention the mode in use with respect to the goddess whom they regard as the greatest, and honour with the chiefest festival. When they have flayed their steer they pray, and when their prayer is ended they take the paunch of the animal out entire, leaving the intestines and the fat inside the body; they then cut off the legs, the end of the loins, the shoulders, and the neck; and having so done, they fill the body of the steer with clean bread, honey, raisins, figs, frankincense, myrrh, and other aromatics. Thus filled, they burn the body, pouring over it great quantities of oil. Before offering the sacrifice they fast, and while the bodies of the victims are being consumed they beat themselves. Afterwards, when they have concluded this part of the ceremony, they have the other parts of the victim served up to them for a repast.

The male kine, therefore, if clean, and the male calves, are used for sacrifice by the Egyptians universally; but the female they are not allowed to sacrifice, since they are sacred to Isis. The statue of this goddess has the form of a woman but with horns like a cow, resembling thus the Greek representations of Io; and the Egyptians, one and all, venerate cows much more highly than any other animal. This is the reason why no native of Egypt, whether man or woman, will give a Greek a kiss, or use the knife of a Greek, or his spit, or his cauldron, or taste the flesh of an ox, known to be pure, if it has been cut with a Greek knife. When kine die, the following is the manner of their sepulture: The females are thrown into the river; the males are buried in the suburbs of the towns, with one or both of their horns appearing above the surface of the ground to mark the place. When the bodies are decayed, a boat comes, at an appointed time, from the island called Prosopitis, which is a portion of the Delta, sixty miles in circumference, — and calls at the several cities in turn to collect the bones of the oxen. Prosopitis is a district containing several cities; the name of that from which the boats come is Atarbechis. Aphrodite has a temple there of much sanctity. Great numbers of men go forth from this city and proceed to the other towns, where they dig up the bones, which they take away with them and bury together in one place. The same practice prevails with respect to the interment of all other cattle — the law so determining; they do not slaughter any of them.

Such Egyptians as possess a temple of the Theban Zeus, or live in the Thebaic nome, offer no sheep in sacrifice, but only goats; for the Egyptians do not all worship the same gods, excepting Isis and Osiris, the latter of whom they say is the Grecian Dionysus. Those, on the contrary, who possess a temple dedicated to Mendes, or belong to the Mendesian canton, abstain from offering goats, and sacrifice sheep instead. The Thebans, and such as imitate them in their practice, give the following account of the origin of the custom, "Heracles," they say, "wished of all things to see Zeus, but Zeus did not choose to be seen of him. At length, when Heracles persisted, Zeus hit on a device — to flay a ram, and, cutting off his head, hold the head before him, and cover himself with the fleece. In this guise he showed himself to Heracles." Therefore the Egyptians give their statues of Zeus the face of a ram; and from them the practice has passed to the Ammonians, who are a joint colony of Egyptians and Ethiopians, speaking a language between the two; hence also, in my opinion, the latter people took their name of Ammonians, since the

Egyptian name for Zeus is Amun. Such then is the reason why the Thebans do not sacrifice rams, but consider them sacred animals. Upon one day in the year, however, at the festival of Zeus, they slay a single ram, and stripping off the fleece, cover with it the statue of that god, as he once covered himself, and then bring up to the statue of Zeus an image of Heracles. When this has been done, the whole assembly beat their breasts in mourning for the ram, and afterwards bury him in a holy sepulchre.

The account which I received of this Heracles makes him one of the twelve gods. Of the other Heracles, with whom the Greeks are familiar, I could hear nothing in any part of Egypt. That the Greeks, however (those I mean who gave the son of Amphitryon that name), took the name from the Egyptians, and not the Egyptians from the Greeks, is I think clearly proved, among other arguments, by the fact that both the parents of Heracles, Amphitryon as well as Alcmena, were of Egyptian origin. Again, the Egyptians disclaim all knowledge of the names of Poseidon and the Dioscuri, and do not include them in the number of their gods; but had they adopted the name of any god from the Greeks, these would have been the likeliest to obtain notice, since the Egyptians, as I am well convinced, practised navigation at that time, and the Greeks also were some of them mariners, so that they would have been more likely to know the names of these gods than that of Heracles. But the Egyptian Heracles is one of their ancient gods. Seventeen thousand years before the reign of Amasis, the twelve gods were, they affirm, produced from the eight: and of these twelve, Heracles is one.

In the wish to get the best information that I could on these matters, I made a voyage to Tyre in Phoenicia, hearing there was a temple of Heracles at that place, very highly venerated. I visited the temple, and found it richly adorned with a number of offerings, among which were two pillars, one of pure gold, the other of emerald, shining with great brilliancy at night. In a conversation which I held with the priests, I inquired how long their temple had been built, and found by their answer that they too differed from the Greeks. They said that the temple was built at the same time that the city was founded, and that the foundation of the city took place 2300 years ago. In Tyre I remarked another temple where the same god was worshipped as the Thasian Heracles. So I went on to Thasos, where I found a temple of Heracles which had been built by the Phoenicians who colonized that island when they sailed in search of Europa. Even this was five generations earlier than the time when Heracles, son of Amphitryon, was born in Greece. These researches show plainly that there is an ancient god Heracles; and my own opinion is, that those Greeks act most wisely who build and maintain two temples of Heracles, in the one of which the Heracles worshipped is known by the name of Olympian, and has sacrifice offered to him as an immortal, while in the other the honours paid are such as are due to a hero.

The Greeks tell many tales without due investigation, and among them the following silly fable respecting Heracles. "Heracles," they say, "went once to Egypt, and there the inhabitants took him, and putting a chaplet on his head, led him out in solemn procession, intending to offer him a sacrifice to Zeus. For a while he submitted quietly; but when they led him up to the altar, and began the ceremonies, he put forth his strength and slew them all." Now to me it seems that such a story proves the Greeks to be utterly ignorant of the character and customs of the people. The Egyptians do not think it allowable even to sacrifice cattle, excepting sheep, and the male kine and calves, provided they be pure, and also geese. How then can it be believed that they would sacrifice men? And again, how would it have been possible for Heracles alone, and, as they confess, a mere mortal, to destroy so many thousands? In saying thus much concerning these matters, may I incur no displeasure either of god or hero!

I mentioned above that some of the Egyptians abstain from sacrificing goats, either male or female. The reason is the following: These Egyptians, who are the Mendesians, consider Pan to be one of the eight gods who existed before the twelve, and Pan is represented in Egypt by the painters and the sculptors, just as he is in Greece, with the face and legs of a goat. They do not, however, believe this to be his shape, or consider him in any respect unlike the other gods; but they represent him thus for a reason which I prefer not to relate. The Mendesians hold all goats in veneration, but the male more than the female, giving the goatherds of the males especial honour. One is venerated more highly than all the rest, and when he dies there is a great mourning throughout all the Mendesian nome. In Egyptian, the goat and Pan are both called Mendes. In my own lifetime a monstrous thing took place in this nome when a woman had intercourse with a goat in public so that it became a matter of common knowledge.

The pig is regarded among them as an unclean animal, so much so that if a man in passing accidentally touch a pig, he instantly hurries to the river, and plunges in with all his clothes on. Hence too the swineherds, notwithstanding that they are of pure Egyptian blood, are forbidden to enter into any of the temples, which are open to all other Egyptians; and further, no one will give his daughter in marriage to a swineherd, or take a wife from among them, so that the swineherds are forced to intermarry among themselves. They do not offer swine in sacrifice to any of their gods, excepting Dionysus and the Moon, whom they honour in this way at the same time, sacrificing pigs to both of them at the same full moon, and afterwards eating of the flesh. There is a reason alleged by them for their detestation of swine at all other seasons, and their use of them at this festival, with which I am well acquainted, but which I do not think it proper to mention. The following is the mode in which they sacrifice the swine to the Moon: As soon as the victim is slain, the tip of the tail, the spleen, and the caul are put together, and having been covered with all the fat that has been found in the animal's belly, are straightway burnt. The remainder of the flesh is eaten on the same day that the sacrifice is offered, which is the day of the full moon: at any other time they would not so much as taste it. The poorer sort, who cannot afford live pigs, form pigs of dough, which they bake and offer in sacrifice.

To Dionysus, on the eve of his feast, every Egyptian sacrifices a hog before the door of his house, which is then given back to the swineherd by whom it was furnished, and by him carried away. In other respects the festival is celebrated almost exactly as Dionysiac festivals are in Greece, excepting that the Egyptians have no choral dances. They also use instead of phalli another invention, consisting of images eighteen inches high, pulled by strings, which the women carry round to the villages. These images have male members of about the same size also operated by strings. A piper goes in front, and the women follow, singing hymns in honour of Dionysus. They give a religious reason for the peculiarities of the image.

Melampus, the son of Amytheon, cannot (I think) have been ignorant of this ceremony — nay, he must, I should conceive, have been well acquainted with it. He it was who introduced into Greece the name of Dionysus, the ceremonial of his worship, and the procession of the phallus. He did not, however, so completely apprehend the whole doctrine as to be able to communicate it entirely, but various sages since his time have carried out his teaching to greater perfection. Still it is certain that Melampus introduced the phallus, and that the Greeks learnt from him the ceremonies which they now practise. I therefore maintain that Melampus, who was a wise man, and had acquired the art of divination, having become acquainted with the worship of Dionysus through knowledge derived from Egypt, introduced it into Greece, with a few slight changes, at the same time that he brought in various other practices. For I can by no means allow that it is by mere coincidence that the ceremonies of Dionysus in Greece are so nearly the same as the Egyptian — they would then have been more Greek in their character, and less recent in their origin. Much less can I admit that the Egyptians borrowed these customs, or any other, from the Greeks. My belief is that Melampus got his knowledge of them from Cadmus the Tyrian, and the followers whom he brought from Phoenicia into the country which is now called Boeotia.

Almost all the names of the gods came into Greece from Egypt. My inquiries prove that they were all derived from a foreign source, and my opinion is that Egypt furnished the greater number. For with the exception of Poseidon and the Dioscuri, whom I mentioned above, and Hera, Hestia, Themis, the Graces, and the Nereids, the other gods have been known from time immemorial in Egypt. This I assert on the authority of the Egyptians themselves. The gods, with whose names they profess themselves unacquainted, the Greeks received, I believe, from the Pelasgi, except Poseidon. Of him they got their knowledge from the Libyans, by whom he has been always honoured, and who were anciently the only people that had a god

of the name. The Egyptians differ from the Greeks also in paying
no divine honours to heroes.

Besides these which have been here mentioned, there are many
other practices whereof I shall speak hereafter, which the Greeks
have borrowed from Egypt. The erection of the phallus, however,
which they observe in their statues of Hermes they did not derive
from the Egyptians, but from the Pelasgi; from them the Athenians
first adopted it, and afterwards it passed from the Athenians to the
other Greeks. For just at the time when the Athenians were entering into the Hellenic body, the Pelasgi came to live with them in
their country, whence it was that the latter came first to be regarded
as Greeks. Whoever has been initiated into the mysteries of the
Cabeiri will understand what I mean. The Samothracians received
these mysteries from the Pelasgi, who, before they went to live in
Attica, were dwellers in Samothrace, and imparted their religious
ceremonies to the inhabitants. The Athenians, then, who were the
first of all the Greeks to make their statues of Hermes with phallus
erect, learnt the practice from the Pelasgians; and by this people a
religious account of the matter is given, which is explained in the
Samothracian mysteries.

In early times the Pelasgi, as I know by information which I got
at Dodona, offered sacrifices of all kinds, and prayed to the gods,
but had no distinct names or appellations for them, since they had
never heard of any. They called them gods, because they had disposed and arranged all things in such a beautiful order. After a long
lapse of time the names of the gods came to Greece from Egypt, and
the Pelasgi learnt them, only as yet they knew nothing of Dionysus,
of whom they first heard at a much later date. Not long after the
arrival of the names they sent to consult the oracle at Dodona about
them. This is the most ancient oracle in Greece, and at that time
there was no other. To their question, "Whether they should adopt
the names that had been imported from the foreigners?" the oracle
replied by recommending their use. Thenceforth in their sacrifices
the Pelasgi made use of the names of the gods, and from them the
names passed afterwards to the Greeks.

Whence the gods severally sprang, whether or no they had all
existed from eternity, what forms they bore — these are questions of
which the Greeks knew nothing until the other day, so to speak.
For Homer and Hesiod were the first to compose genealogies and
give the gods their epithets, to allot them their several offices and
occupations, and describe their forms; and they lived but 400 years
before my time, as I believe. As for the poets, who are thought by
some to be earlier than these, they are, in my judgment, decidedly
later writers. In these matters I have the authority of the priestesses
of Dodona for the former portion of my statements; what I have
said of Homer and Hesiod is my own opinion.

The following tale is commonly told in Egypt concerning the
oracle of Dodona in Greece, and that of Ammon in Libya. My in-
formants on the point were the priests of Zeus at Thebes. They said

that two of the sacred women were once carried off from Thebes by the Phoenicians, and that the story went that one of them was sold into Libya, and the other into Greece, and these women were the first founders of the oracles in the two countries.   On my inquiring how they came to know so exactly what became of the women, they answered, that diligent search had been made after them at the time, but that it had not been found possible to discover where they were; afterwards, however, they received the information which they had given me.

This was what I heard from the priests at Thebes; at Dodona, however, the women who deliver the oracles relate the matter as follows, "Two black doves flew away from Egyptian Thebes, and while one directed its flight to Libya, the other came to them.   She alighted on an oak, and sitting there began to speak with a human voice, and told them that on the spot where she was, there should thenceforth be an oracle of Zeus.   They understood the announcement to be from heaven, so they set to work at once and erected the shrine. The dove which flew to Libya bade the Libyans to establish there the oracle of Ammon."   This likewise is an oracle of Zeus.   The persons from whom I received these particulars were three priestesses of the Dodonaeans, the eldest Promeneia, the next Timarete, and the youngest Nicandra — what they said was confirmed by the other Dodonaeans who dwell around the temple.

My own opinion of these matters is as follows: I think that, if it be true that the Phoenicians carried off the holy women, and sold them for slaves, the one into Libya and the other into Greece, or Pelasgia (as it was then called), this last must have been sold to the Thesprotians.   Afterwards, while undergoing servitude in those parts, she built under a real oak a temple to Jupiter, her thoughts in her new abode reverting — as it was likely they would do, if she had been an attendant in a temple of Zeus at Thebes — to that particular god.   Then, having acquired a knowledge of the Greek tongue, she set up an oracle.   She also mentioned that her sister had been sold for a slave into Libya by the same persons as herself.

The Dodonaeans called the women doves because they were foreigners, and seemed to them to make a noise like birds.   After a while the dove spoke with a human voice, because the woman, whose foreign talk had previously sounded to them like the chattering of a bird, acquired the power of speaking what they could understand. For how can it be conceived possible that a dove should really speak with the voice of a man?   Lastly, by calling the dove black the Dodonaeans indicated that the woman was an Egyptian.   And certainly the character of the oracles at Thebes and Dodona is very similar.   Besides this form of divination, the Greeks learnt also divination by means of victims from the Egyptians.

[II. 35–57, tr. G. Rawlinson]

[Cambyses succeeded in conquering Egypt, but (Herodotus tells us) he went mad, as a punishment for his impious treatment of the Egyptian divinities.   He had his younger brother, Smerdis, secretly murdered on the suspicion of seeking the throne for himself. Shortly thereafter, two of the Magi (a tribe of the Medes) usurped the throne of Persia, one of them claiming to be the dead Smerdis. On the way back to quell this rebellion Cambyses died by his own hand (522 B.C.), and the Magi maintained themselves in power for seven months, until the identity of the false Smerdis was discovered; the two Magi were killed by seven noble Persians, among whom was Darius, son of Hystaspes, the legal heir to the throne.

The debate over the adoption of a constitution, which is reported in the following selection, is probably not historical, but the narrative is an interesting example of Greek political theory in the age of the Sophists.]

FORMS OF GOVERNMENT

And now when five days were gone, and the hubbub had settled down, the conspirators met together to consult about the situation of affairs. At this meeting speeches were made, to which many of the Greeks give no credence, but they were made nevertheless. Otanes recommended that the management of public affairs should be entrusted to the whole nation. "To me," he said, "it seems advisable, that we should no longer have a single man to rule over us — the rule of one is neither good nor pleasant. You cannot have forgotten to what lengths Cambyses went in his haughty tyranny, and the haughtiness of the Magi you have experienced. How indeed is it possible that monarchy should be a well adjusted thing, when it allows a man to do as he likes without being answerable? Such licence is enough to stir strange and unwonted thoughts in the heart of the worthiest of men. Give a person this power, and straightway his manifold good things puff him up with pride, while envy is so natural to human kind that it cannot but arise in him. But pride and envy together include all wickedness; both leading on to deeds of savage violence. True it is that kings, possessing as they do all that heart can desire, ought to be void of envy, but the contrary is seen in their conduct towards the citizens. They are jealous of the most virtuous among their subjects, and wish their death; while they take delight in the meanest and basest, being ever ready to listen to the tales of slanderers. A king, besides, is beyond all other men inconsistent with himself. Pay him court in moderation, and he is angry because you do not show him more profound respect — show him profound respect, and he is offended again, because (as he says) you fawn on him. But the worst of all is, that he sets aside the laws of the land, puts men to death without trial, and rapes women. The rule of the many, on the other hand, has, in the first place, the fairest of names, equality before the law; and further it is free from all those outrages which a king is wont to commit. There, places are given by lot, the magistrate is answerable for what he does, and measures rest with the commonalty. I vote, therefore, that we do away with monarchy, and raise the people to power. For the people are all in all."

Such were the sentiments of Otanes. Megabyzus spoke next, and advised the setting up of an oligarchy, "In all that Otanes has said to persuade you to put down monarchy," he observed, "I fully concur; but his recommendation that we should call the people to power seems to me not the best advice. For there is nothing so void of understanding, nothing so full of wantonness as the unwieldly rabble. It were folly not to be borne for men, while seeking to escape the wantonness of a tyrant, to give themselves up to the wantonness of a rude unbridled mob. The tyrant, in all his doings, at least knows what he is about, but a mob is altogether devoid of knowledge; for how should there be any knowledge in a rabble, untaught, and with no natural sense of what is right and fit? It rushes wildly into state affairs with all the fury of a stream swollen in the winter, and confuses everything. Let the enemies of the Persians be ruled by democracies; but let us choose out from the citizens a certain number of the worthiest, and put the government into their hands. For thus both we ourselves shall be among the governors, and power being entrusted to the best men, it is likely that the best counsels will prevail in the state."

This was the advice which Megabyzus gave, and after him Darius came forward, and spoke as follows, "All that Megabyzus said against democracy was well said, I think; but about oligarchy he did not speak advisedly; for take these three forms of government, democracy, oligarchy, and monarchy, and let them each be at their best, I maintain that monarchy far surpasses the other two. What government can possibly be better than that of the very best man in the whole state? The counsels of such a man are like himself, and so he governs the mass of the people to their heart's content; while at the same time his measures against evil-doers are kept more secret than in other states. Contrariwise, in oligarchies, where men vie with each other in the service of the commonwealth, fierce enmities are apt to arise between man and man, each wishing to be leader, and to carry his own measures; whence violent quarrels come, which lead to open strife, often ending in bloodshed. Then monarchy is sure to follow; and this too shows how far that rule surpasses all others. Again, in a democracy, it is impossible but that there will be malpractices: these malpractices, however, do not lead to enmities, but to close friendships, which are formed among those engaged in them, who must hold well together to carry on their villanies. And so things go on until a man stands forth as champion of the commonalty, and puts down the evil-doers. Straightway the author of so great a service is admired by all, and from being admired soon comes to be appointed king; so that here too it is plain that monarchy is the best government. Lastly, to sum up all in a word, whence, I ask, was it that we got the freedom which we enjoy? — did democracy give it us, or oligarchy, or a monarch? As a single man recovered our freedom for us, my sentence is that we keep to the rule of one. Even apart from this, we ought not to change the laws of our forefathers when they work fairly; for to do so, is not well."

Such were the three opinions brought forward at this meeting; the four other Persians voted in favour of the last. Otanes, who wished to give his countrymen a democracy, when he found the decision against him, arose a second time, and spoke thus before the assembly, "Brother conspirators, it is plain that the king who is to be chosen will be one of ourselves, whether we make the choice by casting lots for the prize, or by letting the people decide which of us they will have to rule over them, or in any other way. Now, as I have neither a mind to rule nor to be ruled, I shall not enter the lists with you in this matter. I withdraw, however, on one condition — none of you shall claim to exercise rule over me or my seed for ever." The six agreed to these terms, and Otanes withdrew and stood aloof from the contest. And still to this day the family of Otanes continues to be the only free family in Persia; those who belong to it submit to the rule of the king only so far as they themselves choose; they are bound, however, to observe the laws of the land like the other Persians.

After this the six took counsel together, as to the fairest way of setting up a king: and first, with respect to Otanes, they resolved, that if any of their own number got the kingdom, Otanes and his seed after him should receive year by year, as a mark of special honour, a Median robe, and all such other gifts as are accounted the most honourable in Persia. And these they resolved to give him, because he was the man who first planned the outbreak, and who brought the seven together. These privileges, therefore, were assigned specially to Otanes. The following were made common to them all: It was to be free to each, whenever he pleased, to enter the palace unannounced, unless the king were sleeping with a woman; and the king was to be bound to marry into no family excepting those of the conspirators. Concerning the appointment of a king, the resolve to which they came was the following: They would ride out together next morning into the skirts of the city, and he whose steed first neighed after the sun was up should have the kingdom.

Now Darius had a sharp-witted groom called Oebares. After the meeting had broken up, Darius sent for him, and said, "Oebares, this is the way in which the king is to be chosen — we are to mount our horses, and the man whose horse first neighs after the sun is up is to have the kingdom. If then you have any cleverness, contrive a plan whereby the prize may fall to us, and not go to another." "Truly, master," Oebares answered, "if it depends on this whether you shall be king or no, set your heart at ease, and fear nothing: I have a charm which is sure not to fail." "If you really have anything of the kind," said Darius, "hasten to get it ready. The matter does not brook delay, for the trial is to be to-morrow." So Oebares when he heard that, did as follows: When night came, he took one of the mares, the chief favourite of the horse which Darius rode, and tethering it in the suburb, brought his master's horse to the place; then, after leading him round and round the mare several times, nearer and nearer at each circuit, he ended by letting him cover her.

And now, when the morning broke, the six Persians, according to agreement, met together on horseback, and rode out to the suburb. As they went along they neared the spot where the mare was tethered the night before, whereupon the horse of Darius sprang forward and neighed. Just at the same time, though the sky was clear and bright, there was a flash of lightning, followed by a thunder-clap. It seemed as if the heavens conspired with Darius, and hereby inaugurated him king: so the five other nobles leaped with one accord from their steeds, and bowed down before him and owned him for their king.

This is the account which some of the Persians gave of the contrivance of Oebares; but there are others who relate the matter differently. They say that in the morning he stroked the mare's genitals with his hand, which he then hid in his trousers until the sun rose and the horses were about to start, when he suddenly drew his hand forth and put it to the nostrils of his master's horse, which immediately snorted and neighed.

[III. 80–87, tr. G. RAWLINSON]

[After securing the throne, Darius reunited the Persian Empire and extended its sway to Europe by the conquest of Thrace. However, the Ionian Greeks of Asia Minor revolted in 499 B.C. and attempted to throw off the Persian yoke. They requested aid from the leading cities of Greece proper; Athens and Eretria, one of the principal cities of Euboea, supported them and sent ships and troops which joined the Ionians in an attack on Sardis, the capital of the Persian satrapy; the city was captured and burnt to the ground — an act for which Darius never forgave the Athenians, as Herodotus tells us in a charming tale: Darius "bade one of his slaves every day, when his dinner was spread, three times repeat these words to him, 'Lord, remember the Athenians.'"

The Ionian Revolt was finally suppressed in 494, and in 490 Darius sent a punitive expedition of six hundred ships, including horse-transports, to Greece under two generals, Datis and Artaphernes, to capture Athens and Eretria. With them went the son of Pisistratus, Hippias, the former tyrant of Athens, who had been expelled in 511. No doubt the Persians meant to restore Hippias and leave him as ruler of Athens in the King's name. The expedition sailed first to Eretria, which was captured and sacked after a siege of six days. The Persians then sailed over to Marathon, not (as Herodotus says) because no other place in Attica was convenient for their horse (indeed, the cavalry didn't figure in the battle at all, and may have been left behind in Eretria), but probably because Hippias believed that the Hillsmen around Marathon, his father's old supporters, would rise to welcome him back as the ruler of Athens and would join the Persians in the attack on the young democracy.]

MARATHON

The Persians, having thus brought Eretria into subjection after waiting a few days, sailed for Attica, greatly straitening the Athenians as they approached, and thinking to deal with them as they had dealt with the people of Eretria. And because there was no place in all Attica so convenient for their horse as Marathon, and it lay moreover quite close to Eretria, therefore Hippias, the son of Pisistratus, conducted them thither.

When intelligence of this reached the Athenians, they likewise marched their troops to Marathon, and there stood on the defensive, having at their head ten generals, of whom one was Miltiades.

Now this man's father, Cimon, the son of Stesagoras, was banished from Athens by Pisistratus, the son of Hippocrates. In his banishment it was his fortune to win the four-horse chariot-race at Olympia, whereby he gained the very same honour which had before been carried off by Miltiades, his half-brother on the mother's side. At the next Olympiad he won the prize again with the same mares, upon which he caused Pisistratus to be proclaimed the winner, having made an agreement with him that on yielding him this honour he should be allowed to come back to his country. Afterwards, still with the same mares, he won the prize a third time, whereupon he was put to death by the sons of Pisistratus, whose father was no longer living. They set men to lie in wait for him secretly, and these men slew him near the town-hall in the night-time. He was buried outside the city, beyond what is called the Valley Road, and right opposite his tomb were buried the mares which had won the three prizes. The same success had likewise been achieved once previously, to wit, by the mares of Evagoras the Lacedaemonian, but never except by them. At the time of Cimon's death, Stesagoras, the elder of his two sons, was in the Chersonese, where he lived with Miltiades his uncle; the younger, who was called Miltiades after the founder of the Chersonesite colony, was with his father in Athens.

It was this Miltiades who now commanded the Athenians, after escaping from the Chersonese, and twice nearly losing his life. First he was chased as far as Imbrus by the Phoenicians, who had a great desire to take him and carry him up to the king; and when he had avoided this danger, and, having reached his own country, thought himself to be altogether in safety, he found his enemies waiting for him, and was cited by them before a court and impeached for his tyranny in the Chersonese. But he came off victorious here likewise, and was thereupon made general of the Athenians by the free choice of the people.

And first, before they left the city, the generals sent off to Sparta a herald, one Philippides, who was by birth an Athenian, and by profession and practice a trained runner. This man, according to the account which he gave to the Athenians on his return, when he was near Mount Parthenium, above Tegea, fell in with the god Pan, who called him by his name, and bade him ask the Athenians, "Why they neglected him so entirely, when he was kindly disposed towards them, and had often helped them in times past, and would do so again in time to come?" The Athenians, entirely believing in the truth of this report, as soon as their affairs were once more in good order, set up a temple to Pan under the Acropolis, and, in return for the message which I have recorded, established in his honour yearly sacrifices and a torch-race.

On the occasion of which we speak, when Philippides was sent by the Athenian generals, and, according to his own account, saw

Pan on his journey, he reached Sparta on the very next day after quitting the city of Athens. Upon his arrival he went before the rulers, and said:

"Men of Lacedaemon, the Athenians beseech you to hasten to their aid, and not allow that state, which is the most ancient in all Greece, to be enslaved by the barbarians. Eretria is already carried away captive, and Greece weakened by the loss of no mean city."

Thus did Philippides deliver the message committed to him. And the Spartans wished to help the Athenians, but were unable to give them any present aid, as they did not like to break their established law. It was the ninth day of the month, and they could not march out of Sparta on the ninth, when the moon had not reached the full. So they waited for the full of the moon.

The barbarians were conducted to Marathon by Hippias, the son of Pisistratus, who the night before had seen a strange vision in his sleep. He seemed to have intercourse with his mother, and conjectured the dream to mean that he would be restored to Athens, recover the power which he had lost, and afterwards live to a good old age in his native country. Such was the sense in which he interpreted the vision. He now proceeded to act as guide to the Persians, and in the first place he landed the prisoners taken from Eretria upon the island that is called Aegileia, belonging to the Styreans, after which he brought the fleet to anchor off Marathon, and marshalled the bands of the barbarians as they disembarked. As he was thus employed it chanced that he sneezed and at the same time coughed with more violence than was his wont. Now as he was a man advanced in years, and the greater number of his teeth were loose, it so happened that one of them was driven out with the force of the cough, and fell down into the sand. Hippias took all the pains he could to find it, but the tooth was nowhere to be seen; whereupon he fetched a deep sigh, and said to the bystanders, "After all the land is not ours, and we shall never be able to bring it under. All my share in it is the portion of which my tooth has possession."

So Hippias believed that this fulfilled his dream.

The Athenians were drawn up in order of battle in a precinct belonging to Heracles when they were joined by the Plataeans, who came in full force to their aid. Some time before, the Plataeans had put themselves under the rule of the Athenians, and these last had already undertaken many labours on their behalf. The occasion of the surrender was the following. The Plataeans suffered grievous things at the hands of the men of Thebes; so, as it chanced that Cleomenes, the son of Anaxandridas, and the Lacedaemonians were in their neighbourhood, they first of all offered to surrender themselves to them. But the Lacedaemonians refused to receive them, and said, "We dwell too far off from you, and ours would be but cold comfort. You might oftentimes be carried into slavery before one of us heard of it. We counsel you rather to give yourselves up to the Athenians, who are your next neighbours, and well able to shelter you."

This they said, not so much out of good will towards the Plataeans as because they wished to involve the Athenians in trouble by engaging them in wars with the Boeotians. The Plataeans, however, when the Lacedaemonians gave them this counsel, complied at once; and when the sacrifice to the Twelve Gods was being offered at Athens, they came and sat as suppliants about the altar, and gave themselves up to the Athenians. The Thebans no sooner learnt what the Plataeans had done than instantly they marched out against them, while the Athenians sent troops to their aid. As the two armies were about to join battle, the Corinthians, who chanced to be at hand, would not allow them to engage; both sides consented to take them for arbitrators, whereupon they made up the quarrel, and fixed the boundary-line between the two states upon this condition: that if any of the Boeotians wished no longer to belong to Boeotia, the Thebans should allow them to follow their own inclinations. The Corinthians, when they had thus decreed, departed to their homes; the Athenians likewise set off on their return, but the Boeotians fell upon them during the march, and a battle was fought wherein they were worsted by the Athenians. Hereupon these last would not be bound by the line which the Corinthians had fixed, but advanced beyond those limits, and made the Asopus the boundary-line between the country of the Thebans and that of the Plataeans and Hysians. Under such circumstances did the Plataeans give themselves up to Athens; and now they were come to Marathon to aid the Athenians.

The Athenian generals were divided in their opinions; and some advised not to risk a battle, because they were too few to engage such a host as that of the Medes; while others were for fighting at once, and among these last was Miltiades. He therefore, seeing that opinions were thus divided, and that the less worthy counsel appeared likely to prevail, resolved to go to the polemarch, and have a conference with him. For the man on whom the lot fell to be polemarch, at Athens was entitled to give his vote with the ten generals, since anciently the Athenians allowed him an equal right of voting with them. The polemarch at this juncture was Callimachus of Aphidnae; to him therefore Miltiades went, and said:

"With you it rests, Callimachus, either to bring Athens to slavery, or, by securing her freedom, to leave behind to all future generations a memory beyond even Harmodius and Aristogeiton. For never since the time that the Athenians became a people were they in so great a danger as now. If they bow their necks beneath the yoke of the Medes, the woes which they will have to suffer when given into the power of Hippias are already determined on; if, on the other hand, they fight and overcome, Athens may rise to be the very first city in Greece. How it comes to pass that these things are likely to happen, and how the determining of them in some sort rests with thee, I will now proceed to make clear. We generals are ten in number, and our votes are divided; half of us wish to engage, half to avoid a combat. Now, if we do not fight, I look to see a great disturbance at Athens which will shake men's resolutions, and then

I fear they will submit themselves; but if we fight the battle before any unsoundness show itself among our citizens, let the gods but give us fair play, and we are well able to overcome the enemy. On you therefore we depend in this matter, which lies wholly in your own power. You have only to add your vote to my side and your country will be free, and not free only, but the first state in Greece. Or, if you prefer to give your vote to them who would decline the combat, then the reverse will follow."

Miltiades by these words gained Callimachus; and the addition of the polemarch's vote caused the decision to be in favour of fighting. Hereupon all those generals who had been desirous of hazarding a battle, when their turn came to command the army, gave up their right to Miltiades. He however, though he accepted their offers, nevertheless waited, and would not fight, until his own day of command arrived in due course.

Then at length, when his own turn was come, the Athenian battle was set in array, and this was the order of it. Callimachus the polemarch led the right wing, for it was at that time a rule with the Athenians to give the right wing to the polemarch. After this followed the tribes, according as they were numbered, in an unbroken line; while last of all came the Plataeans, forming the left wing. And ever since that day it has been a custom with the Athenians, in the sacrifices and assemblies held each fifth year at Athens, for the Athenian herald to implore the blessing of the gods on the Plataeans conjointly with the Athenians. Now as they marshalled the host upon the field of Marathon, in order that the Athenian front might be of equal length with the Median, the ranks of the centre were diminished, and it became the weakest part of the line, while the wings were both made strong with a depth of many ranks.

So when the battle was set in array, and the victims showed themselves favourable, instantly the Athenians, so soon as they were let go, charged the barbarians at a run. Now the distance between the two armies was little short of a mile. The Persians, therefore, when they saw the Greeks coming on at speed, made ready to receive them, although it seemed to them that the Athenians were bereft of their senses, and bent upon their own destruction; for they saw a mere handful of men coming on at a run without either horsemen or archers. Such was the opinion of the barbarians; but the Athenians in close array fell upon them, and fought in a manner worthy of being recorded. They were the first of the Greeks, so far as I know, who introduced the custom of charging the enemy at a run, and they were likewise the first who dared to look upon the Median garb, and to face men clad in that fashion. Until this time the very name of the Medes had been a terror to the Greeks to hear.

The two armies fought together on the plain of Marathon for a length of time; and in the mid battle, where the Persians themselves and the Sacae had their place, the barbarians were victorious, and broke and pursued the Greeks into the inner country; but on the two wings the Athenians and the Plataeans defeated the enemy. Having so done, they suffered the routed barbarians to fly at their ease, and joining the two wings in one, fell upon those who had broken their own centre, and fought and conquered them. These likewise fled, and now the Athenians hung upon the runaways and cut them down, chasing them all the way to the shore, on reaching which they laid hold of the ships and called aloud for fire.

It was in the struggle here that Callimachus the polemarch, after greatly distinguishing himself, lost his life; Stesilaus too, the son of Thrasilaus, one of the generals, was slain; and Cynaegirus,* the son of Euphorion, having seized on a vessel of the enemy's by the ornament at the stern, had his hand cut off by the blow of an axe, and so perished; as likewise did many other Athenians of note and name.

Nevertheless the Athenians secured in this way seven of the vessels, while with the remainder the barbarians pushed off, and taking aboard their Eretrian prisoners from the island where they had left them, doubled Cape Sunium, hoping to reach Athens before the return of the Athenians. The Alcmaeonidae were accused by their countrymen of suggesting this course to them; they had, it was said, an understanding with the Persians, and made a signal to them, by raising a shield, after they were embarked in their ships.

The Persians accordingly sailed round Sunium. But the Athenians with all possible speed marched away to the defence of their city, and succeeded in reaching Athens before the appearance of the barbarians; and as their camp at Marathon had been pitched in a precinct of Heracles, so now they encamped in another precinct of the same god at Cynosarges. The barbarian fleet arrived, and lay to off Phalerum, which was at that time the haven of Athens; but after resting awhile upon their oars, they departed and sailed away to Asia.

There fell in this battle of Marathon, on the side of the barbarians, about 6,400 men; on that of the Athenians, 192. Such was the number of the slain on the one side and the other. A strange prodigy likewise happened at this fight. Epizelus, the son of Cuphagoras, an Athenian, was in the thick of the fray, and behaving himself as a brave man should, when suddenly he was stricken with blindness, without blow of sword or dart, and this blindness continued thenceforth during the whole of his after life. The following is the account which he himself, as I have heard, gave of the matter: he said that a gigantic warrior, with a huge beard, which shaded all his shield, stood over against him, but the ghostly semblance passed him by, and slew the man at his side. Such, as I understand, was the tale which Epizelus told.

Datis meanwhile was on his way back to Asia, and had reached Myconus, when he saw in his sleep a vision. What it was is not known; but no sooner was day come than he caused strict search to be made throughout the whole fleet, and finding on board a Phoenician vessel an image of Apollo overlaid with gold, he inquired from whence it had been taken, and learning to what temple it belonged, he took it with him in his own ship to Delos, and placed it in the

* Brother of the poet Aeschylus.

temple there, enjoining the Delians, who had now come back to their island, to restore the image to the Theban Delium, which lies on the coast over against Chalcis.   Having left these injunctions, he sailed away; but the Delians failed to restore the statue, and it was not till twenty years afterwards that the Thebans, warned by an oracle, themselves brought it back to Delium.

As for the Eretrians, whom Datis and Artaphernes had carried away captive, when the fleet reached Asia, they were taken up to Susa. Now king Darius, before they were made his prisoners, nourished a fierce anger against these men for having injured him without provocation; but now that he saw them brought into his presence, and become his subjects, he did them no other harm, but only settled them at one of his own stations in Cissia, a place called Ardericca, twenty-six miles distant from Susa, and five miles from the well which yields produce of three different kinds.   For from this well they get bitumen, salt, and oil, procuring it in the way that I will now describe: they draw with a swipe, and instead of a bucket make use of the half of a wine-skin; with this the man dips, and after drawing, pours the liquid into a reservoir, wherefrom it passes into another, and there takes three different shapes.   The salt and the bitumen forthwith collect and harden, while the oil is drawn off into casks.   It is called by the Persians rhadinace,* is black, and has an unpleasant smell.   Here then king Darius established the Eretrians, and here they continued to my time, and still spoke their old language.   So thus it fared with the Eretrians.

After the full of the moon 2,000 Lacedaemonians came to Athens. So eager had they been to arrive in time, that they took but three days to reach Attica from Sparta.   They came, however, too late for the battle; yet, as they had a longing to behold the Medes, they continued their march to Marathon and there viewed the slain.   Then, after giving the Athenians all praise for their achievement, they departed and returned home.

[VI. 102–120, tr. G. RAWLINSON]

[Darius' preparations for another expedition to Greece were interrupted by a revolt in Egypt in 487 B.C.   The following year he died, and his plans were carried out by his son, Xerxes, who in 480 B.C. undertook a full-scale invasion of Greece by land and by sea.   The details of this expedition — the digging of a canal through Athos, the flogging and bridging of the Hellespont, the fantastic numbers of the King's army — have become the legendary commonplaces of Ancient History.

The Greek plan of defense seems to have been to hold Xerxes' land army in check while the Greek fleet sought a decision by sea.   This plan was doubtless inspired by Themistocles, who had increased the Athenian navy in the decade after Marathon, and used the famous oracle about the "wooden walls" to persuade the Athenians to put their trust in their ships.   The Greeks first attempted to hold Thessaly by occupying the pass at Tempe, but Xerxes entered Thessaly by another route and the Greeks were forced to withdraw.   They then determined to send a hold-

* Petroleum.

ing force to Thermopylae and to engage the Persian fleet at Artemisium, the northern point of Euboea, in the straits between the island and the mainland. In the meantime, Xerxes passed through Thessaly and Achaea (where he spent a few days in sight-seeing and horse-racing) and arrived at Malis, before the pass of Thermopylae. He was several days in advance of his fleet, which always operated together with his land forces; this is probably the real reason why he waited four days before attacking the Greek detachment under Leonidas.]

THERMOPYLAE

Such were the doings of Xerxes in Thessaly and in Achaea. From hence he passed on into Malis, along the shores of a bay, in which there is an ebb and flow of the tide daily. By the side of this bay lies a piece of flat land, in one part broad, but in another very narrow indeed, around which runs a range of lofty hills, impossible to climb, enclosing all Malis within them, and called the Trachinian Cliffs. The first city upon the bay, as you come from Achaea, is Anticyra, near which the river Spercheius, flowing down from the country of the Enianians, empties itself into the sea. About two miles from this stream there is a second river, called the Dyras, which is said to have appeared first to help Heracles when he was burning. Again, at the distance of about two miles, there is a stream called the Melas, near which, within half a mile, stands the city of Trachis.

At the point where this city is built, the plain between the hills and the sea is broader than at any other, for it there measures 420 miles.* South of Trachis there is a cleft in the mountain-range which shuts in the territory of Trachinia, and the river Asopus issuing from this cleft flows for a while along the foot of the hills.

Further to the south, another river, called the Phoenix, which has no great body of water, flows from the same hills, and falls into the Asopus. Here is the narrowest place of all, for in this part there is only a causeway wide enough for a single carriage. From the river Phoenix to Thermopylae is a distance of two miles; and in this space is situated the village called Anthela, which the river Asopus passes before it reaches the sea. The space about Anthela is of some width, and contains a temple of Amphictyonian Demeter, as well as the seats of the Amphictyonic deputies, and a temple of Amphictyon himself.

King Xerxes pitched his camp in the region of Malis called Trachinia, while on their side the Greeks occupied the straits. These straits the Greeks in general call Thermopylae (the Hot Gates); but the natives and those who dwell in the neighbourhood, call them Pylae (the Gates). Here then the two armies took their stand; the one master of all the region lying north of Trachis, the other of the country extending southward of that place to the verge of the continent.

The Greeks who at this spot awaited the coming of Xerxes were the

---

* This is certainly an incorrect reading. The plain is even now, at the utmost, seven miles across. It is possible to understand the passage as the whole of the plain area.

following: From Sparta, 300 men-at-arms: from Arcadia, 1000 Tegeans and Mantineans, 500 of each people; 120 Orchomenians, from the Arcadian Orchomenus; and 1000 from other cities: from Corinth, 400 men: from Phlius, 200: and from Mycenae eighty. Such was the number from the Peloponnese. There were also present, from Boeotia, 700 Thespians and 400 Thebans.

Besides these troops, the Locrians of Opus and the Phocians had obeyed the call of their countrymen, and sent, the former all the force they had, the latter 1000 men. For envoys had gone from the Greeks at Thermopylae among the Locrians and Phocians, to call on them for assistance, and to say, "They were themselves but the vanguard of the host, sent to precede the main body, which might every day be expected to follow them. The sea was in good keeping, watched by the Athenians, the Aeginetans, and the rest of the fleet. There was no cause why they should fear; for after all the invader was not a god but a man; and there never had been, and never would be, a man who was not liable to misfortunes from the very day of his birth, and those greater in proportion to his own greatness. The assailant therefore, being only a mortal, must needs fall from his glory." Thus urged, the Locrians and the Phocians had come with their troops to Trachis.

The various nations had each captains of their own under whom they served; but the one to whom all especially looked up, and who had the command of the entire force, was the Lacedaemonian, Leonidas. Now Leonidas was the son of Anaxandridas, who was the son of Leo, who was the son of Eurycratidas, who was the son of Anaxander, who was the son of Eurycrates, who was the son of Polydorus, who was the son of Alcamenes, who was the son of Telecles, who was the son of Archelaus, who was the son of Agesilaus, who was the son of Doryssus, who was the son of Labotas, who was the son of Echestratus, who was the son of Agis, who was the son of Eurysthenes, who was the son of Aristodemus, who was the son of Aristomachus, who was the son of Cleodaeus, who was the son of Hyllus, who was the son of Heracles.

Leonidas had come to be king of Sparta quite unexpectedly.

Having two elder brothers, Cleomenes and Dorieus, he had no thought of ever mounting the throne. However when Cleomenes died without male offspring, as Dorieus was likewise deceased, having perished in Sicily, the crown fell to Leonidas, who was older than Cleombrotus, the youngest of the sons of Anaxandridas, and, moreover, was married to the daughter of Cleomenes. He had now come to Thermopylae, accompanied by the 300 men which the law assigned him, whom he had himself chosen from among the citizens, and who were all of them fathers with sons living. On his way he had taken the troops from Thebes, whose number I have already mentioned, and who were under the command of Leontiades the son of Eurymachus. The reason why he made a point of taking troops from Thebes and Thebes only was, that the Thebans were strongly suspected of being well inclined to the Medes. Leonidas therefore called on them to come with him to the war, wishing to see whether they would comply with his demand, or openly refuse, and disclaim the Greek alliance. They, however, though their wishes leant the other way, nevertheless sent the men.

The force with Leonidas was sent forward by the Spartans in advance of their main body, that the sight of them might encourage the allies to fight, and hinder them from going over to the Medes, as it was likely they might have done had they seen Sparta backward. They intended presently, when they had celebrated the Carneian festival, which was what now kept them at home, to leave a garrison in Sparta, and hasten in full force to join the army. The rest of the allies also intended to act similarly; for it happened that the Olympic festival fell exactly at this same period. None of them looked to see the contest at Thermopylae decided so speedily; wherefore they were content to send forward a mere advanced guard. Such accordingly were the intentions of the allies.

The Greek forces at Thermopylae, when the Persian army drew near to the entrance of the pass, were seized with fear, and a council was held to consider about a retreat. It was the wish of the Peloponnesians generally that the army should fall back upon the Peloponnese, and there guard the Isthmus. But Leonidas, who saw with what indignation the Phocians and Locrians heard of this plan, gave his voice for remaining where they were, while they sent envoys to the several cities to ask for help, since they were too few to make a stand against an army like that of the Medes.

While this debate was going on, Xerxes sent a mounted spy to observe the Greeks, and note how many they were, and what they were doing. He had heard, before he came out of Thessaly, that a few men were assembled at this place, and that at their head were certain Lacedaemonians, under Leonidas, a descendant of Heracles. The horseman rode up to the camp, and looked about him, but did not see the whole army; for such as were on the further side of the wall (which had been rebuilt and was now carefully guarded) it was not possible for him to behold; but he observed those on the outside, who were encamped in front of the rampart. It chanced that at this time the Lacedaemonians held the outer guard, and were seen by the spy, some of them engaged in gymnastic exercises, others combing their long hair. At this the spy greatly marvelled, but he counted their number, and when he had taken accurate note of everything, he rode back quietly; for no one pursued after him, or paid any heed to his visit. So he returned, and told Xerxes all that he had seen.

Upon this, Xerxes, who had no means of surmising the truth — namely, that the Spartans were preparing to do or die manfully — but thought it laughable that they should be engaged in such employments, sent and called to his presence Demaratus the son of Ariston, who still remained with the army. When he appeared, Xerxes told him all that he had heard, and questioned him concerning the news, since he was anxious to understand the meaning of such behaviour on the part of the Spartans. Then Demaratus said, "I spoke to you, O king, concerning these men long since, when we had but just begun our march upon Greece; you, however, only laughed at my words, when I told you of all this, which I saw would come to pass. Earnestly do I struggle at all times to speak truth to you, sire; and now listen to it once more. These men have come to dispute the pass with us, and it is for this that they are now making ready. It is their custom, when they are about to hazard their lives, to adorn their heads with care. Be assured, however, that if you can subdue the men who are here and the Lacedaemonians who remain in Sparta, there is no other nation in all the world which will venture to lift a hand in their defence. You have now to deal with the first kingdom and town in Greece, and with the bravest men."

Then Xerxes, to whom what Demaratus said seemed altogether to surpass belief, asked further, "How it was possible for so small an army to contend with his?"

"O king," Demaratus answered, "let me be treated as a liar, if matters fall not out as I say."

But Xerxes was not persuaded any the more. Four whole days he suffered to go by, expecting that the Greeks would run away. When, however, he found on the fifth that they were not gone, thinking that their firm stand was mere impudence and recklessness, he grew wroth, and sent against them the Medes and Cissians, with orders to take them alive and bring them into his presence. Then the Medes rushed forward and charged the Greeks, but fell in vast numbers: others however took the places of the slain, and would not be beaten off, though they suffered terrible losses. In this way it became clear to all, and especially to the king, that though he had plenty of combatants, he had but very few warriors. The struggle, however, continued during the whole day.

Then the Medes, having met so rough a reception, withdrew from the fight; and their place was taken by the band of Persians under Hydarnes, whom the king called his Immortals: they, it was thought, would soon finish the business. But when they joined battle with the Greeks, it was with no better success than the Median detachment — things went much as before — the two armies fighting in a narrow space, and the barbarians using shorter spears than the Greeks, and having no advantage from their numbers. The Lacedaemonians fought in a way worthy of note, and showed themselves far more skilful in fight than their adversaries, often turning their backs, and making as though they were all flying away, on which the barbarians would rush after them with much noise and shouting, when the Spartans at their approach would wheel round and face their pursuers, in this way destroying vast numbers of the enemy. Some Spartans likewise fell in these encounters, but only a very few. At last the Persians, finding that all their efforts to gain the pass availed nothing, and that whether they attacked by divisions or in any other way, it was to no purpose, withdrew to their own quarters.

During these assaults, it is said that Xerxes, who was watching the battle, thrice leaped from the throne on which he sat, in terror for his army.

Next day the combat was renewed, but with no better success on the part of the barbarians. The Greeks were so few that the barbarians hoped to find them disabled, by reason of their wounds, from offering any further resistance; and so they once more attacked them. But the Greeks were drawn up in detachments according to their cities, and bore the brunt of the battle in turns, all except the Phocians, who had been stationed on the mountain to guard the pathway. So when the Persians found no difference between that day and the preceding, they again retired to their quarters.

Now, as the king was at a loss, and knew not how he should deal with the emergency, Ephialtes, the son of Eurydemus, a man of Malis, came to him and was admitted to a conference. Stirred by the hope of receiving a rich reward at the king's hands, he had come to tell him of the pathway which led across the mountain to Thermopylae; by which disclosure he brought destruction on the band of Greeks who had there withstood the barbarians. This Ephialtes afterwards, from fear of the Lacedaemonians, fled into Thessaly; and during his exile, in an assembly of the Amphictyons held at Pylae, a price was set upon his head by the Pylagorae. When some time had gone by, he returned from exile, and went to Anticyra, where he was slain by Athenades, a native of Trachis. Athenades did not slay him for his treachery, but for another reason, which I shall mention in a later part of my history: yet still the Lacedaemonians honoured him none the less. Thus then did Ephialtes perish a long time afterwards.

Besides this there is another story told, which I do not at all believe, that Onetas the son of Phanagoras, a native of Carystus, and Corydallus, a man of Anticyra, were the persons who spoke on this matter to the king, and took the Persians across the mountain. One may guess which story is true, from the fact that the deputies of the Greeks, the Pylagorae, who must have had the best means of ascertaining the truth, did not offer the reward for the heads of Onetas and Corydallus, but for that of Ephialtes of Trachis; and again from the flight of Ephialtes, which we know to have been on this account. Onetas, I allow, although he was not a Malian, might have been acquainted with the path, if he had lived much in that part of the country; but as Ephialtes was the person who actually led the Persians round the mountain by the pathway, I leave his name on record as that of the man who did the deed.

Great was the joy of Xerxes on this occasion; and as he approved highly of the enterprise which Ephialtes undertook to accomplish, he forthwith sent upon the errand Hydarnes, and the Persians under him. The troops left the camp about the time of the lighting of the lamps. The pathway along which they went was first discovered by the Malians of these parts, who soon afterwards led the Thessalians by it to attack the Phocians, at the time when the Phocians fortified the pass with a wall, and so put themselves under covert from danger.

And ever since, the path has always been put to an ill use by the Malians.

The course which it takes is the following: Beginning at the Asopus, where that stream flows through the cleft in the hills, it runs along the ridge of the mountain (which is called, like the pathway over it, Anopaea), and ends at the city of Alpenus — the first Locrian town as you come from Malis — by the stone called Black-buttock and the seats of the Cercopians. Here it is as narrow as at any other point.

The Persians took this path, and crossing the Asopus, continued their march through the whole of the night, having the mountains of Oeta on their right hand, and on their left those of Trachis. At dawn of day they found themselves close to the summit. Now the hill was guarded, as I have already said, by 1000 Phocian men-at-arms, who were placed there to defend the pathway, and at the same time to secure their own country. They had been given the guard of the mountain path, while the other Greeks defended the pass below, because they had volunteered for the service, and had pledged themselves to Leonidas to maintain the post.

The ascent of the Persians became known to the Phocians in the following manner: During all the time that they were making their way up, the Greeks remained unconscious of it, inasmuch as the whole mountain was covered with groves of oak; but it happened that the air was very still, and the leaves which the Persians stirred with their feet made, as it was likely they would, a loud rustling, whereupon the Phocians jumped up and flew to seize their arms. In a moment the barbarians came in sight, and perceiving men arming themselves, were greatly amazed; for they had fallen in with an enemy when they expected no opposition. Hydarnes, alarmed at the sight, and fearing lest the Phocians might be Lacedaemonians, inquired of Ephialtes to what nation these troops belonged. Ephialtes told him the exact truth, whereupon he arrayed his Persians for battle. The Phocians, galled by the showers of arrows to which they were exposed, and imagining themselves the special object of the Persian attack, fled hastily to the crest of the mountain, and there made ready to meet death; but while their mistake continued, the Persians, with Ephialtes and Hydarnes, not thinking it worth their while to delay on account of Phocians, passed on and descended the mountain with all possible speed.

The Greeks at Thermopylae received the first warning of the destruction which the dawn would bring on them from the seer Megistias, who read their fate in the victims as he was sacrificing. After this deserters came in, and brought the news that the Persians were marching round by the hills: it was still night when these men arrived. Last of all, the scouts came running down from the heights, and brought in the same accounts, when the day was just beginning to break. Then the Greeks held a council to consider what they should do, and here opinions were divided: some were strong against quitting their post, while others contended to the contrary. So when the council had broken up, part of the troops departed and went their ways homeward to their several states; part however resolved to remain, and to stand by Leonidas to the last.

It is said that Leonidas himself sent away the troops who departed, because he tendered their safety, but thought it unseemly that either he or his Spartans should quit the post which they had been especially sent to guard. For my own part, I incline to think that Leonidas gave the order, because he perceived the allies to be out of heart and unwilling to encounter the danger to which his own mind was made up. He therefore commanded them to retreat, but said that he himself could not draw back with honour; knowing that, if he stayed, glory awaited him, and that Sparta in that case would not lose her prosperity. For when the Spartans, at the very beginning of the war, sent to consult the oracle concerning it, the answer which they received from the priestess was that either Sparta must be overthrown by the barbarians, or one of her kings must perish. The prophecy was delivered in hexameter verse, and ran thus:

Oh! ye men who dwell in the streets of broad Lacedaemon,
Either your glorious town shall be sacked by the children of Perseus,
Or, in exchange, must all through the whole Laconian country
Mourn for the loss of a king, descendant of great Heracles.
He cannot be withstood by the courage of bulls or of lions,
Strive as they may; he is mighty as Zeus; there is nought that shall stay
    him,
Till he have got for his prey your king, or your glorious city.

The remembrance of this answer, I think, and the wish to secure the whole glory for the Spartans, caused Leonidas to send the allies away. This is more likely than that they quarrelled with him, and took their departure in such unruly fashion.

To me it seems no small argument in favour of this view, that the seer also who accompanied the army, Megistias, the Acarnanian, said to have been of the blood of Melampus, and the same who was led by the appearance of the victims to warn the Greeks of the danger which threatened them, received orders to retire (as it is certain he did) from Leonidas, that he might escape the coming destruction. Megistias, however, though bidden to depart, refused, and stayed with the army; but he had an only son present with the expedition, whom he now sent away.

So the allies, when Leonidas ordered them to retire, obeyed him and forthwith departed. Only the Thespians and the Thebans remained with the Spartans; and of these the Thebans were kept back by Leonidas as hostages, very much against their will. The Thespians, on the contrary, stayed entirely of their own accord, refusing to retreat, and declaring that they would not forsake Leonidas and his followers. So they abode with the Spartans, and died with them. Their leader was Demophilus, the son of Diadromes.

At sunrise Xerxes made libations, after which he waited until the time when the market-place is wont to fill, and then began his advance. Ephialtes had instructed him thus, as the descent of the mountain is much quicker, and the distance much shorter, than the way round the hills, and the ascent. So the barbarians under Xerxes began to draw nigh; and the Greeks under Leonidas, as they now went forth determined to die, advanced much further than on previous days, until they reached the more open portion of the pass. Hitherto they had held their station within the wall, and from this had gone forth to fight at the point where the pass was the narrowest. Now they joined battle beyond the defile, and carried slaughter among the barbarians, who fell in heaps. Behind them the captains of the squadrons, armed with whips, urged their men forward with continual blows. Many were thrust into the sea, and there perished; a still greater number were trampled to death by their own soldiers; no one heeded the dying. For the Greeks, reckless of their own safety and desperate, since they knew that, as the mountain had been crossed, their destruction was nigh at hand, exerted themselves with the most furious valour against the barbarians.

By this time the spears of the greater number were all shivered, and with their swords they hewed down the ranks of the Persians; and here, as they strove, Leonidas fell fighting bravely, together with many other famous Spartans, whose names I have taken care to learn on account of their great worthiness, as indeed I have those of all the 300. There fell too at the same time very many famous Persians: among them, two sons of Darius, Abrocomes and Hyperanthes, his children by Phratagune, the daughter of Artanes. Artanes was brother of King Darius, being a son of Hystaspes, the son of Arsames; and when he gave his daughter to the king, he made him heir likewise of all his substance; for she was his only child.

Thus two brothers of Xerxes here fought and fell. And now there arose a fierce struggle between the Persians and the Lacedaemonians over the body of Leonidas, in which the Greeks four times drove back the enemy, and at last by their great bravery succeeded in bearing off the body. This combat was scarcely ended when the Persians with Ephialtes approached; and the Greeks, informed that they drew nigh, made a change in the manner of their fighting. Drawing back into the narrowest part of the pass, and retreating even behind the cross wall, they posted themselves upon a hillock, where they stood all drawn up together in one close body, except only the Thebans. The hillock whereof I speak is at the entrance of the straits, where the stone lion stands which was set up in honour of Leonidas. Here they defended themselves to the last, such as still had swords using them, and the others resisting with their hands and teeth; till the barbarians, who in part had pulled down the wall and attacked them in front, in part had gone round and now encircled them upon every side, overwhelmed and buried the remnant left beneath showers of missile weapons.

Thus nobly did the whole body of Lacedaemonians and Thespians behave, but nevertheless one man is said to have distinguished himself above all the rest, to wit, Dieneces the Spartan. A speech which he made before the Greeks engaged the Medes, remains on record. One of the Trachinians told him, "Such was the number of the barbarians, that when they shot forth their arrows the sun would be darkened by their multitude." Dieneces, not at all frightened at these words, but making light of the Median numbers, answered, "Our Trachinian friend brings us excellent tidings. If the Medes darken the sun, we shall have our fight in the shade." Other sayings too of a like nature are said to have been left on record by this same person.

Next to him two brothers, Lacedaemonians, are reputed to have made themselves conspicuous: they were named Alpheus and Maro, and were the sons of Orsiphantus. There was also a Thespian who gained greater glory than any of his countrymen: he was a man called Dithyrambus, the son of Harmatidas.

The slain were buried where they fell; and in their honour, nor less in honour of those who died before Leonidas sent the allies away, an inscription was set up, which said:

> Here did four thousand men from Pelops' land
> Against three hundred myriads bravely stand.

This was in honour of all. Another was for the Spartans alone:

> Go, stranger, and to Lacedaemon tell
> That here, obeying her behests, we fell.

This was for the Lacedaemonians. The seer had the following:

> The great Megistias' tomb you here may view,
> Whom slew the Medes, fresh from Spercheius' fords.
> Well the wise seer the coming death foreknew,
> Yet scorned he to forsake his Spartan lords.

These inscriptions, and the pillars likewise, were all set up by the Amphictyons, except that in honour of Megistias, which was inscribed to him (on account of their sworn friendship) by Simonides, the son of Leoprepes.

[VII. 198–228, tr. G. Rawlinson]

[During the fighting at Thermopylae, the Greek fleet at Artemisium had several inconclusive engagements with the enemy. When the news of the taking of the pass reached them, they withdrew to Salamis, an island off the coast of Attica. While the enemy marched through Phocis and Boeotia toward Athens, plundering as he went, the Athenians evacuated their city and left it for the Barbarian to sack. Xerxes entered the almost vacant city, seized the Acropolis (which was slightly defended), and plundered and fired all the temples. At this moment, the Greeks in the allied fleet were so dismayed that they nearly broke up and set sail for home, each contingent thinking only of defending its native city. Only by the most urgent pleas, and by threatening to withdraw the Athenian fleet entirely, was Themistocles able to persuade Eurybiades, the Spartan admiral in command of the allied navy, to stand and engage the Persians before Salamis. In the chapters which immediately precede our selection, Herodotus tells us that the Peloponnesian army was hastily building a wall across the Isthmus of Corinth to check the advance of the Persian land forces.]

SALAMIS

So the Greeks at the Isthmus toiled unceasingly as though in the greatest peril; since they never imagined that any great success would be gained by the fleet. The Greeks at Salamis, on the other hand, when they heard what the rest were about, felt greatly alarmed; but their fear was not so much for themselves, as for the Peloponnese. At first they conversed together in low tones, each man with his fellow, secretly, and marvelled at the folly shown by Eurybiades; but presently the smothered feeling broke out, and another assembly was held; whereat the old subjects provoked much talk from the speakers, one side maintaining that it was best to sail to the Peloponnese and risk battle for that, instead of abiding at Salamis and fighting for a land already taken by the enemy; while the other, which consisted of the Athenians, Aeginetans, and Megarians, was urgent to remain and have the battle fought where they were.

Then Themistocles, when he saw that the Peloponnesians would carry the vote against him, went out secretly from the council, and instructing a certain man what he should say, sent him on board a merchant ship to the fleet of the Medes. The man's name was Sicinnus; he was one of Themistocles' household slaves, and acted as tutor to his sons; in after times, when the Thespians were admitting persons to citizenship, Themistocles made him a Thespian, and a rich man to boot. The ship brought Sicinnus to the Persian fleet, and there he delivered his message to the leaders in these words:

"The Athenian commander has sent me to you without the knowledge of the other Greeks. He is a well-wisher to the king's cause, and would rather success should attend on you than on his countrymen; wherefore he bids me tell you, that fear has seized the Greeks and they are meditating a hasty flight. Now then it is open to you to achieve the best feat you ever accomplished, if only you hinder their escaping. They no longer agree among themselves, so that they will not now make any resistance — indeed you may see a fight already begun between such as favour and such as oppose your cause." The messenger, when he had thus expressed himself, departed and was seen no more.

Then the captains, believing all that the messenger had said, proceeded to land a large body of Persian troops on the islet of Psyttaleia, which lies between Salamis and the mainland; after which, about the hour of midnight, they advanced their western wing towards Salamis, so as to inclose the Greeks. At the same time the force stationed about Ceos and Cynosura moved forward, and filled the whole strait as far as Munychia with their ships. This advance was made to prevent the Greeks from escaping by flight, and to block them up in Salamis, where it was thought that vengeance might be taken upon them for the battles fought near Artemisium. The Persian troops were landed on the islet of Psyttaleia, because, as soon as the battle began, the men and wrecks were likely to be drifted thither, as the isle lay in the very path of the coming fight, and they would thus be able to save their own men and destroy those of the enemy. All these movements were made in silence, that the Greeks might have no knowledge of them; and they occupied the whole night, so that the men had no time to get their sleep.

I cannot say that there is no truth in prophecies, or feel inclined to call in question those which speak with clearness, when I think of the following:

When they shall bridge with their ships to the sacred strand of Artemis
Girt with the golden falchion, and eke to marine Cynosura,
Mad hope swelling their hearts at the downfall of beautiful Athens —
Then shall godlike Right extinguish haughty Presumption,
Insult's furious offspring, who thinketh to overthrow all things.
Brass with brass shall mingle, and Ares with blood shall empurple
Ocean's waves. Then — then shall the day of Grecia's freedom
Come from Victory fair, and Cronus' son all-seeing.

When I look to this, and perceive how clearly Bacis spoke, I neither venture myself to say anything against prophecies, nor do I approve of others impugning them.

Meanwhile, among the captains at Salamis, the strife of words grew fierce. As yet they did not know that they were encompassed, but imagined that the barbarians remained in the same places where they had seen them the day before.

In the midst of their contention, Aristides, the son of Lysimachus, who had crossed from Aegina, arrived in Salamis. He was an Athenian, and had been ostracised by the commonalty; yet I believe, from what I have heard concerning his character, that there was not in all Athens a man so worthy or so just as he. He now came to the council, and standing outside, called for Themistocles. Now Themistocles was not his friend, but his most determined enemy. However, under the pressure of the great dangers impending, Aristides forgot their feud, and called Themistocles out of the council, since he wished to confer with him. He had heard before his arrival of the impatience of the Peloponnesians to withdraw the fleet to the Isthmus. As soon therefore as Themistocles came forth, Aristides addressed him in these words, "Our rivalry at all times, and especially at the present season, ought to be a struggle, which of us shall most advantage our country. Let me then say to you, that so far as regards the departure of the Peloponnesians from this place, much talk and little will be found precisely alike. I have seen with my own eyes that which I now report; that, however much the Corinthians or Eurybiades himself may wish it, they cannot now retreat; for we are inclosed on every side by the enemy. Go in to them, and make this known."

"Your advice is excellent," answered the other, "and your tidings are also good. That which I earnestly desired to happen, your eyes have beheld accomplished. Know that what the Medes have now done was at my instance; for it was necessary, as our men would not fight here at their own free will, to make them fight whether they

would or no. But come now, as you have brought the good news,
go in and tell it. For if I speak to them, they will think it a feigned
tale, and will not believe that the barbarians have inclosed us around.
Therefore you go to them, and inform them how matters stand. If
they believe you, it will be for the best; but if otherwise, it will not
harm. For it is impossible that they should now flee away, if we are
indeed shut in on all sides, as you say."

Then Aristides entered the assembly, and spoke to the captains: he
had come, he told them, from Aegina, and had but barely escaped the
blockading vessels — the Greek fleet was entirely inclosed by the ships
of Xerxes — and he advised them to get themselves in readiness to
resist the foe. Having said so much, he withdrew. And now another contest arose, for the greater part of the captains would not
believe the tidings.

But while they still doubted, a Tenian trireme, commanded by
Panaetius the son of Sosimenes, deserted from the Persians and joined
the Greeks, bringing full intelligence. For this reason the Tenians
were inscribed upon the tripod at Delphi among those who overthrew
the barbarians. With this ship, which deserted to their side at
Salamis, and the Lemnian vessel which came over before at Artemisium, the Greek fleet was brought to the full number of 380 ships;
otherwise it fell short by two of that amount.

The Greeks now, not doubting what the Tenians told them, made
ready for the coming fight. At the dawn of day, all the men-at-arms
were assembled together, and speeches were made to them, of which
the best was that of Themistocles; who throughout contrasted what
was noble with what was base, and bade them, in all that came within
the range of man's nature and constitution, always to make choice
of the nobler part. Having thus wound up his discourse, he told
them to go at once on board their ships, which they accordingly did;
and about this time the trireme, that had been sent to Aegina for the
Aeacidae, returned; whereupon the Greeks put to sea with all their
fleet.

The fleet had scarce left the land when they were attacked by the
barbarians. At once most of the Greeks began to back water, and
were about touching the shore, when Ameinias of Pallene, one of the
Athenian captains, darted forth in front of the line, and charged a
ship of the enemy. The two vessels became entangled, and could not
separate, whereupon the rest of the fleet came up to help Ameinias,
and engaged with the Persians. Such is the account which the
Athenians give of the way in which the battle began; but the Aeginetans maintain that the vessel which had been to Aegina for the
Aeacidae, was the one that brought on the fight. It is also reported,
that a phantom in the form of a woman appeared to the Greeks, and,
in a voice that was heard from end to end of the fleet, cheered them on
to the fight; first, however, rebuking them, and saying, "Strange men,
how long are you going to back water?"

Against the Athenians, who held the western extremity of the line
towards Eleusis, were placed the Phoenicians; against the Lacedaemo-

nians, whose station was eastward towards the Piraeus, the Ionians. Of these last a few only followed the advice of Themistocles, to fight backwardly; the greater number did far otherwise. I could mention here the names of many captains who took vessels from the Greeks, but I shall pass over all excepting Theomestor the son of Androdamus, and Phylacus the son of Histiaeus, both Samians. I show this preference to them, inasmuch as for this service Theomestor was made tyrant of Samos by the Persians, while Phylacus was enrolled among the king's benefactors, and presented with a large estate in land. In the Persian tongue the king's benefactors are called Orosangs.

Far the greater number of the Persian ships engaged in this battle were disabled — either by the Athenians or by the Aeginetans. For as the Greeks fought in order and kept their line, while the barbarians were in confusion and had no plan in anything that they did, the issue of the battle could scarce be other than it was. Yet the Persians fought far more bravely here than at Euboea, and indeed surpassed themselves; each did his utmost through fear of Xerxes, for each thought that the king's eye was upon himself.

What part the several nations, whether Greek or barbarian, took in the combat, I am not able to say for certain; Artemisia, however, I know, distinguished herself in such a way as raised her even higher than she stood before in the esteem of the king. For after confusion had spread throughout the whole of the king's fleet, and her ship was closely pursued by an Athenian trireme, she, having no way to fly, since in front of her were a number of friendly vessels, and she was nearest of all the Persians to the enemy, resolved on a measure which in fact proved her safety. Pressed by the Athenian pursuer, she bore straight against one of the ships of her own party, a Calyndian, which had Damasithymus, the Calyndian king, himself on board. I cannot say whether she had had any quarrel with the man while the fleet was at the Hellespont, or no — neither can I decide whether she of set purpose attacked his vessel, or whether it merely chanced that the Calyndian ship came in her way — but certain it is that she bore down upon his vessel and sank it, and that thereby she had the good fortune to procure herself a double advantage. For the commander of the Athenian trireme, when he saw her bear down on one of the enemy's fleet, thought immediately that her vessel was a Greek, or else had deserted from the Persians, and was now fighting on the Greek side; he therefore gave up the chase, and turned away to attack others.

Thus in the first place she saved her life by the action, and was enabled to get clear off from the battle; while further, it fell out that in the very act of doing the king an injury she raised herself to a greater height than ever in his esteem. For as Xerxes beheld the fight, he remarked (it is said) the destruction of the vessel, whereupon the bystanders observed to him, "Do you see, master, how well Artemisia fights, and how she has just sunk a ship of the enemy?" Then Xerxes asked if it were really Artemisia's doing; and they answered, "Certainly; for they knew her ensign": while all made

sure that the sunken vessel belonged to the opposite side. Every
thing, it is said, conspired to prosper the queen — it was especially
fortunate for her, that not one of those on board the Calyndian ship
survived to become her accuser. Xerxes, they say, in reply to the
remarks made to him, observed, "My men have behaved like women,
and my women like men!"

There fell in this combat Ariabignes, one of the chief commanders
of the fleet, who was son of Darius and brother of Xerxes, and with
him perished a vast number of men of high repute, Persians, Medes,
and allies. Of the Greeks there died only a few; for as they were
able to swim, all those that were not slain outright by the enemy
escaped from the sinking vessels and swam across to Salamis. But on
the side of the barbarians more perished by drowning than in any
other way, since they did not know how to swim. The great destruction took place when the ships which had been first engaged began
to fly; for they who were stationed in the rear, anxious to display
their valour before the eyes of the king, made every effort to force
their way to the front, and thus became entangled with such of
their own vessels as were retreating.

In this confusion the following event occurred: certain Phoenicians belonging to the ships which had thus perished made their
appearance before the king, and laid the blame of their loss on the
Ionians, declaring that they were traitors, and had wilfully destroyed
the vessels. But the upshot of this complaint was, that the Ionian
captains escaped the death which threatened them, while their Phoenician accusers received death as their reward. For it happened that,
exactly as they spoke, a Samothracian vessel bore down on an Athenian and sank it, but was attacked and crippled immediately by one of
the Aeginetan squadron. Now the Samothracians were expert with
the javelin, and aimed their weapons so well, that they cleared the
deck of the vessel which had disabled their own, after which they
sprang on board, and took it. This saved the Ionians. Xerxes,
when he saw the exploit, turned fiercely on the Phoenicians (he was
ready, in his extreme vexation, to find fault with any one) and
ordered their heads to be cut off, to prevent them, he said, from casting the blame of their own misconduct upon braver men. During
the whole time of the battle Xerxes sat at the base of the hill called
Aegaleos, over against Salamis; and whenever he saw any of his own
captains perform any worthy exploit he inquired concerning him;
and the man's name was taken down by his scribes, together with
the names of his father and his city. Ariaramnes too, a Persian, who
was a friend of the Ionians, and present at the time whereof I speak,
had a share in bringing about the punishment of the Phoenicians.

When the rout of the barbarians began, and they sought to make
their escape to Phalerum, the Aeginetans, awaiting them in the
channel, performed exploits worthy to be recorded. Through the
whole of the confused struggle the Athenians employed themselves
in destroying such ships as either made resistance or fled to shore,
while the Aeginetans dealt with those which endeavoured to escape

down the straits; so that the Persian vessels were no sooner clear of the Athenians than straightway they fell into the hands of the Aeginetan squadron.

[VIII. 74-91, tr. G. Rawlinson]

THUCYDIDES

(*ca.* 460–*ca.* 400 B.C.)

THE PELOPONNESIAN WAR

Thucydides, an Athenian, wrote the history of the war in which the Peloponnesians and the Athenians fought against one another. He began to write when they first took up arms, believing that it would be great and memorable above any previous war. For he argued that both states were then at the full height of their military power, and he saw the rest of the Hellenes either siding or intending to side with one or other of them. No movement ever stirred Hellas more deeply than this; it was shared by many of the Barbarians, and might be said even to affect the world at large. The character of the events which preceded, whether immediately or in more remote antiquity, owing to the lapse of time cannot be made out with certainty. But, judging from the evidence which I am able to trust after most careful enquiry, I should imagine that former ages were not great either in their wars or in anything else.

The country which is now called Hellas was not regularly settled in ancient times. The people were migratory, and readily left their homes whenever they were overpowered by numbers. There was no commerce, and they could not safely hold intercourse with one another either by land or sea. The several tribes cultivated their own soil just enough to obtain a maintenance from it. But they had no accumulations of wealth, and did not plant the ground; for, being without walls, they were never sure than an invader might not come and despoil them. Living in this manner and knowing that they could anywhere obtain a bare subsistence, they were always ready to migrate; so that they had neither great cities nor any considerable resources. The richest districts were most constantly changing their inhabitants; for example, the countries which are now called Thessaly and Boeotia, the greater part of the Peloponnesus with the exception of Arcadia, and all the best parts of Hellas. For the productiveness of the land increased the power of individuals; this in turn was a source of quarrels by which communities were ruined, while at the same time they were more exposed to attacks from without. Certainly Attica, of which the soil was poor and thin, enjoyed a long freedom from civil strife, and therefore retained its original inhabitants. And a striking confirmation of my argument is afforded by the fact that Attica through immigration increased in population more than any other region. For the leading men of Hellas, when driven out of their own country by war or revolution, sought an asylum at Athens; and from the very earliest times, being admitted to rights of citizenship, so greatly increased the number of inhabitants that Attica became incapable of containing them, and was at last obliged to send out colonies to Ionia.

The feebleness of antiquity is further proved to me by the circumstance that there appears to have been no common action in Hellas before the Trojan War. And I am inclined to think that the very name was not as yet given to the whole country, and in fact did not exist at all before the time of Hellen, the son of Deucalion; the different tribes, of which the Pelasgian was the most widely spread, gave their own names to different districts. But when Hellen and his sons became powerful in Phthiotis, their aid was invoked by other cities, and those who associated with them gradually began to be called Hellenes, though a long time elapsed before the name prevailed over the whole country. Of this Homer affords the best evidence; for he, although he lived long after the Trojan War, nowhere uses this name collectively, but confines it to the followers of Achilles from Phthiotis, who were the original Hellenes; when speaking of the entire host he calls them Danaans, or Argives, or Achaeans. Neither is there any mention of Barbarians in his poems, clearly because there were as yet no Hellenes opposed to them by a common distinctive name. Thus the several Hellenic tribes (and I mean by the term Hellenes those who, while forming separate communities, had a common language, and were afterwards called by a common name), owing to their weakness and isolation, were never united in any great enterprise before the Trojan War. And they only made the expedition against Troy after they had gained considerable experience of the sea.

Minos is the first to whom tradition ascribes the possession of a navy. He made himself master of a great part of what is now termed the Hellenic sea; he conquered the Cyclades, and was the first coloniser of most of them, expelling the Carians and appointing his own sons to govern in them. Lastly, it was he who, from a natural desire to protect his growing revenues, sought, as far as he was able, to clear the sea of pirates.

For in ancient times both Hellenes and Barbarians, as well the inhabitants of the coast as of the islands, when they began to find their way to one another by sea had recourse to piracy. They were commanded by powerful chiefs, who took this means of increasing their wealth and providing for their poorer followers. They would fall upon the unwalled and straggling towns, or rather villages, which they plundered, and maintained themselves by the plunder of them; for, as yet, such an occupation was held to be honourable and not disgraceful. This is proved by the practice of certain tribes on the mainland who, to the present day, glory in piratical exploits, and by the witness of the ancient poets, in whose verses the question is invariably asked of newly-arrived voyagers, whether they are pirates; which implies that neither those who are questioned disclaim, nor those who are interested in knowing censure the occupation. The land too was infested by robbers; and there are parts of Hellas in which the old practices still continue, as for example among the

Ozolian Locrians, Aetolians, Acarnanians, and the adjacent regions of the continent. The fashion of wearing arms among these continental tribes is a relic of their old predatory habits. For in ancient times all Hellenes carried weapons because their homes were undefended and intercourse was unsafe; like the Barbarians they went armed in their every-day life. And the continuance of the custom in certain parts of the country proves that it once prevailed everywhere.

The Athenians were the first who laid aside arms and adopted an easier and more luxurious way of life. Quite recently the old-fashioned refinement of dress still lingered among the elder men of their richer class, who wore under-garments of linen, and bound back their hair in a knot with golden clasps in the form of grasshoppers; and the same customs long survived among the elders of Ionia, having been derived from their Athenian ancestors. On the other hand, the simple dress which is now common was first worn at Sparta; and there, more than anywhere else, the life of the rich was assimilated to that of the people. The Lacedaemonians too were the first who in their athletic exercises stripped naked and rubbed themselves over with oil. But this was not the ancient custom; athletes formerly, even when they were contending at Olympia, wore girdles about their loins, a practice which lasted until quite lately, and still prevails among the Barbarians, especially those of Asia, where the combatants at boxing and wrestling matches wear girdles. And many other customs which are now confined to the Barbarians might be shown to have existed formerly in Hellas.

In later times, when navigation had become general and wealth was beginning to accumulate, cities were built upon the sea-shore and fortified; peninsulas too were occupied and walled-off with a view to commerce and defence against the neighbouring tribes. But the older towns both in the islands and on the continent, in order to protect themselves against the piracy which so long prevailed, were built inland; and there they remain to this day. For the piratical tribes plundered, not only one another, but all those who, without being sailors, lived on the sea-coast.

The islanders were even more addicted to piracy than the inhabitants of the mainland. They were mostly Carian or Phoenician settlers. This is proved by the fact that when the Athenians purified Delos during the Peloponnesian War and the tombs of the dead were opened, more than half of them were found to be Carians. They were known by the fashion of their arms which were buried with them, and by their mode of burial, the same which is still practised among them.

After Minos had established his navy, communication by sea became more general. For, he having expelled the pirates when he colonised the greater part of the islands, the dwellers on the sea-coast began to grow richer and to live in a more settled manner; and some of them, finding their wealth increase beyond their expectations, surrounded their towns with walls. The love of gain made the weaker willing to serve the stronger, and the command of wealth enabled

the more powerful to subjugate the lesser cities. This was the state
of society which was beginning to prevail at the time of the Trojan
War.

I am inclined to think that Agamemnon succeeded in collecting
the expedition, not because the suitors of Helen had bound themselves
by oath to Tyndareus, but because he was the most powerful king
of his time. Those Peloponnesians who possess the most accurate
traditions say that originally Pelops gained his power by the great
wealth which he brought with him from Asia into a poor country,
whereby he was enabled, although a stranger, to give his name to
the Peloponnesus; and that still greater fortune attended his descendants after the death of Eurystheus, king of Mycenae, who was slain
in Attica by the Heracleidae. For Atreus the son of Pelops was the
maternal uncle of Eurystheus, who, when he went on the expedition,
naturally committed to his charge the kingdom of Mycenae. Now
Atreus had been banished by his father on account of the murder of
Chrysippus. But Eurystheus never returned; and the Mycenaeans,
dreading the Heracleidae, were ready to welcome Atreus, who was
considered a powerful man and had ingratiated himself with the
multitude. So he succeeded to the throne of Mycenae and the other
dominions of Eurystheus. Thus the house of Pelops prevailed over
that of Perseus.

And it was, as I believe, because Agamemnon inherited this power
and also because he was the greatest naval potentate of his time that
he was able to assemble the expedition; and the other princes followed him, not from good-will, but from fear. Of the chiefs who
came to Troy, he, if the witness of Homer be accepted, brought the
greatest number of ships himself, besides supplying the Arcadians
with them. In the "Handing down of the Sceptre" he is described
as, "The king of many islands, and of all Argos." * But, living on
the mainland, he could not have ruled over any except the adjacent
islands (which would not be many) unless he had possessed a considerable navy. From this expedition we must form our conjec-
tures about the character of still earlier times.

When it is said that Mycenae was but a small place, or that any
other city which existed in those days is inconsiderable in our own,
this argument will hardly prove that the expedition was not as great
as the poets relate and as is commonly imagined. Suppose the city
of Sparta to be deserted, and nothing left but the temples and the
ground-plan, distant ages would be very unwilling to believe that
the power of the Lacedaemonians was at all equal to their fame. And
yet they own two-fifths of the Peloponnesus, and are acknowledged
leaders of the whole, as well as of numerous allies in the rest of
Hellas. But their city is not regularly built, and has no splendid
temples or other edifices; it rather resembles a straggling village like
the ancient towns of Hellas, and would therefore make a poor show.
Whereas, if the same fate befell the Athenians, the ruins of Athens
would strike the eye, and we should infer their power to have been

* *Iliad*, ii. 108.

twice as great as it really is. We ought not then to be unduly sceptical. The greatness of cities should be estimated by their real power and not by appearances. And we may fairly suppose the Trojan expedition to have been greater than any which preceded it, although according to Homer, if we may once more appeal to his testimony, not equal to those of our own day. He was a poet, and may therefore be expected to exaggerate; yet, even upon his showing, the expedition was comparatively small. For it numbered, as he tells us, 1200 ships, those of the Boeotians carrying 120 men each, those of Philoctetes fifty; and by these numbers he may be presumed to indicate the largest and the smallest ships; else why in the catalogue is nothing said about the size of any others? That the crews were all fighting men as well as rowers he clearly implies when speaking of the ships of Philoctetes; for he tells us that all the oarsmen were likewise archers And it is not to be supposed that many who were not sailors would accompany the expedition, except the kings and principal officers; for the troops had to cross the sea, bringing with them the materials of war, in vessels without decks, built after the old piratical fashion. Now if we take a mean between the crews, the invading forces will appear not to have been very numerous when we remember that they were drawn from the whole of Hellas.

The cause of the inferiority was not so much the want of men as the want of money; the invading army was limited by the difficulty of obtaining supplies to such a number as might be expected to live on the country in which they were to fight. After their arrival at Troy, when they had won a battle (as they clearly did, for otherwise they could not have fortified their camp), even then they appear not to have used the whole of their force, but to have been driven by want of provisions to the cultivation of the Chersonese and to pillage. And in consequence of this dispersion of their forces, the Trojans were enabled to hold out against them during the whole ten years, being always a match for those who remained on the spot. Whereas if the besieging army had brought abundant supplies, and, instead of betaking themselves to agriculture or pillage, had carried on the war persistently with all their forces, they would easily have been masters of the field and have taken the city; since, even divided as they were, and with only a part of their army available at any one time, they held their ground. Or, again, they might have regularly invested Troy, and the place would have been captured in less time and with less trouble. Poverty was the real reason why the achievements of former ages were insignificant, and why the Trojan War, the most celebrated of them all, when brought to the test of facts, falls short of its fame and of the prevailing traditions to which the poets have given authority.

Even in the age which followed the Trojan War, Hellas was still in process of ferment and settlement, and had no time for peaceful growth. The return of the Hellenes from Troy after their long absence led to many changes: quarrels too arose in nearly every city, and those who were expelled by them went and founded other cities.

Thus in the sixtieth year after the fall of Troy, the Boeotian people, having been expelled from Arnè by the Thessalians, settled in the country formerly called Cadmeis, but now Boeotia: a portion of the tribe already dwelt there, and some of these had joined in the Trojan expedition. In the eightieth year after the war, the Dorians led by the Heracleidae conquered the Peloponnesus. A considerable time elapsed before Hellas became finally settled; after a while, however, she recovered tranquillity and began to send out colonies. The Athenians colonised Ionia and most of the islands; the Peloponnesians the greater part of Italy and Sicily, and various places in Hellas. These colonies were all founded after the Trojan War.

As Hellas grew more powerful and the acquisition of wealth became more and more rapid, the revenues of her cities increased, and in most of them tyrannies were established; they had hitherto been ruled by hereditary kings, having fixed prerogatives. The Hellenes likewise began to build navies and to make the sea their element. The Corinthians are said to have first adopted something like the modern style of ship-building, and the oldest Hellenic triremes to have been constructed at Corinth. A Corinthian ship-builder, Ameinocles, appears to have built four ships for the Samians; he went to Samos about 300 years before the end of the Peloponnesian War. And the earliest naval engagement on record is that between the Corinthians and Corcyraeans which occurred about forty years later. Corinth, being seated on an isthmus, was naturally from the first a centre of commerce; for the Hellenes within and without the Peloponnese in the old days, when they communicated chiefly by land, had to pass through her territory in order to reach one another. Her wealth too was a source of power, as the ancient poets testify, who speak of Corinth the Rich. When navigation grew more common, the Corinthians, having already acquired a fleet, were able to put down piracy; they offered a market both by sea and land, and with the increase of riches the power of their city increased yet more. Later, in the time of Cyrus, the first Persian king, and of Cambyses his son, the Ionians had a large navy; they fought with Cyrus, and were for a time masters of the sea around their own coasts. Polycrates, too, who was tyrant of Samos in the reign of Cambyses, had a powerful navy and subdued several of the islands, among them Rhenea, which he dedicated to the Delian Apollo. And the Phocaeans, when they were colonising Massalia, defeated the Carthaginians in a sea-fight.

These were the most powerful navies, and even these, which came into existence many generations after the Trojan War, appear to have consisted chiefly of fifty-oared vessels and galleys of war, as in the days of Troy; as yet triremes were not common. But a little before the Persian War and the death of Darius, who succeeded Cambyses, the Sicilian tyrants and the Corcyraeans had them in considerable numbers. No other maritime powers of any consequence arose in Hellas before the expedition of Xerxes. The Aeginetans, Athenians, and a few more had small fleets, and these mostly consisted of fifty-oared galleys. Even the ships which the Athenians built quite recently at the instigation of Themistocles, when they were at war with the Aeginetans and in expectation of the Barbarian, even these ships with which they fought at Salamis were not completely decked.

So inconsiderable were the Hellenic navies in recent as well as in more ancient times. And yet those who applied their energies to the sea obtained a great accession of strength by the increase of their revenues and the extension of their domain. For they attacked and subjugated the islands, especially when the pressure of population was felt by them. Whereas by land, no conflict of any kind which brought increase of power ever occurred; what wars they had were mere border feuds. Foreign and distant expeditions of conquest the Hellenes never undertook; they were not as yet ranged under the command of the great states, nor did they form voluntary leagues or make expeditions on an equal footing. Their wars were only the wars of the several neighbouring tribes with one another. It was in the ancient conflict between the Chalcidians and the Eretrians that the rest of Hellas was most divided and took the greatest part.

There were different impediments to the progress of the different states. The Ionians had attained great prosperity when Cyrus and the Persians, having overthrown Croesus and subdued the countries between the river Halys and the sea, made war against them and enslaved the cities on the mainland. Some time afterwards, Darius, strong in the possession of the Phoenician fleet, conquered the islands also.

Nor again did the tyrants of the Hellenic cities extend their thoughts beyond their own interest, that is, the security of their persons, and the aggrandisement of themselves and their families. They were extremely cautious in the administration of their government, and nothing considerable was ever effected by them; they only fought with their neighbours, as in Sicily, where their power attained its greatest height. Thus for a long time everything conspired to prevent Hellas from uniting in any great action and to paralyse enterprise in the individual states.

At length the tyrants of Athens and of the rest of Hellas (which had been under their dominion long before Athens), at least the greater number of them, and with the exception of the Sicilian the last who ever ruled, were put down by the Lacedaemonians. For although Lacedaemon, after the settlement of the country by the Dorians who now inhabit it, long suffered from factions, and indeed longer than any country which we know, nevertheless she obtained good laws at an earlier period than any other, and has never been subject to tyrants; she has preserved the same form of government for rather more than four hundred years, reckoning to the end of the Peloponnesian War. It was the excellence of her constitution which gave her power, and thus enabled her to regulate the affairs of other states. Not long after the overthrow of the tyrants by the Lacedaemonians, the battle of Marathon was fought between the

Athenians and the Persians; ten years later, the Barbarian returned with the vast armament which was to enslave Hellas. In the greatness of the impending danger, the Lacedaemonians, who were the most powerful state in Hellas, assumed the lead of the confederates. The Athenians, as the Persian host advanced, resolved to forsake their city, broke up their homes, and, taking to their ships, became sailors. The Barbarian was repelled by a common effort; but soon the Hellenes, as well those who had revolted from the King as those who formed the original confederacy, took different sides and became the allies, either of the Athenians or of the Lacedaemonians; for these were now the two leading powers, the one strong by land and the other by sea. The league between them was of short duration; they speedily quarrelled and, with their respective allies, went to war. Any of the other Hellenes who had differences of their own now resorted to one or other of them. So that from the Persian to the Peloponnesian War, the Lacedaemonians and the Athenians were perpetually fighting or making peace, either with one another or with their own revolted allies; thus they attained military efficiency, and learned experience in the school of danger.

The Lacedaemonians did not make tributaries of those who acknowledged their leadership, but took care that they should be governed by oligarchies in the exclusive interest of Sparta. The Athenians, on the other hand, after a time deprived the subject cities of their ships and made all of them pay a fixed tribute, except Chios and Lesbos. And the single power of Athens at the beginning of this war was greater than that of Athens and Sparta together at their greatest, while the confederacy remained intact.

Such are the results of my enquiry into the early state of Hellas. They will not readily be believed upon a bare recital of all the proofs of them. Men do not discriminate, and are too ready to receive ancient traditions about their own as well as about other countries. For example, most Athenians think that Hipparchus was actually tyrant when he was slain by Harmodius and Aristogeiton; they are not aware that Hippias was the eldest of the sons of Peisistratus, and succeeded him, and that Hipparchus and Thessalus were only his brothers. At the last moment, Harmodius and Aristogeiton suddenly suspected that Hippias had been forewarned by some of their accomplices. They therefore abstained from attacking him, but, wishing to do something before they were seized, and not to risk their lives in vain, they slew Hipparchus, with whom they fell in near the temple called Leocorium as he was marshalling the Panathenaic procession. There are many other matters, not obscured by time, but contemporary, about which the other Hellenes are equally mistaken. For example, they imagine that the kings of Lacedaemon in their council have not one but two votes each and that in the army of the Lacedaemonians there is a division called the Pitanate division; * whereas they never had anything of the sort. So little

* Herodotus, vi. 57 and ix. 53.

fact they despised the Corinthians, for they were more than a match for them in military strength, and as rich as any state then existing in Hellas. They would often boast that on the sea they were very far superior to them, and would appropriate to themselves the naval renown of the Phaeacians, who were the ancient inhabitants of the island. Such feelings led them more and more to strengthen their navy, which was by no means despicable; for they had 120 triremes when the war broke out.

Irritated by these causes of offence, the Corinthians were too happy to assist Epidamnus; accordingly they invited any one who was willing to settle there, and for the protection of the colonists dispatched with them Ambracian and Leucadian troops and a force of their own. All these they sent by land as far as Apollonia, which is a colony of theirs, fearing that if they went by sea the Corcyraeans might oppose their passage. Great was the rage of the Corcyraeans when they discovered that the settlers and the troops had entered Epidamnus and that the colony had been given up to the Corinthians. They immediately set sail with twenty-five ships, followed by a second fleet, and in insulting terms bade the Epidamnians receive the exiled oligarchs, who had gone to Corcyra and implored the Corcyraeans to restore them, appealing to the tie of kindred and pointing to the sepulchres of their common ancestors. They also bade them send away the troops and the new settlers. But the Epidamnians would not listen to their demands. Whereupon the Corcyraeans attacked them with forty ships. They were accompanied by the exiles whom they were to restore, and had the assistance of the native Illyrian troops. They sat down before the city, and made proclamation that any Epidamnian who chose, and the foreigners, might depart in safety, but that all who remained would be treated as enemies. Being met by a refusal, the Corcyraeans proceeded to invest the city, which is built upon an isthmus.

When the news reached the Corinthians that Epidamnus was besieged, they equipped an army and proclaimed that a colony was to be sent thither; all who wished might go and enjoy equal rights of citizenship; but any one who was unwilling to sail at once might remain at Corinth, and, if he made a deposit of fifty Corinthian drachmas, might still have a share in the colony. Many sailed, and many deposited the money. The Corinthians also sent and requested the Megarians to furnish them with a convoy in case the Corcyraeans should intercept the colonists on their voyage. The Megarians accordingly provided eight ships, and the Cephallenians of Pale four; the Epidaurians, of whom they made a similar request, five; the Hermionians one; the Troezenians two; the Leucadians ten; and the Ambraciots eight. Of the Thebans and Phliasians they begged money, and of the Eleans money, and ships without crews. On their own account they equipped thirty ships and 3000 hoplites.

When the Corcyraeans heard of their preparations they came to Corinth, taking with them Lacedaemonian and Sicyonian envoys, and summoned the Corinthians to withdraw the troops and the colonists, telling them that they had nothing to do with Epidamnus. If they made any claim to it, the Corcyraeans expressed themselves willing to refer the cause for arbitration to such Peloponnesian states as both parties should agree upon, and their decision was to be final; or, they were willing to leave the matter in the hands of the Delphic oracle. But they deprecated war, and declared that, if war there must be, they would be compelled by the Corinthians in self-defence to discard their present friends and seek others whom they would rather not, for help they must have. The Corinthians replied that if the Corcyraeans would withdraw the ships and the barbarian troops they would consider the matter, but that it would not do for them to be litigating while Epidamnus and the colonists were in a state of siege. The Corcyraeans rejoined that they would consent to this proposal if the Corinthians on their part would withdraw their forces from Epidamnus: or again, they were willing that both parties should remain on the spot, and that a truce should be made until the decision was given.

The Corinthians turned a deaf ear to all these overtures, and, when their vessels were manned and their allies had arrived, they sent a herald before them to declare war, and set sail for Epidamnus with seventy-five ships and 2000 hoplites, intending to give battle to the Corcyraeans. Their fleet was commanded by Aristeus the son of Pellichus, Callicrates the son of Callias, and Timanor the son of Timanthes; the land forces by Archetimus the son of Eurytimus, and Isarchidas the son of Isarchus. When they arrived at Actium in the territory of Anactorium, at the mouth of the Ambracian gulf, where the temple of Apollo stands, the Corcyraeans sent a herald to them in a small boat forbidding them to come on. Meanwhile their crews got on board; they had previously equipped their fleet, strengthening the old ships with cross-timbers, so as to make them serviceable. The herald brought back no message of peace from the Corinthians. The Corcyraean ships, numbering eighty (for forty out of the hundred and twenty were engaged in the blockade of Epidamnus), were now fully manned; these sailed out against the Corinthians and, forming line, fought and won a complete victory over them, and destroyed fifteen of their ships. On the very same day the forces besieging Epidamnus succeeded in compelling the city to capitulate, the terms being that the Corinthians until their fate was determined should be imprisoned and the strangers sold.

After the sea-fight the Corcyraeans raised a trophy on Leucimme, a promontory of Corcyra, and put to death all their prisoners with the exception of the Corinthians, whom they kept in chains. The defeated Corinthians and their allies then returned home, and the Corcyraeans (who were now masters of the Ionian sea), sailing to Leucas, a Corinthian colony, devastated the country. They also burnt Cyllene, where the Eleans had their docks, because they had supplied the Corinthians with money and ships. And, during the greater part of the summer after the battle, they retained the command of the sea and sailed about plundering the allies of the Corinthians. But, before the season was over, the Corinthians, perceiving that their allies were suffering, sent out a fleet and formed a camp at Actium and near the promontory of Cheimerium in Thesprotia, that they might protect Leucas and other friendly places. The Corcyraeans with their fleet and army stationed themselves on the opposite coast of Leucimme. Neither party attacked the other, but during the remainder of the summer they maintained their respective positions, and at the approach of winter returned home.

For the whole year after the battle, and for a year after that, the Corinthians, exasperated by their defeat, were busy in building ships. They took the utmost pains to create a great navy: rowers were collected from the Peloponnesus and from the rest of Hellas by the attraction of pay. The Corcyraeans were alarmed at the report of their preparations. They reflected that they had not enrolled themselves in the league either of the Athenians or of the Lacedaemonians, and that allies in Hellas they had none. They determined to go to Athens, join the Athenian alliance, and get what help they could from them. The Corinthians, hearing of their intentions, also sent ambassadors to Athens, fearing lest the combination of the Athenian and Corcyraean navies might prevent them from bringing the war to a satisfactory termination. Accordingly an assembly was held at which both parties came forward to plead their respective causes; and first the Corcyraeans spoke as follows:

"Men of Athens, those who, like ourselves, come to others who are not their allies and to whom they have never rendered any considerable service and ask help of them, are bound to show, in the first place, that the granting of their request is expedient, or at any rate not inexpedient, and, secondly, that their gratitude will be lasting. If they fulfil neither requirement they have no right to complain of a refusal. Now the Corcyraeans, when they sent us hither to ask for an alliance, were confident that they could establish to your satisfaction both these points. But, unfortunately, we have had a practice alike inconsistent with the request which we are about to make and contrary to our own interest at the present moment: Inconsistent; for hitherto we have never, if we could avoid it, been the allies of others, and now we come and ask you to enter into an alliance with us: Contrary to our interest; for through this practice we find ourselves isolated in our war with the Corinthians. The policy of not making alliances lest they should endanger us at another's bidding, instead of being wisdom, as we once fancied, has now unmistakably proved to be weakness and folly. True, in the last naval engagement we repelled the Corinthians single-handed. But now they are on the point of attacking us with a much greater force which they have drawn together from the Peloponnesus and from all Hellas. We know that we are too weak to resist them unaided, and may expect the worst if we fall into their hands. We are therefore compelled to ask assistance of you and of all the world; and you must not be hard upon us if now, renouncing the neutrality of isolation which was an error but not a crime, we dare to be inconsistent.

"To you at this moment the request which we are making offers a glorious opportunity. In the first place, you will assist the oppressed and not the oppressors; secondly, you will admit us to your alliance at a time when our vital interests are at stake, and will lay up a treasure of gratitude in our memories which will have the most abiding of all records. Lastly, we have a navy greater than any but your own. Reflect; what good fortune can be more extraordinary, what more annoying to your enemies than the voluntary accession of a power for whose alliance you would have given any amount of money and could never have been too thankful? This power now places herself at your disposal; you are to incur no danger and no expense, and she brings you a good name in the world, gratitude from those who seek your aid, and an increase of your own strength. Few have ever had all these advantages offered them at once; equally few when they come asking an alliance are able to give in the way of security and honour as much as they hope to receive.

"And if any one thinks that the war in which our services may be needed will never arrive, he is mistaken. He does not see that the Lacedaemonians, fearing the growth of your empire, are eager to take up arms, and that the Corinthians, who are your enemies, are all-powerful with them. They begin with us, but they will go on to you, that we may not stand united against them in the bond of a common enmity; they will not miss the chance of weakening us and strengthening themselves. And it is our business to strike first, we offering and you accepting our alliance, and to forestall their designs instead of waiting to counteract them.

"If they say that we are their colony and that therefore you have no right to receive us, they should be made to understand that all colonies honour their mother-city when she treats them well, but are estranged from her by injustice. For colonists are not meant to be the servants but the equals of those who remain at home. And the injustice of their conduct to us is manifest: for we proposed an arbitration in the matter of Epidamnus, but they insisted on prosecuting their quarrel by arms and would not hear of a legal trial. When you see how they treat us who are their own kinsmen, take warning: if they try deception, do not be misled by them; and if they make a direct request of you, refuse. For he passes through life most securely who has least reason to reproach himself with complaisance to his enemies.

"But again, you will not break the treaty with the Lacedaemonians by receiving us: for we are not allies either of you or of them. What says the treaty? — 'Any Hellenic city which is the ally of no one may join whichever league it pleases.' And how monstrous, that they should man their ships, not only from their own confederacy, but from Hellas in general, nay, even from your subjects, while they would debar us from the alliance which naturally offers and from every other, and will denounce it as a crime if you accede to our request. With far better reason shall we complain of you if you refuse. For you will be thrusting away us who are not your enemies and are in peril; and, far from restraining the enemy and the aggressor, you will be allowing him to gather fresh forces out of your own dominions. How unjust is this! Surely if you would be impartial you should either prevent the Corinthians from hiring soldiers in your dominions, or send to us also such help as you can be induced to send; but it would be best of all if you would openly receive and assist us. Many, as we have already intimated, are the advantages which we offer. Above all, our enemies are your enemies, which is the best guarantee of fidelity in an ally; and they are not weak but well able to injure those who secede from them. Again, when the proffered alliance is that of a maritime and not of an inland power, it is a far more serious matter to refuse. You should, if possible, allow no one to have a fleet but yourselves; or, if this is impossible, whoever is strongest at sea, make him your friend.

"Some one may think that the course which we recommend is expedient, but he may be afraid that if he is convinced by our arguments he will break the treaty. To him we reply, that if he will only strengthen himself he may make a present of his fears to the enemy, but that if he reject the alliance he will be weak, and then his confidence, however reassuring to himself, will be anything but terrifying to enemies who are strong. It is Athens about which he is advising, and not Corcyra: will he be providing for her best interests if, when war is imminent and almost at the door, he is so anxious about the chances of the hour that he hesitates to attach to him a state which cannot be made a friend or enemy without momentous consequences? Corcyra, besides offering many other advantages, is conveniently situated for the coast voyage to Italy and Sicily; it stands in the way of any fleet coming from thence to the Peloponnesus, and can also protect a fleet on its way to Sicily. One word more, which is the sum of all we have to say, and should convince you that you must not abandon us. Hellas has only three considerable navies: there is ours, and there is yours, and there is the Corinthian. Now, if the Corinthians get hold of ours, and you allow the two to become one, you will have to fight against the united navies of Corcyra and the Peloponnesus. But, if you make us your allies, you will have our navy in addition to your own ranged at your side in the impending conflict."

Thus spoke the Corcyraeans: the Corinthians replied as follows:

"Since these Corcyraeans have chosen to speak, not only of their reception into your alliance, but of our misdoings and of the unjust war which has been forced upon them by us, we too must touch on these two points before we proceed to our main argument, that you may be better prepared to appreciate our claim upon you, and may have a good reason for rejecting their petition. They pretend that they have hitherto refused to make alliances from a wise moderation, but they really adopted this policy from a mean and not from a high motive. They did not want to have an ally who might go and tell of their crimes, and who would put them to the blush whenever they called him in. Their insular position makes them judges of their own offences against others, and they can therefore afford to dispense with judges appointed under treaties; for they hardly ever visit their neighbours, but foreign ships are constantly driven to their shores by stress of weather. And all the time they screen themselves under the specious name of neutrality, making believe that they are unwilling to be the accomplices of other men's crimes. But the truth is that they wish to keep their own criminal courses to themselves: where they are strong, to oppress; where they cannot be found out, to defraud; and whatever they may contrive to appropriate, never to be ashamed. If they were really upright men, as they profess to be, the greater their immunity from attack the more clearly they might have made their honesty appear by a willingness to submit differences to arbitration.

"But such they have not shown themselves either towards us or towards others. Although they are our colony they have always stood aloof from us, and now they are fighting against us on the plea that they were not sent out to be ill used. To which we rejoin that we did not send them out to be insulted by them, but that we might be recognised as their leaders and receive proper respect. At any rate our other colonies honour us; no city is more beloved by her colonies than Corinth. That we are popular with the majority proves that the Corcyraeans have no reason to dislike us; and, if it seems extraordinary that we should go to war with them, our defence is that the injury which they are doing us is unexampled. Even if we had been misled by passion, it would have been honourable in them to make allowance for us, and dishonourable in us to use violence when they showed moderation. But they have wronged us over and over again in their insolence and pride of wealth; and now there is our colony of Epidamnus which they would not acknowledge in her distress, but when we came to her rescue, they seized and are now holding by force.

"They pretend that they first offered to have the matter decided by arbitration. The appeal to justice might have some meaning in the mouth of one who before he had recourse to arms acted honourably, as he now talks fairly, but not when it is made from a position of security and advantage. Whereas these men began by laying siege to Epidamnus, and not until they feared our vengeance did they put forward their specious offer of arbitration. And as if the wrong which they have themselves done at Epidamnus were not enough, they now come hither and ask you to be, not their allies, but their accomplices in crime, and would have you receive them when they are at enmity with us. But they ought to have come when they were out of all danger, not at a time when we are smarting under an injury and they have good reason to be afraid. You have never derived any benefit from their power, but they will now be benefited by yours, and, although innocent of their crimes, you will equally be held responsible by us. If you were to have shared the consequences with them, they ought long ago to have shared the power with you.

"We have shown that our complaints are justified and that our adversaries are tyrannical and dishonest; we will now prove to you that you have no right to receive them. Admitting that the treaty allows any unenrolled cities to join either league, this provision does not apply to those who have in view the injury of others, but only to him who is in need of protection, certainly not to one who forsakes his allegiance and who will bring war instead of peace to those who receive him, or rather, if they are wise, will not receive him on such terms. And war the Corcyraeans will bring to you if you listen to them and not to us. For if you become the allies of the Corcyraeans you will be no longer at peace with us, but will be converted into enemies; and we must, if you take their part, in defending ourselves against them, defend ourselves against you. But you ought in common justice to stand aloof from both; or, if you must join either, you should join us and go to war with them; to Corinth you are at all events bound by treaty, but with Corcyra you never even entered into a temporary negotiation. And do not set the precedent of receiving the rebellious subjects of others. At the revolt of Samos, when the other Peloponnesians were divided upon the question of giving aid to the rebels, we voted in your favour and expressly maintained 'that every one should be allowed to chastise his own allies.' If you mean to receive and assist evil-doers, we shall assuredly gain as many allies of yours as you will of ours; and you will establish a principle which will tell against yourselves more than against us.

"Such are the grounds of right which we urge; and they are sufficient according to Hellenic law. And may we venture to recall to your minds an obligation of which we claim the repayment in our present need, we and you being not enemies who seek one another's hurt, nor yet friends who freely give and take? There was a time before the Persian invasion when you were in want of ships for the Aeginetan war, and we Corinthians lent you twenty: the service which we then rendered to you gave you the victory over the Aeginetans, as the other, which prevented the Peloponnesians from aiding the Samians, enabled you to punish Samos. Both benefits were conferred on one of those critical occasions when men in the act of attacking their enemies are utterly regardless of everything but victory, and deem him who assists them a friend though he may have previously been a foe, him who opposes them a foe, even though he may happen to be a friend; nay, they will often neglect their own interests in the excitement of the struggle.

"Think of these things; let the younger be informed of them by their elders, and resolve all of you to render like for like. Do not say to yourselves that this is just, but that in the event of war something else is expedient; for the true path of expediency is the path of right. The war with which the Corcyraeans would frighten you into doing wrong is distant, and may never come; is it worth while to be so carried away by the prospect of it, that you bring upon yourselves the hatred of the Corinthians which is both near and certain? Would you not be wiser in seeking to mitigate the ill-feeling which your treatment of the Megarians has already inspired? The later kindness done in season, though small in comparison, may cancel a greater previous wrong. And do not be attracted by their offer of a great naval alliance; for to do no wrong to a neighbour is a surer source of strength than to gain a perilous advantage under the influence of a momentary illusion.

"We are now ourselves in the same situation in which you were, when we declared at Sparta that every one so placed should be allowed to chastise his own allies; and we claim to receive the same measure at your hands. You profited by our vote, and we ought not to be injured by yours. Pay what you owe, knowing that this is our time of need, in which a man's best friend is he who does him a service, he who opposes him, his worst enemy. Do not receive these Corcyraeans into alliance in despite of us, and do not support them in injustice. In acting thus you will act rightly, and will consult your own true interests."

Such were the words of the Corinthians. The Athenians heard both sides, and they held two assemblies; in the first of them they were more influenced by the words of the Corinthians, but in the second they changed their minds and inclined towards the Corcyraeans. They would not go so far as to make an alliance both offensive and defensive with them; for then, if the Corcyraeans had required them to join in an expedition against Corinth, the treaty with the Peloponnesians would have been broken. But they concluded a defensive league, by which the two states promised to aid each other if an attack were made on the territory or on the allies of either. For they knew that in any case the war with Peloponnesus was inevitable, and they had no mind to let Corcyra and her navy fall into the hands of the Corinthians. Their plan was to embroil them more and more with one another, and then, when the war came, the Corinthians and the other naval powers would be weaker. They also considered that Corcyra was conveniently situated for the coast voyage to Italy and Sicily.

Under the influence of these feelings, they received the Corcyraeans into alliance; the Corinthians departed; and the Athenians now despatched to Corcyra ten ships commanded by Lacedaemonius, the son of Cimon, Diotimus the son of Strombichus, and Proteas the son of Epicles. The commanders received orders not to engage with the Corinthians unless they sailed against Corcyra or to any place belonging to the Corcyraeans, and attempted to land there, in which case they were to resist them to the utmost. These orders were intended to prevent a breach of the treaty.

[I. 1-45, tr. B. JOWETT]

[Despite these orders, the Athenian and Corinthian ships fought against each other in a sea-battle off Corcyra; and this was the first immediate cause of the Peloponnesian War. Other causes followed: Potidaea, a tributary ally of Athens, but originally a Corinthian colony, revolted from the Athenian Empire, at the instigation of Corinth, and Athens sent a large force to subdue the rebellion; the Athenians also passed a set of decrees by which they excluded the Megarians from all markets in the Athenian

Empire. Urged on by the Corinthians, the Spartans and their allies declared war and invaded Attica in the spring of 431 B.C.

During the next winter, following the ancestral practice, the Athenians
held a funeral at the public charge for those who had fallen in the first
year of the war, and the customary funeral oration was delivered by Pericles. In the speech which Thucydides here puts into the statesman's
mouth, he gives an idealized picture of the Athenian democracy at its
zenith, to remind his readers of what Athens had meant to those who
had fought and died for her.]

THE FUNERAL ORATION OF PERICLES

"Most of those who have spoken here before me have commended
the lawgiver who added this oration to our other funeral customs;
it seemed to them a worthy thing that such an honour should be given
at their burial to the dead who have fallen on the field of battle. But
I should have preferred that, when men's deeds have been brave, they
should be honoured in deed only, and with such an honour as this
public funeral, which you are now witnessing. Then the reputation
of many would not have been imperilled on the eloquence or want of
eloquence of one, and their virtues believed or not as he spoke well or
ill. For it is difficult to say neither too little nor too much; and even
moderation is apt not to give the impression of truthfulness. The
friend of the dead who knows the facts is likely to think that the
words of the speaker fall short of his knowledge and of his wishes;
another who is not so well informed, when he hears of anything
which surpasses his own powers, will be envious and will suspect
exaggeration. Mankind are tolerant of the praises of others so long
as each hearer thinks that he can do as well or nearly as well himself,
but, when the deed is beyond him, jealousy is aroused and he begins
to be incredulous. However, since our ancestors have set the seal of
their approval upon the practice, I must obey, and to the utmost of my
power shall endeavour to satisfy the wishes and beliefs of all who hear
me.

"I will speak first of our ancestors, for it is right and becoming that
now, when we are lamenting the dead, a tribute should be paid to
their memory. There has never been a time when they did not inhabit this land, which by their valour they have handed down from
generation to generation, and we have received from them a free state.
But if they were worthy of praise, still more were our fathers, who
added to their inheritance, and after many a struggle transmitted to
us their sons this great empire. And we ourselves assembled here
to-day, who are still most of us in the vigour of life, have chiefly done
the work of improvement, and have richly endowed our city with all
things, so that she is sufficient for herself both in peace and war. Of
the military exploits by which our various possessions were acquired,
or of the energy with which we or our fathers drove back the tide of
war, Hellenic or barbarian, I will not speak; for the tale would be
long and is familiar to you. But before I praise the dead, I should
like to point out by what principles of action we rose to power, and

under what institutions and through what manner of life our empire became great. For I conceive that such thoughts are not unsuited to the occasion, and that this numerous assembly of citizens and strangers may profitably listen to them.

"Our form of government does not enter into rivalry with the institutions of others. We do not copy our neighbours, but are an example to them. It is true that we are called a democracy, for the administration is in the hands of the many and not of the few. But while the law secures equal justice to all alike in their private disputes, the claim of excellence is also recognised; and when a citizen is in any way distinguished, he is preferred to the public service, not as a matter of privilege, but as the reward of merit. Neither is poverty a bar, but a man may benefit his country whatever be the obscurity of his condition. There is no exclusiveness in our public life, and in our private intercourse we are not suspicious of one another, nor angry with our neighbour if he does what he likes; we do not put on sour looks at him which, though harmless, are not pleasant. While we are thus unconstrained in our private intercourse, a spirit of reverence pervades our public acts; we are prevented from doing wrong by respect for authority and for the laws, having an especial regard to those which are ordained for the protection of the injured as well as to those unwritten laws which bring upon the transgressor of them the reprobation of the general sentiment.

"And we have not forgotten to provide for our weary spirits many relaxations from toil; we have regular games and sacrifices throughout the year; at home the style of our life is refined; and the delight which we daily feel in all these things helps to banish melancholy. Because of the greatness of our city the fruits of the whole earth flow in upon us; so that we enjoy the goods of other countries as freely as of our own.

"Then, again, our military training is in many respects superior to that of our adversaries. Our city is thrown open to the world, and we never expel a foreigner or prevent him from seeing or learning anything of which the secret if revealed to an enemy might profit him. We rely not upon management or trickery, but upon our own hearts and hands. And in the matter of education, whereas they from early youth are always undergoing laborious exercises which are to make them brave, we live at ease, and yet are equally ready to face the perils which they face. And here is the proof. The Lacedaemonians come into Attica not by themselves, but with their whole confederacy following; we go alone into a neighbour's country; and although our opponents are fighting for their homes and we on a foreign soil, we have seldom any difficulty in overcoming them. Our enemies have never yet felt our united strength; the care of a navy divides our attention, and on land we are obliged to send our own citizens everywhere. But they, if they meet and defeat a part of our army, are as proud as if they had routed us all, and when defeated they pretend to have been vanquished by us all.

"If then we prefer to meet danger with a light heart but without laborious training, and with a courage which is gained by habit and not enforced by law, are we not greatly the gainers? Since we do not anticipate the pain, although, when the hour comes, we can be as brave as those who never allow themselves to rest; and thus too our city is equally admirable in peace and in war. For we are lovers of the beautiful, yet with economy, and we cultivate the mind without loss of manliness. Wealth we employ, not for talk and ostentation, but when there is a real use for it. To avow poverty with us is no disgrace; the true disgrace is in doing nothing to avoid it. An Athenian citizen does not neglect the state because he takes care of his own household; and even those of us who are engaged in business have a very fair idea of politics. We alone regard a man who takes no interest in public affairs, not as a harmless, but as a useless character; and if few of us are originators, we are all sound judges of a policy. The great impediment to action is, in our opinion, not discussion, but the want of that knowledge which is gained by discussion preparatory to action. For we have a peculiar power of thinking before we act and of acting too, whereas other men are courageous from ignorance but hesitate upon reflection. And they are surely to be esteemed the bravest spirits who, having the clearest sense both of the pains and pleasures of life, do not on that account shrink from danger. In doing good, again, we are unlike others; we make our friends by conferring, not by receiving favours. Now he who confers a favour is the firmer friend, because he would fain by kindness keep alive the memory of an obligation; but the recipient is colder in his feelings, because he knows that in requiting another's generosity he will not be winning gratitude but only paying a debt. We alone do good to our neighbours not upon a calculation of interest, but in the confidence of freedom and in a frank and fearless spirit.

"To sum up: I say that Athens is the school of Hellas, and that the individual Athenian in his own person seems to have the power of adapting himself to the most varied forms of action with the utmost versatility and grace. This is no passing and idle word, but truth and fact; and the assertion is verified by the position to which these qualities have raised the state. For in the hour of trial Athens alone among her contemporaries is superior to the report of her. No enemy who comes against her is indignant at the reverses which he sustains at the hands of such a city; no subject complains that his masters are unworthy of him. And we shall assuredly not be without witnesses; there are mighty monuments of our power which will make us the wonder of this and of succeeding ages; we shall not need the praises of Homer or of any other panegyrist whose poetry may please for the moment, although his representation of the facts will not bear the light of day. For we have compelled every land and every sea to open a path for our valour, and have everywhere planted eternal memorials of our friendship and of our enmity. Such is the city for whose sake these men nobly fought and died; they could not bear the thought that she might be taken from them; and every one of us who survive should gladly toil on her behalf.

"I have dwelt upon the greatness of Athens because I want to show you that we are contending for a higher prize than those who enjoy none of these privileges, and to establish by manifest proof the merit of these men whom I am now commemorating. Their loftiest praise has been already spoken. For in magnifying the city I have magnified them, and men like them whose virtues made her glorious. And of how few Hellenes can it be said as of them, that their deeds when weighed in the balance have been found equal to their fame! It seems to me that a death such as theirs has been gives the true measure of a man's worth; it may be the first revelation of his virtues, but is at any rate their final seal. For even those who come short in other ways may justly plead the valour with which they have fought for their country; they have blotted out the evil with the good, and have benefited the state more by their public services than they have injured her by their private actions. None of these men were enervated by wealth or hesitated to resign the pleasures of life; none of them put off the evil day in the hope, natural to poverty, that a man, though poor, may one day become rich. But, deeming that the punishment of their enemies was sweeter than any of these things, and that they could fall in no nobler cause, they determined at the hazard of their lives to be honourably avenged, and to leave the rest. They resigned to hope their unknown chance of happiness; but in the face of death they resolved to rely upon themselves alone. And when the moment came they were minded to resist and suffer, rather than to fly and save their lives; they ran away from the word of dishonour, but on the battle-field their feet stood fast, and in an instant, at the height of their fortune, they passed away from the scene, not of their fear, but of their glory.

"Such was the end of these men; they were worthy of Athens, and the living need not desire to have a more heroic spirit, although they may pray for a less fatal issue. The value of such a spirit is not to be expressed in words. Any one can discourse to you for ever about the advantages of a brave defence which you know already. But instead of listening to him I would have you day by day fix your eyes upon the greatness of Athens, until you become filled with the love of her; and when you are impressed by the spectacle of her glory, reflect that this empire has been acquired by men who knew their duty and had the courage to do it, who in the hour of conflict had the fear of dishonour always present to them, and who, if ever they failed in an enterprize, would not allow their virtues to be lost to their country, but freely gave their lives to her as the fairest offering which they could present at her feast. The sacrifice which they collectively made was individually repaid to them; for they received again each one for himself a praise which grows not old, and the noblest of all sepulchres— I speak not of that in which their remains are laid, but of that in which their glory survives, and is proclaimed always and on every fitting occasion both in word and deed. For the whole earth is the sepulchre of famous men; not only are they commemorated by columns and inscriptions in their own country, but in foreign lands there dwell also an unwritten memorial of them, graven not on stone but in the hearts of men. Make them your examples, and esteeming courage to be freedom and freedom to be happiness, do not weigh too nicely the perils of war. The unfortunate who has no hope of a change for the better has less reason to throw away his life than the prosperous who, if he survive, is always liable to a change for the worse, and to whom any accidental fall makes the most serious difference. To a man of spirit, cowardice and disaster coming together are far more bitter than death striking him unperceived at a time when he is full of courage and animated by the general hope.

"Wherefore I do not now commiserate the parents of the dead who stand here; I would rather comfort them. You know that your life has been passed amid manifold vicissitudes; and that they may be deemed fortunate who have gained most honour, whether an honourable death like theirs, or an honourable sorrow like yours, and whose days have been so ordered that the term of their happiness is likewise the term of their life. I know how hard it is to make you feel this, when the good fortune of others will too often remind you of the gladness which once lightened your hearts. And sorrow is felt at the want of those blessings, not which a man never knew, but which were a part of his life before they were taken from him. Some of you are of an age at which they may hope to have other children, and they ought to bear their sorrow better; not only will the children who may hereafter be born make them forget their own lost ones, but the city will be doubly a gainer. She will not be left desolate, and she will be safer. For a man's counsel cannot have equal weight or worth, when he alone has no children to risk in the general danger. To those of you who have passed their prime, I say, 'Congratulate yourselves that you have been happy during the greater part of your days; remember that your life of sorrow will not last long, and be comforted by the glory of those who are gone. For the love of honour alone is ever young, and not riches, as some say, but honour is the delight of men when they are old and useless.'

"To you who are the sons and brothers of the departed, I see that the struggle to emulate them will be an arduous one. For all men praise the dead, and, however pre-eminent your virtue may be, hardly will you be thought, I do not say to equal, but even to approach them. The living have their rivals and detractors, but when a man is out of the way, the honour and good-will which he receives is unalloyed. And, if I am to speak of womanly virtues to those of you who will henceforth be widows, let me sum them up in one short admonition: To a woman not to show more weakness than is natural to her sex is a great glory, and not to be talked about for good or for evil among men.

"I have paid the required tribute, in obedience to the law, making use of such fitting words as I had. The tribute of deeds has been paid in part; for the dead have been honourably interred, and it remains only that their children should be maintained at the public charge until they are grown up: this is the solid prize with which, as with a garland, Athens crowns her sons living and dead, after a struggle like theirs. For where the rewards of virtue are greatest, there the noblest citizens are enlisted in the service of the state. And now, when you have duly lamented, every one his own dead, you may depart."

[II. 35–46, tr. B. Jowett]

[The first phase of the war ended in 421 B.C. with the Peace of Nicias. Although Athens and Sparta were officially at peace for the next six years, the time was spent in diplomatic warfare, as each side sought to improve its position. The expedition against Melos in 416 B.C., which is described below, is important not so much for its military results as for the light which it throws on Greek political morality. By the device of a debate between the Athenian envoys and the Melian leaders Thucydides reveals in all its nakedness the brutal policy of "Might makes Right"; what he is expressing here is the Sophists' doctrine of "the law of nature" that the strong shall rule. It must not be supposed, however, that Thucydides necessarily approves of the sentiments which he places in the mouths of the Athenians; he simply exhibits, without comment, what seemed to him to be the underlying, if unspoken, principles of Greek political action.]

THE MELIAN DIALOGUE

In the ensuing summer, Alcibiades sailed to Argos with twenty ships, and seized any of the Argives who were still suspected to be of the Lacedaemonian faction, 300 in number; and the Athenians deposited them in the subject islands near at hand. The Athenians next made an expedition against the island of Melos with thirty ships of their own, six Chian, and two Lesbian, 1200 hoplites and 300 archers besides twenty mounted archers of their own, and about 1500 hoplites furnished by their allies in the islands. The Melians are colonists of the Lacedaemonians who would not submit to Athens like the other islanders. At first they were neutral and took no part. But when the Athenians tried to coerce them by ravaging their lands, they were driven into open hostilities. The generals, Cleomedes the son of Lycomedes and Tisias the son of Tisimachus, encamped with the Athenian forces on the island. But before they did the country any harm they sent envoys to negotiate with the Melians. Instead of bringing these envoys before the people, the Melians desired them to explain their errand to the magistrates and to the chief men. They spoke as follows:

"Since we are not allowed to speak to the people, lest, forsooth, they should be deceived by seductive and unanswerable arguments which they would hear set forth in a single uninterrupted oration (for we are perfectly aware that this is what you mean in bringing us before a select few), you who are sitting here may as well make assurance yet surer. Let us have no set speeches at all, but do you reply to each several statement of which you disprove, and criticise it at once. Say first of all how you like this mode of proceeding."

The Melian representatives answered: "The quiet interchange of explanations is a reasonable thing, and we do not object to that. But your warlike movements, which are present not only to our fears but to our eyes, seem to belie your words. We see that, although you may reason with us, you mean to be our judges; and that at the end of the discussion, if the justice of our cause prevail and we therefore refuse to yield, we may expect war; if we are convinced by you, slavery."

Athenians: Nay, but if you are only going to argue from fancies about the future, or if you meet us with any other purpose than that of looking your circumstances in the face and saving your city, we have done; but if this is your intention we will proceed.

Melians: It is an excusable and natural thing that men in our position should have much to say and should indulge in many fancies. But we admit that this conference has met to consider the question of our preservation; and therefore let the argument proceed in the manner which you propose.

Athenians: Well, then, we Athenians will use no fine words; we will not go out of our way to prove at length that we have a right to rule, because we overthrew the Persians; or that we attack you now because we are suffering any injury at your hands. We should not convince you if we did; nor must you expect to convince us by arguing that, although a colony of the Lacedaemonians, you have taken no part in their expeditions, or that you have never done us any wrong. But you and we should say what we really think, and aim only at what is possible, for we both alike know that into the discussion of human affairs the question of justice only enters where the pressure of necessity is equal, and that the powerful exact what they can, and the weak grant what they must.

Melians: Well, then, since you set aside justice and invite us to speak of expediency, in our judgment it is certainly expedient that you should respect a principle which is for the common good; and that to every man when in peril a reasonable claim should be accounted a claim of right, and any plea which he is disposed to urge, even if failing of the point a little, should help his cause. Your interest in this principle is quite as great as ours, inasmuch as you, if you fall, will incur the heaviest vengeance, and will be the most terrible example to mankind.

Athenians: The fall of our empire, if it should fall, is not an event to which we look forward with dismay; for ruling states such as Lacedaemon are not cruel to their vanquished enemies. And we are fighting not so much against the Lacedaemonians, as against our own subjects who may some day rise up and overcome their former masters. But this is a danger which you may leave to us. And we will now endeavour to show that we have come in the interests of our empire, and that in what we are about to say we are only seeking the preservation of your city. For we want to make you ours with the least trouble to ourselves, and it is for the interests of us both that you should not be destroyed.

Melians: It may be your interest to be our masters, but how can it be ours to be your slaves?

Athenians: To you the gain will be that by submission you will avert the worst; and we shall be all the richer for your preservation.

Melians: But must we be your enemies? Will you not receive us as friends if we are neutral and remain at peace with you?

Athenians: No, your enmity is not half so mischievous to us as your friendship; for the one is in the eyes of our subjects an argument of our power, the other of our weakness.

Melians: But are your subjects really unable to distinguish between states in which you have no concern, and those which are chiefly your own colonies, and in some cases have revolted and been subdued by you?

Athenians: Why, they do not doubt that both of them have a good deal to say for themselves on the score of justice, but they think that states like yours are left free because they are able to defend themselves, and that we do not attack them because we dare not. So that your subjection will give us an increase of security, as well as an extension of empire. For we are masters of the sea, and you who are islanders, and insignificant islanders too, must not be allowed to escape us.

Melians: But do you not recognise another danger? For, once more, since you drive us from the plea of justice and press upon us your doctrine of expediency, we must show you what is for our interest, and, if it be for yours also, may hope to convince you. Will you not be making enemies of all who are now neutrals? When they see how you are treating us they will expect you some day to turn against them; and if so, are you not strengthening the enemies whom you already have, and bringing upon you others who, if they could help, would never dream of being your enemies at all?

Athenians: We do not consider our really dangerous enemies to be any of the peoples inhabiting the mainland who, secure in their freedom, may defer indefinitely any measures of precaution which they take against us, but islanders who, like you, happen to be under no control, and all who may be already irritated by the necessity of submission to our empire — these are our real enemies, for they are the most reckless and most likely to bring themselves as well as us into a danger which they cannot but foresee.

Melians: Surely then, if you and your subjects will brave all this risk, you to preserve your empire and they to be quit of it, how base and cowardly would it be in us, who retain our freedom, not to do and suffer anything rather than be your slaves.

Athenians: Not so, if you calmly reflect: for you are not fighting against equals to whom you cannot yield without disgrace, but you are taking counsel whether or no you shall resist an overwhelming force. The question is not one of honour but of prudence.

Melians: But we know that the fortune of war is sometimes impartial, and not always on the side of numbers. If we yield now, all is over; but if we fight, there is yet a hope that we may stand upright.

Athenians: Hope is a good comforter in the hour of danger, and when men have something else to depend upon, although hurtful, she is not ruinous. But when her spendthrift nature has induced them to stake their all, they see her as she is in the moment of their fall, and not till then. While the knowledge of her might enable them to beware of her, she never fails. You are weak and a single turn of the scale might be your ruin. Do not you be thus deluded; avoid the error of which so many are guilty, who, although they might still be saved if they would take the natural means, when visible grounds of confidence forsake them, have recourse to the invisible, to prophecies and oracles and the like, which ruin men by the hopes which they inspire in them.

Melians: We know only too well how hard the struggle must be against your power, and against fortune, if she does not mean to be impartial. Nevertheless we do not despair of fortune; for we hope to stand as high as you in the favour of heaven, because we are righteous, and you against whom we contend are unrighteous; and we are satisfied that our deficiency in power will be compensated by the aid of our allies the Lacedaemonians; they cannot refuse to help us, if only because we are their kinsmen, and for the sake of their own honour. And therefore our confidence is not so utterly blind as you suppose.

Athenians: As for the gods, we expect to have quite as much of their favour as you: for we are not doing or claiming anything which goes beyond common opinion about divine or men's desires about human things. Of the gods we believe, and of men we know, that by a law of their nature wherever they can rule they will. This law was not made by us, and we are not the first who have acted upon it; we did but inherit it, and shall bequeath it to all time, and we know that you and all mankind, if you were as strong as we are, would do as we do. So much for the gods; we have told you why we expect to stand as high in their good opinion as you. And then as to the Lacedaemonians — when you imagine that out of very shame they will assist you, we admire the simplicity of your idea, but we do not envy you the folly of it. The Lacedaemonians are exceedingly virtuous among themselves, and according to their national standard of morality. But, in respect of their dealings with others, although many things might be said, a word is enough to describe them, of all men whom we know they are the most notorious for identifying what is pleasant with what is honourable, and what is expedient with what is just. But how inconsistent is such a character with your present blind hope of deliverance!

Melians: That is the very reason why we trust them; they will look to their interest, and therefore will not be willing to betray the Melians, who are their own colonists, lest they should be distrusted by their friends in Hellas and play into the hands of their enemies.

Athenians: But do you not see that the path of expediency is safe, whereas justice and honour involve danger in practice, and such dangers the Lacedaemonians seldom care to face?

Melians: On the other hand, we think that whatever perils there may be, they will be ready to face them for our sakes, and will consider danger less dangerous where we are concerned. For if they need to act we are close at hand, and they can better trust our loyal feeling because we are their kinsmen.

Athenians: Yes, but what encourages men who are invited to join in a conflict is clearly not the good-will of those who summon them to their side, but a decided superiority in real power. To this no men look more keenly than the Lacedaemonians; so little confidence have they in their own resources, that they only attack their neighbours when they have numerous allies, and therefore they are not likely to find their way by themselves to an island, when we are masters of the sea.

Melians: But they may send their allies: the Cretan sea is a large place; and the masters of the sea will have more difficulty in overtaking vessels which want to escape than the pursued in escaping. If the attempt should fail they may invade Attica itself, and find their way to allies of yours whom Brasidas did not reach: and then you will have to fight, not for the conquest of a land in which you have no concern, but nearer home, for the preservation of your confederacy and of your own territory.

Athenians: Help may come from Lacedaemon to you as it has come to others, and should you ever have actual experience of it, then you will know that never once have the Athenians retired from a siege through fear of a foe elsewhere. You told us that the safety of your city would be your first care, but we remark that, in this long discussion, not a word has been uttered by you which would give a reasonable man expectation of deliverance. Your strongest grounds are hopes deferred, and what power you have is not to be compared with that which is already arrayed against you. Unless after we have withdrawn you mean to come, as even now you may, to a wiser conclusion, you are showing a great want of sense. For surely you cannot dream of flying to that false sense of honour which has been the ruin of so many when danger and dishonour were staring them in the face. Many men with their eyes still open to the consequences have found the word honour too much for them, and have suffered a mere name to lure them on, until it has drawn down upon them real and irretrievable calamities; through their own folly they have incurred a worse dishonour than fortune would have inflicted upon them. If you are wise you will not run this risk; you ought to see that there can be no disgrace in yielding to a great city which invites you to become her ally on reasonable terms, keeping your own land, and merely paying tribute; and that you will certainly gain no honour if, having to choose between two alternatives, safety and war, you obstinately prefer the worse. To maintain our rights against equals, to be politic with superiors, and to be moderate towards inferiors is the path of safety. Reflect once more when we have withdrawn, and say to yourselves over and over again that you are deliberating about your one and only country, which may be saved or may be destroyed by a single decision.

The Athenians left the conference: the Melians, after consulting among themselves, resolved to persevere in their refusal, and answered as follows, "Men of Athens, our resolution is unchanged; and we will not in a moment surrender that liberty which our city, founded 700 years ago, still enjoys; we will trust to the good-fortune which, by the favour of the gods, has hitherto preserved us, and for human help to the Lacedaemonians, and endeavour to save ourselves. We are ready however to be your friends, and the enemies neither of you nor of the Lacedaemonians, and we ask you to leave our country when you have made such a peace as may appear to be in the interest of both parties."

Such was the answer of the Melians; the Athenians, as they quitted the conference, spoke as follows, "Well, we must say, judging from the decision at which you have arrived, that you are the only men who deem the future to be more certain than the present, and regard things unseen as already realised in your fond anticipation, and that the more you cast yourselves upon the Lacedaemonians and fortune, and hope, and trust them, the more complete will be your ruin."

The Athenian envoys returned to the army; and the generals, when they found that the Melians would not yield, immediately commenced hostilities. They surrounded the town of Melos with a wall, dividing the work among the several contingents. They then left troops of their own and of their allies to keep guard both by land and by sea, and retired with the greater part of their army; the remainder carried on the blockade.

About the same time the Argives made an inroad into Phliasia, and lost nearly eighty men, who were caught in an ambuscade by the Phliasians and the Argive exiles. The Athenian garrison in Pylos took much spoil from the Lacedaemonians; nevertheless the latter did not renounce the peace and go to war, but only notified by a proclamation that if any one of their own people had a mind to make reprisals on the Athenians he might. The Corinthians next declared war upon the Athenians on some private grounds, but the rest of the Peloponnesians did not join them. The Melians took that part of the Athenian wall which looked towards the agora by a night assault, killed a few men, and brought in as much corn and other necessaries as they could; they then retreated and remained inactive. After this the Athenians set a better watch. So the summer ended.

In the following winter the Lacedaemonians had intended to make an expedition into the Argive territory, but finding that the sacrifices which they offered at the frontier were unfavourable they returned home. The Argives, suspecting that the threatened invasion was instigated by citizens of their own, apprehended some of them; others however escaped.

About the same time the Melians took another part of the Athenian wall; for the fortifications were insufficiently guarded. Whereupon the Athenians sent fresh troops, under the command of Philocrates the son of Demeas. The place was now closely invested, and there was treachery among the citizens themselves. So the Melians were

induced to surrender at discretion. The Athenians thereupon put
to death all who were of military age, and made slaves of the women
and children. They then colonised the island, sending thither 500
settlers of their own.

[v. 84–116, tr. B. Jowett]

[In the spring of 415 b.c., Athens took advantage of an unimportant
quarrel between two cities of Sicily to intervene in the affairs of that island.
They sent a large expedition, the avowed object of which was to support
their ally, Segesta; but the real purpose, Thucydides tells us, was to conquer Syracuse, the strongest city of the island, and bring all Sicily into
the Athenian Empire.

The history of this venture, the famous and ill-fated Sicilian Expedition,
fills two books of Thucydides' work, forming a self-contained unit which
may have been published as a separate monograph. The complete an-
nihilation of the Athenian force, described below, was largely responsible
for the final defeat of Athens nine years later.

The Athenian had wasted the first year in Sicily in minor operations,
mainly because of the caution of Nicias, the Athenian commander, who
was ill-suited for an expedition requiring imagination and initiative. The
second summer they began the siege of Syracuse, but failed to invest the
city completely; the Syracusans, led by Gylippus, a Spartan general who
had been sent to help, erected a series of counter-walls and cut the Athenians off from Catana, their only base in Sicily. In the following year
(413 b.c.) the Syracusans mustered a fleet and twice defeated the Athenian
navy, which was moored in the Great Harbour of Syracuse. After the
second battle, they blocked the mouth of the harbour with a barricade
of boats, determined to prevent the escape of the Athenians. The Athenians then decided to make one more trial by sea and to attempt to break
through the blockade at the mouth of the harbour; before manning their
ships, both sides were addressed by their commanding officers.]

THE END OF THE SICILIAN EXPEDITION

When Gylippus and the other Syracusan generals had, like Nicias,
encouraged their troops, perceiving the Athenians to be manning
their ships, they presently did the same. Nicias, overwhelmed by
the situation, and seeing how great and how near the peril was (for
the ships were on the very point of rowing out), feeling too, as men
do on the eve of a great struggle, that all which he had done was
nothing, and that he had not said half enough, again addressed the
captains, and calling each of them by his father's name, and his own
name, and the name of his tribe, he entreated those who had made
any reputation for themselves not to be false to it, and those whose
ancestors were eminent not to tarnish their hereditary fame. He
reminded them that they were the inhabitants of the freest country
in the world, and how in Athens there was no interference with the
daily life of any man. He spoke to them of their wives and children
and their fathers' Gods, as men will at such a time; for then they do
not care whether their commonplace phrases seem to be out of date
or not, but loudly reiterate the old appeals, believing that they may
be of some service at the awful moment. When he thought that he

had exhorted them, not enough, but as much as the scanty time allowed, he retired, and led the land-forces to the shore, extending the line as far as he could, so that they might be of the greatest use in encouraging the combatants on board ship. Demosthenes, Menander, and Euthydemus, who had gone on board the Athenian fleet to take the command, now quitted their own station, and proceeded straight to the closed mouth of the harbour, intending to force their way to the open sea where a passage was still left.

The Syracusans and their allies had already put out with nearly the same number of ships as before. A detachment of them guarded the entrance of the harbour; the remainder were disposed all round it in such a manner that they might fall on the Athenians from every side at once, and that their land-forces might at the same time be able to co-operate wherever the ships retreated to the shore. Sicanus and Agatharchus commanded the Syracusan fleet, each of them a wing; Pythen and the Corinthians occupied the centre. When the Athenians approached the closed mouth of the harbour the violence of their onset overpowered the ships which were stationed there; they then attempted to loosen the fastenings. Whereupon from all sides the Syracusans and their allies came bearing down upon them, and the conflict was no longer confined to the entrance, but extended throughout the harbour. No previous engagement had been so fierce and obstinate. Great was the eagerness with which the rowers on both sides rushed upon their enemies whenever the word of command was given; and keen was the contest between the pilots as they manoeuvred one against another. The marines too were full of anxiety that, when ship struck ship, the service on deck should not fall short of the rest; every one in the place assigned to him was eager to be foremost among his fellows. Many vessels meeting — and never did so many fight in so small a space, for the two fleets together amounted to nearly 200 — they were seldom able to strike in the regular manner, because they had no opportunity of first retiring or breaking the line; they generally fouled one another as ship dashed against ship in the hurry of flight or pursuit. All the time that another vessel was bearing down, the men on deck poured showers of javelins and arrows and stones upon the enemy; and when the two closed, the marines fought hand to hand, and endeavoured to board. In many places, owing to the want of room, they who had struck another found that they were struck themselves; often two or even more vessels were unavoidably entangled about one, and the pilots had to make plans of attack and defence, not against one adversary only, but against several coming from different sides. The crash of so many ships dashing against one another took away the wits of the sailors, and made it impossible to hear the boatswains, whose voices in both fleets rose high, as they gave directions to the rowers, or cheered them on in the excitement of the struggle. On the Athenian side they were shouting to their men that they must force a passage and seize the opportunity now or never of returning in safety to their native land. To the Syracusans and their allies was represented the glory of preventing the escape of their enemies, and of a victory by which every man would exalt the honour of his own city. The commanders too, when they saw any ship backing water without necessity, would call the captain by his name, and ask, of the Athenians, whether they were retreating because they expected to be more at home upon the land of their bitterest foes than upon that sea which had been their own so long; on the Syracusan side, whether, when they knew perfectly well that the Athenians were only eager to find some means of flight, they would themselves fly from the fugitives.

While the naval engagement hung in the balance the two armies on shore had great trial and conflict of soul. The Sicilian soldier was animated by the hope of increasing the glory which he had already won, while the invader was tormented by the fear that his fortunes might sink lower still. The last chance of the Athenians lay in their ships, and their anxiety was dreadful. The fortune of the battle varied; and it was not possible that the spectators on the shore should all receive the same impression of it. Being quite close and having different points of view, they would some of them see their own ships victorious; their courage would then revive, and they would earnestly call upon the Gods not to take from them their hope of deliverance. But others, who saw their ships worsted, cried and shrieked aloud, and were by the sight alone more utterly unnerved than the defeated combatants themselves. Others again, who had fixed their gaze on some part of the struggle which was undecided, were in a state of excitement still more terrible; they kept swaying their bodies to and fro in an agony of hope and fear as the stubborn conflict went on and on; for at every instant they were all but saved or all but lost. And while the strife hung in the balance you might hear in the Athenian army at once lamentation, shouting, cries of victory or defeat, and all the various sounds which are wrung from a great host in extremity of danger. Not less agonising were the feelings of those on board. At length the Syracusans and their allies, after a protracted struggle, put the Athenians to flight, and triumphantly bearing down upon them, and encouraging one another with loud cries and exhortations, drove them to land. Then that part of the navy which had not been taken in the deep water fell back in confusion to the shore, and the crews rushed out of the ships into the camp. And the land-forces, no longer now divided in feeling, but uttering one universal groan of intolerable anguish, ran, some of them to save the ships, others to defend what remained of the wall; but the greater number began to look to themselves and to their own safety. Never had there been a greater panic in an Athenian army than at that moment. They now suffered what they had done to others at Pylos. For at Pylos the Lacedaemonians, when they saw their ships destroyed, knew that their friends who had crossed over into the island of Sphacteria were lost with them. And so now the Athenians, after the rout of their fleet, knew that they had no hope of saving themselves by land unless events took some extraordinary turn.

Thus, after a fierce battle and a great destruction of ships and men on both sides, the Syracusans and their allies gained the victory. They gathered up the wrecks and bodies of the dead, and sailing back to the city, erected a trophy. The Athenians, overwhelmed by their misery, never so much as thought of recovering their wrecks or of asking leave to collect their dead. Their intention was to retreat that very night. Demosthenes came to Nicias and proposed that they should once more man their remaining vessels and endeavour to force the passage at daybreak, saying that they had more ships fit for service than the enemy. For the Athenian fleet still numbered sixty, but the enemy had less than fifty. Nicias approved of his proposal, and they would have manned the ships, but the sailors refused to embark; for they were paralysed by their defeat, and had no longer any hope of succeeding. So the Athenians all made up their minds to escape by land.

Hermocrates the Syracusan suspected their intention, and dreading what might happen if their vast army, retreating by land and settling somewhere in Sicily, should choose to renew the war, he went to the authorities, and represented to them that they ought not to allow the Athenians to withdraw by night (mentioning his own suspicion of their intentions), but that all the Syracusans and their allies should march out before them, wall up the roads, and occupy the passes with a guard. They thought very much as he did, and wanted to carry out his plan, but doubted whether their men, who were too glad to repose after a great battle, and in time of festival — for there happened on that very day to be a sacrifice to Heracles — could be induced to obey. Most of them, in the exultation of victory, were drinking and keeping holiday, and at such a time how could they ever be expected to take up arms and go forth at the order of the generals? On these grounds the authorities decided that the thing was impossible. Whereupon Hermocrates himself, fearing lest the Athenians should gain a start and quietly pass the most difficult places in the night, contrived the following plan: when it was growing dark he sent certain of his own acquaintances, accompanied by a few horsemen, to the Athenian camp. They rode up within earshot, and pretending to be friends (there were known to be men in the city who gave information to Nicias of what went on) called to some of the soldiers, and bade them tell him not to withdraw his army during the night, for the Syracusans were guarding the roads; he should make preparation at leisure and retire by day. Having delivered their message they departed, and those who had heard them informed the Athenian generals.

On receiving this message, which they supposed to be genuine, they remained during the night. And having once given up the intention of starting immediately, they decided to remain during the next day, that the soldiers might, as well as they could, put together their baggage in the most convenient form, and depart, taking with them the bare necessaries of life, but nothing else.

Meanwhile the Syracusans and Gylippus, going forth before them with their land-forces, blocked the roads in the country by which the Athenians were likely to pass, guarded the fords of the rivers and streams, and posted themselves at the best points for receiving and stopping them. Their sailors rowed up to the beach and dragged away the Athenian ships. The Athenians themselves burnt a few of them, as they had intended, but the rest the Syracusans towed away, unmolested and at their leisure, from the places where they had severally run aground, and conveyed them to the city.

On the third day after the sea-fight, when Nicias and Demosthenes thought that their preparations were complete, the army began to move. They were in a dreadful condition; not only was there the great fact that they had lost their whole fleet, and instead of their expected triumph had brought the utmost peril upon Athens as well as upon themselves, but also the sights which presented themselves as they quitted the camp were painful to every eye and mind. The dead were unburied, and when any one saw the body of a friend lying on the ground he was smitten with sorrow and dread, while the sick or wounded who still survived but had to be left were even a greater trial to the living, and more to be pitied than those who were gone. Their prayers and lamentations drove their companions to distraction; they would beg that they might be taken with them, and call by name any friend or relation whom they saw passing; they would hang upon their departing comrades and follow as far as they could, and when their limbs and strength failed them and they dropped behind many were the imprecations and cries which they uttered. So that the whole army was in tears, and such was their despair that they could hardly make up their minds to stir, although they were leaving an enemy's country, having suffered calamities too great for tears already, and dreading miseries yet greater in the unknown future. There was also a general feeling of shame and self-reproach, — indeed they seemed, not like an army, but like the fugitive population of a city captured after a siege; and of a great city too. For the whole multitude who were marching together numbered not less than 40,000. Each of them took with him anything he could carry which was likely to be of use. Even the heavy-armed and cavalry, contrary to their practice when under arms, conveyed about their persons their own food, some because they had no attendants, others because they could not trust them; for they had long been deserting, and most of them had gone off all at once. Nor was the food which they carried sufficient; for the supplies of the camp had failed. Their disgrace and the universality of the misery, although there might be some consolation in the very community of suffering, was nevertheless at that moment hard to bear, especially when they remembered from what pomp and splendour they had fallen into their present low estate. Never had an Hellenic army experienced such a reverse. They had come intending to enslave others, and they were going away in fear that they would be themselves enslaved. Instead of the prayers and hymns with which they had put to sea, they were now departing amid appeals to heaven of another sort. They were no longer sailors but landsmen, depending, not upon their fleet, but upon their infantry. Yet in face of the great danger which still threatened them all these things appeared endurable.

Nicias, seeing the army disheartened at their terrible fall, went along the ranks and encouraged and consoled them as well as he could. In his fervour he raised his voice as he passed from one to another and spoke louder and louder, desiring that the benefit of his words might reach as far as possible:

"Even now, Athenians and allies, we must hope: men have been delivered out of worse straits than these, and I would not have you judge yourselves too severely on account either of the reverses which you have sustained or of your present undeserved miseries. I too am as weak as any of you; for I am quite prostrated by my disease, as you see. And although there was a time when I might have been thought equal to the best of you in the happiness of my private and public life, I am now in as great danger, and as much at the mercy of fortune, as the meanest. Yet my days have been passed in the performance of many a religious duty, and of many a just and blameless action. Therefore my hope of the future remains unshaken, and our calamities do not appall me as they might. Who knows that they may not be lightened? For our enemies have had their full share of success, and if our expedition provoked the jealousy of any god, by this time we have been punished enough. Others ere now have attacked their neighbours; they have done as men will do, and suffered what men can bear. We may therefore begin to hope that the gods will be more merciful to us; for we now invite their pity rather than their jealousy. And look at your own well-armed ranks; see how many brave soldiers you are, marching in solid array, and do not be dismayed; bear in mind that wherever you plant yourselves you are a city already, and that no city of Sicily will find it easy to resist your attack, or can dislodge you if you choose to settle. Provide for the safety and good order of your own march, and remember every one of you that on whatever spot a man is compelled to fight, there if he conquer he may find a home and a fortress. We must press forward day and night, for our supplies are but scanty. The Sicels through fear of the Syracusans still adhere to us, and if we can only reach any part of their territory we shall be among friends, and you may consider yourselves secure. We have sent to them, and they have been told to meet us and bring food. In a word, soldiers, let me tell you that you must be brave; there is no place near to which a coward can fly. And if you now escape your enemies, those of you who are not Athenians may see once more the home for which they long, while you Athenians will again rear aloft the fallen greatness of Athens. For men, and not walls or ships in which are no men, constitute a state."

Thus exhorting his troops Nicias passed through the army, and wherever he saw gaps in the ranks or the men dropping out of line, he brought them back to their proper place. Demosthenes did the same for the troops under his command, and gave them similar exhortations. The army marched disposed in a hollow oblong: the division of Nicias leading, and that of Demosthenes following; the hoplites enclosed within their ranks the baggage-bearers and the rest of the army. When they arrived at the ford of the river Anapus they found a force of the Syracusans and of their allies drawn up to meet them; these they put to flight, and getting command of the ford, proceeded on their march. The Syracusans continually harassed them, the cavalry riding alongside, and the light-armed troops hurling darts at them. On this day the Athenians proceeded about four and a half miles and encamped at a hill. On the next day they started early, and, having advanced more than two miles, descended into a level plain, and encamped. The country was inhabited, and they were desirous of obtaining food from the houses, and also water which they might carry with them, as there was little to be had for many miles in the country which lay before them. Meanwhile the Syracusans had gone on before them, and at a point where the road ascends a steep hill called the Acraean height, and there is a precipitous ravine on either side, were blocking up the pass by a wall. On the next day the Athenians advanced, although again impeded by the numbers of the enemy's cavalry who rode along-side, and of their javelin-men who threw darts at them. For a long time the Athenians maintained the struggle, but at last retired to their own encampment. Their supplies were now cut off, because the horsemen circumscribed their movements.

In the morning they started early and resumed their march. They pressed onwards to the hill where the way was barred, and found in front of them the Syracusan infantry drawn up to defend the wall, in deep array, for the pass was narrow. Whereupon the Athenians advanced and assaulted the barrier, but the enemy, who were numerous and had the advantage of position, threw missiles upon them from the hill, which was steep, and so, not being able to force their way, they again retired and rested. During the conflict, as is often the case in the fall of the year, there came on a storm of rain and thunder, whereby the Athenians were yet more disheartened, for they thought that everything was conspiring to their destruction. While they were resting, Gylippus and the Syracusans despatched a division of their army to raise a wall behind them across the road by which they had come; but the Athenians sent some of their own troops and frustrated their intention. They then retired with their whole army in the direction of the plain and passed the night. On the following day they again advanced. The Syracusans now surrounded and attacked them on every side, and wounded many of them. If the Athenians advanced they retreated, but charged them when they retired, falling especially upon the hindermost of them, in the hope that, if they could put to flight a few at a time, they might strike a panic into the whole army. In this fashion the Athenians struggled on for a long time, and having advanced about three-quarters of a mile rested in the plain. The Syracusans then left them and returned to their own encampment.

The army was now in a miserable plight, being in want of every necessary; and by the continual assaults of the enemy great numbers of the soldiers had been wounded. Nicias and Demosthenes, perceiving their condition, resolved during the night to light as many watch-fires as possible and to lead off their forces. They intended to take another route and march towards the sea in the direction opposite to that from which the Syracusans were watching them. Now their whole line of march lay, not towards Catana, but towards the other side of Sicily, in the direction of Camarina and Gela, and the cities, Hellenic or barbarian, of that region. So they lighted numerous fires and departed in the night. And then, as constantly happens in armies, especially in very great ones, and as might be expected when they were marching by night in an enemy's country, and with the enemy from whom they were flying not far off, there arose a panic among them, and they fell into confusion. The army of Nicias, which led the way, kept together, and was considerably in advance, but that of Demosthenes, which was the larger half, got severed from the other division, and marched in less order. At daybreak they succeeded in reaching the sea, and striking into the Helorine road marched along it, intending as soon as they arrived at the river Cacyparis to follow up the stream through the interior of the island. They were expecting that the Sicels for whom they had sent would meet them on this road. When they had reached the river they found there also a guard of the Syracusans cutting off the passage by a wall and palisade. They forced their way through, and crossing the river, passed on towards another river which is called the Erineus, this being the direction in which their guides led them.

When daylight broke and the Syracusans and their allies saw that the Athenians had departed, most of them thought that Gylippus had let them go on purpose, and were very angry with him. They easily found the line of their retreat, and quickly following, came up with them about the time of the midday meal. The troops of Demosthenes were last; they were marching slowly and in disorder, not having recovered from the panic of the previous night, when they were overtaken by the Syracusans, who immediately fell upon them and fought. Separated as they were from the others, they were easily hemmed in by the Syracusan cavalry and driven into a narrow space. The division of Nicias was as much as six miles in advance, for he marched faster, thinking that their safety depended at such a time, not in remaining and fighting, if they could avoid it, but in retreating as quickly as they could, and resisting only when they were positively compelled. Demosthenes, on the other hand, who had been more incessantly harassed throughout the retreat, because marching last he was first attacked by the enemy, now, when he saw the Syracusans pursuing him, instead of pressing onward, had ranged his army in order of battle. Thus lingering he was surrounded, and he and the Athenians under his command were in the greatest danger and confusion. For they were crushed into a walled enclosure, having a road on both sides and planted thickly with olive-trees, and missiles were hurled at them from all points. The Syracusans naturally preferred this mode of attack to a regular engagement. For to risk themselves against desperate men would have been only playing into the hands of the Athenians. Moreover, every one was sparing of his life; their good fortune was already assured, and they did not want to fall in the hour of victory. Even by this irregular mode of fighting they thought that they could overpower and capture the Athenians.

And so when they had gone on all day assailing them with missiles from every quarter, and saw that they were quite worn out with their wounds and all their other sufferings, Gylippus and the Syracusans made a proclamation, first of all to the islanders, that any of them who pleased might come over to them and have their freedom. But only a few cities accepted the offer. At length an agreement was made for the entire force under Demosthenes. Their arms were to be surrendered, but no one was to suffer death, either from violence or from imprisonment, or from want of the bare means of life. So they all surrendered, being in number 6000, and gave up what money they had. This they threw into the hollows of shields and filled four. The captives were at once taken to the city. On the same day Nicias and his division reached the river Erineus, which he crossed, and halted his army on a rising ground.

On the following day he was overtaken by the Syracusans, who told him that Demosthenes had surrendered, and bade him do the same. He, not believing them, procured a truce while he sent a horseman to go and see. Upon the return of the horseman bringing assurance of the fact, he sent a herald to Gylippus and the Syracusans, saying that he would agree, on behalf of the Athenian state, to pay the expenses which the Syracusans had incurred in the war, on condition that they should let his army go; until the money was paid he would give Athenian citizens as hostages, a man for a talent. Gylippus and the Syracusans would not accept these proposals, but attacked and surrounded this division of the army as well as the other, and hurled missiles at them from every side until the evening. They too were grievously in want of food and necessaries. Nevertheless they meant to wait for the dead of the night and then to proceed. They were just resuming their arms, when the Syracusans discovered them and raised the paean. The Athenians, perceiving that they were detected, laid down their arms again, with the exception of about 300 men who broke through the enemy's guard, and made their escape in the darkness as best they could.

When the day dawned Nicias led forward his army, and the Syracusans and the allies again assailed them on every side, hurling javelins and other missiles at them. The Athenians hurried on to the river Assinarus. They hoped to gain a little relief if they forded the river, for the mass of horsemen and other troops overwhelmed and crushed them; and they were worn out by fatigue and thirst. But no sooner did they reach the water than they lost all order and rushed in; every man was trying to cross first, and, the enemy pressing upon them at the same time, the passage of the river became hopeless.   Being compelled to keep close together they fell one upon another, and trampled each other under foot: some at once perished, pierced by their own spears; others got entangled in the baggage and were carried down the stream.   The Syracusans stood upon the further bank of the river, which was steep, and hurled missiles from above on the Athenians, who were huddled together in the deep bed of the stream and for the most part were drinking greedily.   The Peloponnesians came down the bank and slaughtered them, falling chiefly upon those who were in the river.   Whereupon the water at once became foul, but was drunk all the same, although muddy and dyed with blood, and the crowd fought for it.

At last, when the dead bodies were lying in heaps upon one another in the water and the army was utterly undone, some perishing in the river, and any who escaped being cut off by the cavalry, Nicias surrendered to Gylippus, in whom he had more confidence than in the Syracusans.   He entreated him and the Lacedaemonians to do what they pleased with himself, but not to go on killing the men. So Gylippus gave the word to make prisoners.   Thereupon the survivors, not including however a large number whom the soldiers concealed, were brought in alive.   As for the 300 who had broken through the guard in the night, the Syracusans sent in pursuit and seized them.   The total of the public prisoners when collected was not great; for many were appropriated by the soldiers, and the whole of Sicily was full of them, they not having capitulated like the troops under Demosthenes.   A large number also perished; the slaughter at the river being very great, quite as great as any which took place in the Sicilian war; and not a few had fallen in the frequent attacks which were made upon the Athenians during their march.   Still many escaped, some at the time, others ran away after an interval of slavery, and all these found refuge at Catana.

The Syracusans and their allies collected their forces and returned with the spoil, and as many prisoners as they could take with them, into the city.   The captive Athenians and allies they deposited in the quarries, which they thought would be the safest place of confinement.   Nicias and Demosthenes they put to the sword, although against the will of Gylippus.   For Gylippus thought that to carry home with him to Lacedaemon the generals of the enemy, over and above all his other successes, would be a brilliant triumph.   One of them, Demosthenes, happened to be the greatest foe, and the other the greatest friend of the Lacedaemonians, both in the same matter of Pylos and Sphacteria.   For Nicias had taken up their cause, and had persuaded the Athenians to make the peace which set at liberty the prisoners taken in the island.   The Lacedaemonians were grateful to him for the service, and this was the main reason why he trusted Gylippus and surrendered himself to him.   But certain Syracusans, who had been in communication with him, were afraid (such was the report) that on some suspicion of their guilt he might be put to the torture and bring trouble on them in the hour of their prosperity.   Others, and especially the Corinthians, feared that, being rich, he might by bribery escape and do them further mischief.   So the Syracusans gained the consent of the allies and had him executed. For these or the like reasons he suffered death.   No one of the Hellenes in my time was less deserving of so miserable an end; for he lived in the practice of every customary virtue.

Those who were imprisoned in the quarries were at the beginning of their captivity harshly treated by the Syracusans.   There were great numbers of them, and they were crowded in a deep and narrow place.   At first the sun by day was still scorching and suffocating, for they had no roof over their heads, while the autumn nights were cold, and the extremes of temperature engendered violent disorders. Being cramped for room they had to do everything on the same spot. The corpses of those who died from their wounds, exposure to the weather, and the like, lay heaped one upon another.   The smells were intolerable; and they were at the same time afflicted by hunger and thirst.   During eight months they were allowed only about half a pint of water and a pint of food a day.   Every kind of misery which could befall man in such a place befell them.   This was the condition of all the captives for about ten weeks.   At length the Syracusans sold them, with the exception of the Athenians and of any Sicilian or Italian Greeks who had sided with them in the war. The whole number of the public prisoners is not accurately known, but they were not less than 7000.

Of all the Hellenic actions which took place in this war, or indeed of all Hellenic actions which are on record, this was the greatest — the most glorious to the victors, the most ruinous to the vanquished; for they were utterly and at all points defeated, and their sufferings were prodigious.   Fleet and army perished from the face of the earth; nothing was saved, and of the many who went forth few returned home.

Thus ended the Sicilian expedition.

[VII. 69-87, tr. B. JOWETT]

XENOPHON

(*ca.* 430–*ca.* 358 B.C.)

THE ANABASIS

A SKETCH OF CYRUS THE YOUNGER

[The *Anabasis* is a record of the adventures of the Greek mercenaries who accompanied Cyrus on his expedition against his brother Artaxerxes II, King of Persia, 405–362 B.C.   After the death of Cyrus in the battle against the King's army at Cunaxa (401 B.C.), Xenophon tells how the famous Ten Thousand marched safely through the hostile Persian Empire until they reached the shores of the Black Sea — an exploit which did much to damage the prestige of the Persian arms.

After his description of the battle of Cunaxa, Xenophon inserts the following laudatory sketch of Cyrus' character.]

So died Cyrus; a man the kingliest and most worthy to rule of all the Persians who have lived since the elder Cyrus: according to the concurrent testimony of all who are reputed to have known him intimately.   To begin from the beginning, when still a boy, and while being brought up with his brother and the other lads, his unrivalled excellence was recognised.   For the sons of the noblest Persians, it must be known, are brought up, one and all, at the king's court. Here lessons of sobriety and self-control may be learned, while there is nothing base to see or hear.   There is the daily spectacle ever before the boys of some receiving honour from the king, and again of others receiving dishonour; and the tale of all this is in their ears, so that from earliest boyhood they learn how to rule and to be ruled.

In this training Cyrus was held to be first a paragon of modesty among his fellows, rendering an obedience to his elders which exceeded that of many of his own inferiors; and next he bore away the palm for skill in horsemanship and for love of the animal itself. Likewise in matters of war, in the use of the bow and the javelin, he was held by men in general to be at once the aptest of learners and the most eager practiser.   As soon as his age permitted, the same preeminence showed itself in his fondness for the chase, not without a certain appetite for perilous adventure in facing the wild beasts themselves.   Once a bear made a furious rush at him, and without wincing he grappled with her, and was pulled from his horse, receiving wounds the scars of which were visible through life; but in the end he slew the creature, nor did he forget him who first came to his aid, but made him enviable in the eyes of many.

After he had been sent down by his father to be satrap of Lydia and Great Phrygia and Cappadocia, and had been appointed general of the forces, whose business it is to muster in the plain of the Castolus, nothing was more noticeable in his conduct than the importance which he attached to the faithful fulfilment of every treaty or compact or undertaking entered into with others. He would tell no lies to any one. Thus doubtless it was that he won the confidence alike of individuals and of the communities entrusted to his care; or in case of hostility, a treaty made with Cyrus was a guarantee sufficient to the combatant that he would suffer nothing contrary to its terms. Therefore, in the war with Tissaphernes, all the states of their own accord choose Cyrus rather than Tissaphernes, except only the men of Miletus, and these were only alienated through fear of him, because he refused to abandon their exiled citizens; and his deeds and words bore emphatic witness to his principle: even if they were weakened in number or in fortune, he would never abandon those who had once become his friends.

He made no secret of his endeavour to outdo his friends and his foes alike in reciprocity of conduct. The prayer has been attributed to him, "God grant I may live long enough to recompense my friends and requite my foes with a strong arm." However this may be, no one, at least in our days, ever drew together so ardent a following of friends, eager to lay at his feet their money, their cities, their own lives and persons; nor is it to be inferred from this that he suffered the malefactor and the wrongdoer to laugh him to scorn; on the contrary, these he punished most unflinchingly. It was no rare sight to see on the well-trodden highways, men who had forfeited hand or foot or eye; the result being that throughout the satrapy of Cyrus any one, Hellene or barbarian, provided he were innocent, might fearlessly travel wherever he pleased, and take with him whatever he felt disposed. However, as all allowed, it was for the brave in war that he reserved especial honour. To take the first instance to hand, he had a war with the Pisidians and Mysians. Being himself at the head of an expedition into those territories, he could observe those who voluntarily encountered risks; these he made rulers of the territory which he subjected, and afterwards honoured them with other gifts. So that, if the good and brave were set on a pinnacle of fortune, cowards were recognised as their natural slaves; and so it befel that Cyrus never had lack of volunteers in any service of danger, whenever it was expected that his eye would be upon them.

So again, wherever he might discover any one ready to distinguish himself in the service of uprightness, his delight was to make this man richer than those who seek for gain by unfair means. On the same principle, his own administration was in all respects uprightly conducted, and, in particular, he secured the services of an army worthy of the name. Generals, and Captains alike, came to him from across the seas, not merely to make money, but because they saw that loyalty to Cyrus was a more profitable investment than so much pay a month. Let any man whatsoever render him willing service, such enthusiasm was sure to win its reward. And so Cyrus could always command the service of the best assistants, it was said, whatever the work might be.

Or if he saw any skilful and just steward who furnished well the country over which he ruled, and created revenues, so far from robbing him at any time, to him who had, he delighted to give more. So that toil was a pleasure, and gains were amassed with confidence, and least of all from Cyrus would a man conceal the amount of his possessions, seeing that he showed no jealousy of wealth openly avowed, but his endeavour was rather to turn to account the riches of those who kept them secret. Towards the friends he had made, whose kindliness he knew, or whose fitness as fellow-workers with himself, in anything which he might wish to carry out, he had tested, he showed himself in turn an adept in the arts of courtesy. Just in proportion as he felt the need of this friend or that to help him, so he tried to help each of them in return in whatever seemed to be their desire.

Many were the gifts bestowed on him, for many and diverse reasons; no one man, perhaps, ever received more; no one, certainly, was ever more ready to bestow them on others, with an eye ever to the taste of each, so as to gratify what he saw to be the individual requirement. Many of these presents were sent to him to serve as personal adornments of the body or for battle; and as touching these he would say, "How am I to deck myself out in all these? To my mind a man's chief ornament is the adornment of nobly-adorned friends." Indeed, that he should triumph over his friends in the great matters of welldoing is not surprising, seeing that he was much more powerful than they, but that he should go beyond them in minute attentions, and in an eager desire to give pleasure, seems to me, I must confess, more admirable. Frequently when he had tasted some specially excellent wine, he would send the half remaining flagon to some friend with a message to say, "Cyrus says, this is the best wine he has tasted for a long time, that is his excuse for sending it to you. He hopes you will drink it up to-day with a choice party of friends." Or, perhaps, he would send the remainder of a dish of geese, half loaves of bread, and so forth, the bearer being instructed to say, "This is Cyrus' favourite dish, he hopes you will taste it yourself." Or, perhaps, there was a great dearth of fodder, when, through the number of his servants and his own careful forethought, he was enabled to get supplies for himself; at such times he would send to his friends in different parts, bidding them feed their horses on his hay, since it would not do for the horses that carried his friends to go starving. Then, on any long march or expedition, where the crowd of lookers-on would be large, he would call his friends to him and entertain them with serious talk, as much as to say, "These I delight to honour."

So that, for myself, and from all that I can hear, I should be disposed to say that no one, Greek or barbarian, was ever so beloved. In proof of this, I may cite the fact that, though Cyrus was the king's vassal and slave, no one ever forsook him to join his master, if I may except the attempt of Orontas. That man, indeed, had to learn that Cyrus was closer to the heart of him on whose fidelity he relied than he himself was. On the other hand, many a man revolted from the king to Cyrus, after they went to war with one another; nor were these nobodies, but rather persons high in the king's affection; yet for all that, they believed that their virtues would obtain a reward more adequate from Cyrus than from the king. Another great proof at once of his own worth and of his capacity rightly to discern all loyal, loving, and firm friendship is afforded by an incident which belongs to the last moment of his life. He was slain, but fighting for his life beside him fell also every one of his faithful bodyguard of friends and table-companions, with the sole exception of Ariaeus, who was in command of the cavalry on the left, and he no sooner perceived the fall of Cyrus than he betook himself to flight, with the whole body of troops under his lead.

[I. 9, tr. H. G. Dakyns]

POLYBIUS

(*ca.* 208–*ca.* 125 B.C.)

HISTORIES

[Polybius' *Histories* deal with the events of the Mediterranean world between the years 220 and 146 B.C. — the period during which Rome established her supremacy over Carthage and the Greek east.

After carrying his narrative down to the year 216 (the date of the disastrous Roman defeat at Cannae), Polybius inserts a long digression on the institutions and customs of Rome. He takes up this subject at the moment when Rome's fortunes were at their lowest point and asserts that her recovery and later conquest of the civilized world were due to her excellent constitution and superior management of military affairs.]

ON CONSTITUTIONS

I am aware that some will be at a loss to account for my interrupting the course of my narrative for the sake of entering upon the following disquisition on the Roman constitution. But I think that I have already in many passages made it fully evident that this particular branch of my work was one of the necessities imposed on me by the nature of my original design; and I pointed this out with special clearness in the preface which explained the scope of my history. I there stated that the feature of my work which was at once the best in itself, and the most instructive to the students of it, was that it would enable them to know and fully realise in what manner, and under what kind of constitution, it came about that nearly the whole world fell under the power of Rome in somewhat less than fifty-three years, — an event certainly without precedent. This being my settled purpose, I could see no more fitting period than the present for making a pause, and examining the truth of the remarks about to be made on this constitution. In private life if you wish to satisfy yourself as to the badness or goodness of particular persons, you would not, if you wish to get a genuine test, examine their conduct at a time of uneventful repose, but in the hour of brilliant success or conspicuous reverse. For the true test of a perfect man is the power of bearing with spirit and dignity violent changes of fortune. An examination of a constitution should be conducted in the same way: and therefore being unable to find in our day a more rapid or more signal change than that which has happened to Rome, I reserved my disquisition on its constitution for this place. . .

What is really educational and beneficial to students of history is the clear view of the causes of events, and the consequent power of choosing the better policy in a particular case. Now in every practical undertaking by a state we must regard as the most powerful agent for success or failure the form of its constitution; for from this as from a fountain head all conceptions and plans of action not only proceed, but attain their consummation. . .

Of the Greek republics, which have again and again risen to greatness and fallen into insignificance, it is not difficult to speak, whether we recount their past history or venture an opinion on their future. For to report what is already known is an easy task, nor is it hard to guess what is to come from our knowledge of what has been. But in regard to the Romans it is neither an easy matter to describe their present state, owing to the complexity of their constitution; nor to speak with confidence of their future, from our inadequate acquaintance with their peculiar institutions in the past whether affecting their public or their private life. It will require then no ordinary attention and study to get a clear and comprehensive conception of the distinctive features of this constitution.

Now, it is undoubtedly the case that most of those who profess to give us authoritative instruction on this subject distinguish three kinds of constitutions, which they designate *kingship, aristocracy, democracy*. But in my opinion the question might fairly be put to them, whether they name these as being the *only* ones, or as the *best*. In either case I think they are wrong. For it is plain that we must regard as the *best* constitution that which partakes of all these three elements. And this is no mere assertion, but has been proved by the example of Lycurgus, who was the first to construct a constitution — that of Sparta — on this principle. Nor can we admit that these are the *only* forms: for we have had before now examples of absolute and tyrannical forms of government, which, while differing as widely as possible from kingship, yet appear to have some points of resemblance to it; on which account all absolute rulers falsely assume and use, as far as they can, the title of king. Again there have been many instances of oligarchical governments having in appearance some analogy to aristocracies, which are, if I may say so, as different from them as it is possible to be. The same also holds good about democracy.

I will illustrate the truth of what I say. We cannot hold every absolute government to be a kingship, but only that which is accepted voluntarily, and is directed by an appeal to reason rather than to fear and force. Nor again is every oligarchy to be regarded as an aristocracy; the latter exists only where the power is wielded by the justest and wisest men selected on their merits. Similarly, it is not enough to constitute a democracy that the whole crowd of citizens should have the right to do whatever they wish or propose. But where reverence to the gods, succour of parents, respect to elders, obedience to laws, are traditional and habitual, in such communities, if the will of the majority prevail, we may speak of the form of government as a democracy. — So then we enumerate six forms of government, — the three commonly spoken of which I have just mentioned, and three more allied forms, I mean *despotism, oligarchy* and *mob-rule*. The first of these arises without artificial aid and in the natural order of events. Next to this, and produced from it by the aid of art and adjustment, comes *kingship*; which degenerating into the evil form allied to it, by which I mean *tyranny*, both are once more destroyed and *aristocracy* produced. Again the latter being in the course of nature perverted to *oligarchy*, and the people passionately avenging the unjust acts of their rulers, *democracy* comes into existence; which again by its violence and contempt of law becomes sheer *mob-rule*. No clearer proof of the truth of what I say could be obtained than by a careful observation of the natural origin, genesis and decadence of these several forms of government. For it is only by seeing distinctly how each of them is produced that a distinct view can also be obtained of its growth, zenith, and decadence, and the time, circumstance, and place in which each of these may be expected to recur. This method I have assumed to be especially applicable to the Roman constitution, because its origin and growth have from the first followed natural causes.

Now the natural laws which regulate the merging of one form of government into another are perhaps discussed with greater accuracy by Plato and some other philosophers. But their treatment, from its intricacy and exhaustiveness, is only within the capacity of a few. I will therefore endeavour to give a summary of the subject, just so far as I suppose it to fall within the scope of a practical history and the intelligence of ordinary people. For if my exposition appear in any way inadequate, owing to the general terms in which it is expressed, the details contained in what is immediately to follow will amply atone for what is left for the present unsolved.

What is the origin then of a constitution, and whence is it produced? Suppose that from floods, pestilences, failure of crops, or some such causes the race of man is reduced almost to extinction. Such things we are told have happened, and it is reasonable to think will happen again. Suppose accordingly all knowledge of social habits and arts to have been lost. Suppose that from the survivors, as from seeds, the race of man to have again multiplied. In that case, I presume they would, like the animals, herd together; for it is but reasonable to suppose that bodily weakness would induce them to seek those of their own kind to herd with. And in that case too, as with the animals, he who was superior to the rest in strength of body or courage of soul would lead and rule them. For what we see happen in the case of animals that are without the faculty of reason, such as bulls, goats, and cocks — among whom there can be no dispute that the strongest take the lead — that we must regard as in the truest sense the teaching of nature. Originally then it is probable that the condition of life among men was this — herding together like animals and following the strongest and bravest as leaders. The limit of this authority would be physical strength, and the name we should give it would be despotism. But as soon as the idea of family ties and social relation has arisen amongst such agglomerations of men, then is born also the idea of kingship, and then for the first time mankind conceives the notion of goodness and justice and their reverse.

The way in which such conceptions originate and come into existence is this. The intercourse of the sexes is an instinct of nature, and the result is the birth of children. Now, if any one of these children who have been brought up, when arrived at maturity, is ungrateful and makes no return to those by whom he was nurtured, but on the contrary presumes to injure them by word and deed, it is plain that he will probably offend and annoy such as are present, and have seen the care and trouble bestowed by the parents on the nurture and bringing up of their children. For seeing that men differ from the other animals in being the only creatures possessed of reasoning powers, it is clear that such a difference of conduct is not likely to escape their observation; but that they will remark it when it occurs, and express their displeasure on the spot: because they will have an eye to the future, and will reason on the likelihood of the same occurring to each of themselves. Again, if a man has been rescued or helped in an hour of danger, and, instead of showing gratitude to his preserver, seeks to do him harm, it is clearly probable that the rest will be displeased and offended with him, when they know it: sympathising with their neighbour and imagining themselves in his case. Hence arises a notion in every breast of the meaning and theory of duty, which is in fact the beginning and end of justice. Similarly, again, when any one man stands out as the champion of all in a time of danger, and braves with firm courage the onslaught of the most powerful wild beasts, it is probable that such a man would meet with marks of favour and pre-eminence from the common people; while he who acted in a contrary way would fall under their contempt and dislike. From this, once more, it is reasonable to suppose that there would arise in the minds of the multitude a theory of the disgraceful and the honourable, and of the difference between them; and that one should be sought and imitated for its advantages, the other shunned. When, therefore, the leading and most powerful man among his people ever encourages such persons in accordance with the popular sentiment, and thereby assumes in the eyes of his subject the appearance of being the distributor to each man according to his deserts, they no longer obey him and support his rule from fear of violence, but rather from conviction of its utility, however old he may be, rallying round him with one heart and soul, and fighting against all who form designs against his government. In this way he becomes a *king* instead of a *despot* by imperceptible degrees, reason having ousted brute courage and bodily strength from their supremacy.

This then is the natural process of formation among mankind of the notion of goodness and justice, and their opposites; and this is the origin and genesis of genuine kingship: for people do not only keep up the government of such men personally, but for their descendants also for many generations; from the conviction that those who are born from and educated by men of this kind will have principles also like theirs. But if they subsequently become displeased with their descendants, they do not any longer decide their choice of rulers and kings by their physical strength or brute courage; but by the differences of their intellectual and reasoning faculties, from practical experience of the decisive importance of such a distinction. In old times, then, those who were once thus selected, and obtained this office, grew old in their royal functions, making magnificent strongholds and surrounding them with walls and extending their frontiers, partly for the security of their subjects, and partly to provide them with abundance of the necessaries of life; and while engaged in these works they were exempt from all vituperation or jealousy; because they did not make their distinctive dress, food, or drink, at all conspicuous, but lived very much like the rest, and joined in the everyday employments of the common people. But when their royal power became hereditary in their family, and they found every necessary for security ready to their hands, as well as more than was necessary for their personal support, then they gave the rein to their appetites; imagined that rulers must needs wear different clothes from those of subjects; have different and elaborate luxuries of the table; and must even seek sensual indulgence, however unlawful the source, without fear of denial. These things having given rise in the one case to jealousy and offence, in the other to outburst of hatred and passionate resentment, the kingship became a tyranny: the first step in disintegration was taken; and plots began to be formed against the government, which did not now proceed from the worst men but from the noblest, most high-minded, and most courageous, because these are the men who can least submit to the tyrannical acts of their rulers.

But as soon as the people got leaders, they co-operated with them against the dynasty for the reasons I have mentioned; and then *kingship* and *despotism* were alike entirely abolished, and *aristocracy* once more began to revive and start afresh. For in their immediate gratitude to those who had deposed the despots, the people employed them as leaders, and entrusted their interests to them; who, looking upon this charge at first as a great privilege, made the public advantage their chief concern, and conducted all kinds of business, public or private, with diligence and caution. But when the sons of these men received the same position of authority from their fathers, — having had no experience of misfortunes, and none at all of civil equality and freedom of speech, but having been bred up from the first under the shadow of their fathers' authority and lofty position, — some of them gave themselves up with passion to avarice and unscrupulous love of money, others to drinking and the boundless debaucheries which accompany it, and others to the violation of women or the forcible appropriation of boys; and so they turned an *aristocracy* into an *oligarchy*. But it was not long before they roused in the minds of the people the same feelings as before; and their fall therefore was very like the disaster which befel the tyrants.

For no sooner had the knowledge of the jealousy and hatred exist-ing in the citizens against them emboldened some one to oppose the government by word or deed, than he was sure to find the whole people ready and prepared to take his side. Having then got rid of these rulers by assassination or exile, they do not venture to set up a king again, being still in terror of the injustice to which this led before; nor dare they intrust the common interests again to more than one, considering the recent example of their misconduct: and therefore, as the only sound hope left them is that which depends upon themselves, they are driven to take refuge in that; and so changed the constitution from an oligarchy to a *democracy,* and took upon themselves the superintendence and charge of the state. And as long as any survive who have had experience of oligarchical supremacy and domination, they regard their present constitution as a blessing, and hold equality and freedom as of the utmost value. But as soon as a new generation has arisen, and the democracy has descended to their children's children, long association weakens their value for equality and freedom, and some seek to become more powerful than the ordinary citizens; and the most liable to this temptation are the rich. So when they begin to be fond of office, and find themselves unable to obtain it by their own unassisted efforts and their own merits, they ruin their estates, while enticing and corrupting the common people in every possible way. By which means when, in their senseless mania for reputation, they have made the populace ready and greedy to receive bribes, the virtue of demo-cracy is destroyed, and it is transformed into a government of vio-lence and the strong hand. For the mob, habituated to feed at the expense of others, and to have its hopes of a livelihood in the property of its neighbours, as soon as it has got a leader sufficiently ambitious and daring, being excluded by poverty from the sweets of civil honours, produces a reign of mere violence. Then comes tumul-tuous assemblies, massacres, banishments, redivisions of land; until, after losing all trace of civilisation, it has once more found a master and a despot.

This is the regular cycle of constitutional revolutions, and the natural order in which constitutions change, are transformed, and return again to their original stage. If a man have a clear grasp of these principles he may perhaps make a mistake as to the dates at which this or that will happen to a particular constitution; but he will rarely be entirely mistaken as to the stage of growth or decay at which it has arrived, or as to the point at which it will undergo some revolutionary change. However, it is in the case of the Roman constitution that this method of inquiry will most fully teach us its formation, its growth, and zenith, as well as the changes awaiting it in the future; for this, if any constitution ever did, owed, as I said just now, its original foundation and growth to natural causes, and to natural causes will owe its decay. My subsequent narrative will be the illustration of what I say.

For the present I will make a brief reference to the legislation of

Lycurgus: for such a discussion is not at all alien to my subject. That statesman was fully aware that all those changes which I have enumerated come about by an undeviating law of nature; and reflected that every form of government that was unmixed, and rested on one species of power, was unstable; because it was swiftly perverted into that particular form of evil peculiar to it and inherent in its nature. For just as rust is the natural dissolvent of iron, woodworms and grubs to timber, by which they are destroyed without any external injury, but by that which is engendered in themselves; so in each constitution there is naturally engendered a particular vice inseparable from it: in kingship it is absolutism; in aristocracy it is oligarchy; in democracy lawless ferocity and violence; and to these vicious states all these forms of government are, as I have lately shown, inevitably transformed. Lycurgus, I say, saw all this, and accordingly combined together all the excellences and distinctive features of the best constitutions, that no part should become unduly predominant, and be perverted into its kindred vice; and that, each power being checked by the others, no one part should turn the scale or decisively out-balance the others; but that, by being accurately adjusted and in exact equilibrium, the whole might remain long steady like a ship sailing close to the wind. The royal power was prevented from growing insolent by fear of the people, which had also assigned to it an adequate share in the constitution. The people in their turn were restrained from a bold contempt of the kings by fear of the Gerusia: the members of which, being selected on grounds of merit, were certain to throw their influence on the side of justice in every question that arose; and thus the party placed at a disadvantage by its conservative tendency was always strengthened and supported by the weight and influence of the Gerusia. The result of this combination has been that the Lacedaemonians retained their freedom for the longest period of any people with which we are acquainted.

Lycurgus however established his constitution without the discipline of adversity, because he was able to foresee by the light of reason the course which events naturally take and the source from which they come. But though the Romans have arrived at the same result in framing their commonwealth, they have not done so by means of abstract reasoning, but through many struggles and difficulties, and by continually adopting reforms from knowledge gained in disaster. The result has been a constitution like that of Lycurgus, and the best of any existing in my time. . .

I have given an account of the constitution of Lycurgus, I will now endeavour to describe that of Rome at the period of their disastrous defeat at Cannae.

I am fully conscious that to those who actually live under this constitution I shall appear to give an inadequate account of it by the omission of certain details. Knowing accurately every portion of it from personal experience, and from having been bred up in its customs and laws from childhood, they will not be struck so much by the accuracy of the description, as annoyed by its omissions; nor will they believe that the historian has purposely omitted unimportant distinctions, but will attribute his silence upon the origin of existing institutions or other important facts to ignorance. What is told they depreciate as insignificant or beside the purpose; what is omitted they desiderate as vital to the question: their object being to appear to know more than the writers. But a good critic should not judge a writer by what he leaves unsaid, but from what he says: if he detects mis-statement in the latter, he may then feel certain that ignorance accounts for the former; but if what he says is accurate, his omissions ought to be attributed to deliberate judgment and not to ignorance. So much for those whose criticisms are prompted by personal ambition rather than by justice. . .

Another requisite for obtaining a judicious approval for an historical disquisition, is that it should be germane to the matter in hand; if this is not observed, though its style may be excellent and its matter irreproachable, it will seem out of place, and disgust rather than please. . .

As for the Roman constitution, it had three elements, each of them possessing sovereign powers: and their respective share of power in the whole state had been regulated with such a scrupulous regard to equality and equilibrium, that no one could say for certain, not even a native, whether the constitution as a whole were an aristocracy or democracy or despotism. And no wonder: for if we confine our observation to the power of the Consuls we should be inclined to regard it as despotic; if on that of the Senate, as aristocratic; and if finally one looks at the power possessed by the people it would seem a clear case of a democracy. What the exact powers of these several parts were, and still, with slight modifications, are, I will now state.

The Consuls, before leading out the legions, remain in Rome, and are supreme masters of the administration. All other magistrates, except the Tribunes, are under them and take their orders. They introduce foreign ambassadors to the Senate; bring matters requiring deliberation before it; and see to the execution of its decrees. If, again, there are any matters of state which require the authorisation of the people, it is their business to see to them, to summon the popular meetings, to bring the proposals before them, and to carry out the decrees of the majority. In the preparations for war also, and in a word in the entire administration of a campaign, they have all but absolute power. It is competent to them to impose on the allies such levies as they think good, to appoint the Military Tribunes, to make up the roll for soldiers and select those that are suitable. Besides they have absolute power of inflicting punishment on all who are under their command while on active service: and they have authority to expend as much of the public money as they choose, being accompanied by a quaestor who is entirely at their orders. A survey of these powers would in fact justify our describing the constitution as despotic — a clear case of royal government. Nor will it affect the truth of my description, if any of the institutions I have described are changed in our time, or in that of our posterity: and the same remarks apply to what follows.

The Senate has first of all the control of the treasury, and regulates the receipts and disbursements alike. For the Quaestors cannot issue any public money for the various departments of the state without a decree of the Senate, except for the service of the Consuls. The Senate controls also what is by far the largest and most important expenditure, that, namely, which is made by the censors every *lustrum* for the repair or construction of public buildings; this money cannot be obtained by the censors except by the grant of the Senate. Similarly all crimes committed in Italy requiring a public investigation, such as treason, conspiracy, poisoning, or wilful murder, are in the hands of the Senate. Besides, if any individual or state among the Italian allies requires a controversy to be settled, a penalty to be assessed, help or protection to be afforded — all this is the province of the Senate. Or again, outside Italy, if it is necessary to send an embassy to reconcile warring communities, or to remind them of their duty, or sometimes to impose requisitions upon them, or to receive their submission, or finally to proclaim war against them — this too is the business of the Senate. In like manner the reception to be given to foreign ambassadors in Rome, and the answers to be returned to them, are decided by the Senate. With such business the people have nothing to do. Consequently, if one were staying at Rome when the Consuls were not in town, one would imagine the constitution to be a complete aristocracy: and this has been the idea entertained by many Greeks, and by many kings as well, from the fact that nearly all the business they had with Rome was settled by the Senate.

After this one would naturally be inclined to ask what part is left for the people in the constitution, when the Senate has these various functions, especially the control of the receipts and expenditure of the exchequer; and when the Consuls, again, have absolute power over the details of military preparation, and an absolute authority in the field? There is, however, a part left the people, and it is a most important one. For the people is the sole fountain of honour and of punishment; and it is by these two things and these alone that dynasties and constitutions and, in a word, human society are held together: for where the distinction between them is not sharply drawn both in theory and practice, there no undertaking can be properly administered — as indeed we might expect when good and bad are held in exactly the same honour. The people then are the only court to decide matters of life and death; and even in cases where the penalty is money, if the sum to be assessed is sufficiently serious, and especially when the accused have held the higher magistracies. And in regard to this arrangement there is one point deserving especial commendation and record. Men who are on trial for their lives at Rome, while sentence is in process of being voted — if even only one of the tribes whose votes are needed to ratify the sentence has not voted — have the privilege at Rome of openly departing and condemning themselves to a voluntary exile. Such men are safe at Naples or Praeneste or at Tibur, and at other towns with which this arrangement has been duly ratified on oath.

Again, it is the people who bestow offices on the deserving, which are the most honourable rewards of virtue. It has also the absolute power of passing or repealing laws; and, most important of all, it is the people who deliberate on the question of peace or war. And when provisional terms are made for alliance, suspension of hostilities, or treaties, it is the people who ratify them or the reverse.

These considerations again would lead one to say that the chief power in the state was the people's, and that the constitution was a democracy.

Such, then, is the distribution of power between the several parts of the state. I must now show how each of these several parts can, when they choose, oppose or support each other.

The Consul, then, when he has started on an expedition with the powers I have described, is to all appearance absolute in the administration of the business in hand; still he has need of the support of both people and Senate, and, without them, is quite unable to bring the matter to a successful conclusion. For it is plain that he must have supplies sent to his legions from time to time; but without a decree of the Senate they can be supplied neither with corn, nor clothes, nor pay, so that all the plans of a commander must be futile, if the Senate is resolved either to shrink from danger or hamper his plans. And again, whether a Consul shall bring any undertaking to a conclusion or no depends entirely upon the Senate: for it has absolute authority at the end of a year to send another Consul to supersede him, or to continue the existing one in his command. Again, even to the successes of the generals the Senate has the power to add distinction and glory, and on the other hand to obscure their merits and lower their credit. For these high achievements are brought in tangible form before the eyes of the citizens by what are called "triumphs." But these triumphs the commanders cannot celebrate with proper pomp, or in some cases celebrate at all, unless the Senate concurs and grants the necessary money. As for the people, the Consuls are pre-eminently obliged to court their favour, however distant from home may be the field of their operations; for it is the people, as I have said before, that ratifies, or refuses to ratify, terms of peace and treaties; but most of all because when laying down their office they have to give an account of their administration before it. Therefore in no case is it safe for the Consuls to neglect either the Senate or the good-will of the people.

As for the Senate, which possesses the immense power I have described, in the first place it is obliged in public affairs to take the multitude into account, and respect the wishes of the people; and it cannot put into execution the penalty of offences against the republic, which are punishable with death, unless the people first ratify its decrees. Similarly even in matters which directly affect the senators, — for instance, in the case of a law diminishing the Senate's traditional authority, or depriving senators of certain dignities and offices, or even actually cutting down their property — even in such cases the people have the sole power of passing or rejecting the law. But most important of all is the fact that, if the Tribunes interpose their veto, the Senate not only are unable to pass a decree, but cannot even hold a meeting at all, whether formal or informal. Now, the Tribunes are always bound to carry out the decree of the people, and above all things to have regard to their wishes: therefore, for all these reasons the Senate stands in awe of the multitude, and cannot neglect the feelings of the people.

In like manner the people on its part is far from being independent of the Senate, and is bound to take its wishes into account both collectively and individually. For contracts too numerous to count are given out by the censors in all parts of Italy for the repairs or construction of public buildings; there is also the collection of revenue from many rivers, harbours, gardens, mines, and land — everything, in a word, that comes under the control of the Roman government: and in all these the people at large are engaged; so that there is scarcely a man, so to speak, who is not interested either as a contractor or as being employed in the works. For some purchase the contracts from the censors for themselves; and others go partners with them; while others again go security for these contractors, or actually pledge their property to the treasury for them. Now over all these transactions the Senate has absolute control. It can grant an extension of time; and in case of unforeseen accident can relieve the contractors from a portion of their obligation, or release them from it altogether, if they are absolutely unable to fulfil it. And there are many details in which the Senate can inflict great hardships, or, on the other hand, grant great indulgences to the contractors: for in every case the appeal is to it. But the most important point of all is that the judges are taken from its members in the majority of trials, whether public or private, in which the charges are heavy. Consequently, all citizens are much at its mercy; and being alarmed at the uncertainty as to when they may need its aid, are cautious about resisting or actively opposing its will. And for a similar reason men do not rashly resist the wishes of the Consuls, because one and all may become subject to their absolute authority on a campaign.

The result of this power of the several estates for mutual help or harm is a union sufficiently firm for all emergencies, and a constitution than which it is impossible to find a better. For whenever any danger from without compels them to unite and work together, the strength which is developed by the State is so extraordinary, that everything required is unfailingly carried out by the eager rivalry shown by all classes to devote their whole minds to the need of the hour, and to secure that any determination come to should not fail for want of promptitude; while each individual works, privately and publicly alike, for the accomplishment of the business in hand. Accordingly, the peculiar constitution of the State makes it irresistible, and certain of obtaining whatever it determines to attempt. Nay, even when these external alarms are past, and the people are enjoying their good fortune and the fruits of their victories, and, as usually happens, growing corrupted by flattery and idleness, show a tendency to violence and arrogance — it is in these circumstances, more than ever, that the constitution is seen to possess within itself the power of correcting abuses. For when any one of the three classes becomes puffed up, and manifests an inclination to be contentious and unduly encroaching, the mutual interdependency of all the three, and the possibility of the pretensions of any one being checked and thwarted by the others, must plainly check this tendency; and so the proper equilibrium is maintained by the impulsiveness of the one part being checked by its fear of the other. . .

[VI. 1–18, tr. E. S. SHUCKBURGH]

[A description of the Roman army and camp follows. Polybius then compares the Roman constitution with others, particularly that of Sparta, and he then adds the following suggestive remarks on the condition of Rome and Carthage at the time of the Second Punic War.]

ROME AND CARTHAGE

Now the Carthaginian constitution seems to me originally to have been well contrived in these most distinctively important particulars. For they had kings, and the Gerusia had the powers of an aristocracy, and the multitude were supreme in such things as affected them; and on the whole the adjustment of its several parts was very like that of Rome and Sparta. But about the period of its entering on the Hannibalian war the political state of Carthage was on the decline, that of Rome improving. For whereas there is in every body, or polity, or business a natural stage of growth, zenith, and decay; and whereas everything in them is at its best at the zenith; we may thereby judge of the difference between these two constitutions as they existed at that period. For exactly so far as the strength and prosperity of Carthage preceded that of Rome in point of time, by so much was Carthage then past its prime, while Rome was exactly at its zenith, as far as its political constitution was concerned. In Carthage therefore the influence of the people in the policy of the state had already risen to be supreme, while at Rome the Senate was at the height of its power: and so, as in the one measures were deliberated upon by the many, in the other by the best men, the policy of the Romans in all public undertakings proved the stronger; on which account, though they met with capital disasters, by force of prudent counsels they finally conquered the Carthaginians in the war.

[VI. 51, tr. E. S. SHUCKBURGH]

[The *Histories* close with the fall of Carthage and the capture of Corinth in 146 B.C.; both events marked the complete supremacy of Rome in the Mediterranean. Scipio Africanus the younger, a close friend and a former pupil of Polybius, brought the Third Punic War to an end by the capture of Carthage, which is described in the following selection. The famous picture of Scipio weeping at the fall of Rome's ancient enemy is intended to supplement Polybius' theories of the cycles in constitutions and the growth and decline of states; the gloomy quotation from Homer is both an epitaph for Carthage and a prophecy for Rome.]

THE FALL OF CARTHAGE

Having got within the walls, while the Carthaginians still held out on the citadel, Scipio found that the arm of the sea which intervened was not at all deep; and upon Polybius advising him to set it with iron spikes or drive sharp wooden stakes into it, to prevent the enemy crossing it and attacking the mole, he said that, having taken the walls and got inside the city, it would be ridiculous to take measures to avoid fighting the enemy. . .

The pompous Hasdrubal threw himself on his knees before the Roman commander, quite forgetful of his proud language. . .

When the Carthaginian commander thus threw himself as a suppliant at Scipio's knees, the proconsul with a glance at those present said: "See what Fortune is, gentlemen! What an example she makes of irrational men! This is the Hasdrubal who but the other day disdained the large favours which I offered him, and said that the most glorious funeral pyre was one's country and its burning ruins. Now he comes with suppliant wreaths, beseeching us for bare life and resting all his hopes on us. Who would not learn from such a spectacle that a mere man should never say or do anything presumptuous?" Then some of the deserters came to the edge of the roof and begged the front ranks of the assailants to hold their hands for a little; and, on Scipio ordering a halt, they began abusing Hasdrubal, some for his perjury, declaring that he had sworn again and again on the altars that he would never abandon them, and others for his cowardice and utter baseness: and they did this in the most unsparing language, and with the bitterest terms of abuse. And just at this moment Hasdrubal's wife, seeing him seated in front of the enemy with Scipio, advanced in front of the deserters, dressed in noble and dignified attire herself, but holding in her hands, on either side, her two boys dressed only in short tunics and shielded under her own robes. First she addressed Hasdrubal by his name, and when he said nothing but remained with his head bowed to the ground, she began by calling on the name of the gods, and next thanked Scipio warmly because, as far as he could secure it, both she and her children were saved. And then, pausing for a short time, she asked Hasdrubal how he had had the heart to secure this favour from the Roman general for himself alone . . . and, leaving his fellow-citizens who trusted in him in the most miserable plight, had gone over secretly to the enemy? And how he had the assurance to be sitting there holding suppliant boughs, in the face of the very men to whom he had frequently said that the day would never come in which the sun would see Hasdrubal alive and his native city in flames. . .

After an interview with [Scipio], in which he was kindly treated,

Hasdrubal desired leave to go away from the town. . .

At the sight of the city utterly perishing amidst the flames Scipio burst into tears, and stood long reflecting on the inevitable change which awaits cities, nations, and dynasties, one and all, as it does every one of us men. This, he thought, had befallen Ilium, once a powerful city, and the once mighty empires of the Assyrians, Medes, Persians, and that of Macedonia lately so splendid. And unintentionally or purposely he quoted — the words perhaps escaping him unconsciously, —

> "The day shall be when holy Troy shall fall
> And Priam, lord of spears, and Priam's folk." *

And on my asking him boldly (for I had been his tutor) what he meant by these words, he did not name Rome distinctly, but was evidently fearing for her, from this sight of the mutability of human affairs. . .

Another still more remarkable saying of his I may record. . . [When he had given the order for firing the town] he immediately turned round and grasped me by the hand and said: "O Polybius, it is a grand thing, but, I know not how, I feel a terror and dread, lest some one should one day give the same order about my own native city." . . . Any observation more practical or sensible it is not easy to make. For in the midst of supreme success for one's self and of disaster for the enemy, to take thought of one's own position and of the possible reverse which may come, and in a word to keep well in mind in the midst of prosperity the mutability of Fortune, is the characteristic of a great man, a man free from weaknesses and worthy to be remembered. . .

[XXXIX. 3-5, tr. E. S. SHUCKBURGH]

* Homer, *Iliad* vi. 448.

ORATORY

Although oratory flourished in Greece from earliest times, as the many well-wrought speeches in Homer show, the creation of oratory as a literary art was the work of the fifth century. It was the ideal of the growing democracies of this age that every citizen should take an active part in political life; the ability to speak effectively in public became the surest method of gaining political influence, and was indeed often necessary for personal safety, since every citizen was expected to present his own case in the law-courts. As a result of this situation, teachers of rhetoric, sophists like Protagoras, Gorgias, and Prodicus, undertook to instruct men in the general rules of rhetoric and to give them a repertory of commonplaces which would enable them to speak well on any subject at a moment's notice. At the same time, other professional rhetoricians, like Antiphon of Athens, helped their fellow-citizens by composing speeches for the unskilled litigant to deliver in court. The final step in the creation of oratory as a separate literary form came when such writers began to publish their speeches, not only as examples of their skill and as models for their pupils but also for their intrinsic literary merit. During the same period, writers like Gorgias and Thrasymachus were making bold experiments in composition to raise prose to the level of poetry as an artistic means of expression, by the use of such devices as rhythm and end-rhymes, *antithesis,* and *isocola* (*i.e.,* an equal number of syllables in successive clauses).

The most skilful and successful craftsman in this elaborate style was Isocrates, and all of the devices just noted may be abundantly illustrated in the selections from his *Panegyric* given below. Isocrates was an Athenian who took up the profession of rhetoric after the close of the Peloponnesian War; for some years he earned his living by writing speeches for others, but about 388 B.C. he opened a school of rhetoric and "practical philosophy," which he conducted with great success until his death in 338. Most of his best speeches were composed during these years; and since he lacked the voice and self-assurance necessary for public appearances, his speeches were published as pamphlets for the reading public. In both his writings and in his teaching Isocrates always insisted that the proper subjects of oratory were national, panhellenic affairs, such as he treats in his *Panegyric:* and no writer did more to spread the idea of national unity, even though he was sometimes out of touch with reality. As a stylist, Isocrates is a supreme artist in the construction of rounded, periodic sentences, all richly ornamented with the various rhetorical devices mentioned above; every idea or clause has its complement, nothing is left unexpressed, everything is polished and clear. As a result, Isocrates lacks force and is likely to pall on the reader.

In contrast with Isocrates, no Greek writer is more forceful than Demosthenes. He was born in 384 or 383 B.C.; his father, a wealthy manufacturer, died when Demosthenes was a child, and when the boy came of age he found that his guardians had cheated him of most of his inheritance. At the age of twenty he started a series of lawsuits to recover his property, and thus gained his oratorical training through hard and bitter experience. For some years he was, like Isocrates, a writer of speeches for others; but about 355 he turned to political life, and it was his activity as a statesman that produced his greatest oratory. His name is inevitably associated with that of Athens' great opponent, Philip of Macedon, whose part in Greek history is set forth in the brief historical sketch at the end of this introduction. Depending solely on his eloquence, Demosthenes roused his indolent countrymen to a valiant effort to recapture their position as the leading state of Greece; and in the struggle with Philip he developed an ideal of Panhellenism which was not unworthy of Athens in her best days and went far beyond the ideas of Isocrates: to Demosthenes, Panhellenism meant a voluntary union of free and independent Greek states to repel the Macedonian intruder, not the surrender of Athens' rights in order to follow the leadership of Macedon against Persia.

In his style Demosthenes is always lively and vigorous; he can speak in the periodic style of Isocrates when he wishes, but he varies his presentation with short, staccato sentences, frequent questions, and occasional metaphors and vivid similes. His pages abound in unforgettable phrases and pictures: the people at Athens going around asking one another for news (*Phil.* I), the amusing image of the barbarian boxer and his futile attempts to protect himself (*Phil.* I), or the magnificent oath by the dead of Marathon and Plataea in the speech *On the Crown.* To all the devices of rhetoric Demosthenes adds an intensity of feeling and a moral earnestness which raise his orations above the level of all other ancient orators. In the words of an ancient critic (*On the Sublime* XII. 4): "Our orator, owing to the fact that in his vehemence, — and in his speed, power, and intensity, — he can as it were consume by fire and carry away all before him, may be compared to a thunderbolt or a flash of lightning."

In order to understand the selections which follow, the reader must keep in mind some of the events of the fourth century B.C. Although the period is one of great confusion, most of the facts can be apprehended under two general headings: first, the struggle of the Greeks to achieve and maintain a stable balance of power among the various city-states; and second, the rise of the Macedonian power which eventually dominated Greece.

The Peloponnesian War ended (in 404 B.C.) with Sparta in control of Greece, but her former allies, Thebes and Corinth, now attacked her, and Athens joined in the war which followed (The Corinthian War, 395–387). The Spartans, who had been fighting the Persians in Asia Minor, finally came to terms with Persia and with the aid of the ancient enemy of Greece imposed the infamous Peace of Antalcidas on the other Greeks. This treaty, which had been dictated by the Great King, ceded the Greek cities in Asia to the King and declared all other Greek cities free and independent. Sparta, who acted as the executor of the Peace, used the latter provision as an excuse to interfere in the affairs of other cities and to break up any leagues or alliances which seemed dangerous to her interests; she reduced the strong Arcadian city of Mantinea to a group of scattered villages, she broke up the Chalcidian League, she treacherously and without provocation threw a garrison into the citadel of Thebes. It was at this moment (381–0 B.C.) that Isocrates came forward with his most famous speech, the *Panegyric,* urging the union of all the Greeks in a war against Persia, with Sparta and Athens sharing the command; although this idea of a united Greek crusade against Persia was constantly discussed during the fourth century and was eventually achieved under Alexander, Isocrates cannot be considered as a far-sighted statesman for advocating such an expedition at this time: the possibility of Sparta's sharing the leadership of Greece with anyone was, to say the least, remote. What small amount of union and cooperation the Greek states did achieve at this moment was directed not against Persia but against Sparta. The Athenians formed a new league, the purpose of which was (in the words of the decree which founded the confederacy): "To force the Lacedaemonians to allow the Greeks to enjoy peace in freedom and independence." Through this league Athens restored in part her old maritime empire and became once more the dominant sea-power in the Aegaean. In 371 B.C. Thebes crushed the Spartans at the battle of Leuctra and for ten years assumed the leadership; but Athens, alarmed at the increasing power of her northern neighbour, now allied herself with Sparta against Thebes. The battle of Mantinea in 361 cost Thebes her only first-rate statesman and general, Epaminondas, who died on the field, and the Theban domination gradually dwindled away. After 360 there was no single dominating power in Greece, and the center of historical interest now shifts to the northern kingdom of Macedon.

The events which form the background for Demosthenes' attacks on the Macedonian power in his *Philippics* may be summarized briefly as follows: Philip II began to rule Macedon in 359 B.C., and almost immediately set out to make this backward, only partially Hellenized nation a ruling power in Greek affairs. After reducing to submission the barbaric tribes which harassed his borders, he turned eastward to the Thracian coast, in order to secure an outlet to the sea and access to the rich gold mines of Thrace. Here he came into conflict with the interests of Athens, who controlled the Chersonese and still hoped to regain Amphipolis, the city on the Strymon which had been lost in 424. Philip duped the Athenians by promising to take Amphipolis and hand it over to them in exchange for Pydna, an ally of Athens on the gulf of Therma; but after capturing Amphipolis (357) he kept it for himself, and later also took Pydna (356), Potidaea, and Methone (353); by this time the Athenians had lost most of her northern allies to Philip, while her most powerful island allies had revolted and left her confederacy (357–5). Philip now turned to Thessaly, which he brought under his control in 352; at this time he would have moved into central Greece, had not the Athenians promptly occupied the pass at Thermopylae. Philip immediately marched back to Thrace, where he overthrew the Thracian king, Cersobleptes, the last barrier between Macedon and the vital Athenian possessions in the Chersonese. At the same time he was building a fleet, and his vessels attacked the Athenian grain-ships and even raided the coasts of Euboea and Attica.

Shortly after conquering Thrace, Philip fell ill and the Athenians had a short respite. It was probably at this moment that Demosthenes came forward with his *First Philippic,* in which he tried to arouse the Athenians to effective action against Philip. Part of Athens' difficulty was caused by her dependence on mercenary forces, and Demosthenes' proposal that the citizens themselves serve in the field was well-nigh revolutionary. For the moment, however, nothing was done, and when Philip recovered he attacked and destroyed the Chalcidian League and its principal city, Olynthus (349–348). The Athenians, now thoroughly alarmed and spurred on by Demosthenes' orations, sent help, but it arrived too late. Athens was financially exhausted by the long war with Philip and now negotiated a peace — the Peace of Philocrates (346 B.C.), which permitted each side to keep what it held. The Peace included the allies of both parties, but excluded the Phocians, who had seized the temple at Delphi (*ca.* 355) and were at war with Thebes and the other members of the Amphictyonic League. Although the Phocians were not formally allied to Athens, they were friendly and the Athenians had long supported them against Thebes. Consequently they were disappointed and enraged when Philip, immediately after signing the Peace, led his army into central Greece as the champion of the Amphictyonic League and crushed the Phocians. Philip received the Phocians' seat in the Amphictyonic Council and thus gained a permanent place in the affairs of central Greece.

During the next few years Demosthenes and the anti-Macedonian party in Athens worked vigorously to strengthen the position and resources of the city and to form a panhellenic union against Macedon. When the final clash with Philip came, in 339–338, Athens was joined by a large number of allies, including her former enemy, Thebes. This alliance, which ended the Theban cooperation with Philip, was the master stroke of Demosthenes' Hellenic diplomacy. None the less, Philip crushed the allies at Chaeronea (338 B.C.), and the old system of independent, small city-states came to an end. All the cities except Sparta joined a new Hellenic Confederacy, of which Macedon was the virtual master, and Philip began his plans to implement the favourite idea of Isocrates, a Greek crusade against Persia — plans which were carried out by his son Alexander.

It only remains to note the circumstances of Demosthenes' speech *On the Crown.* After the defeat at Chaeronea, Demosthenes served as commissioner in charge of repairing the fortifications of Athens.

His friend Ctesiphon proposed a bill to honour the orator for his services by presenting him publicly with a golden crown (a customary tribute in that age); Aeschines, who led the pro-Macedonian party at Athens, indicted Ctesiphon and his bill as unconstitutional. Undoubtedly part of the proposal was illegal for technical reasons, but Aeschines also attacked a statement in the bill that Demosthenes "consistently does and says what is best for the city and is eager to do whatever good he can." The main issue of the trial therefore turned on Demosthenes' policies. For various reasons the trial was postponed until 330 B.C.; Philip had been dead for six years, Alexander had crushed an attempted revolt of the Greek city-states and was now sweeping through the Persian Empire at the head of his combined Greek and Macedonian army, and all of Greece was irrevocably committed to the new order. These facts give an air of finality and almost of unreality to the proceedings at the trial: the Athenians, now that their independence was gone, were called upon to examine the events of ten to twenty years before and to judge the policies of the statesman who had led them then in the light of their present situation. The speech of Demosthenes gives an impression not unlike one of those mythological tragedies in which the fated end is foreknown to all the audience. No doubt, in view of the triumphs of Philip and Alexander, Aeschines expected a belated acknowledgement of the wisdom of his own pro-Macedonian policy. But in this hope he was disappointed; the Athenians retained their independence of judgment even in adversity, and Demosthenes was triumphantly vindicated: the jury acquitted Ctesiphon, and Aeschines received less than a fifth of the votes; in accordance with the usual penalty for the accuser in such cases, he was partially disenfranchised and left Athens.

Some modern "scientific" historians have tried to reverse the verdict of Demosthenes' fellow-citizens, and have blamed the orator for not following a policy of collaboration with Macedon in securing the control of the rest of Greece. Such critics have been answered in advance by the celebrated passage of the *Crown* which is printed below (pp. 819–821).

ISOCRATES

(436–338 B.C.)

PANEGYRICUS

[In his introduction Isocrates promises to do full justice to the importance of his subject, and he then points out that previous speakers on this theme have failed to start from the proper basis: they advise the Greeks to make up their enmities and to turn against Persia, but they do not bring forward any arguments to persuade the two most important Greek states, Athens and Sparta, to whom most of the other Hellenes are subject, to reconcile their differences and share equally in the leadership of the Greeks. The Spartans claim the undisputed leadership, but actually this honour belongs rather to Athens for the reasons which Isocrates sets forth in the following passage, notable for its rich and elaborate ornamentation.]

Now other speakers ought to have started from this basis, and not to have given advice about matters of common agreement before instructing us on disputed points; but I especially am bound, for two reasons, to give most of my attention to this matter: first, if possible, that some useful result may be attained, and that we may cease from our mutual rivalry and unite in a war against the barbarians; and, secondly, if that is impossible, that I may point out who are those that stand in the way of the happiness of Hellas, and that it may be made clear to all that, as previously the old maritime empire of Athens was based on a just title, so now she has a good right to dispute the leadership. For, on the one hand, if the men who deserve honour in each sphere of action are those who have the most experience and the greatest power, it is beyond dispute that we have a right to recover the leadership which we formerly used to possess; for no one can point to any other state that is so pre-eminent in war by land as ours excels in maritime enterprises. And, on the other hand, if any think that this is not a fair criterion, but that fortune is too changeable for such a conclusion (since power never continues in the same hands), and claim that leadership, like any other prize, should be held either by those who first won this honour, or by those who have conferred the most benefits upon Hellas, I think that these too are on our side; for the further back one examines both these qualifications, the more we shall leave behind those who dispute our claim. For it is allowed that our commonwealth is the most ancient and the largest and most renowned in all the world; and, good as is this foundation of our claim, for what follows we have still greater right to be honoured. For we did not win the country we dwell in by expelling others from it, or by seizing it when uninhabited, nor are we a mixed race collected together from many nations, but so noble and genuine is our descent, that we have continued for all time in possession of the land from which we sprang, being

802

children of our native soil, and able to address our city by the same titles that we give to our nearest relations; for we alone among the Hellenes have the right to call our city at once nurse and fatherland and mother. Yet our origin is but such as should be possessed by a people who indulge in a reasonable pride, who have a just claim to the leadership of Hellas, and who bring to frequent remembrance their ancestral glories.

This will show the magnitude of the gifts with which fortune originally endowed us; the great benefits we have conferred upon others we shall best examine by a detailed narrative of the early history and achievements of our city; for we shall find that she has not only led the way in warlike enterprises, but is also the founder of nearly all the established institutions among which we dwell, and under which we carry on our public life, and by means of which we are enabled to live. Now of useful services we must of necessity prefer, not such as on account of their insignificance escape notice and are passed over in silence, but such as on account of their importance are spoken of and kept in memory by all men, both in former times and at the present day and in every place.

In the first place, then, the first need of our nature was supplied by the agency of our state; for even though the story is a mythical one, yet it is fit to be told even at the present day. When Demeter came into the country in her wandering, after the rape of Persephone, and was kindly disposed to our forefathers on account of the services they rendered her, which can be told to none but the initiated, she bestowed two gifts which surpass all others: the fruits of the earth, which have saved us from the life of wild beasts, and the mystic rite,* the partakers in which have brighter hopes concerning the end of life and the eternity beyond — under these circumstances Athens showed such love for men, as well as for the gods, that, when she became mistress of these great blessings, she did not grudge them to the rest of the world, but shared her advantages with all. Now as to the festival, we to this day celebrate it every year; and as to the fruits of the earth, Athens has once for all taught the uses to which they can be put, the operations which they require, and the benefits which arise from them. Indeed no one will venture to disbelieve this statement, after I have made a few additional remarks. For in the first place, the very considerations which would lead a man to despise the story on account of its antiquity, would give him probable reason to suppose that the events had actually happened; for that many have told the story of these events, and all have heard it, should make us regard it, though not recent, yet as worthy of belief. In the second place, we can not only take refuge in the fact that we have received the tradition and rumour from a distant period, but we can also produce greater proofs than this of these things. For most of the cities of Hellas, as a memorial of our old services, send to us each year first-fruits of their corn, and those that omit to do so have often been commanded by the Pythia to pay the due proportion of their

* The Eleusinian Mysteries.

produce and perform their ancestral duties to our state. Yet can anything have stronger claims on our belief than that which is the subject of divine ordinance and of widespread approval in Hellas, where ancient story bears common witness to present deeds, and modern events agree with the legends of men of old? Besides this, if we leave all this out of consideration and take a survey from the beginning, we shall find that those who first appeared upon the earth did not at once find life in its present condition, but little by little procured for themselves its advantages. Whom then should we think most likely either to receive it as a gift from the gods or to win it by their own efforts? Surely those who are admitted to have been the first to exist, and are at once most highly gifted for the pursuits of life and most piously disposed towards the gods. Now what high honour ought to accrue to those who have produced such great blessings, it were a superfluous task to point out; for no one could find a reward commensurate with what has been achieved.

So much then concerning the greatest of our good works, first accomplished and most universal in its effects. But, in the same period, Athens, seeing the barbarians occupying the greater part of the country, and the Hellenes confined in a small space and driven by scarcity of land into intestine conspiracies and civil wars, and perishing, either from want of daily necessities or in war, was not content to leave things so, but sent forth leaders into the states who took those most in need of subsistence, made themselves their generals and conquered the barbarians in war, founded many states on both continents, colonized all the islands, and saved both those who followed them and those who stayed behind; for to the latter they left the home country sufficient for their needs, and the former they provided with more territory than they already possessed; for they acquired all the surrounding districts of which we are now in occupation. In this way too they afforded great facilities to those who in later times wished to send out colonists and to imitate our state; for it was not necessary for them to run risk in acquiring new territory, but they could go and live on land which we had marked out. Now who can show a leadership more ancestral than one which arose before most Hellenic cities were founded, or more beneficial than one which drove the barbarians from their homes, and led on the Hellenes to such prosperity?

Yet, after aiding in the accomplishment of the most pressing duties, Athens did not neglect the rest, but deemed it the first step only in a career of beneficence to find food for those in want, a step which is incumbent upon a people who aim at good government generally, and thinking that life which was limited to mere subsistence was not enough to make men desire to live, she devoted such close attention to the other interests of man, that of all the benefits which men enjoy, not derived from the gods but which we owe to our fellow-men, none have arisen without the aid of Athens, and most of them have been brought about by her agency. For finding the Hellenes living in lawlessness and dwelling in a scattered fashion, oppressed by tyrannies or being destroyed by anarchy, she also released them from these evils, either by becoming mistress of them or by making herself an example; for she was the first to lay down laws and establish a constitution. This is clear from the fact that, when men in the earliest times introduced indictments for homicide, and determined to settle their mutual disputes by arguments and not by violence, they followed our laws in the mode of trial which they adopted.

Nay more, the arts also, whether useful for the necessities of life or contrived for pleasure, were by her either invented or put to proof and offered to the rest of the world for their use. In other respects, moreover, she ordered her administration in such a spirit of welcome to strangers and of friendliness to all, as to suit both those who were in want of money and those who desired to enjoy the wealth they possessed, and not to fail in serving either the prosperous, or those who were unfortunate in their own states, but so that each of these classes finds with us a delightful sojourn or a safe refuge. And further, since the territory possessed by the several states was not in every case self-sufficing, but was defective in some products and bore more than was sufficient of others, and much embarrassment arose where to dispose of the latter, and from whence to import the former, she provided a remedy for these troubles also; for she established the Piraeus as a market in the centre of Hellas, of such superlative excellence that articles, which it is difficult for the several states to supply to each other one by one, can all be easily procured from Athens.

Now those who established the great festivals are justly praised for handing down to us a custom which leads us to make treaties with one another, to reconcile the enmities that exist among us, and to assemble in one place; besides that, in making common prayers and sacrifices we are reminded of the original bond of kinship between us, and are more kindly disposed towards each other for the future, we renew old friendships and make new ones. And neither for ordinary men nor for those of distinguished qualities is the time idly spent, but by the concourse of Hellenes opportunity arises for the latter to display their natural excellences, and for the former to be spectators of their mutual contests, and neither spend their time dissatisfied, but each has whereof to be proud, the spectators when they see the competitors toiling on their behalf, and the competitors when they think that everyone has come to look at them. Great then as are the benefits we derive from the assemblies, in these respects, too, our state is not left behind. For indeed she can show many most beautiful spectacles, some passing all bounds in expenditure, others of high artistic repute, and some excelling in both these respects; then, the multitude of strangers who visit us is so great, that if there is any advantage in mutual intercourse, that also has been compassed by her. In addition to this, you can find with us the truest friendships and the most varied acquaintanceships; and, moreover, see contests not merely of speed and strength, but also of oratory and mind, and in all other productions of art, and for these the greatest prizes. For in addition to those which the state herself offers, she also helps to persuade others to bestow the like; for those recognised by us receive such credit as to be universally approved. Apart from this, whereas the other festivals are assembled at long intervals and soon dispersed, our state, on the contrary, is for those who visit her one long festival without ceasing.

Practical philosophy, moreover, which helped to discover and establish all these institutions, which at once educated us for action and softened our mutual intercourse, which distinguished calamities due to ignorance from those which spring from necessity, and taught us to avoid the former and nobly to endure the latter, was introduced by Athens; she also paid honour to eloquence, which all men desire, and begrudge to those who are skilled in it: for she was aware that this is the only distinguishing characteristic which we of all creatures possess, and that by this we have won our position of superiority to all the rest of them; she saw that in other spheres of action men's fortunes are so capricious that often in them the wise fail and the foolish succeed, and that the proper and skilful use of language is beyond the reach of men of poor capacity, but is the function of a soul of sound wisdom, and that those who are considered clever or stupid differ from each other mainly in this respect; she saw, besides, that men who have received a liberal education from the very first are not to be known by courage, or wealth, or such-like advantages, but are most clearly recognised by their speech, and that this is the surest token which is manifested of the education of each one of us, and that those who make good use of language are not only influential in their own states, but also held in honour among other people. So far has Athens left the rest of mankind behind in thought and expression that her pupils have become the teachers of the world, and she has made the name of Hellas distinctive no longer of race but of intellect, and the title of Hellene a badge of education rather than of common descent.

But that I may not seem to be lingering over details of my subject when I proposed to treat of the whole, nor to be eulogizing Athens on these grounds from inability to praise her for her achievements in war, I will say no more to those who take pride in what I have mentioned; but I think that our forefathers deserve to be honoured as much for the dangers they incurred as for the rest of their services. Neither small nor few nor obscure were the struggles they endured, but many and terrible and great, some for their own country, others for the general liberty; for during the whole time they did not cease to open their state to all, and were the champions of those among the Hellenes who from time to time were the victims of oppression. For that very reason some accuse us of a foolish policy, in that we have been accustomed to support the weaker, as if such arguments did not rather justify our admirers. For it was not in ignorance of the superiority of great alliances in regard to security that we took these counsels concerning them, but, while knowing much more accurately than other men the results of such a course, we nevertheless preferred

to help the weak even against our interest rather than for profit's sake
to join in the oppressions of the strong.

[19-53, tr. J. H. FREESE]

[After completing his argument that the leadership of Greece belongs
rightfully to Athens, Isocrates outlines the iniquities of the present situation under the domination of Sparta, and he inveighs against the interference of Persia in the affairs of Greece. He then argues that Persia is
weak and an easy prey. The remainder of the speech, which is printed
here, is devoted to showing the advantages of an attack on the barbarians
at the earliest opportunity.]

I wonder that those who are in power in our states consider that
it befits them to hold their heads high, when they have never yet
been able by word or thought to help in matters of such importance.
For, were they worthy of their present reputation, they ought, neglecting everything else, to have made proposals and taken counsel
concerning the war against the barbarians. For by chance they
might together have accomplished something; and even had they
abandoned the attempt from weariness, yet they would at least have
left their words behind them as oracles for the future. But as it
is, those who are in the highest positions of honour concern themselves with small matters, and have left it to us who stand aloof from
public life to give advice on such weighty affairs.

Nevertheless the more narrow-minded our leaders prove to be, the
more vigorously must the rest of us consider how to be rid of our
present enmity. As things are, it is to no purpose that we make our
treaties of peace; for we do not settle our wars, but only defer them,
and wait for the time when we shall be able to inflict some irremediable injury on one another. Our duty, on the contrary, is to put
aside these plottings and apply ourselves to those undertakings which
will enable us both to dwell in greater security in our cities and to
feel greater confidence in one another. Now the word to be said
on this subject is a simple and easy one; we cannot enjoy a sure peace
unless we make war in common against the barbarians, nor can Hellas be made of one mind until we secure our advantages from the
same enemies and meet our perils in the face of the same foes. When
these things are achieved, when we have removed the poverty surrounding our life, which breaks up friendships, perverts to enmity
the ties of kindred, and throws all mankind into wars and seditions,
it must follow that we shall be of one mind and our mutual goodwill
will be real. For these reasons we must consider it all-important as
speedily as possible to banish our domestic war to the continent, since
the one advantage we can derive from our internal struggles would
be the resolve to use against the barbarian the lessons of experience
we have gained from them.

But, it will be said, may it not be best on account of the treaty *
to wait a little and not to press on and make the expedition too
quickly? It is the states which have been liberated through this

* The Peace of Antalcidas, 387 B.C.

treaty that feel gratitude to the King, on the ground that they have obtained this independence through him, while those which have been given up to the barbarians reproach mainly the Lacedaemonians, and in a lesser degree all the others who were parties to the peace, on the ground that by them they have been forced into slavery. Must it not therefore be right to dissolve this agreement, from which such a feeling has arisen that it is the barbarian who cares for Hellas and is the guardian of her peace, and that among us are to be found those who outrage and ill-use her? But the most ridiculous thing of all is, that of the terms written in the agreements it is the worst that we find ourselves guarding. For those which restore to independence the islands and the states in Europe have long been broken and remain idly on the records; but those which bring us shame and have given up many of our allies, remain in force and all hold them binding. These we must destroy and not leave them for a single day, considering them to be dictates, not agreements. For who does not know that those are agreements which stand equally and fairly to both sides, but that those are dictates which unjustly put one side at a disadvantage? For this reason, too, we could justly complain of those who negotiated this peace, that, although sent by Hellas, they made the treaty in the interest of the barbarians. For whether it was determined that we should each keep our own country, or should also extend our rule over the territory conquered in war, or should retain what we were already in possession of at the time of the peace, their duty was to define some one of these courses, lay down a common principle of justice, and on that basis conclude the treaty. But in fact they allotted no distinction to our state or to Lacedaemon, but established the barbarian as lord of all Asia, as if we had gone to war on his behalf, or as if the Persian empire were of old standing and we but recent inhabitants of our cities, and it were not rather the fact that they have but lately held this high position, while we have for all time been the ruling powers in Hellas. I think, however, that I shall better show the want of respect that has befallen us and the preference which has been shown to the King by putting the matter in this way. Whereas the whole earth lying beneath the firmament is divided into two portions, the one called Asia and the other Europe, he has taken by the treaty one half, as if he were dividing the world with Zeus instead of making an agreement with men. And this is the agreement which he has compelled us to inscribe on pillars of stone and to dedicate in our common temples, a far fairer trophy than any to be won in battles; for the trophies of battle are on account of small events and isolated successes, but this agreement is established to commemorate the whole war and concerns the whole of Hellas.

For these things it is but right that we should feel indignation and consider how we shall take vengeance for the past and set the future on a right footing. For it is a disgrace that, while in private life we think it fitting to use the barbarians as domestic servants, we should in public affairs suffer so many of our allies to be in slavery to them, and that, whereas those who lived in the time of the Trojan war did for the rape of one woman all join so heartily in the indignation of those who had suffered the wrong, that they did not cease to carry on the war until they had laid in ruins the city of the man who had dared to commit the offence, we on the contrary wreak no public vengeance for outrages which are being inflicted upon the whole of Hellas, though it is in our power to achieve things worthy of aspiration. For it is only a war of this kind which is better than peace, a war more like a sacred embassy than a campaign, and to the interest of both parties, both those who prefer to live in quiet and those who desire to go to war; for it would enable the former to reap in security the fruits of their own possessions, and the latter to acquire great riches out of the possessions of others.

Now in many directions it will be found on consideration that this course of action is most to our profit. For consider: against whom should war be made by those who desire no selfish aggression, but look to justice alone? Surely against those who formerly did injury to Hellas, are now scheming against us, and always entertain hostile feelings towards us. Against whom may envy be fairly cherished by men who are not altogether given over to an unmanly jealousy, but indulge this feeling with discretion? Surely against those who have encompassed themselves with power too great for men to hold, and yet are deserving of less than those who are unfortunate in our country. Against whom should a campaign be conducted by those who wish to act as pious men and at the same time desire their own advantage? Surely against those who are both our natural and our ancestral enemies, who possess the highest prosperity with the smallest power of striking a blow in its defence. Now the Persians are open to all these reproaches. Moreover, we shall not even trouble the states by levying soldiers from them, which is now a most severe burden to them in our civil war; for I think that far fewer will wish to stay behind than will desire to follow in our train. For who, be he young or old, has a heart so unmoved that he will not wish to take his part in this expedition, an expedition generalled by Athenians and Lacedaemonians, mustering on behalf of the freedom of the allies, going forth at the bidding of all Hellas, and marching to the chastisement of the barbarians? What fame, and name, and glory must we deem that these men, who have been foremost in so great an enterprise, will enjoy while living, or dying, will leave behind them? For whereas they who fought against Alexander * and took one city were deemed worthy of such praises, what eulogies must we expect will be won by the conquerors of all Asia? For surely everyone who has the gift of poetry or the power of speech will toil and study in the wish to leave behind him for all time a memorial at once of his own genius and of their valour?

Now I do not find myself of the same opinion at the present moment as at the beginning of my speech. Then I thought I should be able to speak in a fashion worthy of my subject; now I cannot

* Paris.

attain to its magnitude, and much that I thought of has escaped me. You must then for yourselves consider together what happiness we should gain by turning against the inhabitants of the continent the war which now besets us here, and by transferring to Europe the happiness of Asia. You must not go away hearers and no more, but the men of action should with mutual exhortation endeavour to reconcile our state to that of the Lacedaemonians, while those who dispute the palm of oratory should cease to write concerning fiduciary deposit and the other trifling subjects of their conversation, and should rather direct their rivalry against this discourse, and consider how to speak better than I have done on the same subject, reflecting that it does not befit those who promise great things to occupy themselves with trifles, nor to engage in arguments from which the lives of their audience will gain no advantage by conviction, but to employ discussions, by the realization of which they will not only themselves be relieved from their present embarrassment, but will also be regarded as the source of great blessings to others.

[170–189, tr. J. H. Freese]

DEMOSTHENES

(384?–322 B.C.)

THE FIRST PHILIPPIC

If some new subject were being brought before us, men of Athens,
I would have waited until most of your ordinary advisers had declared their opinion; and if anything that they said were satisfactory
to me, I would have remained silent, and only if it were not so, would
I have attempted to express my own view. But since we find ourselves once more considering a question upon which they have often
spoken, I think I may reasonably be pardoned for rising first of all.
For if their advice to you in the past had been what it ought to have
been, you would have had no occasion for the present debate.

In the first place, men of Athens, we must not be downhearted at
our present situation, however wretched it may seem to be. For in
the worst feature of the past lies our best hope for the future — in the
fact, that is, that we are in our present plight because you are not
doing your duty in any respect; for if you were doing all that you
should do, and we were still in this evil case, we could not then even
hope for any improvement. In the second place, you must bear in
mind (what some of you have heard from others, and those who
know can recollect for themselves), how powerful the Spartans were,
not long ago, and yet how noble and patriotic your own conduct was,
when instead of doing anything unworthy of your country you faced
the war with Sparta in defence of the right.* Now why do I remind
you of these things? It is because, men of Athens, I wish you to see
and to realize, that so long as you are on your guard you have nothing
to fear; but that if you are indifferent, nothing can be as you would
wish: for this is exemplified for you both by the powers of Sparta
in those days, to which you rose superior because you gave your minds
to your affairs; and by the insolence of Philip to-day, which troubles
us because we care nothing for the things which should concern us.
If, however, any of you, men of Athens, when he considers the immense force now at Philip's command, and the city's loss of all her
strongholds, thinks that Philip is a foe hard to conquer, I ask him
(right though he is in his belief) to reflect also that there was a
time when we possessed Pydna and Potidaea and Methone; when
all the surrounding country was our own, and many of the tribes
which are now on his side were free and independent, and more inclined to be friendly to us than to him. Now if in those days Philip
had made up his mind that it was a hard thing to fight against the
Athenians, with all their fortified outposts on his own frontiers, while
he was destitute of allies, he would have achieved none of his recent successes, nor acquired this great power. But Philip saw quite
clearly, men of Athens, that all these strongholds were prizes of war,

* 378–371 B.C.

displayed for competition. He saw that in the nature of things the property of the absent belongs to those who are on the spot, and that of the negligent to those who are ready for toil and danger. It is, as you know, by acting upon this belief, that he has brought all those places under his power, and now holds them — some of them by right of capture in war, others in virtue of alliances and friendly understandings; for every one is willing to grant alliance and to give attention to those whom they see to be prepared and ready to take action as is necessary. If then, men of Athens, you also will resolve to adopt this principle to-day — the principle which you have never observed before — if each of you can henceforward be relied upon to throw aside all this pretence of incapacity, and to act where his duty bids him, and where his services can be of use to his country; if he who has money will contribute, and he who is of military age will join the campaign; if, in one plain word, you will resolve henceforth to depend absolutely on yourselves, each man no longer hoping that he will need to do nothing himself, and that his neighbour will do everything for him; then, God willing, you will recover your own; you will take back all that your indolence has lost, and you will have your revenge upon Philip. Do not imagine that his fortune is built to last for ever, as if he were a God. He also has those who hate him and fear him, men of Athens, and envy him too, even among those who now seem to be his closest friends. All the feelings that exist in any other body of men must be supposed to exist in Philip's supporters. Now, however, all such feelings are cowed before him: your slothful apathy has taken away their only rallying point; and it is this apathy that I bid you put off to-day. Mark the situation, men of Athens: mark the pitch which the man's outrageous insolence has reached, when he does not even give you a choice between action and inaction, but threatens you, and utters (as we are told) haughty language: for he is not the man to rest content in possession of his conquests: he is always casting his net wider; and while we procrastinate and sit idle, he is setting his toils around us on every side. When, then, men of Athens, when, I say, will you take the action that is required? What are you waiting for? "We are waiting," you say, "till it is necessary." But what must we think of all that is happening at this present time? Surely the strongest necessity that a free people can experience is the shame which they must feel at their position! What? Do you want to go round asking one another, "Is there any news?" Could there be any stranger news than that a man of Macedonia is defeating Athenians in war, and ordering the affairs of the Hellenes? "Is Philip dead?" "No, but he is sick." And what difference does it make to you? For if anything should happen to him, you will soon raise up for yourselves a second Philip, if it is thus that you attend to your interests. Indeed, Philip himself has not risen to this excessive height through his own strength, so much as through our neglect. I go even further. If anything happened to Philip — if the operation of Fortune, who always cares for us better than we care for ourselves, were to effect this too for us —

you know that if you were at hand, you could descend upon the general confusion and order everything as you wished; but in your present condition, even if circumstances offered you Amphipolis, you could not take it; for your forces and your minds alike are far away.

Well, I say no more of the obligation which rests upon you all to be willing and ready to do your duty; I will assume that you are resolved and convinced. But the nature of the armament which, I believe, will set you free from such troubles as these, the numbers of the force, the source from which we must obtain funds, and the best and quickest way, as it seems to me, of making all further preparations — all this, men of Athens, I will at once endeavour to explain when I have made one request of you. Give your verdict on my proposal when you have heard the whole of it; do not prejudge it before I have done; and if at first the force which I propose appears unprecedented, do not think that I am merely creating delays. It is not those whose cry is "At once," "To-day," whose proposals will meet our need; for what has already happened cannot be prevented by any expedition now. It is rather he who can show the nature, the magnitude, and the financial possibility of a force which when provided will be able to continue in existence either until we are persuaded to break off the war, or until we have overcome the enemy; for thus only can we escape further calamity for the future. These things I believe I can show, though I would not stand in the way of any other speaker's professions. It is no less a promise than this that I make; the event will soon test its fulfilment, and you will be the judges of it.

First then, men of Athens, I say that fifty warships must at once be got in readiness: and next, that you must be in such a frame of mind that, if any need arises, you will embark in person and sail. In addition, you must prepare transports for half our cavalry, and a sufficient number of boats. These, I think, should be in readiness to meet those sudden sallies of his from his own country against Thermopylae, the Chersonese, Olynthus, and any other place which he may select. For we must make him realize that there is a possibility of your rousing yourself out of your excessive indifference, just as when once you went to Euboea, and before that (as we are told) to Haliartus, and finally, only the other day, to Thermopylae.* Such a possibility, even if you are unlikely to make it a reality, as I think you ought to do, is not one which he can treat lightly; and you may thus secure one of two objects. On the one hand, he may know that you are on the alert — he will in fact know it well enough: there are only too many persons, I assure you, in Athens itself, who report to him all that happens here: and in that case his apprehensions will ensure his inactivity. But if, on the other hand, he neglects the warning, he may be taken off his guard; for there will be nothing to hinder you from sailing to his country, if he gives you the opportunity.

---

* In 358/7, Athens aided Euboea in obtaining freedom from Thebes; in 395, she sent a force to Haliartus to aid Thebes against the Spartans; in 352 she kept Philip out of central Greece by occupying the pass at Thermopylae.

These are the measures upon which I say you should all be resolved, and your preparations for them made. But before this, men of Athens, you must make ready a force which will fight without intermission, and do him damage. Do not speak to me of ten thousand or twenty thousand mercenaries. I will have none of your paper-armies. Give me an army which will be the army of Athens, and will obey and follow the general whom you elect, be there one general or more, be he one particular individual, or be he who he may. You must also provide maintenance for this force. Now what is this force to be? how large is it to be? how is it to be maintained? how will it consent to act in this manner? I will answer these questions point by point. The number of mercenaries — but you must not repeat the mistake which has so often injured you, the mistake of, first, thinking any measures inadequate, and so voting for the largest proposal, and then, when the time for action comes, not even executing the smaller one; you must rather carry out and make provision for the smaller measure, and add to it, if it proves too small — the total number of soldiers, I say, must be two thousand, and of these five hundred must be Athenians, beginning from whatever age you think good: they must serve for a definite period — not a long one, but one to be fixed at your discretion — and in relays. The rest must be mercenaries. With these must be cavalry, two hundred in number, of whom at least fifty must be Athenians, as with the infantry; and the conditions of service must be the same. You must also find transports for these. And what next? Ten swift ships of war. For as he has a fleet, we need swift-sailing warships too, to secure the safe passage of the army. And how is maintenance to be provided for these? This also I will state and demonstrate, as soon as I have given you my reasons for thinking that a force of this size is sufficient, and for insisting that those who serve in it shall be citizens.

The size of the force, men of Athens, is determined by the fact that we cannot at present provide an army capable of meeting Philip in the open field; we must make plundering forays, and our warfare must at first be of a predatory nature. Consequently the force must not be over-big — we could then neither pay nor feed it — any more than it must be wholly insignificant. The presence of citizens in the force that sails I require for the following reasons. I am told that Athens once maintained a mercenary force in Corinth,* under the command of Polystratus, Iphicrates, Chabrias and others, and that you yourselves joined in the campaign with them; and I remember hearing that these mercenaries, when they took the field with you, and you with them, were victorious over the Spartans. But ever since your mercenary forces have gone to war alone, it is your friends and allies that they conquer, while your enemies have grown more powerful than they should be. After a casual glance at the war to which Athens has sent them, they sail off to Artabazus, or anywhere rather than to the war; and the general follows them naturally enough, for his power over them is gone when he can give them no

* In the Corinthian War, 394–387 B.C.

pay. You ask what I bid you do. I bid you take away their excuses both from the general and the soldiers, by supplying pay and placing citizen-soldiers at their side as spectators of these mysteries of generalship; for our present methods are a mere mockery. Imagine the question to be put to you, men of Athens, whether you are at peace or no. "At peace?" you would say; "Of course not! We are at war with Philip." Now have you not all along been electing from among your own countrymen ten captains and generals, and cavalry-officers, and two masters-of-the-horse? and what are they doing? Except the one single individual whom you happen to send to the seat of war, they all marshalling your processions for you with the commissioners of festivals. You are no better than men modelling puppets of clay. Your captains and your cavalry-officers are elected to be displayed in the streets, not to be sent to the war. Surely, men of Athens, your captains should be elected from among yourselves, and your master-of-the-horse from among yourselves; your officers should be your own countrymen, if the force is to be really the army of Athens. As it is, the master-of-the-horse who is one of yourselves has to sail to Lemnos; while the master-of-the-horse with the army that is fighting to defend the possessions of Athens is Menelaus. I do not wish to disparage that gentleman; but whoever holds that office ought to have been elected by you.

Perhaps, however, while agreeing with all that I have said, you are mainly anxious to hear my financial proposals, which will tell you the amount and the sources of the funds required. I proceed, therefore, with these at once. First for the sum. The cost of the bare rations for the crews, with such a force, will be 90 talents and a little over — 40 talents for ten swift ships, and 20 minae a month for each ship; and for the soldiers as much again, each soldier to receive rations to the value of 10 drachmae a month; and for the cavalry (two hundred in number, each to receive 30 drachmae a month) twelve talents. It may be said that the supply of bare rations to the members of the force is an insufficient initial provision; but this is a mistake. I am quite certain, that, given so much, the army will provide everything else for itself from the proceeds of war, without injury to a single Hellene or ally of ours, and that the full pay will be made upon these means. I am ready to sail as a volunteer and to suffer the worst, if my words are untrue. The next question then is of ways and means, in so far as the funds are to come from yourselves. I will explain this at once.

[*A schedule of ways and means is read.*]

This, men of Athens, is what we have been able to devise; and when you put our proposals to the vote, you will pass them, if you approve of them; that so your war with Philip may be a war, not of resolutions and dispatches, but of actions.

I believe that the value of your deliberations about the war and the armament as a whole would be greatly enhanced, if you were to bear in mind the situation of the country against which you are fighting, remembering that most of Philip's plans are successfully carried out because he takes advantage of winds and seasons; for he waits for the Etesian winds or the winter-season, and only attacks when it would be impossible for us to effect a passage to the scene of action. Bearing this in mind, we must not carry on the war by means of isolated expeditions; we shall always be too late. We must have a permanent force and armament. As our winter-stations for the army we have Lemnos, Thasos, Sciathos, and the islands in that region, which have harbours and corn, and are well supplied with all that an army needs. And as to the time of year, whenever it is easy to approach the shore and the winds are not dangerous, our force can without difficulty lie close to the Macedonian coast itself, and block the mouths of the ports.

How and when he will employ the force is a matter to be determined, when the time comes, by the commander whom you put in control of it. What must be provided from Athens is described in the scheme which I have drafted. If, men of Athens, you first supply the sum I have mentioned, and then, after making ready the rest of the armament — soldiers, ships, cavalry — bind the whole force in its entirety, by law, to remain at the seat of war; if you become your own paymasters, your own commissioners of supply, but require your general to account for the actual operations; then there will be an end of these perpetual discussions of one and the same theme, which end in nothing but discussion: and in addition to this, men of Athens, you will, in the first place, deprive him of his chief source of supply. For what is this? Why, he carries on the war at the cost of your own allies, harrying and plundering those who sail the seas! And what will you gain besides this? You will place yourselves out of reach of disaster. It will not be as it was in the past, when he descended upon Lemnos and Imbros, and went off, with your fellow-citizens as his prisoners of war, or when he seized the vessels off Geraestus, and levied an enormous sum from them; or when (last of all) he landed at Marathon, seized the sacred trireme,* and carried it off from the country; while all the time you can neither prevent these aggressions, nor yet send an expedition which will arrive when you intend it to arrive. But for what reason do you think, men of Athens, do the festival of the Panathenaea and the festival of the Dionysia always take place at the proper time, whether those to whom the charge of either festival is allotted are specially qualified persons or not — festivals upon which you spend larger sums of money than upon any armament whatsoever, and which involve an amount of trouble and preparation, which are unique, so far as I know, in the whole world — ; and yet your armaments are always behind the time — at Methone, at Pagasae, at Potidaea? It is because for the festivals all is arranged by law. Each of you knows long beforehand who is to supply the chorus, and who is to be steward of the games, for his tribe: he knows what he is to receive, and when,

---

* The *Paralus*, a vessel used by the Athenians to carry religious deputations and important messages of state.

and from whom, and what he is to do with it. No detail is here neglected, nothing is left indefinite. But in all that concerns war and our preparation for it, there is no organization, no revision, no definiteness. Consequently it is not until the news comes that we appoint our trierarchs and institute exchanges of property for them, and inquire into ways and means. When that is done, we first resolve that the resident aliens and the independent freedmen shall go on board; then we change our minds and say that citizens shall embark; then that we will send substitutes; and while all these delays are occurring, the object of the expedition is already lost. For we spend on preparation the time when we should be acting, and the opportunities which events afford will not wait for our slothful evasions; while as for the forces on which we think we can rely in the meantime, when the critical moment comes, they are tried and found wanting. And Philip's insolence has reached such a pitch, that he has sent such a letter as the following to the Euboeans.

[The letter is read.]

The greater part of the statements that have been read are true, men of Athens; and they ought not to be true! but I admit that they may possibly be unpleasant to hear; and if the course of future events would pass over all that a speaker passes over in his speech, to avoid giving pain, we should be right in speaking with a view to your pleasure. But if attractive words, spoken out of season, bring their punishment in actual reality, then it is disgraceful to blind our eyes to the truth, to put off everything that is unpleasant, to refuse to understand even so much as this, that those who conduct war rightly must not follow in the wake of events, but must be beforehand with them. for just as a general may be expected to lead his army, so those who debate must lead the course of affairs, in order that what they resolve upon may be done, and that they may not be forced to follow at the heels of events. You, men of Athens, have the greatest power in the world — warships, infantry, cavalry, revenue. But none of these elements of power have you used as you ought, down to this very day. The method of your warfare with Philip is just that of barbarians in a boxing-match. Hit one of them, and he hugs the place; hit him on the other side, and there go his hands; but as for guarding, or looking his opponent in the face, he neither can nor will do it. It is the same with you. If you hear that Philip is in the Chersonese, you resolve to make an expedition there; if he is at Thermopylae, you send one there; and wherever else he may be, you run up and down in his steps. It is he that leads your forces. You have never of yourselves come to any salutary decision in regard to the war. No single event do you ever discern before it occurs — before you have heard that something has happened or is happening. Perhaps there was room for this backwardness until now; but now we are at the very crisis, and such an attitude is possible no longer. Surely, men of Athens, it is one of the gods — one who blushes for Athens, as he sees the course which events are taking — that has inspired Philip with this restless activity. If he were content to remain at peace, in possession of all that he has won by conquest or by forestalling us — if he had no further plans — even then, the record against us as a people, a record of shame and cowardice and all that is most dishonourable, would, I think, seem complete enough to some of you. But now he is always making some new attempt, always grasping after something more; and unless your spirit has utterly departed, his conduct will perhaps bring you out into the field. It amazes me, men of Athens, that not one of you remembers with any indignation, that this war had its origin in our intention to punish Philip; and that now, at the end of it, the question is, how we are to escape disaster at his hands. But that he will not stay his progress until some one arrests it is plain enough. Are we then to wait for that? Do you think that all is right, when you dispatch nothing but empty ships and somebody's hopes? Shall we not embark? Shall we not now, if never before, go forth ourselves, and provide at least some small proportion of Athenian soldiers? Shall we not sail to the enemy's country? But I heard the question, "At what point on his coast are we to anchor?" The war itself, men of Athens, if you take it in hand, will discover his weak points: but if we sit at home listening to the mutual abuse and recriminations of our orators, you can never realize any of the results that you ought to realize. I believe that whenever any portion of Athens is sent with the forces, even if the whole city does not go, the favour of Heaven and of Fortune fights on our side. But whenever you dispatch anywhere a general with an empty resolution and some platform-hopes to support him, then you achieve nothing that you ought to achieve, your enemies laugh at you, and your allies are in deadly fear of all such armaments. It is impossible, utterly impossible, that any one man should be able to effect all that you wish for you. He can give undertakings and promises; he can accuse this man and that; and the result is that your fortunes are ruined. For when the general is at the head of wretched, unpaid mercenaries, and when there are those in Athens who lie to you light-heartedly about all that he does, and, on the strength of the tales that you hear, you pass decrees at random, what must you expect?

How then can this state of things be terminated? Only, men of Athens, when you expressly make the same men soldiers, witnesses of their general's actions, and judges at his examination when they return home; for then the issue of your fortunes will not be a tale which you hear, but a thing which you will be on the spot to see. So shameful is the pass which matters have now reached, that each of your generals is tried for his life before you two or three times, but does not dare to fight in mortal combat with the enemy even once. They prefer the death of kidnappers and brigands to that of a general. For it is a felon's death, to die by sentence of the court: the death of a general is to fall in battle with the enemy. Some of us go about saying that Philip is negotiating with Sparta for the overthrow of the Thebans and the breaking up of the free states; others, that he has sent ambassadors to the king; others, that he is fortifying cities in Illyria. We all go about inventing each his own tale. I quite believe, men of Athens, that he is intoxicated with the greatness of his successes, and entertains many such visions in his mind; for he sees that there are none to hinder him, and he is elated at his achievements. But I do not believe that he has chosen to act in such a way that the most foolish persons in Athens can know what he intends to do; for no persons are so foolish as newsmongers. But if we dismiss all such tales, and attend only to the certainty—that the man is our enemy, that he is robbing us of our own, that he has insulted us for a long time, that all that we ever expected any one to do for us has proved to be against us, that the future is in our own hands, that if we will not fight him now in his own country we shall perhaps be obliged to do so in ours — if, I say, we are assured of this, then we shall have made up our minds aright, and shall be quit of idle words. For you have not to speculate what the future may be: you have only to be assured that the future must be evil, unless you give heed and are ready to do your duty.

Well, I have never yet chosen to gratify you by saying anything which I have not felt certain would be for your good; and to-day I have spoken freely and without concealment, just what I believe. I could wish to be as sure of the good that a speaker will gain by giving you the best advice as of that which you will gain by listening to him. I should then have been far happier than I am. As it is, I do not know what will happen to me, for what I said: but I have chosen to speak in the sure conviction that if you carry out my proposals, it will be for your good; and may the victory rest with that policy which will be for the good of all!

[tr. A. W. Pickard-Cambridge]

ON THE CROWN

[In defending his foreign policy against the attacks of Aeschines, Demosthenes relates the events which led to the alliance of Thebes and Athens in 339 B.C., and argues that his diplomacy provided the only possible means of safety for the city; as for the issue of the war, the events on the battlefield of Chaeronea lay outside his control. He then turns on his opponent with the following paradox and in one of the most elevated and famous passages of ancient oratory shows that no other course was possible for Athens, even if the result had been foreknown.]

But since he bears so hardly upon the results, I desire to say what may even be a paradox; and let no one, in the name of Heaven, be amazed at the length to which I go, but give a kindly consideration to what I say. Even if what was to come was plain to all beforehand; even if all foreknew it; even if you, Aeschines, had been crying with a loud voice in warning and protestation — you who uttered not so much as a sound; even then, I say, it was not right for the city to abandon her course, if she had any regard for her fame, or for our forefathers, or for the ages to come. As it is, she is thought, no doubt, to have failed to secure her object — as happens to all alike, whenever God wills it: but then, by abandoning in favour of Philip her claim to take the lead of others, she must have incurred the blame of having betrayed them all. Had she surrendered without a struggle those claims in defence of which our forefathers faced every imaginable peril, who would not have cast scorn upon you, Aeschines — upon you, I say; not, I trust, upon Athens nor upon me? In God's name, with what faces should we have looked upon those who came to visit the city, if events had come round to the same conclusion as they now have — if Philip had been chosen as commander and lord of all, and we had stood apart, while others carried on the struggle to prevent these things; and that, although the city had never yet in time past preferred an inglorious security to the hazardous vindication of a noble cause? What Hellene, what foreigner, does not know, that the Thebans, and the Spartans, who were powerful still earlier, and the Persian king would all gratefully and gladly have allowed Athens to take what she liked and keep all that was her own, if she would do the bidding of another, and let another take the first place in Hellas? But this was not, it appears, the tradition of the Athenians; it was not tolerable; it was not in their nature. From the beginning of time no one had ever yet succeeded in persuading the city to throw in her lot with those who were strong, but unrighteous in their dealings, and to enjoy the security of servitude. Throughout all time she has maintained her perilous struggle for pre-eminence, honour, and glory. And this policy you look upon as so lofty, so proper to your own national character, that, of your forefathers also, it is those who have acted thus that you praise most highly. And naturally. For who would not admire the courage of those men, who did not fear to leave their land and their city,* and to embark upon their ships, that they might not do the bidding of another; who chose for their general Themistocles (who had counselled them thus), and stoned Cyrsilus to death, when he gave his voice for submission to a master's orders — and not him alone, for your wives stoned his wife also to death. For the Athenians of that day did not look for an orator or a general who would enable them to live in happy servitude; they cared not to live at all, unless they might live in freedom. For every one of them felt that he had come into being, not for his father and his mother alone, but also for his country. And wherein lies the difference? He who thinks he was born for his parents alone awaits the death which destiny assigns him in the course of nature: but he who thinks he was born for his country also will be willing to die, that he may not see her in bondage, and will look upon the outrages and the indignities that he must needs bear in a city that is in bondage as more to be dreaded than death.

Now were I attempting to argue that I had induced you to show a spirit worthy of your forefathers, there is not a man who might not rebuke me with good reason. But in fact, I am declaring that such

* In 480 B.C. when the Athenians abandoned their city to the Persians before the battle of Salamis.

principles as these are your own; I am showing that *before* my time the city displayed this spirit, though I claim that I, too, have had some share, as your servant, in carrying out your policy in detail. But in denouncing the policy as a whole, in bidding you be harsh with me, as one who has brought terrors and dangers upon the city, the prosecutor, in his eagerness to deprive me of my distinction at the present moment, is trying to rob you of praises that will last throughout all time. For if you condemn the defendant on the ground that my policy was not for the best, men will think that your own judgment has been wrong, and that it was not through the unkindness of fortune that you suffered what befell you. But it cannot, it cannot be that you were wrong, men of Athens, when you took upon you the struggle for freedom and deliverance. No! by those who at Marathon bore the brunt of the peril — our forefathers. No! by those who at Plataeae drew up their battle-line, by those who at Salamis, by those who off Artemisium fought the fight at sea, by the many who lie in the sepulchres where the People laid them, brave men, all alike deemed worthy by their country, Aeschines, of the same honour and the same obsequies — not the successful or the victorious alone! And she acted justly. For all these have done that which it was the duty of brave men to do; but their fortune has been that which Heaven assigned to each. Accursed, poring pedant! if you, in your anxiety to deprive me of the honour and the kindness shown to me by my countrymen, recounted trophies and battles and deeds of long ago — and of which of them did this present trial demand the mention? — what spirit was I to take upon me, when I mounted the platform, I who came forward to advise the city how she should maintain her pre-eminence? Tell me, third-rate actor! The spirit of one who would propose things unworthy of this people? I should indeed have deserved to die! For you too, men of Athens, ought not to judge private suits and public in the same spirit. The business transactions of everyday life must be viewed in the light of the special law and practice associated with each; but the public policy of statesmen must be judged by the principles that your forefathers set before them. And if you believe that you should act worthily of them, then, whenever you come into court to try a public suit, each of you must imagine that with his staff and his ticket * there is entrusted to him also the spirit of his country.

[199–210, tr. A. W. Pickard-Cambridge]

[In conclusion, Demosthenes enters a general defense of his own statesmanship and compares his services to Athens with those of Aeschines. He then concludes with the following noble affirmation of his devotion to his country.]

For mark this. Not when my surrender was demanded, not when I was called to account before the Amphictyons, not in face either of threats or of promises, not when these accursed men were hounded

---

* "The colour of the staff indicated the court in which the juror was to sit; the ticket was exchanged for his pay at the end of the day." [Translator's note.]

on against me like wild beasts, have I ever been false to my loyalty towards you.   For from the very first, I chose the straight and honest path in public life: I chose to foster the honour, the supremacy, the good name of my country, to seek to enhance them, and to stand or fall with them.   I do not walk through the market, cheerful and exultant over the success of strangers, holding out my hand and giving the good tidings to any whom I expect to report my conduct yonder, but shuddering, groaning, bowing myself to the earth, when I hear of the city's good fortune, as do these impious men, who make a mock of the city — not remembering that in so doing they are mocking themselves — while they direct their gaze abroad, and, whenever another has gained success through the failure of the Hellenes, belaud that state of things, and declare that we must see that it endures for all time.

Never, O all of ye gods, may any of you consent to their desire! If it can be, may you implant even in these men a better mind and heart.   But if they are verily beyond all cure, then bring them and them alone to utter and early destruction, by land and sea.   And to us who remain, grant the speediest release from the fears that hang over us, and safety that naught can shake!

[322–324, tr. A. W. Pickard-Cambridge]

CHARACTER STUDY, MIME, AND ROMANCE

The modern reader, who usually approaches Greek literature through the great authors, such as Homer, the tragedians, and Plato, may receive the impression that the Greeks were interested exclusively in great figures, the noble, semi-divine heroes and kings, and in the great events of their legendary careers. The unexciting yet absorbing and meaningful events in the daily lives of ordinary people, a casual reader might suppose, were apparently regarded as beneath the notice of the creative artist. This is true to some extent, yet there are certain branches of Greek literature which concentrate attention on the common man; a few examples of such works are gathered together in this section. The three types of literature represented here have, of course, no formal relationship with one another, but all of them are connected through their interest in the character and existence of the ordinary individual of real life. The treatment is essentially realistic in all these forms, despite the generous admixture of romantic flavour in the prose romances.

Theophrastus, the pupil and successor of Aristotle as head of the Peripatetic school, was famous in his lifetime as a philosopher and scientist, especially in the field of botany. But later ages remember him chiefly for his fascinating little studies called *Characters* (*i.e.,* distinguishing traits). It is impossible to discover now whether these sketches were written as an independent work or whether they are excerpts from a larger work (*e.g.,* a series of lectures on ethics or rhetoric). It is not improbable that they were composed for the private entertainment of the philosopher's friends and pupils, and later were introduced into the schools as models of character drawing for the budding orator. It has often been remarked that these skits have much in common with New Comedy; many of the types, such as the Flatterer and the Boor, appear on the comic stage. Likewise they are closely connected with Aristotle's ethical thinking, since they imply a mean or a norm of conduct, deviations from which lead to vice or absurdity. Both the *Nicomachean Ethics* and the *Rhetoric* of Aristotle contain sections delineating ethical types in general terms; Theophrastus has particularized these types, added realistic traits, and the result is a fascinating and tantalizing glimpse of Athenian daily life in the late fourth century.

Of Herodas' life we know almost nothing, except that he wrote in the reign of Ptolemy II Philadelphus. The *mime* was developed in the fifth century B.C. by Sophron of Syracuse; originally it was a prose form, but Herodas composed in the style and meter of Hipponax, an early satiric poet. His mimes show a coarseness of tone and an unpleasant "photographic" realism which is unusual even in the Alexandrian Age: bawds, brothel-keepers, slaves, and foul-mouthed women fill his pages. This form of literary mime is closely related to the dramatic mime which later became so popular at Rome and all but drove the more respectable dramatic forms from the stage.

The prose novel, or romance, appeared late in the history of Greek literature, the earliest example being dated probably in the first century of our era. There were, of course, numerous precursors of the form: the idealized biography of Cyrus by Xenophon, the romantic narratives of later historians, and collections of short amatory tales. The plots of these prose romances are concerned with thwarted love; usually pirates and kidnappers supply the means of separating the young lovers, and the virtue of the girl is miraculously preserved through a series of perils; the length of the novel is limited only by the ability of the author to invent wild and fantastic incidents before uniting the love-lorn couple. The novel of Longus, *Daphnis and Chloe,* which was probably written in the third century after Christ, is by far the best of these romances; the incidents are not too wildly improbable and the author had some idea of psychology. The work portrays the awakening of young and innocent love in a charming fashion. Theocritus and the pastoral poets have contributed largely to the setting, and New Comedy has supplied the frame-work of the plot, with its conventional details of the exposed infants and the happy recognition at the end. In such works as *Daphnis and Chloe,* as well as in pastoral poetry, we clearly see the existence of romantic traits which are often mistakenly denied to the Greeks.

THEOPHRASTUS

(*ca.* 372–*ca.* 287 B.C.)

GARRULITY

Garrulity is the delivering of talk that is irrelevant, or long and unconsidered; and the Garrulous man is one that will sit down close beside somebody he does not know, and begin talk with a eulogy of his own wife, and then relate a dream he had the night before, and after that tell dish by dish what he had for supper. As he warms to his work he will remark that we are by no means the men we were, and the price of wheat has gone down, and there's a great many strangers in town, and that the ships will be able to put to sea after the Dionysia. Next he will surmise that the crops would be all the better for some more rain, and tell him what he is going to grow on his farm next year, adding that it is difficult to make both ends meet, and Damippus' torch was the largest set up at the Mysteries, and how many pillars there are in the Hall of Music, and "I vomited yesterday," and "What day is it to-day?" and that the Mysteries are in September, and the Apaturia in October, and the country-Dionysia in December. And if you let him go on he will never stop.

[tr. J. M. EDMONDS]

LOQUACITY

Loquacity, should you wish to define it, would seem to be an incontinence of speech; and the Loquacious man will say to any that meets him, if he but open his lips, "You are wrong; I know all about it, and if you will listen to me you shall learn the truth." And in the midst of the other's answer he whispers him such words as these: "Pray bethink you what you are about to say"; or "I thank you for reminding me"; or "There's nothing like a talk, is there?" or "I forgot to say"; or "You have taken long to understand it"; or "I had long expected you would come round to my way of thinking"; and provides himself other such openings, so that his friend can hardly get his breath. And when he has worn out such as go singly, he is prone to march upon those who stand together in troops, and put them to flight in the midst of their business. It is a habit of his to go into the schools and wrestling-places and keep the children from learning their tasks, he talks so much to their teachers and trainers. And if you say you must go your ways, he loves to bear you company and see you to your doorstep. And when he has news of the meetings of the Assembly he retails it, with the addition of an account of the famous battle of the orators, and the speeches he too was used to make there so greatly to his credit, all this interlarded with tirades against democracy, till his listeners forget what it is all about, or fall half-asleep, or get up and leave him to his talk. On a jury this man hinders your verdict, at the play your entertainment, at the table your eating, with the plea that it is hard for the talkative to hold his peace, or that the tongue grows in a wet soil, or he could not cease though he should outbabble the very swallows. And he is content to be the butt of his own children, who when it is late and he would fain be sleeping and bids them do likewise, cry "Talk to us, daddy, and then we shall go to sleep."

[tr. J. M. Edmonds]

SUPERSTITIOUSNESS

Superstitiousness, I need hardly say, would seem to be a sort of cowardice with respect to the divine; and your Superstitious man such as will not sally forth for the day till he have washed his hands and sprinkled himself at the Nine Springs, and put a bit of bay-leaf from a temple in his mouth. And if a cat cross his path he will not proceed on his way till someone else be gone by, or he have cast three stones across the street. Should he espy a snake in his house, if it be one of the red sort he will call upon Sabazius, if of the sacred, build a shrine then and there. When he passes one of the smooth stones set up at crossroads he anoints it with oil from his flask, and will not go his ways till he have knelt down and worshipped it. If a mouse gnaw a bag of his meal, he will off to the wizard's and ask what he must do, and if the answer be "send it to the cobbler's to be patched," he neglects the advice and frees himself of the ill by rites of aversion. He is for ever purifying his house on the plea that Hecate has been drawn thither. Should owls hoot when he is abroad, he is much put about, and will not on his way till he have cried "Athena forfend!" Set foot on a tomb he will not, nor come nigh a dead body nor a woman in childbed; he must keep himself unpolluted. On the fourth and seventh days of every month he has wine mulled for his household, and goes out to buy myrtle-boughs, frankincense, and a holy picture, and then returning spends the livelong day doing sacrifice to the Hermaphrodites and putting garlands about them. He never has a dream but he flies to a diviner, or a soothsayer, or an interpreter of visions, to ask what God or Goddess he should appease; and when he is about to be initiated into the holy orders of Orpheus, he visits the priests every month and his wife with him, or if she have not the time, the nurse and children. He would seem to be one of those who are for ever going to the seaside to besprinkle themselves; and if ever he see one of the figures of Hecate at the crossroads wreathed with garlic, he is off home to wash his head and summon priestesses whom he bids purify him with the carrying around him of a squill or a puppy-dog. If he catch sight of a madman or an epilept, he shudders and spits in his bosom.

[tr. J. M. Edmonds]

NASTINESS

Nastiness is a neglect of the person which is painful to others; and your Nasty fellow such as will walk the town with the scall and the scab upon him and with bad nails, and boast that these ailments are hereditary; his father and his grandfather had them before him and 'tis no easy matter to be foisted into *his* family. He is like also, I warrant you, to have gatherings on his shins and sores on his toes, and seek no remedy, but rather let them grow rank. He will keep himself as shaggy as a beast, with hair well-nigh all over his body, and his teeth all black and rotten. These also are marks of the man: — to blow his nose at table; to bite his nails when he is sacrificing with you; to spit from his mouth when he is talking with you; when he has drunken with you, to hiccup in your face. He will go to bed with his wife with hands unwashed and his shoes on; spit on himself at the baths when his oil is rancid; and go forth to the market-place clad in a thick shirt and a very thin coat, and this covered with stains.

[tr. J. M. EDMONDS]

HERODAS

(*fl.* 240 B.C.)

A JEALOUS LADY

[SCENE: *A lady's chamber in a house in Ephesus.* BITINNA *the lady harangues* GASTRON, *her slave, also her unfaithful paramour.* KYDILLA, *her confidential slave-girl, is also present.*]

BI.: Tell me Gastron, art so surfeited, that it sufficeth thee not to stir my legs, but must woo Amphytaea, Meno's woman?

GA.: Amphytaea? I. Have I e'en seen her of whom thou speakest?

BI.: Excuse on excuse all day long!

GA.: Bitinna, thy slave am I: use me as thou wilt, ne sup my blood day and night.

BI.: And what a tongue hast gotten, slave! Kydilla, where is Pyrrhies? Call him to me.

PY.: What is it?

BI.: Bind this fellow — what? Standest still? — loosing anon the rope of the bucket. An I mar thee not and set thee as an example to the countriesyde, la! call me no woman. Am I not rather an Eunuch? 'Tis I, Gastron, I that fault herein, that I set thee among men. But, an I erred then, thou shalt find Bitinna a fool now no moe, for all thou thinkest. Come, thou, bind him unayded when thou hast stripped him of his smock.

GA.: Nay, nay Bitinna — by thy knees, prithee.

BI.: Strip him, I repeat. Must wot that art a slave and that I payd for thee three minae. Ah! ill betyde that day that brought thee hither. Shalt rue it, Pyrrhies — I see that dost aught els save bind him. Truss his arms; bind till they be perdy severed.

GA.: Bitinna, forgive me this errour. Mortal am I, I have erred; but an thou find me moe doing aught thou woldest not, then tatto me.

BI.: Playne not to me, but to Amphytaea with whom thou lyest, and needs must I <your> foot towell <be . . .>.

PY.: Thou hast him well bound.

BI.: See he escape not loose. Take him to the abode of torment to Hermon, and bid him hammer thousand stripes into his back and thousand into's belly.

GA.: Wilt kill me, Bitinna, ne try first an it be sooth or false?

BI.: What of thine own tongues utteraunce "Bitinna forgive me this errour"?

GA.: Aye, for I wolde quench your choler.

BI.: Standest agape, and leadest him not where I bid thee? Kydilla, dint this losells beak, and thou, Drechon, follow now by the way thy fellow leadeth. Slave, wilt give a rag to this curst fellow to hyde his bestiall nakedness, that he be not seen bare through the market? Once moe a second time I cry thee Pyrrhies to tell Hermon that he lay on thousand here and thousand there: hast heard?

Soothly an thou traverse aught of my orders thou shalt thine own self pay debt and interest. Walk on and lead him not by Mrs. Smallwaies but on the Mall. But I mind — run, slave-girl, and call them, call them ere they be afar.

KY.: Pyrrhies, deaf wretche, she calleth thee. La, one mote deme 'twas no fellow-slave he mauleth, but a grave-robber: look how dost drag him perforce to the torments, Pyrrhies. La! 'tis thee that Kydilla will live to see with this pair of eyne in five daies time rubbing with thine ankles at Antidorus abode those Achaean gyves that but yestereen didst doff.

BI.: Ho there, come back bringing him bound even as dost lead him out, and enjoyne Kosis the tattooer to come with needles and ink. Thou must be spotted attone. Let him be taught to cringe as low as his honour Davus.

KY.: Nay, mamma, but now — e'en as thou hopest Batyllis may live and maiest one day see her come to a mans house, and maiest lift her children in thine arms — now let him be: this one errour —

BI.: Kydilla, vex me not, all of you: or will flee the habitaunce. Am I to let be this slave of slaves? Who then that encountred me wolde not rightly spit in my face? Nay by the Queen, but since, though mortal he be, he knoweth not himself, soon shall he know it with this inscripcioun on his forehead.

KY.: But 'tis the twentieth, and but four days to the Gerenia.

BI.: Now shall I let thee be, and be thankfull to this girl whom I love as Batyllis and in mine own hands did noursle. But whenas we have done libacioun to those that sleep, then shalt have unhonied festivall on festivall.

[tr. A. D. KNOX]

A PRIVATE CHAT

[SCENE: *Ephesus? The house of* KORITTO, *a lady. Her friend* METRO *bursts in unannounced. A slave-girl is present.*]

KO.: Sit down, Metro — Arise and set a chayre for the lady! Must I bid thee myself do all thy devoyrs, and thou woldest do naught of thine own self? La! thou'rt a stone in the house, not a slave-girl: but an thou takest thy measure of wheat, each crumb thou tellest, and an ne'er so litell driblet escape, the walls burst with thy day-long playnts and lamentaciouns. So thou dost wipe it and render it clean now, thou thief, when need is? I counsell thee render oblacioun to this lady: els had I given thee taste of my handes.

ME.: Deare Koritto, thou'rt galled by the same yoke as I. I too day and night long yap like a dog gnashing at these bestiall wenches. But for my errand —

KO.: Get ye gone, ye slightfull ones; naught but ears and tongues, and the rest of ye idlenes —

ME.: Prithee, lie not, Koritto deare? Who did stitch thee the scarlet baubon?

KO.: Where hast seen it, Metro?

ME.: Nossis, Erinna's childe, had it two daies agone. La! a fayre gift.

KO.: Nossis! Whence gat she it?

ME.: Wilt bewray an I tell thee?

KO.: By these sweet eyne, Metro deare, none shall hear from Koritto's mouth aught thou saiest.

ME.: Eubule, wife of Bitas, gave it her and bade her that none discover it.

KO.: Oh womankind, this woman shall one day fordo me. I granted her prayers, and gave it her, Metro, ere I used it myself: and she seized it like trove, and gives it to whom she ought not. To such an one, dere, bid I long farewell, and let her quest hence-forward other friends in my room. To Nossis, wife of Medokes — I speke beyond due limit and may Adrasteia hearken not — though I had a thousand yet wolde I not lend one that were rotten.

ME.: Prithee, Koritto, let not ire sit anon on thy nostrils an thou hear word of no fayre import. Gentle woman sholde suffer all things. 'Tis I that fault herein for speking o'ermuch: I sholde cut out my tongue. But — to my main intendiment — who did stitch it? Say, an thou love me. Why these mowes at me? Hast neer seen Metro before? What mene these bashings? I adjure thee, Koritto, false me not, but say who stitched it.

KO.: La! why adjure? 'Twas Kerdon.

ME.: Which Kerdon? Tell me. There are two Kerdons, one of grey eyne, neighbour of Myrtaline daughter of Kylaithis: but yon note stitch plectre for lyre. The other has habitaunce forby the tenement of Hermodorus as one quitteth the Broad Way: of mark once but now eld hath him. Him had Kylaithis, who is now at peace. May her kin memorize her.

KO.: 'Tis neither of these, Metro. This one haileth from Chios or Erythrae, I wot not which: bald and short: a very Prexinos motest say: fig to fig notest so compare: but whenas he prateth thou'lt ken him to be Kerdon not Prexinos. At home he werketh bartering by stealth, for every door now shuddereth at the tax-gatherers. "But what werkes is he werker?" Athenes own handes woldest deme to see, not Kerdons. I — for he came with twain of them, Metro — at first glaunce were mine eyne extent: e'en straighter than the livelihed — none listeth — : nay moe — as soft as sleep, and the thonglets no thongs but wool: kinder cobbler to feminitee notest find, quest how thou wilt.

ME.: How gattest not the other?

KO.: All things tryed I: all persuasiouns trayned: kissing, stroking his bald pate, flagons of mead, fond names, albut surrendring mine own bodie.

ME.: But an he asked, e'en this sholdest have given.

KO.: Aye — but all things in tyde. Eubule wife of Bitas was grinding before us. For day and night long doth she weare our stone into scrapings, enaunter she pay a grote to set her own.

ME.: And how found he his way hither to thee, deare Koritto?   Eke herein false me not.

KO.: Artemis, wife of Kandas the tanner, sent him hither, shewing the house.

ME.: Artemis will aye find some new device drinking deep down in bawdy bottles.   But sin notest salve the twain, algates sholdest have found who bid the other.

KO.: I besought but he swore he nould say: for he was charmed with her and she with him, Metro.

ME.: Thy tale speedeth me: now hie I to Artemis to know what man Kerdon be.   Fare thee well, Koritto: one hungereth and I must move off.

KO.: Shut the door — ho you there, chick-girl — and tell an the hens be safe, and toss darnel to them.   For indeed the bird-thieves spoyle e'en an one rear abosom.

[tr. A. D. Knox]

LONGUS

[DATE UNKNOWN]

DAPHNIS AND CHLOE

[Lamo, a goatherd of Mytilene, finds an infant boy exposed in a glade, takes him home, and names him Daphnis. Two years later Dryas, a shepherd, finds a baby girl, whom he brings up, calling her Chloe. When the children are fifteen and thirteen respectively, their foster-parents send them out to tend their flocks; the children fall in love, but being young and innocent have no idea what is troubling them. Dorco, an oxherd, tries to win Chloe away from Daphnis and asks Dryas for her hand in marriage, but all in vain. He then tries to gain her by force: disguised in a wolf-skin he lies in ambush near a fountain, but the sheep-dogs fall upon him and nearly tear him to pieces before Daphnis rescues him.]

Thus came Dorco out of great danger, and he that was saved from the jaws, not of the wolf in the adage, but of the dog, went home and dressed his wounds. But Daphnis and Chloe had much ado to get together, before it was late in the evening, their scattered straggling sheep and goats. For they were terrified with the wolfskin and the fierce barking and baying of the dogs, and some ran up the steep crags, some ran on rucks and hurried down to the seashore, although they were taught not only to obey the voice and be quieted by the pipe, but to be driven up together even by the clapping of the hands. But fear had cast in an oblivion of all, so that at length with much stir, following their steps like hares by the foot, they drave them home to their own folds.

That night alone Daphnis and Chloe slept soundly, and found that weariness was some kind of remedy for the passion of love. But as soon as the day appeared they fell again to these fits. When they saw one another they were passing joyful, and sad if it chanced that they were parted. They desired, and yet they knew not what they would have. Only this one thing they knew, that kissing had destroyed Daphnis and bathing had undone Chloe.

Now besides this, the season of the year inflamed and burnt them. For now the cooler spring was ended and the summer was come on, and all things were got to their highest flourishing, the trees with their fruits, the fields with standing corn. Sweet then was the singing of the grasshoppers, sweet was the odour of the fruits, and not unpleasant the very blating of the sheep. A man would have thought that the very rivers, by their gentle gliding away, did sing; and that the softer gales of wind did play and whistle on the pines; that the apples, as languishing with love, fell down upon the ground; and that the Sun, as a lover of beauty unveiled, did strive to undress and turn the rurals all naked. By all these was Daphnis inflamed, and therefore often he goes to the rivers and brooks, there to bathe and cool himself, or to chase the fish that went to and fro in the water.

832

And often he drinks of the clear purls, as thinking by that to quench his inward caum and scorching.

When Chloe had milked the sheep and most of the goats and had spent much time and labour (because the flies were importune and vexatious, and would sting if one chased them) to curdle and press the milk into cheeses, she would wash herself and crown her head with pine-twigs, and when she had girt her fawnskin about her, take her piggin and with wine and milk make a sillibub for her dear Daphnis and herself.

When it grew towards noon they would fall to their catching of one another by their eyes. For Chloe, seeing Daphnis naked, was all eyes for his beauty to view it every whit; and therefore could not choose but melt, as being not able to find in him the least moment to dislike or blame. Daphnis again, if he saw Chloe, in her fawn-skin and her pine cornet, give him the sillibub to drink, thought he saw one of the Nymphs of the holy cave. Therefore taking off her pine and kissing it o'er and o'er, he would put it on his own head; and Chloe, when he was naked and bathing, would in her turn take up his vest, and when she kissed it, put it on upon herself. Sometimes now they flung apples at one another, and dressed and distinguished one another's hair into curious trammels and locks. And Chloe likened Daphnis his hair to the myrtle because it was black; Daphnis, again, because her face was white and ruddy, compared it to the fairest apple. He taught her too to play on the pipe, and always when she began to blow would catch the pipe away from her lips and run it presently o'er with his. He seemed to teach her when she was out, but with that specious pretext, by the pipe, he kissed Chloe.

But it happened, when he played on his pipe at noon and the cattle took shade, that Chloe fell unawares asleep. Daphnis observed it and laid down his pipe, and without shame or fear was bold to view her, all over and every limb, insatiably; and withal spoke softly thus: "What sweet eyes are those that sleep! How sweetly breathes that rosy mouth! The apples smell not like to it, nor the flowery lawns and thickets. But I am afraid to kiss her. For her kiss stings to my heart and makes me mad like new honey. Besides, I fear lest a kiss should chance to wake her. Oh the prating grasshoppers! they make a noise to break her sleep. And the goats besides are fighting, and they clatter with their horns. Oh the wolves, worse dastards than the foxes, that they have not ravished them away!"

While he was muttering this passion, a grasshopper that fled from a swallow took sanctuary in Chloe's bosom. And the pursuer could not take her, but her wing by reason of her close pursuit slapped the girl upon the cheek. And she not knowing what was done cried out, and started from her sleep. But when she saw the swallow fly-ing near by and Daphnis laughing at her fear, she began to give it over and rub her eyes that yet would be sleeping. The grasshopper sang out of her bosom, as if her suppliant were now giving thanks for the protection. Therefore Chloe again squeaked out; but Daphnis could not hold laughing, nor pass the opportunity to put his hand into her bosom and draw forth friend Grasshopper, which still did sing even in his hand. When Chloe saw it she was pleased and kissed it, and took and put it in her bosom again, and it prattled all the way. But besides these the stock-dove did delight them too, and sang from the woods her country song. But Chloe, desiring to know, asked Daphnis what that complaint of the stock-dove meant. And he told her the tradition of the ancient shepherds: "There was once, maiden, a very fair maid who kept many cattle in the woods. She was skilful in music, and her herds were so taken with her voice and pipe, that they needed not the discipline of the staff or goad, but sitting under a pine and wearing a coronet of the same she would sing of Pan and the Pine, and her cows would never wander out of her voice. There was a youth that kept his herd not far off, and he also was fair and musical, but as he tried with all his skill to emulate her notes and tones, he played a louder strain as a male, and yet sweet as being young, and so allured from the maid's herd eight of her best cows to his own. She took it ill that her herd was so diminished and in very deep disdain that she was his inferior at the art, and presently prayed to the Gods that she might be transformed to a bird before she did return home. The Gods consent, and turned her thus into a mountain bird, because the maid did haunt there, and musical as she had been. And singing still to this day she publishes her heavy chance and demands her truant cows again."

[I. 22–27, tr. G. Thornley— J. M. Edmonds]

THE SATIRICAL DIALOGUE

LUCIAN

(*ca.* 120–200 A.D.)

The approximate dates of Lucian's life are from A.D. 120 to A.D. 200. Living from the reign of Hadrian on through the troubled days of the end of the century, Lucian witnessed the Roman world in its epoch of moribund splendour until its terrifying collapse after the death of Marcus Aurelius. Lucian was born in Samosata on the Euphrates River, spent some time as a sculptor's apprentice and then undertook the career of a rhetorician. He traveled widely throughout the empire but finally at middle age he settled in Athens, devoting himself to philosophy and to the composition of the satirical dialogues to which he owes his fame. The selections which follow are from his *Dialogues of the Gods* and *Dialogues of the Dead,* from which we can gather Lucian's view of life and the world.

It is interesting to contrast the reaction of Marcus Aurelius to this second-century Roman world with that of Lucian. Any attentive reader of the *Meditations* can see that the Emperor is haunted by a gloomy pessimism. Lucian, in contrast, expressed his reaction in the medium of satire. Instead of giving over to pessimism he laughed at the disproportions which he saw in life and attacked them with the weapon of his wit. Lucian is no respecter of persons. He is always the arch enemy of that which is sham, false, hypocritical and cheating. It makes no difference to him where the sham manifests itself — in low stations or in high — Lucian is quick to sense it and to attack it in his satire. Since he was so quick to sense it and since he found it wherever he turned, it is not strange that his skepticism is virtually complete. In this skepticism Lucian is caught in the snare of his age, in very much the same way as Marcus Aurelius was caught. Though Lucian skeptically laughed at his world and the Emperor painfully and faithfully tried to understand it, though their reactions are radically different, they both reach the same position. They gravely doubt that life has any meaning and seem to believe that all man can do is to endure life with fortitude.

The skeptical and satirical attitude can point out sham and can teach man to endure. But it would be a mistake to see only this in the *Dialogues* of Lucian. Many of them are intensely amusing and we find Lucian exploiting to the full for his humorous purposes the inherent incongruities of anthropomorphism. Lucian never tires of making fun of the ludicrous consequences of the myths concerning the orthodox Greek gods, and likewise he makes great capital of the myths dealing with life after death. It should be noted, however, that his treatment of these myths is always undertaken to throw light upon the essential conditions of human life and the predicament in which man finds himself. The penetration of Lucian's insights has always found admirers in all ages of the western literary tradition.

DIALOGUES OF THE GODS

II

Eros. Zeus

Eros. You might let me off, Zeus! I suppose it *was* rather too bad of me; but there! — I am but a child; a wayward child.

Zeus. A child, and born before Iapetus was ever thought of? You bad old man! Just because you have no beard, and no white hairs, are you going to pass yourself off for a child?

Eros. Well, and what such mighty harm has the old man ever done you, that you should talk of chains?

Zeus. Ask your own guilty conscience, what harm. The pranks you have played me! Satyr, bull, swan, eagle, shower of gold, — I have been everything in my time; and I have you to thank for it. You never by any chance make the women in love with *me*; no one is ever smitten with *my* charms, that I have noticed. No, there must be magic in it always; I must be kept well out of sight. They like the bull or the swan well enough: but once let them set eyes on *me*, and they are frightened out of their lives.

Eros. Well, of course. They are but mortals; the sight of Zeus is too much for them.

Zeus. Then why are Branchus and Hyacinth so fond of Apollo?

Eros. Daphne ran away from him, anyhow; in spite of his beautiful hair and his smooth chin. Now, shall I tell you the way to win hearts? Keep that aegis of yours quiet, and leave the thunderbolt at home; make yourself as smart as you can; curl your hair and tie it up with a bit of ribbon, get a purple cloak, and gold-bespangled shoes, and march forth to the music of flute and drum; — and see if you don't get a finer following than Dionysus, for all his Maenads.

Zeus. Pooh! I'll win no hearts on such terms.

Eros. Oh, in that case, don't fall in love. Nothing could be simpler.

Zeus. I dare say; but I *like* being in love, only I don't like all this fuss. Now mind; if I let you off, it is on this understanding.

[tr. F. G. Fowler]

VI

Hera. Zeus

Hera. Zeus! What is your opinion of this man Ixion?

Zeus. Why, my dear, I think he is a very good sort of man; and the best of company. Indeed, if he were unworthy of our company, he would not be here.

Hera. He *is* unworthy! He is a villain! Discard him!

Zeus. Eh? What has he been after? I must know about this.

Hera. Certainly you must; though I scarce know how to tell you. The wretch!

Zeus. Oh, oh; if he is a 'wretch,' you must certainly tell me all about it. I know what 'wretch' means, on your discreet tongue. What, he has been making love?

Hera. And to me! to me of all people! It has been going on for a long time. At first, when he would keep looking at me, I had no idea —. And then he would sigh and groan; and when I handed my cup to Ganymede after drinking, he would insist on having it, and would stop drinking to kiss it, and lift it up to his eyes; and then he would look at me again. And then of course I knew. For a long time I didn't like to say anything to you; I thought his mad fit would pass. But when he actually dared to *speak* to me, I left him weeping and grovelling about, and stopped my ears, so that I might not hear his impertinences, and came to tell you. It is for you to consider what steps you will take.

Zeus. Whew! I have a rival, I find; and with my own lawful wife. Here is a rascal who has tippled nectar to some purpose. Well, we have no one but ourselves to blame for it: we make too much of these mortals, admitting them to our table like this. When they drink of our nectar, and behold the beauties of Heaven (so different from those of Earth!), 'tis no wonder if they fall in love, and form ambitious schemes! Yes, Love is all-powerful; and not with mortals only: we Gods have sometimes fallen beneath his sway.

Hera. He has made himself master of *you*; no doubt of that. He does what he likes with you; — leads you by the nose. You follow him whither he chooses, and assume every shape at his command; you are his chattel, his toy. I know how it will be: you are going to let Ixion off, because you have had relations with his wife; she is the mother of Peirithous.

Zeus. Why, what a memory you have for these little outings of mine! — Now, my idea about Ixion is this. It would never do to punish him, or to exclude him from our table; that would not look well. No; as he is so fond of you, so hard hit — even to weeping point, you tell me, —

Hera. Zeus! What *are* you going to say?

Zeus. Don't be alarmed. Let us make a cloud-phantom in your likeness, and after dinner, as he lies awake (which of course he will do, being in love), let us take it and lay it by his side. 'Twill put him out of his pain: he will fancy he has attained his desire.

Hera. Never! The presumptuous villain!

Zeus. Yes, I know. But what harm can it do to you, if Ixion makes a conquest of a cloud?

Hera. But he will think that *I* am the cloud; he will be working his wicked will upon *me* for all he can tell.

Zeus. Now you are talking nonsense. The cloud is not Hera, and Hera is not the cloud. Ixion will be deceived; that is all.

Hera. Yes, but these men are all alike — they have no delicacy.

I suppose, when he goes home, he will boast to every one of how he has enjoyed the embraces of Hera, the wife of Zeus! Why, he may tell them that *I* am in love with *him*! And they will believe it; *they* will know nothing about the cloud.

Zeus. If he says anything of the kind he shall soon find himself in Hades, spinning round on a wheel for all eternity. That will keep him busy! And serve him right; not for falling in love — I see no great harm in that — but for letting his tongue wag.

[tr. F. G. Fowler]

VIII

Hephaestus. Zeus

Heph. What are your orders, Zeus? You sent for me, and here I am; with such an edge to my axe as would cleave a stone at one blow.

Zeus. Ah; that's right, Hephaestus. Just split my head in half, will you?

Heph. You think I am mad, perhaps? — Seriously, now, what can I do for you?

Zeus. What I say: crack my skull. Any insubordination, now, and you shall taste my resentment; it will not be the first time. Come, a good lusty stroke, and quick about it. I am in the pangs of travail; my brain is in a whirl.

Heph. Mind you, the consequences may be serious: the axe is sharp, and will prove but a rough midwife.

Zeus. Hew away, and fear nothing. I know what I am about.

Heph. H'm. I don't like it: however, one must obey orders. . . Why, what have we here? A maiden in full armour! This is no joke, Zeus. You might well be waspish, with this great girl growing up beneath your *pia mater*; in armour, too! You have been carrying a regular barracks on your shoulders all this time. So active too! See, she is dancing a war-dance, with shield and spear in full swing. She is like one inspired; and (what is more to the point) she is extremely pretty, and has come to marriageable years in these few minutes; those grey eyes, even, look well beneath a helmet. Zeus, I claim her as the fee for my midwifery.

Zeus. Impossible! She is determined to remain a maid for ever. Not that *I* have any objection, personally.

Heph. That is all I want. You can leave the rest to me. I'll carry her off this moment.

Zeus. Well, if you think it so easy. But I am sure it is a hopeless case.

[tr. F. G. Fowler]

XVI

Hera. Leto

Hera. I must congratulate you, madam, on the children with whom you have presented Zeus.

Leto. Ah, madam; we cannot all be the proud mothers of He-phaestuses.

Hera. My boy may be a cripple, but at least he is of some use. He is a wonderful smith, and has made Heaven look another place; and Aphrodite thought him worth marrying, and dotes on him still. But those two of yours! — that girl is wild and mannish to a degree; and now she has gone off to Scythia, and her doings *there* are no secret; she is as bad as any Scythian herself, — butchering strangers and eating them! Apollo, too, who pretends to be so clever, with his bow and his lyre and his medicine and his prophecies; those oracle-shops that he has opened at Delphi, and Clarus, and Dindyma, are a cheat; he takes good care to be on the safe side by giving ambiguous answers that no one can understand, and makes money out of it, for there are plenty of fools who like being imposed upon, — but sensible people know well enough that most of it is clap-trap. The prophet did not know that he was to kill his favourite with a quoit; he never foresaw that Daphne would run away from him, so handsome as he is, too, such beautiful hair! I am not sure, after all, that there is much to choose between your children and Niobe's.

Leto. Oh, of course; my children are butchers and impostors. I know how you hate the sight of them. You cannot bear to hear my girl complimented on her looks, or my boy's playing admired by the company.

Hera. His playing, madam! — excuse a smile; — why, if the Muses had not favoured him, his contest with Marsyas would have cost him his skin; poor Marsyas was shamefully used on that occasion; 'twas a judicial murder. — As for your charming daughter, when Actaeon once caught sight of her charms, she had to set the dogs upon him, for fear he should tell all he knew: I forbear to ask where the innocent child picked up her knowledge of obstetrics.

Leto. You set no small value on yourself, madam, because you are the wife of Zeus, and share his throne; you may insult whom you please. But there will be tears presently, when the next bull or swan sets out on his travels, and you are left neglected.

[tr. F. G. FOWLER]

XX

The Judgment of Paris

Zeus.   Hermes.   Hera.   Athene.   Aphrodite.   Paris

Zeus. Hermes, take this apple, and go with it to Phrygia; on the Gargaran peak of Ida you will find Priam's son, the herdsman. Give him this message: "Paris, because you are handsome, and wise in the things of love, Zeus commands you to judge between the Goddesses, and say which is the most beautiful. And the prize shall be this apple." — Now, you three, there is no time to be lost: away with you to your judge. I will have nothing to do with the matter: I love you all exactly alike, and I only wish you could all three win. If I were to give the prize to one of you, the other two would hate me, of course. In these circumstances, I am ill qualified to be your judge. But this young Phrygian to whom you are going is of the royal blood — a relation of Ganymede's, — and at the same time a simple country-man; so that we need have no hesitation in trusting his eyes.

Aph. As far as I am concerned, Zeus, Momus himself might be our judge; *I* should not be afraid to show myself. What fault could he find with *me*? But the others must agree too.

Hera. Oh, we are under no alarm, thank you, — though your admirer Ares should be appointed. But Paris will do; whoever Paris is.

Zeus. And my little Athene; have we her approval? Nay, never blush, nor hide your face. Well, well, maidens will be coy; 'tis a delicate subject. But there, she nods consent. Now, off with you; and mind, the beaten ones must not be cross with the judge; I will not have the poor lad harmed. The prize of beauty can be but one.

Herm. Now for Phrygia. I will show the way; keep close behind me, ladies, and don't be nervous. I know Paris well: he is a charming young man; a great gallant, and an admirable judge of beauty. Depend on it, he will make a good award.

Aph. I am glad to hear that; I ask for nothing better than a just judge. — Has he a wife, Hermes, or is he a bachelor?

Herm. Not exactly a bachelor.

Aph. What do you mean?

Herm. I believe there is a wife, as it were; a good enough sort of girl — a native of those parts — but sadly countrified! I fancy he does not care very much about her. — Why do you ask?

Aph. I just wanted to know.

Ath. Now, Hermes, that is not fair. No whispering with Aphrodite.

Herm. It was nothing, Athene; nothing about you. She only asked me whether Paris was a bachelor.

Ath. What business is that of hers?

Herm. None that I know of. She meant nothing by the question; she just wanted to know.

Ath. Well, and is he?

Herm. Why, no.

Ath. And does he care for military glory? has he ambition? or is he a *mere* neatherd?

Herm. I couldn't say for certain. But he is a young man, so it is to be presumed that distinction on the field of battle is among his desires.

Aph. There, you see; *I* don't complain; I say nothing when you whisper with *her*. Aphrodite is not so particular as some people.

Herm. Athene asked me almost exactly the same as you did; so don't be cross. It will do you no harm, my answering a plain ques-tion. — Meanwhile, we have left the stars far behind us, and are al-most over Phrygia. There is Ida: I can make out the peak of Gar-garum quite plainly; and if I am not mistaken, there is Paris himself.

Hera. Where is he?   I don't see him.

Herm. Look over there to the left, Hera: not on the top, but down the side, by that cave where you see the herd.

Hera. But I *don't* see the herd.

Herm. What, don't you see them coming out from between the rocks, — where I am pointing, look — and the man running down from the crag, and keeping them together with his staff?

Hera. I see him now; if he it is.

Herm. Oh, that is Paris.   But we are getting near; it is time to alight and walk.   He might be frightened, if we were to descend upon him so suddenly.

Hera. Yes; very well.   And now that we are on the earth, you might go on ahead, Aphrodite, and show us the way.   You know the country, of course, having been here so often to see Anchises; or so I have heard.

Aph. Your sneers are thrown away on me, Hera.

Herm. Come; I'll lead the way myself.   I spent some time on Ida, while Zeus was courting Ganymede.   Many is the time that I have been sent here to keep watch over the boy; and when at last the eagle came, I flew by his side, and helped him with his lovely burden. This is the very rock, if I remember; yes, Ganymede was piping to his sheep, when down swooped the eagle behind him, and tenderly, oh, so tenderly, caught him up in those talons, and with the turban in his beak bore him off, the frightened boy straining his neck the while to see his captor.   I picked up his pipes — he had dropped them in his fright — and — ah! here is our umpire, close at hand.   Let us accost him. — Good-morrow, herdsman!

Par. Good-morrow, youngster.   And who may you be, who come thus far afield?   And these dames?   They are over comely, to be wandering on the mountain-side.

Herm. "These dames," good Paris, are Hera, Athene, and Aphrodite; and I am Hermes, with a message from Zeus.   Why so pale and tremulous?   Compose yourself; there is nothing the matter. Zeus appoints you the judge of their beauty.   "Because you are handsome, and wise in the things of love" (so runs the message), "I leave the decision to you; and for the prize, — read the inscription on the apple."

Par. Let me see what it is about.   FOR THE FAIR, it says.   But, my lord Hermes, how shall a mortal and a rustic like myself be judge of such unparalleled beauty?   This is no sight for a herdsman's eyes; let the fine city folk decide on such matters.   As for me, I can tell you which of two goats is the fairer beast; or I can judge betwixt heifer and heifer; — 'tis my trade.   But here, where all are beautiful alike, I know not how a man may leave looking at one, to look upon another.   Where my eyes fall, there they fasten, — for there is beauty: I move them, and what do I find? more loveliness!   I am fixed again, yet distracted by neighbouring charms.   I bathe in beauty: I am enthralled: ah, why am I not *all* eyes like Argus?   Methinks it were a fair award, to give the apple to all three. Then again: one is the wife and sister of Zeus; the others are his daughters. Take it where you will, 'tis a hard matter to judge.

Herm. So it is, Paris. At the same time — Zeus's orders! There is no way out of it.

Par. Well, please point out to them, Hermes, that the losers must not be angry with me; the fault will be in my eyes only.

Herm. That is quite understood. And now to work.

Par. I must do what I can; there is no help for it. But first let me ask, — am I just to look at them as they are, or must I go into the matter thoroughly?

Herm. That is for you to decide, in virtue of your office. You have only to give your orders; it is as you think best.

Par. As I think best? Then I will be thorough.

Herm. Get ready, ladies. Now, Mr. Umpire. — I will look the other way.

Hera. I approve your decision, Paris. I will be the first to submit myself to your inspection. You shall see that I have more to boast of than white arms and large eyes: nought of me but is beautiful.

Par. Aphrodite, will you also prepare?

Ath. Oh, Paris, — make her take off that girdle, first; there is magic in it; she will bewitch you. For that matter, she has no right to come thus tricked out and painted, — just like a courtesan! She ought to show herself unadorned.

Par. They are right about the girdle, madam; it must go.

Aph. Oh, very well, Athene: then take off that helmet, and show your head bare, instead of trying to intimidate the judge with that waving plume. I suppose you are afraid the colour of your eyes may be noticed, without their formidable surroundings.

Ath. Oh, here is my helmet.

Aph. And here is my girdle.

Hera. Now then.

Par. God of wonders! What loveliness is here! Oh, rapture! How exquisite these maiden charms! How dazzling the majesty of Heaven's true queen! And oh, how sweet, how enthralling is Aphrodite's smile! 'Tis too much, too much of happiness. — But perhaps it would be well for me to view each in detail; for as yet I doubt, and know not where to look; my eyes are drawn all ways at once.

Aph. Yes, that will be best.

Par. Withdraw then, you and Athene; and let Hera remain.

Hera. So be it; and when you have finished your scrutiny, you have next to consider, how you would like the present which I offer you. Paris, give me the prize of beauty, and you shall be lord of all Asia.

Par. I will take no presents. Withdraw. I shall judge as I think right. Approach, Athene.

Ath. Behold. And, Paris, if you will say that I am the fairest, I will make you a great warrior and conqueror, and you shall always win, in every one of your battles.

Par. But I have nothing to do with fighting, Athene. As you see, there is peace throughout all Lydia and Phrygia, and my father's dominion is uncontested. But never mind: I am not going to take your present, but you shall have fair play. You can robe again and put on your helmet; I have seen. And now for Aphrodite.

Aph. Here I am; take your time, and examine carefully; let nothing escape your vigilance. And I have something else to say to you, handsome Paris. Yes, you handsome boy, I have long had an eye on you; I think you must be the handsomest young fellow in all Phrygia. But it is such a pity that you don't leave these rocks and crags, and live in a town: you will lose all your beauty in this desert. What have you to do with mountains? What satisfaction can your beauty give to a lot of cows? You ought to have been married long ago; not to any of these dowdy women hereabouts, but to some Greek girl; an Argive, perhaps, or a Corinthian, or a Spartan; Helen, now, is a Spartan, and such a pretty girl — quite as pretty as I am — and so susceptible! Why, if she once caught sight of *you,* she would give up everything, I am sure, to go with you, and a most devoted wife she would be. But you have heard of Helen, of course?

Par. No, ma'am; but I should like to hear all about her now.

Aph. Well, she is the daughter of Leda, the beautiful woman, you know, whom Zeus visited in the disguise of a swan.

Par. And what is she like?

Aph. She is fair, as might be expected from the swan, soft as down (she was hatched from an egg, you know), and such a lithe, graceful figure; and only think, she is so much admired, that there was a war because Theseus ran away with her; and she was a mere child then. And when she grew up, the very first men in Greece were suitors for her hand, and she was given to Menelaus, who is descended from Pelops. — Now, if you like, she shall be your wife.

Par. What, when she is married already?

Aph. Tut, child, you are a simpleton: *I* understand these things.

Par. I should like to understand them too.

Aph. You will set out for Greece on a tour of inspection: and when you get to Sparta, Helen will see you; and for the rest — her falling in love, and going back with you — that will be my affair.

Par. But that is what I cannot believe, — that she will forsake her husband to cross the seas with a stranger, a barbarian.

Aph. Trust me for that. I have two beautiful children, Love and Desire. They shall be your guides. Love will assail her in all his might, and compel her to love you: Desire will encompass you about, and make you desirable and lovely as himself; and I will be there to help. I can get the Graces to come too, and between us we shall prevail.

Par. How this will end, I know not. All I do know is, that I am in love with Helen already. I see her before me — I sail for Greece — I am in Sparta — I am on my homeward journey, with her at my side! Ah, why is none of it true?

Aph. Wait. Do not fall in love yet. You have first to secure my

interest with the bride, by your award. The union must be graced
with my victorious presence: your marriage-feast shall be my feast of
victory. Love, beauty, wedlock; all these you may purchase at the
price of yonder apple.

Par. But perhaps after the award you will forget all about *me*?

Aph. Shall I swear?

Par. No; but promise once more.

Aph. I promise that you shall have Helen to wife; that she shall
follow you, and make Troy her home; and I will be present with you,
and help you in all.

Par. And bring Love, and Desire, and the Graces?

Aph. Assuredly; and Passion and Hymen as well.

Par. Take the apple: it is yours.

[tr. F. G. FOWLER]

DIALOGUES OF THE DEAD

I

Diogenes. Pollux

Diog. Pollux, I have a commission for you; next time you go up —
and I think it is your turn for earth to-morrow — if you come across
Menippus the Cynic — you will find him about the Craneum at Corinth, or in the Lyceum, laughing at the philosophers' disputes — well,
give him this message: — Menippus, Diogenes advises you, if mortal
subjects for laughter begin to pall, to come down below, and find
much richer material; where you are now, there is always a dash of
uncertainty in it; the question will always intrude — who can be quite
sure about the hereafter? Here, you can have your laugh out in
security, like me; it is the best of sport to see millionaires, governors,
despots, now mean and insignificant; you can only tell them by their
lamentations, and the spiritless despondency which is the legacy of
better days. Tell him this, and mention that he had better stuff his
wallet with plenty of lupines, and any unconsidered trifles he can
snap up in the way of pauper doles or lustral eggs.

Pol. I will tell him, Diogenes. But give me some idea of his appearance.

Diog. Old, bald, with a cloak that allows him plenty of light and
ventilation, and is patched all colours of the rainbow; always laughing, and usually gibing at pretentious philosophers.

Pol. Ah, I cannot mistake him now.

Diog. May I give you another message to those same philosophers?

Pol. Oh, I don't mind; go on.

Diog. Charge them generally to give up playing the fool, quarrelling over metaphysics, tricking each other with horn and crocodile
puzzles, and teaching people to waste wit on such absurdities.

Pol. Oh, but if I say anything against their wisdom, they will call
me an ignorant blockhead.

Diog. Then tell them from me to go to the devil.

Pol. Very well; rely upon me.

Diog. And then, my most obliging of Polluxes, there is this for the rich:— O vain fools, why hoard gold? why all these pains over interest sums and the adding of hundred to hundred, when you must shortly come to us with nothing beyond the dead-penny?

Pol. They shall have their message too.

Diog. Ah, and a word to the handsome and strong; Megillus of Corinth, and Damoxenus the wrestler will do. Inform them that auburn locks, eyes bright or black, rosy cheeks, are as little in fashion here as tense muscles or mighty shoulders; man and man are as like as two peas, tell them, when it comes to bare skull and no beauty.

Pol. That is to the handsome and strong; yes, I can manage that.

Diog. Yes, my Spartan, and here is for the poor. There are a great many of them, very sorry for themselves and resentful of their helplessness. Tell them to dry their tears and cease their cries; explain to them that here one man is as good as another, and they will find those who were rich on earth no better than themselves. As for your Spartans, you will not mind scolding them, from me, upon their present degeneracy?

Pol. No, no, Diogenes; leave Sparta alone; that is going too far; your other commissions I will execute.

Diog. Oh, well, let them off, if you care about it; but tell all the others what I said.

[tr. H. W. Fowler]

XXII

Charon. Menippus. Hermes

Ch. Your fare, you rascal.

Me. Bawl away, Charon, if it gives you any pleasure.

Ch. I brought you across: give me my fare.

Me. I can't, if I haven't got it.

Ch. And who is so poor that he has not got a penny?

Me. I for one; I don't know who else.

Ch. Pay: or, by Pluto, I'll strangle you.

Me. And I'll crack your skull with this stick.

Ch. So you are to come all that way for nothing?

Me. Let Hermes pay for me: he put me on board.

Her. I dare say! A fine time I shall have of it, if I am to pay for the shades.

Ch. I'm not going to let you off.

Me. You can haul up your ship and wait, for all I care. If I have not got the money, I can't pay you, can I?

Ch. You knew you ought to bring it?

Me. I knew that: but I hadn't got it. What would you have? I ought not to have died, I suppose?

Ch. So you are to have the distinction of being the only passenger that ever crossed gratis?

Me. Oh, come now: gratis! I took an oar, and I baled; and I didn't cry, which is more than can be said for any of the others.

Ch. That's neither here nor there. I must have my penny; it's only right.

Me. Well, you had better take me back again to life.

Ch. Yes, and get a thrashing from Aeacus for my pains! I like that.

Me. Well, don't bother me.

Ch. Let me see what you have got in that wallet.

Me. Beans: have some? — and a Hecate's supper.

Ch. Where did you pick up this Cynic, Hermes? The noise he made on the crossing, too! laughing and jeering at all the rest, and singing, when every one else was at his lamentations.

Her. Ah, Charon, you little know your passenger! Independence, every inch of him: he cares for no one. 'Tis Menippus.

Ch. Wait till I catch you —

Me. Precisely; I'll wait — till you catch me again.

[tr. F. G. Fowler]

BIOGRAPHY

PLUTARCH

(*ca.* 45–*ca.* 125 A.D.)

As a result of Shakespeare's use of the *Parallel Lives* as sources for *Coriolanus, Julius Caesar,* and *Antony and Cleopatra,* Plutarch will always have a special interest for English readers. Plutarch was a native of Chaeronea, a small town in Boeotia; after a long and successful career at Athens and Rome as a popular lecturer on morals and philosophy, he retired to his birthplace and spent the last years of his life there engaged in writing. It will be noted that his later years coincide with one of the most prosperous periods of ancient times, the age of the Antonines, when the Roman Empire reached its greatest heights of material comfort and political stability. The age fostered education and the arts; schools and universities flourished under imperial patronage; interest in literature and philosophy was widespread. But it was not a period of great creative power, and the quality of most of its literature suggests that it was drawing on the accumulated spiritual reserves of the past. Thus, Plutarch turned to the past for inspiration and found in the lives of the great figures of Greek and Roman history moral values for his own times. Yet he brings to this task no profound insight or philosophic vision; he merely passes judgment on his subjects in accordance with the traditional and conventional moral standards of antiquity.

The works of Plutarch fall into two groups: the *Moralia,* a collection of miscellaneous essays on philosophic and ethical subjects; and the *Lives,* a collection of fifty biographies of notable Greeks and Romans, which are, for the most part, arranged in pairs, a Greek followed by a Roman counterpart (e.g., Demosthenes and Cicero, Alexander and Caesar); and the pair of lives is usually followed by a short comparison of the two men. Since Plutarch's fame rests chiefly on these lives, the rest of this introduction must be devoted to a short consideration of biographical literature in antiquity. For an adequate understanding of the following selections, two points must be treated: first, Plutarch's predecessors in this form, and second, Plutarch's own aims and methods in writing biography.

Although what has aptly been called the commemorative spirit is apparent from the earliest period of Greek literature (as, for example, in the mourning for Hector at the end of the *Iliad*), formal biography was a product of the fourth century B.C., the first great era of individualism in Greek history. The tendency of this age may be seen in the sketch of Agesilaus by Xenophon or the encomium of Evagoras by Isocrates, although both works are probably closer to an earlier poetic form, the lyric *encomion,* than to biography in our sense. Philosophy contributed largely to the new trend: for Socrates had been one of the first thinkers to shift the emphasis of philosophy to the individual man and his inner, or spiritual life. Later in the fourth century, Aristotle turned philosophy to the study of individual things; and in his *Ethics* he carefully classifies and analyzes the various types of men and the aspects of man as a moral being. His pupil and successor, Theophrastus, carried this kind of analysis one step further in the *Characters,* in which the type has been individualized by the addition of certain realistic details. But in keeping with the Aristotelian tradition, Theophrastus' emphasis is still on morality; for in these little sketches he is conveying moral criticism in the manner of satire. The step from this sort of character sketch to formal biography is easy and natural; instead of the particularized type, the writer can portray the real, historical individual. Among the followers of Aristotle, the Peripatetics, a type of biographical writing developed in which the author aimed at giving a complete picture of the subject, the individual man, as a moral being, whose true nature was to be found in his moral activity. Biography thus preserves the moral emphasis of philosophy, and there is, as a result, a conviction that the reader would derive moral benefit from the contemplation of others' lives when portrayed in this fashion.

Plutarch clearly belongs to this tradition of ancient biography. He warns us not to expect full and accurate historical treatments. "It must be borne in mind (he writes) that my design is not to write histories, but lives. And the most glorious exploits do not always furnish us with the clearest discoveries of virtue or vice in men; sometimes a matter of less moment, an expression or a jest, informs us better of their characters and inclinations than the most famous sieges, the greatest armaments, or the bloodiest battles whatsoever. Therefore as portrait-painters are more exact in the lines and features of the face, in which the character is seen, than in the other parts of the body, so I must be allowed to give my more particular attention to the marks and indications of the souls of men, and while I endeavour by these to portray their lives, may be free to leave more weighty matters and great battles to be treated of by others." (*Alexander,* Preface.) To Plutarch, the significant actions of men are those which reveal moral characteristics; for example, the little anecdote about Caesar's desire for an unexpected death (see p. 871) tells us more about Caesar's character than a detailed discussion of the battle of Pharsalus. Not that Plutarch was ignorant of history: he had read widely, but not critically, and he could never resist a good story. More well-known anecdotes about the famous men of antiquity come from his pages than from any other single source; and this fact will serve to explain his extraordinary popularity in Western culture.

Plutarch has no doubts about the moral benefits to be derived from the study of biography. "It was for the sake of others that I first commenced writing biographies; but I find myself proceeding and attaching myself to it for my own; the virtues of these great men serving me as a sort of looking-glass, in which I may see how to adjust and adorn my own life. Indeed, it can be compared to nothing but daily living and associating together; we receive, as it were, in our inquiry, and entertain each successive guest, view 'their stature and their qualities,' and select from their actions all that is noblest and worthiest to know. 'Ah, and what greater pleasure can one have?' . . . My method is, by the study of history, and by the familiarity acquired in writing, to habituate my memory to receive and retain images of the best and worthiest characters. I am thus able to free myself from any ignoble, base, or vicious impressions, contracted from the contagion of ill company that I may be unavoidably engaged in, by the remedy of turning my thoughts in a happy and calm temper to view these noble examples." (*Timoleon,* Preface.) This is a refreshing point of view and worth considering in an age which has come to believe that the chief purpose of biography is to put down the mighty from their seats.

In conclusion, it should be mentioned that Plutarch was a deeply pious man. He held a priesthood of the Delphic Apollo and took his duties seriously. He had a serene assurance that virtue triumphs in the end, whether in this world or the next, and he remained confident that the universe is governed by a divine and just Providence. In philosophy he was an eclectic, but he was strongly attracted to the quasi-religious mysticism of Plato, which formed the religion of many educated men of his time.

LYCURGUS

[Lycurgus was the semi-legendary king and lawgiver of Sparta, to whom all the peculiar institutions of the Spartans were ascribed. Since few details of his life were known for certain, the greater part of this biography is devoted to a sympathetic and highly imaginative description of the Lacedaemonian way of life — a description that possibly reflects more of Plato's ideal Republic than of the actual conditions in historic Sparta. The selections which follow deal with the famous Spartan education and discipline.]

Lycurgus would never reduce his laws into writing; nay there is a Rhetra expressly to forbid it. For he thought that the most material points, and such as most directly tended to the public welfare, being imprinted on the hearts of their youth by a good discipline, would be sure to remain, and would find a stronger security, than any compulsion would be, in the principles of action formed in them by their best lawgiver, education. And as for things of lesser importance, as pecuniary contracts, and such like, the forms of which have to be changed as occasion requires, he thought it the best way to prescribe no positive rule or inviolable usage in such cases, willing that their manner and form should be altered according to the circumstances of time, and determinations of men of sound judgment. Every end and object of law and enactment it was his design education should effect. . .

In order to the good education of their youth (which, as I said before, he thought the most important and noblest work of a lawgiver), he went so far back as to take into consideration their very conception and birth, by regulating their marriages. For Aristotle is wrong in saying, that, after he had tried all ways to reduce the women to more modesty and sobriety, he was at last forced to leave them as they were, because that in the absence of their husbands, who spent the best part of their lives in the wars, their wives, whom they were obliged to leave absolute mistresses at home, took great liberties and assumed the superiority; and were treated with overmuch respect and called by the title of lady or queen. The truth is, he took in their case, also, all the care that was possible; he ordered the maidens to exercise themselves with wrestling, running, throwing the quoit, and casting the dart, to the end that the fruit they conceived might, in strong and healthy bodies, take firmer root and find better growth, and withal that they, with this greater vigour, might be the more able to undergo the pains of child-bearing. And to the end he might take away their overgreat tenderness and fear of exposure to the air, and all acquired womanishness, he ordered that the young women should go naked in the processions, as well as the young men, and dance, too, in that condition, at certain solemn feasts, singing certain songs, whilst the young men stood around, seeing and hearing them. On these occasions they now and then made, by jests, a befitting reflection upon those who had misbehaved themselves in the wars; and again sang encomiums upon those who had done any gallant action, and by these means inspired the younger sort with an emulation of their glory. Those that were thus commended went away proud, elated, and gratified with their honour among the maidens; and those who were rallied were as sensibly touched with it as if they had been formally reprimanded; and so much the more, because the kings and the elders, as well as the rest of the city, saw and heard all that passed. Nor was there anything shameful in this nakedness of the young women; modesty attended them, and all wantonness was excluded. It taught them simplicity and a care for good health, and gave them some taste of higher feelings, admitted as they thus were to the field of noble action and glory. Hence it was natural for them to think and speak as Gorgo, for example, the wife of Leonidas, is said to have done, when some foreign lady, as it would seem, told her that the women of Lacedæmon were the only women in the world who could rule men; "With good reason," she said, "for we are the only women who bring forth men."

These public processions of the maidens, and their appearing naked in their exercises and dancings, were incitements to marriage, operating upon the young with the rigour and certainty, as Plato says, of love, if not of mathematics. But besides all this, to promote it yet more effectually, those who continued bachelors were in a degree disfranchised by law; for they were excluded from the sight of those public processions in which the young men and maidens danced naked, and, in winter-time, the officers compelled them to march naked themselves round the market-place, singing as they went a certain song to their own disgrace, that they justly suffered this punishment for disobeying the laws. Moreover, they were denied that respect and observance which the younger men paid their elders; and no man, for example, found fault with what was said to Dercyllidas, though so eminent a commander; upon whose approach one day, a young man, instead of rising, retained his seat, remarking, "No child of yours will make room for me."

In their marriages, the husband carried off his bride by a sort of force; nor were their brides ever small and of tender years, but in their full bloom and ripeness. After this, she who superintended the wedding comes and clips the hair of the bride close round her head, dresses her up in man's clothes, and leaves her upon a mattress in the dark; afterwards comes the bridegroom, in his everyday clothes, sober and composed, as having supped at the common table, and, entering privately into the room where the bride lies, unties her virgin zone, and takes her to himself; and, after staying some time together, he returns composedly to his own apartment, to sleep as usual with the other young men. And so he continues to do, spending his days, and, indeed, his nights, with them, visiting his bride in fear and shame, and with circumspection, when he thought he should not be observed; she, also, on her part, using her wit to help and find favourable opportunities for their meeting, when company was out of the way. In this manner they lived a long time, insomuch that they sometimes had children by their wives before ever they saw their faces by daylight. Their interviews, being thus difficult and rare, served not only for continual exercise of their self-control, but brought them together with their bodies healthy and vigorous, and their affections fresh and lively, unsated and undulled by easy access and long continuance with each other; while their partings were always early enough to leave behind unextinguished in each of them some remaining fire of longing and mutual delight. After guarding marriage with this modesty and reserve, he was equally careful to banish empty and womanish jealousy. For this object, excluding all licentious disorders, he made it, nevertheless, honourable for men to give the use of their wives to those whom they should think fit, that so they might have children by them; ridiculing those in whose opinion such favours are so unfit for participation as to fight and shed blood and go to war about it. Lycurgus allowed a man who was advanced in years and had a young wife to recommend some virtuous and approved young man, that she might have a child by him, who might inherit the good qualities of the father, and be a son to himself. On the other side, an honest man who had love for a married woman upon account of her modesty and the well-favouredness of her children, might, without formality, beg her company of her husband, that he might raise, as it were, from this plot of good ground, worthy and well-allied children for himself. And indeed, Lycurgus was of a persuasion that children were not so much the property of their parents as of the whole commonwealth, and, therefore, would not have his citizens begot by the first-comers, but by the best men that could be found; the laws of other nations seemed to him very absurd and inconsistent, where people would be so solicitous for their dogs and horses as to exert interest and to pay money to procure fine breeding, and yet kept their wives shut up, to be made mothers only by themselves, who might be foolish, infirm, or diseased; as if it were not apparent that children of a bad breed would prove their bad qualities first upon those who kept and were rearing them, and well-born children, in like manner, their good qualities. These regulations, founded on natural and social grounds, were certainly so far from that scandalous liberty which was afterwards charged upon their women, that they knew not what adultery meant. It is told, for instance, of Geradas, a very ancient Spartan, that, being asked by a stranger what punishment their law had appointed for adulterers, he answered, "There are no adulterers in our country." "But," replied the stranger, "suppose there were?" "Then," answered he, "the offender would have to give the plaintiff a bull with a neck so long as that he might drink from the top of Taygetus of the Eurotas river below it." The man, surprised at this, said, "Why, 'tis impossible to find such a bull." Geradas smiling replied, " 'Tis as possible as to find an adulterer in Sparta." So much I had to say of their marriages.

Nor was it in the power of the father to dispose of the child as he thought fit; he was obliged to carry it before certain triers at a place called Lesche; these were some of the elders of the tribe to which the child belonged; their business it was carefully to view the infant, and, if they found it stout and well made, they gave order for its rearing, and allotted to it one of the nine thousand shares of land above mentioned for its maintenance, but, if they found it puny and ill-shaped, ordered it to be taken to what was called the Apothetæ, a sort of chasm under Taygetus; as thinking it neither for the good of the child itself, nor for the public interest, that it should be brought up, if it did not, from the very outset, appear made to be healthy and vigorous. Upon the same account, the women did not bathe the new-born children with water, as is the custom in all other countries, but with wine, to prove the temper and complexion of their bodies; from a notion they had that epileptic and weakly children faint and waste away upon their being thus bathed, while, on the contrary, those of a strong and vigorous habit acquire firmness and get a temper by it, like steel. There was much care and art, too, used by the nurses; they had no swaddling bands; the children grew up free and unconstrained in limb and form, and not dainty and fanciful about their food; not afraid in the dark, or of being left alone; and without peevishness, or ill-humour, or crying. Upon this account Spartan nurses were often bought up, or hired by people of other countries; and it is recorded that she who suckled Alcibiades was a Spartan; who, however, if fortunate in his nurse, was not so in his preceptor; his guardian, Pericles, as Plato tells us, chose a servant for that office called Zopyrus, no better than any common slave.

Lycurgus was of another mind; he would not have masters bought out of the market for his young Spartans, nor such as should sell their pains; nor was it lawful, indeed, for the father himself to breed up the children after his own fancy; but as soon as they were seven years old they were to be enrolled in certain companies and classes, where they all lived under the same order and discipline, doing their exercises and taking their play together. Of these, he who showed the most conduct and courage was made captain; they had their eyes always upon him, obeyed his orders, and underwent patiently whatsoever punishment he inflicted; so that the whole course of their education was one continued exercise of a ready and perfect obedience. The old men, too, were spectators of their performances, and often raised quarrels and disputes among them, to have a good opportunity of finding out their different characters, and of seeing which would be valiant, which a coward, when they should come to more dangerous encounters. Reading and writing they gave them, just enough to serve their turn; their chief care was to make them good subjects, and to teach them to endure pain and conquer in battle. To this end, as they grew in years, their discipline was proportionately increased; their heads were close-clipped, they were accustomed to go barefoot, and for the most part to play naked.

After they were twelve years old, they were no longer allowed to wear any undergarments; they had one coat to serve them a year; their bodies were hard and dry, with but little acquaintance of baths and unguents; these human indulgences they were allowed only on some few particular days in the year. They lodged together in little bands upon beds made of the rushes which grew by the banks of the river Eurotas, which they were to break off with their hands without a knife; if it were winter, they mingled some thistle-down with their rushes, which it was thought had the property of giving warmth. By the time they were come to this age there was not any of the more hopeful boys who had not a lover to bear him company. The old men, too, had an eye upon them, coming often to the grounds to hear and see them contend either in wit or strength with one another, and this as seriously and with as much concern as if they were their fathers, their tutors, or their magistrates; so that there scarcely was any time or place without some one present to put them in mind of their duty, and punish them if they had neglected it.

Besides all this, there was always one of the best and honestest men in the city appointed to undertake the charge and governance of them; he again arranged them into their several bands, and set over each of them for their captain the most temperate and boldest of those they called Irens, who were usually twenty years old, two years out of the boys; and the oldest of the boys, again, were Mell-Irens, as much as to say, who would shortly be men. This young man, therefore, was their captain when they fought and their master at home, using them for the offices of his house; sending the eldest of them to fetch wood, and the weaker and less able to gather salads and herbs, and these they must either go without or steal; which they did by creeping into the gardens, or conveying themselves cunningly and closely into the eating-houses; if they were taken in the fact, they were whipped without mercy, for thieving so ill and awkwardly.

They stole, too, all other meat they could lay their hands on, looking out and watching all opportunities, when people were asleep or more careless than usual. If they were caught, they were not only punished with whipping, but hunger, too, being reduced to their ordinary allowance, which was but very slender, and so contrived on purpose, that they might set about to help themselves, and be forced to exercise their energy and address. This was the principal design of their hard fare; there was another not inconsiderable, that they might grow taller; for the vital spirits, not being overburdened and oppressed by too great a quantity of nourishment, which necessarily discharges itself into thickness and breadth, do, by their natural lightness, rise; and the body, giving and yielding because it is pliant, grows in height. The same thing seems, also, to conduce to beauty of shape; a dry and lean habit is a better subject for nature's configuration, which the gross and over-fed are too heavy to submit to properly. Just as we find that women who take physic whilst they are with child, bear leaner and smaller but better-shaped and prettier children; the material they come of having been more pliable and easily moulded. The reason, however, I leave others to determine.

To return from whence we have digressed. So seriously did the Lacedæmonian children go about their stealing, that a youth, having stolen a young fox and hid it under his coat, suffered it to tear out his very bowels with its teeth and claws and died upon the place, rather than let it be seen. What is practised to this very day in Lacedæmon is enough to gain credit to this story, for I myself have seen several of the youths endure whipping to death at the foot of the altar of Diana surnamed Orthia.

The Iren, or under-master, used to stay a little with them after supper, and one of them he bade to sing a song, to another he put a question which required an advised and deliberate answer; for example, Who was the best man in the city? What he thought of such an action of such a man? They used them thus early to pass a right judgment upon persons and things, and to inform themselves of the abilities or defects of their countrymen. If they had not an answer ready to the question, Who was a good or who an ill-reputed citizen, they were looked upon as of a dull and careless disposition, and to have little or no sense of virtue and honour; besides this, they were to give a good reason for what they said, and in as few words and as comprehensive as might be; he that failed of this, or answered not to the purpose, had his thumb bit by the master. Sometimes the Iren did this in the presence of the old men and magistrates, that they might see whether he punished them justly and in due measure or not, and when he did amiss, they would not reprove him before the boys, but, when they were gone, he was called to an account and underwent correction, if he had run far into either of the extremes of indulgence or severity.

Their lovers and favourers, too, had a share in the young boy's honour or disgrace; and there goes a story that one of them was fined by the magistrate, because the lad whom he loved cried out

effeminately as he was fighting. And though this sort of love was
so approved among them, that the most virtuous matrons would make
professions of it to young girls, yet rivalry did not exist, and if several
men's fancies met in one person, it was rather the beginning of an
intimate friendship, whilst they all jointly conspired to render the
object of their effection as accomplished as possible.

[13–18, tr. DRYDEN-CLOUGH]

To return to the Lacedæmonians. Their discipline continued still
after they were full-grown men. No one was allowed to live after
his own fancy; but the city was a sort of camp, in which every man
had his share of provisions and business set out, and looked upon
himself not so much born to serve his own ends as the interest of his
country. Therefore if they were commanded nothing else, they went
to see the boys perform their exercises, to teach them something useful or to learn it themselves of those who knew better. And indeed
one of the greatest and highest blessings Lycurgus procured his people was the abundance of leisure which proceeded from his forbidding
to them the exercise of any mean and mechanical trade. Of the
money-making that depends on troublesome going about and seeing
people and doing business, they had no need at all in a state where
wealth obtained no honour or respect. The Helots tilled their
ground for them, and paid them yearly in kind the appointed quantity, without any trouble of theirs. To this purpose there goes a
story of a Lacedæmonian who, happening to be at Athens when the
courts were sitting, was told of a citizen that had been fined for living
an idle life, and was being escorted home in much distress of mind by
his condoling friends; the Lacedæmonian was much surprised at it
and desired his friend to show him the man who was condemned
for living like a freeman. So much beneath them did they esteem
the frivolous devotion of time and attention to the mechanical arts
and to money-making.

It need not be said that upon the prohibition of gold and silver, all
lawsuits immediately ceased, for there was now neither avarice nor
poverty amongst them, but equality, where every one's wants were
supplied, and independence, because those wants were so small. All
their time, except when they were in the field, was taken up by the
choral dances and the festivals, in hunting, and in attendance on the
exercise-grounds and the places of public conversation. Those who
were under thirty years of age were not allowed to go into the
market-place, but had the necessaries of their family supplied by the
care of their relations and lovers; nor was it for the credit of elderly
men to be seen too often in the market-place; it was esteemed more
suitable for them to frequent the exercise-grounds and places of conversation, where they spent their leisure rationally in conversation,
not on money-making and market-prices, but for the most part in
passing judgment on some action worth considering; extolling the
good, and censuring those who were otherwise, and that in a light
and sportive manner, conveying, without too much gravity, lessons

of advice and improvement. Nor was Lycurgus himself unduly
austere; it was he who dedicated, says Sosibius, the little statue of
Laughter. Mirth, introduced seasonably at their suppers and places
of common entertainment, was to serve as a sort of sweetmeat to
accompany their strict and hard life. To conclude, he bred up his
citizens in such a way that they neither would nor could live by themselves; they were to make themselves one with the public good, and,
clustering like bees around their commander, be by their zeal and
public spirit carried all but out of themselves, and devoted wholly to
their country. What their sentiments were will better appear by a
few of their sayings. Pædaretus, not being admitted into the list of
the three hundred, returned home with a joyful face, well pleased to
find that there were in Sparta three hundred better men than himself.
And Polycratidas, being sent with some others ambassador to the
lieutenants of the king of Persia, being asked by them whether they
came in a private or in a public character, answered, "In a public, if
we succeed; if not, in a private character." Argileonis, asking some
who came from Amphipolis if her son Brasidas died courageously
and as became a Spartan, on their beginning to praise him to a high
degree, and saying there was not such another left in Sparta, answered,
"Do not say so; Brasidas was a good and brave man, but there are
in Sparta many better than he."

The senate, as I said before, consisted of those who were Lycurgus's
chief aiders and assistants in his plans. The vacancies he ordered to
be supplied out of the best and most deserving men past sixty years
old, and we need not wonder if there was much striving for it; for
what more glorious competition could there be amongst men, than
one in which it was not contested who was swiftest among the swift
or strongest of the strong, but who of many wise and good was wisest
and best, and fittest to be intrusted for ever after, as the reward of
his merits, with the supreme authority of the commonwealth, and
with power over the lives, franchises, and highest interests of all his
countrymen? The manner of their election was as follows: The
people being called together, some selected persons were locked up
in a room near the place of election, so contrived that they could
neither see nor be seen, but could only hear the noise of the assembly
without; for they decided this, as most other affairs of moment, by the
shouts of the people. This done, the competitors were not brought
in and presented all together, but one after another by lot, and passed
in order through the assembly without speaking a word. Those
who were locked up had writing-tables with them, in which they
recorded and marked each shout by its loudness, without knowing in
favour of which candidate each of them was made, but merely that
they came first, second, third, and so forth. He who was found to
have the most and loudest acclamations was declared senator duly
elected. Upon this he had a garland set upon his head, and went in
procession to all the temples to give thanks to the gods; a great number of young men followed him with applauses, and women, also,
singing verses in his honour, and extolling the virtue and happiness

of his life. As he went round the city in this manner, each of his relations and friends set a table before him, saying "The city honours you with this banquet"; but he, instead of accepting, passed round to the common table where he formerly used to eat, and was served as before, excepting that now he had a second allowance, which he took and put by. By the time supper was ended, the women who were of kin to him had come about the door; and he, beckoning to her whom he most esteemed, presented to her the portion he had saved, saying, that it had been a mark of esteem to him, and was so now to her; upon which she was triumphantly waited upon home by the women.

Touching burials, Lycurgus made very wise regulations; for, first of all, to cut off all superstition, he allowed them to bury their dead within the city, and even round about their temples, to the end that their youth might be accustomed to such spectacles, and not be afraid to see a dead body, or imagine that to touch a corpse or to tread upon a grave would defile a man. In the next place, he commanded them to put nothing into the ground with them, except, if they pleased, a few olive leaves, and the scarlet cloth that they were wrapped in. He would not suffer the names to be inscribed, except only of men who fell in the wars, or women who died in a sacred office. The time, too, appointed for mourning, was very short, eleven days; on the twelfth, they were to do sacrifice to Ceres, and leave it off; so that we may see, that as he cut off all superfluity, so in things necessary there was nothing so small and trivial which did not express some homage of virtue or scorn of vice. He filled Lacedæmon all through with proofs and examples of good conduct; with the constant sight of which from their youth up the people would hardly fail to be gradually formed and advanced in virtue.

And this was the reason why he forbade them to travel abroad, and go about acquainting themselves with foreign rules of morality, the habits of ill-educated people, and different views of government. Withal he banished from Lacedæmon all strangers who would not give a very good reason for their coming thither; not because he was afraid lest they should inform themselves of and imitate his manner of government (as Thucydides says), or learn anything to their good; but rather lest they should introduce something contrary to good manners. With strange people, strange words must be admitted; these novelties produce novelties in thought; and on these follow views and feelings whose discordant character destroys the harmony of the state. He was as careful to save his city from the infection of foreign bad habits, as men usually are to prevent the introduction of a pestilence.

Hitherto I, for my part, see no sign of injustice or want of equity in the laws of Lycurgus, though some who admit them to be well contrived to make good soldiers, pronounce them defective in point of justice. The Cryptia, perhaps (if it were one of Lycurgus's ordinances, as Aristotle says it was), gave both him and Plato, too, this opinion alike of the lawgiver and his government. By this ordinance, the magistrates despatched privately some of the ablest of the young men into the country, from time to time, armed only with their daggers, and taking a little necessary provision with them; in the daytime, they hid themselves in out-of-the-way places, and there lay close, but in the night issued out into the highways, and killed all the Helots they could light upon; sometimes they set upon them by day, as they were at work in the fields, and murdered them. As, also, Thucydides, in his history of the Peloponnesian war, tells us, that a good number of them, after being singled out for their bravery by the Spartans, garlanded, as enfranchised persons, and led about to all the temples in token of honours, shortly after disappeared all of a sudden, being about the number of two thousand; and no man either then or since could give an account how they came by their deaths. And Aristotle, in particular, adds, that the ephori, so soon as they were entered into their office, used to declare war against them, that they might be massacred without a breach of religion. It is confessed, on all hands, that the Spartans dealt with them very hardly; for it was a common thing to force them to drink to excess, and to lead them in that condition into their public halls, that the children might see what a sight a drunken man is; they made them to dance low dances, and sing ridiculous songs, forbidding them expressly to meddle with any of a better kind. And accordingly, when the Thebans made their invasion into Laconia,* and took a great number of the Helots, they could by no means persuade them to sing the verses of Terpander, Alcman, or Spendon, "For," said they, "the masters do not like it." So that it was truly observed by one, that in Sparta he who was free was most so, and he that was a slave there, the greatest slave in the world. For my part, I am of opinion that these outrages and cruelties began to be exercised in Sparta at a later time, especially after the great earthquake, when the Helots made a general insurrection, and, joining with the Messenians, laid the country waste, and brought the greatest danger upon the city. For I cannot persuade myself to ascribe to Lycurgus so wicked and barbarous a course, judging of him from the gentleness of his disposition and justice upon all other occasions; to which the oracle also testified.

[24–28, tr. DRYDEN-CLOUGH]

SOLON

[The great Athenian lawgiver was made sole archon (probably 594 B.C.) to relieve the oppressed debtor class and to reform the constitution. In this biography Plutarch tells how he might have seized and held the government as tyrant, and then quotes some lines of Solon himself, in which he says that the people mocked him for letting such an opportunity slip.]

Thus he makes the many and the low people speak of him. Yet, though he refused the government, he was not too mild in the affair; he did not show himself mean and submissive to the powerful, nor make his laws to pleasure those that chose him. For where it was

* In 370 B.C. after the battle of Leuctra.

well before, he applied no remedy, nor altered anything, for fear lest —

"Overthrowing altogether and disordering the state,"

he should be too weak to new-model and recompose it to a tolerable condition; but what he thought he could effect by persuasion upon the pliable, and by force upon the stubborn, this he did, as he himself says —

"With force and justice working both in one."

And, therefore, when he was afterwards asked if he had left the Athenians the best laws that could be given, he replied, "The best they could receive." The way which, the moderns say, the Athenians have of softening the badness of a thing, by ingeniously giving it some pretty and innocent appellation, calling harlots, for example, mistresses, tributes customs, a garrison a guard, and the jail the chamber, seem originally to have been Solon's contrivance, who called cancelling debts Seisacthea, a relief, or disencumbrance. For the first thing which he settled was, that what debts remained should be forgiven, and no man, for the future, should engage the body of his debtor for security. Though some, as Androtion, affirm that the debts were not cancelled, but the interest only lessened, which sufficiently pleased the people; so that they named this benefit the Seisacthea, together with the enlarging their measures, and raising the value of their money; for he made a pound, which before passed for seventy-three drachmas, go for a hundred; so that, though the number of pieces in the payment was equal, the value was less; which proved a considerable benefit to those that were to discharge great debts, and no loss to the creditors. But most agree that it was the taking off the debts that was called Seisacthea, which is confirmed by some places in his poem, where he takes honour to himself, that —

"The mortgage-stones that covered her, by me
Removed, — the land that was a slave is free:"

that some who had been seized for their debts he had brought back from other countries, where —

" — so far their lot to roam,
They had forgot the language of their home;"

and some he had set at liberty —

"Who here in shameful servitude were held." *

While he was designing this, a most vexatious thing happened; for when he had resolved to take off the debts, and was considering the proper form and fit beginning for it, he told some of his friends, Conon, Clinias, and Hipponicus, in whom he had a great deal of confidence, that he would not meddle with the lands, but only free the people from their debts; upon which they, using their advantage,

* Cf. Solon, *The Cancelling of Debts*, p. 977.

made haste and borrowed some considerable sums of money, and purchased some large farms; and when the law was enacted, they kept the possessions, and would not return the money; which brought Solon into great suspicion and dislike, as if he himself had not been abused, but was concerned in the contrivance. But he presently stopped this suspicion, by releasing his debtors of five talents (for he had lent so much), according to the law; others, as Polyzelus the Rhodian, say fifteen; his friends, however, were ever afterward called Chreocopidæ, repudiators.

In this he pleased neither party, for the rich were angry for their money, and the poor that the land was not divided, and, as Lycurgus ordered in his commonwealth, all men reduced to equality. He, it is true, being the eleventh from Hercules, and having reigned many years in Lacedæmon, had got a great reputation and friends and power, which he could use in modelling his state; and applying force more than persuasion, insomuch that he lost his eye in the scuffle, was able to employ the most effectual means for the safety and harmony of a state, by not permitting any to be poor or rich in his common-wealth. Solon could not rise to that in his polity, being but a citizen of the middle classes; yet he acted fully up to the height of his power, having nothing but the good-will and good opinion of his citizens to rely on; and that he offended the most part, who looked for another result, he declares in the words —

"Formerly they boasted of me vainly; with averted eyes
Now they look askance upon me; friends no more, but enemies."

And yet had any other man, he says, received the same power —

"He would not have forborne, nor let alone,
But made the fattest of the milk his own."

Soon, however, becoming sensible of the good that was done, they laid by their grudges, made a public sacrifice, calling it Seisacthea, and chose Solon to new-model and make laws for the commonwealth, giving him the entire power over everything, their magistracies, their assemblies, courts, and councils; that he should appoint the number, times of meeting, and what estate they must have that could be capable of these, and dissolve or continue any of the present constitutions, according to his pleasure.

[15-16, tr. DRYDEN-CLOUGH]

[For the setting of this famous interview between Solon and Croesus, see the selection from Herodotus printed on pp. 703-705.]

That Solon should discourse with Crœsus, some think not agreeable with chronology; but I cannot reject so famous and well-attested a narrative, and, what is more, so agreeable to Solon's temper, and so worthy his wisdom and greatness of mind, because, forsooth, it does not agree with some chronological canons, which thousands have endeavoured to regulate, and yet, to this day, could never bring their differing opinions to any agreement. They say, therefore, that Solon, coming to Crœsus at his request, was in the same condition as an inland man when first he goes to see the sea; for as he fancies every river he meets with to be the ocean, so Solon, as he passed through the court, and saw a great many nobles richly dressed, and proudly attended with a multitude of guards and footboys, thought every one had been the king, till he was brought to Crœsus, who was decked with every possible rarity and curiosity, in ornaments of jewels, purple, and gold, that could make a grand and gorgeous spectacle of him. Now when Solon came before him, and seemed not at all surprised, nor gave Crœsus those compliments he expected, but showed himself to all discerning eyes to be a man that despised the gaudiness and petty ostentation of it, he commanded them to open all his treasure houses, and carry him to see his sumptuous furniture and luxuries, though he did not wish it; Solon could judge of him well enough by the first sight of him; and, when he returned from viewing all, Crœsus asked him if ever he had known a happier man than he. And when Solon answered that he had known one Tellus, a fellow-citizen of his own, and told him that this Tellus had been an honest man, had had good children, a competent estate, and died bravely in battle for his country, Crœsus took him for an ill-bred fellow and a fool, for not measuring happiness by the abundance of gold and silver, and preferring the life and death of a private and mean man before so much power and empire. He asked him, however, again, if, besides Tellus, he knew any other man more happy. And Solon replying, Yes, Cleobis and Biton, who were loving brothers, and extremely dutiful sons to their mother, and, when the oxen delayed her, harnessed themselves to the waggon, and drew her to Juno's temple, her neighbours all calling her happy, and she herself rejoicing; then, after sacrificing and feasting, they went to rest, and never rose again, but died in the midst of their honour a painless and tranquil death. "What," said Crœsus, angrily, "and dost not thou reckon us amongst the happy men at all?" Solon, unwilling either to flatter or exasperate him more, replied, "The gods, O king, have given the Greeks all other gifts in moderate degree; and so our wisdom, too, is a cheerful and a homely, not a noble and kingly wisdom; and this, observing the numerous misfortunes that attend all conditions, forbids us to grow insolent upon our present enjoyments, or to admire any man's happiness that may yet, in course of time, suffer change. For the uncertain future has yet to come, with every possible variety of fortune; and him only to whom the divinity has continued happiness unto the end we call happy; to salute as happy one that is still in the midst of life and hazard, we think as little safe and conclusive as to crown and proclaim as victorious the wrestler that is yet in the ring." After this, he was dismissed, having given Crœsus some pain, but no instruction.

Æsop, who wrote the fables, being then at Sardis upon Crœsus's invitation, and very much esteemed, was concerned that Solon was so ill received, and gave him this advice: "Solon, let your converse with kings be either short or seasonable." "Nay, rather," replied Solon, "either short or reasonable." So at this time Crœsus despised Solon; but when he was overcome by Cyrus, had lost his city, was taken alive, condemned to be burnt, and laid bound upon the pile before all the Persians and Cyrus himself, he cried out as loud as possibly he could three times, "O Solon!" and Cyrus being surprised, and sending some to inquire what man or god this Solon was, who alone he invoked in this extremity, Crœsus told him the whole story, saying, "He was one of the wise men of Greece, whom I sent for, not to be instructed, or to learn anything that I wanted, but that he should see and be a witness of my happiness; the loss of which was, it seems, to be a greater evil than the enjoyment was a good; for when I had them they were goods only in opinion, but now the loss of them has brought upon me intolerable and real evils. And he, conjecturing from what then was, this that now is, bade look to the end of my life, and not rely and grow proud upon uncertainties." When this was told Cyrus, who was a wiser man than Crœsus, and saw in the present example Solon's maxim confirmed, he not only freed Crœsus from punishment, but honoured him as long as he lived; and Solon had the glory, by the same saying, to save one king and instruct another.

[27–28, tr. DRYDEN-CLOUGH]

PERICLES

[The following selection, a bit of gossip about the famous courtesan Aspasia, is a digression in the midst of Plutarch's account of Pericles' military exploits. In 447 B.C. the Athenian Empire, which had reached its greatest extent, faced a series of revolts: Boeotia defeated an Athenian force and secured its independence; Euboea and Megara then revolted simultaneously. Pericles led an army to Euboea, but at the news that the Peloponnesian army was marching toward Attica, he promptly returned and faced the Spartans. The Lacedaemonians then withdrew, not without some suspicion that their king had been bribed. Pericles then completed the reduction of Euboea and arranged a thirty years' peace with Sparta (446 B.C.). Five years later Samos, one of the strongest allies of Athens, revolted and was reduced by Pericles after a hard struggle. There is no doubt that this step was necessary for the preservation of the Athenian Empire, but ancient scandal-mongers spread the following discreditable story in order to connect the war with Pericles' infatuation for Aspasia.]

After this, having made a truce between the Athenians and Lacedæmonians for thirty years, he ordered, by public decree, the expedition against the isle of Samos, on the ground, that, when they were bid to leave off their war with the Milesians they had not complied. And as these measures against the Samians are thought to have been taken to please Aspasia, this may be a fit point for inquiry about the woman, what art or charming faculty she had that enabled her to captivate, as she did, the greatest statesmen, and to give the philosophers occasion to speak so much about her, and that, too, not to her disparagement. That she was a Milesian by birth, the daughter of Axiochus, is a thing acknowledged. And they say it was in emulation of Thargelia, a courtesan of the old Ionian times, that she made her addresses to men of great power. Thargelia was a great beauty, extremely charming, and at the same time sagacious; she had numerous suitors among the Greeks, and brought all who had to do with her over to the Persian interest, and by their means, being men of the greatest power and station, sowed the seeds of the Median faction up and down in several cities. Aspasia, some say, was courted and caressed by Pericles upon account of her knowledge and skill in politics. Socrates himself would sometimes go to visit her, and some of his acquaintance with him; and those who frequented her company would carry their wives with them to listen to her. Her occupation was anything but creditable, her house being a home for young courtesans. Æschines tells us, also, that Lysicles, a sheep-dealer, a man of low birth and character, by keeping Aspasia company after Pericles's death, came to be a chief man in Athens. And in Plato's Menexenus, though we do not take the introduction as quite serious, still thus much seems to be historical, that she had the repute of being resorted to by many of the Athenians for instruction in the art of speaking. Pericles's inclination for her seems, however, to have rather proceeded from the passion of love. He had a wife that was near of kin to him, who had been married first to Hipponicus, by whom she had Callias, surnamed the Rich; and also she brought Pericles, while she lived with him, two sons, Xanthippus and Paralus. Afterwards, when they did not well agree, nor like to live together, he parted with her, with her own consent, to another man, and himself took Aspasia, and loved her with wonderful affection; every day, both as he went out and as he came in from the market-place, he saluted and kissed her.

In the comedies she goes by the nicknames of the new Omphale and Deianira, and again is styled Juno. Cratinus, in downright terms, calls her a harlot.

> "To find him a Juno the goddess of lust
> Bore that harlot past shame,
> Aspasia by name."

It should seem also that he had a son by her; Eupolis, in his *Demes,* introduced Pericles asking after his safety, and Myronides replying —

> "My son?"   "He lives: a man he had been long,
> But that the harlot-mother did him wrong."

Aspasia, they say, became so celebrated and renowned, that Cyrus also who made war against Artaxerxes for the Persian monarchy, gave her whom he loved the best of all his concubines the name of Aspasia, who before that was called Milto. She was a Phocæan by birth, the daughter of one Hermotimus, and, when Cyrus fell in battle, was carried to the king, and had great influence at court. These things coming into my memory as I am writing this story, it would be unnatural for me to omit them.

[24, tr. DRYDEN-CLOUGH]

MARIUS

[Gaius Marius, the great Roman general and leader of the popular faction, won his reputation by his subjection of Jugurtha (106 B.C.) and his overwhelming defeat of the Cimbri and Teutones, two Germanic tribes that invaded Italy, in 102 B.C. After holding six consulships, however, Marius began to lose his power and influence; in 88 B.C. the Civil War between Marius and Sulla broke out. Sulla marched on Rome with thirty-five thousand loyal and well-trained troops, and Marius took to flight, accompanied by a few friends. The following description of Marius' flight is one of the most vivid passages in Plutarch.]

When Marius and his company were now about twenty furlongs distant from Minturnæ, a city in Italy, they espied a troop of horse making up toward them with all speed, and by chance, also, at the same time, two ships under sail. Accordingly, they ran every one with what speed and strength they could to the sea, and plunging into it swam to the ships. Those that were with Granius, reaching one of them, passed over to an island opposite, called Ænaria; Marius himself, whose body was heavy and unwieldy, was with great pains and difficulty kept above the water by two servants, and put into the other ship. The soldiers were by this time come to the seaside, and from thence called out to the seamen to put to shore, or else to throw out Marius, and then they might go whither they would. Marius besought them with tears to the contrary, and the masters of the ship, after frequent changes, in a short space of time, of their purpose, inclining first to one, then to the other side, resolved at length to answer the soldiers that they would not give up Marius. As soon as they had ridden off in a rage, the seamen, again changing their resolution, came to land, and casting anchor at the mouth of the river Liris, where it overflows and makes a marsh, they advised him to land, refresh himself on shore, and take some care of his discomposed body, till the wind came fairer; which, said they, will happen at such an hour, when the wind from the sea will calm, and that from the marshes rise. Marius, following their advice, did so, and when the seamen had set him on shore, he laid him down in an adjacent field, suspecting nothing less than what was to befall him. They, as soon as they had got into the ship, weighed anchor and departed, as thinking it neither honourable to deliver Marius into the hands of those that sought him, nor safe to protect him.

He thus, deserted by all, lay a good while silently on the shore; at length collecting himself, he advanced with pain and difficulty, without any path, till, wading through deep bogs and ditches full of water and mud, he came upon the hut of an old man that worked in the fens, and falling at his feet besought him to assist and preserve one who, if he escaped the present danger, would make him returns beyond his expectation. The poor man, whether he had formerly known him, or were then moved with his superior aspect, told him that if he wanted only rest his cottage would be convenient; but if he

were flying from anybody's search, he would hide him in a more retired place. Marius desiring him to do so, he carried him into the
fens and bade him hide himself in an hollow place by the river-side,
where he laid upon him a great many reeds, and other things that
were light, and would cover, but not oppress him. But within a very
short time he was disturbed with a noise and tumult from the cottage,
for Geminius had sent several from Terracina in pursuit of him;
some of whom happening to come that way, frightened and threatened the old man for having entertained and hid an enemy of the
Romans. Whereupon Marius, arising and stripping himself, plunged
into a puddle full of thick muddy water; and even there he could not
escape their search, but was pulled out covered with mire, and carried away naked to Minturnæ and delivered to the magistrates. For
there had been orders sent through all the towns to make public
search for Marius, and if they found him to kill him; however, the
magistrates thought convenient to consider a little better of it first,
and sent him prisoner to the house of one Fannia.
     This woman was supposed not very well affected towards him
upon an old account. One Tinnius had formerly married this Fannia; from whom she afterwards, being divorced, demanded her portion, which was considerable, but her husband accused her of adultery; so the controversy was brought before Marius in his sixth
consulship. When the case was examined thoroughly, it appeared
both that Fannia had been incontinent, and that her husband, knowing her to be so, had married and lived a considerable time with her.
So that Marius was severe enough with both, commanding him to
restore her portion, and laying a fine of four copper coins upon her
by way of disgrace. But Fannia did not then behave like a woman
that had been injured, but as soon as she saw Marius, remembered
nothing less than old affronts; took care of him according to her
ability, and comforted him. He made her his returns and told her
he did not despair, for he had met with a lucky omen, which was
thus. When he was brought to Fannia's house, as soon as the gate
was opened, an ass came running out to drink at a spring hard by,
and giving a bold and encouraging look, first stood still before him,
then brayed aloud and pranced by him. From which Marius drew
his conclusion, and said, that the fates designed his safety, rather by
sea than land, because the ass neglected his dry fodder, and turned
from it to the water. Having told Fannia this story, he bade the
chamber door to be shut and went to rest.
     Meanwhile the magistrates and councillors of Minturnæ consulted
together, and determined not to delay any longer, but immediately
to kill Marius; and when none of their citizens durst undertake the
business, a certain soldier, a Gaulish or Cimbrian horseman (the
story is told both ways), went in with his sword drawn to him. The
room itself was not very light, that part of it especially where he then
lay was dark, from whence Marius's eyes, they say, seemed to the
fellow to dart out flames at him, and a loud voice to say, out of the
dark, "Fellow, darest thou kill Caius Marius?" The barbarian there-

upon immediately fled, and leaving his sword in the place, rushed out of doors, crying only this, "I cannot kill Caius Marius." At which they were all at first astonished, and presently began to feel pity, and remorse, and anger at themselves for making so unjust and ungrateful a decree against one who had preserved Italy, and whom it was bad enough not to assist. "Let him go," said they, "where he please to banishment, and find his fate somewhere else; we only entreat pardon of the gods for thrusting Marius distressed and deserted out of our city."

[37-39, tr. DRYDEN-CLOUGH]

ALEXANDER

[In his conquest of Asia, Alexander invaded Egypt, which was one of the provinces of the Persian Empire; there he laid the foundations of the great city of Alexandria. The visit to the oracle of Zeus Ammon, which is described in the following passage, had far-reaching political consequences: the Hellenistic monarchs who succeeded Alexander adopted the practice of deifying their predecessors and themselves, and this practice led to the custom of Emperor-worship in the Roman Empire.]

He commanded the workmen to proceed, while he went to visit the temple of Ammon.

This was a long and painful, and, in two respects, a dangerous journey; first, if they should lose their provision of water, as for several days none could be obtained; and, secondly, if a violent south wind should rise upon them, while they were travelling through the wide extent of deep sands, as it is said to have done when Cambyses led his army that way, blowing the sand together in heaps, and raising, as it were, the whole desert like a sea upon them, till fifty thousand were swallowed up and destroyed by it. All these difficulties were weighed and represented to him; but Alexander was not easily to be diverted from anything he was bent upon. For fortune having hitherto seconded him in his designs, made him resolute and firm in his opinions, and the boldness of his temper raised a sort of passion in him for surmounting difficulties; as if it were not enough to be always victorious in the field, unless places and seasons and nature herself submitted to him. In this journey, the relief and assistance the gods afforded him in his distresses were more remarkable, and obtained greater belief than the oracles he received afterwards, which, however, were valued and credited the more on account of those occurrences. For first, plentiful rains that fell preserved them from any fear of perishing by drought, and, allaying the extreme dryness of the sand, which now became moist and firm to travel on, cleared and purified the air. Besides this, when they were out of their way, and were wandering up and down, because the marks which were wont to direct the guides were disordered and lost, they were set right again by some ravens, which flew before them when on their march, and waited for them when they lingered and fell behind; and the greatest miracle, as Callisthenes tells us, was that if any of the company went astray in the night, they never ceased croaking and making a noise till by that means they had brought them into the right way again. Having passed through the wilderness, they came to the place where the high priest, at the first salutation, bade Alexander welcome from his father Ammon. And being asked by him whether any of his father's murderers had escaped punishment, he charged him to speak with more respect, since his was not a mortal father. Then Alexander, changing his expression, desired to know of him if any of those who murdered Philip were yet unpunished, and further concerning dominion, whether the empire of the world was reserved for him? This, the god answered, he should obtain, and that Philip's death was fully revenged, which gave him so much satisfaction that he made splendid offerings to Jupiter, and gave the priests very rich presents. This is what most authors write concerning the oracles. But Alexander, in a letter to his mother, tells her there were some secret answers, which at his return he would communicate to her only. Others say that the priest, desirous as a piece of courtesy to address him in Greek, "O Paidion," by a slip in pronunciation ended with the *s* instead of the *n,* and said "O Paidios," * which mistake Alexander was well enough pleased with, and it went for current that the oracle had called him so.

Among the sayings of one Psammon, a philosopher, whom he heard in Egypt, he most approved of this, that all men are governed by God, because in everything, that which is chief and commands is divine. But what he pronounced himself upon this subject was even more like a philosopher, for he said, God was the common father of us all, but more particularly of the best of us. To the barbarians he carried himself very haughtily, as if he were fully persuaded of his divine birth and parentage; but to the Grecians more moderately, and with less affectation of divinity, except it were once in writing to the Athenians about Samos, when he tells them that he should not himself have bestowed upon them that free and glorious city; "You received it," he says, "from the bounty of him who at that time was called my lord and father," meaning Philip. However, afterwards being wounded with an arrow, and feeling much pain, he turned to those about him, and told them, "This, my friends, is real flowing blood, not Ichor —

"Such as immortal gods are wont to shed."

And another time, when it thundered so much that everybody was afraid, and Anaxarchus, the sophist, asked him if he who was Jupiter's son could do anything like this, "Nay," said Alexander, laughing, "I have no desire to be formidable to my friends, as you would have me, who despised my table for being furnished with fish, and not with the heads of governors of provinces." For in fact it is related as true, that Anaxarchus, seeing a present of small fishes, which the king sent to Hephæstion, had used this expression, in a

* *i.e.,* "O Child of Zeus."

sort of irony, and disparagement of those who undergo vast labours and encounter great hazards in pursuit of magnificent objects which after all bring them little more pleasure or enjoyment than what others have. From what I have said upon this subject, it is apparent that Alexander in himself was not foolishly affected, or had the vanity to think himself really a god, but merely used his claims to divinity as a means of maintaining among other people the sense of his superiority.

[26–28, tr. DRYDEN-CLOUGH]

[After his conquest of the far East, Alexander returned to Babylon, where he died in 323 B.C. Plutarch relates several prodigies and portents which preceded his death; all of these greatly disturbed Alexander, whose mind, according to Plutarch's account, was beginning to waver and give way as a result of the excessive adulation to which he was constantly exposed.]

When once Alexander had given way to fears of supernatural influence, his mind grew so disturbed and so easily alarmed that, if the least unusual or extraordinary thing happened, he thought it a prodigy or a presage, and his court was thronged with diviners and priests whose business was to sacrifice and purify and foretell the future. So miserable a thing is incredulity and contempt of divine power on the one hand, and so miserable, also, superstition on the other, which like water, where the level has been lowered, flowing in and never stopping, fills the mind with slavish fears and follies, as now in Alexander's case. But upon some answers which were brought him from the oracle concerning Hephæstion, he laid aside his sorrow, and fell again to sacrificing and drinking; and having given Nearchus a splendid entertainment, after he had bathed, as was his custom, just as he was going to bed, at Medius's request he went to supper with him. Here he drank all the next day, and was attacked with a fever, which seized him, not as some write, after he had drunk of the bowl of Hercules, nor was he taken with any sudden pain in his back, as if he had been struck with a lance, for these are the inventions of some authors who thought it their duty to make the last scene of so great an action as tragical and moving as they could. Aristobulus tells us, that in the rage of his fever and a violent thirst, he took a draught of wine, upon which he fell into delirium, and died on the thirtieth day of the month Dæsius.

But the journals give the following record. On the eighteenth day of the month he slept in the bathing-room on account of his fever. The next day he bathed and removed into his chamber, and spent his time in playing at dice with Medius. In the evening he bathed and sacrificed, and ate freely, and had the fever on him through the night. On the twentieth, after the usual sacrifices and bathing, he lay in the bathing-room and heard Nearchus's narrative of his voyage, and the observations he had made in the great sea. The twenty-first he passed in the same manner, his fever still increasing, and suffered much during the night. The next day the fever was very violent, and he had himself removed and his bed set by the great bath, and discoursed with his principal officers about finding fit men to fill up the vacant places in the army. On the twenty-fourth he was much worse, and was carried out of his bed to assist at the sacrifices, and gave order that the general officers should wait within the court, whilst the inferior officers kept watch without doors. On the twenty-fifth he was removed to his palace on the other side the river, where he slept a little, but his fever did not abate, and when the generals came into his chamber, he was speechless and continued so the following day. The Macedonians, therefore, supposing he was dead, came with great clamours to the gates, and menaced his friends so that they were forced to admit them, and let them all pass through unarmed by his bedside. The same day Python and Seleucus were despatched to the temple of Serapis to inquire if they should bring Alexander thither, and were answered by the god that they should not remove him. On the twenty-eighth, in the evening, he died. This account is most of it word for word as it 's written in the diary.

[75–76, tr. DRYDEN-CLOUGH]

CAESAR

[Plutarch's account of Caesar's death is familiar to most English readers, since Shakespeare has followed Plutarch most faithfully in *Julius Caesar*. The reader should note that Caesar was at this time engaged in planning an attack on the Parthians, who had annihilated a Roman army under Crassus in 53 B.C. The rest of the selection needs no explanation.]

But that which brought upon him the most apparent and mortal hatred was his desire of being king; which gave the common people the first occasion to quarrel with him, and proved the most specious pretence to those who had been his secret enemies all along. Those who would have procured him that title gave it out that it was foretold in the Sibyls' books that the Romans should conquer the Parthians when they fought against them under the conduct of a king, but not before. And one day, as Cæsar was coming down from Alba to Rome, some were so bold as to salute him by the name of king; but he, finding the people disrelish it, seemed to resent it himself, and said his name was Cæsar, not king. Upon this there was a general silence, and he passed on looking not very well pleased or contented. Another time, when the senate had conferred on him some extravagant honours, he chanced to receive the message as he was sitting on the rostra, where, though the consuls and prætors themselves waited on him, attended by the whole body of the senate, he did not rise, but behaved himself to them as if they had been private men, and told them his honours wanted rather to be retrenched than increased. This treatment offended not only the senate, but the commonalty too, as if they thought the affront upon the senate equally reflected upon the whole republic; so that all who could decently leave him went off, looking much discomposed. Cæsar, perceiving the false step he had made, immediately retired home; and laying his throat bare, told his friends that he was ready to offer this to any one who would give the stroke. But afterwards he made the malady from which he suffered the excuse for his sitting, saying that those who are attacked by it lose their presence of mind if they talk much standing; that they presently grow giddy, fall into convulsions, and quite lose their reason. But this was not the reality, for he would willingly have stood up to the senate, had not Cornelius Balbus, one of his friends, or rather flatterers, hindered him. "Will you not remember," said he, "you are Cæsar, and claim the honour which is due to your merit?"

He gave a fresh occasion of resentment by his affront to the tribunes. The Lupercalia were then celebrated, a feast at the first institution belonging, as some writers say, to the shepherds, and having some connection with the Arcadian Lycæ. Many young noblemen and magistrates run up and down the city with their upper garments off, striking all they meet with thongs of hide, by way of sport; and many women, even of the highest rank, place themselves in the way, and hold out their hands to the lash, as boys in a school do to the master, out of a belief that it procures an easy labour to those who are with child, and makes those conceive who are barren. Cæsar, dressed in a triumphal robe, seated himself in a golden chair at the rostra to view this ceremony. Antony, as consul, was one of those who ran this course, and when he came into the forum, and the people made way for him, he went up and reached to Cæsar a diadem wreathed with laurel. Upon this there was a shout, but only a slight one, made by the few who were planted there for that purpose; but when Cæsar refused it, there was universal applause. Upon the second offer, very few, and upon the second refusal, all again applauded. Cæsar finding it would not take, rose up, and ordered the crown to be carried into the capitol. Cæsar's statues were afterwards found with royal diadems on their heads. Flavius and Marullus, two tribunes of the people, went presently and pulled them off, and having apprehended those who first saluted Cæsar as king committed them to prison. The people followed them with acclamations, and called them by the name of Brutus, because Brutus was the first who ended the succession of kings, and transferred the power which before was lodged in one man into the hands of the senate and people. Cæsar so far resented this, that he displaced Marullus and Flavius; and in urging his charges against them, at the same time ridiculed the people, by himself giving the men more than once the names of Bruti and Cumæi.

This made the multitude turn their thoughts to Marcus Brutus, who, by his father's side, was thought to be descended from that first Brutus, and by his mother's side from the Servilii, another noble family, being besides nephew and son-in-law to Cato. But the honours and favours he had received from Cæsar took off the edge from the desires he might himself have felt for overthrowing the new monarchy. For he had not only been pardoned himself after Pompey's defeat at Pharsalia, and had procured the same grace for many of his friends, but was one in whom Cæsar had a particular confidence. He had at that time the most honourable prætorship for the year, and was named for the consulship four years after, being preferred before Cassius, his competitor. Upon the question as to the choice, Cæsar, it is related, said that Cassius had the fairer pretensions, but that he could not pass by Brutus. Nor would he afterwards listen to some who spoke against Brutus, when the conspiracy against him was already afoot, but laying his hand on his body, said to the informers, "Brutus will wait for this skin of mine," intimating that he was worthy to bear rule on account of his virtue, but would not be base and ungrateful to gain it. Those who desired a change, and looked on him as the only, or at least the most proper, person to effect it, did not venture to speak with him; but in the night-time laid papers about his chair of state, where he used to sit and determine causes, with such sentences in them as, "You are asleep, Brutus," "You are no longer Brutus." Cassius, when he perceived his ambition a little raised upon this, was more instant than before to work him yet further, having himself a private grudge against Cæsar for some reasons that we have mentioned in the Life of Brutus. Nor was Cæsar without suspicions of him, and said once to his friends, "What do you think Cassius is aiming at? I don't like him, he looks so pale." And when it was told him that Antony and Dolabella were in a plot against him, he said he did not fear such fat, luxurious men, but rather the pale, lean fellows, meaning Cassius and Brutus.

Fate, however, is to all appearance more unavoidable than unexpected. For many strange prodigies and apparitions are said to have been observed shortly before this event. As to the lights in the heavens, the noises heard in the night, and the wild birds which perched in the forum, these are not perhaps worth taking notice of in so great a case as this. Strabo, the philosopher, tells us that a number of men were seen, looking as if they were heated through with fire, contending with each other; that a quantity of flame issued from the hand of a soldier's servant, so that they who saw it thought he must be burnt, but that after all he had no hurt. As Cæsar was sacrificing, the victim's heart was missing, a very bad omen, because no living creature can subsist without a heart. One finds it also related by many that a soothsayer bade him prepare for some great danger on the Ides of March. When this day was come, Cæsar, as he went to the senate, met this soothsayer, and said to him by way of raillery, "The Ides of March are come," who answered him calmly, "Yes, they are come, but they are not past." The day before his assassination he supped with Marcus Lepidus; and as he was signing some letters according to his custom, as he reclined at table, there arose a question what sort of death was the best. At which he immediately, before any one could speak, said, "A sudden one."

After this, as he was in bed with his wife, all the doors and windows of the house flew open together; he was startled at the noise, and the light which broke into the room, and sat up in his bed, where by the moonshine he perceived Calpurnia fast asleep, but heard her utter in her dream some indistinct words and inarticulate groans. She fancied at that time she was weeping over Cæsar, and holding him butchered in her arms. Others say this was not her dream, but that she dreamed that a pinnacle, which the senate, as Livy relates, had ordered to be raised on Cæsar's house by way of ornament and grandeur, was tumbling down, which was the occasion of her tears and ejaculations. When it was day, she begged of Cæsar, if it were possible, not to stir out, but to adjourn the senate to another time; and if he slighted her dreams, that she would be pleased to consult his fate by sacrifices and other kinds of divination. Nor was he himself without some suspicion and fears; for he never before discovered any womanish superstition in Calpurnia, whom he now saw in such great alarm. Upon the report which the priests made to him, that they had killed several sacrifices, and still found them inauspicious, he resolved to send Antony to dismiss the senate.

In this juncture, Decimus Brutus, surnamed Albinus, one whom Cæsar had such confidence in that he made him his second heir, who nevertheless was engaged in the conspiracy with the other Brutus and Cassius, fearing lest if Cæsar should put off the senate to another day, the business might get wind, spoke scoffingly and in mockery of the diviners, and blamed Cæsar for giving the senate so fair an occasion of saying he had put a slight upon them, for that they were met upon his summons, and were ready to vote unanimously that he should be declared king of all the provinces out of Italy, and might wear a diadem in any other place but Italy, by sea or land. If any one should be sent to tell them they might break up for the present, and meet again when Calpurnia should chance to have better dreams, what would his enemies say? Or who would with any patience hear his friends, if they should presume to defend his government as not arbitrary and tyrannical? But if he was possessed so far as to think this day unfortunate, yet it were more decent to go himself to the senate, and to adjourn it in his own person. Brutus, as he spoke these words, took Cæsar by the hand, and conducted him forth. He was not gone far from the door, when a servant of some other person's made towards him, but not being able to come up to him, on account of the crowd of those who pressed about him, he made his way into the house, and committed himself to Calpurnia, begging of her to secure him till Cæsar returned, because he had matters of great importance to communicate to him.

Artemidorus, a Cnidian, a teacher of Greek logic, and by that means so far acquainted with Brutus and his friends as to have got into the secret, brought Cæsar in a small written memorial the heads of what he had to depose. He had observed that Cæsar, as he received any papers, presently gave them to the servants who attended on him; and therefore came as near to him as he could, and said, "Read this, Cæsar, alone, and quickly, for it contains matter of great importance which nearly concerns you." Cæsar received it, and tried several times to read it, but was still hindered by the crowd of those who came to speak to him. However, he kept it in his hand by itself till he came into the senate. Some say it was another who gave Cæsar this note, and that Artemidorus could not get to him, being all along kept off by the crowd.

All these things might happen by chance. But the place which was destined for the scene of this murder, in which the senate met that day, was the same in which Pompey's statue stood, and was one of the edifices which Pompey had raised and dedicated with his theatre to the use of the public, plainly showing that there was something of a supernatural influence which guided the action and ordered it to that particular place. Cassius, just before the act, is said to have looked towards Pompey's statue, and silently implored his assistance, though he had been inclined to the doctrines of Epicurus. But this occasion, and the instant danger, carried him away out of all his reasonings, and filled him for the time with a sort of inspiration. As for Antony, who was firm to Cæsar, and a strong man, Brutus Albinus kept him outside the house, and delayed him with a long conversation contrived on purpose. When Cæsar entered, the senate stood up to show their respect to him, and of Brutus's confederates, some came about his chair and stood behind it, others met him, pretending to add their petitions to those of Tillius Cimber, in behalf of his brother, who was in exile; and they followed him with their joint applications till he came to his seat. When he was sat down, he refused to comply with their requests, and upon their urging him further began to reproach them severely for their importunities, when Tillius, laying hold of his robe with both his hands, pulled it down from his neck, which was the signal for the assault. Casca gave him the first cut in the neck, which was not mortal nor dangerous, as coming from one who at the beginning of such a bold action was probably very much disturbed; Cæsar immediately turned about, and laid his hand upon the dagger and kept hold of it. And both of them at the same time cried out, he that received the blow, in Latin, "Vile Casca, what does this mean?" and he that gave it, in Greek to his brother, "Brother, help!" Upon this first onset, those who were not privy to the design were astonished, and their horror and amazement at what they saw were so great that they durst not fly nor assist Cæsar, nor so much as speak a word. But those who came prepared for the business enclosed him on every side, with their naked daggers in their hands. Which way soever he turned he met with blows, and saw their swords levelled at his face and eyes, and was encompassed like a wild beast in the toils on every side. For it had been agreed they should each of them make a thrust at him, and flesh themselves with his blood; for which reason Brutus also gave him one stab in the groin. Some say that he fought and resisted all the rest, shifting his body to avoid the blows, and calling out for help, but that when he saw Brutus's sword drawn, he covered his face with his robe and submitted, letting himself fall, whether it were by chance or that he was pushed in that direction by his murderers, at the foot of the pedestal on which Pompey's statue stood, and which was thus wetted with his blood. So that Pompey himself seemed to have presided, as it were, over the revenge done upon his adversary, who lay here at his feet, and breathed out his soul through his multitude of wounds, for they say he received three-and-twenty. And the conspirators themselves were many of them wounded by each other, whilst they all levelled their blows at the same person.

When Cæsar was despatched, Brutus stood forth to give a reason for what they had done, but the senate would not hear him, but flew out of doors in all haste, and filled the people with so much alarm and distraction, that some shut up their houses, others left their counters and shops. All ran one way or the other, some to the place to see the sad spectacle, others back again after they had seen it. Antony and Lepidus, Cæsar's most faithful friends, got off privately, and hid themselves in some friends' houses. Brutus and his followers, being yet hot from the deed, marched in a body from the senate-house to the capitol with their drawn swords, not like persons who thought of escaping, but with an air of confidence and assurance, and as they went along, called to the people to resume their liberty, and invited the company of any more distinguished people whom they met. And some of these joined the procession and went up along with them, as if they also had been of the conspiracy, and could claim a share in the honour of what had been done. As, for example, Caius Octavius and Lentulus Spinther, who suffered afterwards for their vanity, being taken off by Antony and the young Cæsar, and lost the honour they desired, as well as their lives, which it cost them, since no one believed they had any share in the action. For neither did those who punished them profess to revenge the fact, but the ill-will. The day after, Brutus with the rest came down from the capitol and made a speech to the people, who listened without expressing either any pleasure or resentment, but showed by their silence that they pitied Cæsar and respected Brutus. The senate passed acts of oblivion for what was past, and took measures to reconcile all parties. They ordered that Cæsar should be worshipped as a divinity, and nothing, even of the slightest consequence, should be revoked which he had enacted during his government. At the same time they gave Brutus and his followers the command of provinces, and other considerable posts. So that all the people now thought things were well settled, and brought to the happiest adjustment.

But when Cæsar's will was opened, and it was found that he had left a considerable legacy to each one of the Roman citizens, and when his body was seen carried through the market-place all mangled with wounds, the multitude could no longer contain themselves within the bounds of tranquillity and order, but heaped together a pile of benches, bars, and tables, which they placed the corpse on, and setting fire to it, burnt it on them. Then they took brands from the pile and ran some to fire the houses of the conspirators, others up and down the city, to find out the men and tear them to pieces, but met, however, with none of them, they having taken effectual care to secure themselves.

One Cinna, a friend of Cæsar's, chanced the night before to have an odd dream. He fancied that Cæsar invited him to supper, and that upon his refusal to go with him, Cæsar took him by the hand and forced him, though he hung back. Upon hearing the report that Cæsar's body was burning in the market-place, he got up and went thither, out of respect to his memory, though his dream gave him some ill apprehensions, and though he was suffering from a fever. One of the crowd who saw him there asked another who that was, and having learned his name, told it to his neighbour. It presently passed for a certainty that he was one of Cæsar's murderers, as, indeed, there was another Cinna, a conspirator, and they, taking this to be the man, immediately seized him and tore him limb from limb upon the spot.

Brutus and Cassius, frightened at this, within a few days retired out of the city. What they afterwards did and suffered, and how they died, is written in the Life of Brutus. Cæsar died in his fifty-sixth year, not having survived Pompey above four years. That empire and power which he had pursued through the whole course of his life with so much hazard, he did at last with much difficulty compass, but reaped no other fruits from it than the empty name and invidious glory. But the great genius which attended him through his lifetime even after his death remained as the avenger of his murder, pursuing through every sea and land all those who were concerned in it, and suffering none to escape, but reaching all who in any sort or kind were either actually engaged in the fact, or by their counsels any way promoted it.

The most remarkable of mere human coincidences was that which befell Cassius, who, when he was defeated at Philippi, killed himself with the same dagger which he had made use of against Cæsar. The most signal preternatural appearances were the great comet, which shone very bright for seven nights after Cæsar's death, and then disappeared, and the dimness of the sun, whose orb continued pale and dull for the whole of that year, never showing its ordinary radiance at its rising, and giving but a weak and feeble heat. The air consequently was damp and gross for want of stronger rays to open and rarefy it. The fruits, for that reason, never properly ripened, and began to wither and fall off for want of heat before they were fully formed. But above all, the phantom which appeared to Brutus showed the murder was not pleasing to the gods. The story of it is this.

Brutus, being to pass his army from Abydos to the continent on the other side, laid himself down one night, as he used to do, in his tent, and was not asleep, but thinking of his affairs, and what events he might expect. For he is related to have been the least inclined to sleep of all men who have commanded armies, and to have had the greatest natural capacity for continuing awake, and employing himself without need of rest. He thought he heard a noise at the door of his tent, and looking that way, by the light of his lamp, which was almost out, saw a terrible figure, like that of a man, but of unusual stature and severe countenance. He was somewhat frightened at first, but seeing it neither did nor spoke anything to him, only stood silently by his bedside, he asked who it was. The spectre answered him, "Thy evil genius, Brutus, thou shalt see me at Philippi." Brutus answered courageously, "Well, I shall see you," and immediately the appearance vanished. When the time was come, he drew up his army near Philippi against Antony and Cæsar,* and in the first battle won the day, routed the enemy, and plundered Cæsar's camp. The night before the second battle, the same phantom appeared to him again, but spoke not a word. He presently understood his destiny was at hand, and exposed himself to all the danger of the battle. Yet he did not die in the fight, but seeing his men defeated, got up to the top of a rock, and there presenting his sword to his naked breast, and assisted, as they say, by a friend, who helped him to give the thrust, met his death.

[60–69, tr. Dryden-Clough]

ANTONY

[The complete story of Marc Antony and his relations with Augustus belongs to the province of Roman history and lies outside the scope of this work. Here the following facts will suffice: after their defeat at Actium (a defeat partly caused by Cleopatra's sudden flight with sixty ships before the battle was decided) Antony and Cleopatra returned to Alexandria, where they prepared for a final resistance. Cleopatra however carried on secret negotiations with Augustus, in order to save what she could for her children; at the same time she built herself a strong refuge in the form of a tower, or monument, next to the temple of Isis. Augustus held out every hope to Cleopatra, since he was eager to take her alive and also feared that in her desperation she might destroy the immense treasures of the Ptolemies; in the meantime he marched through Asia Minor to Alexandria, which he reached in the spring of 30 B.C. Antony, despite his suspicions of Cleopatra's intentions, resolved to make one more effort to defeat Caesar Augustus by land and sea.

The story continues at this point in Plutarch's own words. The selections relate the events covered in Shakespeare's *Antony and Cleopatra,* Acts IV and V.]

After this, Antony sent a new challenge to Cæsar to fight him hand-to-hand; who made him answer that he might find several other ways to end his life; and he, considering with himself that he could not die more honourably than in battle, resolved to make an effort both by land and sea. At supper, it is said, he bade his servants help him freely, and pour him out wine plentifully, since to-morrow, perhaps, they should not do the same, but be servants to a new master, whilst he should lie on the ground, a dead corpse, and nothing. His friends that were about him wept to hear him talk so; which he perceiving, told them he would not lead them to a battle in which he expected rather an honourable death than either safety or victory. That night, it is related, about the middle of it, when the whole city was in a deep silence and general sadness, expecting the event of the next day, on

* *i.e.,* Octavian, later Augustus.

a sudden was heard the sound of all sorts of instruments, and voices singing in tune, and the cry of a crowd of people shouting and dancing, like a troop of bacchanals on its way. This tumultuous procession seemed to take its course right through the middle of the city to the gate nearest the enemy; here it became the loudest, and suddenly passed out. People who reflected considered this to signify that Bacchus, the god whom Antony had always made it his study to copy and imitate, had now forsaken him.

As soon as it was light, he marched his infantry out of the city, and posted them upon a rising ground, from whence he saw his fleet make up to the enemy. There he stood in expectation of the event; but as soon as the fleets came near to one another, his men saluted Cæsar's with their oars; and on their responding, the whole body of the ships, forming into a single fleet, rowed up direct to the city. Antony had no sooner seen this, but the horse deserted him, and went over to Cæsar; and his foot being defeated, he retired into the city, crying out that Cleopatra had betrayed him to the enemies he had made for her sake. She, being afraid lest in his fury and despair he might do her a mischief, fled to her monument, and letting down the falling doors, which were strong with bars and bolts, she sent messengers who should tell Antony she was dead. He, believing it, cried out, "Now, Antony, why delay longer? Fate has snatched away the only pretext for which you could say you desired yet to live." Going into his chamber, and there loosening and opening his coat of armour, "I am not," said he, "troubled, Cleopatra, to be at present bereaved of you, for I shall soon be with you; but it distresses me that so great a general should be found of a tardier courage than a woman." He had a faithful servant, whose name was Eros; he had engaged him formerly to kill him when he should think it necessary, and now he put him to his promise. Eros drew his sword, as designing to kill him, but, suddenly turning round, he slew himself. And as he fell dead at his feet, "It is well done, Eros," said Antony; "you show your master how to do what you had not the heart to do yourself;" and so he ran himself into the belly, and laid himself upon the couch. The wound, however, was not immediately mortal; and the flow of blood ceasing when he lay down, presently he came to himself, and entreated those that were about him to put him out of his pain; but they all fled out of the chamber, and left him crying out and struggling, until Diomede, Cleopatra's secretary, came to him, having orders from her to bring him into the monument.

When he understood she was alive, he eagerly gave order to the servants to take him up, and in their arms was carried to the door of the building. Cleopatra would not open the door, but, looking from a sort of window, she let down ropes and cords, to which Antony was fastened; and she and her two women, the only persons she had allowed to enter the monument, drew him up. Those that were present say that nothing was ever more sad than this spectacle, to see Antony, covered all over with blood and just expiring, thus drawn up, still holding up his hands to her, and lifting up his body with the little force he had left. As, indeed, it was no easy task for the women; and Cleopatra, with all her force, clinging to the rope, and straining with her head to the ground, with difficulty pulled him up, while those below encouraged her with their cries, and joined in all her efforts and anxiety. When she had got him up, she laid him on the bed, tearing all her clothes, which she spread upon him; and, beating her breast with her hands, lacerating herself, and disfiguring her own face with the blood from his wounds, she called him her lord, her husband, her emperor, and seemed to have pretty nearly forgotten all her own evils, she was so intent upon his misfortunes. Antony, stopping her lamentations as well as he could, called for wine to drink, either that he was thirsty, or that he imagined that it might put him the sooner out of pain. When he had drunk, he advised her to bring her own affairs, so far as might be honourably done, to a safe conclusion, and that, among all the friends of Cæsar, she should rely on Proculeius; that she should not pity him in this last turn of fate, but rather rejoice for him in remembrance of his past happiness, who had been of all men the most illustrious and powerful, and in the end had fallen not ignobly, a Roman by a Roman overcome.

Just as he breathed his last, Proculeius arrived from Cæsar; for when Antony gave himself his wound, and was carried in to Cleopatra, one of his guards, Dercetæus, took up Antony's sword and hid it; and, when he saw his opportunity, stole away to Cæsar, and brought him the first news of Antony's death, and withal showed him the bloody sword. Cæsar, upon this, retired into the inner part of his tent, and giving some tears to the death of one that had been nearly allied to him in marriage, his colleague in empire, and companion in so many wars and dangers, he came out to his friends, and, bringing with him many letters, he read to them with how much reason and moderation he had always addressed himself to Antony, and in return what overbearing and arrogant answers he received. Then he sent Proculeius to use his utmost endeavours to get Cleopatra alive into his power; for he was afraid of losing a great treasure, and, besides, she would be no small addition to the glory of his triumph. She, however, was careful not to put herself in Proculeius's power; but from within her monument, he standing on the outside of a door, on the level of the ground, which was strongly barred, but so that they might well enough hear one another's voice, she held a conference with him; she demanding that her kingdom might be given to her children, and he bidding her to be of good courage, and trust Cæsar in everything.

Having taken particular notice of the place, he returned to Cæsar, and Gallus was sent to parley with her the second time; who, being come to the door, on purpose prolonged the conference, while Proculeius fixed his scaling-ladders in the window through which the women had pulled up Antony. And so entering, with two men to follow him, he went straight down to the door where Cleopatra was discoursing with Gallus. One of the two women who were shut up in the monument with her cried out, "Miserable Cleopatra, you are taken prisoner!" Upon which she turned quick, and, looking at Proculeius, drew out her dagger which she had with her to stab herself. But Proculeius ran up quickly, and, seizing her with both his hands, "For shame," said he, "Cleopatra; you wrong yourself and Cæsar much, who would rob him of so fair an occasion of showing his clemency, and would make the world believe the most gentle of commanders to be a faithless and implacable enemy." And so, taking the dagger out of her hand, he also shook her dress to see if there were any poison hid in it. After this, Cæsar sent Epaphroditus, one of his freedmen, with orders to treat her with all the gentleness and civility possible, but to take the strictest precautions to keep her alive. . .

Many kings and great commanders made petition to Cæsar for the body of Antony, to give him his funeral rites; but he would not take away his corpse from Cleopatra by whose hands he was buried with royal splendour and magnificence, it being granted to her to employ what she pleased on his funeral. In this extremity of grief and sorrow, and having inflamed and ulcerated her breasts with beating them, she fell into a high fever, and was very glad of the occasion, hoping, under this pretext, to abstain from food, and so to die in quiet without interference. She had her own physician, Olympus, to whom she told the truth, and asked his advice and help to put an end to herself, as Olympus himself has told us, in a narrative which he wrote of these events. But Cæsar, suspecting her purpose, took to menacing language about her children, and excited her fears for them, before which engines her purpose shook and gave way, so that she suffered those about her to give her what meat or medicine they pleased.

Some few days after, Cæsar himself came to make her a visit and comfort her. She lay then upon her pallet-bed in undress, and, on his entering, sprang up from off her bed, having nothing on but the one garment next her body, and flung herself at his feet, her hair and face looking wild and disfigured, her voice quivering, and her eyes sunk in her head. The marks of the blows she had given herself were visible about her bosom, and altogether her whole person seemed no less afflicted than her soul. But, for all this, her old charm, and the boldness of her youthful beauty, had not wholly left her, and, in spite of her present condition, still sparkled from within, and let itself appear in all the movements of her countenance. Cæsar, desiring her to repose herself, sat down by her; and, on this opportunity, she said something to justify her actions, attributing what she had done to the necessity she was under, and to her fear of Antony; and when Cæsar, on each point, made his objections, and she found herself confuted, she broke off at once into language of entreaty and deprecation, as if she desired nothing more than to prolong her life. And at last, having by her a list of her treasure, she gave it into his hands; and when Seleucus, one of her stewards, who was by, pointed out that various articles were omitted, and charged her with secreting them, she flew up and caught him by the hair, and struck him several blows on the face. Cæsar smiling and withholding her, "Is it not very hard, Cæsar," said she, "when you do me the honour to visit me in this condition I am in, that I should be accused by one of my own servants of laying by some women's toys, not meant to adorn, be sure, my unhappy self, but that I might have some little present by me to make your Octavia and your Livia, that by their intercession I might hope to find you in some measure disposed to mercy?" Cæsar was pleased to hear her talk thus, being now assured that she was desirous to live. And, therefore, letting her know that the things she had laid by she might dispose of as she pleased, and his usage of her should be honourable above her expectation, he went away, well satisfied that he had overreached her, but, in fact, was himself deceived.

There was a young man of distinction among Cæsar's companions named Cornelius Dolabella. He was not without a certain tenderness for Cleopatra, and sent her word privately, as she had besought him to do, that Cæsar was about to return through Syria, and that she and her children were to be sent on within three days. When she understood this, she made her request to Cæsar that he would be pleased to permit her to make oblations to the departed Antony; which being granted, she ordered herself to be carried to the place where he was buried, and there, accompanied by her women, she embraced his tomb with tears in her eyes, and spoke in this manner: "O, dearest Antony," said she, "it is not long since that with these hands I buried you; then they were free, now I am a captive, and pay these last duties to you with a guard upon me, for fear that my just griefs and sorrows should impair my servile body, and make it less fit to appear in their triumph over you. No further offerings or libations expect from me; these are the last honours that Cleopatra can pay your memory, for she is to be hurried away far from you. Nothing could part us whilst we lived, but death seems to threaten to divide us. You, a Roman born, have found a grave in Egypt; I, an Egyptian, am to seek that favour, and none but that, in your country. But if the gods below, with whom you now are, either can or will do anything (since those above have betrayed us), suffer not your living wife to be abandoned; let me not be led in triumph to your shame, but hide me and bury me here with you, since, amongst all my bitter misfortunes, nothing has afflicted me like this brief time that I have lived away from you."

Having made these lamentations, crowning the tomb with garlands and kissing it, she gave orders to prepare her a bath, and, coming out of the bath, she lay down and made a sumptuous meal. And a country fellow brought her a little basket, which the guards intercepting and asking what it was, the fellow put the leaves which lay uppermost aside, and showed them it was full of figs; and on their admiring the largeness and beauty of the figs, he laughed, and invited them to take some, which they refused, and, suspecting nothing, bade him carry them in. After her repast, Cleopatra sent to Cæsar a letter which she had written and sealed; and, putting everybody out of the monument but her two women, she shut the doors. Cæsar, opening her letter, and finding pathetic prayers and entreaties that she might be buried in the same tomb with Antony, soon guessed what was doing. At first he was going himself in all haste, but, changing his mind, he sent others to see. The thing had been quickly done. The messengers came at full speed, and found the guards apprehensive of nothing; but on opening the doors they saw her stone-dead, lying upon a bed of gold, set out in all her royal ornaments. Iras, one of her women, lay dying at her feet, and Charmion, just ready to fall, scarce able to hold up her head, was adjusting her mistress's diadem. And when one that came in said angrily, "Was this well done of your lady, Charmion?" "Extremely well," she answered, "and as became the descendant of so many kings;" and as she said this, she fell down dead by the bedside.

Some relate that an asp was brought in amongst those figs and covered with the leaves, and that Cleopatra had arranged that it might settle on her before she knew, but, when she took away some of the figs and saw it, she said, "So here it is," and held out her bare arm to be bitten. Others say that it was kept in a vase, and that she vexed and pricked it with a golden spindle till it seized her arm. But what really took place is known to no one, since it was also said that she carried poison in a hollow bodkin, about which she wound her hair; yet there was not so much as a spot found, or any symptom of poison upon her body, nor was the asp seen within the monument; only something like the trail of it was said to have been noticed on the sand by the sea, on the part towards which the building faced and where the windows were. Some relate that two faint puncture-marks were found on Cleopatra's arm, and to this account Cæsar seems to have given credit; for in his triumph there was carried a figure of Cleopatra, with an asp clinging to her. Such are the various accounts. But Cæsar, though much disappointed by her death, yet could not but admire the greatness of her spirit, and gave order that her body should be buried by Antony with royal splendour and magnificence.

[75–79, 82–86, tr. DRYDEN-CLOUGH]

POETRY

EPIC AND DIDACTIC

HESIOD

[DATE UNKNOWN]

Hesiod is the earliest and most distinguished poet of the didactic epic, a form that arose among the Greeks of the mainland, apparently in revolt against the Ionian epics of heroic deeds and romantic adventure. The new form sought to provide instruction in various ways, *e.g.,* by relating the genealogies of gods and heroes, by giving moral precepts, or by setting forth the methods and rules of some useful activity, like farming or divination. The attitude of this new school of poetry is neatly expressed in the oft-quoted words of the Muses to the author of the *Theogony*: "We know how to tell many false tales like to the truth, but we know, when we will, to utter the truth" (*Theogony* 27–8). Accordingly, the emphasis of didactic poetry is decidedly on "truth" and factual information rather than on fiction. Obviously, many of the productions in this *genre* were in poetry only because prose was not yet a recognized medium of expression; but Hesiod, the author of the *Works and Days,* was a poet of great fervour and of real talent; the ancients admired him intensely and invariably coupled his name with Homer's.

We are unable to date his life with any degree of certainty; he was obviously later than Homer, whose poetry he imitated, and earlier than the first of the lyric poets — *i.e.,* he lived between the ninth and the seventh centuries B.C. He tells us that his father, driven by poverty, emigrated from Cyme in Asia Minor to Boeotia, where he settled in the little town of Ascra. The father left the property which he amassed there to his sons, Hesiod and Perses; but Perses, not content with his share, seized and held part of Hesiod's portion too, through the corrupt decisions of the lords (or Kings, as Hesiod calls them) who ruled the district. This quarrel is the external cause of the *Works and Days,* in which Hesiod upbraids his brother and the unjust judges and exhorts Perses to a life of honest work. Besides the *Works and Days,* from which the following selection is taken, the ancients attributed to Hesiod the *Theogony,* a genealogy of the gods from the time of the primeval powers Chaos and Earth. Although the poem is a catalogue, it is not without interest as the earliest account of the Greek polytheistic system; it became the standard or "authorized version" of the myths for all later poets, and thus had a great influence in shaping the theological thinking of the Greeks.

A brief summary of the *Works and Days* will help the reader to grasp the significance of the following selection. After a short invocation, Hesiod begins with the allegory of the two Strifes, one of

which represents useful, wholesome Emulation, the other quarrelsome Bickering. Perses, by his action in seizing Hesiod's portion,
has chosen the wrong Strife, and Hesiod will set him on the right
path — the path of justice and work. The myth of Prometheus
and Pandora which follows is a primitive attempt to explain the
existence of evil in a divinely governed world. An alternative explanation follows in the myth of the Ages of Mankind, which traces
the gradual degeneration of mankind from a Golden Age to the
present Age of Iron. Both myths serve to explain the need for work:
"In the sweat of thy face shalt thou eat bread." The poet next relates the fable of the Hawk and the Nightingale, the moral of which
is contained in the condemnations of violence which follow. Hesiod
then contrasts the blessings which Justice brings to a community with
the punishments which Zeus sends on the unrighteous city. This
section then ends with a series of moral precepts and admonitions.
The next section deals with the work of the farmer and the sailor,
although in no exhaustive fashion. Then, after another series of
miscellaneous maxims and precepts, Hesiod concludes with a sort of
farmer's almanac of lucky and unlucky days. It will be seen that the
work is not primarily a technical handbook on agriculture, like Vergil's *Georgics,* but a moral exhortation. It is unified in a rough
fashion through the two dominant themes of Justice and Work, and
the aim of the poem is to show man how to get along as best he can
in a difficult world.

    Hesiod is important in Western Culture as the first spokesman
for the common man; he represents the poor peasants against the
corrupt nobility of his day, and his passionate demand for equal
justice for all, honestly administered, points the way to the coming
publication of more equitable law-codes by such men as Draco and
Solon. Finally, his moral earnestness and religious fervour give
Hesiod a quality not unlike the Hebrew prophets, with whom he has
often been compared, especially in his denunciations of the unjust
princes and his glowing picture of the blessings of divine justice.

WORKS AND DAYS

    Muses of Pieria who give glory through song, come hither, tell of
Zeus your father and chant his praise. Through him mortal men
are famed or unfamed, sung or unsung alike, as great Zeus wills.
For easily he makes strong, and easily he brings the strong man low;
easily he humbles the proud and raises the obscure, and easily he
straightens the crooked and blasts the proud, — Zeus who thunders
aloft and has his dwelling most high. Attend thou with eye and
ear, and make judgments straight with righteousness. And I, Perses,
would tell of true things.

    So, after all, there was not one kind of Strife alone, but all over the
earth there are two. As for the one, a man would praise her when he
came to understand her; but the other is blameworthy: and they are

wholly different in nature. For one fosters evil war and battle, being cruel: her no man loves; but perforce, through the will of the death-less gods, men pay harsh Strife her honour due. But the other is the elder daughter of dark Night, and the son of Cronos who sits above and dwells in the aether, set her in the roots of the earth: and she is far kinder to men. She stirs up even the shiftless to toil; for a man grows eager to work when he considers his neighbour, a rich man who hastens to plough and plant and put his house in good order; and neighbour vies with his neighbour as he hurries after wealth. This strife is wholesome for men. And potter is angry with potter, and craftsman with craftsman, and beggar is jealous of beggar, and minstrel of minstrel.

Perses, lay up these things in your heart, and do not let that Strife who delights in mischief hold your heart back from work, while you peep and peer and listen to the wrangles of the court-house. Little concern has he with quarrels and courts who has not a year's victuals laid up betimes, even that which the earth bears, Demeter's grain. When you have got plenty of that, you can raise disputes and strive to get another's goods. But you shall have no second chance to deal so again: nay, let us settle our dispute here with true judgment which is of Zeus and is perfect. For we had already divided our inheritance, but you seized the greater share and carried it off, greatly swelling the glory of our bribe-swallowing lords who love to judge such a cause as this. Fools! They know not how much more the half is than the whole, nor what great advantage there is in mallow and asphodel.

For the gods keep hidden from men the means of life. Else you would easily do work enough in a day to supply you for a full year even without working; soon would you put away your rudder over the smoke, and the fields worked by ox and sturdy mule would run to waste. But Zeus in the anger of his heart hid it, because Prome-theus the crafty deceived him; therefore he planned sorrow and mis-chief against men. He hid fire; but that the noble son of Iapetus stole again for men from Zeus the counsellor in a hollow fennel-stalk, so that Zeus who delights in thunder did not see it. But afterwards Zeus who gathers the clouds said to him in anger:

"Son of Iapetus, surpassing all in cunning, you are glad that you have outwitted me and stolen fire — a great plague to you yourself and to men that shall be. But I will give men as the price for fire an evil thing in which they may all be glad of heart while they embrace their own destruction."

So said the father of men and gods, and laughed aloud. And he bade famous Hephaestus make haste and mix earth with water and to put in it the voice and strength of human kind, and fashion a sweet, lovely maiden-shape, like to the immortal goddesses in face; and Athene to teach her needlework and the weaving of the varied web; and golden Aphrodite to shed grace upon her head and cruel longing and cares that weary the limbs. And he charged Hermes the guide, the Slayer of Argus, to put in her a shameless mind and a deceitful nature.

So he ordered. And they obeyed the lord Zeus the son of Cronos. Forthwith the famous Lame God moulded clay in the likeness of a modest maid, as the son of Cronos purposed. And the goddess bright-eyed Athene girded and clothed her, and the divine Graces and queenly Persuasion put necklaces of gold upon her, and the rich-haired Hours crowned her head with spring flowers. And Pallas Athene bedecked her form with all manner of finery. Also The Guide, the Slayer of Argus, contrived within her lies and crafty words and a deceitful nature at the will of loud thundering Zeus, and the Herald of the gods put speech in her. And he called this woman Pandora, because all they who dwelt on Olympus gave each a gift, a plague to men who eat bread.

But when he had finished the sheer, hopeless snare, the Father sent glorious Argus-Slayer, the swift messenger of the gods, to take it to Epimetheus as a gift. And Epimetheus did not think on what Prometheus had said to him, bidding him never take a gift of Olympian Zeus, but to send it back for fear it might prove to be something harmful to men. But he took the gift and afterwards, when the evil thing was already his, he understood.

For ere this the tribes of men lived on earth remote and free from ills and hard toil and heavy sicknesses which bring the Fates upon men; for in misery men grow old quickly. But the woman took off the great lid of the jar with her hands and scattered all these and her thought caused sorrow and mischief to men. Only Hope remained there in an unbreakable home within under the rim of the great jar, and did not fly out at the door; for ere that, the lid of the jar stopped her, by the will of Aegis-holding Zeus who gathers the clouds. But the other countless plagues wander amongst men; for earth is full of evils and the sea is full. Of themselves diseases come upon men continually by day and by night, bringing mischief to mortals silently; for wise Zeus took away speech from them. So is there no way to escape the will of Zeus.

Or if you will, I will sum you up another tale well and skilfully — and do you lay it up in your heart, — how the gods and mortal men sprang from one source.

First of all the deathless gods who dwell on Olympus made a golden race of mortal men who lived in the time of Cronos when he was reigning in heaven. And they lived like gods without sorrow of heart, remote and free from toil and grief: miserable age rested not on them; but with legs and arms never failing they made merry with feasting beyond the reach of all evils. When they died, it was as though they were overcome with sleep, and they had all good things; for the fruitful earth unforced bare them fruit abundantly and without stint. They dwelt in ease and peace upon their lands with many good things, rich in flocks and loved by the blessed gods.

But after the earth had covered this generation — they are called pure spirits dwelling on the earth, and are kindly, delivering from harm, and guardians of mortal men; for they roam everywhere over the earth, clothed in mist and keep watch on judgments and cruel deeds, givers of wealth; for this royal right also they received; — then they who dwell on Olympus made a second generation which was of silver and less noble by far. It was like the golden race neither in body nor in spirit. A child was brought up at his mother's side an hundred years, an utter simpleton, playing childishly in his own home. But when they were full grown and were come to the full measure of their prime, they lived only a little time and that in sorrow because of their foolishness, for they could not keep from sinning and from wronging one another, nor would they serve the immortals, nor sacrifice on the holy altars of the blessed ones as it is right for men to do wherever they dwell. Then Zeus the son of Cronos was angry and put them away, because they would not give honour to the blessed gods who live on Olympus.

But when earth had covered this generation also — they are called blessed spirits of the underworld by men, and, though they are of second order, yet honour attends them also — Zeus the Father made a third generation of mortal men, a brazen race, sprung from ash-trees; and it was in no way equal to the silver age, but was terrible and strong. They loved the lamentable works of Ares and deeds of violence; they ate no bread, but were hard of heart like adamant, fearful men. Great was their strength and unconquerable the arms which grew from their shoulders on their strong limbs. Their armour was of bronze, and their houses of bronze, and of bronze were their implements: there was no black iron. These were destroyed by their own hands and passed to the dank house of chill Hades, and left no name: terrible though they were, black Death seized them, and they left the bright light of the sun.

But when earth had covered this generation also, Zeus the son of Cronos made yet another, the fourth, upon the fruitful earth, which was nobler and more righteous, a god-like race of hero-men who are called demi-gods, the race before our own, throughout the boundless earth. Grim war and dread battle destroyed a part of them, some in the land of Cadmus at seven-gated Thebe when they fought for the flocks of Oedipus, and some, when it had brought them in ships over the great sea gulf to Troy for rich-haired Helen's sake: there death's end enshrouded a part of them. But to the others father Zeus the son of Cronos gave a living and an abode apart from men, and made them dwell at the ends of earth. And they live untouched by sorrow in the islands of the blessed along the shore of deep swirling Ocean, happy heroes for whom the grain-giving earth bears honey-sweet fruit flourishing thrice a year, far from the deathless gods, and Cronos rules over them; for the father of men and gods released him from his bonds. And these last equally have honour and glory.

And again far-seeing Zeus made yet another generation, the fifth, of men who are upon the bounteous earth.

Thereafter, would that I were not among the men of the fifth generation, but either had died before or been born afterwards. For now truly is a race of iron, and men never rest from labour and sorrow by day and from perishing by night; and the gods shall lay sore trouble upon them. But, notwithstanding even these shall have some good mingled with their evils. And Zeus will destroy this race of mortal men also when they come to have grey hair on the temples at their birth. The father will not agree with his children, nor the children with their father, nor guest with his host, nor comrade with comrade; nor will brother be dear to brother as aforetime. Men will dishonour their parents as they grow quickly old, and will carp at them, chiding them with bitter words, hard-hearted they, not knowing the fear of the gods. They will not repay their aged parents the cost of their nurture, for might shall be their right: and one man will sack another's city. There will be no favour for the man who keeps his oath or for the just or for the good; but rather men will praise the evil-doer and his violent dealing. Strength will be right and reverence will cease to be; and the wicked will hurt the worthy man, speaking false words against him, and will swear an oath upon them. Envy, foul-mouthed, delighting in evil, with scowling face, will go along with wretched men one and all. And then Aidôs and Nemesis, with their sweet forms wrapped in white robes, will go from the wide-pathed earth and forsake mankind to join the company of the deathless gods: and bitter sorrows will be left for mortal men, and there will be no help against evil.

And now I will tell a fable for princes, who themselves understand. Thus said the hawk to the nightingale with speckled neck, while he carried her high up among the clouds, gripped fast in his talons, and she, pierced by his crooked talons, cried pitifully. To her he spoke disdainfully: "Miserable thing, why do you cry out? One far stronger than you now holds you fast, and you must go wherever I take you, songstress as you are. And if I please I will make my meal of you, or let you go. He is a fool who tries to withstand the stronger, for he does not get the mastery and suffers pain besides his shame." So said the swiftly flying hawk, the long-winged bird.

But you, Perses, listen to right and do not foster violence; for violence is bad for a poor man. Even the prosperous cannot easily bear its burden, but is weighed down under it when he has fallen into delusion. The better path is to go by on the other side toward justice; for Justice beats Outrage when she comes at length to the end of the race. But only when he has suffered does the fool learn this. For Oath keeps pace with wrong judgments. There is a noise when Justice is being dragged in the way where those who devour bribes and give sentence with crooked judgments, take her. And she, wrapped in mist, follows to the city and haunts of the people, weeping, and bringing mischief to men, even to such as have driven her forth in that they did not deal straightly with her.

But they who give straight judgments to strangers and to the men of the land, and go not aside from what is just, their city flourishes, and the people prosper in it: Peace, the nurse of children, is abroad in their land, and all-seeing Zeus never decrees cruel war against them. Neither famine nor disaster ever haunt men who do true justice; but lightheartedly they tend the fields which are all their care. The earth bears them victual in plenty, and on the mountains the oak bears acorns upon the top and bees in the midst. Their woolly sheep are laden with fleeces; their women bear children like their parents. They flourish continually with good things, and do not travel on ships, for the grain-giving earth bears them fruit.

But for those who practise violence and cruel deeds far-seeing Zeus, the son of Cronos, ordains a punishment. Often even a whole city suffers for a bad man who sins and devises presumptuous deeds, and the son of Cronos lays great troubles upon the people, famine and plague together, so that the men perish away, and their women do not bear children, and their houses become few, through the contriving of Olympian Zeus. And again, at another time, the son of Cronos either destroys their wide army, or their walls, or else makes an end of their ships on the sea.

You princes, mark well this punishment you also; for the deathless gods are near among men and mark all those who oppress their fellows with crooked judgments, and reck not the anger of the gods. For upon the bounteous earth Zeus has thrice ten thousand spirits, watchers of mortal men, and these keep watch on judgments and the deeds of wrong as they roam, clothed in mist, all over the earth. And there is virgin Justice, the daughter of Zeus, who is honoured and reverenced among the gods who dwell on Olympus, and whenever anyone hurts her with lying slander, she sits beside her father, Zeus the son of Cronos, and tells him of men's wicked heart, until the people pay for the mad folly of their princes who, evilly minded, pervert judgment and give sentence crookedly. Keep watch against this, you princes, and make straight your judgments, you who devour bribes; put crooked judgments altogether from your thoughts.

⌈1-264, tr. Hugh G. Evelyn-White⌉

APOLLONIUS OF RHODES

(ca. 295–ca. 215 B.C.)

Apollonius was an Alexandrian Greek of the third century B.C.; he was associated with the great scholars and critics of the Library at Alexandria, but he became involved in a bitter literary quarrel with Callimachus, the leading spirit of the age, and left Alexandria for Rhodes. The quarrel, one of the famous literary feuds of antiquity, arose over the question of the proper length for a poem and whether a long epic poem in the manner of Homer might still be successful. Callimachus maintained the prevailing view of the Alexandrian Age: "A big book is a big nuisance"; and his own poetry was usually that of the shorter forms — the epyllion, the hymn, and the epigram. Apollonius defied the critical taste of his own times in publishing his *Argonautica,* an epic poem in four lengthy books, which was most unfavourably received. Actually, the work fails to substantiate Apollonius' contention that such works could still be written and appreciated, since the *Argonautica* notably lacks the unity and coherence of Homer, and, when read through, seems extremely dull. In certain episodes, however, it is a work of considerable interest and some originality, especially in the story of Jason and Medea, which forms one of the chief sources for Vergil's *Aeneid,* Book IV.

The poem opens with the mustering of the heroes at Pagasae and their departure in quest of the Golden Fleece. The first two books relate their journey, step by step, until they reach Colchis in the Euxine. At this point Apollonius develops with great skill the love-story of Jason and Medea, an episode which reflects the erotic taste of the Alexandrian Age. Medea, the daughter of King Aeetes, falls in love with Jason when he comes to request the Fleece from her father. As a price for the Fleece Aeetes sets a contest for Jason: he must yoke the King's fire-breathing bulls, plough a field with them, and sow the dragon's teeth, from which will spring fully-armed warriors whom Jason must slay. Jason accepts the contest but privately despairs of accomplishing the tasks. But Medea is prevailed upon, through emissaries, to aid Jason and compound a charm to protect him. A meeting between the two is arranged at a shrine of Hecate outside the city, and our selection begins at this point.

THE ARGONAUTS

JASON AND MEDEA

But Medea — her thoughts unto nought else turned, upon nought
    could be stayed,
Howsoever she sang — but never a song, howsoe'er she essayed,
Pleased her, that long its melody winged her feet for the dance;
But ever she faltered amidst them, her eyes ever wandered askance

Away from the throng of her maidens unresting; and over the ways,
Turning aside her cheeks, far off ever strained she her gaze.
O the heart in her breast oft fainted, whenever in fancy she heard
Fleet past her the sound of a footfall, the breath of a breeze as it
    stirred.
But it was not long ere the hero appeared to her yearning eyes
Stately striding, as out of the ocean doth Sirius uprise,
Who climbeth the sky most glorious and clear to discern from afar,
But unto the flocks for measureless mischief a baleful star:
Even so came Aison's son to the maiden glorious to see, —
But with Jason's appearing dawned on her troublous misery.
Then it seemed as her heart dropped out of her bosom; a dark mist
    came
Over her eyes, and hot in her cheeks did the blushes flame.
Nor backward nor forward a step could she stir: all strength was gone
From her knees; and her feet to the earth seemed rooted; and one
    after one
Her handmaidens all drew back, and with him was she left alone.
    So these twain stood — all stirless and wordless stood face to face:
As oaks they seemed, or as pines upsoaring in stately grace,
Which side by side all still mid the mountains rooted stand
When winds are hushed; but by breath of the breeze when at late
    they are fanned,
Stir they with multitudinous murmur and sigh — so they
By love's breath stirred were to pour out all in their hearts that lay.
    Then Aison's son beheld how the maiden's soul was adread
With wilderment heaven-sent, and kindly-courteous he said:
    "Wherefore, O maiden, dost fear me so sorely, alone as I am?
Never was I as the loud-tongued blusterers, void of shame,
No, not when aforetime I dwelt in my fatherland oversea:
Wherefore be thou not, maiden, over-abashed before me,
That thou shouldst not inquire whatsoever thou wilt, or utter thy
    mind.
But, seeing we twain be met with friendly hearts and kind
In a place where sin is of heaven accurst, in a hallowed spot,
Speak thou, and question withal as thou wilt: but beguile me not
With pleasant words, forasmuch as thou gavest thy promise ere while
To thy sister, to give me the charm that I long for, the herbs of guile.
I beseech thee in Hekatê's name — for the sake of thy parents I pray,
And of Zeus, that o'er stranger and suppliant stretcheth his hand
    alway!
Lo, a suppliant am I, a stranger withal, which am come to thee here,
In sore straits bending the knee; for in this my task of fear
Shall I nowise prevail, except I be holpen of thine and thee.
And to thee will I render requital of thanks in the days to be —
As is meet and right for them in a far-away land which dwell —
Making glorious thy name and thy fame, and mine hero-companions
    shall tell
The story of thy renown, when to Hellas again they have won;

Yea, and the heroes' wives and mothers, who now make moan
For us, I ween, on the strand as they sit by the sighing brine:
And to scatter in air their bitter affliction is thine — is thine!
Not I were the first — was Theseus not saved from the ordeal grim
By Minos' child for her kindness' sake which she bare unto him,
Ariadne, born of the Sun-god's daughter Pasiphaê?
But she, when slumbered the wrath of Minos, over the sea
Sailed with the hero, forsaking her land.   The Immortals divine
Loved well that maid: in the midst of the firmament set is her sign,
A crown of stars, which they name Ariadne's diadem,
All night circling amidst of the signs that the heavens begem.
Thou also shalt have of the Gods like thanks, if thou shalt redeem
From destruction so goodly a host of heroes — ah, needs must it seem
That through form so lovely as thine should the beauty of kindness
        beam!"
Extolling her so spake he; and her eyelids drooped, while played
A nectar-smile on her lips; and melted the heart of the maid
By his praising uplifted: her eyes are a moment upraised to his eyes,
And all speech faileth: no word at the first to her lips may rise;
But in one breath yearned she to speak forth all her joy and her pain.
And with hand ungrudging forth from her odorous zone hath she
        ta'en
The charm, and he straightway received it into his hands full fain.
Yea, now would she even have drawn forth all her soul from her
        breast,
And had laid it with joy in his hands for her gift, had he made request,
So wondrously now from the golden head of Aison's son
Did Love out-lighten the witchery-flame; and her sweet eyes shone
With the gleam that he stole therefrom, and her heart glowed
        through and through
Melting for rapture away, from the lips of the rose as the dew
At the sun's kiss melteth away, when the dayspring is kindled anew.
And these twain now on the earth were fixing their eyes abashed,
And anon yet again their glances each on the other they flashed,
As with radiant eyelids they smiled a heart-beguiling smile;
And bespake him the maiden at last, yet scarce after all this while:
   "Give thou heed now, that my counsel may haply be for thine aid.
What time at thy coming my father within thine hands shall have laid
The crop of the serpent's jaws for thy sowing, the teeth of bane,
Then shalt thou watch for the hour when the night is sundered in
        twain.
Then thou, when first in the river's tireless flow thou hast bathed,
Alone, with none other beside thee, in night-hued vesture swathed,
Shalt dig thee a rounded pit, and over the dark earth-bowl
Shalt thou slaughter a ewe, and shalt burn the unsevered carcase
        whole
On a pyre, the which on the very brink of the pit thou hast piled,
And propitiate only-begotten Hekatê, Perses' child,
Out of a chalice pouring the hive-stored toil of the bee.

So when thou hast sought the grace of the Goddess heedfully,
Then turn thee to pass from the pyre, and beware lest any sound
Or of footfalls behind thee startle thee, so that thou turn thee round,
Or of baying of hounds, lest all that is wrought be undone thereby.
And thyself to thine hero-companions never again draw nigh.
And in water at dawn shalt thou steep this herb, and thy limbs shalt
        thou bare,
And even as with oil shalt anoint thee therewith; and prowess there
Shalt thou find, and strength exceeding great: thou wouldst nowise
        say
That with men thou couldst match thee in might, but with Gods that
        abide for aye.
Therewithal be thy lance and thy buckler besprent with the magic dew,
And thy sword: then shall not the spear-heads prevail to pierce thee
        through
Of the Earth-born men, nor the fiery breath of the bulls of bane
Unendurably darting.   Yet no long time shalt thou thus remain,
But only for that same day: notwithstanding flinch not thou
From the toil; and another thing yet for thine help will I tell to thee
        now:
So soon as the mighty bulls thou hast yoked, and by manifold toil
And by strength of thine hands hast sped the share through the stub-
        born soil,
And adown the furrows the bristling harvest of giants shall stand,
Where fell on the dusky clods the serpent's teeth from thine hand,
Even as thou mark'st them in throngs through the fallows up-
        bursting to day,
Cast thou in their midst unawares a massy stone: and they,
As ravening hounds o'er a gobbet of flesh that wrangle, shall slay
Each one his fellow: thou also in battle-fury shalt fall
On the rout.   So the Golden Fleece unto Hellas, if this be all,
From Aia afar shalt thou bear: — O yea, turn thou and depart
Whithersoever it pleaseth thee: seek the desire of thine heart!"
    She spake, and her eyes to the earth at her feet in silence she cast;
And her cheeks divinely fair were wet as her tears fell fast,
As she sorrowed because that far and afar from her side o'er the main
He must wander away.   And she looked in his eyes, and she spake
        yet again
With mournful word, and his right hand now hath she ta'en in her
        own;
For the shamefastness now from her eyes on the wings of love had
        flown:
    "But O remember, if ever thou com'st to thine home afar,
Medea's name: and in like wise I, when sundered we are,
Will forget thee not.   But tell, of thy good will, where is thine home,
Whitherward bound thou wilt fare in thy galley over the foam.
Is it unto Orchomenus' wealthy burg that thy feet shall go?
Or anigh to Aiaia's isle?   Of the maiden fain would I know,
Some maiden far-renowned, whom thou namedst the daughter, I wis,

Of Pasiphaê: kinswoman unto my sire that lady is."
  So did she speak; and over him stole, as the maiden wept,
Love the victorious; and answering speech to his lips hath leapt:
  "Yea, verily, never by night, I ween, and by day nevermore
Shalt thou be forgotten of me, if unto Achaia's shore
Unscathed I shall 'scape indeed, and Aiêtes before me set,
For mine hands to achieve, none other toil more desperate yet.
But if this hath pleased thee, to learn what land I call mine own,
I will tell thee — yea, and mine own heart biddeth me make it known.
A country there is — steep mountain-ramparts around it run —
A land of streams and of pastures, wherein Iapetus' son,
Even Prometheus, begat the valiant Deukalion,
Who of all men was first that builded a city, or reared a fane
To the Deathless, and first was he of the kings over men that reign.
That land do the folk that around it dwell Haimonia call.
Therein is my city Iolkos found: therein withal
Stand many beside, where not so much have they heard as the name
Of Aiaia's isle: but rumour hath told how Minyas came
Thereout, even Minyas Aiolus' son, and builded the town
Of Orchomenus; over the marches Kadmeian her towers look down.
Yet why should I speak things vain as the wild winds' empty sound
Of our home, of the daughter of Minos, the princess far-renowned
Ariadne — the glorious name whereby that heart's desire
Was called among men, the maiden of whom thou dost inquire?
Would God that, even as Minos his heart unto Theseus inclined
For her sake, so would thy father with me be in friendship joined!"
  So spake he, with tender words and caressing the maiden to woo.
But anguish exceeding bitter was thrilling the heart of her through:
And in sorrow of spirit with vehement words she made reply:
  "O haply in Hellas 'tis good to be heedful of friendship's tie:
But Aiêtes is not such a man among men as thou saidst but now
Was Minos, Pasiphaê's lord; and with Ariadne, I trow,
May I nowise compare me: wherefore of guest-love speak not thou.
Only remember thou me, when safe thou hast sped thy flight
To Iolkos; and I will remember — yea, in my parents' despite
Will remember thee: and from far may a rumour come unto me,
Or a messenger-bird with the tidings, when I am forgotten of thee!
Or me, even me, may the swift-wingèd blasts from the earth's breast
        tear,
And away hence over the sea to the land of Iolkos bear,
That so I might cast reproaches on thee, yea, unto thy face,
And remind thee that all by mine help thou escapedst — but oh that
        my place
That day were of right in thine halls, the place of a queen at the
        board!"
  So spake she, and down her cheeks the piteous tears aye poured.
But he caught up her words even there, and with comforting speech
        did he say:
  "O stricken one, leave thou the empty blasts at their will stray,

And the messenger-bird to roam, for thy words are but vanity!
But if ever thou come unto those abodes, if Hellas thou see,
Honour and worship of men and of women then shall be thine;
Yea, they shall reverence thee as a very presence divine,
Because that again to their homes did the sons of the Hellenes win
By thy devising, yea, and the brethren of these, and their kin;
And many a stalwart husband of thee hath received his life.
Then shalt thou enter the bridal bower with me — my wife;
And nothing shall come between our love, and nothing shall sunder,
Till death's shroud fold us around, and our hearts are chilled there-
    under."
    He spake, and to hear him her soul was melted within her then:
Yet she shuddered to see the deeds whose end was beyond her ken.
Ah hapless! — not long was she doomed to refuse a home in the land
Of Hellas, for hereunto was she guided of Hêra's hand,
To the end that for Pelias' bane Aiaian Medea might come
Unto Iolkos the hallowed, forsaking her fatherland-home.
    But by this from afar were the handmaids glancing towards these
        twain
Full oft in disquiet; for need was now, as the day 'gan wane,
That the maiden unto her mother should turn her homeward again.
But she thought not yet of departing, such joy did her spirit take
Alike in his goodlihead, and the winsome words that he spake.
But Aison's son took heed, and late and at last did he say:
    "Lo now, it is time to depart, lest the sun's light fade away
Before we be ware, and lest some stranger should haply espy
All this. Yet again will we meet, coming hitherward, thou and I."
                                    [III. 948–1145, tr. A. S. Way]

HYMNS

The Greeks developed two types of hymns: one a branch of choral lyric poetry, the other "rhapsodic," — *i.e.,* performed by a rhapsode, or reciter of epic. Of this latter type, which was written in the style and meter of Homer, we have extant thirty-three examples, composed by the post-Homeric bards between the eighth and the fifth centuries B.C. These so-called Homeric Hymns were technically called "preludes" in antiquity; and the closing formula in many of them ("And so farewell . . . ; but I will remember you and another song also.") suggests the most probable origin of the form: the rhapsode, before beginning his recitation of Homer, might invoke one of the gods in a short prelude. This short prelude might, on occasion, be developed to considerable length by the insertion of myths about the god invoked; and there can be no doubt that a composition as long as the *Hymn to Hermes,* for example, formed a complete recitation in itself. Of the present selections, the *Hymn to Hermes* is the earliest in date, perhaps coming from the first part of the sixth century B.C. This delightful poem, with its humorous and completely non-moral picture of the gods, is well known to English readers through Shelley's translation. The two brief hymns, *To Earth* and *To Selene,* are noteworthy for their keen appreciation of the beauties of nature.

The *Hymn to Apollo* of Callimachus, which follows, is in the same form, but is far different in spirit. Callimachus, who has already been mentioned in the introduction to Apollonius of Rhodes, is one of the most important figures in the history of later Greek literature. A native of Cyrene, he spent most of his life at Alexandria under the Ptolemies, engaged in scholarly pursuits and writing in the great royal library there. More than any other single man he imposed on later Greek literature those qualities which have come to be called "Alexandrian" in various other literatures: perfection of form, delicacy and refinement, meticulous avoidance of the commonplace, and abundant use of learned allusions. Few of his many works survived the Middle Ages; besides a few recently discovered papyrus fragments, we have about sixty epigrams (for which, see below p. 1033) and six hymns, in the form and style of the Homeric Hymns. But there is no longer any connection with the rhapsode's performance; the *Hymn to Apollo,* for example, pretends to be sung by a chorus of youths at the Dorian festival of the Carneia, although it is hardly likely that this fiction is to be taken seriously. At any rate, what we have in this poem smacks of the lamp and the study; Callimachus describes the glory of the god with great ingenuity and learning, but without much genuine poetic inspiration. The poem is included here partly for comparison with the earlier hymns, partly as a good example of what Alexandrianism means when separated from the genius of a Theocritus.

HERMES

Of Hermes sing, O Muse, the son of Zeus and Maia, Lord of Cyllene, and Arcadia rich in sheep, the fortune-bearing Herald of the Gods, him whom Maia bore, the fair-tressed nymph, that lay in the arms of Zeus; a shamefaced nymph was she, shunning the assembly of the blessed Gods, dwelling within a shadowy cave. Therein was Cronion wont to embrace the fair-tressed nymph in the deep of night, when sweet sleep held white-armed Hera, the immortal Gods knowing it not, nor mortal men.

But when the mind of great Zeus was fulfilled, and over her the tenth moon stood in the sky, the babe was born to light, and all was made manifest; yea, then she bore a child of many a wile and cunning counsel, a robber, a driver of the kine, a captain of raiders, a watcher of the night, a thief of the gates, who soon should show forth deeds renowned among the deathless Gods. Born in the dawn, by midday well he harped, and in the evening stole the cattle of Apollo the Fardarter, on that fourth day of the month wherein lady Maia bore him. Who, when he leaped from the immortal knees of his mother, lay not long in the sacred cradle, but sped forth to seek the cattle of Apollo, crossing the threshold of the high-roofed cave. There found he a tortoise, and won endless delight, for lo, it was Hermes that first made of the tortoise a minstrel. The creature met him at the outer door, as she fed on the rich grass in front of the dwelling, waddling along, at sight whereof the luck-bringing son of Zeus laughed, and straightway spoke, saying:

"Lo, a lucky omen for me, not by me to be mocked! Hail, darling and dancer, friend of the feast, welcome art thou! whence gatst thou the gay garment, a speckled shell, thou, a mountain-dwelling tortoise? Nay, I will carry thee within, and a boon shalt thou be to me, not by me to be scorned, nay, thou shalt first serve my turn. Best it is to bide at home, since danger is abroad. Living shalt thou be a spell against ill witchery, and dead, then a right sweet music-maker."

So spake he, and raising in both hands the tortoise, went back within the dwelling, bearing the glad treasure. Then he choked the creature, and with a gouge of grey iron he scooped out the marrow of the hill tortoise. And as a swift thought wings through the breast of one that crowding cares are haunting, or as bright glances fleet from the eyes, so swiftly devised renowned Hermes both deed and word. He cut to measure stalks of reed, and fixed them in through holes bored in the stony shell of the tortoise, and cunningly stretched round it the hide of an ox, and put in the horns of the lyre, and to both he fitted the bridge, and stretched seven harmonious chords of sheep-gut.

Then took he his treasure, when he had fashioned it, and touched the strings in turn with the *plectrum,* and wondrously it sounded under his hand, and fair sang the God to the notes, improvising his chant as he played, like lads exchanging taunts at festivals. Of Zeus Cronides and fair-sandalled Maia he sang how they had lived in loving dalliance, and he told out the tale of his begetting, and sang the handmaids and the goodly halls of the nymph, and the tripods in the house, and the store of cauldrons. So then he sang, but dreamed of other deeds; then bore he the hollow lyre and laid it in the sacred cradle, then, in longing for flesh of kine he sped from the fragrant hall to a place of outlook, with such a design in his heart as reiving men pursue in the dark of night.

The sun had sunk down beneath earth into ocean, with horses and chariot, when Hermes came running to the shadowy hills of Pieria, where the deathless kine of the blessed Gods had ever their haunt; there fed they on the fair unshorn meadows. From their number did the keen-sighted Argeiphontes, son of Maia, cut off fifty loud-lowing kine, and drove them hither and thither over the sandy land, reversing their tracks, and, mindful of his cunning, confused the hoof-marks, the front behind, the hind in front, and himself fared down again. Straightway he wove sandals on the sea-sand (things undreamed he wrought, works wonderful, unspeakable) mingling myrtle twigs and tamarisk, then binding together a bundle of the fresh young wood, he shrewdly fastened it for light sandals beneath his feet, leaves and all — brushwood that the renowned slayer of Argos had plucked on his way from Pieria [being, as he was, in haste, down the long way].

Then an old man that was labouring a fruitful vineyard, marked the God faring down to the plain through grassy Onchestus, and to him spoke first the son of renowned Maia:

"Old man that bowest thy shoulders over thy hoeing, verily thou shalt have wine enough when all these vines are bearing. . . See thou, and see not; hear thou, and hear not; be silent, so long as naught of thine is harmed."

Therewith he drave on together the sturdy heads of cattle. And over many a shadowy hill, and through echoing corries and flowering plains drave renowned Hermes. Then stayed for the more part his darkling ally, the sacred Night, and swiftly came morning when men can work, and sacred Selene, daughter of Pallas, mighty prince, clomb to a new place of outlook, and then the strong son of Zeus drave the broad-browed kine of Phoebus Apollo to the river Alpheius. Unwearied they came to the high-roofed stall and the watering-places in front of the fair meadow. There, when he had foddered the deep-voiced kine, he herded them huddled together into the byre, munching lotus and dewy marsh marigold; next brought he much wood, and set himself to the craft of fire-kindling. Taking a goodly shoot of the daphne, he peeled it with the knife, fitting it to his hand, and the hot vapour of smoke arose. [Lo, it was Hermes first who gave fire, and the fire-sticks.] Then took he many dry faggots, great plenty, and piled them in the trench, and flame began to break, sending far the breath of burning fire. And when the force of renowned

Hephaestus kept the fire aflame, then downward dragged he, so mighty his strength, two bellowing kine of twisted horn: close up to the fire he dragged them, and cast them both panting upon their backs to the ground. [Then bending over them he turned them upwards and cut their throats] . . . task upon task, and sliced off the fat meat, pierced it with spits of wood, and broiled it — flesh, and chine, the joint of honour, and blood in the bowels, all together; — then laid all there in its place. The hides he stretched out on a broken rock, as even now they are used, such as are to be enduring: long, and long after that ancient day. Anon glad Hermes dragged the fat portions on to a smooth ledge, and cut twelve messes sorted out by lot, to each its due meed he gave. Then a longing for the rite of the sacrifice of flesh came on renowned Hermes: for the sweet savour irked him, immortal as he was, but not even so did his strong heart yield. . . The fat and flesh he placed in the high-roofed stall, the rest he swiftly raised aloft, a trophy of his reiving, and, gathering dry faggots, he burned heads and feet entire with the vapour of flame. Anon when the God had duly finished all, he cast his sandals into the deep swirling pool of Alpheius, quenched the embers, and all night long spread smooth the black dust: Selene lighting him with her lovely light. Back to the crests of Cyllene came the God at dawn, nor blessed God, on that long way, nor mortal man encountered him; nay, and no dog barked. Then Hermes, son of Zeus, bearer of boon, bowed his head, and entered the hall through the hole of the bolt, like mist on the breath of autumn. Then, standing erect, he sped to the rich inmost chamber of the cave, lightly treading noiseless on the floor. Quickly to his cradle came glorious Hermes and wrapped the swaddling bands about his shoulders, like a witless babe, playing with the wrapper about his knees. So lay he, guarding his dear lyre at his left hand. But his Goddess mother the God did not deceive; she spake, saying:

"Wherefore, thou cunning one, and whence comest thou in the night, thou clad in shamelessness? Anon, methinks, thou wilt go forth at Apollo's hands with bonds about thy sides that may not be broken, sooner than be a robber in the glens. Go to, wretch, thy Father begat thee for a trouble to deathless Gods and mortal men."

But Hermes answered her with words of guile: "Mother mine, why wouldst thou scare me so, as though I were a redeless child, with little craft in his heart, a trembling babe that dreads his mother's chidings? Nay, but I will essay the wiliest craft to feed thee and me for ever. We twain are not to endure to abide here, of all the death-less Gods alone unapproached with sacrifice and prayer, as thou com-mandest. Better it is eternally to be conversant with Immortals, richly, nobly, well seen in wealth of grain, than to be homekeepers in a darkling cave. And for honour, I too will have my dues of sacrifice, even as Apollo. Even if my Father give it me not I will endeavour, for I am of avail, to be a captain of reivers. And if the son of re-nowned Leto make inquest for me, methinks some worse thing will befall him. For to Pytho I will go, to break into his great house, whence I shall sack goodly tripods and cauldrons enough, and gold, and gleaming iron, and much raiment. Thyself, if thou hast a mind, shalt see it."

So held they converse one with another, the son of Zeus of the Aegis, and Lady Maia. Then Morning the Daughter of Dawn was arising from the deep stream of Oceanus, bearing light to mortals, what time Apollo came to Onchestus in his journeying, the gracious grove, a holy place of the loud Girdler of the Earth: there he found an old man grazing his ox, the stay of his vineyard, on the roadside. Him first bespoke the son of renowned Leto.

"Old man, hedger of grassy Onchestus; hither am I come seeking cattle from Pieria, all the crook-horned kine out of my herd: my black bull was wont to graze apart from the rest, and my four bright-eyed hounds followed, four of them, wise as men and all of one mind. These were left, the hounds and the bull, a marvel; but the kine wandered away from their soft meadow and sweet pasture, at the going down of the sun. Tell me, thou old man of ancient days, if thou hast seen any man faring after these cattle?"

Then to him the old man spake and answered:

"My friend, hard it were to tell all that a man may see: for many wayfarers go by, some full of ill intent, and some of good: and it is difficult to be certain regarding each. Nevertheless, the whole day long till sunset I was digging about my vineyard plot, and methought I marked — but I know not surely — a child that went after the horned kine; right young he was, and held a staff, and kept going from side to side, and backwards he drove the kine, their faces fronting him."

So spake the old man, but Apollo heard, and went fleeter on his path. Then marked he a bird long of wing, and anon he knew that the thief had been the son of Zeus Cronion. Swiftly sped the Prince, Apollo, son of Zeus, to goodly Pylos, seeking the shambling kine, while his broad shoulders were swathed in purple cloud. Then the Far-darter marked the tracks, and spake:

"Verily, a great marvel mine eyes behold! These be the tracks of high-horned kine, but all are turned back to the meadow of asphodel. But these are not the footsteps of a man, nay, nor of a woman, nor of grey wolves, nor bears, nor lions, nor, methinks, of a shaggy-maned Centaur, whosoever with fleet feet makes such mighty strides! Dread to see they are that backwards go, more dread they that go forwards."

So speaking, the Prince sped on, Apollo, son of Zeus. To the Cyllenian hill he came, that is clad in forests, to the deep shadow of the hollow rock, where the deathless nymph brought forth the child of Zeus Cronion. A fragrance sweet was spread about the goodly hill, and many tall sheep were grazing the grass. Thence he went fleetly over the stone threshold into the dusky cave, even Apollo, the Far-darter.

Now when the son of Zeus and Maia beheld Apollo thus in wrath for his kine, he sank down within his fragrant swaddling bands, being covered as piled embers of burnt tree-roots are covered by thick ashes, so Hermes coiled himself up, when he saw the Far-darter; and curled himself, feet, head, and hands, into small space [summoning sweet sleep], though of a verity wide awake, and his tortoise-shell he kept beneath his armpit. But the son of Zeus and Leto marked them well, the lovely mountain nymph and her dear son, a little babe, all wrapped in cunning wiles. Gazing round all the chamber of the vasty dwelling, Apollo opened three aumbries with the shining key; full were they of nectar and glad ambrosia, and much gold and silver lay within, and much raiment of the Nymph, purple and glistering, such as are within the dwellings of the mighty Gods. Anon, when he had searched out the chambers of the great hall, the son of Leto spake to renowned Hermes:

"Child, in the cradle lying, tell me straightway of my kine: or speedily between us twain will be unseemly strife. For I will seize thee and cast thee into murky Tartarus, into the darkness of doom where none is of avail. Nor shall thy father or mother redeem thee to the light: nay, under earth shalt thou roam, a reiver among folk fordone."

Then Hermes answered with words of craft: "Apollo, what ungentle word hast thou spoken? And is it thy cattle of the homestead thou comest here to seek? I saw them not, heard not of them, gave ear to no word of them: of them I can tell no tidings, nor win the fee of him who tells. Not like a lifter of cattle, a stalwart man, am I: no task is this of mine: hitherto I have other cares; sleep, and mother's milk, and about my shoulders swaddling bands, and warmed baths. Let none know whence this feud arose! And verily great marvel among the Immortals it would be, that a new-born child should cross the threshold after kine of the homestead; a silly rede of thine. Yesterday was I born, my feet are tender, and rough is the earth below. But if thou wilt I shall swear the great oath by my father's head, that neither I myself am to blame, nor have I seen any other thief of thy kine: be kine what they may, for I know but by hearsay."

So spake he with twinkling eyes, and twisted brows, glancing hither and thither, with long-drawn whistling breath, hearing Apollo's word as a vain thing. Then lightly laughing spake Apollo the Fardarter:

"Oh, thou rogue, thou crafty one; verily methinks that many a time thou wilt break into stablished homes, and by night leave many a man bare, silently pilling through his house, such is thy speech to-day! And many herdsmen of the steadings wilt thou vex in the mountain glens, when in lust for flesh thou comest on the herds and sheep thick of fleece. Nay come, lest thou sleep the last and longest slumber, come forth from thy cradle, thou companion of black night! For surely this honour hereafter thou shalt have among the Immortals, to be called for ever the captain of reivers."

So spake Phoebus Apollo, and lifted the child, but even then strong Argus-bane had his device, and, in the hands of the God, let forth an Omen, an evil belly-tenant, with tidings of worse, and a

speedy sneeze thereafter. Apollo heard, and dropped renowned
Hermes on the ground, then sat down before him, eager as he was
to be gone, chiding Hermes, and thus he spoke:

"Take heart, swaddling one, child of Zeus and Maia. By these
thine Omens shall I find anon the sturdy kine, and thou shalt lead
the way."

So spake he, but swiftly arose Cyllenian Hermes, and swiftly fared,
pulling about his ears his swaddling bands that were his shoulder
wrapping. Then spake he:

"Whither bearest thou me, Far-darter, of Gods most vehement? Is
it for wrath about thy kine that thou thus provokest me? Would
that the race of kine might perish, for thy cattle have I not stolen,
nor seen another steal, whatsoever kine may be; I know but by hearsay, I! But let our suit be judged before Zeus Cronion."

Now were lone Hermes and the splendid son of Leto point by point
disputing their pleas, Apollo with sure knowledge was righteously
seeking to convict renowned Hermes for the sake of his kine, but he
with craft and cunning words sought to beguile, — the Cyllenian to
beguile the God of the Silver Bow. But when the wily one found
one as wily, then speedily he strode forward through the sand in
front, while behind came the son of Zeus and Leto. Swiftly they
came to the crests of fragrant Olympus, to father Cronion they came,
these goodly sons of Zeus, for there were set for them the balances
of doom. Quiet was snowy Olympus, but they who know not decay
or death were gathering after gold-throned Dawn. Then stood
Hermes and Apollo of the Silver Bow before the knees of Zeus, the
Thunderer, who inquired of his glorious Son, saying:

"Phoebus, whence drivest thou such mighty spoil, a new-born babe
like a Herald? A mighty matter this, to come before the gathering
of the Gods!"

Then answered him the Prince, Apollo the Far-darter:

"Father, anon shalt thou hear no empty tale; tauntest thou me, as
though I were the only lover of booty? This boy have I found, a
finished reiver, in the hills of Cyllene, a long way to wander; so fine a
knave as I know not among Gods or men, of all robbers on earth.
My kine he stole from the meadows, and went driving them at even-
tide along the loud sea shores, straight to Pylos. Wondrous were the
tracks, a thing to marvel on, work of a glorious god. For the black
dust showed the tracks of the kine making backward to the mead of
asphodel; but this child intractable fared neither on hands nor feet,
through the sandy land, but this other strange craft had he, to tread
the paths as if shod on with oaken shoots. While he drove the kine
through a land of sand, right plain to discern were all the tracks in
the dust, but when he had crossed the great tract of sand, straightway
on hard ground his traces and those of the kine were ill to discern.
But a mortal man beheld him, driving straight to Pylos the cattle
broad of brow. Now when he had stalled the kine in quiet, and
confused his tracks on either side the way, he lay dark as night in his
cradle, in the dusk of a shadowy cave. The keenest eagle could not

have spied him, and much he rubbed his eyes, with crafty purpose, and bluntly spake his word:

" 'I saw not, I heard not aught, nor learned another's tale; nor tidings could I give, nor win reward of tidings.' "

Therewith Phoebus Apollo sat him down, but another tale did Hermes tell, among the Immortals, addressing Cronion, the master of all Gods:

"Father Zeus, verily the truth will I tell thee: for true am I, nor know the way of falsehood. To-day at sunrise came Apollo to our house, seeking his shambling kine. No witnesses of the Gods brought he, nor no Gods who had seen the fact. But he bade me declare the thing under duress, threatening oft to cast me into wide Tartarus, for he wears the tender flower of glorious youth, but I was born but yesterday, as well himself doth know, and in naught am I like a stalwart lifter of kine. Believe, for thou givest thyself out to be my father, that may I never be well if I drove home the kine, nay, or crossed the threshold. This I say for sooth! The Sun I greatly revere, and other gods, and Thee I love, and *him* I dread. Nay, thyself knowest that I am not to blame; and thereto I will add a great oath: by these fair-wrought porches of the Gods I am guiltless, and one day yet I shall avenge me on him for this pitiless accusation, mighty as he is; but do thou aid the younger!"

So spake Cyllenian Argus-bane, and winked, with his wrapping on his arm: he did not cast it down. But Zeus laughed aloud at the sight of his evil-witted child, so well and wittily he pled denial about the kine. Then bade he them both be of one mind, and so seek the cattle, with Hermes as guide to lead the way, and show without guile where he had hidden the sturdy kine. The Son of Cronos nodded, and glorious Hermes obeyed, for lightly persuadeth the counsel of Zeus of the Aegis.

Then sped both of them, the fair children of Zeus, to sandy Pylos, at the ford of Alpheius, and to the fields they came, and the stall of lofty roof, where the booty was tended in the season of darkness. There anon Hermes went to the side of the rocky cave, and began driving the sturdy cattle into the light. But the son of Leto, glancing aside, saw the flayed skins on the high rock, and quickly asked renowned Hermes:

"How wert thou of avail, oh crafty one, to flay two kine; new-born and childish as thou art? For time to come I dread thy might: no need for thee to be growing long, thou son of Maia!"

[So spake he, and round his hands, twisted strong bands of withes, but they at his feet were soon intertwined, each with other, and lightly were they woven over all the kine of the field, by the counsel of thievish Hermes, but Apollo marvelled at that he saw.]

Then the strong Argus-bane with twinkling glances looked down at the ground, wishful to hide his purpose. But that harsh son of renowned Leto, the Far-darter, did he lightly soothe to his will; taking his lyre in his left hand he tuned it with the *plectrum*: and wondrously it rang beneath his hand. Thereat Phoebus Apollo laughed

and was glad, and the winsome note passed through to his very soul
as he heard. Then Maia's son took courage, and sweetly harping
with his harp he stood at Apollo's left side, playing his prelude, and
thereon followed his winsome voice. He sang the renowns of the
deathless Gods, and the dark Earth, how all things were at the first,
and how each God gat his portion.

To Mnemosyne first of Gods he gave the meed of minstrelsy, to the
Mother of the Muses, for the Muse came upon the Son of Maia.

Then all the rest of the Immortals, in order of rank and birth,
did he honour, the splendid son of Zeus, telling duly all the tale, as
he struck the lyre on his arm. But on Apollo's heart in his breast
came the stress of desire, who spake to him winged words:

"Thou crafty slayer of kine, thou comrade of the feast; thy song
is worth the price of fifty oxen! Henceforth, methinks, shall we be
peacefully made at one. But, come now, tell me this, thou wily Son
of Maia, have these marvels been with thee even since thy birth, or
is it that some immortal, or some mortal man, has given thee the
glorious gift and shown thee song divine? For marvellous is this
new song in mine ears, such as, methinks, none hath known, either
of men, or of Immortals who have mansions in Olympus, save thyself, thou reiver, thou Son of Zeus and Maia! What art is this, what
charm against the stress of cares? What a path of song! for verily
here is choice of all three things, joy, and love, and sweet sleep. For
truly though I be conversant with the Olympian Muses, to whom
dances are a charge, and the bright minstrel hymn, and rich song, and
the lovesome sound of flutes, yet never yet hath aught else been so
dear to my heart, dear as the skill in the festivals of the Gods. I
marvel, Son of Zeus, at this, the music of thy minstrelsy. But now
since, despite thy youth, thou hast such glorious skill, to thee and to
thy Mother I speak this word of sooth: verily, by this shaft of cornel
wood, I shall lead thee renowned and fortunate among the Immortals, and give thee glorious gifts, nor in the end deceive thee."

Then Hermes answered him with cunning words:

"Shrewdly thou questionest me, Far-darter, nor do I grudge thee
to enter upon mine art. This day shalt thou know it: and to thee
would I fain be kind in word and will: but within thyself thou well
knowest all things, for first among the Immortals, Son of Zeus, is
thy place. Mighty art thou and strong, and Zeus of wise counsels
loves thee well with reverence due, and hath given thee honour and
goodly gifts. Nay, they tell that thou knowest soothsaying, Far-
darter, by the voice of Zeus: for from Zeus are all oracles, wherein I
myself now know thee to be all-wise. Thy province it is to know
what so thou wilt. Since, then, thy heart bids thee play the lyre,
harp thou and sing, and let joys be thy care, taking this gift from me;
and to me, friend, gain glory. Sweetly sing with my shrill comrade
in thy hands, that knoweth speech good and fair and in order due.
Freely do thou bear it hereafter into the glad feast, and the winsome
dance, and the glorious revel, a joy by night and day. Whatsoever
skilled hand shall inquire of it artfully and wisely, surely its voice

shall teach him all things joyous, being easily played by gentle practice, fleeing dull toil. But if an unskilled hand first impetuously
inquires of it, vain and discordant shall the false notes sound. But
thine it is of nature to know what things thou wilt: so to thee will I
give this lyre, thou glorious son of Zeus. But we for our part will
let graze thy cattle of the field on the pastures of hill and plain, thou
Far-darter. So shall the kine, consorting with the bulls, bring forth
calves male and female, great store, and no need there is that thou,
wise as thou art, should be vehement in anger."

So spake he, and held forth the lyre that Phoebus Apollo took, and
pledged his shining whip in the hands of Hermes, and set him over
the herds. Gladly the son of Maia received it; while the glorious son
of Leto, Apollo, the Prince, the Far-darter, held the lyre in his left
hand, and tuned it orderly with the *plectrum*. Sweetly it sounded
to his hand, and fair thereto was the song of the God.

Thence anon the twain turned the kine to the rich meadow, but
themselves, the glorious children of Zeus, hastened back to snow-clad
Olympus, rejoicing in the lyre: ay, and Zeus, the counsellor, was
glad of it. [Both did he make one in love, and Hermes loved Leto's
son constantly, even as now, since when in knowledge of his love he
pledged to the Far-darter the winsome lyre, who held it on his arm
and played thereon.] But Hermes withal invented the skill of a new
art, the far-heard music of the reed pipes.

Then spake the son of Leto to Hermes thus:

"I fear me, Son of Maia, thou leader, thou crafty one, lest thou
steal from me both my lyre and my bent bow. For this meed thou
hast from Zeus, to establish the ways of barter among men on the
fruitful earth. Wherefore would that thou shouldst endure to swear
me the great oath of the Gods, with a nod of the head or by the
showering waters of Styx, that thy doings shall ever to my heart be
kind and dear."

Then, with a nod of his head, did Maia's son vow that never would
he steal the possessions of the Far-darter, nor draw nigh his strong
dwelling. And Leto's son made vow and band of love and alliance,
that none other among the Gods should be dearer of Gods or men
the seed of Zeus. [And I shall make, with thee, a perfect token of
a Covenant of all Gods and all men, loyal to my heart and honoured.]
"Thereafter shall I give thee a fair wand of wealth and fortune, a
golden wand, three-pointed, which shall guard thee harmless, accomplishing all things good of word and deed that it is mine to
learn from the voice of Zeus. But as touching the art prophetic, oh
best of fosterlings of Zeus, concerning which thou inquirest, for thee
it is not fit to learn that art, nay, nor for any other Immortal. That
lies in the mind of Zeus alone. Myself did make pledge, and promise,
and strong oath, that, save me, none other of the eternal Gods should
know the secret counsel of Zeus. And thou, my brother of the
Golden Wand, bid me not tell thee what awful purposes is planning
the far-seeing Zeus.

"One mortal shall I harm, and another shall I bless, with many a turn of fortune among hapless men. Of mine oracle shall he have profit whosoever comes in the wake of wings and voice of birds of omen: he shall have profit of mine oracle: him I will not deceive. But whoso, trusting birds not ominous, approaches mine oracle, to inquire beyond my will, and know more than the eternal Gods, shall come, I say, on a bootless journey, yet his gifts shall I receive. Yet another thing will I tell thee, thou Son of renowned Maia and of Zeus of the Aegis, thou bringer of boon; there be certain Thriae, sisters born, three maidens rejoicing in swift wings. Their heads are sprinkled with white barley flour, and they dwell beneath a glade of Parnassus, apart they dwell, teachers of soothsaying. This art I learned while yet a boy I tended the kine, and my Father heeded not. Thence they flit continually hither and thither, feeding on honeycombs and bringing all things to fulfilment. They, when they are full of the spirit of soothsaying, having eaten of the wan honey, delight to speak forth the truth. But if they be bereft of the sweet food divine, then lie they all confusedly. These I bestow on thee, and do thou, inquiring clearly, delight thine own heart, and if thou instruct any man, he will often harken to thine oracle, if he have the good fortune. These be thine, O Son of Maia, and the cattle of the field with twisted horn do thou tend, and horses, and toilsome mules. . . And be lord over the burning eyes of lions, and white-toothed swine, and dogs, and sheep that wide earth nourishes, and over all flocks be glorious Hermes lord. And let him alone be herald appointed to Hades, who, though he be giftless, will give him highest gift of honour."

With such love, in all kindness, did Apollo pledge the Son of Maia, and thereto Cronion added grace. With all mortals and immortals he consorts. Somewhat doth he bless, but ever through the dark night he beguiles the tribes of mortal men.

Hail to thee thus, Son of Zeus and Maia, of thee shall I be mindful and of another lay.

[tr. Andrew Lang]

TO EARTH, THE MOTHER OF ALL

Concerning Earth, the mother of all, shall I sing, firm Earth, eldest of Gods, that nourishes all things in the world; all things that fare on the sacred land, all things in the sea, all flying things, all are fed out of her store. Through thee, revered Goddess, are men happy in their children and fortunate in their harvest. Thine it is to give or to take life from mortal men. Happy is he whom thou honourest with favouring heart; to him all good things are present innumerable: his fertile field is laden, his meadows are rich in cattle, his house filled with all good things. Such men rule righteously in cities of fair women, great wealth and riches are theirs, their children grow glorious in fresh delights: their maidens joyfully dance and sport through the soft meadow flowers in floral revelry. Such are those that thou honourest, holy Goddess, kindly spirit. Hail, Mother of the Gods, thou wife of starry Ouranos, and freely in return for my ode give me sufficient livelihood. Anon will I be mindful of thee and of another lay.

[tr. ANDREW LANG]

TO THE MOON

Ye Muses, sing of the fair-faced, wide-winded Moon; ye sweet-voiced daughters of Zeus son of Cronos, accomplished in song! The heavenly gleam from her immortal head circles the earth, and all beauty arises under her glowing light, and the lampless air beams from her golden crown, and the rays dwell lingering when she has bathed her fair body in the ocean stream, and clad her in shining raiment, divine Selene, yoking her strong-necked glittering steeds. Then forward with speed she drives her deep-maned horses in the evening of the mid-month when her mighty orb is full; then her beams are brightest in the sky as she waxes, a token and a signal to mortal men. With her once was Cronion wedded in love, and she conceived, and brought forth Pandia the maiden, preeminent in beauty among the immortal Gods. Hail, Queen, white-armed Goddess, divine Selene, gentle of heart and fair of tress. Beginning from thee shall I sing the renown of heroes half divine whose deeds do minstrels chant from their charmed lips; these ministers of the Muses.

[tr. ANDREW LANG]

CALLIMACHUS

(*ca.* 310–*ca.* 240 B.C.)

TO APOLLO

Lo, how have Apollo's bay-boughs shaken stormily!
How hath his whole fane shivered!   Afar, ye unhallowed ones, flee!
Lo, clasheth the door at the coming of Phoebus' radiant feet —
Dost mark not?   The Delian palm breathed sudden odours sweet!
O hearken! — the swan in the clear air ravishingly doth sing!
O bolts, by no hands touched do ye suddenly backward spring,
And ye, O locks!   Full nigh in this hour is the God, I trow.
O youthful choir, for the song and the dance make ready now!
Apollo appears not to all, to the good alone and the brave.
Who hath seen him, great man is he; who hath seen not, to sin is he
    slave.
We will look upon thee, Far-worker, to sin will we never be thrall.
Never hushed be the voice of thy lyre, nor unheard be thy footstep's
    fall.
When Phoebus descendeth amidst of his children awhile to abide,
When they fain would accomplish a bridal, or mourn for the old
    which have died,
Or establish on ancient foundations a city's ramparts strong,
Happy I count them.   The lyre for thy sons is not silent long.
Break forth into praise, ye who hear them acclaim Apollo in song.
Yea, the sea breaks forth into praise, when bards of the God's lyre
    sing
Or the bow, which Lycorean Phoebus about his shoulders doth sling.
Yea, Thetis forbeareth her woeful wail for Achilles slain
When she heareth "Iê Paiêon!" the chanted Paean's refrain.
Yea, and the Crag of Weeping the load of its anguish doth cast,
The tear-streaming rock that in Phrygia-land is stablished fast,
The woman made into marble,* whose parted lips from lament never
    rest —
Sing loud the refrain of the Paean! — Ill is it to strive with the Blest!
Whoso fighteth against the Blessèd, against my king let him fight:
Whoso fighteth against my king, let him brave Apollo's might!
Apollo shall honour his chorus, for sweet to his soul is their strain,
And he can, for throned on high at Zeus' right hand doth he reign.
Nor the chorus shall sing the praises of Phoebus one only day;
It hath store of hymns.   Who would chant not gladly to Phoebus
    the lay?
Of gold is Apollo's vesture, the brooch whereby 'tis upcaught,
His lyre, and his Lyctian bow, and his quiver arrow-fraught;
And of gold be his sandals; for gold-abounding Apollo is,
And exceeding wealthy: from Pytho thou mightest divine all this.

* Niobe.

Ever lovely he is, ever young: his cheeks as a woman's are fair
And smooth; never came the down, not in smallest measure, there.
The oil from his tresses that streams the plain with its fragrance fills:
No earthly unguent is that from Apollo's locks that distils,
But the true Panacea it is. In the city whose ways are besprayed
With its dewdrops as earthward they fall, incorruptible all things are
    made.
He is lord over many a craft — there is none like Apollo the King —
His vassal the archer is, he inspireth the bard to sing,
For Phoebus' prerogative is it the bow and the lay to teach:
Of him divination and prophecy are: from Phoebus the leech
Learneth the lore of healing and holding death at bay.
The Lord of the Pastures we name him withal; they be his for aye
Since the days when he nurtured the yoke-bearing steeds on Am-
    phrysia's plain,
What time for the love of Admetus the young his spirit was fain.
Ah, well might it prosper, the feeding of cattle: and multiplied fast
Were the offspring of bleating goats, over which Apollo cast
His glance as they pastured, nor ever the fountains of milk would run
Dry in the udders of ewes, and barren among them was none;
But she that had borne one lamb was suddenly mother of two.
By Phoebus' guidance the builders the lines of their town-walls drew;
For Phoebus delighteth ever the cities of men to raise.
Like the webs of a weaver, himself their broad foundations lays.
He established a city's foundations first in the God's fourth year
In Ortygia the lovely: it stands yet nigh to the rounded mere.
The heads of Cynthian goats the Huntress Artemis brought
To her brother in plenty: an altar therewith Apollo wrought;
For he builded its base with their horns, and he fashioned the altar
    throughout
Of horns, and with walls of horns did he compass his altar about.
Thus Phoebus devised how the first foundations of cities should
    stand:
By him taught, Battus founded my city mid fertile land.
As they entered Libya, in form as a raven at his right hand
Was he guide to his people and founder; and unto our kings he swore
To give walled cities: Apollo keepeth his oaths evermore.
O Apollo, many there be that name thee the Driver of Kine,
And the Clarian many: in all lands many a name is thine.
But I — the Carneian I call thee; mine ancestors so named thee.
Sparta is thine, O Carneian; by thee first founded was she,
The second was Thera, the third was Cyrene. The sixth in descent
Of Oedipus' line with thee at his side from Sparta went
Forth to the founding of Thera. From Thera the vehement-souled
Aristoteles brought to Asbystian soil thine image of gold.
And a royal temple and fair did he rear thee and there did ordain
In the city a yearly feast where bulls full many are slain
In this the latest of thine abodes, O Archer-king.
"Iê!" Carneian of many a prayer! Thine altars in spring

Bear burdens of garlanded flowers, all flowers of manifold hue
That the Hours lure forth into bloom when the West-wind breatheth
 dew,
And in winter the crocus sweet.   The fire thereon burns aye,
And never the ashes smother the brands of yesterday.
Greatly did Phoebus rejoice when the War-queen's belted band
Danced with the daughters golden-haired of Libya-land,
When the feast Carneian returned in the season due of the year.
Not then to the Fountain of Cyre could Dorian men draw near,
But these in Azilis with glens deep-furrowed were dwelling then;
And my King in Cyrene beheld them, and showed to its Nymph the
 men
As he stood on Myrtusa's horn-crest, where towering full-height he
 had slain
The lion that long had been of Eurypylus' oxen the bane.
No goodlier dance than that had Apollo looked upon.
On no city he showered such constant boons as Cyrene won,
For he ever remembered that woodland spoil: and of Battus' line
Was none more honoured than Phoebus of all the Powers divine.
"Iê! Iê! Paion!" — we hear it, the hymnal shout
Which first unto thee from the lips of the Delphian folk rang out
When thou showedst forth the far-flying range of thy golden bow.
At thy coming to Pytho there met thee the monster, the Gods' grim
 foe,
The terrible serpent. Thou slewest him: shaft upon keen shaft came
From thy bowstring raining on him, and the people raised the ac-
 claim —
"Iê Paiêon! Speed thou the arrow! Thy mother bore
Truly a Helper in thee!" So hymned art thou since evermore.
 In the ears of Apollo Envy murmured secretly:
"I admire not the bard who can sing not myriad-voiced as the sea."
With his foot did the God spurn Envy away, and thus he replied:
"Great is the flood of Assyria's river, but bears on its tide
Many of earth's pollutions, and much foul wreckage is there.
But not from all sources the Bee-nymphs to Deo their water bear,
But such as is pure; and, albeit it stealeth scantily
From its holy fountain, is taintless, quintessence of purity."
Hail, King!   To destruction's lair let Censure return from thee! *
           [tr. A. S. WAY]

* The traditional explanation of this puzzling passage is that Callimachus is replying
to critics who jeered at him for writing only short poems.

SATIRIC POETRY

One of the most significant developments of Greek literature in the post-Homeric age was the appearance of the satiric and critical spirit in poetry. The Greeks, so to speak, turned the edge of their genius against themselves and their literature, and the satiric poetry which resulted is one of several signs of their increasing self-consciousness in both life and art. On the one side, this tendency led to the literary parody, of which *The Battle of the Frogs and Mice* is the best surviving example. In this amusing work, which was probably written about the end of the sixth century B.C., the old heroic style and meter of Homer is retained, and the humour of the piece lies in the extreme incongruity between language and subject-matter. No serious criticism of Homer is intended, of course; but obviously such a poem could never have been produced while the heroic age, with its semidivine heroes and Olympian gods mingling with mortals, was taken seriously.

The other side of the Greek critical spirit manifested itself in the poetry of personal invective and abuse. We may be sure that the free-spoken, satiric lampoon had existed among the Greeks from earliest times, but the first poet to impose form and literary artistry on such impromptu outbursts was Archilochus of Paros, who lived in the first half of the seventh century. His vitrolic attacks on various individuals earned him a tremendous reputation as a satirist and "scold" in antiquity, and the well-known legend that his faithless fiancée and her father Lycambes hanged themselves as a result of his verses attests the stinging quality of his lampoons. Archilochus says of himself, in a significant and threatening phrase: "One great thing I know, to requite the man who wrongs me with dreadful punishment." More interesting to modern readers is his frank and uninhibited self-revelation; in an artistocratic age, when only the clan mattered very much, Archilochus asserts that he himself, a single individual, his experiences and moods, his likes and dislikes, are of the utmost importance. He tells us of his life as a soldier of fortune, describes the kind of officer whom he dislikes, and candidly admits that he enjoys a flask of wine to help pass the weary hours of guard-duty. He seems to take a positive delight in flouting the conventions and the aristocratic code of his day: to lose one's shield in battle was a serious disgrace, yet Archilochus, after losing his, joked about it in a poem (*The Poet's Shield*) which is doubly entertaining through its use of heroic Homeric phrases in the midst of this description of his most unheroic action. Finally, in some of his more reflective poems, Archilochus shows himself as a serious thinker who had pondered deeply over the meaning of life and the place of the individual in the world, and finally reached an attitude of patience and manly endurance (as in *Be Still, My Soul*).

Every line which Archilochus wrote is stamped with his original genius and brilliant, complex personality. The remains of the other

Greek satiric poets are on a much lower level of poetic achievement. The satire on women by Semonides of Amorgos, a poet of the late seventh century, which is included here, is a good example. The use of animals to illustrate the qualities, mostly unpleasant, of certain women perhaps derives from the beast-fable, a popular form which had been introduced into Greek literature by Hesiod and Archilochus. It should be noted that Semonides' satire deals with types, not individuals, and thus marks a step toward the more general satire of the Romans. The tradition of direct, personal satire on living persons continued among the Greeks and in the fifth century formed one of the most characteristic elements in early Athenian comedy.

ANONYMOUS

THE BATTLE OF THE FROGS AND MICE

NAMES OF THE MICE

PSYCARPAX, one who plunders granaries.

TROXARTES, a bread-eater.

LYCHOMYLE, a licker of meal.

PTERNOTROCTAS, a bacon-eater.

LYCHOPINAX, a licker of dishes.

EMBASICHYTROS, a creeper into pots.

LYCHENOR, a name from licking.

TROGLODYTES, one who runs into holes.

ARTOPHAGUS, who feeds on bread.

TYROGLYPHUS, a cheese-scooper.

PTERNOGLYPHUS, a bacon-scooper.

PTERNOPHAGUS, a bacon-eater.

CNISSODIOCTES, one who follows the steam of kitchens.

SITOPHAGUS, an eater of wheat.

MERIDARPAX, one who plunders his share.

NAMES OF THE FROGS

PHYSIGNATHUS, one who swells his cheeks.

PELEUS, a name from mud.

HYDROMEDUSE, a ruler in the waters.

HYPSIBOAS, a loud bawler.

PELION, from mud.

SEUTLAEUS, called from the beets.

POLYPHONUS, a great babbler.

LYMNOCHARIS, one who loves the lake.

CRAMBOPHAGUS, a cabbage-eater.

LYMNISIUS, called from the lake.

CALAMINTHIUS, from the herb.

HYDROCHARIS, who loves the water.

BORBOROCOETES, who lies in the mud.

PRASSOPHAGUS, an eater of garlick.

PELUSIUS, from mud.

PELOBATES, who walks in the dirt.

PRASSAEUS, called from garlick.

CRAUGASIDES, from croaking.

But when aloft the curling water rides,
And wets with azure wave his downy sides,
His thoughts grow conscious of approaching woe,
His idle tears with vain repentance flow;
His locks he rends, his trembling feet he rears,
Thick beats his heart with unaccustom'd fears;
He sighs, and chill'd with danger, longs for shore:
His tail extended forms a fruitless oar,
Half drench'd in liquid death his prayers he spake,
And thus bemoan'd him from the dreadful lake.

"So pass'd Europa through the rapid sea,
Trembling and fainting all the venturous way;
With oary feet the bull triumphant row'd,
And safe in Crete depos'd his lovely load.
Ah safe at last! may thus the frog support
My trembling limbs to reach his ample court."

As thus he sorrows, death ambiguous grows,
Lo! from the deep a water-hydra rose;
He rolls his sanguin'd eyes, his bosom heaves,
And darts with active rage along the waves.
Confus'd the monarch sees his hissing foe,
And dives, to shun the sable fates, below.
Forgetful frog!   The friend thy shoulders bore,
Unskill'd in swimming, floats remote from shore.
He grasps with fruitless hands to find relief,
Supinely falls, and grinds his teeth with grief;
Plunging he sinks, and struggling mounts again,
And sinks, and strives, but strives with fate in vain.
The weighty moisture clogs his hairy vest,
And thus the prince his dying rage express'd.

"Nor thou, that fling'st me floundering from thy back,
As from hard rocks rebounds the shattering wrack,
Nor thou shalt 'scape thy due, perfidious king!
Pursu'd by vengeance on the swiftest wing:
At land thy strength could never equal mine,
At sea to conquer, and by craft, was thine.
But heaven has gods, and gods have searching eyes:
Ye mice, ye mice, my great avengers, rise!"

Thi. said, he sighing gasp'd, and gasping died.
His death the young Lychopinax espied,
As on the flowery brink he pass'd the day,
Bask'd in the beams, and loiter'd life away.
Loud shrieks the mouse, his shrieks the shores repeat;
The nibbling nation learn their hero's fate:
Grief, dismal grief ensues; deep murmurs sound,
And shriller fury fills the deafen'd ground.

From lodge to lodge the sacred heralds run,
To fix their council with the rising sun;
Where great Troxartes crown'd in glory reigns,
And winds his lengthening court beneath the plains:
Psycarpax' father, father now no more!
For poor Psycarpax lies remote from shore;
Supine he lies! the silent waters stand,
And no kind billow wafts the dead to land!

BOOK II

When rosy-finger'd morn had ting'd the clouds,
Around their monarch-mouse the nation crowds;
Slow rose the sovereign, heav'd his anxious breast,
And thus the council, fill'd with rage, address'd.

"For lost Psycarpax much my soul endures,
'Tis mine the private grief, the public, yours.
Three warlike sons adorn'd my nuptial bed,
Three sons, alas! before their father dead!
Our eldest perish'd by the ravening cat,
As near my court the prince unheedful sat.
Our next, an engine fraught with danger drew,
The portal gap'd, the bait was hung in view,
Dire arts assist the trap, the fates decoy,
And men unpitying kill'd my gallant boy.
The last, his country's hope, his parents' pride,
Plung'd in the lake by Physignathus, died.
Rouse all the war, my friends! avenge the deed
And bleed that monarch, and his nation bleed."

His words in every breast inspir'd alarms,
And careful Mars supplied their host with arms.
In verdant hulls despoil'd of all their beans,
The buskin'd warriors stalk'd along the plains:
Quills aptly bound, their bracing corselet made,
Fac'd with the plunder of a cat they flay'd;
The lamp's round boss affords their ample shield;
Large shells of nuts their covering helmet yield;
And o'er the region with reflected rays,
Tall groves of needles for their lances blaze.
Dreadful in arms the marching mice appear;
The wondering frogs perceive the tumult near,
Forsake the waters, thickening form a ring,
And ask and hearken, whence the noises spring.
When near the crowd, disclos'd to public view,
The valiant chief Embasichytros drew:
The sacred herald's sceptre grac'd his hand,
And thus his words express'd his king's command.

"Ye frogs! the mice, with vengeance fir'd, advance.
And deck'd in armour shake the shining lance:
Their hapless prince by Physignathus slain,
Extends incumbent on the watery plain.
Then arm your host, the doubtful battle try;
Lead forth those frogs that have the soul to die."

The chief retires, the crowd the challenge hear,
And proudly-swelling yet perplex'd appear:
Much they resent, yet much their monarch blame,
Who rising, spoke to clear his tainted fame.

"O friends, I never forc'd the mouse to death.
Nor saw the gasping of his latest breath.
He, vain of youth, our art of swimming tried,
And venturous, in the lake the wanton died.
To vengeance now by false appearance led,
They point their anger at my guiltless head.
But wage the rising war by deep device,
And turn its fury on the crafty mice.
Your king directs the way; my thoughts elate
With hopes of conquest, form design of fate.
Where high the banks their verdant surface heave,
And the steep sides confine the sleeping wave,
There, near the margin, clad in armour bright,
Sustain the first impetuous shocks of fight:
Then, where the dancing feather joins the crest,
Let each brave frog his obvious mouse arrest;
Each strongly grasping, headlong plunge a foe,
Till countless circles whirl the lake below;
Down sink the mice in yielding waters drown'd;
Loud flash the waters; and the shores resound:
The frogs triumphant tread the conquer'd plain,
And raise their glorious trophies of the slain."

He spake no more: his prudent scheme imparts
Redoubling ardour to the boldest hearts.
Green was the suit his arming heroes chose,
Around their legs the greaves of mallows close;
Green were the beets about their shoulders laid,
And green the colewort, which the target made;
Form'd of the varied shells the waters yield.
Their glossy helmets glisten'd o'er the field;
And tapering sea-reeds for the polish'd spear,
With upright order pierc'd the ambient air.
Thus dress'd for war, they take th' appointed height,
Poise the long arms, and urge the promis'd fight.

But now, where Jove's irradiate spires arise,
With stars surrounded in ethereal skies,

(A solemn council call'd) the brazen gates
Unbar; the gods assume their golden seats:
The sire superior leans, and points to show
What wondrous combats mortals wage below:
How strong, how large, the numerous heroes stride;
What length of lance they shake with warlike pride;
What eager fire, their rapid march reveals;
So the fierce Centaurs ravag'd o'er the dales;
And so confirm'd, the daring Titans rose,
Heap'd hills on hills, and bid the gods be foes.

This seen, the Power his sacred visage rears,
He casts a pitying smile on worldly cares,
And asks what heavenly guardians take the list,
Or who the mice, or who the frogs assist?

Then thus to Pallas. "If my daughter's mind
Have join'd the mice, why stays she still behind?
Drawn forth by savoury steams they wind their way,
And sure attendance round thine altar pay,
Where while the victims gratify their taste,
They sport to please the goddess of the feast."
Thus spake the ruler of the spacious skies;
But thus, resolv'd, the blue-ey'd maid replies.
"In vain, my father! all their dangers plead;
To such, thy Pallas never grants her aid.
My flowery wreaths they petulantly spoil,
And rob my crystal lamps of feeding oil,
Ills following ills: but what afflicts me more,
My veil, that idle race profanely tore.
The web was curious, wrought with art divine;
Relentless wretches! all the work was mine;
Along the loom the purple warp I spread,
Cast the light shoot, and cross'd the silver thread.
In this their teeth a thousand breaches tear;
The thousand breaches skilful hands repair;
For which, vile earthly duns thy daughter grieve;
The gods, that use no coin, have none to give;
And learning's goddess never less can owe:
Neglected learning gains no wealth below.
Nor let the frogs to win my succour sue,
Those clamorous fools have lost my favour too.
For late, when all the conflict ceas'd at night,
When my stretch'd sinews work'd with eager fight;
When spent with glorious toil, I left the field,
And sunk for slumber on my swelling shield;
Lo from the deep, repelling sweet repose,
With noisy croakings half the nation rose:
Devoid of rest, with aching brows I lay,

Till cocks proclaim'd the crimson dawn of day.
Let all, like me, from either host forbear,
Nor tempt the flying furies of the spear;
Let heavenly blood, or what for blood may flow,
Adorn the conquest of a meaner foe.
Some daring mouse may meet the wondrous odds,
Though gods oppose, and brave the wounded gods.
O'er gilded clouds reclin'd, the danger view,
And be the wars of mortals scenes for you."

So mov'd the blue-ey'd queen; her words persuade.
Great Jove assented, and the rest obey'd.

BOOK III

Now front to front the marching armies shine,
Halt ere they meet, and form the lengthening line:
The chiefs conspicuous seen and heard afar,
Give the loud signal to the rushing war;
Their dreadful trumpets deep-mouth'd hornets sound
The sounded charge remurmurs o'er the ground;
E'en Jove proclaims a field of horror nigh,
And rolls low thunder through the troubled sky.

First to the fight the large Hypsiboas flew,
And brave Lychenor with a javelin slew.
The luckless warrior fill'd with generous flame,
Stood foremost glittering in the post of fame;
When in his liver struck, the javelin hung;
The mouse fell thundering, and the target rung;
Prone to the ground he sinks his closing eye,
And soil'd in dust his lovely tresses lie.

A spear at Pelion Troglodytes cast,
The missive spear within the bosom past;
Death's sable shades the fainting frog surround,
And life's red tide runs ebbing from the wound.
Embasichytros felt Seutlaeus' dart
Transfix and quiver in his panting heart;
But great Artophagus aveng'd the slain,
And big Seutlaeus tumbling loads the plain,
And Polyphonus dies, a frog renown'd
For boastful speech and turbulence of sound;
Deep through the belly pierc'd, supine he lay,
And breath'd his soul against the face of day.

The strong Lymnocharis, who view'd with ire
A victor triumph, and a friend expire;
With heaving arms a rocky fragment caught,
And fiercely flung where Troglodytes fought;

A warrior vers'd in arts, of sure retreat,
But arts in vain elude impending fate;
Full on his sinewy neck the fragment fell,
And o'er his eyelids clouds eternal dwell.
Lychenor, second of the glorious name,
Striding advanc'd, and took no wandering aim;
Through all the frog the shining javelin flies,
And near the vanquish'd mouse the victor dies.

The dreadful stroke Crambophagus affrights,
Long bred to banquets, less inur'd to fights;
Heedless he runs, and stumbles o'er the steep,
And wildly floundering flashes up the deep:
Lychenor following with a downward blow,
Reach'd in the lake his unrecover'd foe;
Gasping he rolls, a purple stream of blood
Distains the surface of the silver flood;
Through the wide wound the rushing entrails throng,
And slow the breathless carcass floats along.
Lymnisius good Tyroglyphus assails,
Prince of the mice that haunt the flowery vales,
Lost to the milky fares and rural seat,
He came to perish on the bank of fate.

The dread Pternoglyphus demands the fight,
Which tender Calaminthius shuns by flight,
Drops the green target, springing quits the foe.
Glides through the lake, and safely dives below.
But dire Pternophagus divides his way
Through breaking ranks, and leads the dreadful day.
No nibbling prince excell'd in fierceness more,
His parents fed him on the savage boar;
But where his lance the field with blood imbru'd,
Swift as he mov'd, Hydrocharis pursu'd,
Till fallen in death he lies; a shattering stone
Sounds on the neck, and crushes all the bone;
His blood pollutes the verdure of the plain,
And from his nostrils bursts the gushing brain.

Lychopinax with Borb'rocoetes fights,
A blameless frog whom humbler life delights;
The fatal javelin unrelenting flies,
And darkness seals the gentle croaker's eyes.

Incens'd Prassophagus, with sprightly bound,
Bears Cnissodioctes off the rising ground,
Then drags him o'er the lake depriv'd of breath,
And downward plunging, sinks his soul to death.
But now the great Psycarpax shines afar,
(Scarce he so great whose loss provok'd the war),

Swift to revenge his fatal javelin fled,
And through the liver struck Pelusius dead;
His freckled corpse before the victor fell,
His soul indignant sought the shades of hell.

This saw Pelobates, and from the flood
Heav'd with both hands a monstrous mass of mud:
The cloud obscene o'er all the hero flies,
Dishonours his brown face, and blots his eyes.
Enrag'd, and wildly spluttering, from the shore
A stone immense of size the warrior bore,
A load for labouring earth, whose bulk to raise,
Asks ten degenerate mice of modern days:
Full on the leg arrives the crushing wound;
The frog supportless writhes upon the ground.

Thus flush'd, the victor wars with matchless force,
Till loud Craugasides arrests his course:
Hoarse-croaking threats precede; with fatal speed
Deep through the belly ran the pointed reed.
Then strongly tugg'd, return'd imbru'd with gore;
And on the pile his reeking entrails bore.

The lame Sitophagus, oppress'd with pain,
Creeps from the desperate dangers of the plain;
And where the ditches rising weeds supply
To spread their lowly shades beneath the sky,
There lurks the silent mouse reliev'd from heat,
And safe embower'd, avoids the chance of fate.

But here Troxartes, Physignathus there,
Whirl the dire furies of the pointed spear:
But where the foot around its ankle plies,
Troxartes wounds, and Physignathus flies,
Halts to the pool, a safe retreat to find,
And trails a dangling length of leg behind.
The mouse still urges, still the frog retires,
And half in anguish of the flight expires.

Then pious ardour young Prassaeus brings,
Betwixt the fortunes of contending kings:
Lank, harmless frog! with forces hardly grown,
He darts the reed in combats not his own,
Which faintly tinkling on Troxartes' shield,
Hangs at the point, and drops upon the field.

Now nobly towering o'er the rest appears
A gallant prince that far transcends his years,
Pride of his sire, and glory of his house,
And more a Mars in combat than a mouse;

His action bold, robust his ample frame,
And Meridarpax his resounding name.
The warrior singled from the fighting crowd,
Boasts the dire honours of his arms aloud;
Then strutting near the lake, with looks elate,
To all its nations threats approaching fate
And such his strength, the silver lakes around
Might roll their waters o'er unpeopled ground;
But powerful Jove, who shows no less his grace
To frogs that perish, than to human race,
Felt soft compassion rising in his soul,
And shook his sacred head, that shook the pole.
Then thus to all the gazing powers began
The sire of gods, and frogs, and mice, and man.

"What seas of blood I view! what worlds of slain!
An Iliad rising from a day's campaign!
How fierce his javelin o'er the trembling lakes
The black-furr'd hero Meridarpax shakes!
Unless some favouring deity descends,
Soon will the frog's loquacious empire end.
Let dreadful Pallas wing'd with pity fly,
And make her aegis blaze before his eye:
While Mars refulgent on his rattling car,
Arrests his raging rival of the war."

He ceas'd, reclining with attentive head,
When thus the glorious god of combats said.
"Nor Pallas, Jove! though Pallas take the field,
With all the terrors of her hissing shield,
Nor Mars himself, though Mars in armour bright
Ascend his car, and wheel amidst the fight;
Not these can drive the desperate mouse afar,
Or change the fortunes of the bleeding war.
Let all go forth, all heaven in arms arise;
Or launch thy own red thunder from the skies;
Such ardent bolts as flew that wondrous day,
When heaps of Titans mix'd with mountains lay,
When all the giants race enormous fell,
And huge Enceladus was hurl'd to hell."

'Twas thus th' armipotent advis'd the gods,
When from his throne the cloud-compeller nods;
Deep lengthening thunders run from pole to pole,
Olympus trembles as the thunders roll.
Then swift he whirls the brandish'd bolt around
And headlong darts it at the distant ground;
The bolt discharg'd inwrapp'd with lightning flies,
And rends its flaming passage through the skies:
Then earth's inhabitants, the nibblers, shake,

And frogs, the dwellers in the waters, quake.
Yet still the mice advance their dread design,
And the last danger threats the croaking line,
Till Jove, that inly mourn'd the loss they bore,
With strange assistants fill'd the frighted shore.

Pour'd from the neighb'ring strand, deform'd to view,
They march, a sudden unexpected crew!
Strong suits of armour round their bodies close,
Which, like thick anvils, blunt the force of blows;
In wheeling marches turn'd, oblique they go;
With harpy claws their limbs divide below;
Fell sheers the passage to their mouth command;
From out the flesh their bones by nature stand;
Broad spread their backs, their shining shoulders rise;
Unnumber'd joints distort their lengthen'd thighs,
With nervous cords their hands are firmly brac'd;
Their round black eyeballs in their bosom plac'd;
On eight long feet the wondrous warriors tread;
And either end alike supplies a head.
These, mortal wits to call the crabs agree,
The gods have other names for things than we.

Now, where the jointures from their loins depend,
The heroes' tails with severing grasps they rend.
Here, short of feet, depriv'd the power to fly,
There, without hands, upon the field they lie.
Wrench'd from their holds, and scatter'd all around,
The bended lances heap the cumber'd ground.
Helpless amazement, fear pursuing fear,
And mad confusion through their host appear:
O'er the wild waste with headlong flight they go,
Or creep conceal'd in vaulted holes below.

But down Olympus to the western seas
Far-shooting Phoebus drove with fainter rays;
And a whole war (so Jove ordain'd) begun,
Was fought, and ceas'd, in one revolving sun.

                              [tr. THOMAS PARNELL]

ARCHILOCHUS

(*fl.* 648 B.C.)

THE POET'S SHIELD

Some Thracian strutteth with my shield,
    For, being somewhat flurried,
I left it by a wayside bush,
    As from the field I hurried;

A right good targe, but I got off,
    The deuce may take the shield;
I'll get another just as good
    When next I go afield.

                  [6, tr. PAUL SHOREY]

BE STILL, MY SOUL

Heart, my heart, with griefs confounded whence you no deliv'rance
    find,
Up against them! guard yourself and show the foe a gallant breast;
Take your stand among the foremost where the spears of battle fly
Gallantly. Nor when you conquer make your pleasure manifest,
Nor in turn, if you are conquered, lie down in your home and cry.
Take your joy when life is joyful, and in sorrow do not mind
Overmuch, but know what ups and downs belong to humankind.

                  [67, tr. C. M. BOWRA]

THERE IS NOTHING STRANGE

Never man again may swear, things shall be as once they were;
Never more in wonder stare, since the Olympian thunderer
Bade the Sun's meridian splendour hide in shade of murky night;
While affrighted nations started, trembling at the sudden sight.
Who shall dare to doubt hereafter, whatsoever man may say?
Who refuse with stupid laughter credence to the wildest lay?
Though for pasture dolphins ranging leap the hills and scour the
    wood,
And fierce wolves, their nature changing, dive beneath th' astonished
    flood.

            [74, after J. H. MERIVALE]

SEMONIDES OF AMORGUS

(*fl.* 630 B.C.)

ON WOMEN

In the beginning God made woman's mind apart from man's.

One made He of a bristly Sow; all that is in her house lies disorderly, defiled with dirt, and rolling upon the floor, and she groweth fat a-sitting among the middens in garments as unwashed as herself.

Another did God make of a knavish Vixen, a woman knowing in all things, who taketh note of all, be it bad or good; for the bad often calleth she good and the good bad; and she hath now this mood and now that.

Another of a Bitch, a busybody like her mother, one that would fain hear all, know all, and peering and prying everywhere barketh e'en though she see nobody; a man cannot check her with threats, no, not if in anger he dash her teeth out with a stone, nor yet though he speak gently with her, even though she be sitting among strangers — she must needs keep up her idle baying.

Another the Olympians fashioned of Earth, and gave to her husband all wanting in wits; such a woman knoweth neither evil nor good; her only art is to eat; and never though God give a bad winter draweth she her stool nigher the fire for the cold.

Another of the Sea, whose thoughts are in two minds; one day she laughs and is gay — a stranger seeing her within will praise her, saying "There's no better wife in all the world, nay, nor comelier"; the next she is intolerable to behold or draw nigh to, for then she rageth unapproachably, like a bitch with young; implacable and nasty is she to all, alike foe and friend. Even as the sea in summertime often will stand calm and harmless, to the great joy of the mariners, yet often rage and toss with roaring waves, most like unto it is such a woman in disposition, nor hath the ocean a nature of other sort than hers.

Another's made of a stubborn and belaboured She-Ass; everything she doeth is hardly done, of necessity and after threats, and then 'tis left unfinished; meanwhile eateth she day in day out, in bower and in hall, and all men alike are welcome to her bed.

Another of a Cat, a woeful and miserable sort; for in her there's nought of fair or lovely or pleasant or desirable; she is mad for a love-mate, and yet when she hath him turneth his stomach; she doeth her neighbours much harm underhand, and often eateth up unaccepted offerings.

Another is the child of a dainty long-maned Mare; she refuseth menial tasks and toil; she'll neither set hand to mill nor take up sieve, nor cast forth the muck, nor, for that she shunneth the soot, will she sit beside the oven. She taketh a mate only of necessity. Every day will she wash herself twice, or even thrice, and anointeth her with unguents. She ever weareth her hair deep-combed and wreathed with flowers. Such a wife may be a fair sight for other men, but she's an ill to her husband if he be not a despot or a king, such as take pride in adornments like to her.

Another cometh of an Ape; she is the greatest ill of all Zeus giveth man. Foul of face, such a woman maketh laughter for all men as she goeth through the town; short in neck, she moveth hardly, hipless, lean-shanked — alas for the wretched man that claspeth such a mischief! Like an ape she knoweth all arts and wiles, nor recketh of men's laughter. Neither will she do a man any kindness; all her care, all her considering, is how she shall do the greatest ill she may.

Another of a Bee; and happy he that getteth her. On her alone alighteth there no blame, and life doth flourish and increase because of her; loving and loved groweth she old with her husband, the mother of a fair and name-honoured progeny; she is preeminent among all the women, and a divine grace pervadeth her; neither taketh she delight in sitting among women where they tell tales of venery. Such wives are the best and wisest that Zeus bestoweth upon men; these other kinds, thanks unto Him, both are and will ever be a mischief in the world.

For this is the greatest ill that Zeus hath made, women. Even though they may seem to advantage us, a wife is more than all else a mischief to him that possesseth her; for whoso dwelleth with a woman, he never passeth a whole day glad, nor quickly shall he thrust out of doors Hunger the hated housefellow and hostile deity. But when a man thinketh within-doors to be gladdest at heart by grace of God or favour of man, then of all times will she find cause for blame and gird herself for battle. For where a woman is, they e'en cannot receive a stranger heartily. And she that most seemeth to be discreet, she is all the time doing the greatest harm; her husband is all agape for her, but the neighbours rejoice that yet another is deceived. And no man but will praise his own wife when he speaketh of her, and blame another's, yet we cannot see that we be all alike. Aye, this is the greatest ill that Zeus hath made, this hath he put about us as the bondage of a fetter irrefragable, ever since Death received them that went a-warring for a woman.

[7, tr. J. M. EDMONDS]

PASTORAL POETRY

The remote origin of the pastoral probably lies in the songs of shepherds sung to pass the time as they were guarding their flocks, but this type of spontaneous production is far different from the literary pastoral. The latter form, though indebted in large measure to its primitive origin, depends fundamentally upon the existence of urban communities and the resultant contrast between the life of the city and the life of the country. As J. S. Phillimore has pointed out in his essay on *Pastoral and Allegory,** in Greek literature we have to wait for the poetry of Aristophanes to find the first expression of the mood and spirit of the literary pastoral. By then the folk of the city were conscious of the difference between their life and that of their rural neighbours, and at the same time were artistically developed enough to be able to formulate the difference in verse. Phillimore correctly maintains that the choruses of Aristophanes' *Acharnians* and *Peace* are the first authentic ancestors of Theocritus.

The founder of the independent form of the literary pastoral was Theocritus. His *floruit* in approximately 270 B.C. makes him a contemporary of the Hellenistic Age at its highest point. Born probably at Syracuse, he lived both at Cos and at Alexandria, the brilliant capital of Hellenistic culture under Ptolemy Philadelphus. Theocritus' poetry is perhaps the most perfect representative of this Hellenistic Age. Here was a period well after the great creative epoch of the fifth century. In the field of letters it was generally agreed that in Homer and tragedy a height had been reached which could never be surpassed. Consequently technical scholarship developed, involving analysis and criticism of the masterpieces of the past while creative artists sought to express themselves in new forms, in works of slighter scale, and by exploiting material derived from the byways of myth and legend which the research of their scholarly *confrères* had uncovered.

Hellenistic culture is further characterized by the development of individualism. Stemming first perhaps from the impetus of Aristotle's scientific and philosophical concern for the reality of the individual thing, the individualistic tendency grew in the first part of the third century B.C. Its manifestations in the poetry of Theocritus are found in his generous use of realistic detail, in a kind of proto-romantic interest in the world of external nature, and in a preoccupation with the emotions of individual human beings. As a result we find a curious compound in the Theocritean idyl. It is poetry which combines an artificiality and artistic sophistication appearing so often in the tradition of the pastoral (a temper exhibited in a later day when Marie Antoinette played the shepherdess in the gardens of the *Petit-Trianon*) with the realism of a *Character* of Theophrastus and with a genuine love for nature and rural life. Only

* Oxford, Clarendon Press, 1925, p. 4.

a poet of great powers like Theocritus could take these elements and
fuse them together into works of art whose appeal is unmistakable.

In the selections which follow the reader will find examples of the
various kinds of Theocritean verse. In the first idyl two rustics
meet, talk of the ideal shepherd, Daphnis, whose loves and death
became the subject of a song which one of them sings. The second
idyl studies the intense emotion of a maiden who has been thwarted
in her love and by the use of magic spells seeks to bind her recreant
lover to her. The seventh is the famous pastoral masquerade. Theocritus, who assumes the name of Simichidas in the poem, refers to
real characters in the literary world of the time and in a tissue of a
quasi-allegory creates a work, one of whose purposes is to produce in
the mind of the reader the mood and emotion peculiar to the pastoral type. The eleventh tells of the love of the Cyclops for the fair
sea nymph, Galatea. Here is a typical illustration of the Hellenistic
poet's effort to achieve originality by employing the grotesque and
the erotic in combination. The fifteenth is a literary mime obviously
akin to the works of Herodas. The twentieth idyl exhibits the Alexandrian tendency towards realism, while the twenty-seventh in true
romantic fashion develops an erotic theme.

Of Bion and Moschus as individuals we know but little. They
continued the pastoral tradition of Theocritus, and the two present
selections reveal in its most perfect form the elegiac mood of the
pastoral. Bion's *Lament for Adonis* skilfully weaves together the
several pastoral conventions, while the *Lament for Bion* (which
cannot be certainly ascribed to Moschus) more than any other single
poem influenced the later tradition in Vergil, Milton, Shelley and
Arnold. In fact, convention in a literary form has rarely exerted a
more powerful influence than it has in the pastoral. Consequently
the reader who is familiar with these selections from Theocritus and
his successors can approach such a masterpiece as Milton's *Lycidas*
with a fresh and deeper understanding.

THEOCRITUS

(*ca.* 316–*ca.* 260 B.C.)

IDYL I

THE DAPHNIS SONG

The shepherd Thyrsis meets a goatherd, in a shady place beside a spring, and at his invitation sings the Song of Daphnis. *This ideal hero of Greek pastoral song had won for his bride the fairest of the Nymphs. Confident in the strength of his passion, he boasted that Love could never subdue him to a new affection. Love avenged himself by making Daphnis desire a strange maiden, but to this temptation he never yielded, and so died a constant lover. The song tells how the cattle and the wild things of the wood bewailed him, how Hermes and Priapus gave him counsel in vain, and how with his last breath he retorted the taunts of the implacable Aphrodite. The scene is in Sicily.*

Thyrsis. Sweet, meseems, is the whispering sound of yonder pine tree, goatherd, that murmureth by the wells of water; and sweet are thy pipings. After Pan the second prize shalt thou bear away, and if he take the hornéd goat, the she-goat shalt thou win; but if he choose the she-goat for his meed, the kid falls to thee, and dainty is the flesh of kids e'er the age when thou milkest them.

The Goatherd. Sweeter, O shepherd, is thy song than the music of yonder water that is poured from the high face of the rock! Yea, if the Muses take the young ewe for their gift, a stall-fed lamb shalt thou receive for thy meed; but if it please them to take the lamb, thou shalt lead away the ewe for the second prize.

Thyrsis. Wilt thou, goatherd, in the nymphs' name, wilt thou sit thee down here, among the tamarisks, on this sloping knoll, and pipe while in this place I watch thy flocks?

Goatherd. Nay, shepherd, it may not be; we may not pipe in the noontide. 'Tis Pan we dread, who truly at this hour rests weary from the chase; and bitter of mood is he, the keen wrath sitting ever at his nostrils. But, Thyrsis, for that thou surely wert wont to sing *The Affliction of Daphnis,* and hast most deeply meditated the pastoral muse, come hither, and beneath yonder elm let us sit down, in face of Priapus and the fountain fairies, where is that resting-place of the shepherds, and where the oak trees are. Ah! if thou wilt but sing as on that day thou sangest in thy match with Chromis out of Libya, I will let thee milk, ay, three times, a goat that is the mother of twins, and even when she has suckled her kids her milk doth fill two pails. A deep bowl of ivy-wood, too, I will give thee, rubbed with sweet bees'-wax, a twy-eared bowl newly wrought, smacking still of the knife of the graver. Round its upper edges goes the ivy winding, ivy besprent with golden flowers; and about it is a tendril

929

twisted that joys in its saffron fruit. Within is designed a maiden, as fair a thing as the gods could fashion, arrayed in a sweeping robe, and a snood on her head. Beside her two youths with fair love-locks are contending from either side, with alternate speech, but her heart thereby is all untouched. And now on one she glances, smiling, and anon she lightly flings the other a thought, while by reason of the long vigils of love their eyes are heavy, but their labour is all in vain.

Beyond these an ancient fisherman and a rock are fashioned, a rugged rock, whereon with might and main the old man drags a great net for his cast, as one that labours stoutly. Thou wouldst say that he is fishing with all the might of his limbs, so big the sinews swell all about his neck, grey-haired though he be, but his strength is as the strength of youth. Now divided but a little space from the sea-worn old man is a vineyard laden well with fire-red clusters, and on the rough wall a little lad watches the vineyard, sitting there. Round him two she-foxes are skulking, and one goes along the vine-rows to devour the ripe grapes, and the other brings all her cunning to bear against the scrip, and vows she will never leave the lad, till she strand him bare and breakfastless. But the boy is plaiting a pretty locust-cage with stalks of asphodel, and fitting it with reeds, and less care of his scrip has he, and of the vines, than delight in his plaiting.

All about the cup is spread the soft acanthus, a miracle of varied work, a thing for thee to marvel on. For this bowl I paid to a Caly-donian ferryman a goat and a great white cream cheese. Never has its lip touched mine, but it still lies maiden for me. Gladly with this cup would I gain thee to my desire, if thou, my friend, wilt sing me that delightful song. Nay, I grudge it thee not at all. Begin, my friend, for be sure thou canst in no wise carry thy song with thee to Hades, that puts all things out of mind!

The Song of Thyrsis

Begin, ye Muses dear, begin the pastoral song! Thyrsis of Etna am I, and this is the voice of Thyrsis. Where, ah! where were ye when Daphnis was languishing; ye Nymphs, where were ye? By Peneus's beautiful dells, or by dells of Pindus? for surely ye dwelt not by the great stream of the river Anapus, nor on the watch-tower of Etna, nor by the sacred water of Acis.

Begin, ye Muses dear, begin the pastoral song!

For him the jackals, for him the wolves did cry; for him did even the lion out of the forest lament. Kine and bulls by his feet right many, and heifers plenty, with the young calves bewailed him.

Begin, ye Muses dear, begin the pastoral song!

Came Hermes first from the hill, and said, 'Daphnis, who is it that torments thee; child, whom dost thou love with so great desire?' The neatherds came, and the shepherds; the goatherds came: all they asked what ailed him. Came also Priapus, —

Begin, ye Muses dear, begin the pastoral song!

And said: 'Unhappy Daphnis, wherefore dost thou languish, while for thee the maiden by all the fountains, through all the glades is fleeting, in search of thee? Ah! thou art too laggard a lover, and thou nothing availest! A neatherd wert thou named, and now thou art like the goatherd:

Begin, ye Muses dear, begin the pastoral song!

'For the goatherd, when he marks the young goats at their pastime, looks on with yearning eyes, and fain would be even as they; and thou, when thou beholdest the laughter of maidens, dost gaze with yearning eyes, for that thou dost not join their dances.'

Begin, ye Muses dear, begin the pastoral song!

Yet these the herdsman answered not again, but he bare his bitter love to the end, yea, to the fated end he bare it.

Begin, ye Muses dear, begin the pastoral song!

Ay, but she too came, the sweetly smiling Cypris, craftily smiling she came, yet keeping her heavy anger; and she spake, saying: 'Daphnis, methinks thou didst boast that thou wouldst throw Love a fall, nay, is it not thyself that has been thrown by grievous Love?'

Begin, ye Muses dear, begin the pastoral song!

But to her Daphnis answered again: 'Implacable Cypris, Cypris terrible, Cypris of mortals detested, already dost thou deem that my latest sun has set; nay, Daphnis even in Hades shall prove great sorrow to Love.

Begin, ye Muses dear, begin the pastoral song!

'Where it is told how the herdsman with Cypris —— Get thee to Ida, get thee to Anchises! There are oak trees — here only galingale blows, here sweetly hum the bees about the hives!

Begin, ye Muses dear, begin the pastoral song!

'Thine Adonis, too, is in his bloom, for he herds the sheep and slays the hares, and he chases all the wild beasts. Nay, go and confront Diomedes again, and say, "The herdsman Daphnis I conquered, do thou join battle with me."

Begin, ye Muses dear, begin the pastoral song!

'Ye wolves, ye jackals, and ye bears in the mountain caves, farewell! The herdsman Daphnis ye never shall see again, no more in the dells, no more in the groves, no more in the woodlands. Farewell Arethusa, ye rivers, good-night, that pour down Thymbris your beautiful waters.

Begin, ye Muses dear, begin the pastoral song!

'That Daphnis am I who here do herd the kine, Daphnis who water here the bulls and calves.

'O Pan, Pan! whether thou art on the high hills of Lycaeus, or rangest mighty Maenalus, haste hither to the Sicilian isle! Leave the

tomb of Helice, leave that high cairn of the son of Lycaon, which
seems wondrous fair, even in the eyes of the blessed.
Give o'er, ye Muses, come, give o'er the pastoral song!

'Come hither, my prince, and take this fair pipe, honey-breathed
with wax-stopped joints; and well it fits thy lip: for verily I, even I,
by Love am now haled to Hades.
Give o'er, ye Muses, come, give o'er the pastoral song!

'Now violets bear, ye brambles, ye thorns bear violets; and let fair
narcissus bloom on the boughs of juniper! Let all things with all
be confounded, — from pines let men gather pears, for Daphnis is
dying! Let the stag drag down the hounds, let owls from the hills
contend in song with the nightingales.'
Give o'er, ye Muses, come, give o'er the pastoral song!

So Daphnis spake, and ended; but fain would Aphrodite have
given him back to life. Nay, spun was all the thread that the Fates
assigned, and Daphnis went down the stream. The whirling wave
closed over the man the Muses loved, the man not hated of the
nymphs.
Give o'er, ye Muses, come, give o'er the pastoral song!

And thou, give me the bowl, and the she-goat, that I may milk her
and pour forth a libation to the Muses. Farewell, oh, farewells manifold, ye Muses, and I, some future day, will sing you yet a sweeter
song.
The Goatherd. Filled may thy fair mouth be with honey, Thyrsis,
and filled with the honeycomb; and the sweet dried fig mayst thou
eat of Aegilus, for thou vanquishest the cicala in song! Lo here is
thy cup, see, my friend, of how pleasant a savour! Thou wilt think
it has been dipped in the well-spring of the Hours. Hither, hither,
Cissaetha: do thou milk her, Thyrsis. And you young she-goats,
wanton not so wildly lest you bring up the he-goat against you.
[tr. ANDREW LANG]

IDYL II

THE PHARMACEUTRIA

*Simaetha, madly in love with Delphis, who has forsaken her, en-
deavours to subdue him to her by magic, and by invoking the Moon,
in her character of Hecate, and of Selene. She tells the tale of the
growth of her passion, and vows vengeance if her magic arts are
unsuccessful.*
*The scene is probably some garden beneath the moonlit sky, near the
town, and within sound of the sea. The characters are Simaetha, and
Thestylis, her handmaid.*

Where are my laurel leaves? come, bring them, Thestylis; and
where are the love-charms? Wreath the bowl with bright-red wool,

that I may knit the witch-knots against my grievous lover, who for twelve days, oh cruel, has never come hither, nor knows whether I am alive or dead, nor has once knocked at my door, unkind that he is! Hath Love flown off with his light desires by some other path — Love and Aphrodite? To-morrow I will go to the wrestling school of Timagetus, to see my love and to reproach him with all the wrong he is doing me. But now I will bewitch him with my enchantments! Do thou, Selene, shine clear and fair, for softly, Goddess, to thee will I sing, and to Hecate of hell. The very whelps shiver before her as she fares through black blood and across the barrows of the dead.

Hail, awful Hecate! to the end be thou of our company, and make this medicine of mine no weaker than the spells of Circe, or of Medea, or of Perimede of the golden hair.
My magic wheel, draw home to me the man I love!

Lo, how the barley grain first smoulders in the fire, — nay, toss on the barley, Thestylis! Miserable maid, where are thy wits wandering? Even to thee, wretched that I am, have I become a laughing-stock, even to thee? Scatter the grain, and cry thus the while, ' 'Tis the bones of Delphis I am scattering!'
My magic wheel, draw home to me the man I love!

Delphis troubled me, and I against Delphis am burning this laurel; and even as it crackles loudly when it has caught the flame, and suddenly is burned up, and we see not even the dust thereof, lo, even thus may the flesh of Delphis waste in the burning!
My magic wheel, draw home to me the man I love!

Even as I melt this wax, with the god to aid, so speedily may he by love be molten, the Myndian Delphis! And as whirls this brazen wheel, so restless, under Aphrodite's spell, may he turn and turn about my doors.
My magic wheel, draw home to me the man I love!

Now will I burn the husks, and thou, O Artemis, hast power to move hell's adamantine gates, and all else that is as stubborn. Thestylis, hark, 'tis so; the hounds are baying up and down the town! The Goddess stands where the three ways meet! Hasten, and clash the brazen cymbals.
My magic wheel, draw home to me the man I love!

Lo, silent is the deep, and silent the winds, but never silent the torment in my breast. Nay, I am all on fire for him that made me, miserable me, no wife but a shameful thing, a girl no more a maiden.
My magic wheel, draw home to me the man I love!

Three times do I pour libation, and thrice, my Lady Moon, I speak this spell: — Be it with a friend that he lingers, be it with a leman he lies, may he as clean forget them as Theseus, of old, in Dia — so legends tell — did utterly forget the fair-tressed Ariadne.
My magic wheel, draw home to me the man I love!

Coltsfoot is an Arcadian weed that maddens, on the hills, the young stallions and fleet-footed mares. Ah! even as these may I see Delphis; and to this house of mine, may he speed like a madman, leaving the bright palaestra.

My magic wheel, draw home to me the man I love!

This fringe from his cloak Delphis lost; that now I shred and cast into the cruel flame. Ah, ah, thou torturing Love, why clingest thou to me like a leech of the fen, and drainest all the black blood from my body?

My magic wheel, draw home to me the man I love!

Lo, I will crush an eft, and a venomous draught to-morrow I will bring thee!

But now, Thestylis, take these magic herbs and secretly smear the juice on the jambs of his gate (whereat, even now, my heart is captive, though nothing he recks of me), and spit and whisper, ' 'Tis the bones of Delphis that I smear.'

My magic wheel, draw home to me the man I love!

And now that I am alone, whence shall I begin to bewail my love? Whence shall I take up the tale: who brought on me this sorrow? The maiden-bearer of the mystic vessel came our way, Anaxo, daughter of Eubulus, to the grove of Artemis; and behold, she had many other wild beasts paraded for that time, in the sacred show, and among them a lioness.

Bethink thee of my love, and whence it came, my Lady Moon!

And the Thracian servant of Theucharidas, — my nurse that is but lately dead, and who then dwelt at our doors, — besought me and implored me to come and see the show. And I went with her, wretched woman that I am, clad about in a fair and sweeping linen stole, over which I had thrown the holiday dress of Clearista.

Bethink thee of my love, and whence it came, my Lady Moon!

Lo! I was now come to the mid-point of the highway, near the dwelling of Lycon, and there I saw Delphis and Eudamippus walking together. Their beards were more golden than the golden flower of the ivy; their breasts (they coming fresh from the glorious wrestler's toil) were brighter of sheen than thyself, Selene!

Bethink thee of my love, and whence it came, my Lady Moon!

Even as I looked I loved, loved madly, and all my heart was wounded, woe is me, and my beauty began to wane. No more heed took I of that show, and how I came home I know not; but some parching fever utterly overthrew me, and I lay a-bed ten days and ten nights.

Bethink thee of my love, and whence it came, my Lady Moon!

And oftentimes my skin waxed wan as the colour of boxwood, and all my hair was falling from my head, and what was left of me was but skin and bones. Was there a wizard to whom I did not seek, or a crone to whose house I did not resort, of them that have art magical? But this was no light malady, and the time went fleeting on.

Bethink thee of my love, and whence it came, my Lady Moon!

Thus I told the true story to my maiden, and said, 'Go, Thestylis, and find me some remedy for this sore disease. Ah me, the Myndian possesses me, body and soul! Nay, depart, and watch by the wrestling-ground of Timagetus, for there is his resort, and there he loves to loiter.

Bethink thee of my love, and whence it came, my Lady Moon!

'And when thou art sure he is alone, nod to him secretly, and say, "Simaetha bids thee to come to her," and lead him hither privily.' So I spoke; and she went and brought the bright-limbed Delphis to my house. But I, when I beheld him just crossing the threshold of the door, with his light step, —

Bethink thee of my love, and whence it came, my Lady Moon!

Grew colder all than snow, and the sweat streamed from my brow like the dank dews, and I had no strength to speak, nay, nor to utter as much as children murmur in their slumber, calling to their mother dear: and all my fair body turned stiff as a puppet of wax.

Bethink thee of my love, and whence it came, my Lady Moon!

Then when he had gazed on me, he that knows not love, he fixed his eyes on the ground, and sat down on my bed, and spake as he sat him down: 'Truly, Simaetha, thou didst by no more outrun mine own coming hither, when thou badst me to thy roof, than of late I outran in the race the beautiful Philinus:

Bethink thee of my love, and whence it came, my Lady Moon!

'For I should have come; yea, by sweet Love, I should have come, with friends of mine, two or three, as soon as night drew on, bearing in my breast the apples of Dionysus, and on my head silvery poplar leaves, the holy boughs of Heracles, all twined with bands of purple.

Bethink thee of my love, and whence it came, my Lady Moon!

'And if you had received me, they would have taken it well, for among all the youths unwed I have a name for beauty and speed of foot. With one kiss of thy lovely mouth I had been content; but an if ye had thrust me forth, and the door had been fastened with the bar, then truly should torch and axe have broken in upon you.

Bethink thee of my love, and whence it came, my Lady Moon!

'And now to Cypris first, methinks, my thanks are due, and after Cypris it is thou that hast caught me, lady, from the burning, in that thou badst me come to this thy house, half consumed as I am! Yea, Love, 'tis plain, lights oft a fiercer blaze than Hephaestus the God of Lipara.

Bethink thee of my love, and whence it came, my Lady Moon!

'With his madness dire, he scares both the maiden from her bower and the bride from the bridal bed, yet warm with the body of her lord!'

So he spake, and I, that was easy to win, took his hand, and drew him down on the soft bed beside me. And immediately body from body caught fire, and our faces glowed as they had not done, and sweetly we murmured. And now, dear Selene, to tell thee no long tale, the great rites were accomplished, and we twain came to our desire. Faultless was I in his sight, till yesterday, and he, again, in mine. But there came to me the mother of Philista, my flute player, and the mother of Melixo, to-day, when the horses of the Sun were climbing the sky, bearing Dawn of the rosy arms from the ocean stream. Many another thing she told me; and chiefly this, that Delphis is a lover, and whom he loves she vowed she knew not surely, but this only, that ever he filled up his cup with the unmixed wine, to drink a toast to his dearest. And at last he went off hastily, saying that he would cover with garlands the dwelling of his love.

This news my visitor told me, and she speaks the truth. For indeed, at other seasons, he would come to me thrice, or four times, in the day, and often would leave with me his Dorian oil flask. But now it is the twelfth day since I have even looked on him! Can it be that he has not some other delight, and has forgotten me? Now with magic rites I will strive to bind him, but if still he vexes me, he shall beat, by the Fates I vow it, at the gate of Hell. Such evil medicines I store against him in a certain coffer, the use whereof, my lady, an Assyrian stranger taught me.

But do thou farewell, and turn thy steeds to Ocean, Lady, and my pain I will bear, as even till now I have endured it. Farewell, Selene bright and fair, farewell ye other stars, that follow the wheels of quiet Night.

[tr. ANDREW LANG]

IDYL VII

THE HARVEST-HOME

The poet making his way through the noonday heat, with two friends, to a harvest feast, meets the goatherd, Lycidas. To humour the poet, Lycidas sings a love song of his own, and the other replies with verses about the passion of Aratus, the famous writer of didactic verse. After a courteous parting from Lycidas, the poet and his two friends repair to the orchard, where Demeter is being gratified with the first-fruits of harvest and vintaging.
In this idyl, Theocritus, speaking of himself by the name of Simichidas, alludes to his teachers in poetry, and, perhaps, to some of the literary quarrels of the time.
The scene is in the isle of Cos.

The Harvest-Feast

It fell upon a time when Eucritus and I were walking from the city to the Hales water, and Amyntas was the third in our company. The harvest-feast of Deo was then being held by Phrasidemus and Antigenes, two sons of Lycopeus (if aught there be of noble and old descent), whose lineage dates from Clytia, and Chalcon himself — Chalcon, beneath whose foot the fountain sprang, the well of Buriné. He set his knee stoutly against the rock, and straightway by the spring poplars and elm trees showed a shadowy glade, arched overhead they grew, and pleached with leaves of green. We had not yet reached the mid-point of the way, nor was the tomb of Brasilas yet risen upon our sight, when, — thanks be to the Muses — we met a certain wayfarer, the best of men, a Cydonian. Lycidas was his name, a goatherd was he, nor could any that saw him have taken him for other than he was, for all about him bespoke the goatherd. Stripped from the roughest of he-goats was the tawny skin he wore on his shoulders, the smell of rennet clinging to it still, and about his breast an old cloak was buckled with a plaited belt, and in his right hand he carried a crooked staff of wild olive; and quietly he accosted me, with a smile, a twinkling eye, and a laugh still on his lips: —

'Simichidas, whither, pray, through the noon dost thou trail thy feet, when even the very lizard on the rough stone wall is sleeping, and the crested larks no longer fare afield? Art thou hastening to a feast, a bidden guest, or art thou for treading a townsman's wine-press? For such is thy speed that every stone upon the way spins singing from thy boots!'

'Dear Lycidas,' I answered him, 'they all say that thou among herdsmen, yea, and reapers art far the chiefest flute-player. In sooth this greatly rejoices our hearts, and yet, to my conceit, meseems I can vie with thee. But as to this journey, we are going to the harvest-feast, for, look you some friends of ours are paying a festival to fair-robed Demeter, out of the first-fruits of their increase, for verily in rich measure has the goddess filled their threshing-floor with barley grain. But come, for the way and the day are thine alike and mine, come, let us vie in pastoral song, perchance each will make the other delight. For I, too, am a clear-voiced mouth of the Muses, and they all call me the best of minstrels, but I am not so credulous; no, by Earth, for to my mind I cannot as yet conquer in song that great Sicelidas — the Samian — nay, nor yet Philetas. 'Tis a match of frog against cicala!'

So I spoke, to win my end, and the goatherd with his sweet laugh, said, 'I give thee this staff, because thou art a sapling of Zeus, and in thee is no guile. For as I hate your builders that try to raise a house as high as the mountain summit of Oromedon, so I hate all birds of the Muses that vainly toil with their cackling notes against the Minstrel of Chios! But come, Simichidas, without more ado let us begin the pastoral song. And I — nay, see friend — if it please thee at all, this ditty that I lately fashioned on the mountain side!'

The Song of Lycidas

Fair voyaging befall Ageanax to Mytilene, both when the *Kids* are westering, and the south wind the wet waves chases, and when Orion holds his feet above the Ocean! Fair voyaging betide him, if he saves Lycidas from the fire of Aphrodite, for hot is the love that consumes me.

The halcyons will lull the waves, and lull the deep, and the south wind, and the east, that stirs the sea-weeds on the farthest shores, the halcyons that are dearest to the green-haired mermaids, of all the birds that take their prey from the salt sea. Let all things smile on Ageanax to Mytilene sailing, and may he come to a friendly haven. And I, on that day, will go crowned with anise, or with a rosy wreath, or a garland of white violets, and the fine wine of Ptelea I will dip from the bowl as I lie by the fire, while one shall roast beans for me, in the embers. And elbow-deep shall the flowery bed be thickly strewn, with fragrant leaves and with asphodel, and with curled parsley; and softly will I drink, toasting Ageanax with lips clinging fast to the cup, and draining it even to the lees.

Two shepherds shall be my flute-players, one from Acharnae, one from Lycope, and hard by Tityrus shall sing, how the herdsman Daphnis once loved a strange maiden, and how on the hill he wandered, and how the oak trees sang his dirge — the oaks that grow by the banks of the river Himeras — while he was wasting like any snow under high Haemus, or Athos, or Rhodope, or Caucasus at the world's end.

And he shall sing how, once upon a time, the great chest prisoned the living goatherd, by his lord's infatuate and evil will, and how the blunt-faced bees, as they came up from the meadow to the fragrant cedar chest, fed him with food of tender flowers, because the Muse still dropped sweet nectar on his lips.

O blessed Comatas, surely these joyful things befell thee, and thou wast enclosed within the chest, and feeding on the honeycomb through the springtime didst thou serve out thy bondage. Ah, would that in my days thou hadst been numbered with the living, how gladly on the hills would I have herded thy pretty she-goats, and listened to thy voice, whilst thou, under oaks or pine trees lying, didst sweetly sing, divine Comatas!

When he had chanted thus much he ceased, and I followed after him again, with some such words as these: —

'Dear Lycidas, many another song the Nymphs have taught me also, as I followed my herds upon the hillside, bright songs that Rumour, perchance, has brought even to the throne of Zeus. But of them all this is far the most excellent, wherewith I will begin to do thee honour: nay listen as thou art dear to the Muses.'

The Song of Simichidas

For Simichidas the Loves have sneezed, for truly the wretch loves Myrto as dearly as goats love the spring. But Aratus, far the dearest of my friends, deep, deep in his heart he keeps Desire, — and Aratus's love is young! Aristis knows it, an honourable man, nay of men the best, whom even Phoebus would permit to stand and sing lyre in hand, by his tripods. Aristis knows how deeply love is burning Aratus to the bone. Ah, Pan, thou lord of the beautiful plain of Homole, bring, I pray thee, the darling of Aratus unbidden to his arms, whosoe'er it be that he loves. If this thou dost, dear Pan, then never may the boys of Arcady flog thy sides and shoulders with sting-ing herbs, when scanty meats are left them on thine altar. But if thou shouldst otherwise decree, then may all thy skin be frayed and torn with thy nails, yea, and in nettles mayst thou couch! In the hills of the Edonians mayst thou dwell in mid-winter time, by the river Hebrus, close neighbour to the Polar star! But in summer mayst thou range with the uttermost Æthiopians beneath the rock of the Blemyes, whence Nile no more is seen.

And you, leave ye the sweet fountain of Hyetis and Byblis, and ye that dwell in the steep home of golden Dione, ye Loves as rosy as red apples, strike me with your arrows, the desired, the beloved; strike, for that ill-starred one pities not my friend, my host! And yet assur-edly the pear is over-ripe, and the maidens cry 'alas, alas, thy fair bloom fades away!'

Come, no more let us mount guard by these gates, Aratus, nor wear our feet away with knocking there. Nay, let the crowing of the morning cock give others over to the bitter cold of dawn. Let Molon alone, my friend, bear the torment at that school of passion! For us, let us secure a quiet life, and some old crone to spit on us for luck, and so keep all unlovely things away.

Thus I sang, and sweetly smiling, as before, he gave me the staff, a pledge of brotherhood in the Muses. Then he bent his way to the left, and took the road to Pyxa, while I and Eucritus, with beautiful Amyntas, turned to the farm of Phrasidemus. There we reclined on deep beds of fragrant lentisk, lowly strown, and rejoicing we lay in new stript leaves of the vine. And high above our heads waved many a poplar, many an elm tree, while close at hand the sacred water from the nymphs' own cave welled forth with murmurs musical. On shadowy boughs the burnt cicalas kept their chattering toil, far off the little owl cried in the thick thorn brake, the larks and finches were singing, the ring-dove moaned, the yellow bees were flitting about the springs. All breathed the scent of the opulent summer, of the season of fruits; pears at our feet and apples by our sides were rolling plentiful, the tender branches, with wild plums laden, were earthward bowed, and the four-year-old pitch seal was loosened from the mouth of the wine-jars.

Ye nymphs of Castaly that hold the steep of Parnassus, say, was it ever a bowl like this that old Chiron set before Heracles in the rocky

cave of Pholus? Was it nectar like this that beguiled the shepherd
to dance and foot it about his folds, the shepherd that dwelt by
Anapus, on a time, the strong Polyphemus who hurled at ships with
mountains? Had these ever such a draught as ye nymphs bade flow
for us by the altar of Demeter of the threshing-floor?

Ah, once again may I plant the great fan on her corn-heap, while
she stands smiling by, with sheaves and poppies in her hands.

[tr. ANDREW LANG]

IDYL XI

THE CYCLOPS IN LOVE

*Nicias, the physician and poet, being in love, Theocritus reminds him
that in song lies the only remedy. It was by song, he says, that the
Cyclops, Polyphemus, got him some ease, when he was in love with
Galatea, the sea-nymph.*

*The idyl displays, in the most graceful manner, the Alexandrian taste
for turning Greek mythology into love stories. No creature could
be more remote from love than the original Polyphemus, the canni-
bal giant of the Odyssey.*

There is none other medicine, Nicias, against Love, neither unguent, methinks, nor salve to sprinkle, — none, save the Muses of
Pieria! Now a delicate thing is their minstrelsy in man's life, and
a sweet, but hard to procure. Methinks thou know'st this well, who
art thyself a leech, and beyond all men art plainly dear to the Muses
nine.

'Twas surely thus the Cyclops fleeted his life most easily, he that
dwelt among us, — Polyphemus of old time, — when the beard was
yet young on his cheek and chin; and he loved Galatea. He loved,
not with apples, not roses, nor locks of hair, but with fatal frenzy, and
all things else he held but trifles by the way. Many a time from the
green pastures would his ewes stray back, self-shepherded, to the fold.
But he was singing of Galatea, and pining in his place he sat by the
sea-weed of the beach, from the dawn of day, with the direst hurt
beneath his breast of mighty Cypris's sending, — the wound of her
arrow in his heart!

Yet this remedy he found, and sitting on the crest of the tall cliff,
and looking to the deep, 'twas thus he would sing: —

Song of the Cyclops

O milk-white Galatea, why cast off him that loves thee? More
white than is pressed milk to look upon, more delicate than the lamb
art thou, than the young calf wantoner, more sleek than the unripened grape! Here dost thou resort, even so, when sweet sleep possesses me, and home straightway dost thou depart when sweet sleep
lets me go, fleeing me like an ewe that has seen the grey wolf.

I fell in love with thee, maiden, I, on the day when first thou camest, with my mother, and didst wish to pluck the hyacinths from the hill, and I was thy guide on the way. But to leave loving thee, when once I had seen thee, neither afterward, nor now at all, have I the strength, even from that hour. But to thee all this is as nothing, by Zeus, nay, nothing at all!

I know, thou gracious maiden, why it is that thou dost shun me. It is all for the shaggy brow that spans all my forehead, from this to the other ear, one long unbroken eyebrow. And but one eye is on my forehead, and broad is the nose that overhangs my lip. Yet I (even such as thou seest me) feed a thousand cattle, and from these I draw and drink the best milk in the world. And cheese I never lack, in summer time or autumn, nay, nor in the dead of winter, but my baskets are always overladen.

Also I am skilled in piping, as none other of the Cyclopes here, and of thee, my love, my sweet-apple, and of myself too I sing, many a time, deep in the night. And for thee I tend eleven fawns, all crescent-browed, and four young whelps of the bear.

Nay, come thou to me, and thou shalt lack nothing that now thou hast. Leave the grey sea to roll against the land; more sweetly, in this cavern, shalt thou fleet the night with me! Thereby the laurels grow, and there the slender cypresses, there is the ivy dun, and the sweet clustered grapes; there is chill water, that for me deep-wooded Ætna sends down from the white snow, a draught divine! Ah who, in place of these, would choose the sea to dwell in, or the waves of the sea?

But if thou dost refuse because my body seems shaggy and rough, well, I have faggots of oakwood, and beneath the ashes is fire unwearied, and I would endure to let thee burn my very soul, and this my one eye, the dearest thing that is mine.

Ah me, that my mother bore me not a finny thing, so would I have gone down to thee, and kissed thy hand, if thy lips thou would not suffer me to kiss! And I would have brought thee either white lilies, or the soft poppy with its scarlet petals. Nay, these are summer's flowers, and those are flowers of winter, so I could not have brought thee them all at one time.

Now, verily, maiden, now and here will I learn to swim, if perchance some stranger come hither, sailing with his ship, that I may see why it is so dear to thee, to have thy dwelling in the deep.

Come forth, Galatea, and forget as thou comest, even as I that sit here have forgotten, the homeward way! Nay, choose with me to go shepherding, with me to milk the flocks, and to pour the sharp rennet in, and to fix the cheeses.

There is none that wrongs me but that mother of mine, and her do I blame. Never, nay, never once has she spoken a kind word for me to thee, and that though day by day she beholds me wasting. I will tell her that my head, and both my feet are throbbing, that she may somewhat suffer, since I too am suffering.

O Cyclops, Cyclops, whither are thy wits wandering? Ah that

thou wouldst go, and weave thy wicker-work, and gather broken boughs to carry to thy lambs: in faith, if thou didst this, far wiser wouldst thou be!

Milk the ewe that thou hast, why pursue the thing that shuns thee? Thou wilt find, perchance, another, and a fairer Galatea. Many be the girls that bid me play with them through the night, and softly they all laugh, if perchance I answer them. On land it is plain that I too seem to be somebody!

Lo, thus Polyphemus still shepherded his love with song, and lived lighter than if he had given gold for ease.

[tr. ANDREW LANG]

IDYL XV

THE SYRACUSAN WOMEN

This famous idyl should rather, perhaps, be called a mimus. *It describes the visit paid by two Syracusan women residing in Alexandria, to the festival of the resurrection of Adonis. The festival is given by Arsinoë, wife and sister of Ptolemy Philadelphus, and the poem cannot have been written earlier than his marriage, in* 266 B.C. [?] *Nothing can be more gay and natural than the chatter of the women, which has changed no more in two thousand years than the song of birds. Theocritus is believed to have had a model for this idyl in the* Isthmiazusae *of Sophron, an older poet. In the* Isthmiazusae *two ladies described the spectacle of the Isthmian games.*

Gorgo. Is Praxinoë at home?

Praxinoë. Dear Gorgo, how long it is since you have been here! She *is* at home. The wonder is that you have got here at last! Eunoë, see that she has a chair. Throw a cushion on it too.

Gorgo. It does most charmingly as it is.

Praxinoë. Do sit down.

Gorgo. Oh, what a thing spirit is! I have scarcely got to you alive, Praxinoë! What a huge crowd, what hosts of four-in-hands! Everywhere cavalry boots, everywhere men in uniform! And the road is endless: yes, you really live *too* far away!

Praxinoë. It is all the fault of that madman of mine. Here he came to the ends of the earth and took — a hole, not a house, and all that we might not be neighbours. The jealous wretch, always the same, ever for spite!

Gorgo. Don't talk of your husband, Dinon, like that, my dear girl, before the little boy, — look how he is staring at you! Never mind, Zopyrion, sweet child, she is not speaking about papa.

Praxinoë. Our Lady! the child takes notice.

Gorgo. Nice papa!

Praxinoë. That papa of his the other day — we call every day 'the other day' — went to get soap and rouge at the shop, and back he came to me with salt — the great big endless fellow!

Gorgo. Mine has the same trick, too, a perfect spendthrift — Diocleides! Yesterday he got what he meant for five fleeces, and paid
seven shillings a piece for — what do you suppose? — dogskins,
shreds of old leather wallets, mere trash — trouble on trouble. But
come, take your cloak and shawl. Let us be off to the palace of rich
Ptolemy, the King, to see the Adonis; I hear the Queen has provided
something splendid!

Praxinoë. Fine folks do everything finely.

Gorgo. What a tale you will have to tell about the things you have
seen, to any one who has not seen them! It seems nearly time to go.

Praxinoë. Idlers have always holiday. Eunoë, bring the water
and put it down in the middle of the room, lazy creature that you
are. Cats like always to sleep soft! Come, bustle, bring the water;
quicker. I want water first, and how she carries it! give it me all
the same; don't pour out so much, you extravagant thing. Stupid
girl! Why are you wetting my dress? There, stop, I have washed
my hands, as heaven would have it. Where is the key of the big
chest? Bring it here.

Gorgo. Praxinoë, that full body becomes you wonderfully. Tell
me how much did the stuff cost you just off the loom?

Praxinoë. Don't speak of it, Gorgo! More than eight pounds in
good silver money, — and the work on it! I nearly slaved my soul
out over it!

Gorgo. Well, it is *most* successful; all you could wish.

Praxinoë. Thanks for the pretty speech! Bring my shawl, and set
my hat on my head, the fashionable way. No, child, I don't mean
to take you. Boo! Bogies! There's a horse that bites! Cry as
much as you please, but I cannot have you lamed. Let us be moving.
Phrygia take the child, and keep him amused, call in the dog, and
shut the street door.

[*They go into the street.*

Ye gods, what a crowd! How on earth are we ever to get through
this coil? They are like ants that no one can measure or number.
Many a good deed have you done, Ptolemy; since your father joined
the immortals, there's never a malefactor to spoil the passer-by, creeping on him in Egyptian fashion — oh! the tricks those perfect rascals
used to play. Birds of a feather, ill jesters, scoundrels all! Dear
Gorgo, what will become of us? Here come the King's war-horses!
My dear man, don't trample on me. Look, the bay's rearing, see,
what temper! Eunoë, you foolhardy girl, will you never keep out
of the way? The beast will kill the man that's leading him. What
a good thing it is for me that my brat stays safe at home.

Gorgo. Courage, Praxinoë. We are safe behind them, now, and
they have gone to their station.

Praxinoë. There! I begin to be myself again. Ever since I was a
child I have feared nothing so much as horses and the chilly snake.
Come along, the huge mob is overflowing us.

Gorgo (*to an old Woman*). Are you from the Court, mother?

Old Woman. I am, my child.

Praxinoë. Is it easy to get there?

Old Woman. The Achaeans got into Troy by trying, my prettiest of ladies. Trying will do everything in the long run.

Gorgo. The old wife has spoken her oracles, and off she goes.

Praxinoë. Women know everything, yes, and how Zeus married Hera!

Gorgo. See, Praxinoë, what a crowd there is about the doors.

Praxinoë. Monstrous, Gorgo! Give me your hand, and you, Eunoë, catch hold of Eutychis; never lose hold of her, for fear lest you get lost. Let us all go in together; Eunoë, clutch tight to me. Oh, how tiresome. Gorgo, my muslin veil is torn in two already! For heaven's sake, sir, if you ever wish to be fortunate, take care of my shawl!

Stranger. I can hardly help myself, but for all that I will be as careful as I can.

Praxinoë. How close-packed the mob is, they hustle like a herd of swine.

Stranger. Courage, lady, all is well with us now.

Praxinoë. Both this year and for ever may all be well with you, my dear sir, for your care of us. A good kind man! We're letting Eunoë get squeezed — come, wretched girl, push your way through. That is the way. We are all on the right side of the door, quoth the bridegroom, when he had shut himself in with his bride.

Gorgo. Do come here, Praxinoë. Look first at these embroideries. How light and how lovely! You will call them the garments of the gods.

Praxinoë. Lady Athene, what spinning women wrought them, what painters designed these drawings, so true they are? How naturally they stand and move, like living creatures, not patterns woven. What a clever thing is man! Ah, and himself — Adonis — how beautiful to behold he lies on his silver couch, with the first down on his cheeks, the thrice-beloved Adonis, — Adonis beloved even among the dead.

A Stranger. You weariful women, do cease your endless cooing talk! They bore one to death with their eternal broad vowels!

Gorgo. Indeed! And where may this person come from? What is it to you if we are chatterboxes! Give orders to your own servants, sir. Do you pretend to command ladies of Syracuse? If you must know, we are Corinthians by descent, like Bellerophon himself, and we speak Peloponnesian. Dorian women may lawfully speak Doric, I presume?

Praxinoë. Lady Persephone, never may we have more than one master. I am not afraid of *your* putting me on short commons.

Gorgo. Hush, hush, Praxinoë — the Argive woman's daughter, the great singer, is beginning the *Adonis*; she that won the prize last year for dirge-singing. I am sure she will give us something lovely; see, she is preluding with her airs and graces.

The Psalm of Adonis

O Queen that lovest Golgi, and Idalium, and the steep of Eryx,
O Aphrodite, that playest with gold, lo, from the stream eternal of
Acheron they have brought back to thee Adonis — even in the
twelfth month they have brought him, the dainty-footed Hours.
Tardiest of the Immortals are the beloved Hours, but dear and desired they come, for always, to all mortals, they bring some gift with
them. O Cypris, daughter of Diônê, from mortal to immortal, so
men tell, thou hast changed Berenice, dropping softly in the woman's
breast the stuff of immortality.

Therefore, for thy delight, O thou of many names and many temples, doth the daughter of Berenice, even Arsinoë, lovely as Helen,
cherish Adonis with all things beautiful.

Before him lie all ripe fruits that the tall trees' branches bear, and
the delicate gardens, arrayed in baskets of silver, and the golden
vessels are full of incense of Syria. And all the dainty cakes that
women fashion in the kneading-tray, mingling blossoms manifold
with the white wheaten flour, all that is wrought of honey sweet, and
in soft olive oil, all cakes fashioned in the semblance of things that
fly, and of things that creep, lo, here they are set before him.

Here are built for him shadowy bowers of green, all laden with
tender anise, and children flit overhead — the little Loves — as the
young nightingales perched upon the trees fly forth and try their
wings from bough to bough.

O the ebony, O the gold, O the twin eagles of white ivory that carry
to Zeus the son of Cronos his darling, his cup-bearer! O the purple
coverlet strewn above, more soft than sleep! So Miletus will say, and
whoso feeds sheep in Samos.

Another bed is strewn for beautiful Adonis, one bed Cypris keeps,
and one the rosy-armed Adonis. A bridegroom of eighteen or nineteen years is he, his kisses are not rough, the golden down being yet
upon his lips! And now, good-night to Cypris, in the arms of her
lover! But lo, in the morning we will all of us gather with the dew,
and carry him forth among the waves that break upon the beach, and
with locks unloosed, and ungirt raiment falling to the ankles, and
bosoms bare will we begin our shrill sweet song.

Thou only, dear Adonis, so men tell, thou only of the demigods
dost visit both this world and the stream of Acheron. For Agamemnon had no such lot, nor Aias, that mighty lord of the terrible anger,
nor Hector, the eldest born of the twenty sons of Hecabe, nor Patroclus, nor Pyrrhus, that returned out of Troyland, nor the heroes of
yet more ancient days, the Lapithae and Deucalion's sons, nor the
sons of Pelops, and the chiefs of Pelasgian Argos. Be gracious now,
dear Adonis, and propitious even in the coming year. Dear to us has
thine advent been, Adonis, and dear shall it be when thou comest
again.

Gorgo. Praxinoë, the woman is cleverer than we fancied! Happy
woman to know so much, thrice happy to have so sweet a voice.

Well, all the same, it is time to be making for home. Diocleides has not had his dinner, and the man is all vinegar, — don't venture near him when he is kept waiting for dinner. Farewell, beloved Adonis, may you find us glad at your next coming!

[tr. ANDREW LANG]

IDYL XX

THE NEATHERD'S LAMENT

A herdsman, who had been contemptuously rejected by Eunica, a girl of the town, protests that he is beautiful, and that Eunica is prouder than Cybele, Selene, and Aphrodite, all of whom loved mortal herdsmen. For grammatical and other reasons, some critics consider this idyl apocryphal.

Eunica laughed out at me when sweetly I would have kissed her, and taunting me, thus she spoke: 'Get thee gone from me! Wouldst thou kiss me, wretch; thou — a neatherd? I never learned to kiss in country fashion, but to press lips with city gentlefolks. Never hope to kiss my lovely mouth, nay, not even in a dream. How thou dost look, what chatter is thine, how countrified thy tricks are, how delicate thy talk, how easy thy tattle! And then thy beard — so soft! thy elegant hair! Why, thy lips are like some sick man's, thy hands are black, and thou art of evil savour. Away with thee, lest thy presence soil me!' These taunts she mouthed, and thrice spat in the breast of her gown, and stared at me all over from head to feet; shooting out her lips, and glancing with half-shut eyes, writhing her beautiful body, and so sneered, and laughed me to scorn. And instantly my blood boiled, and I grew red under the sting, as a rose with dew. And she went off and left me, but I bear angry pride deep in my heart, that I, the handsome shepherd, should have been mocked by a wretched light-o'-love.

Shepherds, tell me the very truth; am I not beautiful? Has some God changed me suddenly to another man? Surely a sweet grace ever blossomed round me, till this hour, like ivy round a tree, and covered my chin, and about my temples fell my locks, like curling parsley-leaves, and white shone my forehead above my dark eyebrows. Mine eyes were brighter far than the glance of the grey-eyed Athene, my mouth than even pressed milk was sweeter, and from my lips my voice flowed sweeter than honey from the honeycomb. Sweet too, is my music, whether I make melody on pipe, or discourse on the flute, or reed, or flageolet. And all the mountain-maidens call me beautiful, and they would kiss me, all of them. But the city girl did not kiss me, but ran past me, because I am a neatherd, and she never heard how fair Dionysus in the dells doth drive the calves, and knows not that Cypris was wild with love for a herdsman, and drove afield in the mountains of Phrygia; ay, and Adonis himself, — in the oakwood she kissed, in the oakwood she bewailed him. And what was Endymion? was he not a neatherd? whom nevertheless as he watched his herds Selene saw and loved, and from Olympus descending she came to the Latmian glade, and lay in one couch with the boy; and thou, Rhea, dost weep for thy herdsman.

And didst not thou, too, Son of Cronos, take the shape of a wandering bird, and all for a cowherd boy?

But Eunica alone would not kiss the herdsman; Eunica, she that is greater than Cybele, and Cypris, and Selene!

Well, Cypris, never mayst thou, in city or on hillside, kiss thy darling, and lonely all the long night mayst thou sleep!

[tr. ANDREW LANG]

IDYL XXVII

THE WOOING OF DAPHNIS

The authenticity of this idyl has been denied, partly because the Daphnis of the poem is not identical in character with the Daphnis of the first idyl.   But the piece is certainly worthy of a place beside the work of Theocritus.   The dialogue is here arranged as in the text of Fritzsche.

The Maiden. Helen the wise did Paris, another neatherd, ravish!

Daphnis. 'Tis rather this Helen that kisses her shepherd, even me!

The Maiden. Boast not, little satyr, for kisses they call an empty favour.

Daphnis. Nay, even in empty kisses there is a sweet delight.

The Maiden. I wash my lips, I blow away from me thy kisses!

Daphnis. Dost thou wash thy lips?   Then give me them again to kiss!

The Maiden. 'Tis for thee to caress thy kine, not a maiden unwed.

Daphnis. Boast not, for swiftly thy youth flits by thee, like a dream.

The Maiden. The grapes turn to raisins, not wholly will the dry rose perish.

Daphnis. Come hither, beneath the wild olives, that I may tell thee a tale.

The Maiden. I will not come; ay, ere now with a sweet tale didst thou beguile me.

Daphnis. Come hither, beneath the elms, to listen to my pipe!

The Maiden. Nay, please thyself, no woful tune delights me.

Daphnis. Ah maiden, see that thou too shun the anger of the Paphian.

The Maiden. Good-bye to the Paphian, let Artemis only be friendly!

Daphnis. Say not so, lest she smite thee, and thou fall into a trap whence there is no escape.

The Maiden. Let her smite an she will; Artemis again would be my defender.   Lay no hand on me; nay, if thou do more, and touch me with thy lips, I will bite thee.

Daphnis. From Love thou dost not flee, whom never yet maiden fled.

The Maiden. Escape him, by Pan, I do, but thou dost ever bear his yoke.

Daphnis. This is ever my fear lest he even give thee to a meaner man.

The Maiden. Many have been my wooers, but none has won my heart.

Daphnis. Yea I, out of many chosen, come here thy wooer.

The Maiden. Dear love, what can I do? Marriage has much annoy.

Daphnis. Nor pain nor sorrow has marriage, but mirth and dancing.

The Maiden. Ay, but they say that women dread their lords.

Daphnis. Nay, rather they always rule them, — whom do women fear?

The Maiden. Travail I dread, and sharp is the shaft of Eilithyia.

Daphnis. But thy queen is Artemis, that lightens labour.

The Maiden. But I fear childbirth, lest, perchance, I lose my beauty.

Daphnis. Nay, if thou bearest dear children thou wilt see the light revive in thy sons.

The Maiden. And what wedding gift dost thou bring me if I consent?

Daphnis. My whole flock, all my groves, and all my pasture land shall be thine.

The Maiden. Swear that thou wilt not win me, and then depart and leave me forlorn.

Daphnis. So help me Pan I would not leave thee, didst thou even choose to banish me!

The Maiden. Dost thou build me bowers, and a house, and folds for flocks?

Daphnis. Yea, bowers I build thee, the flocks I tend are fair.

The Maiden. But to my grey old father, what tale, ah what, shall I tell?

Daphnis. He will approve thy wedlock when he has heard my name.

The Maiden. Prithee, tell me that name of thine; in a name there is often delight.

Daphnis. Daphnis am I, Lycidas is my father, and Nomaea is my mother.

The Maiden. Thou comest of men well-born, but there I am thy match.

Daphnis. I know it, thou art of high degree, for thy father is Menalcas.

The Maiden. Show me thy grove, wherein is thy cattle-stall.

Daphnis. See here, how they bloom, my slender cypress-trees.

The Maiden. Graze on, my goats, I go to learn the herdsman's labours.

Daphnis. Feed fair, my bulls, while I show my woodlands to my lady!

The Maiden. What dost thou, little satyr; why dost thou touch my breast?

Daphnis. I will show thee that these earliest apples are ripe.

The Maiden. By Pan, I swoon; away, take back thy hand.

Daphnis. Courage, dear girl, why fearest thou me, thou art over fearful!

The Maiden. Thou makest me lie down by the water-course, defiling my fair raiment!

Daphnis. Nay, see, 'neath thy raiment fair I am throwing this soft fleece.

The Maiden. Ah, ah, thou hast snatched my girdle too; why hast thou loosed my girdle?

Daphnis. These first-fruits I offer, a gift to the Paphian.

The Maiden. Stay, wretch, hark; surely a stranger cometh; nay, I hear a sound.

Daphnis. The cypresses do but whisper to each other of thy wedding.

The Maiden. Thou hast torn my mantle, and unclad am I.

Daphnis. Another mantle I will give thee, and an ampler far than thine.

The Maiden. Thou dost promise all things, but soon thou wilt not give me even a grain of salt.

Daphnis. Ah, would that I could give thee my very life.

The Maiden. Artemis, be not wrathful, thy votary breaks her vow.

Daphnis. I will slay a calf for Love, and for Aphrodite herself a heifer.

The Maiden. A maiden I came hither, a woman shall I go homeward.

Daphnis. Nay, a wife and a mother of children shalt thou be, no more a maiden.

So, each to each, in the joy of their young fresh limbs they were murmuring: it was the hour of secret love. Then she arose, and stole to herd her sheep; with shamefast eyes she went, but her heart was comforted within her. And he went to his herds of kine, rejoicing in his wedlock.

[tr. ANDREW LANG]

BION

(*fl.* 120? B.C.)

I

THE LAMENT FOR ADONIS

This poem was probably intended to be sung at one of the spring celebrations of the festival of Adonis, like that described by Theocritus in his fifteenth idyl.

Woe, woe for Adonis, he hath perished, the beauteous Adonis, dead is the beauteous Adonis, the Loves join in the lament. No more in thy purple raiment, Cypris, do thou sleep; arise, thou wretched one, sable-stoled, and beat thy breasts, and say to all, 'He hath perished, the lovely Adonis!'

Woe, woe for Adonis, the Loves join in the lament!

Low on the hills is lying the lovely Adonis, and his thigh with the boar's tusk, his white thigh with the boar's tusk is wounded, and sorrow on Cypris he brings, as softly he breathes his life away.

His dark blood drips down his skin of snow, beneath his brows his eyes wax heavy and dim, and the rose flees from his lip, and thereon the very kiss is dying, the kiss that Cypris will never forego.

To Cypris his kiss is dear, though he lives no longer, but Adonis knew not that she kissed him as he died.

Woe, woe for Adonis, the Loves join in the lament!

A cruel, cruel wound on his thigh hath Adonis, but a deeper wound in her heart doth Cytherea bear. About him his dear hounds are loudly baying, and the nymphs of the wild wood wail him; but Aphrodite with unbound locks through the glades goes wandering, — wretched, with hair unbraided, with feet unsandaled, and the thorns as she passes wound her and pluck the blossom of her sacred blood. Shrill she wails as down the long woodlands she is borne, lamenting her Assyrian lord, and again calling him, and again. But round his navel the dark blood leapt forth, with blood from his thighs his chest was scarlet, and beneath Adonis's breast, the spaces that afore were snow-white, were purple with blood.

Woe, woe for Cytherea, the Loves join in the lament!

She hath lost her lovely lord, with him she hath lost her sacred beauty. Fair was the form of Cypris, while Adonis was living, but her beauty has died with Adonis! *Woe, woe for Cypris,* the mountains all are saying, and the oak-trees answer, *Woe for Adonis.* And the rivers bewail the sorrows of Aphrodite, and the wells are weeping Adonis on the mountains. The flowers flush red for anguish, and Cytherea through all the mountain-knees, through every dell doth shrill the piteous dirge.

Woe, woe for Cytherea, he hath perished, the lovely Adonis!

And Echo cried in answer, *He hath perished, the lovely Adonis.*
Nay, who but would have lamented the grievous love of Cypris?
When she saw, when she marked the unstaunched wounds of Adonis,
when she saw the bright red blood about his languid thigh, she cast
her arms abroad and moaned, 'Abide with me, Adonis, hapless
Adonis abide, that this last time of all I may possess thee, that I may
cast myself about thee, and lips with lips may mingle. Awake,
Adonis, for a little while, and kiss me yet again, the latest kiss! Nay
kiss me but a moment, but the lifetime of a kiss, till from thine inmost soul into my lips, into my heart, thy life-breath ebb, and till
I drain thy sweet love-philtre, and drink down all thy love. This
kiss will I treasure, even as thyself, Adonis, since, ah ill-fated, thou
art fleeing me, thou art fleeing far, Adonis, and art faring to Acheron,
to that hateful king and cruel, while wretched I yet live, being a
goddess, and may not follow thee! Persephone, take thou my lover,
my lord, for thy self art stronger than I, and all lovely things drift
down to thee. But I am ill-fated, inconsolable is my anguish, and
I lament mine Adonis, dead to me, and I have no rest for sorrow.

'Thou diest, O thrice-desired, and my desire hath flown away as
a dream. Nay, widowed is Cytherea, and idle are the Loves along
the halls! With thee has the girdle of my beauty perished. For
why, ah overbold, didst thou follow the chase, and being so fair, why
wert thou thus overhardy to fight with beasts?'

So Cypris bewailed her, the Loves join in the lament:
Woe, woe for Cytherea, he hath perished, the lovely Adonis!

A tear the Paphian sheds for each blood-drop of Adonis, and tears
and blood on the earth are turned to flowers. The blood brings forth
the rose, the tears, the wind-flower.
Woe, woe for Adonis, he hath perished, the lovely Adonis!

No more in the oak-woods, Cypris, lament thy lord. It is no fair
couch for Adonis, the lonely bed of leaves! Thine own bed, Cytherea, let him now possess, — the dead Adonis. Ah, even in death
he is beautiful, beautiful in death, as one that hath fallen on sleep.
Now lay him down to sleep in his own soft coverlets, wherein with
thee through the night he shared the holy slumber in a couch all of
gold, that yearns for Adonis, though sad is he to look upon. Cast on
him garlands and blossoms: all things have perished in his death,
yea all the flowers are faded. Sprinkle him with ointments of Syria,
sprinkle him with unguents of myrrh. Nay, perish all perfumes, for
Adonis, who was thy perfume, hath perished.

He reclines, the delicate Adonis, in his raiment of purple, and
around him the Loves are weeping, and groaning aloud, clipping
their locks for Adonis. And one upon his shafts, another on his
bow is treading, and one hath loosed the sandal of Adonis, and another hath broken his own feathered quiver, and one in a golden
vessel bears water, and another laves the wound, and another from
behind him with his wings is fanning Adonis.
Woe, woe for Cytherea, the Loves join in the lament!

Every torch on the lintels of the door has Hymenaeus quenched, and hath torn to shreds the bridal crown, and *Hymen* no more, *Hymen* no more is the song, but a new song is sung of wailing.

'*Woe, woe for Adonis,*' rather than the nuptial song the Graces are shrilling, lamenting the son of Cinyras, and one to the other declaring, *He hath perished, the lovely Adonis.*

And *woe, woe for Adonis*, shrilly cry the Muses, neglecting Paeon, and they lament Adonis aloud, and songs they chant to him, but he does not heed them, not that he is loth to hear, but that the Maiden of Hades doth not let him go.

Cease, Cytherea, from thy lamentations, to-day refrain from thy dirges. Thou must again bewail him, again must weep for him another year.

[tr. Andrew Lang]

MOSCHUS

(*fl.* 150? B.C.)

IDYL III

THE LAMENT FOR BION

Wail, let me hear you wail, ye woodland glades, and thou Dorian water; and weep ye rivers, for Bion, the well beloved! Now all ye green things mourn, and now ye groves lament him, ye flowers now in sad clusters breathe yourselves away. Now redden ye roses in your sorrow, and now wax red ye wind-flowers, now thou hyacinth, whisper the letters on thee graven, and add a deeper *ai ai* to thy petals; he is dead, the beautiful singer.

Begin, ye Sicilian Muses, begin the dirge.

Ye nightingales that lament among the thick leaves of the trees, tell ye to the Sicilian waters of Arethusa the tidings that Bion the herdsman is dead, and that with Bion song too has died, and perished hath the Dorian minstrelsy.

Begin, ye Sicilian Muses, begin the dirge.

Ye Strymonian swans, sadly wail ye by the waters, and chant with melancholy notes the dolorous song, even such a song as in his time with voice like yours he was wont to sing. And tell again to the Œagrian maidens, tell to all the Nymphs Bistonian, how that he hath perished, the Dorian Orpheus.

Begin, ye Sicilian Muses, begin the dirge.

No more to his herds he sings, that beloved herdsman, no more 'neath the lonely oaks he sits and sings, nay, but by Pluteus's side he chants a refrain of oblivion. The mountains too are voiceless: and the heifers that wander by the bulls lament and refuse their pasture.

Begin, ye Sicilian Muses, begin the dirge.

Thy sudden doom, O Bion, Apollo himself lamented, and the Satyrs mourned thee, and the Priapi in sable raiment, and the Panes sorrow for thy song, and the fountain fairies in the wood made moan, and their tears turned to rivers of waters. And Echo in the rocks laments that thou art silent, and no more she mimics thy voice. And in sorrow for thy fall the trees cast down their fruit, and all the flowers have faded. From the ewes hath flowed no fair milk, nor honey from the hives, nay, it hath perished for mere sorrow in the wax, for now hath thy honey perished, and no more it behoves men to gather the honey of the bees.

Begin, ye Sicilian Muses, begin the dirge.

Not so much did the dolphin mourn beside the sea-banks, nor ever sang so sweet the nightingale on the cliffs, nor so much lamented the swallow on the long ranges of the hills, nor shrilled so loud the halcyon o'er his sorrows;

(Begin, ye Sicilian Muses, begin the dirge.)

Nor so much, by the grey sea-waves, did ever the sea-bird sing, nor so much in the dells of dawn did the bird of Memnon bewail the son of the Morning, fluttering around his tomb, as they lamented for Bion dead.

Nightingales, and all the swallows that once he was wont to delight, that he would teach to speak, they sat over against each other on the boughs and kept moaning, and the birds sang in answer, 'Wail, ye wretched ones, even ye!'

Begin, ye Sicilian Muses, begin the dirge.

Who, ah who will ever make music on thy pipe, O thrice desired Bion, and who will put his mouth to the reeds of thine instrument? who is so bold?

For still thy lips and still thy breath survive, and Echo, among the reeds, doth still feed upon thy songs. To Pan shall I bear the pipe? Nay, perchance even he would fear to set his mouth to it, lest, after thee, he should win but the second prize.

Begin, ye Sicilian Muses, begin the dirge.

Yea, and Galatea laments thy song, she whom once thou wouldst delight, as with thee she sat by the sea-banks. For not like the Cyclops didst thou sing — him fair Galatea ever fled, but on thee she still looked more kindly than on the salt water. And now hath she forgotten the wave, and sits on the lonely sands, but still she keeps thy kine.

Begin, ye Sicilian Muses, begin the dirge.

All the gifts of the Muses, herdsman, have died with thee, the delightful kisses of maidens, the lips of boys; and woful round thy tomb the loves are weeping. But Cypris loves thee far more than the kiss wherewith she kissed the dying Adonis.

Begin, ye Sicilian Muses, begin the dirge.

This, O most musical of rivers, is thy second sorrow, this, Meles, thy new woe. Of old didst thou lose Homer, that sweet mouth of Calliope, and men say thou didst bewail thy goodly son with streams of many tears, and didst fill all the salt sea with the voice of thy lamentation — now again another son thou weepest, and in a new sorrow art thou wasting away.

Begin, ye Sicilian Muses, begin the dirge.

Both were beloved of the fountains, and one ever drank of the Pegasean fount, but the other would drain a draught of Arethusa. And the one sang the fair daughter of Tyndarus, and the mighty son of Thetis, and Menelaus Atreus's son, but that other, — not of wars, not of tears, but of Pan, would he sing, and of herdsmen would he chant, and so singing, he tended the herds. And pipes he would fashion, and would milk the sweet heifer, and taught lads how to kiss, and Love he cherished in his bosom and woke the passion of Aphrodite.

Begin, ye Sicilian Muses, begin the dirge.

Every famous city laments thee, Bion, and all the towns. Ascra laments thee far more than her Hesiod, and Pindar is less regretted by the forests of Boeotia. Nor so much did pleasant Lesbos mourn for Alcaeus, nor did the Teian town so greatly bewail her poet, while for thee more than for Archilochus doth Paros yearn, and not for Sappho, but still for thee doth Mytilene wail her musical lament;

[Here seven verses are lost.]

And in Syracuse Theocritus; but I sing thee the dirge of an Ausonian sorrow, I that am no stranger to the pastoral song, but heir of the Doric Muse which thou didst teach thy pupils. This was thy gift to me; to others didst thou leave thy wealth, to me thy minstrelsy.

Begin, ye Sicilian Muses, begin the dirge.

Ah me, when the mallows wither in the garden, and the green parsley, and the curled tendrils of the anise, on a later day they live again, and spring in another year; but we men, we, the great and mighty, or wise, when once we have died, in hollow earth we sleep, gone down into silence; a right long, and endless, and unawakening sleep. And thou too, in the earth wilt be lapped in silence, but the nymphs have thought good that the frog should eternally sing. Nay, him I would not envy, for 'tis no sweet song he singeth.

Begin, ye Sicilian Muses, begin the dirge.

Poison came, Bion, to thy mouth, thou didst know poison. To such lips as thine did it come, and was not sweetened? What mortal was so cruel that could mix poison for thee, or who could give thee the venom that heard thy voice? surely he had no music in his soul.

Begin, ye Sicilian Muses, begin the dirge.

But justice hath overtaken them all. Still for this sorrow I weep, and bewail thy ruin. But ah, if I might have gone down like Orpheus to Tartarus, or as once Odysseus, or Alcides of yore, I too would speedily have come to the house of Pluteus, that thee perchance I might behold, and if thou singest to Pluteus, that I might hear what is thy song. Nay, sing to the Maiden some strain of Sicily, sing some sweet pastoral lay.

And she too is Sicilian, and on the shores by Aetna she was wont to play, and she knew the Dorian strain. Not unrewarded will the singing be; and as once to Orpheus's sweet minstrelsy she gave Eurydice to return with him, even so will she send thee too, Bion, to the hills. But if I, even I, and my piping had aught availed, before Pluteus I too would have sung.

[tr. ANDREW LANG]

LYRIC AND REFLECTIVE POETRY

Three distinct types of poetry are included in this final section; two are true lyric forms (*i.e.,* poems to be sung to the accompaniment of the lyre), *viz.,* choral lyric and monodic, or solo, lyric. The third type, which is included here under the term "reflective," was classified in antiquity simply as elegiac, according to its metrical scheme of a hexameter verse alternating with a so-called pentameter. Since both subject-matter and manner of treatment were to a large extent determined by the form which the poet used, it will be necessary to say a few words on the origins and characteristics of each of these three types.

The origins of choral lyric are primarily religious and social; almost all early peoples sing in groups, if they sing at all, to honour their gods, to mourn their dead, or to celebrate social events. Homer mentions various types as familiar in his time: hymns, dirges, wedding-songs, and "maiden-songs." Many other types developed in the eighth and seventh centuries B.C. in response to the needs of the Greek communal life: some of the most important of these are the Paean, or Hymn to Apollo; the Dithyramb, or narrative song in honour of Dionysus; the Epinician, or song to celebrate an athletic victory; and the Encomion, or Song of Praise for a mortal. The differences between such types were mainly functional; as far as external form is concerned, all were more or less identical. They were performed by a chorus which both sang and danced; it should be remembered, therefore, in reading any choral poem that we have only one element — the words — left, music and dancing being irrevocably lost. Almost all choral lyrics contain a myth which celebrates the god of the festival or illustrates some general truth of human life. The myth is usually followed by a gnomic section, in which the poet assumes the role of priest and teacher: this section may include some personal references to the poet himself or to the various members of the chorus. Thus, in the first selection from Alcman, who lived and wrote in seventh-century Sparta, we have the ending of a long Maiden-Song which originally contained a myth and a moralizing section; then, in the portion of the poem which is printed here, the maidens of the chorus turn to jesting among themselves and express elaborate compliments to their leaders, Hagesichora and Hagido. The other choral poets included in this volume (Simonides, Pindar, and Bacchylides) are dealt with in more detail later; but all show these constant elements — the myth and the religious or moral reflections.

Monodic lyric probably stems from folksongs, and originally had no function except to express the personal feelings of the singer. Monodic poems are, on the whole, briefer and more simple than the choral lyrics, and need not include the elements of myth and moralizing, since they have less didactic purpose than any other branch of

Greek poetry. The earliest and greatest names in this field are those of Sappho (for whom, see below, p. 968) and Alcaeus. The latter was a poet of Mytilene in Lesbos, where monodic lyric reached its greatest heights; he represents the aristocratic point of view against the democratic faction and its leaders, the so-called tyrants, in the late seventh century. Besides his passionate outbursts of hatred against all the opponents of the aristocracy, his poetry includes some excellent drinking-songs. The Latin poet Horace chose him as his model for his civic odes and some of his best convivial songs. Anacreon is the third note-worthy poet in this form; he was an Ionian by birth and spent most of his life at the courts of various sixth-century tyrants; his simple and polished songs reflect the Ionian love of elegance and the pleasure-loving society which flourished at such royal courts.

Elegy was originally merely a song accompanied by the ancient reed-flute; since the flute was a favourite instrument both in military surroundings and at banquets, the earliest elegies which we possess are either military or convivial in character. Furthermore, early elegy is characteristically addressed to a specific audience, whose presence must be felt by the reader in interpreting the poem. Thus, the poet Archilochus (who has already been met in the satiric section) wrote elegies addressed to his comrades-in-arms. But the military character of the elegy is most clearly seen in the poetry of Tyrtaeus, who lived and wrote in Sparta during the Second Messenian War (seventh century B.C.); his elegies are exhortations addressed to the Spartan soldiers and citizens, and no writer has more clearly expressed the ideals and nature of the Spartan character. Callinus of Ephesus writes the same type of elegy; the selection included here implies an audience of young men lying about in idleness at a feast instead of taking up arms to defend their native land. The convivial character of the elegiac form is well illustrated by Mimnermus, an Ionian Greek of Colophon, with his melancholy observations on the shortness of life and the transitory pleasures of love. He was the first Greek to turn the elegy to the expression of love's joys and sorrows, and as such is the remote literary ancestor of the Roman elegiac poets, Tibullus, Propertius, and Ovid. The nature of the elegies of Solon and Theognis is discussed later in separate introductions, but it may be noted here that Solon's poems are addressed to the citizen-body of Athens and are the Athenian counterpart of the martial elegies of the Spartan Tyrtaeus.

One more important use of the elegy remains to be mentioned; from early times the elegiac couplet was found suitable for epigrams — *i.e.,* epitaphs and brief inscriptions on monuments and dedications. The short epigram of Anacreon, *For a Slain Warrior,* is the earliest example in this book. The most notable poet of this type was Simonides, to whom many of the best epigrams of the fifth century are ascribed. In later times, particularly in the Alexandrian Age, the inscriptional epigram developed into the purely literary epigram freed from its associations with epitaphs and monuments. In the hands of Callimachus, Asclepiades, Leonidas, and Meleager, such epigrams were used to express any sort of personal feeling — *e.g.*, the woes of a lover, laments for lost friends, or theories of literary criticism. From such epigrams of personal feeling stem the Roman epigrams of Catullus and Martial.

A few additional remarks may help the reader to appreciate the important place which lyric poetry (and, indeed, all poetry) held in the life of the Greeks. In the first place, the reader should remember that almost all poetry before the Alexandrian Age was composed to be sung or recited, not to be read. All forms of lyric and elegiac poetry were intimately connected with the social and religious needs of the community and therefore became the vehicles for the most profound truths and observations of human experience. Furthermore, the Greeks never had a well-organized priesthood with a body of sacerdotal wisdom; religious thinking and teaching was done primarily by the poets. Particularly in the case of the choral lyricists, who composed for the great religious festivals of the city-states, the poet was regarded as the inspired mouthpiece of the gods and the interpreter of divine wisdom. And while the poets thus filled the place of a priesthood in their teaching, on another side they became the earliest philosophers: up to the end of the fifth century and the rise of prose literature, the Greeks tended to think in mythical rather than in conceptual or abstract terms. Thus by means of myths the best Greek poets imparted great and moving ideas in a way which is impossible for the poet of an age when all serious thinking is performed in logical prose and in abstract philosophical terms.

These facts will serve to explain the extraordinary vitality of Greek lyric poetry and the sense of richness, depth, and immediacy which it imparts. The poets of Greece were assured of an honourable and important place in the life of their communities; it was only when the old system of small, independent city-states began to disintegrate and was finally destroyed by the Macedonians that poetry moved into the study and the library, where scholars wrote for other scholars and for a relatively small reading public.

[Note on the reference-numbers which follow each of the selections given below:

Numbers not preceded by a letter refer to the numbering in E. Diehl, *Anthologica Lyrica Graeca,* 2nd. ed., Leipsig, 1936.

Carm. Pop. = ibid., vol. II (*Carmina Popularia*).

An. = Anacreontea in J. M. Edmonds, *Elegy and Iambus,* vol. II, Loeb Classical Library, 1931.

A.P. = the traditional numbering of the *Greek Anthology.*

T.G.F. = A. Nauck, *Tragicorum Graecorum Fragmenta.*]

TYRTAEUS

(*fl.* 685–668 B.C.)

HOW CAN MAN DIE BETTER

Noble is he who falls in front of battle
  bravely fighting for his native land;
and wretchedest the man who begs, a recreant,
  citiless, from fertile acres fled.
Dear mother, ageing father, little children
  drift beside him, and his wedded wife;
unwelcome he shall be, wherever turning,
  press'd by want and hateful penury;
he shames his folk and cheats his glorious manhood:
  all disgrace attends him, all despite.
Come then, — if beggars go unheard, uncared for,
  spurn'd in life and in their children spurn'd —
with courage let us battle for our country,
  freely spending life to save our sons.
Young men, stand firm and fight, stand one by other;
  base retreat and rout let none begin.
Be high of heart, be strong in pride of combat;
  grapple, self-forgetting, man to man.
Forbear to fly, deserting men grown older —
  stiff about the knees, in honour old.
O foul reproach, when fallen with the foremost
  lies an elder, hindermost the young —
a man whose head is white, whose beard is hoary,
  breathing out his strong soul in the dust,
in nakedness his blood-wet members clutching —
  foul reproach, a sight no gods condone!
Naked he lies where youth were better lying —
  sweet-flow'r'd youth, that nothing misbecomes.
Grown men regard the young, women desire them —
  fair in life, in noble death still fair.
Be steadfast then, be strong and firmly rooted,
  grip the ground astride, press teeth to lip.

[6–7, tr. T. F. HIGHAM]

MARCHING SONG

Up, in free-born hardihood,
Soldiers born of Spartan blood!
Guard your left with shields a-swinging;
High the gallant spear-shafts flinging.
Hoard not life nor stint to pay:
Such was never Sparta's way.

[Carm. Pop. 18, tr. C. M. BOWRA]

CALLINUS

(*fl.* 660 B.C.)

A CALL TO ACTION

How long, young men, unsoldiered, disregarding,
    laze you, scorned by neighbours round about?
Slack to the bone, on peace resolved, supinely
    careless in a land where all is war?

. . .

    hurl in death your javelins once again.
For great and glorious is a man defending
    home and children and his wedded wife
against the enemy. At Fate's own moment
    snaps his thread of life. So forward all
with spear in poise, crouching to shields that cover
    hearts courageous, soon as battle's joined.
There's no escaping death: that destination
    men must face — ev'n of immortal seed.
Many from war and ringing lance have sheltered,
    homeward fled: at home death finds them out.
But these the people love not, none regrets them:
    brave men fallen great and small lament.
The whole land mourns a man of heart heroic
    dead: in life a demigod he seems.
His strength is as a tower to all beholders —
    work for many hands he does alone.

                  [1, tr. T. F. HIGHAM]

ALCMAN

(*fl.* 630 B.C.)

HAGESICHORA

Vengeance is God's: he will repay.
Lucky who, without a tear,
fills the pattern of one day
with gaiety.

            And now, give ear!
Of radiant Agido my lay
shall be — her radiance as clear
as the sun, whose morning ray
she conjures to appear.

               I hear,
but any praise or any blame of her
is silenced by our fair chief-chorister

whose beauty seems as high and rare
as if with brutes one should compare
a sturdy thundering horse, a champion,
of wingèd dreams the son.

There's the likeness, plain to see:
steed of proud Enetic race,
and my cousin — fair is she
and her tresses have the grace
of a golden filigree;
beneath the gold, a silver face —
shall I say whose it must be?

It is Hagesichora's.
In beauty they shall be competitors —
a Lydian horse to pace a Scythian horse.
For while we make our offering
the Pleiades arise and sing
in rivalry, like Sirius burning bright
in the ambrosial night.

Not the wealth of crimson dress
makes our choir victorious,
nor do golden snakes that press
wrist and neck embolden us;
Lydian coif brings not success —
veiling our luxurious
maiden-eyes — nor Nanno's tress
nor Arete the beauteous.
Sylakis, or Kleesisera? nay —
Nor at the school of Ainesimbrote
can you say 'My saviour is
Philylla, or Astaphis,
lovely Vianthemis, Damareta —'
'tis Hagesichora!

Look, beside me sings my friend,
my cousin, of the ankles small:
Agido and she commend
alike our ceremonial.
Immortals, who possess the end
of every action, hear their call
with favour, as their voices blend!
For my own singing is the squall
which the owl screeches foolishly above
the rooftree; though my heart would dearly love
to please the goddess Dawn who brings
comfort for our sufferings.
Yet Hagesichora leads us with song
to peace, for which we long.

The chariot obediently
follows the outrunning steed;
men obey the helmsman's cry,
when on shipboard, with all speed.
Our own leader's melody
though it surpasses not, indeed,
the Sirens — they are gods — will vie
with ten or more of mortal breed.
Her voice is like a swan upon the streams
of Xanthus river; and the golden gleams
in her companion's hair. . .

[1, tr. GILBERT HIGHET]

THE HALCYONS

No more, O maiden voices, sweet as honey, soft as love is,
No more my limbs sustain me. — A halcyon on the wing
Flying o'er the foam-flowers, in the halcyon coveys,
Would I were, and knew not care, the sea-blue bird of spring!

[94, tr. H. T. WADE-GERY]

ON THE MOUNTAINS

Where, on the mountain peaks high up,
Their torch-lit feasts the gods amuse,
Often you took a great gold cup,
A vessel such as shepherds use,
And milked a lioness with your hands, to make
A round of silver-bright cheese-cake.

[37, tr. C. M. BOWRA]

NIGHT

The far peaks sleep, the great ravines,
The foot-hills, and the streams.
Asleep are trees, and hived bees,
The mountain beasts, and all that dark earth teems,
The glooming seas, the monsters in their deeps:
And every bird, its wide wings folded, sleeps.

[58, tr. H. T. WADE-GERY]

MIMNERMUS

(*fl.* 630 B.C.)

SINE AMORE NIL EST JUCUNDUM

O Golden Love, what life, what joy but thine?
   Come death when thou art gone and make an end!
When gifts and tokens are no longer mine,
   Nor the sweet intimacies of a friend.
These are the flowers of youth.   But painful age,

The bane of beauty, following swiftly on,
Wearies the heart of man with sad presage
  And takes away his pleasure in the sun.
Hateful is he to maiden and to boy,
  And fashioned by the gods for our annoy.

[1, tr. G. Lowes Dickinson]

WE ALL DO FAIL AS A LEAF

We are as leaves in jewelled springtime growing
  That open to the sunlight's quickening rays;
So joy we in our span of youth, unknowing
  If God shall bring us good or evil days.

Two fates beside thee stand; the one hath sorrow,
  Dull age's fruit, that other gives the boon
Of Death, for youth's fair flower hath no to-morrow,
  And lives but as a sunlit afternoon.

And when thine hour is spent, and passeth by thee,
  Surely to die were better than to live,
Ere grief or evil fortune come anigh thee,
  And penury that hath but ill to give.

Who longs for children's love, for all his yearning
  Shall haply pass to death anhungered still;
Or pain shall come, his life to anguish turning,
  Zeus hath for all an endless store of ill.

[2, tr. J. A. Pott]

THE SUN'S GOLDEN BOWL

Toil is the Sun-god's portion, toil all the livelong day,
Day in, day out, forever; there is no stop, no stay —
So soon as Dawn leaves Ocean, and, rosyfingered, speeds
Upon her journey skyward — for him, nor for his steeds.
For when his course is ended, back through the dusky deep
A hollow couch goes faring, wherein he lies asleep.
A mighty bowl this couch is, and lovely to behold,
The gift of wise Hephaistos, who wrought it all in gold,
And furnished it with pinions. It darts across the seas,
Skimming the crested waves from the far Hesperides
Back to the ruddy Sun-folk, where steeds and car remain
Till Morning's own dear daughter, the Dawn, comes up again.
The Sun then mounts his chariot, seeks that far western shore
And rushing, rushing onward, gives us the day once more.

[10, tr. Kirby Flower Smith]

ANONYMOUS

SWALLOW SONG

The swallow comes winging
Her way to us here;
Fair weather she's bringing,
And a happy new year.
White is her breast,
And black all the rest.

Roll us out a plum-cake,
For the swallow's sake,
From the house of your plenty;
And wine in a flasket,
And cheese in a basket;
Or a bakie she'll eat
Of your pease or your wheat,
She's not over-dainty!

Will you give us?   Or shall we go?
If you will, — why, rest you so;
But and if you shall say us nay,
Then we will carry the door away,
Or the lintel above it, or, easiest of all,
Your wife within, for she is but small.
Give us our need
And take God speed.
Open the door to the swallow, then,
For we are children and not old men.

[*Carm. Pop.* 32, tr. VARIOUS HANDS]

ALCAEUS

(*fl.* 600? B.C.)

STORM AT SEA

(*i*)

The quarrelling winds perplex me.   On this side
One wave rolls up, on that a different tide,
   And the black ship, whereon we sail,
   Shifts with the shifting of the gale.

We are exhausted by the fearful blast:
Round the mast's foot the bilge is rising fast.
   And all the sail is thin and worn,
   With great holes gaping, rent and torn.

(*ii*)

On top of all the rest comes on a new
Wave up, and that will give us much to do. . .
   Patch up with haste the gaping side
   And into a safe harbour ride!

Let no soft fear lay hold of anyone;
Before us lies a great task to be done.
   Remembering the past and how
   We suffered, prove our manhood now!

[46A + 119, tr. C. M. Bowra]

DRINKING SONGS

(*i*)

Zeus rains; a storm comes in its might
From heav'n, and freezes rivers tight. . .

Put down the storm! Pile up the fire,
Mix the sweet wine to your desire,
   And round your forehead set
   A dainty coronet.

To woe the heart must not give in.
In grief's no help. One medicine,
   My friend, alone is fit —
   Wine —, and get drunk on it.

(*ii*)

   Now bind the woven necklaces
   Of dill about your throat
   And let the smell of frankincense
   Into your bosom float.

(*iii*)

Drink! Why wait for lamps? The day
Has not another inch to fall.
Fetch the biggest beakers — they
Hang on pegs along the wall.

Bacchus, son of Semelê
And of Zeus, discovered wine
Giving it to man to be
Care's oblivious anodyne.

   Pour in water two to one,
   Fill them full to overflowing;
   When the first is drained and done,
   Set another cup a-going!

(iv)

Soak your lungs with wine, for now
The Dog Star's at the turn.
How the summer wounds, and how
All must thirst and burn.

In the bushes, strong and clear
Now the cricket sings,
And sweet music fills the air
From beneath his wings.

Now is all the earth at song
In the summer's fire,
And the girasole is strong.
Now does wild desire

Make the girls most amorous.
But the men won't please;
For the fire of Sirius
Withers heads and knees.

(v)

On my long-suffering head let the sweet myrrh flow,
Let it flow on my breast where the white hairs show.
[90-1, 92, 96, 94, 86, tr. C. M. Bowra]

IMMORTALIA NE SPERES

Drink, Melanippus, and be drunk with me.
How can you think that you will ever see,

Once over Acheron, the pure bright day
Again? Come, throw such proud desires away.

Sisyphus, wisest of men, thought he could find
An artifice that should leave death behind,

But fate decreed his wisdom should not save
Him from twice crossing Acheron's rough wave,

And Cronus' son gave him great sufferings
Below the dark earth. Hope not for such things,

While we are young. Now is the moment, now,
To take what happiness the gods allow.
[73, tr. C. M. Bowra]

HELEN AND THETIS

Not thee, O world's desire
Did Peleus bear away
As bride from her sea-sire;
When on his wedding day

He bade the immortals come
And feast in Cheiron's home.
No; but a maiden chaste
Was she whom he embraced,
   A princess of the sea;
And when a year had passed
   She bare a son, and he
Of demigods was best,
Driving his chestnut yoke,
   A charioteer of pride;
But Troy, and all her folk,
   Because of Helen, died.

[74, tr. SIR WILLIAM MARRIS]

SAPPHO

(*fl.* 590 B.C.)

The few certain facts about the life of Sappho are these: she was born on the island of Lesbos about 612 B.C., or perhaps a little earlier, of an aristocratic family. Like Alcaeus and many other nobles of Mytilene, she was exiled for a time during the fierce struggles between the nobility and the tyrants. But she spent most of her life in Mytilene as the leader and teacher of an educational institution which trained young girls for marriage and for a life in the best circles. She was married and had a daughter, the child Cleis mentioned in the selection, *A Girl*. The date of her death is unknown.

These facts should suffice to rescue Sappho's name from some of the unsavoury scandal often attached to it. None the less, the nature of her poetry requires an explanation for the modern reader. The school which Sappho directed was much more than a modern finishing school; it was a religious organization devoted to the cult of Aphrodite and the Muses, from which men were excluded. The girls lived together in an atmosphere of emotional intimacy, and their thoughts were naturally directed toward love. For many of these girls Sappho felt a deep affection, which she expressed not in terms of motherly or sisterly love, but in the language of the deepest passion. In estimating the meaning of her passionate addresses to her pupils, the reader must take into account both the unusual environment in which these girls were placed, and the unreserved, ardent temperament of Sappho herself.

Three types of poetry may be distinguished in Sappho's work. Most of her poems are intensely personal addresses to the maidens around her: thus, in the famous prayer, *To Aphrodite,* Sappho is in love again with one of her young pupils, who is not named, as she is among the group to whom the poem is sung. *To a Bride* probably reveals Sappho's feelings as one of her girls leaves her for marriage and sits beside the bridegroom at the wedding feast. Other works of Sappho are more objective and reveal the influence of folk-song; these popular love-songs are represented here by the selections *Night* and *Mother, I Cannot Mind my Wheel.* Finally, there are the weddingsongs which Sappho wrote for her maidens when they left her circle for marriage. These were sung by a chorus of the bride's friends, and (perhaps) by the groom's friends also; it is most regrettable that we possess only short fragments of Sappho's work in this form. Perhaps the best way to gain an idea of Sappho's style in her wedding-songs is to read the two complete *epithalamia* of Catullus (61, 62), where the Latin poet has neatly blended Roman elements with reminiscences of the Lesbian poetess. The short passages included here contain the traditional mockery of the groom and his best-man, and laments made by the chorus of girls for the passing flower of maidenhood.

No translation will ever recapture all the grace and charm of Sappho's poetry, and the English reader, at first sight, may find it hard to understand her tremendous reputation among the ancients, who called her the Tenth Muse and ranked her with Homer. Her style is graceful and easy and her choice of words inevitably right. In antiquity only Catullus can approach her happy gift of making the highest art seem like the spontaneous, unstudied utterance of a passionate soul. Her simplicity is saved from banality by the intensity and directness of her emotions, and by a keen eye for the beauty which she worshipped. Other Greek poets who treat of love, as one can see from the selections of Alcaeus, Mimnermus, and Anacreon, consider it a pleasant pastime to be reserved for one's leisure moments; Sappho alone treats it with seriousness and dignity.

TO APHRODITE

Immortal on thy many-splendoured throne
    Hear, Aphrodite Queen, that art
Zeus' witching daughter; and with pain and moan
    Break not my heart!

But come, if ever thou hast caught of old
    My distant cry and heard my plea,
And left thy father's palaces of gold
    To visit me;

And yoked thy chariot, and from heaven forth
    Driven thy sparrows fleet and fair
With whirr of wings above the swarthy earth
    Through middle air.

How fast they came! Then, Blessed One, didst thou
    With lips divinely smiling ask:
"What new mischance is come upon thee now?
    Unto what task

Have I been called? what is the dearest aim
    Of thy mad heart? who is to be
Persuaded to thy passion? Sappho, name
    Thine enemy!

For whoso flies thee now shall soon pursue;
    Who spurns thy gifts shall give anon;
And whoso loves thee not, whate'er she do,
    Shall love thee soon."

Ah, come then, and release me from alarms
    That crush me: all I long to see
Fulfilled, fulfil! A very mate-in-arms
    Be thou to me.

[1, tr. SIR WILLIAM MARRIS]

TO A BRIDE

Blest beyond earth's bliss, with heaven I deem him
  Blest, the man that in thy presence near thee
Face to face may sit, and while thou speakest,
  Listening may hear thee,

And thy sweet-voiced laughter: — In my bosom
  The rapt heart so troubleth, wildly stirred:
Let me see thee, but a glimpse — and straightway
  Utterance of word

Fails me; no voice comes; my tongue is palsied;
  Thrilling fire through all my flesh hath run;
Mine eyes cannot see, mine ears make dinning
  Noises that stun;

The sweat streameth down, — my whole frame seized with
  Shivering, — and wan paleness o'er me spread,
Greener than the grass; I seem with faintness
  Almost as dead.

                                    [2, tr. WALTER HEADLAM]

THE MOON

Bright stars, around the fair Selene peering,
No more their beauty to the night discover
When she, at full, her silver light ensphering,
    Floods the world over.

                                    [4, tr. T. F. HIGHAM]

GARDEN OF THE NYMPHS

Cool waters tumble, singing as they go
Through appled boughs.   Softly the leaves are dancing.
Down streams a slumber on the drowsy flow,
    My soul entrancing.

                                    [5, tr. T. F. HIGHAM]

TO AN UNCULTIVATED WOMAN

Ever dead shalt thou lie under the earth; none shall remember thee
As time passeth; for thou never hast shared aught in the roses dear,
Those Pierian blooms. Wherefore obscure thou shalt in Death's
    house be,
Wand'ring, flitting amidst shades without fame, unhonoured there
    as here.

                                    [58, tr. C. T. MURPHY]

FLOWERS FOR THE GRACES

Weave garlands, maiden, from the strands
Of dill, and with soft gentle hands
Set the delicious leafage round your head.

The Goddess and the happy Graces
Love to look on flower-crown'd faces,
But turn aside from the ungarlanded.

[80, tr. C. M. Bowra]

TO ATTHIS

I loved you, Atthis, once, long, long ago. . .
You seemed to me a small, ungainly child.

[40–1, tr. C. M. Bowra]

PARTING

Truly I want to die.
Such was her weeping when she said Good-bye.

These words she said to me:
"What sad calamity!
Sappho, I leave you most unwillingly."

To her I made reply:
"Go with good heart, but try
Not to forget our love in days gone by.

Else let me call to mind,
If your heart proves unkind,
The soft delightful ways you leave behind.

Many a coronet
Of rose and violet,
Crocus and dill upon your brow you set:

Many a necklace too
Round your soft throat you threw,
Woven with me from buds of ravishing hue,

And often balm you spread
Of myrrh upon my head,
And royal ointment on my hair you shed."

[96, tr. C. M. Bowra]

AN ABSENT FRIEND

A glorious goddess in her eyes
Were you, her comrade, and your songs
Above all other songs she'd prize.

With Lydian women now she dwells
Surpassing them, as when day dies
The rosy-fingered moon excels

The host of stars, and light illumes
The salt sea and the cornland glows
With light upon its thousand blooms.

In loveliness the dew spills over
And with new strength revives the rose,
Slim grasses and the flowering clover.

But sadly up and down she goes,
Remembering Atthis, once her lover,
And in her heart sick longing grows.

[98, tr. C. M. Bowra]

LOVE

Love has unbound my limbs and set me shaking,
A monster bitter-sweet and my unmaking.

[137, tr. C. M. Bowra]

A GIRL

I have a child; so fair
As golden flowers is she,
My Cleïs, all my care.
I'd not give her away
For Lydia's wide sway
Nor lands men long to see.

[152, tr. C. M. Bowra]

NIGHT

The Moon is gone
And the Pleiads set,
Midnight is nigh;
Time passes on,
And passes, yet
Alone I lie.

[94, tr. J. M. Edmonds]

MOTHER, I CANNOT MIND MY WHEEL

Sweet mother, let the weaving be,
My hand is faint to move.
Frail Aphrodite masters me;
I long for my young love.

[114, tr. T. F. Higham]

THE NIGHTINGALE

The dear good angel of the spring
The nightingale.

[121, tr. Ben Jonson]

WEDDING SONGS

(i)

BRIDE.   Maidenhood, O Maidenhood
Where art thou flown away from me?

MAIDENHOOD.   Never again shall I come back,
                 Never again back to thee.
                            [131, tr. C. M. BOWRA]

(ii)

Bridegroom dear, to what shall I compare thee?
   To a slim green rod best do I compare thee.
                            [127, tr. ANON.]

A YOUNG BRIDE

(i)

Like the sweet apple which reddens upon the topmost bough,
A-top on the topmost twig, — which the pluckers forgot somehow, —
Forgot it not, nay, but got it not, for none could get it till now.

(ii)

Like the wild hyacinth flower, which on the hills is found,
Which the passing feet of the shepherds for ever tear and wound,
Until the purple blossom is trodden into the ground.
                       [116 + 117, tr. D. G. ROSSETTI]

EVENING

    Thou, Hesper, bringest homeward all
      That radiant dawn sped far and wide,
    The sheep to fold, the goat to stall,
      The children to their mother's side.
                    [120, tr. SIR RENNELL RODD]

ANDROMACHE'S WEDDING

"Hector and his men bring the girl, her eyes gleaming,
From Thebe the Holy, from Placia fount unfailing,
Andromache the beautiful, over the salt sea sailing
With whorls and roundlets golden, with robes for her arraying
Purple embroidered daintily, away on the wind streaming;
And silver cups uncountable and carven ivory."
   This was the herald's story.
And Hector's father heard it, and gay he rose, and the saying
Went the round of Troy Town for all friends' knowing.
Then the men of Troy put their mules into harnessing
Back against the chariots, and then mounted pressing
The rout of young women, and of lightfoot girls going,
Then Priams's daughters apart; and then the soldiers
Were harnessing their horses under the chariot rim,
The young men in their prime. . .

And the sweet piping with lyreplay was blending,
With castanets clashing; and the maidens high singing

Sang the holy song to heaven ascending
With strange din ringing. . .

There were myrrh and cassia with frankincense smoking;
There the elder women their chant were choiring;
There all the men sang their high song invoking
The God far-darting, Paean of the lyring,
Singing for Hector and for Andromache divine.

[55, tr. GEORGE ALLEN]

SOLON

(ca. 634–ca. 560 B.C.)

Solon's activity as a statesman and legislator overshadows in the minds of modern readers his great gifts as a poet and thinker. He was born of an aristocratic Athenian family, during a period when the old land-owning nobles were gradually reducing the free peasantry of Attica to the condition of serfs, and the people were murmuring against oppressive debts and political disabilities. In 594 B.C. Solon received the office of sole archon, with the task of reforming the laws and finding some acceptable settlement for the vexing political and economic questions of the day. His first measure was the cancellation of debts referred to in one of the selections that follow; the actual details of this measure are much debated, but it certainly freed the debt-ridden farmers from the mortgages that encumbered their lands. His other measures were a skilful compromise, and although he himself was far from wishing to establish an unrestricted democracy, he boldly championed the fundamental rights of the individual citizen — the right to a fair trial before his peers, a minimum share in the government of the city, and freedom from the penalty of slavery for his debts. Later Athenians were not far wrong in considering him the founder of the Athenian democracy.

Solon is the first Athenian poet or writer whom we know, and he reveals the versatility and richness of thought that mark the Athenians of the next century. The first group of selections chosen for this work deal with his political ideas and activities. In the first selection note how clearly he conceives of Justice as an active force in the state; retribution comes upon the unjust state in the form of party feuds and civil war. This is "the first objective statement of the universal truth that the violation of justice means the disruption of the life of the community." * In other selections he defends his policies as legislator and answers those who sneered at him for not making himself tyrant.

In the last three selections Solon's reflections are more general. In the somewhat prosaic but charming *Ages of Man* we may see a connection with earlier attempts to find one single *areté,* or excellence for man. The Spartan Tyrtaeus had recently proclaimed courage in battle to be man's sole *areté;* Solon, the typical Athenian, finds many ways in which the individual can fulfil himself and show forth his excellence in the course of a complete life. The *Prayer to the Muses* is perhaps Solon's greatest poem; here he wrestles with the problem of man's destiny and his responsibility for his own fate. In the first part of the poem he declares that man is responsible for his own sufferings: arrogance and injustice lead to ruin, and Zeus brings punishment without fail either on the sinner himself or on his descendants. Yet Solon cannot bring himself to leave the problem

* Jaeger, *Paideia,* p. 139.

here; all human activities are uncertain, and the ways of the gods are inscrutable. Hence even a good man *may* fall into evil plight. No matter how unsatisfactory this answer may seem to the theologian, Solon's attempt to grapple with the problem and the noble language in which he clothes his thought mark him as a significant and worthy forerunner of the great Athenian tragic poets.

ATHENS

If on our city ruin comes, it will never be by the dispensation of Zeus and the purpose of the blessed immortal gods, so powerful is our great-hearted guardian, born of mighty sire, Pallas Athene, who holds over it her hands. It is the people themselves who in their folly seek to destroy our great city, prompted by desire for wealth; and their leaders, unjust of heart, for whom awaits the suffering of many woes, the fruit of their great arrogance, since they know not how to check their greed, and to enjoy with order and sobriety the pleasures set before them at the feast. . . They have wealth through their following of unjust works and ways. . . Neither the sacred treasure nor that of the state do they spare in any wise, but they steal, each in his own corner, like men pillaging. They take no heed of the holy foundations of Justice, who in silence marks what happens and what has been, and who in course of time comes without fail to exact the penalty. Behold, there is coming now upon the whole state an injury that cannot be avoided; she has fallen swiftly into the evil of servitude, which awakens civil strife and war from their sleep — war that destroys many men in the bloom of their youth. By the work of the disaffected, swiftly our lovely city is being worn away, in those gatherings which are dear to unjust men.

Such are the ills that are rife within our state; while of the poor great numbers are journeying to foreign lands, sold into slavery, and bound with shameful fetters. [They bear perforce the accursed yoke of slavery.] Thus the public ill comes home to every single man, and no longer do his court-yard gates avail to hold it back; high though the wall be, it leaps over, and finds him out unfailingly, even though in his flight he be hid in the farthest corner of his chamber.

These are the lessons which my heart bids me teach the Athenians, how that lawlessness brings innumerable ills to the state, but obedience to the law shows forth all things in order and harmony and at the same time sets shackles on the unjust. It smoothes what is rough, checks greed, dims arrogance, withers the opening blooms of ruinous folly, makes straight the crooked judgment, tames the deeds of insolence, puts a stop to the works of civil dissension, and ends the wrath of bitter strife. Under its rule all things among mankind are sane and wise.

[3, tr. KATHLEEN FREEMAN]

THE DISTRIBUTION OF WEALTH

For many unworthy men are rich, while good men are poor; but we will not barter with them our worth for their wealth, since the one stands ever unshaken, whereas riches pass now into one man's hands, now into another's.

[4, lines 9–12, tr. KATHLEEN FREEMAN]

THE RIGHTS OF THE PEOPLE

To the people I have given just as much power as suffices, neither taking away from their due nor offering more; while for those who had power and were honoured for wealth I have taken thought likewise, that they should suffer nothing unseemly. I stand with strong shield flung around both parties, and have allowed neither to win an unjust victory.

[5, tr. KATHLEEN FREEMAN]

SOLON AND HIS COUNTRY

If I spared my native land, and did not defile and dishonour my good repute by laying hands on a tyranny of cruel violence, I feel no shame at all; for in this way I believe that I shall win a greater triumph — over all mankind.

[23, lines 8–12, tr. KATHLEEN FREEMAN]

THE CANCELLING OF DEBTS

Those who came as pillagers had lavish hopes; every man of them believed he would light on a great fortune, and that I, though I coaxed so smoothly, would soon reveal a harsh purpose. Vain were their imaginings then, and now in their anger against me they all eye me askance as if I were an enemy. It is undeserved; for that which I promised I have fulfilled, by heaven's aid; and other things I undertook, not without success. To achieve aught by violence of tyranny is not to my mind; nor that the unworthy should have an equal share with the good in the rich soil of my native land.

. . . Whereas I, before the people had attained to any of the things for the sake of which they had drawn my chariot, brought it to a standstill. A witness I have who will support this claim full well in the tribunal of Time — the mighty mother of the Olympian deities, black Earth, from whose bosom once I drew out the pillars everywhere implanted; and she who was formerly enslaved is now free. Many men I restored to Athens, their native city divinely-founded, men who justly or unjustly had been sold abroad, and others who through pressure of need had gone into exile, and who through wanderings far and wide no longer spoke the Attic tongue. Those here at home who were reduced to shameful slavery, and trembled at the caprices of their masters, I made free. These things I wrought by main strength, fashioning the blend of force and justice that is law, and I went through to the close as I had promised. And ordinances for noble and base alike I wrote, fitting a rule of jurisdiction straight and true to every man. Had another, a villainous and covetous man, grasped the goad as I did, he would not have held the people back. Had I complied with the wishes of my opponents then, or at a later time with the designs of the other party against them, this city would have been bereaved of many sons. Wherefore I stood at bay, defending myself on every side, like a wolf among a pack of hounds.

[23, lines 13–21, 24, tr. KATHLEEN FREEMAN]

BEWARE THE DESPOT

From the cloud comes the violent snow- and hail-storm, and the thunder springs from the lightning-flash; so from the men of rank comes ruin to the state, and the people through their ignorance fall into the servitude of rule by one man. When a man has risen too high, it is not easy to check him after; now is the time to take heed of everything.

[10, tr. KATHLEEN FREEMAN]

PRAYER TO THE MUSES

Ye glorious children of Memory and Olympian Zeus, Muses of Pieria, hear me as I pray. Grant me from the blessed gods prosperity, and from all mankind the possession ever of good repute; and that I may thus be a delight to my friends, and an affliction to my foes, by the first revered, by the others beheld with dread. Wealth I do desire to possess, but to gain it unjustly I have no wish; without fail in after-time comes retribution. The wealth that the gods give stays with a man firmplanted from bottom-most foundation to summit; whereas that which men pursue through arrogance comes not in orderly wise, but, under constraint of unjust deeds, against her will she follows; and swiftly is ruin mingled therewith. The beginning, as of a fire, arises from little; negligible at first, in its end it is without remedy; the works of men's arrogance have no long life. Zeus watches over the end of all things; and all at once, like a wind, that suddenly scatters the clouds, a wind of spring, that having stirred the deeps of the many-billowed unharvested sea, and razed the fair works of husbandry over the wheat-bearing earth, reaches the abode of the gods, the lofty sky, and makes it bright again to behold; and the sun in his might shines fair over the rich earth, and no longer is any cloud to be seen — such is the retribution of Zeus. Not over single happenings, like a mortal, does he show himself swift to wrath; yet no man who has a sinful heart escapes his eye for ever; in the end without fail he is brought to light. But one man pays the penalty straightway, another at a later time; and if the offenders themselves escape, and the fate of the gods in its oncoming alight not on them, yet it comes without fail at another time; the innocent pay for those deeds, either the children or the generations that come after.

We mortals, good and bad alike, think thus — each one has a good opinion of himself, before he comes to grief; then at once he begins to lament; but up to that moment in gaping folly we gloat over our vain hopes. The man who is crushed by cruel disease sets his thought on the hope of becoming well. [Another who is a coward thinks himself a brave man, and the uncomely man thinks himself handsome.] The needy man, whom the works of poverty constrain, thinks that he will assuredly win great wealth. One man spends his effort in one direction, another in another. One wanders over the sea, home of fishes, striving to bring back gain in ships, borne along by the fierce winds, having no mercy on his life. Another, one of those whose business is with curved ploughs, cleaves the earth rich in trees, doing service throughout the year. Another, skilled in the works of Athene and Hephaistos the able craftsman, collects a living by means of his two hands. Another, trained in the gifts of the Olympian Muses, has knowledge of lovely poesy's measure. Another the Lord Apollo, worker from afar, has appointed to be a seer, and he if he be one whom the gods accompany, discerns the distant evil coming upon a man; yet that which is fated assuredly neither omen of bird nor of victim shall avert. Others, who follow the profession of Paion, god of medicines, are physicians; and for their work, too, no certain issue is set; often from a slight pain comes great suffering, nor can any one relieve it by the giving of soothing medicines; again, when a man is afflicted with disease fell and fierce, by a touch of his hands at once the physician makes him whole. Verily, Fate brings to mortals both evil and good; the gifts of the immortal gods may not be declined. In every kind of activity there is risk, and no man can tell, when a thing is beginning, what way it is destined to take. One man trying to do his work well, falls unexpectedly into great and bitter ruin; to another who blunders in his work the god grants good luck in everything, to save him from his folly. In wealth no limit is set up within man's view; those of us who now have the largest fortune are doubling our efforts; what amount would satisfy the greed of all? Gain is granted to mankind by the immortals; but from it arises disastrous Folly, and when Zeus sends her to exact retribution, she comes now to this man, now to that.

[1, tr. KATHLEEN FREEMAN]

THE LOT OF MAN

No mortal is blest with happiness; wretched are all human souls on whom the sun looks down.

[15, tr. KATHLEEN FREEMAN]

THE AGES OF MAN

A boy, before he has reached adolescence, while still a child, grows and casts out his "fence of teeth" within the first seven years. When the god brings to an end the next seven years, he puts forth the signs of adolescence. In the third period, while his limbs are still growing, the down of the beard appears, and his complexion loses its bloom. In the fourth hebdomad, every man is in the prime of his strength; this men have as a sign of their worth. In the fifth, it is seasonable for a man to take thought on marriage, and to seek after a breed of sons to succeed him. In the sixth, the mind of a man is in all things fully trained, and he no longer feels the same impulse towards wild behaviour. In the seventh seven he is at his prime in mind and tongue, and in the eighth, the sum of the two being fourteen years. In the ninth, though he still has some strength, his tongue and his wisdom are too feeble for works of mighty worth. If he complete the tenth and reach its full measure, not untimely is it if he meets the fate of death.

[19, tr. KATHLEEN FREEMAN]

ANACREON

(*ca.* 563–478 B.C)

TO ARTEMIS

To Artemis I kneel, whose bow
Finds the stag and lays him low,
    The Queen whom beasts obey —
O child of Zeus, his golden daughter,
From Lethaeus whirling water
Thine eyes on men brave-hearted rest
With joy; for these thou shepherdest
    Have learnt the gentler way.
        [1, tr. T. F. HIGHAM]

TO DIONYSUS

Roving god, whose playfellows
Over the mountains' airy brows
    In happy chase are led;
Where Love, who breaks the heart of pride,
Or Nymphs amuse thee, violet-eyed,
Or Aphrodite keeps thy side,
    The goddess rosy-red —
Lord Dionyse, I kneel to thee;
Stoop to me of thy charity
    And this my prayer receive:
Dear Lord, thy best persuasion use,
Bid Cleobulus not refuse
    The gift of love I give.
        [2, tr. T. F. HIGHAM]

TO CLEOBULUS

Soft-eyed, a girl's, your face is. . .
    Unheard I plead: unknown
My soul takes on the traces
    And moves by you alone.
        [4, tr. T. F. HIGHAM]

LOVE

Once more the Lad with golden hair
His purple ball across the air
    Flings at me, true to aim;
And light her broidered slippers go,
That Lesbian lass, — my playfellow
    As Love would set the game.
O Lesbos isle is tight and trim. . .
She's not the breed to pleasure him,

Another game she plays;
My hair mislikes her, grown so white;
There's someone lovelier in her sight
  Who draws that callow gaze.

[5, tr. T. F. HIGHAM]

THE GOLDEN MEAN

No Amalthea's horn for me!
    Riches I disdain;
Nor in Tarshish would I be,
To king it for a century
    And half as long again.

[8, tr. T. F. HIGHAM]

OLD AGE

Sweet Youth no more will tarry,
    My friend a while ago;
Now white's the head I carry,
    And grey my temples grow,
    My teeth — a ragged row.

To taste the joy of living
    But little space have I,
And torn with sick misgiving
    I can but sob and sigh,
    So deep the dead men lie.

So deep their place and dismal,
    All means, be sure, they lack
Down in the murk abysmal
    To scale the upward track
    And win their journey back.

[44, tr. T. F. HIGHAM]

NUNC EST BIBENDUM

Water bring, and bring me wine,
Bring the wreaths where flowers entwine;
Hasten, lad; our fists we try,
Matched together, Love and I.

Come, a wassail I would keep,
Drinking pledges flagon-deep.
Pour me wine, five measures, lad;
Measures ten of water add;
So good manners shall remain
In your Bacchant, foxed again.

Drink, good fellows, drink no more
With a clutter and uproar;
Thus, when Scythians hold a bout,

Wine goes in and tongues let out.
Gentlemen observe a mean,
Tippling with good songs between.

[43, tr. T. F. Higham]

TAKE HER, BREAK HER

Ah tell me why you turn and fly,
My little Thracian filly shy?
    Why turn askance
    That cruel glance,
And think that such a dunce am I?

O I am blest with ample wit
To fix the bridle and the bit,
    And make thee bend
    Each turning-end
In harness all the course of it.

But now 'tis yet the meadow free
And frisking it with merry glee;
    The master yet
    Has not been met
To mount the car and manage thee.

[88, tr. Walter Headlam]

ON A SLAIN WARRIOR

Well fought Timocritus, and has this grave:
For battle spares the coward, not the brave.

[101, tr. Hugh Macnaghten]

ANACREONTEA

The collection of *Anacreontea* (or *Anacreontics*) is a group of light songs in the manner and favourite meter of Anacreon; although the ancient compiler of the collection did not explicitly claim that the poems were written by Anacreon, many ancient and modern readers (as late as the eighteenth century) accepted these slight imitations as genuine works of the genial Ionian poet. The earliest poems in the collections may be dated perhaps as early as the second century B.C., the latest in the Byzantine Age (after 529 A.D.). They were composed to be sung at drinking-feasts, and deal almost exclusively with drinking, love, and regrets for lost youth; in tone, they are light and pretty rather than beautiful, and they lack the earnestness and sincerity of the best Greek poetry.

None the less, the poems have had a great and lasting effect on modern European literature; they were constantly translated and imitated by poets of the sixteenth and seventeenth centuries, in English notably by Thomas Moore and Robert Herrick, whose *Hesperides* abound in reminiscences of these little songs.

GIVE ME HOMER'S LYRE

Comrades, give me Homer's lyre,
But change the chord of blood and fire;
   Bring cups to-day
   Of laws, not wine,
   That so I may
   The drink divine
   Mingle in
   Due 'rithmetic,
   Not too thin
   Nor yet too thick.
   I'ld tippling be
   And dance and sing
   (But decently)
   To th' merry string.
Comrades, give me Homer's lyre,
But change the chord of blood and fire.

              [*An*. 2, tr. J. M. EDMONDS]

YOU'RE OLD, ANACREON

"You're old, Anacreon,"
   The ladies say; "look on
Your forehead in the glass, and see
   How thin your love-locks be."

As for my hair, I wot
Not whe'r 'tis thin or not;

But this I know, the nigher Death's day
The more should old men play.
[An. 7, tr. J. M. Edmonds]

TO A PAINTER

Come, master of the Rhodian art
And draw the darling of my heart;
She's absent, but your paint lay on
To her swain's dictation.
Make soft and black the hair of her
And, if brush may, to smell of myrrh;
Make her full-face, the locks of jet
Over ivory temples set;
Her eyebrows neither join nor sever,
But make (as 'tis) that selvage never
Clearly one nor surely two;
Her glance be fire (no mimic hue)
Like Pallas grey, like Venus tender;
For her cheeks and nose to render
Mingle rose-leaves with the cream;
And that the lip like hers may seem,
Make it what Persuasion's is,
Provocation to a kiss;
And then beneath a shapely chin
Let every Grace fly out and in
About a marble throat; the rest
Be in a chastened purple drest,
But let her flesh peep here and there
The lines of beauty to declare.
You've limned her to the life, so take your price;
You, colours, will be speaking in a trice.
[An. 16, tr. J. M. Edmonds]

TO THE SWALLOW

Gentle Swallow, thou we know
Every year dost come and go,
In the Spring thy nest thou mak'st;
In the Winter it forsak'st,
And divert'st thy self awhile
Near the Memphian Towers, or Nile;
But Love in my suff'ring breast
Builds, and never quits his nest;
First one Love's hatcht; when that flies,
In the shell another lies;
Then a third is half expos'd;
Then a whole brood is disclos'd,
Which for meat still peeping cry,
Whilst the others that can fly

Do their callow brethren feed,
And grown up, they young ones breed.
What then will become of me,
Bound to pain incessantly,
Whilst so many Loves conspire
On my heart by turns to tire?

[*An.* 25, tr. THOMAS STANLEY]

LET'S DRINK AND LOVE

On lotus-leaves and myrtles fine
  I'll lean, and the Love-lad
    In apron clad
Shall stand and serve me wine.

Like wheels our running lives are sped,
  And lie we shall and must
    A little dust
Of bones uncemented.

Why at my grave your unguents pour?
  Why vain anoilment give?
    While yet I live
Embalm my forehead o'er.

Bring roses, and some maiden fair;
  For ere to join I go
    The rout below
I fain would banish care.

[*An.* 32, tr. J. M. EDMONDS]

AT THE MID HOUR OF NIGHT

Downward was the wheeling Bear
Driven by the Waggoner;
Men by powerful sleep opprest,
Gave their busie troubles rest:
Love, in this still depth of night,
Lately at my house did light;
Where perceiving all fast lockt,
At the door he boldly knockt.
"Who's that," said I, "that does keep
Such a noise, and breaks my sleep?"
"Ope," saith Love, "for pity hear;
'Tis a childe, thou need'st not fear,
Wet and weary, from his way
Led by this dark night astray."
With compassion this I heard;
Light I struck; the door unbarr'd:
Where a little Boy appears,
Who wings, bow, and quiver bears;
Near the fire I made him stand,

With my own I chaft his hand;
And with kindly busie care
Wrung the chill drops from his hair:
When well warm'd he was, and dry,
"Now," saith he, " 'tis time to try
If my bow no hurt did get,
For me thinks the string is wet."
With that, drawing it, a dart
He let fly that pierc'd my heart:
Leaping then, and laughing said,
"Come, my friend, with me be glad;
For my Bow thou see'st is sound,
Since thy heart hath got a wound."

[*An.* 33, tr. Thomas Stanley]

CICADA

We bless you, cicada,
When out of the tree-tops
Having sipped of the dew
Like a king you are singing:
And indeed you are king of
These meadows around us,
And the woodland's all yours.
Man's dear little neighbour,
And midsummer's envoy,
The Muses all love you,
And Apollo himself does —
He gave you your music.
Age cannot wither you,
Tiny philosopher,
Earth-child, musician;
The world, flesh and devil
Accost you so little,
That you might be a god.

[*An.* 34, tr. Edmund Blunden]

THEOGNIS

(*fl.* 530 B.C.)

Theognis has had the misfortune to become a literary problem, and almost every statement that can be made about him and his poetry is open to dispute; because of limitations of space it is necessary to confine this notice to a brief and somewhat dogmatic statement of the facts as accepted by the majority of Hellenists.

Theognis was a Megarian noble who lived in the second half of the sixth century; in the struggle between aristocrats and commoners, which marks this era in almost all Greek city-states, he lost his lands and suffered exile. He composed a series of precepts in elegiac verse, embodying the aristocratic code of ethics and views on life, which he addressed to a noble youth, Cyrnus, son of Polypaus, to whom he was deeply attached. The book of Theognis became the nucleus of a larger collection of elegiac verses on similar themes, written by various hands and preserved in aristocratic circles as a sort of song-book; selections from this book were sung to the flute during the drinking after dinner.

The verses which are unquestionably by Theognis himself reveal to us a strong-minded, unbending aristocrat of the old school. He despises the poor peasants, who, as he says, used to wear goatskins and pasture outside the city like deer; even more he hates the new rich — the commercial class which was gaining wealth and power at this time, and (to make matters worse) was marrying into the old, noble families. In the good old days, wealth and birth were inseparable, but in Theognis' time the landowning class was losing its monopoly of economic and social privilege; many of the nobles became poor and the old test of wealth or poverty no longer sufficed to establish a man's true worth, or his *areté*. The question of the relation of wealth to *areté* greatly disturbs Theognis; sometimes, in a mood of bitter irony or of genuine despair, he declares that wealth is all that matters; at other times, he says, "In right-doing lies all man's worth" — that is, in doing nothing contrary to the code of the aristocrats. In a series of maxims he tries to convey this code to Cyrnus; his instruction covers ethics and good manners, and was intended to instil that moderation and self-control which was the constant ideal of Greek ethical teaching.

Theognis is hardly a great poet by modern standards: he is frankly didactic and somewhat dry, but he feels deeply the importance of what he has to say, and he expresses his thoughts clearly and forcibly. Finally, in his epilogue to Cyrnus (*Immortality Conferred in Vain*) he reveals a genuine lyric gift; few poets have expressed this commonplace of the immortality conferred by poetry in more vivid and lofty language; the reader may well compare the more famous ode of Horace, *Exegi monumentum* (*Odes* III. 30).

ON CHOOSING FRIENDS

With base-born men let not thy converse be,
But ever cleave to those of high degree:
With these recline, and eat and drink with these;
The man of great resources seek to please.

"Good friends impart good sense."   But mean and low
Companions spoil what wit thou now dost show.
[31–36, tr. C. T. MURPHY]

REPROACH NO MAN FOR POVERTY

Rail not at grinding Poverty, nor curse
A man hard-driven for his empty purse;
As dips the balance, Zeus from day to day
Gives great possessions, or takes all away.
[155–8, tr. T. F. HIGHAM]

THE BANE OF POVERTY

Poverty, Kyrnos, breaks a gallant man
More than white hairs or shivering fevers can.
To flee it, Kyrnos, in the deep sea drown,
Or from a towering precipice leap down;
Broken by poverty, a man's denied
All power of speech and act: his tongue is tied.
[173–8, tr. T. F. HIGHAM]

EUGENICS

Ram, ass, and horse, my Kyrnos, we look over
With care, and seek good stock for good to cover;
And yet the best men make no argument,
But wed, for money, runts of poor descent.
So too a woman will demean her state
And spurn the better for the richer mate.
Money's the cry.   Good stock to bad is wed
And bad to good, till all the world's cross-bred.
No wonder if the country's breed declines, —
Mixed metal, Kyrnos, that but dimly shines.
[183–92, tr. T. F. HIGHAM]

ALL THINGS TO ALL MEN

Be versatile, my Kyrnos; make a blend
Of tone and temper suited to each friend.
Study the writhen cuttle where he lies
Toned to his fellow rock, and cheats our eyes.
Match every colour, follow every move, —
Wisdom is supple: folly keeps a groove.
[213–18, tr. T. F. HIGHAM]

IMMORTALITY CONFERRED IN VAIN

I've given thee wings shall waft thee forth with ease
High o'er the land, high o'er the boundless seas;
No feast shall ever be but thou'lt be there
Couch'd on men's lips, for oft the young and fair
With ordered sweetness clear shall sing thy praise
To the clear flute; and when in after-days
To the dark and dolorous land thou com'st below,
Ne'er even in death shalt thou thy fame forgo,
But men will keep in memory unchanging
The name of Cyrnus, who shalt, all Greece ranging,
Mainland and island, pass the unharvested
Home of the fish, not Pegasus-wise, but sped
By the grand gifts of Them of the Violet Crown,
To all that ope their doors, and up and down
While Sun and Earth endure, world without end,
Shalt live a song to men; — yet I, sweet friend,
I have no honour small or great with thee,
But, like a child, with words thou cheatest me.

[237–54, tr. J. M. Edmonds]

MAY I DRINK THE BLOOD OF MY ENEMIES

Olympian Zeus, a timely prayer fulfil
And grant good fortune may reprieve me still.
Come death, if I from ill find no relief
And vex not those that vex me, grief for grief.
There lies just measure.   Now, in vain I wait
To smite the spoilers, lords of my estate,
Who stript me, — like a dog I scrambled past
The rain-swol'n torrent and shook free at last!
O let me drink their dark blood down!   Take heed
Some kindly Spirit, and fulfil my need.

[341–50, tr. T. F. Higham]

REFINED GOLD

So dress me down and douse me as you will,
From head to foot shall flow clear water still.
In all I do assay me: you shall find
Pure gold, in red upon the touchstone sign'd —
A grain no rust can foul, nor any trace
Of soiling mould its perfect bloom deface.

[447–52, tr. T. F. Higham]

PUT MONEY IN THY PURSE

Save up.   Your very death won't dim an eye
If none perceive a heritage put by.

[931–2, tr. T. F. Higham]

A FAITHLESS FRIEND

You stole my friend, a sneakthief manifest,
Driving the old road that you still have driven
With that cold spotted snake claspt to your breast —
O damned — by man a knave, a fiend by heaven!

[599–602, tr. T. F. HIGHAM]

WEEP FOR YOUTH'S PASSING

What fools men are to weep the dead and gone!
Unwept, youth drops its petals one by one.

[1069–70, tr. T. F. HIGHAM]

PRIDE OF THE FLESH

Pride it was that laid Magnesia low,
And Kolophon and Smyrna. Well I know,
Kyrnos, the way that you and yours shall go.

[1103–4, tr. T. F. HIGHAM]

THE DEAD FEEL NOT

That my dead bones should lie in royal state
I wish not, but would live more fortunate.
Lie hard, lie soft, all's one: when we are dead
Rugs are no richer than a quick-thorn bed.

[1191–4, tr. T. F. HIGHAM]

THE CRANE'S MESSAGE

I heard the crane cry unto men his greeting,
    To tell them it was time to drive the plough:
Ah, friend! he set my sorry heart a-beating,
    For others have my fertile acres now.

[1197–1200, tr. SIR WILLIAM MARRIS]

SIMONIDES

(556–467 B.C.)

Simonides of Ceos is noteworthy for his many-sided genius and the variety of his verse. He lived a long and extraordinarily full life: he was in Athens at the court of Hippias and Hipparchus; after the murder of the latter he went to Thessaly to live with the noble family of the Scopadae; he was in Athens again at the time of the Persian Wars, and tradition represents him as the friend and associate of the great statesman, Themistocles. At the age of eighty he went to Sicily to enjoy the patronage of Hiero, tyrant of Syracuse. He was the first Greek poet whose verses were definitely the means of his livelihood; later Greeks represented him as overly fond of money, which probably means merely that he accepted honoraria from the nobles whom he celebrated in his poems. His wandering existence and his ability to make his way among the great and wealthy families, coupled with a broad, worldly wisdom, earned him the reputation of being "the first of the Sophists." There is some truth in this view, since Simonides, like the later Sophists, was keenly interested in "political *areté,*" that is, civic virtue, or the excellence proper to a man who lives in a *polis* (city-state): thus, in the first selection below, he declares, ". . . who is not bad . . . who knows the right that makes the city stand — a sound man he." In this and in the following selection (*The Climb to Virtue*) Simonides combats the aristocratic belief that *areté* depends solely on birth, wealth, and a position of honour.

Simonides wrote in many different poetic forms. The first eight selections printed here are true lyrics, poems to be sung either by a chorus or by a single voice, accompanied by the lyre. Some of the more important types should be noted: *Human Imperfection* is probably a *scolion* (drinking-song). *The Greek Dead at Thermopylae* comes perhaps from a choral hymn. *The Turn of a Dragonfly's Wing* and *Danae* are fragments of *threnoi* (dirges), a type in which Simonides excelled; and in *Danae* we may see that gift for pathos which all ancient criticism ascribes to him. He is also credited with "inventing" or developing the *epinician,* an ode to celebrate a victory in the games, but no certain fragment of this type has been included here.

The rest of the selections are sepulchral epigrams, in the elegiac meter; and although some of the epigrams ascribed to him may not have been written by Simonides, it is for these poems that he is best remembered today. For in his epitaphs commemorating the dead of the Persian Wars Simonides became the very Voice of Greece and is the first poet after Homer to write for a Panhellenic audience. Note the simple dignity with which he states the essential facts, and the high art which rescues these bare statements from banality — it may be a reminder of the great cause for which the dead gave their lives, or it may be nothing more than a well-chosen epithet, or the picturesque and appropriate scenery in the epitaph for the hunting-dog, Lycas.

HUMAN IMPERFECTION

Hard it is wholly to win worthy manhood,
with hand and foot and heart alike to be foursquare,
an ashlar cut without a flaw.
Who is not bad, not all a niddering, who knows
the right that makes the city stand —
a sound man he: not I indeed
will ever fault him, for of fools
the generation's endless.   All, all is fair
that is not mingled with the base.

Harmony sings not in Pittacus' proverb,
nay, not for me, although a wight of wisdom spake
the word, that *to excel is hard*.
A god alone could have such a privilege: a man
undone by a resistless fate
must needs be bad.   Yes: every man
is worthy if his luck is good,
and bad if it goes badly.   They most excel
who are belovèd by the gods.

Therefore I seek no impossible being,
I squander not my life's allotted term, in vain,
on an impracticable hope —
faultless humanity — beyond their power who win
the bread of life from spacious earth;
when 'tis discovered, I shall tell.
Honour and love to every man
who wills to do no baseness; but not the gods
themselves oppose necessity.

[4, tr. GILBERT HIGHET]

THE CLIMB TO VIRTUE

Virtue dwells, so runs the tale,
On precipices hard to scale.
Swift holy Nymphs attend her place;
No mortal eyes may see her face,
But only he, who with distress
Of soul and sweating heart can press
On to the height in manliness.

[37, tr. C. M. BOWRA]

THE GREEK DEAD AT THERMOPYLAE

Great are the fallen of Thermopylae,
Nobly they ended, high their destination —

Beneath an altar laid, no more a tomb,
Where none with pity comes or lamentation,
    But praise and memory —
    A splendour of oblation
No rust shall blot nor wreckful Time consume.

The ground is holy: here the brave are resting,
And here Greek Honour keeps her chosen shrine.
Here too is one the worth of all attesting —
Leonidas, of Sparta's royal line,
Who left behind a gem-like heritage
    Of courage and renown,
    A name that shall go down
      From age to age.

               [5, tr. T. F. Higham]

THE TURN OF A DRAGONFLY'S WING

Being but man, forbear to say
Beyond to-night what thing shall be,
And date no man's felicity.
    For know, all things
    Make briefer stay
Than dragonflies, whose slender wings
    Hover, and whip away.

               [6, tr. T. F. Higham]

DANAE

The wind blew fresh and seaward made,
The water stirred and lifted;
She, in carven coffer laid,
Rode the sea, and drifted.

Stolen upon her cheek tear-wet
Fear in that hour came preying;
But Perseus in her arm she set
And held him to her, saying:

"Child, my heart is faint with care . . .
You lie quiet, unaware,
    Drowsing still, dream-possest,
All the world a mother's breast.

In this vessel brute and bare,
Brazen-clamped and timbered tight,
    Stark your bed, wrapt about
With the darkness of our night
And the raven gloom without.

Spindrift comes and then is gone
Dashing your hair with deepening brine,
And the wind howls — all in vain.

Safe you rest, sleeping on
In your cloak of purple stain,
Cheek laid up to cheek of mine.

Child, if fear to you were fear,
Soon would turn that dainty ear
To my words attending;
Now I bid you nothing hear —
    Sleep, my babe, sleep, O sea,
Sleep, my pain unending.

Father Zeus, I call to thee.
Lighten our adversity,
Turning evil into good.
Oh, forgive my hardihood
If I speak offending."

[13, tr. T. F. HIGHAM]

ORPHEUS

And over his head
Birds without number are flying.   Fishes leap around
Out of the deep blue waters won by the tuneful sound.

[27, tr. J. STERLING]

STILLNESS AND SOUND

No breath of a wind rose then
To stir the leaves of the trees,
Nor any quivering breeze
To stay the sweet note of his song
From traveling straight along
To be fixed to the ears of men.

[40, tr. C. M. BOWRA]

MONUMENTS PERISH

Thoughtful men their praise withhold
From Lindian Cleobûlus.   He defied
Running rivers, spring flowers, burning gold
Of sun and moon, and swirling ocean pools
In strength to outbide
A stone.
The gods are strong alone.
Marble our hands can break to bits.
Those Lindian wits
Are but a fool's.

[48, tr. T. F. HIGHAM]

THE ATHENIAN DEAD

On Dirphys' wrinkled side we fell;
    And where the Narrow Waters drift

Our countrymen, to mark us well,
  Raised up this cairn, their gift.

A gift deserved; for youth is sweet,
  And youth we gave, nor turned away,
Though sharp the storm of battle beat
  That darkened all our day.

[87, tr. T. F. Higham]

AT THERMOPYLAE

Tell them in Lakedaimon, passer-by,
That here obedient to their word we lie.

[92, tr. Various Hands]

THE POET'S FRIEND

This is the grave of famed Megistias, whom
  Beside Spercheius' stream the Persian slew:
A seer he, who dared to share the doom
  Of Sparta's leaders, though that doom he knew.

[83, tr. G. B. Grundy]

PLATAEA

(i) *The Spartan Monument*

Into the dark death cloud they passed, to set
  Fame on their own dear land for fadeless wreath,
And dying died not.   Valour lifts them yet
  Into the splendour from the night beneath.

[121, tr. H. Macnaghten]

(ii) *The Athenian Monument*

If Valour's best be gallantly to die,
  Fortune to us of all men grants it now.
We to set Freedom's crown on Hellas' brow
  Laboured, and here in ageless honour lie.

[118, tr. W. C. Lawton]

TEGËA

(i) *A Cenotaph*

No cloud of smoke, from Tegëa thrown
In blaze of ruin, smote the sky;
Such men were these, she holds her own,
  And wide her acres lie.

As counting freedom hard to lose,
To sons they left her prime unspent;
Themselves the battle's front they chose,
  And went to death content.

[122, tr. T. F. Higham]

Not dead thou art,
Harmodius, dear heart,
But gone, men say, to islands of the blest, —
For all his speed
Achilles there finds rest,
And Tydeus' child, the gallant Diomede.

The blade I bear
A myrtle spray shall wear;
Harmodius and Aristogeiton drest
The brand even so,
When at Athena's feast
They laid Hipparchus, that great tyrant, low.

Dear hearts, your worth
Has deathless fame on earth, —
Harmodius and Aristogeiton, ye
Who blade in hand
Dealt death to tyranny
And liberated our Athenian land.

[SCOLIA 10–13, tr. GILBERT HIGHET, T. F. HIGHAM]

PINDAR AND BACCHYLIDES

Pindar is without doubt the greatest lyric poet of antiquity, and we are fortunate in possessing a large amount of his work, since four complete books of his poems survived the Middle Ages. All of these poems, as well as most of the work of Bacchylides, are *epinician* odes, poems to celebrate a victory in one of the Greek national games (the Olympian, Pythian, Nemean, and Isthmian Games). The question naturally rises in the mind of a modern reader: "Can athletic contests supply the material for great poetry?" The following remarks are intended to suggest the means by which Pindar transforms his subject-matter and attains the lofty heights of great poetry.

Pindar, a Theban noble who claimed kinship with one of the royal houses of Sparta, was the last great aristocrat in the course of Greek poetry, and he expresses more ardently than any other poet the ideals of the noble families. They believed that *areté*, that excellence or virtue which Greek thought was ever seeking to define, was the peculiar, inborn possession of the nobles; they traced their ancestry back to some god, and their *areté* was the product of the divine blood which still flowed in their veins. This *areté*, conceived of as an ideal union of physical and spiritual excellences, was most clearly revealed at the moment of victory in one of the great games. Athletic contests were originally an aristocratic diversion; the twenty-third book of the *Iliad* shows the importance which the great Achaean warriors placed on such sports. Naturally, in the post-Homeric world, participation in the games was not limited to the nobles, but up to the middle of the fifth century the great families took a leading part in them, since they alone could expend the time and money necessary for training.

With such a background, Pindar was able to raise his songs of victory to the level of hymns, with an exalted religious tone and a divine message to the victor. The method by which he achieved this elevation can best be understood by considering the form of a typical *epinician* ode. The *proem*, or introduction, is a splendid, dazzling prelude, which usually concludes with some mention of the occasion for the song, the victory; Pindar seldom dwells on the details of the contest but passes quickly to the legendary past, the *myth*, which is the core of the poem. This myth is connected with the occasion in a variety of ways: the setting of the victory (as in *Olympian* I), some event in the contest, some characteristic of the athlete or his family may remind Pindar of a legend. Frequently the myth is drawn from the saga of the victor's ancestors (as in *Olympian* II); thus, the present is connected with the heroic age when men lived close to their gods, and the victor becomes the worthy heir to the proud traditions of his family and to the *areté* bequeathed him by his divine forebears. The *epilogue*, or conclusion, is usually a personal address to the victor, filled with aristocratic wis-

dom and advice. Pindar can address his noble patrons with absolute freedom: not only is he their social equal but he feels keenly
his position as the divine mouthpiece of the Muses. Not infre-
quently he mentions himself and vaunts his poetic skill and inspiration.

An outline of the *Fourth Pythian,* Pindar's longest poem, may
serve as an example. Arkesilaos, King of Cyrene, traced his descent
from Battos, the founder of the colony. In the *proem* (1–69) Pindar invokes the Muse and relates the prophecy of Medea, which tells
how Thera and Cyrene were to be colonized by the descendants of
Euphamos, one of the Argonauts. At the end of this lengthy introduction, he returns to Arkesilaos and mentions his victory in the
chariot-race — in one brief line. The *myth* proper follows (70–262),
the story of the quest of the Golden Fleece. In the conclusion (263–
299) the poet tactfully pleads for Damophilos, an exiled noble of
Cyrene, at whose request this poem was composed by Pindar, "the
fair fountain of immortal words" (as he proudly says), who had
entertained the exile at Thebes.

Pindar's art is not easily apprehended, nor will the modern reader
grasp at one perusal the nobility and stately beauty of these poems;
they are as free from mere prettiness as the stiff archaic sculpture of
Pindar's own day. Unfriendly critics in all ages have stressed his
obscurity — a charge that Pindar himself answers: "Many swift arrows have I under my arm, within my quiver — arrows that speak
to the wise; but for the mob they need interpreters" (*O.* II. 83–6).
But Pindar never condescends to be his own interpreter. This alleged obscurity is the result of several factors: first, his allusive, lyrical method of telling his story. The local legends and variants in
the myth, which seem obscure to us, were, of course, well known
to his audience; he speaks as a friend among equals, alluding to
stories that need no explanation, since they are drawn from the annals
of the victor's own family and home. Second, Pindar moves with
great swiftness: he seldom lingers over details or elaborates an idea
to any length. While his brevity may at times seem baffling and
blind to us, nevertheless, as a result of his constant movement and
concentration of thought, he gives an impression of strength and richness that is unequalled by any other poet. Pindar is like a runner
who is never forced to extend himself: he always has an abundance
of power in reserve. Third, Pindar is a master of brilliant and constantly shifting metaphors: for example, his poetry is "a gale of
songs," "a fountain of immortal words," "a shaft mighty in strength,"
he "shoots forth shafts of good fame from the quiver of a kindly
heart." Hiero "culls the crests of all virtues," Theron is "a bulwark
of Acragas," "the choicest flower of a famous line of sires." This
bold identification of object and image, in place of the more leisurely
comparison by similes, is the very hall-mark of Pindar's art.

Bacchylides is comparatively easy to understand, since his odes
follow the same pattern but lack the intense concentration of Pindar's. He is graceful, smooth, and elegant where Pindar is stiff,

harsh, and majestic. He was a younger contemporary of Pindar, and the nephew of Simonides of Ceos, who took him to Sicily and secured for him the patronage of Hiero; he appears to have been more successful than Pindar in flattering the tyrant, and eventually supplanted him in his favour. His work was known to the modern world only in small fragments until 1897, when a papyrus was discovered in Egypt which contained nineteen more or less complete poems of Bacchylides — thirteen *epinicians* and six *dithyrambs,* one of which, the *Theseus,* is given below. The discovery serves to confirm the judgment of the best of ancient critics, the so-called Longinus (*On the Sublime,* XXXIII. 5): "In lyric poetry, would you prefer to be Bacchylides rather than Pindar? And in tragedy to be Ion of Chios rather than Sophocles? It is true that Bacchylides and Ion are faultless and entirely elegant writers of the polished school, while Pindar and Sophocles, although at times they burn everything before them as it were in their swift career, are often extinguished unaccountably and fail most lamentably. But would anyone in his senses regard all the compositions of Ion put together as an equivalent for the single play of the *Oedipus?*" And (we might add) all nineteen poems of Bacchylides would not be too high a price to pay for the *First Olympian* of Pindar.

PINDAR

(522?–448? B.C.)

THE FIRST OLYMPIAN

For Hiero, tyrant of Syracuse, on a victory won by his horse Pherenikus, 476 B.C.

(*Strophe* 1)

Chiefest is water of all things, for streaming
    Therefrom all life and existence came;
And all proud treasure of princes the gleaming
    Splendour of gold outshines, as the flame
Of a great fire flings through the night its rays.
But, heart of mine, if thou fain wouldst praise
    Triumphs in athlete-contests won,
Search not, when day with his glory is glowing,
For a radiant star more life-bestowing
    In the whole void sky, than the kingly sun.
Even so shall we find no brighter crown
    Than Olympia giveth whereof to sing;
For thence doth the chant of high renown
    O'er the spirits of bards its perfume fling,
When, the praise of Kronion in song resounding,
Unto Hiero's blest heart wealth-abounding
    The hymn of his praise they bring.

(Antistrophe 1)

Hiero!—yea, for the rod of his power
  Is a sceptre of righteousness stretched o'er the land
Of the myriad flocks; and the choice of the flower
  Of chivalry ever is plucked by his hand.
Yea, and he also is garlanded
With the blossom of song enstarring his head,
  The song that with gladsome voices now
We singers chant, at the banquet meeting
Of the Prince who giveth us friendship's greeting.
  Now, O my Muse, from its rest take thou
The lyre that is strung to the Dorian strain,
  If the glory of fleet Pherenikus, he
Who triumphed in Pisa's Olympian plain,
  Haply with rapture of song thrilled thee,
When flashed in the course by Alpheus' river
His body by lash or by goad touched never,
    And wedded to victory.

(Epode 1)

His lord, the ruler of Syracuse-town,
  The king who joyeth in gallant steeds,
Flasheth afar his name's renown,
  Flasheth from Sicily far over sea
  Where Pelops, the exile from Lydia's meads,
  Founded a hero-colony—
Pelops, beloved of the Earth-enfolder,
  Poseidon the strong, when the Fate of the Thread
Drew him resplendent with ivory shoulder
  From the undefiled laver, whom men deemed dead.
There be legends full many; and fables hoary
  With inventions manifold broidered o'er
Falsify legend, I wot, with a story
    Wherein truth liveth no more.

(Str. 2)

But the Grace of Beauty, which aye is weaving
  All manner of charm round the souls of men,
Taketh these tales unworthy believing,
  And arrays them in honour: so cometh it then
That man with unwavering credence clings
To a false-feigned tale of impossible things.
  But the after-days are witnesses
That be wisest.   Reverent speech beseemeth
The mortal who uttereth that which he deemeth
  Of the Gods—so shall his reproach be less.
O Tantalus' son, I will speak not as they
  Who told thy story in days of old!
But thy father bade thee a guest that day

To a banquet arrayed by the righteous-souled
Upon Sipylus' loved height — so he tendered
To the Gods requittal for boons they had rendered.
    On a sudden the chariot of gold

                                        (*Ant. 2*)

Of the Lord of the Trident gleaming splendid,
    Whose soul was with love for thy youth overcome,
Bare thee, as up through the blue ye ascended,
    To imperial Zeus's glory-home,
Whither also came in the after-day
Ganymedes ravished from earth away
    In halls celestial the nectar to pour.
But when viewless thus from the earth they had caught thee,
Nor the questers that far and near had sought thee
    To the arms of thy mother could thee restore,
Then spake some neighbour in envious spite
    A whispered slander of sin and shame,
How that over the boiling water's might
    Which hissed in the bronze that bestrode the flame
Did they carve thy flesh with the knife, and seethe it,
And served at the feast, and — dare lips breathe it? —
    That the God-guests ate of the same.

                                        (*Ep. 2*)

But impossible is it for me to call
    Any Blest One man-eater — with loathing and scorn
I recoil! Oh, the profit is passing small
    That the dealer in slander hath ofttimes found.
    But if ever a man on the earth was born
    Whom the Watchers from Heaven with honour crowned,
That man was Tantalus: yet of their favour
    No profit he had, nor of that high bliss.
But the man's proud stomach was drunk with its savour
    And gorged with pride; and by reason of this
He drew on him ruin utter-crashing;
    For Zeus hung o'er him a huge black scaur,
And he cowers from it aye on his head down-rushing
    From happiness exiled far.

                                        (*Str. 3*)

And there unto torment fettered for ever
    Living on, living on in eternal despair
He abides with the Three * on whom hope dawns never,
    He who from the feast of the Gods could dare
To steal the ambrosia and nectar whereby
They had given him immortality,
    That the guests of his wine-cup might revel thereon!

* Tityus, Sisyphus, and Ixion.

But who thinketh to hide his evil doing
From God, he errs to his bitter ruing!
  So then the Immortals sent back his son
Exiled to earth from the heavenly home,
    Thenceforth with the sons of a day to abide.
But in process of time, when Pelops was come
  To the flower-bright season of life's springtide,
When the soft rose-tint of his cheek 'gan darken,
To the whisper of love did his spirit hearken,
    And he dreamed of the world-famed bride

(Ant. 3)

Hippodameia, the glorious daughter
  Of the Lord of Pisa, a prize for him
Who could win her. Alone by the surf-white water
  Of the sea he stood in the darkness dim.
To the Thunder-voiced he cried o'er the wave,
To the Lord of the Trident mighty to save:
  And lo, at his side did the God appear.
And "O Poseidon," he spake imploring,
"If the gifts of the Cyprian Queen's outpouring
  To thy spirit, O King, be in any wise dear,
His bronze lance let not Oenomaus lift
  To mine hurt, but cause me to Elis to ride
On a god-given chariot passing swift:
  There throne thou me by victory's side.
For lovers by that spear merciless-slaying
Have died thirteen, and he still is delaying
    To bestow his child as a bride.

(Ep. 3)

In the path doth a mighty peril lie;
  To the craven soul no welcome it gives.
But, seeing a man must needs once die,
    Wherefore should I unto old age screen
    From peril a life that only *lives,*
    Sitting nameless and fameless in darkness unseen,
In the deeds of the valiant never sharing?
  Nay, lies at my feet the challenge now:
I will accept it for doing and daring!
  Good speed to mine heart's desire grant thou!"
Not fruitless the cry of his heart's desiring
  Was uttered. The God heard gracious-souled,
And crowned him with honour. Winged steeds untiring
    He gave, and a chariot of gold.

(Str. 4)

So he won for his bride that maiden peerless;
  For her terrible father he overcame.

And she bare to him six sons battle-fearless,
   Captains of war-hosts, thirsting for fame.
And his portion assured hath Pelops still
Where the priests the blood of the sacrifice spill;
   And unto his tomb resorteth the throng
Of strangers from far who have heard his story.
From his grave-mound his spirit beholdeth the glory
   Of the mighty Olympian strife of the strong
In the course that from Pelops its name hath ta'en,
   Wherein be contending the swift to run
And the thews that be mighty in wrestling-strain.
   And whoso therein hath the victory won,
Thereafter on through his life-days ever
Sweetly his peace shall flow as a river
     Blissfully gliding on

                                              (Ant. 4)

For those Games' sake. Yea, the good that unceasing
   On man's lot daily as dew droppeth down
Is that which to each is most well-pleasing.
   Now is it my bounden duty to crown
With a strain wherein hoof-beats triumphant ring
In Aeolian mood Sicilia's King.
   And hereof is my spirit assured past doubt
That amidst all men on the wide earth dwelling
There is found no host whom with prouder-swelling
   Notes in many a winding bout
Of noble song I may glorify;
   Yea, none more learned in honour's lore,
None who showeth therein more potency.
   The God who guardeth thee watcheth o'er
Thine hopes and thine aims, that no evil assail thee;
And if — O nay, but he cannot fail thee! —
     I trust ere long once more

                                              (Ep. 4)

To chant a triumph than all more sweet,
   Inspiration-wafted, as one that flies
In a chariot, on paths of utterance meet,
   Till I win unto Kronos' Hill sunbright.
   O yea, in my Muses' quiver lies
   A song-arrow winged for stronger flight.*
By diverse paths men upward aspire:
   Earth's highest summit by kings is attained.
Thou therefore look to attain no higher

---

* Pindar is here expressing the hope that Hiero will win the more important four-horse chariot victory at Olympia, and that he will commission Pindar to write the victory-ode. Hiero did achieve this distinction, in 468 B.C., but Bacchylides wrote the ode for the occasion; see *infra* p. 1022.

Than earth.   Be it thine on the height thou hast gained
To pace mid splendour of royal achieving
   Thy life through: mine be it no less long
To consort with victors, from Hellas receiving
    The world o'er praise for my song.

[tr. A. S. Way]

SECOND OLYMPIAN

For Theron, tyrant of Akragas, for a victory in the chariot-race,
476 B.C.

(*Str.* 1)

Songs, lords of the lyre! what God shall we hymn? — what hero's
   praises? —
  What man's fame publish afar?
Pisa doth Zeus own; Herakles stablished Olympia's races
   With the regal spoils of his war;
Theron, who honours the guest, whose four steeds raced victorious,
Akragas' stay, let us chant, full flower of an ancestry glorious,
   His city's saviour-star.

(*Ant.* 1)

Toils bravely his fathers endured, and a hallowed home by the river
   They reared: they were Sicily's eye.
And to crown their inborn worth, Fair Fortune attended them, giver
   Of wealth and of dignity.
Son of Kronos and Rhea, enthroned in Olympus, thou lord of the
   choicest
Of contests by Alpheus' ford, guard, since in our song thou rejoicest,
   For their sons ever graciously

(*Ep* 1)

Their fatherland-soil!   When for right or for wrong hath been
   woven the tissue
Of our deeds, not Time the father of all can reverse the issue.
   Yet oblivion may come of the past
With the dawn of a happier day; for overmastered and slain
By the sunlight of happiness oft is memory's rankling pain,
   When broad and high at the last

(*Str.* 2)

Prosperity grows by the fiat of God.   Yea, of Kadmus' daughters
   This thing I have said proved true: —
Sore anguish they suffered, yet mightier blessings from out of the
   waters
   Of affliction the stricken ones drew.
Mid thunder-crash Semele perished, yet lives in heavenly star-land;

And Pallas and Zeus and her son, who is crowned with the ivy-
garland,
  Enfold her with love ever new.

(Ant. 2)

With the sea-maids, the daughters of Nereus, to Ino a life unending
  In the deep is ordained for aye.
But to mortals no date is appointed whereon death's bolt descending
  Shall smite; nor can any man say
When one day, child of the sun, shall in calm peace close with un-
broken
Blessing. With sorrow and joy run life's streams, giving no token
  How their mutable courses will stray.

(Ep. 2)

So Destiny, she who the line of the fathers of Theron hath guided
To happiness, yet for their god-given bliss hath also provided
  In its season a bitter reverse,
Since the hour when met in his journeying Laius was, and killed
By his doom-driven son, and the word that from Pytho went forth
was fulfilled,
  The old-time prophecy-curse.

(Str. 3)

Swift Erinys beheld it, and slew by hands with a brother's blood gory
  His warrior sons. When died
Polyneikes, Thersander was left to win in a new war glory,
  The Adrastids' saviour and pride.
From him these trace their descent; and the son of a prince most
meetly
With all praises of song triumphant and lyres outpealing sweetly
  This day shall be magnified.

(Ant. 3)

Olympia's guerdon he won, and at Pytho and Isthmus the Graces,
  Who his kindred have evermore blessed,
Brought to his brother the crowns of the twelve-course four-horse
races.
  Ay, triumph to pain bringeth rest.
Riches with nobleness graced of many things bring fruition,
And they kindle the deep-glowing fire of the huntress of honour,
Ambition,
  Within their possessor's breast,

(Ep. 3)

A lodestar that beacons afar, by whose light men steer most surely,
If he who doth hold by it knoweth what shall be — that they which
impurely

Here lived, shall when they have died
Suffer the penalty: sins that in Zeus's realm of light
Were committed shall One judge there in the underworld Kingdom
    of Night,
    And their awful doom shall decide.

                                                    (Str. 4)

But through sunlitten nights and days a life of bliss untoiling
    Is ordained for the righteous-souled.
No more for a meagre pittance they labour the land sore moiling,
    Nor on stormy seas are they rolled;
But with them that be honoured of Gods, who had pleasure in leal
    oath-keeping,
They have joy of a tearless life, while the wicked are endlessly reaping
    Sin harvests too dread to behold.

                                                      (Ant. 4)

But they that through those three lives have endured, their spirits
    refraining
    From sin upon each side of death,*
These traverse the pathway of Zeus, to the tower of Kronos attaining,
    Where the breezes of Ocean breathe
Round the Isles of the Blest, where flowers all-golden like flames are
    glowing,
Which are drooping from trees of splendour, or float on the flood
    soft-flowing;
    And their heads and their hands they enwreathe,

                                                      (Ep. 4)

As it standeth by just Rhadamanthus decreed, the eternal assessor
Of Kronos the husband of Rhea, of her who is throned possessor
    Of dominion the universe o'er.
And Peleus and Kadmus are numbered amidst the glorified there;
And the heart of Zeus by Thetis' petition was swayed, that she bare
    Achilles to that blest shore,

                                                      (Str. 5)

Him who slew the invincible Hector, and Troy's strong pillar did
    shiver,
    And of whom was Kyknus slain
And the Dawn-queen's Aethiop son. Many swift shafts lie in my
    quiver;
    To the wise is their meaning plain;
For the common herd need they interpreters. Who is by nature
    discerning

---

* Pindar here refers to a doctrine of transmigration: those who pass through three
lives without sin are released from the cycle of birth and death and are sent to the
Isles of the Blest. Compare the form of the doctrine in Plato, *Phaedrus* 248–9.

Is the poet inspired; but the vehement babblers of other men's learn-
    ing
    Croak vanity — crows be the twain! — *

                                    (*Ant.* 5)

At the hallowed eagle of Zeus! O my soul, on the bow be thou
    aiming —
    And at whom in all love wilt thou speed
The renowned arrow? To Akragas send thou it, boldly proclaim-
    ing —
Bidding Truth of thine oath take heed —
That through years five-score no city on earth hath been known to
    rear on
Her breast any son more kindly in spirit to friends than Theron,
    None of more liberal deed.

                                    (*Ep.* 5)

Yet praise is by spite ever dogged, wherein never is justice abiding,
But from grasping envy it springs; with its slanders it fain would
    be hiding
    In darkness the good deeds done
By the noble of heart. But, as no man can number the great sea's
    sands,
So the joys on his fellow-men showered by Theron with lavish hands,
    Who telleth the tale of them? None!

                               [tr. A. S. WAY]

FOURTH PYTHIAN

For Arkesilas of Kyrene, Winner in the Chariot-race.   462 B.C.

THE PRELUDE: MEDEA'S PROPHECY

I

Today, Muse, you must stand by the side of a friend,
By the King of Kyrene, the land of good horses:
And when Arkesilas holds his triumph
Swell the gale of your songs,
Paying your debt to Lato's Twins, and to Pytho,
Where once, when Apollo was in his land,
The priestess — she who sits by God's gold eagles —
Ordained Battos a leader of men
Into fruitful Libya.
He must straightway leave his holy island
And build a city
Of Charioteers
On a silver breast of the earth,

---

   * Explained by the ancient commentators as a jibe at Pindar's rivals, Simonides
and Bacchylides. The eagle, of course, is Pindar.

To bring back the word of Medea
In the seventeenth generation,
Which at Thera once Aietes' terrible child
Breathed from immortal lips, the Colchians' Queen —
And thus she spoke
To the seed of Gods, the sailors of Jason the fighter:
"Hear, sons of high-hearted men and of Gods!
I tell you, from this wave-beaten land shall go
A stock, and shall beteem the daughter of Epaphos,*
And cities shall rise
And the world shall know it
In the place where Zeus Ammon stands.

Instead of the short-finned dolphins
They shall have swift horses, and reins for oars:
They shall drive the stormfoot chariots.
The Omen, that shall make
Thera mother-city of mighty cities,
Was given, where Lake Tritonis flows to the sea,
To Euphamos once
(A guest-gift from the God in a man's likeness)
A *Clod*: Euphamos, alighting from the bows,
Took it, and Father Zeus, the son of Krones,
Well pleased rang out in thunder.

                        II

He found us slinging the bronze-jawed anchor
Beside the prow, swift Argo's bridle.
I had bidden them haul her, our sea-timber, ashore,
And we had borne her from Ocean
Twelve days across earth's lonely ridges.
Out of his solitudes then
The God appeared
Clothed in the bright shape of a reverend lord:
And friendly words he began,
As a good host,
When strangers come,
Starts with his offers of supper:

But we spoke of our sweet road home
And could not stay. He told us his name
Eurypylos, son of the undying
    Shaker and Holder of Earth.
And he knew our hurry: and there and then
Took a clod in his right hand, fain to offer what gift he could:
And the hero did not refuse it.
He leaped to the beach, and clasping hand in hand
Took the piece of earth divine. —
But a wave broke,

* Libya.

I hear, and washed it
Overboard into the sea

At evening, and it went with the waters of the deep.
O often I bade the servants we had for our ease
Keep it safe: but their souls forgot.
So now against this isle has been washed
The undying seed of Libya's wide meadows,
Out of due time.
For had he come home, and cast it beside Hell's mouth in the earth,
Had he come to holy Tainaron, — he
Euphamos, son of Poseidon the captain of the horse,
Born on Kaphisos' banks of Europa, Tityos' child, —

III

Then the blood of his grandsons' grandsons after him,
With a Danaan host, had taken that wide mainland.
For then, behold!
Men coming from great Lakedaimon,
From the gulf of Argos and from Mykenai!
— But now, he shall lie with foreign women
And get a chosen race: who shall come to this island
      (for the Gods will care for them)
And have a son to be lord of those dark-clouded plains.
Him one day
In that gold-stored House
Phoebos shall tell in oracles

(When in later days he comes down to the Pythian shrine)
To carry cities in ships
To the land where Neilos dwells, the son of Kronos."
   Medea's words filed past: and the godlike heroes
Kept silent and still, and bowed their heads,
Listening to her deep wisdom.
   O happy son of Polymnastos! *
To you, as was here foretold,
The oracle of the Delphic Bee gave glory
In her unprompted cry,
Bidding you three times "Hail!"
Foreshown
Kyrene's King to be.

(You were asking
About your stammering tongue, might the Gods release you.)
And later in time, even today,
There flowers, as when spring puts out her reddest blossom,
The eighth generation, Arkesilas.

   * Battos.

VI

You have heard the sum of my story.
But where
Is the house of my fathers that rode white horses?
Good citizens, tell me clearly.
I am Aison's son, a man of the land,
Nor am I come to a strange country belonging to others.
By my name Jason the godlike Beast addressed me."
　He spoke: and when he went in, his father's eyes
Knew him, and tears bubbled down
From his old eyelids:
For in his soul
He was glad, seeing
His chosen son, the fairest of men.

And his two brothers came to that house
At the fame of the man.　From near
Pheres came, leaving the fountain Hyperia,
From Messene Amythaon.
And soon Admetos came and Melampos,
For their hearts yearned to their cousin.
— With due feasting, and words honeysweet,
Jason their host made pleasant entertainment
And long-stretched-out delight, five nights
Without ceasing
And five days
Gathering the great luxurious hours.

But on the sixth day, with sober words
He let his kinsmen know all from the beginning:
And they gave him heed.
And he leaped up quick from his couch, and they with him,
And went to Pelias' hall and made haste and stood within.
When the King heard them, himself came forth to them,
The son of Tyro, lovely-haired queen:
And Jason with soft voice let smooth words fall,
Laying a foundation of wise speech: —
"Son of Poseidon of the Rock,

VII

The hearts of men are perhaps too quick
At choosing a smart advantage rather than right
(Though the next day the taste is wry in the mouth).
But I and you must rule our wrath
And weave our future fortune.
You know as well as I, one womb
Bore Kretheus and Salmoneus hardy in cunning,
From whom in the third generation ourselves sprang,
Who look on the golden strength of the sun.
— The Fates recoil

When men of one blood
Hating each other, lose sight of shame.

We must not take, you and I,
Swords of biting bronze or javelins
To divide our fathers' honours.
The sheep and the tawny herds of oxen
I yield you, and all the fields,
Which you stole from my parents and live on, fattening your sub-
    stance.
Nourish with these your house, it yearns me little.
But there is the sceptre of absolute rule,
And the throne on which the son of Kretheus sat
And gave straight judgments
To a people of horsemen.
To spare both of us sorrow

Let me have these;
And no fresh evil come of them!"
— So he spoke: and gently too Pelias answered him:
"I will do as you say.
But already the sere end of life attends me
And your youth bursts into flower.
You have power to lay the wrath of those in earth.
Phrixos is calling, that someone redeem his ghost,
And, going to the halls of Aietes, fetch
The thick-piled Fleece
Of the Ram, by whom he was saved of old
From the sea,

VIII

And from the godless knives of his stepmother.
A marvellous dream came and told me of this.
I have asked the oracle at Kastalia
Should I follow this up? and he bids me find
At once, the crew for a ship.
— Achieve this task, so please you: and I swear
I will let you be sole ruler and king.
Let Him be our strong oath,
Zeus the Witness, the father of both our races."
So they approved
This covenant:
And those two parted: but as for Jason, already

He was sending messengers everywhere
That a quest was afoot.
— And soon there came, that never tired of battle,
The sons of Zeus Kronidas,
Of Alkmena of the dancing eyelids and of Leda:
And two tall-crested men, the Earth-Shaker's seed
In the proudness of valour,

From Pylos and Cape Tainaron:
—Fair was the fame they won,
Euphamos, and you, strong Periklymenos.
From Apollo's house
The lute-player came,
The father of songs, ever-worshipped Orpheus.

Hermes of the golden wand
Sent his twin sons to that long stretch of labour,
Echion one (O loud exultation of youth),
The other Erytos.   Quick came two
Who dwelt round the roots of Pangaion:
For gladly with laughing heart and swiftly
Their father Boreas, King of Winds,
Sent Zetes and Kalais, — men,
Yet scarlet feathers ruffled upon their backs.
    And in these sons of Gods Hera kindled
That all-persuading sweet desire

IX

For the ship Argo, that none be left behind
To nurse at his mother's side a ventureless life,
But, even though he die,
Find in his own valour the fairest enchantment
With others young as he.
    They came to the port of Iolchos, the finest of sailors,
And Jason marshalled all, and approved them.
And the seer Mopsos, that watched God's will for him
In birds and the holy taking of lots,
Bade with good heart
The host be started.
They hung the anchor over the prow: and then

The Captain at the stern
Held in his hands a gold cup, and called
On the Father of the Sons of Heaven,
Zeus, whose spear is the lightning,
On the swift rushing of the waves, the winds,
On the nights and the paths of the sea;
For days of kind weather, and the sweet road home at last.
From the clouds answered back to him
The assenting voice of thunder,
And lightnings flashed and tore the sky.
The heroes found fresh breath of courage,
For they believed
The omens of God.
The Seer of signs called to them

To fall to the oars,
And he put sweet hopes into them: under their rapid hands
The oars insatiably fell and rose.

A south wind blew, and before it they reached the Unwelcoming Sea.
They marked a holy acre there
For Poseidon of the Deep,
And there was a red herd of Thracian bulls
And an altar basin newly fashioned of stone.
   They were running toward deep danger
And prayed to the Lord of Ships

x

To escape the awful onset
Of the Clashing Rocks.   Two they were, and alive,
And they rolled swifter
Than the howling winds charge past.
But that sailing of the sons of Gods
Brought them to an end.
   After that they came to the River Phasis
And matched their might
Among the dark-faced Kolchians, yea
In the presence of Aietes.
But from Olympos the Queen of sharpest arrows
Bound past loosing
The dappled wryneck
To the four spokes of a wheel: *

She, the Kypros-born, for the first time brought
The maddening bird to men.
She taught Aison's wise son
What sorceries he must chant, and Medea forget
To honour those who begot her,
And her heart be all on fire for lovely Hellas
And tremble under the lash of love.
She showed him at once
How to achieve her father's tasks:
With olive-oil she made an enchantment against hard pains
And gave it to him for anointing.
And they swore to make a sweet marriage one with another.

But when Aietes
Dragged forth the adamantine plough in the midst of them
And the oxen who breathed from yellow nostrils a flame of burning
       fire,
And hoof after bronze-shod hoof ripped up the ground, —
He took them and forced them to the yoke
Alone, and straight was the furrow he ploughed as he drove them:
He cast up the clods, and clove earth's back
A fathom deep; and thus he spoke:
"Let the King do this, the captain of the ship!
Let him do this, I say,
And have for his own the immortal coverlet,

* This was a common type of love-charm in antiquity; see Theocritus, Idyl II, pp. 932.

XI

The Fleece, glowing with matted skeins of gold."
He spoke, and Jason
Threw off his saffron clothing, and trusting God
Assayed the task.
And the fire did not make him flinch,
Through the strange woman's words, that strong enchantress.
He, grasping the plough,
Harnessed perforce the oxen's necks, and driving
In those huge flanks a steady goad
With violence he achieved the appointed distance.
And, speechless though
His grief, Aietes
Howled in amazement at his might.

To the mighty man his comrades
Stretched out their hands, and gathered grass to crown him:
With sweet words they caressed him.
Then the Sun's wondrous child
Told him where the shining Skin
Had been stretched by Phrixos' sword (and there
Was a labour *where,* he hoped, *he yet might fail*).
It lay in a snake's den,
Caught on the monster's raging teeth
That was thicker and longer
Than a ship
Of fifty oars
Made by the smiting iron.

The journey is long on the high road:
Time presses me, and I know a short path
(In the wisdom of song I am the leader of many).
— He slew by cunning
The snake with glaring eyes and bright-scaled back;
O Arkesilas,
He stole Medea, she willing, — she, who was Pelias' death.
They came to the depths of Ocean, to the Red Sea,
To the Land of Lemnians,
Women the slayers of men.
There in bodily games they proved their might
(A garment for the prize)

XII

And there they wedded. Then it was, in foreign furrows
A day, or a night,
Received the destined seed
Of your house's sunlike fortune.
For then the race of Euphamos took root,
Growing thereafter always higher.

They mixed first in Lakedaimon's dwellings,
Then went to live in the island
Once called Loveliest.
And after that Lato's son
Gave you Libya's plain, for the Gods love you,
To enrich and govern
The holy city
Of Kyrene on her throne of gold,

Since judgment and right counsel are yours.

THE CONCLUSION: DAMOPHILOS

Try now the Art of Oedipus.
If a man with a keen axe-blade
Lops the branches of a great oak,
Defiling the beauty that men gazed at, —
Though its fruit has perished, yet it gives
Witness of itself when it comes at last
In winter to the fire,
Or rests on the upright pillars of a master,
Doing sad labour
In a stranger's house,
While its own house is desolate.

— But you can heal in the very nick of time.
You give light, and Paian adds honour to it.
Stretch out a gentle hand, to tend
A sore wound.
It is easy even for weaker men than you
To shake a city, but hard indeed
To set it back in the land,
Unless God be suddenly there, the Pilot of Kings.
For you
The web of these bright years is being woven.
Have patience for the sake of Kyrene's happiness
To give it all your care.

XIII

Remember a saying of Homer's, and cherish it —
"*A good messenger,*" he said, "*heightens the honour of any errand.*"
Even the Muse's stature
Is more, if she be well reported.
There was known in Kyrene and to that most famous hall of Battos
A man of just heart, Damophilos.
Young in the eyes of boys, but in counsel
An old man with a hundred garner'd years,
He robs of loudness
The slanderous tongue.
He has learnt to hate the insolent,

He does not strive counter to the good,
None of his purposes tarry: for very swift is the Moment for a man.
He has seen it: Time is his servant now, and not running away.
— They say there is nothing more sorrowful
Than to see joy and stand perforce outside.
Atlas indeed still wrestles with the sky
Far from his father's country and his possessions:
Yet deathless Zeus
Set free the Titans.
In time the wind sags, and we hoist

New sails. — But now, he cries,
He has done with foul illness at last, and he sees home.
Near Apollo's fountain
He shall lie at the feast, and yield his heart to youth
Often, and playing his painted lyre,
Where men know music, shall touch the hands of peace:
Giving sorrow to none, and having no wrong from his fellow-
     townsmen.
And perhaps he will tell, Arkesilas,
What a well of immortal words he found
When lately a guest in Thebes.

[tr. H. T. WADE-GERY, C. M. BOWRA]

BACCHYLIDES

(505–450 B.C.)

Victor in the Four-horse chariot-race at Olympia. 468 B.C.

(Str. 1*)*

Sing, Klio, thou giver of guerdons of sweetness,
  Her who doth o'er fair-fruited Sicilia reign,
And her pansy-crowned Daughter; and chant me the fleetness
  Of Hiero's steeds on Olympia's plain.

(Ant. 1*)*

Glory went with them, and triumph victorious,
  As by wide-swirling Alpheus onward they sped,
And the name of Deinomenes' son they made glorious
  With garlands of victory wreathing his head.

(Ep. 1*)*

And the folk of Achaia-land shouted aloud:
  "Hail, hero-king, thou in thy lot thrice-blest,
Thou whom the bounty of Zeus hath endowed
  With lordship o'er Hellenes most kingliest,
Who hast wisdom, whereby thou dost ne'er overcloud
Thy tower-like weal as with sable shroud!"

(Str. 2*)*

Aglow are the temples with burnt sacrifices,
  With guest-welcome aglow are the streets of the land;
Far flashes the gold of cunning devices
  On the tripods afront of the temple that stand

(Ant. 2*)*

Where of Phoebus' wide precinct the Delphians are tenders,
Where the Fountain of Castaly showers its spray.
To the God, to the God highest honours who renders,
  The surest foundation of bliss doth he lay.

(Ep. 2*)*

So was it with Croesus, who reigned of old
  Over Lydia whose warriors the wild steed quell;
When by Zeus's decree, of whom the earth is controlled,
  Sardis 'neath might of the Persians fell,
Over him did the Lord of the Falchion of Gold,
Apollo, his shield of protection hold.

(Str. 3)

For he brooked not, a king, in his day of disaster,
  The day that his soul never dreamed should befall,
To weep as a slave 'neath the lash of a master:
  But a pyre in his court of the brazen wall

(Ant. 3)

He upreared, and thereon with his queen he ascended
  And his daughters who tore their beautiful hair,
And wailed for the life in such pangs to be ended;
  And to high heaven raised he his hands in prayer:

(Ep. 3)

"What thank for mine offerings now have I,"
  Cried he, "O tyrannous God and unjust?
O King, son of Leto, wilt thou not draw nigh?
  Alyattes' house is ruinward thrust,
Though your altars were ever with gifts heaped high,
Though our sacrifice-smoke ever soared to your sky!

(Str. 4)

Lo, how hath it ceased, the golden city!
  The swirls of Pactolus our blood crimsoneth:
Forth of their chambers fair-built without pity
  Our women are haled unto worse than death!

(Ant. 4)

What was hideous is sweet — I meet death with glad hailing!
  Ho, kindle the pyre!" to the eunuch he cried.
Then the maidens his daughters with shrieking and wailing
  Clasped wildly their mother, and clung to her side.

(Ep. 4)

For death is most awful when full in our sight
  He draws nearer and nearer the shuddering frame.
And now, even now was the terrible might
  Of the fire climbing upward, the glare of the flame.
Then, then Zeus brought o'er them in heaven's mid-height
Black cloud-palls, and quenched that fire's red light.

(Str. 5)

Our faith shall not stagger, what purpose soever
  Is framed by the Gods. For thence on that day
To the Rest-land Auroral where north winds blow never
  By Apollo the old king was wafted away

(Ant. 5)

With his slim-ankled daughters, for aye to be dwelling
  At peace, for his piety's fitting reward,
For that gifts in abundance, all mortals excelling,
  Had Croesus in Pytho most holy outpoured.

(*Ep.* 5)

And thou, O Hiero, worthy to be
  Highly extolled, of all in the land
Of Hellas hath no man outrivalled thee —
  None dares so boast — in the lavish hand
That gave gold gifts so abundantly
As thou sentest to Loxias' shrine oversea.

(*Str.* 6)

Whoso batteneth not upon jealousy's poison
  Must needs praise a steed-loving warrior king
Whom Zeus, Lord of Justice, upholds, who hath foison
  Of wealth, whose praises the Song-queens sing.

(*Ant.* 6)

Mortals see not so far as from evening to morning;
  But hope with far visions our hearts doth delude.
Yet Admetus received from Apollo wise warning:
  "Being mortal, of thee be life diversely viewed: —

(*Ep.* 6)

Be thy first thought: I may see the light of the sun
  For the last time tomorrow; thy second thought this:
I may live till years fifty their courses have run,
  Years brimmed up full-measure with wealth and with bliss.
Live righteously then and glad-heartedly; none
Of life's prizes but is by contentment outdone."

(*Str.* 7)

Plain be my words unto whoso discerneth: —
  The heaven's blue depths are for aye undefiled:
To corruption the sea's salt flood never turneth:
  Of gold the mother is gladness the child.

(*Ant.* 7)

No man may put off from him eld with his hoary
  Hairs, and recall youth's bloom fled away;
But not with our frames wastes virtue's glory;
  Nay, the Song-goddess keepeth it young for aye.

(*Ep.* 7)

To the world, O Hiero, thou hast revealed
  The fairest flowers that ever have blown
In prosperity's garden. If lips be sealed,
  How shall thy good deads' glory be known?
Nay, the nightingale's notes that from Keos have pealed
In thy praises shall share: never truth is concealed.

[3, tr. A. S. WAY]

Victor in the Boys' wrestling match at the Pythian Games.

(*Str.* 1)

O Victory, whose feet are shod with triumph sweet,
  Allfather throned in majesty divine
Hath empowered thee to be sole Queen of Rivalry,
  And where with gold Olympus' mansions shine,
At Zeus's side thou bidest, and aye as thou decidest
  As touching deeds of valour and of might,
The Gods who live forever and mortals murmur never
  At the sentence that is righteous in thy sight.

  Smile, Daughter of Styx the splendour-tressed
    Who judgeth in equity!   Thou
  Hast filled Metapontum the burg heaven-blest
    With joy, as her fair sons now
  Sing, sing the renown of the Pythian crown
    On Phaïskus' scion's brow.

(*Ant.* 1)

Unto him the Delian King gave gracious welcoming,
  The God whom royal-girded Leto bare;
And garlands of bright flowers fell on his head in showers
  For strong Alexidamus' triumph there
In that Arena glorious, by the wrestler's might victorious
  O'er rivals in the mighty tug and strain,
When Helios, all-beholder, ne'er saw our champion's shoulder
  Bowed earthward to the dust of Kirrha's plain.

  This too will I say — on the hallowed ground
    Of Pelops by Alpheus' stream
  Fair-flowing, there had he also bound
    His brows with the silvery gleam
  Of the olive that haileth whoever prevaileth
    In the contest as victor supreme.

(*Ep.* 1)

So in triumph would he stand in the heifer-rearing land,
  Had the judges not from justice gone astray: —
Yet I charge not on these the trickster's knaveries
  Who in lovely Elis stole his prize away.
Nay, their wisdom in discerning was a God to folly turning
  Peradventure, or, since hearts of mortal men,
False guiding-stars obeying, into error still are straying,
  These robbed him off his glory-guerdon then.

  But the Bow-queen now of the arrow of gold,
    The Huntress, the Gracious One,
  Giveth victory, she unto whom of old

An altar by Abas' son
And his daughters was reared, for their prayers had she heard,
And the spell of the Curse had undone.

(*Str.* 2)

For Hera's cruel might had constrained them in affright
To leave the well-belovèd home behind;
For a fearful yoke she laid upon each tormented maid,
Even madness overmastering the mind.
For they went in childish folly to the temple-precinct holy
Of the Goddess of the purple zone, and there,
By her majesty undaunted, with idle lips they vaunted
That their father's wealth was greater past compare

Than the riches of Zeus' bride golden-tressed.
Then Hera in anger smote
Their spirits with madness distracting the breast
With visions of dreadful note;
And they sped their flight to a forest-clad height,
And they howled from a bestial throat.

(*Ant.* 2)

So fled they soul-appalled from Tiryns titan-walled,
From the streets of dwellings reared by hands divine; —
Seeing ten years now were told since the Heroes aweless-souled,
Bronze-bucklered, with the prince of Abas' line
Left Argos dear to Heaven for the habitation given
To their king, the cynosure of envyings.
For a feud past all assuaging had from childhood up been raging
'Twixt Proitus and Akrisius, brother-kings.

And by this contention of Abas' seed
Did a people divided stand
With the warring princes arrayed, to bleed
And die by spear and brand,
Till they made petition — "Now make ye division
Of this wheat-wealthy land:

(*Ep.* 2)

Let the younger of you twain in Tiryns' city reign,
Ere your feet be trapped in ruin's fatal snare."
And Zeus Kronion willed that the storm of strife be stilled,
That the agony of hate be ended there.
For with honour he befriended the mighty line descended
From Danaus and Lynkeus chariot-lord.
And Cyclopes might-abounding upreared the walls surrounding
That city whose renown they were to ward.

And the world-famed heroes through after days
There dwelt, who forsook the land

Of steeds, fair Argos whom all men praise: —
  Even thence by the dread curse banned
Those maids dark-haired fled horror-scared
  With madness by Hera's command.

                                    (*Str.* 3)

Then pierced with sorrow's dart was their father Proitus' heart;
  Weird thoughts turmoiled his soul in wild unrest;
And he drew the whetted blade from its scabbard and essayed
  To bury it within his tortured breast;
Nor from death had they refrained him, but his spearman-guards
      restrained him
  By gentle pleading with the lord they loved;
Yea, their clinging hands compelled him, and from Hades gate
      withheld him.
  But his madness-goaded daughters blindly roved

For months thirteen through the forest-shades,
  And mid Arcady's flocks strayed wide;
And their sire, as he followed the frenzied maids,
  Came at last where Lusus doth glide.
To the stream fair-plashing he bowed, and washing
  His hands, he upraised them, and cried

                                    (*Ant.* 3)

To the daughter lovely-eyed of the crimson-snooded bride
  Of Zeus, and to heaven stretched his hands,
Unto where the splendour shone of the swift steeds of the sun,
  Imploring her to loose the madness-bands
On his daughters' spirits lying, and a vow he added, crying,
  "I will sacrifice unto thee twenty kine
Ruddy-hided, and unbroken to the yoke."   The vow was spoken:
  And the mighty-fathered Huntress-maid divine

Hearkened, and Hera's wrath she appeased,
  And the unblest madness-pain
Of the blossom-garlanded maidens ceased.
  Then they built her an altar and fane,
And they slew sheep there, and dances fair
  Of women did they ordain.

                                    (*Ep.* 3)

Thence didst thou cross the sea with Achaia's chivalry
  To where the gallant steed is nurtured well.
Came Good Fortune in thy train, and in Metapontum's fane,
  O golden Queen of Nations, dost thou dwell.
And there by Kasa river that flows in beauty ever
  Those first forefathers of a noble race
With a lovely grove surrounded the temple they had founded,
  O Goddess, unto thee in Priam's days,

What time with Atreus' sons bronze-mailed —
  By the blest Gods' will was it done —
Proud Troy they had smitten, and homeward sailed.
  Yea, justice-lovers shall own
How measureless glory through all time's story
  Is by prowess Achaian won.

[10, tr. A. S. Way]

THESEUS. A DITHYRAMB

(Str. 1)

The dark-prowed ship through surges cleft her way
  To Crete, and battle-bider Theseus bare
With all those doomed to be the man-bull's prey,
  Twice seven Ionian children passing-fair.
The north wind smote on her far-gleaming sail
  By grace of Pallas, aegis-brandisher.
Then goads of love-crowned Kypris, stings of bale,
  Began in Minos' tyrant heart to stir,
That he refrained him not from outrage proud,
  But on the cheek on one white girl he laid
A wanton hand.   Eriboia shrieked aloud
  Unto Pandion's scion bronze-arrayed.
And Theseus saw the deed: full height he sprung;
  Sudden beneath his brows flashed his dark eye,
As indignation's bitter anguish stung
  His soul, and unto Minos did he cry:
"Ha! <i>thou</i> a son of Zeus most mightiest —
  Or base-born churl that knoweth not to rein
In righteousness the brute within his breast?
  From outrage arrogant those hands refrain!

(Ant. 1)

What weird soever the resistless Fate
  God-sent, and scales of Justice, shall ordain,
That cup, what time it cometh, soon or late,
  Will we receive, and to the dregs will drain.
But now—forbear thy caitiff purpose thou!
  If Phoinix' noble child of gracious name
Bare thee indeed to Zeus 'neath Ida's brow
  To be the chief of men in power and fame,
Me too the child of Pittheus wealth-renowned
  In union with Poseidon the Sea-king
Bare to a God.   The Nereids violet-crowned
  Over her head a golden veil did fling.
Therefore, thou captain of Crete's war-array,
  I warn thee, this thy wantonness refrain
That breeds but grief; for verily I would pray

Never to see dawn's lovesome light again,
If thou by force hadst wrought thy foul intent
On any of this fair young company.
Nay, we will try the steel's arbitrament
Ere then!   The issue shall with Heaven lie."

(*Ep.* 1)

Thus far he spake, that hero battle-peerless;
And all the shipmen with amazement heard
The warrior's stern defiance utter-fearless.
But Helios' kinsman's * wrath was fury-stirred.
A web whose warp and woof held life's perdition
He wove, and cried: "Supreme in might, hear me,
Zeus, father!   If the white-armed maid Phoenician
In very truth did bear me unto thee,
Now unto me do thou send down from heaven
A token none shall fail to understand,
Thy swift bolt of the fiery-streaming levin!
But thou — if to the Shaker of the land
Aithra the maid Troezenian truly bore thee,
For proof thereof, this golden signet-ring
Whose splendour flashes on mine hand before thee,
Up from the dark deep sea-floor do thou bring.
Ay, cast thy body down to thy sire's dwelling!
So shalt thou know if He doth hear my prayer,
Kronion, lord of thunder terror-kneeling,
Whose sway is over all things everywhere."

(*Str.* 2)

That daring prayer by Zeus the all-puissant one
Was heard, and he vouchsafed to Minos then
Transcendent honour, to his own dear son
Granting a grace all-manifest to men.
The lightning flashed.   He saw that welcome sign:
To glorious heaven the king war-steadfast raised
His hands — "Thou seest, Theseus, yon divine
Boon wherewith Zeus," he cried, "his son hath graced.
Thou then into the thunder-tolling sea
Leap! so shall Kronos' son who gave thee birth
Poseidon, the Sea-king, bestow on thee
Renown transcendent through the green-vestured earth."
So spake: shrank Theseus' heart from that essay
No whit; upon the strong-knit stern he stood
And leapt.   The sea's white-blossomed mead straightway
Welcomed him in, and closed o'er him the flood.
Then gladness thrilled the soul of Zeus's son.
He gave command to hold adown the wind

---

* Minos was the son-in-law of the Sun-god.

The goodly-fashioned ship fast flying on —
But Fate prepared far other ways to find.

(Ant. 2)

Hard-thrusting blew the North astern; the pine
  Sped fast. But Athens' children quaked with fear,
Deeming he leapt to death beneath the brine,
  And from their flower-bright eyes shed many a tear.
But dolphins, haunters of the watery ways,
  Upstayed the mighty Theseus: onward fast
They bore the hero to the dwelling-place
  Of his Sire, Lord of Steeds. And so he passed
Into the palace-halls where Gods abode;
  And there with trembling awe he looked upon
Blest Nereus' glorious daughters. Far and wide
  Flame-like a splendour from their bright limbs shone.
And twined about the glory of their hair
  Did fillets golden-braided gleam and glance;
And joyance filled their hearts, as here, as there
  Softly their feet were floating in the dance.
And there he saw his sire's belovèd bride
  Throned in that goodly palace of the sea:
Imperial Amphitrite lovely-eyed
  Clad him in purple-rippling bravery.

(Ep 2)

She laid withal a wreath of rich adorning
  On his crisped hair, of fadeless roses wrought
Dark-splendid, which upon her bridal morning
  She of the love-wiles, Aphrodite, brought.
No miracle of the high Gods' devising
  To men whose hearts are right, is past belief.
By that ship's taper stern from sea-gulfs rising
  There was he! With what thoughts he smote the chief
Of Cnossian men aghast, when midst the plashing
  Wave-crests he rose unwetted! Oh, he seemed
A marvel! On his limbs the sunlight-flashing
  Gifts of the Gods with heavenly radiance gleamed.
And up from the hyaline halls there came a crying,
  The chanting of the Sea-maids splendour-throned
In new-born rapture. The great deep replying
  Echoed their joy with voices thunder-toned.
And from the deck hard by they sang the paean,
  Those youths and maids in accents sweetly blent.
O Delian, may thy soul by choir-hymns Keian
  Glow gladdened! Grant fair fortune heaven-sent!

[16, tr. A. S. WAY]

ARISTOPHANES

(*ca.* 447–*ca.* 385 B.C.)

SONG OF THE CLOUDS

[In the *Clouds* Aristophanes satirizes the new philosophy of the Sophists. Strepsiades, an ignorant peasant, goes to the "Thinking-shop" of Socrates to learn rhetoric, so he may be able to evade his creditors. Socrates first instructs him in the theology of the new physicists: Zeus and the Olympians are no more; the Gods of the philosophers are Vortex, Aether, and the Clouds (appropriate divinities for men who are popularly supposed to have their heads "up in the clouds"). Socrates summons the Clouds, who form the chorus of the play, to assist in the education of the neophyte; they enter the orchestra with the following charming song:]

Chorus

Clouds, ever drifting in air,
Rise, O dewy anatomies, shine to the world in splendour.
Upward from thundering Ocean who fathered us
rise, make way to the forested pinnacles.
There let us gaze upon
summits aërial opening under us;
Earth, most holy, and fruits of our watering;
rivers melodious, rich in divinity;
seas, deep-throated, of echo reverberant.
Rise, for his Eye, many-splendoured, unwearying,
burns in the front of Heaven.
Shake as a cloak from our heavenly essences
vapour and rain, and at Earth in our purity
with far-seeing eye let us wonder.

Maidens that minister rain,
Come, gaze down on the city of Pallas, the land of Cecrops.
O for the lustre, the manhood, the charm of her!
There are the Rites unspoken, inviolate, —
holy solemnities
calling the faithful to Mysteries visible.
Treasures of marble in high-roofed sanctuaries
honour the Blessèd; and holy processionals,
feast and blood-offering, wreathing of flower on flower
praise everlasting give them.
Merrily also the choirs of Bromios
herald the Spring with a battle of melody
and music of clarinet droning.

[*Clouds*, 275–90, 299–313, tr. T. F. HIGHAM]

PLATO

(429–347 B.C.)

TO ASTER

Thou wert the morning-star among the living,
  Ere thy fair light had fled;
But now thou art as Hesperus, giving
  New splendour to the dead.

[5, tr. P. B. Shelley]

CHAEREMON

(*fl.* 350? B.C.)

MAIDENS AT REST

One lay lit by the moon, breast white and bare,
Her strap off shoulder fallen. There a dancer
  From dancing showed her left flank naked in air
  Visible, picture living to declare
Of dazzling white to shadow making answer.

And one her arms and dainty wrists revealed
  Twining them round the neck of playmate fair;
One — for being torn the pleated dress must yield —
  Her thigh: and love, for lover to despair,
Deep on her laughing summer time was sealed.

They fell in sleep on elecampanon lying,
  Or bruising the violets' plumage darkly flying,
And yellow crocus, by their robes concealed
  Yet still the underweave with sun's grain dyeing,
As they leaned their necks upon the gentle field.

[*T.G.F.* 14, tr. George Allen]

THE ANTHOLOGY

All the selections that follow (except the one by Cercidas) are taken from the Greek Anthology, often called the Palatine Anthology from the sole manuscript of the work in the Palatine Library at Heidelberg. Cephalas, a Byzantine scholar, compiled the collection in the tenth century from a number of earlier anthologies, the oldest and most important of which was the *Garland* of Meleager, a Syrian Greek of the early first century B.C., and a writer of exquisite amatory epigrams; the *Garland* included the best Greek epigrams from the seventh to the third century B.C. and some of Meleager's own. We owe to his collection the epigrams of Simonides quoted above (pp. 994–998). Cephalas also drew on the *Cycle* of Agathias, a functionary at the court of Justinian (527–565 A.D.); his collection apparently included only the poems of his own contemporaries, notably his father-in-law, Paul the Silentiary, another imperial official. The work represents the last flowering of Greek culture at Constantinople.

The best of these little poems come from the earlier period; and it may be fairly said that the epigram shows the Alexandrian writers at their best. The brevity of the form suited well with Callimachus' dislike of long poems; there is less room for the cumbersome learning that burdens Callimachus' Hymns; the emphasis on perfection of form and the light touch are characteristics of an age which mistrusted its own ability and felt incapable of saying anything of an importance to equal the great classic writers of the past.

Callimachus ranks second only to Simonides as a writer of epigrams; nothing could surpass the eloquent simplicity of his epitaph for Nicoteles, and his lines on Heraclitus have become the most familiar of all Greek epigrams to English readers through the paraphrase of William Cory. Of Asclepiades and Leonidas, the other representatives of the Alexandrian Age, it should be sufficient to note that they were innovators who helped to usher in the new era in literature through their emphasis on erotic themes and the use of minute realism in the description of daily life. Leonidas, it might be added, appears in Theocritus' *Seventh Idyl,* under the name of Lycidas, masquerading as a goatherd on the island of Cos.

CALLIMACHUS

(310–*ca.* 240 B.C.)

HERACLITUS

One told me, Heraclitus, you were dead.
I wept: and thought how oft we two have sped
The sun with talking. Carian friend, you must
Be lying now an old, old heap of dust.

Ay, but your nightingales yet live: on those
Death's hand, that plunders all, shall never close.
[A.P. VII. 80, tr. G. M. YOUNG]

[The beautiful paraphrase of William Cory has become an English classic in its own right:

"They told me, Heraclitus, they told me you were dead,
They brought me bitter news to hear and bitter tears to shed.
I wept as I remember'd how often you and I
Had tired the sun with talking and sent him down the sky.

And now that thou art lying, my dear old Carian guest,
A handful of grey ashes, long, long ago at rest,
Still are thy pleasant voices, thy nightingales, awake:
For Death, he taketh all away, but these he cannot take."]

TIMON

"Timon, now dead, is life or death more drear?
Pray tell us." "Death; since more of you are here."
[A.P. VII. 317, tr. G. M. YOUNG]

NICOTELES

Here Philip laid Nicoteles, who died
When he was twelve, his father's hope and pride.
[A.P. VII. 453, tr. G. M. YOUNG]

CLEOMBROTUS

Cleombrotus the Ambraciot called out "O Sun, good-bye,"
And from a lofty parapet leapt to eternity.
It was no grief unbearable that made him seek that goal:
He had but read a single work of Plato's, "On the Soul."
[A.P. VII. 471, tr. G. M. YOUNG]

BROTHER AND SISTER

Ere daybreak Melanippus passed away,
And while the sun was setting, the same day,
The maiden Basilo, his sister, took
With her own hand the life she could not brook
After she laid his body on the flame.
Thus to their father Aristippus came
A double grief, o'ershadowing his estate,
And all Cyrene mourned to see the fate
That left that goodly house of children desolate.
[A.P. VII. 517, tr. G. M. YOUNG]

CALLIGNOTUS AND IONIS

"Ionis, I swear it, there never shall be
A man, or a woman, more precious to me."

Thus swore Callignotus: But oaths made in love —
The proverb is true — go unheeded above.

Poor girl! His first flame, since he burns with a second,
Is like the Megarians, unmentioned, unreckoned.
[A.P. v. 6, tr. G. M. YOUNG]

CONOPION

As I contrive to slumber by your will
On this cold doorstep! May you have such rest
As you allow your lover, cruellest!
O may you sleep, mosquito girl, as ill.
Can you not pity? Nay, you do not know
What pity means, although the neighbours show
Pity enough. But grizzled hair ere long
Will teach you to remember all this wrong.
[A.P. v. 23, tr. G. M. YOUNG]

A STATUE OF BERENICE

The Graces are four,
For lately one more
Was fashioned to be
A mate to the three.
The myrrh still bedews her,
Oh who would not choose her,
In beauty serene,
Berenice the queen?
There are not even three
Without her! 'Tis she —
So lovely her face is —
That graces the Graces.
[A.P. v. 145, tr. G. M. YOUNG]

LOVE'S CHASE

Over the mountains will the hunter go
Through frost and snow,
My Epicydes, tracking everywhere
Gazelle and hare.
If any say, "Lo, here a beast lies shot,"
He takes it not.
Like him, my heart to all that flees apace
Gives eager chase,
And will not stay to pouch the game that lies
Before my eyes.
[A.P. XII. 102, tr. G. M. YOUNG]

THE CYCLOPS

How excellent an antidote for Love's inoculation
The Cyclops found. By Mother Earth, the Polypheme had wit!

The Muses, Philip mine, reduce the arrow's inflammation,
  The sovereign cure is verse, if you of women would be quit.
While, if your heart is plagued with boys, the treatment is starvation·
  That kills the germ — to me it seems its only benefit!
So we may say with confidence, in either situation,
  To Love the Bully, "Little boy, we fear you not a bit,
Go, clip your silly wings: for now, whichever complication
  Your wound begets, we keep at home the remedy for it."

[A.P. XII. 150, tr. G. M. YOUNG]

THE BACCHANTE'S OFFERING

These gifts to Aphrodite
  Simon, the wanton gave:
Her effigy, the girdle
  That to her bosom clave,
The torch — ah me! — and thyrsus
  That once she used to wave.

[A.P. XIII. 24, tr. G. M. YOUNG]

ASCLEPIADES

(*fl.* 290 B.C.)

THERE IS NO LOVING AFTER DEATH

Why hoard your maidenhood? There'll not be found
A lad to love you, girl, under the ground.
Love's joys are for the quick; but when we're dead
It's dust and ashes, girl, will go to bed.

[A.P. v. 85, tr. R. A. FURNESS]

THE POWER OF LOVE

Snow, hail, make darkness, lighten, thunder, shake out on the earth all thy black clouds! If thou slayest me, then shall I cease, but if thou lettest me live, though I pass through worse than this, I will go with music to her doors; for the god compels me who is thy master too, Zeus, he at whose bidding thou, turned to gold, didst pierce the brazen chamber.

[A.P. v. 64, tr. W. R. PATON]

DIDYME

Didyme by the branch she waved at me has carried me clean away, alas! and looking on her beauty, I melt like wax before the fire. And if she is dusky, what is that to me? So are the coals, but when we light them, they shine as bright as roses.

[A.P. v. 210, tr. W. R. PATON]

LOVE IS BEST

Sweet is the snow to drink in summer heat
For one athirst; and, after winter, sweet

Spring's pledge, the starry Crown, to mariners.
But this is sweetest, when two lovers meet,
Two loving hearts beneath one mantle beat,
And praise of love is on his lips and hers.

[A.P. v. 169, tr. HUGH MACNAGHTEN]

LEONIDAS OF TARENTUM

(*fl.* 274 B.C.)

TIME

Measureless time or ever thy years, O man, were reckon'd;
    Measureless time shall run over thee low in the ground.
And thy life between is — what? The flick of a flying second,
    A flash, a point — or less, if a lesser thing can be found.

[A.P. VII. 472, 1–4, tr. EDWYN BEVAN]

CERCIDAS

(*fl.* 250 B.C.)

THE VOYAGE OF LOVE

Aphrodite has a son
    with azure wings:
he breathes a gentle breath on one
    (so the poet sings)
on others he blows harsh and strong —
Demonomus, you know the song.

When he sends a happy breeze
    from friendly lip,
Love voyages in tranquil ease
    and the prudent ship
letting safe Obedience steer
finds the ocean mild and clear.

But whenever he unbinds
    the hurricane
of fierce Desire, its wanton winds
    infuriate the main:
then Love must sail on perilous seas
    — Truly said, Euripides!

Choose the favorable wind;
    call to the wheel
Obedience, let the temperate mind
    keep us on steady keel.
So shall we voyage fair and far
setting our course by Love's high star.

[2, tr. GILBERT HIGHET]

MELEAGER

(*fl.* 90 B.C.)

A BRIDE

Bridegroom none but death alone
Has my Clearista won,
So to loose her virgin zone.

Yester eve the flutes blew sweet,
Bridegroom and the bride to greet,
And the bridal doors were beat.

Now at dawn they sound again,
But another sadder strain,
Hymen's song is hushed in pain;

And the torch that flared so gay,
Lighting up her bride's array,
Lit the dead her downward way.

[A.P. VII. 182, tr. H. C. BEECHING]

ZENOPHILA

Thou sleepest, Zenophila, tender flower. Would I were Sleep,
though wingless, to creep under thy lashes, so that not even he who
lulls the eyes of Zeus might visit thee, but I might have thee all to
myself.

[A.P. V. 174, tr. W. R. PATON]

PALLADAS

(*ca.* 360–430 A.D.)

NAKED I CAME

Naked I reached the world at birth;
Naked I pass beneath the earth:
Why toil I, then, in vain distress,
Seeing the end is nakedness?

[A.P. X. 58, tr. A. J. BUTLER]

RUFINUS

(DATE UNKNOWN)

GOLDEN EYES

Ah, Golden Eyes, to win you yet,
I bring mine April coronet.
The lovely blossoms of the spring,
For you I weave, to you I bring: —

These roses with the lilies wet,
The dewy dark-eyed violet,
Narcissus, and the wind-flower wet.
Wilt thou disdain mine offering,
    Ah, Golden Eyes?
Crowned with thy lover's flowers, forget
The pride wherein thy heart is set;
For thou, like these or anything,
Hast but thine hour of blossoming,
Thy spring, and then — the long regret,
    Ah, Golden Eyes!

[A.P. v. 74, tr. ANDREW LANG]

PAULUS SILENTIARIUS

(*fl.* 563 A.D.)

THE TEARS OF FEAR

Sweet is my Lais' smile, and sweet the tide
  Of tears that floods her eyes alive with meaning:
Now yesterday without a cause she sighed,
  Her head a long time on my shoulder leaning:
I kissed her as she wept, but tear on tear
  Fell on our meeting lips like fountain dew:
I asked her why she cried.   She said, 'For fear
  You will desert me: men are never true.'

[A.P. v. 250, tr. SIR WILLIAM MARRIS]

AGATHIAS SCHOLASTICUS

(*ca.* 536–582 A.D.)

LEAVE A KISS WITHIN THE CUP

I love not wine; yet if thou'ldst make
  A sad man merry, sip first sup,
  And when thou giv'st I'll take the cup:
If thy lip touch it, for thy sake
  No more may I be stiff and staid
  And the luscious jug evade:
The cup convoys thy kiss to me,
And tells the joy it had of thee.

[A.P. v. 261, tr. J. M. EDMONDS]